W9-DAX-105

RETAILING
MANAGEMENT

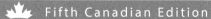 Fifth Canadian Edition

Michael Levy, Ph.D.
Babson College

Barton A. Weitz, Ph.D.
University of Florida

Dea Watson, MBA
Conestoga College

Michael Madore, MBA
University of Lethbridge

Humber College Library
3199 Lakeshore Blvd. West
Toronto, ON   M8V 1K8

DISCARD

Mc
Graw
Hill
Education

RETAILING MANAGEMENT
Fifth Canadian Edition

Copyright © 2017, 2014, 2011, 2008, 2005 by McGraw-Hill Ryerson Limited. Copyright © 2014, 2012, 2009, 2007 by McGraw-Hill Education LLC. All rights reserved. No part of this publication may be reproduced or transmitted in any form or by any means, or stored in a database or retrieval system, without the prior written permission of McGraw-Hill Ryerson Limited, or in the case of photocopying or other reprographic copying, a license from The Canadian Copyright Licensing Agency (Access Copyright). For an Access Copyright license, visit www.accesscopyright.ca or call toll free to 1-800-893-5777.

The Internet addresses listed in the text were accurate at the time of publication. The inclusion of a website does not indicate an endorsement by the authors or McGraw-Hill Ryerson, and McGraw-Hill Ryerson does not guarantee the accuracy of the information presented at these sites.

ISBN-13: 978-1-25-926920-2
ISBN-10: 1-25-926920-5

1 2 3 4 5 6 7 8 9 WEB 1 2 3 4 5 6 7

Printed and bound in Canada.

Care has been taken to trace ownership of copyright material contained in this text; however, the publisher will welcome any information that enables them to rectify any reference or credit for subsequent editions.

Portfolio and Program Manager: *Karen Fozard*
Product Manager: *Sara Braithwaite*
Executive Marketing Manager: *Joy Armitage Taylor*
Product Developer: *Sara Braithwaite / Loula March*
Senior Product Team Associate: *Marina Seguin*
Supervising Editor: *Stephanie Gibson*
Copy Editor: *Janice Dyer*
Photo/Permissions Researcher: *Marnie Lamb*
Plant Production Coordinator: *Scott Morrison*
Manufacturing Production Coordinator: *Sheryl MacAdam*
Cover and eBook Interior Design: *Michelle Losier*
Cover Image: *Anna Frajtova / Getty Images*
Print Interior Design: *Lightbox Visual Communications Inc.*
Page Layout: *Aptara®, Inc.*
Printer: *Webcom, Ltd.*

*To Jacquie Levy, the best Mom in the world—
loving, elegant, and with a will to live driven by
her need to give of herself. — Michael Levy*

*To Shirley Weitz, the best wife in the world, whose
love and enthusiasm enrich our lives. — Bart Weitz*

*To my amazing colleagues and students at
Conestoga College Institute of Technology and
Advanced Learning, thank you for making such a
profound impact on my life. — Dea Watson*

*To my wonderful family—Lara, Matthew, Nicole,
Logan, and Oliver. This would not have been
possible without your love and support over
the years. — Michael Madore*

ABOUT THE AUTHORS

Michael Levy, Ph.D., is the Charles Clarke Reynolds Professor of Marketing and Director of the Retail Supply Chain Institute at Babson College (http://www.babson.edu/retail). He received his Ph.D. in business administration from The Ohio State University and his undergraduate and MS degrees in business administration from the University of Colorado at Boulder. He taught at Southern Methodist University before joining the faculty as professor and chair of the marketing department at the University of Miami.

Professor Levy received the 2009 Lifetime Achievement Award by the American Marketing Association Retailing Special Interest Group. He has developed a strong stream of research in retailing, business logistics, financial retailing strategy, pricing, and sales management. He has published over 50 articles in leading marketing and logistics journals, including the *Journal of Retailing, Journal of Marketing, Journal of the Academy of Marketing Science,* and *Journal of Marketing Research.* He currently serves on the editorial review boards of the *Journal of Retailing, International Journal of Logistics Management, International Journal of Logistics and Materials Management,* and *European Business Review.* He is co-author of *Marketing* (3e, 2012) and *M-Marketing* (2e, 2011), both with McGraw-Hill/Irwin. Professor Levy was co-editor of *Journal of Retailing* from 2001 to 2007. He co-chaired the 1993 Academy of Marketing Science conference and the 2006 Summer AMA conference.

Professor Levy has worked in retailing and related disciplines throughout his professional life. Prior to his academic career, he worked for several retailers and a housewares distributor in Colorado. He has performed research projects with many retailers and retail technology firms, including Accenture, Federated Department Stores, Khimetrics (SAP), Mervyn's, Neiman Marcus, ProfitLogic (Oracle), Zale Corporation, and numerous law firms.

Barton A. Weitz, Ph.D., received an undergraduate degree in electrical engineering from MIT and an MBA and a Ph.D. in business administration from Stanford University. He has been a member of the faculty at the UCLA Graduate School of Business and the Wharton School at the University of Pennsylvania, and is presently the JCPenney Eminent Scholar Chair in Retail Management in the Warrington College of Business Administration at the University of Florida.

Professor Weitz is the founder of the David F. Miller Center for Retailing Education and Research at the University of Florida (http://www.cba.ufl.edu/mkt/retail-center). The activities of the centre are supported by contributions from 35 retailers and firms in the retail industry, including JCPenney, Macy's, Walmart, Office Depot, Walgreens, Target, Build-A-Bear, Brown Shoe, NPD, and the International Council of Shopping Centers. Each year, the centre places more than 250 undergraduates in paid summer internships and management trainee positions with retail firms and funds research on retailing issues and problems.

Professor Weitz has won awards for teaching excellence and made numerous presentations to industry and academic groups. He has published over 50 articles in leading academic journals on channel relationships, electronic retailing, store design, salesperson effectiveness, and salesforce and human resource management. His research has been recognized with two Louis Stern Awards for his contributions to channel management research and a Paul Root Award for the *Journal of Marketing* article that makes the greatest contribution to marketing practice. He serves on the editorial review boards of the *Journal of Retailing, Journal of Marketing, International Journal of Research in Marketing, Marketing Science,* and *Journal of Marketing Research.* He is a former editor of the *Journal of Marketing Research.*

Professor Weitz has been the chair of the American Marketing Association and a member of the board of directors of the National Retail Federation, the National Retail Foundation, and the American Marketing Association. In 1989, he was honoured as the AMA/Irwin Distinguished Educator in recognition of his contributions to the marketing discipline. He was selected by the National Retail Federation as Retail Educator of the Year in 2005 and been recognized for lifetime achievements by American Marketing Association Retailing, Sales, and Inter-Organizational Special Interests Groups.

Dea Watson, MBA, has been a faculty member at Conestoga College Institute of Technology & Advanced Learning in Kitchener, Ontario, for 11 years. Dea holds an undergraduate degree in sociology from Wilfrid Laurier University and an MBA in retailing from the Retail Institute at the University of Stirling, Scotland.

Prior to her academic career, she had a variety of opportunities in Canadian retail over a 15-year span. She spent a significant amount of time delivering a national customer service training program and managed a variety of multi-million dollar soft goods departments for several major Canadian department stores.

As a professor and program coordinator for business marketing programs at Conestoga College, she possesses a passion for the retail industry and a wealth of practical experience. Dea coaches the college's Retail Case team for the Ontario Colleges Marketing Competition, which consists of industry judges who determine the most viable, realistic business solutions to pre-determined real-world cases. The competition includes a minimum of 16 competing Ontario colleges marketing student teams. A founding member of the charity Jessica's Footprint, Dea has used her knowledge of marketing and sponsorship to raise money to fund paediatric brain cancer research at the Hospital for Sick Children in Toronto. With Dea's help, the charity has achieved an impressive $1.4 million in donations since its inception in 2005.

Michael Madore, MBA, has been an educator for over 25 years, with the past nine as a faculty member at the University of Lethbridge, Alberta. Michael holds an undergraduate degree in education from the University of New Brunswick and an MBA in marketing from City University in Seattle, Washington. Michael is currently enrolled in an M.Ed. specializing in Educational Leadership with the hopes of completing a doctorate in this area in the future.

Michael has been involved in retailing for over 30 years. An entrepreneur at heart, Michael operated his first retail service business while in high school and currently operates three retail e-commerce businesses, all of which have a global reach. He also provides marketing and educational consulting services to organizations across Canada.

As a professor and program director for IME (Integrated Management Experience) at the University of Lethbridge, Michael's knowledge stems from both his academic and practical experience, which he successfully leverages in his classroom. The IME program works with non-profit organizations in the Lethbridge community, helping them with managerial decisions and organizing fundraising activities. Michael has coached the U of L's JDC marketing case team for six years. The team competes against 11 other teams in Western Canada. During Michael's tenure as coach, the team has placed first, third, and fourth.

BRIEF CONTENTS

CONTENTS

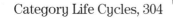

Retailing is a high-tech, global growth industry that plays a vital economic role in Canadian society. The objective in this Fifth Canadian Edition is to stimulate student interest in retailing courses and careers by capturing the exciting, challenging, and rewarding opportunities facing both retailers and firms that sell their products to retailers. To this end, the authors have concentrated on tracking the evolving role of the Internet and social media on the retail industry.

As with previous editions, *Retailing Management* reflects the evolving nature of retailing, including up-to-date data, current and Canadian examples, and cutting-edge information on trends in retailing.

Basic Philosophy

The Fifth Canadian Edition of *Retailing Management* focuses on the broad spectrum of Canadian and international retailers, both large and small, that sells merchandise or services. The text examines key strategic issues with an emphasis on the financial considerations and store management issues that are particular to the Canadian experience. We include descriptive, how-to, and conceptual material to demonstrate key concepts and core principles.

Broad Spectrum of Retailing In this text, we define retailing as the set of business activities that add value to the products and services sold to consumers for their personal or family use. Thus, in addition to products in stores, this text examines the issues facing services retailers such as Starbucks and non-store retailers such as eBay and Lands' End.

Strategic Perspective The entire textbook is organized around a model of strategic decision making. Each section and chapter is related back to this overarching strategic framework. In addition, the book focuses on critical strategic decisions such as selecting target markets, developing a sustainable competitive advantage, building an organizational structure and information and distribution systems to support the strategic direction, building customer loyalty, and managing customer relationships.

Financial Analysis The financial aspects of retailing are becoming increasingly important. The financial problems experienced by some of the largest retail firms highlight the need for a thorough understanding of the financial implications of retail decisions. Financial analysis is emphasized in Chapters 8, 10, 11, and 12. Financial issues are also raised in the sections on trade area decisions and site assessment (Chapter 5), compensating salespeople (Chapter 13), and developing a communication budget (Chapter 15). In-text Concept Checks are provided to help students evaluate their grasp of essential topics in financial analysis for the retail environment; answers to the Concept Checks are available on Connect.

Operations and Store Management Traditionally, retailers have exalted the merchant prince—the buyer who knew what the hot trends were going to be. By devoting an entire chapter to information systems and supply chain management and an entire section to store management, this text reflects the changes that have occurred over the past ten years—the shift in emphasis from merchandise management to the block and tackling of getting merchandise to the stores and customers and providing excellent customer services and an exciting shopping experience. Due to this shift toward store management, most students embarking on retail careers now go into store management rather than merchandise buying.

Balanced Approach

The Fifth Canadian Edition continues to offer a balanced approach to teaching an introductory retailing course by including descriptive, how-to, and conceptual information in a highly readable format.

Descriptive Information Students can learn about the vocabulary and practice of retailing from the descriptive information provided throughout the text. Examples of this material are:

- Leading North American and international retailers
- Management decisions made by retailers
- Types of store-based and non-store retailers

- Approaches to entering international markets
- Issues concerning retail locations
- Organizational structure of typical retailers
- Flow of information and merchandise
- Branding strategies
- Methods of communicating with customers
- Store layout options and merchandise display equipment
- Technological advancement that is affecting the industry
- Adoption of environmental practices

How-to Information *Retailing Management* goes beyond this descriptive information to illustrate how and why retailers, large and small, make decisions. Step-by-step procedures with examples are provided for making the following decisions:

- Comparison shopping
- Managing a multichannel outreach to customers
- Scanning the environment and developing a retail strategy
- Analyzing the financial implications of retail strategy
- Evaluating location decisions
- Developing a merchandise assortment and budget plan
- Negotiating with vendors
- Pricing merchandise
- Recruiting, selecting, training, evaluating, and compensating sales associates
- Designing the layout for a store

Conceptual Information *Retailing Management* also includes conceptual information that enables students to understand why decisions are made as outlined in the text. As Mark Twain said, "There is nothing as practical as a good theory." Students need to know these basic concepts so that they can make effective decisions in new situations. Examples of this conceptual information in the Fifth Canadian Edition include:

- Retail evolution theories
- Customers' decision-making process
- Market attractiveness/competitive position matrix for evaluating strategic alternatives

- Activity-based costing analysis of merchandise categories
- The strategic profit model
- Price theory and marginal analysis
- The gaps model for service quality management

Unique Aspects of *Retailing Management*, Fifth Canadian Edition

Customer Relationship Management Chapter 14 examines how retailers are using customer databases to build repeat business and realize a greater share of wallet from key customers. These customer relationship management activities exploit the 80–20 rule—20 percent of the customers account for 80 percent of the sales and profits. In this chapter, we discuss how retailers identify their best customers and target these customers with special promotions and customer services. The topics covered in this chapter include:

- Why retailers want to provide special services to their best customers
- How retailers use customer databases to determine who their best customers are
- How retailers build loyalty from their best customers
- What retailers do to increase their share of wallet
- How retailers balance customer privacy concerns with the provision of personalized promotions and services

Evolving Role of the Internet Integrated coverage includes the opportunities and challenges retailers face interacting with customers through multiple channels—stores, catalogues, Internet, social media, and mobile. Ten years ago, many experts thought that the consumer would abandon the mall and shop for most products and services using the Internet. Now it is clear that the Internet is not transforming the retail industry, but rather facilitating the activities undertaken by traditional retailers—retailers that use multiple channels—to interact with their customers. In the Fifth Canadian Edition, we have increased our treatment of how these multichannel retailers provide information and sell products and services to customers. We discuss multichannel retailing, omnichannel retailing, and Internet retailing applications throughout the textbook, including:

- The distinctive customer benefits offered to customers by the different channels—stores, catalogues, social media, mobile, and the Internet
- How multichannel and omnichannel retailers offer more value to their customers by providing a seamless interface so that customers can interact with retailers anytime, anywhere
- Factors that will affect the growth of the Internet channel
- The key success factors in multichannel and omnichannel retailing
- The impact of social networks on buying behaviour
- The use of the Internet for recruitment and training
- Communicating with customers through m-commerce, social shopping, email, and websites
- Providing information and customer service through Web-enabled kiosks and POS terminals
- Internet-based digital signage in stores

New Ways to Communicate with Customers

Retailers communicate with customers using a mix of methods, such as advertising, sales, promotion, publicity, email, and social media using Twitter, Facebook, YouTube, and blogs. Although many traditional methods, such as advertising, have been used for decades, Internet-enabling technology has changed the way retailers use their promotional budgets and communicate with customers, including:

- The impact of social networks on buying behaviour
- The increased use of smartphones to allow customers to make price comparisons, locate merchandise, receive coupons, and buy merchandise
- The use of blogs, Twitter, Facebook, and YouTube to promote retailers and specific merchandise, as well as to collect customer attitudes about retailers and reviews of their product
- The use of the technology to customize and deliver coupons and other targeted promotions to customers, who also use Internet sites to find coupons to redeem at their favourite retailers

Social Responsibility of Retailers

Retail institutions are pervasive in our society and thus have a major impact on the welfare of their customers, suppliers, and employees. Given the importance of their societal role, both consumers and retailers are becoming more concerned about societal issues facing the world, such as global warming, immigration, health care, and working conditions in less developed economies. Some of these social responsibility issues are discussed in the Fifth Canadian Edition, including:

- Consumer interest in green products
- Issues in sourcing merchandise globally
- Considering sustainability issues in store operations

Expanded Treatment of Brand Development Issues

To differentiate their offerings and build a competitive advantage, retailers are devoting more resources to the development of exclusive products—whether products that the retailer designs (private label) or exclusive brands produced by national brand manufacturers. For example, Club Monaco founder Joseph Mimran personally oversees the design and development of the extensive Joe Fresh clothing range for the Loblaws group.

Retailers are placing more emphasis on developing their brand image, building a strong image for their private-label merchandise, and extending their image to new retail formats. These exclusive brands, as the term implies, are available only from the retailer, and thus customers loyal to these brands can find them only in one store. Some examples of our extended treatment of exclusive brands in this edition are:

- Strategic importance of private labels
- Private-label approaches and types
- Process for developing and sourcing private labels
- Building a strong brand image

Emphasis on International Retailing

Retailing is a global industry and it is imperative that students understand how firms adapt their business practices to the cultural and infrastructural differences in international markets. With a greater emphasis being placed on private-label merchandise, retailers are working with manufacturers located throughout the world to acquire merchandise. In addition, retailers are increasingly looking to international markets for growth opportunities. We examine international retailing strategies, ranging from those used to enter new international markets to the global sourcing of merchandise.

Active Learning and Application Concept Checks are found in the chapters that deal with financial analysis, pricing, and HR management. These stopping points allow students to reflect on the mathematical components of various types of analysis and test their knowledge. Solutions are provided to students on Connect so they can self-assess as they study.

The Get Out & Do It! exercises suggest projects that students can undertake by either visiting local retail stores or using the Internet. The exercises are designed to provide a hands-on learning experience for students. The Discussion Questions and Problems allow students to critically analyze the chapter material in a particular scenario or context.

End-of-text cases and video cases provide discussion questions for a comprehensive examination of a scenario or case covering multiple topics and chapters. These use current and exciting examples of retailers students see every day. New cases in this edition include companies such as Target, Staples Inc., and Starbucks.

New Features in the Fifth Canadian Edition

Up-to-Date and Cutting Edge!   Many of the Spotlight on Retailing vignettes have been replaced with new examples and photos to help put the text material into a real-world context. The Did You Know? boxes throughout and the cases at the end of the text have been updated for currency.

Chapter-By-Chapter Updates

In addition to reorganization within some chapters to improve flow and structure, the following changes have been made for the Fifth Canadian Edition.

Chapter 1
- New Spotlight on Retailing on Luxury Goods entering the Canadian retail market: "Luxury expands into Canada!"
- New Retailing View 1.1: "Global Consumers are willing to put Their Money Where Their Heart is when it comes to Goods and Services from Companies Committed to Social Responsibility"
- Updated listing of Canada's leading retail corporations (Exhibit 1–6)
- Updated Canadian industry statistics

Chapter 2
- Updated exhibit of Canadian franchises
- Expanded content includes online retail in Canada, m-commerce, and the rise of omni-channel retailing

Chapter 3
- New Spotlight on Retailing: "What's up with mPayments?"
- New Retailing View 3.3: "Retailing to Generation Z"

Chapter 4
- Updated Spotlight on Retailing: "Mobile Delivering Magic Results for Retailers"
- New Retailing Views 4.4: "Why Target failed in Canada"

Chapter 5
- New Spotlight on Retailing: "Study: Luxury Brands Choosing Canadian Malls Over High Street"
- New Retailing View 5.1: "Ten Most Expensive Retail Shopping Strips"

Chapter 6
- New Spotlight on Retailing: "Microsoft retail flagship opens doors in NY"
- New Retailing Views
  - 6.3: "Why do retail stores still have cash registers?"
  - 6.7: "BMO Launches Beautiful figure3-designed Flagship at Canada's Financial Crossroads"
- Updated Retailing View 6.1: "Mission Hill Enters a Different World"

Chapter 7
- New Retailing Views
  - 7.1: "An Empire State of Mind"
  - 7.3: "For all those Jibes about Shopping, Indian Men Buy More Clothes than Women"

Chapter 8
- Revised Spotlight on Retailing: "*easyhome* Ltd."
- New Retailing View 8.1: "Why Private Equity likes Mid-Sized Companies such as Town Shoes"
- Revised Retailing View 8.2: "Dollarama and Nordstrom: Retailers Targeting Customers at the Opposite Ends of the Income Distribution Spectrum"

Chapter 9
- New Retailing Views
  - 9.1: "Shhh . . . Zara's Got a Secret . . . and It's All about Supply Chain Management"
  - 9.2: "Netflix: The Evolution of a Company"

Chapter 10
- Revised Spotlight on Retailing: "ALDO Group Inc.: Canadian Global Success Story"
- New Retailing View 10.2: "Athleisure—Fad or Fashion for the Long Haul?"
- Revised Retailing Views
  - 10.1: "Fast Fashion at Mango"
  - 10.3: "Costco Goes for Variety, or Does It?"

Chapter 11
- New Retailing View 11.3: "Consumers Care About Buying From Socially Responsible"
- Revised Strategic Sales Planning section that includes more detailed strategic material on the selling and negotiation process with retail partners

Chapter 12
- Revised Spotlight on Retailing: "Pricing without Borders"

Chapter 13
- New Spotlight on Retailing: "ATB Developing a Positive Employee Experience"

- New Retailing Views
  - 13.4: "Social Media Recruiting: Understand the Legal Guidelines!"
  - 13.5: "Social Media and Hiring: When Potential New Hires are Searching YOU"
- New section outlining how social media recruiting can impact job opportunities from both an employee's and employer's perspective

Chapter 14
- Revised Retailing View 14.6: "Adoption Problems Plague Digital Wallets"
- Updated discussion about mobile applications and their impact on CRM programs
- Updated definition of what a customer is from L.L. Bean website

Chapter 15
- New Spotlight on Retailing: "Mobile in the New Millennium (Brands and Millennials)"
- New Retailing Views:
  - 15.2: "Harnessing the Power of Social Media to Make Customers Happy"
  - 15.3: "Trending Mobile Marketing Themes"
- New discussion on mobile marketing and on-line marketing

Cases
- New cases
  - **Case 1:** The Last Days of Target
  - **Case 5:** Staples Inc.
  - **Case 6:** Starbucks' Expansion into China
  - **Case 7:** Build-A-Bear Workshop: Where Best Friends Are Made
  - **Case 9:** Blue Tomato: Internationalization of a Multichannel Retailer
  - **Case 17:** Walmart: Pioneer in Supply Chain Management

ABOUT RETAILING MANAGEMENT: GUIDED TOUR

Spotlight on Retailing:
Each chapter opens with a brief vignette, highlighting a retailer or retailing trend that is related to the material in the chapter. These spotlights illustrate how successful organizations view the industry and provide students with first-hand information about what people in retailing do and their successes and challenges. Ten of the Spotlight on Retailers boxes are either new or have been revised for the Fifth Canadian Edition.

JSMimages/Alamy.

Did You Know? Boxes:
Highlighted boxes in the margin of each chapter contain interesting facts about retailing. For instance, did you know that expensive toilet paper sells better during the holiday season between Thanksgiving and New Year's, since people have guests in their homes?

> ### DID YOU KNOW?
> **68 percent.** The percent of Canadians who owned a smartphone in 2015, up 13 percent from the previous year.[3]

Key Terms:
Found in the margins of the chapter content—key terms are defined as students encounter them, making for easy, on-the-spot referencing. For example:

net sales
A small selling space offering a limited merchandise assortment.

mixed-use development (MXD)
Development that combines several uses in one complex—for example, shopping centre, office tower, hotel, residential complex, civic centre, and convention centre.

Retailing Views:
The chapter vignettes called Retailing Views relate concepts to activities and decisions made by retailers such as Walmart, Costco, and IKEA. They also discuss innovative retailers—including Mango and Zara—and provide interesting facts about Generation Z. The majority of the vignettes are either new or revised in this edition.

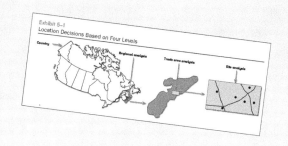

3.3 | RETAILING VIEW

Retailing to Generation Z
Meet the most complex yet most critical shopper of all time—Generation Z. By 2020, today's 16–21 year olds (Gen Z) will be the largest group of consumers worldwide, making up 40 percent of the US, Europe, and BRIC countries, and 10 percent in the rest of the world. The needs and behaviours of this group will inform not only the next generation of shoppers, but the future of mainstream retail.

There's A New Wave of Shoppers in Town
Though they live and shop among us, these new shoppers are happier with access than with ownership. Shrewd

Exhibits:
Charts, illustrations, and tables give visual meaning to complex subject matter and provide easy reference for students.

Exhibit 5–1
Location Decisions Based on Four Levels

Concept Checks:

These boxes allow students to take a look at some of the more challenging math-related concepts they have been introduced to, test their knowledge, and then check the solutions on Connect.

8.1 CONCEPT CHECK

1. Set up a skeletal income statement given the following information:

Net sales	$525 000
Gross margin	44.6%
Expenses	45.0%

Summary:

Chapter summaries recap the chapter content—a great tool for studying!

SUMMARY

Financial management involves a thorough understanding of the importance of return on investment and how this relates to the retailer's image. Clearly defined quantifiable performance objectives are essential to evaluating business strategies and making changes to correct problems.

This chapter explains some basic elements of retailing financial strategy and examines how retailing strategy affects the financial performance of a firm. We used the strategic profit model as a vehicle for understanding the complex interrelations between financial ratios and retailing strategy. Different types of retailers have different financial operating characteristics. Specifically, jewellery store chains such as Birks generally have higher profit margins and lower turnover than discount stores such as Walmart. Yet, when margin and turnover are combined into return on assets, it's possible to achieve similar financial performance.

Get Out and Do It!:

At the end of each chapter, these exercises suggest hands-on projects that students can complete either by visiting a local retailer or using the Internet.

GET OUT & DO IT!

1. **INTERNET EXERCISE** Go to **http://www.hoovers.com**, **http://www.google.com/finance**, or the company's latest annual reports (Walmart and Birks) and use the financial information to update the numbers in the profit margin model in Exhibit 8–5 and the asset turnover model in Exhibit 8–8. Use these two models to develop the strategic profit model in Exhibit 8–11 for Walmart and Birks. Then repeat the process for Amazon and Bally Total Fitness.

for this chapter. The SPM tutorial is designed to provide a refresher for the basic financial ratios leading to return on assets. The tutorial walks you through it step-by-step. A "calculation page" is also included that will calculate all the ratios. You can type in the numbers from a firm's balance sheet and income statement to see the financial results that are produced with the current financial figures. You can also access an Excel spreadsheet for doing SPM calculations. The calculation page or the Excel spreadsheet can be used for the case

DISCUSSION QUESTIONS AND PROBLEMS

1. Why must retailers use multiple performance measures to evaluate their performance?

2. Describe how a multiple-store retailer would set its annual performance objectives.

3. Buyers' performance is often measured by their gross margin. Why is this figure more appropriate than net

4. How does the strategic profit model (SPM) help retailers plan and evaluate marketing and financial strategies?

5. Holt Renfrew (a high-service department store) and Costco (a chain of warehouse clubs) target different groups of customers. Which should have the higher asset turnover, net profit margin, and return on as-

Discussion Questions and Problems:

These questions propose thoughtful questions and encourage analysis and application of the text material.

End-of-Text Cases:

Thirty-two comprehensive cases and accompanying questions are provided at the end of the text, including 6 brand new cases. The inclusion of some longer cases provides students with an opportunity to explore important concepts in greater depth.

CASES

Case	Title	Chapter
1	The Last Days of Target	2
2	Retailing in India—Impact of Hypermarkets	3
3	Sobeys Finds Its Fit with the Urban Crowd: Customer Behaviour	3, 4, 13
4	Attracting Generation Y to a Retail Career	9
5	Staples Inc.	5, 7
6	Starbucks' Expansion into China	4
7	Build-A-Bear Workshop: Where Best Friends Are Made	

Source: Joe Castaldo, "The Last Days of Target," *Canadian Business*, http://www.canadianbusiness.com/the-last-days-of-target-canada/ (accessed June 14, 2016).

SUPPLEMENTS

Learn without Limits

McGraw-Hill connect®

McGraw-Hill Connect® is an award-winning digital teaching and learning platform that gives students the means to better connect with their coursework, with their instructors, and with the important concepts that they will need to know for success now and in the future. With Connect, instructors can take advantage of McGraw-Hill's trusted content to seamlessly deliver assignments, quizzes and tests online. McGraw-Hill Connect is a learning platform that continually adapts to each student, delivering precisely what they need, when they need it, so class time is more engaging and effective. Connect makes teaching and learning personal, easy, and proven.

Connect Key Features:

McGraw-Hill SMARTBOOK™

As the first and only adaptive reading experience, SmartBook is changing the way students read and learn. SmartBook creates a personalized reading experience by highlighting the most important concepts students need to learn at that moment in time. As students engage with SmartBook, the reading experience continuously adapts by highlighting content based on what each student knows and doesn't know. This ensures that students focus on the content needed to close specific knowledge gaps, while simultaneously promoting long-term learning.

McGraw-Hill connect INSIGHT

Connect Insight is Connect's new one-of-a-kind visual analytics dashboard—now available for instructors—that provides at-a-glance information regarding student performance, which is immediately actionable. By presenting assignment, assessment, and topical performance results together with a time metric that is easily visible for aggregate or individual results, Connect Insight gives instructors the ability to take a just-in-time approach to teaching and learning, which was never before available. Connect Insight presents data that helps instructors improve class performance in a way that is efficient and effective.

Simple Assignment Management   With Connect, creating assignments is easier than ever, so instructors can spend more time teaching and less time managing.

- Assign SmartBook learning modules.
- Edit existing questions and create new questions.
- Draw from a variety of text specific questions, resources, and test bank material to assign online.
- Streamline lesson planning, student progress reporting, and assignment grading to make classroom management more efficient than ever.

Smart Grading   When it comes to studying, time is precious. Connect helps students learn more efficiently by providing feedback and practice material when they need it, where they need it.

- Automatically score assignments, giving students immediate feedback on their work and comparisons with correct answers.
- Access and review each response; manually change grades or leave comments for students to review.
- Track individual student performance—by question, assignment, or in relation to the class overall—with detailed grade reports.
- Reinforce classroom concepts with practice tests and instant quizzes.
- Integrate grade reports easily with Learning Management Systems including Blackboard, D2L, and Moodle.

Instructor Library   The Connect Instructor Library is a repository for additional resources to improve student engagement in and out of the class. It provides all the critical resources instructors need to build their course.

- Access Instructor resources.
- View assignments and resources created for past sections.
- Post your own resources for students to use.

Supplements for Instructors

The following instructor supplements are available on Connect.

Instructor's Manual and Video Notes These supplements include an annotated outline and notes, answers to Discussion Questions and Problems, ancillary lectures and exercises, and notes for the end-of-text and video cases.

Videos A wealth of video segments are available to illustrate issues addressed in the text.

Computerized Test Bank The test bank includes multiple-choice, essay, fill-in-the-blank, and short answer questions. Professors may use this software to create, edit, and print a variety of tests.

Microsoft PowerPoint® Lecture Slides These supplements support and organize lectures.

Superior Learning Solutions and Support

The McGraw-Hill team is ready to help you assess and integrate any of our products, technology, and services into your course for optimal teaching and learning performance. Whether helping your students improve their grades, or putting your entire course online, the McGraw-Hill team is here to help you do it. Contact your Learning Solutions Consultant today to learn how to maximize all of McGraw-Hill's resources!

For more information on the latest technology and Learning Solutions offered by McGraw-Hill and its partners, please visit us online: **http://www. mcgrawhill.ca/he/solutions**.

ACKNOWLEDGEMENTS

As the "new kid on the block," this project was a huge learning curve for me. I am indebted to the team at McGraw-Hill Education—Karen Fozard, Portfolio and Program Manager; Sara Braithwaite, Product Manager; Stephanie Gibson, Supervising Editor; Marnie Lamb, Permissions Editor; Loula March, Product Developer; and Janice Dyer, Copy Editor. The professionalism of the McGraw-Hill Education team made my job so much easier. Thank you for your hard work and dedication to this project.

As well, a special thanks to the Retail Council of Canada and the CSCA for generously allowing the use of several excerpts and articles in this Fifth Canadian Edition.

Reviewers from across Canada provided support and recommendations throughout the development process. I would like to thank them for their invaluable feedback and guidance:

Patrick Charlton, *Algonquin College*
Drew Evans, *Red River College*
Seung Hwan (Mark) Lee, *Ryerson University*
Kathleen Leslie, *Centennial College*
Ken Kwong-Kay Wong, *Seneca College and University of Toronto*

Michael Madore

CHAPTER ONE

Introduction to the world of retailing

LEARNING OBJECTIVES

Lo1   Define retailing.

Lo2   Understand the role retailers play in the distribution channel and the functions they perform.

Lo3   Know the economic significance of retailing in Canada.

Lo4   Examine the various career and entrepreneurial opportunities retail offers.

Lo5   Discuss different types of decisions retail managers make.

Lo6   Understand the meaning of ethics and social responsibility and how they relate to the individual, retailer, and society.

SPOTLIGHT ON RETAILING

LUXURY EXPANDS INTO CANADA!

Regardless of the type of retail organization, growth is required to ensure longevity. Companies need to continue to build their brands and engage in expansion activities. Expansion is considered modification of place (location), a marketing mix element that is related to a firm's retail marketing strategy.

Who's Joining the Party?

Even as the sun sets on Target's expansion plans in Canada, other international retailers are eager to enter. Take Nordstrom, for instance, a retail giant in the US marketplace with over 320 stores. Nordstrom has decided to enter the retail market in Canada by opening stores in various strategic locations across Canada. Their initial rollout includes stores in Toronto, Vancouver, Calgary, and Ottawa.

Blake Nordstrom has indicated that "many Canadians are already familiar with the upscale department store chain, with 15 000 of them already holding a Nordstrom credit card." He says, "From what we know, it's pretty evident that your economy has been stronger and more robust [than the US]." Mr. Nordstrom adds that Canadians have fewer choices and less retail space than Americans do, with 50 percent less retail square footage per capita than the US.

And Nordstrom is not alone. Other US retailers, such as Jimmy Choo, Versace, and international retailer Ladurée, have also entered the Canadian marketplace. They have stores up and running in major metropolitan areas, including Toronto and Vancouver.

Why Canada?

The question you may be asking is why? With a much small population (a tenth of the US population), Canada doesn't seem like a "retail hotbed." Why would all these luxury retailers want to come to here?

"Some of the country's wealthy spend tens or hundreds of thousands of dollars annually on luxury goods and if they're not shopping at mono-brand designer boutiques, Holt Renfrew or Harry Rosen, they're buying online or travelling internationally," says Farla Efros, Executive Vice President and COO of HRC Advisory, a retail advisory firm based in Toronto and Chicago. Efros goes on to say, "Luxury retailers are increasingly recognizing Canada as a lucrative market, and are opening stores accordingly."

The burning question is, will this last? With a small affluent target segment in Canada, how many luxury brands can be established and maintained?

The catch is that not only are the affluent making these luxury purchases, the middle income class consumer is also desirous of these material goods. According to Ms. Efros, "there's a trend among many women, especially those in urban centres, to splurge on luxury footwear and handbags—even more than on pricey ready-to-wear."

The End Result?

Time and consumer debt loads will provide insight as to much many of these luxury brands will become established and be able to maintain a presence in our market. With median incomes actually on the decline (approximately 3 percent in Toronto and Vancouver), it seems this desire to move into a Canadian market may be questionable, with some luxury brands following a path similar to the fate of Target.

© Paul Mckinnon | Dreamstime.com.

Sources: http://business.financialpost.com/news/retail-marketing/nordstrom-opening-stores-in-toronto-ottawa-calgary-and-vancouver (accessed November 25, 2015); http://www.retail-insider.com/retail-insider/2014/9/peregrine (accessed November 25, 2015); http://www.retail-insider.com/retail-insider/2015/2/why-luxury (accessed November 25, 2015); http://www.macleans.ca/economy/whats-behind-canadas-newfound-lust-for-luxury/(accessed November 25, 2015).

Retailing is a global high-tech industry. Walmart is the world's largest corporation, with retail sales of $482.2 billion for the fiscal year 2015 and over 11 500 stores in 28 countries worldwide. French-based Carrefour, the world's second-largest retailer, operates 10 860 stores in 34 countries (but not in Canada or the United States). The largest retailer in Canada, Loblaws, with annual sales of $31.6 billion, has over 2300 corporate, franchised, and associated banner stores. It offers over 8000 private label products, is Canada's largest wholesale food distributor, and employs 192 000 full- and part-time employees.

Retailing in Canada is a vibrant industry, with total retail sales in 2014 of $505 billion. The retail sector is one of the largest employers nationally, employing almost two million Canadians. Success in retailing is about understanding and engaging your customers. Retailers use sophisticated technologies and information systems to improve their customers' shopping experience, reduce costs, and provide better value. Small local retailers such as Grassroots Environmental Products, a retailer of eco-friendly products with one store in Toronto and a full-service e-commerce site, offer customers the opportunity to shop in their store as well as online, thus expanding their market share. Customers today want to interact with retailers as they seek information and buy merchandise ranging from concert tickets to a new iPod, shopping through multiple channels, such as smartphones, tablets, computers, Web-enabled kiosks, telephone lines to call centres, and retail stores. In addition to selling merchandise, retailers use the Internet to build brand images, provide customer service, and manage their employees. Retailers such as Amazon.ca use advanced analytical techniques and data warehousing to customize approaches to online customers, suggesting books and products that might be of interest based on previous sales.

retailing A set of business activities that adds value to the products and services sold to consumers for their personal or family use.

To compete against non-store retailers, stores are becoming more than just places to buy products. They are offering entertaining and educational experiences to their customers. For example, Running Room operates 117 stores across Canada and the United States and connects to its customers with a Learn to Run program that offers advice to the novice runner. As well, Running Room produces a free magazine (currently published six times a year) to advise 200 000 customers of new products and community runs.[1] These features enhance customers' visual experiences, provide them with educational information, and enhance sales potential by enabling them to "try before they buy."

Retailing is such an integral part of our everyday lives that it's often taken for granted. Customers often aren't aware of the sophisticated business decisions retail managers make and the technologies they use to provide goods and services. Retail managers must make complex decisions in selecting target markets and retail locations, determining what merchandise and services to offer, negotiating with suppliers and distributing merchandise to stores, training and motivating sales associates, and deciding how to price, promote, and present merchandise. Considerable skill and knowledge are required to make these decisions effectively. Working in this highly competitive, rapidly changing environment is challenging and exciting, and offers significant financial rewards.

This book describes the world of retailing and provides principles for effectively managing businesses in this challenging environment. Knowledge of retailing principles and practices will help you develop management skills you can apply in many business contexts. For example, Procter & Gamble and Hewlett-Packard brand managers need to have a thorough understanding of how retailers operate and make money so that they can get their products on retail shelves and work with retailers to sell them to consumers. Financial and health care institutions use retail principles to develop a variety of services, improve customer service, and make their offerings available at convenient locations for their customers. Thus, any student interested in professional business-to-consumer (B2C) selling, marketing management, or finance will find this book useful.

Lo1 What Is Retailing?

Retailing is the set of business activities that add value to the products and services sold to consumers for their personal or family use. Often, people think of retailing only as the sale of products in stores. However, retailing also involves the sale of services: overnight lodging in a motel, a doctor's exam, a haircut, a movie rental, or a home-delivered pizza. Not all retailing is done in stores. Examples of non-store retailing are Internet

DID YOU KNOW?

68 percent. The percent of Canadians who owned a smartphone in 2015, up 13 percent from the previous year.[3]

sales of books and music, direct sales of cosmetics by Avon, catalogue sales by Canadian Tire, and DVD rentals through Redbox kiosks.

Lo2   A Retailer's Role in a Distribution Channel

A **retailer** is a business that sells products or services, or both, to consumers for their personal or family use. Retailers attempt to satisfy consumer needs by having the *right merchandise,* at the *right price,* at the *right place,* in the *right quantities,* and at the *right time* when the consumer wants it. Retailers also provide markets for producers to sell their merchandise. Retailers are the final business in a distribution channel that links manufacturers to consumers. A **distribution channel** is a set of firms that facilitate the movement of products from the point of production to the point of sale to the ultimate consumer. Exhibit 1–1 shows the retailer's position within a distribution channel.[2]

Manufacturers typically make products and sell them to retailers or wholesalers. When manufacturers such as Roots and Dell Computers sell directly to consumers, they are performing both the production and retailing business activities. Wholesalers, in contrast, engage in buying, taking title to, often storing, and physically handling goods in large quantities, then reselling the goods (usually in smaller quantities) to retailers or industrial or business users. Wholesalers and retailers may perform many of the same functions, but wholesalers uniquely satisfy retailers' needs, whereas retailers direct their efforts to satisfying the needs of ultimate consumers. Some retail chains, such as Rona, Loblaws, and Costco, function as both retailers and wholesalers. They are performing retailing activities when they sell to consumers and wholesaling activities when they sell to other businesses such as building contractors, independent grocers, or restaurant owners.

In some distribution channels, the manufacturing, wholesaling, and retailing activities are performed by independent firms, but most distribution channels feature some vertical integration.

Vertical integration means that a firm performs more than one set of activities in the channel, such as investments by retailers in wholesaling or manufacturing. *Backward integration* arises when a retailer performs some distribution and manufacturing activities, such as operating warehouses or designing private-label merchandise. *Forward integration* occurs when a manufacturer undertakes retailing activities, such as Roots operating its own retail stores.

Most large retailers—such as Walmart and Staples—engage in both wholesaling and retailing activities. They buy directly from manufacturers, have merchandise shipped to their warehouses for storage, and then distribute the merchandise to their stores. Other retailers, such as The Gap, Aritzia, Aldo, and Joe Fresh, are even more vertically integrated. They also design the merchandise they sell and then contract with manufacturers to produce it exclusively for them.

Functions Performed by Retailers

Why are retailers necessary? After all, wouldn't it be easier and cheaper to buy directly from those who produce the products? The answer is, generally no. Although there are situations where it is easier and cheaper to buy directly from manufacturers, such as at a farmers' market or from Dell Computer, retailers provide important functions that increase the value of the products and services they sell to consumers and facilitate the distribution of those products and services for those who produce them. These value-creating functions are:

- providing an assortment of products and services
- breaking bulk
- holding inventory
- providing service and services

retailer A business that sells products and services to consumers for their personal or family use.

distribution channel A set of firms that facilitate the movement of products from the point of production to the point of sale to the ultimate consumer.

vertical integration An example of diversification by retailers involving investments by retailers in wholesaling or manufacturing merchandise.

Exhibit 1–1
Example of a Distribution Channel

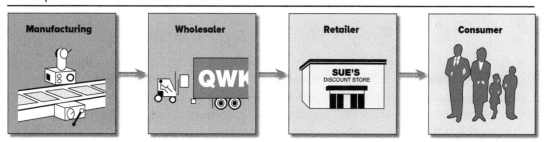

| Manufacturing | Wholesaler | Retailer | Consumer |

Providing Assortments Supermarkets typically carry 20 000 to 30 000 different items made by over 500 companies. Offering an assortment enables customers to choose from a wide selection of brands, designs, sizes, colours, and prices in one location. Manufacturers specialize in producing specific types of products. For example, Campbell makes soup, Kraft makes dairy products, Kellogg makes breakfast cereals, and McCormick makes spices. If each of these manufacturers had its own stores that sold only its own products, consumers would have to go to many different stores to buy groceries to prepare a single meal.

All retailers offer assortments of products, but they specialize in the assortments they offer. Supermarkets provide assortments of food, health and beauty care, and household products, whereas Club Monaco provides assortments of clothing and accessories. Most consumers are well aware of the product assortments retailers offer; even small children tend to know where to buy different types of products. But new types of retailers offering unique assortments appear each year. WineStyles is a wine store that arranges wine by taste category instead of region or type of wine, and provides extensive information to reduce the complexity of buying wines. Gold Grass Home sells a wide assortment of environmentally healthy products such as housewares, furniture and decor, and building supplies.

Breaking Bulk To reduce transportation costs, manufacturers and wholesalers typically ship cases of frozen dinners or cartons of shirts to retailers. Retailers then offer the products in smaller quantities tailored to the individual consumer's and household's consumption patterns. This is called **breaking bulk**. Breaking bulk is important to both manufacturers and consumers. It is cost-effective for manufacturers to package and ship merchandise in larger rather than smaller quantities. It is also easier for consumers to purchase merchandise in the smaller, more manageable quantities they prefer.

breaking bulk A function performed by retailers or wholesalers in which they receive large quantities of merchandise.

corporate social responsibility (CSR) Voluntary actions taken by a company to address the ethical, social, and environmental impacts of its business operations and the concerns of its stakeholders.

Holding Inventory A major function of retailers is to keep inventory that is already broken into user-friendly sizes so that products will be available when consumers want them. By maintaining an inventory, retailers provide a benefit to consumers—they reduce the consumer's cost of storing products. This function is particularly important to consumers with limited storage space and when purchasing perishable merchandise such as meat and produce.

Providing Service and Services Retailers provide services that make it easier for customers to buy and use products. They offer various methods of payment, including debit, direct, and credit payment, as well as various payment plans so that customers can have a product now and pay for it later, thus encouraging sales. Retailers display products so that consumers can see and test them before buying. Increasingly, retailers must have knowledgeable sales staff on hand to answer questions and provide information about products. Multichannel retailers offer flexibility to the customer by answering questions online and enabling buying any time, day or night.

By providing assortments, breaking bulk, holding inventory, and providing services, retailers increase the value consumers receive from their products and services. To illustrate, consider a closet door in a shipping crate in a manufacturer's warehouse. The door won't satisfy the needs of a do-it-yourselfer who wants to replace a closet door today. For the customer, a conveniently located home improvement centre such as Rona sells one door that is available when the customer wants it. The home improvement centre helps the customer select the door by displaying doors so that they can be examined before they are purchased. An employee is available to explain which door is best for closets and how the door should be hung. The centre has an assortment of hardware, paint, and tools that the customer will need for the job. Thus, retailers can increase the value of products and services bought by their customers.

Social and Economic Significance of Retailing
Social Responsibility

Most retailers try to be socially responsible. **Corporate social responsibility (CSR)** describes the voluntary actions taken by a company to address the ethical, social, and environmental impacts of its business operations and the concerns of its stakeholders.[4]

As corporate social responsibility continues to grow in popularity within the Canadian retail industry, more significance is being placed on the need for retailers to explain the impact of their business practices and to implement suitable strategies to seize the related opportunities.[5] Firms typically go through several stages before they fully integrate corporate social responsibility into their strategy. Companies in the first stage engage only in CSR activities required by law. In this stage, companies are not actually convinced of the importance of CSR actions. In the second stage, companies go beyond activities required by law to engage in CSR activities that provide a short-term financial benefit to the company. For example, a retailer might reduce the energy consumption of its stores just because doing so costs less. In the third stage, companies operate responsibly because they believe this is the "right thing" to do. Companies in the fourth and final stage engage in socially and environmentally responsible actions because they believe these activities must be done for the "well being" of everyone. These companies have truly incorporated the concept of CSR into their business strategy.[6] Retailing View 1.1 illustrates how retailers provide value to their communities and society, as well as to their customers.

DID YOU KNOW?

1 000 000 (and counting). The number of children who have participated in Canadian Tire's "Jumpstart" program since 2005.[7]

Lo3 Retail Sales in Canada

Retail is a driving force of Canada's economy and affects every facet of life. Just think of how much contact you have with retailers when you eat meals, furnish your apartment, have your car fixed, or buy clothing for a party or a job interview. In 2014, total retail sales in Canada amounted to $505 billion, up 4.6 percent from 2013 and 15.1 percent over a five-year period. Ontario (35 percent) and Quebec (21.4 percent) contributed the largest share of retail sales, followed by Alberta (15.6 percent) and British Columbia (13.1 percent). Canada's leading retailers tend to concentrate their operations in these four provinces as they include the country's largest cities.

Sales in the retail sector were dominated by the motor vehicle and parts sub-sector, which totalled $119.7 billion in sales in 2014, or 23.7 percent of market share, and the food and beverage stores sub-sector, which totalled $107.7 billion, or 21.9 percent of market share. Exhibit 1–2 shows a list of total sales by retail sub-sector in Canada for 2014.

Large retail chains dominate many segments in the Canadian market place. The top 100 retail organizations still control 75 percent of the non-automotive retail sales.[8] In 2014, there were a total of 30 organizations with at least one billion in total sales, and this "billion dollar club" (BDC) accounted for 88 percent, or $213 billion, of non-automotive retail sales in Canada for 2014. BDC retailers control a network of approximately

Exhibit 1–2
Retail Sales by Trade Group, Canada: 2014 (Unadjusted*)

Retail Trade Group	Sales 2013 ($ millions)	Sales 2014 ($ millions)	Annual Growth (%)	2014 Share of Sales
Motor Vehicle and Parts Dealers	111 751.9	119 729.7	6.7	23.7
Gasoline Stations	61 406.7	64 282.9	4.5	12.7
Furniture and Home Furnishings Stores	15 349.9	15 911.9	3.5	3.2
Electronics and Appliance Stores	14 656.2	14 848.6	1.3	2.9
Building Material and Garden Equipment and Supplies Dealers	26 993.7	27 036.1	0.2	5.8
Food and Beverage Stores	107 720.7	110 827.2	2.8	21.9
Health and Personal Care Stores	34 985.2	36 242.8	3.5	7.2
Clothing and Clothing Accessories Stores	169.4	28 095.4	3.3	5.6
General Merchandise Stores	58 593.2	58 794.7	0.4	12.5
Sporting Goods, Hobby, Book and Music Stores	10 844.5	11 455.0	5.3	2.3
Miscellaneous Store Retailers	11 607.8	11 608.4	0.0	2.3
Total Retail Sales (Unadjusted)	482 997.9	505 007.7	4.4	100.0

*Chart contains raw unadjusted data accessed November 2015.

Source: Statistics Canada. *Table 080-0020 Retail Sales, by Industry* (table). CANSIM (database). Reproduced and distributed on an "as is" basis with the permission of Statistics Canada.

Global Consumers are Willing to Put their Money Where Their Heart Is when It Comes to Goods and Services from Companies Committed to Social Responsibility

NEW YORK – June 17, 2014 – Fifty-five percent of global online consumers across 60 countries say they are willing to pay more for products and services provided by companies that are committed to positive social and environmental impact, according to a new study by Nielsen. The propensity to buy socially responsible brands is strongest in Asia-Pacific (64 percent), Latin America (63 percent), and Middle East/Africa (63 percent). The numbers for North America and Europe are 42 and 40 percent, respectively.

"Consumers around the world are saying loud and clear that a brand's social purpose is among the factors that influence purchase decisions," said Amy Fenton, global leader of public development and sustainability, Nielsen. "This behaviour is on the rise and it provides opportunities for meaningful impact in our communities, in addition to helping to grow share for brands."

The Nielsen Global Survey on Corporate Social Responsibility polled 30 000 consumers in 60 countries to understand: how passionate consumers are about sustainable practices when it comes to purchase considerations; which consumer segments are most supportive of ecological or other socially responsible efforts; and which social issues/causes are attracting the most concern.

More than half of global respondents (52 percent) say they have purchased at least one product or service in the past six months from a socially responsible company, with respondents in Latin America (65 percent), Asia-Pacific (59 percent), and Middle East/Africa (59 percent) exceeding the global average. Four in 10 respondents in North America and Europe say they have made a sustainable purchase in the past six months.

Sustainability and Corporate Social Responsibility Efforts Can Boost the Bottom Line Finding consumers around the world who say they care about the environment or extreme poverty is relatively easy. But does care about issues convert to action when it comes to buying decisions?

Some 52 percent of global respondents in Nielsen's survey say their purchase decisions are partly dependent on the packaging—they check the labelling first before buying to ensure the brand is committed to positive social and environmental impact. Sustainable purchase considerations are most influenced by the packaging in

18 322 stores and almost 420 000 square feet of retail store space. The BDC accounts for 88 percent of the Centre for the Study of Commercial Activity (CSCA) Retail 100 total sales, 66 percent of Canadian non-automotive total sales, and 48 percent of total retail sales in 2014 (see Exhibits 1–3, 1–4, and 1–5). In most countries, when the market concentration percentage for a particular industry or industry sub-sector reaches 40 percent, oligopolistic behaviour becomes likely in the marketplace.[9]

Exhibit 1–5 demonstrates that four of the nine retail sub-sectors have concentration ratio levels higher than 55 percent amongst the top three retailers in each sub-sector. This group of large retailers, identified by their relative dominance of Canadian retail market segments, includes Weston Group

(30.9 percent *health and personal care* and 29.82 percent *grocery*), Empire Company Limited (21.24 percent *grocery*), Walmart (44.12 percent *general merchandise*), and Costco Wholesale (30.04 percent *general merchandise*).[10]

The list of the top 100 leading retailers (Exhibit 1–6) shows that the top three retailers in Canada (Weston Group [Shoppers, The Real Canadian super Store], Walmart, and the Empire Company [Sobeys, IGA, and Safeway]) control almost 40 percent of the non-automotive retail market and have more than 4900 retail locations between them.

The Canadian retail market continues to evolve and change as foreign-owned retailers continue to increase their presence within the Canadian marketplace. In 2014, Canadian-controlled conglomerates accounted for 60.9 percent of the CSCA Retail sales

Asia-Pacific (63 percent), Latin America (62 percent), and Middle East/Africa (62 percent), and to a lesser extent in Europe (36 percent) and North America (32 percent).

To determine if the sentiments expressed by respondents are supported by actual retail performance, Nielsen also reviewed retail sales data for a cross-section of both consumable and non-consumable categories across 20 brands in nine countries. These brands either included sustainability claims on packaging or actively promoted their sustainability actions through marketing efforts. The results from a March 2014 year-over-year analysis show an average annual sales increase of two percent for products with sustainability claims on the packaging and a lift of five percent for products that promoted sustainability actions through marketing programs. A review of 14 other brands without sustainability claims or marketing shows a sales rise of only one percent.

The "Sustainable Mainstream"

In an effort to separate the passive eco-friendly consumer from the passionate, Natural Marketing Institute (NMI), a Nielsen strategic business collaborator, conducted a nine-country online study to understand how global attitudes and behaviours about sustainability engagement are changing. Consumers were clustered into five segments to quantify what attracts them to sustainability actions.

The findings reveal that two-thirds of the "sustainable mainstream" population (a cluster of three of the five segments) will choose products from sustainable sources over other conventional products. These consumers will buy as many eco-friendly products as they can and have personally changed their behavior to minimize their impact on global climate change. Additionally, these consumers are more likely to buy products repeatedly from a company if they know the company is mindful of its impact on the environment and society.

Millennials (age 21–34) appear more responsive to sustainability actions. Among global respondents in Nielsen's survey who are responsive to sustainability actions, half are Millennials; they represent 51 percent of those who will pay extra for sustainable products and 51 percent of those who check the packaging for sustainable labelling.

Regionally, there are wide gaps between younger and older respondents in the Asia-Pacific and Middle East/Africa regions. In these largely developing regions, Millennial respondents in favour of sustainability actions are three times more agreeable, on average, to sustainability actions than Generation X (age 35–49) respondents and 12 times more agreeable, on average, than Baby Boomer (age 50–64) respondents.

Said Fenton, "It's no longer a question if consumers care about social impact. Consumers do care and show they do through their actions. Now the focus is on determining how your brand can effectively create shared value by marrying the appropriate social cause and consumer segments."

Source: "Global Consumers Are Willing to Put Their Money Where Their Heart Is When It Comes to Goods and Services from Companies Committed to Social Responsibility," *Nielsen*, June 17, 2014, http://www.nielsen.com/ca/en/press-room/2014/global-consumers-are-willing-to-put-their-money-where-their-heart-is.html (accessed December 15, 2015). Copyright Nielsen.

in Canada.[11] American retailers account for 37.3 percent of retail sales by foreign retailers in Canada (see Exhibit 1–7).[12] The American presence is significant, as Exhibit 1–6 demonstrates. Nine out of the top 20 retailers (by sales) in Canada are American, with four of these companies being among the top ten retailers operating in the country. Notable US retailers that have expanded operations into Canada include Lowe's, Marshall's, Nordstrom, Jimmy Choo, and Versace, among others. The increased presence of foreign, especially US-based, retailers is expected to benefit Canadian consumers by providing important advantages, such as a wider variety of products, more convenient locations and

Exhibit 1–3

Comparison of Distribution of CSCA 100 Retail Sales (in $ billions): 2014 and the Rest of Canada (Adjusted)

CSCA - Retail Top 100 Profiles: Fiscal 2014			
Sector		**Sales (billions)**	
Non-Automotive (NA)	Top 30 CSCA retailers	213	88%
All Others (NA)	Remaining 70 CSCA retailers	29	12%
Total	**Top 100 CSCA retailers**	**242**	**100%**
2014 Canada Wide Retail Sales (including Automotive)			
Sector		**Sales (billions)**	
Total Retail Sales Canada		505	100%
Total CSCA Top 100 (NA)		242	47.8%
Remaining Retail Landscape		263	52.1%

Source: C. Daniel and T. Hernandez (2015) CSCA Retail 100, Centre for the Study of Commercial Activity, Ryerson University, Toronto, Canada; http://www.statcan.gc.ca/tables-tableaux/sum-som/l01/cst01/trad15a-eng.htm.

formats, and the potential for a more competitive pricing environment.

Exhibit 1–5 illustrates the profound impact US retailers have had on the Canadian retail landscape, as many of these retailers have captured significant market share of retail sales across many sub-sectors. Walmart and Costco cumulatively own approximately 74 percent of the general merchandise sector. Best Buy and Apple account for almost 40 percent of the electronics and appliances sector. However, as mentioned above, Canadian-based retailers still dominate the grocery (with 60.9 percent among Weston Group, Empire Company, and Metro) and pharmaceutical sectors (with 41.59 percent among Weston Group and Jean Coutu) of the Canadian retail industry.

Canadian retailers have yet to experience the same level of success with expansion into the United States and abroad. That being said, there are some great Canadian success stories, such as Couche Tard, Fruits & Passion, Aldo, Lululemon,

Exhibit 1–4
Retail Sales Distribution (in $ billions) (NAICS): 2014

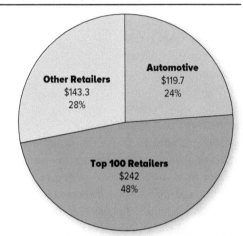

Source: C. Daniel and T. Hernandez (2015). CSCA Retail 100, Centre for the Study of Commercial Activity, Ryerson University, Toronto, Canada; http://www.statcan.gc.ca/tables-tableaux/sum-som/l01/cst01/trad15a-eng.htm.

Exhibit 1–5
Market Concentration (CR4) by NAICS: 2014, 2013

NAICS	Sector	2014 Sales (millions)	%	First	%	Second	%	Third	%	Fourth	CR4 2014 %	CR4 2013 %
442	Furniture and Home Furnishings	$15 912	14.75	Leon's furniture Ltd.	10.29	IKEA	4.40	Groupe BMTC Inc.	4.36	The TJX Companies, Inc.	33.80	32.39
443	Electronics and Appliance	$14 849	29.08	Best Buy Co. Inc.	10.80	Apple Inc.	3.43	GameStop Corp.	3.35	BCE Inc.	45.94	49.24
444	Home Improvement	$28 262	25.29	The Home Depot Inc.	19.46	Home Hardware Stores Ltd.	17.70	Rona Inc.	7.30	Tim-Br Marts Ltd.	69.76	71.73
445	Grocery	$110 827	29.82	Weston Group	21.24	Empire Company Limited	9.83	Metro Inc.	3.97	The Jim Pattison Group	64.86	61.75
446	Pharmacy and Personal Care	$36 243	30.09	Weston Group	13.47	McKesson Corporation	11.50	Le Groupe Jean Coutu (PJC) Inc.	9.41	Katz Group Inc.	64.49	65.23
448	Clothing and Accessory	$28 095	8.49	The TJX Companies Inc.	4.31	The Gap, Inc.	3.99	Canadian Tire Corp. Ltd.	3.71	YM Inc.	20.50	19.88
451	Hobby Stores	$11 455	16.63	Canadian Tire Corp. Ltd.	8.38	Toys "R" Us Inc.	7.81	Indigo Books & Music Inc.	4.80	OMERS Administration Corporation	37.62	36.65
452	General Merchandise	$63 744	44.12	Walmart Stores Inc.	30.04	Costco Wholesale Corp	9.83	Canadian Tire Corp. Ltd.	5.19	Sears Holdings Corporation	89.18	90.27
453	Miscellaneous	$11 608	24.79	Staples Inc.	3.86	Petsmart Inc.	2.84	Savers, Inc.	2.44	Roark Capital Group	33.93	33.99

Source: C. Daniel and T. Hernandez (2015) CSCA Retail100, Centre for the Study of Commercial Activity, Ryerson University, Toronto, Canada.

Exhibit 1–6

The CSCA Retail 100 Profiles, 2014

Rank	Rank Change	Corporate Ownership	Selected Banners	Capital Control	Retail Sales ($ Millions)	Cum % Sales	No of Chains	Footage Sq ft (000s)	Employees Total No	No of Stores	Activity (NAICS)	Sales Growth
1	0	Weston Group	Shoppers Drug Mart, The Real Canadian Superstore, No Frills	CAN	44,460	13.85%	34	66,645	1,94,973	2,746	445, 446, 448	37.35
2	0	Wal-Mart Stores, Inc.	Wal-Mart Supercenters, Wal-Mart	USA	28,122	22.61%	2	56,815	94,000	389	452	3.71
3	0	Empire Company Limited	IGA, Sobeys, Safeway	CAN	23,929	30.07%	19	38,808	1,20,309	1,864	445, 446	34.74
4	0	Costco Wholesale Corp	Costco	USA	19,149	36.03%	1	12,100	24,759	88	452	9.85
5	0	Metro Inc.	Metro, Food Basics, Super C	CAN	11,590	39.64%	12	21,489	65,000	979	445, 446	1.65
6	1	Canadian Tire Corporation Limited	Canadian Tire, Mark's Work Wearhouse, Sport Chek	CAN	9,296	42.54%	13	31,106	85,000	1,327	448, 451, 452	7.67
7	1	The Home Depot, Inc.	The Home Depot	USA	7,148	44.77%	1	19,005	29,592	181	444	5.06
8	2	Home Hardware Stores Limited	Home Hardware, Home Building Centre	CAN	5,700	46.54%	4	10,915	18,556	1,082	442, 444	5.56
9	2	Rona Inc.	Rona, Rona Home & Garden, Rona Warehouse/ L'Entrepot	CAN	5,314	48.20%	13	15,645	24,000	873	444, 452, 453	-0.8
10	3	McKesson Corporation	IDA Pharmacy, HealthCare Pharmacy, Proxim	USA	4,882	49.72%	6	4,987	13,548	1,398	446	3.14
11	5	The Jim Pattison Group	Save On Foods & Drugs, AG Foods, Overwaitea Foods	CAN	4,401	51.09%	11	7,236	21,135	220	445	17.85
12	0	Best Buy Co., Inc.	Future Shop, Best Buy, Best Buy Mobile	USA	4,319	52.43%	3	5,802	15,051	260	443	-9.33
13	2	Le Groupe Jean Coutu (PJC) Inc.	Jean Coutu Pharmacy, PJC Clinic/Clinique, PJC Sante Beaute	CAN	4,175	53.73%	3	3,203	21,237	415	446	2.83
14	0	Sears Holdings Corporation	Sears Store, Sears Whole Home Furniture, Sears Outlet Store	USA	3,695	54.89%	6	18,575	21,919	404	442, 443, 452	-11.51
15	2	Katz Group Inc.	Rexall Pharma Plus, Rexall Drug Store	CAN	3,410	55.95%	2	3,310	5,506	455	446	9.85
16	3	The TJX Companies, Inc.	Winners, HomeSense, Marshalls	USA	3,078	56.91%	3	10,230	20,820	368	442, 448	5.89
17	3	Pharmasave Drugs (National) Ltd.	Pharmasave	CAN	2,975	57.83%	1	3,190	5,901	493	446	5.57
18	0	Staples Inc.	Staples	USA	2,878	58.73%	1	8,159	13,623	315	453	-2.84
19	2	NRDC Equity Partners	Hudson's Bay, Home Outfitters, Zellers	USA	2,810	59.61%	4	18,863	25,822	162	442, 452	3.11
20	2	HY Louie Group	London Drugs, MarketPlace IGA, Fresh St. Market	CAN	2,752	60.46%	3	3,521	9,413	115	445, 446	2.2
21	5	Leon's Furniture Ltd.	The Brick, Leon's Furniture, United Furniture Warehouse	CAN	2,348	61.19%	7	14,246	13,951	306	442	15.15
22	3	Dollarama Inc.	Dollarama	CAN	2,331	61.92%	1	9,464	18,400	955	452	12.89
23	1	Uniprix Inc	Uniprix, Clinique Sante, Unipharm	CAN	2,159	62.59%	4	1,948	4,347	367	446	-12.81
24	-1	Tim-Br Marts Ltd.	Tim-Br Mart, BMR, IRLY Building Centres	CAN	2,064	63.24%	5	4,801	11,676	547	444	-21.75
25	5	Target Corporation	Target	USA	2,030	63.87%	1	14,607	17,600	133	452	N.A.
26	1	Alimentation Couche-Tard Inc.	Mac's, Couche-Tard, Daisy Mart	CAN	1,808	64.43%	5	3,344	14,077	1,513	445	-2.19
27	1	Ikea	Ikea	SWE	1,637	64.94%	1	3,240	3,888	12	442	3.81
28	1	Apple Inc.	Apple Store	USA	1,497	65.41%	1	203	3,066	29	443	1.8
29	2	Lowe's Companies Inc.	Lowe's	USA	1,463	65.86%	1	4,903	5,365	37	444	15.23
30	2	The Gap, Inc.	Old Navy, Gap, Banana Republic	USA	1,210	66.24%	7	3,063	11,336	289	448	6.5
31	3	Familiprix Inc.	Familiprix Extra, Familiprix Pharmacy, Familiprix Clinique	CAN	973	66.54%	3	1,460	4,457	312	446	4.83
32	3	Toys 'R' Us Inc.	Toys 'R' Us, Toys 'R' Us Express, Wonderlab	USA	960	66.84%	3	3,025	4,177	95	451	3.51
33	0	The Reitman Group	Reitmans, Penningtons, Addition-Elle	CAN	939	67.14%	9	3,885	8,899	823	448	-2.19
34	2	YM Inc.	Urban Planet, Suzy Shier, Bluenotes	CAN	898	67.42%	12	2,740	6,685	543	448	-0.4
35	3	International Clothiers Inc.	Stockhomme, Fairweather, International Clothiers	CAN	898	67.69%	15	1,918	2,966	249	448, 452	3.65
36	1	Indigo Books & Music Inc.	Chapters, Indigo Books & Music, Coles The Book People	CAN	895	67.97%	6	2,541	6,346	225	451	3.2
37	2	Seven-Eleven Japan Co. Ltd.	7-Eleven Food Stores	JPN	820	68.23%	1	1,062	5,693	494	445	5.67
38	2	Groupe BMTC Inc.	Brault & Martineau, Tanguay Ameublements, EconoMax	CAN	701	68.45%	6	1,863	2,214	45	442	0.95
39	3	Calgary Co-operative Association Ltd.	Calgary Co-op	CAN	644	68.65%	1	1,272	3,700	24	445	4.51
40	1	The North West Company Inc.	Northern Stores, Northmart	CAN	643	68.85%	2	806	2,792	127	445	-3.98
41	5	L Brands, Inc.	La Senza, Bath & Body Works, Victoria's Secret	USA	639	69.05%	5	981	6,809	278	446, 448	13.79
42	5	Bulk Barn Foods Limited	Bulk Barn	CAN	618	69.24%	1	1,016	1,525	231	445	12.18
43	0	Longo Brothers Fruit Markets Inc.	Longo's	CAN	607	69.43%	1	998	3,382	26	445	-1.33
44	0	The ALDO Group Inc.	Globo Shoes, Aldo, Spring	CAN	570	69.61%	10	1,004	4,309	384	448	-6.92
45	3	L'Aubainerie	L'Aubainerie Concept Mode, L'Aubainerie Entrepot	CAN	567	69.78%	2	1,462	4,343	58	448	3.15
46	-1	Giant Tiger Stores Ltd.	Giant Tiger	CAN	557	69.96%	1	5,259	6,521	198	452	-3.61
47	2	OMERS Administration Corporation	Golf Town	CAN	549	70.13%	1	1,036	2,456	57	451	5.2
48	2	J.D. Irving Ltd.	Kent Building Supplies	CAN	538	70.30%	1	1,968	984	41	444	5.27
49	6	Bain Capital Partners	Michaels, Gymboree	USA	527	70.46%	2	2,211	5,199	166	448, 451	10.51
50	2	Castle Building Centres Group Ltd.	Castle Building Centres	CAN	522	70.62%	1	2,607	4,693	273	444	3.94
51	5	GameStop Corp.	EB Games, GameStop	USA	508	70.78%	2	507	2,648	331	443	7.38
52	-1	BCE Inc.	The Source	CAN	497	70.94%	1	854	2,460	657	443	-2.61
53	0	M & M Meat Shops Ltd	M & M Meat Shops	CAN	484	71.09%	1	560	2,402	400	445	-1.71
54	3	Lululemon Athletica Inc.	Lululemon, ivivva athletica	CAN	464	71.23%	2	180	2,822	61	448	1.04
55	3	Visions Electronics	Visions Electronic	CAN	454	71.37%	1	480	1,483	32	443	-0.39
56	-2	Arden Holdings Inc.	Ardene	CAN	454	71.51%	1	1,169	3,471	403	448	-7.08
57	3	Petsmart Inc.	PetSmart	USA	448	71.65%	1	1,598	2,972	94	453	10.94
58	1	H & M Hennes & Mauritz AB	H & M	SWE	447	71.79%	1	1,235	1,264	72	448	9.8
59	3	Laura Canada Inc.	Laura, Laura Petites, Melanie Lyne	CAN	438	71.93%	5	1,545	6,221	296	448	18.55
60	5	Sleep Country Canada Holdings Inc.	Sleep Country Canada, Dormez - Vous	CAN	396	72.05%	2	1,078	1,121	210	442	11.92
61	2	Trivestment Holdings Limited	Fabricland/Fabricville	CAN	371	72.17%	1	1,240	3,311	124	451	2.72
62	-1	Golden Gate Capital	Payless ShoeSource, Eddie Bauer	USA	370	72.28%	2	1,088	2,212	304	448	-3.84
63	15	Bed Bath & Beyond Inc.	Bed Bath & Beyond	USA	360	72.40%	1	1,223	1,705	44	442	18.87
64	3	Groupe Dynomite	Garage, Dynamite, Garage Outlet	CAN	343	72.50%	3	883	2,623	254	448	4.53
65	12	Whole Foods Market, Inc.	Whole Foods	USA	338	72.61%	1	342	1,968	9	445	11.03
66	4	Mountain Equipment Co-operative	Mountain Equipment Co-op	CAN	336	72.71%	1	441	1,936	18	451	4.72
67	-1	The B&C Group	Bowring, The Bombay Company, Benix & Co. Stores	CAN	335	72.82%	4	743	1,252	129	442	-3.69
68	1	Gestion Francois Roberge Inc	La Vie En Rose, La Vie En Rose Outlet, La Vie en Rose Aqua	CAN	335	72.92%	4	863	2,562	207	448	4.23
69	5	Savers, Inc.	Value Village/Village Valeurs	USA	330	73.02%	1	3,250	5,525	130	453	7.27
70	-2	The Men's Wearhouse, Inc.	Moores	USA	328	73.13%	1	775	2,007	123	448	1.75
71	1	Town Shoes Ltd.	The Shoe Company, Shoe Warehouse Store, Town Shoes	CAN	322	73.23%	4	831	2,466	193	448	2.69
72	7	Gordon Brothers Group	Tip Top, George Richards Mr Big & Tall, Mr. Big 'N Tall	USA	319	73.33%	4	767	2,423	184	448, 453	5.56
73	2	LVMH MoÙt Hennessy Louis Vuitton SA	Sephora, Louis Vuitton	FRA	315	73.42%	2	250	905	52	446, 448	2.93
74	-1	Foot Locker, Inc.	Foot Locker, Champs Sports	USA	308	73.52%	2	520	1,768	156	448	-1.54
75	-4	Signet Jewelers Limited	Peoples Jewellers, Mappins Jewellers	GBR	307	73.62%	2	306	1,464	190	448	-4.06
76	14	Dollar Tree, INC.	Dollar Tree	USA	302	73.71%	1	1,915	2,957	210	452	21.7
77	3	La Maison Simons	Simons	CAN	295	73.80%	1	618	1,131	9	452	-1.67
78	5	Roark Capital Group	Pet Valu, Paulmac's Pet Food	USA	283	73.89%	2	804	2,638	377	453	3.96
79	-3	Hilco UK	HMV Canada	GBR	280	73.98%	1	494	1,915	105	443	-8.72
80	6	American Eagle Outfitters, Inc.	American Eagle Outfitters, Aerie, American Eagle Outlet	USA	278	74.06%	3	525	3,152	96	448	4.47
81	-17	Apax Partners LLP	Ricki's, Bootlegger, Cleo	USA	275	74.15%	5	1,463	3,433	345	442, 448	-23.07
82	-1	Genuity Capital Markets	The Bargain! Shop, Red Apple Clearance Centre	CAN	270	74.23%	2	1,970	1,778	165	448, 452	-3.15
83	4	Boutique Marie Claire Inc	Mode Le Grenier, Boutique Marie Claire, Claire France	CAN	262	74.32%	8	974	2,708	319	448	-1.06
84	5	Sports Distributors of Canada Limited	Source For Sports	CAN	260	74.40%	1	869	2,320	158	451	4.54
85	-1	Roots Canada Ltd.	Roots 73 Outlet Store, Roots, Roots Kids	CAN	258	74.48%	4	446	988	110	442, 448	-3.5
86	-1	Guess?, Inc.	Guess, Guess Factory Store, Guess by Marciano	USA	254	74.56%	4	519	2,333	117	448	-4.61
87	9	Inditex Group	Zara, Massimo Dutti, Zara Home	SPN	252	74.63%	3	379	1,381	33	442, 448	22.37
88	3	The Children's Place Retail Stores, Inc.	The Children's Place, The Children's Place Outlet	USA	248	74.71%	2	669	1,954	134	448	3.46
89	3	JYSK A/S	JYSK Linen 'n' Furniture	DEN	244	74.79%	1	1,215	1,580	54	442	7.81
90	-8	Le Chateau Inc.	Le Chateau, Le Chateau Outlet	CAN	238	74.86%	2	1,215	2,488	221	448	-13.14
91	2	Nygard Enterprises Ltd	Tan Jay, Alia, Nygard Store	CAN	232	74.93%	6	557	2,557	240	448	3.17
92	N.A.	Cabela's Incorporated	Cabela's	USA	231	75.01%	1	410	1,147	7	451	56.4
93	N.A.	Bass Pro Inc	Bass Pro Shops	USA	226	75.08%	1	390	507	3	451	57.8
94	1	The Gores Group	Mexx, Mexx Kids, Mexx Outlet	USA	217	75.14%	3	558	1,658	113	448	2.78
95	-1	Bouclair Inc.	BouClair Home	CAN	215	75.21%	1	1,069	1,390	108	442	0.11
96	4	Sally Beauty Holdings, Inc.	Cosmo Prof, Sally Beauty Supply	USA	208	75.28%	2	427	1,320	199	446	13.75
97	N.A.	Farm Boy Inc.	Farm Boy	CAN	207	75.34%	1	338	1,025	15	445	9.81
98	1	Ashley Furniture Industries Inc.	Ashley Furniture Homestore	USA	206	75.40%	1	1,024	1,331	32	442	10.73
99	-2	Bentley Leathers Inc.	Bentley Leathers, Access Luggage, Unic	CAN	201	75.47%	8	518	1,541	390	448	-2.08
100	N.A	TSC Stores Ltd.	TSC Stores	CAN	200	75.53%	1	1,000	1,050	50	444	11.26

Source: C. Daniel and T. Hernandez (2015) CSCA Retail100, Centre for the Study of Commercial Activity, Ryerson University, Toronto, Canada.

Exhibit 1–7
Market Control by Origin of Capital, 2014
(in $ billions)

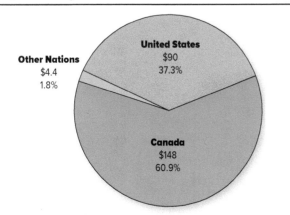

Other Nations
$4.4
1.8%

United States
$90
37.3%

Canada
$148
60.9%

Source: C. Daniel and T. Hernandez (2015) CSCA Retail 100, Centre for the Study of Commercial Activity, Ryerson University, Toronto, Canada.

Joe Fresh, and Aritzia. These companies have successfully expanded globally through a mix of corporate and franchise stores. Joe Fresh is a stand-out: in 2012 they signed a deal with JCPenney to open 700 shops within 1100 of its locations in the United States.[13]

Global Retailers

Retailing is becoming a global industry, as more and more retailers pursue growth by expanding their operations to other countries. The large retail firms are becoming increasingly international in the geographical scope of their operations. For example, Amway, Avon, Ace Hardware, and Inditex (Zara) operate in more than 20 countries. The share of the global retail market accounted for by retailers operating in more than one country is also increasing because these global retailers are growing at an even faster rate than are global retail sales. International operations account for a larger proportion of sales by these large firms, as is particularly apparent in European firms with their longer internationalization experience. The percentage of retail revenue generated from global operations for the top ten global retailers is approximately 29.7 percent of the overall global retail revenue. As a group, the top ten have a much larger geographic footprint than the top 250 overall. The average revenue derived from foreign operations for the big ten is approximately 32.5 percent of their overall income. Exhibit 7–5 (in Chapter 7) lists the ten largest global retailers along with Canada's top entries in

the top 250 as published by Deloitte. (To see the entire list, go to http://www2.deloitte.com/content/dam/Deloitte/global/Documents/Consumer-Business/gx-cb-global-powers-of-retailing.pdf) These large retailers operate in 16.5 countries, on average, nearly twice as many as the average for the entire group (nine countries).[14] In 2011, for the first time, the share of North American top 250 retailers that remained single-country operators fell to less than half.

With worldwide retail revenue estimated at $4.4 trillion, the ten largest global retailers represent a 29.7 percent share of the world market.[15] The average size of the top 250 global retailers in 2015, as measured by retail revenue, topped $17.4 billion. The threshold to join the top 250 in 2013 was $3.7 billion. Canada has nine retailers that broke that threshold: Loblaw ($30.7 billion), Empire Company ($19.8 billion), Metro Inc. ($11.2 billion), Shoppers Drug Mart ($10.7 billion), Canadian Tire Corporation ($10.4 billion), Hudson's Bay Company ($5.0 billion), RONA Inc. ($4.0 billion), LCBO ($3.8 billion), and Overwaitea Food Group ($3.7 billion).

DID YOU KNOW?

The acronym IKEA is made up of the initials of the founder's name (Ingvar Kamprad) plus those of Elmtaryd, his family farm, and the nearby village of Agunnard.[17]

Of the top global retailers, 31.6 percent are headquartered in the United States, 36 percent in Europe, 12.4 percent in Japan, and 3.6 percent in Canada.[16] Walmart remains the undisputed leader in the retail world, with sales more than three times as great as those of Costco Wholesale Corporation, the second-largest retailer, and accounting for more than 10 percent of the total top 250 retailers' worldwide revenue.

LO4 Opportunities in Retailing

Management Opportunities

To cope with a highly competitive and challenging environment, retailers are hiring and promoting people with a wide range of skills and interests. Students often view retailing as part of marketing because management of distribution channels is part of a manufacturer's marketing function. Retailers undertake most of the traditional business activities: raising capital from financial institutions; purchasing goods and services; developing accounting and management information systems to control operations; managing warehouses and distribution systems; designing and developing new products; and undertaking marketing activities such as advertising, promotions, sales force management, and market research. Thus, retailers employ people with expertise and interest in finance, accounting, human resources management, logistics, and computer systems, as well as marketing.

Retail managers often are given considerable responsibility early in their careers. Retail management is also financially rewarding. After completing a management training program in retailing, managers can increase their starting salary in three to five years if they perform well. Aspects of retail careers are discussed in Appendix 1A, available on Connect.

Entrepreneurial Opportunities

Retailing also provides opportunities for people wishing to start their own businesses. Some of the most successful people are retail entrepreneurs, such as Canada's John Forzani. Some are household names because their names appear over the stores' doors; these include Tim Horton (Tim Hortons), Eddie Black (Black's Cameras), and John Holt and G.R. Renfrew (Holt Renfrew). Some other innovative retail entrepreneurs include John Stanton, John Forzani, Jeff Bezos, and Ingvar Kamprad. Retailing View 1.2 examines the importance of the Retail Council of Canada and its effect on career opportunities in retailing.

Lo5 The Retail Management Decision Process

Understanding the World of Retailing

The first step in the retail management decision-making process is understanding the world of retailing. Retail managers need to understand their environment, especially their customers and competition, before they can develop and implement effective strategies. The first section of this book provides a general overview of the retailing industry and its customers.

The critical environmental factors in the world of retailing are the macro-environment and the micro-environment. The impacts of the macro-environment—including technological, social, and ethical/legal/political factors on retailing—are discussed throughout the book. Successful retailers will react to changes in the macro-environment. Huge technological changes in the macro-environment are having a significant impact on retailers, enabling database marketing to provide information about consumers, the Internet to connect to customers, and radio-frequency identification (RFID) technology to increase retail efficiencies. The retailer's micro-environment focuses specifically on its competitors and customers.

Competitors At first glance, identifying competitors appears easy. A retailer's primary competitors are those with the same format. Thus, department stores compete against other department stores and supermarkets against other supermarkets. This competition between retailers of the same type is called **intratype competition**.

To appeal to a broader group of consumers and provide one-stop shopping, many retailers are increasing their variety of merchandise. **Variety** is the number of different merchandise categories within a store or department. By offering greater variety in one store, retailers can offer one-stop shopping to satisfy more of the needs of their target market. For example, clothing and food are now available in grocery, department, and discount stores and drugstores. Fast food is available at McDonald's and convenience stores. The offering of merchandise not typically associated with the store type, such as clothing in a drugstore, is called **scrambled merchandising**. Scrambled merchandising increases **intertype competition**—competition between retailers that sell similar merchandise using different formats, such as discount and department stores.

Increasingly, intertype competition has made it harder for retailers to identify and monitor their competition. In one sense, all retailers compete against each other for the dollars consumers spend on goods and services. But the intensity of competition is greatest among retailers located close together with retail offerings that are viewed as very similar, such as in a shopping mall.

intratype competition Competition between retailers of the same type (e.g., Loblaws versus Sobeys).

variety The number of different merchandise categories within a store or department; also called *breadth*.

scrambled merchandising The offering of merchandise not typically associated with the store type, such as clothing in a drugstore.

intertype competition Competition between retailers that sell similar merchandise using different formats, such as discount and department stores.

Retail Council of Canada

Since 1963, the Retail Council of Canada (RCC) has been the voice of retail in Canada. RCC is an industry-funded, not-for-profit association that represents more than 40 000 members across the country. The association provides support to merchants, vendors, and suppliers so that they in turn are able to meet the challenges of offering goods and services to consumers in a competitive marketplace.

RCC members become a part of a national network of retailers, participate in money-saving benefit programs, access industry research and information, and make their collective voices heard through government lobbying. The RCC also provides members with a full range of services and programs, including education and training, benchmarking, best practices, and networking.

The RCC works with all levels of government and other stakeholders as a strong advocate for retailing in Canada. The organization supports career opportunities and employment growth in retail, improves consumer choice and industry competitiveness, and supports and sustains retail investments in Canadian communities from coast to coast.

The retail agenda is put on the radar screens of Canada's policy-makers at the federal and provincial levels by RCC's Government Relations Team. The team has been a united voice for retail in Canada since the RCC was called upon to represent retailers' interests in the 1960s, when credit cards were first introduced into retail operations. That early success led to other policy challenges, including the introduction of UPC codes and bilingual packaging requirements in the 1970s; negotiations of the General Agreement on Tariffs and Trade and the North American Free Trade Agreement in the 1980s; the introduction of the goods and services tax, debit cards, and e-commerce in the 1990s; and gift card, environmental, and consumer privacy legislation in the 2000s. The agenda going forward includes a variety of topics including, but not limited to, issues relating to taxation, human resources training, employment and labour relations, international trade, environmental protection, and market practices.

Retailers recognize the growing importance of employing skilled people at every level of their organizations. In response, the RCC has a team that oversees training and certification programs through the Canadian Retail Institute. As a division of the RCC, the Canadian Retail Institute promotes retail as a rewarding career through educational programs, scholarships, and partnerships with post-secondary institutions offering retail programs across the country. They focus their efforts on strengthening the industry by encouraging retail education, increasing career awareness, and advancing professional designation programs such as First Level Manager Certification and Retail Sales Associate Certification.

In partnership with industry sponsors, RCC awards more than $80 000 in scholarships and benefits to students entering or currently enrolled in a business, marketing, or retail-related program at a Canadian post-secondary institution. Students who receive the scholarships not only benefit from the financial assistance for their post-secondary education, but also are invited to attend the annual STORE conference in Toronto. This gives the winners the opportunity to network with the brightest retail professionals in the Canadian retail industry. For more information about these retail scholarships, go to http://www.retaileducation.ca.

In today's competitive environment, it is fundamental that retailers are able to tap into key trends and developments and access information in a variety of formats. The RCC's Communications team publishes the country's retail magazine, *Canadian Retailer*, as well as industry newsletters in electronic format. Additionally, RCC's website is a gateway to Canada's retail world, offering white papers, current events, retail statistics, and a plethora of other relevant retail information.

Source: Retail Council of Canada.

Management's view of competition may differ depending on the manager's position within the retail firm. For example, the manager of Hudson's Bay's women's sportswear department in Toronto views the other women's sportswear specialty stores in Yorkdale Mall as her major mall competitors. But the store manager for Hudson's Bay views the Holt Renfrew store in the mall as her strongest competitor. These differences in perspective arise because the department sales manager is primarily concerned with customers for a specific category of merchandise, whereas the

DID YOU KNOW?

Leon's Furniture was founded in 1909. It was named Distinguished Canadian Retailer of the Year by the Retail Council of Canada for 2015. It supports the Boys & Girls Clubs of Canada.[18,19]

store manager is concerned with customers seeking the entire selection of all merchandise and services offered by a department store. The CEO of a retail chain, in contrast, views competition from a much broader geographic perspective. For example, Shoppers Drug Mart might identify its strongest competitor as London Drugs in the west, the Katz Group (Rexall, Pharma Plus) in central Canada, and Jean Coutu in Quebec. The CEO may also take a broader strategic perspective and recognize that other activities compete for consumers' disposable income. For example, Loblaw's CEO adopts the consumer's perspective and recognizes that grocery stores are competing with drugstores, convenience stores, and restaurants for customers' food dollars.

Retailing is intensely competitive. Understanding the different types of retailers and how they compete with each other is critical to developing and implementing a retail strategy.

Customers The second factor in the micro-environment is customers. Customer needs are changing at an ever-increasing rate. Retailers are responding to broad demographic and lifestyle trends in our society, such as the growth in the elderly and minority segments of the Canadian population and the increasing importance of shopping convenience to the rising number of two-income families. To develop and implement an effective strategy, retailers need to understand why customers shop, how they select a store, and how they select among that store's merchandise.

McGraw-Hill Education.

Developing a Retail Strategy

The next stages in the retail management decision-making process, formulating and implementing a retail strategy, are based on an understanding of the macro- and micro-environments. Section 2 in this book focuses on decisions related to developing a retail strategy.

The **retail strategy** indicates how the firm plans to focus its resources to accomplish its objectives. It identifies:

- the target market, or markets, toward which the retailer will direct its efforts

- the nature of the merchandise and/or services the retailer will offer to satisfy needs of the target market

- how the retailer will build a long-term advantage over competitors

The nature of a retail strategy can be illustrated by comparing strategies of Walmart and Toys "R" Us. Walmart offers name-brand merchandise at low prices in a broad array of categories, ranging from laundry detergent to girls' dresses. Although Walmart stores have many different categories of merchandise, selection in each

retail strategy A statement that indicates (1) the target market toward which a retailer plans to commit its resources, (2) the nature of the retail offering that the retailer plans to use to satisfy the needs of the target market, and (3) the bases upon which the retailer will attempt to build a sustainable competitive advantage over competitors.

category is limited. A store might have only three brands of detergents in two sizes, while a supermarket carries eight brands in five sizes.

In contrast, Toys "R" Us identifies its target as consumers living in suburban areas of large cities. Rather than carrying a broad array of merchandise categories, Toys "R" Us stores specialize in toys, games, bicycles, and furniture for children. Although Toys "R" Us has limited categories of merchandise, it has almost all the different types and brands of toys and games currently available in the market.

Both Walmart and Toys "R" Us emphasize self-service. Customers select their merchandise, bring it to the checkout line, and then carry it to their cars. Customers may even assemble the merchandise at home.

Since Walmart and Toys "R" Us emphasize competitive prices, they have made strategic decisions to develop a cost advantage over competitors. Both firms have sophisticated distribution and management information systems to manage inventory. Their strong relationships with suppliers enable them to buy merchandise at low prices.

Strategic Decision Areas   The key strategic decision areas for a retailer involve determining a market strategy, a financial strategy, a location strategy, organizational structure and human resources strategies, information systems and supply chain strategies, and customer relationship management strategies.

The selection of a retail *market strategy* is based on analyzing the environment and the firm's strengths and weaknesses. When major environmental changes occur, the current strategy and the reasoning behind it are re-examined. The retailer then decides what, if any, strategy changes are needed to take advantage of new opportunities or avoid new threats in the environment.

The retailer's market strategy must be consistent with the firm's *financial objectives*. Financial variables such as sales, costs, expenses, profits, assets, liabilities, and owner's equity are used to evaluate the market strategy and its implementation.

Decisions regarding *location strategy* are important for both consumer and competitive reasons. First, location is typically consumers' top consideration when selecting a store. Generally, consumers buy gas at the closest service station and patronize the shopping mall that's most convenient to their home or office. Second, location offers an opportunity to gain long-term advantage over competition. When a retailer has the best location, a competing retailer has to settle for the second-best location.

DID YOU KNOW?

One plastic bag can take up to 500 years to decay in a landfill.[20]

A retailer's *organization design and human resources management strategies* are intimately related to its market strategy. For example, retailers that attempt to serve national or regional markets must make trade-offs between the efficiency of centralized buying and the need to tailor merchandise and services to local needs. Retailers that focus on customer segments seeking high-quality customer service must motivate and enable sales associates to provide the expected levels of service. The organization structure and human resources policies coordinate the implementation of the retailing strategy by buyers, store managers, and sales associates.

Retail information and supply chain management systems will offer a significant opportunity for retailers to gain strategic advantage in the coming decade. Retailers are developing sophisticated computer and distribution systems to monitor flows of information and merchandise from vendors to retail distribution centres to retail stores. Point-of-sale (POS) terminals read price and product information that is coded into Universal Product Codes (UPCs) affixed to the merchandise. This information is then transmitted to distribution centres or directly to vendors electronically, computer to computer. These technologies are part of an overall inventory management system that enables retailers:

- to give customers a more complete selection of merchandise
- to increase awareness of inventory levels
- to decrease inventory investment

Basic to any strategy is understanding the customers in order to provide them with the goods and services they want. And even more important is to understand and cater to the wants of the retailer's most-valued customers. After all, these customers account for the major share of a retailer's sales and profits. **Customer relationship management (CRM)** is a business philosophy and set of strategies, programs, and systems that focus on identifying and building loyalty with a firm's most-valued

customer relationship management (CRM) A business philosophy and set of strategies, programs, and systems that focuses on identifying and building loyalty with a retailer's most valued customers.

Exhibit 1–8
Elements in the Retail Mix

Element	Description	Detail
Product	Intensity, assortment	Types of merchandise/services offered
Place	Movement, flow of goods, distribution channels	Length of channels, hybrid channel approaches, types of distribution channels
Physical	Atmosphere, climate	Theme of the store, emotional attachment customer derives from the store, layout, design; measure of what it is like to shop in the store
Price	Quality, value, price	Value perception
People	Knowledge, service	Product knowledge and policies; getting customers in and out efficiently
Promotion	Promotional communication mix	Public relations, sales promotion, advertising, direct marketing, personal selling
Process	Standards, protocols, variability	Ensure consistent behaviours and performance; includes internal and external processes

customers. Retailers use data analysis to identify their most-valued customers. Once they have identified these customers, retailers design special programs to build their loyalty.

Implementing the Retail Strategy

To implement a retail strategy, management develops a retail mix that satisfies the needs of its target market better than that of its competitors. The retail mix includes the decision variables retailers use to satisfy customer needs and influence their purchase decisions. Elements in the retail mix (Exhibit 1–8) include the types of merchandise and services offered, merchandise pricing, the communication program, convenience of the store's location and its layout and design, people (assistance to customers provided by salespeople), HR training programs, and logistical processes.

Managers in the organization must decide how much and what types of merchandise to buy; the vendors to use and the purchase terms; the retail prices to set; how to advertise; a theme for their stores; where and how merchandise will be displayed; how to promote merchandise; and how to move goods via channels of distribution. Store managers must determine how to recruit, select, motivate, and train sales associates, how to monitor organizational consistency, and the nature of services to provide customers (see Exhibit 1–9).

Lo6 Ethical and Legal Considerations

When making the strategic and tactical decisions discussed previously, managers need to consider

Exhibit 1–9
Retail Strategy

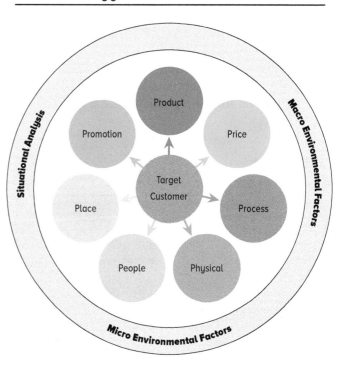

the ethical and legal implications of their decisions, in addition to the effects those decisions have on the profitability of their firms and the satisfaction of their customers. **Ethics** are the principles governing the behaviour of individuals and companies to establish appropriate behaviour and indicate what is right and wrong. Defining the term is easy, but determining

ethics A system or code of conduct based on universal moral duties and obligations that indicate how one should behave.

what the principles are is difficult. What one person thinks is right, another may consider wrong.

What is ethical can vary from country to country and from industry to industry. For example, offering bribes to overcome bureaucratic roadblocks is an accepted practice in some countries, but is considered unethical, and even illegal, in Canada. An ethical principle also can change over time. For example, some years ago, doctors and lawyers who advertised their services were considered unethical. Today, such advertising is accepted.

Some examples of difficult situations that retail managers face are:

- Should a retailer sell merchandise it suspects was made using child labour?
- Should a retailer advertise that its prices are the lowest available in the market even though some items are not?
- Should a retail buyer accept an expensive gift from a vendor?
- Should retail salespeople use a high-pressure sales approach when they know the product is not the best for the customer's needs?

- Should a retailer give preference to minorities when making promotion decisions?
- Should a retailer treat some customers better than others?

Laws dictate which activities society has deemed to be clearly wrong—those activities for which retailers and their employees will be punished through the federal or provincial legal systems. However, most business decisions are not regulated by laws. Often, retail managers have to rely on their firm's and industry's code of ethics and/or their own code of ethics to determine the right thing to do.

Many companies have a code of ethics to provide guidelines for their employees in making their ethical decisions. These ethical policies provide a clear sense of right and wrong so that companies and their customers can depend on their employees when questionable situations arise. However, in many situations, retail managers need to rely on their personal code of ethics—their personal sense of what is right or wrong.

Exhibit 1–10 lists some questions you can ask yourself to determine whether a behaviour or

Exhibit 1–10
The Six Tests of Ethical Action

The Publicity Test
- Would I want to see this action that I'm about to take described on the front page of the local paper or in a national magazine?
- How would I feel about having done this if everyone were to find out all about it, including the people I love and care about the most?

The Moral Mentor Test
- What would the person I admire the most do in this situation?

The Admired Observer Test
- Would I want the person I admire most to see me doing this?
- Would I be proud of this action in the presence of a person whose life and character I really admire?
- What would make the person I admire most proud of me in this situation?

The Transparency Test
- Could I give a clear explanation for the action I'm contemplating, including an honest and transparent account of all my motives, that would satisfy a fair and dispassionate moral judge?

The Person in the Mirror Test
- Will I be able to look at myself in the mirror and respect the person I see there?

The Golden Rule Test
- Would I like to be on the receiving end of this action and all its potential consequences?
- Am I treating others the way I'd want to be treated?

Source: Tom Morris, *The Art of Achievement: Mastering the 7 Cs of Success in Business and Life,* Andrews McMeel Publishing, 2002.

activity is unethical. The questions emphasize that ethical behaviour is determined by widely accepted views of what is right and wrong. Thus, you should engage only in activities about which you would be proud to tell your family, friends, employer, and customers.

If the answer to any of these questions is yes, the behaviour or activity is probably unethical, and you should not do it.

Your firm can strongly affect the ethical choices you will have to make. When you view your firm's policies or requests as improper, you have three choices:

1. Ignore your personal values and do what your company asks you to do. Self-respect suffers when you have to compromise your principles to please an employer. If you take this path, you will probably feel guilty and be dissatisfied with your job in the long run.

2. Take a stand and tell your employer what you think. Try to influence the decisions and policies of your company and supervisors.

3. Refuse to compromise your principles. Taking this path may mean you will get fired or be forced to quit.

You should not take a job with a company whose products, policies, and conduct conflict with your standards. Before taking a job, investigate the company's procedures and selling approach to see if they conflict with your personal ethical standards. In this text, we will highlight the legal and ethical issues associated with the retail decisions made by managers.

SUMMARY

This chapter provides an overview of the importance of the retailing sector to the Canadian economy. The retailing process is the final stage in the distribution of merchandise and is one of the most important sectors of the Canadian economy, producing annual retail sales of approximately $505 billion in 2014. In that year, sales in the retail sector were dominated by the motor vehicle and parts sub-sector, which totalled $119.7 billion in sales in 2014, or 23.7 percent of market share, and the food and beverage stores sub-sector, which totalled $107.7 billion, or 21.9 percent of market share.

The Canadian retail industry has witnessed a number of dramatic changes in recent years as big-box stores and power centres hit our landscape, and information and communication technology grow in sophistication. Retailing in Canada has responded with diversity, with many types of stores competing in this dynamic marketplace; speciality retailers compete against category killers, and traditional department stores battle for market share with mass merchandisers. The examples in this chapter provide real-life examples of what is happening.

The retail management decision process involves developing a strategy for creating a competitive advantage in the marketplace and then developing a retail mix to implement that strategy. The strategic decisions involve selecting a target market, defining the nature of the retailer's offering, and building a competitive advantage through location, human resources management, information and supply chain management systems, and customer relationship management programs. The tactical decisions for implementing the strategy involve selecting a merchandise assortment, buying merchandise, setting prices, communicating with customers, managing the store, presenting merchandise in stores, and providing customer service. There is no doubt that the nature of retailing has changed, as sophisticated technologies create efficiency of product distribution and improve daily operations to satisfy customer needs.

The key to successful retailing is offering the right product, at the right price, in the right place, in the right quantities, at the right time, and making a profit. To accomplish all this, retailers must understand what customers want and what competitors are offering now and in the future. Retailers' wide range of decisions extend from setting a sweater's price to determining whether a new multi-million dollar store should be built in a mall.

Retailing offers opportunities for exciting, challenging careers, either by working for a retail firm or starting your own business. Aspects of retail careers are discussed in **Appendix 1A,** available on Connect.

KEY TERMS

breaking bulk
corporate social responsibility (CSR)
customer relationship management
   (CRM)
distribution channel

ethics
intertype competition
intratype competition
retail strategy
retailer

retailing
scrambled merchandising
variety
vertical integration

1. GO SHOPPING Visit your favourite multichannel retailer by going to a store and going to its Internet site. Evaluate how well the company has integrated these channels into one seamless strategy.

2. GO SHOPPING Visit a local retail store and describe each of the elements in its retail mix.

3. GO TO CAREER WEBSITES Visit the career sites for Best Buy (http://www.bestbuy.ca/en-CA/careers.aspx), Hudson's Bay (http://www.hbc.monstermediaworks.ca), and the Canadian Retail Institute (http://www.retaileducation.ca). Find information about retail careers with these companies and within your area. In which positions would you be interested? Which positions are not of interest to you? Which company would interest you? Why?

DISCUSSION QUESTIONS AND PROBLEMS

1. Read the Spot Light on Retailing "Luxury expands into Canada."
   a) What do you think about all these different luxury brands coming to Canada?
   b) What chance do they have of being successful? Why do you feel this way?

2. Choose one clearly identifiable item (e.g., a pair of jeans, a white shirt). Visit one big-box retailer (e.g., Costco, Walmart) or a department store, one speciality chain retailer, and one online retailer.
   a) Conduct a price comparison and determine which is the better buy.
   b) Observe customers in the store. Take notes. Be prepared to discuss your research.

3. Does Walmart contribute to or detract from the communities in which it operates stores? Check out http://www.walmart.ca. From their home page go to the bottom of the home page and click on the link "Charity & Communities" under the section titled "About Us."

4. How might managers at different levels of a retail organization define their competition?

5. Explain the marketing mix strategy used by your favourite retailer.

6. Choose one of Canada's top 20 retailers. Go to the company's website and find out how the company started and how it has changed over time.

7. You are familiar with The Gap as a retailer currently undergoing changes to attract more customers. You have been given $150 to go shopping. Go to The Gap online (http://www.gapcanada.ca) and go through the process of picking your product. Describe your experience.

8. Retailing View 1.1 describes how some retailers are acting socially responsibly. Take the perspective of a stockholder in the company. What effect will these activities have on the value of its stock? Why might they have a positive or negative effect?

CHAPTER TWO

Types of retailers

LEARNING OBJECTIVES

Lo1   Explore various trends that are shaping today's retailers.

Lo2   Compare and contrast the different types of retailers.

Lo3   Examine how retailers differ in terms of how they meet the needs of their customers.

Lo4   Review how services retailers differ from merchandise retailers.

Lo5   Explore how multichannel retailers provide more value to their customers.

Lo6   Recognize the key success factors in multichannel retailing.

Lo7   Identify the types of ownership for retail firms.

SPOTLIGHT ON RETAILING

COMMITMENT TO CUSTOMER KEY TO GROCER'S SUCCESS

Bill McEwan started in the grocery business as a 15-year-old high school student in his hometown of Trail, British Columbia He worked evenings and weekends—stocking shelves, sweeping floors, cleaning washrooms, bagging groceries, and carrying them to the car for the customer. In short, he did everything that needed to be done, and then some.

Four full and rewarding decades later, 55-year-old McEwan took his leave of a business he loved, having done just about everything there was to do in grocery. By then, he was president and CEO of Sobeys Inc., the Stellarton, Nova Scotia-based retail giant that boasts annual revenues of $16 billion and either owns or oversees 1350 stores that operate under five different banners from coast to coast.

"I was fascinated with the business as a teenager and I still have the same fascination with how it all comes together," says McEwan, who is stepping aside for health reasons. "I'm going to miss the industry terribly and I'm going to miss the company."

McEwan received a number of accolades and honours upon his retirement, including the Retail Council of Canada's (RCC) Lifetime Achievement Award. The award recognizes senior executives who have a minimum of 25 years of continuous service in retail and who have demonstrated outstanding business success and community service.

"RCC is proud to honour Bill McEwan," says Diane J. Brisebois, president and CEO of RCC. "Over his 40 years in the industry, Bill's visionary leadership, driven by his passion for the grocery business, has inspired all those who have had the opportunity to work with him. His business success is exceeded only by the inspiration and influence he has had on the countless individuals he has worked with throughout his career."

Bill McEwan spent the early years of his career with the family-owned business Ferraro Foods, where he had worked as a high school student. In 1989, he began working for Coca-Cola, where he stayed until 1993, gaining invaluable experience and insights from a world leader in marketing, branding, manufacturing, and consumer research. And then the grocery industry came knocking again in 1994 when he joined A&P Canada as senior vice-president of marketing.

When McEwan took over Sobeys, the entire retail industry was going through a fundamental change. Retailers began moving beyond traditional boundaries and introduced entirely new lines of merchandise.

Some of the national drugstore chains, for example, added substantial grocery departments. Grocers beefed up their pharmacy departments, added outdoor garden centres in the spring and summer, and, in some cases, built warehouse-sized stores in order to introduce a broad assortment of general merchandise.

Under McEwan's stewardship, however, Sobeys went against the prevailing winds. The company made a strategic decision to stick to a pure grocery offering in smaller format stores. Even in large urban and suburban centres, Sobeys stores top out at 45 000 to 50 000 square feet, whereas some competitors have built 100 000-square-foot grocery and general merchandise outlets.

"We're all about food," he said. "We decided we were going to stick with what we know and love. We don't sell pipe wrenches and dishwashers and hammocks. That wasn't considered the right strategy at the time. A lot of people questioned why we weren't doing what others were doing. But it proved to be the right approach."

Sobeys decided to follow the customer, rather than join the rush to create a new market for consumers. The company also recognized the fact that there is no single shopper, and Sobeys has positioned its various banners—Sobeys, IGA, Foodland, FreshCo, and Urban Fresh—to address the demands of various markets.

"We identified a food consumer who didn't want to walk around a 100 000-square-foot store to buy milk and fresh peppers," he says. "We always said we want the right size stores, not the biggest."

As he departed the industry, McEwan had some simple, straightforward advice for anyone considering a career in retail: go for it. "There's so much to choose from, so much diversity," he says. "There's real estate, finance, purchasing, and merchandising, among other things. I think it's unrivalled as a career."

And he has a special affection for the grocery business. "I love the rhythm and seasonality of it," he says. "There's summer merchandise and fall merchandise and all the holidays and special events—Halloween, Christmas, Easter. You become a big part of the lives of your customers."

Indeed, listening to McEwan talk about the business, it's easy to understand why he's going to miss it.

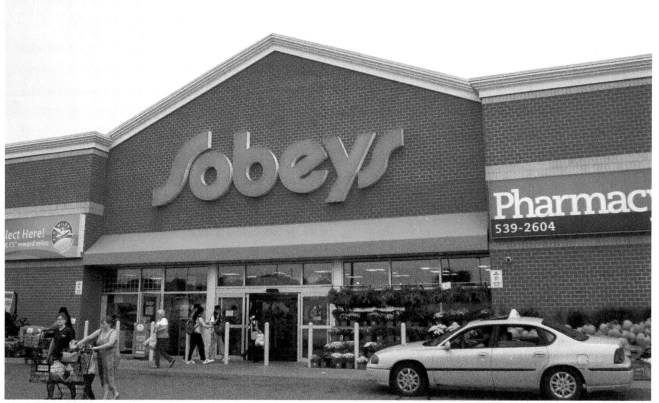

Lee Brown/Alamy.

Source: D'Arcy Jenish, "Commitment to Customer—Key to Grocer's Success," *Canadian Retailer*, Store 2012, Volume 22, Issue 4, pp. 30–31. Canadian Retailer, a publication of Retail Council of Canada.

To develop and implement a retail strategy, retailers need to understand the nature of competition in the retail marketplace. This chapter describes the different types of retailers—both store- and non-store–based retailers. Retailers differ in terms of the types of merchandise and services they offer to customers, the nature of the retail mix used to satisfy customer needs, the degree to which their offerings emphasize services versus merchandise, the prices charged, and the ownership of the firm.

Lo1 Growing Diversity of Retail Formats

As discussed in Boston Consulting Group's *Retail 2020* report, the following ten trends are profoundly changing the retail industry:

1. *Empowered, discriminating consumers.* Consumers can make informed decisions with the increased access to product information, price comparisons, and user reviews, and then widely share their experiences with others. These empowered, discriminating consumers are putting pressure on retailers to add meaningful value to what they can find for themselves, both online and in stores.

2. *Ubiquitous connectivity.* It has never been more critical for retailers to integrate digital opportunities into the shopping experience, with the Internet available at work, at home, and on the go (mobile). Digital and physical experiences are converging, with shoppers expecting interactive, value-added experiences anytime, anywhere, and through any channel.

3. *Buying local, going green.* Consumers want to consume in a responsible, sustainable way. Retailers are responding by embracing the issues and helping customers and suppliers do the same.

4. *Explosion of consumer data.* The enormous amount of data generated by points of sale, social media, corporate websites, and tracking URLs is greater than the ability of many retailers to exploit the potential value of this input.

5. *New age of marketing.* With increasing amounts of data available on customers, their online activities, and their purchasing patterns, retailers are able to create more targeted marketing campaigns.

6. *Scientific retailing.* By applying smart algorithms and deep, data-driven analytics to the massive amounts of data, retailers are able to maximize all aspects of their business, including pricing, assortments, shelf displays, staffing, and warehouse space.

7. *Growing retailer power.* The top five grocery stores in Canada now have 67 percent share of the market, with Loblaw Companies Ltd. dominating with 29.9 percent. Canadian Tire's recent acquisition of the Forzani Group is a critical component of its strategy to maintain leading market share in sporting goods in Canada.

8. *Maturing retail technologies.* A wide range of maturing technologies is allowing companies to streamline backroom functions and increase efficiency, helping to offset higher labour costs.

9. *Blurring boundaries among channels, formats, and brands.* Shoppers Drug Mart is selling food; Loblaws has in-house bank branches; and Indigo has Starbucks cafés in stores. Retailers are evolving into a more integrated business model where all channels share a common strategy for profitable growth.

10. *Challenged store economics.* Physical stores turning into showrooms in the minds of consumers and the rise of online buying are forcing retailers to rethink their costly real-estate assets and merchandising formats.[1]

As consumer needs and competition have changed, new retail formats have been created and continue to evolve. Consider the theory of natural selection and its relevance for explaining change in retailing. It follows Charles Darwin's view that organisms evolve and grow on the basis of the *survival of the fittest*. In retailing, those businesses best able to adapt to change in customer demands, technological advances, and increased competition have the greatest chance of success.

Expanding Retail Breadth

Over the past 20 years, many new retail formats have been developed. Consumers now can purchase the same merchandise from a wide variety of retailers. The initial category specialists in toys, consumer electronics, and home improvement supplies have been joined by a host of specialists including Sport Chek (sportswear), Bed Bath & Beyond (home decor), and PetSmart (pet supplies). Grocery stores such as Loblaws have added

© Joshuaraineyphotography | Dreamstime.com.

pharmacies, clothing (Joe Fresh), and home decor products to expand their retail mix; Shoppers Drug Mart has added shelves full of grocery products to the traditional health and beauty options. Rental companies represent an interesting retail format that has evolved from simple car or equipment rental to Netflix (movie rentals) and *easyhome* (sales and lease ownership firm). The Internet has spawned a new set of retailers offering consumers the opportunity to buy merchandise and services (http://www.alibaba.com), participate in auctions (http://www.ebay.com), or submit "take-it-or-leave-it" bids (http://www.priceline.com).

Many new types of retailers coexist with traditional retailers. Each type of retailer offers a different set of benefits. Thus, consumers patronize different retailers for different purchase occasions. For example, a consumer might purchase a pair of pants from a catalogue as a gift for a friend in another city, and then visit a local store to try on and buy the same pants for himself. The greater diversity of retail formats increases competition in the industry and also enables consumers to buy merchandise and services from a retailer that better satisfies their needs for the specific purchase.

Increasing Industry Concentration

Although the number of different types of retailers has grown, the number of competitors within each format is decreasing. The Canadian marketplace is powered by a small number of large retailers who dominate in their specific retail category. For example, Walmart (which entered the Canadian market in 1994) and Canadian Tire are the major mass merchandisers, and Shoppers Drug Mart is the largest drugstore chain. In Canada, the consumer electronics specialist is Best Buy. The dominant warehouse club Costco has little direct competition since Sam's Club closed its Canadian locations in winter 2009. Three major department stores dominate the Canadian retail landscape: Holt Renfrew, Hudson's Bay, and Sears (a subsidiary of Sears Roebuck and Co. in the United States). Weston Group (Loblaws and its subsidiaries, which includes The Real Canadian Superstore, No Frills, Zehrs, Extra Foods, Wholesale Club, and SaveEasy chains) is Canada's largest grocery chain, with $33 billion in sales and a 29.8 percent grocery market share in Canada. Its nearest national competitor is the Empire Company and its Sobeys chain with sales of $23.5 billion and a 21.2 percent market share. Metro is the third-largest grocery player in Canada with sales of $10.9 billion and a 9.83 percent market share.[2] Dominant in home improvement retailing are American giant Home Depot and Quebec retailer Rona. Both have had rapid growth across Canada.

The trend toward a blurring of retail channels will continue: Drugstores have moved into high-end cosmetics, traditionally the territory of department stores; grocery stores have invaded the pharmacy business. Meanwhile, banks have a problem—more and more customers are not coming into their branches. Banking online or by phone is now the norm. In addition, there is competition from retailers (including Loblaws and Canadian Tire) offering banking services that include mortgages and loans that extend the customer relationship. In response, progressive banks are luring customers with plasma TVs, iPads, and comfy chairs to attract more profitable clients to invest in financial advisory services. Ultimately, it will be the customer who makes the retail decisions.

Retailer Characteristics

Store-based retailers range from street vendors selling hot dogs to large corporations such as Staples that offer products in their stores and through catalogue and Internet channels. Each retailer survives and prospers by satisfying a group of

Exhibit 2–1
NAICS Codes for Retailers

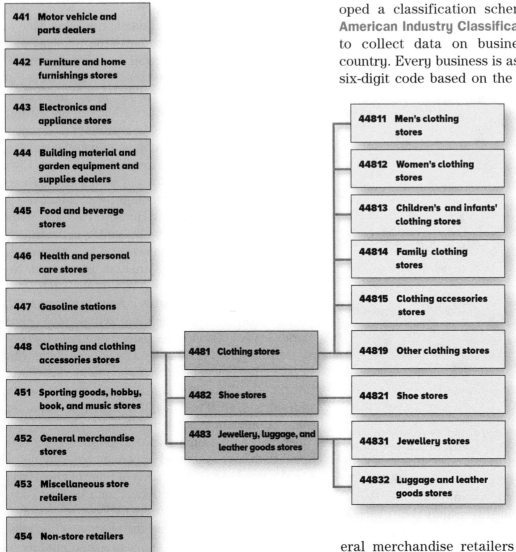

441	**Motor vehicle and parts dealers**
442	**Furniture and home furnishings stores**
443	**Electronics and appliance stores**
444	**Building material and garden equipment and supplies dealers**
445	**Food and beverage stores**
446	**Health and personal care stores**
447	**Gasoline stations**
448	**Clothing and clothing accessories stores**
451	**Sporting goods, hobby, book, and music stores**
452	**General merchandise stores**
453	**Miscellaneous store retailers**
454	**Non-store retailers**

4481	**Clothing stores**
4482	**Shoe stores**
4483	**Jewellery, luggage, and leather goods stores**

44811	**Men's clothing stores**
44812	**Women's clothing stores**
44813	**Children's and infants' clothing stores**
44814	**Family clothing stores**
44815	**Clothing accessories stores**
44819	**Other clothing stores**
44821	**Shoe stores**
44831	**Jewellery stores**
44832	**Luggage and leather goods stores**

Type of Merchandise

The United States, Canada, and Mexico have developed a classification scheme, called the **North American Industry Classification System (NAICS)**, to collect data on business activity in each country. Every business is assigned a hierarchical, six-digit code based on the type of products and services it produces and sells. The first two digits identify the firm's business sector, and the remaining four digits identify various sub-sectors.

The classifications for retail firms selling merchandise, based largely on the type of merchandise sold, are illustrated in Exhibit 2–1. Merchandise retailers constitute sectors 44 and 45, and the third digit breaks down these retailers further. For example, retailers selling clothing and clothing accessories are in classification 448, whereas general merchandise retailers are in classification 452. The fourth and fifth digits provide a finer classification. The fourth digit subdivides clothing and accessories retailers (448) into clothing stores (4481), shoe stores (4482), and jewellery, luggage, and leather goods stores (4483). The fifth digit provides a further breakdown into men's clothing stores (44811) and women's clothing stores (44812). The sixth digit, not illustrated in Exhibit 2–1, captures differences in the three North American countries using the classification scheme.

Most services retailers appear in sectors 71 (arts, entertainment, and recreation) and 72 (accommodation and food services). For example, food services and drinking places are in category 722, which gets subdivided into full-service restaurants (7221) and limited-service eating places like fast-food restaurants (7222).

consumers' needs more effectively than its competitors. Over time, different types of retailers have emerged and prospered because they have attracted and maintained a significant customer base.

The most basic characteristic of a retailer is its retail mix—the elements used by a retailer to satisfy its customers' needs (see Exhibits 1–8 and 1–9).

Four elements of the retail mix are particularly useful for classifying retailers:

- type of merchandise/services offered
- breadth and depth of merchandise offered
- level of customer service
- price of merchandise

North American Industry Classification System (NAICS) Classification of retail firms into a hierarchical set of six-digit codes based on the types of products and services they produce and sell.

Breadth and Depth

Even if retailers sell the same type of merchandise, they might not compete directly. For example, the primary classification for retailers selling clothing and clothing accessories is 448. But clothing can be purchased in sporting goods stores (45111), department stores (4521), warehouse clubs and supercentres (45291), and electronic shopping and mail-order houses (4541). These different types of retailers do not compete directly because they appeal to different customer needs and thus offer different assortments and varieties of merchandise and services. Variety (breadth of merchandise) is the number of merchandise categories a retailer offers. **Depth of merchandise** is the number of different items in a merchandise category. Breadth of merchandise means that the retailer carries a number of different product lines. For example, large department stores carry a wide range of different types of products (shoes, appliances, apparel, and cosmetics). Depth of merchandise is the number of *items* within each product line. For example, the shoe department in a department store offers a large assortment of shoes (running shoes, dress shoes, children's shoes, walking shoes). Retailers can have product/service assortment strategies that range from wide and deep (many merchandise categories and a large assortment in each category) like Hudson's Bay; wide and shallow (many merchandise categories and a limited assortment in each category) like Walmart; narrow and deep (limited number of merchandise categories and a large assortment in each category) like House of Knives; or a narrow and shallow strategy (few merchandise categories and a limited assortment in each category) like M&M Meat Shops (see Exhibit 2–2).

Each different *item* of merchandise is called a **SKU (stock keeping unit)**. For example, a 3.7 kg box of Tide laundry detergent and a white, button-down-collar Tommy Hilfiger shirt, size 16–33, are both SKUs.

Warehouse club stores (Costco), discount stores (Walmart, Giant Tiger), and toy stores all sell toys. However, warehouse clubs and discount stores sell many other categories of merchandise in addition to toys; they have greater variety or breadth of merchandise. Stores specializing in toys stock more types of toys (more SKUs). For each type of toy, such as dolls, the specialty toy retailer offers more assortment or depth of merchandise (more models, sizes, and brands, and deeper assortment) than general merchants such as warehouse clubs or discount stores.

© Courtesy of Eastern Mountain Sports.

depth of merchandise The number of SKUs within a merchandise category; also called *assortment and depth of stock*.

SKU (stock keeping unit) The smallest unit available for keeping inventory control. In soft goods merchandise, an SKU usually means size, colour, and style.

Exhibit 2–2
Breadth versus Depth of Merchandise Lines

	Breadth: Number of different product lines			
	Shoes	**Appliances**	**Houseware**	**Men's clothing**
Depth: Number of items within each product line	Nike running shoes Florsheim dress shoes Top Sider boat shoes Adidas tennis shoes	Sony TV sets Samsung Blu Ray Player General Electric dishwashers Sharp microwave ovens	Glassware Cutlery Coffee cups Tableware	Suits Ties Jackets Overcoats Socks Shirts

Exhibit 2–3
Breadth and Depth of Kayaks in Different Retail Outlets

Retailer	Brand	White-Water	Recreational	Sea Touring	Fishing
EMS (Eastern Mountain Sports)	Necky		X	X	
	Wilderness Systems		X	X	X
	Hurricane			X	
	Perception		X		
	Old Town		X		
	Airis				X
			7 SKUs $489–$1209	14 SKUs $1259–$1695	3 SKUs $975–$1365
Outdoorplay.com	Axiom	X			
	Axis	X			
	WaveSport	X			
	Dagger	X	X	X	
	Airis	X	X		
	NRS	X			
	Wilderness Systems		X	X	X
	Perception		X	X	
	Necky		X	X	
	Advanced Elements		X		
	Ocean Kayak				X
	Freedom Hawk				X
		27 SKUs $649–$1538	23 SKUs $449–$1299	20 SKUs $794–$1699	12 SKUs $849–$1999
Walmart	K2			X	
	Waterquest		X		
	Airhead		X		
	Coleman		X		
			4 SKUs $299.98–$377.99	1 SKU $349.99	

Exhibit 2–3 shows the breadth and depth of kayaks carried by EMS (Eastern Mountain Sports), an outdoor gear and equipment specialist; Outdoorplay.com, an Internet kayak specialty retailer; and Walmart, a full-line discount store. Although EMS carries many of the same brands as Outdoorplay.com, EMS offers a narrower assortment—only four of the five categories—than Outdoorplay.com. Outdoorplay.com carries a deeper assortment of kayaks. Walmart has the least variety (only two categories) and the shallowest assortment, offering only 5 SKUs compared with 24 at EMS and 82 at Outdoorplay.com.

Customer Services

Retailers differ in the services they offer customers. For example, EMS offers assistance in selecting the appropriate kayak as well as repairing kayaks. Outdoorplay.com and Walmart do not provide these services. Customers expect retailers to provide some services: accepting credit and debit payment, providing parking, and being open at convenient hours. Some retailers charge customers for additional services, such as home delivery and gift wrapping. Retailers that cater to service-oriented consumers offer most of these services at no charge.

Cost of Offering Breadth and Depth of Merchandise and Services

Stocking a deep assortment like EMS's kayak offering is appealing to customers but costly for retailers. When a retailer offers customers many SKUs, inventory investment increases because the retailer must have backup stock for each SKU.

Similarly, services attract customers to the retailer, but they are also costly. More salespeople are needed to provide information and assist customers, to alter merchandise to meet customers' needs, and to demonstrate merchandise. Child care facilities, washrooms, dressing rooms, and check rooms take up valuable store space that could be used to stock and display merchandise. Offering delayed billing, credit, and instalment payments requires a financial investment that could be used to buy more merchandise.

To make a profit, retailers that offer broader variety, deeper assortments, and/or additional services need to charge higher prices. For example, department stores have higher prices because of their higher costs, which result from stocking a lot of fashionable and seasonal merchandise, discounting merchandise when they make errors in forecasting consumer tastes, providing some personal sales service, and having expensive mall locations. In contrast, discount stores appeal to customers who are looking for lower prices and are less interested in services but want to see a broad range of merchandise brands and models. Thus, a critical retail decision involves the trade-off between the costs and benefits of maintaining additional inventory or providing additional services.

To compare their offering with competitive offerings, retailers often shop their competitors' stores. In the next section, we discuss the different types of general merchandise, then food retailers and non-store retailers. Exhibit 2–4 includes information about the size and growth rates for each of these retail sectors.

Lo2 Lo3 General Merchandise Retailers

Types of general merchandise retailers include discount stores, specialty stores, category specialists, department stores, home improvement centres, off-price retailers, and value retailers. Exhibit 2–5 summarizes characteristics of general merchandise retailers that sell through stores. Many of these general merchandise retailers sell through multichannels, such as stores, online, catalogues, call centres, social networking, digital displays, and mobile.

DID YOU KNOW?

Hudson's Bay Company, the oldest retailer in North America, conquered the Canadian wilderness by trading furs over 300 years ago.[3]

Discount Stores

A **discount store** is a retailer that offers a broad variety of merchandise, limited service, and low prices. Discount stores offer both private labels and national brands. Discount stores can also be referred to as *mass merchandisers* or *full-line discount stores*. Examples include Dollarama, Giant Tiger, and Walmart.

Walmart alone accounts for almost 67 percent of full-line discount store retail sales, so the most significant trend in this sector is Walmart's conversion of discount stores to supercentres. This change in emphasis is the result of the increased competition faced by full-line discount stores and the operating efficiencies of supercentres. Full-line discount stores experience intense competition from discount specialty stores that focus on a single category of merchandise, such as Golf Town, Staples, HomeSense, Sport Chek, and Rona. They also compete with Old Navy and Hudson's Bay for apparel, Sears for home furnishings, and Shoppers Drug Mart for health and beauty products. To respond to this competitive environment, discount stores have created more attractive shopping environments, placed more emphasis on apparel, and developed strong private-label merchandise programs.

Walmart pioneered the everyday low price concept. And its efficient operations have allowed it to offer the lowest-priced basket of merchandise in every market in which it competes. This doesn't mean that Walmart has the lowest price on every item in every market. But it tries to be the lowest across a wide variety of things. Many scholars of business believe Walmart has the best and most sophisticated supply chain and information systems in the industry, allowing for retail efficiency and lower prices.

There is no doubt that Walmart's global success has been a matter of efficiency and timing. However, a *lack* of timing and efficiencies can spell disaster for a company as well. Take Target, for example. Less than two years after their entry into the Canadian market, and after opening 133 stores across the country, they gathered $2.5 billion in pre-tax losses and left Canada. The erosion of the Canadian

DID YOU KNOW?

"The first Dollarama store opens in April, 1992 in Matane, Quebec with all items offered for $1. The company grows the store base by converting existing Rossy stores to the Dollarama concept and opening new locations. The company opens its first store outside Quebec in Grand Falls, New Brunswick."[4]

discount store A general merchandise retailer that offers a wide variety of merchandise, limited service, and low prices; also called *mass merchandiser* and *full-line discount store*.

Exhibit 2-4

Canadian Retail Sales by Type of Store

To September 2015	$ Billions Last 12 Months	YEAR-OVER-YEAR % CHANGE			
		Sept. 2015	2015 Year- to-Date	Last 3 Months	Last 12 Months
Total Location-Based Retail	**$512.7**	**2.5%**	**2.1%**	**2.2%**	**2.6%**
Store retail	**$330.0**	**3.8%**	**3.9%**	**3.0%**	**4.0%**
Food & drug	$150.8	3.2%	3.4%	2.6%	3.6%
Store merchandise	$179.2	4.2%	4.3%	3.3%	4.4%
Automotive & related	**$182.8**	**0.4%**	**−0.9%**	**0.9%**	**0.2%**
Food & Drug Sector	**$150.8**	**3.2%**	**3.4%**	**2.6%**	**3.6%**
Food & beverage stores	**$113.2**	**2.7%**	**2.9%**	**1.9%**	**3.4%**
Grocery stores	$86.1	1.2%	2.5%	0.8%	3.1%
Supermarkets & other grocery stores	$78.9	0.8%	2.2%	0.3%	2.8%
Convenience stores	$7.2	5.0%	6.7%	5.5%	6.8%
Specialty food stores	$6.1	3.4%	3.5%	3.1%	3.2%
Beer, wine, & liquor stores	$21.0	8.8%	4.5%	6.2%	4.6%
Health & personal care stores	**$37.5**	**4.9%**	**4.9%**	**4.6%**	**4.0%**
Store Merchandise Sector	**$179.2**	**4.2%**	**4.3%**	**3.3%**	**4.4%**
General merchandise stores	**$65.1**	**3.7%**	**3.1%**	**2.2%**	**3.6%**
Department stores	$27.7	2.6%	2.2%	1.5%	2.2%
Other general merchandise stores	$37.4	4.5%	3.7%	2.8%	4.7%
Clothing & clothing accessories stores	**$29.4**	**7.5%**	**6.7%**	**6.9%**	**6.0%**
Clothing stores	$23.0	6.9%	6.5%	6.1%	6.0%
Shoe stores	$3.3	11.0%	8.3%	10.8%	7.1%
Jewellery, luggage, & leather goods stores	$3.0	7.6%	6.7%	8.1%	4.8%
Furniture & home furnishings stores	**$16.5**	**5.6%**	**5.5%**	**5.1%**	**5.6%**
Furniture stores	$10.5	7.3%	5.4%	5.0%	5.7%
Home furnishings stores	$6.1	2.7%	5.7%	5.3%	5.3%
Electronics & appliance stores	**$14.9**	**−1.6%**	**0.7%**	**−1.0%**	**1.7%**
Building material & garden equipment/supplies	**$29.7**	**5.7%**	**6.8%**	**3.1%**	**6.5%**
Other stores	**$23.6**	**2.5%**	**3.1%**	**3.4%**	**3.2%**
Sporting goods, hobby, book, & music stores	$11.7	0.2%	3.5%	2.9%	4.5%
Miscellaneous store retailers	$11.8	4.8%	2.6%	3.9%	2.0%
Automotive & Related Sector	**$182.8**	**0.4%**	**−0.9%**	**0.9%**	**0.2%**
Motor vehicle & parts dealers	**$125.9**	**7.8%**	**6.7%**	**7.2%**	**7.2%**
Automobile dealers	$110.0	8.2%	7.0%	7.7%	7.6%
New car dealers	$102.5	6.9%	6.2%	6.5%	7.0%
Used car dealers	$7.5	28.4%	19.8%	28.0%	16.3%
Other motor vehicle dealers	$7.8	8.4%	5.7%	5.5%	6.1%
Automotive parts, accessories & tire stores	$8.1	1.3%	3.7%	1.9%	3.5%
Gasoline stations	**$56.9**	**−14.3%**	**−14.9%**	**−11.4%**	**−12.5%**

Sources: Statistics Canada, data to September 2015 (preliminary). NAICS (North American Industrial Classification System) basis. Not seasonally adjusted. Reproduced and distributed on an "as is" basis with the permission of Statistics Canada. Prepared by Ed Strapagiel, Consultant, 20 November 2015.

Exhibit 2–5
Characteristics of General Merchandise Retailers

Type	Variety	Assortment	Service	Prices	Size (000 sq. ft.)	SKUs (000)	Location
Department stores	Broad	Deep to average	Average to high	Average to high	100–200	100	Regional malls
Discount stores	Broad	Average to shallow	Low	Low	60–80	30	Stand-alone, power strip centres
Category specialists	Narrow	Very deep	Low to high	Low	50–100	20–40	Stand-alone, power strip centres
Specialty stores	Narrow	Deep	High	High	4–12	5	Regional malls
Home improvement centres	Narrow	Very deep	Low to high	Low	80–120	20–40	Stand-alone, power strip centres
Drugstores	Narrow	Very deep	Average	Average to high	3–15	10–20	Stand-alone, strip centres
Off-price stores	Average	Deep but varying	Low	Low	20–30	50	Outlet malls
Extreme-value retailers	Average	Average and varying	Low	Low	7–15	3–4	Urban, strip

economy along with poor inventory systems and an overly-zealous launch (124 stores in year one) were all ingredients that lead to their downfall.[5] Organizations must be leery of macro-environmental forces, keeping these forces in mind when considering modifications of their retail marketing strategy in relation to timing and distribution efficiencies.

Specialty Stores

A **specialty store** concentrates on a limited number of complementary merchandise categories and provides a high level of service in an area typically under 8000 square feet. For example, Pro Hockey Life, owned by Sports Gilbert Rousseau Inc. of Montreal, and Hockey Experts, a subsidiary of Canadian Tire, are examples of hockey chains that specialize in hockey gear, ranging from relatively inexpensive to higher end.

Issues in Specialty Store Retailing Specialty stores tailor their retail strategy toward a very specific market segment by offering deep but narrow assortments along with knowledgeable sales staff. For example, West 49 retails action sports clothing that had its origins with young skateboard enthusiasts. West 49 has very specific strategies to make sure that it appeals to the under-16 demographic. For example, the mall is a perfect location for this retailer because the target age group does not drive and usually relies on a parent to drop them off at the shopping centre.

Sephora, France's leading cosmetic chain and a division of the luxury goods conglomerate LVMH (Louis Vuitton–Moet Hennessy), is an example of an innovative specialty store concept. In Canada, prestige cosmetics were historically sold in department stores. Sephora is a cosmetic and perfume specialty store offering a deep assortment of merchandise in a 6000- to 9000-square-foot self-serve retail environment. Each cosmetic brand has a separate counter with testers and sales staff available to answer

specialty store Store concentrating on a limited number of complementary merchandise categories and providing a high level of service in an area typically under 8000 square feet.

Sephora offers a unique shopping experience, differentiating it from other specialty stores selling beauty products.

© Murdock2013 | Dreamstime.com.

questions. The concept is extremely popular with customers, who are encouraged to browse and experiment in a friendly environment. Its stores offer over 15 000 SKUs and more than 200 brands, including its own private-label brand. Merchandise is grouped by product category, with the brands displayed alphabetically so that customers can locate them easily. Customers are free to shop and experiment on their own. Sampling is encouraged. Knowledgeable salespeople are available to assist customers. The low-key, open-sell environment results in customers spending more time shopping.

Because specialty retailers focus on specific market segments, they are vulnerable to shifts in consumer tastes and preferences. For example, mall-based specialty retailers are affected by consumers who prefer the convenience of shopping in retail locations outside the mall. Ease of parking and time saving are two factors that influence the consumer. Apparel and footwear specialty retailers are capturing fewer consumers' dollars because consumers are spending more on necessities such as rent or mortgage, school expenses, and transportation costs and are enjoying eating out, concerts, or clubs.

category specialist A discount retailer that offers a narrow but deep assortment of merchandise in a category and thus dominates the category from the customers' perspective. Also called *category killer*.

Europe-based apparel specialty stores Zara (Spain) and H&M (short for Hennes & Mauritz, in Sweden) are very successful in Europe, and are expanding into Canada. Zara's philosophy is "fashion on demand." At the end of every day in each of the chain's more than 1000 shops around the world, the manager goes online to company headquarters in Spain and describes which items were moving and which weren't. Using this simple method as a guide, designers can get a newly-created item on the racks within little more than a week, compared to as long as six months for The Gap. In the fickle and fast-changing world of fashion, agility means success. Zara produces more than half of its own clothes and makes 40 percent of its own fabric. H&M also responds quickly to fashion trends. In contrast, however, H&M has 800 suppliers and does not own factories.[6] H&M also competes at lower price points than both Zara and The Gap. Its philosophy is "disposable chic," and its merchandise is so inexpensive that it doesn't matter if it goes out of style quickly.[7]

Fast-fashion companies like H&M introduce new products two to three times per week, compared with 10 to 12 times per year at traditional specialty stores, to ensure that they offer the most trendy and up-to-date fashions. Because of the constantly fresh atmosphere, customers develop "buy it now" shopping behaviour; next week, the store will have different merchandise. As a result, fast-fashion retailers actually sell 85 percent of their merchandise at full price compared with only 60 percent at traditional stores.

Many manufacturers have opened their own specialty stores in recent years. Tired of being at the mercy of retailers to purchase and merchandise their products, these manufacturers and specialty retailers can control their own destiny by operating their own stores. Consider, for instance, Apple (computers and phones) and Lucky Brand (jeans and apparel).

Category Specialist/Category Killer

Bass Pro Shops' Outdoor World is a **category specialist** offering merchandise for outdoor recreational activities. The stores offer everything a person needs for hunting and fishing—from 27-cent plastic bait to boats and recreational vehicles costing $45 000. Sales associates are knowledgeable outdoors people. Each is hired for a particular department that matches that person's expertise. All private-branded products are field tested by Bass Pro Shops' professional teams: Redhead Pro Hunting Team and Tracker Pro Fishing Team.

Interior of a Bass Pro Shops sporting goods store.
© Clewisleake | Dreamstime.com.

DID YOU KNOW?

"According to Visa Canada's new quarterly report, the Visa Canada Digital Commerce Index, just over one-quarter (26 percent) of Canadians have used a mobile device to make an online purchase over the past three months (November 18, 2014)."[8]

Many of these category killers are operating in a big-box format. These large format stores typically range in size from about 40 000 to 200 000 square feet. But it must be noted that it is the size of the store in comparison to its competitors that would qualify it as a big-box category killer, as shown in Exhibit 2–6.

Issues for Category Specialists Most category specialist chains started in one region of the country and saturated that region before expanding to other regions. During this period of expansion, competition between specialists in a category was limited.

Competition between specialists in each category becomes intense as firms expand into regions originally dominated by another firm. In many merchandise categories, the major firms are now in direct competition across the country. This direct competition focuses on price, resulting in reduced profits because the competitors have difficulty differentiating themselves on other elements of the retail mix. All the competitors in a category provide similar assortments since they have similar access to national brands. These sophisticated big-box, category killer venues are often grouped together in power centres, dominating the industry with their low prices, extensive product offerings, and ample customer parking.[9]

In response to this increasing competitive intensity, the category killers continue to concentrate on reducing costs by increasing operating efficiency and acquiring smaller chains to gain scale economies. Where appropriate, category specialists have attempted to differentiate themselves with service. For example, Home Depot, Rona, and Lowe's hire licensed contractors as sales associates to help customers with electrical and plumbing repairs. They also provide classes to train home owners in tiling, painting, and other tasks to give shoppers the confidence to tackle their do-it-yourself (DIY) projects on their own.

As retailers try to satisfy today's ever-changing consumer, many are realizing that big is not always better. More and more North American retailers are turning to the smaller format concepts that have been trending in Europe, Asia, and Latin America for several reasons: Real estate is not always

Exhibit 2–6
Big-Box Comparative Size Advantage

- Superstores—3 times the traditional supermarket
- Home Depot—18 times the traditional hardware store
- Chapters—12 times the traditional book store
- Winners—6 times the traditional fashion store
- Staples—5 times the traditional office supply store
- Michaels Craft Stores—9 times the traditional arts and crafts store
- Sport Chek—6 times the traditional sporting goods store

available for big-box players; populations are shifting; and the Web is having a significant impact on consumer in-store expectations and shopping processes. Rona is moving to reduce the number of its big-box locations from 80 to 57 and is focusing its expansion efforts on smaller-format neighbourhood stores. Best Buy is responding to the shift by reducing the footprint of new store builds by 10 000 square feet and launching new mobile device stores that are less than 3000 square feet. However, the days of the big-box experience are not over, says Nick Jones, executive vice-president and retail practice lead for Leo Burnett/Arc Worldwide in Chicago. He says, "The big box will survive. But only by virtue of how it addresses the competitive advantage of physical retail over e-tail. But, in either channel, the most successful retailers will deliver real shopper experiences that entertain and inspire shoppers and give them ideas and solutions, not just product."[10]

Department Stores

A **department store** is a retailer that carries a broad variety and deep assortment of stock, offers some customer services, and is organized into separate departments for displaying merchandise. The largest department store chains in Canada are Sears Canada and Hudson's Bay, bought in 2006 by Jerry Zucker, US billionaire investor,[11] and then sold again in 2008 to the owners of US-based Lord and Taylor, NRDC Equity partners. Department store chains are very diverse and can be categorized into three tiers. The first tier includes upscale, high-fashion chains with exclusive designer merchandise and excellent customer service, such as

department store A retailer that carries a wide variety and deep assortment, offers considerable customer services, and is organized into separate departments for displaying merchandise.

© The Canadian Press/Mario Beauregard.

a POS terminal to transact and record sales, and salespeople to assist customers. The department store often resembles a collection of specialty shops. The major departments are women's, men's, and children's clothing and accessories; home furnishings and furniture; kitchenware and small appliances; and cosmetics and fragrances.

In some situations, departments in a department store or discount store are leased and operated by an independent company. A **leased department** is an area in a retail store that is leased or rented to an independent firm. The leaseholder is typically responsible for all retail mix decisions involved in operating the department and pays the store a percentage of its sales as rent. Retailers lease departments when they feel they lack expertise to operate the department efficiently. Commonly leased departments in Canadian stores are beauty salons, pharmacies, shoes, jewellery, furs, photography studios, and repair services.

Department stores are unique in terms of the shopping experience they offer, the services they provide, and the atmosphere of the store. They offer a full range of services from altering clothing to home delivery. To create excitement, apparel is displayed on mannequins, attention is drawn to displays with theatrical lighting, and sales associates are frequently stationed throughout the store demonstrating products. Department stores also emphasize special promotions such as elaborate displays during the Christmas season and other holidays.

Issues in Department Store Retailing Department stores' overall sales have stagnated and market share has fallen in recent years due to increased competition from discount stores and specialty stores, as well as a decline in perceived value for merchandise and services. Department stores, which started in the nineteenth century, attracted consumers by offering them ambience, attentive service, and a wide variety of merchandise under one roof. They still account for some of retailing's romance—its parades, its Santa Claus lands, and its holiday windows. Department stores also offer designer brands that are not available at other retailers.

leased department An area in a retail store leased or rented to an independent company. The leaseholder is typically responsible for all retail mix decisions involved in operating the department and pays the store a percentage of its sales as rent.

Holt Renfrew in Canada and Nordstrom in the United States (and now in Canada). Hudson's Bay represents the second tier of upscale department stores, in which retailers sell more modestly-priced merchandise with less customer service. The value-oriented third tier—Sears Canada—caters to more price-conscious consumers. Holt Renfrew in the first tier has had an established, clearly defined, differentiated position for years, whereas the value-oriented tier has been facing significant competitive challenges from discount stores.

The entire category, including the first tier, is getting a big shake-up with American luxury retailer Nordstrom moving into Canadian malls (Pacific Centre in Vancouver, Chinook Centre in Calgary, Rideau Centre in Ottawa, and Sherway Gardens in Toronto). Further, it is rumoured that department store Bloomingdale's is considering moving into the Canadian retail marketplace. Only time will tell how significantly these stores will affect department store retailing in Canada and the Canadian luxury market.[12]

Traditionally, department stores attracted customers by offering a pleasing ambience, attentive service, and a wide variety of merchandise under one roof. They sell both soft goods (apparel and bedding) and hard goods (appliances, furniture, and consumer electronics). Each department within the store has a specific selling space allocated to it,

Unfortunately, many consumers believe that department stores are no longer romantic or convenient. Many believe that they are difficult to get to because they are located in large malls, that it is difficult to find specific merchandise because the same category is often located in several designer departments, and that it is difficult to get professional sales assistance because of labour cutbacks. At the same time, department stores typically charge higher prices than their discount and specialty store competitors.

To deal with eroding market share, department stores are (1) attempting to increase the amount of exclusive merchandise they sell, (2) undertaking marketing campaigns to develop strong images for their stores and brands, and (3) expanding their online presence.

Drugstores

A **drugstore** is a specialty store that concentrates on health and personal grooming merchandise. Pharmaceuticals often represent over 50 percent of drugstore sales and an even greater percentage of their profits. The largest drugstore chain in Canada is Shoppers Drug Mart (owned by Weston Group) with a market share of 30.1 percent.[13]

Pharmaprix retail pharmacy chain in Quebec, which is part of Shoppers Drug Mart, Canada's largest pharmacy chain.
© The Canadian Press/Mario Beauregard.

> **DID YOU KNOW?**
>
> **460.** The approximate number of Rexall stores across the country. Rexall is considered one of the country's largest pharmacy chains.[15]

> **DID YOU KNOW?**
>
> North Americans rate pharmacists as the most trusted profession.

Issues in Drugstore Retailing Drugstores, particularly the national chains, are experiencing sustained sales growth because the aging population requires more prescription drugs and the profit margins for prescription pharmaceuticals are higher than for other drugstore merchandise. The non-prescription side of drugstores is also being squeezed by considerable competition from pharmacies in discount stores and supermarkets, as well as from prescription mail-order retailers.

In response, the major drugstore chains are building larger stand-alone stores offering a wider assortment of merchandise, more frequently-purchased food items, and drive-through windows for picking up prescriptions.[14] To build customer loyalty, the chains are also changing the role of their pharmacists from dispensing pills (referred to as count, pour, lick, and stick) to providing health care assistance.

Shoppers Drug Mart, Canada's largest pharmacy, operates 1259 Shoppers Drug Mart/Pharmaprix drugstores, 56 medical clinic pharmacies called Shoppers Simply Pharmacy, 56 Shoppers Health Care stores, and 5 luxury beauty destinations operating as Murale.[16,17] Shoppers has launched beauty boutiques by adding prestige cosmetics and fragrance brands. Following suit, London Drugs and Jean Coutu are also giving their cosmetics sections a major makeover, borrowing ideas from the department stores to chase new revenue opportunities.

Off-Price Retailers

An **off-price retailer** offers an inconsistent assortment of brand-name, fashion-oriented soft goods at low prices. Winners—launched in Canada in 1982—had grown to over 234 stores across the country by the end of 2014.[18] The company, which is owned by US-based TJX Companies (which owns T.J. Maxx, Marshalls, and other off-price retailers), has 70 buyers worldwide in Canada, Hong Kong, New York, Los Angeles, and London searching for the best buys in fashion. The flagship store, which opened in 2003 at the College Park location in Toronto, receives about 10 000 new items a week and is a shopper's dream.[19,20] In 2005, Winners arrived on fashionable Bloor Street in Toronto, not far from Tiffany, Chanel, and Holt Renfrew. The off-price concept appeals to the Canadian shopper and the company is cashing in with its Winners (apparel), HomeSense (home), and StyleSense (accessories) formats.

drugstore Specialty retail store that concentrates on pharmaceuticals and health and personal grooming merchandise.

off-price retailer A retailer that offers an inconsistent assortment of brand-name, fashion-oriented soft goods at low prices.

closeout retailers Off-price retailers that sell a broad but inconsistent assortment of general merchandise as well as apparel and soft home goods, obtained through retail liquidations and bankruptcy proceedings.

outlet stores Off-price retailers owned by a manufacturer or a department or specialty store chain.

factory outlets Outlet stores owned by a manufacturer.

value retailers General merchandise discount stores that are found in low-income urban or rural areas and are much smaller than traditional discount stores, less than 9000 square feet.

As announced in 2010, TJX Companies brought the Marshalls' banner to Canada in 2011 to operate alongside sister chains Winners and HomeSense. Similar to the Winners chain, Marshalls offers current fashions at discount prices, with a stronger focus on clothing selections for the entire family, compared to the Winners selection that is more oriented toward women. TJX opened six Marshalls stores in the Greater Toronto Area in 2011 and sees the chain as the next growth vehicle for its Canadian operations. Marshalls managed 38 stores in Canada at 2014's year end, averaging 30 000 square feet in size.[21]

Off-price retailers can sell brand-name and even designer-label merchandise at low prices due to their unique buying and merchandising practices. Most merchandise is bought opportunistically from manufacturers or other retailers with excess inventory at the end of the season. This merchandise might be in odd sizes or unpopular colours and styles, or it might be irregular (having minor mistakes in construction). Typically, merchandise is purchased at one-fourth to one-fifth of the original wholesale price. Off-price retailers can buy at low prices because they don't ask suppliers for advertising allowances, return privileges, markdown adjustments, or delayed payments. For a different take on off-price retailing, Retailing View 2.1 describes Bag Borrow or Steal, which rents luxury products.

Due to this pattern of opportunistic buying, customers can't be confident that the same type of merchandise will be in stock each time they visit the store. Different bargains will be available on each visit. To improve their offerings' consistency, some off-price retailers complement opportunistically bought merchandise with merchandise purchased at regular wholesale prices. Two special types of off-price retailers are closeout and outlet stores.

- **Closeout retailers** are off-price retailers that sell a broad but inconsistent assortment of merchandise usually obtained from a store closing or bankruptcy, consisting of general merchandise, apparel, and home furnishings. Factory Direct, which owns over 20 stores in Ontario, is an example of this type of merchandiser.[22]

- **Outlet stores** are off-price retailers owned by manufacturers or retailers. Outlet stores owned by manufacturers are referred to as **factory outlets**. Outlet stores can be found clustered together in a geographic area, such as the Southworks Outlet Mall in Cambridge, Ontario. Maps are often distributed to shoppers to indicate outlet locations. The outlet mall provides a shopping location that includes added services such as food and beverages, parking, and a climate-controlled environment, along with the bargains of off-price merchandise.

Manufacturers view outlet stores as an opportunity to sell irregulars, production overruns, and merchandise returned by retailers. Outlet stores also allow manufacturers some control over where their branded merchandise is sold at discount prices.

Retailers with strong brand names, such as Holt Renfrew, also operate outlet stores (HR2). By selling excess merchandise in outlet stores rather than selling it at markdown prices in their primary stores, these department and specialty store chains can maintain an image of offering desirable merchandise at full price.

Canadian retailers operating outlet stores include Roots (outdoor apparel), Club Monaco (trendy urban apparel), and Danier Leather. Problems occur as traditional mall landlords dispute with tenants who are opening branches in power centres located close to their shopping centres. Fashion retailers are selling identical merchandise and price points of clothes at their power centre stores and their mall locations. The end result: The consumer is confused, assumes there are higher prices at the mall, and thus avoids shopping at the traditional shopping centre.

Value Retailers

Value retailers are general merchandise discount stores that are found in either lower-income urban or middle-income suburbs, or in rural areas, and are much smaller than traditional discount stores. Value retailers are the fastest-growing

DID YOU KNOW?

The rapidly growing Canadian dollar-store industry—estimated at roughly $35 billion in 2009—will expand by more than 60 percent over the next decade and double in size by 2025.[23]

Rent Some Luxury

DETAILS

Designers   Chloe   Chloe Paddington Satchel

CHLOE

Chloe Paddington Satchel
SKU# BBOS5828

A chic little bag with a funky edge. The Chloe Paddington has a whiskey colored pebbled leather exterior with a large padlock closure, and its thick round straps are easy on the shoulders. Soft, tan fabric interior has a secure zip pocket. Dimensions: 13"L x 7"W x 8"H, 7" drop handle.

This item is not available at this time. Click below to add it to your Wait List and it will be shipped to you as soon as it becomes available.

WAIT LIST

Can't afford this purse? Just rent it from Bag Borrow or Steal.
Courtesy of Bag Borrow or Steal TM.

Bag Borrow or Steal, founded in 2004 (http://www.BagBorrowOrSteal.com) rents luxury products such as handbags, jewellery, watches, and sunglasses to more than 1 million members. Customers have the option of becoming members by paying a monthly subscription fee that allows them to rent items for 20 percent off the listed prices and provides additional perks such as priority access to certain merchandise and reward points. For example, a BCBG clutch is available for about $9 a week or $25 a month for non-members, but members get 20 percent off. On the higher end, a Chloe Small Paddington Satchel bag that retails for about $1300 rents for about $100 a week or $250 a month for non-members, and about $65 a week and $200 a month for members. If a customer "falls in love" with an item, she has the option of paying a reduced price for it based on its condition and age. The website also offers an outlet store that sells items at 40 to 85 percent off the suggested retail price, depending on their condition.

When it was just getting started, 70 percent of Bag Borrow or Steal's sales were from its opening price point bags, those under $500, and included many well-known brands such as Kate Spade and Coach. Now about 80 percent of its sales are from the bags that retail for $1500 and up from well-known designers like Gucci and Prada. The business has grown considerably; a typical wholesale buy from a vendor is from $500 000 to $750 000, an amount rare for even the biggest luxury retailers like Bergdorf Goodman.

Many of their customers already have designer bags or other high-end accessories but cannot afford to buy the selection that is available to them through Bag Borrow or Steal. A bag, for instance, is an accessory item for which many consumers are willing to spend up to their limit, or above, because of its "noticeability" compared with other articles of clothing. "Fashionistas" especially value the ability to carry many designer bags throughout the year rather than just one or two.

Sources: http://fora.tv/2009/02/13/Weathering_the_Storm_Retail_Solutions_for_All_Seasons#Bag_Borrow_or_Steal_Fashion_Meets_Online_Innovation (accessed October 6, 2009); Paul Demery, "New Capital Wave," InternetRetailer.com, September 2008; Sarah Lacy, "The Tech Beat," *BusinessWeek*, March 7, 2006; Kate M. Jackson, "Renting a Handful of Luxury," *Boston Globe,* October 13, 2005; http://www.bagborrowsteal.com (accessed October 6, 2009).

© Payphoto | Dreamstime.com.

segment in Canadian retailing.[24] Many value retailers target low-income consumers, whose shopping behaviour differs from typical discount store or warehouse club customers. For instance, although these consumers demand well-known national brands, they often can't afford to buy large-size packages. Since this segment of the retail industry is growing rapidly and is known to pay its bills on time, vendors are creating special smaller packages for these people.

Value retailers follow a variety of business models. Although most cater to low-income groups, some draw from multiple-income groups and are generally located in suburban strip malls. They specialize in giftware, party, and craft items rather than consumables. Despite some of these chains' names, few just sell merchandise for a dollar. The $1 price is the focus, but the chains carry many different price points, all rounded off in even dollars. Your Dollar Store With More, a Kelowna, BC, franchise chain, has grown to 150 stores in five years and uses a similar pricing strategy. Dollar stores are attracting the "tween" market with low-cost, trendy cosmetics and jewellery for girls ages 8 to 13. The names imply a *good value*, while not limiting the customer to the arbitrary dollar price point.

Pop-Up Stores

So-called pop-up stores—temporary stores—are creating retail buzz as they respond to customers by reaching out in non-traditional ways and locations such as unfinished space. These stores pop up unexpectedly for hours, days, or months, draw word-of-mouth crowds, then vanish and may resurface someplace else. Subscribers are usually given notice via email as to time and place of the event. Smart retailers must be prepared to cater aggressively to their customers anywhere and anytime.

It is not enough for retailers to build a store and expect customers will find them. Strong retailers are reaching customers through touch points. Pop-up stores can also act as an effective promotional medium. These stores most often exist for a defined period of time in a place where the target customer will be focused. For example, a garden centre may open a temporary site to attract customers during the spring months to capture additional sales. Mobile wireless technology allows retailers to provide a full range of POS services to their non-permanent locations.

Pop-up stores are the perfect embodiment of a here today, replaced tomorrow retail ethic, which has built-in obsolescence at the core of the consumer dynamic. Brands and retailers love them because they create buzz, provide an incubator for new ideas, and permit targeted market research. Pop-ups can also provide benefits to a community, turning a forgotten neighbourhood into a destination or, like old-fashioned craft shows, allowing market exposure for those who can't afford the retail infrastructure.

In July 2015, Soma Beauty (a service business which offers massage therapy and cosmetic acupuncture) negotiated a three month lease as a pop up store in a Holt Renfrew franchise located in downtown Calgary with hopes of extending its lease if the business model concept was successful. The strategy for Soma was required as retail rental space along with a downturn in the economy forced the company to come up with a creative solution to identify a location (Place) for their business operations.[25]

Food Retailers

Ten years ago, people purchased food primarily at conventional grocery stores. Today, however, discount stores and warehouse clubs are significantly changing consumers' food purchasing patterns because they also sell food (see Exhibit 2–7). At the same time, traditional food retailers carry many

Exhibit 2–7
Canadian Food Retail Sales 2009–2013

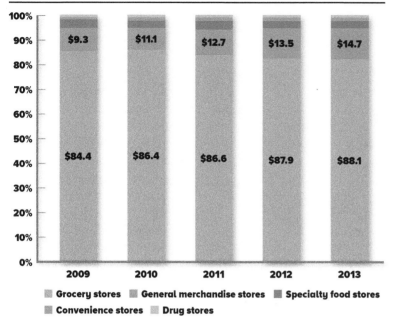

Source: Kenric S. Tyghe and Krisztina Katai, *Grocery as Science, Data as Art,* Raymond James, Oct. 24, 2014, p. 4. Courtesy of Raymond James.

Exhibit 2–8
Food Market Shares of the Top Canadian Grocers – 2008 and 2013

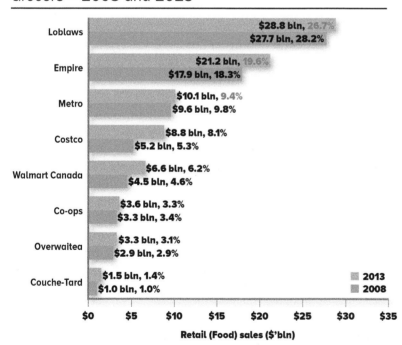

Source: Kenric S. Tyghe and Krisztina Katai, *Grocery as Science, Data as Art,* Raymond James, Oct. 24, 2014, p. 4. Courtesy of Raymond James.

non-food items, plus many have pharmacies, photo processing centres, banks, and cafés.

The world's largest food retailer is Walmart, with sales in the United States alone equalling $188 billion in 2013. The next-largest world food retailers that follow include: Tesco (United Kingdom), Carrefour (France), Costco (United States), Kroger (United States), Schwartz Group (Germany), and Metro Group (Germany). As shown in Exhibit 2-8, the largest grocery store chains in Canada are Loblaws, Empire (Sobeys), and Metro.[26, 27]

Loblaws (Weston Group) continues to achieve success with the President's Choice brand. It is also building convenience convergence by forming strategic alliances with coffee shops, fitness studios, photo marts, wine shops, dry cleaners, and other companies to provide its customers with the convenience of one-stop shopping. The addition of a community room that is available to local groups and charities, and which can be used for cooking classes by local chefs, is a popular community connection in Loblaws' newer stores. The experiences are all designed to build loyalty and stimulate sales.[28]

It is now easy to see that we can't easily answer the question, When is a food retailer really not a food retailer? Nonetheless, our discussion of food and **combination stores** will include conventional supermarkets, big-box food retailers, and convenience stores. Exhibit 2–9 shows the sales revenues and retail mixes for different types of food retailers.

combination stores Retailers that sell both food and non-food items.

conventional supermarket A self-service food store that offers groceries, meat, and produce with limited sales of non-food items, such as health and beauty aids and general merchandise.

Supermarkets

A **conventional supermarket** is a large, self-service retail food store offering groceries, meat, and produce, as well as non-food items such as health and beauty aids and general merchandise.[29] Perishables, including meat, produce, baked goods, and dairy products, account for 44 percent of supermarket sales and typically have higher margins than packaged goods.[30]

Exhibit 2-9
Characteristics of Food Retailers

	Conventional Supermarket	Limited-Assortment Supermarket	Supercentre	Warehouse Club	Convenience Store
Percentage food	70–80	80–90	30–40	60	90
Size (000 sq. ft.)	35–40	7–10	160–200	100–150	3–5
SKUs (000)	30–40	1–1.5	100–150	20	2–3
Variety	Average	Narrow	Broad	Broad	Narrow
Assortment	Average	Shallow	Deep	Shallow	Shallow
Ambience	Pleasant	Minimal	Average	Minimal	Average
Service	Modest	Limited	Limited	Limited	Limited
Prices	Average	Lowest	Low	Low	High
Gross margin (%)	20–22	10–12	15–18	12–15	25–30

limited-assortment supermarkets Supermarkets offering a limited number of SKUs; also called *extreme-value food retailers.*

superstore A large supermarket between 35 000 and 45 000 square feet in size.

power perimeter The area around the outside walls of a supermarket that have fresh-merchandise categories.

fair trade Purchasing practices that require producers to pay workers a living wage, well more than the prevailing minimum wage, and offer other benefits, such as on-site medical treatment.

locavore movement A movement whose adherents' primary source of food originates within a specified radius of where they live.

Whereas conventional supermarkets carry about 30 000 SKUs, **limited-assortment supermarkets** (also called *extreme-value food retailers*) stock only about 2000 SKUs.[31] Canadian retailer M&M Meat Shops is a good example of a successful limited-assortment supermarket. Each store is set up with one convenient aisle and large, glass-door freezers to display the entire selection. Certified product consultants serve the counter, answer questions, and provide helpful preparation tips and meal suggestions. M&M Meat Shops offer approximately 375 products, the majority of which are flash-frozen.[32] Dollar Tree Canada is another example of an extreme-value food retailer, with almost half of its product mix being food and drink, including perishable items such as milk and ice cream. A **superstore** is a larger conventional supermarket with expanded-service deli, bakery, seafood, and non-food sections.[33]

To compete successfully against other food retailing formats, conventional supermarkets are differentiating their offerings by (1) emphasizing fresh perishables, (2) targeting health-conscious and ethnic consumers, (3) providing a better in-store experience, and (4) offering more private-label brands.

Fresh Merchandise Fresh-merchandise categories are the areas around the outer walls of a supermarket, known as the **power perimeter**, that include dairy, bakery, meat, florist, produce, deli, and coffee bar. These departments attract consumers and are very profitable. The dairy and produce sections in particular are high-need items that, if of high quality and priced competitively, can increase store loyalty among customers. Conventional supermarkets are building on this strength by devoting more space to fresh merchandise with cooking exhibitions and "action" stations, such as store-made sushi and freshly grilled meat.

Another example of emphasis on "fresh" is the offering of meal solutions for time-pressured consumers. Canadian retailers such as Sobeys have introduced fresh formats like Sobeys Urban Fresh in an effort to boost their presence in urban markets. The largest store is 10 000 square feet, but the average is only about 3900 square feet, offering a broad assortment of grocery items in a much smaller footprint.

Health/Organic Merchandise Conventional supermarkets are also offering more natural, organic, and fair-trade foods for the growing segment of consumers who are health and environmentally conscious.[34] **Fair trade** means purchasing from factories that pay workers a living wage—considerably more than the prevailing minimum wage—and that offer other benefits such as on-site medical treatment. Although Whole Foods continues to be the world's largest retailer of natural and organic foods with stores throughout North America, other supermarket chains such as Loblaws and Metro are devoting significant space to natural and organic foods.

A related food retailing trend is offering locally grown products, a trend brought about in response to environmental concerns and the increasing financial costs (e.g., fuel) of transporting food long distances. The **locavore movement** focuses on reducing the carbon footprint caused by the transportation of food throughout the world. Food miles are calculated using the distance that food travels from the farm to the plate. Many Canadians appreciate the idea of supporting local businesses, but they also want the variety of products they can find in their grocery store. It is difficult to maintain a balance between buying locally and maintaining such variety. Leading the growing movement toward buying local and satisfying consumer demand when it comes to sourcing food, Loblaws launched the "Ontario Grown—Picked at Its Peak" produce program in 2007 across all Ontario Loblaws, Fortinos, Zehrs, Valu-Mart, and Your Independent Grocer stores.

© AP Photo-Lisa Poole/The Canadian Press.

Private-Label Merchandise Conventional supermarket chains are leveraging their quality reputation to offer more private-label merchandise. Private-label brands benefit both customers and retailers. The benefits to customers include having more choices and finding the same ingredients and quality as in national brands at a lower price. The benefits of private-label brands to retailers include increased store loyalty, the ability to differentiate themselves from the competition, lower promotional costs, and higher gross margins compared with national brands. In Canada, just over 40 percent of consumers think that private-label brands are a good alternative to national brands, versus 37 percent of Americans.[35] According to a March 2011 report by Nielsen, titled *The Rise of the Value-Conscious Shopper*, 60 percent of Canadians indicated that their purchase of private-label products increased during the recession, while 95 percent indicated that they will continue purchasing private-label products post-recession.[36]

Loblaws' private-label products (with more than 8000 products marketed under private-label brands such as President's Choice, no name, Blue Menu, Mini Chefs, and more) have traditionally performed well, accounting for 26.9 percent of the company's sales in 2010. Loblaws continues in its strategy to leverage its private-label capabilities and scale with the launch of its Black Label line.[37] Premium private label (as evidenced by Tesco's success in the UK with Tesco Finest) is the fastest-growing segment within the private-label category. PC Black Label represents affordable indulgence and targets the so-called cross-shopping between Loblaws stores, which range in price point and selection from hard discount (No Frills) to superstore (Real Canadian Superstores) and supermarket (Loblaws), and specialty grocers like Whole Foods Market, Pusateri's, and Urban Fare.[38]

Improving the Shopping Experience Creating an enjoyable experience through better store ambience and customer service is another approach that supermarket chains use to differentiate themselves from low-cost, low-price competitors. Grocery stores are increasingly incorporating "food as theatre" concepts, such as open-air market designs, cooking and nutrition classes, demonstrations, babysitting services, and food tasting.

Big-Box Food Retailers

Over the past 25 years, supermarkets have increased in size and have begun to sell a broader variety of merchandise.

Supercentres are 160 000 to 200 000 square feet in size and offer a wide variety of food (30–40 percent) and non-food merchandise (60–70 percent).[39] They are the fastest-growing retail category. Supercentres stock between 100 000 and 150 000 individual items (SKUs). With the popularity of the superstore concept in Canada in the 1990s, Loblaws expanded its product offering by including clothing, pharmaceuticals, and other non-food items. By maintaining its quality and position through a three-part strategy of innovation, market domination, and reduction of costs, Loblaws remains relatively unchallenged in the Canadian grocery retail marketplace.[40]

supercentres Large stores (160 000 to 200 000 square feet) combining a discount store with a supermarket.

DID YOU KNOW?

Loblaw Groceterias in Toronto was the first self-serve and cash and carry grocery retailer in Canada, opening in 1919.[43]

By offering broad assortments of grocery and general merchandise under one roof, supercentres provide a one-stop shopping experience. Customers will typically drive farther to shop at these stores than to visit conventional grocery stores (which offer a smaller selection). General merchandise items (non-food items) are often purchased on impulse when customers' primary reason for coming to the store is to buy groceries. The general merchandise has higher margins, enabling the supercentres to price food items more aggressively. However, since supercentres are very large, some customers find them frustrating because it can take a long time to find the items they want.

Hypermarkets are also large (greater than 200 000 square feet) combination food (60–70 percent) and general merchandise (30–40 percent) retailers. Hypermarkets typically stock less than supercentres, between 40 000 and 60 000 items ranging from groceries, hardware, and sports equipment, to furniture and appliances, computers, and electronics.[41]

Hypermarkets were created in France after the Second World War. By building large stores on the outskirts of metropolitan areas, French retailers could attract customers and not violate strict land-use laws. They have spread throughout Europe and are popular in some South American countries such as Argentina and Brazil. Consider, for instance, France-based Auchan. It is a hypermarket chain with a workforce of 145 000 operating in 14 countries, including Taiwan, China, Argentina, the United States, Mexico, and most European countries. A typical store is 250 000 square feet and has 60 checkout counters, more than 100 000 food and non-food items, and 2000 shopping carts. Auchan offers everything from fresh produce to groceries to housewares to electronics.

hypermarkets Large combination food (60–70 percent) and general merchandise (30–40 percent) retailers.

big-box stores Large, limited-service retailers.

warehouse club A retailer that offers a limited assortment of food and general merchandise with little service and low prices to ultimate consumers and small businesses.

Supercentres versus Hypermarkets Hypermarkets, per se, are not prevalent in North America,[42] although the differences between a French hypermarket and a Walmart are sometimes difficult to distinguish. Both hypermarkets and supercentres are large, carry grocery and general merchandise categories, are self-service, and are located in warehouse-type structures with large parking facilities. However, hypermarkets carry a larger proportion of food items than supercentres, with a greater emphasis on perishables—produce, meat, fish, and bakery items. Supercentres, in contrast, have a larger percentage of non-food items and focus more on dry groceries, such as breakfast cereal and canned goods, instead of fresh items.

Although supercentres and hypermarkets are the fastest-growing segments in food retailing, they face challenges in finding locations for new, large, limited-service **big-box stores**. In Europe and Japan, land for building large stores is limited and expensive. New supercentres and hypermarkets in these areas often have to be multi-storey, which increases operating costs and reduces shopper convenience. Furthermore, some countries place restrictions on the size of new retail outlets. In both Canada and the United States, there has been a backlash against large retail stores, particularly Walmart outlets. These opposing sentiments are based on local views that big-box stores drive local retailers out of business.

DID YOU KNOW?

Statistics from the industry magazine *Canadian Grocer* suggest that Chinese Canadians source and consume about 20 percent of their meals out-of-home, while the national average lingers around 15 percent.[44]

DID YOU KNOW?

Of the largest 100 retailers worldwide, over 89 percent are from France, Germany, Japan, the United Kingdom, and the United States.

Warehouse Club A **warehouse club** is a retailer that offers a limited assortment of food and general merchandise with little service at low prices to ultimate consumers and small businesses. Stores are large (100 000 to 150 000 square feet)[45] and located in low-rent districts. They have simple interiors and concrete floors. Aisles are wide so that forklifts can pick up pallets of merchandise and arrange them on the selling floor. Little service is offered. Customers pick merchandise off shipping pallets, take it to checkout lines in the front of the store, and pay with cash, credit, or debit. The largest warehouse club chains are Costco and US-based Sam's Club, a division of Walmart. Costco is the fifth-largest food retailer in Canada, with estimated food sales of $8.9 billion in 2013.[46]

Merchandise in warehouse clubs is about half food and half general merchandise. Specific brands and items may differ from time to time because the stores buy merchandise available on special promotions from manufacturers. Warehouse clubs reduce prices by using low-cost locations and store designs. They reduce inventory holding costs by carrying a limited assortment of fast-selling items. Merchandise usually is sold before the clubs need to pay for it.

Most warehouse clubs have two types of members: wholesale members who own small businesses, and individual members who purchase for their own use. For example, many small restaurants are wholesale customers who buy their supplies, food ingredients, and desserts from a warehouse club rather than from food distributors. Members usually pay an annual fee of $55 to $110. In some stores, individual members pay no fee but instead pay 5 percent over an item's ticketed price. Wholesale members typically represent less than 30 percent of the customer base but account for over 70 percent of sales. The membership fee–driven warehouse club is a US-based phenomenon.

Convenience and Drug Stores

Convenience stores provide a limited variety and assortment of merchandise at a convenient location in a 3000- to 5000-square-foot store with speedy checkout. They are the modern version of the neighbourhood mom-and-pop grocery/general store.

Enable consumers to make purchases quickly, without having to search through a large store and wait in a long checkout line. Over half the items bought are consumed within 30 minutes of purchase. Due to their small size and high sales, convenience and drug stores typically receive deliveries every day.

Convenience and drug stores offer a limited breadth and depth, and they charge higher prices than supermarkets. Milk, eggs, and bread once represented the majority of their sales. Now almost all convenience stores in non-urban areas sell gasoline as well, which accounts for over 55 percent of annual sales.

Although the convenience store concept has stagnated a bit in Canada and Europe, it has been growing throughout Japan, the rest of Asia, and in parts of Latin America. The reason is that the stores are so convenient. In many Asian countries,

Traditional food retailers are competing with convenience stores for customers who want prepared meals.
© The Canadian Press/Lars Hagberg.

consumers face space constraints at home, so they prefer buying in smaller quantities at neighbourhood locations. Additionally, many e-tailers in Asia use convenience stores as distribution points. Customers buy online and pick up at the store.[47] The largest convenience store retailer in Canada is Alimentation Couche-Tard with $37.9 billion in revenue (worldwide) in 2014.[48] The company operates a network of over 6241 stores in North America, and approximately 4750 of the stores sell motor fuel. Grouped under three main brands—Couche-Tard, Mac's, and Circle K —its neighbourhood stores feature a friendly, modern setting, with the majority of the stores open 24/7.[49]

convenience stores Stores that provide a limited variety and assortment of merchandise at a convenient location with speedy checkout.

Convenience stores also face increased competition from other formats. Sales tend to increase during periods of rising gasoline prices, but their dependency on gasoline sales is a problem because gasoline sales have low margins. In addition, supercentre and supermarket chains are attempting to increase customer store visits by offering gasoline and tying gasoline sales to their frequent shopper programs (e.g., Walmart, Canadian Tire, Real Canadian Superstore). Full-line discount stores also are setting up easily accessed areas of their stores with convenience store merchandise (e.g., Walmart).

Issues in Food Retailing

The primary issue facing food retailers in general, and supermarket and convenience store retailers in particular, is the increasing level of competition from other types of retailers. As mentioned earlier, supercentres in North America and hypermarkets in the rest of the world are growing at a rapid pace. In Canada, this growth has been spurred by Walmart's aggressive supercentre strategy. Competition is coming from other sources as well. Other retailers such as department stores, drugstores, convenience stores, gas stations, and even dollar stores are increasingly displaying food items on their shelves. In addition, fast-food restaurants such as Subway sandwich shops have positioned themselves as a healthy food alternative.

In response to these competitive pressures, convenience stores are taking steps to decrease their dependency on gasoline sales, tailoring assortments to local markets, and making their stores even more convenient to shop. To get gasoline customers to spend more on other merchandise and services, convenience stores are offering more fresh food and healthy fast food that appeals to today's on-the-go consumers, especially women and young adults. For example, Mac's combines a convenience store and takeout restaurant. Mac's has ready-to-heat meals, a sandwich bar, salads, and a ready-to-eat section. It also offers fresh produce, beverages, snacks, and other food. Customers can park, walk in, pick up tonight's dinner and tomorrow's breakfast, and be back in their cars in 10 minutes.[50]

electronic retailing A retail format in which the retailers communicate with customers and offer products and services for sale over the Internet. Also called *e-tailing, online retailing,* and *Internet retailing.*

The UK supermarket giant Tesco's Fresh & Easy stores sell fresh produce, meats, and ready-to-eat meals targeted at customers who do not want to visit a regular grocery store or spend too much time cooking.[51] Finally, convenience stores are adding new services, such as financial service kiosks that give customers the opportunity to cash cheques, pay bills, and buy prepaid telephone minutes, theatre tickets, and gift cards.

DID YOU KNOW?

According to Mintel, 73 percent of Canadian consumers shop at least once per week, and Statistics Canada reports that food purchases directly from retail stores comprise 77 percent of all food expenditures in Canada.[54]

Traditional grocery chains are fighting back by making significant investments in providing meal solutions, either hot food or partially cooked entrées. The market for prepared foods can be quite profitable. Profit margins on prepared foods are higher than most other grocery categories. Also, although shoppers rarely visit a supermarket in search of prepared foods alone, those who do spend almost 40 percent more than those who seldom or never purchase prepared foods.[52] Imagine being greeted by chefs in white hats tossing fresh pasta, with a dining area in the grocery store. The store could offer an extensive variety of prepared meals ranging from Caesar salads to Chinese food made by chefs in full view of its customers, and a satisfied customer saying, "They have the drama. I ask for a fresh salmon sautéed with a little lemon, browse ten minutes in the store, and take it home for dinner."[53]

Non-Store Retail Formats

In the preceding sections, we examined retailers whose *primary* modes of operation are bricks-and-mortar stores. In this section, we will discuss types of retailers that operate primarily in non-store environments. The major types of non-store retailers are electronic retailers, catalogue and direct-mail retailers, direct selling, television home shopping, and vending machines.

Electronic Retailing

Electronic retailing (also called *e-tailing, online retailing,* and *Internet retailing*) is a retail format in which the retailers communicate with customers and offer products and services for sale over the Internet. Shopping over the Internet provides the safety and convenience of catalogues and other non-store formats. However, the Internet, compared with store and catalogue channels, also has the potential to offer a greater selection of products and more personalized information about products and services.

Broader and Deeper Assortments One benefit of the Internet channel, compared with other channels, is the vast number of alternatives that consumers can consider. The number of SKUs available in a store is limited by the store's size. The number of pages in a catalogue limits that channel.

More Timely Information for Evaluating Merchandise An important service offered to customers is providing information that helps them make better buying decisions. The retail channels differ in terms of how much information customers can access. The amount of information available

Helping Couples Get Ready for the Big Day

The typical engagement and wedding planning process lasts 14 months, costs almost $25 000, and involves many emotionally charged decisions, such as how many and which people to invite, what print style to use on the invitations, where to hold the reception, what music to play during the ceremony, and what gifts to list in the bridal registry. Traditionally, the bride's family managed the wedding planning process. With more couples getting married when they are older, both working, and living farther from their parents, planning a wedding has become much more challenging.

Internet wedding sites, such as The Knot (http://www.theknot.com) and mywedding (http://www.mywedding.com/), offer couples

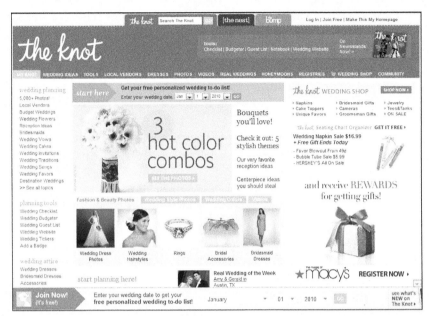

TheKnot.com offers information and merchandise to help couples prepare for their weddings.
Courtesy of The Knot Inc., www.theknot.com.

and their families planning guides and advice. A budgeting tool allows the couple to enter a dollar amount (say, $9000) and the number of guests (30), and it calculates, on the basis of national averages, how much they can spend on elements such as the bride's dress ($540) and bouquet ($68). With the tool, couples can also enter what they have actually spent, and it recalculates the sums that can be spent elsewhere. A planning tool is available to make sure arrangements are made, and reminders are emailed to the couple when key dates loom.

Couples can chat with experts and other couples on issues such as dealing with a micromanaging mother-in-law

or divorced parents. Gift registries can be created at different retailers and broadcast to guests through email. Couples can collect information from home rather than having to make visits to different suppliers. They can narrow the list of potential places for the reception by looking at photos on the Web, and they can download bands' audio clips from the Web instead of going to hear different bands play. Hotel reservations for out-of-town guests can be made over the Internet, and maps can be created to show those guests how to get to the hotel and reception. Finally, couples can have their own personal site on which they post their wedding pictures.

Sources: http://www.weddingchannel.com; http://www.theknot.com (accessed January 10, 2010).

---

through the store channel is limited by the number of sales associates and the space for signage. Similarly, the information available through a catalogue channel is limited by the number of pages in the catalogue. In contrast, the information provided through the Internet channel is unlimited. The vast amount of information available through the Internet channel enables customers using this channel to solve problems rather than just get information about specific products.

In addition to providing more information, the Internet channel offers customers more current

information whenever they want it. Retailing View 2.2 describes an Internet site that offers products plus information, some of which is generated by customers, which can help couples solve the problems associated with planning a wedding.

Finally, consumers can access information from other consumers through the Internet channel—information that may be viewed as less biased than information provided by a retailer or manufacturer. Many retailers provide an opportunity for customers to post reviews of products or services they have bought.

Personalization   Due to the Web's interactive nature, the most significant potential benefit of the Internet channel is its ability to personalize merchandise offerings and information for each customer electronically. Customers control some of this personalization. Customers shopping on an Internet channel can drill down through Web pages until they have enough information to make a purchase decision. In addition, when using the Internet channel, customers can format the information so that it can be effectively used when they are comparing alternatives.

The retailer can play a more proactive role in personalizing merchandise and information through the Internet channel. For example, many retailers offer live chats: Customers can click a button at any time and have an instant messaging, email, or voice conversation with a customer service representative. This technology also enables retailers to send a proactive chat invitation automatically to customers on the site. The timing of these invitations can be based on the time the visitor has spent on the site, the specific page the customer is viewing, or a product on which the customer has clicked. At Bluefly.com, for example, if a visitor searches for more than three items in five minutes, thereby demonstrating more than a passing interest, Bluefly will display a pop-up window with a friendly face offering help.

The interactive nature of the Internet also provides an opportunity for retailers to personalize their offerings for each of their customers. For example, Amazon provides customers with a personalized landing page with information about books and other products of interest based on the customer's past purchases and search behaviour on the website. Amazon also sends interested customers customized email messages that notify them that their favourite author or recording artist has published a new book or released a new CD. Another personalization opportunity is presenting customers with recommendations of complementary merchandise. Just as a well-trained salesperson would make recommendations to customers before checkout, an interactive Web page can make suggestions to shoppers about additional items that they might like to consider.

Exhibit 2–10

Retail e-Commerce Sales in Canada 2014–2019, Billions of C$, % Change and % of Total Retail Sales

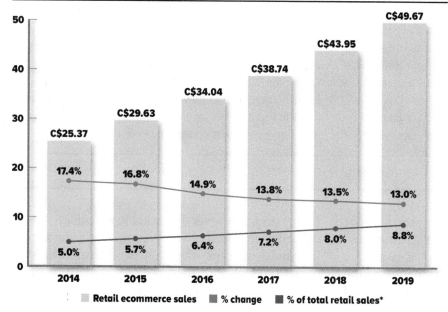

Legend: Retail ecommerce sales   % change   % of total retail sales*

Note: includes products or services ordered using the internet via any device, regardless of the method of payment or fulfillment; excludes travel and event tickets; *eMarketer benchmarks its Canada total retail sales figures against Statistics Canada (StatCan) data, for which the last full year measured was 2014
Source: eMarketer, July 2015

Source: "In Canada, Retail Ecommerce Sales to Rise by Double Digits Through 2019," *eMarketer. com*, July 24, 2015, http://www.emarketer.com/Article/Canada-Retail-Ecommerce-Sales-Rise-by-Double-Digits-Through-2019/1012771 (accessed December 22, 2015). Courtesy of eMarketer.com.

Online Retail in Canada   Despite Canada's reputation as one of the world's most wired and digitally social people, Canadians were projected to spend $25.37 billion online in 2015, or just 5.9 percent of total retail sales (Exhibit 2–10), according to eMarketer.[55] Even though Canadians spend more time online compared with all other countries, with the average being 24 hours per week, online sales in Canada have some catching up to do. The online market is not as mature as the United States, where a long history of catalogue sales, better shipping infrastructure, and other factors have made online buying a fast friend to many consumers. In the United States, sales for 2015 were projected to be approximately $349 billion.[56,57]

Large Canadian retailers have struggled to serve their customers on the Web: Canadian Tire abandoned online selling

Exhibit 2-11
Canadian Shopping Trends

Canadian shopping trends

68%
made their first online purchase
more than three years ago

42%
of millennials buy online monthly

The main reason for shopping online?
46% say 'convenience'

Computer, tablet or mobile

Top products customers **research** online	66% consumer electronics and computers
	63% books, music, movies and video games
	53% household appliances
S Top products customers **purchase** online	52% books, music, movies and video games
	28% consumer electronics and computers
	23% clothing and footware

In-store

Top products customers **research** in-store	51% grocery
	38% furniture and homeware
	36% clothing and footware
S Top products customers **purchase** in-store	82% do-it-yourself/home improvement
	72% furniture and homeware
	71% household appliances

Source: PwC Canada.

three years ago, and while it now has plans to return, the only thing customers can buy through its website are tires. Hudson's Bay Company is back online after shutting down its online efforts in 2009, and Shoppers Drug Mart offers only e-flyers and directions to their nearest stores online. Their US peers, meanwhile, operate full e-stores.[58]

Some blame the lack of a catalogue-buying tradition in Canada; others blame our sprawling geography that can make shipping slow and expensive. Four in ten dollars spent online in Canada goes abroad, meaning a large portion of spending isn't going back into the Canadian economy.[60] Getting e-commerce right needs to be part of making the Canadian retail sector more productive and competitive. Exhibit 2–11 shows information about Canadian online shopping trends.

DID YOU KNOW?

63 percent. Percent of Canadians more likely to continue doing business with a company that has a loyalty program.[59]

Catalogue Channel

The **catalogue channel** is a non-store retail channel in which the retail offering is communicated to customers through a catalogue, whereas direct-mail retailers communicate with their customers using letters and brochures. Historically, catalogue and direct-mail retailing were most successful with rural consumers, who lacked ready access to retail stores. Today's consumers enjoy the convenience of shopping by catalogue. The major catalogue retailers have embraced a multichannel strategy by integrating the Internet into their catalogue operations. Customers often get a catalogue in the mail, look it over, and go to the Internet for more information and to place an order. The merchandise categories with the greatest catalogue sales are drugs and beauty aids, computers and software, clothing and accessories, furniture and housewares, and books, music, and magazines.[61]

In recent years, a new breed of catalogue has sprung up to give this old form of retailing a new look—niche catalogue retailing. These retailers are focused on niche markets, such as retired middle-class women or young mothers. Artigiano, for example, sells high-end Italian fashion from catalogues and the Web, while the US-based Lollipop Moon sells hard-to-find, trendy baby clothing. The success of these retailers comes down to a number of factors: People are increasingly prepared to pay more for quality products; they prefer niche to mass-market brands; and they like the convenience of being able to shop and order from home.

catalogue channel
A non-store retail format in which the retailer communicates directly with customers using catalogues sent through the mail.

Exhibit 2–12

Capabilities Needed to Successfully Sell Merchandise Online

Capabilities	Electronic-only Retailers	Catalogue Retailers	Store-based Retailers	Merchandise Manufacturers
Strong brand name and image to build traffic and reduce customers' perceived risk	Low	Medium to high	High	Medium to high
Availability of customer information to tailor presentations	Medium to high	High	Medium to high	Low
Providing and managing complementary merchandise and services	High	High	High	Medium
Offering unique merchandise	Low	Medium to high	Medium to high	High
Presenting merchandise and information in electronic format	High	High	Medium to high	Medium
Efficient distribution system to deliver merchandise to homes and accept returns	Low	Medium to high	High	Low

As indicated in Exhibit 2–12, catalogue retailers are best positioned to exploit an electronic retail channel. They have very efficient systems for taking orders from individual customers, packaging the merchandise ordered for shipping, delivering it to homes, and handling returned merchandise. They also have extensive information about their customers and database management strategies to effectively personalize service. Finally, the visual merchandising skills necessary for preparing catalogues are similar to those needed in setting up an effective website.

The IKEA catalogue, considered to be the main marketing tool of the company, was first published in Sweden in 1951 and is distributed both by mail and in-store for no charge to its customers. The Swedish home furnishing retailer printed and distributed its IKEA catalogue to over 219 million consumers worldwide in 34 languages and 49 countries in 2016, and inspired people around the world to create homes that they love.[62] IKEA customers have also been able to access the catalogue online since 2011 and can now also use the IKEA Catalogue App on their smartphone and tablet to scan select pages to unlock films, interactive experiences, photo galleries, and more home furnishing inspiration.[63]

The Internet has become a natural extension to most cataloguers' selling strategy; 95 percent of catalogues describe themselves as multichannel retailers, with 53 percent defining their companies as catalogue/Internet/retail and 42 percent as catalogue/Internet.[64] Although firms spend millions of dollars mailing catalogues, only about 1.3 percent of the catalogues mailed generate a direct sale.[65] The use of catalogues is coming under attack from consumer groups that believe that catalogues are an unnecessary waste of natural resources. In the United States, catalogues account for 3 percent of the roughly 80 million tonnes of paper products used annually. That is more than either magazines or books.[66] Further, catalogues' share of sales is declining relative to the Internet. But catalogues are not going away. Analysts believe that their role is shifting from primarily generating sales to driving traffic to the Internet and physical stores.

Direct-mail retailers typically mail brochures and pamphlets to sell a specific product or service to customers at one point in time. For example, American Express sells a broad array of financial services targeted to the consumer. In addition to the focus on a specific product or service, most direct-mail retailers are primarily interested in making a single sale from a specific mailing, whereas catalogue retailers typically maintain relationships with customers over time.

The catalogue channel provides some benefits to customers, such as safety and convenience, that are associated with all non-store channels. However, catalogues also have some unique convenience advantages over other non-store formats.

Safety Security in malls and shopping areas is becoming an important concern for many shoppers, particularly the elderly. Non-store retail channels enable customers to review merchandise and place orders from a safe environment—their home.[67]

Convenience Catalogues offer the convenience of looking at merchandise and placing an order from almost anywhere 24/7. However, catalogues are easier to browse through than websites. Consumers can refer to the information in a catalogue anytime by simply picking it up from the coffee table. They can take a catalogue to the beach and browse through it without an Internet connection.

Finally, the information in a catalogue is easily accessible for a long period of time. However, it is important to note that the use of smartphones and tablets has changed how consumers can access and view information.

Direct Selling

Direct selling is a retail channel in which salespeople interact with customers face-to-face in a convenient location, either at the customer's home or at work. Direct salespeople demonstrate merchandise benefits and/or explain a service, take an order, and deliver the merchandise. Direct selling is a highly interactive retail channel in which considerable information is conveyed to customers through face-to-face discussions. However, providing this high level of information, including extensive demonstrations, is costly. Home parties organized by associates of the Pampered Chef are a method used to sell kitchenware.

The Canadian Direct Sellers Association (DSA) represents 50 companies with sales revenue of over $2 billion annually and accounts for over 16 percent of non-store retail sales in Canada.[68] According to the Canadian DSA, over 900 000 Canadians are associated with the direct selling industry, and 91 percent of direct sellers in this country are women.[69] Annual US sales through direct selling are over $30 billion; worldwide, they are more than $100 billion.[70] The largest categories of merchandise sold through direct selling are personal care (e.g., cosmetics, fragrances), home and family care (e.g., cooking, kitchenware), wellness (e.g., weight loss products, vitamins), and leisure and educational items (e.g., books, videos, toys).

Similar to catalogue retailers and television shopping networks, direct sellers are using the Internet to complement their face-to-face selling. Approximately 73 percent of all direct sales are made face-to-face, mostly in homes.[71] Salespeople who work in direct sales are independent agents who are not employed by the direct sales firms, but rather act as independent distributors, buying merchandise from the firms and then reselling it to customers. In addition, 87 percent of direct salespeople work part-time (fewer than 30 hours per week). In most cases, direct salespeople may sell their merchandise to anyone, but some companies, such as Avon, assign territories to salespeople who regularly contact households in their territory.

Two special types of direct selling are the party plan and multilevel systems. About one-quarter of

> **direct selling** A retail format in which a salesperson, frequently an independent distributor, contacts a customer directly in a convenient location (either at a customer's home or at work), demonstrates merchandise benefits, takes an order, and delivers the merchandise to the customer.

Courtesy of IKEA Canada.

party plan system
Salespeople encourage people to act as hosts and invite friends or co-workers to a "party" at which the merchandise is demonstrated. The host or hostess receives a gift or commission for arranging the meeting.

multilevel system A retail format in which people serve as master distributors, recruiting other people to become distributors in their network.

pyramid scheme When a firm and its program are designed to sell merchandise and services to other distributors rather than to end users.

television home shopping A retail format in which customers watch a TV program demonstrating merchandise and then place orders for the merchandise by phone; also called *teleshopping*.

infomercials TV programs, typically 30 minutes long, that mix entertainment with product demonstrations and solicit orders placed by telephone from consumers.

direct-response advertising Advertisements on TV and radio that describe products and provide an opportunity for customers to order them.

all direct sales are made using a **party plan system**. Salespeople encourage customers to act as hosts and invite friends or co-workers to a "party" at which the merchandise is demonstrated.[72] Sales made at the party are influenced by the social relationship of the people attending with the host or hostess, who receives a gift or commission for arranging the party. At the party, the merchandise is demonstrated and attendees place orders. A party system can be, but does not have to be, used in a multilevel network.

Almost three-quarters of all direct sales are made through multilevel sales networks. In a **multilevel system**, independent businesspeople serve as master distributors, recruiting other people to become distributors in their network. The master distributors either buy merchandise from the firm and resell it to their distributors or receive a commission on all merchandise purchased by the distributors in their network. In addition to selling merchandise themselves, the master distributors are involved in recruiting and training other distributors.

Some multilevel direct selling firms are illegal pyramid schemes. A **pyramid scheme** develops when the firm and its program are designed to sell merchandise and services to other distributors rather than to end users. The founders and initial distributors in pyramid schemes profit from the inventory bought by later participants, but little merchandise is sold to consumers who use it.

Television Home Shopping

Television home shopping, also known as *T-commerce* or *teleshopping*, is a retail format in which customers watch a TV program demonstrating merchandise and then place orders for the merchandise by telephone. Recent technology advances even allow viewers to purchase products using their TV's remote control.[73] The three forms of electronic home shopping retailing are:

- cable channels dedicated to television shopping
- infomercials
- direct-response advertising

Infomercials are TV programs, typically 30 minutes long, that mix entertainment with product demonstrations and then solicit orders placed by telephone. **Direct-response advertising** includes advertisements on TV and radio that describe products and provide an opportunity for consumers to order them.

The Shopping Channel Facts

364:	The number of days the channel broadcasts live (every day but Christmas).
18:	The number of hours the channel broadcasts live each day.
10 000:	The number of phone calls/ emails/ chats received in a day.
2 802 262:	The number of phone calls/ emails/ chats received in 2012.
8 500 000:	The number of homes The Shopping Channel programming reaches in Canada.
3 966 103:	The number of items shipped in 2012.
16 000:	The average number of packages the distribution centre ships a day.
208 727:	The number of videos viewed on TheShoppingChannel.com on average per month.
3500:	The number of BlackBerry PlayBooks sold in one day.
800:	The number of products presented each week.
26 115:	The number of videos the channel currently holds as resource material.
200:	The number of operators in the channel's customer care centre.
24:	The number of hours those operators staff the customer care centre.
6552:	The hours of live TV produced by the channel each year.

Source: Paul Irish, "The Shopping Channel can be an alternative to crowded mall at Christmas," *Toronto Star*, December 6, 2012, http://www.thestar.com/life/2012/12/06/the_shopping_channel_can_be_an_alternative_to_crowded_mall_at_christmas.html. Reprinted with permission – Torstar Syndication Services.

The Shopping Channel is located in Mississauga, Ontario, and on any given day the business can move thousands of units of a single item, such as a necklace. The potential sales volume of the daily show stopper—the station's version of a door crasher—is staggering. For example, the company moved $4 million in Dell computers in one day. The Shopping Channel broadcasts 18 hours of live broadcasting a day. This multichannel retailer offers up bargains through TV cable/satellite households, website, catalogue, and soon via interactive television that combines television with a computer.

The logistical issues connected with television retailing are apparent when you consider 10 000 products in stock and between 200 to 1000 new items arriving each week. Every item must be photographed, video-taped, catalogued, and made ready for television and to accommodate online sales through http://www.theshoppingchannel.com.

Competitors to the Canadian Shopping Channel are home shopping networks out of the United States that broadcast through infomercials and online, Amazon and eBay, and Sears Canada, which offers a department store selection.

The major advantage of TV home shopping compared to catalogue retailing is that customers can see the merchandise demonstrated on the TV screen. However, customers can't examine a particular type of merchandise or a specific item when they want to, as they can with catalogues. They have to wait until the merchandise shows up on the screen. To address this limitation, home shopping networks schedule categories of merchandise for specific times so that customers looking for specific merchandise can plan their viewing time.

Vending Machine Retailing

Vending machine retailing is a non-store format in which merchandise or services are stored in a machine and dispensed to customers when they deposit cash or use a credit card. Vending machines are placed at convenient, high-traffic locations such as in the workplace, at the airport, or on university campuses, and primarily contain snacks or drinks.

Although $25.6 billion in goods is sold annually through vending machines in North America, vending machine sales growth is relatively slow, less than 5 percent, and closely mirrors the growth in

DID YOU KNOW?

Smartphones have become so important that 33 percent of consumers would rather give up TV than their smartphone.[74]

the economy.[76] Vending machine sales growth has been declining during the past few years. The vast majority of vending machine sales are cold beverages, candy, and snacks, but sales in these categories are being adversely affected by growing concerns among consumers about healthy eating habits.

DID YOU KNOW?

Japan has 5.4 million vending machines—one machine for every 23 people. Unlike the packaged-food and soft-drink offerings in North America, products in Japan range from rice crackers and eyebrow shapers, to micro radios and condoms.[75]

Technological developments in vending machine design may result in long-term sales growth. New video kiosk vending machines enable consumers to see the merchandise in use, get information about it, and use their credit cards to make a purchase. The new vending machine designs also enable the retailers to increase the productivity of the machines. Electronic systems in the machine keep track of inventory, cash, and other operating conditions. Then radio devices transmit data back to a host computer. These data are analyzed, and communications are sent to route drivers telling them when stockouts and malfunctions occur.[77]

Svetlana Uduslivaia, senior research analyst with Euromonitor International, says vending operators are branching out from the traditional vending offerings of snacks and beverages in order to stay relevant to today's consumers. "Products that have not traditionally been a stronghold of the vending industry, for instance, consumer electronics (Apple and Best Buy) and skin care products (Sephora and Pro Active), are now starting to be sold through vending machines in the US and Canada. Consumers are seeing them in airports, shopping malls, grocery stores, and department stores."[78]

A current trend in Canada is to offer a healthier alternative in vending machines. The problem is these healthier alternatives end up costing more since they have a shorter shelf life and they are not as profitable as sugary treats. Thus consumers have to pay more for healthier food alternatives in vending machines.[79]

"DVD rentals [through vending machines], which have been fairly successful in the US, are now coming into Canada as well. With the closure of Blockbuster locations and the general lack of extensive DVD rentals, industries

vending machine retailing A non-store format in which merchandise or services are stored in a machine and dispensed to customers when they deposit cash or use a credit card.

are trying to see if they can fill the void and benefit from that," Uduslivaia says.

LO4 Services Retailing

The retail firms discussed in the previous sections sell products to consumers. However, **services retailers**, firms selling primarily services rather than merchandise, are a large and growing part of the retail industry. Consider a typical Saturday. After a bagel and cup of coffee at a nearby Tim Hortons, you go to the laundromat to wash and dry your clothes, drop a suit off at a dry cleaner, leave film to be developed at a Shoppers Drug Mart, and make your way to the Jiffy Lube to have your car's oil changed. Since you are in a hurry, you drive through a Taco Bell so that you can eat lunch quickly and not be late for your haircut at 1 p.m. By mid-afternoon, you're ready for a swim at your health club. After stopping at home for a change of clothes, you're off to dinner, a movie, and dancing with a friend. Finally, you end your day with a caffé latte at Starbucks, having interacted with ten different services retailers during the day.

There are several trends that suggest considerable future growth in services retailing. For example, the aging of the population will increase demand for health services. Younger people too are spending increasing amounts of time and money on health and fitness. Parents in two-income families are willing to pay to have their homes cleaned, lawns maintained, clothes washed and pressed, and meals prepared so that they can spend more time with their families.

There is a wide variety of services retailers. These companies are retailers because they sell goods and services to consumers. However, some of these companies are not just retailers. For example, airlines, banks, hotels, and insurance and express mail companies sell their services to businesses as well as consumers. Also, a large number of services retailers, such as lawyers, doctors, and dry cleaners, focus on local markets and do not have a Canada-wide presence.

Many organizations—such as banks, hospitals, health spas, legal clinics, entertainment firms, and universities—that offer services to consumers traditionally haven't considered themselves as retailers. Due to increased competition, these organizations are adopting retailing principles to attract customers and satisfy their needs.

All retailers provide goods and services for their customers. However, the emphasis placed on the merchandise versus the services differs across retail formats, as Exhibit 2–13 shows. On the left side of the exhibit are supermarkets and warehouse clubs. These retail formats consist of self-service stores that offer very few services. However, these formats do offer a few services, such as cheque cashing and some assistance from store employees. Moving along the continuum from left to right, we find category specialists, which also emphasize self-service but have employees who can answer questions, demonstrate merchandise, and make recommendations. Next, department and specialty stores provide even higher levels of service. In addition to assistance from sales associates, these stores offer services such as gift wrapping, bridal registries, and alterations.

Optical centres and restaurants lie somewhere in the middle of the merchandise/service continuum. In addition to selling frames, eyeglasses, and contact lenses, optical centres also provide important services such as eye examinations and eyeglass fittings. Similarly, restaurants offer food plus a place to eat, music in the background, a pleasant

services retailer
Organization that offers consumers services rather than merchandise. Examples include banks, hospitals, health spas, doctors, legal clinics, entertainment firms, and universities.

© John Lund/Marc Romanelli/ Blend Images LLC.

© Hiya Images/Corbis.

Purestock/SuperStock.

These are retailers, too. You start the day with a bagel, go to the bank, and then burn off the calories at the fitness centre.

Exhibit 2–13
Merchandise/Service Continuum

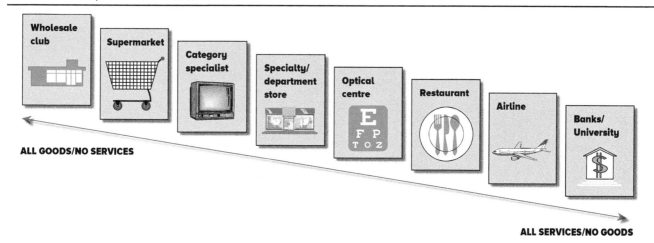

ALL GOODS/NO SERVICES

Wholesale club · Supermarket · Category specialist · Specialty/department store · Optical centre · Restaurant · Airline · Banks/University

ALL SERVICES/NO GOODS

ambience, and table service. As we move to the right end of the continuum, we encounter retailers whose offering is primarily services. However, even these retailers have some products associated with the services offered, such as a meal on the airplane or a chequebook at a bank. Services retailers are defined as retailers for which the major aspect of their offerings is services versus merchandise.

Differences between Services and Merchandise Retailers

As a retailer falls more to the right on the merchandise/service continuum, services become a more important aspect of the retailer's offering. Four important differences in the nature of the offering provided by services and merchandise retailers are as follows:

- intangibility
- simultaneous production and consumption
- perishability
- inconsistency of the offering to customers[80]

Intangibility Services are generally intangible—customers cannot see, touch, or feel them. They are performances or actions rather than objects. For example, health care services cannot be seen or touched by a patient. Even after diagnosis and treatment, the patient may not realize the full extent of the service that has been performed. Services retailers also have difficulty in evaluating the quality of services they are providing. To evaluate the quality of their offering, services retailers emphasize soliciting customer evaluations and complaints.

Simultaneous Production and Consumption Products are typically made in a factory, stored and sold by a retailer, and then used by consumers in their homes. Service providers, on the other hand, create and deliver the service as the customer is consuming it. For example, when you eat at a restaurant, the meal is prepared and consumed almost at the same time.

Because services are produced and consumed at the same time, it is difficult to reduce costs through mass production. For this reason, most services retailers are small, local firms. Large national retailers are able to reduce costs by "industrializing" the services they offer. They make substantial investments in equipment and training to provide a uniform service. For example, McDonald's has a detailed procedure for cooking french fries and hamburgers to make sure they come out the same whether cooked in Paris, France; Paris, Ontario; or Paris, Illinois.

Perishability Because the creation and consumption of services are inseparable, services are perishable. They can't be saved, stored, or resold. This is in contrast to merchandise that can be held in inventory until a customer is ready to buy it. Due to the perishability of services, an important aspect of services retailing is matching supply and demand. Most services retailers have a capacity constraint, and the capacity cannot be easily changed. There is a fixed number of tables in a restaurant, seats in a classroom, and beds in a hospital, as well as a finite amount of electricity that can be generated by a power plant. To increase capacity, services retailers need to make major investments such as buying more airplanes.

In addition, demand for service varies considerably over time. Consumers are most likely to fly on airplanes during holidays and the summer, and eat in restaurants at lunch and dinner time. Thus, services retailers often have times when their services are underused and other times when they have to turn customers away because they can't accommodate them.

multichannel retailer
Retailer that sells merchandise or services through more than one channel.

Services retailers use a variety of programs to match demand and supply. For example, airlines and hotels set lower prices on weekends when they have excess capacity because businesspeople aren't travelling.

Inconsistency Merchandise is often produced by machines with very tight quality control so that customers are reasonably assured that, for example, all boxes of a cereal will be identical. Because services are performances produced by people (employees and customers), no two services will be identical. The waiter at a restaurant can be in a bad mood and make your dining experience a disaster. Thus, an important challenge for services retailers is to provide consistently high-quality services. Services retailers expend considerable time and effort selecting, training, managing, and motivating their service providers.

Lo5 Multichannel Retailing

Retailers were classified either as store-based or non-store (electronic, catalogue/direct mail, direct selling, TV home shopping, and vending machine)

retailers. However, many retail firms use more than one channel to reach their customers. For example, Gateway started as an electronic retailer and has opened up stores; Amazon.com now distributes a catalogue; and Eddie Bauer and Sears interface with customers through their stores, catalogues, and websites.

A **multichannel retailer** is a retailer that sells merchandise or services through more than one channel. Single-channel retailers are evolving into multichannel retailers to attract and satisfy more customers. By using a combination of channels, retailers can exploit the unique benefits provided by each channel.

Exhibit 2–14 lists the unique benefits of stores, catalogues, and the Internet. These benefits illustrate how the channels can be used to complement each other.[81]

Store Channel

Stores offer a number of benefits to customers that they cannot get when shopping through catalogues and the Internet.

Personal Service Although shoppers can be critical of the personal service they get in stores, sales associates still have the capability of providing meaningful, personalized information.

Cash Payment Stores are the only channel that accepts cash payments.

Immediate Gratification Stores have the advantage of allowing customers to get the merchandise immediately after they buy it.

Entertainment and Social Experience In-store shopping can be a stimulating experience for some people, providing a break in their daily routine and enabling them to interact with friends. Paco Underhill, author of *How We Shop*, points out, "Stores are a social experience. I don't care how many chat rooms there are on a site, they will never provide what the experience of bricks-and-mortar shopping provides for all five senses, if not six or seven."[82]

Exhibit 2–14
Channel Benefits

Stores	Catalogue	Internet
• Browsing • Touching and feeling products • Personal service • Cash payment • Immediate gratification • Entertainment and social interaction	• Convenience • Portability; easily accessible • Safety • Visual presentation	• Convenience • Safety • Broad selection • Detailed information • Personalization • Problem-solving information

DID YOU KNOW?

Mountain Equipment Co-op (MEC) has close to 3.8 million members throughout Canada, including 565 000 in Quebec. MEC operates 16 stores in six provinces, and also serves customers online at mec.ca and through the new Shop MEC app.[83]

DID YOU KNOW?

Consumers report that information about the availability of merchandise in a local store is the most useful feature on a retail website.[84]

Convenience All non-store formats offer the convenience of looking at merchandise and placing an order any day at any time from almost anywhere.

Safety Non-store retail formats have an advantage over store-based retailers by enabling customers to review merchandise and place orders from a safe environment—their homes.[85]

Quality of Visual Presentation The photographs of merchandise in catalogues, although not as useful as in-store presentations, are superior to the visual information that can be displayed on a LCD screen.

LO6 Tuning into the Multichannel Universe

Consumers desire a seamless experience when interacting with multichannel retailers. They want to be recognized, whether they interact with a sales associate or kiosk in-store; log on to the retailer's website through a PC, smartphone, or tablet; or contact the retailer's call centre by telephone. Customers may want to buy a product through the retailer's Internet or catalogue channel, and pick it up or return it to a local store; find out if a product offered on the Internet channel is available at a local store; and, when unable to find a product in a store, determine whether it is available for home delivery through the retailer's Internet channel.

Retailers also benefit by using multiple channels synergistically. Multichannel retailers can use one channel to promote the services offered by other channels. For example, the URL of a store's website can be advertised on in-store signs, shopping bags, credit card billing statements, point-of-sale (POS) receipts, and the print or broadcast advertising used to promote the store. The physical stores and catalogues are also advertisements for a retailer's other channels. The retailer's electronic channel can be used to stimulate store visits by announcing special store events and promotions. Multichannel retailers can leverage their stores to lower the cost of fulfilling orders and processing returned merchandise. They can use their stores as "warehouses" for gathering merchandise for delivery to customers. Customers also can be offered the opportunity to pick up and return merchandise at the retailer's stores rather than pay shipping charges. Many retailers will waive shipping charges when orders are placed online or through the catalogue if the customer physically comes into the store.

The retail store is not dead and it's not going away. But it will evolve as the lines between the physical and virtual worlds continue to blur and customers demand an integrated experience across channels.[86] However, providing this seamless experience for customers and exploiting the synergies between channels is challenging. Retailers need to consider how to connect with customers across channels to provide them with an immersive and meaningful brand experience.

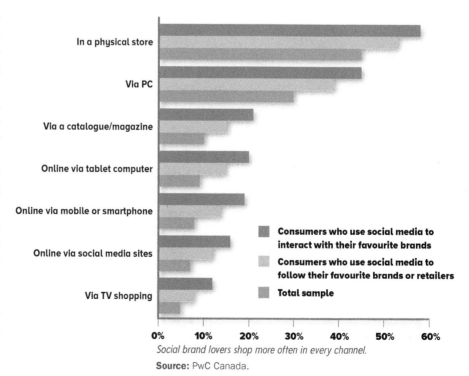

Social brand lovers shop more often in every channel.

Source: PwC Canada.

After all, consumers think of "shopping"—whether it is online, in-store, with a catalogue, or on mobile device—as one shopping experience, and therefore, so must retailers.[87]

M-commerce

Customers can access a retailer's Internet channel using a variety of devices, ranging from a desktop computer to a mobile phone or tablet. Due to the rapid growth of domestic and international broadband access through mobile devices, retailers are very interested in developing **m-commerce**—the purchase of products and services through mobile devices. In addition, retailers have developed apps—small computer programs—that enable mobile device users to engage in an activity such as shopping. For example, The Brick, working with the development company Imagiu Software Ltd., has an app that allows consumers to scan QR codes on furniture tags and size the furniture against a photo of a room in their home.

m-commerce The purchase of products and services through mobile devices.

The adoption of mobile devices by consumers is growing at a rapid rate. According to research conducted by Deloitte Consulting LLP, digital influence factors (defined as smartphones, tablets, and laptops) accounted for 36 percent (1.1 trillion) of all retail store sales in the United States in 2013.[88] Mobile is a natural fit for the Canadian consumer, as Canadians are adopting mobile technology at a similar pace to the United States. Many retailers are currently focusing on optimizing their websites for mobile devices. Strategies vary from having a mobile site with the same functionality as their websites, to developing sites that focus on what consumers would mainly need to access when they are out and about doing their shopping (for example, store locations, store hours, store contact information, etc.). According to Deloitte's research and analysis, the impact of smartphones isn't just on direct sales generated through the mobile channel, but also on the influence they exert over traditional in-store sales to drive in-store conversion and in-store average order size.[89]

- As of 2015, 68 percent of Canadians have smartphones, and it is estimated that "around 3 million Canadians bought their first smartphone in the past six months."[90]
- Roughly 58 percent of consumers who own a smartphone have used it for store-related shopping.
- Twenty-three percent of smartphone users who mobile-shop will research on the smartphone, visit the store to check out the product, and then purchase online (using a computer or Internet-enabled device).[91]
- Among smartphone shoppers, the percentage who use their smartphones for shopping varies by store category, from 49 percent in electronics and appliances stores to 19 percent in convenience stores and gas stations.
- Once consumers start using their smartphones for shopping, they tend to use them a lot—typically for 50 to 60 percent of their store shopping trips, depending on the store category.

Mobile's influence is expected to grow exponentially over the next few years, driven by a perfect storm of rising smartphone penetration, increased adoption by shoppers, decreasing

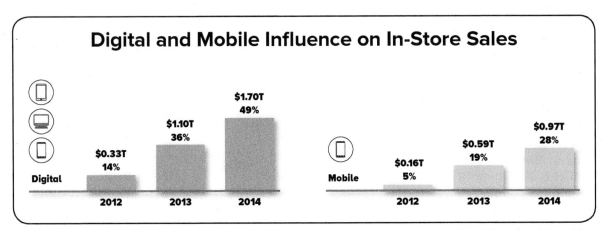

Digital and Mobile Influence on In-Store Sales

Digital: 2012 $0.33T 14%, 2013 $1.10T 36%, 2014 $1.70T 49%

Mobile: 2012 $0.16T 5%, 2013 $0.59T 19%, 2014 $0.97T 28%

Source: Deloitte Digital, "Navigating the New Digital Divide: Capitalizing on Digital Influence in Retail," 2015, Figure 3, p. 6, http://www2.deloitte.com/content/dam/Deloitte/us/Documents/consumer-business/us-cb-navigating-the-new-digital-divide-v2-051315.pdf.

The Impact of Social Media

 Shoppers are **29 percent more likely** to make a purchase the same day when they use social media to help shop either before or during their trip (90 percent vs. 70 percent conversion).

 Consumers who use social media during their shopping process are ≈ **4x more likely** than non-users to spend more or significantly more on purchases as a result of a digital shopping experience.[8]

 Respondents who consider themselves somewhat or very influenced by social media are **6x more likely** to spend significantly more than non-users (42 percent vs. 7 percent) due to their digital shopping experiences.[8]

Source: Deloitte Digital, "Navigating the New Digital Divide: Capitalizing on Digital Influence in Retail," 2015, Figure 8, p. 16, http://www2.deloitte.com/content/dam/Deloitte/us/Documents/consumer-business/us-cb-navigating-the-new-digital-divide-v2-051315.pdf.

barriers to use, and improved mobile functionality for retail applications.[92] In 2015, 76 percent of customers surveyed used digital devices to shop prior to going to the store.[93] Store-based retailers should consider mobile as a strategic imperative because it can impact the entire business, not just online or m-commerce. Retailers need to understand how their consumers may use their mobile devices, whether it is as simple as store locations or as complex as understanding what subset of their inventory consumers would be likely to buy through a mobile device.

Social media continues to impact the retail shopping experience as well, specifically regarding the amount a consumer is willing to spend.

Consumer needs vary by product and shopping trip, and retailers need to customize mobile app capabilities accordingly. Smartphones are most likely to be used for store-related shopping when the customer is close to or at the point of making a purchase, rather than as a passive shopping device. Deloitte's Mobile Influence Survey 2012 indicated that over 60 percent of mobile shoppers use their smartphones while in a store, and another 76 percent while on the way to a store. Retail analysts suggest that today's consumers merely use retail stores as a showroom before buying elsewhere. Deloitte's survey results echoed this threat, finding that 37 percent of shoppers surveyed who used a smartphone on their last trip used an external app or website (such as a price comparison tool or deal finder).[94,95] This indicates consumers often use other websites or mobile apps due to the retailer being unable to provide the appropriate digital tools to aid in the consumer's purchase decision process.

The mobile landscape is changing at a rapid rate, and retailers need to consider the ways in which they can leverage the mobile capabilities to best serve their customers. Mobile offers retailers a means to influence sales revenue and potentially improve conversion rates by engaging with customers and thereby significantly improving the customer experience. Exhibit 2–15 outlines consumer behaviour, trends, and statistics regarding mobile retail sales.

The Rise of Omni-Channel Retailing

This new phrase has surfaced recently in retail and is being hyped as "the next big trend." Omni-channel is definitely an iteration of multichannel as it is still a marketing strategy in which the retailer offers multiple ways for shoppers to buy its products, but with a stronger focus on a seamless approach to the customer experience through all available shopping channels. Multichannel means that the retailer and its branded products are on a variety of the key channels (store, online, mobile, TV, catalogue, or whichever medium the customer is interested in buying). **Omni-channel retailing** requires *seamless integration* between all channels so that shoppers can shop any way they want with the *exact same results*.

In a blog post on Econsultancy, Darren Hitchcock defines omni-channel retailing as "an integrated sales experience that melds the advantages of physical stores with the information-rich

DID YOU KNOW?

The Shopping Channel continues to grow in prestige year after year as one of Canada's foremost e-commerce retailers. E-commerce sales account for nearly 40 percent of the company's sales.[96]

omni-channel retailing Seamless integration between all channels so that shoppers can shop any way they want with the exact same results.

Exhibit 2–15
Mobile Retail Sales – Consumer's Behaviour, Trends, and Stats

Moment	Definition	Finding
Find Inspiration	The customer informally gathers information from a variety of trusted sources: family, friends, blogs, social media, and traditional media.	Seventy percent of consumers are now leading their own shopping journey (becoming aware of products through means outside of retailer or brand communications), while only 30 percent get their initial inspiration from a retailer or brand's advertisement.
Browse and Research	The customer begins to match the inspiration to a group of physical products that meet his/her need. He/she gathers additional information on the options available for sale.	Sixty-seven percent of shoppers browse retailer sites prior to shopping in stores, but nearly as many (61 percent) are using search engines for their browsing and research activities.
Select and Validate	The customer continues to narrow down his/her consideration set, eventually reducing the choices to only a few options. Then, he/she makes a selection and validates that the choice will best meet his/her need.	Sixty-seven percent of consumers read product reviews during their shopping journey. The reviews they read are split equally across retailers' sites or apps and third-party sites or apps.
Purchase and Pay	The customer locates the product (online or in a physical store) and determines how he/she would like to pay for and receive the item.	Thirteen percent of shoppers use the 'buy online, pick up in store' (or BOPUS) method to purchase and pay for their items. Twenty-five percent of consumers indicate that this is their preferred method for receiving their purchases in the future.
Return and Service	The customer returns to the original place or channel of purchase to seek follow-up related to the item.	Nearly 20 percent of shoppers would like to initiate a product return or refund from their personal digital device.

Source: Deloitte Digital, "Navigating the New Digital Divide: Capitalizing on Digital Influence in Retail," 2015, p. 10, http://www2.deloitte.com/content/dam/Deloitte/us/Documents/consumer-business/us-cb-navigating-the-new-digital-divide-v2-051315.pdf.

experience of online shopping."[97] With an omni-channel strategy, retailers allow customers to experience the brand, not a channel within the brand. Merchandise, promotions, pricing, customer service, and communications are not channel specific, but rather are consistent across all of the retail channels, not just one or two. That means that whatever channel the customers touch, they will see the same stock at the same price with the same promotions merchandised in the same way, and that connection is made and updated in real time.[98] The physical stores and e-commerce sites become an extension of the supply chain in which consumers can make purchases, but they are researched through other "channels" of communication.[99]

A retail study developed by Deloitte and the Retail Council of Canada in 2014 indicated that omni-channel retailing is slow to be employed as a retail strategy in Canada. Two key factors influencing this slow pace include current information systems and organizational culture. The study states:

"Historically, retailers have not invested in technology, leaving them with legacy systems that predate some of their employees, and some tough decisions on how to best move forward."[100] Peter Higgins, president and chocolate scientist for Purdy Chocolates indicates, "One significant challenge is around the question of whether you can effectively move forward with the systems you have in place today. Will they continue to be a match with the organization's future goals? In an omni-channel environment, systems and goals must be closely interrelated."[101] An organization's IT department must be working in conjunction with all departments in the organization to ensure fluidity. Organizations that work in silos will not be successful with implementing a omni-channel strategy.[102]

In order to employ a successful omni-channel retail strategy, an organization must consider the following five factors:

- Evaluate synergies across channels.
- Find the best operating methods.
- Choose technologies/processes for each operating method.
- Define optimal flow paths.
- Choose specific technologies.[103]

DID YOU KNOW?

Since 2013, Canadian Tire has spent over $300 million dollars setting up an omni-channel marketing system based out of Winnipeg, MB.

5 Examples of Omni-channel Retailing Done Right

- **Crate & Barrel** – The company recognizes that many shoppers switch from Web to smartphone to tablet when conducting research and completing purchases, so when customers are signed in, the C&B app saves their shopping cart so they can access their information across multiple devices and browsers. This enables them to pick up where they left off no matter where they are in the shopping process.
- **Oasis** – UK fashion retailer Oasis has an e-commerce site, a mobile app, and several brick-and-mortar locations, and it does a pretty good job in fusing those channels to give people a great shopping experience. Oasis arms its in-store associates with iPads to give shoppers on-the-spot information on product availability. This also allows the staff to ring up customers from anywhere in the shop. And if an item isn't in-stock, the staff can use their iPads to place online orders for the customer. A similar service is made available for online shoppers. If an item is sold out online, customers can use Oasis' "Seek & Send" service where the retailer searches its stores for the product and ships it to the shopper. Once the item is located, Oasis will send an email to notify shoppers and let them track their goods.
- **Starbucks** – The Starbucks rewards app is frequently mentioned in "top" lists of omni-channel efforts and for good reason: the coffee company does an excellent job in providing a seamless user experience across all channels. Customers have the option of checking and reloading their Starbucks card balance through their phone, the Starbucks website, or when they are at the store. Any balance or profile changes are also updated in real-time, across all channels, letting users stay in-the-know no matter where they are or what device they are using. Plus, any earned rewards are automatically reflected in the account without any action on the user's part.
- **Sephora** – Through its "My Beauty Bag" program, cosmetics retailer Sephora makes it easy for its loyal customers to manage their "loved" products and purchase history from any device. Sephora's Beauty Insiders (i.e., members of its reward program) can use their Beauty Bag on their phone or on their computer to view and track their purchases and rewards. They can add items to their shopping list, view their buying history, save items for future purchases, and easily re-order items. Shopping is a breeze with the ability for users to purchase products right from the app itself. Alternatively, when they are in the store, they can use Sephora's app to access their shopping list to complement their in-store experience.
- **Chipotle** – Chipotle Mexican Grill is using multiple channels to enable customers to place orders wherever they are. People can place an order online for pick-up at the nearest Chipotle location, and they can also use its official mobile app to order on the go. Plus, if they create an account, users can track past orders and save their favourites for faster ordering in the future. Account information can be accessed both online and using the app.

Source: Excerpt from Jason Trout, "5 Excellent Examples of Omnichannel Retailing Done Right," May 14, 2014, http://multichannelmerchant.com/must-reads/5-excellent-examples-omnichannel-retailing-done-right-14052014/ (accessed December 27, 2015).

With an omni-channel strategy, each channel needs to be *aware* of the other if the experience is to be seamless, as can be seen in Exhibit 2-16. The retail industry is already dominated by performance marketing, which includes site optimization, monetization modelling, search engine optimization, and paid search. An omni-channel strategy requires retailers to pay more attention to tagging and reporting, and then pulling all of the data collected together to build a sophisticated consumer profile. Awareness and seamlessness are possible only if retailers are integrating that customer and shopping data with behavioural profiling and preferences and being rigorous about adding to it at every opportunity. Consumers move from channel to channel on a regular basis, often to perform the same task, and they have expectations that what they do in one place will influence the experience in another. The challenge for retailers is to tell a continuous story that plays out whenever or wherever the consumer interacts with their brand.[104]

in-store kiosks Spaces located within stores containing a computer connected to the store's central offices or to the Internet.

In-Store Electronic Kiosks

Another multichannel approach to retailing is the addition of the electronic kiosk. **In-store kiosks** are spaces located within stores containing a computer

Exhibit 2-16
Designing Distribution Centres for Omni-Channel Fulfillment

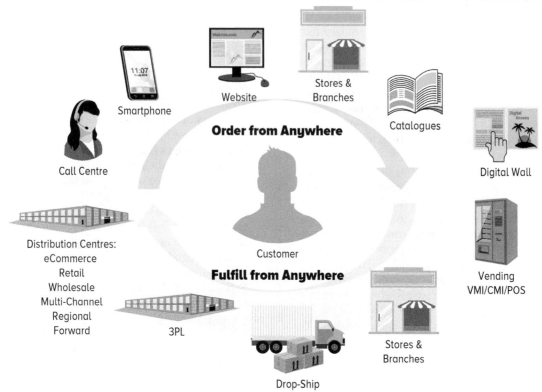

Source: *5 Steps to Designing Omni-channel Fulfillment Operations,* Fortna, http://www.fortna.com/whitepapers/designing-omnichannel-fulfillment-operations-en.pdf, p. 3 (accessed Dec. 27, 2015). Courtesy of Fortna Inc.

connected to the store's central offices or to the Internet. Customers or salespeople can use in-store kiosks to order merchandise through a retailer's electronic channel, check on product availability at distribution centres or other stores, get more information about the merchandise, and scan bar codes to check the prices. Retailers are interested in installing these kiosks because they create a synergy between the store and the Internet site. Kiosks provide additional assortment choices that aren't available in stores. For instance, The Source makes slower-moving electronic accessories available at its kiosks so that it doesn't have to carry them in its stores.[105] The typical Staples store has 9000 SKUs, compared to 100 000 offered via in-store kiosks.[106]

Do kiosks cannibalize store sales? Yes, but only initially. Shoppers who purchase in stores and online from an in-store kiosk tend to buy more. When REI installed in-store kiosks, it found that customers who shop both online and in the store spend 22 percent more than those who buy only from traditional stores.[107] Staples provided an incentive to

store managers to push the use of kiosks: Online sales are credited to the stores from which they are placed.[108]

There are downsides to making investments in these kiosks, however. First, they can be expensive—anywhere from $3000 to $25 000 per kiosk.[109] Second, once the investment is made, there is no guarantee that customers will use them. Gap Inc. abandoned its program because shoppers didn't use them enough.[110] Finally, there are significant costs in maintaining the kiosks—making sure they are working properly.

Customer Service Using Technology Many retailers are installing kiosks with broadband Internet access in the stores. In addition to offering customers the opportunity to order merchandise not available in the store, kiosks can provide routine customer service, freeing employees to deal with more demanding customer requests and problems. For example, customers can use kiosks to locate merchandise in the store and to inquire whether specific products, brands, and sizes are available in the store. Kiosks can also be used to automate existing store services such as gift registry management, rain checks, film drop-off, and credit applications, and to preorder service for bakeries and delicatessens.

Customers can use a kiosk to find out more information about products and how they are used. A Best Buy customer can use a kiosk to provide side-by-side comparisons of two high-definition TVs and to find more detailed information than is available from the shelf tag or from a sales associate. The customer can also access evaluations of the models as reported by *Consumer Reports*. The information provided by the kiosk could be tailored to specific customers by accessing the retailer's customer database. For example, a customer who is considering a new set of speakers might not remember the preamplifier purchased previously from Best Buy. This customer might not know whether the speakers are compatible with the preamplifier or what cables are needed to connect the new speakers. These concerns could be addressed by accessing the retailer's customer database through the kiosk.

Kiosks can also be used to provide customized solutions. For example, suppose a customer, perhaps with the assistance of a salesperson, wants to design a home entertainment system. A kiosk could allow the customer to see what the system would look like after setup. Finally, customers could use a kiosk to see how different colours of cosmetics would look on them without having to apply the cosmetics. These types of applications could complement the efforts of salespeople and improve the service they can offer to customers.[112]

DID YOU KNOW?

In January 2013, Sport Chek opened a concept store in Toronto with more than 140 digital screens to experiment with a mixed digital and retail experience.[111]

Integrated Concept   In summary, to provide this same face to a customer across multiple channels, retailers need to integrate their customer databases and systems used to support each channel.[113] In addition to the information technology issues, other critical issues facing retailers that want to provide an integrated, customer-centric offering include the following:

- centralized customer database
- brand image
- merchandise assortment
- pricing[114]

Centralized Customer Database   While there are differences in opinion about whether to integrate or separately manage many key multichannel activities, there is a general consensus on the need to establish a centralized customer data warehouse with a complete history of each customer's interaction with the retailer.[115] The centralized customer data warehouse is crucial for exploiting the ability to collect detailed customer data through the Internet channel and providing a seamless experience for customers when they interact with the retailer through multiple channels.

Brand Image   Multichannel retailers need to project the same image to their customers through all channels. For example, Talbots reinforces its image of classic-style apparel and excellent customer service in its stores, catalogues, and website. On the website, customers can consult an online style guide offering seasonal fashion tips and articles about how to buy the right size swimsuit, the art of layering, and petite sizing. Talbots' commitment to "friendly" service is reinforced by the availability of 24/7 personal service.

DID YOU KNOW?

According to the Deloitte Mobile Influence Survey (March 2012 and 2015), over 60 percent of mobile shoppers use their smartphones while in a store, and over 70 percent use them prior to shopping in a store.

Mountain Equipment Co-op (MEC) reinforces its image of selling high-quality, environmentally friendly sports equipment, not fashion, in the descriptions of MEC products. MEC's concerns about the environment are communicated by carefully engineered stores and using recycled polyester in many of its clothes, as well as only organic, rather than pesticide-intensive, cotton. Its web blog, blog.mec.ca, is dedicated to essays and other features on sports, innovative design, and environmental activism.

Merchandise Assortment   Typically, customers expect that everything they see in a retailer's store will also be available on its website. A significant product overlap across channels reinforces the one-brand image in the customer's mind. The trend now is to integrate the merchandise offerings across channels.

Multichannel retailers often offer a broader and deeper merchandise assortment through their Internet channel than through their store channel. The Internet channel is more efficient for selling merchandise that does not have broad appeal. The channels also differ in terms of their effectiveness in generating sales for types of merchandise. For example, the store channel is better suited for selling products with important "touch-and-feel" attributes such as the fit of a shirt, the taste of an ice cream flavour, or the smell of a perfume. On the other hand, an Internet channel might be just as effective as a store channel for selling products with important "look-and-see" attributes such as price, colour, and grams of fat. Evaluating these products does not require senses beyond sight. Because of the problems of providing touch-and-feel information, apparel retailers experience return rates of more than 20 percent on purchases made through an electronic channel but only 10 percent on purchases made in-store.

Pricing Pricing is another difficult decision for a multichannel retailer. Customers expect pricing consistency across channels (excluding shipping charges and sales tax). However, in some cases, retailers need to adjust their pricing strategy because of the competition they face in different channels. For example, chapters.indigo.ca offers lower prices over its electronic channel to compete effectively against Amazon.ca.

Retailers with stores in multiple markets often set different prices for the same merchandise to deal with differences in local competition. Typical customers do not notice these price differences because they are exposed only to the prices in their local markets. Multichannel retailers may have difficulties sustaining these regional price differences when customers can easily check prices on the Internet.

Multichannel retailers are beginning to offer new types of pricing, such as auctions, that take advantage of the unique properties of the Internet.

Reduction of Channel Migration The availability of an Internet channel enables customers to easily search for information about products and their prices. Browsing on the Internet channel and purchasing the merchandise at a store is the most common use of multiple channels during a shopping episode. Many consumers are now simply accessing the Internet on smartphones or tablets to browse social networks or shopping applications to find product information, read customer reviews, compare prices, or buy items.[116] In a recent Deloitte study, 42 percent of shoppers used smartphones for shopping-related activities at least once in the past year

for apparel, while 48 percent used devices to shop for consumer electronics.[117]

However, multichannel retailers want to prevent channel migration—consumers collecting information about products and pricing on their channels and then buying the product from a competitor.[119] Retailers want customers to both search for information and complete the transaction through their channels, but the low cost of searching on the Internet increases the opportunity for channel migration. Thus, customer retention during shopping episodes is a challenge for multichannel retailers. Note that before the Internet and mobile technology, customers typically researched and purchased products during a trip to one store because it was too "costly" to visit multiple stores. Two approaches that multichannel retailers can use to reduce channel migration are to (1) offer uniquely relevant information based on proprietary data the retailer has collected about the customers, and (2) promote private-label or exclusive merchandise that can be purchased only from the retailer.

Retailing View 2.3 describes how Canadian Tire is dealing with e-commerce.

DID YOU KNOW?

79 percent of Canadian smartphone users are unable to leave their homes without their device, and 60 percent have used their smartphone to access a Web page every day over the past seven days. Smartphones can officially be considered Canadian consumers' companions.[118]

Lo7 Types of Ownership

Previous sections of this chapter discussed how retailers are classified in terms of their retail mix (the variety and depth of merchandise and services offered to customers) and the merchandise and services they sell (food, general merchandise, and services). Another way to classify retailers is by their ownership. The major classifications of retail ownership are:

- independent, single-store establishments
- corporate retail chains
- franchises

Independent, Single-Store Establishments

Retailing is one of the few sectors in our economy where entrepreneurial activity is extensive. Over

60 000 new retail businesses are started in North America each year.[120] Many such stores are owner-managed. Thus, management has direct contact with customers and can respond quickly to their needs. Small retailers are also very flexible and can therefore react quickly to market changes and customer needs. They aren't bound by bureaucracies inherent in large retail organizations.

Although single-store retailers can tailor their offerings to their customers' needs, corporate chains can more effectively negotiate lower prices for merchandise and advertising due to their larger size. In addition, corporate chains have a broader management base, with people who specialize in specific retail activities. Single-store retailers typically have to rely on owner–managers' capabilities to make the broad range of necessary retail decisions.

To better compete against corporate chains, some independent retailers join a **wholesale-sponsored voluntary cooperative group**, which is an organization operated by a wholesaler offering a merchandising program to small, independent retailers on a voluntary basis. The Independent Grocers Alliance (IGA) is an example of a wholesale-sponsored voluntary cooperative group. In addition to buying, warehousing, and distribution, these groups offer members services such as store design and layout, site selection, bookkeeping and inventory management systems, and employee training programs.

Corporate Retail Chains

A **retail chain** is a company operating multiple retail units under common ownership and usually has centralized decision making for defining and implementing its strategy. There were about 2688 chains operating in Canada in 2012 with approximately 85 826 chain-store locations across the country.[121] Retail chains can range in size from a drugstore with two stores to retailers with many stores such as Loblaws, No Frills, Zehrs, Fortinos, and Real Canadian Superstore. Some retail chains are divisions of larger corporations or holding companies. For example, Venator owns Foot Locker, Lady Foot Locker, Kids Foot Locker, Foot Locker International, Champs Sports, and Footlocker.com/Eastbay. Champs; Intimate Brands owns Victoria's Secret, La Senza, Bath & Body Works, and The White Barn Candle Co.

There has been considerable concern that corporate retail chains drive independent retailers out of business. For example, Walmart has pursued a strategy of opening full-line discount stores and supercentres on the outskirts of small towns.[122] These stores offer a broader selection of merchandise at much lower prices than previously available from local retailers. Due to scale economies and an efficient distribution system, corporate chains can sell at low prices. This forces some directly competing local retailers out of business and alters the community fabric.

On the other hand, local retailers offering complementary merchandise and services can prosper. When large chain stores open, more consumers are attracted to the community from surrounding areas. Thus, the market for the local stores expands. Although chain stores may have cost advantages over local retailers, large retail chains can be very bureaucratic, stifling managers' creativity with excessive rules and procedures. Often, all stores in the chain have the same merchandise and services, whereas local retailers can provide merchandise compatible with local market needs.

Franchises

Franchising is a contractual agreement between a franchisor and a franchisee that allows the franchisee to operate a retail outlet using a name and format developed and supported by the franchisor. Approximately one-third of all North American retail sales are made by franchisees.

In a franchise contract, the franchisee pays a lump sum plus a royalty on all sales for the right to operate a store in a specific location. The franchisee also agrees to operate the outlet in accordance with procedures prescribed by the franchisor. The franchisor provides assistance in locating and building the store, developing the products or services sold, management training, and advertising. To maintain the franchisee's reputation, the franchisor also makes sure that all outlets provide the same quality of services and products.

wholesale-sponsored voluntary cooperative group An organization operated by a wholesaler offering a merchandising program to small, independent retailers on a voluntary basis.

retail chain A firm that consists of multiple retail units under common ownership and usually has some centralization of decision making in defining and implementing its strategy.

franchising A contractual agreement between a franchisor and a franchisee that allows the franchisee to operate a retail outlet using a name and format developed and supported by the franchisor.

How Canadian Tire is Grappling with the Economics of E-commerce

Technology can be both a blessing and a curse for traditional retailers.

On the one hand, Web, loyalty, and payment technologies provide retailers with deeper, more intelligent data about who their customers are, and what they are buying, segmented right down to a postal code.

On the other hand, Web technology requires a huge commitment, in dollar terms and manpower terms, to stay on top of how retail consumers shop—and the price transparency that brings allows those consumers to pick up the item they want at whichever retailer has it priced the lowest that week.

All the while, questions in the industry still abound as to whether retailers will be able to support a thriving Web operation without putting a serious dent in the profits and sales of their bricks and mortar stores.

That challenge will only grow in 2016: Online shopping in Canada is expected to grow at a pace of 12.9 per cent a year until 2019, according to Forrester Research, when sales will hit an estimated $39.9 billion and account for 10 percent of retail spending excluding autos, up from 6 percent in 2014.

For a legacy retailer like Canadian Tire, which infamously scrapped its original website in 2009 due to poor sales and relaunched it in 2011 with tires and general merchandise last year, getting e-commerce right the second time around has been even more critical.

"We are in the midst of a transformation, because the economics of e-commerce aren't there yet."

This time, the retailer has devoted far more of its resources to its digital initiatives, even though executives admit the unknowns of e-commerce represent both a challenge and an opportunity for the entire retail industry.

"We are in the midst of a transformation, because the economics of e-commerce aren't there yet," Allan MacDonald, Canadian Tire's chief operating officer, said in an interview. "There are still a lot of unanswered questions."

To meet the challenge of trying to answer some of those, Canadian Tire is spending a significant portion of its annual capital expenditures of $600 million to $625 million through to 2017 on digital technology investments. Its technology initiatives to date include launching digital flyers and interactive social media advertising, and opening a digital research hub in Waterloo, Ontario, to work on

Allan MacDonald, Canadian Tire's chief operating officer. The legacy retailer scrapped its original website in 2009 due to poor sales and relaunched it in 2011 with tires and general merchandise last year. Getting e-commerce right the second time around is even more critical.

Material republished with the express permission of: National Post, a division of Postmedia Network Inc.

customer tools including a shopping app and in-store digital tablets and product information screens. The retailer also launched a digital version of its veteran loyalty program, Canadian Tire money, which has grown to more than eight million members since its launch last fall.

Still, MacDonald noted, some of the same questions about the economics of e-commerce have persisted since it began in the 1990s, when so-called "pure play" Internet retailers believed they would upend the model of traditional retail.

At that time those startups reasoned that doing away with the costs of stores—pesky retail leases and customer-facing employees—would make online retailing a cheaper business model for owners, and a more convenient and cheaper way for consumers to shop. That might have been true to a degree for small, lightweight commodities or items with decent product margins—books and small electronics—but it proved untrue for larger, low margin items such as bags of pet food or diapers, and that remains the case.

"Conventional economics would tell you that delivery to home on demand can't possibly be cheaper," MacDonald said. "Should all products be treated equally in the online space? To be able to ship a barbecue to your house cost effectively at the price points that we sell is incredibly difficult—the margin just doesn't support it. And how does a

Material republished with the express permission of: National Post, a division of Postmedia Network Inc.

customer feel about me leaving a barbecue on their doorstep? Then, if need be, how are you going to return it?"

Canadian Tire solved one part of its e-commerce puzzle by using a so-called "click and collect" model for its relaunched site—customers who buy online pick up the products at their closest store, and home delivery of bulkier items is organized at those stores. The model is in use at Ottawa-area Walmart stores for groceries and in test market at a handful of Loblaws stores in the Toronto area.

The click and collect practice helps mitigate return costs, as customers can do a live, point-of-sale inspection for their purchases. Over time it also lowers warehousing costs: Canadian Tire can fill some online orders using store stock, rather than shipping online purchases from a warehouse.

But even in more mature online markets, it is not a given that such a retail model is sustainable. In the summer, UK department store retailer John Lewis introduced an £2 charge for all click-and-collect orders under £30. John Lewis operates in the UK, where e-commerce has grown to 33 percent of total trade from 10 percent over the past eight years and is viewed as a lower cost market than Canada from a fulfillment and supply chain cost perspective, due to the two countries' relative density, size, and distance between major cities.

"There is a huge logistical operation behind this system, and quite frankly it's unsustainable," Andy Street, managing director of John Lewis, told The Guardian in July. "We consider ourselves to be leaders, and we want to take the lead on this." The retailer noted it was expensive for the retailer to ship orders of small, inexpensive items to local stores and ready them for customer pickup.

"Pickup in the store is akin to personal shopping, so there is a cost for that," MacDonald said. In the meantime, he added, Amazon Canada still offers free shipping on orders above $25 for much of its merchandise.

"When you see those two things happening simultaneously to two quite successful companies (John Lewis and Amazon), you realize we are still figuring it out."

All bricks and mortar retailers who offer free home delivery of online orders will have to ultimately weigh the costs at every step of the value chain, he said, in order to see how well the model works for them.

"It's not like Canadian Tire is substantially more profitable than any other retail company in the world. Retail is not a huge margin business."

"They are adding in the step of delivering it to your door, and I am delivering it to a store in a massive 53-foot

Allan MacDonald, chief operating officer of Canadian Tire, at one of the retailer's Toronto stores.

Material republished with the express permission of: National Post, a division of Postmedia Network Inc.

container. They have got to take enough value out that they can deliver it to your door and make an equal amount of money. It's not like Canadian Tire is substantially more profitable than any other retail company in the world. Retail is not a huge margin business."

But operating online and in-store, while having visibility to customers in between—what is known in the industry as omnichannel or multichannel retail—has key cost advantages, too, MacDonald said.

When Canadian Tire began selling tires online in 2011, it prompted customers to put in the make and model year of their car, then would display search results showing tire options and their costs. It also allowed customers to check the stock of the relevant tires at their local stores—all processes that, prior to then, had taken up several minutes' worth of employee time at a store or over the phone.

"Rather than (leaving the process up) to 5000 counter staff across the service group, we just made the reference tool available to all Canadians. That is the brilliance in checking inventory online: instead of you calling the store, you can check the inventory yourself." Customers still have the option to call the store, but the practice is considerably more efficient from a labour standpoint now that many customers do the legwork themselves online.

"The jury is not out as to whether or not e-commerce is here to stay," MacDonald says. "The jury is out on what form it will ultimately take." He also reiterates that a multichannel service model has its advantages in sectors beyond retail. "Look at e-commerce when it comes to banking. Everybody banks online. But there are more branches in Canada open more hours today than any time in history."

Exhibit 2–17
Sampling of Selected Canadian Franchises (2017)

Franchisor	Number of Units Owned in Canada	Number of Franchisees/ Dealers in Canada	Initial Fee	Royalty	Advertising Program	Approximate Investment Required (millions)	Website
Boston Pizza	3	350	$69 000	7%	2.5%	$1.7–$2.2	http://www.bostonpizza.com
Dairy Queen Canada	–	638	$30 000–$45 000	4%	5–6%	$.4+	http://www.dairyqueen.com
McDonald's Restaurants of Canada	230	1213	$45 000	17%, including rent, services fee, and advertising		$.8	http://www.mcdonalds.com
Midas Muffler Shop	0	150	$30 000	5%	5%	$.18–$.43	http://www.midas.com
Tommy Guns's Original Barber Shop	1	51	$30 000	n/a	n/a	$.35+	http://tommyguns.com
Tim Hortons	15	3657	$50 000	4.5%	4%	$.2+	http://www.timhortons.com

Source: Adapted from *Franchise Canada Directory 2010*, Canadian Franchise Association, http://www.cfa.ca.; Look for a franchise http://www.lookforafranchise.ca.

The franchise ownership format attempts to combine advantages of owner-managed businesses with efficiencies of centralized decision making in chain-store operations. Franchisees are motivated to make their store successful because they receive the profits (after the royalty is paid). The franchisor is motivated to develop new products and systems and to promote the franchise because it receives a royalty on all sales. Advertising, product development, and system development are efficiently done by the franchisor, with costs shared by all franchisees (see Exhibit 2–17).

This chapter reviews the types of retailers and ownership classifications and highlights strategies for success in a competitive retail marketplace. Definitions of the retail formats and the examples confirm the diversity and innovation within the retail sector.

Many different types of retailers now offer multichannel approaches to their retail customers in an attempt to gain loyalty. Multichannel is not a format in itself, but rather an additional way of reaching the customer and increasing revenue.

Different types of retailers compete with different retail mixes to sell merchandise and services to customers. To collect statistics about retailing, the federal government classifies retailers by type of merchandise and services sold. But this classification method may not be useful in determining a retailer's major competitors. A more useful approach for understanding the retail marketplace is classifying retailers on the basis of their retail mix, the merchandise variety and assortment, services, location, pricing, and promotion decisions made to attract customers.

Over the past 30 years, North American retail markets have been characterized by the emergence of many new retail institutions. Traditional institutions (supermarkets, convenience, department, discount, and specialty stores) have been joined by category specialists, superstores, convenience stores, warehouse clubs, off-price retailers, catalogue showrooms, and hypermarkets. In addition, there has been substantial growth in services retailing. The inherent differences between services and merchandise result in services retailers emphasizing store management while merchandise retailers emphasize inventory control issues. Traditional retail institutions have changed in response to these new retailers. For example, department stores have increased their emphasis on fashion-oriented apparel and improved the services they offer. Supermarkets are focusing more attention on meal solutions and perishables.

Although the bubble burst for most pure electronic retailers, traditional store-based and catalogue retailers are adding an electronic channel and evolving into integrated, customer-centric, multichannel retailers. This evolution toward multichannel retailing is driven by the increasing desire of customers to communicate with retailers anytime, anywhere, anyplace. Each of the channels (stores, catalogues, and websites) offers unique benefits to customers. The store channel enables customers to touch and feel merchandise and use the products shortly after they are purchased. Catalogues enable customers to browse through a retailer's offering anytime and anyplace. A unique benefit offered by the electronic channel is the opportunity for consumers to search across a broad range of alternatives, develop a smaller set of alternatives based on their needs, and get specific information about the alternatives they want.

By offering multiple channels, retailers overcome the limitations of each channel. Websites can be used to extend the geographical presence and assortment offered by the store channel. Websites also can be used to update the information provided in catalogues. Stores can be used to provide a multisensory experience and an economical distribution capability supporting the electronic channel.

Providing a seamless interface across channels is very challenging for multiple retailers. Meeting customer expectations will require the development and use of common customer databases and integrated systems. In addition, omni-channel retailers will have to make decisions about how to use the different channels to support the retailer's brand image and how to present consistent merchandise assortments and pricing across channels.

big-box stores
catalogue channel
category specialist
closeout retailers
combination stores
convenience stores
conventional supermarket
department store
depth of merchandise
direct-response advertising

direct selling
discount store
drugstore
electronic retailing
factory outlets
fair trade
franchising
hypermarkets
infomercials
in-store kiosks

leased department
limited-assortment supermarkets
locavore movement
m-commerce
multichannel retailer
multilevel system
North American Industry Classification
    System (NAICS)
off-price retailer
omni-channel retailing

outlet stores	SKU (stock keeping unit)	vending machine retailing
party plan system	specialty store	warehouse club
power perimeter	supercentres	wholesale-sponsored voluntary
pyramid scheme	superstore	cooperative group
retail chain	television home shopping	
services retailers	value retailers	

GET OUT & DO IT!

1. **GO SHOPPING** Go to an athletic footwear specialty store such as Foot Locker, a department store, and a discount store. Analyze their variety and assortment of athletic footwear by creating a table similar to Exhibit 2–3.

2. **GO SHOPPING** Keep a diary of where you shop, what you buy, and how much you spend for two weeks. Tabulate your results by type of retailer. Are your shopping habits significantly different from your parents'? Do your and your parents' shopping habits coincide with the trends discussed in this chapter? Explain why or why not.

3. **INTERNET EXERCISE** Two large associations of retailers are the National Retail Federation (http://www.nrf.com) and the Retail Council of Canada (http://www.retailcouncil.org). Visit these sites and report the latest retail developments and issues confronting the industry.

4. **INTERNET EXERCISE** Go to http://corporate. walmart.com. Click on "Our Story," then "Our Business," and then "Walmart U.S." Scroll down to read "Walmart Supercenter." Now go to http://www.groupe-auchan.com and click on "Our Businesses." See if you can determine the differences between a Walmart supercentre and an Auchan hypermarket.

5. **INTERNET EXERCISE** Check out Mark's at http://www.marks.com. Explain why Mark's retail product is a successful addition to Canadian Tire's assortments, broadening the product mix for consumers.

6. **INTERNET EXERCISE** Do an online search for "Craigslist." Explain the popularity of this unique site.

7. **GO SHOPPING AND INTERNET EXERCISE** Compare the merchandise assortment offered and the prices in your favourite store and on the store's website. If there are differences, what is the reason for these differences?

8. **INTERNET EXERCISE** Go to The Gap (http:// www.gap.com), Sears (http://www.sears. ca), and Lands' End (http://www.landsend. com) and shop for a pair of pants. Evaluate your shopping experience at each site. Compare the sites and your shopping experience on characteristics you think are important to consumers.

9. **INTERNET EXERCISE** Examine a variety of on-line stores. Explain what works for you and what doesn't work for you.

10. **INTERNET EXERCISE** Visit http://www.bombay. ca and take a virtual tour of the store. Describe the experience.

1. Distinguish between variety and assortment. Why are these important elements of retail market structure?

2. How can small independent retailers compete against the large national chains?

3. What do off-price retailers need to do to compete against other formats in the future?

4. Compare and contrast the retail mixes of convenience stores, traditional supermarkets, supercentres, hypermarkets, and warehouse stores. Can all of these food retail institutions survive over the long run? Explain why or why not.

5. Why haven't hypermarkets been successful in North America? Do you believe they will be successful in the future?

6. The same brand and model personal computer is sold in specialty computer stores, discount stores, category specialists, and warehouse stores. Why would a customer choose one store over the others?

7. Choose a product category that both you and your parents purchase (e.g., clothing, DVDs, electronic equipment). In which type of store do you typically purchase this merchandise? What about your parents? Explain why there is, or is not, a difference in your store choices.

8. At many optical stores, you can get your eyes checked and purchase glasses or contact lenses. How is the shopping experience different for the service as compared to the product? Design a strategy to get customers to purchase both the service and the product. In so doing, delineate specific actions that should be taken to acquire and retain optical customers.

9. Many experts believe that customer service is one of retailing's most important issues in the coming years. How can retailers that emphasize price (such as discount stores, category specialists, and off-price retailers) improve customer service without increasing costs and, thus, prices?

10. Should a multichannel retailer offer the same assortment of merchandise for sale on its website at the same price as it sells in its stores? Explain why or why not.

CHAPTER THREE

Customer buying behaviour

LEARNING OBJECTIVES

Lo1   Explore how customers make decisions about whether to patronize a retailer and buy merchandise.

Lo2   Determine what social and personal factors affect customer purchase decisions.

Lo3   Investigate how retailers can get customers to visit their stores more frequently and buy more merchandise during each visit.

Lo4   Discuss why and how retailers group customers into market segments.

SPOTLIGHT ON RETAILING

WHAT'S UP WITH mPAYMENTS?

Use of mPayments is on the rise—in fact, there was a four-fold increase over the past year. What are the trends relating to mPayments? As Apple, Samsung, Google, PayPal and others increase their focus on mobile wallet products, paying with phones in stores is going to become common-place. John Heggestuen, from BI Intelligence, has written a mobile payments forecast report to reflect new developments in the market, including the late launch of mobile wallet CurrentC and the considerable impact expected from Samsung Pay.

- In our latest US in-store mobile payments forecast, we find that mobile payment volume will reach $37 billion in 2015.
- By the end of the forecast period in 2019, we expect volume to reach $808 billion, or about 99 percent of the old estimate. Our forecast is still one of the largest in the industry, and we think mobile payments will catch on faster than other research firms suggest: Mobile payment capability is either already offered or about to be implemented at merchants accounting for a huge chunk of US payment volume.
- The number of people who make a mobile payment at least once a year will grow from nearly 8 percent of the US consumer population in 2014 to 65 percent by 2019. The growth in mobile payment users will largely be driven by mobile wallet initiatives from Apple, Samsung, and Google. When these are in place, 90 percent of the forthcoming smartphones in the US will come with mobile wallets pre-installed.

- Samsung Pay will be a huge driver of mobile payment volume. Unlike Apple Pay, when Samsung Pay launches it will be compatible at virtually every payment terminal in the US, thanks to the company's acquisition of LoopPay. This will make it easier for early adopters to make a habit of paying with their phone.
- The sheer number of mobile wallets available or in the works from Apple Pay, Samsung Pay, CurrentC, Google Wallet, and others will drive mobile payment adoption as well. This will largely be the result of competitive pressure building between the companies and the bandwagon effect. Adoption will be self-reinforcing—the more consumers and retailers that use or offer mobile in-store payments, the more the behaviour will catch on among others.

Canadian consumers seem to be slow to adopt this new payment method. Canadian consumers were first introduced to mPayment options back in 2012 via BlackBerry technology with little fanfare. Despite Canadians' attachment to smartphones and the rapid proliferation of all-things digital, the pick-up of mobile payments in Canada to date shows that, once again, sometimes old consumer habits die hard and timing for new products is everything.

© Montgomery Martin / Alamy.

Sources: The Canadian Press, "Apple Pay launches in Canada today," *CBC*, Nov. 17, 2015, http://www.cbc.ca/news/technology/apple-pay-canada-1.3322433" (accessed December 31, 2015); Christina Pellegrini, "'Thought it was going to be a big thing': Canadians haven't been so quick to pay with their smartphones," *Financial Post*, April 29, 2015, http://business.financialpost.com/fp-tech-desk/canada-mobile-payments?__lsa=aebd-faa6 (accessed December 31, 2015); John Heggestuen, "The Mobile Payments Report: Forecasts, user trends, and the companies vying to dominate mobile payments," *Business Insider*, June 19, 2015, http://www.businessinsider.com/the-mobile-payments-report-2015-5 (accessed December 31, 2015).

An effective retail strategy satisfies customer needs better than competitors' strategies. Thus, understanding customer needs and buying behaviour is critical for effective retail decision making. We are not all the same. This is a mistake many marketers make when going after a demographic group, particularly the Boomer segment, a population segment that has over half of the country's discretionary spending potential. Consider the teen population: Not all teens are the same. Some are jocks, others are geeks; some like rap music, others are part of the hipster culture. Retailers are beginning to realize the importance of understanding the subgroups in the marketplace in order to connect with the customer. You cannot be all things to all customers.

This chapter focuses on the needs and buying behaviour of customers and market segments. It describes the stages customers go through to purchase merchandise and the factors that influence the buying process. We then use the information about the buying process to discuss how consumers can be grouped into market segments.[1]

New Consumer Mindset

LS Retail, an international business management software solutions company for retail and hospitality companies, has identified five current and upcoming trends in the retail market that companies will need to consider. What are twenty-first century consumers looking for in their retail shopping experience?

Pre-Tail Access

"The neologism 'pre-tail' means that people want to start shopping before they even enter the store. Retailers have responded to this demand in original ways by using technology. For example, 'shoppable windows' have popped up in New York, which allow customers to purchase products even when the shop is closed through a touch screen in the shop window. The customers are then offered fast home delivery. IKEA, the furniture giant, has implemented new technology which lets customers see how a piece of furniture would look in their home while they are still at the store, before purchase."[2]

Next-Generation Environments

"Consumers are now used to the totalizing shopping and entertainment environments offered online, and increasingly look for the same kind of experience also in traditional stores. Retailers are being pressured to change their game, and shops are transforming into entertainment centres. The increasing demand for Omni-channel shopping means that retailers need to offer an integrated shopping experience which spans across the physical, online, and mobile space. Fashion brand Burberry led the transformation by turning its flagship store in London into a website-like environment. Customers can now interact with the store as if it were a website; the environment is very tactile, and when items are touched they react just as if they were 'clicked' online. The shop is equipped with over 100 video screens and 500 audio speakers which react to touch, providing customers with a 360° shopping experience."[3]

Retail/Hospitality Mash-Ups

"The era of brands is over. Increasingly, customers enter stores looking for an integrated lifestyle experience, one which unites retail and hospitality. A few brands have taken on the challenges of combining hospitality services and a retail environment. The luxury goods Alfred Dunhill stores have opened stylish bars inside their clothing shop in London and Tokyo. Other brands have entered partnerships with the aim of creating special experiences to offer their guests. Uniqlo, the casual wear brand, has renovated its store environments by partnering up with both Starbucks cafés and MoMA. Uniqlo customers can now shop for clothes while sipping a coffee and enjoying a work of modern art."[4]

Social Shopping

"The constant growth in use of social media has made them an integral part of every facet of our lives—including the shopping experience. While shopping, customers use social media to look for validation of their purchases; retailers are starting to realize that this social media validation can be used to increase sales. More and more stores now do not just allow, but actively encourage their customers to take pictures of the clothes they are trying on, and then share their snapshots on social media. Topshop in London went one step further by setting up the 'Helmut Newton machine': shoppers are encouraged to take a picture in the clothes they are trying on as if they were modelling for the famous photographer, and then upload their star-moment snapshot straight to social media. The proliferation of food pictures in social media has led some forward-thinking hospitality operators to realize the advertising possibilities. Some restaurants are now purposely creating so-called 'Instagram moments' by plating up attractive-looking dishes which encourage picture-taking and sharing."[5]

Net-Tech Customer Service

"Increasing customer demands for technological innovations have set the bar very high for companies. The most forward-thinking businesses now use technology to provide around-the-clock, high-quality customer service. Kindle, Amazon's own e-reader, now includes a 'may day button'. By pressing it, users can enter a video conference with Amazon's customer service; Amazon claims that the customer service will respond in an average of 9–10 seconds after a customer has clicked the 'may day button'. Fiat, the car manufacturer, allows its Brazilian customers to video conference with experts at a Fiat dealership. In case of problems or doubts about the car's functions customers can chat with an expert, who will be sitting in the same car make at the dealership, and will be able to show the customer easy and fast what they need to do to effectively use the car."[6]

LoI The Buying Process

Consider your most recent shopping trip as we describe the customer buying process. The **buying process**, the steps consumers go through when buying a product or service, begins when customers recognize an unsatisfied need. They seek information about how to satisfy the need, such as what products might be useful and how they can be bought. Customers evaluate the alternative retailers and channels available for purchasing the merchandise, such as stores, catalogues, and the Internet, and then choose a store or Internet site to visit or a catalogue to review. This encounter with a retailer provides more information and may alert customers to additional needs. After evaluating the retailer's merchandise offering by weighing both objective and subjective criteria, customers may make a purchase or go to another retailer to collect more information.

Eventually, customers make a purchase, use the product, and then decide whether the product satisfies their needs during the post-purchase evaluation stage of the customer buying process.

Exhibit 3–1 outlines the buying process—the stages in selecting a retailer and buying merchandise. Retailers attempt to influence consumers as they go through the buying process to encourage them to buy their merchandise and services. Each stage in the buying process is addressed in the following sections.

Need Recognition

The buying process is triggered when consumers recognize they have an unsatisfied need. An unsatisfied need arises when a customer's desired level of satisfaction differs from his or her present level of satisfaction. Need recognition can be triggered by realizing you need a haircut, by feeling the need for an uplifting experience after a final exam, or by a message from a Facebook group member about an addition to his or her profile.

Types of Needs The needs that motivate customers to go shopping and purchase merchandise can be classified as

buying process The stages customers go through to purchase merchandise or services.

Exhibit 3–1
The Buying Process

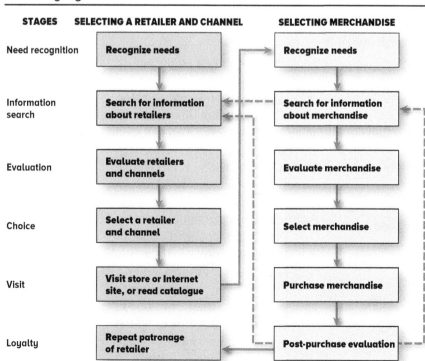

STAGES	SELECTING A RETAILER AND CHANNEL	SELECTING MERCHANDISE
Need recognition	Recognize needs	Recognize needs
Information search	Search for information about retailers	Search for information about merchandise
Evaluation	Evaluate retailers and channels	Evaluate merchandise
Choice	Select a retailer and channel	Select merchandise
Visit	Visit store or Internet site, or read catalogue	Purchase merchandise
Loyalty	Repeat patronage of retailer	Post-purchase evaluation

utilitarian needs Needs motivating consumers to go shopping to accomplish a specific task.

hedonic needs Needs motivating consumers to go shopping for pleasure.

utilitarian or hedonic. When consumers go shopping to accomplish a specific task, such as buying a suit for job interviews, they are seeking to satisfy **utilitarian needs**. When consumers go shopping for pleasure, they are seeking to satisfy their **hedonic needs**—their needs for an entertaining, emotional, and recreational experience. Thus, from the consumer's perspective, utilitarian needs are associated with work, whereas hedonic needs are associated with fun.[7]

Successful retailers attempt to satisfy both the utilitarian and hedonic needs of their customers. Consumers motivated by utilitarian needs typically shop in a more deliberate and efficient manner; thus, retailers need to make the shopping experience easy and effortless for them by providing the desired merchandise in a way that can be easily located and purchased. Some hedonic needs that retailers can satisfy include stimulation, social experience, learning new trends, status and power, self-reward, and adventure.[8]

1. *Stimulation.* Retailers and mall managers use background music, visual displays, scents, and demonstrations in stores and malls to create a carnival-like, stimulating experience for their customers. These environments encourage consumers to take a break from their everyday lives and visit stores.[9] Retailers also attempt to stimulate customers with exciting graphics and photography in their catalogues and on their websites.[10]

2. *Social experience.* Marketplaces traditionally have been centres of social activity, places where people could meet friends and develop new relationships. Regional shopping malls in many communities have replaced open markets as social meeting places, especially for teenagers. Mall developers are focusing on mixed-use developments to satisfy consumers' need for social experiences. Lifestyle centres are allocating significant space to restaurants, movie theatres, outdoor entertainment, and even condominium living. Chapters bookstores host cafés in which customers can discuss novels while sipping lattes. Online retailers provide similar social experiences by enabling customers to email products to their friends, create personal blogs with their shopping lists to be shared with other people, or participate in a particular interest-driven forum. For example, visitors to Amazon.ca can write reviews and opinions about books they have read and make them available to all potential customers on the website.

3. *Learning new trends.* By visiting retailers, people learn about new trends and ideas. These visits satisfy customers' needs to be informed about their environment. For example, teens might go to The Body Shop to learn about new products, as well as ways they can live an environmentally friendly lifestyle. Customers also learn about trends through normal social encounters and surfing the Web.

4. *Status and power.* For some people, a store or a service provider is one of the few places where they get attention and respect. Canyon Ranch offers upscale health resorts in Tucson, Arizona, and Lenox, Massachusetts, as well as spa clubs in Las Vegas, Nevada, and Kissimmee, Florida. All Canyon Ranch resorts and spas make the customer the centre of attention, offering spa services, medical and nutritional consultations and workshops, spiritual pursuits, and healthy gourmet cuisine.

5. *Self-reward.* Customers frequently purchase merchandise to reward themselves when they have accomplished something or want to dispel depression. Perfume, cosmetics, apparel, and jewellery are common self-gifts. Retailers satisfy these needs by, for example, "treating" customers to personalized makeovers while they are in the store.

6. *Adventure.* Often consumers go shopping because they enjoy finding bargains, looking for sales, and finding discounts or low prices. They treat shopping as a game to be "won." Off-price retailers like Winners, warehouse clubs like Costco, discount stores like Walmart, and fast-fashion retailers like Zara and H&M cater to this need by constantly changing their assortment so that customers never know what kind of treasure they will find.

Some people view shopping as a leisure-time activity, just like any other sport. Frequent leisure-time shoppers spend an average of $113.33 per shopping trip, making this segment of consumers

DID YOU KNOW?

Customers who spend 40 minutes in a store are more than twice as likely to buy than someone who spends 10 minutes, and they typically buy twice as many items.[11]

one of the most profitable and informed. They buy primarily apparel, health and beauty aids, entertainment and leisure items, and electronics.[12]

Conflicting Needs   Most customers have multiple needs. Moreover, these needs often conflict. For example, a graduating student would like to wear a DKNY suit, which would enhance her self-image, earn her the admiration of her university friends, and be appropriate for her upcoming job interviews. But this hedonic need conflicts with her budget and her utilitarian need to get a job. Employers might feel that she's not responsible if she wears a suit that is too expensive for an interview for an entry-level position. Typically, customers make trade-offs between their conflicting needs. Later in this chapter, we will discuss a model of how customers make such trade-offs.

Because needs often cannot be satisfied in one store or by one product, consumers may appear to be inconsistent in their shopping behaviour. For example, a skier may purchase expensive Spyder goggles but wear an inexpensive snow suit from Sport Chek. A grocery shopper might buy an inexpensive store brand of paper towels and a premium national brand of orange juice like Tropicana. The pattern of buying both premium and low-priced merchandise or patronizing both expensive, status-oriented retailers and price-oriented retailers is called **cross-shopping**.

Although all cross-shoppers seek value, their perception of value varies across product classes. Thus, a cross-shopper might feel it is worth the money to dine at an expensive restaurant, but believe there is little quality difference between kitchen utensils at Walmart and designer brands at a specialty store. Similarly, consumers may cut back on their vacations at costly resorts but still want to treat themselves to expensive, high-quality jams, mustards, and olive oils from the supermarket. Retailers might not be able to discern how the buying patterns of cross-shoppers make sense, but they certainly make sense to their customers.

Stimulating Need Recognition   As we have noted, customers must recognize unsatisfied needs before they are motivated to visit a store or go online to buy merchandise. Sometimes these needs are stimulated by an event in a person's life. For example, a consumer's department store visit to buy a suit was stimulated by an impending interview, an examination of her current wardrobe, and a visit to BrandHabit.com. Retailers use a variety of approaches to stimulate problem recognition and

Purestock/SuperStock.

motivate customers to visit their stores and buy merchandise. Advertising, Internet promotions, direct mail, publicity, and special events communicate the availability of merchandise or special prices. SeenOn.com stimulates need recognition by showing products that celebrities or television actors have worn. Within the store, visual merchandising and salespeople can stimulate need recognition, such as when a salesperson shows a customer a scarf or tie to stimulate the need for an accessory to complement a new suit.

Information Search

Once customers identify a need, they may seek information about retailers or products to help them satisfy that need. More extended buying processes may involve collecting a lot of information, visiting several retailers, spending more time on the Internet, or deliberating a long time before making a purchase.[13]

Amount of Information Searched   In general, the amount of **information search** depends on the value customers feel they can gain from searching versus the cost of searching. Consumers will often spend more time searching for information when they have little prior experience with the merchandise category. The value of the search stems from how it improves the customer's purchase decision. Will the search help the customer find a lower-priced

> **cross-shopping** A pattern of buying both premium and low-priced merchandise or patronizing expensive, status-oriented retailers and price-oriented retailers.

> **information search** The stage in the buying process in which a customer seeks additional information to satisfy a need.

product or one that will give superior performance? The costs of search include both time and money. Travelling from store to store can cost money for gas and parking, but the major cost incurred is the customer's time.

DID YOU KNOW?

Members of a demographic profile named **Generation Connected** typically use the Internet to start their vehicle research. In fact, 97 percent use the Internet to gather data.[15]

Technology can dramatically reduce the cost of searching for information. For example, NearbyNow. co sends promotions to customers' smartphones via a text message and enables them to search their local malls for products and brands via text messages. This way, customers can save time in the search process by going directly to the retailer that sells the desired product.[14] Vast information about merchandise sold across the world is just a mouse click away. Retailing View 3.1 describes how readily available information on the Web is affecting the automobile buying process.

Factors influencing the amount of information search include (1) the nature and use of the product being purchased, (2) characteristics of the individual customer, and (3) aspects of the market and buying situation in which the purchase is made. Some people search more than others. For example, social shoppers spend more time shopping than other customers, and do so for the sheer enjoyment of the process and interacting with other potential customers and retailer customer service and sales representatives.[16] Also, customers who are self-confident or have prior experience purchasing and using the product or service tend to search less.

Marketplace and situational factors affecting information search include (1) the number of competing brands and retail outlets and (2) the time pressure under which the purchase must be made. When competition is greater and there are more alternatives to consider, the amount of information search increases. However, the amount decreases as time pressure increases.

internal sources of information Information in a customer's memory such as names, images, and past experiences with different stores.

external sources of information Information provided by the media and other people.

Sources of Information

Customers have two sources of information: internal and external. **Internal sources of information** are in a customer's memory, such as names, images, and past experiences with different stores. The major source of internal information is the customer's past shopping experience. Even if they remember only a small fraction of the information to which they are exposed, customers have an extensive internal information bank to draw upon when deciding where to shop and what to buy.

External sources of information refer to information provided by ads and other people. When customers feel that their internal information is inadequate, they turn to external information sources. External sources of information play a major role in the acceptance of fashions, as discussed in Appendix 2A, available on Connect.

The Internet has had a profound impact on consumers' ability to gather external information. If consumers want to search for something specific, they can try specialized search engines such as Google Shopping (http://www.google.com/shopping).[17] The site relies on artificial intelligence technology to search images on the Web and then serves up goods for sale that visually match items on a shopper's wish list. Visitors to the site can search for products in one of two ways. First, they may type in, say, "silver earrings" and they receive pages filled with images that match the description, along with prices and links to the product pages of the websites on which the items are sold. Second, users may browse through selected items in the wardrobes of about a dozen celebrities, including Scarlett Johansson and Jessica Simpson, and choose, perhaps, the dress that Johansson wore on the cover of *Esquire* magazine. The site then searches for similar dresses, returning more than 5000 ranging in price from $40 to $8000.

Two other sites, NearbyNow.com and GPShopper. com, have introduced mobile Internet applications that allow shoppers to use their cellphones and tablets to search inventory and prices while at a particular mall, saving them time and sometimes turning up last-minute bargains and promotions.[18]

However, retailers are concerned that the ease of collecting price information through the Internet will increase price competition. Traditionally, price competition between store-based retailers offering the same merchandise was reduced by geographic constraints. Through the Internet and mobile technology, the number of stores that consumers can visit to compare prices is no longer limited by physical distance.

Increasingly, retailers are encouraging their customers to post information on their websites too, such as product reviews, ratings, and, in some

The Internet has Changed the Car-Buying Process

Ten years ago, if consumers wanted to buy a car, they would visit several dealers, look at different models, test drive the cars sold by each dealer, and then negotiate price and financing with a dealer. Many consumers viewed this traditional process of buying a car as about as pleasurable as a visit to the dentist. But now the Internet is changing this experience, as well as the nature of automobile retailing.

The Internet is giving consumers more control over the car-buying process. Consumers can go to websites such as http://www.autobytel.com, http://www.cars.com, or http://www.edmunds.com; access a wealth of information, including the dealer's costs for cars and options; compare vehicles in a side-by-side chart that lists their price, features, horsepower, mileage, legroom, and options; read multiple reviews for most models; and even take a 360-degree photo tour of car interiors that gives them an idea of what the view looks like from the driver's seat.

Through the sites' relationships with car dealers, consumers can request prices from dealers in their area. A handy calculator tells customers how much the monthly payment would be if they were to buy a car on credit. The sites also have calculators to help car buyers figure out how much they can afford to spend on a car, whether they should buy a new or used car, and whether they should lease or buy. This information enables consumers to walk into a dealership knowing as much as or more than the dealer's salespeople.

The Build Your Own Honda site offers a simple four-step process that customers can use to select a model, a trim level (including exterior colour), and an accessory package. Then, a summary of selections with front and back views of the customer-designed vehicle is generated. Another tool lets users compare Honda products to vehicles from other manufacturers.

CarFax (http://www.carfax.com) enables customers to access a vehicle's history report by typing in its vehicle identification number (VIN). This history describes any accidents the vehicle was in, its past ownership, odometer fraud, and any other events that might be related to the vehicle. Services such as CarFax make it much easier for customers to purchase used cars with confidence.

© Echo/Getty Images.   Courtesy of Edmunds.com Inc.

The Internet has dramatically reduced the time and effort needed to collect information—and increased the quality of information acquired—to make a decision when buying an automobile.

Sources: Geoffrey A. Fowler, John D. Stoll, Scott Morrison, "GM, eBay Will Let Car Buyers Dicker Online," *Wall Street Journal*, Aug. 11, 2009, p. B1; Thomas Pack, "Kicking the Virtual Tires: Car Research on the Web," *Information Today*, Jan. 2009, pp. 44–45; http://www.cars.com (accessed January 21, 2010); http://www.carfax.com (accessed January 21, 2010).

cases, photos and videos.[19] Consumers can also get product reviews from other consumers on retailer sites like Amazon and Golfsmith (http://www.golfsmith.com). The result is that customer reviews are emerging as a prime source for online shoppers as they collect information during the buying process.

Reducing Information Search The retailer's objective at the information search stage of the buying process is to limit the customer's search to its store or website. One measure of a retailer's performance on this objective is the conversion rate, that is, the percentage of customers who enter a store or access a website and then buy a product at the store or website. Each element of the retailing mix can be used to achieve this objective. Category specialists such as Best Buy and Rona provide a very deep assortment of merchandise, everything a customer might want in the category, so that the customer can collect all of the information and make the necessary comparisons in their stores or on their websites.

Services provided by retailers can also limit search to the retailer's location. The availability of credit and delivery may be important for consumers who want to purchase large durable goods, such as furniture and appliances. Salespeople can provide enough information to customers that they don't feel the need to collect additional information by visiting other stores. For example, most men have no idea how to buy lingerie for their girlfriends or wives and are embarrassed to ask female sales associates. So London's Marks & Spencer department store used several "Stocking Fellas" as a one-time holiday promotion to help them shop for these items.[20] Thanks to the Stocking Fellas, lingerie sales are up, and merchandise returns are down.

Everyday low pricing is another way retailers increase the chance that customers will buy in their store and not search for a better price elsewhere. An **everyday low pricing strategy (ELDP)** maintains the continuity of retail prices at a level somewhere between the regular non-sale price and the deep discount sale price of the retailer's competitors. Walmart and The Source have everyday low pricing policies, which make customers confident that they won't find that merchandise at a lower price at another retailer. Many stores

everyday low pricing strategy (EDLP) A pricing strategy that stresses continuity of retail prices at a level somewhere between the regular non-sale price and the deep-discount sale price of the retailer's competitors.

with everyday low pricing offer price-matching guarantees if a competitor offers the same merchandise at a lower price.

Increasingly, consumers are embracing digital technologies and devices in all stages of their buying journey. They are moving from channel to channel on a regular basis, searching for information, and they have expectations that their behaviour in one place will influence the experience in another. The 2015 *Navigating The New Digital Divide*, published by Deloitte, outlines the methods that online shoppers use to shop. Seventy percent of consumers are now leading their own shopping journey (becoming aware of products through means outside of retailer or brand communications), while only 30 percent get their initial inspiration from a retailer or brand's advertisement. Sixty-seven percent of shoppers browse retailer sites prior to shopping in stores, but nearly as many (61 percent) are using search engines for their browsing and research activities. Thirteen percent of shoppers use the "buy online, pick up in store" (or BOPUS) method to purchase and pay for their items. Twenty-five percent of consumers indicated that this is their preferred method for receiving their purchases in the future. As a result, retailers are looking at embracing omni-channel strategies that will require them to build bridges between their online and offline environments for a single customer view.

Retailers need to make use of social media and social communities to entice peer-to-peer communication and help build their brand through consumer discussions and recommendations. Like social media, reviews are powerful advertising tools that retailers can use to help disseminate information to consumers. Reviews and product guides can be available in-store and online, allowing consumers to access information while they shop and use it to help make purchasing decisions. Finally, location-based social media like Foursquare and Facebook Places will allow retailers to link mobile users to their friends via "check-ins," showing who has stopped where and any comments they had about the experience. Retailers can offer coupons, sales alerts, messages about important events, and more, delivering advertising and information to consumers as they go about their daily routines.[21]

Although retailers hope to confine their customers' information search to their stores and websites, they also want to encourage customers to spend as much time shopping in their channels as possible. The more time customers spend shopping, the more they will buy. Stores use food and personal service to create a comfortable environment that encourages customers to keep shopping.[22] For instance, Talbots offers the personal attention of a sales associate, by appointment, along with a light snack. American Eagle Outfitter's Martin + Osa Division, which targets a slightly older audience, serves bottled water and apples. Gymboree provides a television playing videos at the back of its stores to keep its youngest customers occupied while their parents shop.

Evaluation of Alternatives: The Multiattribute Attitude Model

The multiattribute attitude model provides a useful way to summarize how customers use the information they have and collect about alternative products, evaluate the alternatives, and select the one that best satisfies their needs. We discuss it in detail because it offers a framework for developing a retailing strategy.[23]

The **multiattribute attitude model** is based on the notion that customers see a retailer, a product, or a service as a collection of attributes or characteristics. The model is designed to predict a customer's evaluation of a product, service, or retailer based on (1) its performance on relevant attributes and (2) the importance of those attributes to the customer.

Beliefs about Performance To illustrate this model, consider the store choice decision confronting a young, single, professional woman from Mississauga who needs groceries. She considers three alternatives: a supercentre in the next suburb, her local supermarket, or an Internet grocery retailer such as Grocery Gateway (http://www.grocerygateway.com), as shown in Exhibit 3–2.

The customer mentally processes the "objective" information about each grocery retailer in Exhibit 3–2A and forms an impression of the benefits each one provides. Exhibit 3–2B shows the customer's beliefs about these benefits. Notice that some benefits can combine several objective characteristics. For example, the convenience benefit combines travel time, checkout time, and ease of finding products. Grocery prices and delivery cost affect the customer's beliefs about the economy of shopping at the various retail outlets.

The degree to which each retailer provides each benefit is represented on a 10-point scale: 10 means the retailer performs well in providing the benefit; 1 means it performs poorly. Here, no retailer has superior performance on all benefits. The supercentre performs well on economy and assortment but is low on convenience. The Internet grocer offers the best convenience but is weak on economy and assortment.

Importance Weights The young woman in the preceding example forms an overall

multiattribute attitude model A model of customer decision making based on the notion that customers see a retailer or a product as a collection of attributes or characteristics. The model can also be used for evaluating a retailer, product, or vendor. The model uses a weighted average score based on the importance of various issues and performance on those issues.

Exhibit 3–2
Characteristics of Food Retailers

A. INFORMATION ABOUT STORES SELLING GROCERIES			
Store Characteristics	**Supercentre**	**Supermarket**	**Internet Grocer**
Grocery prices	20% below average	average	10% above average
Delivery cost ($)	0	0	10
Total travel time (minutes)	30	15	0
Typical checkout time (minutes)	10	5	2
Number of products, brands, and sizes	40 000	30 000	40 000
Fresh produce	Yes	Yes	Yes
Fresh fish	Yes	Yes	No
Ease of finding products	Difficult	Easy	Easy
Ease of collecting nutritional information about products	Difficult	Difficult	Easy
B. BELIEFS ABOUT STORES' PERFORMANCE BENEFITS*			
Performance Benefits	**Supercentre**	**Supermarket**	**Internet Grocer**
Economy	10	8	6
Convenience	3	5	10
Assortment	9	7	5
Availability of product information	4	4	8

* 10 = excellent, 1 = poor.

Exhibit 3–3
Evaluation of Retailers

	IMPORTANCE WEIGHTS*		PERFORMANCE BELIEFS		
Characteristic	Young Single Woman	Parent with Four Children	Supercentre	Supermarket	Internet Grocer
Economy	4	10	10	8	6
Convenience	10	4	3	5	10
Assortment	5	8	9	7	5
Availability of product information	9	2	4	4	8
OVERALL EVALUATION					
Young single woman			151	153	221
Parent with four children			192	164	156

* 10 = very important, 1 = very unimportant.

evaluation of each alternative on the basis of the importance she places on each benefit the stores provide. The importance she places on a benefit can also be represented using a 10-point rating scale, with 10 indicating the benefit is very important and 1 indicating it's very unimportant. Using this rating scale, the importance of the retailer benefits for the young woman and for a parent with four children are shown in Exhibit 3–3, along with the performance beliefs previously discussed. Notice that the single woman may value convenience and the availability of product information much more than economy and assortment. But the parent may place a lot of importance on economy, assortment is moderately important, and convenience and product information aren't very important.

The importance of a retailer's benefits differs for each customer and also may differ for each shopping trip. For example, the parent with four children may stress economy for major shopping trips but place more importance on convenience for a fill-in trip.

In Exhibit 3–3, the single woman and parent may have the same beliefs about each retailer's performance, but they differ in the importance they place on the benefits the retailers offer. In general, customers can differ in their beliefs about the retailers' performance as well as in their importance weights.

Evaluating Stores Research has shown that a customer's overall evaluation of an alternative (in this situation, two stores and the Internet channel) relates closely to the sum of the performance beliefs multiplied by the importance weights.[24] Thus,

we calculate the young, single woman's overall evaluation or score for the supercentre as follows:

$$4 \times 10 = 40$$
$$10 \times 3 = 30$$
$$5 \times 9 = 45$$
$$9 \times 4 = 36$$
$$\overline{151}$$

Exhibit 3–3 shows the overall evaluation of the three retailers using the importance weights of the single woman and the parent. For the single woman, the Internet grocer has the highest score, 221, and thus the most favourable evaluation. Therefore, on the one hand, she would probably select this retailer for most of her grocery shopping. On the other hand, the supercentre has the highest score, 192, for the parent, who would probably buy the family's weekly groceries there.

Of course, when customers are about to select a retailer, they don't actually go through the process of listing store characteristics, evaluating retailers' performances on these characteristics, determining each characteristic's importance, calculating each store's overall score, and then patronizing the retailer with the highest score! The multiattribute attitude model does not reflect customers' actual decision process, but it does predict their evaluation of alternatives and their choice.[25] In addition, the model provides useful information for designing a retail offering. For example, if the supermarket could increase its performance rating on assortment from 7 to 10 (perhaps by adding a bakery and a wide selection of prepared meals), customers like the parent might shop at the supermarket more often than at the supercentre.

Customers don't thoroughly evaluate all alternatives, as is suggested by the multiattribute attitude model. Instead, they simply buy merchandise that's good enough or very good on one particular attribute. In general, customers don't spend the time necessary to find the very best product. Once they have found a product that satisfies their need, they stop searching.[26]

Implications for Retailers   How can a retailer use the multiattribute attitude model to encourage customers to shop at it more frequently? First, the model indicates what information customers use to decide which retailer to patronize and which channel to use. Second, it suggests tactics that retailers can undertake to influence customer store choices and merchandise selection.

Thus, to develop a program for attracting customers, the retailer must do market research to collect the following information:

1. alternative retailers that customers consider
2. characteristics or benefits that customers consider when evaluating and choosing a retailer
3. customers' ratings of each retailer's performance on the characteristics
4. importance weights that customers attach to the characteristics

Armed with this information, the retailer can use several approaches to influence customers to patronize its store or Internet site.

Getting into the Consideration Set   The retailer needs to make sure that it is included in the customer's **consideration set**, or the set of alternatives the customer evaluates when making a selection. To be included in the consideration set, retailers develop programs to increase the likelihood that customers will remember them when they are about to go shopping. Retailers influence this top-of-the-mind awareness through the Internet, advertising, and location strategies. They get exposure on search engines like Google or Yahoo! by placing ads that are shown on pages related to the search items. Advertising expenditures that stress the retailer's name can increase top-of-the-mind awareness. When a retailer such as Starbucks locates several stores in the same area, customers are exposed more frequently to the store name as they drive through the area.[27]

After ensuring that it is in consumers' consideration set, a retailer can use four methods to increase the chances that customers will select its store for a visit:

> **consideration set** The set of alternatives the customer evaluates when making a merchandise selection.

1. Increase beliefs about the store's performance.
2. Decrease the performance beliefs for competing stores in the consideration set.
3. Increase customers' importance weights.
4. Add a new benefit.

Changing Performance Beliefs   The first approach involves altering customers' beliefs about the retailer's performance by increasing the retailer's performance rating on a characteristic.

For example, the supermarket in Exhibit 3–3 would want to increase its overall rating by improving its rating on all four benefits. The supermarket could improve its rating on economy by lowering prices and its assortment rating by stocking more gourmet and ethnic foods. Retailing View 3.2 illustrates how Lowe's altered the performance beliefs of women for its stores.

Because it can get costly for a retailer to improve its performance on all benefits, retailers must focus on improving their performance on those benefits that are important to customers in their target markets. For example, Best Buy knows that its customers don't want to be without their computers for lengthy

© AP-Brian Bohannon/The Canadian Press.

Do It Herself at Lowe's

You might think that home improvement centres are a retail recreation destination mostly for men. Men visit the stores on the weekends to check out the new tools and buy material for do-it-yourself (DIY) projects. But more than 50 percent of the sales at home improvement centres actually are made to women—who make decisions about what materials to use in home improvement projects and often do much of the work themselves.

Lowe's was early to recognize the importance of female customers—though it is not the only traditionally male-oriented retailer to do so. It redesigned its stores to be brighter, lose the warehouse look, and feature departments more appealing to women. With wider aisles, shoppers can avoid uncomfortable, unintended contact with items on shelves—otherwise known as "butt brush." The shelves also are a bit shorter, to make it easy to reach the easy-to-find products that are well marked by aisle markers and maps.

But these changes need to be restrained, to avoid causing male customers to reject the stores as overly

Lowe's changed its store design to change women's beliefs about the pleasantness of its store environment.
© Photographerlondon | Dreamstime.com.

feminine. Moreover, women express negative views of offerings that seem condescending in their "girlie" appeals. To balance its recent findings with its long-standing performance tactics, Lowe's offers workshops to teach women about tools, rather than carrying tools specifically designed for women.

Sources: Tony Bingham and Pat Galagan, "Training at Lowe's: Let's Learn Something Together," *T + D*, Nov. 2009, pp. 35–41; Amanda Junk, "Women Wield the Tools: Lowe's, Habitat for Humanity Teaches Them How," *McClatchy-Tribune Business News*, July 18, 2009; Cecile B. Corral, "Lowe's Outlines Expansion Plans," *Home Textiles Today*, October 5, 2009, p. 6; and Fara Warner, "Yes, Women Spend (And Saw and Sand)," *The New York Times*, February 29, 2004.

amounts of time when they are in need of repair.[28] So it has a 165 000-square-foot "Geek Squad City" warehouse designed to cut the time it takes to repair and return a PC to one to three days. Inside the facility's sprawling repair room, PC parts and precision tools are spread over the rows and rows of desks where hundreds of computer techs—Geek Squad's "agents"—fix more than 2000 laptops a day. Best Buy recognizes the sizable investment this warehouse requires, but it also believes it is worth it to achieve high ratings on a service attribute that is very important to its customers.

A change in a performance belief about an important benefit results in a large change in customers' overall evaluations. In Exhibit 3–3, the supermarket should attempt to improve its convenience ratings if it wants to attract more young, single women who presently shop on the Internet. If its convenience rating rose from 5 to 8, its overall evaluation among young, single women would increase from 153 to 183 and thus be much higher than their evaluation of supercentres. Note that an increase in the rating from 8 to 10 for a less important benefit, such as economy, would have less effect on the store's overall evaluation. The supermarket might try to improve its rating on convenience by increasing the number of checkout stations, using customer scanning to reduce checkout time, or providing more in-store information so that customers could locate merchandise more easily.

Research further suggests that consumers in Germany, France, and the United Kingdom place different weights on three important attributes—price/value, service/quality, and relationships—when selecting a retailer to patronize. German consumers tend to place more weight on price/value, whereas customer service and product quality are more important for French consumers, and affinity benefits such as loyalty cards and preferred customer programs are more important for English consumers. Thus, in general, retailers that emphasize price and good value will be more successful in Germany than in France or the United Kingdom.[29]

Another approach tries to decrease customers' performance ratings of a competing store. This approach may be illegal and usually isn't very effective, because bad-mouthing competitors generally backfires and customers typically don't believe a firm's negative comments about its competitors anyway.

Changing Importance Weights   Altering customers' importance weights is another approach to influencing store choice. A retailer wants to increase the importance customers place on benefits for which its performance is superior and decrease the importance of benefits for which it has inferior performance. For example, if the supermarket in Exhibit 3–3 tried to attract families who shop at supercentres, it could increase the importance of convenience for them. Typically, changing importance weights is harder than changing performance beliefs, because importance weights reflect customers' personal values.[30]

Adding a New Benefit   Finally, retailers might try to add a new benefit to the set of benefits customers consider when selecting a store. For example, Fair Indigo (http://www.fairindigo.com), along with other retailers, is adding a new benefit that is important to many consumers: social responsibility. Fair Indigo emphasizes that the apparel sold through its multiple channels is made by workers who are paid a fair wage, not just a minimum wage. A fair wage means that workers are able to live relatively comfortably within the context of their local area, with enough money for housing, food, health care, education for their children, and some disposable income. To get a high evaluation on this new benefit, Fair Indigo handpicks the most ethical factories around the globe to make its apparel.[31] The approach of adding a new benefit is often effective, because it's easier to change customer evaluations of new than of old benefits.

Purchasing the Merchandise or Service

Customers don't always purchase a brand or item of merchandise with the highest overall evaluation. The product or service offering the greatest benefits (having the highest evaluation) may not be available in the store, or the customer may feel that its risks outweigh the potential benefits. One measure of retailers' success at converting positive evaluations to purchases is the number of real or virtual abandoned carts in the retailer's store and website.

Retailers use various tactics to increase the chances that customers will convert their positive merchandise or service evaluations into purchases. Retailers can reduce the number of abandoned carts by making it easier to purchase merchandise. They reduce the actual wait time to buy merchandise by having more checkout lanes open and placing them conveniently inside the store. To reduce perceived wait times, they install digital displays to entertain customers waiting in line. On a website, the ease of navigation is critical for decreasing the number of abandoned virtual carts.

> **DID YOU KNOW?**
>
> According to research, eight in ten people aged 18–34 usually read the content of indoor advertising. Of these people, a whopping 91 percent find MiniBoard advertising to be eye-catching and effective in influencing their shopping behaviour.[35]

Customers' perceived risk in making a purchase decision can be reduced by providing sufficient information that reinforces the customer's positive evaluation. For those customers browsing the Internet, retailers offer online reviews.[32] Finally, risks are reduced when retailers offer liberal return policies, money-back guarantees, price-matching policies, and refunds if customers find the same merchandise available at lower prices from another retailer.

Conversion rates are particularly low for consumers using an Internet channel because consumers are able to easily keep track of things they like. They can look at products, throw them in their cart, and delay a purchase decision. Retailers do a few things to encourage customers to make a purchase

satisfaction A post-consumption evaluation of the degree to which a store or product meets or exceeds customer expectations.

post-purchase evaluation The evaluation of merchandise or services after the customer has purchased and consumed them.

extended problem solving A buying process in which customers spend considerable time at each stage of the decision-making process because the decision is important and they have limited knowledge of alternatives.

limited problem solving A purchase-decision process involving a moderate amount of effort and time. Customers engage in this type of buying process when they have some prior experience with the product or service and their risk is moderate.

decision. For example, Zappos.com and Overstock.com create urgency by alerting customers when an item they have put in their shopping cart is almost sold out. Other sites, such as Gilt Groupe, offer items for a specified 36-hour period. While the Internet channel makes it easier for shoppers to delay purchase decisions, it also makes it easier to identify potential customers and encourage them to buy. Petco.com devotes entire sections within each pet category to "top rated" products. Shoppers who browse these products purchase 35 percent more than those who browse assortments arranged in a traditional manner. Those who buy from "top rated" sections spend 40 percent more than those who do not.[33] Many retailers send reminder emails to visitors about items in carts they have abandoned.[34]

Post-Purchase Evaluation

The buying process doesn't end when a customer purchases a product. After making a purchase, the customer uses the product and then evaluates the experience to determine whether it was satisfactory or unsatisfactory. **Satisfaction** is a post-consumption evaluation of how well a store or product meets or exceeds customer expectations. This **post-purchase evaluation** then becomes part of the customer's internal information and affects future store and product decisions. Unsatisfactory experiences can motivate customers to complain to the retailer, patronize other stores, and select different brands in the future.[36] Consistently high levels of satisfaction build store and brand loyalty, important sources of competitive advantage for retailers.

Types of Buying Decisions

In some situations, customers spend considerable time and effort selecting a retailer and evaluating alternative products—going through all the steps in the buying process described in the preceding section. In other situations, buying decisions are made automatically with little thought. Three types of customer decision-making processes are extended problem solving, limited problem solving, and habitual decision making.

Extended Problem Solving

Extended problem solving is a purchase-decision process in which customers devote considerable time and effort to analyzing their alternatives. Customers typically engage in extended problem solving when the purchase decision involves a lot of risk and uncertainty. Financial risks arise when customers purchase an expensive product or service. Physical risks are important when customers feel that a product or service may affect their health or safety. Social risks arise when customers believe a product will affect how others view them. Lasik eye surgery, for instance, involves all three types of risks: It can be expensive, potentially damage the eyes, and change a person's appearance.

Consumers engage in extended problem solving when they are making a buying decision to satisfy an important need or when they have little knowledge about the product or service. Due to the high risk in such situations, customers go beyond their internal knowledge to consult with friends, family members, or experts. They may also visit several retailers before making a purchase decision.

Retailers stimulate sales from customers engaged in extended problem solving by providing the necessary information in a readily available and easily understood manner and by offering money-back guarantees. For example, retailers that sell merchandise involving extended problem solving provide information on their websites describing the merchandise and its specifications, have informational displays in their stores (such as a sofa cut in half to show its construction), and use salespeople to demonstrate features and answer questions.

Limited Problem Solving

Limited problem solving is a purchase-decision process involving a moderate amount of effort and time. Customers engage in this type of buying process when they have had some prior experience with the product or service and their risk is moderate. In such situations, customers tend to rely more on personal knowledge than on external information. They usually choose a retailer they have shopped at before and select merchandise they have bought in the past. The majority of customer purchase decisions involve limited problem solving.

Retailers attempt to reinforce this buying pattern and make it habitual when customers are buying merchandise from them. If customers are shopping elsewhere, however, retailers need to break this buying pattern by introducing new information or offering different merchandise or services.

One type of limited problem solving is impulse buying, or unplanned purchasing, which is a buying decision made by customers on the spot after seeing the merchandise.[37] Retailers encourage impulse-buying behaviour by using prominent point-of-purchase (POP) or point-of-sale (POS) displays to attract customers' attention. Retailers have long recognized that the most valuable real estate in the store is at the point of purchase. An increasing number of non-food retailers are looking to increase impulse buys from customers by offering gum, candy, and mints at their cash registers. Electronic shoppers are also stimulated to purchase impulsively when Internet retailers put special merchandise on their home pages and suggest complementary merchandise just before checkout.

Habitual Decision Making

Habitual decision making is a purchase-decision process involving little or no conscious effort. Today's customers have many demands on their time. One way they cope with these time pressures is by simplifying their decision-making process. When a need arises, customers automatically respond with, "I'll buy the same thing I bought last time from the same store." Typically, this habitual decision-making process occurs when decisions aren't very important to customers and involve familiar merchandise they have bought in the past. When customers are loyal to a brand or a store, they engage in habitual decision making.

Brand loyalty means that customers like and consistently buy a specific brand in a product category. They are reluctant to switch to other brands if their favourite brand isn't available. For example, loyal Coca-Cola drinkers won't buy Pepsi, no matter what. Thus, retailers can satisfy these customers' needs only if they offer the specific brands desired.

Brand loyalty creates both opportunities and problems for retailers. Customers are attracted to stores that carry popular brands, but because retailers must carry these high-loyalty brands, they may not be able to negotiate favourable terms with the suppliers of the popular national brands. If, however, the high-loyalty brands are private-label brands (i.e., brands owned by the retailer), retailer loyalty is heightened.

Retailer loyalty means that customers like and habitually visit the same retailer to purchase a type of merchandise. All retailers would like to increase their customers' loyalty, and they can do so by selecting a convenient location, offering complete assortments of national and private-label brands, reducing the number of stockouts, rewarding customers for frequent purchases, or providing good customer service.

habitual decision making A purchase decision involving little or no conscious effort.

brand loyalty Indicates customers like and consistently buy a specific brand in a product category. They are reluctant to switch to other brands if their favourite brand isn't available.

retailer loyalty Indicates that customers like and habitually visit the same retailer to purchase a type of merchandise.

Lo2 Lo3 Social Factors Influencing Buying Decisions

Exhibit 3–4 illustrates that a customer's buying decisions are influenced by both the customer's beliefs, attitudes, and values *and* factors in the customer's social environment. In this section, we discuss how buying decisions are affected by the customer's social environment—the customer's family, reference groups, and culture.

Family

Many purchase decisions are made for products that the entire family will consume or use. Thus, retailers must understand how families make purchase decisions and how various family members influence these decisions.

Family Decision Making

When families make purchase decisions, they often consider the needs of

DID YOU KNOW?

Negative word of mouth is expensive. Only 6 percent of shoppers who experience a problem with a retailer contact the company, but 31 percent tell someone what happened, and many of those go on to tell others. Overall, if 100 people have a bad experience, a retailer stands to lose between 32 and 36 current or potential customers.

Exhibit 3-4
Factors Affecting Buying Decisions

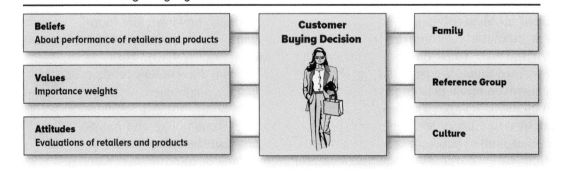

Beliefs — About performance of retailers and products		Customer Buying Decision		Family
Values — Importance weights				Reference Group
Attitudes — Evaluations of retailers and products				Culture

reference group One or more people whom a person uses as a basis of comparison for his or her beliefs, feelings, and behaviours.

all family members.[38] In a situation such as choosing a vacation site, all family members may participate in the decision making. In other situations, one member of the family may assume the role of making the purchase decision. For example, the husband might buy the groceries, the wife uses them to prepare their child's lunch, and the child consumes the lunch in school. In this situation, the store choice decision might be made by the husband, but the brand choice decision might be made by the wife, though greatly influenced by the child.

Children play an important role in family buying decisions.[39] Satisfying the needs of children is particularly important for many Baby Boomers who decide to have children late in life. They often have high disposable income and want to stay in luxury resorts, but they still want to take their children on vacations. Resort hotels now realize they must satisfy children's needs as well as adults'. To meet this need, Hyatt hotels greet families by offering books and games tailored to the children's ages. Parents checking in with infants receive a first-day supply of baby food or formula and diapers at no charge. The hotels also offer babysitting and escort services to attractions for children.[40]

Retailers can attract consumers who shop with other family members by satisfying the needs of all family members. For example, IKEA, a Swedish furniture store chain, has a "ball pit" in which children can play while their parents shop. By accommodating the needs of children who might not be interested in shopping, the family stays in the stores longer and buys more merchandise.[41]

Reference Groups

A **reference group** is composed of two or more people whom a person uses as a basis of comparison for his or her beliefs, feelings, and behaviours. A consumer might have a number of different reference groups, although the most important reference group is the family. These reference groups affect buying decisions by:

- offering information
- providing rewards for specific purchasing behaviours
- enhancing a consumer's self-image

Reference groups provide information to consumers directly through conversation or indirectly through observation. Celebrity sports people can capture the hearts and wallets of

Many purchase decisions consider the needs of family members other than the shopper.
© John Lund/Mark Romanelli/Blend Images LLC.

consumers through product endorsements and retailer relationships. For example, Kaillie Humphries (Olympic Bobsled defending gold medal and world champion) is sponsored by Sports Chek; female golfers might look to Lori Kane or Michelle Wei to guide their purchase decisions; and Canadian hockey hero Wayne Gretzky has added his face to a Canadian Tire's advertising campaign.

By identifying and affiliating with reference groups, consumers create, enhance, and maintain self-image. Customers who want to be seen as members of an elite social class may shop at Holt Renfrew, whereas others who want to create an image of an athletic enthusiast might buy merchandise from Lululemon.

Retailers are particularly interested in identifying and reaching out to those in a reference group who act as store advocates and actively influence others in the group. **Store advocates** are customers who like a store so much that they actively share their positive experiences with family and friends. Because today's consumers see so much advertising, they have become suspicious of the claims being made. As a result, they are relying more on their own social networks for information about stores to patronize and merchandise to buy. Research has found that advocacy for a particular supermarket is not built on low prices. It is stimulated by a store design that enables advocates to find items easily, by courteous and helpful employees, and by having a wide selection of fresh vegetables and fruits.[42]

Alpha moms are good example of store advocates. Educated, tech-savvy, Type A moms have a common goal: mommy excellence.[43] An alpha mom is a multitasker, kidcentric, and hands-on. She may or may not work outside the home, but at home, she views motherhood as a job that can be mastered with diligent research. As the label implies, she is a leader of the pack who influences how other moms spend. She's also wired—online 87 minutes a day, she spends a hefty 7 percent more than the typical Internet user. The impact of her purchases or what she touts can spread on the Internet, far beyond her personal email list or blog.

Canada's Multicultural Market

Visible minorities in Canada have grown threefold over the last two decades and now make up 13 percent of the population. It is predicted that visible minorities will make up 20 percent of Canada's population and 18 percent of the labour force by 2016. Today more than eight out of ten visible minorities are first-generation immigrants. More than 48 percent of Toronto's population is now foreign-born, making it the most ethnically diverse city in the world, and Vancouver is more ethnically diverse than any city in the United States. According to Statistics Canada, in another few years Toronto's population will be more than half foreign-born. Almost a quarter of southern Ontario residents, 37 percent of Vancouver citizens, and approximately 20 percent of people living in Calgary and Montreal are first-generation immigrants. Across Canada, 5.4 million people are first-generation immigrant Canadians. According to Statistics Canada, immigrants from India, Pakistan, south China, the Philippines, and other South Asian countries will represent the largest proportion of new Canadians by 2017.

Canada has evolving societal issues; no one comes here and discards their **culture** (values shared by most members of a society). These people bring unique culture and world views to Canada, and they also bring unique shopping preferences: They like to shop around and haggle with shop owners, and if they don't feel like they can negotiate a better price, they will shop somewhere else. Haggling is about building a relationship. It is all about learning about the product, talking to a shop owner, and negotiating a special price; think of it as a shopping ritual. For South Asians, it is a way of gaining respect. This aspect of Canada's new cultural influx is going to be a challenge for many retailers.

For Canada's large retailers with centralized pricing and buying, it will be difficult to adjust prices and product to meet the needs of individual markets. It may be important to connect to community leaders who can talk to people from their population and find out about retail preferences of the ethnic market. Retailers can also show the market that they are listening to ethnic consumers by acknowledging special times, for example, Chinese New Year.

The one thing that ethnic consumers and aging Boomers have in common is their desire for quality service. They know the value of a dollar and they will not trade away quality. Marketers must

DID YOU KNOW?

Victoria's Secret has the highest percentage of advocates among its customers. Twenty-three percent of its customers are store advocates, compared with an average of 13 percent for other retailers.[44]

store advocates Customers who like a store so much that they actively share their positive experiences with friends and family.

culture The meaning and values shared by most members of a society.

subculture A distinctive group of people within a culture. Members of a subculture share some customs and norms with the overall society but also have some unique perspectives.

understand how new immigrants think before they can market to them, because the solution is not simply to take a commercial and add a voiceover in another language. The way to optimize the multicultural market is to build relationships. It is not just about selling to the market, but rather about serving the market. For example, General Motors Canada capitalizes on the fact that the Chinese culture considers 2, 8, and 9 to be lucky numbers by trying to help customers obtain licence plates reflecting this preference. Walmart began airing ethnic ads in 1998 in Toronto, featuring customers of different ethnicities speaking in their own language.

In this changing marketplace, you cannot afford not to invest in research. Retailers need to keep their research up to date and look at their product mix, fashion sizes, and service and match them to the market preferences. Hiring an ethnically diverse staff will also help retailers understand the market. The reality is, if you don't keep up with the market, someone else will. Two important points to remember:

- Immigrants often arrive in Canada with only money and a suitcase. They need to buy necessary supplies and household items to set up a home.

- Immigrants are often used to sophisticated marketing from their home country and will look to advertising for information, store product, price, and location.

Not only does retailing have to differ for Canadian- and foreign-born market segments, differences can also arise among groups of native Canadians as well. For example, what appeals to the rest of Canada may not work in Quebec. The needs and tastes of the Quebec market are particular to its culture and its self-contained nature. Quebecers differ in their shopping behaviour, and

retailers who are not of Quebec origin generally have a tough time becoming successful in this marketplace. Many non-Quebec retailers who have entered the market have had limited success and subsequently have left the market. Quebecers are loyal to Quebec-based retailers, whether they are francophone or not.

Quebec also represents its own media universe that is unique in Canada; the province has more beauty and fashion publications than the rest of Canada combined. Tween girls have a strong cultural background where pop icons and cultural references are different; for example, when Nicki Minaj is hot, she's hot in Quebec too, but most of the Quebec pop icons are francophone. It is good to tie a product to a spokesperson, but retailers must make sure that they know the market to find the best match for their product. Young Quebecers watch French-language movies and reality shows, and are not fond of clothes displaying big logos and brand names that may be popular in the rest of Canada. Language is responsible for fundamental cultural distinctions.[45]

A **subculture** is a distinctive group of people within a culture. Members of a subculture share some customs and norms with the overall society, but also have some unique perspectives.[46] Subcultures can be based on geography (southerners), age (Baby Boomers), ethnicity (Asian Canadians), or lifestyle (hipster).

Cora Reed/Cutcaster.

DID YOU KNOW?

In 1994, the Swedish furniture retailer IKEA aired the first mainstream TV ad targeted toward the gay subculture by featuring a gay relationship.[47]

Accessibility Accessibility is the ability of the retailer to deliver the appropriate retail mix to the customers in the segment. For instance, customers of Marriott convention hotels and resort hotels are accessed in different ways because they use different sources to collect information about products and services. Convention hotel customers are best reached through newspapers such as the *National Post* and the *Globe and Mail*, whereas resort hotel customers are best reached through ads on TV and in travel and leisure magazines.

LO4 Market Segmentation

The preceding discussion focused on how individual customers evaluate and select stores and merchandise, and factors affecting their decision making. To increase their efficiency, retailers identify groups of customers (market segments) and target their offerings to meet the needs of typical customers in that segment rather than the needs of a specific customer. A **retail market segment** is a group of customers whose needs are satisfied by the same retail mix because they have similar needs. For example, families travelling on a vacation have different needs than do executives on business trips. Thus, Marriott offers hotels with different retail mixes for each of these segments.

The Internet enables retailers to efficiently target individual customers and market products to them on a one-to-one basis.

Criteria for Evaluating Market Segments

Customers are grouped into segments in many different ways. For example, customers can be grouped on the basis of where they live, income, and education, or if they barbecue at home twice a week or more. Exhibit 3–5 shows different methods for segmenting retail markets. There is no simple way to determine which method is best. Four criteria for evaluating whether a retail segment is a viable target market are actionability, identifiability, accessibility, and size.

Actionability The fundamental criteria for evaluating a retail market segment are as follows:

- Customers in the segment must have similar needs, seek similar benefits, and be satisfied by a similar retail offering.

- Those customers' needs must be different from the needs of customers in other segments.

Actionability means that the definition of a segment must clearly indicate what the retailer should do to satisfy its needs. According to this criterion, it makes sense for Addition Elle (which caters to full-figured women) to segment the apparel market on the basis of the demographic characteristic, physical size of women. Customers who wear large sizes have different needs than those who wear small sizes, so they are attracted to a store offering a unique merchandise mix. Plus-size retailers have been striving to offer fashion to this consumer group that wants more than just clothing that fits—they insist on style. The plus-size market has been a growing segment of the women's apparel market over the last few years.

On the other hand, it wouldn't make sense for a supermarket to segment its market on the basis of the customer size. Large and small men and women probably have the same needs, seek the same benefits, and go through the same buying process for groceries. This segmentation approach wouldn't be actionable for a supermarket retailer because the retailer couldn't develop unique mixes for large and small customers. Thus, supermarkets usually segment markets using demographics such as income or ethnic origin to develop their retail mix.

Identifiability Retailers must be able to identify the customers in a target segment. **Identifiability** is important because it permits the retailer to determine the following:

- the segment's size
- with whom the retailer should communicate when promoting its retail offering

accessibility (1) The degree to which customers can easily get into and out of a shopping centre; (2) ability of the retailer to deliver the appropriate retail mix to the customers in the segment.

retail market segment A group of customers whose needs will be satisfied by the same retail offering because they have similar needs and go through similar buying processes.

actionability Means that the definition of a market segment must clearly indicate what the retailer should do to satisfy its needs.

identifiability Permits a retailer to determine a market segment's size and with whom the retailer should communicate when promoting its retail offering.

Exhibit 3–5
Methods for segmenting retail markets

Segmentation Descriptor	Example of Categories
Geographic	
Region	Pacific, Prairies, Central, Maritimes
Population density	Rural, suburban, urban
Climate	Cold, warm
Demographic	
Age	Under 6, 6–12, 13–19, 20–29, 30–49, 50–65, over 65
Gender	Male, female
Family life cycle	Single; married with no children; married with youngest child under 6; married with youngest child over 6; married with children no longer living at home; widowed
Family income	Under $19 999; $20 000–29 999; $30 000–49 999; $50 000–$74 999; over $75 000
Occupation	Professional, clerical sales, craftsperson, retired, student, homemaker
Education	Some high school, high school graduate, some university, university graduate, graduate degree
Religion	Catholic, Protestant, Jewish, Muslim
Race	Caucasian, African American, Hispanic, Asian
Nationality	Canadian, American, Japanese, British, French, German, Italian, Chinese
Psychosocial	
Social class	Lower, middle, upper
Lifestyle	Striver, driver, devotee, intimate, altruist, fun seeker, creative
Personality	Aggressive, shy, emotional
Feelings and Behaviours	
Attitudes	Positive, neutral, negative
Benefit sought	Convenience, economy, prestige
Stage in decision process	Unaware, aware, informed, interested, intend to buy, bought previously
Perceived risk	High, medium, low
Innovativeness	Innovator, early adopter, early majority, late majority, laggard
Loyalty	None, some, complete
Usage rate	None, light, medium, heavy
Usage situation	Home, work, vacation, leisure
User status	Non-user, ex-user, potential user, current user

Accessibility   Is the ability of the retailer to deliver the appropriate retail mix to the customers in a targeted segment. The retailer may have a segment who may wish to purchase the product but are not able to access the product. The evolution of online retailing has helped retailers with this physical constraint to access segments they previously would not have been able to reach. The problem with this, however, is that retailers in other geographical areas now have similar accessibility to segments in the local trading area.

Size   A target segment must be large enough to support a unique retailing mix. For example, in the past, health food and vitamins were found primarily in small, owner-operated stores that catered to a relatively small market. In the wake of higher consciousness about exercise and nutrition, health food stores such as Whole Foods have gained customer loyalty. Supermarkets have also expanded their offering of health foods, vitamins, and organic produce to meet this substantial market segment's needs.

On the other hand, the number of consumers in a target segment may not always be a good indicator of potential sales. For example, international retailers are very interested in China because it has 1.4 billion consumers, expected to rise to 1.54 billion around 2040. Urban migration continues to expand in China. According to a Global Analysis Report, "Half of China's population resided in urban areas, such as Beijing, Shanghai, Guangzhou, Tianjin, and Chongqing, in 2011. This growing urbanization is leading to a greater concentration of urban consumers, who live busier lifestyles and earn high incomes. These urban consumers are increasing demand for imported food products that are convenient and quick, such as ready-meals, and are a key target market for imports."[48] This indicates opportunity to offer products to a "time poverty" consumer, but more research would need to be done prior to entering this market. One market analysis report should not drive a retail marketing strategy. There is no assurance imported products would be successful; a complete market analysis would need to be done first.

Approaches for Segmenting Markets

Exhibit 3–5 illustrates the wide variety of approaches for segmenting retail markets. No single approach is best for all retailers. They must explore various factors that affect customer buying behaviour and determine which factors are most important. Now we will discuss methods for segmenting retail markets.

Geographic Segmentation

Geographic segmentation groups customers by where they live. A retail market can be segmented by country (e.g., Japan, Mexico) and by areas within a country, such as provinces, cities, and neighbourhoods. Since customers typically shop at stores convenient to where they live and work, individual retail outlets usually focus on the customer segment reasonably close to the outlet.

In the United States, many food retailers concentrate on particular regions of the country. For example, HEB concentrates on Texas, while Wegmans concentrates on Western New York. However, in the United Kingdom, supermarket retailing is dominated by national firms such as Sainsbury and Tesco. The Canadian grocery industry is dominated by George Weston Ltd., the country's largest food processor and distributor and owner of Loblaws, the country's biggest grocery chain.

Even though national retailers such as The Gap and Sears have no geographic focus, they do tailor their merchandise selections to different regions of North America—snow sleds don't sell well in Florida, and surfboards don't sell well in Alberta. Even within a metropolitan area, stores in a chain must adjust to the unique needs of customers in different neighbourhoods. For example, supermarkets in affluent neighbourhoods typically have more gourmet foods than stores in less affluent neighbourhoods.

Segments based on geography are identifiable, accessible, and substantial. It's easy to determine who lives in a geographic segment, such as the Paris metropolitan area, and to target communications and locate retail outlets for customers in Paris. When customers in different geographic segments have similar needs, it would be inappropriate to develop unique retail offerings by geographic markets. For example, a fast-food customer in Toronto probably seeks the same benefits as a fast-food customer in Vancouver. Thus, it wouldn't be useful to segment the fast-food market geographically. Even though Hudson's Bay and The Gap vary some merchandise assortments geographically, the majority of their merchandise is identical in all of their stores because customers who buy basic clothing (underwear, slacks, shirts, and blouses) have many of the same needs in all regions of North America. On the other hand, Home Depot and many supermarket chains have significantly different assortments in stores located in the same city.

Demographic Segmentation

Demographics are numbers about people, and this information is collected through a census of the population in Canada by Statistics Canada and in the United States by the US Census Bureau. The law requires that all people living in the country complete the questionnaire accurately. The general demographic information collected is available to all researchers, business people, and students to help in decision making. **Demographic segmentation** groups consumers on the basis of easily measured, objective characteristics such as age, gender, income, and education. Demographic variables are the most common means to define segments because consumers in these segments can be easily identified and accessed. The media used by retailers to communicate with

> **geographic segmentation**
> Segmentation of potential customers by where they live. A retail market can be segmented by countries, provinces, cities, and neighbourhoods.
>
> **demographic segmentation** A method of segmenting a retail market that groups consumers on the basis of easily measured, objective characteristics such as age, sex, income, and education.

© McGraw-Hill Education/Andrew Resek.

customers are defined in terms of demographic profiles. Demographics such as gender are related to differences in shopping behaviour.

Who Is the Male Shopper? It does appear that men are from Mars and women are from Venus when the sexes go shopping. In general, men show little ability or interest in honing their shopping skills, whereas women view the supermarket as a place where they can demonstrate their expertise in getting the most value for their money. Rather than looking for items on sale or making price comparisons, men tend to select well-known brands. They also tend not to pay attention at the checkout register, whereas women watch the cashier to be sure they are charged the right price. Men and women even buy different merchandise. Women buy more health-oriented foods (such as cottage cheese and refrigerated yogourt) and household essentials (such as cleaning and personal health products). Men's shopping baskets contain more beer, cupcakes, ice cream, and hot dogs. Men also do less planning and make numerous last-minute grocery trips: Single men visit supermarkets 99 times a year, while single women make 80 trips a year. These eleventh-hour trips make men more susceptible to impulse purchases such as potato chips and cookies.[49]

The Power of Women Women comprise 52 percent of the North American population and have significant buying power. Women make 85 percent of all retail and service purchases ($3.7 trillion) and buy 51 percent of consumer electronics and 51 percent of all cars (and influence 85 percent of all auto purchases), 50 percent of computers, and 51 percent of all travel.[50] Women bring in half or more of the income in most North American households. Unlike their male counterparts, who rely on promotions to make a purchasing decision, women will seek out a product's credibility or discuss the product's attributes with a friend.

Well-known retailers such as Home Depot are aware of the importance of understanding gender difference in marketing to both sexes. The big-box stores are recognizing that women are wearing the overalls and thus are designing stores with wider aisles, detailed signage, samples of finished projects, and lots of helpful staff to assist with decisions. Even men's clothier Harry Rosen understands the influence of women in closing a sale; you talk to the men but sell to their wives. Women are rapidly surpassing men in starting to use online services, and nearly half of first-time Web buyers are women (Wired.com).

According to GenderMark International, up to 70 percent of women ignore marketing campaigns that don't speak to them, and if they have a bad experience with a product or service, on average, women will tell 28 people. The bottom line is that women want a more intelligent, more honest approach to retailing. Women make up 80 percent of The Shopping Channel's paying customers, and 50 percent of online shoppers are women ages 35 to 54. Even in time spent on social media, (PC, mobile, Web, and apps), women are more deeply engaged than men, spending an average of 8 hours and 37 minutes of social networking time versus 6 hours and 13 minutes for men.[51] It seems that women want it all—made to feel special both online and offline. However, when it comes right down to it, they show no loyalty because price matters more than brand.

Knowledge of Demographics Is Critical Demographics are critical to understanding product demand and defining a retailer's strategy. Demographics can explain the growth of specialty beers and skin care creams, the demand for healthy food, the trends in real estate, and golf memberships. A study by AOL and Bovitz Research Group looked at how women are spending their time online and what they want from the Web. The study broadly categorized Web-savvy women into three distinct behavioural groups. First, *social expressionistas* are community creators who are passionate about spreading the word online and are highly active on social networking sites. Second, *alpha trendsetters* take their social lives and careers seriously and are very brand conscious; these women are the perfect market for retailers of luxury brands that aim their products at women. Finally, *shopsessives* believe they are experts in all areas, ranging from fashion to health, and are shopping online across all product categories; this group of women highly influences the shopping decisions of friends and family.[52]

David Foot—demographer, professor at the University of Toronto, and author of *Boom, Bust & Echo* (followed by *Boom, Bust & Echo 2000*)—has widely discussed the impact of demographics on Canadian life. For example, he explains that one-third of the North American population was born after the Second World War. Known as the Boomers (born from 1946 to 1966), by sheer numbers this large group has had an immense impact on every aspect of social and economic life. By 2015, leading-edge Baby Boomers were staring 70 head-on; trailing-edge Boomers were looking at 50 in the rear-view mirror. If 50 was the new 30, will 70 be the new 50? Retailers need to recognize that Baby Boomers will not go conventionally into maturity, but will in fact continue to redefine older age and retirement, remaining active and involved.[53]

The Digital Generation

This new youth culture is smart, savvy, and the first generation to grow up surrounded by digital media: the Internet, smartphones, tablets, computer games, Blue Ray DVDs, MP3, mobile technology, social media, and digital cameras. The digital generation will epitomize the new mindset of the decade as they have grown up in a world where there are very few physical or psychological barriers to trying new ways of doing things. Everything is interconnected, anything goes, everything is available, and nothing is private. Retailers and suppliers will need to respond by providing this generation with the tools they need to create, co-create, or re-create to suit themselves.[54]

Fancy/SuperStock.

Retailing to Generation Z

Generation Z, those born between 1995 to present, are the fastest-growing segment in Canada. In Canada, the 7.9 million "Zers" influence the $20 billion their parents spend.[55] This phenomenon is known as *kidfluence*, the influence that kids have over the family's purchase decisions. In the United States, Gen Z has approximately $44 billion in purchasing power.[56] See Retailing View 3.3 for more information on this group.

The teens of today are very sophisticated for their young years, primarily because they have been exposed to so much knowledge and information through various media.

However, demographics may not be useful for defining segments for some retailers. For example, demographics are poor predictors of users of active wear such as jogging suits and running shoes. At one time, retailers assumed that active wear would be purchased exclusively by young people, but the health and fitness lifestyle trend has led people of all ages to buy this merchandise. Relatively inactive consumers find active wear to be comfortable. Initially, retailers felt that DVDs would be a luxury product purchased mainly by wealthy customers. But retailers found that low-income customers and families with young children were strongly attracted to DVDs because they offered low-cost, convenient entertainment.

Geodemographic Segmentation **Geodemographic segmentation** uses both geographic and demographic characteristics to classify consumers. This segmentation scheme is based on the principle that "birds of a feather flock together."[57] Consumers in the same neighbourhoods tend to buy the same types of cars, appliances, and apparel and shop at the same types of retailers.

Geodemographers are busy tracking consumer habits across Canada, postal code by postal code. This is the business of data mining. They tabulate and map information from surveys and census data and then fit together a picture of Canadians. Based on information gathered, they are able to formulate a statistical prediction of the likely behaviour the next time someone picks a movie or a restaurant, or hands over a credit card at the shopping mall. Geodemographers do not know you by name, but from juggling postal codes and probabilities they have a good idea of your lifestyle and spending habits.

Environics Analytics specializes in data mining. They break the country down into recognizable clusters of consumer habits, by region, city, and even neighbourhood. They have clients who pay to know what consumers want,

geodemographic segmentation A market segmentation system that uses both geographic and demographic characteristics to classify consumers.

DID YOU KNOW?

Of the 6.3 daily hours Canadians aged 18 to 24 spend daily on media, 78 minutes are spent gaming, 48 minutes on social media, and 60 minutes browsing the Internet.[58]

Retailing to Generation Z

Meet the most complex yet most critical shopper of all time—Generation Z. By 2020, today's 16–21 year olds (Gen Z) will be the largest group of consumers worldwide, making up 40 percent of the US, Europe, and BRIC countries, and 10 percent in the rest of the world. The needs and behaviours of this group will inform not only the next generation of shoppers, but the future of mainstream retail.

There's A New Wave of Shoppers in Town

Though they live and shop among us, these new shoppers are happier with access than with ownership. Shrewd with money and eschewing credit, they have the time and tools to compare produc ts and hunt for the best prices.

These shoppers have the power to hop between retailers—be they physical stores or online destinations—snapping pics and screen grabs as they go, and leaving a trail of hashtags in their wake. Their world is constant, so if they're awake at 3 a.m., they expect you to be too: open all hours, access all areas.

They are as socially-conscious as they are brand-conscious; they have Googled what your brand's about before leaving home—and browse a scrapbook of wants and ideas as they peruse your shelves, all the while getting real-time feedback from friends.

Logged into multiple platforms across a mosaic world of their own making, they live in a constant state of partial attention, but will know about a product problem or promotion way before you do. They are happy to accept a beta product today, with the promise of a better one tomorrow; it will be better because they have co-created it.

Opinionated, connected, and influential in the digital realm, they are expert messaging filterers, resourceful planners, and careful savers, looking for a retail experience with opt-in service, two-way dialogue, and mutual rewards.

Profiling Gen Z Comprised of everyone born after 1995, Gen Z is the most culturally diverse generation to date. These 16–21 year olds have grown up with varied family structures, a more diverse mix of defined ethnic groups, and blurred gender roles. As a result of this and

The purchase decisions of tweens are influenced by family members and friends.
© Fancy Collection/SuperStock.

the global context surrounding their formative years, their relationship and career aspirations differ vastly from those of their X and Y forebears.

While differences in perspective can be seen between developed and developing markets, the general outlook of teens worldwide has been influenced by several global reaching events that have shaped their context and reference points. These events have profoundly influenced Gen Z fears and concerns, while simultaneously

Source: Excerpted from "Gen Z and the Future of Retail," *FITCH,* http://www.fitch.com/think/gen-z-and-the-future-of-retail/ (accessed March 23, 2016).

how to track them down, and how to get their attention. Environics can advise on retail locations, best products to succeed in specific markets, and appropriate advertising strategies.

With each retail transaction, consumers give valuable data that will provide insight into buying behaviour. Retail stores want to track where their customers live and what they purchase, in order to evoking a tendency to dream about making the world a better place, and to believe that they have the power to effect significant change.

Some key issues that concern Gen Z include the following:

- **Climate change**—Three-quarters of teens around the world consider this a greater risk than drugs, violence, or war. Gen Z have a social conscience. Gen Z dream of a world in which good works are not the preserve of volunteers, but rather are an intrinsic part of society, especially in the corporate world.

- **Solitary pursuits**—As teens who have grown up with social media, everything is better as "we," not "me." Gen Z value their community and their ability to cascade messages widely and instantly, recognizing the power and influence this brings.

- **Bankruptcy**—They have seen adults follow society's rules and still lose everything, so they don't trust conventional views on money. Unlike their parents and grandparents before them, Gen Z do not assume that if they study hard they will get a "job for life"; they assume that they will have to shape their own destiny. While instant gratification in shopping was the norm for Generations X and Y, and credit cards were iconic of this attitude, Gen Z are credit cynics. These resourceful savers are careful not to waste their limited financial means, and expect to become self-sufficient entrepreneurs—creators of their own sustainable fortunes.

Some Takeaways:

1. Gen Z were born seamless and expect a similarly seamless retail experience.

2. They are savvy cynics who trust their peers, not marketers, and who won't pay more for ownership if they can pay less for access.

3. They don't expect to be treated differently by store staff because they are young; they expect the same respectful and helpful interaction as older shoppers.

4. They prefer the "good enough" approach. They would rather have a product that is made available quickly and then improved at regular intervals with their input (agile development) than a perfect product with guarantees and warranties in which they have had no involvement.

5. Gen Z use multiple platforms instead of owning multiple devices—they talk about Facebook, Instagram, or Pinterest rather than hardware tech manufacturers such as Nokia or Blackberry—and usernames have replaced avatars as symbols of identity.

6. Gen Z expect constant innovation. Upgrades and updates are always welcomed as signs of progress. In fact, they actively dislike products that aren't constantly changing.

7. Gen Z identify potential purchases via their natural state of seamless multi-tasking and social media scanning.

8. Gen Z will start with Google before doing anything else. They then happily remix style trends, make a digital scrapbook (taking photos with their smartphones in stores and mixing them up with images scraped off Pinterest), and price-check across websites. While most of this activity is digital, they will also plan store visits as excursions—not individually, but en masse with friends.

9. Gen Z will seek approval from their peers, delaying gratification in case something better comes along, while constantly tracking prices using apps. These savvy shoppers may set product ceiling price, buying only when the price falls below that level.

10. Gen Z—cash-poor but savvy—believe there is no shame in using bargain websites such as eBay, nor in picking up a good deal second-hand.

11. Having made their purchase, Gen Z immediately want to connect with their peers, creating, watching, and responding to "haul" videos.

Retail is on the brink of a revolution. Retailers and brand owners need to fundamentally reconsider their proposition if they are going to capture the hearts, minds, wallets, and attention spans of this constantly connected, partially attentive generation.

target the biggest-spending potential buyers. Privacy laws in Canada prevent companies from trading customers' names, so they collect information based on customers' postal codes. The idea is based on the premise that people live and act more or less like their neighbours.

Geodemographers group people into clusters, using census data to determine factors such as age, income, education, and ethnicity, and overlay the findings with consumer purchasing and attitudinal data. In Canada, 66 consumer clusters have been identified; for example, the wealthiest—the *Cosmopolitan Elite*—represent those earning in excess of $330 000 annually, and account for only 0.21 percent of the population. They can be found in Toronto's Forest Hill and Montreal's Westmount. The *Young Digerati* segment consists of tech-savvy singles and couples living in fashionable urban neighbourhoods in a handful of large cities. But by adding social values data, retailers learn that the values of *Young Digerati* are as cutting-edge as their laptops. These young Canadians see themselves as belonging to the global village and show their recognition of the shrinking world in their global ecological consciousness. While they are eager to succeed, they don't want to climb an outdated corporate hierarchy to do so; any marketing campaign should highlight their independent spirit, working on their own outside the cubicles of a large corporation.[59]

The cluster profiles also make a strong case for cultural influences. Environics was able to determine that there are 15 clusters that are unique to Quebec. Quebecers shop differently than other Canadians, and Quebec cities appear as almost uniform groupings, enjoying good wine, fine restaurants, and high-fashion more than the rest of the country. Only 16 Canadian clusters are similar to clusters found in the United States, leaving 50 clusters unique to Canada.

Some interesting tidbits: There are more coffee addicts per capita in Medicine Hat than anywhere else in Canada; more wine connoisseurs in Quebec; more bottle blondes in Oshawa, Ontario; more dieters in Barrie, Ontario; and more gadget-mad consumers in Vancouver.

Geodemographic segmentation is particularly appealing to store-based retailers, because customers typically patronize stores close to their neighbourhood. Thus, retailers can use geodemographic segmentation to select locations for their stores and tailor assortment in the stores to the preferences of the local community.

lifestyle segmentation A method of segmenting a retail market based on consumers' lifestyles.

psychographics Refers to how consumers live, how they spend their time and money, what activities they pursue, and their attitudes and opinions about the world they live in.

Lifestyle Segmentation **Lifestyle segmentation** is a method of segmenting a retail market based on consumers' lifestyle. This method of segmentation is achieved through the study of consumer **psychographics**, which refers to how consumers live, how they spend their time and money, what activities they pursue, and their attitudes and opinions about the world they live in. When you are conducting market research, you want more information than basic market size and growth. You need to understand your market's attitudes, interests, and opinions. The aim is to narrowly define your target market so that you can effectively sell to the customers with the most potential for sales. Retailers today are placing more emphasis on lifestyles than on demographics to define a target segment.

Exhibit 3–6 shows how Canada Post uses a system to divide Canada's population into segments. Canada Post's Snapshot Segmentation System segments Canada's population into five major spending categories: Big Spenders, Beyond Basics, Wannabe Shoppers, Smart Shoppers, and Penny Pinchers. This system is designed to provide information to:

- build direct mail circulated based on target market
- increase relevance of product offerings
- customize marketing according to the target market's lifestyle and preferences

Although psychographics can provide revealing information about a particular market, they can also be the most difficult to access. In Canada, the most readily available psychographics information is in the publication *FP Markets—Canadian Demographics*, produced by the *Financial Post*. This annual publication has two sets of consumer "PSYTE" categories. The first examines lifestyle patterns and segments the population into 60 different categories. For example, The *Affluents* are educated middle-aged executive and professional families with older children and teenagers who live in expensive lightly mortgaged houses in stable, older, executive sections of larger cities. The second set of PSYTE categories provides segmentation based on financial psychographics; for example, the *Mortgages and Minivans* category is a large family with young children. The average household income is above average, but dwelling values are significantly below average. Dual incomes predominate in this group, and jobs are a mix of the white- and grey-collar categories. The tendency toward larger families results in significant expenditures on child care, toys, and sports equipment.

Michael Adams is a social scientist, the president of Environics Research Group, and a bestselling author. In his second book, *Better Happy Than*

Exhibit 3-6
Canada Post's Snapshot Segmentation System

Canada is an extremely diverse multicultural society of more than 32 million people. Canada Post's Snapshot Segmentation System segments Canada's population into five major spending categories: Big Spenders, Beyond Basics, Wannabe Shoppers, Smart Shoppers, and Penny Pinchers. This system is designed to provide information to:

- Build direct mail circulation based on target market
- Increase relevance of product offerings
- Customize marketing according to target market's lifestyle and preferences

BIG SPENDERS

Income: $80 000 plus
High-maintenance lifestyle
Purchase goods to enhance their status
Respond to direct mail
Use Internet for purchases
Hot Spends: home decor, clothing, garden supplies, sporting goods, toys/games/novelties

SMART SHOPPERS

Income: $50 000 to $75 000
Work–life balance important
Respond to direct mail
Shop by catalogue
Look for quality, family-oriented products
Shop around for the best deal
Shop online
Hot Spends: household tools, appliances, home decor, digital camera, garden supplies

BEYOND BASICS

Income: $40 000 to $65 000
Empty nesters
Own their home
Enjoy dining and theatre
More disposable income than other segments
Respond to direct mail
Shop by catalogue
Hot Spends: garden supplies, jewellery, flowers

PENNY PINCHERS

Income: $ 30 000 to $ 50 000
Low income/high aspirations
Like to buy for their children
Respond to direct mail
Spend conservatively
Hot Spends: electronics, kids stuff, household tools, computer, sporting goods

WANNABE SHOPPERS

Income: $35 000 to $50 000
"It's all about me"
Impulsive, want to lead glamorous life
Early adopters of technology and new trends
Shop online
Hot Spends: clothing, DVD equipment and home electronics, computer, music/CDs

Lifestyle segmentation is useful because it identifies what motivates buying behaviour. However, it is difficult to identify and access consumers in specific lifestyle segments.

Rich (2000), Adams looks at money and its changing meaning in the lives of Canadians. He makes the point that today, money has achieved an unprecedented primacy as a lens through which we see ourselves and others. Instead of eroding our values, money is becoming the primary manifestation of our values. The way Canadians earn, spend, invest, and give away their money expresses how they think the world works—and how they would like to see it work.[60] His bestseller *Fire and Ice* (2003) laid to rest the notion that Canadians are simply Americans with snow shovels at the ready. In *Stayin' Alive* (2010), Adams divided the Boomers into four "values" tribes, reasoning that people's beliefs shape our opinions to external forces at least as powerfully as more traditional categories (e.g., age, region, party affiliation). He slots himself into the *Autonomous Rebel* tribe, which most closely resembles the prevailing stereotype of the Boomer as a countercultural hippie.

Looking ahead to the Boomers' dotage, Adams doesn't expect the much-studied generation born between 1946 and 1964 to make a sharp right turn into reactionary old age. The Boomers, his findings further indicate, are not morphing into their parents, and the progressive values of their youth remain intact.[61]

Ingram Publishing.

PSYTE HD, developed by Pitney Bowes Business Insight, is geodemographic data solution software that pulls Canadian information together (household-level data by postal code). Go to http://www.pitney-bowes.com/ca/en/location-intelligence.html and click on "Location Intelligence." You will note various digital solution to help identify what location a retailer may want to consider based on the data set provided. Sometimes it is possible to uncover detailed data free of charge. Check out the following:

- Ipsos (http://www.ipsos.ca)
- Leger Marketing (http://www.legermarketing.com)
- Pollara (http://www.pollara.ca)
  - Decima Research (http://www.decima.ca)
  - Environics (http://www.environics.ca)

Buying Situation Segmentation The buying behaviour of customers with the same demographics or lifestyle can differ depending on their buying situation. Thus, retailers may use **buying situation segmentation**, such as fill-in versus weekly shopping to segment a market. For example, a parent with four children prefers the super-centre to the Internet grocer or supermarket for weekly grocery purchases. But if the parent runs out of milk during the week, he or she would probably go to the convenience store rather than the warehouse club for this fill-in shopping. Convenience would be more important than assortment in the fill-in shopping situation. Similarly, an executive will stay at a convention hotel on a business trip and a resort on a family vacation.

Benefit Segmentation Another approach to defining a target segment is to group customers seeking similar benefits; this is called **benefit segmentation**. In the multiattribute attitude model, customers in the same benefit segment would attach a similar set of importance weights to the attributes of a store or a product. For example, customers who place high importance on fashion and style and low importance on price would form a fashion segment, whereas customers who place more importance on price would form a price segment.

Benefit segments are very actionable. Benefits sought by customers in the target segment clearly indicate how retailers should design their offerings to appeal to the segment. But customers in benefit segments aren't easily identified or accessed. It's hard to look at a person and determine what benefits he or she is seeking. Typically, the audience for media used by retailers is described by demographics rather than by the benefits sought.

Composite Segmentation Approaches

As we have seen, no one approach meets all the criteria for useful customer segmentation. For example, segmenting by demographics and geography is ideal for identifying and accessing customers, but these characteristics often are unrelated to customers' needs. Thus, these approaches may not indicate the actions necessary to attract customers in these segments. On the other hand, knowing what benefits customers are seeking is useful for designing an effective retail offering; the problem is identifying which customers are seeking these benefits. For these reasons, **composite segmentation** plans use multiple variables to identify customers in the target segment.

buying situation segmentation A method of segmenting a retail market based on customer needs in a specific buying situation, such as a fill-in shopping trip versus a weekly shopping trip.

benefit segmentation A method of segmenting a retail market on the basis of similar benefits sought in merchandise or services.

composite segmentation A method of segmenting a retail market using multiple variables, including benefits sought, lifestyles, and demographics.

They define target customers by benefits sought, lifestyles, and demographics.

Best Buy has introduced its "Customer Centricity" program to target five composite segments.[62] Each of these segments, referred by a first name, has a manager responsible for developing a retail strategy for the market segment. *Barrys* are the best customers. They are affluent professional men, 30 to 60 years of age, who make a minimum of $150 000 a year and drive luxury cars. Barry is the kind of guy who walks in to Best Buy, sees a $30 000 home theatre system, and says, "I'll take it." In contrast, *Jills* are the busy suburban moms; *Buzzes* are focused, active younger men; and *Rays* are family men who like their technology practical. The fifth segment consists of small businesses buying their consumer electronics at Best Buy.

Best Buy has redesigned groups of stores to focus on a specific segment or two with significant representation in the local area. For example, Jill stores have personal shoppers and areas for children to play while mom shops, and the soundtrack playing in the background is often children's music. Stores catering to Barrys have special areas to display high-end entertainment systems and experts in mobile technology, while stores for Jills dedicate more inventory to things like learning software and feature softer colours and a children's technology department. The Buzz-oriented stores, by contrast, feature the very latest technologies and video games. They have comfortable places in which customers can sample technologies, complete with sofas and flat-screen televisions for testing video games and consoles. Ray stores focus more on low price.

SUMMARY

This chapter reviews trends that are impacting consumer buying decisions. Based on life stage and lifestyle influences, dominant market segments—for example, the influential tween market and the time-starved working woman—are emerging to reshape the retail environment. The very nature of our multitasking lifestyles will influence how and where we choose to shop in the future.

Understanding consumer buying behaviour is essential to describing a retailer's target market. Awareness of the consumer's needs will help the retailer develop a strategic plan that includes the right product, at the right price, and available at a desired retailer.

To satisfy customer needs, retailers must thoroughly understand how customers make store choice and purchase decisions and the factors they consider when deciding. The six stages in the buying process are need recognition, information search, evaluation of alternatives, choice of alternatives, purchase, and post-purchase evaluation, and retailers can influence their customers at each stage. The importance of the stages depends on the nature of the customer's decision. When decisions are important and risky, the buying process is longer; customers spend more time and effort on information search and evaluating alternatives. When buying decisions are less important to customers, they spend little time in the buying process and their buying behaviour may become habitual. The buying process of consumers is influenced by their personal beliefs, attitudes, and values and by their social environment. The primary social influences are provided by the consumers' families, reference groups, and culture.

To develop cost-effective retail programs, retailers group customers into segments. Some approaches for segmenting markets are based on geography, demographics, geodemographics, lifestyles, usage situations, and benefits sought. Since each approach has its advantages and disadvantages, retailers typically define their target segment by several characteristics.

KEY TERMS

accessibility
actionability
benefit segmentation
brand loyalty
buying process
buying situation segmentation
composite segmentation
consideration set
cross-shopping
culture
demographic segmentation

everyday low pricing strategy (EDLP)
extended problem solving
external sources of information
geodemographic segmentation
geographic segmentation
habitual decision making
hedonic needs
identifiability
information search
internal sources of information
lifestyle segmentation

limited problem solving
multiattribute attitude model
post-purchase evaluation
psychographics
reference group
retail market segment
retailer loyalty
satisfaction
store advocates
subculture
utilitarian needs

GET OUT & DO IT!

1. CONNECT EXERCISE Access Connect to develop a multiattribute attitude model describing your evaluation and decision concerning some relatively expensive product you bought recently, such as a car or consumer electronics. Open the multiattribute attitude model exercise. List the attributes you considered in the left-hand column. List the alternatives you considered in the top row.

Now fill in the importance weight for each attribute in the second column on the left (10—very important, 1—very unimportant). Now fill in your evaluation of each product on each attribute (10—excellent performance, 1—poor performance). Based on your weight and beliefs, the evaluation of each product is shown in the bottom row. Did you buy the product with the highest evaluation?

2. INTERNET EXERCISE Visit SRI's website at http://www.strategic businessinsights.com/vals/presurvey.shtml. Click on the "Take the survey" button near the bottom of the page and answer the questions used to classify people into different VALS segments. When you have completed the survey and click on "submit," you should get a form that states your primary and secondary types. You can read descriptions of the types at http://www.strategicbusinessinsights.com/vals/ustypes.shtml. Type up a two-page, double-spaced report on what the survey said about you and whether you agree with it. How can retailers effectively use the results of this survey when planning and implementing their business strategies?

3. INTERNET EXERCISE Check out http://www.ytv.com and learn more about tweens.

4. INTERNET EXERCISE What are the consumer trends at http://www.trendwatching.com?

DISCUSSION QUESTIONS AND PROBLEMS

1. Does the customer buying process end when a customer buys some merchandise? Explain your answer.

2. What would get a consumer to switch from making a habitual choice decision to eat at Wendy's to making a limited or extended choice decision?

3. Reflect on your decision process in selecting a university or college. (Universities are non-profit service retailers.) Was your decision-making process extensive, limited, or habitual?

4. Considering the steps in the consumer buying process (Exhibit 3–1), describe how you (and your family) used this process to select your college/university. How many schools did you consider? How much time did you invest in this purchase decision? When you were deciding on which school to attend, what objective and subjective criteria did you use in the alternative evaluation portion of the consumer buying process?

5. Why is geodemographic segmentation used by retailers to locate stores?

6. Any retailer's goal is to get a customer in its store to stop searching and buy a product at its outlet. How can a sporting goods retailer ensure that the customer buys athletic equipment at its outlet?

7. A family-owned record store across the street from a major university campus wants to identify the various segments in its market. What approaches might the store owner use to segment its market? List two potential target market segments based on this segmentation approach. Then contrast the retail mix that would be most appropriate for two potential target segments.

8. Develop a demographic profile for two different target market segments for a hardware store. Outline the difference in the retail mixes that would be most appealing to each of these target markets.

9. How would you expect the buying decision process to differ when shopping on the Internet compared to shopping in a store?

10. Using the multiattribute attitude model, identify the probable choice of a local car dealer for a young single woman and for a retired couple with limited income (see the table below). What can the national retail chain do to increase the chances of the retired couple patronizing its dealership? You can use the multiattribute attitude model template at Connect.

	IMPORTANCE WEIGHTS		PERFORMANCE BELIEFS		
Performance Attributes	Young Single Woman	Retired Couple	Local Gas Station	National Service Chain	Local Car Dealer
Price	2	10	9	10	3
Time to complete repair	8	5	5	9	7
Reliability	2	9	2	7	10
Convenience	8	3	3	6	5

CHAPTER FOUR

Retail market strategy

LEARNING OBJECTIVES

Lo1 Review the basic principles of retail strategy.

Lo2 Examine how a retailer can build a sustainable competitive advantage.

Lo3 Identify different strategic opportunities retailers can pursue.

Lo4 Explore the steps retailers go through to develop a strategy.

SPOTLIGHT ON RETAILING

MOBILE DELIVERING MAGIC RESULTS FOR RETAILERS

Retailers are barely scratching the surface of mobile device usage when it comes to customer service. Even though wireless devices have been used in retail operations for such functions as inventory and checkout, the latest iterations of tablets and smartphones promise to be significant game-changers in defining the retail experience for both e-commerce and bricks-and-mortar players.

That's in part because service excellence and customer service are emerging as the key focus for retailers, according to a recent survey by American Express Canada. That focus, says Colin D. Temple, vice president of merchant services, is playing into the role of mobile as a means to enrich the customer experience. "Competition is intensifying and a lot of retailers are learning to understand how to differentiate themselves," he says. "Part of that is leveraging new and emerging channels. Mobile enables retailers to extend their reach and connect to a broader base of potential customers."

Retailers are definitely becoming mesmerized by the thought of leveraging mobile to enhance the consumer experience, notes Robert Passikoff, founder and president of Brand Keys Inc. in New York. "Retail looks to anything it can get its hands on to create a different type of retail experience. In some cases, it's less about inventory control as much as it is a way to present options in a way that's cool."

A mobile groundswell. It doesn't hurt that penetration of smartphones and tablets has been accelerating at breakneck speed. According to eMarketer, there will be more than 6 million new smartphone users in Canada between 2014 and 2018. At that point, this group will represent nearly 65 percent of the country's overall population.

Retailers can't afford to overlook the burgeoning population of smartphone users, says Robert Levy, president of BrandSpark International, a market research firm specializing in consumer shopping behaviour.

The implications of this are extremely important for retailers seeking new service-related opportunities, notes Mike Dover, research group director for J.C. Williams Group. "Mobile opens the doors to all sorts of applications to improve the in-store experience. For one, it allows retailers to offer deals and make suggestions based on profiles or collaborative filtering consumers."

Dover says the mobile move is taking hold everywhere. "In grocery, Tesco does a great job, for example. Customers can scan an item in-store, the purchase is done electronically, and the items are delivered to the customer's home. In clothing, Wet Seal is doing some interesting things, including social shopping. Target is good for finding a location/ search for inventory, etc. The thing is you can do so many innovative things with these devices."

The power of rapid response. The advent of features in the latest smartphone models is also stretching the possibilities of what retailers can do, from couponing to transaction processing.

When it comes to offline purchases at retail outlets, 68 percent of smartphone owners are aware of Near Field Communication (NFC) or Quick Response (QR) Codes, with 65 percent likely to make NFC or QR payments over the next six months.

With NFC, retailers can communicate with smartphones to advertise, hold contests, or deliver coupons and special offers that are meaningful to customers, he explains. "That's significant when you realize that 96 percent of Canadian shoppers still browse flyers at grocery stores. They like to use those coupons and NFC would make that easier."

E-commerce retailer Well.ca is breaking new ground with its QR code–based shopping trials. The online provider of drugstore sundries wrapped up its virtual store pilot at Union Station in Toronto, which was based on similar retail concepts in Asia targeted at the consumer on the move. Life-size photographs of 120 products included QR codes that commuters could simply scan and enter their delivery information for next-day shipping. "This was about letting Canadians imagine what shopping can become," says J. Paige Malling, vice president of marketing for Well.ca. The response was dramatic, she notes. "Sales of featured products skyrocketed. For example, single-day sales for Tide alone were higher than the entire previous month."

Reaching a moving target. Harry Rosen has added its mobile technology repertoire to improve customer service. Stephen Jackson, the clothier's chief information officer, says that wireless devices were first used in-store to help sales associates connect with a customer's information, including sizing, preferences, and preferred brands. Now the plan is to extend reach even further by using mobile to connect with customers

© Photo by Paul Brown-Rex Features/The Canadian Press.

outside of the store or online. A new E-PICS program, for example, lets associates use their smartphones to take and send pictures of laid-out merchandise to their clients. New initiatives are also in the works to loop store associates with online customers via their mobile devices. When it comes to choosing apps, "It's a matter of finding what adds value and gives them what they really want," Jackson says.

In March 2012, Mac's Convenience and Couche-Tard stores began the first broadcasts of an in-store mobile advertising network from iSIGN Media Solutions Inc. An in-store intelligent antenna detects mobile devices within range of the store and pings them with opt-ins for special offers or loyalty points. "Mobile is the greatest revolution for retail in the last couple of years and creates the perfect advertising point," says Alex Romanoff, iSIGN founder and CEO in Vancouver. He estimates that the program will reach 1.5 million devices a day. In a test site in Japan, he reports that in the space of two years, an electronics store increased sales by 6 percent, loyalty card adoption by 20 percent, and extended warranty sales by 20 percent.

As mobile continues to generate sales numbers, retailers have a veritable ocean of opportunities to explore the mobile front. As Malling says, "The sky's the limit in terms of execution and what this can become."

Sources: Denise Deveau, "Mobile Delivering Magic Results for Retailers," *Canadian Retailer*, Summer 2012, Volume 22, Issue 3, pp. 44–45; eMarketer, "Over Half of Canada's Population to Use Smartphones," January 6, 2015, http://www.emarketer.com/Article/Over-Half-of-Canadas-Population-Use-Smartphones-2015/1011759#sthash.hCr28cAs.dpuf (accessed January 4, 2016); VISA, "Mobile eCommerce Beginning to Take Hold in Canada," November 18, 2014, http://www.visa.ca/en/aboutcan/mediacentre/news/mobile_ecommerce.jsp#.VorVJ_krKHs (accessed January 6, 2015). Canadian Retailer, a publication of Retail Council of Canada.

The growing intensity of retail competition due to the emergence of new competitors, formats, and technologies, as well as shifts in consumer preferences, is forcing retailers to devote more attention to long-term strategic planning. This chapter on retailing strategy is the bridge between understanding the world of retailing—the analysis of the retail environment—and the more tactical merchandise management decisions and store operations activities undertaken to implement the retail strategy. The retail strategy provides the direction retailers need to take to deal effectively with their environment, their customers, and competitors.[2]

Canadian retailers must be innovative and differentiate themselves from their competitors if they are to survive in a marketplace that is characterized by a blurring of retail channels, increasing competition, and changing consumer preferences.

Retailers need to examine every aspect of their business, assessing the "easy-to-navigate" factor of their store layout, merchandise offerings, efficiency of distribution systems, service attributes, loyalty programs, and their position in the retail marketplace.

DID YOU KNOW?

It is projected that by 2018, 98 percent of people between the ages of 18 to 34 will own a smartphone.[1]

LO1 What Is a Retail Strategy?

The term *strategy* is frequently used in retailing. For example, retailers talk about their merchandise strategy, promotion strategy, location strategy, and private-brand strategy. In fact, the term is used so commonly it appears that all retailing decisions are now strategic decisions. But retail strategy isn't just another expression for retail management (see Exhibit 4–1).

target market The market segment(s) toward which the retailer plans to focus its resources and retail mix.

retail format The retailers' type of retail mix (product, price [value], promotion [communication], place, people, and processes).

sustainable competitive advantage A distinct competency of a retailer relative to its competitors that can be maintained over a considerable time period.

Definition of Retail Market Strategy

A retail strategy is a statement identifying the following:

- the retailer's target market

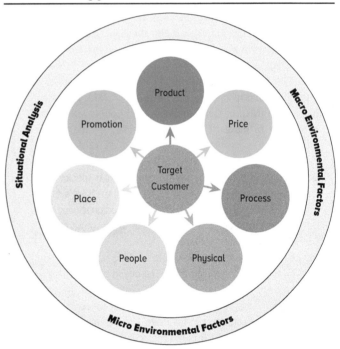

Exhibit 4–1
Retail Strategy

- the format the retailer plans to use to satisfy the target market's needs
- the bases upon which the retailer plans to build a sustainable competitive advantage[3]

The **target market** is the market segment(s) toward which the retailer plans to focus its resources and retail mix. A **retail format** describes the nature of the retailer's operations—that is, the retailer's mix (product, price [value], promotion [communication], place, people, and processes)—that is designed to satisfy the needs of its target market. A **sustainable competitive advantage** is an advantage over competition that cannot be easily copied and can be maintained over a long period of time. Here are two examples of retailing strategies:

- Curves has grown to more than 10 000 franchises in over 70 countries, making it by far the world's top fitness centre in terms of number of clubs. Curves is the market leader in Canada and 23 other countries around the world, including the United States. Over the past 15 years, Curves has been recognized as the fastest-growing franchise in history. Other clubs go after the prized 18-to-34-year-old demographic segment; Curves' customers are aging Baby Boomers, typically living in small towns. This retailer's fitness centres don't have treadmills, saunas, locker rooms, mirrors,

Most fitness centres target the 18-to-34-year-old segment; Curves' retail offering appeals to aging Baby Boomers.
Courtesy of Curves International.

aerobics classes, or free weights. Members work out on 8 to 12 hydraulic resistance machines, stopping between stations to walk or jog in place. The clubs' standard routine is finished in 30 minutes and is designed to burn 500 calories. Club members usually pay $29 a month, far less than conventional fitness clubs. Rather than attract customers from other clubs, Curves generates customers who haven't considered joining a fitness club before.[4]

- Magazine Luiza is one of Brazil's largest non-food retailers. The company targets low-income consumers by selling consumer electronics and appliances on instalment payment plans and offering affordable credit in a country with a significant number of people living in poverty. Customers buying merchandise on credit return to the store each month to make payments in person. Frequently, they are enticed to purchase more merchandise during these visits. In a country where almost half the population does not have a chequing account, the retailer also provides services—including personal loans and insurance policies—that would otherwise be out of reach to most customers. Even though 80 percent of its loans are paid for in instalments, its default rate is 50 percent lower than that of other Brazilian retailers.[5]

Every retail strategy involves the following:

- selecting target market segment(s)
- selecting a retail format
- selecting the elements in the retail mix

- developing a sustainable competitive advantage that enables the retailer to reduce the level of competition it faces

Now let's examine these central concepts in a retail strategy, as shown in Exhibit 4–1.

Target Market and the Retail Mix

The **retailing concept** is a management orientation that focuses a retailer on determining the needs of its target market and satisfying those needs more effectively and efficiently than its competitors. Successful retailers satisfy the needs of customers in their target segment better than the competition does. The selection of a target market focuses the retailer on a group of consumers whose needs it will attempt to satisfy. The selection of a retail format outlines the retail mix to be used to satisfy needs of those customers. The retail strategy determines the markets in which a retailer will compete. Traditional markets, such as a farmers' market, are places where buyers and sellers meet and make transactions—say, a consumer buys six ears of corn from a farmer. But in modern markets, potential buyers and sellers aren't necessarily located in one place; transactions can occur without face-to-face interactions. For example, many customers contact retailers and place orders with a smartphone or tablet.

A **retail market** is a group of consumers with similar needs (a market segment) and a group of retailers using a similar retail format to satisfy those consumer needs.[6] Exhibit 4–2 illustrates a set of retail markets for women's clothing, with a number of retail formats listed down the left-hand column. Each format offers a different retail mix to its customers. Customer market segments are listed in the exhibit's top row. These segments can be defined in terms of the customers' geographic location, demographics, lifestyle, buying situation, or benefits sought. In this illustration, we divide the market into three fashion-related segments: conservative, those who place little importance on fashion and

retailing concept A management orientation that holds that the key task of a retailer is to determine the needs and wants of its target markets and to direct the firm toward satisfying those needs and wants more effectively and efficiently than competitors do.

retail market A group of consumers with similar needs (a market segment) and a group of retailers using a similar retail format to satisfy those consumer needs.

are price-sensitive; traditional, those who want classic styles that are moderately priced; and fashion-forward, those who want the most fashionable merchandise. Each square of the matrix shown in Exhibit 4–2 describes a potential retail market where two or more retailers compete with each other. For example, Sears and Hudson's Bay compete against each other with a department store format targeting the traditional segment looking for moderately-priced fashions.

The women's clothing market in Exhibit 4–2 is just one of several representations that could have been used. Retail formats could be expanded to include outlet stores and electronic retailing. Rather than being segmented by fashion orientation, the market could have been segmented using other approaches. Although Exhibit 4–2 isn't the only way to describe the women's retail clothing market, it does illustrate how retail markets are defined in terms of retail format and customer market segment. Each fashion segment—conservative, traditional, and fashion-forward—is likely to shop multiple retail formats. For example, a fashion-forward customer might shop H&M for casual wear, Holt Renfrew for shoes, and Marshalls for a sweater. Each of these retailers then uses a variation of the retail mix to help build and sustain a competitive advantage.

Basically, the matrix in Exhibit 4–2 describes the battlefield on which women's clothing retailers compete. The position in this battlefield indicates the first two elements of a retailer's strategy: its target market segment and retail format. Consider the situation confronting The Gap as it develops a retail strategy for the women's clothing market. Should The Gap compete in multiple retail markets, or should it focus on a limited set of retail markets? If The Gap decides to focus on a limited set of markets, which should it pursue? The Gap's answers to these questions define its retail strategy and indicate how it plans to focus its resources.

The retailer controls the seven elements of the retailing mix (outlined below), but the strategies for all of the components must be blended for optimum

Exhibit 4–2
Retail Market for Women's Apparel

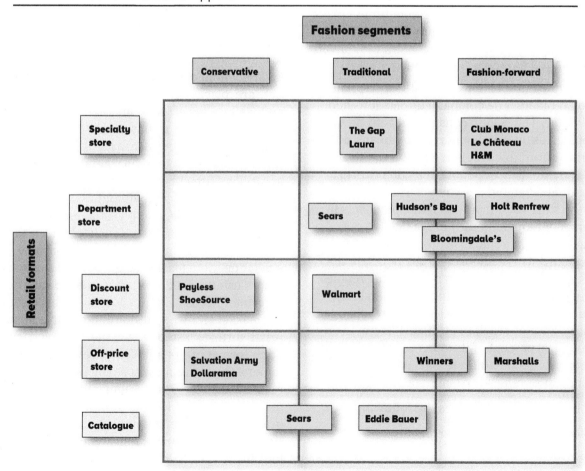

results. Variations in retailing mixes do not occur by chance. By manipulating the components of the mix and focusing on one or two of the elements in particular, retailers can fine-tune their customer offerings to gain advantages over competitors and best serve the wants and needs of their particular target market segment.

- **Product:** Product and/or service, package, warranty, after-sales service, brand name, company image, return policies, and other factors
- **Price (value):** Prestige pricing, competitive (at-the-market) pricing, discount pricing, everyday low pricing (EDLP)
- **Place:** Use of a store or non-store format; placement in a geographic area; database management, retail information system (RIS), data mining, and micromarketing; IT; and physical distribution (collaborative planning, forecasting, and replenishment [CPFR], QR)
- **Promotion:** Communication mix, including advertising, direct marketing, personal selling, sales promotion, and public relations
- **People:** Human resource management (recruiting, selecting, training, recognition, retaining, and supervising), and customer service (personal attention provided)
- **Process:** The systems used to develop the service (inputs, throughputs, and outputs); making the process consistent by reducing variability
- **Physical:** Store design and displays, store atmosphere

Lo2 Building a Sustainable Competitive Advantage

Any business that retailers engage in can be the basis for a competitive advantage, but some advantages are more sustainable over a long period of time.

When developing a retail strategy, two sets of variables that will impact your retail business must be assessed:

- the micro-environment
- the macro-environment

Consider the micro-environment to be all of the things that are within your control and can be changed; this would include the retail product that will be sold, the price at which you will sell the product, the location of your store, the promotion (including the visual image of your store and promotion activities), the processes, and human resource management decisions. Remember that a retailer can change these factors as needed. But it must be understood that these decisions are never made in a vacuum.

The external environment that the retailer cannot control is called the macro-environment. The macro-environment consists of five subsections: competition; economic stability of a trade area; the technology that will make retailing more efficient; the regulatory and ethical environment in which the business operates; and social trends, including consumer behaviour and demographic and lifestyle trends. A SWOT analysis (strengths, weaknesses, opportunities, and threats) is designed to assess both the micro- and macro-environments and the retailer's position relative to these issues.

Developing a proactive position based on the knowledge of what is happening in your retail trade area will help establish a sustainable competitive advantage. Any business activity that a retailer engages in can be a basis for a competitive advantage. However, some advantages are sustainable over a long period of time, while others can be duplicated by competitors almost immediately[7] (see Exhibit 4–3).

For example, it would be hard for Starbucks to get a long-term advantage over Tim Hortons by simply offering the same coffee specialties at lower prices. If Starbucks' lower prices were successful in attracting customers, Tim Hortons would know what Starbucks had done and would match the price reduction. Similarly, it's hard for retailers to develop a long-term advantage by offering broader or deeper merchandise assortments. If broader and deeper assortments attract a lot of customers, competitors will simply go out and buy the same merchandise for their stores.

Establishing a retailer's competitive advantage is similar to building a strong wall around its position in a retail market. If the wall is strong, it will be hard

micro-environment All of the things within the retailer's control, including the retail product that will be sold, the price for the product, the store location, the promotion and visual image of the store, the processes, and human resource management decisions.

macro-environment The external environment that the retailer cannot control, including competition, economic stability of the trade area, the technology that will make retailing more efficient, the regulatory and ethical environment in which the business operates, and social trends, including consumer behaviour and lifestyle and demographic trends.

SWOT analysis An analysis of strengths, weaknesses, opportunities, and threats, designed to assess both the micro- and macro-environments and their relation to the retailer.

Exhibit 4–3
Methods for Developing Competitive Advantage

	SUSTAINABILITY OF ADVANTAGE	
Sources of Advantage	**Less Sustainable**	**More Sustainable**
Customer loyalty	Habitual repeat purchasing; repeat purchases because of limited competition in the local area	Building a brand image with an emotional connection with customers; using databases to develop and utilize a deeper understanding of customers
Location		Convenient locations
Human resource management	More employees	Committed, knowledgeable employees
Distribution and information systems	Bigger warehouses; automated warehouses	Shared systems with vendors
Unique merchandise	More merchandise; greater assortment; lower price; higher advertising budgets; more sales promotions	Exclusive merchandise
Vendor relations	Repeat purchases from vendor due to limited alternatives	Coordination of procurement efforts; ability to get scarce merchandise
Customer service	Hours of operation	Knowledgeable and helpful salespeople

for competitors outside the wall to contact customers in the retailer's target market. If the retailer has built a wall around an attractive market, competitors will attempt to break down the wall. Over time, advantages may be eroded due to these competitive forces; but by building high, thick walls, retailers can sustain their advantage, minimize competitive pressure, and boost profits for a longer time. Thus, establishing a sustainable competitive advantage is the key to positive long-term financial performance.

customer loyalty
Customers' commitment to shopping at a store.

Three approaches for developing a sustainable competitive advantage are (1) building strong relationships with customers, (2) building strong relationships with suppliers, and (3) achieving efficient internal operations. Each of these approaches involves developing an asset—loyal customers, strong vendor relationships, committed effective human resources and efficient systems, and attractive locations—that is not easily duplicated by competitors.[8] Let's look at each of these approaches.

Relationships with Customers

Customer Loyalty

Customer loyalty means that customers are committed to shopping at a particular retailer. For instance, having dedicated employees, unique merchandise, and superior customer service all help solidify a loyal customer base. But having loyal customers is, in and of itself, an important method of sustaining an advantage over competitors.

Loyalty is more than simply preferring one retailer over another.[9] Loyalty means that customers will be reluctant to patronize competitive retailers. For example, loyal customers will continue to shop at Canadian Tire even if Home Depot opens a store nearby and provides a slightly superior assortment or slightly lower prices. Some ways that retailers build loyalty include the following:

- developing clear and precise positioning strategies
- developing a strong brand for the store or store brands
- providing outstanding customer service
- creating an emotional attachment with customers through loyalty programs[10]

In addition, other activities discussed in this section also contribute to developing customer loyalty. For example, providing convenient locations encourages patronage, which can develop into loyalty. Engaging in human resource management practices develops competent, committed sales associates, leading to better customer and subsequent customer loyalty.

Brand Image

Retailers build customer loyalty by developing a well-known attractive image of their brand—their name. For example, when most consumers think about fast food or hamburgers or french fries, they immediately think of McDonald's. Their image of McDonald's includes many favourable impressions, such as fast service, consistent quality, and clean washrooms.

Strong **brand images** facilitate customer loyalty because they reduce the risks associated with purchases. They assure customers that they will receive a consistent level of quality and satisfaction from the retailer. The retailer's image can also create an emotional tie with a customer that leads the customer to trust the retailer. Consumers know, for instance, that when they purchase products from L.L. Bean, the retailer guarantees that its customers will be pleased with their purchases. L.L. Bean guarantees "to give 100 percent satisfaction in every way. Return anything purchased from us at any time if it proves otherwise. Our guarantee is based on something as simple as a handshake—the deal that you'll be satisfied with your purchase, and if you are not, we'll make it right. We guarantee that we'll hold up our end of the bargain. It's just how we do business. If your purchase isn't completely satisfactory, we're happy to accept your exchange or return at any time for items purchased directly from us."[11]

A retail brand, whether it is the name of the retailer or a private label, can create an emotional tie with customers that builds their trust and loyalty. Retail brands also facilitate loyalty because they stand for a predictable level of quality that customers feel comfortable with and often seek. A strong retail brand also becomes part of a retailer's positioning strategy, the topic discussed next.

Positioning

A retailer builds customer loyalty by developing a clear, distinctive image of its retail offering and consistently

reinforcing that image through its merchandise and service. **Positioning** is the design and implementation of a retail mix to create an image of the retailer in the customer's mind relative to its competitors.[12]

Positioning emphasizes that the image in the customer's mind (not the retail manager's mind) is critical. Thus, the retailer needs to research what its image is and make sure it is consistent with what customers in its target market want. A perceptual map is frequently used to represent the customer's image and preference for retailers.

Exhibit 4–4 is a hypothetical perceptual map of retailers selling women's clothing. The two dimensions in this map, fashion/style and service, represent the two primary characteristics that consumers in this example use in forming their impression of retail stores. Perceptual maps are developed so that the distance between two retailers' positions on the map indicates how similar the stores appear to

brand images Sets of associations consumers have about a brand that are usually organized around some meaningful themes.

positioning The design and implementation of a retail mix to create in the customer's mind an image of the retailer relative to its competitors; also called *brand building*.

Exhibit 4–4

Hypothetical Perceptual Map of Women's Apparel Market

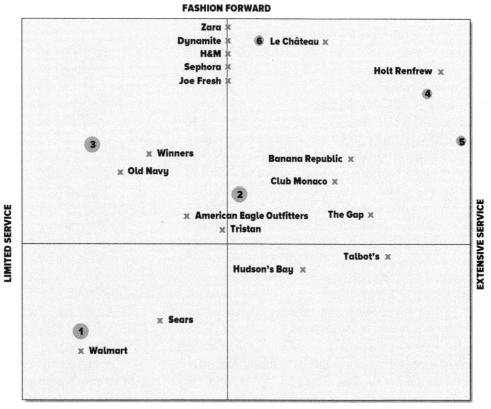

private-label brands
Products developed and marketed by a retailer and available for sale only by that retailer; also called *store brands*.

consumers. For example, Sears and Hudson's Bay are somewhat close to each other on the map because consumers in this illustration see them as offering similar service and fashion. On the other hand, Holt Renfrew and Winners are far apart, indicating that consumers think they are quite different. Note that stores close to each other compete vigorously with each other because consumers feel they provide similar benefits.

According to Exhibit 4–4, The Gap has an image of offering moderately priced fashionable women's clothing with good service. Winners offers more fashionable clothing with less service. Sears is viewed as a retailer offering women's clothing that's less fashionable and has relatively limited service.

The ideal points (marked by green dots on the map) indicate characteristics of an ideal retailer for consumers in different market segments. For example, consumers in Segment 3 prefer a retailer that offers high-fashion merchandise with low service, whereas consumers in Segment 1 want less expensive/more traditional apparel and aren't concerned about service. The ideal points are located so that the distance between the retailer's position (marked with a blue "x") and the ideal point indicates how consumers in the segment evaluate the retailer. Retailers that are closer to an ideal point are evaluated more favourably by the consumers in the segment than retailers located farther away. Thus, consumers in Segment 6 prefer Le Château to Holt Renfrew because their target customers do not require such high service levels.

Customers of The Gap have complained that they can't get the same assortment of high-quality basics—button-down shirts and khaki pants—that made The Gap famous. Probably the biggest problem is that The Gap's success spawned lower-priced imitators, including its own lower-priced chain, Old Navy, which is closer to Segment 2 than The Gap. At the same time, Winners has become more fashion-forward. So both Winners and Old Navy are vying for customers in the huge Segment 2 in Exhibit 4–4. Additionally, The Gap is positioned too far away from Segment 5 to compete successfully with Holt Renfrew on service. In fact, its sister chain, Banana Republic, is closer to Segment 5 and is therefore also siphoning sales from The Gap.[13] Finally, The Gap has two strong competitors for Segment 2, Tristan and American Eagle Outfitters.

Unique Merchandise

It is difficult for retailers to develop a competitive advantage through merchandise because most competitors can purchase and sell the same popular national brands. But many retailers realize a sustainable competitive advantage by developing **private-label brands** (also called *store brands*), which are products developed and marketed by a retailer and available only from that retailer. For example, if you want to buy a Kenmore washer or dryer, you have to buy it from Sears. Loblaws' powerful private-label brand, President's Choice, engenders strong brand loyalty among a significant group of consumers and consequently generates considerable loyalty toward the Loblaws group of stores. The quality image of its private-label products makes a significant contribution to the image of Loblaws. Retailing View 4.1 describes how IKEA builds customer loyalty through its unique merchandise. Store brands now account for one of every five items sold and are achieving new levels of growth every year. The low search associated with electronic shopping increases the importance of unique merchandise as a source of competitive advantage.

Customer Service

Retailers also build a sustainable competitive advantage by offering excellent customer service.[14] Offering good service consistently is difficult because customer service is provided by retail employees—and humans are less consistent than machines. Have you ever received less than perfect service from a salesperson or customer service representative? It is possible that the employee wasn't trained properly, that she didn't like her job, or that he was either inept or just plain rude. It is also possible that you were the 497th customer the salesperson interacted with that day, and she was at the end of her shift. Retailers that offer good customer service instill its importance in their employees over a long period of time. Customer service must become part of the retailer's organizational culture through coaching and training.

It takes considerable time and effort to build a tradition and reputation for customer service, but good service is a valuable strategic asset. Once a retailer has earned a service reputation, it can sustain this advantage for a long time because it's hard for a competitor to develop a comparable reputation.

The IKEA Way

IKEA, a global retailer headquartered in Sweden, offers a wide range of well-designed and functional home-furnishing products at low prices. It's easy to make high-quality products and sell them at a high price or make low-quality products to sell at a low price. But IKEA has to be cost-effective and innovative to sell quality products at low prices.

Creating IKEA's unique merchandise starts on the factory floor. IKEA product developers and designers work closely with suppliers to efficiently use production equipment and raw materials and keep waste to a minimum. For example, an IKEA product developer learned about board-on-frame construction touring a door factory. This technique is cost-effective and environmentally friendly because sheets of wood are layered over a honeycomb core to provide a strong, lightweight structure with minimal wood content. This type of construction is used in many IKEA products, such as its LACK tables.

IKEA's designers go beyond the factory floor to consider transportation costs. Many items IKEA sells are shipped and sold disassembled in flat packs to reduce transportation costs and make it easier for customers to take them home. However, some products, like lamps, take up a lot of space even when disassembled. The LAMPAN illustrates the IKEA way of offering extremely low

IKEA considers all costs when designing its unique, low-cost, fashionable merchandise.

© Evdoha | Dreamstime.com.

price with beautiful design and high quality. This was achieved by developing a new packing method in which the lamp shade could be used as a bucket for the lamp base.

IKEA reduces labour costs in its stores by providing signage with extensive information about its products and their quality, presenting its products in room settings, and prominently displaying price tags. These features enable customers to serve themselves and reduce IKEA's labour costs.

Sources: http://www.IKEA.com (accessed March 30, 2010); "The Man Who Named the Furniture," *Financial Times*, Jan. 16, 2010, p. 30; Yongquan Hu and Huifang Jiang, "Innovation Strategy of Retailers: From the View of Global Value Chains," *6th International Conference on Service Systems and Service Management*, 2009, pp. 340–345.

Loyalty Programs

Loyalty programs are part of an overall customer relationship management (CRM) program. These programs are prevalent in retailing, from airlines and department stores to the corner pizza shop. Popular examples include Canadian Tire Money, Shoppers Optimum Card, HBC Rewards, AIR MILES, and Aeroplan. Approximately 90 percent of Canadians own a loyalty card, with the average Canadian having four loyalty cards on them when they shop. A third of all consumers say that they will buy more if they have an opportunity to earn more points.[15]

DID YOU KNOW?

6 out of 10 Canadians choose loyalty programs that come free-of-charge.[16]

Customer loyalty programs work hand-in-hand with CRM. Members of loyalty programs are identified when they buy because they use some type of loyalty card. The purchase information is stored in a huge database known as a **data warehouse**. From this data warehouse, analysts determine what types of merchandise and services certain groups of customers are buying. Data and information gathered can be used to build store loyalty by targeting promotional activities to specific market

data warehouse The coordinated and periodic copying of data from various sources, both inside and outside the enterprise, into an environment ready for analytical and informational processing. It contains all of the data the firm has collected about its customers and is the foundation for subsequent CRM activities.

Harry Rosen, President, Harry Rosen Menswear

Harry Rosen has been in the business of selling high-priced menswear for more than 60 years and has become a Canadian icon. The business has evolved from a tiny tailor shop in Toronto to 17 stores from Montreal to Vancouver. This retailer, with annual sales of $350 million, accounting for 40 percent of all sales of high-end menswear in Canada, has a celebrity clientele and a long list of honours. Not only is Rosen a dynamic retailer, he's a great corporate citizen, initiating major fund-raising events in support of prostate cancer research. In 2004, Harry Rosen was named to the prestigious Order of Canada.

Harry Rosen at 82 is a psychoanalyst, social anthropologist, businessman, and brilliant marketer. His prize-winning advertisements have become recognized for innovation, such as the series, "What So and So Is Wearing Today" featuring well-known Canadians, from Toronto Blue Jay José Bautista to musician Oscar Peterson to comedian Russell Peters. Always enthusiastic, Rosen once posed nude, except for a strategically placed necktie—all part of a very creative advertising campaign.

Each, Harry Rosen salesperson has a commitment to their customers and can access the firm's data warehouse with customer information from any POS terminal in the store. The database tells what the customer has bought in the past and also provides personal information, such as preferences in style and colour. All sales associates are urged to contribute to the database. Harry

Harry Rosen builds loyalty and competitive advantage by using its customer database to tailor its promotional offerings.
Harry Rosen Inc.

Rosen believes that men are in need of help; they are not like women who like to shop and will make an enlightened choice. Rosen thinks most men appreciate informed assistance and value the knowledge provided by its expert "Clothing Advisors" when choosing quality menswear. The customer database is designed to enable sales associates to advise customers on promotions and develop valuable one-to-one relationships.

Even though only 3 percent of Canadian men actually shop in his stores, the first name that comes to mind when most men dream of buying a special wardrobe is Harry Rosen's. Rosen attributes his success to two things: his commitment to quality clothing and his insistence that staff make sure their clients understand why quality matters.

---

segments, to provide a more focused merchandise mix, and to produce higher profits by efficiently targeting advertising efforts.

Customers may join loyalty programs of competing retailers and continue to patronize multiple retailers. However, the data collected about customer shopping behaviour by these programs can provide insights that enable retailers to build and maintain loyalty. For instance, Harry Rosen, a Canadian specialty retailer selling designer menswear (see Retailing View 4.2), has a system for collecting and saving customer data. Every Harry Rosen salesperson can access the firm's customer database from any point-of-sale (POS) terminal in any store. The database indicates what the customer

has bought in the past and also provides personal information. All sales associates are urged to contribute to the database. If a wife buys a birthday gift for her husband, salespeople are encouraged to find out when his birthday is and how old he is and include this information in the system rather than in their personal notebooks.

The information system improves Harry Rosen's customer service and the targeting of retail promotions. For example, when garments are left in the store for alterations, the system tracks their progress and electronically notifies the salesperson of any delay so that the salesperson can relay this information to the customer. Heavy spenders are identified and invited to special promotional events. When new merchandise arrives, the salesperson can identify customers who have bought that type of merchandise in the past and inform them of the new merchandise.[17] Thus, the data developed through the loyalty program enables a retailer to develop a personal relationship with customers that builds loyalty.

Relationships with Suppliers

A second approach for developing competitive advantage is developing strong relationships with companies that provide merchandise and services to the retailer, such as real estate developers, advertising agencies, and transportation companies. Of these relationships with suppliers, the most important are relationships with vendors.

Vendor Relations

By strengthening relationships with each other, both retailers and vendors can develop mutually beneficial assets and programs that will give the retailer–vendor pair an advantage over competing pairs. These collaborations are win–win situations. By working together, both parties develop a sustainable competitive advantage and increase their sales and profits.

The relationship between Proctor & Gamble (P&G) and Walmart initially focused on improving supply chain efficiencies. Today, the partners in this relationship share sensitive information with each other so that Walmart is better able to plan for the introduction of new P&G products and even develop some unique packaging for P&G's national brands exclusively available at Walmart. Walmart shares its sales data with P&G so that P&G can better plan its production and use a just-in-time inventory management system to reduce the level of inventory in the system. From their initial focus on improving supply chain efficiency, P&G and Walmart now work together on other initiatives, such as Family Moments, to produce family-friendly TV programming.

By developing strong relations with vendors, retailers may gain the following exclusive rights:

- selling merchandise in a specific region
- obtaining special terms of purchase that are not available to competitors who lack such relations
- receiving popular merchandise in short supply

Relationships with vendors, like relationships with customers, are developed over a long time and

may not be easily offset by a competitor.[18] For example, Ahold, the Holland-based food retailer, works very closely with Swiss food giant Nestlé to provide products tailored to meet the local tastes of customers in specific markets.[19]

Efficiency of Internal Operations

In addition to strong relationships with external parties—customers and suppliers—retailers can develop competitive advantages by having more efficient internal operations. Efficient internal operations enable retailers to have a cost advantage over competitors or offer customers more benefits than do competitors at the same cost.

A larger company size typically produces more efficient internal operations. Larger retailers have more bargaining power with vendors and thus can buy merchandise at lower costs. Larger retailers can also invest in developing sophisticated systems and spread the fixed cost of these systems over more sales. In addition to size, other approaches for improving internal operating efficiencies are human resource management and information and supply chain management systems.

Human Resource Management

Retailing is a labour-intensive business. Employees play a major role in providing services for customers and building customer loyalty. Knowledgeable and skilled employees committed to the retailer's objectives are critical assets that support the success of companies such as Harry Rosen, Whole Foods, and Canadian Tire.

Recruiting and retaining great employees is not easy. Retailers gain a sustainable competitive advantage by developing programs to motivate and coordinate employee efforts, providing appropriate incentives, fostering a strong and positive organizational culture and environment, and managing diversity.

Distribution and Information Systems

All retailers strive to reduce operating costs—the costs associated with running the business—and make sure that the right merchandise is available at the right time and place. The use of sophisticated distribution and information systems offers an opportunity for retailers to achieve these

Finding a prime location is a competitive advantage that is not easily duplicated.
© Jeff Whyte | Dreamstime.com.

efficiencies.[20] Through its data sharing about merchandise sales, information flows seamlessly from Walmart to its vendors to facilitate quick and efficient merchandise replenishment that avoids costly stockouts. Walmart's distribution and information systems have enabled it to have a cost advantage that its competitors cannot overcome.

In addition to using information systems to improve supply chain efficiency, the customers' purchase data collected by information systems provide an opportunity for retailers to tailor store merchandise assortments to the market served by each of its stores and to tailor promotion to the specific needs of individual customers. These data about its customers' buying behaviour are a valuable asset, offering an advantage not easily duplicated by competitors.

Location

The classic response to the question, "What are the three most important things in retailing?" is "Location, location, and location." Location is the critical factor in consumer selection of a store. It is also a competitive advantage that is not easily duplicated. For instance, once Shoppers Drug Mart has put a store at the best location of an intersection, other drugstores are relegated to the second-best location. Finding great locations is particularly challenging in older urban locations, where space is limited and tenant turnover is relatively low.

Starbucks has developed a national presence and a strong competitive advantage with its location strategy. It conquers one area of the city at a time and then expands in the region, saturating a major market before entering a new market. Starbucks will frequently open several stores close to one another. It has two stores on two corners of the intersection of Robson and Thurlow in Vancouver. Starbucks has such a high density of stores that it lets the storefront promote the company and does very little media advertising. In heavily trafficked downtown districts, Starbucks often operates kiosks in commercial buildings. Neighbourhood locations that attract customers in the evenings and on weekends are important because they become part of the path of people's weekly shopping experience or their route to work.

By concentrating its locations, Starbucks creates a market presence that is difficult for competition to match. In addition, multiple locations facilitate scale economies that enable frequent deliveries, thereby ensuring fresh merchandise.

In contrast to Starbucks' urban locations, Tim Hortons chooses suburban locations with easy drive-through access in smaller cities, communities, and neighbourhoods across Canada.

Multiple Sources of Advantage

To build a sustainable advantage, retailers typically don't rely on a single approach such as low cost or excellent service.[21] They need multiple approaches to build as high a wall around their position as possible. In addition to its exclusive product and associated customer loyalty, IKEA has a large group of loyal customers due to its strong brand image and the unique shopping experience it provides its customers. Walmart complements its size advantage with strong vendor relationships and its clear positioning as a retailer that offers superior value. Starbucks combines its location advantage with unique products, committed employees, a strong brand name, and strong relationships with coffee growers to build an overall advantage that is very difficult for competitors to erode.

The success of McDonald's is based on providing customers with a good value that meets their expectations, having good customer service, maintaining good vendor relations, and having great locations. By doing all of these things right, McDonald's has developed a huge cadre of loyal customers.

McDonald's has always positioned itself as providing fast food at a good value—customers get a lot for not much money. Its customers don't have extraordinary expectations. They don't expect a meal prepared to their specific tastes. But customers do expect and get hot, fresh food that is reasonably priced.

McDonald's customers also don't expect friendly table service with linen tablecloths and sterling cutlery. Their service expectations, which are typically met, are simple. By developing a system for producing its food and using extensive training for store managers, McDonald's reduces customers' waiting time. This training also means that customers will be handled quickly and courteously.

McDonald's vendor relationships ensure that it will always have quality ingredients. Its distribution and inventory control systems enable it to make sure that the ingredients are available at each location. Furthermore, McDonald's has a strong brand name with very high levels of awareness around the world. When most people think of fast food, they think of McDonald's. The brand also has a number of favourable brand associations, such as Ronald McDonald, fast, clean, and french fries.

Finally, McDonald's has a large number of great locations. It is important for convenience products, such as fast food, to have lots of locations. Given its market power, it has been successful in finding and opening stores in prime retail locations. In every city in which it operates around the world, McDonald's has outstanding locations.

By developing unique capabilities in a number of areas, McDonald's has maintained its position as a service retailer, using a fast-food format directed toward families with young children.

Each of the retail strategies outlined in the chapter involves multiple sources of advantage. For example, Tim Hortons has developed a strong competitive position through its excellent product line with a strong Canadian brand name, high-quality service provided by committed employees, and excellent and plentiful locations. Tim Hortons' donuts are a tradition in all communities across Canada.

Lo3 Growth Strategies

Four types of growth opportunities that retailers may pursue (market penetration, market expansion, retail format development, and diversification)

Exhibit 4–5
Growth Opportunities

TARGET MARKETS

	Existing	New
Existing (Retail Format)	Market Penetration	Market Expansion
New (Retail Format)	Format Development	Diversification (unrelated/related)

are shown in Exhibit 4–5.[22] The vertical axis indicates the synergies between the retailer's present markets and growth-opportunity markets—whether the opportunity involves markets the retailer is presently pursuing or new markets. The horizontal axis indicates the synergies between the retailer's present retail mix and the growth-opportunity retail mix—whether the opportunity exploits the retailer's present format or requires a new format.

Market Penetration

A **market penetration opportunity** involves directing efforts toward existing customers by using the present retailing format. The retailer can achieve this growth strategy either by attracting consumers in its current target market who don't shop at its outlets or by devising strategies that induce current customers to visit a store more often or to buy more merchandise on each visit.

Approaches for increasing market penetration include attracting new customers by opening more stores in the target market and keeping existing stores open for longer hours. Other approaches are displaying merchandise to increase

market penetration opportunity An investment opportunity strategy that focuses on increasing sales to present customers using the present retailing format.

Abercrombie & Fitch

© McGraw-Hill Education/Andrew Resek.

impulse purchases and training salespeople to cross-sell. **Cross-selling** means that sales associates in one department attempt to sell complementary merchandise from other departments to their customers. For example, a sales associate who has just sold a dress to a customer will take the customer to the accessories department to sell her a handbag or scarf that will go with the dress. More cross-selling increases sales from existing customers.

For example, The North West Company—a leading community retailer to underserved rural communities and urban neighbourhood markets in northern Canada, western Canada, rural Alaska, the South Pacific, and the Caribbean—is driven by a strategy aimed at growing "with and within" each market that they serve.

cross-selling When sales associates in one department attempt to sell complementary merchandise from other departments to their customers.

market expansion opportunity A strategic investment opportunity that employs the existing retailing format in new market segments.

retail format development opportunity An investment opportunity strategy in which a retailer offers a new retail format—a format involving a different retail mix—to the same target market.

Market Expansion

A **market expansion opportunity** employs the existing retail format in new market segments. For example, Abercrombie & Fitch (A&F) Co.'s primary target market is university students, not high-schoolers. Since university-aged people don't particularly like to hang out with teens, A&F rolled out a lower-priced chain called Hollister Co. to appeal to teens. Although the merchandise and ambience are slightly different

than A&F, the retail format is essentially the same.[23] When the French hypermarket chain Carrefour expanded into other European and South American countries, it was also employing a market expansion growth strategy because it was entering a new geographic market segment with essentially the same retail format.[24]

Retail Format Development

A **retail format development opportunity** involves offering a new retail format—a format with a different retail mix—to the same target market. For example, Chapters exploited a format development opportunity when it began selling books to its present target market over the Internet (http://www.chapters.indigo.ca).

Another example of a retail format development opportunity occurs when a retailer adds merchandise categories, such as when Amazon.com began selling DVDs and electronics in addition to books. Adjusting the type of merchandise or services offered typically involves a small investment. In contrast, providing an entirely different format, such as a store-based retailer going into electronic retailing, requires a much larger and riskier investment.

Another example of a retail format development opportunity is Best Buy offering professional services to install new high-tech electronic equipment for consumers. Best Buy offers a Geek Squad to customers with 24-hour computer support and service. Although this growth opportunity is directed toward the same customers who buy merchandise in the stores, it involves running a service rather than a merchandise-based retail business.

The UK-based retailer Tesco has employed a retail format development growth strategy by operating several different food store formats that all cater to essentially the same target markets. The smallest Tesco Express is no larger than 3000 square feet. These stores are located close to where customers work and live. Tesco Metro stores are 7000 to 15 000 square feet, bring convenience to city centre locations, and specialize in offering a wide range of ready-to-eat meals. Tesco Superstores (up to 50 000 square feet) are the oldest format. In

> **DID YOU KNOW?**
>
> Amazon.ca has captured up to 7 percent of Canada's $21.6-billion in e-commerce sales, a vastly bigger market share than other retailers who sell online, and more than four times larger than the next-in-line players, Costco.ca (1.6 percent) and Walmart.ca (1.5 percent).[25]

recent years, the company has added non-food products, such as DVDs and books, to improve customer satisfaction. Finally, Tesco Extra stores (more than 60 000 square feet) are designed to be a one-stop destination, with the widest range of food and non-food products, from housewares and clothing to garden furniture.[26]

Canadian Tire's purchase of Forzani Group retailers such as Sport Chek represents an unrelated diversification opportunity.
© Kevinbrine | Dreamstime.com.

Diversification

A **diversification opportunity** occurs when a retailer introduces a new retail format directed toward a market segment that's not currently served, such as when Gap Inc. opened Old Navy to attract to a different demographic profile. Diversification opportunities are either related or unrelated.

Related versus Unrelated Diversification In a **related diversification opportunity**, the present target market or retail format shares something in common with the new opportunity. This commonality might entail purchasing from the same vendors, using the same distribution or management information system, or advertising in the same newspapers to similar target markets. In contrast, an **unrelated diversification** lacks any commonality between the present business and the new business.

Through acquisition, Canadian Tire Corporation purchased the Forzani Group, acquiring younger shoppers in the 18-to-35-year-old demographic who prefer Forzani's banners (Sport Chek, Atmosphere, National Sports, etc.) to Canadian Tire. Many of this new demographic head to enclosed malls, where Forzani chains tend to be located, rather than open-air power centres, where Canadian Tire stores are more commonly based.

Through acquisition, Home Depot built a wholesale building-supply business called HD Supply, which generated over $3 billion annual sales. Management felt that this growth opportunity would be synergistic with the firm's retail business because its stores were already selling similar merchandise to contractors. Thus, Home Depot viewed this growth opportunity as a related diversification, because the targeted customers (i.e., contractors) would be similar, and the new large contractor market could be served using warehouses similar to Home Depot's present retail stores. In addition, Home Depot would realize cost savings by placing larger orders with vendors because it would

be selling to both retail and wholesale customers. However, HD Supply actually was an unrelated diversification. The large contractor market served by HD Supply sold primarily pipes, lumber, and concrete— products with limited sales in Home Depot's retail stores. Selling these supplies to large contractors involved competitive bidding and transporting large bulky orders to job sites—skills that Home Depot lacked. So Home Depot sold this unrelated diversification to concentrate on its core retail small-contractor business.

Unrelated diversifications are considered to be very risky and often don't work, as was the case with Home Depot. As a result, most retailers apply the old adage "stick to your knitting" and seek growth opportunities that are closer in nature to their current operations.

Vertical Integration Vertical integration is diversification by retailers into wholesaling or manufacturing.[28] Examples of vertical integration are The

diversification opportunity A strategic investment opportunity that involves an entirely new retail format directed toward a market segment not presently being served.

related diversification opportunity A diversification opportunity strategy in which the retailer's present offering and market share something in common with the market and format being considered.

unrelated diversification Diversification in which there is no commonality between the present business and the new business.

DID YOU KNOW?

Home Depot has 180 stores in Canada and employs 35 000 people.[27]

Rona

Rona was established in 1939 as a buying group for independent Quebec hardware retailers. Rona has evolved from a dealer-owned chain into a publicly-traded company. The largest Canadian distributor and retailer of hardware, home renovation, and gardening products, the corporation operates a network of close to 800 corporate, franchise, and affiliate stores under several banners and a network of 14 hardware and construction materials distribution centres. With stores in every province, Rona currently owns a 19 percent share in the $36 billion Canadian industry.

In 2000, Rona purchased the 66-store chain Cashway Building Centres; in 2001, Western-based Revelstoke and Revy and Ontario's Lansing were added to the Rona banner. Rona has also purchased the Chester Dawe Ltd. chain of stores in Newfoundland. More recently, the company is benefiting from economic growth in Western Canada.

Rona is a mixed toolbox with a variety of retail formats, including big boxes, franchise stores, and independents. Rona's business plan is focused on three complementary sectors of activity in the hardware, renovation, and construction marketplace: distribution, retail and commercial, and professional.

Rona recognizes that consumers, like dealer-owners, have varying needs and goals, which is why the company has developed a unique business model designed to satisfy different types of customers, as well as different types of dealer-owners. This unique model comprises various store formats that address specific markets or consumer sectors and three ownership formulas. So even dealer-owners who prefer to remain independent can still enjoy all the advantages, energy, and solid foundation that make Rona what it is today.

The battle for the home hardware man, or more often today, woman, continues across Canada with the three major competitors—Rona, Home Depot, and Home Hardware—all doing over $4 billion a year in Canadian sales. The home hardware retail market is extremely competitive, and the entrance of US hardware giant Lowes has pressured all players in the battle for the home hardware consumer.

For years, Rona has been supporting Canadian sports and athletes from both professional and amateur levels. The company acted as a proud national partner of the Canadian Olympic and Paralympic teams from 2006 until 2012.

Rona's aggressive bid to secure a spot as a leader in home improvement retailing in Canada will no doubt continue to keep the company in the headlines.

DID YOU KNOW?

Approximately 1.1 million customers visit IKEA each day, and 150 million Swedish meatballs are served per year, or 41 000 each day.[29]

Limited's acquisition of Mast Industries (a trading company that contracts for private-label manufacturing) and Zale Corporation's manufacturing of jewellery. When retailers integrate by manufacturing products, they are making risky investments because the skills required to make products are different from those associated with retailing. Additionally, retailers and manufacturers have different customers; the immediate customers for a manufacturer's merchandise are retailers, whereas a retailer's customers are consumers. Thus, a manufacturer's marketing activities are very different from those of a retailer. Designing private-label merchandise is a related diversification because it builds on the retailer's knowledge of its customers, but actually making the merchandise is considered an unrelated

diversification. Some manufacturers and designers such as Nike, Prada, and Ralph Lauren forward-integrate into retailing. In this case, the designer/ manufacturer has control of both the manufacturing and distribution processes and makes the strategic decision to move forward and control the retailing process by opening its own stores.

Strategic Opportunities and Competitive Advantage

Typically, retailers have the greatest competitive advantage in opportunities that are similar to their present retail strategy. Thus, retailers would be most successful engaging in market penetration opportunities that don't involve entering new, unfamiliar markets or operating new, unfamiliar retail formats (see Retailing View 4.3).

When retailers pursue market expansion opportunities, they build on their strengths in operating a retail format and apply this competitive advantage to a new market. Those retailers that successfully expand globally are able to translate what they do best—their core competencies—to a new culture and market.

A retail format development opportunity builds on the retailer's reputation and success with present customers. Even if a retailer doesn't have experience and skills in operating the new format, it hopes to attract its loyal customers to it. For example, retailers that have successfully developed multichannel strategies by seamlessly integrating stores, the Internet, and catalogues provide extra convenience and multiple opportunities for their current customers to shop.

Retailers have the least competitive advantage when they pursue diversification opportunities. Thus, these opportunities are generally risky and often don't work, as was the case with Home Depot. Vertical integration, however, albeit risky, often has overwhelming benefits for those large and sophisticated retailers that can invest heavily for the long term. By making direct investments in distribution or manufacturing facilities, these retailers have total control over the entire marketing channel.

Global Growth Opportunities

International expansion is a market growth opportunity that successful retailers find attractive. The most commonly targeted regions are Mexico, Latin America, Europe, China, and Japan. International expansion can be risky because retailers must deal with differences in government regulations, cultural traditions, supply chain considerations, and language.

The issues connected to global expansion are discussed in Chapter 7, International Retailing Strategy.

Lo4 The Strategic Retail Planning Process

The **strategic retail planning process** is the set of steps a retailer goes through to develop a strategic retail plan[30] (see Exhibit 4–6). It describes how retailers select target market segments, determine the appropriate retail format, and build sustainable competitive advantages. It is not always necessary to go through the entire process each time an evaluation is performed. For instance, a retailer could

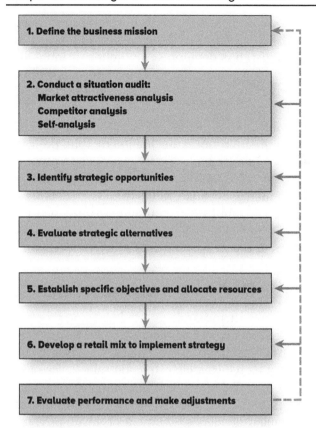

Exhibit 4–6
Steps in Strategic Retail Planning Process

1. Define the business mission

2. Conduct a situation audit:
   Market attractiveness analysis
   Competitor analysis
   Self-analysis

3. Identify strategic opportunities

4. Evaluate strategic alternatives

5. Establish specific objectives and allocate resources

6. Develop a retail mix to implement strategy

7. Evaluate performance and make adjustments

evaluate its performance and go directly to Step 2, conduct a situation audit.

The planning process can be used to formulate strategic plans at different levels within a retail business. For example, the corporate strategic plan of American Express indicates how resources are to be allocated across the corporation's various businesses such as credit cards and travel services. Each business within American Express has its own strategic plan, and then strategies are developed for products within a business, such as the American Express Gold card.

As we discuss the steps in the retail planning process, we will apply each step to the planning process Kelly Bradford is undertaking. Kelly owns Gifts To Go, a small, two-store chain in the Vancouver area. One of her 1000-square-foot stores is located in the downtown area; the other is in an upscale suburban mall. The target market for Gifts To Go is upper-income men and women looking for gifts

strategic retail planning process The steps a retailer goes through to develop a strategic retail plan. It describes how retailers select target market segments, determine the appropriate retail format, and build sustainable competitive advantages.

in the $50 to $500 price range. The stores have an eclectic selection of merchandise, including handmade jewellery and crafts, fine china and glassware, perfume, watches, writing instruments, and a variety of one-of-a-kind items. Gifts To Go also has developed a number of loyal customers who are contacted by sales associates when family anniversaries and birthdays come up. In many cases, customers have a close relationship with a sales associate and enough confidence in the associate's judgment that they tell the associate to pick out an appropriate gift. The turnover of Gifts To Go sales associates is low for the industry because Kelly treats associates as part of the family. The company offers employee benefits for all associates, and they share in the profits of the firm.

Step 1: Define the Business, Mission

The first step in the strategic retail planning process is to define the business mission. The **mission statement** is a broad description of a retailer's objectives and the scope of activities it plans to undertake.[31] The objective of a publicly held firm is to maximize its stockholders' wealth by increasing the value of its stock and paying dividends.[32] Owners of small, privately-held firms frequently have other objectives, such as achieving a specific level of income and avoiding risks rather than maximizing income.

The mission statement should define the general nature of the target segments and retail formats that the firm will consider. For example, the following mission statement of an office supply category specialist is too broad: "Serve the customer, build value for shareholders, and create opportunities for associates." It does not provide a sense of strategic direction. In contrast, Target's vision statement is as follows: "We fulfill the needs and fuel the potential of our guests. That means making Target your preferred shopping destination in all channels by delivering outstanding value, continuous innovation and exceptional experiences—consistently fulfilling our Expect More. Pay Less.® brand promise." The question is, why did Target do such a poor job of fulfilling that vision in Canada? (See Retailing View 4.4 to read about how they did not fulfil their vision statement here in Canada.)

mission statement A broad description of the scope of activities a business plans to undertake.

situation audit An analysis of the opportunities and threats in the retail environment and the strengths and weaknesses of the retail business relative to its competitors.

In developing the mission statement, managers must answer five questions:

- What business are we in?
- What should be our business in the future?
- Who are our customers?
- What are our capabilities?
- What do we want to accomplish?

Gifts To Go's mission statement is "to be the leading retailer of higher-priced gifts in the Vancouver area and provide a stable income of $100 000 per year for the owner."

Because the mission statement defines the retailer's objectives and the scope of activities it plans to undertake, Gifts To Go's mission statement clarifies that its management won't consider retail opportunities outside the Vancouver area, for selling low-priced gifts, or that would jeopardize its ability to generate $100 000 in annual income.[33]

Step 2: Conduct a Situation Audit

After developing a mission statement and setting objectives, the next step in the strategic planning process is to do a situation audit. A **situation audit** or SWOT analysis is an analysis of the strengths and weaknesses of the retail business relative to its competitors and the opportunities and threats in the retail environment. The elements in the situation analysis are shown in Exhibit 4–7.[34]

Market Factors Some critical factors related to consumers and their buying patterns are market size and growth, sales cyclicality, and seasonality. Market size, typically measured in retail sales dollars, is important because it indicates a retailer's opportunity for generating revenues to cover its investment. Large markets are attractive to large retail firms. But they are also attractive to small entrepreneurs because they offer more opportunities to focus on a market segment. Some retailers, however, prefer to concentrate on smaller markets.

Growing markets are typically more attractive than mature or declining markets. For example, retail markets for specialty stores are growing faster than those for department stores. Typically, margins and prices are higher in growing markets because competition is less intense than in mature markets. Since new customers are just beginning to patronize stores in growing markets, they may not have developed strong store loyalties and thus might be easier to attract to a new store. Some

Exhibit 4–7
Elements in Market Analysis/SWOT (Strengths, Weaknesses, Opportunities, and Threats)

MARKET FACTORS

Size

Growth

Seasonality

Business cycles

COMPETITIVE FACTORS

Barriers to entry

Bargaining power of vendors

Competitive rivalry

ENVIRONMENTAL FACTORS

Technology

Economic

Regulatory

Social

ANALYSIS OF STRENGTHS AND WEAKNESSES

Management capabilities

Financial resources

Locations

Operations

Merchandise

Store management

Customer loyalty

---

retailers, however, prefer to locate in mature markets. These locations are attractive when the customer base is stable and competition is weak.

Firms are often interested in minimizing the business cycle's impact on their sales. Thus, retail markets for merchandise affected by economic conditions (such as cars and major appliances) are less attractive than retail markets unaffected by economic conditions (such as food). In general, markets with highly seasonal sales are unattractive because a lot of resources are needed to accommodate the peak season, but then resources are underused the rest of the year. For example, to minimize these problems due to seasonality, ski resorts promote summer vacations to generate sales during all four seasons.

To conduct an analysis of the market factors for Gifts To Go, Kelly Bradford went on the Internet to get information about the size, growth, and cyclical and seasonal nature of the gift market in general and, more specifically, in Vancouver. On the basis of her analysis, she concluded that the market factors were attractive; the market for more-expensive gifts was large, growing, and not vulnerable to business cycles. The only negative aspect was the high seasonality of gifts, with peaks at Valentine's Day, June (due to weddings), Christmas, and other holidays.

Competitive Factors The nature of the competition in retail markets is affected by barriers to entry, bargaining power of vendors, and competitive rivalry.[35] Retail markets are more attractive when competitive entry is costly. **Barriers to entry** are conditions in a retail market that make it difficult for firms to enter the market. These conditions include scale economies, customer loyalty,

and availability of great locations.

Scale economies are cost advantages due to a retailer's size. Markets dominated by large competitors with scale economies are typically unattractive. For example, a small entrepreneur would avoid becoming an office supply category specialist because the market is dominated by Staples. This firm has a considerable cost advantage over the entrepreneur because it can buy merchandise more cheaply and operate more efficiently by investing in the latest technology and spreading its overhead across more stores. Retail markets dominated by a well-established retailer that has developed a loyal group of customers offer limited profit potential. For example, Home Depot's high customer loyalty makes it hard for a competing home improvement centre to enter the same market.

Finally, the availability of locations may impede competitive entry. A retail market with high entry barriers is very attractive to retailers presently competing in that market because those barriers limit competition. However, markets with high entry barriers are unattractive to retailers not already in the market. For example, the lack of good retail locations in Hong Kong makes this market attractive to retailers already in the region, but less attractive to retailers desiring to enter the market.

Another competitive factor is the **bargaining power of vendors**. Markets are less attractive when a few vendors control the merchandise sold in them. In these situations, vendors have an opportunity to dictate prices and other terms (such as delivery dates), reducing the retailer's profits. For example, the market for retailing fashionable cosmetics is less attractive because two suppliers,

barriers to entry Conditions in a retail market that make it difficult for firms to enter the market.

scale economies Cost advantages due to the size of a retailer.

bargaining power of vendors A competitive factor that makes a market unattractive when a few vendors control the merchandise sold in it. In these situations, vendors have an opportunity to dictate prices and other terms, reducing retailer's profits.

Why Target Failed in Canada

On paper, at least, Target Corp.'s ill-fated 2011 decision to enter Canada by paying $1.8 billion for the leases of a few hundred Zellers stores seemed like a no-brainer. Canada, unlike the United States at the time, was a bastion of economic opportunity—or so it appeared. Our banks were healthy, house prices were rising, and consumers were spending more on clothing and housewares than ever before. Best of all, Target's own research showed that as many as 10 percent of Canadians were already crossing the border to shop in its sprawling, red-and-white US stores, and 70 percent were familiar with its "cheap chic" brand.

© The Globe and Mail-Fred Lum/The Canadian Press.

Less than two years later, the Minneapolis-based giant pulled out of Canada after amassing $2.5 billion in pre-tax losses. The collateral damage: 133 stores closed across the country, 17 600 jobs lost, and a huge, $5.4-billion write-down for the US parent company. So much for Target's much-ballyhooed bid to change the face of Canadian retail.

Target's failure to take Canada has been chalked up to an overly ambitious launch, which included the rollout of 124 stores the first year, and problems with inventory control systems that left store shelves bare. Stores struggled to keep key items such as milk and eggs in stock, while photos on Twitter showed empty aisles, save for a few packages of men's underwear. More harmful, though, was the perception—not always supported by fact—that Target was more expensive than rivals like Walmart. Despite a concerted effort to get things back on track in 2014, Target CEO Brian Cornell said in recent blog post that executives were "unable to find a realistic scenario that got Target Canada to profitability until at least 2021."

What's surprising about Target's Canadian misadventure isn't that it ran into unforeseen problems—it's that it didn't think there was any point in trying to fix them. To be sure, the company was being pressured by investors to improve performance following an infamous data breach in 2013. But one could hardly imagine Target abandoning the state of California, with roughly the same population as Canada, just because it experienced a few teething problems.

Although it wasn't cited as a reason in Target Canada's bankruptcy fling, Canada's rapidly deteriorating economic climate almost certainly hastened Target's decision to snap a leash on its bull-terrier mascot and head home. Target's announcement came the same day that Sony Canada closed all 14 of its stores, and federal Finance Minister Joe Oliver announced he was delaying the federal budget because of collapsing oil prices, which threatened to erase surpluses and plunge parts of the country in recession. "They're looking at a lot of different metrics, and consumer spending would be one of them," says Peter Chapman, a former Loblaws executive and retail consultant in Halifax. "What we're seeing in the oil industry and the ripple effect on the economy is huge."

A saturation of the Canadian retail market may have also factored into Target's decision. Twenty years ago, Walmart, a discount chain whose arrival was more likely to generate protests than the fawning newspaper coverage enjoyed by Target, managed to successfully colonize Canada with a similarly rapid expansion after it bought 122 Woolco stores. But much has changed since. A long line of US retailers, from J-Crew to Lowe's, have followed Walmart northward in recent years, each laying a claim to

Source: *Originally published in Maclean's™ magazine on February 2, 2015. Used with permission of Rogers Media Inc. All rights reserved.*

a piece of Canadians' wallets. Target, in other words, may have simply come too late to the party (to the extent there ever was one)—a realization that should have other US retailers thinking twice about tapping Canada for easy growth.

The outlook for the Canadian economy in early 2015 was far worse than it was six months earlier—around the time Target Canada president and company veteran Mark Schindele was readying a turnaround plan for the struggling Canadian operation. Citing the plunge in oil prices, US investment bank Morgan Stanley, for example, downgraded its GDP growth forecast to 1.8 percent in 2015 and 1.5 percent in 2016—a full percentage point lower than its previous estimates. By contrast, most economists expected the US economy to grow at 3 percent over the same period, with falling energy prices acting as a stiff tailwind. In the Prairies, where the collapse in oil prices is wreaking the most havoc, there is even talk about Alberta being thrown into recession, a marked turnaround from previous years when the province led the country in employment growth. Suncor Energy has already laid off 1000 workers and there's likely more pain to come with oil now below US$50 a barrel.

What's more, the oil-induced hangover could be exported elsewhere, with Ontario having become more reliant on manufacturing specialized equipment for the oil sands in recent years. It all adds up to a rather alarming picture, given that Canadian households now owe a record $1.63 for every dollar they earn. Economists have frequently warned that elevated debt levels make Canada vulnerable to economic shocks—such as wild swings in energy prices.

Even before oil prices collapsed, US retailers were taking an increasingly cautious approach to Canada. A report from early 2015 by US commercial real estate firm CBRE found that Canada went from being the sixth-most desirable market for global retail expansion in 2012 to not even on the list in 2014. Nordstrom, for example, decided in 2015 to delay the launch of its discount chain, the Rack, in Canada until 2017.

The growing trepidation is only partly due to the weakening Canadian economy. Foreign retailers—and US chains, in particular—have long assumed Canada is under-served by retailers. The country currently has about 15 sq. feet of leasable shopping-centre square footage for every person in the country, compared to about 25 sq. feet per person in the US, according to Colliers

International. But, despite all the recent arrivals to the Canadian retail scene since the recession, the gap between the two countries has remained fairly constant over the years. We simply don't seem to need new retail space. For every shiny new J-Crew that's popped up in the local shopping mall, there's been a Jacob store that's gone out of business. In recent years, the number of retailers that have announced store closures or ceased operations entirely in Canada include: Sony (14 stores), Smart Set (107 stores), Jacob (92 stores), Mexx Canada (95 stores), Sears Canada (5 stores), Big Lots and Liquidation World (78 stores), and, of course, Zellers, which had its 22 locations sold to Target.

Target's slogan is, "Expect more, pay less." But Target Canada initially appeared to deliver on neither. Although the company's Ontario stores attracted plenty of curious customers after opening in early 2013, it wasn't long before shoppers complained about Target's prices and analysts started asking tough questions. "While shoppers appreciate the higher quality assortment, especially in discretionary categories"—more KitchenAid mixers and cute area rugs—"the complaints on pricing were alarming," Deutsche Bank securities analyst Paul Trussell wrote in 2013.

The problem, it turned out, was that shoppers weren't comparing prices against Target's Canadian competitors, but against its own US stores, which was bound to be a recipe for disappointment in a country where many products can cost up to 25 percent more than in the US. J-Crew, the popular US clothing retailer, ran into a similar snag when it opened its Canadian stores in 2011 and immediately faced a pricing backlash from shoppers accustomed to buying through its US website. The effect was magnified for Target, however, because there had been so much hype prior to the chain's launch. "When Target was coming in, they were only too happy to get the media machine behind them," says David Ian Gray, the founder of DIG360 Consulting in Vancouver. "But when they fell short, it created an even bigger perceptual gap."

Target responded by making sure it was meeting or beating Walmart Canada on everyday products such as toilet paper and breakfast cereal. Even so, Chapman says Target didn't try hard enough to shake its pricey perception among Canadians. "If you're a retailer teetering on the edge, you've got to pile it high at the front of those stores," he says. "They might have narrowed the price with Walmart, but they sure didn't tell anyone about it." In

Continued

part, that's because Target has traditionally eschewed the traditional discount approach in order to give its stores a more organized, higher-end feel—hence, the whole "Tar-zhay" moniker. But that only works if people are already walking through the doors, Chapman says. Another frequent complaint was empty shelves. A report by Reuters suggested that barcodes on products didn't always match up with what was in the computer system, creating backlogs and shortages as staff attempted to sort things out. A post on the website *Gawker,* purportedly written by a "management-level employee," also blamed Target's Minneapolis headquarters for trying to force its processes and procedures on the Canadian operation despite evidence they weren't working. Others, however, heard rumours Target Canada was reluctant to ask Minneapolis for help when it was in over its head. Either way, it was hardly the well-oiled machine many had expected.

Of course, supply chain snafus aren't unheard of in the industry. Loblaws has suffered from them, and so has the Brick. Both recovered. And Target appeared to be on its way to doing the same after Schindele was brought in to replace Tony Fisher as Target Canada's president last spring. But Target had left itself little margin for error after spending $1.8 billion for the Zellers leases and another $2.3 billion to renovate the stores themselves, about double the initial estimate. "The hole was too big," says Scott Mushkin, an analyst at Wolfe Research in New York. He says Target Canada was only selling about US$140 worth of merchandise per square foot when it needed to be moving closer to US$250 a square foot to break even. By comparison, most of Target's US stores manage US$300 a square foot, which is the number Target Canada would have had to hit to realize its stated goal of reaching US$6 billion in sales by 2017.

Interestingly, however, Mushkin doesn't believe Target's supply-chain problems or pricing ultimately led to its undoing. Instead, he argues there simply wasn't sufficient consumer demand for another big discount retailer in Canada, and that Target failed to provide consumers with a compelling reason to switch their shopping allegiances. The initial missteps and the deteriorating economic picture only served to hammer home the point sooner than might have otherwise been the case.

After visiting several stores in Toronto in late 2014, Mushkin wrote in a note to clients that, "Overall, we found the shopping experience in-store quite pleasurable and didn't see any areas of major concern." Similarly, he suggested that pricing comparisons with Walmart Canada suggested Target shoppers were getting a "good deal," once loyalty program discounts were included. Mushkin concluded that the only explanation for Target Canada's poor performance was that Canadian consumers were already well-served by existing players, many of whom had upped their game in preparation for Target's arrival, and that the operation should be mothballed. "In the end, Target is a great retailer," Mushkin says. "But was there a real need in Canada? The answer is no."

Estée Lauder (Estée Lauder, Clinique, Prescriptives, Aramis, Tommy Hilfiger, M.A.C., and Origins)[36] and L'Oréal (Maybelline, Giorgio Armani, Helena Rubinstein, Lancôme, Lanvin, and Ralph Lauren brands),[37] provide the most desired premium brands. Since department stores need these brands to support a fashionable image, these suppliers have the power to sell their products to retailers at high prices.

The final industry factor is the level of competitive rivalry in the retail market. **Competitive rivalry** is the frequency and intensity of reactions to actions undertaken by competitors. When rivalry is high, price wars erupt, advertising and promotion expenses increase, and profit potential falls. Conditions that may lead to intense rivalry include the following:

competitive rivalry The frequency and intensity of reactions to actions undertaken by competitors.

- a large number of competitors that are all about the same size
- slow growth
- high fixed costs
- lack of perceived differences between competing retailers

Tim Hortons, McDonald's, and Starbucks have an intense rivalry in some markets. Starbucks has extended its food/lunch menu, while McDonald's and Tim's is encroaching on Starbucks' gourmet coffee turf. Pricing for similar items is close, though Starbucks is still more expensive. To provide easier accessibility, Starbucks is offering McDonald's/Tim-style drive-through windows in some locations.

When Kelly Bradford started to analyze the competitive factors for Gifts To Go, she realized that identifying her competitors wasn't easy. Although there were no gift stores carrying similar merchandise at the same price points in the Vancouver area, there were various other retailers from which a customer could buy gifts. She identified her primary competitors as department stores, craft galleries, catalogues, and Internet retailers. Kelly felt there were some scale economies in developing customer databases to support gift retailing. The lack of large suppliers meant that vendors' bargaining power wasn't a problem, and competitive rivalry was minimal because the gift business was not a critical part of the department store's overall business. In addition, merchandise carried by the various retailers offered considerable differentiation opportunities.

Macro-environment The macro-environment factors that affect market attractiveness span technological, economic, regulatory, and social changes.[38] When a retail market is going through significant changes in technology, present competitors are vulnerable to new entrants that are skilled at using the new technology. For example, in the late 1990s, many traditional retailers were nervously scrambling to define their space in e-tailing. Thousands of pure-play e-tailers with technological sophistication flooded the Internet. Many of the bricks-and-mortar retailers invested heavily in Internet technology and were able to integrate the Internet with their other selling channels.

Some retailers may be more affected by economic conditions than others. During tough economic times, retailers that offer a perceived high value offering, such as discount, off-price, warehouse clubs, and extreme value retailers, are in a much better position than retailers specializing in luxury goods, such as jewellery stores, designer apparel specialty stores, and gourmet and organic grocers. Harry Rosen employs many well-paid salespeople to provide high-quality customer service. When unemployment is low, costs may increase significantly, as salespeople's wages rise due to the difficulty in hiring qualified people. But retailers such as Walmart that provide little service and have much lower labour costs as a percentage of sales may be less affected by low unemployment.

Government regulations can reduce the attractiveness of a retail market. For example, it is difficult for large retailers to open new stores in France due to size restrictions placed on new stores. Also, many local governments within Canada have tried to stop Walmart from entering their market in an attempt to protect locally owned retailers.[39]

Finally, trends in demographics, lifestyles, attitudes, and personal values affect retail markets' attractiveness. Harry Rosen, for example, has been struggling with several trends simultaneously. Known for traditional suits and dress shirts, the company had to learn how to appeal to younger customers and business people who prefer to dress casually without alienating its traditional customer base.[40]

Retailers need to answer three questions about the macro-environment:

- What new developments or changes might occur, such as new technologies and regulations or different social factors and economic conditions?

- What is the likelihood that these environmental changes will occur? What key factors affect whether these changes will occur?

- How will these changes impact each retail market, the firm, and its competitors?

Kelly Bradford's primary concern when she did an environmental analysis was the potential growth of Internet gift retailers such as RedEnvelope. Gifts seem ideal for an electronic channel, because customers can order the item over the Internet and have it shipped directly to the gift recipient. Kelly also recognized that the electronic channel could effectively collect information about customers and then target promotions and suggestions to them when future gift-giving occasions arose.

Strengths and Weaknesses Analysis The most critical aspect of the situation audit is for a retailer to determine its unique capabilities in terms of its strengths and weaknesses relative to the competition.[41] A **strengths and weaknesses analysis** indicates how well the business can seize opportunities and avoid harm from threats in the environment. Exhibit 4–8 outlines issues to consider in performing a self-analysis.

strengths and weaknesses analysis A critical aspect of the situation audit in which a retailer determines its unique capabilities—its strengths and weaknesses relative to its competition.

Below is Kelly Bradford's analysis of Gifts To Go's strengths and weaknesses:

Management capability	Limited—Two excellent store managers and a relatively inexperienced person helps Kelly buy merchandise. An accounting firm keeps the financial records for the business but has no skills in developing and using customer databases.
Financial resources	Good—Gifts To Go has no debt and has a good relationship with a bank. Kelly has saved $255 000 that she has in liquid securities.
Operations	Poor—While Kelly feels Gifts To Go has relatively low overhead, the company does not have a computer-based inventory control system or management and customer information systems. Her competitors (local department stores, catalogue, and Internet retailers) certainly have superior systems.
Merchandising capabilities	Good—Kelly has a flair for selecting unique gifts, and she has excellent relationships with vendors providing one-of-a-kind merchandise.
Store management capabilities	Excellent—The store managers and sales associates are excellent. They are very attentive to customers and loyal to the firm. Employee and customer theft are kept to a minimum.
Locations	Excellent—Both of Gifts To Go's locations are excellent. The downtown location is convenient for office workers. The suburban mall location is at a heavily trafficked juncture.
Customers	Good—While Gifts To Go does not achieve the sales volume in gifts done in department stores, the company has a loyal base of customers.

Step 3: Identify Strategic Opportunities

After completing the situation audit, the next step is to identify opportunities for increasing retail sales. Some growth opportunities could involve a redefinition of the retailer's mission statement. The strategic opportunities could involve market preparation, market expansion, retail format development, or diversification. Kelly Bradford presently competes in gift retailing using a

DID YOU KNOW?

55 percent of Canadians indicate that they use coupons to purchase grocery items; 36 percent of those reveal that they find their coupons online.[42]

specialty store format. The strategic alternatives she is considering are defined in terms of the growth opportunities in Exhibit 4–5. Note that some of these growth strategies involve a redefinition of her mission.

Step 4: Evaluate Strategic Opportunities

The fourth step in the strategic planning progress is to evaluate opportunities that have been identified in the situation audit. The evaluation determines the retailer's potential to establish a sustainable competitive advantage and reap long-term profits from the opportunities under evaluation. Thus, a retailer must focus on opportunities that use its strengths and its area of competitive advantage. For example, expertise in developing private-label apparel is one of Club Monaco's sources of competitive advantage. Thus, Club Monaco would positively evaluate opportunities that involve development of private-label merchandise. Some of the areas retailers should consider when evaluating new opportunities are shown in Exhibit 4–8.

Both the market attractiveness and the strengths and weaknesses of the retailer need to be considered in evaluating strategic opportunities. The greatest investments should be made in market opportunities where the retailer has a strong competitive position. The table below represents Kelly's informal analysis:

Growth Opportunity	Market Attractiveness	Competitive Position
Increase size of present stores and amount of merchandise in stores	Low	High
Open additional gift stores in Vancouver area	Medium	Medium
Open gift stores outside the Vancouver area (new geographic segment)	Medium	Low
Sell lower-priced gifts in present stores or open new stores selling low-priced gifts (new benefit segment)	Medium	Low
Sell apparel and other non-gift merchandise to same customers in same or new stores	High	Medium
Sell similar gift merchandise to same market segment using the Internet	High	Low
Open apparel stores targeted at teenagers	High	Low
Open a category specialist selling low-priced gifts	High	Low

Exhibit 4–8
Strengths and Weaknesses Analysis

In performing a self-analysis, the retailer considers the potential areas for developing a competitive advantage listed below and answers the following questions:

- At what is our company good?
- In which of these areas is our company better than our competitors?
- In which of these areas does our company's unique capabilities provide a sustainable competitive advantage or a basis for developing one?

MANAGEMENT CAPABILITY

Capabilities and experience of top management

Depth of management—capabilities of middle management

Management's commitment to firm

FINANCIAL RESOURCES

Cash flow from existing business

Ability to raise debt or equity financing

OPERATIONS

Overhead cost structure

Quality of operating systems

Distribution capabilities

Management information systems

Loss prevention systems

Inventory control systems

MERCHANDISING CAPABILITIES

Knowledge and skills of buyers

Relationships with vendors

Capabilities in developing private brands

Advertising and promotion capabilities

STORE MANAGEMENT CAPABILITIES

Management capabilities

Quality of sales associates

Commitment of sales associates to firm

LOCATIONS

CUSTOMERS

Loyalty of customers

Step 5: Establish Specific Objectives and Allocate Resources

After evaluating the strategic investment opportunities, the next step in the strategic planning process is to establish a specific objective for each opportunity. The retailer's overall objective is included in the mission statement. The specific objectives are goals against which progress toward the overall objective can be measured. Thus, these specific objectives have three components:

- the performance sought, including a numerical index against which progress may be measured
- a time frame within which the goal is to be achieved
- the level of investment needed to achieve the objective

Typically, the performance levels are financial criteria such as return on investment, sales, or

profits. Kelly's objective is to increase profits by 20 percent in each of the next five years. She expects she will need to invest an additional $25 000 in her apparel and other non-gift merchandise inventory.

Step 6: Develop a Retail Mix to Implement Strategy

The sixth step in the planning process is to develop a retail mix for each opportunity in which investment will be made and to control and evaluate performance.

Step 7: Evaluate Performance and Make Adjustments

The final step in the planning process is evaluating the results of the strategy and implementation program. If the retailer is meeting or exceeding its objectives, changes aren't needed. But if the retailer fails to meet its objectives, re-analysis is needed. Typically, this re-analysis starts with reviewing the implementation programs; but it may indicate that the strategy (or even the mission statement) needs to be reconsidered. This conclusion would result in starting a new planning process, including a new situation audit. Changes in the macro-environment can force retailers to re-evaluate their strategy. For example, the strategy could involve targeting a new market segment, and tailoring their offering to meet the needs of this new segment.

Strategic Planning in the Real World

The planning process in Exhibit 4–6 indicates that strategic decisions are made in a sequential manner. After the business mission is defined, the situation audit is performed, strategic opportunities are identified, alternatives are evaluated, objectives are set, resources are allocated, the implementation plan is developed, and, finally, performance is evaluated and adjustments are made. But actual planning processes have interactions among the steps. For example, the situation audit may uncover a logical alternative for the firm to consider, even though this alternative isn't included in the mission statement. Thus, the mission statement may need to be reformulated. Development of the implementation plan might reveal that resource allocation to the opportunity is insufficient to achieve the objective. In that case, the objective would need to be changed or the resources would need to be increased, or the retailer might consider not investing in the opportunity at all.

Remember that a situation analysis is an essential part of developing a sustainable retail strategy. The analysis will reveal the retailer's potential for success by analyzing both the macro-environment and the micro-environment to highlight the retailer's unique capabilities. It is a competitive business world and smart retailers are always on alert for a competitive edge. Retail is a game of survival of the fittest!

> ### DID YOU KNOW?
>
> The average sales conversion rate among visitors to Canadian retail websites is 1.7 percent.[43]

A retailer's long-term performance is largely determined by its strategy. A strategy coordinates employees' activities and communicates the direction the retailer plans to take. Thus, retail market strategy describes both the strategic direction and the process by which the strategy is to be developed.

The retail strategy statement includes an identification of the target market and the retail format (its offering) to be directed toward that target market. The statement also needs to indicate the retailer's methods to build a sustainable competitive advantage. Three approaches for developing competitive advantage are (1) building strong relationships with customers, (2) building strong relationships with suppliers, and (3) achieving efficient internal operations. Each of these approaches involves developing an asset—loyal customers, strong vendor relationships, committed effective human resources and efficient systems, and attractive locations—that is not easily duplicated by competitors.

The strategic planning process consists of a sequence of steps, including (1) defining the business mission, (2) conducting a situation audit, (3) identifying strategic opportunities, (4) evaluating the alternatives, (5) establishing specific objectives and allocating resources, (6) developing a retail mix to implement strategy, and (7) evaluating performance and making adjustments.

Strategic planning is an ongoing process. Every day, retailers audit their situations, examine customer trends, study new technologies, and monitor competitive activities. But the retail strategy statement does not change every year or every six months; the strategy statement is reviewed and altered only when major changes in the retailer's environment or capabilities occur.

When a retailer undertakes a major re-examination of its strategy, the process for developing a new strategy statement may take a year or two. Potential strategic directions are generated by people at all levels of the organization, then evaluated by senior executives and operating personnel to ensure that the eventual strategic direction is profitable in the long run and can be implemented.

KEY TERMS

bargaining power of vendors
barriers to entry
brand images
competitive rivalry
cross-selling
customer loyalty
data warehouse
diversification opportunity
macro-environment
market expansion opportunity

market penetration opportunity
micro-environment
mission statement
positioning
private-label brands
related diversification opportunity
retail format
retail format development opportunity
retail market
retailing concept

scale economies
situation audit
strategic retail planning process
strengths and weaknesses analysis
sustainable competitive advantage
SWOT analysis
target market
unrelated diversification

GET OUT & DO IT!

1. **INTERNET EXERCISE** Visit the website for Restoration Hardware (http://www.restorationhardware.com). Does this Internet site reflect the retail strategies for the company as discussed here?

2. **GO SHOPPING** Visit two stores that sell similar merchandise categories and cater to the same target segment(s). How are their retail formats similar? Dissimilar? On what basis do they have a sustainable competitive advantage? Explain which you believe has a stronger position.

3. **GO SHOPPING** Develop a strategic plan for your favourite retailer. Go to the store. Observe and interview the store manager. Supplement your visit with information available online through Hoovers, the store's website (which should include its annual report), and other published sources.

4. Visit the websites for IKEA (http://www.ikea.com) and Starbucks (http://www.starbucks.com). Is the look/feel of these Internet sites consistent with the in-store experience of these stores?

DISCUSSION QUESTIONS AND PROBLEMS

1. What approaches can a retailer use to develop a competitive advantage? Choose a retailer and describe how it has developed a competitive strategic advantage.

2. Give an example of a market penetration, a retail format development, a market expansion, and a diversification growth strategy that Best Buy might use.

3. Draw and explain a positioning map such as that shown in Exhibit 4–4 for the retailers and customer segments (ideal points) for your favourite retailer.

4. View the video "Build-A-Bear Workshop" on Connect and complete a situation analysis identifying the retailer's strategy (see Exhibit 4–1). Detail the micro-environment and the macro-environment in the analysis. What are the strengths and weaknesses? Explain what threats and opportunities exist for this unique retailer.

5. Go to http://www.harryrosen.com and read the profile of Harry Rosen. Identify why Harry has been so successful in marketing to the high-end menswear market segment.

6. Read the Rona profile in Retailing View 4.3. What is Rona's sustainable competitive advantage?

7. Do a situation analysis for McDonald's. What is its mission? What are its strengths and weaknesses? What environmental threats might it face over the next ten years? How could it prepare for these threats?

8. Assume you are interested in opening a restaurant in your town. Go through the steps in the strategic retail planning process shown in Exhibit 4–6. Focus on doing a situation audit of the local restaurant market, identifying alternatives, evaluating alternatives, and selecting a target market and a retail mix for the restaurant.

9. The Gap owns several chains, including Old Navy and Banana Republic. What type of growth opportunity was The Gap pursuing when it opened each of these retail concepts? Which is most synergistic with the original The Gap chain?

10. Identify a store or service provider that you believe has an effective loyalty program. Explain why it is effective.

CHAPTER FIVE

Retail locations strategy—trade area decisions and site assessment

LEARNING OBJECTIVES

Lo1 Examine the four major factors retailers consider when evaluating an area.

Lo2 Consider the three factors retailers consider when evaluating and selecting a specific site.

Lo3 Define what a trade area is for a store and how retailers determine the trade area, and develop an understanding of the nature of consumers in the site's trade area.

Lo4 Review the three approaches for estimating potential sales for a store site.

Lo5 Explore the types of locations that are available to retailers and the relative advantages of each location type.

Lo6 Discuss why some locations are particularly well-suited to specific retail strategies.

SPOTLIGHT ON RETAILING

STUDY: LUXURY BRANDS CHOOSING CANADIAN MALLS OVER HIGH STREET

Luxury brands are increasingly locating in Canadian shopping centres, sometimes at the expense of traditional downtown luxury high streets. As a result of this typically American phenomenon, new luxury retail nodes have been created in several Canadian cities, including the suburbs for the first time. This study ranks Canada's top luxury retail areas, including high streets and shopping centres, based on number of free-standing luxury stores and concessions within larger upscale retailers.

Luxury retail expert Brian Winston, head of Toronto-based WINSTON Collective, notes that luxury brands are increasingly locating within shopping centres. Traditionally, he said, brands have congregated along upscale downtown high streets such as Bloor Street West in Toronto (aka the Mink Mile) and Burrard Street in Vancouver. Toronto's Yorkdale Shopping Centre is the Canadian trailblazer—with 23 luxury brands operating in the mall, it now ranks as Canada's third most exclusive luxury retail node. Furthermore, many luxury brands are entering Canada through Toronto's suburban Yorkdale, with many of its luxury brands unavailable on Toronto's Bloor Street West or, for that matter, anywhere else in Canada.

For the purposes of this study, luxury brands are considered to be those featuring relatively high price, quality, aesthetics, and rarity. Brands such as Coach and Michael Kors are excluded, primarily because their ubiquity. As well, luxury brand concessions within stores are included in this

JSMimages/Alamy.

study, excluding shops-in-stores which are not brand-operated. WINSTON Collective will soon do a follow-up to this article where it will discuss "new luxury" and how it pertains to Canadian Millennials.

The following is the summarized list of WINSTON Collective's 2015 Top-10 List of Canadian luxury retail nodes:

1. Bloor Street West/Yorkville, Toronto (23 free-standing luxury brands, 11 concessions)
2. Vancouver Luxury Zone (21 free-standing luxury brands)
3. Yorkdale Shopping Centre, Toronto (15 free-standing, 8 concessions)
4. Downtown Montreal (4 free-standing, 13 concessions)
5. Pacific Centre/Howe Street, Vancouver (6 free-standing, 9 concessions)
6. The CORE, downtown Calgary (10 concessions)
7. Oakridge Shopping Centre, Vancouver (4 free-standing, 1 concession)
8. Sherway Gardens, Toronto (5 free-standing)
9. Chinook Centre, Calgary (3 free-standing)
10. West Edmonton Mall, Edmonton (2 free-standing)

Remarkably, Toronto and Vancouver are each home to three of Canada's top-10 luxury nodes. Montreal, Edmonton, and Calgary also ranked in the study, with Calgary housing two luxury retail nodes.

WINSTON Collective Founder and Principle, Brian Winston, explained how although luxury brands are increasingly locating in malls, street-front locations will ultimately be prime space for luxury brands as luxury retail continues to evolve in Canada. Luxury brands will continue to seek space in Toronto and Vancouver in particular, according to Mr. Winston, as both cities continue to see increasing numbers of affluent and fashion-forward Asian locals and tourists.

Sources: Brian Winston, "Study: Luxury Brands Choosing Canadian Malls over High Street," *Winston*, August 17, 2015, http://winstoncollective.com/study-luxury-brands/ (accessed January 6, 2016); "Canada Becoming 'Americanized' as Luxury Brands Choose Malls over High Streets," *cpp-luxury.com*, http://www.cpp-luxury.com/canada-becoming-americanized-as-luxury-brands-choose-malls-over-high-streets/ (accessed January 6, 2015); Charlie Smith "Vancouver has Three of Canada's Top 10 Luxury Retail Nodes," *Georgia Straight*, http://www.straight.com/blogra/514701/vancouver-has-three-canadas-top-10-luxury-retail-nodes (accessed August 17, 2016).

region In retail location analysis, refers to a part of the country, a particular city, or a census metropolitan area (CMA).

trade area A geographic sector that contains potential customers for a particular retailer or shopping centre.

For several reasons, store location is often the most important decision made by a retailer. First, location is typically the prime consideration in a customer's store choice. For instance, when choosing where you are going to have your car washed, you usually pick the location closest to your home or work. Second, location decisions have strategic importance because they can be used to develop a sustainable competitive advantage. Retailers can change their pricing, service, and merchandise assortments in a relatively short time. However, location decisions are harder to change because retailers frequently have to either make substantial investments to buy and develop real estate or commit to long-term leases with developers. It's not unusual, for instance, for a national chain store to sign a lease for seven to ten years. If that location is the best in a particular mall or central business district, the retailer then has a strategic advantage competitors can't easily copy, because they are precluded from locating there.

Location decisions have become even more important in recent years. First, there are more retailers opening new locations, making the better locations harder to obtain. This problem is made more complex by a slowdown in both population growth and new shopping centre construction. A retailer may find a suitable location, but high rent, complicated leases, and expensive fixtures and remodelling can make it very costly. Many experts believe that there is too much retail space in Canada and that the best retail locations are already taken. Retailers must consider issues of suitability or compatibility, availability, affordability, accessibility, and visibility.

This chapter describes the types of locations available to retailers and the relative advantages of each. We then examine factors that retailers should consider when choosing a particular location type.

Lo1 Evaluating Specific Areas for Locations

Many types of locations are available for retail stores—each with its own strengths and weaknesses. Choosing a particular location type involves evaluating a series of trade-offs. These trade-offs generally concern the cost of the location versus its value to customers.

Exhibit 5–1 breaks the location decision into four levels: country, region, trade area, and specific site. The country is a decision of international expansion, which will be discussed in Chapter 7. A **region** refers to a part of the country, a particular city, or a census metropolitan area (CMA). A **trade area** is the geographic area encompassing most of the customers who would patronize a specific retail site, and that accounts for the majority of the store's sales and customers. A trade area may be part of a city, or it can extend beyond the city's boundaries, depending on the type of store and the density of potential customers surrounding it. For example, the best locations for a 7-Eleven convenience store are not the best locations for a category specialist such as a Best Buy.

In making store location decisions, retailers must examine all four levels simultaneously. For instance, suppose Pizza Pizza is expanding operations in the Atlantic provinces and has plans to simultaneously open several stores. Its research indicates that competition in the Halifax market is

Exhibit 5–1
Location Decisions Based on Four Levels

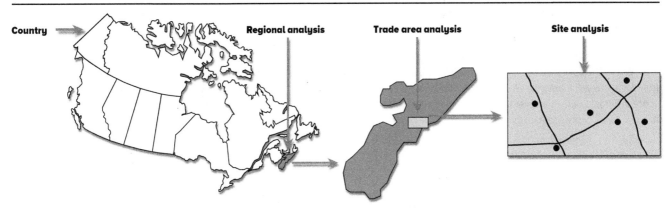

relatively weak, making it an attractive region. But maybe it can't find enough suitable sites, so it must temporarily postpone locating there.

In examining a site, we look at the factors that affect the attractiveness of a particular region and trade area. Then we examine what retailers look for in choosing a particular site.

The best areas for locating stores are those that generate the highest long-term profits for a retailer. Some factors affecting the long-term profit generated by stores that should be considered when evaluating an area include (1) the economic conditions, (2) competition, (3) the strategic fit of the area's population with the retailer's target market, and (4) the costs of operating stores (see Exhibit 5–2). Note that these factors are similar to those that retailers consider when evaluating an investment in a new business opportunity or entry into a foreign market.

Economic Conditions

Because locations involve a commitment of resources over a long time horizon, it is important to examine an area's level and growth of population and employment. In most cases, areas where the general population is growing are preferable to those with declining populations. Some retailers, such as Subway, often go into new strip shopping centres in anticipation that the surrounding suburban area will eventually be built up enough to support demand. Yet population growth alone doesn't tell the whole story.

It's important to examine a market's employment trends because a high level of employment usually means high purchasing power and high levels of retail sales. For instance, Ottawa has become a desirable retail location because of its proximity to government and corporate headquarters. Retail location analysts must determine how long such growth will continue and how it will affect demand for their merchandise. For instance, the economies

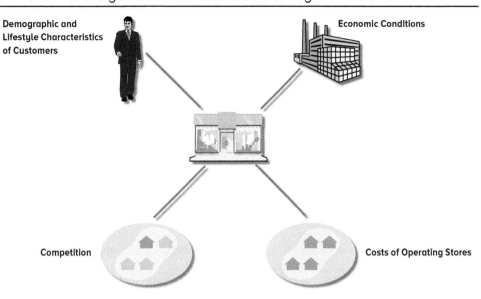

Exhibit 5–2

Factors Affecting Profit Potential within a Region or Trade Area

Demographic and Lifestyle Characteristics of Customers

Economic Conditions

Competition

Costs of Operating Stores

of some cities such as Oshawa and Windsor experience greater peaks and valleys due to their dependence on specific industries such as automobiles (General Motors and Ford).

Employment growth in and of itself isn't enough to ensure a strong retail environment in the future. If growth isn't diversified in a number of industries, the area may suffer from adverse cyclical trends. For instance, many areas that have been traditionally dependent on agriculture have attempted to bring in new industries, either manufacturing or high-tech, to help diversify their economies.

DID YOU KNOW?

Microsoft is opening its stores in close proximity to its rival Apple so that it can attract potential customers interested in technology.[1]

Competition

The level of competition in an area also affects demand for a retailer's merchandise. The level of competition can be defined as saturated, understored, or overstored. A **saturated trade area** offers customers a good selection of goods and services, while allowing competing retailers to make good profits. Since customers are drawn to these areas because of the great selections, retailers who believe they can offer customers a superior retail format in terms of merchandise, pricing, or service may find

saturated trade area A trade area that offers customers a good selection of goods and services, while allowing competing retailers to make good profits.

understored trade area
An area that has too few stores selling a specific good or service to satisfy the needs of the population.

overstored trade area
An area having so many stores selling a specific good or service that some stores will fail.

these areas attractive. Some restaurants such as Burger King seek locations where their major competition—McDonald's—has a strong presence. They believe that it's important to go head-to-head with their strongest competitors so that they can develop methods and systems that will allow them to compete successfully with them. They contend that locating in areas with weak competition allows them to become complacent. The strongest competitor will eventually enter the trade area. By then, however, it will have lost its competitive edge.[2]

Another strategy is to locate in an **understored trade area**—an area that has too few stores selling a specific good or service to satisfy the needs of the population. Walmart's early success was based on a location strategy of opening stores in small towns that were relatively understored. Now these stores experience high market share in their towns and draw from surrounding communities. In effect, these areas have gone from being understored before Walmart arrived to being an **overstored trade area**—having so many stores selling a specific good or service that some stores will fail. Unable to compete head-to-head with Walmart on price or breadth of selection, many family-owned retailers in those cities have had to either reposition their merchandising or service strategies or else go out of business.

Strategic Fit

Population level, growth, and competition alone don't tell the whole story. The area needs to have consumers who are in the retailer's target market—who are attracted to the retailer's offerings and interested in patronizing its stores. Thus, the area must have the right demographic and lifestyle profile. The size and composition of households in an area can be an important determinant of success. For instance, Laura, Laura Petites, and Laura II (a chain of stores specializing in traditional and business apparel for women) generally locate in areas with high-income, dual-career families; household size, however, isn't a particularly critical issue. Toys "R" Us, on the other hand, is interested in locations with heavy concentrations of families with young children.

Finally, lifestyle characteristics of the population may be relevant, depending on the target market(s) that a particular retailer is pursuing. Many college and university students, for instance, have relatively low incomes. However, they may come from well-to-do families, and by the fact that they are in university or college, they are relatively educated. Their lifestyles more closely resemble those of recent graduates in professional jobs making a good income than they do people with similar incomes working odd jobs in a rural area. Thus, the way people spend their money is often as important as how much money people make.

Operating Costs

The cost of operating stores can vary across areas. Operating costs are also affected by the proximity of the area being considered to other areas in which the retailer operates stores. For example, if a store is located near other stores and the retailer's distribution centres, the cost of shipping merchandise to the store is lower, as is the cost and travel time spent by the district manager supervising the stores' operations.

The local and provincial legal and regulatory environment can have a significant effect on operating costs. For example, according to Section 63 of Quebec's French Language Charter, the name of a business must be in French. Some companies have changed their name to comply with the Charter; for example, Kentucky Fried Chicken is known as "Poulet Frit Kentucky" in Quebec. Others are being taken to task by the Office Québécois de la Langue Française to change their signs to either give themselves a French name or add a slogan or explanation that reflects what it is they are selling. Changing signing to comply can be a costly venture for retailers.

Another thing retailers must keep in mind is the cost per square foot for retail space. Retailing View 5.1 identifies how much the rent is for the top 10 highest-rent shopping strips in the world. Keep in mind the location of a city in Canada will drive rental costs. For example in Lethbridge, Alberta, with a population of approximately 100 000 people, rent per square foot can range anywhere from $10 to $30 annually per square foot.

> **DID YOU KNOW?**
>
> "Canadian average rents per square foot range from between $200 to $315 in Vancouver (Robson Street) and Toronto (Bloor Street West), or about $200 000–$315 000 annually for a space of 1000 square feet."[3]

Ten Most Expensive Retail Shopping Strips

"The rent is too damn high," is the motto of a political party from New York City lamenting over the price of housing in their city. They are not alone. One would argue a majority of the retailers in New York city share the same sediment.

Cushman & Wakefield, an international commercial real estate company, prepared a report citing the Big Apple has four of the top ten most expensive real estate annual rental costs (per square foot). The increased rents in New York can be attributed to the increased number of consumers (projected to be over 55 million this year) who come to visit the city due to being known as "one of the world's hottest shopping strips, essential for its brand equity."

Lease and rent costs in the Big Apple aren't cheap. Take Restoration Hardware for example, who last year signed a contract to lease a 70 000 square foot building in the Meatpacking district for $250 million dollars. Forever 21 is also shelling out top dollar for prime real estate. They recently opened a 90 000-square-foot store in the middle of Times Square, where rent averages $2300 per square foot. What makes it hard to comprehend is Forever 21 is selling jeans for $9 a pair!

A number of retailers imply "gateway cities" will be their strategic focus over the coming years. Coach, for example, indicated it would shut down 20 percent of its stores in North America to focus on those "top cities." Internationally, Tiffany & Co laid claims to real estate on the Champs-Elysées in Paris and is currently renting a 10 000 square foot retail space for approximately US$15 million dollars per year.

During the annual convention for the National Retail Federation, David Zoba, who is in charge of real estate for Gap Inc., mentioned his concern about the escalating costs of retail rentals to Bill Taubman, whose family has ownership in a mall development company. Zoba was concerned about how these increased costs could potentially put retailers at risk, forcing them to close stores.

"You're going to see cities grow. It's going to expand—I expect rents to rise. It's simple supply and demand—there's endless demand and not enough supply," said Gene Spiegelman, a vice chairman at Cushman & Wakefield, told *Fortune*. "Rents in places like New York, Hong Kong, Paris, London, Shanghai, and Tokyo should keep rising."

Below is a list of the average annual sales per square foot for the 10 most expensive strips for international retailers (based on sales per square foot).

1. New York City, Upper 5th Avenue – $3500
2. Hong Kong, Causeway Bay – $2735
3. New York, Times Square – $2300
4. Hong Kong, Central – $2164
5. Hong Kong, Tsim Sha Tsui – $2063
6. Paris, Champs-Elysées – $1556
7. New York, Madison Avenue – $1400
8. London, New Bond Street – $1216
9. Sydney, Pitt Street Mall – $1016
10. New York, Lower 5th Avenue – $1000

Sources: Phil Wahba, "Top 10 highest-rent shopping strips in the world," *Fortune*, January 21, 2015, http://fortune.com/2015/01/21/10-highest-rent-shopping-strips-in-the-world/ (accessed January 6, 2015); "Home furnishings retailer inks $250M lease in Meatpacking," *The Real Deal*, October 14, 2014, http://therealdeal.com/2014/10/14/home-furnishings-retailer-inks-250m-lease-in-meatpacking/ (accessed March 22, 2016); *Tiffany & Co.*, http://www.tiffany.ca/WorldOfTiffany/LatestNews/Article.aspx?ArticleID=1597&PageType=2 (accessed March 22, 2016).

Number of Stores in an Area

Having selected an area in which to locate its stores, a retailer's next decision is how many stores to operate in the area. At first glance, you might think that a retailer should choose the one best location in each CMA, but clearly, larger CMAs can support more stores than smaller CMAs. It may therefore be more advantageous to locate several stores in one CMA and none in others. But there is a limit to how many stores can be operated in even the largest of CMAs. When making the decision about how many stores to open in an area, retailers must consider the trade-offs between lower operating costs and potential sales cannibalization from having multiple stores in an area.

Economies of Scale Versus Cannibalization

At first glance, you would expect that a retailer should choose the one best location in a given trade area. But most chains plan to go into an area with a network of stores. After all, promotion and

franchisors The owner of a franchise in a franchise agreement.

franchisees The owner of an individual store in a franchise agreement.

distribution economies of scale can be achieved with multiple locations. The total cost is the same to run a newspaper ad for a retailer with 20 stores in an area as it is if the retailer has only one store. Likewise, chains such as Canadian Tire expand into areas only where they have distribution capabilities designed to support the stores.

The question is: What is the best number of stores to have in an area? The answer depends on who owns the stores. For company-owned stores, the objective is to maximize profits for the entire chain. In this case, the retailer would continue to open stores as long as the marginal revenues achieved by opening a new store are greater than the marginal costs. Home Depot subscribes to this fundamental axiom of site selection: It is better to have two stores producing $75 million each than one store producing $100 million. The company believes that a store can do too much business. The store might be overcrowded, offer poor service, have a hard time staying in stock, and actually be underperforming. Home Depot believes that the solution to an underperforming store is to build another store in the same trade area. Although this strategy may seem illogical at first glance, it works for Home Depot. Best Buy uses a similar location strategy to control the electronics retail market.

For franchise operations, however, each individual franchise owner wants to maximize profits. Some **franchisors** (owners of the franchise) grant their **franchisees** (owners of the individual stores) an exclusive geographic territory so that other stores under the same franchise do not compete directly with them. In other franchise operations, the franchisees have not been afforded this protection and often have been involved in very antagonistic negotiations with the franchisors in an attempt to protect their investment.

Lo2 Retail Site Selection

Retail site selection is a very strategic decision. Opening a store at a site often involves committing to a lease of five years or more, purchasing land and building a store, or buying an existing building, each of which requires a considerable investment. Consider the tragic results if the store's performance is below expectations: The retailer may not be able to find another business to assume the lease, damage to the business credibility can be disastrous, and the investment capital may be very difficult to recover. The difference between moving into a superior trade area and an inferior one can mean the difference between success and failure. Furthermore, even if a retailer finds the "right" neighbourhood, the wrong site can spell disaster.

Consider, for instance, the location of a new doughnut shop. The retailer has the option to locate in two sites, one across the street from the other. One might think that it should simply choose the cheaper site. But one site has easier access and its signs are highly visible to motorists passing by. More importantly, that same site is on the way into the central

Home Depot believes that if a store is underperforming, then it may be overcrowded. So the company builds another store in the same trade area.

© McGraw-Hill Education/Andrew Resek.

business district, whereas the other is on the way to the suburbs. People who enjoy a morning doughnut know that it tastes best on the way to work with a big cup of coffee. Without careful analysis of trade areas and specific sites, multi-million dollar mistakes can be easily made. Fortunately, sophisticated statistical models are available through firms that provide geographic and demographic data and consulting services critical to evaluating specific sites, including Pitney Bowes at http://www.pitneybowes.com/us/location-intelligence.html?products-tab and ACNielsen Canada at http://www.acnielsen.ca.

The following questions will be discussed in assessing the retail site:

- What issues should be considered when determining in which region or trade area to locate a store?
- What is a trade area, and why should a retailer choose one over another?
- What factors should retailers consider when deciding on a particular site?
- How can retailers forecast sales for new store locations?

Evaluating a Site for Locating a Retail Store

Having decided to locate stores in an area, the retailer's next step is to evaluate and select a specific site. In making this decision, retailers consider three factors: (1) the characteristics of the site, (2) the characteristics of the trading area for a store at the site, and (3) the estimated potential sales that can be generated by a store at the site. The first two sets of factors are typically considered in an initial screening of potential sites. The methods used to forecast sales, the third factor, can involve a more complex analytical approach. Each of these factors is discussed in the following sections.

Factors Affecting the Attractiveness of a Site

Some characteristics of a site that affect store sales and thus are considered in selecting a site are traffic flow past the site and accessibility to the site, as well as location characteristics, restrictions, and costs (see Exhibit 5–3).

Exhibit 5–3
Site Characteristics

A. Traffic Flow and Accessibility	C. Restrictions
Vehicular traffic	Zoning
Ease of vehicular access	Signage
Access to major highways	Restrictions on tenant mix
Street congestion	Safety code restrictions
Pedestrian traffic	
Availability of mass transit	
B. Location Characteristics	**D. Costs**
Parking spaces	Rental fee
Access to store entrance and exit	Common area maintenance cost
Visibility of store from street	Local taxes
Access for deliveries	Advertising and promotion fees
Size and shape of store	Length of lease
Condition of building	
Adjacent retailers	

Traffic Flow and Accessibility

The accessibility of a site is the ease with which a customer may get into and out of it. The accessibility analysis has two stages: a macro analysis and then a micro analysis.

Macro Analysis The macro analysis considers the primary trade area, such as the area five to ten kilometres around the site in the case of a supermarket or drugstore. To assess a site's accessibility on a macro level, the retailer simultaneously evaluates several factors, such as road patterns, road conditions, and barriers.

In the macro analysis, the analyst should consider the **road pattern**. The primary trade area needs major arteries or highways so that customers can travel easily to the site. A related factor is the **road condition**, including the age, number of lanes, number of stoplights, congestion, and general state of repair of roads in the primary trade area. For instance, a location on an old, narrow, congested secondary road in disrepair with too many stoplights wouldn't be a particularly good site for a retail store.

Natural barriers, such as rivers or mountains, and **artificial barriers**, such as railroad

road pattern A consideration used in measuring the accessibility of a retail location via major arteries, highways, or roads.

road condition Includes the age, number of lanes, number of stoplights, congestion, and general state of repair of roads in a trade area.

natural barriers Barriers, such as rivers or mountains, that affect accessibility to a site.

artificial barriers In site evaluations for accessibility, barriers such as railroad tracks, major highways, or parks.

visibility The customers' ability to see the store and enter the parking lot safely.

amount and quality of parking facilities A store having enough parking spaces, close enough to the building, so that the store is ideally accessible to customers, but not so many open spaces that the store is viewed as being unpopular. A standard rule of thumb is 5.9 spaces per 1000 square feet of retail store space.

congestion The amount of crowding of either cars or people.

ingress/egress The means of entering/exiting the parking lot of a retail site.

tracks, major highways, or parks, may also affect accessibility. The impact of these barriers on a particular site primarily depends on whether the merchandise or services are available on both sides of the barrier. If, for instance, only one supermarket serves both sides of a highway, people on the opposite side must cross to shop.

Micro Analysis The micro analysis concentrates on issues in the immediate vicinity of the site, such as visibility, traffic flow, parking, congestion, and ingress/egress.

Visibility refers to customers' ability to see the store and enter the parking lot safely. Good visibility is less important for stores with established and loyal customers and for stores with limited market areas because customers know where the store is. Nonetheless, large national retailers such as Canadian Tire insist that there be no impediments to a direct, undisturbed view of their store. In an area with a highly transient population, such as a tourist centre or large city, good visibility from the road is particularly important.

The success of a site with good traffic flow is a question of balance. The site should have a substantial number of cars per day, but not so many that congestion impedes access to the store. To assess the level of vehicular traffic, the analyst can usually obtain data from the regional planning commission or highway department. But the data may have to be adjusted for special situations. As a result, it's sometimes easier and more accurate to do the analysis in-house. For instance, the analyst must consider that the presence of large places of employment, schools, or big trucks may lessen a site's desirability. Also, areas congested during rush hours may have a good traffic flow during the rest of the day when most shopping takes place. Finally, some retailers might wish to adjust the raw traffic counts by excluding out-of-province licence plates or counting only homeward-bound traffic.

The **amount and quality of parking facilities** are critical to a shopping centre's overall accessibility. If

there aren't enough spaces or if they are too far from the stores, customers will be discouraged from entering the area. On the other hand, if there are too many open spaces, the shopping centre may be seen as a failure or as having unpopular stores. It's hard to assess how many parking spaces are enough, although location analysts use parking ratios as a starting point. A standard rule of thumb is 5.9:100 (5.9 spaces per 1000 square feet of retail store space).[4] Nevertheless, there's no good substitute for observing the shopping centre at various times of the day, week, and season. The analyst must also assess the availability of employee parking, the proportion of shoppers using cars, parking by non-shoppers, and the typical length of a shopping trip.

An issue that's closely related to the amount of available parking facilities, but extends into the shopping centre itself, is the relative congestion of the area. **Congestion** can refer to the amount of crowding of either cars or people. There's some optimal range of comfortable congestion for customers. Too much congestion can make shopping slow, irritate customers, and generally discourage sales. On the other hand, a relatively high level of activity in a shopping centre creates excitement and can stimulate sales.[5]

The last factor to consider in the accessibility analysis is **ingress/egress**—the ease of entering and exiting the site's parking lot. Often, medians or one-way streets make entering or exiting difficult from one or more directions, limiting accessibility.

Adjacent Tenants Locations with complementary, as well as competing, adjacent retailers have the potential to build traffic. Complementary retailers target the same market segment but have a different, non-competing merchandise offering. For example, Price Chopper, a limited assortment supermarket targeting price-sensitive consumers, prefers to be co-located with other retailers targeting price-sensitive consumers, such as Dollarama or even Walmart.

Have you ever noticed that competing fast-food restaurants, automobile dealerships, antiques dealers, and even shoe and apparel stores in a mall are located next to one another? Consumers looking for these types of merchandise are involved in convenience or comparison shopping situations. They want to be able to make their choice easily in the case of convenience shopping, or to have a good assortment so that they can "shop around."

This location approach is based on the principle of cumulative attraction, in which a cluster of similar and complementary retailing activities will generally have greater drawing power than isolated stores that engage in the same retailing activities.

Locational Advantages Within a Centre

Once the centre's accessibility is evaluated, the analyst must evaluate the locations within it. Since the better sites cost more, retailers must consider their importance. For instance, in a strip shopping centre, the more expensive locations are closest to the grocery store. A liquor store or a flower shop that may attract impulse buyers should thus be close to the grocery store. But a shoe repair store, which shouldn't expect impulse customers, could be in an inferior location because customers in need of this service will seek out the store.

The same issues apply when evaluating regional multilevel shopping centres. It's advantageous for apparel stores such as Club Monaco to be clustered in the more expensive locations near a department store in a mall. People shopping for clothing may start at the department store and naturally gravitate to stores near it. Yet a store such as Sport Chek, another destination store, needn't be in the most expensive location, since many of its customers know they are in the market for this type of product before they even get to the centre.

Another consideration is to locate stores that appeal to similar target markets close together. In essence, customers want to shop where they will find a good assortment of merchandise. This is based on the principle of **cumulative attraction**, in which a cluster of similar and complementary retailing activities will generally have greater drawing power than isolated stores that engage in the same retailing activities. This is why antiques shops, car dealers, and shoe and clothing stores all seem to do better if they are close to one another. Of course, an area can become overstored when it has too many competing stores to profitably satisfy demand.

The principle of cumulative attraction applies both to stores that sell complementary merchandise and those that compete directly with one another. Thus a good location is one whose tenant mix provides:

- a good selection of merchandise that competes with itself
- complementary merchandise

Lo3 Trade Area Characteristics

After identifying several sites that have acceptable traffic flow, accessibility, and other location characteristics, the next step is to collect information about the trade area that can be used to forecast sales for a store located at the site. Once the trade area is defined, the retailer can use several different information sources to develop a detailed understanding of the nature of consumers in the site's trade area.

Trade Area

A trade area is a contiguous geographic area that accounts for the majority of a store's sales and customers. Trade areas can be divided into two or three zones. Such trade areas are called **polygons** because their boundaries conform to streets and other map features. The zones' exact definitions should be flexible to account for particular areas' nuances.

The **primary zone** is the geographic area from which the store or shopping centre derives 60 to 65 percent of its customers. The **secondary zone** is the geographic area of secondary importance in terms of customer sales, generating about 20 percent of a store's sales. The **tertiary zone** (the outermost ring) includes customers who occasionally shop at the store or shopping centre. There are several reasons for the tertiary zone. First, these customers may lack adequate retail facilities closer to home. Second, there are excellent highway systems to the store or centre so that customers can get there easily. Third, customers may drive near the store or centre on the way to or from work. Finally, customers are drawn to the store or centre because it is in or near a tourist area.

cumulative attraction The principle that a cluster of similar and complementary retailing activities will generally have greater drawing power than isolated stores that engage in the same retailing activities.

polygons Trade areas whose boundaries conform to streets and other map features rather than being concentric circles.

primary zone The geographic area from which the store or shopping centre derives 60 to 65 percent of its customers; also called *primary trade area.*

secondary zone The geographic area of secondary importance in terms of customer sales, generating about 20 percent of a store's sales; also called *secondary trade area.*

tertiary zone The outermost ring of a trade area that includes customers who occasionally shop at the store or shopping centre; also called *tertiary trade area.*

A 7-Eleven convenience store's trade area is small, possibly only a kilometre or two, compared to a Sears store that may draw customers from 50 kilometres away. **(left):** © McGraw-Hill Education/Andrew Resek; **(right):** © Kevinbrine | Dreamstime.com.

Factors Defining Trade Areas The actual boundaries of a trade area are determined by the store's accessibility, natural and physical barriers, type of shopping area, type of store, and competition. Driving time is a useful criterion for defining trade areas because the time it takes to get to a particular shopping area is more important to the potential customer than distance. For example, driving to the retailer's location might take 5 minutes for those in the primary trade area, 10 minutes for those in the secondary trade area, and 20 minutes for those in the tertiary trade area.

Trade area size is also influenced by the type of store or shopping area. A 7-Eleven convenience store's trade area, for example, may extend less than a kilometre, whereas a category specialist such as Toys "R" Us may draw customers from 50 kilometres away. The difference is due to the nature of the merchandise sold and the total size of the assortment offered. Convenience stores succeed because customers can buy products such as milk and bread quickly and easily. If customers must drive great distances, the store is no longer convenient. Category specialists offer a large choice of shopping and specialty products for which customers are willing to put forth additional effort to shop. Thus, customers will generally drive some distance to shop at a category specialist.

Another way of looking at how the type of store influences the size of a trade area is whether it's a destination or a symbiotic store. A destination store is one in which the merchandise, selection, presentation, pricing, or other unique features act as a magnet for customers. A **symbiotic store** is one that does not create its own traffic and whose trade area is determined by the dominant retailer in the shopping centre or retail area. In general, destination stores have larger trade areas than symbiotic stores—people are willing to drive farther to shop there. Hakim Optical would qualify as a destination store due to the exclusive nature of its merchandise. Other examples of destination stores are anchor stores in shopping centres, such as grocery stores or department stores; certain specialty stores, such as RadioShack and Polo/Ralph Lauren; category killers, such as Staples; and some service providers, such as movie theatres.

The level of competition also affects the size and shape of a trade area for a particular store. If two convenience food stores are too close together, their respective trade areas will shrink since they offer the same merchandise. On the other hand, Hakim Optical is one of several optical shops in this business district. Having similar shopping goods stores in the same vicinity generally expands the trade area boundaries; more people are drawn to the area to shop because of its expanded selection. Additionally, a retailer's trade area is limited by a large regional shopping centre that has several stores carrying similar merchandise.

Sources of Information

Three types of information are required to define a trade area:

- Retailers must determine how many people are in the trade area and where they live. For this, retailers use a technique known as *customer spotting*.

symbiotic store A store that does not create its own traffic and whose trade area is determined by the dominant retailer in the shopping centre or retail area; also called a *parasite store*.

- Retailers use the demographic and **geographic information systems (GIS)** data to describe their potential customers in an attempt to assess how much they will buy in the proposed trade area.

- Retailers use the Internet and other published sources to assess their competition. In strongly competitive trade areas, a retailer can expect to achieve a smaller piece of the total market potential for a particular type of merchandise or store.

Customer Spotting The purpose of the customer spotting technique is to spot, or locate, the residences of customers for a store or shopping centre.[6] Data specific to a retailer's customers are usually obtained from information from credit card or cheque purchases or from customer loyalty programs. Retailers can also collect this information manually as part of the checkout process.

Another method is to note automobile licence plates in the parking lot and trace them to the owner by purchasing the information from governments or private research companies. A word of caution, however: This method is thought to be inaccurate and is illegal in some areas. Experts believe that at least 500 plates are necessary to provide a good sample. The plates can be matched against a national vehicle registration database and summarize where the vehicles originate. This approach may, however, be the easiest way to understand the trade area of competitors.

The data collected from customer spotting can be processed in two ways: by manually plotting the location of each customer on a map, or by using a GIS system. Once the customers are spotted, the retailer can delineate a trade area. This process involves a lot of subjectivity, so the guidelines presented earlier in this chapter are helpful.

Statistics Canada A census is taken every five years in Canada. The population of each census tract area can range from 2500 to 8000 people, but the preferred average is 4000 people; city cores will have a higher population density. In Canada, there are 25 census metropolitan areas (CMAs) across the country.

In the census, each household in the country is counted to determine the number of persons per household, household relationships, sex, race, age, and marital status. The information is detailed under the following themes: population, education, earnings, work, income, families, dwellings, and religion. Detailed census information is also available through *GeoPost Plus,* which can be purchased from Canada Post. A report on each building identifies the number of housing units at the address, whether the dwelling is owned or rented, whether the dwelling is owner-occupied, the housing value, the rent, and the vacancy status.

Additional information can be obtained from private companies such as Environics Analytics (http://www.environicsanalytics.ca) (see Exhibit 5–4).

geographic information system (GIS) Computerized systems that enable analysts to visualize information about their customers' demographics, buying behaviour, and other data in a map format.

Location of Consumer Market Segments There are hundreds of private companies specializing in providing retailers with information that will help them make better store-location decisions. Some, known as *data and analytics providers,* such as Environics Analytics, specialize in developing and enhancing census and marketing research data in a format that's easy to understand, easy and quick to obtain, and relatively inexpensive. Since the data from a national census will eventually be dated, these firms construct computer models to generate estimates of current and future population projections, which can then be integrated with behavioural and psychographic characteristics to predict consumer spending.

Measuring Competition Estimating the demand for a retailer's products is a critical success factor, but it tells only half the story. It's equally important to determine the level of competition in the trade area. Earlier in this chapter, we concluded that either a saturated or an understored trade area offers a potentially good location opportunity, but that retailers should avoid trade areas that are overstored. How can a retailer such as Hakim Optical determine the level of saturation of the trade area for a potential new location? In other words, what's the level of trade area competition?

One of the most powerful methods of measuring competition is over the Internet.[7] Most websites list not only all current locations, but future sites as well. Demographic information for prospective sales in other countries might eliminate the need for an in-person visit. A more traditional method of accessing competitive information is through the Yellow Pages of the telephone book. This information is also available through their online search directory. Other sources of competitive information are directories published by trade associations, chambers of commerce, the International Council of Shopping

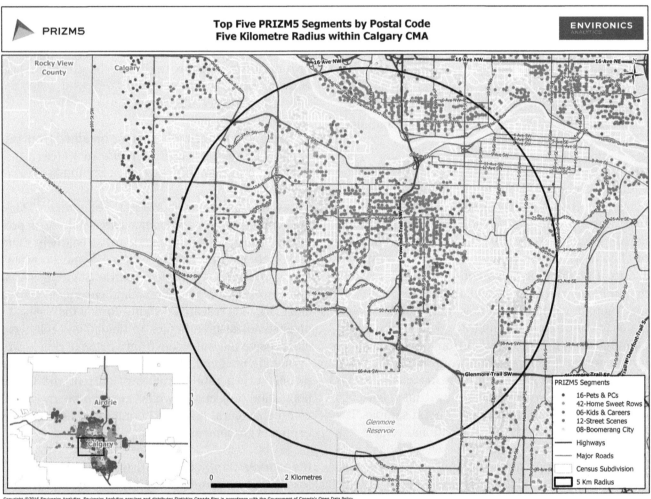

Source: Environics Analytics (www.environicsanalytics.ca).

Centres (shopping centres), the Urban Land Institute (shopping centres), local newspaper advertising departments, municipal and provincial governments, specialized trade magazines, and list brokers.

A relatively easy way to determine level of competition is to calculate the total square footage of retail space devoted to a type of store per household. For example, published sources can estimate the total square feet devoted to optical retailers in their trade area and divide it by the number of households. The higher the ratio, the higher the level of competition will be. Of course, there's no substitute for personal visits, as observation will lend valuable insight to gathering competitive intelligence.

Methods of Estimating Demand

A number of complementary analytical methods are used to estimate the demand for a new store.

One of the most widely used techniques, the analogue approach, was first developed by William Applebaum for the Kroger Company in the 1930s. A more formalized statistical version of the analogue approach uses regression analysis. A third approach, known as Huff's gravity model, is based on Newton's law of gravity. We discuss these location analysis methods below.

The Analogue Approach

The analogue approach could just as easily be called the *similar store approach*. Suppose European Optical wants to open a new location in the southeast quadrant of Calgary, AB. Since its current location in southwest

DID YOU KNOW?

Esri (one of the top international GIS companies) software leverages somewhere between $16 and $19 billion in sales of data, hardware and services. Technology companies put together leverage about $60–75 billion, making the total closer to the $100-billion mark.[8]

Calgary has been very successful, it would like to find a location whose trade area has similar characteristics. It would estimate the size and customer demographic characteristics of its current trade area and then attempt to match those characteristics to new potential locations. Thus, knowledge of customer demographics, the competition, and sales of currently operating stores can be used to predict the size and sales potential of a new location.

Using the analogue approach, European Optical would undertake the following steps:

- Complete a competitive analysis of the optional sites to estimate potential sales for the store sites.

- Define the current trade area based on density of customers to the store, drive zones, major roads, and natural or manmade barriers.

- Determine the trade area characteristics based on demographic research and psychographic profiles.

- Match the characteristics of the current trade area with the potential new store locations to determine the best site.

Step 1: Conduct Competitive Analysis to Estimate Potential Sales Unlike other optical stores, European Optical carries a very exclusive merchandise selection. In general, the higher the trade area potential, the lower the relative competition will be (see Exhibits 5–5 and 5–6).

Step 2: Define the Current Trade Area On the basis of customer spotting data gathered from a data warehouse of current customers, a trade area map can be generated. The trade area map can also be defined based on drive times: 5 minutes for the primary trade area, 10 minutes for the secondary

trade area, and 20 minutes for the tertiary trade area. Major highways and heavily-travelled roads will bring traffic to the area but can also divide a trade area, as can a river or bridge, and may limit trade area potential.

Because European Optical is in a residential district, the trade area will be smaller than it would be if located in a regional shopping centre. The regional shopping centre has complementary stores that attract more people to the area to shop because of the expanded selection of retailers and restaurants.

Step 3: Determine Trade Area Characteristics The Environics Analytics map (see Exhibit 5–4) includes data on population, demographics, marketplace preferences, psychographics, and behavioural characteristics. As we said earlier in this chapter, it is just as important to look at consumer lifestyles or psychographics as it is to examine their demographics. We know that European Optical's trade area is generally affluent, but are the residents the kind of people who would purchase its upscale fashion eyewear?

Exhibit 5–5 summarizes the most prominent lifestyle report for the five-kilometre ring surrounding European Optical. These clusters, described in Exhibit 5–6, indicate an interesting mix of potential customers. Of the five profiles, Urban Digerati, Street Scenes, and Boomerang City clusters account for approximately 32.6 percent of the population and should be drawn to European Optical's high-fashion product lines. Generally, the reports show that the area is affluent and is therefore ideal for selling exclusive and expensive eyewear.

Step 4: Match Characteristics of Current Store with Potential New Store's Location to Determine the Best Site Now that the trade area for European Optical's existing store is defined, the information can be used to choose a new store location. The trick is to find a location whose market area is similar or analogous to its existing store. On the basis of the factors affecting demand described earlier in the chapter, it can be concluded that the five factors that contribute most to the success of European Optical's current location are high income, predominantly white-collar occupations, relatively large percentage of older residents, upscale profile, and relatively low competition for expensive, high-fashion eyewear.

Exhibit 5–7 compares European Optical's current location with four potential locations on these five factors. These locations are pictured in Exhibit 5–8.

Exhibit 5–5
Neighbourhood Lifestyle Clusters for Five-Kilometre Ring Surrounding European Optical

Cluster Classification	Population Count in Five-Kilometer Ring	Percentage of Population in Each Classification
Urban Digerati	6831	6.98
Grads & Pads	18 632	19.04
New World Symphony	7198	7.36
Street Scenes	16 647	17.01
Boomerang City	8416	8.60

Source: Environics Analytics (http://www.environicsanalytics.ca).

Exhibit 5-6
Descriptions of Largest Clusters Surrounding Current European Optical Location

Urban Digerati

Average household Income–$105 803 The most urban of all the segments, Urban Digerati, is a collection of younger, tech-savvy singles concentrated in the downtown apartment buildings of two cities: Toronto and Montreal. Reflecting two emerging demographic trends—the increasing urbanization of Canada and the growth of high-rise neighbourhoods—Urban Digerati offers residents a vibrant vertical world, with bedrooms in the clouds and a lively social scene on the ground. Upper-middle-income, highly educated, and culturally diverse, Urban Digerati neighbourhoods are typically filled with recently built high-rise apartments and condos located near fitness clubs, clothing boutiques, and all types of bars—from wine to coffee to microbrew. Because many residents have yet to start families, they have the time and discretionary income to pursue active social lives, going dancing and bar-hopping, and hitting film festivals and food and wine shows. And they like to look good while on the social scene, taking aerobics and Pilates classes and purchasing the latest fashions and electronics online. But they're not simply acquisitive materialists; many are globally conscious consumers who support the arts and are actively involved in their communities.

In Urban Digerati, residents have used their higher education—more than half hold university degrees—to pursue technology- and information-intensive lifestyles. Their average income, above six figures, allows them to buy tech devices and download plenty of apps. These are the Canadians who sleep with their phones and go online to bank, shop, invest, look for a job, and check out dating services. Digitally-obsessed, they spend less time with printed newspapers and magazines—unless they're alternative weeklies or tech-focused magazines—but stay on top of the latest trends in popular culture by reading online magazines, restaurant guides, and fashion and beauty blogs.

New World Symphony

Average household Income–$82 866 New World Symphony is one of the most culturally diverse of Canada's lifestyles. In this segment, 49 different languages are spoken at home at rates that are more than twice the national average for each language. Often the first neighbourhood for new immigrants, this segment reflects Canada's increasing diversity and urbanization in recent years. More than 40 percent of segment members are foreign born, drawn to city neighbourhoods that are diverse beyond their diversity. New World Symphony consists of singles and couples, old and young, condo owners and apartment renters; half live in high-rise buildings. No one's particularly wealthy, but residents manage to live decently by stretching their lower-middle incomes. They have high rates for listening to classical and jazz music, attending basketball and baseball games, and frequenting live theatre and art galleries. Befitting the wide range in ages, this segment makes a strong market for health club memberships and Pilates, as well as collecting stamps, home shows, and senior citizen's magazines. But nearly everyone goes to the local movie theatres, often enjoying film festivals as well.

Even with the presence of so many languages, New World Symphony neighbourhoods have above-average rates for consuming most media, and members are particularly fond of daily newspapers, magazines, and online channels. They have high rates for reading home décor and news magazines, listening to talk/call-in shows on the radio, and watching soccer, basketball, and infomercials on TV. This is an educated segment—nearly 34 percent have gone to university—and a disproportionate number hold jobs in business, science, and information industries. They also are fluent in digital media, going online to read newspapers, read restaurant reviews, invest in stocks, and purchase group coupons. These newcomers use their smartphones to access newspaper sites and download mobile coupons, and for many, the Internet is their top source for news in their native language.

Grads & Pads

Average household Income–$69 170 The youngest lifestyle type in Canada, Grads & Pads is a collection of young city dwellers living near universities. Present since 2004, segment members have become slightly younger, less affluent, and more likely to be living in low-rise apartments than in the past. But it's still a progressive mix of well-educated singles and couples, students and recent grads, white-collar professionals and service workers—all living in apartments within a short commute to work by public transit or foot. Their incomes aren't high, but these young adults just entering the workforce enjoy the freedom of spending their first paycheques solely on themselves. With two-thirds of the adults unattached, Grads & Pads residents are nightowls who frequent bars, nightclubs, and art galleries. They stay active by jogging, mountain biking, playing squash, and working out at health clubs. They're also the kind of young consumers who, to balance their alcohol-fuelled partying, are health-conscious foodies who prefer organic veggies and patronize grocery stores that offer sustainably sourced products.

Street Scenes

Average household Income–$118 791 Located on the fringes of the downtown core, Street Scenes attracts younger singles and families to well-kept streets with their aging houses, duplexes, and semi-detached houses. Many residents are well educated—nearly 40 percent graduated from a university—with white-collar jobs and active leisure lives. While residents here have above-average incomes, their spending power appears greater because so many households are childless. They open their wallets for music, books, health and beauty items, and consumer electronics. Many engage in athletic activities such as cycling, aerobics, golfing, and downhill skiing. And they frequent stores offering sporting goods and athletic wear such as Mountain Equipment Co-op, Lululemon and Play It Again Sports. Living close to city entertainment districts, they have high rates for going to bars, nightclubs, art galleries, theatres, pop music concerts, and film festivals. They're big fans of professional sports, attending basketball and football games at high rates. Status conscious, they score high for the value of Ostentatious Consumption, which they demonstrate by acquiring the latest in fashion, food, and wine.

Grads & Pads is a magnet for young and footloose singles: nearly a third have moved into their current apartments within the past year. They're also frequent travellers who occasionally spend a lot of money on adventurous trips to Europe, Latin America, and the Middle East. Back home, they're rapidly tuning out traditional media, watching relatively few TV shows and rarely listening to the radio. They're selective in their print media, reading alternative weekly publications and newspapers for the national news and fashion and lifestyle coverage. Few segments exhibit higher Internet use, with residents visiting news, entertainment, and fashion websites. They use their smartphones for texting, updating their status on social media, and finding a date. And they respond to messages that appeal to their progressive views—whether the subject is marijuana legalization or the latest tablet.

Found in big cities like Toronto and Calgary, Street Scenes brings together a unique mix of cultures and households, all in a vibrant city setting: singles and families, single-detached, semi-detached, and row houses, immigrants from Asian and European countries, and adults between 25 and 54. Not surprisingly, their media tastes are just as varied. Many are print fans who read alternative weeklies, computer, science and technology magazines, and newspaper sections that cover business and financial issues. They like to spend their vacation time travelling abroad, whether it's to the United Kingdom, Australia, or the Middle East. But these young Canadians are most comfortable going online to visit magazine websites, research products, listen to streaming audio, or stay connected to friends through LinkedIn.

Boomerang City

Average household Income—$134 693 Reflecting the recent demographic trend of older children still living at home, Boomerang City consists of middle-aged families and older couples aging in place in urban neighbourhoods. A third of the children at home are over the age of 20, and three-quarters of the families live in single-detached homes lining city streets. Found in a number of large cities, including Vancouver, Calgary, Winnipeg, and Toronto, these adults tend to be Baby Boomers who have parlayed good educations—more than 40 percent have graduated or attended university—into well-paying jobs in science, education, government, and the arts. Many maintain active social lives, going to the theatre and ballet, visiting art galleries and music festivals, and frequenting garden and boat shows. And many of these multi-generational households are health conscious, joining health clubs and signing up for Pilates and yoga classes. Because this segment includes so many young adults who have returned to their childhood homes or simply never left, surveys reveal the popularity of a number of youth-centred activities—from soccer and adventure sports to basketball and football—though it's possible the segment's age-denying Boomer parents are enjoying these sports, too. Boomerang City is an engaged and centred group that accepts non-traditional Flexible Families and seeks relationships of equality with young people (Equal Relationship with Youth). With their solid educations and high-paying jobs that give them meaning (Fulfillment Through Work), these Canadians enjoy accessing the world through technology (Enthusiasm for Technology). Many have an Attraction for Crowds and are active participants in their local communities (Community Involvement). They are health conscious, focusing on diet and exercise in an Effort Toward Health. They also embrace living in a cultural mosaic (Culture Sampling), seeking to demonstrate their individuality while embracing opportunities to interact with culturally diverse peers (Pursuit of Originality, Social Learning). With their multi-generational households, their consumer tastes range widely; some members seek practical products to cope with the Time Stress from busy lives; others seek new and modern products in a Pursuit of Novelty and as a way to express Personal Creativity. They look for favourite brands that convey their personality (Importance of Brand, Personal Expression) in part as a means to satisfy their Need for Status Recognition.

Source: Environics Analytics (http://www.environicsanalytics.ca).

Exhibit 5–7

Descriptions of European Optical and Four Potential Locations' Trade Areas

Store Location	Average Household Income (Projected)	White-Collar Occupations	Percentage Residents Age 45 and Over (Projected)	Predominant Profile	Level of Competition
European Optical	$100 000 plus	High	50%	Street Scene and Boomerang City	Low
Site A	85 000	Middle	10	Grads and Pads	Medium
Site B	60 000	Low	31	New World Symphony	Low
Site C	105 000	High	45	Boomerang City	High
Site D	100 000 plus	High	65	Street Scene	Medium

Average household income is estimated projections based on current Stats Canada trends. Level of white-collar occupations is estimated from data in Exhibit 5–6. Percentage of residents 45 years old and over is estimated from Exhibit 5–6. Level of competition was subjectively determined.

Exhibit 5–8

Potential locations for a European Optical Store

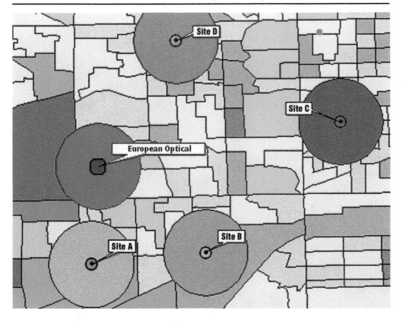

The potential customers of **Site A** typically have white-collar occupations; they have relatively good incomes and tend to support more than one generation, so expensive eyewear may not be a priority purchase. Finally, there's a medium level of competition in the area.

The residents surrounding **Site B** have moderate incomes. Even though competition would be low, these customers are more interested in value than in fashion.

Huff gravity model A trade area analysis model used to determine the probability that a customer residing in a particular area will shop at a particular store or shopping centre.

Site C has strong potential since the residents in the area have a mix of young and middle aged consumers with sufficient disposable income. These

segments also seems to have an interest in fashion. Although they would appreciate European Optical's fashionable assortment, other high-end optical stores are entrenched in the area.

Site D is the best location for European Optical. These "street scene" couples are primarily "empty nesters" and are sophisticated consumers of adult luxuries such as high-fashion eyewear.

Unfortunately, finding analogous situations isn't always as easy as in this example. The weaker the analogy, the more difficult the location decision will be. When a retailer has a relatively small number of outlets (say, 20 or fewer), the analogue approach is often best. Even retailers with just one outlet can use the analogue approach. As the number of stores increases, it becomes more difficult for the analyst to organize the data in a meaningful way. More analytical approaches are necessary.

Lo4 Estimating Potential Sales for a Store

Three approaches for using the information about the trade area to estimate the potential sales for a store at the location are (1) gravitational theory, (2) regression analysis, and (3) the analogue method.

Gravitational Theories

The **Huff gravity model**[9] for estimating the sales of a retail store is based on the concept of gravity: Consumers are attracted to a store location just like Newton's falling apple was attracted to the Earth. In this model, the force of the attraction is based on two factors: the size of the store (larger stores have more pulling power) and the time it takes to travel to the store (stores that take more time to get to have less pulling power). The mathematical formula to predict the probability of a customer going to a specific store location is as follows:

$$P_{ij} = \frac{S_j \div T_{ij}^b}{\sum\limits_{j=1}^{n} S_j \div T_{ij}^b}$$

P_{ij} = probability that customer i shops at location j
S_j = size of the store at location j
T_{ij} = travel time for customer i to get to location j
λ = parameter used to estimate the effect of travel time on different kinds of shopping trips
b = distance decay parameter approximated from empirical observations
n = number of different shopping locations

The formula indicates that the larger the size (S_j) of the store compared with competing stores' sizes, the greater the probability that a customer will shop at the location. A larger size is generally more attractive in consumers' eyes because it means more merchandise assortment and variety. Travel time or distance (T_{ij}) has the opposite effect on the probability that a consumer will shop at the location. The greater the travel time or distance to the consumer, compared with that of competing locations, the lower the probability that the consumer will shop at the location. Generally, customers would rather shop at a close store rather than a distant one.

The exponent λ reflects the relative effect of travel time versus store size. When λ is equal to 1, store size and travel time have an equal but opposite effect on the probability of a consumer shopping at a store location. When λ is greater than 1, travel time has a greater effect, and when λ is less than 1, store size has a greater effect. The value of λ is affected by the nature of the shopping trips consumers generally take when visiting the specific type of store. For instance, travel time or distance is generally more important for convenience goods than for shopping goods because people are less willing to travel a great distance for a litre of milk than

they are for a new pair of shoes. Thus, a larger value for λ is assigned if the store being studied specializes in convenience shopping trips rather than comparison shopping trips. The value of λ is usually estimated statistically using data that describe shopping patterns at existing stores.

To illustrate the use of the Huff model, consider the situations shown in Exhibit 5–9. A small town has two communities: Rock Creek and Oak Hammock. The town currently has one 5000 square-foot drugstore with annual sales of $8 million, $3 million of which come from Oak Hammock residents and $5 million from Rock Creek residents. A competitive chain is considering opening a 10 000 square-foot store. As the exhibit illustrates, the driving time for the average Rock Creek resident to the existing store is 10 minutes, but it would be only 5 minutes to the new store. In contrast, the driving time for the typical Oak Hammock resident to the existing drugstore is 5 minutes and would be 15 minutes to the new store. Based on its past experience, the drugstore chain has found that λ equals 2 for its store locations. Using the Huff formula, the probability of a Rock Creek resident shopping at the new location, P_{RC}, is

$$P_{RC} = \frac{10\ 000/5^2}{10\ 000/5^2 + 5000/10^2} = .889$$

The probability of Oak Hammock residents shopping at the new location, P_{OH}, is

$$P_{OH} = \frac{10\ 000/15^2}{10\ 000/15^2 + 5000/5^2} = .182$$

The expected sales (probability of patronage times market size) for the new location thus would be

$(.889 \times \$5\ \text{million}) + (.182 \times \$3\ \text{million}) = \$4\ 991\ 000$

Exhibit 5–9

Application of Huff Gravity Models for Estimating Store Sales

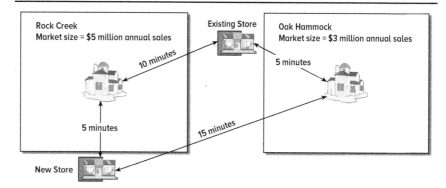

This simple application assumes that the market size for drugstores in the community will remain the same at $8 million with the addition of the new store. We also could have considered that two drugstores would increase the total size of the market. In addition, rather than do the calculations for the average customer located in the middle of each community, we could have calculated the probabilities that each customer in the two communities would go to the new location.

Even though the Huff gravity model considers only two factors affecting store sales—travel time and store size—its predictions are quite accurate because these two factors typically have the greatest effect on store choice.[10]

A marketer named William J. Reilly developed a calculation called **Reilly's law of retail gravitation**. This theory is based on the similar premise as Huff's gravity model in the sense that there is a point where consumers will travel from to obtain goods and services. He believed consumers would travel longer distances to larger retail centres due to the greater attraction they present to customers.

In Reilly's theory, the calculation looks like this:

$$\text{Mab} = \frac{\text{Dab}}{1 + \sqrt{\frac{\text{Pb}}{\text{Pa}}}}$$

$\text{M}ab$ = distance from city a to breaking point or a boundary between the two areas
$\text{D}ab$ = distance in kilometres along a major roadway between cities (communities) A and B
P_a = population of city (community) A
P_b = population of city (community) B

The following is an example showing how a catchment area boundary is drawn using Reilly's law of retail gravitation.

A city (A) has a population of 350 000, and a city (B) has a population of 175 000. City A is 85 kilometres from city B. One would think that the point of indifference between the two cities would be halfway between the two cities (42.5 km). However, the point of indifference is 49.8 kilometres away from city A and 35.2 kilometres away from city B (see Exhibit 5-10).

This method of analysis can provide an idea of the sphere of influence. Breaking points for other surrounding cities or communities can be calculated.

Reilly's law of retail gravitation A model used in trade area analysis to define the relative ability of two cities to attract customers from the area between them.

regression analysis A statistical approach based on the assumption that factors that affect the sales of existing stores in a chain will have the same impact on stores located at new sites.

Exhibit 5–10
Reilly's Law of Retail Gravitation

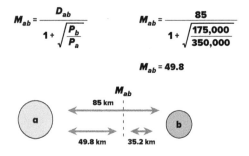

This sphere of influence can be quantified by drawing a series of these breaking points from the other nearby cities (C and D) or communities to form a catchment area boundary.

The regression approach discussed in the next section provides a way to incorporate additional factors into the sales forecast for a store under consideration.

Regression Analysis

The **regression analysis** approach is based on the assumption that factors that affect the sales of existing stores in a chain will have the same impact on stores located at new sites being considered. When using this approach, the retailer employs a technique called multiple regression to estimate a statistical model that predicts sales at existing store locations. The technique can consider the effects of the wide range of factors discussed in this chapter, including site characteristics, such as visibility and access, and characteristics of the trade area, such as demographics and lifestyle segments.

Consider the following example: A chain of sporting goods stores has analyzed the factors affecting sales in its existing stores and found that the following model is the best predictor of store sales (the weights for the factors, such as 275 for the number of households, are estimated using multiple regression):

Store sales = 275 × number of households in trade area (15-minute drive time)
+ 1 800 000 × percentage of households in trade area in children under 15 years of age
+ 2 000 000 × percentage of households in trade area in Tapestry segment "aspiring young"
+ 8 × shopping centre square feet
+ 250 000 if visible from the street
+ 300 000 if Walmart in centre

The sporting goods chain is considering the following two locations:

Variable	Location A	Location B
Households within 15-minute drive time	11 000	15 000
% of households with children under 15 years old	70%	20%
% of households in aspiring young geodemographic segment	60%	10%
Sq ft of shopping centre	200 000	250 000
Visible from street	yes	no
Walmart in shopping centre	yes	no

Using the statistical model, the forecasted sales for location A are:

$$
\begin{aligned}
\text{Store sales at location A} = {} & 275 \times 11\,000 \\
& + 1\,800\,000 \times .7 \\
& + 2\,000\,000 \times .6 \\
& + 8 \times 200\,000 \\
& + 250\,000 \\
& + 300\,000 \\
= {} & \$7\,635\,000
\end{aligned}
$$

And forecasted sales for location B are:

$$
\begin{aligned}
\text{Store sales at location B} = {} & 275 \times 15\,000 \\
& + 1\,800\,000 \times .2 \\
& + 2\,000\,000 \times .1 \\
& + 8 \times 250\,000 \\
= {} & \$6\,685\,000
\end{aligned}
$$

Note that location A has greater forecasted sales, even though it has a smaller trading area population and shopping centre size, because the profile of its target market fits the profile of the trade area better.

Analogue Approach

As discussed, to develop a regression model, a retailer needs data about the trade area and site characteristics from a large number of stores. Because small chains cannot use the regression approach, they use the similar but more subjective analogue approach. When using the **analogue approach**, the retailer simply describes the site and trade area characteristics for its most successful stores and attempts to find a site with similar characteristics.

DID YOU KNOW?

Quebec's European influence within North America makes it an ideal place for European companies to launch new products and a logical location from which North American companies can expand into Europe.[11]

Suppose European Optical was deciding to open another location, this time in Vancouver and had four potential sites as identified in Column 1 of Exhibit 5–11. Using the analogue approach, the retailer undertakes the following steps to estimate potential sales for a store site.

First, estimate the number of eyeglasses sold per person per year in Column 2. The area population is identified in Column 3 (this includes the number of your targeted customers living in the area); these numbers can be taken from Statistics Canada or *Financial Post Markets*. Next, estimate the trade area potential by multiplying Column 2 by Column 3. This will identify the total eyeglasses potential for the area in Column 4.

Column 5 is the rough estimates of the number of eyeglasses sold in the trade areas, based on visits to the competitive stores. Column 6 represents the unit sales potential for eyeglasses in the trade areas (Column 4 minus Column 5). To calculate the trade area potential penetration, divide Column 6 by Column 4. For instance, because the total eyeglasses potential for the current Vancouver store trade area is 17 196 pairs and an additional 9646 pairs could be sold in that trade area, 56.09 percent of the eyeglasses market in the area remains untapped.

In general, the higher the trade area potential, the lower the relative competition will be. Column 8, the relative level of competition, is subjectively estimated on the basis of Column 7. According to the information in Exhibit 5–11, the best location for the new optical store would be Site B. The trade area potential is high and the competition is low.

Choosing the Best Method(s) In any decision, the more information that's available, the better the outcome is likely to be. This is true for research in general and location analysis in particular. Therefore, if a combination of techniques is applied and the same conclusion is reached, the retailer should have more confidence in the decision.

Some methods used for analyzing trade areas are better in certain situations, however. The analogue and gravitational approaches are best when the number of stores with obtainable data is small, usually fewer than 30. These approaches can

analogue approach A method of trade area analysis, also known as the *similar store* or *mapping approach,* that is divided into four steps: (1) describing the current trade areas through the technique of customer spotting; (2) plotting the customers on a map; (3) defining the primary, secondary, and tertiary area zones; and (4) matching the characteristics of stores in the trade areas with the potential new store to estimate its sales potential.

Exhibit 5–11
Competitive Analysis of Potential Locations

Trade Area (1)	Eyeglasses/ Year/ Person (2)	Trade Area Population (3)	Total Eyeglasses Potential (4)	Estimated Eyeglasses Sold (5)	Trade Area Potential Units (6)	Trade Area Potential Percentage (7)	Relative Level of Competition (8)
Vancouver	0.2	85 979	17 196	7 550	9 646	56.09%	Low
Site A	0.2	91 683	18 338	15 800	2 537	13.83	Medium
Site B	0.2	101 972	20 394	12 580	7 814	38.32	Low
Site C	0.2	60 200	12 040	11 300	740	6.15	High
Site D	0.2	81 390	16 278	13 300	2 978	18.29	Medium

shopping centre A group of retail and other commercial establishments that is planned, developed, owned, and managed as a single property.

strip centre A shopping centre that usually has parking directly in front of the stores and does not have enclosed walkways linking the stores.

mall A shopping centre with a pedestrian focus where customers park in outlying areas and walk to the stores.

also be used by small retailers. The regression approach, on the other hand, is best when there are multiple variables expected to explain sales, since it's hard to keep track of multiple predictor variables when using a manual system such as the analogue approach. Also, the Huff gravity model and Reilly's law of retail gravitation explicitly consider the attractiveness of competition and customers' distance or travel time to the store or shopping centre in question. Finally, since Huff's gravity model and Reilly's law usually do not use demographic variables, it's particularly important to use them in conjunction with the analogue or regression methods.

There are three trends that will shape site selection research in the next few decades.[12] First, it will be easier to collect and store data on customers in data warehouses. Second, advanced statistical modelling techniques, such as CHAID (chi square automatic interaction detection) and spatial allocation models, will become more popular. Finally, geographic information systems will become more sophisticated and at the same time more accessible to users.

Lo5 Types of Locations

Retailers have three basic types of locations to choose from: a shopping centre, a city or town location, or a freestanding location. Retailers can also locate in a non-traditional location such as an airport or within another store. The following sections describe each type of location and present criteria for choosing a particular location type.

Shopping Centres

From the 1950s through the 1980s, suburban shopping centres grew as populations shifted to the suburbs. Large shopping centres provide huge assortments for consumers. Combining many stores under one roof creates a synergy that attracts more customers than if the stores had separate locations. It's not uncommon, for instance, for a store's sales to increase after a competing store enters a shopping centre.

The term *shopping centre* has been evolving since the early 1950s. A **shopping centre** is a group of retail and other commercial establishments that is planned, developed, owned, and managed as a single property. The two main configurations of shopping centres are strip centres and enclosed malls. A **strip centre** is a shopping centre that usually has parking directly in front of the stores. A **mall**, on the other hand, is a shopping centre where customers park in outlying areas and walk to the stores. Traditional malls are enclosed, with a climate-controlled walkway between two facing strips of stores. The main shopping centre types are defined in Exhibit 5–12.

The developer and shopping centre management carefully select a set of retailers that are complementary; this tenant mix is planned to attract a specific market segment to the shopping centre. The goal of a successful tenant mix is to provide customers with a one-stop shopping experience by providing a well-balanced assortment of product offerings including retailers, services, and entertainment.

The shopping centre management maintains the common facilities (referred to as common area maintenance [CAM]), such as the parking area, and is

Exhibit 5–12
Shopping Centre Definitions

Type	Concept	Square Feet	Number of Anchors	Types of Anchors	Trade Area*
Strip Centres					
Traditional	General merchandise; convenience	30 000–350 000	One or more	Discount; supermarket; drug; home improvement; large specialty discount apparel	3–7 square miles
Power	Category-dominant anchors; few small tenants	250 000–600 000	Three or more	Category specialist; home improvement; discount; warehouse club; off-price	5–10 square miles
Shopping Malls					
Regional	General merchandise; fashion (typically enclosed)	400 000–800 000	Two or more	Department; discount; fashion apparel; other specialty stores	5–15 square miles
Superregional	Similar to regional but has more variety and assortment	800 000+	Three or more	Department; discount; fashion apparel; other specialty stores	5–25 square miles
Lifestyle	Higher-end, fashion-oriented	Variable	N/A	Higher-end specialty stores and restaurants	5–15 square miles
Fashion/specialty	Higher-end, fashion-oriented	80 000–250 000	N/A	Higher-end fashion and other specialty stores	5–15 square miles
Outlet	Manufacturers' outlet stores	50 000–400 000	N/A	Manufacturer's outlet stores	25–75 square miles
Theme/festival	Leisure; tourist-oriented	80 000–250 000	N/A	Restaurants; entertainment; fashion; other specialty stores	N/A

*The area from which 60 to 80 percent of the centre's sales originate.

responsible for activities such as providing security, parking lot lighting, outdoor signage for the centre, and advertising and special events to attract consumers. The stores in the centre typically pay a negotiated annual fee based on their size to cover the CAM costs. The shopping centre management can also place restrictions on the operating hours, signage, and even the type of merchandise sold in the stores.

Most shopping centres have at least one or two major retailers, referred to as **anchors**. These retailers are courted by the centre developer because they attract a significant number of consumers and consequently make the centre more appealing to other retailers. To get these anchor retailers to locate in a centre in Canada, developers frequently make special deals, such as reduced lease costs, for the anchor tenants. Anchor tenants can pay between about $5 and $10 a square foot annually, while non-anchor tenants pay up to 10 or 15 times more than those amounts.[14]

In strip centres, supermarkets are typically anchors, whereas department stores traditionally anchor shopping malls. A lifestyle centre may not have anchors, whereas power centres are composed primarily of multiple "anchor" stores. The different types of shopping centres are discussed next.

A **traditional strip centre** is a shopping centre that is designed to provide convenient shopping for the day-to-day needs of consumers in their immediate neighbourhood. Smaller strip centres are typically anchored by a supermarket or a drugstore; the larger strips are anchored by discount stores, off-price stores, or category killers selling such items as apparel, home improvement/furnishings, toys, shoes, pet supplies, electronics, and sporting goods. These anchors are supported by stores offering sundries, food, and a variety of personal services such as barber shops and dry cleaners.

Strip Shopping Centres The primary advantages of strip centres or community shopping centres are that they offer customers convenient locations and easy parking, and they entail relatively low rents for retailers. The primary

DID YOU KNOW?

The largest shopping mall in Canada is West Edmonton Mall. The mall has over 29 million visitors per year and averages $727 in retail sales per square foot.[13]

anchors Major retailers located in a shopping centre.

traditional strip centre A shopping centre that is designed to provide convenience shopping for the day-to-day needs of consumers in their immediate neighbourhood.

power centre Shopping centre that is dominated by several large anchors, including discount stores, off-price stores, warehouse clubs, or category specialists.

disadvantages are that there is no protection from the weather, and they offer less assortment and entertainment options for customers than malls. As a result, strip centres do not attract as many customers as larger shopping centres that rely on community participation.

The strip centres of today have a mix of mom-and-pop stores and national tenants such as A Buck or Two and Shoppers Drug Mart. National chains like these are able to compete effectively in strip centres against their rival stores in malls. They can offer lower prices, partly because of the lower rents, plus their customers can drive right up to the door. New spinoff grocery franchises such as No Frills and Price Chopper are popular with value-conscious consumers and are often located in strip centres.

Power Centres

A **power centre** is a shopping centre that is dominated by several big-box retailers, including discount stores (Walmart), off-price stores (Winners), warehouse clubs (Costco), or category specialists such as Home Depot, Staples, Best Buy, and Toys "R" Us. Unlike traditional strip centres, power centres often include several freestanding (unconnected) anchors and only a minimum number of small specialty tenants. They are typically unenclosed in a strip centre configuration. Many power centres are located near an enclosed shopping mall and are becoming major competition for the shopping centres.

Power centres were virtually unknown before the 1990s, but they have steadily grown in number. Many are now larger than some regional malls and attract customers from a large trade area. Why have they become so popular? First and foremost, their tenants have experienced tremendous growth and prosperity. A power centre is a natural location for these large tenants. They don't want to pay the high rents of regional shopping malls, and they benefit from the synergy of being with other big-box stores. Also, shoppers are seeking value alternatives to the stores found in shopping malls.

Shopping Malls

Shopping malls have several advantages over alternative locations. First, because of the many different types of stores, the merchandise assortments

available within those stores, and the opportunity to combine shopping with entertainment, shopping malls have become the Main Street for today's shoppers. Teenagers hang out and meet friends, older citizens in Nikes get their exercise by walking the malls, and families make trips to the mall a form of entertainment. To enhance the total shopping experience, many malls incorporate food and entertainment such as movies and amusement parks.

The second major advantage of locating in a shopping mall is that the tenant mix can be planned. Shopping mall owners control the number of different types of retailers so that customers can have a one-stop shopping experience with a well-balanced assortment of merchandise. For instance, it's important to have several women's clothing stores in a major mall to draw in customers. Mall managers also attempt to create a complementary tenant mix. They like to have all stores that appeal to certain target markets (such as all upscale specialty clothing stores) located together. Thus, customers know what types of merchandise they can expect to find in a particular mall or location within a mall. In addition, managers strive for a good mix between shopping and specialty goods stores. A strong core of shopping goods stores, such as shoe stores, brings people to the mall. Specialty stores, such as computer software stores, also bring shoppers to the mall. While specialty store customers are in the mall, they will likely be attracted to other stores.

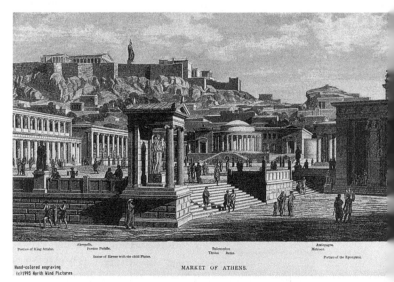

The first shopping centre, a marketplace with retail stores, was the Agora at the foot of the Parthenon in Athens in 600 BCE. It was the centre of all commerce, politics, and entertainment in ancient Greece.

North Wind Picture Archives.

The third advantage of shopping malls is that the retailers and their customers don't have to worry about their external environment. The mall's management takes care of maintenance of common areas. Mall tenants can look forward to a strong level of homogeneity with the other stores. For instance, most major malls enforce uniform hours of operation. Most malls control the external signage used for window displays and sales. Since most shopping malls are enclosed, customers are protected from the Canadian weather.

Although shopping centres are an excellent site option for many retailers, they have some disadvantages. Mall rents are higher than those of some strip centres, freestanding sites, and most central business districts. As a result, retailers that require large stores, such as home improvement centres, typically seek other options. Some tenants may not like mall managers controlling their operations. Mall managers can, for instance, dictate store hours and have strict rules regarding window displays and signage. Finally, competition within shopping centres can be intense. It may be hard for small specialty stores to compete directly with large department stores.

In addition, shopping malls are facing several challenges. First, shopping malls appeal to consumers who have the time to enjoy wandering through stores, punctuated by a leisurely lunch or an afternoon movie. The increasing number of two-income families and families with a single household head is creating more time pressures for consumers, limiting the time they can devote to shopping. Freestanding locations, strip centres, and power centres are more convenient because customers can park in front of a store, go in and buy what they want, and go about their other errands. There is increasing competition from other types of retail location alternatives, such as power and lifestyle centres, catalogues, and the Internet. Many of today's shoppers are looking for value alternatives to stores found in shopping malls. Also, the apparel business, which makes up a large percentage of mall tenants (Exhibit 5–13), has continued to be weak, causing some specialty store chains to close. Finally, many malls are getting old and are in need of major renovation to appeal to consumers.

Exhibit 5–13
Canada's Ten Largest Malls (By ownership of apparel specialty chains, February 1, 2013)

Mall	Apparel Specialty Chains	% Domestic Ownership	% Foreign Ownership
West Edmonton Mall, AB	73	44%	56%
Metropolis, BC	56	61%	39%
Square One, ON	72	56%	44%
Eaton Centre, ON	63	37%	63%
Yorkdale, ON	57	37%	63%
Galeries de la Capitale, QC	61	84%	16%
Bramalea City Centre, ON	60	58%	42%
Pacific Centre, BC	20	30%	70%
Chinook Centre, AB	78	53%	47%
Carrefour Laval, QC	87	71%	29%

According to Trendex research, foreign retailers account for 41 percent of the apparel specialty chains in Canada's ten largest malls.

Source: *Canadian Retailer*, "Canada's Ten Largest Malls," Spring 2013, Volume 23, Issue 2, p. 8. Canadian Retailer, a publication of Retail Council of Canada.

What are they doing about their problems? Some mall owners are turning their centres into traditional town squares with lots of entertainment opportunities.[15] They believe if they can encourage people to spend more time in the mall, they will spend more money there. The owners are renting to non-traditional mall tenants such as dry cleaners, doctors' offices, and even chapels—everything that you would have found in a town square in the 1950s. Others are forging links to their communities by opening wellness centres, libraries, city halls, and children's play areas. In this environment, people can ride the midway, go to a movie, visit the petting zoo, or eat at a theme restaurant.

A more extreme approach to revitalizing a mall is known as demalling.[17] **Demalling** usually involves demolishing a mall's small shops, scrapping its common space and food courts, enlarging the sites once occupied by department stores, and adding more entrances to the parking lot.

Regional Centres A **regional centre** is a shopping mall that provides general merchandise (a large percentage of which

demalling The activity of revitalizing a mall by demolishing a mall's small shops, scrapping its common space and food courts, enlarging the sites once occupied by department stores, and adding more entrances to the parking lot.

regional centre Shopping mall that provides general merchandise (a large percentage of which is apparel) and services in full depth and variety.

One of the world's largest shopping, amusement, and recreation centres is the West Edmonton Mall in Alberta, with 5.3 million square feet of covered space. Image courtesy of West Edmonton Mall.

DID YOU KNOW?

A developer is proposing to build a Lifestyle Mall in the town of Mount Royal, Quebec. It would be 2.5 million square feet and would cost $1.7 billion. It would include such amenities as a water park, a performing arts space with 3000 seats, an indoor cinema complex and outdoor cinema on a green roof, an outdoor skating rink, two hotels, several office towers, as well as restaurants and terraces.[16]

superregional centre Similar to a regional centre, but because of its larger size, it has more anchors and a deeper selection of merchandise, and it draws from a larger population base.

lifestyle centre A shopping centre with an outdoor, traditional streetscape layout with sit-down restaurants and a conglomeration of specialty retailers.

is apparel) and services in full depth and variety. Its main attractions are its anchors, department and discount stores, or fashion specialty stores. A typical regional centre is usually enclosed with an inward orientation of the stores connected by a common walkway, with parking surrounding the outside perimeter.

Superregional Centres
A **superregional centre** is a shopping centre that is similar to a regional centre, but because of its larger size, it has more anchors and a deeper selection of merchandise, and it draws from a larger population base. As with regional centres, the typical configuration is an enclosed mall, frequently with multiple levels.

Canada's largest shopping, amusement, and recreation centre is the West Edmonton Mall in Alberta (top twenty worldwide). It has 5.3 million square feet of covered space, 3.8 million square feet of selling space, more than 800 stores and services, and 110 restaurants. But the mall has more than shopping to attract millions of people a year. It also

sports the Galaxyland Amusement park, a 7.5-acre waterpark, an NHL-size ice arena, submarines, an exact replica of the *Santa Maria* ship, a lagoon, Fantasyland Hotel, a miniature golf course, 26 movie and IMAX theatres, and a casino. Don't worry about parking. It also has the largest parking capacity in the world, enough for 20 000 vehicles.

Located on just under 200 acres north of Toronto, Vaughan Mills features 14 anchor tenants and more than 200 specialty stores, theme restaurants, cinemas, and recreation activities in a 1.1 million square-foot complex. Many of the tenants were the first of their kind in Canada, including Bass Pro Shops Outdoor World, NASCAR SpeedPark, Lucky Strike Lanes, and Hudson's Bay Company's Designer Depot. The centre also features the world's largest Tommy Hilfiger Outlet and the only Holt Renfrew Last Call in Canada. Located at the southeast corner of Highway 400 and Rutherford Road in Vaughan, Ontario, the area is home to 60 percent of Ontario's population (and almost 25 percent of Canada's population), and there are 10 million people within 160 kilometres of the mall (including Buffalo and Niagara Falls, New York). Vaughan Mills is a joint venture between Ivanhoe Cambridge, Canada, and Mills Corp of the United States, and opened in the fall of 2004. It was the first enclosed regional shopping centre build in Canada in more than 16 years.

The design of the mall is innovative and fresh and is based on the design concept "Discover Ontario." The mall is divided into six neighbourhoods based on the themes of lakes, nature, rural living, small towns, city, and fashion. It is estimated that Vaughan Mills and its retailers employ more than 3500 workers on a full- or part-time basis and add approximately $12.5 million in taxes to the local economy annually.[18]

Lifestyle Centres A **lifestyle centre** is an outdoor traditional streetscape layout with sit-down restaurants and a conglomeration of retailers such as Williams-Sonoma, Pottery Barn, and Eddie Bauer. These centres offer shoppers convenience, safety, an optimum tenant mix, and a pleasant atmosphere. Like "Main Street" locations, shoppers go because it's an attractive, energetic place to meet their friends and have fun. Some lifestyle centres consist only of stores and restaurants; some have cinemas and entertainment; and still others mingle retail with homes and offices. Nearly all are located in high-income areas. They have gone into posh neighbourhoods where they depend on a market radius far smaller, but a lot richer, than malls.

Many of the projects are designed to look as though they have been there for decades. Park Place in Barrie, Ontario is an example of a lifestyle centre. This 1.5 million square-foot centre combines commercial office space, retail outlets, entertainment centres, restaurants, bars, and a fitness centre, and is adjacent to the Barrie Molson Centre, home of the Barrie Colts hockey team. High-end retailers are placed alongside big-box discount stores, and green space allows customers to walk between stores on the outside of the centre. Park Place was designed to bring back the fun of shopping.[19]

DID YOU KNOW?

The average income of lifestyle centre customers is about double that of mall shoppers: They visit 2.5 times more often and spend 50 percent more per visit.[20]

Vaughan Mills is where fashion and outlets, plus dining and entertainment, equal something consumers have to experience to believe.
MaximImages/Alamy.

Fashion/Specialty Centres A **fashion/specialty centre** is a shopping centre that is composed mainly of upscale apparel shops, boutiques, and gift shops carrying selected fashions or unique merchandise of high quality and price. These centres need not be anchored, although sometimes gourmet restaurants and theatres can function as anchors. The physical design of these centres is very sophisticated, emphasizing a rich decor and high-quality landscaping.

Fashion/specialty centres are similar to lifestyle centres in terms of the clientele and the types of stores they attract. The difference is that these centres are typically enclosed and are larger than most lifestyle centres. This type of centre is usually found in trade areas having high income levels, in tourist areas, or in some central business districts. Their trade areas may be large because of the specialty nature of the tenants and their products. Customers are more likely to travel great distances to shop for specialty products sold at nationally known shops such as Holt Renfrew and Ralph Lauren/Polo than for other types of goods.

Outlet Centres **Outlet centres** are shopping centres that consist mostly of manufacturers' outlet stores selling their own brands, supposedly at a discount.[21] Outlet centre tenants view this location option as an opportunity to get rid of excess or distressed merchandise, sell more merchandise, and, to a lesser extent, test new merchandise ideas. These centres also sometimes include off-price retailers such as Winners or HomeSense. As a result of the shifting tenant mix in some of these centres, various industry experts now refer to outlet centres as *value centres* or *value megamalls*. Similar to power centres, a strip configuration is most common, although some are enclosed malls, such as Dixie Outlet Mall in Mississauga, Ontario.

Consumer demand for stores in outlet centres is declining. Although customers can shop for an extensive assortment within individual brands and buy below full retail prices every day, they have to deal with broken assortments, distressed or damaged goods, and less convenient locations. Additionally, traditional retailing has become more price-competitive.

Outlet centres have progressed from no-frills warehouses to well-designed buildings with landscaping and food options that make them hard to distinguish from more traditional shopping centres. The newest outlet centres have a strong entertainment component, including movie theatres and theme restaurants, comprising about 15 to 20 percent of the leasable area.[22] Mall developers believe that these entertainment concepts help keep people on the premises longer. Outlet centre tenants have also upgraded their offerings by adding credit, dressing rooms, high-quality fixtures and lighting, and a merchandise return policy.

Outlet centres are often located some distance from regional shopping centres so that outlet tenants don't compete directly for department and specialty store customers, although most manufacturer

fashion/specialty centre A shopping centre that is composed mainly of upscale apparel shops, boutiques, and gift shops carrying selected fashions or unique merchandise of high quality and price.

outlet centres Typically feature stores owned by retail chains or manufacturers that sell excess and out-of-season merchandise at reduced prices.

freestanding site A retail location that is not connected to other retailers.

kiosk A small selling space offering a limited merchandise assortment.

outlets have learned to peacefully coexist with their department and specialty store customers by editing assortments in their outlet stores to minimize overlap. Outlet centres can be located in strong tourist areas. For instance, since shopping is a favourite vacation pastime, and Niagara Falls attracts 15 million tourists per year, the 1.2 million square-foot Factory Outlet megamall in Niagara Falls, New York, is a natural location for an outlet centre. Some centre developers actually organize bus tours to bring people hundreds of kilometres to their malls. As a result, the primary trade area for some outlet centres is 100 kilometres or more.

In August 2013, Premium Outlets, the first of its kind in Canada, opened a 500 000 square-foot mall in Halton Hills west of Toronto. The project is a 50/50 venture of Simon Property Group Inc. and one of the world's largest real estate companies, Ontario-based Calloway Real Estate. The outlet centre houses more than 100 high-quality outlet stores and is seen as the Canadian entry point for selected US retailers and designer brands.[23]

Freestanding Sites Although most retailers locate in strip centres or planned shopping malls, a frequent option for large retailers is a freestanding site. A **freestanding site** is a retail location that's not connected to other retailers, although many are located adjacent to malls. Retailers with large space requirements, such as warehouse clubs and hypermarkets, are often freestanding. Category specialists such as Toys "R" Us also use freestanding sites. Advantages of freestanding locations are greater visibility; lower rents; ample parking; no direct competition; greater convenience for customers; fewer restrictions on signs, hours, or merchandise (which might be imposed in a shopping centre); and ease of expansion. The most serious disadvantage is the lack of synergy with other stores. A retailer in a freestanding location must be a primary destination point for customers. It must offer customers something special in merchandise, price, promotion, or services to get them into the store.

Many retailers report that freestanding stores perform better than stores in malls. Shoppers Drug Mart shifted to freestanding locations because it wanted more space for front-end merchandise.

Other Retail Location Opportunities

Merchandise kiosks, mixed-use developments, airports, resorts, hospitals, and stores within a store are interesting, if not unusual, location alternatives for many retailers.

Merchandise Kiosks Although not a type of shopping mall, merchandise kiosks are found in shopping malls of all types and are a popular location alternative for retailers with small space needs. A merchandise **kiosk** is a small selling space offering a limited merchandise assortment. These selling spaces are typically between 40 and 500 square feet and can be in prime mall locations. Surprisingly, kiosks may be small in size but the rental costs are not—kiosks, because of their central locations, can cost more than a traditional storefront location. It is important to note that rental costs for kiosks vary depending on the province, the mall's location, and customer traffic. They usually have short-term

Merchandise kiosks are found in shopping malls of all types and are a popular location alternative for retailers with small space needs.

Laurence Torao Konishi/Alamy.

leases, shielding tenants from the liability of having to pay long-term rent in case the business fails. Some merchandise kiosks operate seasonally, for instance, selling polar fleece in winter and baseball hats in summer. Of course, vendors also can be evicted on short notice. These alternatives to regular stores are often a great way for small retailers to begin or expand. Kiosks have been the venue of choice for Vivah Jewellery, a retail concept that focuses specifically on fashion jewellery.

Mall operators see these alternative selling spaces as an opportunity to generate rental income in otherwise vacant space. Some of the nation's biggest mall developers are installing merchandise kiosks in every available space. These kiosks sell everything from concert tickets to gift certificates, along with many different kinds of merchandise. They also can generate excitement, leading to additional sales for the entire mall. Mall operators must be sensitive to their regular mall tenants' needs, however. These kiosks can block a store, be incompatible with its image, or actually compete with similar merchandise.

Mixed-Use Developments
A **mixed-use development (MXD)** combines several different uses in one complex, including shopping centres, office towers, hotels, residential complexes, civic centres, and convention centres. MXDs are popular with retailers because they bring additional shoppers to their stores. Developers like MXDs because they use space productively. For instance, land costs the same whether a developer builds a shopping mall by itself or builds an office tower over the mall or parking structure.

Airports
One important high-pedestrian-traffic area that has become popular with national retail chains is airports. After all, what better way to spend waiting time than to have a Second Cup coffee or shop in Victoria's Secret? Sales per square metre at airport malls are often three to four times as high as at regular mall stores.[24] However, rents are at least 20 percent higher than at malls. Also, costs can be higher—hours are longer, and since the location is often inconvenient for workers, the businesses have to pay higher wages. The best airport locations tend to be ones where there are many layovers and international flights. The best-selling products are gifts, necessities, and easy-to-pack items such as books and magazines.

Resorts
Who needs anchor stores to bring in customers when there are mountains or a beach to attract people? Retailers view resorts as prime location opportunities for golf courses, entertainment spas, and complementary retailers. There is a captive audience of well-to-do customers with lots of time on their hands. As noted earlier, outlet malls are popular in tourist areas. Resort retailing also attracts small, unique local retailers, premium national brands such as Tim Hortons or Roots, and can support dozens of art galleries and fashion retailers. Popular resort areas such as Whistler or Big White (near Kelowna) in British Columbia have developed town centres that attract tourists worldwide.

Hospitals
Hospitals are an increasingly popular location alternative. Both patients and their guests often have time to shop. Necessities are important for patients since they can't readily leave. Gift-giving opportunities abound. Chapters has opened retail locations in large hospitals.

Store within a Store
Another non-traditional location for retailers is within other, larger stores. Retailers, particularly department stores, have traditionally leased space to other retailers such as sellers of cosmetics and fine jewellery or furs. Grocery stores have been experimenting with the store-within-a-store concept for years with service providers such as banks, photo processors, and video outlets. Chapters has Starbucks Coffee outlets in many of its stores.

Pop-Up Stores and Other Temporary Locations
Retailers and manufacturers sometimes open **pop-up stores**, which are stores in temporary locations that focus on new products or a limited group of products. A few years ago, pop-up stores were a major investment for retailers because of high start-up costs amortized over a very short lease and relatively high lease costs. Now with retail space more plentiful and less expensive, these stores have become more popular. Retailers and manufacturers are using these spaces to create buzz, test new concepts, or even evaluate a new neighbourhood or city. Clarks (a British shoe brand) opened a pop-up store in Toronto during the Christmas season to create buzz and hype about its brand, which is already sold

mixed-use development (MXD) Development that combines several uses in one complex—for example, shopping centre, office tower, hotel, residential complex, civic centre, and convention centre.

pop-up stores Stores in temporary locations that focus on new products or a limited group of products.

by several Canadian retailers such as Hudson's Bay, Sears, and Soft Moc.

Other retailers, often one-person operations, open temporary stores to take advantage of the holiday season in December or to get visibility and additional sales at festivals or concerts. Local retailers, who pay high rents, aren't necessarily so enthusiastic, because some of the temporary retailers use the same suppliers.

City or Town Locations

Although shopping centres are also located in cities or towns, the locations that are discussed in this section are typically unplanned, have multiple owners, and have access from the street. In particular, we will examine central business districts, downtown locations (or "Main Streets"), and the redevelopment efforts being undertaken in these locations.

Central Business Districts

The **central business district (CBD)** is the traditional downtown business area in a city or town. Due to its business activity, it draws many people into the area during business hours. Also, people must go to the area for work. The CBD is also the hub for public transportation, and there is a high level of pedestrian traffic. Finally, the most successful CBDs for retail trade are those with a large number of residents living in the area.

But many central business district locations in Canada have been declining in popularity with retailers and their customers for years. Retailers can be concerned about CBDs because high security may be required and parking is often limited. Urban decay and no control over the weather can discourage shoppers. Shopping in the evening and on weekends can be particularly slow in many CBDs. Also, unlike modern shopping centres, CBDs tend to suffer from a lack

central business district (CBD) The traditional downtown business area of a city or town.

downtown location The central business district located in the traditional shopping area of smaller towns, or a secondary business district in a suburb or within a larger city, generally featuring lower occupancy costs, fewer people, fewer stores, smaller overall selection of goods or services, and fewer entertainment and recreational activities than more successful primary central business districts.

gentrification A process in which old buildings are torn down or are restored to create new offices, housing developments, and retailers.

of planning. One block may contain upscale boutiques, and the next may be populated with low-income housing, so consumers may not have enough interesting retailers that they can visit on a shopping trip.

Downtown Locations

A **downtown location** is the CBD located in the traditional shopping area of smaller towns, or a secondary business district in a suburb or within a larger city. Downtown locations share most of the characteristics of the primary CBD, but their occupancy costs are generally lower than that of the primary CBD. They do not draw as many people as the primary CBD because fewer people work in the area, and fewer stores generally means a smaller overall selection. Finally, downtown locations typically don't offer the entertainment and recreational activities available in the more successful primary CBDs.

Redevelopment Efforts in City and Town Locations

Some city and town locations have become very attractive location alternatives to shopping centres. Why is this happening?

- Some of these locations have undergone a process of **gentrification**, which is the renewal and rebuilding of offices, housing, and retailers in deteriorating areas, coupled with the influx of more affluent people that often displaces earlier, usually poorer residents. Retailers are simply locating where their customers are.

- Developers aren't building as many malls as before, and it's often hard to find a good location in a successful mall.

- These same chains are finding that occupancy costs in city and town locations compare favourably to malls.

- City and town locations often offer retailers incredible expansion opportunities because of a stable and mature customer base and relatively low competition.

- Cities often provide significant incentives to locate in urban centres. Not only do these retailers bring needed goods and services to the area, but they also bring jobs. If, for instance, a major retailer hires 500 people, there would be more than 100 additional new jobs created to satisfy the retailing needs of that retailer's employees.

- Young professionals and retired empty-nesters are moving to urban centres to enjoy the convenience of shopping, restaurants, and entertainment.

Successful national chain stores such as Staples, Mountain Equipment Co-op, and Tim Hortons need these locations to fuel their expansion. Even big-box stores such as Home Depot and Walmart are opening up city and town locations. Walmart solved the space problem associated with urban locations by opening a three-level store in Los Angeles.[25]

LO6 Location and Retail Strategy

The selection of a location type must reinforce the retailer's strategy. Thus, the location type decision needs to be consistent with the shopping behaviour and size of its target market and the retailer's positioning in its target market. Each of these factors is discussed next.

Shopping Behaviour of Consumers in Retailer's Target Market

A critical factor affecting the location consumers select to visit is the shopping situation in which they are involved. Three types of shopping situations are convenience shopping, comparison shopping, and specialty shopping.

Convenience Shopping When consumers are engaged in convenience shopping situations, they are primarily concerned with minimizing their effort to get the product or service they want. They are indifferent about which brands to buy or the retailer's image and are somewhat insensitive to price. Thus, they don't spend much time evaluating different brands or retailers; they simply want to make the purchase as quickly and as easily as possible. Examples of convenience shopping situations are getting a cup of coffee during a work break or buying milk for breakfast in the morning.

Retailers targeting customers involved in convenience shopping, such as convenience stores, usually locate their stores close to where their customers are and make it easy for them to park, find what they want, and go about their other business. Thus, convenience stores should and generally do locate in neighbourhood strip centres, freestanding spots, and city and town locations. Drugstores and fast-food restaurants also cater to convenience shoppers and thus select locations with easy access, parking, and locations that enable them to offer the additional convenience of a drive-through window. Convenience plays an important role for supermarkets and full-line discount stores as well. Generally, shoppers at these stores are not particularly brand or store loyal and do not find shopping in these stores enjoyable. As a result, these stores typically are also located in neighbourhood strip centres and freestanding locations.

DID YOU KNOW?

Millennial, Baby Boomers, and Generation Z are moving to downtown areas to have easy access to everything and to save on transportation costs.[26]

Comparison Shopping Consumers involved in comparison shopping situations have a general idea about the type of product or service they want, but do not have a strong preference for a brand, model, or specific retailer to patronize. Similar to many convenience shopping situations, consumers are not particularly brand or store loyal. However, the purchase decisions are more important to them, so they seek information and are willing to expend considerable effort planning and making their purchase decisions. Consumers typically engage in this type of shopping behaviour when buying furniture, appliances, apparel, consumer electronics, hand tools, and cameras.

Furniture retailers, for instance, often locate next to each other to create a "furniture row." In Toronto, a number of retailers selling furniture are all located on Dundas Street West. These competing retailers locate near one another because doing so facilitates comparison shopping and thus attracts customers to the locations to compare different types of furniture and prices. The advantage of attracting a large number of shoppers to this area of Dundas Street outweighs the disadvantage of sharing these customers with other retailers.

Enclosed malls offer the same benefits to consumers interested in comparison shopping for fashionable apparel. For example, a customer who is looking for a business suit for job interviews could easily compare the suits offered at Hudson's Bay and Club Monaco with the suits at Sears by simply walking to these other stores located in the same mall. Thus, department stores and specialty apparel retailers locate in enclosed malls for the same reason that houseplant retailers locate together on 6th Avenue in New York City. By co-locating in the same mall, they attract more potential customers interested in comparison shopping for fashionable apparel. Even though the enclosed mall might be inconvenient compared with a freestanding location, comparison shopping is easier after the customers have arrived.

Category specialists offer the same benefit of comparison shopping as a collection of co-located specialty stores such as those described previously. Rather than going to a set of specialty stores when comparison shopping for consumer electronics, consumers know they can see almost all of the brands and models they would want to buy in either Best Buy or Future Shop. Thus, category specialists are **destination stores**, places where consumers will go even if it is inconvenient, just as enclosed malls are destination locations for fashionable apparel comparison shopping. Category specialists locate in power centres primarily to reduce their costs and create awareness of their location and secondarily to benefit from the multiple retailers attracting more consumers and the potential for cross-shopping. Basically, power centres are a collection of destination stores.

Specialty Shopping When consumers are going specialty shopping, they know what they want and will not accept a substitute. They are brand and/or retailer loyal and will pay a premium or spend extra effort, if necessary, to get exactly what they want. Examples of these shopping occasions include buying an expensive designer-brand perfume, adopting a dog from the animal shelter, or buying a dress made by a specific designer. The retailer they patronize when specialty shopping also becomes a destination store. Thus, consumers are willing to travel to an inconvenient location to patronize a unique gourmet restaurant or a health

destination stores
Retail stores in which the merchandise, selection, presentation, pricing, or other unique feature acts as a magnet for customers.

As a destination store, Best Buy offers many brands of merchandise to give consumers the opportunity to comparison shop for consumer electronics.
©Dion Ogust/The Image Works.

food store that specializes in organic vegetables. Having a convenient location is not as important for retailers selling unique merchandise or services. Hudson's Bay's relaunch of the iconic in-store boutique The Room at its Toronto flagship store, in October 2009, hoped to woo back its specialty shoppers. The Room, formerly called the St. Regis Room, used to be the shopping destination for the who's who of Toronto society. There is currently a second location in downtown Vancouver.[27]

Density of Target Market

A second but closely-related factor that affects the choice of location type is the density of the retailer's target market in relation to the location. A good location has many people in the target market that are drawn to it. So, a convenience store located in a CBD (central business district) can be sustained by customers living or working in fairly close proximity to the store. Similarly, a comparison shopping store located next to Hudson's Bay is a potentially good location because Hudson's Bay draws lots of customers from a very large area. It is not as important to have high customer density near a store that sells specialty merchandise because people are willing to search out this type of merchandise. A Porsche dealer, for instance, need not be near other car dealers or in close proximity to its target market because those seeking this luxury car will drive to wherever the dealer may be.

Uniqueness of Retail Offering

Finally, the convenience of their locations is less important for retailers with unique, differentiated offerings than for retailers with an offering similar to other retailers. For example, Bass Pro Shops provides a unique merchandise assortment and store atmosphere. Customers will travel to wherever the store is located, and its location will become a destination.

Each Bass Pro Shops store is unique and offers a truly unforgettable shopping experience—as close to the Great Outdoors as you can get indoors!
Jeff Greenberg 6 of 6/Alamy.

SUMMARY

Location decisions are probably the most important decisions that a retailer will make. Compensation for a poor location may mean lowering prices and spending extra money on advertising to draw customers to the store. Remember that the most important factors in store location are the traffic flow and the demographics of people living in the area. If either attribute is inappropriate for the store location, then the site should be avoided.

Decisions about where to locate a store are critical to any retailer's success. A clear, coherent strategy should specify location goals. A location decision is particularly important because of its high cost and long-term commitment. A location mistake is clearly more devastating to a retailer than a buying mistake, for instance.

Retailers have a plethora of types of sites from which to choose. Many central business districts and downtown locations have become a more viable option than in the past due to gentrification of the areas and lack of suburban mall opportunities. Retailers also have many types of shopping centres from which to choose. They can locate in a strip or power centre, or they can go into a mall. In this chapter, we examined the relative advantages of several types of malls, including regional and superregional centres, lifestyle, fashion/specialty centres, and outlet centres. We also examined the viability of kiosks, free-standing sites, mixed-use developments, and other non-traditional locations.

Retailers have a hard time finding a perfect site. Each site has its own set of advantages and disadvantages. In assessing the viability of a particular site, a retailer must make sure the store's target markets will patronize that location. The location analyst's job isn't finished until terms of occupancy and other legal issues are considered.

Retailers consider several issues when assessing the attractiveness of a particular region, market, or trade area. They want to know about the people living in the area. What are their lifestyles? How wealthy and large are the households? Is the area growing or declining? Does it have a favourable business climate? Importantly, what is the level of competition? Retailers should only locate in areas with heavy competition if they believe their retailing format is superior to that of their competitors. A safer strategy is to locate in an area with little competition. Of course, in today's overbuilt retail environment, such areas are nearly impossible to find. Does a retailer have the ability to manage multiple stores in an area or in multiple areas? What is the most profitable number of stores to operate in a particular area?

In assessing the viability of a particular site, a retailer must consider the location's accessibility as well as locational advantages within the centre.

Trade areas are typically divided into primary, secondary, and tertiary zones. The boundaries of a trade area are determined by how accessible it is to customers, the natural and physical barriers that exist in the area, the type of shopping area in which the store is located, the type of store, and the level of competition.

Retailers have three types of information at their disposal to help them define a trade area. First, they use a customer spotting technique to determine how many people are in their trade area and where they live. Second, they use demographic data and GIS firms and Statistics Canada. Finally, they use the Internet, other sources of secondary information, and a good old-fashioned walk through the neighbourhood to assess their competition.

Once retailers have the data that describes their trade areas, they use several analytical techniques to estimate demand. The analogue approach—one of the easiest to use—can be particularly useful for smaller retailers. Using this method, the retailer makes predictions about the sales of a new store based on sales in stores in similar areas. Regression analysis uses the same logic as the analogue approach but is statistically based and requires more objective data. Finally, the Huff gravity model and Reilly's law of retail gravitation can be used to predict the probability that a customer will frequent a particular store in a trade area. They are based on the premise that customers are more likely to shop at a given store or shopping centre if it's conveniently located and offers a large selection.

amount and quality of parking facilities
analogue approach
anchors
artificial barriers
central business district (CBD)
congestion
cumulative attraction
demalling
destination stores
downtown location
fashion/specialty centre
franchisees
franchisors
freestanding site
gentrification

geographic information systems (GIS)
Huff gravity model
ingress/egress
kiosk
lifestyle centre
mall
mixed-use development (MXD)
natural barriers
outlet centres
overstored trade area
polygons
pop-up stores
power centre
primary zone
region
regional centre

regression analysis
Reilly's law of retail gravitation
road condition
road pattern
saturated trade area
secondary zone
shopping centre
strip centre
superregional centre
symbiotic store
tertiary zone
trade area
traditional strip centre
understored trade area
visibility

GET OUT & DO IT!

1. **INTERNET EXERCISE** The largest mall in Canada is the West Edmonton Mall in Alberta. Go to http://www.wem.ca. Do you think the attractions overshadow the shopping?

2. **GO SHOPPING** Go to your favourite shopping centre and analyze the tenant mix. Do the tenants appear to complement each other? What changes would you make in the tenant mix to increase the overall health of the centre?

3. **INTERNET EXERCISE** Go to http://www.esri.com/what-is-gis (the site for Esri Geographical Information Systems) and click on Overview. After reading the overview, explain how retailers can make better decisions with GIS.

4. **INTERNET EXERCISE** Do a competitive trade area analysis for a store of your choice by going to competitors' corporate websites and determining the probability that they will be entering a particular trade area.

5. **GO SHOPPING** Go to two stores owned by the same chain. Define and evaluate their trade area. Which store do you think is more successful?

6. **GO SHOPPING** Go to a shopping mall. Get or draw a map of the stores. Analyze whether the stores are clustered appropriately. For instance, are all the high-end stores together? Is there a good mix of shopping goods stores adjacent to each other?

DISCUSSION QUESTIONS AND PROBLEMS

1. Why have location decisions become more important in recent years?

2. Pick your favourite store. Explain why you believe it is (or isn't) in the best location, given its target market.

3. Read the Spotlight on Retailing. What is behind the location shift for luxury stores? Why are they moving away from their traditional locations?

4. As a consultant to 7-Eleven convenience stores, American Eagle Outfitters, and BMW car dealerships, what would you say is the single most important factor in choosing a site for these three very different types of stores?

5. Retailers have a tradition of developing shopping centres and freestanding locations in neighbourhoods or central business districts that have suffered decay. Some people have questioned the ethical and social ramifications of this process, which is known as gentrification. What are the benefits and problems associated with gentrification?

6. Staples has a strong multichannel strategy. How does the Internet affect its strategies for locating stores?

7. In many malls, fast-food retailers are located together in an area known as a food court. What are this arrangement's advantages and disadvantages to the fast-food retailer?

8. Why would a Payless ShoeSource store locate in a neighbourhood shopping centre instead of a regional shopping mall?

9. Why would a company such as Coach, a manufacturer of high-quality leather goods, open outlet stores? What are the disadvantages to such a strategy?

10. What are the shape and size of the trade area zones of a shopping centre near your school?

11. When measuring trade areas, why is the analogue approach not a good choice for a retailer with several hundred outlets?

12. True Value Hardware plans to open a new store. Two sites are available, both in middle-income neighbourhood centres. One neighbourhood is 20 years old and has been well maintained. The other was recently built in a newly planned community. Which site is preferable for True Value? Why?

13. Trade areas are often described as concentric circles emanating from the store or shopping centre. Why is this practice used? Suggest an alternative method. Which would you use if you owned a store in need of a trade area analysis?

14. Under what circumstances would a retailer use the analogue approach to estimate demand for a new store? What about regression?

15. Some specialty stores prefer to locate next to or close to an anchor store. But Little Caesars, a takeout pizza retailer typically found in strip centres, wants to be at the end of the centre away from the supermarket anchor. Why?

16. Retailers have a choice of locating on a mall's main floor or second or third level. Typically, the main floor offers the best, but most expensive, locations. Why would specialty stores such as Radio Shack and Foot Locker choose the second or third floor?

17. A drugstore is considering opening a new location at shopping centre A, with hopes of capturing sales from a new neighbourhood under construction. Two nearby shopping centres, C and E, will provide competition. Using the following information and Huff's gravity model, determine the probability that residents of the new neighbourhood will shop at shopping centre A.

Shopping Centre	Size (sq. ft.)	Distance from New Neighbourhood (kilometres)
A	3 500 000	4
C	1 500 000	5
E	300 000	3

Assume that $b = 2$

18. Identify the location strategies for each of the following types of retailers:
   - department stores
   - category killers/specialists
   - specialty apparel stores
   - grocery stores

CHAPTER SIX

Store design, layout, and visual merchandising strategy

LEARNING OBJECTIVES

Lo1   Discuss the potential objectives retailers consider when designing or redesigning a store.

Lo2   Understand the power of the retail environment to influence customers and that retailers need to balance store design elements and generate traffic through feature areas.

Lo3   Examine the factors that retailers consider when deciding how much floor or shelf space to allocate to merchandise categories and brands.

Lo4   Review how stores can increase customer appeal and sales through various merchandise presentation techniques.

Lo5   Describe the atmospheric elements that enhance store environment and strengthen store brand or image.

Lo6   Explore the good design principles that can apply to both physical store and web/mobile sites and the importance of reflecting the retailer's target market.

SPOTLIGHT ON RETAILING

MICROSOFT RETAIL FLAGSHIP OPENS DOORS IN NY

It's opening day today for Microsoft's first flagship retail location on Fifth Avenue in Manhattan, and from all reports it's bound to be a customer experience above the norm given its five floors and lots of interactive features for the Windows device fan.

  The store is the tech giant's first to boast more than one floor and is both a retail site and consumer training and education facility, according to Engadget's report. There is a big community theatre and a big section dedicated just to the gaming console Xbox. PC vendor and longtime partner Dell occupies the third floor. Reports claim there will be more than 15 store associates on hand, providing insight in nearly 20 different languages, a reflection of the diverse shopper population in New York City.

The store boasts an exterior culture wall, for digital imagery representative of the Fifth Avenue shopping district culture, according to a Microsoft post. Called a culture wall—40 feet wide by 20 feet high—the focus is on the vendor integrating into the community as it will display non-commercial, artistic images.

"This is something that is super important to us and really layers back up to the company's mission of how we are helping people achieve more," said Kelly Soligon, general manager, worldwide marketing, Microsoft Retail and Online Stores, in the post. "We really strive to be part of the fabric of every community where we operate."

No word yet on what Microsoft plans for the fifth floor penthouse area and all operations are on the fourth floor.

One very noticeable feature, according to PC World, is a two-story video tower at the 22 000-square-foot site. The retail launch comes with the arrival of Microsoft's new Surface Pro 4 and Surface Book devices.

Randy Duchaine/Alamy.

Source: Retail Customer Experience, "Microsoft retail flagship opens doors in NY," October 26, 2015, http://www.retailcustomerexperience.com/news/microsoft-retail-flagship-opens-doors-in-ny/ (accessed January 13, 2016).

Retail revenue accounts for about 12 percent of Canada's gross domestic product.[1] Retail also represents nearly 50 percent of total household spending in this country. Retailers must ask: "How do I get consumers to stop, shop, and keep coming back to my store?" To solve these challenges, retailers should link store design to their strategic plan.

The environment in a store, the design of the store, and the presentation and location of merchandise in the store have a significant impact on shopping behaviour. The store image that a retailer creates is strategically planned to attract a specific target market's demographic and psychographic profile and to enhance the appeal of merchandise to that customer. The design of a store, website, or mobile site can attract customers to visit the location, increase the time they spend in the store or at the site(s), and increase the amount of merchandise they purchase. Store design can also have long-term effects on building customer loyalty toward the retailer by enhancing the retailer's brand image and providing rewarding shopping experiences that encourage repeat visits.

> **DID YOU KNOW?**
>
> Retailers remodel their stores every five to seven years.[2]

Store managers are responsible for implementing the design and visual merchandising developed by specialists at the retailer's corporate headquarters. They adapt the prototype plans to the unique characteristics of their stores and then make sure the image and experience provided by the design are consistent over time. As discussed in this chapter, store design and visual merchandising are also elements of a retailer's communication mix (as explored in Chapter 15) and play an important role in creating and reinforcing a retailer's brand image.

A good store design should be like a good story.[3] Every story has a beginning, middle, and end, usually in that order. The entrance sets up the story. It creates expectations and contains promises. As for the first impression, the storefront says, "I'm cheap" or "I'm sophisticated" or "I'm cool." Too often, stores launch right into "Here's what we've got to sell. Don't you love it?" A good entrance should entice, hint, and tease. There should be mystery. The cost of making an eye-catching window display doesn't have to be great, but the price of not making the effort could be.

Inside the store comes the middle of the story. It should start off slowly. Customers need a few seconds to orient themselves after the entrance. A single message has a far greater chance of sticking than do a dozen products cluttering the way.

Seventy percent of purchase decisions are made in the store. This statistic is driving in-store marketing trends. Shopping today is less about utility and more about experience. Consumers want and now usually expect more from stores than products lined up neatly on a shelf. Customers need to be led on a journey throughout the store. Using visuals, light, and motion take customers down a path of discovery.

There should, for instance, be visual destinations at the end of a long aisle. Exciting stores should be like Paris. Sighting down the Champs-Elysées, you are enticed by the Arc de Triomphe as a powerful destination. Finally, the cash wrap or checkout counter is the story's climactic finale. It's where retailers can convey subtle messaging without hard selling.

LO1 Store Design Objectives

Retail giants such as Holt Renfrew, Mountain Equipment Co-op, and Home Depot increase store traffic by creating experiences that go beyond attractive sales prices and product samples, from store events and interactive displays to in-store emotional and memorable experiences for shoppers. A growing trend in experiential marketing known as "retailtainment" engages shoppers in various interactive events such as contests, shows, giveaways, and activities. The results are sales increases and long-term customer loyalty. When designing or redesigning a store, some objectives are to (1) implement the retailer's strategy, (2) build loyalty, (3) increase sales on visits, (4) control costs, and (5) meet legal requirements.

Implement Retail Strategy

To meet the first objective, retail managers must define the target customer and then design a store that complements customers' needs.[4] For instance, warehouse clubs, such as Costco, have high ceilings with metal grids and concrete floors instead of tile—all of those things are perceived to indicate low prices. Actually, they are more expensive than some alternatives, but they are used to maintain an image.[5] Nielsen, the world's leading marketing information provider, offers services to help its customers create tailored retail experiences and ultimately increase sales. Customers would find it hard to accurately judge value if the physical environment were inconsistent with the merchandise or prices.

The Apple Store in New York City reinforces the company's image of developing products with innovative features.
© Radekdrewek | Dreamstime.com.

To appeal better to European customers, McDonald's remodelled its stores with lime-green designer chairs and dark leather upholstery to create a more relaxed experience in a sophisticated atmosphere.[6] It also implemented nine different designs for different location types and target markets, ranging from "purely simple," with minimalist decor in neutral colours, to "Qualite," featuring large pictures of lettuces and tomatoes and gleaming stainless kitchen utensils, such as meat grinders. In developing these redesigns, McDonald's had to make sure that the new designs project a more appealing image but still enable customers to recognize the store as a McDonald's and continue to have favourable associations with the McDonald's brand.

The Apple Store on Fifth Avenue in Manhattan reinforces the company's image of developing products with innovative design features. Its most striking feature is a transparent glass cube, 32 feet on each side, marking the entrance to the store. The cube houses a cylindrical glass elevator and a spiral glass staircase leading to a 10 000 square-foot subterranean retail space.[7] Another example is Mission Hill, which received the 2014 Excellence in Retailing Award for In-Store Merchandising (Mid-Size Retailer). Mission Hill is a master at matching its target customer with store design (see Retailing View 6.1).

Build Loyalty

To meet the second design objective of building loyalty and influencing customer buying decisions, retailers concentrate on store layout and space-planning issues. When customers consistently have rewarding experiences when patronizing a retailer's store, website, or mobile app, they are motivated to visit the store or website repeatedly and develop loyalty toward the retailer. Store design plays an important role in making shopping experiences rewarding. Specifically, retailers want the store design to attract customers to the store; enable them to locate merchandise of interest easily;

This McDonald's restaurant in Europe features an innovative design that creates an appealing brand image.
© Tea | Dreamstime.com.

Mission Hill Enters a Different World

Communicating the message and connecting with customers, with the emphasis on merchandise

Family Estate Winery, just outside Kelowna, BC, overlooks Lake Okanagan. From the pictures, the winery looks like the kind of old world winery usually found in the movies, with sweeping panorama views of blue waters and lush green fields, a bell tower, and a 1200-seat Greek-style outdoor amphitheatre. Inside the winery, guests will find an art collection that includes works by Chagall and Leger, along with 2000-year-old antiquities. They will also find some of the best wine in the country—in 2013, the winery received global awards for Best

Courtesy of the Retail Council of Canada.

Pinot Noir and for Winery of the Year. The winery seeks to surprise and delight each of its guests, including with its retail offerings. The challenge became: how to retail merchandise in a way that doesn't interfere with the architectural integrity of the structure? The winery found a solution in the retail strategy they call Enter a Different World.

Surpassing Goals Enter a Different World established clear metrics for the winery. They wanted the shop to increase revenue by 7 percent over the previous year, increase visitors to the winery by 2 percent, and devise a new marketing plan to attract visitors with higher incomes. The results of the program were impressive. The winery ended the season with a 12 percent year-over-year increase and an increase in the average ticket by 15 percent (the average basket contained 5.2 units compared to 4.1 units the previous year). From a retail standpoint, the results were doubly impressive, considering the fact that most visitors to the winery would rather spend their money on wine. But after Enter a Different World, 45 percent of all units sold were not wine and 25 percent of all transactions did not include wine at all. On top of all these good numbers, TripAdvisor comments were overwhelmingly positive, with a 4.5/5 rating for the retailer on the site.

Merchandise Speaks for Itself The retail strategy limits the amount of signage in the store. What signage they do have includes handwritten tags for one-of-a-kind vintage items, handwritten chalk boards for a French bistro feel, and books that act as mini billboards when the store needs to communicate more information about products. The winery also removed supplier fixtures from the store and uses a collection of vintage European and Canadian tables to display many of the goods for sale in the shop.

David Amos, director of retail and merchandising at Mark Anthony Group, says that the biggest learning for him was to focus on the merchandise and not so much the props or signage. "The merchandising can tell the story with much more clarity and impact [than signage can]. Customers react most positively with colour and good organization, balance, and structure of the merchandise. Sound in-store merchandising can make the simple quite extraordinary," he says.

The success of the retail operations has helped to raise revenue and give customers more selection and more reasons to open their wallets. The store also helps to reinforce the winery's key message—they sell some of the best wine in Canada. "We were privileged to be awarded several medals on the global stage for our wines. The in-store merchandising for the award winning wines allowed us to communicate the recognition in a very impactful manner. Creatively, the in-store merchandising was much more powerful than just signage," says Amos.

Source: "Mission Hill Enters a Different World: Communicating the Message and Connecting with Customers, with the Emphasis on Merchandise," *Canadian Retailer,* Store 2014, p. 57, http://www.retailcouncil.org/sites/default/files/In-Store_Merchandising_MID_Mission_Hill.pdf (accessed January 13, 2016). Canadian Retailer, a publication of Retail Council of Canada.

---

motivate them to make unplanned, impulse purchases; and provide them with a satisfying shopping experience.

Customers seek two types of benefits when shopping—utilitarian and hedonic benefits.[8] Store design provides a **utilitarian benefit** when it enables customers to locate and purchase products in an efficient and timely manner with minimum hassle. Utilitarian benefits are becoming increasingly important with the rise of two-income and single head-of-household families. Due to the limited time these families have, they are spending less time shopping. They want to get their shopping done as quickly as possible.

To accommodate these utilitarian-oriented shoppers, Walmart Supercentre stores in Canada have redesigned a section of their checkout areas so that customers with fewer than eight to ten items form a serpentine single line that feeds into multiple cash registers. Although banks and amusement parks have used a similar checkout system for decades, supermarkets and general merchandise retailers have generally favoured the one-line-per-register system, because they are concerned that a long line will scare off shoppers. However, when customers stand in one line that feeds multiple checkout stations, there are no "slow" lines, delayed by a coupon-counting customer or slow cashier. Using this system, the wait can be reduced 50 to 75 percent compared with using a traditional system.

Store design provides a **hedonic benefit** by offering customers an entertaining and enjoyable shopping experience. This shopping experience encourages customers to spend more time in a store because the visit itself is rewarding. For example, Bass Pro Shops, a chain of stores catering to outdoor enthusiasts, provides an educational and entertaining experience with a mix of museum-quality animal displays in colourful dioramas, huge aquariums stocked with native fish, and a shooting gallery providing fun along with the opportunity to learn basic shooting skills in a safe environment. Its stores are known as shopping and tourism destinations, drawing customers not only from the local area but also from hundreds of kilometres away. Similarly, Cinnabon stores attract customers because of the smell of fresh-baked cinnamon buns.

Increase Sales on Visits

A third design objective is to increase sales made to customers on a visit. Store design has a substantial impact on which products customers buy, how long they stay in the store, and how much they spend during a visit. Grocery stores are organized to facilitate the shopping trip and to display as much merchandise as possible to encourage impulse sales. In contrast, boutiques are laid out in a free-form design that allows customers to browse.

Due to the limited time consumers have, they are spending less time planning shopping trips and making more purchase decisions in stores. So retailers are making adjustments to their stores to get people in and out more quickly. The purchase decisions are greatly influenced by what products customers see during their visit, and what they see is affected by the store layout and how the merchandise is presented.

Customers' purchasing behaviour is also influenced, both positively and negatively, by the store's atmosphere. Signs are designed to attract attention. On a more subtle level, Mrs. Fields stores, for example, attract customers because of the smell of cookies. This chapter explores the methods retailers use to positively influence consumers' purchase behaviour and in-store experience.

utilitarian benefit A motivation for shopping in which consumers accomplish a specific task, such as buying a suit for a job interview.

hedonic benefit Shopping for pleasure, entertainment, and/or to achieve an emotional or recreational experience.

Control Costs

Consistent with any retail decision, the fourth design objective is to consider the costs associated with each store design element versus the value received in terms of higher sales and profits. For instance, the free-form design found in many boutiques is much more costly than rows of gondolas in a discount store. (A *gondola* is an island type of self-service counter with tiers of shelves, bins, or pegs.) Also, the best locations within a store are "worth" the most, so they are reserved for certain types of merchandise. For instance, many grocery stores place their produce near the store's entrance because it has a higher margin than other merchandise categories and it creates a nice atmosphere. Retailers develop maps called *planograms* that prescribe the location of merchandise based on profitability and other factors.

The store design can also affect labour costs and inventory shrinkage. Traditional department stores typically are organized into departments that are isolated from one another. This design provides an intimate and comfortable shopping experience that can result in more sales. However, the design prevents sales associates from observing and covering adjacent departments, which makes it necessary to have at least one sales associate permanently stationed in each department to provide customer service and prevent shoplifting. When considering atmospheric issues of store design, retailers must weigh the costs along with the strategy and customer attraction issues. For

instance, certain types of lighting used to highlight expensive jewellery and crystal cost more than rows of bare fluorescent bulbs. Retailing View 6.2 describes how Walmart is building environmentally sensitive stores that reduce energy costs and help build Walmart's image as a socially responsible retailer.

Retailing is a very dynamic business. Competitors might enter a market and cause existing retailers to change the mix of merchandise offered. As

---

6.2 | RETAILING VIEW

Walmart Goes Green and Lowers Its Energy Costs

In an initiative begun several years ago, Walmart continues to design new stores and retrofit older stores to ensure their energy efficiency. These stores are among the "greenest" in the world. The three main design objectives for these stores are reducing the amount of energy and other natural resources required for store operations, minimizing the raw materials used to construct each facility, and using renewable materials whenever possible.

These design elements reflect Walmart's three broad environmental goals: (1) to be supplied 100 percent by renewable energy, (2) to create zero waste, and (3) to sell products that sustain the world's resources and environment. Although such design features reduce the stores' impact on the environment, they also are expensive to build. Initial projections call for the energy used at these new stores to be 25 to 30 percent less than older stores that have not been retrofitted, reducing a store's energy costs by $500 000 annually. Such savings could increase if energy costs continue to climb.

Some of the sustainable features that have passed these steps or are currently being tested include the following:

- A wind turbine on top of a store produces sufficient energy to offset 5 percent of the store's electricity consumption.
- A system to collect and treat rainwater provides nearly all of the water required for irrigation and thus will reduce demands placed on local stormwater systems.
- Grass that does not need irrigation or mowing is used for landscaping .
- LEDs, instead of fluorescent lighting, are used in refrigerated cases. In cold temperatures, fluorescent lights

lose life expectancy every time they are switched on and off; LEDs do not suffer from this limitation. The lights stay off until the customer opens the case. In addition to saving energy, the lights add a theatrical appeal for customers.

- A system captures the heat generated by each building's refrigeration system, then redirects that heat to warm the water in restroom sinks or support new radiant, floor-heating systems located beneath the entries and other areas.

Although many of these changes have been made globally, Walmart also customizes some green design choices by region. For example:

- Brazil: Stores employ smart lights that dim when natural sunlight is available.
- Mexico: Walmart invested 640 million pesos (US$57 million) to convert a 25-acre, 50-foot deep dump into a green mall, which created 1500 jobs. The trash produces energy through a bio-gas burning process. The green mall is now home to a Walmart supercenter, Sam's Club, and Vips and El Porton restaurants.
- Central America: 70 percent of stores have installed skylights to reduce lighting costs, covering approximately 15 percent of the roof space of each store.
- China: Walmart is switching over to LED lighting throughout its stores and integrating lighting controls to reduce energy usage by a target amount of 30 percent in existing stores and 40 percent in prototype stores.
- Japan: Prototype stores use a desiccant temperature and humidity system to reduce energy costs and CO_2 emissions.

Sources: "Taking Sustainability to New Heights," October 15, 2012, http://www.walmartgreeenroom.com; "No Matter the Season, Our Energy Commitment Is Always On," September 28, 2012, http://www.walmartgreenroom.com; Michelle Moran, "Seeing Green," *Progressive Grocer,* March 2010, pp. 16–31; Cathy Jett, "New Design's Goal: To Cut the Clutter," *McClatchy-Tribune Business News,* October 14, 2009; and Aaron Besecker, "Walmart Store Gets Green Light," *McClatchy-Tribune Business News,* August 31, 2009.

the merchandise mix changes, so must the space allocated to merchandise categories and the layout of the store change. Thus, store planners attempt to design stores with maximum flexibility. Flexibility can take two forms: the ability to physically move store components, and the ease with which components can be modified.

For instance, a sporting goods store must be prepared to accommodate seasonal merchandise demands, expanding or contracting space to accommodate the seasonal flux inherent in the sporting goods business. Stores with built-in design flexibility can respond to seasonal changes and renew themselves from an image perspective without the need for large-scale renovations. For example, as much as 30 percent more retail space can be provided for in-season sports equipment or apparel through the use of flexible fixturing systems that are movable and accommodate additional tie-in units and shelves.

Legal Considerations

In the United States, store design or redesign decisions must comply with the 1990 *Americans with Disabilities Act (ADA)*.[9] This law protects people with disabilities from discrimination in employment, transportation, public accommodations, telecommunications, and activities of state and local governments. It affects store design because the act calls for "reasonable access" to merchandise and services in retail stores that were built before 1993. Stores built after 1993 must be fully accessible.

The act also states that retailers should not have to incur "undue burdens" to comply with ADA requirements. Although retailers are concerned about the needs of their disabled customers, they are also worried that making merchandise completely accessible to people in a wheelchair or a motorized cart will result in less space available to display merchandise and thus reduce sales. However, providing for wider aisles and more space around fixtures can result in a more pleasant shopping experience for able-bodied as well as disabled customers.

The ADA does not clearly define critical terms such as "reasonable access," "fully accessible," or "undue burden." So the actual ADA requirements are being defined through a series of court cases in which disabled plaintiffs have filed class action suits against retailers.[10] On the basis of these court cases, retailers are typically required to (1) provide 32-inch-wide pathways in the main aisle; to bathrooms, fitting rooms, and elevators; and around

most fixtures; (2) lower most cash wraps (checkout stations) and fixtures so that they can be reached by a person in a wheelchair; and (3) make bathrooms and fitting rooms fully accessible. These accessibility requirements are somewhat relaxed for retailers in very small spaces and during peak sales periods such as the Christmas holidays.[11]

It has been 25 years since the Canadian federal government spearheaded a National Strategy for the Integration of Persons with Disabilities, and 15 years since the federal, territorial, and provincial First Ministers identified disability issues as a priority.[12] While many smaller pieces of legislation related to the well-being of people with disabilities exist at the federal level in Canada, the possibility of overarching federal disability legislation has been a matter of public debate to a greater or lesser degree for three decades.[13]

In 2005, the Ontario government took a step toward building a more accessible province when it passed the *Accessibility for Ontarians with Disabilities Act (AODA)*, calling for the development of standards for accessibility in five key areas of daily living: customer service, information and communications, employment, transportation, and built environment. As of January 1, 2012, the AODA legally requires all organizations, both public and private, that provide goods and services either directly to the public or to other organizations in Ontario (third parties) and that have one or more employees, to provide accessible customer service to persons of all ability levels.[14]

Retailers were encouraged to review the customer service standards and develop compliance strategies in advance of January 1, 2012. The review included things such as consumer-facing material and customer communication methods to ensure that they take into account potential customer disabilities (e.g., written materials available in Braille or by audio), and websites that can be accessible by the visually impaired.[15]

People with disabilities dine out, work, travel, shop, and do business. People with disabilities have spending power! A Royal Bank study released in the year 2000 estimated the spending power of people with disabilities to be $25 billion a year in Canada. Businesses that are accessible attract more customers and improve services for everyone.[16]

Retailer are taking heed. Canadian Tire, for example, has a policy titled "Customer Service Accessibility Policy," which can be found on their website (http://www.canadiantire.ca/en/customer-service/accessibility-policy.html).

Design Trade-Offs

Typically, a store design cannot achieve all of these objectives, so managers need to make trade-offs among them. Home Depot's traditional warehouse design can efficiently store and display a lot of merchandise with long rows of floor-to-ceiling racks, but this design is not conducive for a pleasant shopping experience, particularly for female customers who account for more than half of the sales in home improvement centres. Women preferred to shop in Lowes' stores. So Home Depot lowered the ceilings, increased the lighting, widened the aisles, and provided better signage—design aspects that tend to appeal to women.[17]

Retailers often make trade-offs between stimulating impulse purchases and making it easy to buy products. For example, supermarkets place milk, a commonly purchased item, at the back of the store to make customers walk through the entire store and thus stimulate more impulse purchases. Realizing that some customers may want to buy only milk, Walgreen's places its milk at the front of the store, enabling it to compete more effectively with convenience stores.

The trade-off between the ease of finding merchandise and providing an interesting shopping experience is determined by the customer's shopping needs. For example, supermarket shoppers typically want to minimize the time they spend shopping, so supermarkets emphasize the ease of locating merchandise. In contrast, customers shopping for specialty goods like a computer, a home entertainment centre, or furniture are more likely to spend time in the store browsing, comparing products, and talking with the salesperson. Thus, specialty store retailers that offer this type of merchandise place more emphasis on encouraging exploration rather than the ease of finding merchandise.

Another trade-off is the balance between giving customers adequate space in which to shop and productively using this scarce resource for displaying merchandise. For instance, customers are attracted to stores with wide aisles and fixtures whose primary purpose is to display rather than hold the merchandise. However, this type of design reduces the amount of merchandise that can be available to buy, which may also reduce impulse purchases and the customers' chances of finding what they are looking for. But too many racks and displays in a store can cause customers to feel uncomfortable and even confused. The issue of overcrowded display fixtures and merchandise is particularly important when retailers consider the special needs of persons with disabilities.

Lo2 Store Design Elements

Three elements in the design of stores are (1) layout, (2) signage, and (3) feature areas. Each of these elements is discussed in this section. Research shows that 70 percent of final retail purchase decisions are made in the store. Increasingly, retailers must understand the power of the retail environment to influence customers at that critical moment when awareness, brand loyalty, and impulse converge.

To develop a good store layout, store designers must balance many objectives—objectives that often conflict. For example, the store layout should entice customers to move around the store to purchase more merchandise than they may have originally planned. However, if the layout is too complex, customers may find it difficult to locate the merchandise they are looking for and decide not to patronize the store. A well-thought-out store layout will increase store traffic, drive sales, and build store loyalty.

The study of customer movement is a science. Research indicates that about 80 to 90 percent of consumers will turn to the right when entering a store unless they have a specific destination. According to Joseph Weisher, international store designer and president of New Vision Studios, it does not seem to matter whether you are right- or left-handed, read from left to right, drive on the left side of the road, or are male or female: Consumers are predisposed to turn right. The reason for this is that we receive and compute information from the left to the right side of our brains.

This right-entry pattern seems to be consistent as consumers enter, scan the space from left to right, and proceed right. At the same time, the head moves in a natural 45-degree turn and the right foot leads into the retail space. Having this knowledge can be an asset when designing a store and positioning high-margin merchandise. Placing fixtures at a 45-degree angle to the entrance of the store will encourage customers to move along a fixed path, exposing maximum merchandise and stimulating impulse sales. For example, The Gap places its new and high-margin merchandise at key points along a path, leading the eyes and the body to the wall.

Traffic patterns are meant to lead the customer from the entrance in and around merchandise, creating various points of interest along the way. The

Sixty percent of sales come from impulse purchases.
Dorothy Alexander/Alamy.

proper distance for visualizing a presentation is up to 26 feet from the point of entry. Larger stores (over 5000 square feet) need to map traffic patterns and place multiple merchandise presentations along the customer's path. The goal is to move the customer from the aisles to the wall, the most important fixture in the store. There is a saying in retail that, "The longer a customer stays in a store, the more he or she will buy."

If customers enter to the right, then they will naturally exit on the left. Placing the cash/transaction area at the end of the shopping trip near the front left—in other words, putting it on the customers' right when they exit—will encourage impulse sales at the point of purchase.[18]

Customers can be enticed to follow what amounts to a yellow brick road, as in *The Wizard of Oz*. For instance, Toys "R" Us uses a layout that almost forces customers to move through sections of inexpensive impulse-purchase products to get to larger, more expensive goods. It takes a strong-willed parent to navigate through the balloons and party favours without making a purchase.

Another method of helping customers move through the store is to provide interesting design elements. For example, antiques stores have little nooks and crannies that entice shoppers to wander around. Off-price retailers intentionally create some degree of messiness so that people will be encouraged to look through the racks for bargains. Another objective of a good layout is to provide a balance between giving customers adequate space in which to shop and productively using this space for merchandise.

To meet their objectives, retailers must decide which design type to use and how to generate traffic through feature areas.

Types of Design

Today's modern retailers use four general types of store layout design: grid, racetrack, free-form, and servuction system.

Grid   The **grid layout** is best illustrated by most grocery and drugstore operations. It contains long gondolas of merchandise and aisles in a repetitive pattern. The grid isn't the most aesthetically pleasing arrangement, but it's very good for shopping trips in which customers need to move throughout the entire store and easily locate and access products they want to buy.

grid layout A store design, typically used by grocery stores, in which merchandise is displayed on long gondolas in aisles with a repetitive pattern.

For instance, when customers do their weekly grocery shopping, they weave in and out of the specific aisles picking up similar products every week. Since they know where everything is, they can minimize the time spent on a task that many don't especially enjoy. The grid layout is also cost-efficient in terms of space and it allows orderly stocking (see Exhibit 6–1).

There is less wasted space with the grid design than with others because the aisles are all the same width and are designed to be just wide enough to accommodate shoppers and their carts. Since the grid design is used with long gondolas that have multiple shelf levels, the amount of merchandise on the floor can be significantly more than with other layouts. Thus, space productivity is enhanced. (Space productivity is discussed later in this chapter.) The grid layout creates natural sightlines, which lead to focal points at the end of aisles. Finally, since the fixtures are generally standardized and repetitive, the fixturing cost is reduced.

Many of the massive superstores opened in the past few years run aisles horizontally. The layout allows a wider central aisle for promotions and

Exhibit 6–1
Grid Layout

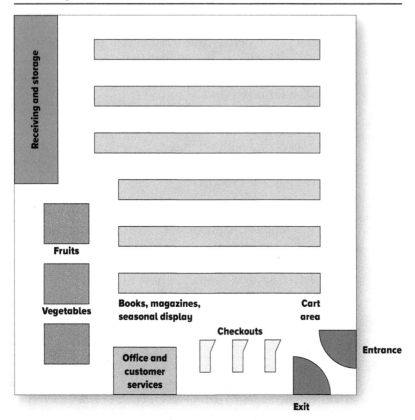

Receiving and storage

Fruits

Vegetables

Books, magazines, seasonal display

Cart area

Checkouts

Office and customer services

Entrance

Exit

breaks up the large expanse with effective endcaps facing the main aisle. Loblaws' addition of the Joe Fresh apparel line to the traditional grocery mix breaks the repetitive grid pattern with a fashion image boutique layout.

Racetrack   One problem with the grid design is that customers aren't exposed to all of the merchandise in the store. This isn't an issue in grocery stores, where most customers have a good notion of what they are going to purchase before they enter the store. But how can design pull customers through stores to encourage them to explore and seek out new and interesting merchandise?

The racetrack layout facilitates the goal of getting customers to visit multiple departments. The **racetrack layout**, also known as a *loop*, is a type of store design that provides a major aisle to facilitate customer traffic, with access to

racetrack layout A type of store layout that provides a major aisle to facilitate customer traffic that has access to the store's multiple entrances. Also known as a *loop*.

free-form layout A store design, used primarily in small specialty stores or within the boutiques of large stores, that arranges fixtures and aisles asymmetrically. Also called *boutique layout*.

the store's multiple entrances. This aisle loops through the store, providing access to all the departments. The racetrack design encourages impulse purchasing. As customers go around the racetrack, their eyes are forced to take different viewing angles rather than looking down one aisle as in the grid design.

Exhibit 6–2 shows the layout of a department store. Since the store has multiple entrances, the loop design tends to place all departments on the main aisle by drawing customers through the store in a series of major and minor loops. To entice customers through the various departments, the design has placed some of the more important departments, such as juniors, toward the rear of the store. The newest items are featured on the aisles to draw customers into departments and around the loop. IKEA's racetrack layout leads the customer in a particular direction using arrows on the floor to move customers throughout the lifestyle vignettes and merchandise groups. To direct customers through the store, the aisles are defined by a change in surface or colour. For instance, the aisle flooring is of marble-like tile, and the departments vary in material, texture, and colour, depending on the desired ambience.

Free-Form   A **free-form layout**, also known as *boutique layout*, arranges fixtures and aisles asymmetrically (Exhibit 6–3). It's successfully used primarily in small specialty stores or within the departments of large stores. In this relaxed environment, customers feel like they are at someone's home, which facilitates shopping and browsing. A pleasant atmosphere isn't inexpensive, however. For one thing, the fixtures are likely to be expensive custom units. Since the customers aren't naturally drawn around the store as they are in the grid and racetrack layouts, personal selling becomes more important. Also, since sales associates can't easily watch adjacent departments, theft is higher than with the grid design. Finally, the store sacrifices some storage and display space to create the more spacious environment. If the free-form layout is carefully designed, however, the increased costs can be easily offset by increased

Exhibit 6–2
Racetrack Layout

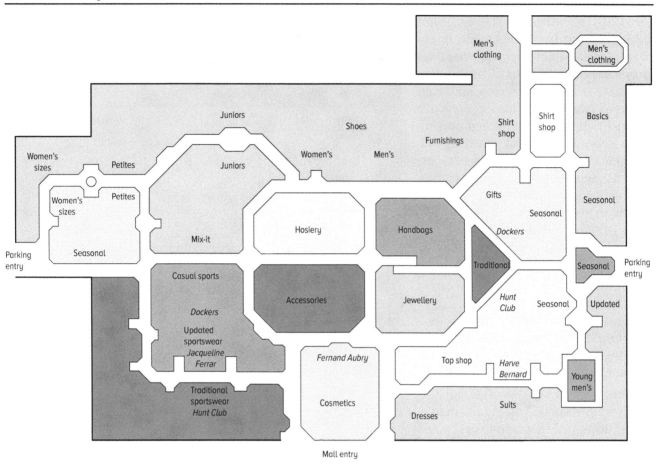

Mall entry

sales and profit margins because the customer feels at home.

To illustrate a free-form boutique within a racetrack layout, consider the image above. The designer's objective was to create a simple, clear space that draws customers into the area. Fixtures with the latest garments are placed along the perimeter of the boutique, yet the flooring and lighting clearly delineate the area from adjacent departments and the walkway.[19]

Servuction System A fourth type of layout is based on the service industry and is call a **servuction system**. This type of design is used by service retails who need to separate employee and consumer space in order to complete a service process. Examples includes restaurants, oil lube companies, and service repair businesses.

In this type of scenario, the employee and customer engage in conversation in the *interaction area* and the consumer makes a service request to the employee. In a restaurant, for example, the consumer would order a meal. The employee who takes the order (a waiter in this instance) then passes this information on to another employee who works in the *service production area* (the chef). In this area, the employee (the chef) physically processes the customer's request. When the process is completed, the employee (waiter) takes the processed service back to the interaction area for the consumer. The consumer, in turn, either consumes the service offering in the *interaction area* or takes it with them to be consumed at a later time, depending on the service process.

Signage and Graphics

Signage and graphics help customers locate specific products and departments, provide product information, and suggest items or special purchases. Graphics, such as photo panels, can reinforce a store's image.

servuction system A design that includes both a visible and invisible area which provides value to the consumer.

Signage is used to identify the location of merchandise categories within a store and the types of products offered in the category. The signs are typically hung from the ceiling to enhance their visibility. Icons rather than words are often used to facilitate communication with customers speaking different languages. Smaller signs are used to identify sale items and provide more information about specific products. Finally, retailers may use images, such as pictures of people and places, to create moods that encourage customers to buy products. Some different types of signs include the following:

- **Category signage.** Used within a particular department or sector of the store, category signs are usually smaller than directional signs. Their purpose is to identify types of products offered; they are usually located near the goods to which they refer.

- **Promotional signage.** This signage describes special offers and may be displayed in windows to entice the customer into the store. For instance, value apparel stores for young women often display large posters in their windows of models wearing the items on special offer.

- **Point-of-sale signage.** Point-of-sale signs are placed near the merchandise they refer to so that customers know its price and other detailed information. Some of this information may already be on product labels or packaging. However, point-of-sale signage can quickly identify for the customer those aspects likely to be of greater interest, such as whether the product is on special offer.

Exhibit 6–3
Free-Form Store Layout

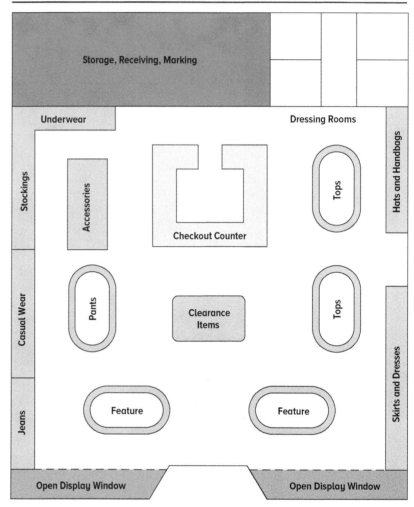

category signage
Signage within a particular department or sector of the store designed to identify types of products offered; usually located near the goods to which they refer.

promotional signage
Describes special offers and may be displayed in windows to entice the customer into the store.

point-of-sale signage
Signs placed near the merchandise they refer to so that customers know the price and other detailed information.

digital signage Signs whose visual content is delivered digitally through a centrally managed and controlled network and displayed on a television monitor or flat-panel screen.

Digital Signage Traditional print signage is typically developed and produced at corporate headquarters, distributed to stores, and installed by store employees or contractors.[20] Many retailers are beginning to replace traditional signage with digital signage systems. **Digital signage** includes signs with visual content that is delivered digitally through a centrally managed and controlled network, distributed to servers in stores, and displayed on a flat-panel screen. The content delivered can range from entertaining video clips to simple displays of the price of merchandise.

Digital signage provides a number of benefits over traditional static-print signage. Due to their dynamic nature, digital signs are more effective in attracting the attention of customers and helping them recall the messages displayed. Digital signage also offers the opportunity to enhance a store's environment by displaying graphics and

© Erik Isakson/Blend Images.

videos to provide an atmosphere that customers find appealing.[21]

Digital signage overcomes the time-to-message hurdle associated with traditional print signage. Changing market developments or events can immediately be incorporated into the digital sign. The ease and speed (flexibility) of content development and deployment of digital signage enables the content to be varied within and across stores at different times of the day or days of the week. For example, the weather could lead to automatic adjustments to digital in-store signage such as automatically advertising cold drinks when the temperature rises above 30 degrees Celsius or advertising sunscreen three days before a weekend that's forecast to be sunny and warm.

Because the content is delivered digitally, it can easily be tailored to a store's market and changed during the week or even

Digital signs are more effective at attracting the attention of shoppers than are traditional statics signs.
Courtesy of Keywest Technology.

the day and hour. For instance, one retailer experimented with changing the content of its storefront digital signage. In the morning, the signage emphasized merchandise with lower price points and sale items. The merchandise at higher price points and more consistent with the retailer's brand image was displayed later in the day.

The ability to control digital signage content centrally ensures that the retailer's strategy for communicating with its customers is properly executed system-wide. Digital signage thus eliminates the challenge facing retailers that send out static signage to stores announcing a special promotion or a new marketing initiative and then find the signage stacked in the storage area, never put out on the selling floor during the promotion. Digital signage ensures that the signage is installed in the right place at the right time.

H&M effectively uses graphic photo panels to enhance its store image.
© Andy Kropa/Redux.

Finally, digital signage eliminates the costs associated with printing, distributing, and installing static signage. In addition, it may decrease store labour costs while improving labour productivity. However, the drawback to using digital signage is the initial cost of the display devices and the system that supports the delivery of the signage.

Visual Communications

Visual communications—composed of graphics, signs, and theatrical effects, both in the store and in windows—help boost sales by providing information on products, special purchases, and value propositions. Signs and graphics also help customers find a department or merchandise. Graphics, such as photo panels, can add personality, beauty, and romance to the store's image.

Retailers should consider the following seven issues when designing visual communications strategies for their stores.

Coordinate Signs and Graphics with the Store's Image Signs and graphics should act as a bridge between the merchandise and the target markets. The colours and tone of the signs and graphics should complement the merchandise. For example, a pastel pink sign in a store selling nautical supplies would not be as appropriate as bold red, white, and blue. Also, a formally worded black-and-white rectangular sign doesn't relate to a children's display as well as a red-and-yellow circus tent design does. Colour combinations should appeal to specific target customers or highlight specific merchandise—primary colours for children, hot vivid colours for teens, pastels for lingerie, brights for sportswear, and so forth. At Athlete's Foot, for instance, sliding graphic panels highlight the lifestyles of the target market while at the same time displaying product and concealing inventory.

Inform the Customer Informative signs and graphics make merchandise more desirable. For

RosaBetancourt 0 people images/Alamy.

example, Athlete's Foot uses a series of freestanding prints to explain its five-step fitting process.[22] The process begins with a foot scanner, which ensures a perfect fit for each customer. Then, after analyzing the customer's activity level, in-store personnel help the individual choose the right shoes and determine the best way to tie shoes to fit the customer's feet.

Use Signs and Graphics as Props   Using signs or graphics that masquerade as props, or vice versa, is a great way to unify a theme and merchandise for an appealing overall presentation. For instance, a store selling educational toys may use lively graphics and props in a unifying theme that is consistent with the store's image.

Keep Signs and Graphics Fresh   Signs shouldn't be left in the store or in windows after displays are removed. Forgotten, faded, and fraught with water spots, such signs do more to disparage a store's image than sell merchandise. Also, new signs imply new merchandise.

Limit the Copy on Signs   As a general rule, signs with too much text won't be read. Customers must be able to quickly grasp the information on the sign as they walk through the store.

Use Appropriate Typefaces on Signs   Different typefaces impart different messages and moods. For instance, carefully done calligraphy in an Old English script provides a very different message than a hastily written price-reduction sign.

Create Theatrical Effects   To heighten store excitement and enhance store image, retailers have borrowed from the theatre. Bold graphic posters, photographs, or fabrics can be hung from ceilings and walls to decorate, provide information, or camouflage less aesthetic areas, such as the ceiling structure.

Feature Areas

Besides the area where most of the merchandise is displayed and stored, there are **feature areas**— areas within a store designed to get the customer's attention. They include end caps, promotional aisles or areas, freestanding fixtures and mannequins that introduce a soft goods department, windows, point-of-sale or cash-wrap areas, and walls.

Entrances   The first impression caused by the entry area affects the customer's image of the store. Department stores typically have cosmetics and fragrance categories at the main entrance because these categories are visually appealing and create a sense of excitement. While the entry area plays a prominent role in creating an image, the first 10 feet of the store is often referred to as the "decompression zone," because customers are making an adjustment to the new environment: escaping from the noisy street or mall, taking off their sunglasses, closing umbrellas, and developing a visual impression of the entire store. Customers are not prepared to evaluate merchandise or make purchase decisions in the decompression zone, so retailers try to keep this area free of merchandise, displays, and signage.[23]

End Caps   The displays located at the end of an aisle are called **end caps**. For instance, a food store's large end-cap display of Coca-Cola is designed to catch consumers' attention. The Coca-Cola is located near the rest of the soft drinks, but is on sale. It's not always necessary to use end caps for sales, however. Due to their high visibility, end caps can also be used to feature special promotional items.

Promotional Aisle or Area   A **promotional aisle or area** is an aisle or area used to display merchandise that is being promoted. Canadian Tire, for instance, uses a promotional aisle to sell seasonal merchandise,

feature areas Areas designed to get the customer's attention that include end caps, promotional aisles or areas, freestanding fixtures and mannequins that introduce a soft goods department, windows, and point-of-sale areas.

end caps Display fixtures located at the end of an aisle.

promotional aisle or area Aisle or area of a store designed to get the customer's attention. An example might be a special "trim-the-tree" department that seems magically to appear right after Halloween every year for the Christmas holidays.

such as lawn and garden in the summer and Christmas decorations in the fall. Apparel stores, such as The Gap, often place their sale merchandise in the back of the store so that customers must wander through the full-price merchandise to get to the sale merchandise.

Freestanding Fixtures and Mannequins Freestanding fixtures and mannequins located on aisles are designed primarily to get customers' attention and bring them into a department. These fixtures often display and store the newest, most exciting merchandise in the department.

Windows Although windows are clearly external to the store, they can be an important component of the store layout. Properly used, window displays can help draw customers into the store. They provide a visual message about the type of merchandise for sale in the store and the type of image the store wishes to portray. Window displays should be tied to the merchandise and other displays in the store window. For instance, if beach towels are displayed in a Hudson's Bay store window, they should also be prominently displayed inside. Otherwise, the drawing power of the window display is lost. Finally, windows can be used to set the shopping mood for a season or holiday such as Christmas or Valentine's Day.

Point-of-Sale (POS) Areas Point-of-sale (POS) areas, also known as *point-of-purchase (POP) areas*, are places in the store where customers can purchase merchandise. Also called **checkout areas** (or *cash-wrap areas*), these areas can be the most valuable piece of real estate in the store because customers often wait there for the transactions to be

In this store, mannequins with the latest garments are placed in the front window to draw customers in.

Lars A. Niki.

completed. While waiting in a long check-out line at a grocery store, notice how people pick up things such as batteries, candy, razors, and magazines. Did they need these items? Not really, but the wait bored them, so they spent the extra time shopping.

As retailers try to rethink their retailer spaces to provide a better shopping experience for consumers, there is a growing movement in the industry to reconsider the need of a POS area altogether. In Apple stores, for example, the POS has been removed. "Associates are equipped with iPhones with card readers. They can literally enable consumers as a POS sale as they are making purchase decisions right where they are standing in store"[24] (see Retailing View 6.3).

Walls Since retail space is often scarce and expensive, many retailers have successfully increased their ability to store extra stock, display merchandise, and creatively present a message by using wall space. Merchandise can be stored on shelving and racks. The merchandise can also be coordinated with displays, photographs, or graphics featuring the merchandise.

The goal of good store design is to get customers to approach the wall. The distance from the main aisle to the wall (or column) should be no more than 20 to 30 feet—beyond this, a customer's visual perception diminishes. The wall is the most important fixture, according to visual merchandiser John Weishar. The wall:

- holds more merchandise
- can present coordinated face-outs with a multiple fashion story in a small space
- facilitates a variety of fixturing methods, such as shelving and hanging
- is the focal point for seasonal merchandise
- can present a feature display to attract the customer
- effectively sells more high-margin merchandise than floor fixtures
- is visible from a distance

freestanding fixtures Fixtures and mannequins located on aisles that are designed primarily to get customers' attention and bring them into a department.

point-of-sale (POS) areas Areas where the customer waits at checkout. This area can be the most valuable piece of real estate in the store, because the customer is almost held captive in that spot; also called *point-of-purchase (POP) areas*.

checkout areas The places in a store where customers can purchase merchandise and have it "wrapped"—placed in a bag; also called *cash-wrap areas*.

Why do Retail Stores Still Have Cash Registers?

Armed with smartphones, consumers have literally become the new POS (Point of Sale). Yet, retailers are still trying to herd them through checkout lanes.

When the consumer can purchase anywhere and anytime, there are a multitude of reasons why retailers can and should rip out POS registers and checkout lanes in stores:

- Checkout lanes take up considerable floor space.
- Security and theft prevention could remain in place with a sensor scan at the exit door.
- Cashiers could be redeployed as associates helping consumers on the floor.
- Associates could also check out consumers in-aisle with smartphones and card readers.
- Consumers could checkout/purchase on their own smartphones with an app.
- Electronic receipts can be emailed to consumers, or printed at portable printers.
- Portable POS devices can still scan bar and QR codes for prices and inventory.
- More sales might result if purchases were made in the aisle while looking at products.
- How many consumers desire/need to pay in cash?

While the centralized checkout lanes have been a highly efficient system for stores, what are the actual costs in terms of lost sales? How many consumers abandon shopping carts because they don't want to wait in line, especially during peak holiday periods? What is the cost in terms of onsumer experience and satisfaction?

Apple's store format is a case study in how an omnichannel retailer has changed the consumer experience by ripping out checkout lanes to enable purchase anywhere on the floor with no wait times.

One could argue that removing POS registers and checkout lanes will not work in a store like Walmart. Really? Why not? With more widespread adoption of RFID tags, an individual can scan a whole cart at once. RFID could also establish an added layer of theft prevention out of the front and back doors.

What retailers have not yet realized is that it will not be their choice to make. The consumer is now the POS, not the store or website. Today's consumers can now decide where to purchase, how much they are willing to pay, how to pay, and whether they would like to ship to their home or pick up in-store.

Retail store survival will depend on providing an experience that is consumer-centric and adds value to the customer first and foremost. The best place to start redesigning both the consumer experience and the profitable store of the future will be to rip out the registers and checkout lanes.

Source: Chris Peterson, "Why Do Retail Stores Still Have Cash Registers?," April 7, 2015, http://www.retailcustomerexperience.com/blogs/the-ultimate-retail-disruptors-shoppers-are-the-new-pos/ (accessed January 17, 2016).

The power wall is usually considered to be the wall space to the right as the customer enters the store or department. Most often associated with the free-form layout, this wall space is capable of generating the highest sales. Skilled visual merchandisers will plan the wall presentation first and then group the floor fixtures. The most successful retailers are those that understand the power of the wall to sell.[25]

Dressing Rooms Dressing rooms are critical spaces in which customers decide whether to purchase an item. Large, clean, and comfortable dressing rooms put customers in the mood to buy merchandise. Retailers are using technologies in their dressing rooms to enhance the buying experience. Interactive mirrors, 3-D scanners, and holographic sales assistants may sound like they belong in a sci-fi movie, but they will likely be part of the shopping experience in the near future. Currently, customers bring five or six items into the dressing room and try to narrow down their selection. Often they cannot remember how they looked in each outfit as they try the items on. By putting an interactive mirror in a dressing room, customers can simultaneously see pictures of themselves in all the items they try on.[26]

By using interactive mirrors and webcams, customers can include friends or parents in their shopping experience. Through RFID tagging, the dressing room registers the items shoppers take in to try on and produces video and images of the merchandise. A touch screen gives shoppers the option to invite friends to participate in the buying

sales per square foot
A measure of space productivity used by most retailers since rent and land purchases are assessed on a per-square-foot basis.

sales per linear foot A measure of space productivity used when most merchandise is displayed on multiple shelves of long gondolas, such as in grocery stores.

process. Through their personal cellphones, they can send an email or text message to friends. By clicking on a URL and logging on to a website, the friends can see the items being tried on and make comments. The website could also suggest other complementary merchandise available from the retailer. Customers can then click on one of the recommendations, and it will appear in the mirror superimposed over their image, as though they were trying on the garment.[27]

Although technology and decor can enhance the experience of trying on clothing, some retailers are cautious about the extent to which they will use technology. The personal attention by sales associates remains the most effective agent for providing customer service.

Lo3 Space Management

Allocation of store space to merchandise categories and brands, the location of the departments in the store, and where to place items to attract attention are a few of store planners' and buyers' most complicated and difficult decisions. They must answer four questions:

1. What items, brands, categories, and departments should be carried?
2. How much of each item should be carried?
3. How much space should the merchandise take?
4. Where should the merchandise be located to create maximum exposure?

Space management thus involves two resource decisions: (1) the allocation of store space to merchandise categories and brands, and (2) the location of departments or merchandise categories in the store.

Space Allocated to Merchandise Categories

Some factors that retailers consider when deciding on how much floor or shelf space to allocate to merchandise categories and brands are (1) the productivity of the allocated space, (2) the merchandise's

inventory turnover, (3) the impact on store sales, and (4) the display needs for the merchandise.

Space Productivity Store planners, in conjunction with buyers, typically start by allocating space based on sales productivity. For instance, if knit shirts represent 15 percent of the total expected sales for the men's clothing department, they will initially get 15 percent of the space. Store planners must then adjust the initial estimate on the basis of the following five factors:

- How profitable is the merchandise?
- How will the planned inventory turnover and the resulting stock-to-sales ratio affect how many SKUs will normally be carried in stock? Buyers and store planners must allocate space on the basis of seasonal fluctuations that recognize space demands during peak times, such as Christmas and back-to-school.
- How will the merchandise be displayed?
- Will the location of certain merchandise draw the customer through the store, thus encouraging sales?
- What items does the retailer wish to emphasize?

Exhibit 6–4 shows typical floor space allocation based on sales potential. The front of the store is a much stronger selling space, with the potential to produce 48 percent of sales, whereas the back of the store generates only 16 percent of store sales. Thus, the newest merchandise should be placed at the front of the store to encourage customer response.

But as the discussion of marginal analysis for advertising allocations in Chapter 15 will indicate, retailers should also allocate space to a merchandise category on the basis of its effect on the profitability of the entire store. In practice, this recommendation means that the men's furnishings department should add more space to the knit shirts section as long as the profitability of the additional space is greater than the profitability of the category from which space was taken away. In this condition, the additional space for knit shirts will increase the profitability of the entire store. However, at some point, it will be more profitable to not take away space from other categories.

Two commonly used measures of space productivity are **sales per square foot** and **sales per linear foot**. Apparel retailers that display most of their merchandise on freestanding fixtures typically measure space productivity as sales per square foot. In supermarkets, most merchandise is displayed on shelves.

Exhibit 6-4
Floor Space Allocation Based on Sales Potential

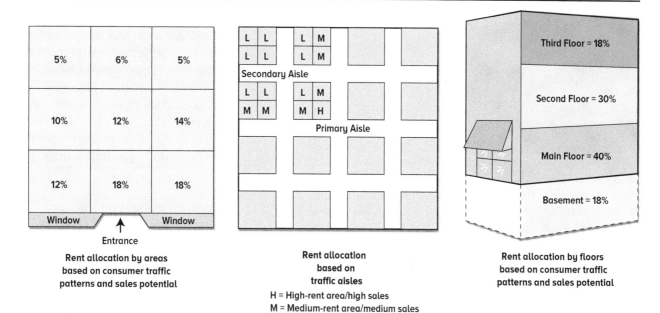

Rent allocation by areas based on consumer traffic patterns and sales potential

Rent allocation based on traffic aisles

H = High-rent area/high sales
M = Medium-rent area/medium sales
L = Low-rent area/low sales

Rent allocation by floors based on consumer traffic patterns and sales potential

---

Because the shelves have approximately the same width, only the length, or the linear dimensions sales per linear foot, is used to assess space productivity.

A more appropriate productivity measure, such as gross margin per square foot, would consider the contribution generated by the merchandise, not just the sales. Thus, if salty snacks generate $400 in gross margin per linear foot and canned soup generates only $300 per linear foot, more space should be allocated to salty snacks. However, factors other than marginal productivity need to be considered when making space allocation decisions. These factors will be discussed in the next section.

In addition, retailers need to allocate space to maximize the profitability of the store, not just a particular merchandise category or department. For instance, supermarkets "over-allocate" space to some low-profitability categories such as milk because an extensive assortment in these categories attracts customers to the store and positively affects the sales of other categories. Retailers might also over-allocate space to categories purchased by their platinum customers, the customers with the highest lifetime value.

Inventory Turnover Inventory turnover affects space allocations in two ways. As will be discussed in Chapter 8, both **inventory turnover** and **gross margin** contribute to **gross margin return on investment (GMROI)**—a measure of the retailer's return on its merchandise inventory investment. Thus,

merchandise categories with higher inventory turnover merit more space than merchandise categories with lower inventory turnover.

Display Considerations The physical limitations of the store and its fixtures affect space allocation. As a result, the store planner needs to provide enough merchandise to fill an entire fixture dedicated to a particular item. A retailer might also decide that it wants to use a merchandise display to build its image. For example, Target has a very appealing offering of its private-label bath towels. To emphasize this offering, it might over-allocate space for bath towels and present a wide range of colours.

Location of Merchandise Categories and Design Elements

As discussed previously, the store layout, signage, and feature areas can guide customers through the

inventory turnover Net sales divided by average retail inventory; used to evaluate how effectively managers use their investment in inventory.

gross margin The difference between the price the customer pays for merchandise and the cost of the merchandise (the price the retailer paid the supplier of the merchandise). More specifically, gross margin = net sales − cost of goods sold (= maintained markup) − alteration cost + cash discounts; also called *gross profit*.

gross margin return on investment (GMROI) A financial ratio that assesses a buyer's contribution to return on assets: gross margin dollars divided by average (cost) inventory.

Why are cosmetics counters typically located near the front of the store?
© McGraw-Hill Education/Gary He.

store. The location of merchandise categories also plays a role in how customers navigate through the store.[28] By strategically placing impulse and demand/destination merchandise throughout the store, retailers increase the chances that customers will shop the entire store and that their attention will be focused on the merchandise that the retailer is most interested in selling—merchandise with a high GMROI. Demand/destination merchandise is products that customers have decided to buy before entering the store.

As customers enter the store and pass through the decompression zone, they are welcomed with introductory displays, including graphics. Once through the decompression zone, they often turn right (Western cultures) and observe the prices and quality of the first items they encounter. This area, referred to as the "strike zone," is critical because it creates the customer's first impression of the store's offering. Thus, retailers display some of their most compelling merchandise in the strike zone.

After passing through the strike zone, the most heavily trafficked and viewed area is the right-hand side of the store. By this point in their journey through the store, customers have become accustomed to the environment, have developed a first impression, and are ready to make purchase decisions. Thus, the right-hand side is a prime area for displaying high GMROI merchandise. For example, supermarkets typically locate the produce section in this area because produce appeals to shoppers' senses. The smell of fresh fruits and vegetables gets a shopper's mouth watering, and the best grocery store customer is a hungry one.

impulse products Products that are purchased by customers without prior plans. These products are almost always located near the front of the store, where they are seen by everyone and may actually draw people into the store.

Impulse Merchandise   The prime store locations for selling merchandise are heavily trafficked areas such as 10 feet beyond the entrance on the right side of the store, the right-hand side of the store, and areas near escalators and cash wraps. In multilevel stores, a space's value decreases the farther it is from the entry-level floor. Thus, **impulse products**—products that are purchased without planning, such as fragrances and cosmetics in department stores and magazines in supermarkets—are almost always located near the front of the store, where they are seen by everyone and may actually draw people into the store.

Demand Merchandise   Some merchandise categories involve a buying process that is best accomplished in a lightly trafficked area. For example, women's lingerie is typically located in a remote area to offer a more private shopping experience.

Categories that require large amounts of floor space, like furniture, are often located in less desirable locations. Some categories, like curtains, need significant wall space, whereas others, like shoes, require easily accessible storage rooms.

Category Adjacencies   Retailers often put complementary categories next to each other to encourage unplanned purchases. For example, men's dress shirts and ties are located next to each other between men's and boy's apparel. Some stores are now combining traditionally separate departments or categories to facilitate multiple purchases using market-basket analysis. Stores are laid out according to the way customers purchase merchandise (by brand, for example, or by lifestyle image), rather than by traditional categories or departments (see Retailing View 6.4).

Seasonal Needs   Some departments need to be more flexible than others. For instance, it's helpful to locate winter coats near sportswear. Extra space in the coat department can be absorbed by sportswear or swimwear in the spring when most of the winter coats have been sold.

Location of Merchandise Within a Category

Retailers use a variety of rules to locate specific SKUs within a category.[29] For instance, supermarkets and drugstores typically place private-label brands to the right of national brands. Because Western consumers read from left to right, they will

Shopping Behaviour and Store Design

Envirosell, a consulting firm in New York, has made a science out of determining the best ways to lay out a department or a store. Although the firm uses lots of hidden video cameras and other high-tech equipment, its most important research tool is a piece of paper called a track sheet in the hands of people called trackers. Trackers follow shoppers and note everything they do. They also make inferences about consumer behaviour on the basis of what they have observed. Examples of their quantitative research findings appear in Exhibits 6–5 and 6–6. Here are just a few of the things that they have learned:

- **Avoid the butt-brush effect.** The "butt-brush effect" was discovered at a New York City Bloomingdale's. The researchers taped shoppers attempting to reach the tie rack while negotiating an entrance during busy times. They noticed that after being bumped once or twice, most shoppers abandoned their search for neckwear. The conclusion: Shoppers don't like to shop when their personal space is invaded.

- **Place merchandise where customers can readily access it.** Toy store designers are, for the most part, still designing stores as if the customer were taller than 5 feet. Designers should be made to get down on their hands and knees (sitting on a skateboard also works quite well) and tour the store from a child's point of view.

- **Make information accessible.** Older shoppers often have a hard time reading the small print on the boxes and the prices. Thus, selective displays should take some of the information off the boxes and enlarge it with a simple 6 foot × 6 foot sign.

Exhibit 6–5
Percentage of Shoppers Visiting Different Areas of the Store

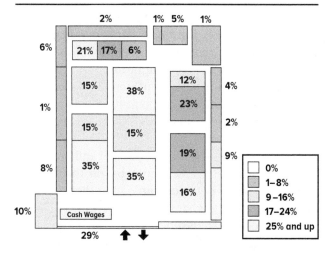

Exhibit 6–6
Number of Shoppers Entering the Store at Different Times of the Day

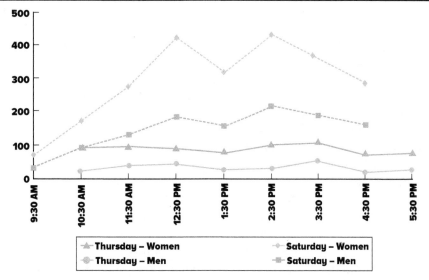

Sources: http://www.envirosell.com (accessed November 19, 2007); "Customer Behavior Insights of Paco Underhill," *Inside Retailing*, November 2, 2007; Paco Underhill, *Call of the Mall: The Geography of Shopping* (New York: Simon & Schuster, 2004); Paco Underhill, *Why We Buy: The Science of Shopping* (New York: Simon & Schuster, 2000).

see the higher-priced national brand first and then see and possibly purchase the lower-priced, higher-margin private-label item on the right that looks similar to the national brand. Produce departments in grocery stores are arranged so that apples are the first item most customers see; apples are a very popular produce item and thus can best initiate a buying pattern.

Supermarkets typically display merchandise on four shelves, with the most profitable merchandise on the third shelf from the floor. The third shelf attracts the most attention because it is at eye level for most adults. Merchandise that appeals to a smaller group of customers is often displayed on the top shelf because reaching for items requires significant effort. Heavy, bulky items are stocked on the bottom shelf for safety reasons.

However, when purchase decisions are influenced by shorter consumers, positioning merchandise on the lower shelves might be more effective. For example, children may influence breakfast cereal purchases when accompanying their parents to the supermarket. Thus, the second shelf from the floor might be a prime location for the most profitable cereal brands. The most appealing and profitable placement for pet treats might be on the bottom shelf to appeal to pets accompanying their pet parents on visits to a pet supply supercentre.

Some tools, discussed in the following section, that retailers use to make decisions on the positioning of items in a category are planograms, videotapes of consumers as they move through the store, and virtual-store software.

Planograms A **planogram** is a diagram that shows how and where specific SKUs should be placed on retail shelves or displays to increase customer purchases. The locations can be illustrated using photographs, computer output, or artists' renderings. In developing the planogram, retailers need to make the category visually appealing, consider the manner in which customers shop (or the manner in which the retailer would like customers to shop), and achieve the retailer's strategic and financial objectives. The technology for computer-generated planograms is quite sophisticated.

Planograms are also useful for merchandise that doesn't fit nicely on shelves in supermarkets or discount stores. Most specialty retailers provide their

planogram A diagram created from photographs, computer output, or artists' renderings that illustrates exactly where every SKU should be placed.

Kimberly-Clark uses virtual-store software that employs a retina-tracking device to record a customer's glances. The information obtained from the software enables the retailer to get a fast read on new product designs and displays without having to conduct real-life tests in the early stages of product development.

Virtual Baby Aisle, © 2005 Kimberly-Clark Worldwide, Inc. Used with permission.

managers with photographs and diagrams of how merchandise should be displayed. Retailing View 6.5 provides an example from the Home Depot planogram playbook.

Videotaping Consumers Another research-method used to assess customer reactions to planograms involves tracking customers in actual store environments. GPS tracking devices are placed in customer shopping carts and on shoppers to determine where customers and carts go in a store. Small video cameras are strapped on the shoppers' foreheads to provide information on their eye movements. These videos can be used to improve layouts and planograms by identifying the causes of slow-moving merchandise, such as poor shelf placement. By studying customers' movements, retailers can also learn where customers pause or move quickly or where there is congestion. This information can help retailers decide, for instance, if the layout and merchandise placement is operating as expected or if new or promoted merchandise is getting the attention it deserves.

Virtual-Store Simulation Virtual-store simulations are another tool used to determine the effects of placing merchandise in different areas of a store and evaluating the potential for the new items.[30] In these simulations, customers stand in front of computer screens that depict a store aisle. Retina-tracking devices record the eye movements of the customers. When the customers push forward on a handle, similar to the handle on a shopping cart, they

Home Depot Truckload Event

FLOORING TRUCKLOAD

We will be featuring great deals on flooring in March to drive traffic in stores and to offer our customers great flooring solutions at great prices. The details are as follows:

Dates:
Thursday, March 23, 2017, to Sunday, March 26, 2017

Applicable Markets:
National

Marketing Support:
Messaging in the flyer (fiscal week seven), call outs on homedepot.ca, direct mail pieces to customers and much more.

Sam Dao/Alamy.

Signage:
All stores will receive signage for this event prior to the start date. It should be placed around the store **(after closing)** on March 22 in an effort to generate excitement.

Merchandising Requirements:
The items listed below are incremental product buys (this means that new inventory will be arriving in your store). Please ensure these articles are placed in the flooring laydown area and merchandised with signage.

Article Number	Description
1000741618	12MM SOHO OAK 12.06 SQFT
1000749920	3/4″ × 1/4″ Oak Gunstock 22SF/CA
1000687267	7MM PLYMOUTH OAK 28.67 SQFT
1000753511	HB 10MM Lisbon Maple 13.78 SQFT
1000724818	12 × 12 Dakota Sand
1000764940	18 × 30 Korhani Coco mats
1000719641	5 × 7 Bound Remnant
1000533897	8 × 10 Assorted Bound Remnant Rug
1000755979	5 × 8 Assorted woven polypropolene rugs
1000776826	28 × 40 assorted shag mats
1000772687	3 × 4 Lexington Assorted 20RIB

progress down the simulated aisle. Customers can virtually reach forward, pick an item off the shelf, look at the packaging, and then place the item in the virtual cart. These virtual shopping trips allow retailers and their suppliers to develop a better understanding of how customers will respond to different planograms.

LO4 Visual Merchandising

Visual merchandising is the presentation of a store and its merchandise in ways that will attract the attention of potential customers.

visual merchandising The presentation of a store and its merchandise in ways that will attract the attention of potential customers.

Many methods are available to retailers for effectively presenting merchandise to the customer. To decide which is best for a particular situation, store planners must consider the following four issues:

- Merchandise should be displayed in a manner consistent with the store's image. For instance, some traditional men's stores display dress shirts by size, so all size 16–34 shirts are together. Thus, the customer can easily determine what's available in his size. This is consistent with a no-nonsense image of the store. Other stores keep all colour/style combinations together. This presentation evokes a more fashion-forward image and is more aesthetically pleasing.

- Store planners must consider the nature of the product. Basic jeans can easily be displayed in stacks, but skirts must be hung so that the customer can more easily examine the design and style.

- Packaging often dictates how the product is displayed. Discount stores sell small packages of nuts and bolts, for example, but some hardware stores still sell individual nuts and bolts. Although the per-unit cost is significantly higher for the packages, self-service operations don't have adequate personnel to weigh and bag these small items.

- A product's profit potential influences display decisions. For example, low-profit, high-turnover items such as back-to-school supplies don't require the same elaborate, expensive displays as Mont Blanc fountain pens.

In this section, we will examine some specific presentation techniques. Then we will describe the fixtures used in these merchandise presentations.

Presentation Techniques

Idea-Oriented Presentation   Some retailers successfully use an **idea-oriented presentation**—a method of presenting merchandise based on a specific idea or the image of the store. Women's fashions, for instance, are often displayed to present an overall image or idea. Also, furniture is combined in room settings to give customers an idea of how it would look in their homes. Individual items are grouped to show customers how the items could be used and combined. This approach encourages the customer to make multiple complementary purchases.

idea-oriented presentation A method of presenting merchandise based on a specific idea or the image of the store.

vertical merchandising A method whereby merchandise is organized to follow the eye's natural up-and-down movement.

Style/Item Presentation   Probably the most common technique of organizing stock is by style or item. Discount stores, grocery stores, hardware stores, and drugstores employ this method for nearly every category of merchandise. Also, many apparel retailers use this technique. When customers look for a particular type of merchandise, such as sweaters, they expect to find all items in the same location.

Arranging items by size is a common method of organizing many types of merchandise, from nuts and bolts to apparel. Since the customer usually knows the desired size, it's easy to locate items organized in this manner.

Colour Presentation   A powerful merchandising technique is referred to as colour blocking. Fashion apparel and home fashion retailers realize that by grouping merchandise by colour not only does the store look more attractive, but also the technique encourages multiple sales. Women are particularly attracted to colour presentation, and most will have strong colour preferences according to personal favourites or fashion dominance. Red is the most noticeable colour and has the ability to grab the customer's attention when used in visual presentation and signage. Home Outfitters uses colour blocking to increase buyer appeal in everything from kitchenware to home fashions.

Price Lining   Organizing merchandise in price categories, or *price lining* (when retailers offer a limited number of predetermined price points within a classification), is a strategy that helps customers easily find merchandise at the price they wish to pay. For instance, men's dress shirts may be organized into three groups selling for $30, $45, and $60. Moore's Clothing has an effective program of price lining: good–better–best.

Vertical Merchandising   Another common way of organizing merchandise is **vertical merchandising**. Here, merchandise is presented vertically using walls and high gondolas. Customers shop much as they read a newspaper—from left to right, going down each column, and top to bottom. Stores can

> **DID YOU KNOW?**
>
> 67 percent of US women purchased clothing online from retailers in the past year.[31]

Exhibit 6–7
Vertical versus Horizontal Presentation

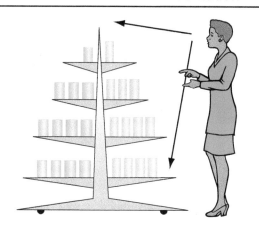

effectively organize merchandise to follow the eye's natural movement. Good vertical merchandising techniques will maximize product visibility as the customer scans from left to right. A poor presentation would be horizontal merchandising, where the customer only sees a small assortment of products for sale. See Exhibit 6–7 for a comparison of vertical and horizontal merchandising.

Retailers take advantage of this tendency in several ways. Many grocery stores put national brands at eye level and store brands on lower shelves because customers scan from eye level down. Finally, retailers often display merchandise in bold vertical bands of an item. For instance, you will see vertical columns of towels of the same colour displayed in a department store or a vertical band of yellow-and-orange boxes of Tide detergent followed by a band of blue Cheer boxes in a supermarket.

By presenting the merchandise vertically, stores show more merchandise per square foot—making better use of floor space by increasing its selling capacity and getting a better return for their money (floor space is expensive). The customer has a category or style of merchandise right in front of her—at eye and hand level—and does not have to run back and forth along the fixture to find what the store has in a given category or style. Customer access to merchandise on the sales floor has positive implications for payroll.

Tonnage Merchandising As the name implies, **tonnage merchandising** is a display technique in which large quantities of merchandise are displayed together. Customers have come to equate tonnage with low price, following the retail adage "stock it high and let it fly." Tonnage merchandising is therefore used to enhance and reinforce a store's price image. Using this display concept, the merchandise itself is the display, and the retailer hopes customers will notice the merchandise and be drawn to it. For instance, before many holidays, grocery stores use an entire end of a gondola (i.e., an end cap) to display six-packs of soft drinks.

Frontal Presentation It is important to show as much of the merchandise as possible. The **frontal presentation** is a method of displaying merchandise in which the retailer exposes as much of the product as possible to catch the customer's eye. Book manufacturers, for instance, make great efforts to create eye-catching covers. But bookstores usually display books exposing only the spine. To create an effective display and break the monotony, book retailers often face the cover out like a billboard to catch the customer's attention. A similar frontal presentation is achieved on a rack of apparel by simply turning one item out to show the merchandise. The goal is to face the merchandise out to the customer's viewpoint whenever possible. For example, clothing on a straight rack may show only the sleeve; using the face-out technique for the garment will show its collar and unique details. Employing merchandise face-outs will encourage sales.

Fixtures

The primary purposes of fixtures are to efficiently hold and display merchandise. At the same time, they must help define areas of a store and encourage traffic flow. Fixtures must be in concert with the other physical aspects of the store, such as floor coverings and lighting, as well as the overall image of the store. For instance, in stores designed to convey a sense of tradition or history, customers automatically expect to see lots of wood rather than plastic or metal fixtures. Wood mixed with metal, acrylic, or stone changes the traditional orientation. The rule of thumb is that the more unexpected the combination of textures, the more contemporary the image.

Fixtures come in an infinite variety of styles, colours, sizes, and textures, but only a few basic types are commonly used. For apparel, retailers use the straight rack, rounder, and four-way. The mainstay fixture for most other merchandise is the gondola.

tonnage merchandising A display technique in which large quantities of merchandise are displayed together.

frontal presentation A method of displaying merchandise in which the retailer exposes as much of the product as possible to catch the customer's eye.

straight rack A type of fixture that consists of a long pipe suspended with supports going to the floor or attached to a wall.

rounder A round fixture that sits on a pedestal. Smaller than the straight rack, it is designed to hold a maximum amount of merchandise. Also known as a *bulk fixture* or *capacity fixture*.

four-way fixture A fixture with two crossbars that sit perpendicular to each other on a pedestal. Also known as a *feature fixture*.

gondola An island type of self-service counter with tiers of shelves, bins, or pegs.

The **straight rack** consists of a long pipe suspended with supports going to the floor or attached to a wall (Exhibit 6–8A). Although the straight rack can hold a lot of apparel, it's hard to feature specific styles or colours. All the customer can see is a sleeve or a pant leg. As a result, straight racks are often found in discount and off-price apparel stores.

A **rounder**, also known as a *bulk fixture* or *capacity fixture*, is a round fixture that sits on a pedestal (Exhibit 6–8B). Although smaller than the straight rack, it's designed to hold a maximum amount of merchandise. Since they are easy to move and they efficiently store apparel, rounders are found in most types of apparel stores. But as with the straight rack, customers can't get a frontal view of the merchandise.

A **four-way fixture**, also known as a *feature fixture*, has two crossbars that sit perpendicular to each other on a pedestal (Exhibit 6–8C). This fixture holds a large amount of merchandise and allows the customer to view the entire garment. The four-way is harder to properly maintain than the rounder or straight rack, however. All merchandise on an arm must be of a similar style and colour, or the customer may become confused. Due to their superior display properties, four-way fixtures are commonly used by fashion-oriented apparel retailers.

A **gondola**, an island type of self-service counter with tiers of shelves, bins, or pegs, is extremely versatile (Exhibit 6–8D). They are used extensively, but not exclusively, in grocery and discount stores to display everything from canned foods to baseball gloves. Gondolas are also used to display towels, sheets, and housewares in department stores. Folded apparel can be efficiently displayed on gondolas, but because the items are folded, it's even harder for customers to view apparel on gondolas than on straight racks.

DID YOU KNOW?

Aldo, the Canadian shoe company, boasts average sales of more than $1000 per square foot, more than double other shoe stores in Canada.[32]

Exhibit 6–8
Four Fixture Types

(A) Straight rack

(B) Rounder

(C) Four-way

(D) Gondola

(all) © Sharon Hoogstraten.

Lo5 Creating an Appealing Store Atmosphere

To provide a rewarding shopping experience, retailers go beyond presenting appealing merchandise. For example, Disney plans to spend about $1 million per store to create a highly entertaining and rewarding experience for its customers using interactive technology. The chain's traditional approach of displaying row after row of toys and apparel geared to Disney franchises will be given a high-tech makeover. Children will be able to watch film clips of their choice in a theatre, participate in karaoke contests, and chat live with Disney stars via satellite. Computer chips embedded in packaging will activate hidden features so that when children walk by a "magic mirror" while holding a princess tiara, Cinderella will appear and say something to them.

Disney will also adopt Apple-like touches, such as mobile checkouts (employees will carry miniature receipt printers in their aprons) and an emphasis on community (Disney's theatre idea is an extension of Apple's lecture spaces). The focus will be on interactivity—parents will even be able to book a Disney cruise on touch-screen kiosks while their children play.[33]

Employees play a major role in creating an appealing store environment. For example, the atmosphere at Pike Place Market in Seattle is unusual. Employees, known as fishmongers, throw fish over the counters to co-workers for wrapping. The fishmongers also invite customers to get in on the action and try to catch fish. What could be a dull retail space is transformed into a place where customers and employees are smiling, laughing, and connecting with one another, while keeping an eye out for flying fish.[34]

In addition to these interactive technologies, retailers are using lighting, colour, music, and scent. **Atmospherics** refers to the design of an environment via visual communications, colour, lighting, music, and scent to stimulate customers' perceptual and emotional responses and ultimately to affect their purchase behaviour.[35] Many retailers have discovered the subtle benefits of developing atmospherics that complement other aspects of the store design and the merchandise. Research has shown that it is important for these atmospheric elements to work together, for example, the right music with the right scent.[36] Now let's explore some basic principles of good atmospheric design and examine a few new, exciting, and somewhat controversial trends.

Lighting

Good lighting in a store involves more than simply illuminating space. Lighting is used to highlight merchandise, sculpt space, and capture a mood or feeling that enhances the store's image. Lighting can also be used to downplay less attractive features that can't be changed. Having the appropriate lighting has been shown to positively influence customer shopping behaviour.[37]

Highlight Merchandise   A good lighting system helps create a sense of excitement in the store. At the same time, lighting must provide an accurate colour rendition of the merchandise so that a green silk tie looks the same colour in the store as outside. Similarly, lighting should complement the customer. A department store's cosmetics area, for instance, requires more expensive lighting than the fluorescent lighting found in many grocery stores because it has to complement the customer and make her skin look natural.

Another key use of lighting is called **popping the merchandise**—focusing spotlights on special feature areas and items. Using lighting to focus on

merchandise moves shoppers' eyes to the merchandise and draws customers strategically through the store. For example, retailers may choose to highlight limited and one-of-a-kind glass sculptures with special lighting.

Capture a Mood and Maintain an Image   Traditionally, North American specialty and department stores have employed incandescent lighting sources to promote a warm and cozy ambience.[38] Overall lighting sources are reduced and accent lighting is added to call attention to merchandise and displays.

European stores have long favoured high light levels, cool colours, and little contrast or accent lighting. European lighting design is bolder, starker, and more minimal than in North America, creating a very different mood and image than the softer incandescent lighting. Lighting can hide errors and outmoded store designs. A popular technique is to focus product lighting very high compared to the rest of the store and paint the ceiling dark to downplay unsightly concrete and ventilation ducts.

Energy-Efficient Lighting   As the price of energy soars and retailers and their customers become more energy-conscious, retailers are looking for ways to cut their energy costs and be more ecologically friendly. One obvious source of energy consumption is the lighting in a store. Stores are switching from incandescent lighting to more energy-efficient fluorescent lights, installing display lights that turn off and on based on customer motion detectors, and cutting energy used to light sales floors by as much as 20 percent. By installing LED lights in storefront signs, retailers use 90 percent less energy than with traditional lighting applications.

Colour

The creative use of colour can enhance a retailer's image and help create a mood. Research has shown that warm colours (red and yellow) produce opposite physiological and psychological effects from cool colours (blue and green), which are opposite on the colour spectrum.[39] Red and other warm

atmospherics The design of an environment via visual communications, lighting, colour, music, and scent to stimulate customers' perceptual and emotional responses and ultimately to affect their purchase behaviour.

popping the merchandise Focusing spotlights on special feature areas and items.

© Maclean's-Peter Bregg/The Canadian Press.

colours have been found to increase blood pressure, respiratory rate, and other physiological responses. As we translate these findings to a retail store environment, warm colours are thought to attract customers and gain attention, yet they can be distracting and even unpleasant if too strong a hue. Fast-food restaurants often use warm colours to facilitate rapid turnover.

In contrast, research indicates that cool colours, such as blue or green, are relaxing, peaceful, calm, and pleasant. Thus, cool colours may be most effective for retailers selling anxiety-causing products, such as expensive shopping goods, or services such as those provided at a dentist's office.

Music

Like colour and lighting, music can either add to or detract from a retailer's total atmospheric package. Unlike other atmospheric elements, however, music can be easily changed. Although research in grocery stores indicates that music's tempo and volume don't significantly influence patrons' shopping time or purchase amount,[40] other research has shown that the presence of music positively affects customers' attitudes toward the store.[41]

Retailers can also use music to affect customers' behaviour. Music can control the pace of store traffic, create an image, and attract or direct consumers' attention. For instance, the Disney Stores pipe in soundtracks from famous Disney movies that are tied directly to the merchandise.

Scent

Researchers say smell can affect a shopper's behaviour, but it's mainly about trying to make sure that shoppers are having a pleasant experience, such as the smell of baby powder in an infant clothing department or the aroma of freshly baked cookies in a model home. As an example, consider the ice cream chain that introduced the smell of waffle cones and saw sales rise by more than a third. Vancouver-based Enhance Air Technologies believes that tapping customers' noses will also open their wallets to beat slow retail sales.

Many buying decisions are based on emotions, and smell has a large impact on our emotions. One researcher indicated that "Smell, more than any other sense, is a straight line to feelings of happiness, hunger, disgust, and nostalgia—the same feelings marketers want to tap."[42] In fact, research indicates that scent, in conjunction with music, has a positive impact on impulse buying behaviour and customer satisfaction.[43] Scents that are neutral were found to produce better perceptions of the store than no scent. As a result, customers in a scented store perceive that they have spent less time in the store than those in a no-scent store. This study suggests that stores using scents may improve customers' subjective shopping experience by making them feel that they are spending less time examining merchandise or waiting for sales help or to check out.

Retailers must carefully plan the scents that they use, depending on their target market. The gender of the target customer should be taken into account when choosing the intensity of the fragrance in a store. Research has shown that women have a better ability to smell than men. Age and ethnic background are also factors. As people get older, their sense of smell decreases. Half of all people over age 65 and three-quarters over age 80 have almost no sense of smell at all.[44] Nevertheless, many retailers are trying to cash in on what the nose knows.

Retailing View 6.6 describes Bank of Montreal's "fresh" approach to service retailing and how it has redesigned itself to appeal to a clients by providing a more relaxing and inviting environment for consumers' senses.

How Exciting Should a Store Be?

Retailers such as REI, Build-A-Bear Workshop, Bass Pro Shops, and Indigo attempt to create an entertaining shopping environment by viewing their stores as theatrical scenes: The floor and walls constitute the stage and scenery; the lighting, fixtures, and displays are the props; and the merchandise represents the performance. This creation of a theatrical experience in stores has resulted in a combination of retailing and entertainment. In contrast, retail chains such as Costco and Home Depot successfully use minimalist, warehouse-style shopping environments.

Does providing an exciting, entertaining store environment lead customers to patronize a store more frequently and spend more time and money during each visit? The answer to this question: It depends.[45]

The impact of the store's environment depends on the customer's shopping goals. The two basic shopping goals are task completion, such as buying a new suit for a job interview, and recreation, such as spending a Saturday afternoon with a friend wandering through a mall. When customers are shopping to complete a task that they view as inherently unrewarding, they prefer to be in a soothing, calming environment—a simple atmosphere with slow music, dimmer lighting, and blue/green colours. However, when customers go shopping for fun, an inherently rewarding activity, they want to be in an exciting atmosphere—a complex environment with fast music, bright lighting, and red/yellow colours.

What does this mean for retailers? They must consider the typical shopping goals for their customers when designing their store environments. For example, grocery shopping is typically viewed as an unpleasant task, thus supermarkets should be designed in soothing colours and use slow background music. In contrast, shopping for fashion apparel is typically viewed as fun, so an arousing environment in apparel retail outlets will have a positive impact on customers' shopping behaviour.

The level of excitement caused by the environment might vary across the store. For example, a consumer electronics retailer might create a low-arousal environment in the accessories area to accommodate customers who typically are task-oriented when shopping for print cartridges and batteries, but then create a high-arousal environment in the home-entertainment area that is typically visited by more pleasure-seeking shopping customers.

Finally, retailers might vary the nature of their websites for customers depending on their shopping goals. For example, research suggests that Amazon should serve up complex, high-arousal websites with rich media to customers who indicate they are browsing, but simpler, low-arousal sites to customers looking for a specific book.[46] Some similar parallels between store and website designs are drawn in the following section.

BMO Launches Beautiful Figure3-Designed Flagship at Canada's Financial Crossroads

Although not the traditional type of retail reported on at *Retail Insider*, the following is a revelation of Bank of Montreal's impressive new 21 000 square foot flagship at Toronto's First Canadian Place.

According to the space's design firm figure3, banks today are facing many of the same challenges as "traditional" retailers: fierce competition for share of mind and wallet—and, as e-commerce expands, more consumers turning to the convenience of online to shop and carry out transactions. figure3 designed a storefront which it says helps in "developing meaningful relationships between businesses and customers, the needs of both can be successfully merged."

In working with BMO, figure3's retail design team was charged with "seeing what others don't," in order to make intelligent, evidence-based decisions for the redesign of the BMO flagship at First Canadian Place.

This meant developing a design strategy that changes the way BMO's customers think, feel, and behave in the new 21 000 square foot branch—a direct function of design research identifying a need for clarity in the banking experience.

"The new First Canadian Place branch is designed with the customer experience in mind, featuring a layout that removes physical barriers and ultimately fosters deeper,

Courtesy of figure3.

more valuable advice-based conversations," said Tony Tintinalli, regional vice president, BMO Bank of Montreal.

The corner of King Street and Bay Street is one of downtown Toronto's busiest and most crowded corners. The illuminated branding (see image at the top of this article), BMO blue racing stripe and digital signage, grabs the attention of passersby, while the floor-to-ceiling windows provide a clear view of what is happening inside.

Once inside, customers are struck by the openness of the bank—"we have pulled back the curtains,"

Sources: Text courtesy of figure3 and Retail Insider. Photos courtesy of figure3.

L06 Website Design

In many, but not all, cases, the good design principles that apply to a physical store can also be applied to a website and/or mobile app.[47] Consider the following examples.

Simplicity Matters

A good store design allows shoppers to move freely, unencumbered by clutter. There is a fine line between providing customers with a good assortment and confusing them with too much merchandise.[48]

Similarly in a website, it is not necessary to mention all the merchandise available at a site on each page. It is better to present a limited selection tailored to the customer's needs and then provide links to related merchandise and alternative assortments. It is also important to include navigation headings and a search engine feature on each page in case a customer gets lost. The search feature in the virtual world is similar to having sales associates readily available in the physical world. Also, less is more. Having a small number of standard links on every page makes it more likely that users can learn the navigation scheme for the site.

Courtesy of figure3.

Courtesy of figure3.

says Marjorie Mackenzie, figure3's VP of retail. No longer is banking something that happens in back rooms—customers immediately feel empowered; like the integral part of the banking experience. By breaking up the long, transactional "us vs. them" counter and offering seating, traditional physical and emotional barriers are reduced and customers are invited to share in a more collaborative interaction with the staff.

The Business Banking area functions as a "bank-within-a-bank." The intimate, seated interaction space allows people to comfortably engage in more comprehensive conversations, encouraging them to stay a little longer and spend time learning about products and services they care about. The inclusion of new omni-channel elements (like the tablets pictured), helps make the transition from online to in-store more streamlined, offering customers a compatible banking experience with direct access to apps and online banking as well as in-store offerings.

The meeting pods are a conscious nod to the delicate balance of transparency and privacy in a banking experience. While the pods are situated within the open environment, the custom furniture offers acoustic and visual privacy in a comfortable, relaxed setting. Added mobile technology allows for movement between pods, streamlining information sharing.

Getting Around

When a store is properly designed, customers should be able to easily find what they are looking for. The products that customers frequently purchase together are often displayed together: umbrellas with raincoats, soft drinks with snack foods, and tomato sauce with pasta. One way to help customers get around a website is by using links to other sections of the site. When establishing local links, websites should connect:

- products that are similar in price
- complementary products

- products that differ from the product shown on some important dimension (e.g., a link to organic produce if the user is looking at natural breakfast cereals)
- different versions of the shown product (e.g., the same blouse in yellow if the customer is viewing a red blouse)

Let Them See It

Stores are designed so that customers can easily view the merchandise and read the signs. But in a store, if the lighting isn't good or a sign is too small to read, the customer can always move around to get a better view. Customers don't have this flexibility on the Internet. Web designers should assume that all potential viewers lack perfect vision. They should strive for realistic colours and sharpness. Some retailers that use the Internet channel have developed interesting ways of viewing merchandise in multiple dimensions (see, for instance, http://www.landsend.com).

Chapters/Indigo has a comfy and creative setting for grown-ups and children alike.

© The Globe and Mail-Fernando Morales/The Canadian Press.

Blend the Website and Devices With the Store

It is important to visually reassure customers that they are going to have the same satisfactory experience on the website and devices that they have in stores. Even if the electronic store is designed for navigation efficiency, some design elements should still be common to both channels. For instance, though different store types, http://www.tiffany.com and http://www.burberry.com each have similar looks and feels to those of their stores.

DID YOU KNOW?

Burberry is regarded as the pioneer in omni-channel retailing.

With the impact of omni-channel retailing, retailers must consider all devices that consumers interact with (tablets, smartphones, and computers) to view merchandise. Failure to do so could impact the shopping experience and result in a loss sale due to the inability to make consumers "feel" they are interacting with brand in a similar fashion that they would in bricks-and-mortar location.

Prioritize

Stores become annoying if everything jumps out at you as if to say, "Buy me! No, buy me!" Other stores are so bland that the merchandise appears boring. Setting priorities for merchandise displays and locations is just as important on the website as it is in a physical store. A common mistake on many Internet sites is that everything is too prominent, resulting from an overuse of colours, animation, blinking, and graphics. If everything is equally prominent, then *nothing* is prominent. Being too bland is

equally troublesome. The site should be designed to advise the customers and guide them to the most important or most promising choices, while also ensuring their freedom to go anywhere they please. Like a newspaper, the most important items or categories should be given the bigger headlines and more prominent placement.

Type of Layout

Some stores are laid out to be functional, like supermarkets and discount stores. They use a grid design to make it easy to locate merchandise. Other stores, like department stores or bookstores, use a more relaxed layout to encourage browsing. The trick is to pick the appropriate layout that matches the typical motives of the shopper.

Here is where store layout and website layout differ. Although many higher-end multichannel retailers experimented with fancy and complex designs in their early years on the Internet, most have become much more simple and utilitarian than their bricks-and-mortar counterparts (see, for instance, http://www.polo.com, http://www.harryrosen.com, and http://www.marks.com). When shopping on the Web, customers are interested in speed, convenience, and ease of navigation, not necessarily fancy graphics.[49]

Store designers also strive to make their stores seem different, to stand out in the crowd. A website, however, must strike a balance between keeping customers' interest and providing them with a basic comfort level based on convention. Users spend most of their time on *other* sites, so that's where they form their expectations about how most sites work.

When trying to make a decision about website design, good designers look at the most visited sites on the Internet to see how they organize their information. If 90 percent or more of the big sites do things in a single way, then it is the de facto standard.

Checkout

Physical stores recognize the perils of long lines at checkout, and some have taken steps to alleviate the problem, as we discussed earlier in this chapter. The problem of abandoned carts at checkout is even more acute with Internet sites. Over half of all online customers abandon their purchases during the checkout process—one of the greatest causes of lost revenue for online retailers.[50] Some tips for lessening the abandoned online cart problem include the following:[51]

DID YOU KNOW?

The average rate of cart abandonment in 2015 was 68 percent. That means that two-thirds of online shoppers add to their basket only to leave the items there.[52]

- **Make the process seem clear and simple.** Make sure customers know what to expect from the checkout process, how long it will take, and what details they must provide. Because customers hate hidden charges and delivery costs, make this information clear at the beginning of the process. Giving some visible signs of progress through the checkout stages also helps.

- **Close off the checkout process.** Remove links to any parts of the site other than the specific stages of the checkout process to focus the customer's mind. Once in the checkout area, there should be only one place customers can go: purchase confirmation.

- **Make the process navigable without threatening the loss of information.** Customers may need to make changes at different stages, so making it possible for them to go back and forth through the process without losing any of the details they have already entered is vital to minimize frustration. Back buttons on the form, which save data when clicked, are a good way to achieve this functionality and offer an alternative to hitting the back button on a browser, which causes customers to lose information. Enabling them to use the browser to navigate through checkout and still not lose their data would be even better.

- **Reinforce trust in the checkout process.** Display clear signs of server security and third-party verification logos. The company's full address and phone number should also be provided, as well as links to information about the terms and conditions, delivery, and payment rules.

SUMMARY

This chapter explains how retailers can set up a series of stimuli through merchandise presentation that will encourage customers to move from point to point in the store until they reach, touch, and make a purchase. Retailers have the ability to control the eye and body movements of their customers. Ultimately, store design shapes the shopping experience and has a tremendous impact on retail sales potential.

Amid the competitive marketplace, retailers are increasingly realizing that the key to success is identity. Now, more than ever, it is important to stand out from the retail crowd and be noticed. Most customers will pass by the front of a retail store in 10 seconds or less. Therefore, understanding and controlling the retail image become essential parts of the retailer's strategic plan.

Store designers, buyers, and merchandise planners are faced with a number of issues to consider. A good store layout helps customers find and purchase merchandise. Retailers commonly use several types of layouts. The grid design is best for stores in which customers are expected to explore the entire store, such as grocery stores and drugstores. Racetrack designs are more common in large upscale stores such as department stores. Free-form designs are usually found in small specialty stores and within large stores' departments. Store planners also must carefully delineate different areas of the store. Feature areas, bulk of stock, and walls each have their own unique purpose, but must also be coordinated to create a unifying theme.

There is more to assigning space to merchandise and departments than just determining where they will fit. Retailers should determine the location of departments based on the overall profitability and inventory turnover goals of the assortment, the type of product, consumer buying behaviour, the relationship with merchandise in other departments, and the physical characteristics of the merchandise. Planograms, both manual and computer-generated, are used to experiment with various space allocation configurations to determine the most productive use of space. When evaluating the productivity of retail space, retailers generally use sales per square foot.

Several tricks of the trade can help retailers present merchandise to facilitate sales. Retailers must attempt to empathize with the shopping experience and answer the following questions: How does the customer expect to find the merchandise? Is it easier to view, understand, and ultimately purchase merchandise when it's presented as a total concept or presented by manufacturer, colour, style, size, or price? Ultimately, retailers must decide on the appropriate type of fixture to use for a particular purpose.

Retailers use various forms of atmospherics—graphics, signs, and theatrical effects—to facilitate sales. Strategies involve lighting, colour, music, and scent. The use of atmospherics can create a calming environment for task-oriented shoppers or an exciting environment for recreational shoppers.

Although a retailer's website is different than its physical store, in many cases, good design principles that apply to a physical store space can also be applied to a website.

KEY TERMS

atmospherics
category signage
checkout areas
digital signage
end caps
feature areas
four-way fixture
free-form layout
freestanding fixtures
frontal presentation
gondola
grid layout

gross margin
gross margin return on investment
  (GMROI)
hedonic benefit
idea-oriented presentation
impulse products
inventory turnover
planogram
point-of-sale (POS) areas
point-of-sale signage
popping the merchandise
promotional aisle or area

promotional signage
racetrack layout
rounder
sales per linear foot
sales per square foot
servuction system
straight rack
tonnage merchandising
utilitarian benefit
vertical merchandising
visual merchandising

1. 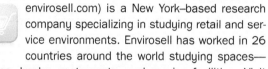 **GO SHOPPING** Go into a store of your choice and evaluate its layout, design, and visual merchandising.

- In general, are the techniques consistent with the exterior image of the store and location?
- Is the store's ambience consistent with the merchandise presented and the target customer?
- Does the store need to be redesigned? Do you think it needs a facelift, update, remodel, or renovation?
- To what extent are the store's layout, design, and merchandising techniques flexible?
- Notice the lighting. Does it do a good job in highlighting merchandise, structuring space, capturing a mood, and downplaying unwanted features?
- Does the layout maximize sales potential?
- Are the fixtures consistent with the merchandise and the overall ambience of the store? Are they flexible?
- Evaluate the store's signage. Does it do an effective job in selling merchandise?
- Has the retailer used any theatrical effects to help sell merchandise?
- Does the layout draw people through the store?
- Evaluate the retailer's use of empty space.
- Has the retailer taken advantage of the opportunity to sell merchandise in feature areas?
- Does the store make creative use of wall space?
- What type of layout does the store use? Is it appropriate for the type of store? Would another type of layout be better?
- Ask the store manager how the profitability of space is evaluated. Is there a better approach?
- Ask the store manager how space is assigned to merchandise. Critically evaluate the answer.
- Ask the store manager if planograms are used. If so, try to determine what factors are considered when putting together a planogram.
- Has the retailer employed any techniques for achieving greater space productivity, such as using the cube, downsizing gondolas and racks, and minimizing non-selling space?
- Are departments in the most appropriate locations? Would you move any departments?
- What method(s) has the retailer used for organizing merchandise? Suggest appropriate changes.

2. INTERNET EXERCISE Envirosell (http://www.envirosell.com) is a New York–based research company specializing in studying retail and service environments. Envirosell has worked in 26 countries around the world studying spaces—stores, banks, restaurants, and service facilities. Visit the website and answer the following questions:

a) Describe the three proprietary research tools used by Envirosell to document and analyze consumer behaviour.

b) In its research, Envirosell collects data to measure shopping behaviour in a retail environment. Identify the specific data that are collected.

c) View the videos on the Envirosell website. Observe and discuss consumer behaviour.

3. INTERNET EXERCISE Go to the following websites and review the white papers by Retail Shelf Planner: http://www.planograms.eu/Documents/White_Paper_-_Planogram_Data_Requirements.pdf and http://www.planograms.eu/Documents/White_Paper_-_Analyzing_your_first_planogram.pdf. What are the five levels at which planograms can be used? How can retailers use planograms to evaluate the best shelf placement for new products in terms of visual impact, consumers' shopping patterns, and financial earnings potential?

DISCUSSION QUESTIONS AND PROBLEMS

1. Name your favourite retail store.
   a) Describe in detail the aspects of store design and merchandise that appeal to you.
   b) Describe how this image attracts the target customer.

2. Assume you have been hired to assess a local discount store's space productivity. What analytical tools would you use to assess the situation? What suggestions would you make to improve the store's space productivity?

3. What are the different types of design that can be used in a store layout? Why are some stores more suited for a particular type of layout than others?

4. Generally speaking, departments located near entrances, on major aisles, and on the main level of multilevel stores have the best profit-generating potential. What additional factors help to determine the location of departments? Give examples of each factor.

5. A department store is building an addition. The merchandise manager for furniture is trying to convince the vice-president to allot this new space to the furniture department. The merchandise manager for men's clothing is also trying to gain the space. What points should each manager use when presenting his or her rationale?

6. Which retailers are particularly good at presenting their store as theatre? Why?

7. Lighting in a store has been said to be similar to makeup on a model. Why?

8. Why do supermarkets put candy at the front of the store, and milk and eggs at the back of the store?

9. One of the fastest-growing sectors of the population is those aged 60 and over, who may have limitations in their vision, hearing, and movement. How can retailers develop store designs with the older population's needs in mind?

10. Name your favourite store. Analyze the merchandise layout with reference to Exhibit 6–3 sales potential.

11. Consider the following types of retail formats that you likely have visited in the past: discount store, department store, office superstore, food store, clothing specialty store, and a card and gift store. Describe which retail formats have implemented the best practices for coordinating signs and graphics with each store's image, and which formats should improve this aspect of their store layout, design, and visual merchandising. What was appealing to you as a shopper in the stores with a coordinated strategy for store signage and retail brand image?

CHAPTER SEVEN

International retailing strategy

LEARNING OBJECTIVES

Lo1   Examine Canada's changing retail marketspace.

Lo2   Review the factors in the marketplace that would encourage a move to international retail expansion.

Lo3   Review the four characteristics of retailers that have successfully exploited international growth opportunities.

Lo4   Identify strategic decisions that must be considered when entering the international marketplace.

Lo5   Discuss the differences between a global retailer and a multinational retailer.

Lo6   Explore the top 250 global retailers.

SPOTLIGHT ON RETAILING

IKEA: BRINGING ITS PHILOSOPHY TO A WORLD MARKET

As it expands globally, IKEA is not just selling products, it's also selling its philosophy: This is how things are done in Sweden. The IKEA concept is based on offering unique, well-designed, functional furniture at low prices. Home furnishing solutions and products are displayed in realistic room settings. Customers are encouraged to get actively involved in the shopping experience by sitting on the sofas and opening and closing drawers. Prices and product information are clearly marked on large, easy-to-read tags, making it easier for customers to serve themselves. Merchandise is purchased in unassembled flat packs. The guiding philosophy is: "You do your part. We do our part. Together, we save money."

Store openings generate tremendous excitement and large crowds. In September 2004, two men were trampled to death and 16 shoppers were injured in a rush by 20 000 people to claim vouchers at the first IKEA in Saudi Arabia. In February 2005, a riot at the opening of a new IKEA in North London forced the store to close just 30 minutes after opening. IKEA currently operates 130 stores in 29 countries.

Other global retailers such as McDonald's make changes to adapt to local preferences; IKEA is less willing to make concessions. For example, there is only one set of instructions to assemble a piece of IKEA furniture, wherever you are in the world. Every store opening begins in the same way: a Swedish breakfast and a traditional log sawing ceremony, which founder Ingvar Kamprad often attends. Every store is decorated in blue and yellow, the colours of Sweden's flag, with a complex layout. One of the most frequently asked questions is how to get out of the store.

When IKEA entered North America in 1987, it discovered that consumers were not buying into its "one size fits all" philosophy, and it had to make some changes. For example, IKEA initially tried to sell its Scandinavian beds in Canada before discovering they were the wrong size for North American bed linens. Its Scandinavian-styled bookshelves were too small to hold a TV for Canadians who wanted shelving for an entertainment system. Even IKEA's European-style bath towels were too small and thin, and its glasses were deemed too small for the super-sized thirsts of North Americans. The European-style sofas were too hard for Canadian bottoms, and the IKEA dining room tables weren't big enough to fit a turkey in the centre on Thanksgiving.

IKEA's system of self-service, self-assembly, and consumer involvement in the whole retail process also was a new concept to many Canadians. However, rather than deviate from its philosophy and sell assembled merchandise, IKEA decided to improve its instructions and offer an assembly service.

DID YOU KNOW?

The name IKEA was derived from the founder's initials plus the first letters of the farm and village where he grew up.

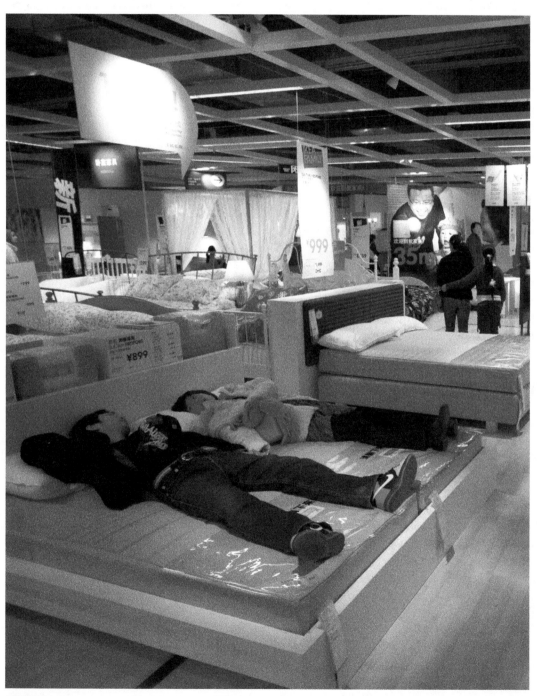

DBURKE/Alamy.

Sources: Elen Lewis, "Is IKEA for Everyone?" *Brandchannel.com*, March 28, 2005; James Scully, "IKEA," *Time*, Summer 2004, pp. 16–19; http://www.IKEA.com.

LO1 International Retailing: Canadian Issues

American Retailers Come to Canada

Faced with an overcrowded domestic market, a growing number of American retailers have looked northward to augment their brands. In 1952, the multimillion-dollar merger of two of the world's largest mail-order companies—Simpsons Ltd. of Toronto and Sears, Roebuck and Co. of Chicago—transpired to create Simpsons-Sears. The Canadian consumer became attracted to Sears and so the Simpsons name was dropped in 1971 to avoid confusion. In 1994, Walmart acquired 120 Canadian Woolco stores and wisely kept the former president of the Woolco chain (who had 28 years of Canadian retail experience and who could provide cultural guidance). Sears and Walmart account for approximately two-thirds of all department store sales in Canada. Walmart continues to catch the public's attention by adding organics to the grocery mix, developing energy-efficient lighting systems for its stores, and setting reduced packaging requirements for its vendors.

The Hudson's Bay Company, Canada's oldest retailer, was acquired in 2006 by American billionaire businessman Jerry Zucker, and was sold and acquired by NRDC Equity Partners in July 2008. The Hudson's Bay Trading Company (HBTC) was formed, which is a leading North American retailer with four divisions: Lord & Taylor, an upscale specialty retailer with 47 stores in 9 states; Fortunoff, a 23-store retail chain specializing in fine jewellery and home furnishings in the New York tri-state area; Creative Design Studios, a fashion design and manufacturing division that creates branded collections for customers throughout North America and internationally; and the Hudson's Bay Company. Hudson's Bay has more than 160 retail outlets across Canada, including Hudson's Bay (90), Home Outfitters (69), and Designer Depot (9).

Free trade also encouraged American retailers to venture north as many retailers regarded Canada as "The Promised Land." The North American Free Trade Agreement (NAFTA, 1994) prompted a surge of big-box retailers and category killers across the border. As a result, by 1995 the Canadian retail industry was in crisis, experiencing a record number of bankruptcies and the descent into receivership of five major Canadian retailers: Eaton's, Woolco, Kmart, Woolworth Inc., and Consumer's Distributing. According to retail analyst John Winter, by the fall of 1997, 15 percent of the Canadian retail sales market was made up of warehouse outlets. The fallout also forced many Canadian retailers who had moved into the American market to withdraw, bringing the failure rate of Canadian retailers expanding into the United States to 90 percent, according to the Centre for the Study of Commercial Activity at Ryerson University.

Then there were the buyouts, where many popular Canadian retailers were acquired by American giants. Examples include Shoppers Drug Mart (acquired in 1999 by Manhattan-based buyout experts Kohlberg Kravis Roberts and Co.), Club Monaco Inc. (purchased in 1999 for $80 million by Polo Ralph Lauren, US), Winners (now owned by TJ Maxx), and Canadian icon Tim Hortons (purchased by American fast-food giant Burger King in 2014).

Success in Canada came quickly, and US retail banners now control approximately 38 percent of all retail sales in Canada. San Francisco's Gap Inc. expanded quickly to include Gap stores, urban chic Banana Republic stores, and the trendy youth-oriented, big-box store, Old Navy.

What is the trouble with Canadian retailing and why is the sector becoming Americanized so quickly? Retail experts are quick to judge, pointing to lack of attention to customer service, lacklustre Canadian stores that need an image update, and sales staff who lack initiative and product knowledge. However, according to experts at the Retail Council of Canada, this is a bad rap as many Canadian retailers at all levels strive to exceed customer expectations and remain very competitive in an increasingly complex marketplace. Still, Nordstrom from the United States, which began opening stores in Canada in 2014, remains the gold standard globally and a tough act to follow, excelling in visual merchandising, knowledgeable staff, and unbeatable customer service.

Perhaps the reality is that Canadian retailers do not have the deep pockets of their southern neighbour. Consider this: When the 127-year-old

> **DID YOU KNOW?**
>
> Burger King paid approximately $12 billion to buy Tim Hortons in 2014.[1]

T. Eaton Co. Ltd. was going through its bankruptcy problems in 1998 and trying desperately to attract customers, a $60 million renovation took place across its 64-store chain. In stark contrast, Marshall Fields in Chicago spent twice that amount on a single store.[2]

Canadian Retailers in the United States

Retailers who have made unsuccessful ventures into the United States include Canadian Tire (twice), Future Shop, Mark's Work Wearhouse, Shoppers Drug Mart, Coles Books, Colour Your World, Second Cup, and La Senza. Cheap-chic fashion retailer Le Chateau and Danier Leather both managed through several difficult years operating a handful of stores in New York. Canadian companies such as Jean Coutu and Alimentation Couche-Tard have had better luck buying existing US stores and turning them around. Canadian retailers often choose to penetrate the United States market because of the close proximity, but are poorly prepared to conquer the market. Some of the problems include the following:

- inability to secure good real estate
- underfunded advertising budgets (US retailers spend about 6 percent of overall sales on advertising compared to 3 percent in Canada)
- underestimating the competitiveness of the US market
- failing to do adequate research
- not devoting enough money and resources to the project

DID YOU KNOW?

There are rumours of Under Armour and Lululemon uniting as a single corporation!

Montreal's Aldo Shoes has 100 shoe stores in several states, and Roots, which has drawn on its popularity resulting from outfitting the US Olympic team, operates six stores in major cities. Unfortunately, Roots's inability to secure the 2010 Canadian Olympic clothing deal had a negative effect on the Roots image globally.

The copycat approach to retail strategy provides no strong basis for being a competitor in the American marketplace and is a formula for disaster. A more successful route for Canadian retailers has been to expand cautiously through:

- acquisition of existing US retailers
- developing a unique product that people want

The Quebec-based, 50-year-old Pharm-Escomptes Jean Coutu pharmacy practically owns the Quebec market, with 269 stores. Looking to expand further into the US market, the company announced in 2004 the purchase of Eckerd drugstores in the eastern United States for $3.1 billion. This strategic move was based on Coutu's long track record of successfully operating in the United States, extending back to 1987 and its takeover of 333 Brooks Pharmacies in seven northeastern states. Coutu's success was built on retaining the old management at Brooks and learning the business before making any major moves.

In Canada, we see very little in the way of Canadian firms buying out American businesses that have already established a presence here in Canada. One buyout of note was Bell Canada purchasing The Source (formerly known as Radio Shack) from the defunct US electronic giant Circuit City.

The Canadian brand Aldo has been successful internationally since 2001; it now has over 1000 Aldo stores operating in 65 countries and more than 160 Aldo Accessories s tores in 19 countries with plans to expand into Italy, Norway, France, and Korea. Aldo sells shoes in the mid-market price range ($59 to $89); the private-label fashion-oriented shoes are designed by and made for the company through a well-established distribution network and licensee agreements.

Joe Fresh, Aritzia, Booster Juice, and Lululemon are other examples of Canadian retailers that not only are succeeding internationally, but that have been able to build global consumer brands (see Retailing View 7.1).

Canadian entrepreneurs are still attempting to open establishments south of the boarder, however. Take Japadog, a Vancouver-based restaurateur that has several portable locations in the downtown area of Vancouver, along with a bricks-and-mortar location on Robson Street. Their first attempted to enter the US market in New York city back in 2011 eventually ended in a closure (2014). The company has remained diligent in their attempt to expand into the US food market, however, and currently has two locations in California, one cart in downtown Los Angles and the other at the Santa Monica pier. Chez Cora is another Canadian franchise considering a move to the south, with sights currently set on Boston, Massachusetts.

An Empire State of Mind

The next time you are in Manhattan, take a stroll up Fifth Avenue and note the change. Walk past the windows of Fossil, Build-A-Bear Workshop, Guess—humdrum chains you can find in any mall in America. Cross north at 49th Street, though, and suddenly it happens: you have passed over into retail wonderland. On one side is the legendary Saks Fifth Avenue, St. John, Fendi; on the other, Botticelli, Prada, Bergdorf Goodman—temples of high fashion, lined up one after the other.

New Yorkers know the distinction well: they call these two retail strips "Lower Fifth" and "Upper Fifth"—two zones, divided by 49th Street, sharing one avenue but existing worlds apart. The corner of Fifth and 49th is the precise intersection where high fashion meets fast fashion, where quality meets quantity, where shopping worlds collide. So it's no coincidence that this is the corner where Aritzia LP, the Vancouver-based women's clothing retailer, recently opened the doors of its biggest store yet.

© The Globe and Mail-Kevin Van Paassen/The Canadian Press.

The two-storey, 13 000-square-foot flagship inside the famed Rockefeller Center showcases a mix of street- and office-wear aimed at stylish women aged 15 to 34. The meticulously stocked boutique is an attempt to mesmerize even the most jaded New York shopper: verdant murals of fruits and nymph-like creatures and rich wood panelling provide an organic backdrop for the clothing, while halogen lights beaming from every direction, even the floor, reflect off a central glass staircase. And all of it dwarfed under the canopy of a fantastical 30-foot-tall mushroom forest carved from cherry wood. The decor, according to the retailer, "revolves around a metaphysical theme inspired by natural phenomena."

But don't let the groovy psychedelia fool you. This Fifth Avenue boutique is Aritzia's stake in the ground, marking its ambition to become a world-class retailer. "We like to think we always target the best of the best locations," Aritzia founder and CEO Brian Hill says. By opening at the corner of upper and lower Fifth, Aritzia has literally and figuratively positioned itself as a destination for a growing segment of the US buying public: aspirational shoppers. They are the style-savvy set who can't quite afford a closet full of luxury garments, but who aren't satisfied with the disposable fare available at the global mega-chains like H&M or Zara.

"Aritzia is the bridge between upscale boutique shopping and fast fashion," says David Ian Gray, a retail expert and founder of Vancouver-based DIG360 Consulting Ltd.

But the US expansion also puts the Vancouver retailer up against some stiff competition. Other bridge labels, including Theory, Sandro, and the Kooples, are also aggressively expanding across the United States, seeking to grab a share of the same market.

Aritzia, financially backed by Boston-based investment house Berkshire Partners LLC, is trying to keep up. Its Fifth Avenue store is the chain's twelfth US location, following openings in Seattle, Chicago, Dallas, and San Francisco.

"The US business has been healthy, so we're planning on continuing opening stores," says Hill. "But we're selective in our real estate." The plan is to "fill in" the northern half of the country with more stores, adding three to four locations a year. Aritzia's current American locations operate mostly in isolation, notes Gray, so upping saturation is key: "The more they can start to fill in a regional geography, so as to start and gain some critical mass, the better."

This Fifth Avenue outpost is the most important signal yet of Aritzia's American intentions: to be a key way station for women on their sartorial journey from H&M to Hermes. The enchanted mushroom forest might mark the way to wonderland. Or it might just be a bad trip.

Source: Stefania Di Verdi, "An Empire State of Mind," *Canadian Business*, March 12, 2013, http://www.canadianbusiness.com/companies-and-industries/an-empire-state-mind/ (accessed March 29, 2016).

From the beginning, Aritzia has pitched its customers on quality. Its tunics, for instance, are almost always silk—not polyester—and pea coats are made with thick wool-and-cashmere blends. That's intentional, according to Gray, who describes a shifting ethos among North American consumers. "The idea of value is now being linked to more durable pieces," he says.

Since opening its first boutique in Vancouver in 1984, Aritzia has grown to 54 stores across North America, with more than 2000 employees. The company has a team of about 30 designers who work on 10 in-house labels, including Wilfred, geared more toward professionals, and TNA, aimed at a sportier teenage market. About 80 percent of Aritzia's merchandise is made up of these in-house labels; the 20 percent the company doesn't make are mostly popular denim brands like J Brand, Citizens of Humanity, and 7 For All Mankind.

"When we first opened 28 years ago, the majority of the business was done carrying other people's brands," says Hill. But featuring mostly in-house brands allowed Aritzia to respond to trends faster, and also provides greater margins. So far, this hybrid strategy has paid off for Hill, a third-generation retailer. His grandfather, John Hill, opened the Hill's of Kerrisdale department store in Vancouver in 1914, which is still in business today. The idea for Aritzia was born when Hill noticed the contemporary women's apparel was doing above-average sales at Kerrisdale. After graduating with an economics degree from Queen's University in 1982, Hill opened the first Aritzia store to target that market more specifically.

"I've been in business a long time. I certainly think you have to go with your gut. That said, your gut has formed its opinion based on more tangible facts and figures," he says.

The facts and figures look good. The most recent batch of data from the American Apparel & Footwear Association suggests a large swath of US consumers is opting for quality over quantity: in 2011, Americans spent 4.9 percent more on apparel, while the number of items purchased dropped 5.3 percent.

Megan Evans, a New York–based image consultant, shops at Aritzia for some of her clients and would recommend the store partly because of its value proposition. "It's a nice middle-of-the-road store," she says. "It's not J. Crew or Banana Republic—it's a step up from that—but it's not high-end like Barneys. It's that in-between store that can work for a lot of people."

Mass market appeal is exactly what Aritzia and its backers are after. Berkshire Partners reportedly bought a majority stake in the company in 2005 for an estimated US$87 million. At the time, Aritzia had projected sales of $100 million for 2006 following "several years of double-digit growth."

Aritzia's current limiting factor appears to be the chain's advertising—more specifically, its lack thereof. "We don't do any US advertising of any consequence," Hill says. For 28 years, Aritzia has instead focused on word-of-mouth and prime storefront locations to reach its shoppers. That strategy has worked well for the company's slow-and-steady growth in Canada. But Gray isn't convinced it will be enough in the cutthroat US market.

"There's a time, when you are just starting out, that works okay," says Gray. "But you've got a lot of dollars on the table now." Stunning retail locations and inventory are not always enough. "You've got to convey that message to shoppers. They need to be a little more open to marketing. It can be done in a brand appropriate way," he says, pointing to Lululemon, which mostly places its print advertising in fitness magazines to grab the true yogis.

Hill appears to pride himself on his track record for zero ad spend. "I think what's happened over the years is the whole advertising, marketing, PR...everything has become quite blurred, particularly with the Internet," he says. Kristi Soomer, a retail consultant with PwC, says retailers can succeed without traditional advertising, even in new markets, because social media has quickened the brand-building process. Her research shows that 59 percent of US consumers follow, discover, and give feedback on brands and retailers using social media.

While it doesn't buy traditional ads, Aritzia has embraced a modern public-relations push by courting style bloggers; building a vigorous, chatty social-media following; and outfitting Hollywood starlets like Rachel Bilson, Jessica Alba, Scarlett Johansson, Reese Witherspoon, and Kristen Stewart. Aritzia took full advantage of the *Twilight* saga filming in its home city of Vancouver by inviting the cast to shop at its store and later posting pictures on Twitter. Before that, Aritzia cleverly suited up Canadian bachelorette Jillian Harris in its Whistler hoodie, an unauthorized reference to the 2010 Vancouver Olympics.

Hill's reluctance to "sell out" with mainstream advertising is understandable. It's taken years for Aritzia to establish its niche in Canada. The brand has resisted the chain mentality in order to position itself as a boutique.

Continued

It's evident in the way delicate dresses are paired with rugged canvas jackets, the way artsy coffee table books are thrown in among the stacks of sweaters. You can even hear it in the in-store music choices, usually well-known songs remixed by obscure artists—another way to embrace pop while trying to maintain an indie edge.

Aritzia, however, is clearly a chain. The store in Edmonton's Kingsway Mall smells just as sweet and earthy as the store at Masonville Place in London, Ontario. The same blazers line the walls in Short Hills, New Jersey, and Toronto. And there's nothing wrong with that—consistency has been the secret sauce of every successful clothing chain. Aritzia's winning formula is that it's ultra-hip and super-accessible at the same time. It's for the shopper who aspires to be a boutique shopper but isn't going to hunt down the latest hip independent shop.

The real problem is that Aritzia is being missed by the very American shoppers it's trying to attract. Take the Fifth Avenue store: directly next door is Ann Taylor, which you can spot from a half-mile away. Aritzia's tiny black signage in cursive font is literally overshadowed. And who could miss Ann Taylor's recent ad campaign, featuring actress Kate Hudson, plastered across North America?

The Fifth Avenue store is, of course, itself a form of advertising. It's "one of the most prime billboards you can have on the planet," says Gray. But with rents on upper Fifth averaging US$3000 per square foot, "you want to be selling enough that you are at least offsetting a good chunk of that rent."

"We don't look at it as just purely an advertising thing," Hill says, though he declined to comment on whether he expects the store to be profitable this year. The American customer "has responded very well, and that has given us the confidence to continue to open stores."

Roughly 800 kilometres northwest of the Fifth Avenue flagship, Aritzia's Bloor Street store in Toronto is sandwiched between Aldo and BCBG Max Azria. Not far down the street are luxury retailers Holt Renfrew, Cole Haan, and Chanel. It's early on a Friday evening, and roughly two dozen women, mostly in their 20s, navigate the racks. Erin Jones, 33, is among them.

"The price points are too high, but the quality is good," she says. She left the store with four new tops. With the typical blouse costing in the neighbourhood of $100, it's clear Aritzia is not trying to be the next H&M. It is, however, trying to wrestle away a select few of the mega-chain's customers. "One of our successes in the past has been staying focused on manageable opportunities and not running in too many directions at the same time," Hill says.

New York is a make-it-or-break-it proposition for Aritzia. If you can make it here, as the song goes, you can make it anywhere: New Yorkers are tastemakers, and success in the Big Apple will fuel appetites in other US markets. In *Alice's Adventures in Wonderland,* a piece of giant mushroom causes Alice's neck to grow. Aritzia is clearly hoping—with the aid of its Fifth Avenue fungal fantasia—that it can repeat the trick.

Lo2 Global Growth Opportunities

As retailers saturate their domestic markets, many find international expansion to be an attractive growth opportunity. Of the 50 largest retailers in the world, only two operate in one country.[3] By expanding internationally, retailers can increase their sales, leverage their knowledge and systems across a greater sales base, and gain more bargaining power with vendors. But international expansion is risky because retailers must deal with different government regulations, cultural traditions, consumer preferences, supply chains, and languages. Retailing View 7.2 describes the substantial differences in apparel preferences for men and women in India compared to those in Western countries.

Attractiveness of International Markets

Two factors that are often used to determine the attractiveness of different international opportunities are (1) the potential size of the retail market in the country, and (2) the degree to which the country can and does support the entry of foreign retailers.[4] Some indicators of these factors are shown in Exhibit 7–1. The (+) or (−) indicates whether the indicator is positively or negatively related to the factor.

The most attractive countries are those with large and growing potential sales as indicated by the level and growth rate of present retail sales and the amount of money people have in the country to spend on services and merchandise as indicated by gross domestic product (GDP), GDP growth rate, and GDP per capita. Income and age distribution

For all those Jibes about Shopping, Indian Men Buy more Clothes than Women

You can now stop forwarding that tired Whatsapp joke about women's penchant for shopping and clothes. The data can't stand that joke.

The men's apparel market in India is worth nearly $2 billion (Rs 12 000 crore) more than that of women, a study by retail consultant Technopak has shown. In comparison, the total sales for men's apparel in the US is half that of women's clothes.

The total size of the men's apparel market in the subcontinent is worth about $17.3 billion (Rs 104 000 crore), whereas the women's segment is sized at $15.5 billion (Rs 93 000 crore). On the other hand, the US men's apparel market registered total sales of $60 billion dollars in 2013 and women's clocked $116 billion.

"In India, spending in women's apparel in rural areas and smaller cities is comparatively lower than men's apparel," said Amit Gugnani, senior vice president, fashion, at Technopak.

"However, it is expected that with increasing urbanization and increasing participation of women in the workforce, the women's apparel market will continue to grow faster than the men's market," he added. During 2013–14, the market for women's clothes grew at 10 percent, marginally more than men's, which grew at 9 percent.

When it comes to women's clothing, sarees and salwar kameez had the biggest share of the market in 2013. For men, ethnic wear is rather unpopular, and shorts and trousers lead the way instead.

Most Indian women prefer to wear traditional garments at work and in social contexts.

© Erica Simone Leeds 2007.

For men, the fastest growing segments are denims and T-shirts at 14 percent and 12 percent, respectively.

Although the traditional saree dominates the women's market right now, it had the slowest growth rate in 2013. Inner wear and western clothes registered the highest growth at 15 percent and 13 percent respectively, indicating a shift in preferences. And as young India become more urbanised and aspirational, expect these categories to grow further in the coming years.

The size of the Indian apparel retail market was $41 billion (Rs 227 000 crores) in 2013.

© 2016 Quartz/Diksha Madhok http://qz.com. http://qz.com/259305/for-all-those-jibes-about-shopping-indian-men-buy-more-clothes-than-women/.

Exhibit 7–1
Indicators of the Attractiveness of International Markets

Country Potential	Country Support
• Population (+)	• Market share of modern retailing (+)
• Population growth rate (+)	• Quality of infrastructure, transportation, and communications (+)
• Gross domestic product (GDP) (+)	• Urban population (+)
• GDP per capita (+)	• Market share of leading domestic retailers (−)
• Retail sales (+)	• Ease of doing business (+)
• Growth rate in retail sales (+)	• Business-friendly laws and regulations (+)
• Retail sales per capita (+)	• Political stability (+)
• Income distribution (+) or (−)	
• Age distribution (+) or (−)	

can be either positively or negatively related to market attractiveness, depending on the type of retailer evaluating the country for entry. For example, a retailer of video games, such as EB Games (GameStop), would find a country with a large percentage of people under 19 to be more attractive than a country with a large percentage of people over 65. High fashion retailers that sell expensive merchandise, such as Nordstrom and Cartier, would find a country that has a significant percentage of the population with high incomes to be more attractive than a country that has a large percentage of people in poverty.

With respect to company support, most retailers considering entry into foreign markets are successful retailers that use sophisticated management practices. Thus they would find countries that support modern retailing, have more advanced infrastructures, and have significant urban populations to be more attractive (see Retailing View 7.3). In addition, countries lacking strong domestic retailers but having a stable economy and political environment would be more attractive.

The factors outlined in Exhibit 7–1 are weighted to develop an attractiveness index. One index ranking the 20 most attractive international retail markets, along with some demographic information about the countries, is shown in Exhibit 7–2. Of the top 30 countries in this ranking, 5 are emerging countries ranked by *Fortune* as countries companies may want to consider investing in. The emerging international markets that receive the most attention from *Fortune* are India, Indonesia, Malaysia, Mexico, and Columbia.[5]

According to the Global Retail Development Index, China, Brazil, India, and Russia are all lucrative retail markets in the emerging economies. However, these countries offer different opportunities and challenges for retailers contemplating entry.

China (ranked 1st) Government regulations for retailing are much less onerous in China than in India, and direct foreign investment is encouraged. Since the lifting of most operational restrictions on international retailers, six global food retailers (Auchan, Carrefour, Ito-Yokado, Metro, Tesco, and

DID YOU KNOW?

Booster Juice, which originated in Sherwood Park, Alberta, now has over 300 locations worldwide. The countries that have a Booster Juice franchise include Canada, the United States, Mexico, Brazil, India, and the Netherlands.

Walmart) have entered China. Although much of this retail development has been in the large eastern cities of Shanghai, Beijing, Guangzhou, and Shenzhen, these tier 1 markets are approaching saturation for hypermarkets; the interior tier 2 and tier 3 markets are very attractive. (However, see Retailing View 7.5, later in this chapter, for a discussion of one area in which supermarkets and hypermarkets in China struggle to compete.)

China is rapidly developing the infrastructure to support modern retailing. Highway density in China is already approaching that in the United States. China has a number of high-quality airports and a rapidly developing sophisticated railroad network.[6] However, doing business in China is still challenging. Operating costs are increasing, managerial talent is becoming more difficult to find and retain, and an underdeveloped and inefficient supply chain predominates.

Brazil (ranked 8th) Brazil has the largest population and strongest economy in Latin America. It is a country of many poor people and few very wealthy families. Brazilian retailers have developed some very innovative practices for retailing to low-income families, including offering credit and instalment purchases. Many low-income customers go from week to week paying their credit card commitments. Most major retailers own their own credit card facility, with "signing up" booths at entrances to their stores. In contrast, the very wealthy Brazilians provide a significant market for luxury goods and retailers. Even though they are approximately 1 percent of the population, this equates to approximately 19 million people, a market just a little smaller than all of Australia.

India (ranked 15th) In India, the retail industry is divided into organized and unorganized sectors. The unorganized retailing includes the small independent retailers—the local *kirana* shops, owner-operated general stores; *paan/beedi* shops, convenience stores; and handcart and street vendors. Most Indians shop in open markets and millions of independent grocery shops called *kirana*. However, India's growing, well-educated, aspirational middle class wants a more sophisticated retail environment and global brands.

While the demand for modern (organized) retailing exists in India, entering the Indian market is challenging. As the world's largest pluralistic democracy, with diverse cultures and 22 official languages, India actually is a conglomeration of

Exhibit 7–2
2015 Global Retail Development Index

2015 rank	Country	Market attractiveness (25%)	Country risk (25%)	Market saturation (25%)	Time pressure (25%)	GRDI score	Change in rank compared to 2014	Population (million)	GDP per capita, PPP (thousand)
1	China	66.7	55.7	42.3	96.6	65.3	1	1,364	13
2	Uruguay	93.3	60.4	68.0	38.9	65.1	1	3	20
3	Chile	98.2	100.0	13.0	37.9	62.3	2	18	23
4	Qatar	100.0	89.4	34.3	12.8	59.1	N/A	2	144
5	Mongolia	22.4	19.9	93.1	100.0	58.8	N/A	3	10
6	Georgia	36.5	39.1	78.8	79.2	58.4	1	5	8
7	United Arab Emirates	97.6	84.0	16.5	33.9	58.0	3	9	65
8	Brazil	98.0	60.4	45.2	28.0	57.9	3	203	15
9	Malaysia	75.6	68.8	29.3	52.7	56.6		30	25
10	Armenia	35.4	37.1	82.1	66.3	55.2	4	3	7
11	Turkey	83.1	48.1	40.2	44.8	54.1		77	20
12	Indonesia	50.6	35.5	55.1	65.9	51.8	3	251	10
13	Kazakhstan	49.6	34.2	72.5	50.7	51.8	−3	17	24
14	Sri Lanka	15.8	34.4	77.8	78.8	51.7	+4	21	10
15	India	30.5	39.8	75.7	58.5	51.1	+5	1,296	6
16	Peru	48.9	43.9	58.6	51.8	50.8	−3	31	12
17	Saudi Arabia	78.6	64.4	30.4	27.0	50.1	−1	31	54
18	Botswana	49.2	62.5	33.3	54.2	49.8	+8	2	16
19	Panama	62.3	46.8	49.7	37.6	49.1	−5	4	20
20	Colombia	55.6	49.3	52.0	39.1	49.0	+1	48	13
21	Russia	94.9	28.4	24.5	46.6	48.6	−9	144	25
22	Azerbaijan	33.9	26.9	82.4	46.8	47.5	+8	10	18
23	Nigeria	19.6	8.3	94.0	66.5	47.1	−4	178	6
24	Philippines	39.6	36.0	51.6	60.7	47.0	−1	100	7
25	Jordan	51.1	35.5	64.2	36.8	46.9	−3	8	12
26	Oman	75.0	77.3	24.9	9.8	46.7	−9	4	44
27	Kuwait	81.0	68.1	33.2	0.0	45.6	−19*	4	71
28	Costa Rica	66.9	49.2	38.7	25.1	45.0	−4	5	15
29	Mexico	82.5	56.1	0.2	38.8	44.4	−4	120	18
30	Angola	22.4	9.2	99.4	45.0	44.0	N/A	22	8

0 = low attractiveness 100 = high attractiveness	0 = high risk 100 = low risk	0 = saturated 100 = not saturated	0 = no time pressure 100 = urgency to enter

Notes: PPP is purchasing power parity. For an interactive map of the GRDI top 30 countries, go to www.atkearney.com/consumer-products-retail/global-retail-development-index.

*The significant decline in Kuwait's position in the GRDI is partially due to a change in country-specific data sources (see page 17 for more details).

Sources: Economist intelligence Unit, Euromoney, international Monetary Fund, Planet Retail, population Reterence Bureau, World Bank, World Economic Forum; A.T. Kearney analysis

Source: 2015 Global Retail Development Index, Copyright A.T. Kearney, 2015. All rights reserved. Reprinted with permission.

Mega-Malls in Asia

Eight of the ten largest malls in the world are located in Asia, and of these, seven were built since 2004 (see Exhibit 7–3). The West Edmonton Mall is the largest mega-mall in North America; the King of Prussia Mall is the largest mega-mall in the United States, but the 11th-largest in the world. The largest mall in the world, the New South China Mall in Dongguan, China, was built in 2005 and has 7.1 million gross leasable square feet. Unfortunately, its poor location was unable to attract retail tenants, and it is currently 99 percent vacant. The Dubai Mall is currently the seventh-largest mega mall in the world, but when completed, it will be the largest in the world.

Mall development is rapidly growing to keep up with the lifestyle and income changes in Asia. Mega-malls are mixed-use centres with retail, dining, entertainment, and residential living.

They house many familiar global luxury brands, including Gucci, Hermes, Versace, and Cartier. The malls, located in places like Singapore, Hong Kong, and Kuala Lumpur, are impressive because of their large size and the entertainment choices they offer (cinemas, bowling alleys, windmills, children's theme parks, skating rinks, and an abundance of restaurants).

When customers get tired of shopping at the Dubai Mall in the United Arab Emirates, they can go skiing inside!

© Maremagnum/Getty Images.

Sources: Stan Sesser, "The New Spot for Giant Malls: Asia," *Wall Street Journal*, September 16, 2006; Tom Van Riper, "World's Largest Malls," *Forbes*, January 9, 2007; http://www.easternct.edu/depts/amerst/MallsWorld.htm (accessed July 25, 2007).

discrete markets. In addition, government regulations impede foreign investment in retailing. Non-Indian firms cannot have a controlling interest in retail firms and thus must partner with an Indian firm. Retailers must comply with a myriad of regulations before opening stores and shipping merchandise. For example, there are taxes for moving goods to different states and even within states. Walmart's entry into India is a partnership with Bharti Enterprises to open wholesale outlets called

Best Price Modern Wholesale. The outlets are allowed to sell only to firms that register by showing tax documents that prove they own retail outlets. The development of organized retailing is being undertaken by industrial conglomerates that have limited expertise in running retail chains.[7]

Russia (ranked 21st) In Russia, the impediments to market entry are less visible but more problematic. Corruption is rampant, with various

Exhibit 7–3
The Largest Mega-Malls

Shopping Mall	Year Opened	GLA* (million sq. ft.)	Total Area (million sq. ft.)	Stores	Comments
1 Jin Yuan (Golden Resources Shopping Mall), Beijing, China	2004	6.0	7.3	1000+	Also known as the "Great Mall of China"; includes six floors; located near the Fourth Ring Road, west of Beijing
2 SM City North EDSA, Philippines	1985	5.0		1100+	
3 Central World Plaza, Bangkok, Thailand	2006	4.6	11	500+	Includes 21-screen cinemas, bowling lanes, and restaurants, as well as a convention centre (not included in the GLA)
4 SM Mall of Asia, Philippines	2006	4.2	4.4	600	
5 West Edmonton Mall, Edmonton, Alberta, Canada	1981	3.8	6.0	800	Largest shopping mall in North America; includes an indoor wave pool, amusement areas, a hotel, restaurants, and 20 000 parking spaces
6 Cevahir Istanbul, Istanbul, Turkey	2005	3.8	4.5	280	Largest shopping mall in Europe; has six floors, cinemas, a roller coaster, and a theatre
7 The Dubai Mall, Dubai, United Arab Emirates	2008	3.77	5.9	600	
8 Berjaya Times Square, Kuala Lumpur, Malaysia	2003	3.5	7.5	1000+	Includes 45 restaurants, a theme park, and a 3D Digi-IMAX theatre
9 Beijing Mall, Beijing, China	2005	3.4	4.7	600	Includes four levels of shopping with interior residences; located near Fifth Ring Road, southeast of Beijing
10 Zhengjia Plaza (Grandview Mall), Guangzhou, China	2005	3.0	4.5		Enclosed in a complex that includes a 48-story hotel and 30-story office building
11 King of Prussia Mall, Philadelphia, Pennsylvania, United States	1962	2.8		327	Created by connecting together three adjacent malls; managed by a single company
12 South Coast Plaza, Costa Mesa, California, United States	1967	2.7		280	Highest revenue volume mall in the United States; home to the Orange Lounge, a branch of the Orange County Museum of Art

*Gross leasable area—the total usable, rental space in a building.

administrative authorities capable of impeding operations if payments are not made. Retailers encounter severe logistical challenges in supporting operations in Russia. There are long delays at borders and ports and a scarcity of containers. Over 70 percent of international container shipments come through the Saint Petersburg port, which is very congested. Retailers often cannot rely on domestic products because the quality of products made in Russia is poor. Finally, much of the purchasing power is concentrated in Moscow, where salaries are about double those in other regions; however, Moscow is already saturated with shopping centres.

Global Consumer Attitudes and Retail Trends

Following changing consumer attitudes and retail trends around the world has provided a unique career for Canadian Anthony Stokan. In his book,

Naked Consumption: Retail Trends Uncovered, he highlights ten global retail trends:

1. *It's a Wally, Wally World*—Walmart will increase its retail power across all income levels.

2. *The Death of Inspiration*—Price emphasis focuses on utilitarian store environments.

3. *Experience Shopping*—Go beyond entertainment to attract niche markets.

4. *Empowered Consumers*—Consumers use the Internet to comparison shop.

5. *Kidopoly*—Kids are a big market opportunity; $25 billion in direct sales and $500 billion worth influencing parents' spending in North America.

6. *Dollar Store Euphoria*—Consumers like the value of low-priced merchandise.

7. *Luxury for All*—Include affordable luxury elements in products for all shoppers.

8. *E-Commerce: Action/Transaction*—Sales online will remain a minor share of overall retail sales.

9. *The Loyalty Myth*—There is value in keeping and growing an existing customer base.

10. *The New Brand Management*—Successful retailers will build their own brands.

Retailers engage in international ventures for many reasons. When the home marketplace is not producing desired sales and profits diminish over time, some of the problems may be attributed to the following factors:

- a saturated home marketplace with no room to grow
- a highly competitive marketplace
- an aging population that spends less and saves more
- an economic recession, which limits consumer spending
- high operating costs including staff wages, rental costs, and taxes
- restrictive policies on retail development
- shareholder pressure

The age factor is a dominant issue in Canada and the United States, where aging populations have put their spending years behind them; the prediction for the future is that the North American economy will be much slower growing. North American retailers who want to maintain growth rates have no alternative but to sell their products in an international arena. The reality is that if you want 8 percent growth in sales, you are forced to go to new growing economies, probably in South America, Mexico, or Chile, where a dominant young population between the ages of 15 and 25 (the desirable demographic) is entering the workplace, producing, and spending.

It should be noted that countries such as Taiwan, South Korea, and Singapore are also now aging quite rapidly. Although younger than Canada, these countries over the next ten years will experience a dramatic slowdown in consumption. China has an immense population of 1.2 billion, and even if you get a small portion of the market, success can be huge. China appears to have stronger retail market potential than India, with a population of 1 billion. China has a one-child-per-family policy, whereas Indians still have an average of three children per family. If a population includes many children, then much of its resources are used for the health care and education of its young people, inevitably putting a taxation burden on those of working age and limiting disposable income for retail purchases.

To succeed as an international retailer, the company must have a thorough understanding of the macro-environment, including cultural differences, government policies, and the economic stability in the international trade area. Other important factors include the sources of product production and the distribution capabilities within the international market. Some of the factors that would encourage a retailer to enter into the international marketplace include:[8]

- limited competition in the international marketplace
- rising numbers of middle-class consumers with improved standard of living
- younger population with purchasing power
- trade agreements and organizations, including North American Free Trade Agreement (NAFTA), World Trade Organization (WTO), European Union (EU)
- relaxed regulatory framework
- favourable operating costs, including lower wages and taxes
- opportunity to diversify
- opportunity to try innovative concepts

Both the micro- and macro-environments must be wisely managed for a retailer to be successful.

Italian designer Giorgio Armani made his first venture into Beijing, China, in 1998. According to Armani, "The Chinese market is growing full steam ahead. We are seeing very good results from Chinese tourists buying in our Hong Kong flagship store and the future possibilities are endless." The designer was well aware of the growing Chinese market for luxury goods; the decision to open a new flagship store in Shanghai in 2004 was part of an ambitious strategy to have 30 stores in China by 2008.[9] By 2013, he had 289 stores in that country.[10]

The World's Largest Shopping District

Officially launched in April 2009, Bawadi, the multi-billion-dollar leisure and tourism destination in Dubailand, has the world's largest shopping experience, with over 110 million square metres (1185 million square feet) of gross leasable area. It has over 400 retail outlets, including numerous international brands. Dubai is one of the United Arab Emirates in the eastern Arabian Peninsula, and Dubai City is the main city.

The world's largest shopping area provides support to the tourism and hospitality industry, which in turn plays a major role in the diversification and development of Dubai's economy. Bawadi includes a 10 kilometre–long hotel and shopping strip, entertainment, convention centres, and residential complexes. The 31 hotels, ranging from three to five star, focuses Dubai as one of the world's premier family destinations.

Dubai's fantastic—even bizarre—previous developments include The Mall of the Emirates, featuring a ski slope in the desert and man-made islands shaped like palm fronds. These strategic marketing tactics helped draw over 10 million tourists in 2014 to this tiny desert land that is fast running out of oil.

Who is Successful and Who Isn't

Retailers—particularly specialty store retailers with strong brand names such as The Gap and Zara, and food and discount retailers such as Walmart, Carrefour, Royal Ahold, and Metro AG—may have a strong competitive advantage when competing globally.

Some retailers, such as Roots and The Gap, have a competitive advantage in global markets because the North American culture is emulated in many countries, particularly by young people. Due to rising prosperity and rapidly increasing access to cable TV with North American programming, fashion trends are spreading to young people in emerging countries. The global MTV generation prefers Coke to tea, athletic shoes to sandals, Chicken McNuggets to rice, and credit cards to cash.[11] In the last few years, China's major cities have sprouted American stores and restaurants, including KFC, Pizza Hut, and McDonald's. Shanghai and Beijing each have more than two dozen Starbucks. Coffee was not the drink of choice until Starbucks came to town. But Chinese urban dwellers go there to impress a friend or because it's a symbol of a new kind of lifestyle. Although Western products and stores have gained a reputation for high quality and good service in China, in some ways it is the American culture that many Chinese want.[12]

On the other hand, some large European and Japanese retailers have considerably more experience operating retail stores in non-domestic markets. For example, France's Carrefour has been operating stores in non-domestic markets for almost 30 years. It is very good at adapting its hypermarket format to local tastes. The company buys many products locally and hires and trains local managers, quickly passing on

> **DID YOU KNOW?**
> Of the largest 20 retailers worldwide, half are from the United States.[14]

> **DID YOU KNOW?**
> Walmart currently operates in 28 different countries worldwide.[15]

© Chris Kerrigan.

globally sustainable competitive advantage One of the characteristics of retailers that have successfully exploited international growth opportunities.

adaptability A company's recognition of cultural differences and adaptation of its core strategy to the needs of local markets.

global culture A company's embracing a multicultural perspective and developing an infrastructure that makes maximal use of local management.

financial resources Resources that enable companies to make strategic decisions, such as expansion into international markets, requiring significant and ongoing financial commitment, often at the expense of short-term profit.

DID YOU KNOW?

The world's largest retailers are likely to be global players. Thirty-nine out of the top 50 global retailers operate in more than one country. The implication: Eventually retailers must go global to keep growing.[16]

power and authority to them. Even though Walmart has a more efficient distribution system, Carrefour has competed effectively against Walmart in Brazil and Argentina.[13]

Category killers and hypermarket retailers may be particularly suited to succeeding internationally because of the expertise they have already developed at home. First, these retailers are leaders in the use of technology to manage inventories, control global logistical systems, and tailor merchandise assortments to local needs. For instance, firms such as Home Depot provide consumers with an assortment of brand-name merchandise procured from sources around the world. This advantage is particularly valuable if brand-name merchandise is important to consumers. Second, retailers such as Walmart and Carrefour have become the low-price provider in every market they enter because of their buying scale economies and efficient distribution systems. Third, despite idiosyncrasies in the international environment, category killers and hypermarket retailers have developed unique systems and standardized formats that facilitate control over multiple stores. These systems and procedures should work well regardless of the country of operation. Fourth, because of the category killer's narrow assortment and focused strategy, communications across national boundaries and cultures are specifically focused, which improves management coordination. Finally, at one time, people felt that consumers outside North America were used to high levels of personalized service and would not accept the self-service concept employed by category killers and hypermarket retailers. However, consumers around the globe are willing to forgo the service for lower prices.[17]

Global expansion is often difficult and full of pitfalls. For instance, The Gap is pulling back on some of its European store base. UK-based Marks & Spencer (M&S) has sold off its Canadian operations, Brooks Brothers, as part of an overall withdrawal from markets outside Britain. Its plan to close its 18 stores in France demonstrates the difficulty of operating in foreign markets. M&S found it was in violation of French labour laws when it announced the closures. The laws require prior consultation with the employees. UK-based J. Sainsbury, on the other hand, got caught up in a geopolitical conflict. It has abandoned expansion plans into Egypt because of a consumer boycott and heavy losses. The Egyptians believe that the company is pro-Israel, despite Sainsbury's denials.[18]

Lo3 Keys to Success

Four characteristics of retailers that have successfully exploited international growth opportunities are:

- **globally sustainable competitive advantage**
- **adaptability**
- **global culture**
- **financial resources**[19]

Globally Sustainable Competitive Advantage ntry into non-domestic markets is most successful when the expansion opportunity is consistent with the retailer's core bases of competitive advantage. Some core competitive advantages for global retailers are shown below.

Core Advantage	Global Retailer
Low cost; efficient operations	Walmart, Carrefour
Strong private brands	Royal Ahold, IKEA, Starbucks
Fashion reputation	The Gap, Zara, H&M (Hennes & Mauritz)
Category dominance	Office Depot, Home Depot
Image	Disney, Warner Brothers

Thus, Walmart and Carrefour are successful in international markets where price plays an important role in consumer decision making and distribution infrastructure is available to enable these firms to exploit their logistical capabilities. On the other hand, The Gap and Zara are successful in international markets that value fashionable merchandise.

Adaptability Successful global retailers build on their core competencies. They also recognize cultural differences and adapt their core strategy to the needs of local markets.[20] Colour preferences, the preferred cut of apparel, and sizes differ between cultures. For example, in China, white is the colour of mourning and brides wear red dresses. Food probably has the greatest diversity of tastes. Ahold operates under nearly 20 brand names around the globe, including Superdiplo in Spain, ICA in Sweden, Albert Heijn in the Netherlands, and Stop & Shop and Giant in the United States. Ahold firmly believes that, like politics, all retailing is local, as customers develop loyalty toward a store brand they have known for decades. Ahold's mantra: "Everything the customer sees, we localize. Everything they don't see, we globalize."[21]

Selling seasons also vary across countries. The Gap's major Canadian selling season is back-to-school in August; however, this is one of the slowest sales periods in Europe because most people are on vacation. Back-to-school in Japan is in April.

Store designs need to be adjusted. In some cultures, social norms dictate that men's and women's clothing cannot be displayed next to each other. In North America, the standard practice is to place low-priced, private-label merchandise on the shelf to the right of national brands, assuming that customers' natural eye movement is from left to right. This merchandising approach does not work in cultures where people read from right to left or up and down. As mentioned earlier, IKEA initially tried to sell its Scandinavian beds in Canada before discovering they were the wrong size for North American bed linens.

Government regulations and cultural values also affect store operations. Some differences such as holidays, hours of operation, and regulations governing part-time employees and terminations are easy to identify. Other factors require a deeper understanding. For example, the Latin American culture is very family oriented. Thus, North American work schedules need to be adjusted so that employees can have more time with their families. Boots, a UK drugstore chain, has the checkout clerks in its Japanese stores standing up because it discovered that Japanese shoppers found it offensive to pay money to a seated clerk. Retailers in Germany must recycle packaging materials sold in their stores.[22] Also in Germany, seasonal sales can be held only during specific weeks and apply to only specific product categories, and discounts are limited. Unlimited guarantees are generally forbidden, which is why Lands' End may not describe such a guarantee on its goods in an ad and may only talk about it if customers ask for it first.[23]

Global Culture To be global, companies have to think globally. It is not sufficient to transplant a home-country culture and infrastructure into another country. In this regard, Carrefour is truly global. In the early years of its international expansion, it started in each country slowly, which reduced the company's ethnocentrism. Further enriching its global perspective, Carrefour has always encouraged rapid development of local management and retains few expatriates in its overseas operations. Carrefour's management ranks are truly international. One is just as likely to run across a Portuguese regional manager in Hong Kong as a French or Chinese one. Finally, Carrefour discourages the classic overseas "tour of duty" mentality often found in North American firms. International assignments are important in themselves, not just as stepping stones to ultimate career advancement back in France. The globalization of Carrefour's culture is perhaps most evident in the speed with which ideas flow throughout the organization. A global management structure of regional "committees," which meet regularly, advances the awareness and implementation of global best practices.

The proof of Carrefour's global commitment is in the numbers. It has had almost 30 years of international experience in 21 countries—both developed and developing.[25]

Financial Resources Expansion into international markets requires a long-term commitment and considerable upfront planning. Retailers find it very difficult to generate short-term profit when they make the transition to global retailing. Although firms such as Walmart, Carrefour, Staples, and Costco often initially have difficulty achieving success in new global markets, these large firms generally are in a strong financial position and therefore have the ability to keep investing in projects long enough to become successful. Walmart's US$8.2 billion cash flow and 48 percent share of the US$225 billion discount store industry in the United States provides the financial ability to maintain this type of staying power.[26] Walmart is the world's largest retailer, and the second-largest retailer in Canada (behind Weston Group), but as a single banner store it ranks number one in Canada with sales of 27.1 billion (from almost 400 stores in Canada).[27]

> **DID YOU KNOW?**
>
> Retail revenue for the Top 250 Global Powers of Retailing totalled almost US$4.5 trillion in fiscal 2014, with an average of nearly US$18 billion per company.[24]

LO4 Entry Strategies

Retailers take four approaches when entering non-domestic markets:

- direct investment
- joint venture
- strategic alliance
- franchising[28]

direct investment The investment and ownership by a retail firm or a division or subsidiary that builds and operates stores in a foreign country.

joint venture An entity formed when the entering retailer pools its resources with a local retailer to form a new company in which ownership, control, and profits are shared.

strategic alliance Collaborative relationship between independent firms. For example, a foreign retailer might enter an international market through direct investment but develop an alliance with a local firm to perform logistical and warehousing activities.

tariff A tax placed by a government upon imports; also called *duty*.

Direct Investment Direct investment involves a retail firm investing in and owning a division or subsidiary that builds and operates stores in a foreign country. This entry strategy requires the highest level of investment and exposes the retailer to significant risks, but it has the highest potential returns. One advantage of direct investment is that the retailer has complete control of the operations. For example, McDonald's chose this entry strategy for the UK market, building a plant to produce buns when local suppliers could not meet its specifications.

Joint Venture A **joint venture** is formed when the entering retailer pools its resources with a local retailer to form a new company in which ownership, control, and profits are shared. Examples of successful joint ventures are Royal Ahold (the Netherlands) and Velox Holdings (Argentina); Metro AG (Germany) and Koc Group's Migros (Turkey); Carrefour and Sabanci Holding (Turkey); Metro AG (Germany) and Marubeni (Japan); and Monsoon (United Kingdom) and Charming Shoppes (United States).[29]

A joint venture reduces the entrant's risks. Besides sharing the financial burden, the local partner understands the market and has access to resources—vendors and real estate. Many foreign countries, such as China, require joint ownership, although these restrictions may loosen as a result of World Trade Organization (WTO) negotiations.[30] Problems with this entry approach can arise if the partners disagree or the government places restrictions on the repatriation of profits.

Strategic Alliance A **strategic alliance** is a collaborative relationship between independent firms. For example, a foreign retailer might enter an international market through direct investment but develop an alliance with a local firm to perform logistical and warehousing activities.

Franchising Franchising offers the lowest risk and requires the least investment. However, the entrant has limited control over the retail operations in the foreign country, potential profit is reduced, and the risk of assisting in the creation of a local domestic competitor is increased. UK-based Marks & Spencer, for example, has 136 franchised stores in 27 countries, including Cyprus (8), Greece (28), Indonesia (10), and Thailand (10).[31]

Costs Associated with Global Decisions

Retailers use production facilities located in developing economies for much of their private-label merchandise because of the very low labour costs in these countries. To counterbalance the lower acquisition costs, however, there are other more subtle expenses that increase the costs of sourcing private-label merchandise from other countries. These costs include foreign currency fluctuations, tariffs, longer lead times, and increased transportation costs.

Fluctuations in currency exchange rates can increase costs. For example, if the Indian rupee increases relative to the Canadian dollar, the cost of private-label merchandise produced in India and imported for sale into Canada will increase. If this increase occurs between the time the order is placed and when it is delivered, Canadian retailers will have to pay more for the merchandise than planned. Most retailers use financial instruments such as options and futures contracts to minimize the effects of currency fluctuations.

Tariffs, also known as *duties*, are taxes placed by a government on imports that increase the cost of merchandise imported from international sources. Import tariffs have been used to shield domestic manufacturers from foreign competition. Because tariffs raise the cost of imported merchandise, retailers have a strong incentive to use their political clout to reduce them.

Inventory turnover is likely to be lower when purchasing from suppliers outside the United States than from domestic suppliers, which will result in

Direct Selling in China

While sales growth through the direct selling channel is limited in the United States, companies like Avon and Mary Kay have effectively used this channel to sell products in less developed countries. Using the direct selling channel is particularly effective in less developed countries because an extensive infrastructure to supply stores is not required. Products are sent to hundreds of thousands of sales representatives in small villages. They pay for the products when they sell them.

The direct selling channel also is part of a movement around the world for women to have more economic independence. For example, Zhang Xiaoying, a 19-year-old woman from Guizhou, one of China's poorest regions, says, "I love the corporate culture of Mary Kay. This company teaches you to aspire to a higher level."

The direct selling channel is particularly effective in less developed areas that lack the infrastructure to support retail stores.
© Bloomberg via Getty Images.

Before joining the company, many Mary Kay sales agents in China held low-paying jobs as secretaries, cashiers, and rural schoolteachers. Many were looking for a new focus in their lives. "Because my husband is a businessman, and he is busy, we talked less and less," says Lu Laidi, a Mary Kay sales director. "I felt my life was boring. I stayed home and barely dressed up."

The use of a direct selling channel has been controversial in China. Many direct sellers have been accused of operating sophisticated pyramid schemes and other sales swindles. In response to these concerns, China banned direct selling in 1998, saying that it was often a cover for "evil cults, secret societies and lawless and superstitious activities." In 2006, after heavy lobbying from American companies, China lifted its ban, and since then direct selling has grown into an $8 billion industry.

Sources: David Barboza, "Direct Selling Flourishes in China," *New York Times*, December 26, 2009; J. Alex Tarquinio, "Selling Beauty on a Global Scale," *New York Times*, November 1, 2008, p. B2.

DID YOU KNOW?

Canada's major trading partner is the United States. In 2014, the value of trade with them was worth approximately $33.8 billion.[32]

higher inventory carrying costs. Consider The Spoke bicycle store in Aspen, Colorado, which is buying Moots bicycles manufactured in Steamboat Springs, Colorado. The Spoke buyer knows that the lead time—the amount of time between the recognition that an order needs to be placed and the point at which the merchandise arrives in the store and is ready for sale—is usually two weeks, plus or minus three days. But if The Spoke ordered bikes from Italy, the lead time might be three months, plus or minus three weeks. Since lead times are longer, retailers using foreign sources must maintain larger inventories to ensure that merchandise is available when the customer wants it. Larger inventories mean larger inventory carrying costs.

International Human Resources Issues The legal-political system in countries often dictates the human resource management practices that retailers can use. For example, Canada has led the world in eliminating workplace discrimination. However, in Singapore it is perfectly legal to place an employment ad specifying that candidates must be male, between the ages of 25 and 40, and ethnic Chinese. In the Netherlands, a retailer can make a substantial reduction in its workforce only if it demonstrates to the government that the cutback is absolutely necessary. In addition, a Dutch retailer must develop a plan for the cutback, which must then be approved by unions and other involved parties.

In countries with a collectivist culture such as China and Japan, employees downplay individual desires and focus on the needs of the group. Thus, group-based evaluations and incentives are more effective in those countries.

Finally, the staffing of management positions in foreign countries raises a wide set of issues. Should management be local or should expatriates be used? How should the local managers or expatriates be selected, trained, and compensated? Cole Peterson, during his tenure as vice-president of the People Division of Walmart, said its biggest problem with international expansion was its lack of "human capital." Walmart makes every effort to replace expatriates with locals, and in every overseas country except China, its operations are now led by a non-American. Yet Walmart is expanding faster than it can train people internally, and the company has lost high-quality local managers to rivals.[33]

Lo5 Global versus Multinational Retailers

A McDonald's in China looks the same as a McDonald's in Calgary or in Chicago: It has the same visual concept with the golden arches and the always popular Big Mac and fries. But worldwide, there may be some differences. In Germany, the restaurant looks the same but beer is added to the menu; and in Japan, the same predictable Big Mac and fries is accompanied by an unusual blue drink. The same holds true with The Gap and The Body Shop throughout the world. These retailers use a **global strategy**, which means that they replicate their standard retail format and centralized management throughout the world in each new market. Often the global retailer will develop franchising initiatives based on its standardized form of doing business in return for a substantial franchise fee. The global retailer can expand rapidly but it is learning little from its internationalization.[34]

Retailers who change their products and image to reflect the international marketplace use a **multinational strategy**. These retailers use a decentralized format, learning about the country's culture and changing their retail concept to adapt to cultural differences and cater to local market demands. Each country they enter enhances their knowledge portfolio. The greater the cultural diversity, the more likely the multinational retailer is to enter a joint venture with a company from the host country. The Spanish retailer Zara has opened at the Eaton Centre in Toronto. The trendy fashions are ordered daily with the newest fabrics and styles to appeal to the trend-conscious Canadian consumer. Zara's just-in-time small production facilities are able to cater to specific market demands with quick turnaround time.[35]

Global Location Issues

Many of the issues and procedures used for making global location decisions are the same as we discussed in the previous chapter.[36] The retailer needs to decide on a region, a trade area within that region, and a specific site. The retailer still needs to examine competition, population characteristics, traffic patterns, and the like. What makes global location decisions more difficult and potentially interesting is that those in charge of making these decisions are typically not as familiar with the nuances of the foreign location issues as they are with the same issues in their home country. Furthermore, national chains in Canada typically have close working relationships with a handful of major developers. These developers work with retailers on a strategic level while the malls are still on the drawing board.

Although similar developer–retailer relationships are growing worldwide, often retailers must deal with landlords directly—and cope with a confusing world of site requirements, red tape, and restrictions. For example, a retailer may be surprised to learn that the local government requires a $1-million key payment upfront, or a landlord may demand a 25-year lease. And if there's to be construction, it's likely to be a slow, politically charged process. Traditional shopping behaviours can also influence place strategy as can be seen in Retailing View 7.5.

Real estate selection is where many grand global designs ultimately succeed or fail. A retailer may devote months to targeting a region—Latin America, for instance—before choosing a country to enter. From that point, a city must be chosen. But when it comes to picking an exact site within that city—a decision that often demands knowing local **traffic flow**, the most desirable side of a street, or urban development patterns—the decision is sometimes rushed and made without the

global strategy
Replicating a retailer's standard retail format and centralized management throughout the world in each new market.

multinational strategy
A strategy that involves changing a retailer's products and image to reflect the international marketplace, using a decentralized format, learning about the country's culture, and changing the retail concept to adapt to cultural differences and cater to local market demands.

traffic flow The balance between a substantial number of cars and not so many that congestion impedes access to the store.

Wet Markets in Shanghai

Shanghai, with more than 23 million inhabitants, is the largest city by population in the world. It is a sophisticated international city, like New York, London, and Tokyo, with substantial influence in global commerce, culture, finance, media, fashion, technology, and transportation. It is a major financial centre and the busiest container port in the world. The major international food retailers (Walmart, Carrefour, Metro, and Tesco) have opened more than 200 Western-style hypermarkets in Shanghai. In addition, there are more than 2000 modern supermarkets operated mostly by Chinese firms. But the majority of perishable goods (fish, meat, chicken, pork, vegetables, and fruit) are still sold in traditional wet markets.

Wet markets are buildings divided into small stalls lined along narrow corridors with small, independent retailers selling perishables in the stalls. The retailers lease the stalls from market operators. They buy the perishables from various sources, including wholesale markets, rural merchants, and farmers' cooperatives, and then sort, clean, and package the perishables for sale to their customers. These markets are called "wet markets" because the concrete floor is constantly wet from the spraying of perishables and cleaning of live meat and fish. There are more than 900 wet markets in Shanghai.

The Chinese government would like to close all wet markets because they do not reflect the modern China and because they pose health risks due to poor hygiene. But Chinese urban consumers cross-format shop for groceries: They buy manufactured goods in supermarkets and hypermarkets but perishables in wet markets.

Even though there are many modern supermarkets and hypermarkets in Shanghai, the majority of perishable groceries are still bought at traditional wet markets.

© Jean Claude Toung Cheong | Dreamstime.com.

Two factors contribute to this preference for wet markets. First, Chinese consumers place great importance on freshness. Perishables sold at supermarkets and hypermarkets usually get to the store around 8 p.m. the night before and have been shelved for at least half a day before reaching consumers. At wet markets, vendors buy their perishables around 4 a.m. and constantly trim, spray, clean, and sort the perishables to keep them fresh. Also, wet-market vendors do not have or use refrigerators for storage; thus, they have to replenish their inventory with fresh supplies every day. The modern-format retailers simply cannot win the freshness contest.

Second, for logistical reasons, most Chinese consumers shop for groceries every day and buy just enough to prepare for that day's meals. In their small homes, the average kitchen size is about 60 square feet, leaving little room to store any items for extended periods, especially perishable foods that require refrigeration. Furthermore, though the automotive market is growing in China, many families still travel by other means. In Shanghai for example, bicycles (20 percent), buses (30 percent), and walking (40 percent) are more common means of transport for shopping trips. In these locations, the small wet markets provide far more convenient locations than larger supermarkets or hypermarkets.

Sources: "Buying the Store," *China Economic Review*, June 14, 2012; Louise Herring, Daniel Hui, Paul Morgan, and Caroline Tufft, *Inside China's Hypermarkets: Past and Prospects* (Hong Kong: McKinsey By McKinsey, 2012); Qian Forrest Zhang and Zi Pan, *The Transformation of Urban Vegetable Retail in China: Wet Markets, Supermarkets, and Informal Markets in Shanghai*, Research Collection School of Social Sciences, 2012.

right knowledge. As with many locations in Canada, particularly congested urban areas, if the retailer chooses the wrong side of the street, it may fail.

Costs can also be troublesome. Compared to North American locations, occupancy costs in cities such as London, Paris, or Tokyo are extremely high. Retailers have to be extremely high-volume to

DID YOU KNOW?

Organized retailing, such as multi-unit, self-service supermarkets, accounts for just 4 percent of retail sales in India.[37]

DID YOU KNOW?

H&M opened three stores ranging from 15 000 to 35 000 square feet in the Toronto area, and receives merchandise daily from Europe. As of 2014, the company had over 93 000 employees in 3011 stores across 28 countries worldwide, including 72 stores in Canada.[38]

survive. Real estate rental costs are 30 percent more in the United Kingdom than they are in Germany, which are 30 percent more than they are in the United States, which are 30 percent more than they are in Canada.

Real estate restrictions also complicate international location decisions. For instance, tough European laws make it difficult for big-box retailers to open large stores that have historically required a large piece of property. Solutions occasionally demand a little ingenuity and flexibility. Costco Wholesale's solution, for example, has been to modify store formats in some overseas markets—most notably, the adoption of two-level operations in Korea and Taiwan. Some retailers prefer to open locations within a mall setting, and for some, the bigger the mall, the better. See Exhibit 7–3 for a list of the world's largest shopping malls.

Although there continues to be talk of a downturn for the outlet centre model in North America, their popularity is still very good in other parts of the world such as Japan and Europe. Japan is particularly attractive given its large population, love for American brands, and growing consumer enthusiasm for value retailing concepts. Compared to American outlet centres, current European centres are smaller, have fewer entertainment options, and have fewer well-known manufacturer outlets of European brands due to concern about channel conflict. These centres are growing more slowly in Europe, but there definitely seems to be an upward trend for this model in Europe.

Lo6 The Top 250 Global Retailers

Deloitte publishes an annual report called *Global Powers of Retailing*. This report identifies the 250 largest retailers around the world based on publicly available data for the companies' fiscal year (for example, see Exhibit 7–4 for information based on

Exhibit 7–4

Top 250 Quick Stats, 2014

Quick Facts about the Top 250 Retailers in 2014

- $4.48 trillion: aggregate retail revenue
- $17.91 billion: average size
- $3.65 billion: minimum retail revenue required to be among the top 250 retailers
- 4.3%: composite year-over-year retail revenue growth
- 4.9%: composite compound annual growth rate in retail
- 2.8%: composite net profit margin
- 4.3%: composite return on assets
- 23.4%: percent of top 250 retail revenue from foreign operations
- 10.4: average number of countries in which top 250 companies have retail operations

Source: Deloitte, *Global Powers of Retailing 2016: Retail Beyond*, January 2016, p. 21, http://www2.deloitte.com/sg/en/pages/consumer-business/articles/global-powers-of-retailing.html (accessed January 20, 2016).

2014 data). Exhibit 7–5 lists the ten largest global retailers in 2014 from this report. With worldwide retail sales estimated at US$4.5 trillion, four retailers generated more than $100 billion in sales (US dollars), with the top ten garnering 31.5 percent of the total top 250 sales.[39]

As a group, the ten largest global retailers have a much larger geographic footprint than the top 250 global retailers overall. These large retailers (see Exhibit 7–5) operate on average in 16.7 countries, which is nearly twice as many as the average for the entire group of 250 retailers. The revenue from foreign operations, according to the Deloitte report, accounts for nearly one-third of the total top ten global retailers' retail revenue.[40]

Macro environmental forces (oil prices) are currently impacting the level of growth in retail markets. Though there was still growth (retail revenue grew 4.3 percent in 2014), it lagged when comparing numbers from 2010 to 2014. Weak exports and investing has slowed grow in China, which has had a ripple affect in global retail markets.[41]

Kroger, the third largest retailer world wide, had the highest level of growth in 2014, at 10.3 percent. This was partly due to the buy out of Harris Teeter Supermarkets and the acquisition of Vitacost.com, an online vitamin retailer.[42]

According to the study by Deloitte, the top 250 retailers continued to extend their global reach in 2014. Sixty-six percent (165) of the top 250 retailers operated in more than one country in 2014. It is important to point out that these numbers are based

Exhibit 7-5
Top 10 Retailers Worldwide

Top 250 rank	Name of company	Country of origin	FY2014 retail revenue (US$M)	FY2014 retail revenue growth	FY2014 net profit margin	FY2014 return on assets	FY2009–2014 retail revenue CAGR*	# countries of operation	% retail revenue from foreign operations
1	Walmart Stores Inc.	US	485 651	2.0%	3.5%	8.4%	3.5%	28	28.3%
2	Costco Wholesale Corporation	US	112 640	7.1%	1.9%	6.3%	9.5%	10	28.6%
3	The Kroger Co.	US	108 465	10.3%	1.6%	5.7%	7.2%	1	0.0%
4	Schwarz Unternehmenstreuhand KG	Germany	102 694*	7.2%	n/a	n/a	7.7%	26	59.2%
5	Tesco PLC	UK	99 713	−2.1%	−9.3%	−13.0%	1.8%	13	30.0%
6	Carrefour S.A.	France	98 497	−0.3%	1.8%	3.0%	−2.8%	34	52.7%
7	Aldi Elnkauf GmbH & Co. oHG	Germany	86 470*	6.6%	n/a	n/a	6.8%	17	57.1%
8	Metro Ag	Germany	85 570	−4.0%	0.3%	0.6%	−0.8%	32	59.3%
9	The Home Depot Inc.	US	83 176	5.5%	7.6%	15.9%	4.7%	4	10.2%
10	Walgreen Co.	US	76 392	5.8%	2.7%	5.5%	3.8%	2	1.5%
Top 10[1]			**1 339 267**	**3.2%**	**1.9%**	**4.3%**	**3.8%**	**16.7[2]**	**31.5%**
Top 250[1]			**4 478 205**	**4.3%**	**2.8%**	**4.3%**	**4.9%**	**10.4[2]**	**23.4%**

Top 10 share of Top 250 retail revenue   **29.9%**

e = estimate
n/a = not available
* Compound annual growth rate
[1] **Sales-weighted, currency-adjusted composites** [2] **Average**
Source: Deloitte, *Global Powers of Retailing 2016: Retail Beyond,* January 2016, p. 23, http://www2.deloitte.com/sg/en/pages/consumer-business/articles/global-powers-of-retailing.html (accessed January 20, 2016).

on the information available to Deloitte at the time of the study and may not capture all activity. Twenty-six percent of the top 250 retail revenue was less than US$5.0 billion.[43]

The apparel and accessories retailer sector was the most profitable and fastest growing section in both 2013 and 2014. Composite new profit grew to 8.1 percent, while composite retail revenue grew 6.7 percent in 2014. Eighty-five percent (41 out of 48 Top 250 accessories and apparel) operated internationally in 2014. The average retail revenue for this sector was US$9.1 billion.[44]

For 2014, 173 of the top 250 retailers had e-commerce enabled websites that contain information available for consumers to view (i.e., information websites). Of these e-tailers, 140 had e-commerce enabled websites. Online sales for these 140 companies grew at a composite rate of 20.3 percent over a one year period.[45]

Deloitte also created a list of the top 50 e-retailing retailers in 2014. Most of the top 50 (39) were omnichannel retailers that have bricks-and-mortar locations, online, and other types of non-store retail formats. Of this e-50 group, 11 were "pure click" companies, with Amazon being the largest with sales greater than US$70 billion (largest of the top e-50).[46]

The majority of the largest global retailers are involved in the food sector and other fast-moving consumer goods. More than half of the top 250 companies are fast-moving consumer good retailers accounting for more than two-thirds of top 250 sales. In addition to being the most numerous, these retailers are also the biggest with average 2014 retail sales of US$24 billion.[47]

The number of US companies in the top 250 and their share of sales dropped to 84 in 2008, to 76 in 2011, and then went up to 77 in 2014. Walmart alone represented 10.8 percent of the top 250 sales. In

DID YOU KNOW?

Tim Hortons currently has approximately 950 stores in the United States.[48]

DID YOU KNOW?

India's working age population is expected to grow by 335 million by 2030. This increase is equal to the working age population of the European Union and the United States combined.[49]

2014, five of the top ten retailers were from the United States, three were from Germany, one was from the United Kingdom, and one was from France. Canada represented a 3 percent share of the top 250 retailers by region/country, and a 2.2 percent share of the top 250 sales by region/country, in 2014.

The CSCA Retail 100 report indicates that Canadian-controlled retail remains relatively strong in the Canadian retail sector as a whole, with about 61 percent of Canada's total retail sales coming from domestic retailers, 37 percent of sales from American firms, and the remaining 2 percent coming from other foreign firms such as Zara and H&M.[50]

Historically, a large consumer market and relatively abundant land have kept many Canadian retailers from seeking global expansion. But with domestic markets reaching saturation, companies are seeking opportunities abroad. Still, North American companies have not caught up to the largest European firms, which operate in an average of seven countries.

Structure of Retailing and Distribution Channels Around the World

The nature of retailing and distribution channels in North America is unique. Some critical differences between Canadian, US, European, and Japanese retailing and distribution systems are summarized in Exhibit 7–6.

The US distribution system has the greatest retail density and the greatest concentration of large retail firms. Some people think that North America is overstored. Many retail firms are large enough to operate their own warehouses, eliminating the need for wholesalers. The fastest-growing types of retailers sell through large stores with over 20 000 square feet. The combination of large stores and large firms results in a very efficient distribution system.

In contrast, the Japanese distribution system is characterized by small stores operated by relatively small firms and a large independent wholesale industry. To make daily deliveries efficiently to these small retailers, merchandise often moves through

Exhibit 7–6

Comparison of Retailing and Distribution Channels Across the World

Characteristic	Canada	U.S.	U.K.	Belgium	France	Germany	Spain	Italy	Hungary	Czech	Japan
			EUROPE								
			NORTHWEST				SOUTHERN		CENTRAL		
Concentration (% of retail sales in category by top three firms)	High	High	High				Low		Very Low		Medium
Number of outlets per 1000 people	Medium	Medium	Medium				High		Low		High
Retail density (sq. ft. of retail space per person)	High	High	Medium				Low		Low		Medium
Store size (% of retail sales made in stores over 10 000 square feet)	High	High	Medium				Low		Low		Low
Role of wholesaling (wholesale sales as a % of retail sales)	Low	Low	Medium				Medium		High		High
Distribution Inefficiency (average maintained markup–distribution costs as a % of retail price)	Low	Low	Medium				High		High		High

three distributors between the manufacturer and retailer. This difference in efficiency results in a much larger percentage of the Japanese labour force being employed in distribution and retailing than in Canada.

The European distribution system falls between the North American and Japanese systems on this continuum of efficiency and scale. However, the northern, southern, and central parts of Europe have to be distinguished, with northern European retailing being the most similar to the North American system. In northern Europe, concentration levels are high—in some national markets, 80 percent or more of sales in a sector such as food or home improvements are accounted for by 5 or fewer firms. Southern European retailing is more fragmented across all sectors. For example, traditional farmers' market retailing is still important in some sectors, operating alongside large "big-box" formats. In central Europe, the privatization of retail trade has resulted in a change from a previously highly-concentrated government-controlled structure to one of extreme fragmentation characterized by many small family-owned retailers.

Some factors that have created these differences in distribution systems in the major markets are:

- **Social and political objectives.** A top priority of the Japanese economic policy is to reduce unemployment by protecting small businesses such as neighbourhood retailers. Japan's *Large Scale Retail Stores Law* regulates the locations and openings of stores of over 5000 square feet. Several European countries have also passed laws protecting small retailers. For example, in 1996, France tightened its existing laws to constrain the opening of stores of over 3000 square feet. European governments have also passed strict zoning laws to preserve green spaces, protect town centres, and inhibit the development of large-scale retailing in the suburbs.

- **Geography.** The population density in Canada is much lower than in Europe and Japan. Thus, Europe and Japan have less low-cost real estate available for building large stores.

- **Market size.** The North American retail market is larger than Japan or any single European country. In Europe, distribution centres and retail chains typically operate within a single country and are therefore not able to achieve the scale economies of North American retailers serving a broader customer base. Even

with the euro and other initiatives designed to make trade within European countries easier and more efficient, barriers to trade still exist that are not found in the Canadian and American marketplaces.

Counterfeiting is a Global Threat

Counterfeit merchandise is imitation or fake, usually made with the intent to deceptively represent its contents or origins. Counterfeiting usually involves forged currency or documents, but can also describe clothing, software, electronic stock shares or certificates, pharmaceuticals, watches, or more recently, auto parts, cars, and motorcycles. Often this results in patent infringement and trademark infringement. Widespread use of counterfeit products undermines the North American system of standards, testing, and certification that is designed to protect consumers, retailers, manufacturers, and regulators.

The term **bootleg** is more often used when there is little or no attempt to hide the fact that it is a counterfeit product, such as CDs, DVDs, computer software, and toys. The user is fully aware of its illegal status. By contrast, a **knockoff** item may imitate a well-known brand, may be sold for a lower price, and may be of inferior quality, but there is usually no attempt to deceive the buyer or infringe upon the original product.

The appearance of counterfeit products in North America has increased dramatically in recent years. According to Manny Gratz, manager of

counterfeit merchandise Goods that are made and sold without permission of the owner of a trademark, a copyright, or a patented invention that is legally protected in the country where it is marketed.

bootleg The sale of imitation goods where there is little or no attempt to hide the fact that the product is counterfeit.

knockoff A copy of the latest styles displayed at designer fashion shows and sold in exclusive specialty stores. These copies are sold at lower prices through retailers targeting a broader market.

DID YOU KNOW?

The city of Yimu in China is known as "Counterfeit Central" and international buyers come to purchase retail merchandise/ product knockoffs in bulk. Some 40 000 wholesale shops sell about 100 000 products that are up to 90 percent fake.[51]

DID YOU KNOW?

Chinese counterfeiting now costs foreign firms an estimated $20 billion a year in lost profits. "In the case of one consumer goods manufacturer, as much as 70 percent of the goods on the market are counterfeits."[52]

Anti-Counterfeiting & Intellectual Property Enforcement, the manufacture and distribution of counterfeit products have been linked to organized crime. He feels that people who deliberately choose to buy counterfeit products are not victims; instead, they support the criminally deceptive practices of counterfeiters by creating a built-in market for their goods.

Retailers knowingly selling counterfeit merchandise in Canada can face fines, lawsuits, and court costs. For example, a retailer in British Columbia incurred court costs of over $1 million for selling counterfeit Louis Vuitton accessories. In another instance, Microsoft Corporation received a total judgement of $700 000 from a Quebec court after another company pirated and sold its software.[53]

So what impact, if any, does this have on Canadian consumers purchasing counterfeit products in Canada? The RCMP website in Canada says: When you commit to buy a counterfeit product:

- You could be putting your family at risk. There is no quality control, and counterfeiters are not concerned about what happens to the people who buy and use counterfeit products. For example, "Counterfeit electrical devices have caught fire causing injury and serious damage to property; counterfeit pharmaceutical products often contain no active ingredients or, worse still, toxic ingredients, and have caused death; counterfeit children's clothing often contain no fire retardant."

- You could be funding terrorists or organized crime.

- You could be impacting the economy, which may result in the loss of jobs/tax revenue.[54]

This chapter provides an overview of international retailing. Understanding the macro-environment becomes increasingly critical in making strategic decisions to expand internationally. Questions about the local economy, legal environment, technological capabilities, consumer behaviour, and the retail competition must be answered. Business laws and regulations will not only impact the ability to conduct business, but will also dictate how to function operationally in a global marketplace. The macro-environment is different for each country and must be constantly monitored.

Issues of global location strategy will impact retailing success or failure on a day-to-day basis. International retailers must be intimately aware of the cultural climate in domestic markets and respond to the market demands of the micro-environment. Understanding the importance of place, including the retail location and store environment, product mix, price, and management decisions is critical. Retailing is geographically tied and must therefore gain insight into the direct-to-customer link.

Global retailers will develop strength through centralized management and a standardized image, whereas multinational retailers gain success by adapting to the local environment through decentralized management and a more flexible approach to retail store design.

Key Terms

adaptability
bootleg
counterfeit merchandise
direct investment
financial resources

global culture
global strategy
globally sustainable competitive
    advantage
joint venture

knockoff
multinational strategy
strategic alliance
tariffs
traffic flow

GET OUT & DO IT!

1. INTERNET EXERCISE Go to the websites for Walmart (http://www.walmartstores.com), Carrefour (http://www.carrefour.com), Royal Ahold (http://www.ahold.com), and Metro AG (http://www.metro.de). Which chain has the most global strategy? Justify your answer.

2. INTERNET EXERCISE Choose your favourite national retail chain. Pick a country for it to enter where it is not currently operating. Using information found on the Internet, collect information on that country and the retailer. Develop a report that analyzes whether the retailer should enter the country, and if so, how it should do so.

3. INTERNET EXERCISE

a) Go to http://www.counterfeitchic.com. Review recent blogs.

b) Read the paper by Renée Richardson Gosline, "The Real Value of Fakes," at http://gradworks.umi.com/3371273.pdf; the article by Meg Tirrell, "Fake Louis Vuitton Bags Look Fake Without a Tony Aura (Update1)," at http://www.bloomberg.com/news/articles/2009-12-02/fake-louis-vuittons-look-fake-without-a-tony-aura-study-says; and the blog entry by Felix Salmon, "Those Weirdly Persistent Counterfeiting Statistics," at http://blogs.reuters.com/felix-salmon/2009/12/06/those-weirdly-persistent-counterfeiting-statistics. Discuss the economic impact of counterfeiting, taking the unique perspective and research findings of Gosline into consideration.

c) Explain the economic impact of counterfeiting.

DISCUSSION QUESTIONS AND PROBLEMS

1. Read "IKEA: Bringing its Philosophy to a World Market" at the beginning of the chapter and visit http://www.ikea.com.

   a) Explain why IKEA has had such strong appeal in the global marketplace.

   b) Why does the philosophy "one size fits all" not work in global markets? Suggest situations where this policy is problematic.

2. Explain how global culture can impact the success or failure of a global retailer such as Toys "R" Us.

3. What advantages does a multinational retailer such as Avon have over a global retailer?

4. Why are global companies such as McDonald's Restaurants gaining worldwide customer appeal?

5. Explain the strengths and weaknesses of global companies versus multinational retailers.

6. Why is a joint venture alliance often a favourable approach to facilitating an international retail venture?

7. Why is it important to understand the macro-environment when making decisions about an international retail venture?

8. Explain the importance of understanding the micro-environment when planning to open a retail store in an international location.

9. Complete a research study to determine what laws and regulations exist for opening a retail store in the following countries:

   - China
   - India
   - Russia
   - Mexico

10. Choose a retailer that you believe would be, but is not yet, successful in other countries. Explain why you think it would be successful.

CHAPTER EIGHT

Financial strategy

LEARNING OBJECTIVES

Lo1   Explore why retailers need to evaluate their performance.

Lo2   Identify the measures retailers use to assess their performance.

Lo3   Explore the strategic profit model and examine how it is used.

Lo4   Examine how retail strategy is reflected in retailers' financial objectives.

SPOTLIGHT ON RETAILING

goeasy Ltd.

goeasy Ltd. offers Canadian customers alternatives that may not be available from other retailers or financial institutions. *goeasy Ltd.* currently operates through two business units: *easyhome* Leasing, and *easyfinancial* Services.

easyhome is Canada's largest merchandise leasing retailer and provides its customers with access to brand-name household goods (furnishings, appliances, and electronic products) under weekly or monthly leasing agreements. They provide lease programs for customers who wish to lease merchandise on a short-term basis to try a product before making a purchase decision, or to obtain a product they may not otherwise be able to have as a result of being either cash- or credit-constrained. The retailer began operations in 1990 and currently operates 151 corporate and 27 franchised stores for a total of 178 stores in Canada. *easyhome* generated $152.6 million in revenues in 2015.

easyfinancial offers personal loans from $500 up to $15 000 in the alternative financial services space to customers who have limited access to funds from traditional financial institutions including banks. *easyfinancial* began operations in 2006 to fill the gap in the market between banks and payday lenders by providing a more affordable option to consumers who have limited financial options. The business was initially developed using a kiosk that was physically located within an existing *easyhome* location. The business grew quickly and by 2011, the company determined that the *easyfinancial* business would scale more successfully by operating out of stand-alone locations that were physically separated from the *easyhome* stores. As of December 2015, the company operated 51 kiosk locations and 150 stand-alone locations, as well as one national loan office. Revenue for the year ending December 31, 2015 increased to $151.7 million from $100.8 million in 2014, an increase of $50.8 million or 50.4 percent.

David Ingram took over as chief operating officer of RTO Enterprises (now *goeasy* Ltd.) in late 2000. The then 100-store rent-to-own company had grown rapidly through acquisitions, but was relying on extremely expensive debt for funding and simply wasn't generating enough revenue to keep it in business. He saved the company from imminent bankruptcy by initiating a rights issue that allowed existing shareholders to reinvest at a very low share price. The proceeds—some $10 million—went to pay down high-interest debt and positioned the company for growth.

Ingram and his management team isolated three key factors that had led to RTO's financial situation. First, they determined that due to growth through acquisition, the company did not have a cohesive brand identity—it had 6 different brands across 100 stores. The six different brands had nothing particularly unique about them as the product offered was the same, the pricing was the same, and the service(s) offered was the same. They determined that it was an inefficient strategy as they could not market a single brand message with six different brands in the marketplace.

The team worked on building the single, unified brand we see today by looking at the products sold; the name, organization, and location of stores; and consumer insights through focus groups. The team developed the company's new name, *easyhome*, by writing down the key words used by focus group participants. According to Ingram, two words kept recurring: "easy," because customers wanted something that would make life easier for them, and "home," the cherished place where they could be with family. "We put those two words together and we came up with *easyhome*," says Ingram.

Second, the management team determined that customers did not want access to second-tier merchandise simply because they were looking for alternative payment opportunities. To grow the business, the team seriously addressed consumers' desire to access premium-brand goods, particularly electronics. The team worked with brand leaders to become suppliers. Today, the company offers brands such as Ashley, Dynasty, Eztia, and Serta mattresses; Samsung and Whirlpool appliances; Sony, Samsung, LG, and Toshiba home electronics; and Dell, HP, Acer, and Toshiba computers. In order to keep the higher-priced merchandise manageable, *easyhome* offers customers the flexibility of paying for products weekly, bi-weekly, or monthly over 18 to 36 months.

Finally, at the beginning of 2002, Ingram and his team considered the look and feel of the stores, from window presentation to signage, lighting, and even location. They determined that stores required

Courtesy of *goeasy* Ltd.

a facelift to bring them up to date and connect with *easyhome*'s average customer. In order to appeal to young to middle-aged women with children, they incorporated wide aisles that could accommodate strollers and revamped stores to make them brightly lit, secure, and inviting, with a modern appeal. "Our customers wanted to have the same shopping experience as they'd expect from a decent furniture retail or electronics store," says Ingram. "They wanted a place they could feel proud of, where they wouldn't worry about bringing young children."

The new *easyhome* brand (name, in-store look, and pricing structure) was tested in ten stores and was rolled out to all (110) stores in April 2003. The rebranding effort took three months as Ingram believed that a drawn-out rollout would not allow the company to get the momentum and traction they required from the rebrand.

Since then, the company has achieved 14 consecutive years of revenue growth fuelled primarily by the *easyfinancial* business, which in 2016 will eclipse *easyhome* in revenues for the first time.

As the company grew over the years, there was a need to establish an evolved brand strategy, which came in 2014 with the launch of a newly created master brand: *goeasy*. The objective was to create one umbrella brand that would be used to promote both sub-brands while more broadly positing the organization for growth and scale. The success of the master brand launch ultimately led to the company's name change in 2015 to *goeasy Ltd.*

Since Ingram took over the top spot in 2001, the company has almost doubled in size, achieving 17.4 percent total revenue growth and 16.3 percent same-store sales growth.

Sources: easyhome Ltd., *Annual Report 2015*, March 6, 2012, http://www.investorx.ca/Doc/XS5AU08SQ9/2015/04/13/easyhome-ltd/annual-report-english (accessed January 26, 2016); Camilla Cornell, "Easyhome: A Forward Regression," *Canadian Retailer*, Spring 2012, Volume 22, Issue 2, pp. 52–54; http://investors.easyhome.ca/phoenix.zhtml?c=83047&p=RssLanding_pf&cat=news&id=2002520 (accessed January 26, 2016).

Financial decisions are an integral component in every aspect of a retailer's strategy. In this chapter, we look at financial tools retailers use to measure and evaluate their performance.

Retail store owners need to know how well they are doing because they want to be successful and stay in business. Retailers are aware of how many customers enter their stores and count up the receipts at the end of the day to see how much has been sold. Unfortunately, these simple measures aren't enough. For instance, sometimes a retailer finds that sales are good, but it still can't afford to buy new merchandise. When things are good, retailers often don't think about their retail strategy; but when things go bad, they think about nothing else.

Based on strategies the retailer sets, it is important to establish quantifiable performance objectives. If the retailer is achieving objectives, changes in strategy or implementation programs aren't needed. But if the performance information indicates that objectives aren't being met, the retailer needs to re-analyze plans and programs. For example, after reviewing the accountant's financial report, the retailer might conclude that it is not earning a fair return on the time and money invested in the stores. Based on this evaluation, the retailer might consider changing the strategy by appealing to a different target market and lowering the average price point of the merchandise in order to improve the turnover rate.

return on assets (ROA) Net profit after taxes divided by total assets.

Lo1 Objectives and Goals

As we discussed in Chapter 4, the first step in the strategic planning process involves articulating the retailer's strategy and the scope of activities it plans to undertake to be successful. Three types of objectives that a retailer might have are (1) financial, (2) societal, and (3) personal.[1]

Financial Objectives

When assessing financial performance, most people focus on profits: What were the retailer's profits or profit margin (profit as a percentage of sales) last year, and what will they be this year and into the future? But the appropriate financial performance measure is not profits, but rather return on investment (ROI). For example, Kelly Bradford, the owner of Gifts To Go, whom we introduced in Chapter 4, set a financial objective of making a profit of at least $100 000 a year. However, she really needs to consider how much she needs to invest to make the $100 000 profit she desires from her investment.

Think of the decisions you might make when planning how to invest some money you might have. In making this investment, you want to determine the highest percentage return you can—the highest interest rate or greatest percentage increase in stock price—not the absolute amount of the return. You can always get a greater absolute return by investing more money. For example, Kelly Bradford would be delighted if she made $100 000 and only needed to invest $500 000 (a 20 percent ROI) in the business, but disappointed if she had to invest $2 000 000 to make $100 000 profit (a 5 percent ROI). A commonly used measure of return on investment is **return on assets (ROA)**, or the profit return on all the assets possessed by the firm.

Societal Objectives

Societal objectives are related to broader issues about providing benefits to society—making the world a better place to live. For example, retailers might be concerned about providing employment opportunities for people in a particular area, or more specifically for minorities or persons with disabilities. Other societal objectives might include offering people unique merchandise, such as environmentally sensitive products, providing an innovative service to improve personal health, such as weight reduction programs, or sponsoring community events.

For example, McDonald's values diversity among its employees and suppliers. The company ensures diversity among its corporate employees by including it in the business planning process. "As business units and corporate departments put together their business plans, diversity is included in them. We have diversity business planning guidelines that we provide to the McDonald's leadership so that they're incorporated in the strategic planning process," explains Chief Diversity Officer Pat Harris. McDonald's also values diversity in its supply chain and has been recognized by *Fortune* magazine as the leading purchaser from minority suppliers, with more than $3 billion a year (27 percent of it its total purchases) acquired from minority suppliers.[2]

Performance with respect to societal objectives is more difficult to measure than financial objectives. But explicit societal goals can be set, such as the percentage of executives or store managers that are women or minorities or the percentage of profits donated to worthy charities.

Personal Objectives

Many retailers, particularly owners of small, independent businesses, have important personal objectives, including self-gratification, status, and respect. For example, Lululemon Athletica believes that its core values and distinctive corporate culture allow it to attract passionate and motivated employees who are driven to succeed and share its vision. Lululemon provides its employees with a supportive, goal-oriented environment and encourages them to reach their full professional, health, and personal potential. The company offers programs such as personal development workshops and goal-coaching to help its employees realize their long-term personal objectives.[3]

Whereas societal and personal objectives are important to some retailers, financial objectives should be the primary focus of managers of publicly-held retailers—retailers whose stocks are listed on and bought through a stock market. Investors in publicly-held companies, namely, the people who buy stock in a company, are primarily interested in getting a return on their investment, and the managers of these companies must have the same objectives as the investors. Therefore, the remaining sections of this chapter focus on financial objectives and the factors affecting a retailer's ability to achieve financial goals. (Retailing View 8.1 discusses the impact of private equity investment in retailers.)

Ratio Analysis

In order to fully appreciate the concepts of finance, it is necessary to understand material from the accounting area. The analysis of a retailer's financial statements—income statement and balance sheet—is based on the knowledge and use of ratios. The income statement measures the profitability of a retailer over a time period (quarter or year), while the balance sheet indicates the retailer's holdings and obligations at a point in time (usually fiscal year end).[4]

A ratio is a numerator divided by a denominator. The resulting calculation could be a ratio of one of three types: (1) a percent (e.g., ROA, net

profit or expense), (2) a multiplier (e.g., asset turnover, inventory turnover), or (3) a number of days. It is important to understand the ratio to know the unit of the answer. For example, you do not want to calculate a ratio of .59 and convert it to a percent when it is supposed to be a multiplier (asset turnover).

Ratio analysis is more than just the application of a formula to financial data; it is "the measure of the inter-relationship between different sections of the financial statements, which then is compared with the budgeted or forecasted results, prior year results"[5] and or industry results. In other words, it is the interpretation of the ratio value that is important.

There are three types of ratio comparisons that can be made: cross-sectional, time-series, or a combination of the two. A **cross-sectional ratio analysis** is where a retailer compares its company's ratios to another company's or to the industry ratios. It is important to note that cross-sectional ratios must be calculated for the same time period—the same year or quarter—to be relevant. **Time-series analysis** evaluates performance over time. Retailers compare ratios for the most recent fiscal year or quarter with previous ratios to determine whether they are meeting financial objectives. By using time-series comparisons, retailers can identify developing trends and use the knowledge of these trends to assist in future planning. The third type of ratio comparison is one that combines cross-sectional and time-series analyses. By combining these two analyses, the retailer can evaluate its performance over time, as well as assess its performance against the industry average.[6]

Lo2 Overview: Strategic Profit Model

The **strategic profit model**, illustrated in Exhibit 8–1, is a method for summarizing the factors found in the income statement and balance sheet that affect a firm's financial performance, as measured by

> **cross-sectional ratio analysis** The analysis of a financial ratio of a company with the same ratio of different companies in the same industry.
>
> **time-series analysis** A comparison of a variable to itself over time.
>
> **strategic profit model (SPM)** A tool used for planning a retailer's financial strategy based on both margin management (net profit margin), asset management (asset turnover), and financial leverage management (financial leverage ratio). Using the SPM, a retailer's objective is to achieve a target return on owners' equity.

Why Private Equity Likes Mid-sized Companies such as Town Shoes

Canadians who wander by a Town Shoes store might see a nice pair of boots or heels in the window. Private equity investors might see something different—an example of a mid-market company that's a good investment target.

Private equity funds, both Canadian and international, have become increasingly interested in Canada's mid-market sector. The interest can be mutually beneficial—profitable for the private equity investors and helpful for growth to mid-sized firms, which typically have between 50 and 500 employees and at least $5-million a year in revenue.

Town Shoes is a good example, explains Michael Akkawi, a partner at Torys LLP in Toronto and head of the firm's Private Equity Group. The chain, now a giant, got started in 1952 by then-22-year-old Leonard Simpson, who was persuaded to open a store in what turned out to be Canada's first strip mall, at Bayview and Eglinton avenues in Toronto. By 2012, the chain had grown to 116 stores across Canada, with good positions in both high-end retail markets because of its locations in fashionable areas, and in the discount sector because it also owned The Shoe Company stores.

As a strong, viable business, its only real limits were: how to make the transition from a family-founded mid-sized company into a big firm; and how to have access to the capital needed to do so.

In 2012, the founders sold controlling interest to Alberta Investment Management Corp. (AIMCO) and Callisto Capital, the latter a Toronto private equity firm, with the Simpsons' management team continuing to run the company. This type of private equity deal is a win–win situation for both the buyer and the seller, Mr. Akkawi says. "It's a great example of how private equity works," he explains. The buyers acquire a well-run business that has room to grow, while "from the owner's side, they make a good return on the sale and retain some of their equity."

The story didn't end there. By this year, the chain had 182 stores under both brands, with annual sales last year of $291 million. Earlier this year, US giant DSW Inc. bought a 44 percent stake in Town Shoes for US$62 million, with options to buy the rest of the company after four years.

Private equity firms are looking more eagerly at Canadian mid-sized firms of all types for investment opportunities, says Sophia Tolias, an associate at Torys who has worked on similar private equity transactions. "It's partly because of changing Canadian demographics. The population is aging. Baby boomers are retiring in the next few years, and they're looking to transition their businesses. The private equity firms see

Source: David Israelson, "Why Private Equity Likes Mid-Sized Companies such as Town Shoes," *Globe and Mail,* December 15, 2014, http://www.theglobeandmail.com/report-on-business/economy/growth/why-private-equity-likes-mid-sized-companies-such-as-town-shoes/article21874593/(accessed January 26, 2016). Reprinted with permission of David Israelson.

return on assets. Return on assets (ROA) determines how much profit can be generated from the retailer's investment in assets. The model decomposes ROA into two components: (1) net profit margin and (2) asset turnover. The **net profit margin** is simply how much profit (after tax) a firm makes divided by its net sales. Thus, it reflects the profits generated from each dollar of sales. For example, if a retailer's net profit margin is 5 percent, it makes $.05 for every dollar of merchandise or services it sells.

Asset turnover is the retailer's net sales divided by its assets. This financial measure assesses the productivity of a

net profit margin The profit (after tax) a firm makes divided by its net sales.

asset turnover Net sales divided by total assets.

Exhibit 8–1

Components of the Strategic Profit Model

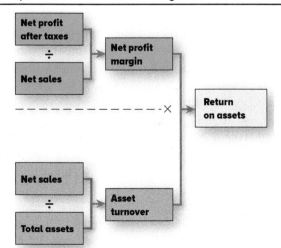

opportunities, which, in turn, creates more opportunities," she says.

Together with Torys partner Guy Berman, Ms. Tolias and Mr. Akkawi published a review of Canada's private equity market in 2012. (They are updating their data and publishing a new review soon.) They found that mid-market transactions were rich territory for private equity firms in 2012. "The vast majority of private equity transactions in Canada in 2012 remained in the low- to mid-market, with deals of less than $500-million accounting for 80 percent of the disclosed deal values, similar to the experience in US private equity markets. Canadian transactions were predominantly less than $100 million," their review said.

Among trends the experts are seeing now in the Canadian transaction market are that private equity firms are searching for and buying more mid-market companies than they were two years ago. In 2012 there was more selling than buying, as private equity firms sought to realize returns on their investment. Now there's more interest in finding good Canadian mid-sized businesses and investing, Mr. Berman says. "Everybody's all over them," he explains.

The understanding of the strengths of Canadian mid-sized companies has changed, he adds. A few years ago, funds saw Canadian mid-sized firms as a way to gain a toehold in the Canadian economy without too much risk; now they want a bigger perch. "The funds aren't looking at [these companies] as just a Canadian play any more,

they're looking at it as a North American play," Mr. Berman says.

Investors are sharpening their business strategies, too, Mr. Akkawi adds. "One of the big focuses that we're seeing from our clients in their investment strategies is to focus on platform assets," he says. By this he means that private equity investors are trying to build businesses, rather than simply parking money in the hope of a large profit later.

Town Shoes is an example, Mr. Akkawi says. "They [private equity firms] will buy a shoe retailer and acquire a good solid base by building a national chain. Typically, our clients are real experts in a select number of industries. They have the expertise, they're looking for the platform investment, and then they'll build on that," he says.

Pros and cons Taking on private equity can have upsides and downsides for mid-sized businesses. Pros and cons include:

Control – Dynamic mid-sized firms usually draw their energy from entrepreneurs. Private equity investment can take this energy away, unless the investors reach a deal to keep the founders as managers or co-owners for a while.

Transition – Private equity can help owners build their business methodically, and it can eliminate family feuds that often spring up when it's time to pass on the company or make it bigger.

---

firm's investment in its assets and indicates how many sales dollars are generated by each dollar of assets. Thus, if a retailer's asset turnover is 3.0, it generates $3 in sales for each dollar invested in the firm's assets.

The retailer's ROA is determined by either: multiplying net profit margin by asset turnover or dividing net profit by total assets. The option you choose will be based on the variable presents. The two alternatives to calculate ROA are shown below:

Alternative 1:

$$\text{Net profit margin} \times \text{Asset turnover} = \text{Return on assets (ROA)}$$

Alternative 2:

$$\frac{\text{Net profit}}{\text{Net sales}} \times \frac{\text{Net sales}}{\text{Total assets}} = \frac{\text{Net profit}}{\text{Total assets}}$$

These two components of the strategic profit model illustrate that return on assets (ROA) is determined by two sets of activities, profit margin management and asset management, and that a high ROA can be achieved by various combinations of net profit margin and asset turnover. Specifically, retailers have two paths available to achieve a high level of performance: the profit path and the turnover path. Different retailers, however, pursue different strategies, resulting in different types of financial performance (see Retailing View 8.2).

The two paths are combined into the strategic profit model to illustrate that retailers using very different strategies and financial performance characteristics can both be financially successful. As a vehicle for discussion, we will compare the financial performance of two very different retailers: Birks (a national jewellery store chain) and Walmart (the world's largest retailer). Then we will discuss how retailers set performance objectives and how different performance measures are used throughout the organization. For a description of activity-based costing and how it is used to make retailing decisions, see Appendix 8A on Connect.

We begin our examination of corporate-level performance measures by looking at the strategic profit model.

Exhibit 8-2
Return on Assets Model for a Bakery and a Jewellery Store

	Net profit margin	× Asset turnover	= Return on assets
La Madeline Bakery	1%	10 times	10%
Kalame Jewellery	10%	1 time	10%

	PROFIT PATH	TURNOVER PATH

$$\text{Return on assets (ROA)} = \text{Net profit margin} \times \text{Asset turnover}$$

$$= \frac{\text{Net profit}}{\text{Net sales}} \times \frac{\text{Net sales}}{\text{Total assets}}$$

$$= \frac{\text{Net profit}}{\text{Total assets}}$$

To illustrate how the strategic profit model works, consider the two very different hypothetical retailers in Exhibit 8–2. La Madeline Bakery has a net profit margin of 1 percent and asset turnover of ten times, resulting in a return on assets of 10 percent. The profit margin is low due to the competitive nature of this commodity-type business. Asset turnover is relatively high because the firm doesn't have its own credit card system (no accounts receivable). Also, it rents its store, so fixed assets are relatively low, and it has a very fast inventory turnover—in fact, its inventory turns every day!

On the other hand, Kalame Jewellery has a net profit margin of 10 percent and an asset turnover of one time, again resulting in a return on assets of 10 percent. The difference is that even though the jewellery store has higher operating expenses than the bakery, its gross margin is much more—it may double the cost of jewellery to arrive at a retail price. Kalame's asset turnover is so low compared to the bakery's because Kalame has very expensive fixtures and precision jewellery-manufacturing equipment (fixed assets), offers liberal credit to customers (accounts receivable), and has very slow inventory turnover—possibly only one-half to

one turn per year. In sum, these two very different types of retailers could have exactly the same return on assets.

Thus, La Madeline is achieving its 10 percent return on assets by having a relatively high asset turnover—the *turnover path*. Kalame Jewellery, on the other hand, achieves its return on assets with a relatively high net profit margin—the *profit path*. We will examine the relationship between these ratios and retailing strategy and describe where the information can be found in traditional accounting records.

One way to define financial success is to provide the owners of the firm with a good return on their investment. Although retailers pursue similar financial goals, they employ different strategies. For instance, Birks has broad assortments of jewellery and gifts, exceptionally high levels of service, and a beautiful store image. Birks concentrates on the profit path. Walmart takes the opposite approach. It concentrates on the turnover path. Walmart has narrow assortments, relatively little service, and functional decor. Based on this description, why would anyone shop at Walmart? The answer is that Walmart strives for and maintains everyday low prices. The strategic profit model is used to evaluate the performance of different retailers that, like Birks and Walmart, may employ very different strategies.

DID YOU KNOW?

Lululemon believes its culture and community-based business approach provides the retailer with competitive advantages that are responsible for its strong financial performance. Net revenue increased from $40.7 million in fiscal 2004 to $1.8 billion in fiscal 2014.[7]

The Profit Path

The information used to analyze a firm's profit path comes from the income statement. The income statement summarizes a firm's financial performance over a period of time, typically a quarter or a year. To capture all the sales, gift card purchases, and returns from the holiday season, many retailers set their fiscal year as beginning on February 1 and ending on January 31 of the following year. Exhibit 8–3

Exhibit 8–3

Hypothetical Income Statements for Walmart Stores, Inc., and Birks, 2017 ($ in millions)

	Walmart	Birks
Net sales	219 812	171 562
Less: Cost of goods sold	1 607	663
Gross margin	48 250	944
Less: Operating expense	36 173	634
Less: Interest expense	1 326	20
Total expense	37 499	653
Net profit, pretax	10 751	291
Less: Taxes*	3 897	116
Tax rate	36.25%	39.79%
Net profit after tax	6 854	175

*Effective tax rates often differ among corporations due to different tax breaks and advantages.

shows income statements in a hypothetical situation for Walmart and Birks. The profit path portion of the strategic profit model that uses such income statement data appears in Exhibit 8–4. Let's look at each item in the income statement. (Throughout this chapter, dollar figures are expressed in millions.)

Exhibit 8–4

Profit Margin Models for Walmart Stores, Inc., and Birks, 2017 ($ in millions)

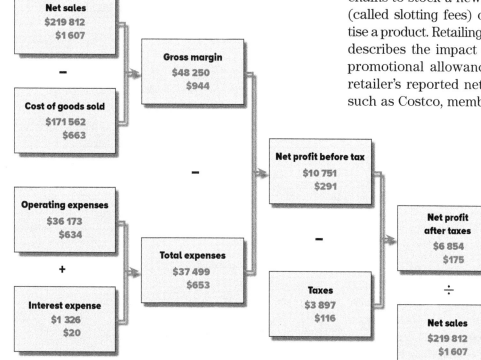

Top number = Walmart
Bottom number = Birks

Net Sales

The four main components in the profit margin management path are net sales, cost of goods sold (COGS), gross margin, and operating profit margin. The term **net sales** refers to the total number of dollars received by a retailer after all refunds have been paid to customers for returned merchandise:

$$\text{Net sales} = \text{Gross amount of sales} + \text{Promotional allowance} - \text{Customer returns}$$

Customer returns represent the value of merchandise that customers return and for which they receive a refund of cash or a credit. To calculate customer returns percentage, divide the dollar sum of customer returns by gross sales. (This is the only time that a retail ratio is calculated on gross sales.) **Promotional allowances** are payments made by vendors to retailers in exchange for the retailer promoting the vendor's merchandise. For example, consumer packaged-goods manufacturers will frequently pay supermarket chains to stock a new product (called slotting fees) or advertise a product. Retailing View 8.2 describes the impact of these promotional allowances on a retailer's reported net sales. For warehouse clubs such as Costco, membership fees are an additional

DID YOU KNOW?

Over 14 million Canadians shop at a Loblaw Companies store every week.[8]

net sales The total number of dollars received by a retailer after all refunds have been paid to customers for returned merchandise.

customer returns The value of merchandise that customers return because it is damaged, it doesn't fit, and so forth.

promotional allowances Payments made by vendors to retailers to compensate the latter for money spent in advertising a particular item.

Dollarama and Nordstrom: Retailers Targeting Customers at the Opposite Ends of the Income Distribution Spectrum

Dollarama and Nordstrom both have a high ROA but they achieve this high level of financial performance with significantly different retail strategies (see Exhibit 8–5). Canadian-owned and -operated since the first store opened in 1992 in Matane, Quebec, Dollarama is a value retailer with over 900 stores across the country, employing nearly 15 000 people. The firm has differentiated itself from other value retailers by offering a more consistent product selection, which includes everyday household needs and a selection of nationally branded products, as well as an assortment of unique and seasonal items. Merchandise is sold in individual or multiple units at select fixed price points up to $3.

Stores are all corporately managed, providing a consistent shopping experience, and nearly all are located in high-traffic areas, such as strip malls and shopping centres in various locations including metropolitan areas, mid-sized cities, and small towns. Dollarama continues to pursue its original vision of operating relatively convenient-sized (average 9905 square feet), self-service, no-frills store environments to offer a compelling value proposition on a wide variety of everyday merchandise to a broad base of customers.

Exhibit 8–5
Retail Strategy Comparison: Dollarama versus Nordstrom

Dollarama (2014)			Nordstrom (2014)		
Income Statement	**Balance Sheet**	**Key Stats and Ratios**	**Income Statement**	**Balance Sheet**	**Key Stats and Ratios**
Revenue: $2 064	Inventory: $364	Net profit margin: 12.1%	Revenue: $13 110	Inventory: $1 733	Net profit margin: 5.5%
Cost of goods: $1 299	Total assets: $1 566	Operating Expenses: 17.6%	Cost of goods: $8 406	Total assets: $9 245	Operating expenses: 28.8%
Gross profit: $765	Total liabilities: $702	Return on assets: 16%	Gross profit: $4 704	Total liabilities: $5 931	Return on assets: 8.1%
SG&A: $363	Total equity: $864	Inventory turnover: 5.9 times	SG&A: $3 777	Total equity: $2 440	Inventory Turnover: 4.67%
Income before tax: $324		Employees: 14 824	Income before tax: $1 323		Employees: 67 000
Income after tax: $250			Income after tax: $720		

Note: SG&A refers to selling, general, and administrative expenses. All figures are in $ millions, except for margins and employee numbers.

Sources: Robert Spector and Patrick McCarthy, *The Nordstrom Way to Customer Service Excellence* (Hoboken, NJ: Wiley, 2005); "Our History," Dollarama.com, http://www.dollarama.com/about_us/our_history (accessed January 27, 2016); "Dollarama Inc. Annual Information Form," April 27, 2012, http://www.dollarama.com/wp-content/uploads/2014/04/Fourth-Quarter-Financial-Statements.pdf (accessed January 27, 2016); http://investor.nordstrom.com/phoenix.zhtml?c=93295&p=irol-reportsannual (accessed January 27, 2016); http://shop.nordstrom.com/c/about-us (accessed April 1, 2010).

cost of goods sold Amount on an income statement that represents the cost of purchasing raw materials and manufacturing finished products.

source of revenue. About 4 percent of Costco's $48 billion in sales are from membership fees.

Sales are an important measure of performance because they indicate the activity level of the merchandising function. Retailers are particularly interested in sales growth due to its direct link to the firm's overall profitability.

Cost of Goods Sold

Cost of goods sold is a major component in determining a retailer's operating profit. Cash discounts, alteration/workroom costs, billed costs of

© Jerry Coli | Dreamstime.com.

© Oliver7perez/Dreamstime.com/GetStock.com.

Nordstrom is an upscale department store chain in the United States. It operates over 121 Nordstrom department stores, its online store at http://www.nordstrom.com, 194 Nordstrom Rack off-price stores, and five Trunk club warehouses, in 39 states. Its other retail channels include its online private-sale subsidiary HauteLook, its two Jeffrey boutiques,and one clearance store that operates under the name Last Chance.

Nordstrom currently has three stores in Canada and plans to have three more in the province of Ontario by 2017. The three current locations include premier shopping malls in Calgary, Ottawa, and Vancouver. The three shopping malls are: Pacific Centre in Vancouver, Calgary's Chinook Centre, and Rideau Centre in Ottawa.

John W. Nordstrom opened the first Nordstrom store in 1887 in Seattle, which continues to be Nordstrom's headquarters and the site of its flagship store. While the initial store was a shoe retailer, today the stores also sell clothing, accessories, handbags, jewellery, cosmetics, fragrances, and, in some locations, home furnishings. However, Nordstrom continues to carry an extraordinarily deep and broad assortment of shoes—about 15 000 SKUs in a typical department store.

Nordstrom is known for its outstanding customer service. Its customer-centric organizational culture is epitomized by its "handbook" that is given to new employees. The original handbook was a single 5- by 8-inch grey card containing 75 words:

WELCOME TO NORDSTROM

We're glad to have you with our Company. Our number one goal is to provide outstanding customer service. Set both your personal and professional goals high. We have great confidence in your ability to achieve them.

Nordstrom Rules: Rule #1: Use good judgment in all situations. There will be no additional rules. Please feel free to ask your department manager, store manager, or division general manager any questions at any time.

Now, in addition to this card, a full handbook of other more specific rules and legal regulations is given to new employees.

merchandise, and transportation costs all influence total cost of merchandise sold. In order to maintain or improve profit, retailers must figure ways to control these factors.

Gross Margin

Gross margin = Net sales − Cost of goods sold

Gross margin, also called *gross profit*, is an important measure in retailing. It gives the retailer a measure of how much profit it's making on merchandise sales without considering the expenses associated with operating the store. Gross margin is the amount that retailers use to cover expenses and provide profit for the organization.

Gross margin, like other performance measures, is also expressed as a percentage of net sales so that retailers can compare performances of various types of merchandise and their own performance with other retailers with higher or lower levels of sales.

$$\frac{\text{Gross margin}}{\text{Net sales}} = \text{Gross margin}\%$$

Walmart: $\dfrac{\$48\,250}{\$219\,812} = 21.95\%$

Birks: $\dfrac{\$944}{\$1607} = 58.75\%$

expenses Costs incurred in the normal course of doing business to generate revenues.

operating expenses Costs, other than the cost of merchandise, incurred in the normal course of doing business, such as salaries for sales associates and managers, advertising, utilities, office supplies, and rent.

selling, general, and administrative expenses (SG&A) Operating expenses, plus the depreciation and amortization of assets.

interest The amount charged by a financial institution to borrow money.

interest income The income a retailer can generate through proprietary credit cards, bank deposits, bonds, treasury bills, fixed income investments, and other investments.

Superficially, Birks appears to outperform Walmart on gross margin. However, further analysis will show that other factors interact with gross margin to determine overall performance. But first, let's consider the factors that contribute to differences in gross margin performance.

Discount stores such as Walmart generally have lower gross margins than jewellery stores because discount stores pursue a deliberate strategy of offering merchandise at everyday low prices with minimal service to several cost-oriented market segments. Discount stores have tried to increase their average gross margin by adding specialty products and departments such as gourmet foods and jewellery. Discount stores grow profit based on volume of sales.

Expenses

Expenses are costs incurred in the normal course of doing business to generate revenues. Types of

retail operating expenses are broken down in Exhibit 8–6 and are further defined in the hypothetical balance sheet in Exhibit 8–7. **Operating expenses** are the **selling, general, and administrative expenses (SG&A)**, plus the depreciation and amortization of assets. The SG&A includes costs, other than the cost of merchandise, incurred in the normal course of doing business, such as salaries for sales associates and managers, advertising, utilities, office supplies, information technology, and rent. Retailing View 8.3 reviews the creative ways that Costco reduces its SG&A costs.

DID YOU KNOW?

A retail outlet producing $400 000 in sales yields a net profit of only 2 percent or 3 percent, often as a result of SG&A costs, which typically are between 40 percent and 50 percent of sales.[9]

$$\frac{\text{Operating expenses}}{\text{Net sales}} = \text{Operating expenses}\%$$

Walmart: $\dfrac{\$36\,173}{\$219\,812} = 16.56\%$

Birks: $\dfrac{\$634}{\$1607} = 39.45\%$

Another major expense category, **interest**, is the cost of financing everything from inventory to the purchase of a new store location. For instance, if a bank charges Birks 10 percent interest, Birks pays $49 million in interest to borrow $490 million. Offsetting the interest expense is the **interest income** a retailer can generate through proprietary credit cards, bank deposits, bonds, fixed income investments, and other investments.

Most retailers incur expenses for interest and taxes. However, these costs of doing business may not reflect the retailer's performance in its primary business activity, which is selling its merchandise and services. That is, the interest expense is a financial, not an operating, decision, based on the evaluation of the relative cost of borrowing money or raising funds by selling more stock in the company. Taxes can be affected by the retailer's losses in the previous year and/or changes in government regulations and laws.

Exhibit 8–6
Types of Retail Operating Expenses

Selling expenses	= Sales staff salaries + Commissions + Benefits
General expenses	= Rent + Utilities + Miscellaneous expenses
Administrative expenses	= Salaries of all employees other than salespeople + Operations of buying offices + Other administrative expenses

Exhibit 8–7

Hypothetical Balance Sheets for Walmart Stores, Inc., and Birks ($ in millions)

	Walmart (as of 1/31/17)	Birks (as of 1/31/17)
ASSETS		
Current assets		
Accounts receivable	$ 2 000	$ 99
Merchandise inventory	22 614	612
Cash	2 161	174
Other current assets	1 471	71
Total current assets	28 246	955
Fixed assets		
Building, equipment, and other fixed assets, less depreciation	55 205	675
Total assets	$ 83 451	$1 630
LIABILITIES		
Current liabilities	$ 27 282	$ 341
Long-term liabilities	18 732	221
Other liabilities	2 335	30
Total liabilities	$ 48 349	$ 593
OWNERS' EQUITY		
Common shares	$ 1 929	$ 332
Retained earnings	33 173	705
Total owners' equity	$ 35 102	$1 037
Total liabilities and owners' equity	$ 83 451	$1 630

Birks has significantly higher total expenses as a percentage of net sales than Walmart. Like gross margin, total expenses are also expressed as a percentage of net sales to facilitate comparisons across items and departments within firms.

$$\frac{\text{Total expenses}}{\text{Net sales}} = \text{Total expenses/Net sales ratio}$$

Walmart: $\dfrac{\$37\ 499}{\$219\ 812} = 17.06\%$

Birks: $\dfrac{\$634}{\$1607} = 40.65$

The total expenses to net sales ratio is only approximately 17 percent for Walmart; at Birks, it's over 40 percent. This difference is to be expected. Discount stores have relatively low selling expenses. They are also typically located on comparatively inexpensive real estate, so rent is relatively low. Finally, discount stores operate with a smaller administrative staff than a store like Birks. For instance, buying expenses are much lower for discount stores. Their buyers don't have to travel very far, and much of the purchasing consists of re-buying staple merchandise that is already in the stores. On the other hand, a jewellery store's total expenses are much higher because its large, experienced sales staff requires a modest salary plus commission and benefits. Unlike Walmart stores' locations that are usually suburban or in rural areas, Birks stores are in some of the most expensive areas in the country. Birks locations therefore command high rent and incur other expenses.

Net Operating Income

Due to the lack of control over taxes, interest, and extraordinary expenses, a commonly-used profit measure is the net profit percentage before interest expenses/income, taxes, and extraordinary expenses. Like the gross margin and operating expenses, net operating income is often expressed as a percentage of net sales to facilitate comparisons across items, merchandise categories, and departments with different sales levels.

$$\frac{\text{Gross margin} - \text{Operating expenses}}{\text{Net sales}} = \frac{\text{Net operating}}{\text{income\%}}$$

Walmart: $\dfrac{\$48\ 250 - \$36\ 173}{\$219\ 812} = 5.49\%$

Birks: $\dfrac{\$944 - \$634}{\$1607} = 19.29\%$

Cutting Costs at Costco Wholesale

Costco's retail strategy focuses on offering its customer a good value—quality products at a reasonable price—on a wide merchandise assortment ranging from wheels of Parmesan cheese to 60-inch flat-screen TVs. Keeping prices low is challenging in light of increasing commodity prices, so Costco works with its vendors to control costs.

For example, Costco typically buys 70 percent of the large, premium macadamia nuts produced by Mauna Loa, a division of Hershey, leaving Mauna Loa with an inventory of small nuts. Costco buyers have worked with Mauna Loa to use smaller nuts in a new chocolate-nut cluster that will be sold exclusively at Costco. Because Mauna Loa won't have to face the uncertainty of selling those smaller nuts at a steep discount, it can afford to offer Costco better prices for its premium nuts.

Simple packaging changes can result in cost savings. For example, packaging cashews into square containers instead of traditional round ones enables Costco to increase the number of units it can stack on a pallet from 280 to 426. This relatively minor change to a product selling $100 million a year decreases the number of pallets shipped annually by 24 000 and decreases the number of truck trips by 600.

However, Costco does not scrimp on its employees. Eighty-six percent of its employees get health care and other benefits, even though half of its employees are

Changing this jar of nuts from a round shape to a square shape made a significant reduction in Costco's SG&A.
Courtesy of Costco.

part-timers. The average compensation of store employees is $20 an hour, more than 50 percent higher than the industry average. No Costco employees were laid off as a result of the recent recession. Costco believes that treating its employees well actually reduces labour costs in the long run. Its employee turnover is only 13 percent, among the lowest in the retail industry.

Sources: Zeynep Ton, "Why 'Good Jobs' Are Good for Retailers," *Harvard Business Review*, January–February 2012; Christopher Matthews, "Future of Retail: Companies That Profit by Investing in Employees," *Time*, June 18, 2012; "Costco's Artful Discounts," *Business Week*, October 20, 2008.

Net Profit

Net profit is a measure of the firm's overall performance:

$$\text{Net profit} = \text{Gross margin} - \text{Expenses}$$

Net profit can be expressed either before or after taxes. Generally, it's more useful to express net profit after taxes, since this is the amount of money left over to reinvest in the business, disburse as dividends to stockholders or owners, or repay debt.

net profit A measure of the overall performance of a firm; revenues (sales) minus expenses and losses for the period.

Net profit margin, like gross margin, is often expressed as a percentage of net sales:

$$\text{Net profit percentage} = \frac{\text{Net profit}}{\text{Net sales}}$$

However, net profit measures the profitability of the entire firm, whereas gross margin measures the profitability of merchandising activities. In Exhibit 8–5, the after-tax net profit margin is 3.12 percent for Walmart and 10.89 percent for Birks. From a profit perspective alone, Birks, with 70 stores in Canada, is outperforming Walmart. Even though Birks has a higher total expenses/net sales ratio, its gross margin percentage is so large compared to Walmart's that it still surpasses the discount store's profit performance in this scenario.

Skeletal Income Statement Using the profit path information discussed above and incorporating it into a series of skeletal statements will help provide a better understanding of the relationship between sales volume, cost of merchandise sold, and expenses, the basic merchandising factors found in an income statement. A **skeletal statement** demonstrates these three basic merchandising factors, plus gross margin and profit results. In working with basic income statement numbers in a skeletal format, the results of these three relationships can be demonstrated. To check the two columns for accuracy, add up from the bottom; the correlation between the numbers becomes more evident, in both dollars and percents.

Example of a skeletal statement	$	%
Net sales	48 000	100.00
(*minus*) Cost of goods sold	24 280	50.58
Gross margin	23 720	49.42
(*minus*) Expenses	12 360	25.75
Operating profit/loss	11 360	23.67

Even if some of the data were missing from the above skeletal statement, it could still be completed by setting up the relationships among the basic merchandising factors (net sales, cost of goods sold, and expenses). To find the percent of any one factor, divide the dollar amount of that factor by net sales. (Remember that net profit percent always equals 100 percent unless working with customer returns, when gross sales represent 100 percent.)

Example of a skeletal statement	$	%
Net sales	b.	100.00
(*minus*) Cost of goods sold	c.	d.
Gross margin	23 720	e.
(*minus*) Expenses	12 360	f.
Operating profit/loss	a.	23.67

The form can be "filled" by completing the following calculations:

Completing a skeletal statement

Calculations

a. **Operating Profit** = $23 720 − $12 360 = **$11 360**

b. **Net sales** = $11 360 ÷ 23.67% = **$48 000 (rounded)**

c. **Cost of goods sold** = $48 000 − $23 720 = **$24 280**

d. **Cost of goods sold %** = $24 280 ÷ $48 000 = **50.58%**

e. **Gross margin %** = $23 720 ÷ $48 000 = **49.42%**

f. **Expense %** = $12 360 ÷ $48 000 = **25.75%**

The Turnover Path

The information used to analyze a firm's turnover path comes primarily from the balance sheet. Whereas the income statement summarizes the financial performance over a period of time (usually a year or quarter), the balance sheet summarizes a retailer's financial position at a given point in time, typically the end of its fiscal year. The balance sheet shows the following relationship:

$$\text{Assets} = \text{Liabilities} + \text{Owners' equity}$$

Assets are economic resources (such as inventory, buildings, or store fixtures) owned or controlled by an enterprise as a result of past transactions or events. There are two types of assets: current and fixed. **Liabilities** are an enterprise's obligations (such as accounts or notes payable) to pay cash or other economic resources in return for past, current, or future benefits. **Owners' equity** (owners' investment in the business) is the difference between assets and liabilities. It represents the amount of assets belonging to the owners of the retail firm after all obligations (liabilities) have been met.

Exhibit 8–7 shows a hypothetical balance sheet for Birks and Walmart Stores, Inc. (in $ millions). The turnover path portion of the strategic profit model is shown in Exhibit 8–8's asset turnover model.

Current Assets

By accounting definition, **current assets** are those that can normally be converted to cash within one year. In retailing, current assets are primarily cash, accounts receivable, and merchandise inventory.

$$\frac{\text{Accounts}}{\text{receivable}} + \frac{\text{Merchandise}}{\text{inventory}} + \text{Cash} + \frac{\text{Other}}{\text{current}}_{\text{assets}} = \frac{\text{Current}}{\text{assets}}$$

Accounts Receivable

Accounts receivable are monies due to the retailer from selling merchandise on credit. This current

skeletal statement An analysis of the five key categories found in all operating statements.

assets Economic resources, such as inventory or store fixtures, owned or controlled by an enterprise as a result of past transactions or events.

liabilities Obligations of a retail enterprise to pay cash or other economic resources in return for past, present, or future benefits.

owners' equity The amount of assets belonging to the owners of the retail firm after all obligations (liabilities) have been met; also known as *net worth* and *shareholders' equity*.

current assets Cash or any assets that can normally be converted into cash within one year.

accounts receivable The amount of money due to the retailer from selling merchandise on credit.

Exhibit 8-8

Asset Turnover Model for Walmart Stores, Inc., and Birks (in $ millions)

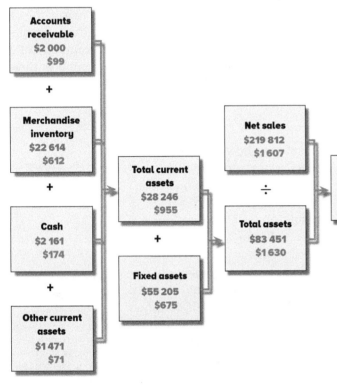

Accounts receivable
$2 000
$99

+

Merchandise inventory
$22 614
$612

+

Cash
$2 161
$174

+

Other current assets
$1 471
$71

Total current assets
$28 246
$955

+

Fixed assets
$55 205
$675

Net sales
$219 812
$1 607

÷

Total assets
$83 451
$1 630

Asset turnover
2.63
0.99

Top number = Walmart
Bottom number = Birks

difference between making or losing a sale. Paying cash for a sizable purchase such as a diamond engagement ring or car may be difficult for many people.

Unfortunately, having a large amount of accounts receivable is expensive for retailers, who of course would like to sell a product for cash and immediately reinvest the cash in new merchandise. When merchandise is sold on credit, proceeds of the sale are tied up as accounts receivable until collection is made. The money invested in accounts receivable costs the retailer interest expense and keeps the retailer from investing proceeds of the sale elsewhere. To ease the financial burden of carrying accounts receivable, retailers can use third-party credit cards such as Visa or MasterCard, give discounts to customers who pay with cash, discourage credit sales, and control delinquent accounts.

Merchandise Inventory

Merchandise inventory is a retailer's lifeblood, representing 27.10 percent of total assets for Walmart and 37.53 percent of total assets for Birks. An

asset is substantial for some retailers. For example, Walmart's investment in accounts receivable is proportionally much smaller than Birks' due to Walmart customers' high propensity to pay cash or use third-party credit cards such as Visa or MasterCard. Here are their accounts receivable:

Walmart: $2000, or 0.9 percent of sales

Birks: $99, or 6.1 percent of sales

From a marketing perspective, the accounts receivable generated from credit sales may be the result of an important service provided to customers. A **proprietary store credit card system**, also known as an *in-house credit system*, is one in which credit cards have the store's name on them, and the accounts receivable are administered by the retailer, not a credit card company like Visa or MasterCard or a financial institution.[10] The retailer's ability to provide credit, particularly at low interest rates, could make the

proprietary store credit card system A system in which credit cards have the store's name on them and the accounts receivable are administered by the retailer; also known as an *in-house credit system*.

8.1 CONCEPT CHECK

1. Set up a skeletal income statement given the following information:

Net sales	$525 000
Gross margin	44.6%
Expenses	45.0%

2. Set up a skeletal income statement, given the following information:

Gross margin	$118 500
Expenses	$52 930
Profit	26.44%

3. Determine the percent of gross margin necessary for Staples to achieve a net profit of 4.89 percent. Estimated net sales are $319 607; estimated operating expenses are $54 333.

4. Set up a skeletal income statement, given the following information:

Gross sales	$385 620
Customer returns	6.85%
Cost of goods sold	35.84%
Expenses	$152 078

Since credit card sales can be expensive for retailers, why do they take them?
© Blend Images/Getty Images.

Think of inventory as "merchandise in motion." The faster it moves through the store, the greater the inventory turnover.
© DreamPictures/Shannon Faulk/Blend Images LLC.

exception to this generalization is service retailers such as Sears Pest Control Service, Marriott Hotels, and your local barber shop/beauty salon, which carry little or no merchandise inventory.

$$\frac{\text{Inventory}}{\text{Total assets}}$$

Walmart: $\dfrac{\$22\ 614}{\$83\ 451} = 27.10\%$

Birks: $\dfrac{\$612}{\$1630} = 37.53\%$

Inventory turnover measures how effectively managers use their investment in inventory; it can be figured on the basis of retail, cost, or units of merchandise. Turnover includes stock purchase, sale, and repurchase, as demonstrated in Exhibit 8–9. The cost method of calculating inventory turnover is not often used because most retailers keep their merchandise records at retail. To calculate inventory at cost, both stock and sales figures (cost of goods sold) must be cost values. (Cost of goods sold divided by average inventory at cost equals inventory turnover at cost.) Inventory turnover by unit is impractical with categories of merchandise consisting of many small items, but becomes practical with large or high-priced items like furniture, fine jewellery, and major electronics. Calculating inventory turnover at retail is the most common method, and if not

otherwise stated, most inventory turnover ratios are at retail. Inventory turnover is defined as follows:

$$\text{Inventory turnover} = \frac{\text{Net sales}}{\text{Average inventory}}$$

Think of inventory as a measure of the productivity of inventory—how many sales dollars can be generated from $1 invested in inventory. Generally, the larger the inventory turnover, the better. Exhibit 8–9 illustrates the concept of inventory turnover. Inventory is delivered to the store, spends some time in the store, and then is sold. We can think of inventory turnover as how many times, on average, the inventory cycles through the store during a specific period of time (usually a year). Inventory turnover can vary from less than 2 to over 20 turns depending upon the type of merchandise. Merchandise that is purchased frequently, like gasoline or perishable grocery items, tends to have a

Exhibit 8–9
Inventory Turnover

high turnover; more specialized goods, like furniture or fine jewellery, have a much lower inventory turn. Not only is it important to determine how many sales dollars can be generated from one dollar invested in inventory, but keep in mind the gross margin generated on each sales dollar.

Walmart's inventory turnover is about seven times Birks': 7.59 compared to 1.08.[11]

$$\frac{\text{Net sales}}{\text{Average inventory}} = \text{Inventory turnover}$$

Walmart: $\dfrac{\$219812}{\$28974} = 7.59$

Birks: $\dfrac{\$1607}{\$1484} = 1.08$

	Margin	**Turnover**
Birks	High	Low
Walmart	Low	High

Walmart's faster inventory turnover is expected due to the nature of discount and grocery stores. First, most items in Walmart are commodities and staples such as batteries, housewares, and basic apparel items. Its new superstores also carry grocery products such as baked goods, frozen meat, and produce. Birks, on the other hand, specializes in unique luxury items. Second, since Walmart-type merchandise is available at other discount and grocery stores, it competes by offering lower prices, which results in rapid turnover. Third, discount stores carry a simpler stock selection than jewellery stores do. In a Walmart store, for example, there may be only two brands of ketchup, each in two sizes, which represents four inventory items. High-end jewellery stores, on the other hand, may stock 100 distinctly different types of necklaces. Finally, due to Birks' unique positioning strategy, much of its inventory, particularly the jewellery, is made especially for it in other countries, requiring buyers to place orders several months in advance of delivery. Discount stores, on the other hand, order items daily or weekly. These factors, when taken together, explain why Walmart has a faster inventory turnover than Birks.

Measuring Inventory Turnover

The notion of inventory turnover was introduced as "merchandise in motion." Jeans are delivered to the store through the loading dock in the back, spend some time in the store on the racks, and then are sold and go out the front door. The faster this process takes place, the higher the inventory turnover will be. We thus can think of inventory turnover as how many times, on average, the jeans cycle through the store during a specific period of time, usually one year. It's a measure of the productivity of inventory—that is, how many sales dollars can be generated from a dollar invested in jeans.

Again, inventory turnover can be defined as follows:

A. Inventory turnover $= \dfrac{\text{Net sales}}{\text{Average inventory at retail}}$

or

B. Inventory turnover $= \dfrac{\text{Cost of goods sold}}{\text{Average inventory at cost}}$

Since most retailers tend to think of their inventory at retail, the first definition is preferable. Arithmetically there's no difference between these two definitions; they yield the same result.[12] Be careful, however; since both the numerator and denominator must be at retail or at cost, it is different than the sales-to-stock ratio where the inventory is always expressed at cost. To illustrate:

Sales-to-stock ratio $= \dfrac{\text{Net sales}}{\text{Average cost inventory}}$

So if Sales = \$100 000 and Average cost inventory = \$33 333, then

Sales-to-stock ratio $= \dfrac{\$100\,000}{\$33\,333} = 3$

Thus,[13]

Inventory turnover = Sales-to-stock ratio
$\times$ (100% − Gross margin%)

Continuing the example, if gross margin = 40 percent, then
Inventory turnover = 3 × (100% − 40%) = 1.8

Retailers normally express inventory turnover rates on an annual basis rather than for parts of a year. Suppose the net sales used in an inventory turnover calculation are for a three-month season. If turnover for a quarter is calculated as 2.3 turns, then annual turnover will be four times that number (9.2). Thus, to convert an inventory turnover calculation based on part of a year to an annual figure, multiply it by the number of such time periods in the year. Exhibit 8–10 shows inventory turnover ratios for selected departments from discount stores. The range is from 7 (food) to 2 (jewellery and furniture). There are no real surprises in these data. One would expect food to have the highest turnover.

DID YOU KNOW?

Zara, Spain's fashion giant, believes that in a perfect world a store would never have anything in it that it wasn't going to sell that very day. Zara isn't perfect, but its inventory turnover is three times as fast as The Gap.[14]

Exhibit 8–10

Gross Margin Percentage, Inventory Turnover, and GMROI for Selected Departments in Discount Stores

Category	Gross Margin (%)	Inventory Turnover	GMROI
Apparel	37	4	235
Housewares	35	3	162
Food	20	7	175
Jewellery	38	2	123
Furniture	31	2	90
Health and beauty	22	4	113
Consumer electronics	21	4	106

Food is either sold quickly or it spoils; it is perishable. By the same token, being a luxury item, jewellery turns relatively slowly. Furniture achieves a low turnover because a relatively large assortment of expensive items is needed to support the sales level.

Calculating Average Inventory Average inventory is calculated by dividing the inventory at the beginning of the month (BOM) for each of several months, plus the inventory at the end of the month (EOM), divided by the total number of months plus 1.

Average inventory (1 month)

$$= \frac{\text{BOM inventory} + \text{EOM inventory}}{2}$$

Average inventory (6 month)

$$= \frac{\text{BOM inventory for each of the 6 months} + \text{EOM inventory for last month}}{7}$$

Average inventory (1 year)

$$= \frac{\text{BOM inventory for each of the 12 months} + \text{Last month's EOM}}{13}$$

For example, if a variety store had $330 000 of inventory at the beginning of January and $370 000 of inventory at the beginning of February, what was the store owner's average inventory for the month of January?

Average inventory

$$= \frac{\text{BOM inventory} + \text{EOM inventory for last month}}{\text{Number of months} + 1}$$

$$= \frac{330\ 000 + 370\ 000}{2}$$

$$= \$350\ 000$$

If the variety store owner had sales of $156 000 for the month of January, what would the variety store's inventory turnover be for the month?

Inventory turnover

$$= \text{Net sales} \div \text{Average inventory}$$
$$= \$156\ 000 \div \$350\ 000$$
$$= 0.45 \text{ for the month}$$

What if the owner of the same variety store wanted to find out what his inventory turnover for the four-month period from January through April was with reported net sales for the period being $545 000?

Month	BOM Inventory
January	$330 000
February	$370 000
March	$350 000
April	$345 000
May	$320 000

Average inventory =

$$\frac{\text{BOM inventory for each month} + \text{EOM inventory for last month}}{\text{Number of months} + 1}$$

$$= \frac{\$330\ 000 + \$370\ 000 + \$350\ 000 + \$345\ 000 + \$320\ 000}{5}$$

$$= \$343\ 000$$

Inventory turnover $= \text{Net sales} \div \text{Average inventory}$
$$= \$545\ 000 \div \$343\ 000$$
$$= 1.59 \text{ times in the four-month time frame}$$

Given the above information, it can be determined that if inventory turnover equals net sales divided by average inventory, then average inventory can also be calculated by taking net sales and dividing by inventory turnover.

Average inventory $= \text{Net sales} \div \text{Inventory turnover}$

Most retailers no longer need to use physical counts to determine average inventory. Point-of-sale (POS) terminals capture daily sales and automatically subtract them from on-hand inventory. Retailers with POS systems can get accurate average inventory estimates by averaging the inventory on hand for each day in the year. Retailers do typically take occasional physical inventories, usually twice a year, to determine the amount of inventory shrinkage due to theft or paperwork/entry mistakes.

Advantages of High Inventory Turnover Retailers want rapid inventory turnover—but not too rapid, as we will soon see. Advantages of rapid inventory turnover include increased sales volume, less risk of obsolescence and markdowns, improved salesperson morale, more money for market opportunities, decreased operating expenses, and increased asset turnover.[15]

Increased Sales Volume A rapid inventory turnover increases sales volume since fresh merchandise is available to customers, and fresh merchandise sells better and faster than old, shopworn merchandise. Fresh merchandise encourages customers to visit the store more frequently because they see new things. Also, notice the produce next time you're in a less-than-successful supermarket... brown bananas! Since turnover is slow, the produce is old, which makes it even harder to sell.

Quick response delivery systems are inventory management systems designed to reduce retailers' lead time for receiving merchandise. Retailers order less merchandise, more often, so merchandise supply is more closely aligned with demand. As a result, inventory turnover rises since inventory investment falls, and sales climb since the retailer is out of stock less often.

Less Risk of Obsolescence and Markdowns The value of fashion and other perishable merchandise is said to start declining as soon as it's placed on display. When inventory is selling quickly, merchandise isn't in the store long enough to become obsolete. As a result, markdowns are reduced and gross margins increase.

Improved Salesperson Morale With rapid inventory turnover and the fresh merchandise that results, salesperson morale stays high. No one likes to sell yesterday's merchandise. Salespeople are excited over new merchandise, the assortment of sizes is still complete, and the merchandise isn't shopworn. When salespeople's morale is high, they try harder so sales increase—increasing inventory turnover even further.

More Money for Market Opportunities When inventory turnover is high, money previously tied up in inventory is freed to buy more merchandise. Having money available to buy merchandise late in a fashion season can open tremendous profit opportunities. Suppose Levi Strauss overestimates demand for its seasonal products. It has two choices:

- Hold the inventory until next season.
- Sell it to retailers at a lower-than-normal price.

If retailers have money available because of rapid turnover, they can take advantage of this special price. Retailers can pocket the additional markup or choose to maintain their high-turnover strategy by offering the special merchandise at a reduced cost to the consumer. In either case, sales and gross margin increase.

Decreased Operating Expenses An increase in turnover may mean that a lower level of inventory is supporting the same level of sales. And lower inventory means lower inventory carrying costs, which is an operating expense. For instance, if a retailer has $1 million in inventory and the cost to carry the inventory—including money borrowed from a bank, insurance, and taxes—is 20 percent a year, the inventory carrying cost is $200 000. Lowering inventory can therefore represent a significant savings.

Increased Asset Turnover Finally, since inventory is a current asset, and if assets decrease and sales stay the same or increase, then asset turnover increases. This directly affects return on assets, the key performance measure for top management.

Disadvantages of Too High an Inventory Turnover Retailers should strike a balance in their rate of inventory turnover. An excessively rapid inventory turnover can hurt the firm due to a lower sales volume, an increase in the cost of goods sold, and an increase in operating expenses.

Lowered Sales Volume One way to increase turnover is to limit the number of merchandise categories or the number of SKUs within a category. But if customers can't find the size or colour they seek—or even worse, if they can't find the product line at all—a sale is lost. Customers who are disappointed on a regular basis will shop elsewhere and will possibly urge their friends to do the same. In this case, not only is a sale lost, but so are the customers and their friends.

Increased Cost of Goods Sold To achieve rapid turnover, merchandise must be bought more often and in smaller quantities, which reduces average inventory without reducing sales. But by buying smaller quantities, the buyer can't take advantage of quantity discounts and transportation

1. What is the inventory turnover if a store has $48 000 of BOM inventory for June and $38 000 for July. Net sales for June were $18 275.

2. Calculate the average inventory for a store with annual sales of $550 000 and an annual inventory turnover of 3.8.

3. Determine the average inventory of a store for its third quarter (August to October) given the following inventory information:

Month	Sales	BOM inventory
February	$ 12 000	$ 22 000
March	$ 10 000	$ 16 000
April	$ 7 000	$ 15 500
May	$ 16 000	$ 25 000
June	$ 14 425	$ 26 250
July	$ 18 000	$ 36 000
August	$ 17 000	$ 22 250
September	$ 13 000	$ 20 000
October	$ 21 575	$ 28 800
November	$ 25 250	$ 29 400
December	$ 30 370	$ 36 000
January	$ 15 000	$ 24 000

4. Using the information from the previous question, determine the inventory turnover for the following time frames:
   a. Month of June
   b. Six-month spring-summer season (February to July)

---

economies of scale. It may be possible, for instance, to buy a year's supply of Levi's at a quantity discount that offsets the high costs of carrying a large inventory.

Retailers who pay transportation costs must consider that the more merchandise shipped and the slower the mode of transportation, the smaller the per-unit transportation expense. For instance, to ship a 10-kilogram package of jeans from Toronto to Halifax, overnight delivery, would cost about $50 ($5 per kilogram). If the retailer could order 50 kilograms of jeans at the same time and could wait 5 to 10 days for delivery, the cost would be only about $30 (60 cents per kilogram). In this example, it costs over eight times more to ship small packages quickly.

Increased Operating Expenses Economies of scale can also be gained when a retailer purchases

large quantities. A buyer spends about the same amount of time meeting with vendors and writing orders whether the order is large or small. It also takes about the same amount of time, for both large and small orders, to print invoices, receive merchandise, and pay invoices—all factors that increase merchandise's cost.

In summary, rapid inventory turnover is generally preferred to slow turnover. But the turnover rate can be pushed to the point of diminishing returns, a key concern for merchandise managers in all retail sectors.

Cash and Other Current Assets

It is important to know how much cash a company has access to in order to pay bills in a timely fashion.

Cash = Monies on hand
   + Demand and savings accounts in banks to which a retailer has immediate access
   + Marketable securities such as treasury bills

Other current assets = Prepaid expenses + Supplies

Walmart reports cash of about 0.98 percent of sales, whereas Birks' cash percentage is 10.81 percent.

Fixed Assets

Fixed assets are assets that require more than a year to convert to cash. In retailing,

Fixed assets = Buildings (if store property is owned rather than leased)
   + Fixtures (such as display racks)
   + Equipment (such as computers or delivery trucks)
   + Long-term investments such as real estate or stock in other firms

In retailing, the principal fixed assets are buildings (if store property is owned rather than leased), fixtures (e.g., display racks), equipment (e.g., computers, delivery trucks), and other long-term investments such as stock in other forms.

Typically, large retailers such as Walmart and Home Depot own their store locations.[16] Other retailers rent their retail space and use the money they would have used to buy the land to remodel stores or buy merchandise. Yet ownership appeals to many retailers, because it enables them to secure their costs and avoid the possibility of increasing

fixed assets Assets that require more than a year to convert to cash.

rents. When a retailer owns, however, the area around the location may change and become unattractive, which would force the retailer to sell the location at a loss.

Fixed assets represent 66.15 percent and 41.44 percent of total assets for Walmart and Birks, respectively. Walmart's fixed assets are relatively higher than Birks' because they have vast real estate holdings in stores and distribution centres, whereas Birks typically rents space in malls and has direct store delivery.

$$\text{Asset cost} - \text{Depreciation} = \text{Fixed assets}$$

Since most fixed assets have a limited useful life, the value of those assets should be less over time—in other words, they are depreciated. For instance, Birks stores require refurbishing every few years due to general wear-and-tear. So, carpet and some fixtures are depreciated over three to five years, whereas a building may be depreciated over 25 years.

Asset Turnover

Asset turnover is an overall performance measure from the asset side of the balance sheet.

$$\frac{\text{Net sales}}{\text{Total assets}} = \text{Asset turnover}$$

Although fixed assets don't turn over as quickly as inventory, asset turnover can be used to evaluate and compare how effectively managers use their assets. When a retailer redecorates a store, for example, old fixtures, carpeting, and lights are removed and replaced with new ones. Thus, like inventory, these assets cycle through the store. The difference is that the process is a lot slower. The life of a fixture in a Birks store may be five years (instead of five months, as it might be for a diamond ring in the store's inventory), yet the concept of turnover is the same. When a retailer decides to invest in a fixed asset, it should determine how many sales dollars can be generated from that asset.

Suppose that Birks needs to purchase a new fixture for displaying dinnerware. It has a choice of buying an expensive antique display cabinet for $5000 or having a simple plywood display constructed for $500. Using the expensive antique, it forecasts sales of $50 000 in the first year, whereas

current liabilities
Debts that are expected to be paid in less than one year.

accounts payable The amount of money owed to vendors, primarily for merchandise inventory.

the plywood display is expected to generate only $40 000. Ignoring all other assets for a moment,

$$\frac{\text{Net sales}}{\text{Total assets}} = \text{Asset turnover}$$

Antique cabinet: $\dfrac{\$50\,000}{\$5000} = 10$

Plywood cabinet: $\dfrac{\$40\,000}{\$500} = 80$

The antique cabinet will certainly help create an atmosphere conducive to selling expensive dinnerwear. Exclusively from a marketing perspective, the antique would thus appear appropriate. But it costs much more than the plywood shelves. From a strictly financial perspective, Birks should examine how much additional sales can be expected to be generated from the added expenditure in assets. Clearly, by considering only asset turnover, the plywood shelves are the way to go. In the end, a combination of marketing and financial factors should be considered when making the asset purchase decision.[17]

In this case, Walmart's asset turnover is 2.7 times Birks'. The asset turnover is 2.63 for Walmart and 0.99 for Birks. This finding is consistent with the different strategies each firm is implementing. We saw earlier that Walmart has a higher inventory turnover. Its other assets are relatively lower than Birks' as well. For instance, the fixed assets involved in outfitting a store (such as fixtures, lighting, and mannequins) would be relatively lower for a discount store than a jewellery store.

The other side of the balance sheet equation from assets involves liabilities and owners' equity. Now let's look at the major liabilities and components of owners' equity.

Liabilities and Owners' Equity

Current Liabilities Like current assets, **current liabilities** are debts that are expected to be paid in less than one year. The most important current liabilities are accounts payable, notes payable, and accrued liabilities. Current liabilities as a percentage of net sales are 12.41 percent for Walmart and 21.24 percent for Birks.

Accounts Payable Accounts payable refers to the amount of money owed to vendors, primarily for merchandise inventory. Accounts payable is an important source of short-term financing. Retailers buy merchandise on credit from vendors. The longer the period of time they have to pay for that merchandise, the larger their accounts payable—and the less they need to borrow from financial

To provide a more attractive store environment, department store retailers (top) have higher fixed assets than warehouse club retailers (bottom).

(top) © Jackbluee | Dreamstime.com; (bottom) © Cafebeanzphoto/ Dreamstime.com/GetStock.com

institutions (notes payable), issue bonds or shares, or finance internally through retained earnings. Since retailers normally don't have to pay interest to vendors on their accounts payable, they have strong incentive to negotiate for a long time period before payment for merchandise is due.

Accounts payable management can play an important role in a retailer's profit strategy. This is the case for many European hypermarkets such as Carrefour. Hypermarkets are similar to Canadian-style supercentres but have some key differences. Hypermarkets are primarily food-based and emphasize fresh products to drive customer traffic, whereas supercentres are primarily non-food retailers that focus on dry goods. Carrefour is able to negotiate extended supplier terms because, like most European food retailers, it has national scope and is able to exert significant influence over its suppliers. As a result, Carrefour manages its accounts payable as a profit centre. For example, Carrefour

typically has about 42 days of inventory on hand and roughly 90 days in payables. That 48-day float generates income that contributes as much as 25 to 35 percent to Carrefour's operating profit.[18]

Notes Payable Under the current liabilities section of the balance sheet, **notes payable** are the principal and interest the retailer owes to financial institutions (banks) that are due and payable in less than a year. Retailers borrow money from financial institutions to pay for current assets, such as inventory.

notes payable Current liabilities representing principal and interest the retailer owes to financial institutions (banks) that are due and payable in less than a year.

accrued liabilities Liabilities that accumulate daily but are paid only at the end of a period.

long-term liabilities Debts that will be paid after one year.

shareholders' equity The amount of assets belonging to the owners of the retail firm after all obligations (liabilities) have been met.

Accrued Liabilities **Accrued liabilities** include taxes, salaries, rent, utilities, and other incurred obligations that haven't yet been paid. These are called accrued liabilities because they usually accumulate daily but are only paid at the end of a time period, such as a month.

Long-Term Liabilities **Long-term liabilities** are debts that will be paid after one year. The notes payable entry in the long-term liability section of the balance sheet is similar to the one in the current liability section except that it's due to be paid in more than one year. Other long-term liabilities include bonds and mortgages on real estate.

Owners' Equity Owners' equity, also known as **shareholders' equity**, represents the amount of assets belonging to the owners of the retail firm after all obligations (liabilities) have been met. In accounting terms, the relationship can be expressed as

$$\text{Owners' equity} = \text{Total assets} - \text{Total liabilities}$$

Although there are several entries in the owners' equity category, two of the most common are common shares and retained earnings.

Common shares are the type of shares most frequently issued by corporations.[19] Owners of common shares usually have voting rights in the retail corporation. They also have the right to share in distributed corporate earnings. If the firm is liquidated, common share owners have the right to share in the sale of its assets. Finally, they have the right to purchase additional shares to maintain the same percentage ownership if new shares are issued.

retained earnings The portion of owners' equity that has accumulated over time through profits but has not been paid out in dividends to owners.

Retained earnings refers to the portion of owners' equity that has accumulated over time through profits but hasn't been paid out in dividends to owners. The decision of how much of the retailer's earnings should be retained in the firm and how much should be returned to the owners in the form of dividends is related to the firm's growth potential. Specifically, retailers with a propensity toward and opportunities for growth will retain and reinvest their profits to fund growth opportunities. For example, a high-growth retailer such as Walmart retains most of its earnings to pay for the new stores, inventory, and expenses associated with its growth.

In the case discussed, total owners' equity is over $35 102 million for Walmart and over $1 037 million for Birks.

Lo3 Examining the Strategic Profit Model

The previous sections defined the most important balance sheet and income statement entries, as well as the most useful performance ratios. Yet many of these items are interrelated, and when examined alone they can be confusing. More importantly, it's hard to compare the performance of retailers with different operating characteristics, such as Birks and Walmart. The strategic profit model (Exhibit 8–11) combines the two performance ratios from the income statement and balance sheets: net profit margin and asset turnover. By multiplying these ratios together, you get return on assets.

Return on Assets

Overall performance, as measured by return on assets (ROA), is determined by considering the effects of both paths by multiplying the net profit margin by asset turnover. Return on assets determines how much profit can be generated from the retailer's investment in assets.

$$\text{Return on assets} = \text{Net profit margin} \times \text{Asset turnover}$$
$$= \frac{\text{Net profit}}{\text{Net sales}} \times \frac{\text{Net sales}}{\text{Total assets}}$$
$$= \frac{\text{Net profit}}{\text{Total assets}}$$

(Note that when we multiply net profit margin by asset turnover, net sales drops out of the equation.)

Exhibit 8–11
The Strategic Profit Model

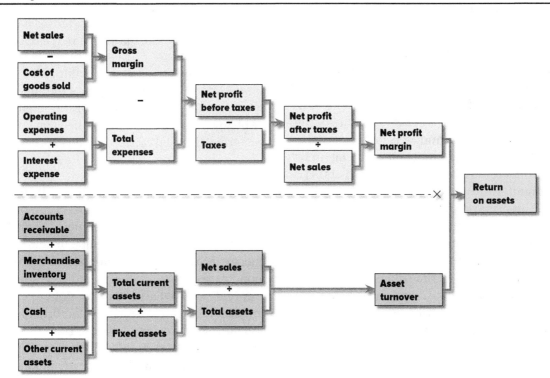

The most important issue associated with return on assets is that the money that would be invested in retailing could also be invested in any other asset, such as a CD or Canada Savings Bond. For instance, if a retailer can achieve 9 percent return on assets by opening a new store and 10 percent by investing in a nearly risk-free savings bond, the retailer should take the higher-yield, lower-risk investment. In fact, should the ROA of another investment with similar risk be greater, it would be the manager's fiduciary duty to invest in the other asset. In general, return on assets is effective in evaluating the profitability of individual investments in assets because it can easily be compared with yields of other investments with similar risk. It has also been shown to be an effective predictor of business failures.[20]

$$\frac{\text{Net profit}}{\text{Total assets}} = \text{Return on assets}$$

Walmart: $\dfrac{\$6854}{\$83\,451} = 8.21\%$

Birks: $\dfrac{\$175}{\$1630} = 10.74\%$

Return on assets for Birks and Walmart are very similar! Birks generated a larger net profit margin, 10.89 percent, compared to 3.12 percent for Walmart (Exhibit 8–5). But Walmart outperformed Birks on asset turnover, 2.63 compared to 0.99, respectively (Exhibit 8–8).

The strategic profit model illustrates two important issues. First, retailers and investors need to consider both net profit margin and asset turnover when evaluating their financial performance. Firms can achieve high performance (high ROA) by effectively managing both net profit margins and asset turnover. Second, retailers need to consider the implications of their strategic decisions on both components of the strategic profit model. For example, simply increasing prices will increase the gross margin and net profit margins (profit margin management path). However, increasing prices will result in fewer sales, and assuming the level of assets stays the same, asset turnover will decrease. Thus, profit margin increases, asset turnover decreases, and the effect on ROA depends on how much the profit margin increases compared with the decrease in asset turnover.

Exhibit 8–12 shows strategic profit model (SPM) ratios for a variety of retailers. The exhibit illustrates that supermarket and discount chains typically have higher ROA and lower net profit margin percentages; while the exact opposite holds true for the banking sector. Even though earnings before interest, taxes, depreciation, and amortization (EBITDA) isn't a formula used in the exercises in this chapter, it is interesting to see how it compares to net profit margin calculation. An EBITDA margin percentage can provide an investor with a concrete view of a company's main profitability since it doesn't include depreciation and amortization. Take a few minutes to compare it to net profit margin for each store, the banks especially!

The next section examines the performance measure on which the merchandise plan is evaluated. This measure, GMROI (gross margin/return on investment), is composed of two ratios: inventory turnover and gross margin percentage. The section concludes with a discussion of how retailers forecast sales.

Putting Margin, Sales, and Turnover Together: GMROI

At the corporate level, return on assets is used to plan and evaluate performance of overall retail operations.

$$\text{Return on assets} = \text{Net profit margin} \times \text{Asset turnover}$$
$$= \frac{\text{Net profit}}{\text{Net sales}} \times \frac{\text{Net sales}}{\text{Total assets}}$$
$$= \frac{\text{Net profit}}{\text{Total assets}}$$

With the strategic profit model, we can use return on assets to plan and compare the performance of executives since they are responsible for managing all of the retailer's assets and realizing a return based on these assets.

But merchandise managers only have control over the merchandise they buy and manage. Buyers generally have control over gross margin but not expenses involved with the operation of the stores and the management of the retailer's human resources, locations, and systems. As a result, the financial ratio that is useful for planning and measuring merchandising performance is a return on investment measure called gross margin return on inventory investment, or GMROI.[21] It measures how many gross margin dollars are earned on every dollar of inventory investment.

GMROI is a similar concept to return on assets, only its components are under the control of the

Exhibit 8–12
Strategic Profit Models for Selected Retailers as of 2015

	Net Profit Margin (%)	EBITDA Margin (%)	Return on Assets (%)
	Net profit / Net sales	EBITDA / Total Revenue	Net profit margin × asset turnover
Discount Stores			
Best Buy Co., Inc.	3.09%	5.2%	8.51%
Costco Wholesale Corp.	2.07%	4.09%	7.25%
Walmart Stores, Inc.	3.46%	7.48%	8.24%
Grocery			
Empire Co. Ltd./Sobeys	1.82%	4.82%	3.69%
Metro Inc.	4.25%	7.07%	9.74%
Banking			
Bank of Montreal	24.29%	44.37%	0.72%
Royal Bank	28.39%	45.57%	n/a
Toronto Dominion	27.41%	46.50%	0.74%
CIBC	25.91%	40.03%	0.82%
Specialty			
Cineplex Inc./Galaxy	6.18%	15.96%	4.77%
Indigo Inc./Chapters	−0.39%	2.4%	−0.67%
Leon's Furniture	3.83%	8.23%	4.83%
Lululemon Athletica Inc.	13.3%	24.17%	18.76%
Reitmans Canada Ltd.	1.43%	7.08%	n/a
Home Improvement			
Canadian Tire Corp., Ltd.	5.13%	11.04%	4.54%
Home Depot, Inc.	7.63%	14.73%	15.77%
Rona Inc.	1.88%	2.82	3.29%
Lowes	4.8%	11.39%	8.36%

Sources: Company filings for fiscal 2015, http://www.google.ca/finance.

buyer rather than other managers. Instead of combining net profit margin and asset turnover, GMROI uses gross margin percentage and the sales-to-stock ratio, which is similar to inventory turnover.

$$\text{GMROI} = \text{Gross margin percentage} \times \text{Sales-to-stock ratio}$$

$$= \frac{\text{Gross margin}}{\text{Net sales}} \times \frac{\text{Net sales}}{\text{Average inventory}}$$

$$= \frac{\text{Gross margin}}{\text{Average inventory}}$$

Average inventory in GMROI is measured at cost, because a retailer's investment in inventory is the cost of the inventory, not its retail value.

Like return on assets, GMROI combines the effects of both profits and turnover. It's important to use a measure that considers both of these factors so that departments with different margin/turnover profiles can be compared and evaluated. For instance, within a grocery store, some departments (such as wine) are high margin/low turnover, whereas other departments (such as dairy products) are low margin/high turnover. If the wine department's performance is compared to that of dairy products using inventory turnover alone, the contribution of wine to the grocery store's performance will be undervalued. On the other hand, if only gross margin is used, wine's contribution will be overvalued.

Consider the situation in Exhibit 8–13. Here a grocery store manager wants to evaluate performance of two classifications: bread and ready-to-eat prepared foods. If evaluated on gross margin percentage or sales alone, prepared foods is certainly the winner with a 50 percent gross margin and sales of $300 000 compared to bread's gross

Exhibit 8–13
Illustration of GMROI

				Bread	Prepared Foods		
		Gross margin		$2 000	$150 000		
		Sales		$150 000	$300 000		
		Average inventory		$1 000	$75 000		
Bread	GMROI =	$\dfrac{\text{Gross margin}}{\text{Net sales}}$	×	$\dfrac{\text{Net sales}}{\text{Average inventory}}$	=	$\dfrac{\text{Gross margin}}{\text{Average inventory}}$	
	GMROI =	$\dfrac{\$2000}{\$150\,000}$	×	$\dfrac{\$150\,000}{\$1000}$	=	$\dfrac{\$2000}{\$1000}$	
		= 1.333 %	×	150 times	=	200%	
Prepared Foods	GMROI =	$\dfrac{\$150\,000}{\$300\,000}$	×	$\dfrac{\$300\,000}{\$75\,000}$	=	$\dfrac{\$150\,000}{\$75\,000}$	
		= 50%	×	4	=	200%	

margin of 1.333 percent and sales of $150 000. Yet prepared foods turns (sales-to-stock ratio) only four times a year, whereas bread turns 150 times a year. Using GMROI, both classifications achieve a GMROI of 200 percent and so are equal performers from a return on investment perspective.

GMROI is used as a return on investment profitability measure to evaluate departments,

8.3 CONCEPT CHECK

1. Calculate the GMROI if average inventory at cost is $84 250 and gross margin is $240 500.

2. Determine the GMROI given net sales of $280 000, average inventory at cost of $80 000, and gross margin of 42 percent.

3. If net sales for July are $162 000, beginning of the month inventory at cost is $36 000, closing inventory at cost is $38 000, and gross margin is 46 percent, what is the GMROI?

4. Calculate asset turnover for a retailer who has total current assets of $46 282, fixed assets of $51 438, gross sales of $812 912, and customer returns of $89 426.

5. Calculate the ROA for an organization with a net profit of $89 345 and $12 260 in total assets.

6. Determine the ROA for a retailer with the following information:

Gross margin	$800 811
Expenses	$180 925
Profit	44%
Current assets	$64 270
Total assets	$98 694

merchandise classifications, vendor lines, and items. It's also useful for management in evaluating buyers' performance since it can be related to the retailer's overall return on investment. As we just demonstrated, merchandise with different margin/turnover characteristics can be compared. Exhibit 8–10 shows GMROI percentages for selected departments from discount stores. The range is from 235 (for apparel) to 90 (for furniture). It's no wonder that many discount stores are placing so much emphasis on apparel and that some have discontinued furniture. They continue to carry consumer electronics and health and beauty products—both with low GMROIs—because they have traditionally brought customers into the store. The retailers hope that while there, customers will purchase higher-GMROI items.

The gross margin component of GMROI is affected by pricing decisions. GMROI answers the question: For each dollar at cost, how many dollars of gross profit will I generate in one year? GMROI is traditionally calculated by using one year's gross profit against the average of 12 or 13 units of inventory at cost. A rule of thumb is that a GMROI of at least 3.2 is the break-even point for a business.

Recap of the Strategic Profit Model

The strategic profit model is useful to retailers because it combines two decision-making areas—margin management and asset management—so managers can examine interrelationships between them. The strategic profit model uses return on

top-down planning One side of the process of developing an overall retail strategy where goals are set at the top of the organization and filter down through the operating levels.

bottom-up planning When goals are set at the bottom of the organization and filter up through the operating levels.

assets as the primary criterion for planning and evaluating a firm's financial performance.

The strategic profit model can also be used to evaluate financial implications of new strategies before they are implemented. For instance, suppose a retailer wishes to increase sales by 10 percent. Using the strategic profit model, the retailer can estimate this action's impact on other parts of the strategic profit model. For instance, to increase sales, the retailer may choose to have a sale. Lowering prices will reduce gross margin. In addition, the retailer would have to advertise the sale and hire additional sales help, thus increasing operating expenses. So, although the retailer may be able to achieve the 10 percent sales increase, net profit margin might go down.

Looking at the turnover path, increasing sales without an appreciable change in inventory will increase inventory turnover. Assuming other assets aren't affected, asset turnover will also increase. When multiplying the lower net profit margin by the higher asset turnover, the resulting return on assets may remain unchanged.

LO4 Setting Performance Objectives

Setting performance objectives is a necessary component of any firm's strategic planning process. How would a retailer know how it has performed if it doesn't have specific objectives in mind to compare actual performance against? Performance objectives should include:

- the performance sought, including a numerical index against which progress may be measured

- a time frame within which the goal is to be achieved

- the resources needed to achieve the objective

For example, "earning reasonable profits" isn't a good objective because it doesn't provide specific goals that can be used to evaluate performance. What's reasonable? When do you want to realize the profits? A better objective would be "earning $100 000 in profit during calendar year 2017 on $500 000 investment in inventory and building."

Top-Down versus Bottom-Up Processes

Setting objectives in large retail organizations entails a combination of the top-down and bottom-up approaches to planning.

Top-down planning means that goals get set at the top of the organization and are passed down to the lower operating levels. In a retailing organization, top-down planning involves corporate officers developing an overall retail strategy and assessing broad economic, competitive, and consumer trends. With this information, they develop performance objectives for the corporation. These overall objectives are then broken down into specific objectives for each buyer and merchandise category and for each region, store, and even each department within stores and the sales associates working in those departments.

The overall strategy determines the merchandise variety, assortment, and product availability, plus the store size, location, and level of customer service. Then the merchandise vice presidents decide which types of merchandise are expected to grow, stay the same, or shrink. Next, performance goals are established for each buyer and merchandise manager.

Similarly, regional store vice presidents translate the company's performance objectives into objectives for each district manager, who then develop objectives with their store managers. The process then trickles down to department managers in the stores and individual sales associates.

This top-down planning is complemented by a bottom-up planning approach. **Bottom-up planning** involves lower levels in the company developing performance objectives that are aggregated up to develop overall company objectives. Buyers and store managers estimate what they can achieve, and their estimates are transmitted up the organization to the corporate executives.

Frequently there are disagreements between the goals that have trickled down from the top and those set by lower-level employees of the organization. For example, a store manager may not be able to achieve the 10 percent sales growth set for his or her region because a major employer in the area has announced plans to lay off 2000 employees. These differences between bottom-up and top-down plans are resolved through a negotiation process involving corporate executives and operating managers. If the operating managers aren't involved in the objective setting process, they won't accept the objectives and thus will be less motivated to achieve them.

Accountable for Performance

At each level of the retail organization, the business unit and its manager should be held accountable only for the revenues, expenses, and contribution to ROA that they can control. Thus, expenses that affect several levels of the organization (e.g., labour and capital expenses associated with operating a corporate headquarters) shouldn't be arbitrarily assigned to lower levels. In the case of a store, for example, it may be appropriate to set performance objectives based on sales, sales associate productivity, store inventory shrinkage due to employee theft and shoplifting, and energy costs. If the buyer lowers prices to get rid of merchandise and therefore profits suffer, it is not fair to assess a store manager's performance on the basis of the resulting decline in store profit.

Performance objectives and measures can be used to pinpoint problem areas. The reasons that performance may be above or below planned levels must be examined. Perhaps the managers involved in setting the objectives aren't very good at making estimates. If so, they may need to be trained in forecasting. Also, buyers may misrepresent their business unit's ability to contribute to the firm's financial goals to get a larger inventory budget than is warranted and consequently earn a higher bonus. In either case, investment funds would be misallocated.

Actual performance may be different than the plan predicts due to circumstances beyond the manager's control. For example, there may have been a recession. Assuming the recession wasn't predicted, or was more severe or lasted longer than anticipated, there are several relevant questions: How quickly were plans adjusted? How rapidly and appropriately were pricing and promotional policies modified? In short, did the manager react to salvage an adverse situation, or did those reactions worsen the situation?

Performance Objectives and Measures

Many factors contribute to a retailer's overall performance, which makes it hard to find a single measure to evaluate performance. For instance, sales is a global measure of a retail store's activity

level. However, a store manager could easily increase sales by lowering prices, but the profit realized on that merchandise (gross margin) would suffer as a result. Clearly, an attempt to maximize one measure may lower another. Managers must therefore understand how their actions affect multiple performance measures. It's usually unwise to use only one measure, because it rarely tells the whole story.

The measures used to evaluate retail operations vary depending on (1) the level of the organization at which the decision is made and (2) the resources the manager controls. For example, the principal resources controlled by store managers are space and money for operating expenses (such as wages for sales associates and utility payments to light and heat the store). Thus, store managers focus on performance measures like sales per square foot and employee cost as a percent of sales.

input measure A performance measure used to assess the amount of resources or money used by the retailer to achieve outputs.

output measure Measure that assesses the results of retailers' investment decisions.

productivity measure The ratio of an output to an input determining how effectively a firm uses a resource.

Types of Measures

Exhibit 8–14 breaks down a variety of retailers' performance measures into three types: input measures, output measures, and productivity measures. An **input measure** represents the resources or money allocated by a retailer to achieve outputs, or results. For example, the amount and selection of merchandise inventory, the number of stores, the size of the stores, the employees, advertising, markdowns, store hours, and promotions are managerial decisions involving resource allocations.

An **output measure** assesses the results of a retailer's investment decisions. For example, sales revenue, gross margin, and net profit margin are all output measures and ways to evaluate a retailer's input or resource allocations decisions. A **productivity measure** (the ratio of an output to an input) determines how effectively retailers use their resources—what return they get on their investments.

In general, since productivity measures are a ratio of outputs to inputs, they can be used to compare different business units. Suppose a retail chain's two stores are different sizes: One has 5000 square feet

Exhibit 8-14
Performance Objectives and Measures Used by Retailers

Level of Organization	Output	Input	Productivity (output/input)
Corporate (measures for entire corporation)	Net sales Net profits Growth in sales, profits, comparable store sales	Square footage of store space Number of employees Inventory Advertising expenditures	Return on assets Asset turnover Sales per employee Sales per square foot
Merchandise management (measures for a merchandise category)	Net sales Gross margin Growth in sales	Inventory level Markdowns Advertising expenses Cost of merchandise	Gross margin return on investment (GMROI) Inventory turnover Advertising as a percentage of sales* Markdown as a percentage of sales*
Store operations (measures for a store or department within a store)	Net sales Gross margin Growth in sales	Square footage of selling areas Expenses for utilities Number of sales associates	Net sales per square foot Net sales per sales associate or per selling hour Utility expenses as a percentage of sales* Inventory shrinkage*

*These productivity measures are commonly expressed as an input/output ratio.

and the other has 10 000 square feet. It's hard to compare stores' performances using just output or input measures. The larger store will probably generate more sales and have higher expenses. But if the larger store generates $180 net sales per square foot and the smaller store generates $300 per square foot, the retailer knows that the smaller store is operating more efficiently even though it's generating lower sales.

Productivity Measures

Corporate Performance At a corporate level, retail executives have three critical resources (inputs)—merchandise inventory, store space, and employees—that they can manage to generate sales and profits (outputs). Thus, effective productivity measures of the use of these assets include asset and inventory turnover, sales per square foot of selling space, and sales per employee.

As we have discussed, ROA is an overall productivity measure combining the profit margin percentage and asset turnover management. **Comparable store sales growth** (also called *same-store sales growth*) is a commonly used measure of a retailer's performance. There are two sources of annual sales

comparable store sales growth The sales growth in stores that have been open for over one year; also called *same-store sales growth*.

growth: sales from new stores opened during the year and sales growth from stores that were open during the previous year. Comparable store sales growth is the sales growth in stores that have been open for at least a year—the second source of sales growth. Thus, growth in comparable store sales assesses how well the retailer is doing with its core business strategy and execution.

Comparable store sales growth is a preferable measure to overall sales growth because the inclusion of new store sales clouds the long-term performance assessment. For example, overall sales might be increasing because the retailer is opening new stores, but over time, the sales in the retailer's stores, new and existing, is decreasing. Thus, when the new store openings slow down, the retailer will experience negative sales growth. By excluding the sales from new stores, retailers and investors can better assess how the overall strategy and implantation are working. Comparable store sales growth assesses how well the retailer's fundamental business approach is being received by its customers.

Merchandise Management Measures The critical resource (input) controlled by merchandise managers is merchandise inventory. Merchandise managers also have the authority to set initial prices and lower prices when merchandise is not selling (i.e., take a markdown). Finally, they negotiate with vendors over the paid price for merchandise.

Inventory turnover is a productivity measure of the management of inventory; higher turnover means greater inventory management productivity. Gross margin percentage indicates the performance of merchandise managers in negotiating with vendors and buying merchandise that can generate a profit. Discounts (markdowns) as a percentage of sales are also a measure of the quality of the merchandise buying decisions. If merchandise managers have a high percentage of markdowns, they may not be buying the right merchandise or the right quantities, because they weren't able to sell some of it at its original retail price. Note that gross margin and discount percentages are productivity measures, but they are typically expressed as an input divided by an output as opposed to the typical productivity measures that are outputs divided by inputs.

Store Operations Measures The critical assets controlled by store managers are the use of the store space and the management of the store's employees. Thus, measures of store operations productivity include sales per square foot of selling space and sales per employee (or sales per employee working hour, to take into account that some employees work part-time). Store management is also responsible for controlling theft by employees and customers (referred to as inventory shrinkage), store maintenance, and energy costs (lighting, heating, and air conditioning). Thus, some other productivity measures used to assess the performance of store managers are inventory shrinkage and energy costs as a percentage of sales.

Assessing Performance: The Role of Benchmarks

As we have discussed, the financial measures used to assess performance reflect the retailer's market strategy. For example, because Costco has a different business strategy than Hudson's Bay, it has a lower profit margin (see Exhibit 8–15). It earns an acceptable ROA because it increases its inventory and asset turnovers by stocking a more limited merchandise assortment of less fashionable, staple items. In contrast, Hudson's Bay specializes in apparel and accessories, which requires a broad and deep merchandise assortment. Thus, it has lower inventory and asset turnover but achieves an acceptable ROA through its higher profit margins. In other words, the performance of a retailer cannot be assessed accurately simply by looking at isolated measures, because they are affected by the retailer's strategy. To get a better assessment of a retailer's performance, we need to compare it to a benchmark. Two commonly used benchmarks are (1) the performance of the retailer over time and (2) the performance of the retailer compared with that of its competitors.

Performance over Time (Time-Series Analysis)
One useful approach for assessing a retailer's performance compares its recent performance in the preceding months, quarters, or years. Exhibit 8–15 shows the performance measures for Costco over a three-year period.

Costco experiences greater inventory turnover and sales per square foot due to the type of merchandise sold (food and staples versus fashion

Exhibit 8–15
Costco Wholesale Corporation

METRICS	2015	2014	2013
Revenue	$116 199	$112 640	$105 156
Net Income	$2 377	$2 058	$2 039
Net Profit Margin	2.0%	1.8%	1.9%
Total Assets	$33 428	$33 024	$30 283
Asset Turnover	3.47	3.41	3.47
ROA	6.94%	6.1%	6.6%
Total Common Shares Outstanding	437.95	437.68	436.84

Note: All amounts expressed in USD millions, except for margins.

Sources: Company filings for fiscal 2015, http://www.google.ca/finance.

apparel). Costco also has lower sales per employee due to its self-service offering compared with the customer service provided by the sales associates at a retailer such as Hudson's Bay. In terms of the strategic profit model components, Costco's ROA shows a general upward trend.

Performance Compared to Competitors (Cross-Sectional Ratio Analysis) A second approach

for assessing a retailer's performance involves comparing it with that of its competitors. Exhibit 8–16 compares the performance of Best Buy Co., Inc., and Walmart Stores, Inc. How does this data then compare to the Costco Wholesale Corporation data in Exhibit 8–15?

Exhibit 8–16
Performance Compared to Competitors

METRICS	BEST BUY CO., INC.			WALMART STORES, INC.		
	2015	2014	2013	2015	2014	2013
Revenue	$40 339	$40 611	$38 252	$485 651	$476 294	$421 849
Net Income	$1 233	$532	($441)	$16 363	$16 022	$16 999
Net Profit Margin	2.7%	2.6%	–2.4%	3.4%	3.4%	4.0%
Total Assets	$15 256	$14 013	$16 787	$203 490	$204 751	$203 105
Asset Turnover	2.64	2.89	2.27	2.38	2.33	2.08
ROA	7.1%	7.5%	5.4%	7.9%	7.9%	8.3%

Note: All $ expressed in USD millions, except for margins.

Sources: Company filings for fiscal 2015, http://www.google.ca/finance.

Financial management involves a thorough understanding of the importance of return on investment and how this relates to the retailer's image. Clearly defined quantifiable performance objectives are essential to evaluating business strategies and making changes to correct problems.

This chapter explains some basic elements of retailing financial strategy and examines how retailing strategy affects the financial performance of a firm. We used the strategic profit model as a vehicle for understanding the complex interrelations between financial ratios and retailing strategy. Different types of retailers have different financial operating characteristics. Specifically, jewellery store chains such as Birks generally have higher profit margins and lower turnover than discount stores such as Walmart. Yet, when margin and turnover are combined into return on assets, it's possible to achieve similar financial performance.

A number of financial performance measures are used to evaluate different aspects of a retailing organization. Although the return on assets ratio in the strategic profit model is appropriate for evaluating the performance of retail operating managers, other measures are more appropriate for more specific activities. For instance, gross margin return on investment (GMROI) is appropriate for buyers, whereas store managers should be concerned with sales or gross margin per square foot.

KEY TERMS

accounts payable
accounts receivable
accrued liabilities
asset turnover
assets
bottom-up planning
comparable store sales growth
cost of goods sold
cross-sectional ratio analysis
current assets
current liabilities
customer returns
expenses

fixed assets
input measure
interest
interest income
liabilities
long-term liabilities
net profit
net profit margin
net sales
notes payable
operating expenses
output measure
owners' equity

productivity measure
promotional allowances
proprietary store credit card system
retained earnings
return on assets (ROA)
selling, general, and administrative
    expenses (SG&A)
shareholders' equity
skeletal statement
strategic profit model (SPM)
time-series analysis
top-down planning

GET OUT & DO IT!

1. **INTERNET EXERCISE** Go to **http://www.hoovers.com**, **http://www.google.com/finance**, or the company's latest annual reports (Walmart and Birks) and use the financial information to update the numbers in the profit margin model in Exhibit 8–5 and the asset turnover model in Exhibit 8–8. Use these two models to develop the strategic profit model in Exhibit 8–11 for Walmart and Birks. Then repeat the process for Amazon and Bally Total Fitness. Have there been any significant changes in their financial performance? Why are the key financial ratios for these four retailers so different?

2. **GO SHOPPING** Go to your favourite store and interview the manager. Determine how the retailer sets its performance objectives. Evaluate its procedures relative to the procedures presented in the text.

3. **INTERNET EXERCISE/GO SHOPPING** Get balance sheet and income statement information for your favourite publicly-traded retailer by going to **http://www.hoovers.com**, **http://www.google.com/finance**, or the retailer's annual report, or by visiting the store and interviewing the owner/manager. Construct a strategic profit model and evaluate its financial performance. Explain why you believe its ratios are or are not consistent with its strategy.

4. **CONNECT EXERCISE** Access Connect and go to the Strategic Profit Model (SPM) under additional resources for this chapter. The SPM tutorial is designed to provide a refresher for the basic financial ratios leading to return on assets. The tutorial walks you through it step-by-step. A "calculation page" is also included that will calculate all the ratios. You can type in the numbers from a firm's balance sheet and income statement to see the financial results that are produced with the current financial figures. You can also access an Excel spreadsheet for doing SPM calculations. The calculation page or the Excel spreadsheet can be used for the case on Blue Nile and Tiffany's.

5. **INTERNET EXERCISE** Go to **http://www.retailowner. com**. Under the Benchmarks menu, click on each of the following and then compare GMROI:

   a) General Merchandiser Stores – Department Stores
   b) Bldg. Materials, Garden Supplies Dealers – Building Materials Dealers
   c) Apparel, Accessories Stores – Jewelry Stores
   d) Motor Vehicles, Parts Dealers – Motorcycle Dealers

6. **INTERNET EXERCISE** Go to **http://www.bizstats.com**. Compare industry benchmarks with the retailer results found in Exhibit 8–12 by clicking on Industry Financials/Corporations/Retail Trade and then the applicable NAICS category (i.e., food and beverage). What are your findings?

DISCUSSION QUESTIONS AND PROBLEMS

1. Why must retailers use multiple performance measures to evaluate their performance?

2. Describe how a multiple-store retailer would set its annual performance objectives.

3. Buyers' performance is often measured by their gross margin. Why is this figure more appropriate than net profit or loss?

4. How does the strategic profit model (SPM) help retailers plan and evaluate marketing and financial strategies?

5. Holt Renfrew (a high-service department store) and Costco (a chain of warehouse clubs) target different groups of customers. Which should have the higher asset turnover, net profit margin, and return on assets? Why?

6. Given the following information, construct an income statement and determine if there is a profit or loss. (Figures are in $000.)

Sales	$3 015 534
Cost of goods sold	2 020 954
Operating expenses	193 628
Interest expense	15 188
Taxes	67 807

7. Using the following information taken from Sharper Image Corporation's balance sheet, determine the asset turnover. (Figures are in $000.)

Net sales	$383 222
Total assets	162 338
Total liabilities	67 595

8. Using the following information taken from a balance sheet and income statement for Lululemon, develop a strategic profit model. (Figures are in $000.)

Sales	$1 000 839
Cost of goods	431 569
Gross profit	569 270
Operating expense	282 312
Interest expenses	0
Income	286 958
Net income	184 964
Inventory	104 100
Accounts receivable	5 200
Total assets	734 630
Total liabilities	133 260

9. Assume Sears is planning a special promotion for the upcoming holiday season. It has purchased 2.5 million Santa Bears, stuffed teddy bears dressed like Santa Claus, from a vendor in Taiwan. The GMROI for the bears is expected to be 144 percent (gross margin = 24 percent and sales-to-stock ratio = 6), about average for a seasonal promotion. Besides the invoice cost of the bears, Sears will incur import fees, transportation costs from Taiwan to distribution centres and then to stores, and distribution centre and store costs such as marking and handling. Since the bears arrived early in April, additional storage facilities are needed until they are shipped to the stores the first week of October. Is GMROI an adequate measure for evaluating the performance of Santa Bears? Explain your answer.

10. Increasing inventory turnover is an important goal for a retail manager. What are the consequences of turnover that is too slow?

11. The fine jewellery department in a department store has the same GMROI as the small appliances department even though characteristics of the merchandise are quite different. Explain this situation.

12. Calculate GMROI and inventory turnover given:

Annual sales	$20 000
Average inventory (at cost)	$75 000
Gross margin	45%

13. Calculate GMROI and inventory turnover given:

Annual sales	$12 000
Average inventory (at cost)	$4 000
Gross margin	35%

14. Using the following information taken from a balance sheet and income statement for Loblaw Companies Ltd., develop a strategic profit model. (Figures are in $000.) You can access an Excel spreadsheet for SPM calculations on the student side of the book's website.

Net sales	$31 250
Cost of goods sold	23 894
Operating expenses	5 972
Interest expenses	0
Inventory	2 025
Accounts receivable	2 568
Current assets	6 462
Total assets	17 428
Total liabilities	11 421

CHAPTER NINE

Information systems and supply chain management

LEARNING OBJECTIVES

Lo1   Explore how retailers create strategic advantage through supply management and information systems.

Lo2   Examine how merchandise and information flow from the vendor to the retailer to consumers.

Lo3   Explore the activities undertaken in a distribution centre.

Lo4   Identify various IT developments that are facilitating vendor–retailer communications.

Lo5   Review how collaboration on supply chain management benefits vendors and retailers.

Lo6   Discuss electronic communication tools which aid inventory and the buying process.

SPOTLIGHT ON RETAILING

LIFTING SPIRITS: CLOUD-BASED SOFTWARE SMOOTHS LCBO'S PURCHASE ORDER AND DELIVERY OPERATIONS

Step-by-step, the Liquor Control Board of Ontario (LCBO) is making business flow better by moving some core supply chain procedures into the cloud.

The Ontario government agency, responsible for purchasing and retailing wine and spirits in the province, has been steadily looking for ways to streamline procedures, reduce errors, and free up staff from clerical duties so that they can perform more complex, higher-value work. To that end, the LCBO has completely reworked both its purchase order and inbound delivery scheduling systems, and turned them from laborious, inefficient, paper-, fax- and telephone-based processes into web-based, automated, self-serve systems.

The LCBO buys alcoholic beverages from roughly 2700 suppliers in 75 countries. Some suppliers are major, multinational organizations. Others are small artisanal producers who sell only a few cases of wine to the LCBO every year. In total, the agency issues about 40 000 purchase orders (POs) annually. Implementing a system that was both robust enough to handle the number of purchase orders the LCBO issues and simple enough that it could be used by its entire supplier base made choosing the type of platform a pretty easy decision.

"We knew it needed to be web-based. We knew it needed to be accessible from anywhere in the world, around the clock. It had to provide that PO visibility. It had to be secure and have a secure protocol for access, and it had to provide online training for problem issues and support problem resolution 24/7. We also needed it to provide good audit-trail tracking, exception reporting, and real-time visibility," says Lisa MacGregor, director of supply chain for the LCBO.

The LCBO was already using a few applications, including its new submission system (NISS), developed and hosted by the Mississauga, Ontario-based QLogitek division of Logitek Data Sciences Ltd., so it returned to that company to create a web-based purchase-order management system, referred to inside the LCBO as WEB PO. WEB PO, however, was much larger in scope and was to be the first step in a more integrated supply chain management solution.

Because of the vast changes this system would bring, the LCBO knew it had to invest a great deal in supplier training and preparation before the system could go live, says project manager David Collins. "With 2700 suppliers around the world, getting them registered was a big

© Mike Clegg | Dreamstime.com.

task before rollout. That was the main hurdle for the WEB PO rollout. We developed our own in-house application for them to register. We had them sign up as an administrator. They would provide an email address and background information. We would verify that. We held back all the passwords and user IDs until the weekend before we actually rolled out, so they didn't lose them ahead of time. After they became an administrator, they could sign up additional people from their own office."

One of the challenges facing the LCBO was the multilingual nature of its supplier base. The software itself is available only in English, but suppliers who had problems due to language were able to call the QLogitek-run support line and receive assistance delivered in their native languages.

WEB PO has all but eliminated phone calls and faxes for regular transactions. Now, only exception-based incidents need to be dealt with manually. The software handles the rest of the normal, everyday transactions.

"If we issue a purchase order to a supplier for 1000 cases to be delivered by September 1, the supplier can request a change and say, 'I only have 800 cases and I can't make September 1, but I can make September 15.' That then comes back to us for us to approve or reject, and it's all automated. We don't have to deal with that manually. An alert goes to our LCBO staff. It's up to them to accept or reject, but it's still in the system," says MacGregor.

"They'll actually re-issue the PO, and then it goes back through the normal channels, and the supplier will see a revised PO come through," adds Collins.

Beyond its automated order-handling capabilities, MacGregor says one of WEB PO's biggest advantages is it now gives the LCBO the ability to track supplier performance.

"We have the audit trail, so we know if suppliers aren't meeting demands or time frames. That was a key point for us in terms of being able to have good data to track a supplier's performance. It's done by data extraction to a vendor scorecard. That process is a little more manual in terms of data extraction, but at least now we have the data in terms of being able to identify problem vendors."

Source: Carolyn Gruske, "Lifting Spirits," *Materials Management & Distribution*, October 30, 2012.

Joe Jackson wakes up in the morning, takes a shower, dresses, and goes to his kitchen to make a cup of coffee and toast a bagel. He slices the bagel and puts it in his toaster oven, but, to his dismay, the toaster oven is not working. As he reads the newspaper and eats his untoasted bagel with his coffee, he notices that Canadian Tire is having a sale on Sunbeam toaster ovens. The toaster ovens look great. So, on his way home from work, he stops at a Canadian Tire store to buy one. He finds the advertised Sunbeam model on the shelf and buys it.

Joe expected to find the Sunbeam toaster oven, as well as other models, available at Canadian Tire, but he probably didn't realize that a lot of behind-the-scene activities were going on to get those toaster ovens to the store. Canadian Tire uses sophisticated information and supply chain management systems to make sure that the Sunbeam toaster ovens and other brands are available in its stores whenever Joe and other customers want them. When Joe bought the toaster oven, the information about his transaction was automatically forwarded by the information systems to Canadian Tire's regional distribution centre, the home appliance planner at Canadian Tire's corporate headquarters in Toronto, and the toaster oven manufacturer in China. A computer information system monitors all toaster oven sales and inventory levels in every Canadian Tire store and indicates when to have toaster ovens shipped from the manufacturer in China to the regional distribution centres and then from the centres to the stores. Shipments to the distribution centres and stores are monitored using a satellite tracking system that locates the ships and trucks transporting the toaster ovens.

Of course, Canadian Tire could ensure the availability of toaster ovens and other merchandise by simply keeping a large number of units in the stores at all times. But stocking a large number of each SKU would require much more space to store the items and a significant investment in additional inventory. So the challenge for Canadian Tire is to limit its inventory and space investment but still make sure products are always available when customers want them.

distribution centre A warehouse that receives merchandise from multiple vendors and distributes it to multiple stores.

supply chain management The set of approaches and techniques firms employ to efficiently and effectively integrate their suppliers, manufacturers, warehouses, stores, and transportation intermediaries to efficiently have the right quantities at the right locations, and at the right time.

This chapter begins by outlining how retailers can gain a strategic advantage through supply chain management and information systems. Then the chapter describes information and product flows in the supply chain and the activities undertaken in distribution centres. Next, it examines a set of decisions that retailers make to determine the structure of the supply chain, such as whether to use distribution centres or direct store deliveries and whether to outsource some supply chain functions. The chapter continues with a discussion of how vendors and retailers work together to efficiently manage the movement of merchandise from the vendor through the retailer's distribution centres to its stores and customers. The chapter concludes with a discussion of a new technology, radio frequency identification (RFID), being used to improve supply chain efficiency.

LO1 Creating Strategic Advantage through Supply Management and Information Systems

As discussed in Chapter 1, retailers are the connection between customers and product manufacturers. It is the retailer's responsibility to gauge customers' wants and needs and work with the other members of the supply chain—distributors, vendors, and transportation companies—to make sure the merchandise that customers want is available when they want it. A simplified supply chain is illustrated in Exhibit 9–1. Vendors ship merchandise either to a **distribution centre** (as is the case for vendors V_1 and V_3) or directly to stores (as is the case for vendor V_2). The factors considered in deciding to ship directly to stores versus to distribution centres are discussed later in this chapter.

Supply chain management is a set of activities and techniques firms employ to efficiently and effectively manage the flow of merchandise from the vendors to the retailer's customers. These activities ensure that customers are able to purchase merchandise in the desired quantities at a preferred location and appropriate time.[1]

Retailers are increasingly taking a leadership role in managing their supply chains. When retailers were predominantly small businesses, larger manufacturers and distributors dictated when, where, and how merchandise was delivered. But

Exhibit 9–1
Illustration of a Supply Chain

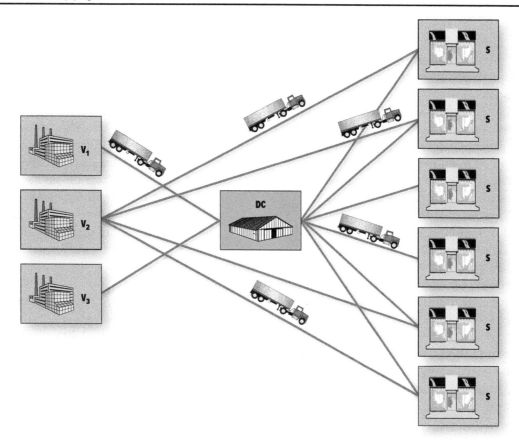

with the consolidation and emergence of large, international retail chains, retailers now play an active role in coordinating supply chain management activities. The size of these international retailers typically makes them more knowledgeable and powerful than their vendors and thus better able to control their supply chains. Retailers are in a unique position to collect information about customer shopping behaviour and purchases. As we will discuss later in the chapter, this information is shared with suppliers to plan production, promotions, deliveries, assortments, and inventory levels. Efficient supply chain management is important to retailers because it can provide a strategic advantage that increases product availability and an inventory turnover that produces a higher return on assets.

Strategic Advantage

As we discussed in Chapter 4, strategic advantage is the unique and sustainable advantage that enables retailers to realize a higher-than-average return on their assets. Of course, all retailers strive to develop

a competitive advantage, but not all retailers can develop a competitive advantage from their information and supply chain systems. However, if they do develop such an advantage, the advantage is sustainable because it is difficult for competitors to duplicate it.

For example, a critical factor in Walmart's success is its information and supply chain management systems. Even though competitors recognize this advantage, they have difficulty achieving the same level of performance as Walmart's systems for four reasons. First, Walmart has made substantial initial and continuing investments in developing its systems over a long time period. Second, it has the scale economies to justify these investments. Third, the

> **DID YOU KNOW?**
>
> One in every six consumers (16.6 percent) shopping in grocery and household goods retailers who experience a stockout situation do not purchase a substitute product.[2]

> **DID YOU KNOW?**
>
> The actual stockout rate experienced by consumers is about 17.8 percent, which is 123 percent higher than the stockout rate claimed by retailers.[3]

stockout A situation occurring when an SKU that a customer wants is not available.

supply chain activities take place within the firm and are not easily known or copied by competitors. Its systems are not simply software packages that any firm can buy from a software supplier. Through its continuous learning process, Walmart is always refining its systems to improve its performance. Fourth, the effective use of these systems requires top management support and the coordinated effort of employees and functional areas throughout the company.

Walmart's systems are so well regarded that retailers in emerging economies are anxious to partner with Walmart in the hopes of acquiring some of these skills. For example, Bharti Enterprises in India has a joint venture with Walmart to wholesale food and other products to small Indian retailers. With Walmart's supply chain management systems in place, farmers and small manufacturers are directly linked to retailers, thus streamlining the supply chain.[4]

To understand the complexity of the tasks performed by these systems and the need for coordinated efforts, consider the various activities that retailers undertake to keep merchandise in stock:

- Accurately forecast sales and needed inventory levels for each category and SKU.
- Monitor sales to detect derivations from the forecast.
- Transport the right amount of merchandise from the distribution centres to each store.
- Make sure that accurate information is available that indicates where the merchandise is—either in the vendor's warehouse, the distribution centre, the store, sold to customer, or in transit.
- Place accurate, timely orders with vendors and distribution centres.
- Replenish merchandise from distribution centres with the right quantities when the stores need it.
- Ensure that buyers and marketing managers coordinate merchandise delivery with special sales and promotional materials.
- Collect and process returned merchandise.

Improved Product Availability

Efficient supply chain management provides two benefits to retailers and their customers: (1) fewer stock-outs and (2) tailored assortments. These benefits translate into greater sales, lower costs, higher inventory turnover, and lower markdowns for retailers.

Fewer Stockouts A **stockout** occurs when an SKU that a customer wants is not available. What would happen if Joe went to the Canadian Tire store and the store did not have Sunbeam toaster ovens because the distribution centre did not ship enough to the store? The store would give Joe a rain check so that he could come back and still pay the sale price when the store receives a new shipment. But Joe would not be pleased because he would have made a wasted trip to the store. As a result of the stockout, Joe might decide to buy another model, or he might go to a nearby Walmart to buy a toaster oven. While at Walmart, he could buy other items in addition to the toaster oven. He also might be reluctant to shop at Target in the future and might tell all of his friends about the negative experience he had. This bad experience could have been avoided if Target had done a better job of managing its supply chain.

In general, stockouts have significant short- and long-term effects on sales and profits. Data show that the first time customers experience a stockout, they will purchase a substitute item 70 percent of the time. With a second out-of-stock occurrence, that rate drops to 50 percent, with customers going to a competitor the other 50 percent of the time. By the third instance, there is a 70 percent chance that the retailer has lost the sale entirely and, most likely, the customers' loyalty as well. Customers may never come back.[5]

Tailored Assortments Another benefit provided by information systems that support supply chain systems is making sure that the right merchandise is available at the right store. Most national retail chains adjust assortments in their stores on the basis of climate—stocking more wool sweaters during the winter and cotton sweaters in fall. Some retailers are now using sophisticated statistical methods to analyze sales transaction data and adjust store assortments for a wide range of merchandise on the basis of the characteristics of customers in each store's local market.

Higher Return on Assets

From the retailer's perspective, an efficient supply chain and information system can improve its return on assets (ROA) because the system increases sales and net profit margins, without increasing inventory. Net sales increase because customers are offered more attractive, tailored assortments that are in stock. Consider Joe Jackson's toaster oven purchase. Canadian Tire, with its information systems, could accurately estimate how many Sunbeam toaster ovens each store would sell during the special promotion. Using its supply chain management system, it would make sure sufficient stock was available at Joe's store so that all customers who wanted to buy one could.

Net profit margin is improved by increasing the gross margin and lowering expenses. An information system that coordinates buyers and vendors allows retailers to take advantage of special buying opportunities and obtain the merchandise at a lower cost, thus improving their gross margins. Retailers also can lower their operating expenses by coordinating deliveries, thus reducing transportation expenses. With more efficient distribution centres, merchandise can be received, prepared for sale, and shipped to stores with minimum handling, further reducing expenses.

By efficiently managing their supply chains, retailers can carry less backup inventory yet still avoid stockouts. Thus, inventory levels are lower, and with a lower inventory investment, total assets are also lower, so the asset and inventory turnovers are both higher. Retailing View 9.1 describes how supply chain management is changing the way fashion comes to market.

Lo2 The Flow of Information and Products in a Supply Chain

The complexities of the flow of merchandise and of information in a typical multistore chain are illustrated in Exhibit 9–2. Although the flow of information and of merchandise are intertwined, in the following sections we describe first how information about customer demand is captured at the store, which triggers a series of responses from buyers and planners, distribution centres, and vendors. This information is used to make sure that merchandise

Exhibit 9–2
Flow of Information and of Merchandise

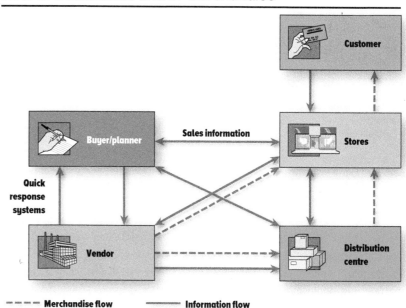

is available at the store when the customer wants it. Then we discuss the physical movement of merchandise from vendors through distribution centres to the stores.

Information Flows

When Joe Jackson bought his toaster oven at Canadian Tire, he initiated the information flows illustrated in Exhibit 9–3. (The numbers in circles refer to the path in the exhibit.)

The Target cashier scans the **Universal Product Code (UPC)** tag on the toaster oven box (1), and a sales receipt is generated for Joe. The UPC tag is a black-and-white bar code containing a 13-digit code that indicates the manufacturer of the item, a description of the item, information about special packaging, and special promotions. The codes for all products are issued by GS1 US, formerly the Uniform Code Council. In the future, RFID tags, discussed later in this chapter, may replace UPC tags.

Universal Product Code (UPC) The black-and-white bar code found on most merchandise that is used to collect sales information at the point of sale using computer terminals that read the code. This information is transmitted computer to computer to buyers, distribution centres, and then to vendors, who in turn quickly ship replenishment merchandise.

DID YOU KNOW?

Shortly after 8 a.m. on June 26, 1974, the first UPC tag was scanned in Troy, Ohio, when Clyde Dawson bought a 10-pack of Wrigley's Juicy Fruit gum for 67 cents in a Marsh supermarket. Now, over 10 billion items are scanned each day.[6]

Shhhh . . . Zara's Got a Secret . . . and It's all about Supply Chain Management

DID YOU KNOW?

Zara was originally named Zorba, but the title was changed because a local bar in Spain had the same name.[7]

With sales of 19.2 billion by fiscal year-end of January 2015, Zara continues to flourish. With 7013 stores (of which 330 were new in 2014), 153 000 employees, and a 15 percent increase in sales over 2014, Zara is a global retailer leader in the garment industry and an international power house.

You may find their numbers somewhat surprising. With global retail industry growth projected to be approximately 5 percent during the same time frame, Zara's figures are somewhat robust in comparison. The question, is how do they do it?

If you were to analyze their competitive strengths based on their marketing mix, several "Ps" stand out, with a key being their distribution network.

Place (Distribution) Within two weeks of displaying their clothing at a fashion show on a catwalk, the same items can be found in retail stores, ready for consumers to buy. Every week two sets of orders are sent out to Zara outlets on specific days and times. This means trucks are leaving at specific times and merchandise is then also arriving at guaranteed times. Garments have already been labelled and priced, so when they reach their destination they can simply be placed on the retail floor.

Zara's efficient distribution chain enables the company to deliver garments to its European retailers within 24 hours, and to its Asian and US retailers in less than 40 hours.

The culture of Zara is defined in such a manner that all employees, from buying, manufacturing, and logistics to retail, appreciate the importance of the company's timeline and how each member in the channel impacts the flow of goods. This also includes consumers who know that new garments arrive on a regular basis and in limited quantities.

Product Zara's mantra is *fast fashion* (new pieces of clothing are designed daily, as much as three to four pieces), but they also provide only a limited quantity of the clothing they release to market. Consumers understand that if they don't first buy the item when they see it in the store, it may not be available the next time they visit the store.

Zara completes much of their production in-house and ensures their factories reserve 85 percent of capacity for in-season adjustments. If a certain design or

Sources: Clara Lu, "Zara's Secret to Retail Success - Its Supply Chain," *Trade Gecko,* December 4, 2014, https://www.tradegecko.com/blog/zara-supply-chain-its-secret-to-retail-success (accessed February 2, 2016); eMarketer, "Retail Sales Worldwide Will Top $22 Trillion This Year Ecommerce Eclipses $1.3 Trillion, Led by China and US," December 23, 2014, http://www.emarketer.com/Article/Retail-Sales-Worldwide-Will-Top-22-Trillion-This-Year/1011765 (accessed June 21, 2016); Walter Loeb, "Zara Leads In Fast Fashion," *Forbes,* March 30, 2015,

Exhibit 9–3
Information Flows

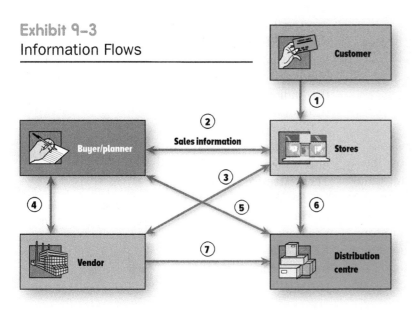

The information about the transaction is captured at the point-of-sale (POS) terminal and sent to Target's information system, where it can be accessed by the planner for the toaster oven product category (2). The planner uses this information to monitor and analyze sales and decide when to reorder more toaster ovens or reduce their prices if sales are below expectations.

The sales transaction data also are sent to Target's distribution centre (6). When the store inventory drops to a specified level, more toaster ovens are shipped to the store, and the shipment information is sent to the Target computer style suddenly is in high demand, Zara can quickly react and design new styles, getting the garments into Zara outlets while the fashion is still reaching its peak.

Zara produces approximately 450 million retail pieces a year. About 150 million garments go through their main centre in Arteixo, Spain, which boasts a 5 million-square-foot main distribution centre.

Price In terms of the clothing that Zara sells, 85 percent of it is sold at full price. The average for the industry is approximately 65 percent. When looking at unsold items, Zara has less than 10 percent of their merchandise fall into that category, while the industry average is somewhere between 17 percent and 20 percent.

People The people who work for Zara in Europe are better paid than industry counterparts, thus enhancing the work culture and making workers feel as if they are a valuable resource. Managers who work for Zara are constantly in contact with customers and pass the feedback they have gathered to Zara's production department,

Zara's competitive advantage in specialty apparel retailing is based on its efficient supply chain that delivers fashionable merchandise to its stores frequently.

© AP Photo/Denis Doyle.

which starts developing sketches of new garments to bring to market right way.

Final Thought By proper management of several key components of the marketing mix, Zara has been able to become an industry leader, setting the bench market for *fast fashion*. It doesn't look like they will be relinquishing the title anytime soon.

http://www.forbes.com/sites/walterloeb/2015/03/30/zara-leads-in-fast-fashion/#960d01b61d79 (accessed June 21, 2015); Kevin O'Marah, "Zara Uses Supply Chain To Win Again," *Forbes*, March 9, 2016, http://www.forbes.com/sites/kevinomarah/2016/03/09/zara-uses-supply-chain-to-win-again/#420cd36e63ae (accessed June 21, 2016); Susan Berfield and Manuel Baigorri, "Zara's Fast-Fashion Edge," *Bloomberg*, November 2013, http://www.bloomberg.com/news/articles/2013-11-14/2014-outlook-zaras-fashion-supply-chain-edge (accessed June 21, 2016).

system (5) so that the planner knows the inventory level that remains in the distribution centre.

When the inventory drops to a specified level in the distribution centre (4), the planner negotiates terms and shipping dates and places an order with the manufacturer of the toaster ovens. The planner then informs the distribution centre about the new order and when the store can expect delivery (5).

When the manufacturer ships the toaster ovens to the Target distribution centre, it sends an advanced shipping notice to the distribution centre (7). An **advance shipping notice (ASN)** is a document that tells the distribution centre what specifically is being shipped and when it will be delivered. The distribution centre then makes appointments for trucks to make the delivery at a specific time, date, and loading dock. When the shipment is received at the distribution centre, the planner is notified (5) and then authorizes payment to the vendor.

In some situations, discussed later in this chapter, the sales transaction data are sent directly from the store to the vendor (3), and the vendor decides when to ship more merchandise to the distribution centre and stores. The fulfillment of sales from non-store channels may involve the vendor shipping merchandise directly to the customer. In other situations, especially when merchandise

advance shipping notice (ASN) An electronic document received by a retailer's computer from a supplier in advance of a shipment.

Exhibit 9–4
Retail Data Warehouse

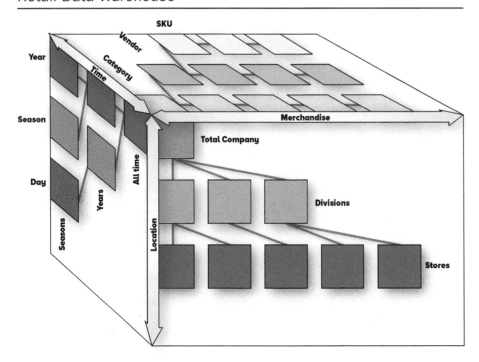

is reordered frequently, the ordering process is done automatically, bypassing the planners.

Data Warehouse Purchase data collected at the point of sale goes into a database known as a *data warehouse*. The information stored in the data warehouse is accessible on various dimensions and levels, as depicted in the data cube in Exhibit 9–4.

As shown on the horizontal axis, data can be accessed according to the level of merchandise aggregation—SKU (item), vendor, category (dresses), department (women's apparel), or all merchandise. Along the vertical axis, data can be accessed by level of the company—store, division, or total company. Finally, along the third dimension, data can be accessed by point in time—day, season, or year.

The CEO might be interested in how the corporation is generally doing and could look at the data aggregated by quarter for a merchandise division, a region of the country, or the total corporation. A buyer may be more interested in a particular vendor in a

specific store on a particular day. Analysts from various levels of the retail operation extract information from the data warehouse to make a plethora of retailing decisions about developing and replenishing merchandise assortments.

Data warehouses also contain detailed information about customers, which is used to target promotions and group products together in stores. These applications are discussed in Chapter 14. To economically collect this information, most of the communication between vendors and retailers and within the retailer is done via electronic data interchange (EDI).

Electronic Data Interchange In the past, retailer–vendor information flows were accomplished by sending handwritten or typed documents through the mail or by fax. Now, most communications between vendors and retailers occur via electronic data interchange. **Electronic data interchange (EDI)** is the computer-to-computer exchange of business documents in a standardized format. To facilitate the adoption of EDI, the retail industry agreed to use specific symbols to delineate the purchase order number, the vendor's name, the address the merchandise is being shipped to, and so forth.

Retailers also have developed standards for exchanging information about purchase order changes, order status, transportation routings, advance shipping notices, on-hand inventory status, and vendor promotions, as well as information that enables vendors to put price tags on merchandise. The development and use of these standards is critical to the use of EDI because they enable all retailers to use the same format when transmitting data to their vendors.

EDI transmissions between retailers and vendors occur over the Internet. Because the Internet is a publicly-accessible network, its use to communicate internally and externally with vendors and customers raises security issues. Some potential implications of security failures are the loss of business data essential to conducting business, disputes with vendors and customers, loss of public

electronic data interchange (EDI) The computer-to-computer exchange of business documents from retailer to vendor and back.

DID YOU KNOW?

By analyzing its customer database, Walmart knows that sales of strawberry Pop Tarts increase by 700 percent in areas facing the arrival of a hurricane.[8]

confidence and its effect on brand image, bad publicity, and loss of revenue from customers using an electronic channel.

To help secure information, retailers have incorporated security policies. A **security policy** is the set of rules that applies to activities involving computer and communication resources that belong to an organization. Retailers also train employees and add the necessary software and hardware to enforce the rules. The objectives of a security policy are as follows:

- **Authentication.** The system ensures or verifies that the person or computer at the other end of the communication really is who or what it claims to be.

- **Authorization.** The system ensures that the person or computer at the other end of the comunication has permission to carry out the request.

- **Integrity.** The system ensures that the arriving information is the same as that sent, which means that the data have been protected from unauthorized changes or tampering through a data encryption process.

The Physical Flow of Merchandise—Logistics

Exhibit 9–5 illustrates the physical flow of merchandise within the supply chain.

1. Merchandise flows from vendor to distribution centre.

2. Merchandise goes from distribution centre to stores.

3. Alternatively, merchandise can go from vendor directly to stores or even the customer.

Logistics is the aspect of supply chain management that refers to the planning, implementation, and control of the efficient flow and storage of goods, services, and related information from the point of origin to the point of consumption to meet customers' needs.[9] In addition to managing inbound and outbound transportation, logistics involves the activities undertaken in the retailer's distribution centre. For example, sometimes merchandise is temporarily stored at the distribution centre; other times it just passes through the centre from an inbound to an outbound truck. Merchandise shipments might be prepared for stores in the centre. For example, the centre might break down received

Exhibit 9–5
Merchandise Flow

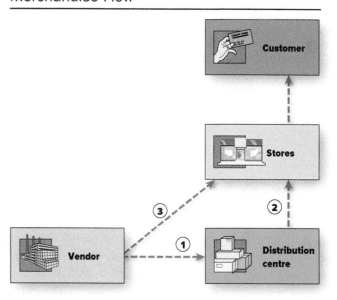

shipping cartons into smaller quantities that can be more readily used by the individual stores and/or apply price tags and the retailer's labels. The following section describes activities undertaken in a distribution centre.

Lo3 The Distribution Centre

The distribution centre performs the following activities: coordinating inbound transportation; receiving, checking, storing, and cross-docking; getting merchandise "floor-ready"; and coordinating outbound transportation. To illustrate these activities, we shall follow a shipment of Sony PlayStation systems that is arriving at a Sears distribution centre.

Management of Inbound Transportation

When working with vendors, buyers traditionally focused their efforts on developing merchandise assortments, negotiating prices, and arranging joint promotions. Now, buyers and planners are much more involved in coordinating the physical flow of merchandise to the stores. The Sears game buyer has arranged for a truckload of systems to be

security policy The set of rules that applies to activities in the computer and communications resources that belong to an organization.

logistics Part of the supply chain process that plans, implements, and controls the efficient, effective flow and storage of goods, services, and related information from the point of origin to the point of consumption to meet customers' requirements.

dispatcher A person who coordinates deliveries from the vendor to the distribution centre or stores, or from the distribution centre to stores.

receiving The process of filling out paperwork to record the receipt of merchandise that arrives at a store or distribution centre.

checking The process of going through goods upon receipt to make sure that they arrived undamaged and that the merchandise received matches the merchandise ordered.

cross-docked Items that are unloaded from the shippers' truck and within a few hours reloaded onto trucks going to stores. These items are prepackaged by the vendor for a specific store, such that the UPC labels on a carton indicate the store to which it is to be sent.

delivered to its St. Laurent, Quebec, distribution centre on Monday between 1 p.m. and 3 p.m. The buyer has also specified the particular way that the merchandise should be placed on pallets for easy unloading.

The truck must arrive within the specified time because the distribution centre has all of its 100 receiving docks allocated throughout the day and much of the merchandise on this particular truck is going to be shipped to stores that evening. Unfortunately, the truck was delayed in a snowstorm. The **dispatcher**—the person who coordinates deliveries to the distribution centre—reassigns the truck delivering the Sony game stations to a Wednesday morning delivery slot, notifies the planner, and charges the firm several hundred dollars for missing its delivery time. Although many manufacturers pay transportation expenses, some retailers negotiate with their vendors to absorb this expense.

Receiving and Checking

Receiving is the process of recording the receipt of merchandise as it arrives at a distribution centre. **Checking** is the process of going through the goods on receipt to make sure that they arrived undamaged and that the merchandise ordered was the merchandise received.

Checking merchandise is a very labour-intensive and time-consuming task. When retailers have developed good relationships with vendors, they often do not check the number of items received compared to the number sent as indicated on the vendor's ASN for all merchandise received. Instead, they randomly check a sample of shipments to monitor the accuracy of the vendor's ASNs. In the future, retailers may be able to automatically check the contents of each carton by detecting signals sent from RFID chips placed on each item of merchandise in a carton.

Storing and Cross-Docking

After the PlayStations are received and checked, they are either stored or cross-docked. When PlayStations are stored, the cartons are transported by a conveyor system and forklift trucks to racks that go from the distribution centre's floor to its ceiling. Then, when the PlayStations are needed in the stores, a forklift driver goes to the rack, picks up the carton, and places it on a conveyor system that routes the carton to the loading dock of a truck going to the stores.

Cross-Docking PlayStation cartons that are **cross-docked** are prepackaged by Sony for a specific store. The UPC label on each carton indicates the store to which it is to be sent. Sony may also affix a price tag to each item in the carton. The PlayStation cartons are placed on a conveyor system that routes them from the unloading dock at which they were received to the loading dock for the truck going to the specific store—thus, the term *cross-docked*. The cartons are automatically routed on the conveyor system by sensors that read the UPC labels on the cartons. These cross-docked cartons are only in the distribution centre for a few hours before they are shipped to the stores.

The size, sales rate, and vendor performance typically determine whether cartons are cross-docked or stored. Merchandise is cross-docked only if an entire carton can be shipped to a store. For example, it would be inefficient to cross-dock toothbrush cartons if a received carton contained 500 units but a store only sold 50 units a day. In this situation, the received toothbrush carton would be

Important activities undertaken in distribution centres are ticketing and marking merchandise so that it is floor-ready.

Charles Gupton.

opened and a smaller number of units, along with other merchandise, would be put in a carton going to a store. Finally, when cross-docking cartons, retailers are assuming that the number and type of merchandise, as well as the store designation, are correctly encoded in the vendor's UPC labels. Thus, retailers are reluctant to cross-dock merchandise from unreliable vendors because it is very costly to correct errors that are not discovered until the cartons are first opened in stores.

Getting Merchandise Floor-Ready

For some merchandise, additional tasks are undertaken in the distribution centre to make the merchandise floor-ready. **Floor-ready merchandise** is merchandise that is ready to be placed on the selling floor. Getting merchandise floor-ready entails ticketing, marking, and, in the case of some apparel, placing garments on hangers.

Ticketing and marking refer to affixing price and identification labels to the merchandise. It is more efficient for a retailer to perform these activities at a distribution centre than in its stores. In a distribution centre, an area can be set aside and a process implemented to efficiently add labels and put apparel on hangers. Conversely, getting merchandise floor-ready in stores can block aisles and divert salespeople's attention from their customers. An even better approach from the retailer's perspective is to get vendors to ship floor-ready merchandise, thus totally eliminating the expensive, time-consuming ticketing and marking process.

Preparing to Ship Merchandise to a Store

At the beginning of the day, the computer system in the distribution centre generates a list of items to be shipped to each store on that day. For each item, a pick ticket and shipping label are generated. The **pick ticket** is a document or display on a screen in a forklift truck that indicates how much of each item to get from specific storage areas. The forklift driver goes to the storage area, picks up the number of cartons indicated on the pick ticket, places UPC shipping labels on the cartons that indicate the stores to which the items are to be shipped, and puts the cartons on the conveyor system, where they are automatically routed to the loading dock for the truck going to the stores.

Pick tickets and labels are also generated for the break pack area. In the break pack area,

cartons with too many items to be shipped to a single store (like the toothbrushes discussed above) are packaged for the store. Using the pick ticket, employees select items from open cartons and put them into a new carton. When all the items have been picked, a shipping label indicating the store's destination is attached to the carton, which is then placed on the conveyor system and routed to the appropriate loading dock.

So the conveyor system feeds cartons from three sources to the loading dock for a truck going to a specific store: (1) cross-docked cartons directly from the vendor's delivery trucks, (2) cartons stored in the distribution centre, and (3) cartons from the break pack area. These cartons are then loaded onto the trucks by employees.

Management of Outbound Transportation

The management of outbound transportation from distribution centre to stores is quite complex. Most distribution centres run 50 to 100 outbound truck routes each day. To handle this complex transportation problem, the centres use sophisticated routing and scheduling computer systems that consider the locations of the stores, road conditions, and

An automated conveyor system moves most cartons to outbound trucks for delivery to stores.
Courtesy of Walmart.

floor-ready merchandise Merchandise received at the store ready to be sold, without the need for any additional preparation by retail employees.

ticketing and marking Procedures for making price labels and placing them on the merchandise.

pick ticket A document that tells the order filler how much of each item to get from the storage area.

transportation operating constraints to develop the most efficient routes possible. As a result, stores are provided with an accurate estimated time of arrival, and vehicle use is maximized.

Retailers also need to determine the mode of transportation—planes, ships, or trucks. Some retailers mix modes of transportation to reduce overall costs and time delays. For example, many Chinese vendors send Europe-bound cargo by ship to the US West Coast. From there, the cargo is flown to its final destination in Europe. By combining the two modes of transport, sea and air, the entire trip takes about two weeks, as opposed to four or five weeks with an all-water route, and the cost is about half that of an all-air route.

Dollar General, an extreme-value, full-line discount store in the Untied States, developed an interesting, low-tech approach for dealing with a challenge it faced with outbound transportation to its stores. Controlling cost and distributing merchandise efficiently to its 8000 stores is key to maintaining its low prices and still making a profit. Each week, more than 2000 cartons are delivered to a typical store, and 12 person-hours are required to unload a delivery truck—time the employees could have spent helping customers. Labour scheduling is a real problem because store managers have to schedule additional staff on truck days and then, in some cases, the drivers cannot make deliveries at the preplanned time. In addition, many of the stores are located in urban areas that make it difficult to park delivery trucks at a convenient location for an extended time period.

To address these challenges, Dollar General invested $100 million in a delivery system called *EZ store*. The EZ store system involves packing merchandise for shipment to stores in easy-to-move containers called *roll-tainers*. Instead of having store staff unload the truck when it arrives, the truck drivers alone can unload the 25 roll-tainers for the typical store in about 90 minutes. Store employees no longer need to wait for the truck to arrive and then walk 5 to 13 kilometres, lifting over 2700 kilograms of merchandise, on truck days. Instead, they can unpack merchandise from the roll-tainers and stock it on shelves during slow times in the day. The roll-tainers are also designed to protect the merchandise. When drivers make their next delivery, they offload the filled roll-tainers and pick up the empty ones. The system has led to significant reductions in employee injuries and turnover, reduced labour hours, and greater customer satisfaction.[10]

Retailing View 9.2 describes how Netflix has evolved from a tangible DVD movie distributor to an online streaming heavyweight. Netflix hasn't just changed their distribution strategy to mirror competitors initiatives; one might argue they are blazing the trail for distribution of online data streaming.

LO4 System Design Issues

This section reviews the factors affecting the decisions made by retailers concerning their supply chains. These decisions involve determining what activities, if any, should be outsourced to independent firms; what merchandise, if any, should be delivered directly to the store, bypassing the distribution centre; and how shipments directly to customers should be made.

Outsourcing Logistics

To streamline their operations and make more productive use of their assets and personnel, some retailers **outsource** supply chain functions. Many independent companies are very efficient at performing individual activities or all the supply chain activities. A large number of companies are available to transport merchandise from the vendor to distribution centres or from the centres to the retailer's stores. Rather than owning warehouses to store merchandise, retailers can use **public warehouses** that are owned and operated by an independent company. Rather than outsource specific activities, retailers can use freight forwarders to arrange for the storage and shipping of their merchandise. **Freight forwarders** usually provide a full range of services including tracking inland transportation, preparing shipping and export documents, warehousing, booking cargo space, negotiating freight charges, consolidating freight, insuring cargo, and filing insurance claims.[11]

Advantages and Disadvantages of Outsourcing Supply Chain Activities The primary benefit of outsourcing is that the independent firms can perform the activity at a lower cost or more efficiently

outsource Obtain a service from outside the company that had previously been done by the firm itself.

public warehouses Warehouses that are owned and operated by a third party.

freight forwarders Companies that purchase transport services. They then consolidate small shipments from a number of shippers into large shipments that move at a lower freight rate.

Netflix: The Evolution of a Company

If ever you need an example of a business that has managed to keep up with—and even help define—the times, look no further than Netflix. The multimedia powerhouse enjoys the kind of dominance in the film industry that all but ensures it will never go out of style. But its ascent to the top of the celluloid food chain is anything but chance; indeed, the company owes its success to a carefully executed business strategy that has evolved with the years. By examining Netflix, we can understand how enterprises can—and should—exist in a state of constant innovation.

Tracing the Three Major Shifts Remember Blockbuster Video? Or Hollywood Video, for that matter? If you are anything like us, then Friday afternoons were spent perusing their aisles, looking for DVDs or perhaps even a VHS tape. As *The New Yorker* points out, Netflix first emerged during this time, an era when rentals were still a thriving industry and the term "streaming" hadn't yet entered the film lexicon. But that was 17 years ago, and in the intervening years the entire film medium—not to mention modes of viewership—has experienced a tectonic shift. No longer do we rent movies. No longer are there Blockbusters and Hollywoods (the one in my town is now a Planet Fitness); today it's all about streaming. And Netflix endures.

How has Netflix stood the test of time while other rental services faltered and finally failed? As James Surowiecki explains in *The New Yorker* piece, it's all about adaptability. Whereas stores like Blockbuster were unable to change in order to meet evolving customer demands, Netflix not only evolved, but also helped lay the foundation for that evolution. Beginning as a rental service, Netflix effortlessly parlayed its business into online streaming, something that hadn't been done on a large scale before. The shift has fundamentally changed the nature of film and television viewership. After all, how many people do you know who watch TV shows at the appointed hour? Instead, people just wait till it "hits Netflix."

But the multimedia titan didn't stop with streaming. In the third (though likely not final) stage of its evolution, the company launched its own line of original content, including the hugely popular "Orange is the New Black" and "House of Cards." By doing this, Netflix's business model now closely resembles that of HBO. Yet it seems this latter company has also been influenced by the former, since *The*

Netflix's semi-automated system for processing rented DVDs gave it a competitive advantage. Now they stream!
(both) Courtesy of Netflix

New Yorker points out that HBO plans to debut HBO Go as its own streaming service. Meanwhile, Netflix's original content line couldn't be in a better place, with new seasons of both "Orange" and "Cards" planned, as well as a host of other shows. And as if that weren't enough, the business has recruited Happy Gilmore himself, Mr. Adam Sandler, to make four movies exclusively for Netflix. This begs the question: Is Netflix's fourth phase going to be the gradual supplanting of the movie theatre? Honestly, we hope not. To us, Netflix and cinema can harmoniously coexist, and neither one needs to negate the other. At the end of the day, we enjoy the trip to the theatre to see "Gone Girl" as much as a weekend spent binging on "Orange."

As far as your business goes, here's one way to pave the road for adaptability: implement a unified communications solution. By having a UC strategy in place, your business will be equipped with the tools to keep up with the times, from video conferencing and chat to advanced email solutions.

Source: Fonality, "Netflix: The evolution of a company," November 7, 2014, http://www.fonality.com/blog/netflix-the-evolution-of-a-company (accessed February 8, 2016).

than the retailer. Independent firms typically have a lower cost because they perform the activity for many retailers and thus realize scale economies. For example, independent trucking firms have more opportunities to fill their trucks on the return trip (backhaul) with merchandise for other retailers after delivering merchandise to one retailer's stores. In addition, when there are many independent firms available to undertake the activity, retailers can have the firms bid against each other to undertake the activity and thus drive down the costs.

However, when retailers outsource a supply chain activity, they can no longer develop a competitive advantage based on the performance of this activity. If the retailer's competitor discovers that the retailer is significantly reducing its costs or improving its efficiency by using an independent firm, the competitor can match the performance improvement by contracting with the same provider.[12]

Pull and Push Supply Chains

Another supply chain decision retailers make is determining whether merchandise will be pushed from the distribution centres to the stores or pulled from the distribution centres to the stores. Information and merchandise flows such as those described in Exhibit 9–2 illustrate a **pull supply chain**—a supply chain in which requests for merchandise are generated at the store level on the basis of sales data captured by POS terminals. Basically, in this type of supply chain, the demand for an item pulls it through the supply chain. An alternate and less sophisticated approach is a **push supply chain**, in which merchandise is allocated to stores on the basis of forecasted demand. Once a forecast is developed, specified quantities of merchandise are shipped (pushed) to distribution centres and stores at predetermined time intervals.

In a pull supply chain, there is less likelihood of being overstocked or out of stock because the store's requests for merchandise are based on customer demand. A pull approach increases inventory turnover and is more responsive to changes in customer demand. As a result, it becomes even more efficient than a push approach when demand is uncertain and difficult to forecast.[13]

Although generally more desirable, a pull approach is not the most effective in all situations. First, a pull approach requires a more costly and sophisticated information system to support it. Second, for some merchandise, retailers do not have the flexibility to adjust inventory levels on the basis of demand. For example, commitments must be made months in advance for fashion and private-label apparel. Because these commitments cannot be easily changed, the merchandise has to be allocated to the stores at the time the orders are formulated. Third, push supply chains are efficient for merchandise that has steady, predictable demand, such as milk and eggs, basic men's underwear, and bath towels. Because both pull and push supply chains have their advantages, most retailers use a combination of these approaches.

Distribution Centres versus Direct Store Delivery

As indicated in Exhibit 9–5, retailers can have merchandise shipped directly to their stores—direct store delivery (path 3)—or to their distribution centres (paths 1 and 2). **Direct store delivery (DSD)** is a method of delivering merchandise to stores in which vendors distribute merchandise directly to the stores.[14]

The vendors offering DSD also undertake additional services such as merchandising (arranging merchandise on racks or shelves) and information gathering about inventory levels. As part of the DSD process, vendor employees visit the retailer's store several times a week. In those store visits, trained personnel assess stock levels and backroom inventory to determine the right order amount, replenish the order, and display products based on local preferences.

The decision to use DSD or distribution centres depends on the characteristics of the merchandise and the nature of demand. To determine which distribution system is more efficient, retailers balance the total cost of each alternative and the impact of the alternatives on customer satisfaction.

Distribution centres lower inventory levels because the amount of backup stock needed in a

pull supply chain Strategy in which orders for merchandise are generated at store level on the basis of demand data captured by point-of-sale terminals.

push supply chain Strategy in which merchandise is allocated to stores on the basis of historical demand, the inventory position at the distribution centre, and the stores' needs.

direct store delivery (DSD) A method of delivering merchandise to stores in which vendors distribute merchandise directly to the stores rather than going through distribution centres.

centralized distribution centre is less than the amount of backup stock needed in all the stores served by the centre. For example, to achieve the desired product availability with direct delivery, each store might need to stock 10 Sunbeam toaster ovens for a total of 500 units in the 50 stores served by a distribution centre. By delivering products to a distribution centre and feeding the 50 stores from the centre, the retailer could achieve the same level of product availability with only 350 toaster ovens (5 in each store and 100 in the distribution centre). Since the stores get frequent deliveries from the distribution centre, they need to carry relatively less extra merchandise as backup stock. Thus, distribution centres enable the retailer to carry less merchandise in the individual stores, and this results in lower inventory investments systemwide. In addition, retail store space is typically much more expensive than space at a distribution centre. Distribution centres are typically located in remote areas near highways, while stores are located in more expensive areas near customers' homes. Distribution centres are also more efficient than direct store delivery when retailers need to prepare merchandise for sale, such as affixing price labels. When preparation is done in a centre, several employees can be trained to perform the activity efficiently rather than having 50 people (one in each store) do the preparation along with other duties.

However, distribution centres aren't appropriate for all retailers. If retailers have only a few outlets, the expense of a distribution centre is probably unwarranted. Also, direct store delivery gets merchandise to the stores faster and thus is used for perishable goods (meat and produce), items that help create the retailer's image of being the first to sell the latest product (e.g., video games), or fad items. DSD also is most efficient for fragile products for which freshness is important, such as salty snacks, bread, milk, and ice cream. For example, by

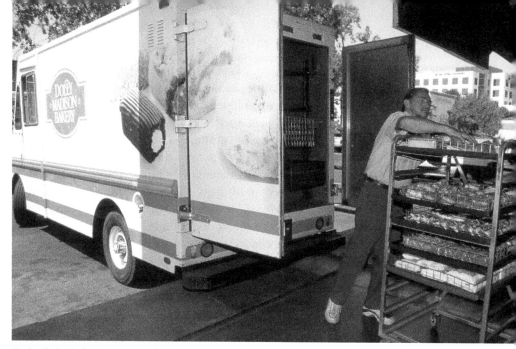

Having Dolly Madison's products delivered directly to stores, bypassing the supermarkets' distribution centres, enables customers to get fresher baked goods.
Spencer Grant/PhotoEdit.

developing a supply chain that bypasses the distribution centre, ProFlowers reduced the time from flower cutting to store delivery from 12 to 3 days. Finally, some vendors provide direct store delivery for retailers to ensure that their products are on the store's shelves, properly displayed, and fresh. For instance, employees delivering Frito-Lay snacks directly to supermarkets replace products that have been on the shelf too long and are stale, replenish products that have been sold, and arrange products so that they are neatly displayed.

Reverse Logistics

Reverse logistics is the process of capturing value from and/or properly disposing of merchandise returned by customers and/or stores. The reverse-logistics system processes merchandise that is returned because it is damaged, has been recalled, is no longer sold to customers because its selling season has ended or the product has been discontinued, or has excessive inventory. Packaging and shipping materials are also processed through the reverse-logistics system. The returned merchandise might involve returns from a customer to a retail store, from a retail store to a distribution centre, or from a distribution centre to a vendor.[16]

Reverse-logistics systems are challenging. The returned items may be damaged or lack the original shipping carton and thus require special

reverse logistics The process of capturing value from and/or properly disposing of merchandise returned by customers and/or stores.

DID YOU KNOW?

Customer returns can reduce a retailer's or manufacturer's profitability by an average of 3.8 percent.[15]

DID YOU KNOW?

According to the Reverse Logistics Association, the volume of returns annually via reverse logistics is estimated to be between $150 and $200 billion in the United States.[17]

drop-shipping A supply chain system in which retailers receive orders from customers and relay these orders to a vendor and then the vendor ships the merchandise ordered directly to the customer; also called *consumer direct fulfillment.*

handling. Transportation costs are high because items are shipped back in small quantities. Of the 48 million units shipped by L.L. Bean each year, 6 million are returned. About 85 percent of these returns are refunds and 15 percent are exchanges. For whatever reason, the products have disappointed the customer. L.L. Bean is committed to getting it right the second time. Although the returned merchandise moves through its system on a conveyor belt, one person handles each returned item from the time it is picked up off the conveyor to be scanned, processed, and prepped to the time it is sorted and placed back on the conveyor for reintroduction into the inventory system. This process has streamlined the return process and reduced errors.

Supply Chain for Fulfilling Catalogue and Internet Orders

The distribution centres and supply chains for supporting catalogue and Internet channels are very different from those supporting a store channel. The typical retail distribution centre supporting a store channel is designed to receive cartons from vendors and ship cartons to a limited number of stores. In contrast, distribution centres supporting non-store channels are designed to receive cartons and ship individual orders to a large number of customers. Since completely different distribution centre designs are required for supporting the different channels, multichannel retailers either have different distribution centres for the channels or designate separate areas within a single centre devoted to the different channels.

When the dot-com boom started, a number of store-based retailers lacked the capability to efficiently fulfill individual orders placed through their electronic channels. Thus they initially outsourced the fulfillment function when they added an Internet channel. For example, Toys "R" Us turned to Amazon for help after a disastrous 1999 holiday season when many of its customers did not receive their orders on

time, creating many unhappy customers on Christmas morning. Toys "R" Us entered into a ten-year agreement outsourcing the fulfillment of its orders. Even though Amazon's fulfillment capability is very efficient, over time Toys "R" Us acquired this capability and found that outsourcing its electronic channel was an impediment to creating a unified, multichannel offering. As a result, Toys "R" Us terminated its outsourcing contract with Amazon.[18]

Drop-Shipping

Drop-shipping, also called consumer direct fulfillment, is a system in which retailers receive orders from customers and relay these orders to vendors and then the vendors ship the merchandise ordered directly to the customer. Drop-shipping has been used for years by companies that sell bulky products such as lumber, iron, and petroleum, as well as by catalogue and mail-order companies.[19]

From the retailer's perspective, drop-shipping reduces the retailer's supply chain costs and investment because the vendor, rather than the retailer, assumes the costs and risks of supplying merchandise to customers. The vendor has to build and operate the distribution centres, hire and pay for employees to pick and pack individual orders, and manage inventory. Drop-shipping is particularly attractive for retailers that do not have distribution centres capable of fulfilling individual orders from customers. However, drop-shipping can lengthen delivery times and increase costs, particularly for customers who order multiple items from different vendors. In addition, retailers do not have control over an aspect of their offering that is of importance to their customer—how and when orders are delivered.

DID YOU KNOW?

A third of online retailers (including those on marketplaces such as Amazon and eBay) have converted to drop-shipping because it eliminates a lot of headaches associated with fulfillment, such as stocking, packaging, and shipping.[20]

Lo5 Collaboration between Retailers and Vendors in Supply Chain Management

As we discussed previously, retailers' and vendors' objectives for supply chain management are to minimize investments in inventory and costs and still make sure that merchandise is available when and where customers want it. Retailing View 9.1 at the beginning of this chapter illustrated how fast-fashion specialty retailers, such as Zara and H&M, excel at coordinating their stores, designers, and production capability to achieve these objectives.

Benefits of Coordination

Supply chain efficiency dramatically improves when vendors and retailers share information and work together. By collaborating, vendors can plan their purchases of raw materials and their production processes to match the retailer's merchandise needs. Thus, vendors can make sure that the merchandise is available "just in time," when the retailer needs it, without having to stock excessive inventory in the vendor's warehouse or the retailer's distribution centres or stores.

When retailers and vendors do not coordinate their supply chain management activities, excess inventory builds up in the system, even if the retail sales rate for the merchandise is relatively constant. This buildup of inventory in an uncoordinated channel is called the **bullwhip effect.** The effect was first discovered by Procter & Gamble, which saw that its orders from retailers for Pampers disposable diapers were shaped like a bullwhip, with wide swings in quantity ordered, even though retail sales were relatively constant (see Exhibit 9–6). Its retailers were ordering, on average, more inventory than they really needed.[22]

Research has found that the bullwhip effect in an uncoordinated supply chain is caused by the following factors:

- **Delays in transmitting orders and receiving merchandise.** Even when retailers can forecast sales accurately, there are delays in getting orders to the vendor and receiving those orders from the vendor. In an uncoordinated supply chain, retailers might not know how fast they can get the merchandise, and thus they overorder to prevent stockouts.

DID YOU KNOW?

Organizations that engage with suppliers at any level of supply chain collaboration are 38 percent more likely to achieve or surpass their expectations and have their initiatives result in cost reductions.[21]

Exhibit 9–6
Bullwhip Effect in Uncoordinated Supply Chain

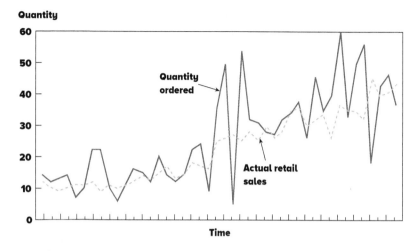

- **Overreacting to shortages.** When retailers find it difficult to get the merchandise they want, they begin to play the shortage game. They order more than they need to prevent stockouts, hoping they will receive a larger partial shipment. So, on average, the vendor ships more than the retailer really needs.

- **Ordering in batches.** Rather than generating a number of small orders, retailers wait and place larger orders to reduce order processing and transportation costs and take advantage of quantity discounts.[23]

These factors cause the bullwhip effect even when sales are fairly constant. However, for many retailers, sales are not constant. They go up dramatically when retailers put merchandise on sale and during special gift-giving times of the year. These irregularities in sales heighten the bullwhip effect and the buildup of inventory in the supply chain. Retailing View 9.3 describes the historical forces motivating retailers and vendors to collaborate on supply chain management.

bullwhip effect The buildup of inventory in an uncoordinated channel.

Vendors and retailers have found that by working together, they can reduce the level of inventory in the supply chain and the number of stockouts in the stores. Four approaches for coordinating supply chain activities, in order of the level of collaboration, are (1) using electronic data interchange (EDI); (2) exchanging information; (3) using vendor-managed inventory; and (4) employing collaborative planning, forecasting, and replenishment.[24]

Quick Response and Efficient Consumer Response

Retailer–vendor collaboration in supply chain management grew out of activities undertaken by apparel manufacturers and retailers, called *quick response (QR)*, and by consumer packaged goods (CPG) manufacturers and supermarket retailers, called *efficient consumer response (ECR)*. In the mid-1980s, Milliken, a US textile manufacturer facing severe price competition from imports, developed a strategy to compete on its speed to market rather than price. At the time, it took 66 weeks for the apparel industry to go from yarn at the manufacturer to clothing on a retail store fixture. Because no one in the supply chain knew what would be selling in a month, much less a year, the cost of that lengthy supply cycle was devastating. The apparel industry as a whole lost billions of dollars each year through price reductions on items customers didn't want and because they did not have enough of what they did want.

To address this supply chain inefficiency, Milliken joined with a children's apparel maker and large retail department store chain to compete through what it called "quick response." Quick response was modelled after the just-in-time (JIT) initiatives undertaken by Japanese automobile makers. The department store developed a sales forecast for a season. Milliken manufactured the fabric to meet the forecast but kept most of the fabric as "grey goods" that could be dyed different colours when orders for the specific colours came in. The apparel manufacturer cut and sewed a small initial assortment of garments and shipped them to the department store. The department store monitored the initial sales of colours and sizes and then transmitted this information to the manufacturer and Milliken so that the remaining fabric could be dyed, cut, and sewed in the colours and sizes that consumers were buying.

Walmart and other discount store chains were the motivating force for collaboration between CPG manufacturers and supermarket retailers. Through the Food Marketing Institute, supermarkets, facing price competition from discount stores, commissioned Kurt Salmon Associates (KSA) to find out how they could compete more effectively. KSA found that the supermarkets had a significant cost disadvantage due to their inefficient supply chains. When CPG manufacturers held special trade promotions (discounting the wholesale price), supermarket chains would buy a six-month supply of the products, leaving them with $30 billion of excess inventory in their distribution centres. In 1993, the KSA report recommended a multipronged efficient consumer response approach, which involved collaboration between manufacturers and retailers to achieve efficient replenishment and promotions.

Since these initiatives were launched, the grocery industry has made greater strides in improving its supply chain efficiencies than has the apparel industry because the manufacturing process for apparel is more complex and the number of SKUs is significantly larger.

Sources: Kurt Salmon Associates, *Efficient Consumer Response: Enhancing Customer Value in the Grocery Industry* (Washington, DC: The Food Marketing Institute, 1993); Sameer Kumar, "A Study of the Supermarket Industry and Its Growing Logistics Capabilities," *International Journal of Retail & Distribution Management* 36, no. 3 (2008), pp. 192–211; T.C.E Cheng and T. M. Choi, "Innovative Quick Response Programs in Logistics and Supply Chain Management," in *International Handbooks on Information Systems*, eds. Edwin Cheng and Tsan-Ming Choi (New York: Springer, 2010).

DID YOU KNOW?

For orders (B2B) *received* from customers (Sales Orders), 55 percent are received via EDI (either totally integrated or requiring minimal manual intervention). Only 10 percent are received via a portal and 7 percent are received via exchanges. The rest are sent via other, including manual, methods.[26]

Using EDI

The use of EDI to transmit purchase order information reduces the time it takes for retailers to place orders and for vendors to acknowledge the receipt of orders and communicate delivery information about those orders. In addition, EDI facilitates the implementation of other collaborative approaches discussed in the following sections.

However, the use of EDI without other collaborative approaches only addresses one factor discussed previously—the delay in transmitting and receiving orders—that causes the buildup of inventory in the supply chain.

Sharing Information

One of the major factors causing excessive inventory in the supply chain is the inability of vendors to know what the actual level of retail sales are.

For instance, suppose a consumer packaged goods vendor offered discounts to retailers several times a year, hoping that the price reduction would be passed on to customers.[25] Instead, however, the retailers purchased extra inventory and kept the extra discounts to increase their margins. Just looking at the orders it received, the vendor might think that demand for its products had increased significantly and therefore increase its production, causing an inventory buildup. To reduce this effect, vendors can use the retailer's sales records and give discounts based on sales rather than orders placed.

Sharing sales data with vendors is an important first step in improving supply chain efficiency. With the sales data, vendors can improve their sales forecasts, improve production efficiency, and reduce the need for excessive backup inventory. But additional levels of collaboration are needed to use this information effectively. The sales data reflect historical data, not what the retailer's plans are for the future. For example, the retailer might decide to delete a vendor's SKU from its assortment—a decision that clearly affects future sales. The two approaches discussed in the next sections introduce a forward-looking collaborative perspective.

Vendor-Managed Inventory

Vendor-managed inventory (VMI) is an approach for improving supply chain efficiency in which the vendor is responsible for maintaining the retailer's inventory levels. The vendor determines a reorder point—a level of inventory at which more merchandise is ordered. The retailer shares sales and inventory data with the vendor via EDI. When inventory drops to the order point, the vendor generates the order and delivers the merchandise.

In ideal conditions, the vendor replenishes inventories in quantities that meet the retailer's immediate demand and reduce stockouts with minimal inventory. In addition to better matching retail demand to supply, VMI can reduce the vendor's and the retailer's costs. Vendor salespeople no longer need to spend time generating orders on items that are already in the stores, and their role shifts to selling new items and maintaining relationships. Retail buyers and planners no longer need to monitor inventory levels and place orders.

For example, TAL Apparel Ltd., a Hong Kong shirt maker, produces garments for labels such as J. Crew, Calvin Klein, Banana Republic, and JCPenney. It supplies one in seven dress shirts sold in the United States and manages JCPenney's men's dress shirt inventory. TAL collects POS data for JCPenney's shirts directly from stores in North America and then runs the numbers through a computer model it designed. Next, TAL decides how many shirts to make and in what styles, colours, and sizes. It sends the shirts directly to each JCPenney store, bypassing the retailer's distribution centres and merchandise managers. Because TAL manages the entire process, from design to the ordering of yarn, it can bring a new style from the testing stage to full retail rollout in four months, much faster than Penney could on its own. The system, in effect, lets consumers, not merchandise managers, choose the styles.[28]

The use of VMI is not a new approach. Frito-Lay and other snack food, candy, and beverage vendors have used direct store delivery to manage the inventory of their products on supermarket VMI and shelves for a long time. However, technological advances have increased the sophistication of VMI. The sharing of POS transaction data, for instance, allows vendors to sell merchandise on **consignment**; the vendor owns the merchandise until it is sold by the retailer, at which time the retailer pays for the merchandise. Consignment selling provides an incentive for the vendor to pick SKUs and inventory levels that will minimize inventory and generate sales. Because the vendor is bearing the financial cost of owning the inventory, retailers are more willing to allow the vendor to be responsible for determining the inventory plan and appropriate assortment for each store.

Although it is a more advanced level of collaboration than simply using EDI and sharing information, VMI has its limitations. While the vendor coordinates the supply chain for its specific products, it does not know what other actions the retailer is taking that might affect the sales of its products in the future. For example, Pepsi might not know that a supermarket will be having a big promotion in three weeks for a new beverage

> **DID YOU KNOW?**
>
> Improvements in vendor-managed inventory can result in the elimination of between 20 and 30 percent of the previously required supply chain inventory.[27]

vendor-managed inventory (VMI) An approach for improving supply chain efficiency in which the vendor is responsible for maintaining the retailer's inventory levels in each of its stores.

consignment When the vendor owns the merchandise until it is sold by the retailer, at which time the retailer pays for the merchandise.

introduced by Coca-Cola. Without this knowledge, Pepsi would ship too much merchandise to the supermarket.

Collaborative Planning, Forecasting, and Replenishment

Collaborative planning, forecasting, and replenishment (CPFR) is the sharing of forecasts and related business information and collaborative planning between retailers and vendors to improve supply chain efficiency and product replenishment.[29] Although retailers share sales and inventory data when using a VMI approach, the vendor remains responsible for managing the inventory. In contrast, CPFR is a more advanced form of retailer–vendor collaboration that involves sharing proprietary information such as business strategies, promotion plans, new product developments and introductions, production schedules, and lead-time information. Retailing View 9.4 illustrates how West Marine uses CPFR to improve its supply chain efficiency.

Quick Response Delivery Systems

There are only two groups of retail businesses today: the quick and the dead.[30]

A **quick response (QR) delivery system** is an inventory management system designed to reduce the retailer's lead time for receiving merchandise, thereby lowering inventory investment, improving customer service levels, and reducing logistics expenses. QR is the integrating link between the information and the merchandise flows depicted in Exhibit 9–2.

Many of the concepts that comprise QR systems have been previously discussed in this chapter. In this section, however, we describe how they all work together. The origins of the present QR systems were derived from just-in-time (JIT) initiatives undertaken by manufacturers and adapted for retailing. QR is part of the efficient consumer response (ECR) initiatives undertaken by packaged goods manufacturers and food goods manufacturers and food

collaborative planning, forecasting, and replenishment (CPFR) A collaborative inventory management system in which a retailer shares information with vendors. CPFR software uses data to construct a computer-generated replenishment forecast that is shared by the retailer and vendor before it's executed.

quick response (QR) delivery system A system designed to reduce the lead time for receiving merchandise, thereby lowering inventory investment, improving customer service levels, and reducing distribution expenses; also known as a *just-in-time inventory management system.*

and drugstore retailers.[33] EDI facilitates the exchange of data between retailer and vendors.

Originally, quick response delivery systems seemed better suited to basic items—such as underwear, paper towels, or toothpaste—than to high fashion. By its nature, however, fashion dictates being able to adjust quickly to the changing seasons as well as to new colours and styles. Thus, quick response is as important in managing fashion inventories as in managing basic-item inventories. Fashion retailers need to determine what's selling (so it can be reordered quickly) and what isn't selling (so it can be marked down).

To illustrate a QR system, consider how the system works at Zara, which we discussed in Retailing View 9.1 earlier in this chapter.[34] Zara, located in Galicia, Spain, is now the third-largest clothing retailer in the world, with profits growing at 30 percent per year. It operates over 500 stores in 31 countries, including nine Canadian stores—in Toronto, Montreal, Quebec City, Calgary, and Vancouver.

Benefits of a QR System The benefits of a QR system are reduced lead time, increased product availability, lower inventory investment, and reduced logistics expenses.

Reduces Lead Time By eliminating the need for paper transactions using the mail, overnight deliveries, or even fax, EDI in the QR system reduces lead time. Lead time is the amount of time between the recognition that an order needs to be placed and its arrival in the store, ready for sale. Since the vendor's computer acquires the data electronically, no manual data entry is required on the recipient's end. As a result, lead time is reduced even more, and vendor recording errors are eliminated. Thus, use of EDI in the QR system can cut lead time by a week or more. Shorter lead times further reduce the need for inventory because the shorter the lead time, the easier it is to forecast demand; therefore, the retailer needs less inventory.

> **DID YOU KNOW?**
>
> A precursor to the Internet-based systems used for CPFR occurred in 1987 when Walmart and Procter & Gamble forged a partnership to control their inventory. The partnership program improved product availability, decreased inventory, and reduced costs, which Walmart passed on as savings to its customers in the form of lower prices.

> **DID YOU KNOW?**
>
> The QR code was invented in 1994 by the Denso Wave company to track the vehicle manufacturing process.[31]

West Marine Uses CPFR to Build a Competitive Advantage

Apparently, at one time, retailers believed that boaters liked dark, poorly organized stores and staffers who were better at telling stories than locating necessary items. Boating supply stores were just like that for many years—until West Marine decided to change the rules of the game.

The founder of the company, Randy Repass, envisioned great customer service provided to boaters who could stop by a single source for all their boating needs. The vision was clearly a good one, and West Marine has grown into a chain with more than 400 North American stores. These stores, along with West Marine's catalogue and Internet channels, provide everything from ropes to electronics, covering more than 50 000 SKUs.

For most boaters, the time to buy these supplies is during boating season: April through October. Unlike most retailers, which enjoy sales peaks during the holiday season, West Marine looks forward every year to the first long weekend of the summer. However, promotions offered frequently by suppliers also helped create substantial uncertainty in West Marine's demand predictions, which in turn led to lost sales due to supply chain inefficiencies.

West Marine uses CPFR to engage in collaborative planning and supply chain management with its vendors.

Courtesy of West Marine.

To deal with these inefficiencies and demand challenges, West Marine adopted collaborative planning, forecasting, and replenishment (CPFR) programs, in conjunction with most of its key suppliers. To start, it met with its key suppliers so that together they could develop better forecasts. The result was a system that collects daily SKU-level sales, together with store-level inventory information, then generates a year-long forecast that is specific to the level of demand that day, by store, and by SKU. West Marine then sends the forecast to its suppliers to help them schedule their production, and together they use the information to time their marketing and promotional events.

Because CPFR has become so integral to West Marine's merchandising and planning, it also has revised the retailer's organizational structure. Every category manager (CM) for West Marine works closely with a merchandise planner (MP). While the CM takes responsibility for vendor strategies and marketing links, the MP directs supply chain relationships. Together, these MPs and CMs host quarterly meetings with suppliers to update their supply chain planning, keeping the marketing, production, distribution, and transportation departments from both firms closely in the loop. In monthly meetings—to which all team members are invited—the planners also review recent CPFR results to identify any supply chain hindrances, plan new initiatives, and resolve any remaining concerns.

Sources: http://www.westmarine.com; Joel Wisner, Keah-Choon Tan, and G. Keong Leong, *Principles of Supply Chain Management: A Balanced Approach*, 3rd ed. (Mason, OH: Southwestern, 2011); T. Schoenherr and V. M. R. Tummala, "Best Practices for the Implementation of Supply Chain Management Initiatives," *International Journal of Logistics Systems and Management* 4, no. 4 (2008), pp. 391–410.

DID YOU KNOW?

More than 55 percent of Canadian retailers achieve on-time shipments of Canadian and US products, but only 4 percent of retailers achieve on-time shipments through low-cost country sourcing (LCCS).[32]

DID YOU KNOW?

Almost all food items are marked with a UPC bar code. In fact, Walmart's buying office has a sign reading:

IF YOUR PRODUCT DOESN'T HAVE A BAR CODE, DON'T BOTHER TO TAKE A CHAIR IN OUR WAITING ROOM.

radio frequency identification (RFID) A technology that allows an object or person to be identified at a distance by means of radio waves.

Increases Product Availability and Lowers Inventory Investment In general, as a retailer's ability to satisfy customer demand by being in stock increases, so does its inventory investment. Yet with QR, the ability to satisfy demand can actually increase while inventory decreases! Since the retailer can make purchase commitments or produce merchandise closer to the time of sale, its inventory investment is reduced. Stores need less inventory because they are getting less merchandise on each order, but they receive shipments more often. Inventory is further reduced because the retailer isn't forecasting sales so far into the future. For instance, fashion retailers that don't use QR make purchase commitments as much as six months in advance and receive merchandise far in advance of actual sales. QR systems align deliveries more closely with sales. The ability to satisfy customer demand by being in stock also increases in QR systems as a result of the more frequent shipments.

Reduces Logistics Expenses QR systems also have the potential to significantly reduce logistics expenses. Many retailers receive merchandise in their distribution centres, store it, consolidate shipments from multiple vendors, attach price labels and theft prevention devices, and then reship the merchandise to stores. Retailers have two options for reducing these logistics expenses using QR systems. They can either use a cross-docking warehouse system or they can negotiate a direct store delivery system. Cross-docking eliminates storage and some handling costs. Direct store delivery eliminates all distribution centre costs and transportation costs from the distibution centre to stores. If the merchandise is floor-ready, there's no need to devote expensive retail space to receiving and processing merchandise in the store, and sales associates can devote all of their attention to their customers.

Costs of a QR System Although retailers achieve great benefits from a QR system, it's not without costs. The logistics function has become much more complicated with more frequent deliveries. With greater order frequency come smaller orders, which are more expensive to transport. The greater order frequency also makes deliveries and transportation more difficult to coordinate.

QR systems also require a strong commitment by the retailer and its vendors to cooperate, share data, and develop systems such as EDI and CPFR. Successful QR systems not only require financial support from top management, but also a psychological commitment to become partners with their vendors. Large retailers often apply their power to get their vendors to absorb many of these expensive logistics costs.

Lo6 Electronic Communication Tools

Radio Frequency Identification

Radio frequency identification (RFID) is a technology that allows an object or person to be identified at a distance by means of radio waves. The RFID devices or tags are attached to containers, shipping cartons, or even behind labels on individual items. They then transmit data about the object in which they are embedded. RFID technology has two advantages over bar codes. First, the devices can hold more data and update the data stored. For instance, the device can keep track of where an item has been in the supply chain and even where it is stored in a distribution centre. Second, the data on the devices can be acquired in harsh environments without a visual line of sight—an environment in which bar-code labels won't work. Thus, RFID enables the accurate, real-time tracking of every single product, from manufacturer to checkout in the store. It also eliminates the manual point-and-read operations needed to get data from UPC bar codes. As a result, RFID can significantly decrease warehouse, distribution, and inventory costs; increase margins; and provide better in-stock positions.

Several retailers are already taking advantage of this new technology. Walmart has requested that its top suppliers put RFID tags on all pallets, cases, cartons, and high-margin items.[37] Metro (Germany's largest retailer), Target, Best Buy, and Albertson's are also experimenting with RFID programs.[38] To meet these demands, vendors have been forced to make significant investments to acquire the necessary technology and equipment.

Retailing View 9.5 describes how American Apparel innovated use of RFID on

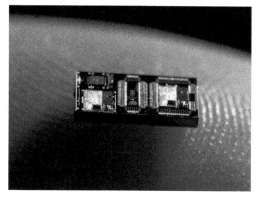

Data about an item or carton can be encoded into an RFID chip which then can be accessed remotely to determine the presence of the item and where it should be.

© Agencia Estado via AP Images.

individual items instead of cartons or pallets, which are the typical current application in retailing.

Types of RFID Tags

There are three types of RFID tags: active, semi-passive, and passive tags. Active and semi-passive RFID tags use internal batteries to power their circuitry. An active tag also uses its battery to broadcast radio waves to a reader, whereas a

---

9.5 **RETAILING VIEW**

RFID at American Apparel

Known for its "Made in Downtown LA" motto, American Apparel is accustomed to turning heads. The Los Angeles–based company's RFID push began with a pilot program at one of the firm's New York stores. Every one of the roughly 40 000 items in the store, from basic T-shirts to shiny gold lamé hot shorts, was RFID-tagged.

The objective of American Apparel's RFID system is to provide improved inventory accuracy and better-stocked sales floors. American Apparel has an unusual approach to merchandising. It puts only one of everything on the floor to give the appearance of selling unique merchandise—customers can buy something no one else will be wearing. But that means that once an item is sold, that particular SKU is out of stock on the sales floor. To restock the store, employees would periodically take a list of items sold from the POS system and make trips to the stockroom, where they would search for each item.

American Apparel saw quick benefits from the technology. As an item leaves the sales floor—because it has been sold, accidentally returned to the stockroom, or stolen—its departure is displayed at stockroom

American Apparel is experimenting with placing RFID tags on each item to ensure that all items are on display on store fixtures.

© Getty Images.

workstations, enabling workers to quickly get the item restocked. Personnel can easily keep the sales floor fully stocked. The time required to do the weekly process of taking inventory of items in the store was reduced from 32 to 4 hours. This gives employees more time to assist customers directly and carry out other tasks.

Sources: Claire Swedberg, "American Apparel Adds RFID to Two More Stores, Switches RFID Software," *RFID Journal*, Janurary 12, 2010; and Mary Catherine O'Connor, "American Apparel Makes a Bold Fashion Statement with RFID," *RFID Journal*, August 14, 2008.

DID YOU KNOW?

The average retailer's reverse logistics costs for consumer goods are equal to an average 8.1 percent of total sales.[35]

semi-passive tag relies on the reader to supply its power for broadcasting. Because these tags involve more hardware than passive RFID tags, they are more expensive.

Active and semi-passive tags are mostly used for costly items that require tracking from about 30 metres (100 feet) or more. When tags must be read from even farther away, additional batteries can increase a tag's range to over 90 metres (300 feet).

Passive RFID tags can be read from up to 6 metres (20 feet) away, and they have lower production costs, ranging from 7 to 20 cents each. The RFID industry is aiming to get the cost of a passive RFID tag down to 5 cents each once more retailers adopt them. These tags can be applied to less expensive merchandise such as cosmetics and some clothes. These tags are manufactured to be disposable, along with the disposable consumer goods on which they are placed.

DID YOU KNOW?

The smallest RFID tag is manufactured by Hitachi. It is 0.25 mm (.01 inches) square.[36]

Benefits of RFID

Some of the benefits of RFID include the following:

- **Reduced warehouse and distribution labour costs.** Warehouse and distribution costs typically represent 2 to 4 percent of operating expenses for retailers. Replacing point-and-read, labour-intensive operations with sensors that track pallets, cases, cartons, and individual products anywhere in the facility can significantly reduce labour costs by as much as 30 percent.

- **Reduced point-of-sale labour costs.** Using RFID at the product level can help retailers reduce the labour costs needed for checking shelf inventory. In addition, RFID-enabled products will improve self-scan checkouts and increase the use of self-scans, thus shortening checkout times and reducing employee fraud.

- **Inventory savings.** RFID reduces inventory errors, ensuring that the inventory recorded is actually available. By tracking pieces more exactly, companies have more accurate information about what was sold and what inventory is actually needed.

- **Elimination of counterfeit merchandise.** Using RFID on individual items can help eliminate counterfeit merchandise.[41] For example, California planned for pharmaceutical manufacturers to use RFID technology starting in January 2009 for its mass serialization and e-pedigree requirements; however, the deal was delayed and is scheduled to go into effect in a phased manner between 2015 and 2017. A drug pedigree is a statement of origin that identifies each prior sale, purchase, or trade of a drug, including the date of the transactions and the names and addresses of all parties to them.[42] The primary purpose of an e-pedigree is to protect consumers from contaminated medicine or counterfeit drugs. As the product moves down the supply chain, each company is required to carry forward all previous e-pedigree information. In this way, the final point of sale has the complete lineage of every unit. Such a system would require fairly significant changes to the company's data interchange. The use of RFID forms the basis of such a secured supply chain system. Oregon and New York, as well as France, Japan, and Spain, are all making moves toward similar legislation.

- **Reduced theft.** With RFID, products can be tracked through the supply chain to pinpoint where a product is at all times; this helps reduce theft in transportation, at distribution centres, or in stores. RFID has already been successfully deployed in stores, particularly on costly items prone to theft, such as Gillette Mach 3 razor blades.

- **Reduced out-of-stock conditions.** Because RFID facilitates accurate product tracking, forecasts are more accurate and thus stock-outs decrease. Using RFID, store managers can be automatically notified when specific SKUs are not on the shelves and need to be stocked, as noted in Retailing View 9.5.[43]

Impediments to the Adoption of RFID

A major obstacle to the widespread adoption of RFID has been the high costs, which make the present return on investment low. The cost of a passive RFID tag is 7 to 15 cents per tag.[44] However, with demand increasing and tag production costs declining, the tags are expected to reach only 5 cents per tag, and they may be reusable in some applications.

Another reason RFID has not been adopted by more retailers is that it generates more data than can be efficiently processed. As a result, retailers find it difficult to justify the implementation costs. Most retailers are not capable of transmitting, storing, and processing the data that would be available about the location of pallets, cases, cartons, totes, and individual products in the supply chain.

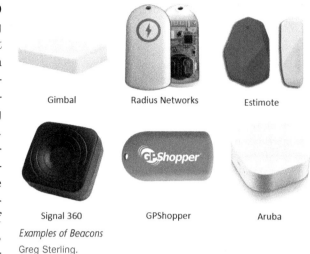

Gimbal Radius Networks Estimote

Signal 360 GPShopper Aruba

Examples of Beacons
Greg Sterling.

DID YOU KNOW?

Walmart found there were 21 percent fewer stockouts in test stores using RFID tags than in stores not using them.[39]

DID YOU KNOW?

Levi Strauss has been piloting the Intel Retail Sensor Platform—designed to make RFID deployments easier and provide real-time inventory data—in Levi's Plaza store, located at its headquarters in San Francisco.[40]

Vendors are pushing back as well. Some claim that instead of saving labour, RFID tagging actually increases it. Bar codes are printed on cases at the factory, but because most manufacturers have yet to adopt RFID, those tags have to be put on by hand at the warehouse.

Finally, consumers, particularly in the United States, are wary that once the tags are on individual items, they could be used to track individual buyers—an obvious invasion of privacy.[45] The problem is less acute in the European Union, where retailers have educated consumers on RFID use and changed procedures to accommodate consumers' fears by developing tag-removal policies. Germany's Metro and England's Marks & Spencer are both using item-level RFID on a limited basis.

Beacon Technology

Beacon technology is a new technology currently being considered by retailers across North America. This technology works with a consumer's smartphone (Bluetooth) and a electronic enabler (beacon) that the retailer locates on store shelves. These beacons read a consumer's smartphone from approximately 50 to 100 feet away. The device sends a message to the smartphone alerting the consumer of various promotions based on the proximity of the beacon.

Canadians seem to be ready for this new technology. Research by the Canadian Marketing Association (CMA) shows that consumers are ready to use beacon technology and understand the benefits. Of those surveyed, 56 percent said they have used the technology and 60 percent said they are more likely to engage with a retailer's location-based service app if they can set timing preferences on when notifications are sent.[46]

A few additional highlights from the research:

- An average of 86 percent of consumers are aware of beacons (rising to 91 percent of Gen Y and Gen X consumers).
- Consumers understand the benefits of beacon technology, and say the top benefit is receiving rewards relevant to their location (62 percent), followed by receiving alerts (56 percent).
- Almost half (45 percent) of mobile users who have used a device in-store said it led them to make an immediate purchase.[47]

Beacons and location-based services offer an opportunity for businesses looking to take their mobile messaging strategy to the next level. From a marketing perspective, it's about talking to your customers at the right time, place, and medium.[48]

Examples of beacons being used in Canada include the following:

- One of AIR MILES' partners launched a new program that uses in-store beacons to send its members exclusive mobile offers, allowing them to collect extra points on products at select locations in Toronto.
- Partygoers at the Maple Leafs team's draft party in June 2015 who had the Leaf app received special offers and were able to win prizes and interact with activities happening at the event.
- *Marketing* magazine reported in August 2014 that HBC was implementing beacons in five of its Canadian stores to shoppers who have downloaded the HBC gift registry app. The Retail Council of Canada points to a broader implementation throughout the stores more recently.[49]

SUMMARY

Supply chain management and information systems have become important tools for achieving a sustainable competitive advantage. Developing more efficient methods of distributing merchandise creates an opportunity to reduce costs and prices and ensure that the right merchandise is available when and where customers want it.

The systems used to control the flow of information to buyers and then on to vendors have become quite sophisticated. Retailers have developed data warehouses that provide them with intimate knowledge of who their customers are and what they like to buy. The data warehouses are being used to strengthen the relationships with their customers and improve the productivity of their marketing and inventory management efforts.

Most large retailers own and operate their own distribution centres. Some of the activities performed by the centre are managing inbound and outbound transportation, receiving and checking merchandise shipments, storing and cross-docking, and getting merchandise floor-ready.

In designing their supply chain management systems, retailers make decisions about what activities to outsource, when to use a push or pull system for replenishing stores, what merchandise to cross-dock, and whether to ship merchandise to stores through a distribution centre, use direct store delivery, or have products drop-shipped to customers.

Retailers and vendors are collaborating to improve supply chain efficiency. Electronic data interchange enables retailers to communicate electronically with their vendors. The Internet has accelerated the adoption of EDI. Other more involved and effective collaborative approaches include information sharing, VMI, CPFR, and QR. These approaches represent the nexus of information systems and logistics management. They reduce lead time, increase product availability, lower inventory investments, and reduce overall logistics expenses.

Finally, RFID has the potential of further streamlining the supply chain. The small RFID devices are affixed to pallets, cartons, and individual items and can be used to track merchandise through the supply chain and store information, such as when an item was shipped to a distribution centre. Although still relatively expensive to be placed on all items, RFID technology can reduce labour, theft, and inventory costs.

KEY TERMS

advance shipping notice (ASN)
bullwhip effect
checking
collaborative planning, forecasting,
    and replenishment (CPFR)
consignment
cross-docked
direct store delivery (DSD)
dispatcher
distribution centre

drop-shipping
electronic data interchange (EDI)
floor-ready merchandise
freight forwarders
logistics
outsource
pick ticket
public warehouses
pull supply chain
push supply chain

quick response (QR) delivery system
radio frequency identification (RFID)
receiving
reverse logistics
security policy
stockout
supply chain management
ticketing and marking
Universal Product Code (UPC)
vendor-managed inventory (VMI)

1. Interview the store manager working for a retailer. Write a report that describes and evaluates the retailer's information and supply chain systems. Use this chapter as a basis for developing a set of questions to ask the manager. For example: Where is the store's distribution centre? Does the retailer use direct store delivery from vendors? How frequently are deliveries made to the store? Does the merchandise come in ready for sale? What is the store's percentage of stockouts? Does the retailer use a push or pull system? Does the store get involved in determining what merchandise is in the store and in what quantities? Does the retailer use VMI, EDI, CPFR, or RFID?

2. INTERNET EXERCISE Go to Barcoding Incorporated's website at **http://www.barcoding. com** and search for retail, warehouse management, and RFID. How is this company using technology to support retailers with information systems and supply chain management?

3. INTERNET EXERCISE Go to the website of *Stores Magazine* at **http://www.stores.org** and search for supply chain in the current issue. Summarize one of the recent articles, and explain how the key concept(s) described could make the shopping experience better for consumers and improve efficiency in the supply chain.

4. INTERNET EXERCISE Go to the website of Vendor Managed Inventory at **http://www. vendormanagedinventory.com/index.php** and answer the following questions: What is vendor-managed inventory? What are the benefits and limitations of a vendor-managed inventory approach?

DISCUSSION QUESTIONS AND PROBLEMS

1. Retail system acronyms include DSD, VMI, EDI, CPFR, and RFID. How are these terms related to one another?

2. Explain how an efficient supply chain system can increase a retailer's level of product availability and decrease its inventory investment.

3. This chapter presents some trends in logistics and information systems that benefit retailers. How do vendors benefit from these trends?

4. What type of merchandise is most likely to be cross-docked at retailers' distribution centres? Why is this often the case?

5. Why haven't more fashion retailers adopted an integrated supply chain system similar to Zara's?

6. Explain the differences between pull and push supply chains.

7. Consumers have five key reactions to stockouts: buy the item at another store, substitute a different brand, substitute the same brand, delay the purchase, or do not purchase the item. Consider your own purchasing behaviour, and describe how various categories of merchandise would result in different reactions to a stockout.

8. Abandoned purchases as a result of stockouts can mean millions of dollars a year in lost sales. How are retailers and manufacturers using technology to reduce stockouts and improve sales?

9. What is a Universal Product Code (UPC)? How does this code enable manufacturers, distributors, and retailers to track merchandise throughout the supply chain?

10. Reread Retailing View 9.2 about Netflix. How has this online retailer modified their marketing strategy to stay current with the times?

CHAPTER TEN

Merchandise management

BUY NOW

LEARNING OBJECTIVES

Lo1   Examine how the buying process is organized.

Lo2   Examine the types of merchandise management planning processes retailers use to manage merchandise categories.

Lo3   Explore how retailers forecast sales.

Lo4   Determine what trade-offs retailers must make to ensure that stores carry the appropriate type and amount of merchandise.

Lo5   Review how retailers plan their assortments.

Lo6   Explore merchandise budget plans and open-to-buy systems, and how they are prepared.

Lo7   Review how multistore retailers allocate merchandise to stores.

Lo8   Explore how retailers analyze the profitability of their merchandising decisions.

SPOTLIGHT ON RETAILING

ALDO GROUP INC.: CANADIAN GLOBAL SUCCESS STORY

Aldo is a household name in Canada that is synonymous with trendy shoes, but it is also "the most successful global retailer that Canada has ever built," according to Tim McGuire, a senior partner at consultancy McKinsey & Co., which has advised Aldo. Aldo Bensadoun, the son of a retailer who operated a small chain of shoe stores in France and Morocco and the grandson of a cobbler, completed his university studies at McGill University in Montreal. A degree in economics led him to a marketing research position, which found Bensadoun doing a project for a regional shoe chain. Eventually, the combination of past family history in the shoe business, knowledge of Canadian population trends, and smart business sense led him to open his own company.

The company had humble beginnings in 1972 in Montreal as a concession within Le Chateau clothing stores. By the end of 1972 his brand had reached several provinces including Quebec (Montreal and Quebec City), Ontario (Ottawa), and Manitoba (Winnipeg). He started his Aldo chain in 1980, rushing to find the next new fashion at an affordable cost—in effect, practising fast fashion before the industry coined the term. Today, Aldo is still a privately-held company, operating over 1900 stores across all continents except Antarctica. The Canadian, American, Irish, and UK stores are corporate stores, while the other international stores are franchises. The Aldo Group currently has five brands, each catering to a distinct market segment: Aldo (the flagship brand, which represents approximately 1450 of the 1900 stores), Aldo Rise, Mr. B's, Call it Spring, and Globo. Further, the company boasts average sales per square foot of more than $1000 in Canada, which is more than twice that of other mall shoe chains.

Aldo primarily sells private-label, fashion-oriented shoes designed and made for the company banners. Analyzing population groups provides design inspiration; in fact, trends are often influenced by the environment, politics, and economics. The design team researches clothing designs and magazines to interpret the trends in footwear. Once it finds a workable idea, the Aldo Group requires a mere 5 to 12 weeks to get shoes to stores, compared with an industry average of 17 weeks.

Here in North America, the Aldo Group's rapidly increasing competition, such as Payless ShoeSource, Walmart, H&M, and Zara, is putting pressure on the company to find new avenues for growth and sharpen its fast-fashion (cheap-chic) strategy. Head office now receives hourly—rather than weekly—sales data, allowing it to make faster decisions about restocking top sellers and ditching losers. The speedy updates also shave the time it takes to get shoes on the shelf by as much as 30 percent.

© Wing Ho Tsang | Dreamstime.com.

Wanting to expand in North America without the huge spending required to open new stores, Mr. Bensadoun's solution was to wholesale products to other retailers. In 2011, he struck deals with Kohl's, JCPenney, Hudson's Bay, and Zappos.com to supply private-label and exclusive footwear and accessories. For instance, in hopes of attracting the 12- to 25-year-old demographic that is fashion obsessed and budget savvy, JCPenney launched a new 350- to 500-square-foot in-house shop that sells some 300 styles of women's and men's Aldo Call It Spring line. The in-house shop includes a line of Aldo handbags in addition to an Aldo shoe collection with the most expensive piece topping out at $59.99.

In March 2015, Joe Fresh announced a global licence agreement that will see Aldo Group design, produce, and distribute its line of shoes. Montreal-based Aldo Group will deliver lines of women's, men's and children's footwear in time for the Spring 2016 season. The designs will include casual and fashion styles, as well as boots.

Truly a success story, Aldo Bensadoun is one of Canada's richest retailers with revenue of almost $2 billion in 2013. Bensadoun continues to grow his fast-fashion shoe empire with quality and cutting-edge trends at affordable prices, season after season, in Canada and around the world.

Sources: Marina Strauss, "Aldo's Global Footprint," *The Globe and Mail*, September 3, 2010, http://www.theglobeandmail.com/report-on-business/small-business/sb-growth/going-global/aldos-global-footprint/article601117/?page=all (accessed September 27, 2012); "Aldo Culture," Aldo, http://www.aldoshoes.com/ca-eng/culture (accessed September 27, 2012); Sarah St. Lifer, "JCPenney Launches 'Call It Spring' Collection with Aldo Shoes," *StyleList*, March 2, 2011, http://main.stylelist.com/2011/03/02/jcpenney-launches-call-it-spring-collection-with-aldo-shoes/ (accessed September 27, 2012); http://www.Aldoshoes.com (accessed February 6, 2016); *CBC News*, March 26, 2015, http://www.cbc.ca/news/business/aldo-group-makes-deal-to-design-shoe-line-for-joe-fresh-1.3010625 (accessed Febrary 6, 2016); http://www.aldogroup.com/timeline.html (accessed April 21, 2016).

LO1 Organizing the Buying Process

Merchandise management activities are undertaken primarily by buyers and their superiors, divisional merchandise managers (DMMs), and general merchandise managers (GMMs). Many people view these jobs as very exciting and glamorous. They think that buyers spend most of their time trying to identify the latest fashions and trends, attending designer shows replete with celebrities in Paris and Milan, and going to rock concerts and other glamorous events to see what the trendsetters are wearing. But in reality, the lives of retail buyers are more like those of Wall Street investment analysts than globe-trotting trend spotters.

Investment analysts manage a portfolio of stocks. They buy stocks in companies they think will increase in value and sell stocks in companies they believe do not have a promising future. They continuously monitor the performance of the stocks they own to see which are increasing in value and which are decreasing. Sometimes they make mistakes and invest in companies that do not perform well. So they sell their stock in these companies and lose money, but they use the money from the sold stocks to buy more attractive stocks. Other times, the stocks they buy increase dramatically in price, and they wish they had bought more shares.

Rather than managing a portfolio of stocks, retail buyers manage a portfolio of merchandise inventory. They buy merchandise they think will be popular with their customers. Like investment analysts, they use an information system to monitor the performance of their merchandise portfolio—to see what is selling and what is not. Retail buyers also make mistakes. When the merchandise they bought is not selling well, they get rid of it by putting it on sale so that they can use the money to buy better-selling merchandise. However, they also might take a chance and buy a lot of a new product and be rewarded when it sells well, while competitors, who were more conservative, don't have enough of the product.

Merchandise management is the process by which a retailer attempts to offer the right quantity of the right merchandise in the right place at the right time and meet the

merchandise management The process by which a retailer attempts to offer the right quantity of the right merchandise in the right place at the right time while meeting the company's financial goal.

company's financial goals. Buyers need to be in touch with and anticipate what customers will want to buy, but this ability to sense market trends is just one skill needed to manage merchandise inventory effectively. Perhaps an even more important skill is the ability to analyze sales data continually and make appropriate adjustments in prices and inventory levels.

The first part of this chapter provides the background needed to understand the merchandise management process. In this introduction, we discuss how the process is organized, who makes the merchandise decisions, and how merchandise management performance is evaluated. The last part of the chapter examines the steps in the merchandise management process—forecasting sales, formulating an assortment plan, determining the appropriate inventory level, developing a merchandise management plan, allocating merchandise to stores, and monitoring performance. Other activities involved in merchandise management are reviewed in subsequent chapters, including buying merchandise (Chapter 11) and pricing (Chapter 12).

Merchandise Management Overview

This section provides an overview of the merchandise management process, including the organization of a retailer's merchandise management activities, the objectives and measures used to evaluate merchandise management performance, the differences in the process for managing fashion and seasonal merchandise versus basic merchandise, and the steps in the merchandise management process. In the following section, we review each of the steps in the merchandise management process.

The Buying Organization

Every retailer has its own system for grouping categories of merchandise, but the basic structure of the buying organization is similar for most retailers. Exhibit 10–1 illustrates this basic structure by depicting the organization of the merchandise division for a department store chain such as Holt Renfrew or Hudson's Bay. Exhibit 10–1 shows the organization of buyers in the merchandise division. A similar structure for planners parallels the structure for buyers.

Exhibit 10–1

Standard Merchandise Classification Scheme and Organizational Chart

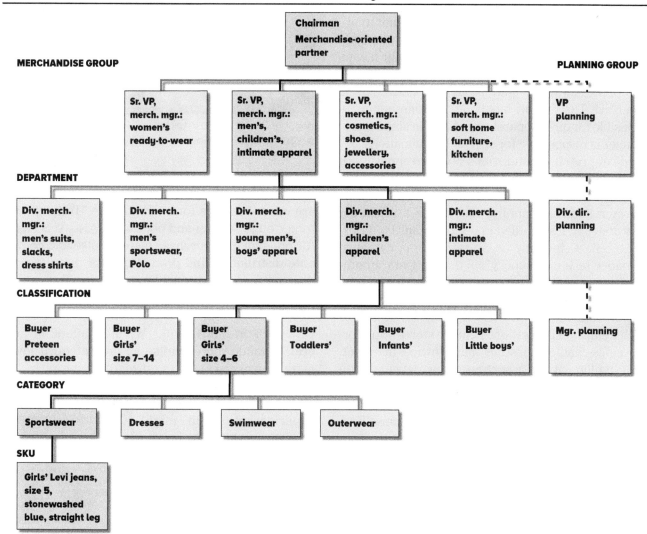

Merchandise Group The highest classification level is the **merchandise group**. The organizational chart shown in Exhibit 10–1 has four merchandise groups: (1) women's apparel; (2) men's, children's, and intimate apparel; (3) cosmetics, shoes, jewellery, and accessories; and (4) home and kitchen. Each of the four merchandise groups is managed by a general merchandise manager (GMM), who is often a senior vice president in the firm. Each of the GMMs is responsible for several departments. For example, the GMM for men's, children's, and intimate apparel makes decisions about how the merchandise inventory is managed in five departments: men's dress apparel, men's sportswear, young men's apparel, children's apparel, and intimate apparel.

Department The second level in the merchandise classification scheme is the **department**. Departments are managed by divisional merchandise managers

(DMMs). For example, the DMM highlighted in Exhibit 10–1 is in charge of children's apparel and manages the buyers responsible for six merchandise departments.

Classification The classification is the third level for categorizing merchandise and organizing merchandise management activities. Each divisional merchandise manager is responsible for a number of buyers or category managers. The children's apparel divisional merchandise manager in the exhibit is responsible for six buyers. Each buyer purchases a **classification**—a

merchandise group
A group within an organization managed by the senior vice presidents of merchandise and responsible for several departments.

department A segment of a store with merchandise that represents a group of classifications the consumer views as being complementary.

classification
A group of items or SKUs for the same type of merchandise, such as pants (as opposed to jackets or suits), supplied by different vendors.

group of items or SKUs for the same type of merchandise (such as men's pants as opposed to men's jackets or suits) supplied by different vendors. A stock keeping unit (SKU) is the smallest unit available for keeping inventory control. In soft goods merchandise, for instance, an SKU usually means size, colour, and style. For example, a pair of girls' size 5, stonewashed blue, straight-legged Levi's is one SKU. The exhibit highlights the one buyer responsible for girls' apparel sizes 4 to 6. In some cases, a buyer is responsible for several classifications.

Many retail organizations divide responsibility for buying merchandise between a buyer or category manager and a merchandise planner. Since the merchandise planning function is a relatively new concept, it's handled in various ways by different retailers. In some organizations, the category manager or buyer supervises the planners; in others, they are equal partners.

The planners' role is more analytical. They are responsible for buying the correct quantities of each item, allocating those items to stores, monitoring sales, and suggesting markdowns. In effect, they implement the assortment plan developed by the buyer. Together, the buyer and planner are the merchandising team. This team attempts to maximize the sales and profits of the entire classification, not just a particular category or brand.

Merchandise Category: The Planning Unit

The merchandise category is the basic unit of analysis for making merchandising management decisions. A **merchandise category** is an assortment of items that customers see as substitutes for one another. For example, a department store might offer a wide variety of girls' dresses sizes 4 to 6 in different colours, styles, and brand names. A mother buying a dress for her daughter might consider the entire set of dresses when making her purchase decision. Lowering the price on one dress may increase the sales of that dress but also decrease the sales of other dresses. Thus, the buyers' decisions about pricing and promoting specific SKUs in the category will affect the sales of other SKUs in the same category.

Some retailers may define categories in terms of brands. For example, Tommy Hilfiger might be one category and Polo/Ralph Lauren another

merchandise category
An assortment of items (SKUs) the customer sees as reasonable substitutes for each other.

How many SKUs are there in this picture?
Courtesy of Fleming Companies, Inc.

category because the retailer feels that the brands are not substitutes for each other. A "Tommy" customer buys Tommy and not Ralph. Also, it is easier for one buyer to purchase merchandise and coordinate distribution and promotions for the merchandise offered by a national-brand vendor. Typically, a buyer manages several categories of merchandise.

Category Management While retailers, in general, manage merchandise at the category level, many supermarkets organize their merchandise management around brands or vendors. For instance, a supermarket chain might have three different buyers for breakfast cereals—one each for Kellogg's, General Mills, and General Foods.[2] Managing merchandise within a category by brand can lead to inefficiencies because it fails to consider the interdependencies between SKUs in the category. For example, the three breakfast cereal buyers for a supermarket chain, one for each major brand, might each decide to stock a new product line of gluten-free breakfast cereals offered by Kellogg, General Mills, and General Foods. However, if the brand-organized buyers had taken a category-level perspective, they would have realized that the market for wheat-free cereals is limited and that the supermarket would generate more sales by stocking one brand of gluten-free cereals and using the space set aside for the other wheat-free cereal brands to stock a locally-produced cereal that has a strong following among some customers. The category management approach to managing merchandise assigns one buyer or

DID YOU KNOW?

Days inventory outstanding measures the average number of days that a company holds its inventory before selling it. Nordstrom's days inventory outstanding of 68.01 is much lower than that of its peers. For instance, Neiman Marcus and Macy's have days inventory outstanding of 121.30 and 118.23, respectively.[1]

category manager to oversee all merchandising activities for the entire category. **Category management** can help ensure that the store's assortment includes the "best" combination of sizes and vendors—the one that will get the most profit from the allocated space.[3]

Category Captain   Some retailers select a vendor to help them manage a particular category. The vendor, known as the **category captain**, works with the retailer to develop a better understanding of shopping behaviour, create assortments that satisfy consumer needs, and improve the profitability of the merchandise category.[4] Selecting vendors as category captains has its advantages for retailers. It makes merchandise management tasks easier and can increase profits. Vendors are often in a better position to manage a category than are retailers as they have superior information because of their focus on a specific category. In addition, they have acquired insights from managing the category for other retailers.

A potential problem with establishing a vendor as a category captain is that the vendor could take advantage of its position. Suppose, for example, that Frito-Lay chose to maximize its own sales, rather than the retailer's sales, in managing the salty snack category. It could suggest an assortment plan that included most of its SKUs and exclude SKUs that are more profitable to the retailer, such as high-margin, private-label SKUs. Thus, retailers are becoming increasingly reluctant to turn over these important decisions to their vendors. They have found that working with their vendors and carefully evaluating their suggestions is a much more prudent approach.[5] There are also antitrust considerations. The vendor category captain could collude with the retailer to fix prices. It could also block other brands, particularly smaller ones, from access to shelf space.[6]

Stock Keeping Unit (SKU)   A **stock keeping unit (SKU)** is the smallest unit available for inventory control. In soft-goods merchandise, for instance, an SKU usually means a particular size, colour, and style. For example, a pair of size 5, stonewashed, blue, straight-legged Levi's jeans is an SKU.

Lo2   Merchandise Management Process

Buyers forecast category sales, develop an assortment plan for merchandise in the category, and determine the amount of inventory needed to support the forecasted sales and assortment plan. Then, buyers develop a plan outlining the sales expected for each month, the inventory needed to support the sales, and the money that can be spent on replenishing sold merchandise and buying new merchandise. Along with developing the plan, the buyers or planners decide what type and how much merchandise should be allocated to each store. Having developed the plan, the buyer negotiates with vendors and buys the merchandise. Merchandise buying activities are reviewed in Chapter 11.

Finally, buyers continually monitor the sales of merchandise in the category and make adjustments. For example, if category sales are less than the forecast in the plan and the projected gross margin return on inventory investment (GMROI) for the category falls below the buyer's goal, the buyer may decide to dispose of some merchandise by putting it on sale. The buyer would then use the money generated to buy merchandise with greater sales potential or to reduce the number of SKUs in the assortment to increase inventory turnover.

Although Exhibit 10–2 suggests that these decisions follow each other sequentially, in practice some decisions may be made at the same time or in a different order. For example, a buyer might first decide on the amount of inventory to invest in the category, and this decision might determine the number of SKUs that can be offered in the category.

Retailers use different types of merchandise management planning systems for managing staple merchandise categories compared to fashion and seasonal merchandise categories.

Staple Merchandise Categories   A **staple merchandise category**, also called a basic merchandise category, is a category that is in continuous demand over an extended time period. While consumer packaged-goods companies introduce many line extensions each year, the number of really new product introductions each year in these categories

category management The process of managing a retail business with the objective of maximizing the sales and profits of a category.

category captain A supplier that forms an alliance with a retailer to help gain consumer insight, satisfy consumer needs, and improve the performance and profit potential across the entire category.

stock keeping unit (SKU) The smallest unit available for keeping inventory control. In soft goods merchandise, an SKU usually means a size, colour, and style.

staple merchandise category A category of inventory that has continuous demand by customers over an extended period of time; also called *basic merchandise category.*

Exhibit 10–2
Merchandise Planning Process

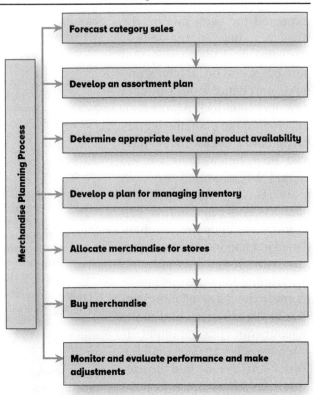

Merchandise Planning Process

- Forecast category sales
- Develop an assortment plan
- Determine appropriate level and product availability
- Develop a plan for managing inventory
- Allocate merchandise for stores
- Buy merchandise
- Monitor and evaluate performance and make adjustments

continuous replenishment A system of continuously monitoring merchandise sales and generating replacement orders, often automatically, when inventory levels drop below predetermined levels.

fashion merchandise category Category of merchandise that typically lasts several seasons, and sales can vary dramatically from one season to the next.

seasonal merchandise category Category of inventory whose sales fluctuate dramatically according to the time of the year.

is limited. Some examples of staple merchandise categories include most categories sold in supermarkets, as well as white paint, copy paper, basic casual apparel such as T-shirts, and men's underwear.

Because sales of staple merchandise are fairly steady from week to week, it is relatively easy to forecast demand, and the consequences of making mistakes in forecasting are not great. For example, if a buyer overestimates the demand for canned soup and buys too much, the retailer will have excess inventory for a short period of time. Eventually, the canned soup will be sold without having to resort to discounts or special marketing efforts. Because the demand for staple merchandise is predictable, merchandise planning systems for staple categories often involve **continuous replenishment**. These systems involve continuously monitoring merchandise sales and generating replacement orders, often automatically, when inventory levels drop below predetermined levels.

DID YOU KNOW?

A smartphone has an average life expectancy of approximately 24 months.

Fashion Merchandise Categories A **fashion merchandise category** is in demand only for a relatively short period of time. New products are continually introduced into these categories, making the existing products obsolete. In some cases, the basic product does not change, but the colours and styles change to reflect what is "hot" that season. Some examples of fashion merchandise categories are athletic shoes, smartphones, and women's apparel. Retailing View 10.1 describes how Mango creates and manages its fashion merchandise assortments.

Forecasting the sales for fashion merchandise categories is much more challenging than for staple categories. Buyers for fashion merchandise categories have much less flexibility in correcting forecasting errors. For example, if the laptop computer buyer for Best Buy buys too many units of a particular model, the excess inventory cannot be easily sold when a new upgraded model is introduced. Due to the short selling season for fashion merchandise, buyers often do not have a chance to reorder additional merchandise after an initial order is placed. So, if buyers initially order too little fashion merchandise, the retailer may not be able to satisfy the demand for the merchandise and will develop a reputation for not having the most popular merchandise in stock. Thus, an important objective of merchandise planning systems for fashion merchandise categories is to be as close to out of stock as possible at the same time that the SKUs become out of fashion.

Seasonal Merchandise Categories A **seasonal merchandise category** consists of items whose sales fluctuate dramatically depending on the time of year. Some examples of seasonal merchandise are Halloween candy, Christmas ornaments, swimwear, and snow shovels. Both staple and fashion merchandise can be seasonal categories. For example, swimwear is a fashion merchandise category, and snow shovels are a staple merchandise category. Thus, seasonal merchandise

DID YOU KNOW?

Even toilet paper has seasonal influences. Fancy toilet paper sells better during the holiday season between Thanksgiving and New Year's, since people have guests in their homes.

Fast Fashion at Mango

"We know how to improvise," says David Egea, Mango's merchandising director and a top executive. "To react and have what people want, we have to break some rules." Mango/MNG Holding SL, with over 2060 stores in 104 countries, including the United States and Canada, typifies the new retail trend of "fast fashion," pioneered by Spain's Zara and Sweden's H&M. These chains fill their racks with a steady stream of new, gotta-have-it merchandise. The company's retail strategy combines stylistic and technological resources built on flexibility and speed, from design sketch to the store shelf.

Mango is famous for an eclectic mix of body-hugging styles. A black pinstriped jacket sells for $60 and a black mini-dress for $40. The retailer maintains tight controls over the design and manufacturing of its private-label merchandise. Last-minute changes, like substituting a fabric or dropping a hemline, are a built-in part of the creative process. As long as the company has fabric in stock, it can move a design from sketchpad to store in four weeks.

Mango's merchandise planning cycle begins every three months when designers meet to discuss important new trends for each of its main collections, which contain five or six mini-collections. So, shops receive a near-constant stream of new merchandise, ranging from short dresses to office-wear and sparkly evening gowns. New items are sent to its stores once a week, roughly six times as often as the typical North American clothing chain.

To get ideas for each collection, designers attend the traditional fashion shows and trade fairs. But they also stay close to the customer. They take photos of stylish young women and note what people are wearing on the streets and in nightclubs. "To see what everyone's going to do for next season is very easy," says Egea. "But that doesn't mean this is the thing that is going to catch on." Hoping to stay *au courant*, design teams meet each week to adjust to ever-changing trends. Mango commissioned Penelope Cruz and her sister Monica to design a 25-piece collection to compete with the other fast-fashion companies that have used celebrities as designers. For example, Top Shop released its Kate Moss collection and H&M came out with a Madonna collection.

When collection designs are set, Mango's product management and distribution team assigns them personality

Mango stocks high-fashion, trendy merchandise to attract its target shoppers.
© Getty Images.

traits, denoting SKUs as trendy, dressy, or suitable for hot weather. Depending on an item's personality, it heads to one of Mango's 2060 stores, which also has its own set of traits, such as the climate, where the shop is located, and whether large or small sizes sell best. A proprietary computer program then matches compatible shops and styles.

Orders are sent to a distribution centre where clothes are scanned and dropped into one of 466 store-specific slots. Then they are boxed and shipped to shops, where managers can adjust store layouts daily on the basis of input from regional supervisors and headquarters. Mango stores display only a limited merchandise assortment. On each rack, only one size per item is hung. This policy encourages a sense of urgency by playing on customers' worst fear: Maybe your size is going to run out.

Sources: Erin White, "For Retailer Mango, Frenzied 'Fast Fashion' Proves Sweet," *Wall Street Journal*, May 28, 2004; http://www.mangoshop.com (accessed September 18, 2007); Beth Wilson, "Mango's Fast-Fashion Approach To Expansion," *WWD*, December 7, 2006, p. 23; Sally Raikes, "Cruz Control," *Scotland on Sunday*, September 16, 2007 (accessed September 18, 2007); Mango Worldwide, http://shop.mango.com/iframe.faces?state=she_404_IN (accessed February 7, 2016).

has characteristics of both fashion and staple merchandise.

However, from a merchandise planning perspective, retailers buy seasonal merchandise in much the same way that they buy fashion merchandise. Retailers could store unsold snow shovels at the end of the winter season and sell them the next winter, but it is typically more profitable to sell the shovels at a steep discount near the end of the season rather than incur the cost of carrying this excess inventory until the beginning of the next season. Thus, plans for seasonal merchandise, like fashion merchandise, zero out merchandise at the end of the season.

These two different merchandise planning systems affect the nature of the approaches used to forecast and manage inventory.

Lo4 Forecasting Sales

As indicated in Exhibit 10–2, the first step in merchandise management planning is to develop a forecast for category sales. The methods and information used for forecasting staple and fashion merchandise categories are discussed in this section.

Category Life Cycles

When developing a sales forecast, a retailer must be able to predict how well product categories will sell over time. Product categories typically follow a predictable sales pattern—sales start off low, increase, plateau, and then ultimately decline. Yet the shape of that pattern varies considerably from category to category and will help buyers forecast sales. This section describes the most fundamental form of sales pattern: the category life cycle. Using the category life cycle as a basis, we will examine some commonly found variations on it: fad, fashion, staple, and seasonal.

In the retail industry, **forecast** is the term used for forecasting short-term sales and other financial factors based on current business conditions. For example, a six-month merchandise plan is created six to nine months

forecast To estimate or calculate in advance; predict the future.

category life cycle A merchandise category's sales pattern over time.

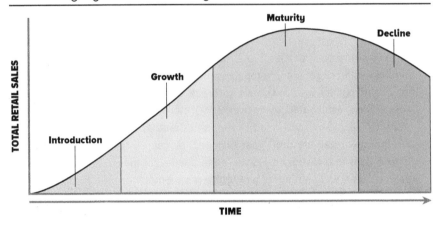

Exhibit 10–3
The Category Product Life Cycle

prior to the beginning of the season. As the season begins and business starts to occur, planners will forecast sales, markdowns, etc. for the current month and perhaps the following two months as well. This process measures the actual results against the original plan and helps the merchandise teams manage and assess their original plan objectives. In summary, the term often used is *plan* or *budget*.

The **category life cycle** describes a merchandise category's sales pattern over time. The category life cycle (Exhibit 10–3) is divided into four stages: introduction, growth, maturity, and decline. Knowing where a category, or specific item within a category, is in its life cycle is important in developing a sales forecast and merchandising strategy.

When personal digital assistants (PDAs) were first introduced in 1996, the target market was businesspeople who were high-tech aficionados, people who wanted to be first in adopting an innovation and were willing to pay for the convenience of having a very small computer.[7] PDAs were very expensive compared to paper address and appointment books, and they weren't available at all stores that normally sell office supplies or computers. PDAs were next marketed to doctors, stockbrokers, and business executives, who used them for access to medical databases, stock markets, and email. As categories reach the growth and maturity stages, they usually appeal to broader, mass-market customers who patronize discount stores and category specialists.

Knowing where a category is in its life cycle is useful for predicting sales. However, the shape of the life cycle can be affected by the activities undertaken by retailers and vendors. For instance, a vendor might set a low introductory price for a new product to increase the adoption rate of the product, or set a high price to increase profits even though sales might not grow as quickly. Care must be taken, however, that use of the category life cycle as a predictive tool does not adversely affect sales. If a product is classified as being in decline, it's likely that retailers will stock less variety and limit promotions. Naturally, sales will go down. Thus, the decline classification may actually become a self-fulfilling prophecy. Many products have been successfully maintained at the maturity stage because their buyers have maintained innovative strategies that are consistent with a mature product. For instance, Kellogg's Corn Flakes has been the best-selling ready-to-eat cereal over many decades because it has innovative advertising and competitive pricing.

Variations on the Category Life Cycle

Most categories follow the basic form of the category life cycle: sales increase, peak, and then decline. Variations on the category life cycle—fad, fashion, staple, and seasonal—are shown in Exhibit 10–4. The distinguishing characteristics between them are whether the category lasts for many seasons, whether a specific style sells for many seasons, and whether sales vary dramatically from one season to the next. Life cycle trends can impact many different categories. For example, consider the popular colours for kitchen appliances, cars, and paint for home items such as bathroom fixtures that have now become jewellery for the home. A *fad* is a merchandise category that generates a lot of sales for a relatively short time—often less than a season. Examples are Pogs, Furbys, Pokémon, butterfly hair clips, and some licensed characters such as Star Wars action figures. More mainstream examples are certain computer games, new electronic equipment, and some apparel, such as cropped and flared jeans. Fads are primarily aimed at children and teens.

Fads are often illogical and unpredictable. The art of managing a fad comes in recognizing the fad in its earliest stages and immediately locking up distribution rights for merchandise to stores nationwide before the competition does. Marketing fads is one of the riskiest ventures in retailing because even if the company properly identifies a fad, it must still have the sixth sense to recognize the peak

Exhibit 10–4

Variations in Category Life Cycles

	FAD	FASHION	STAPLE
Sales over many seasons	No	Yes	Yes
Sales of a specific style over many seasons	No	No	Yes
Sales vary dramatically from one season to the next	No	Yes	No
Illustration (Sales against Time)			

so that it can bail out before it's stuck with a warehouse full of merchandise.

Unlike a fad, a *fashion* is a category of merchandise that typically lasts several seasons, and sales can vary dramatically from one season to the next. A fashion is similar to a fad in that a specific style or SKU sells for one season or less. A fashion's lifespan depends on the type of category and the target market. For instance, double-breasted suits for men or certain colours are fashions with a life that may last several years. On the other hand, fashions such as see-through track shoes may last only a season or two. Retailing View 10.1, from earlier in this chapter, describes how Mango creates and manages fashion merchandise.

Some questions that help buyers distinguish between fads and more enduring fashions are as follows:

- **Is it compatible with a change in consumer lifestyles?** Innovations that are consistent with lifestyles will endure. For example, certain jeans are an enduring fashion because they are comfortable to wear and can be worn on multiple occasions. Leather pants, on the other hand, can be hot and heavy, and are typically worn in the evening. They are a fad.

- **Does the innovation provide real benefits?** The switch to poultry and fish from beef is not a fad because it provides real benefits to a health-conscious society.

- **Is the innovation compatible with other changes in the marketplace?** For example, shorter skirts that resulted in a greater emphasis on women's hosiery are declining due to the growing emphasis on casual apparel.

Athleisure—Fad or Fashion for the Long Haul?

A fleeting trend or a cultural shift? That is the question everyone is asking about the popularity of athleisure clothing. It is everywhere—in gyms, yoga studios, coffee shops, grocery stores, restaurants, playgrounds, shopping malls, and airports. It can even be found in some shape or form in the workplace.

But in three to five years, will consumers grow tired of this category and cast it aside for something entirely different? No one is absolutely sure how long the athleisure trend will be around, but most agree it has room to grow and could morph into other categories.

"The real trends that last, I think, come from deeper things and typically fill a void," said Jane Buckingham, president of Trendera, a Beverly Hills trend forecasting and brand-strategy company. "I think this athleisure category is actually filling a void and, therefore, will stick around for a while. The void it fills is that area in between workwear and casualwear that is shorts, T-shirts, and really unattractive sweatpants."

In some ways, the athleisure category got its first peek at fashion when Pamela Skaist-Levy and Gela Nash-Taylor launched Juicy Couture in Los Angeles in 1997. Those bedazzled velour track suits sold for $200 and were worn by everyone who was anyone—from celebrity and model Paris Hilton to megawatt entertainer Madonna. The brightly hued suits were accessorized with lots of bling and high-rise heels and were accepted everywhere.

© The Canadian Press/Darryl Dyck.

Yoga saw a renewed surge in popularity in the United States about a decade ago. As yoga pants became a staple in many women's (and men's) wardrobes, a new trend called athleisure began to take root.

And every designer seems to be adding his or her twist to the trend. Kate Spade has partnered with Beyond Yoga to produce a clothing line featuring 16 new items, including leggings, bras, and camis, debuting in 2016.

Stella McCartney and Adidas have collaborated on fashionable fitness collections for years, but earlier this year, the designer and the athletic brand joined forces to launch a new, more-affordable athleisure line called StellaSport.

Staying Power? But how long will this trend continue? "I think athleisure is here to stay in one form or

---

- **Who adopted the trend?** If it is not adopted by large, growing segments such as working mothers, Baby Boomers, Generation Y, or the elderly, it is not likely to endure. Alternatively, if it is being adopted by teenagers, who are known to be fickle in their tastes, it is likely to fade quickly.

Items within the *staple* merchandise, also called basic merchandise, category are in continuous demand over an extended period of time. Even certain brands of basic merchandise, however, ultimately go into decline. Most merchandise in grocery stores, as well as housewares, hosiery, and women's intimate apparel are considered to be staple merchandise.

another," noted Clare Varga, director of active at British trend forecaster WGSN. "The reason I think that is because athleisure is a cultural trend and not a fashion trend. It is underpinned by a cultural change to healthy lifestyles and a demand for clothing that is comfortable and functional and will take you from desk to disco. That is what gives it its longevity."

Varga said athleisure is now a natural way of dressing for the millennial generation between the ages of 18 and 34. "They grew up with health and well-being," Varga said.

People have fitness apps on their smartphones and smart watches and wear bracelets that measure their heart rate. Juice bars are popping up on every corner, and organic food is now part of mainstream grocery stores.

Trend forecasters observe that athleisure is a natural sweet spot between fashion and sportswear, which hasn't been lost on big retail chains such as Dillard's. The Arkansas-based chain just launched Trina Turk Recreation, created by the Los Angeles designer who lends her name to the label. "It is very colourful, great quality, and eye catching," said Annemarie Dillard, the store's director of contemporary sportswear and online experience.

With many years of watching trends, Dillard doesn't see athleisure as a trend but rather as a shift in the evolution of people's wardrobes. "I think it has staying power and fits with the whole movement that is going on in the modern woman's life—focusing on health and wellness in general. Apparel is a part of the transformation," she said.

With more than 300 outposts across the country, Dillard's is launching its own athleisure component with its private label Gianni Bini. "Athleisure is just as popular in middle America as anywhere. I can tell you that," Dillard said. "We are pleased with its growth."

The athleisure category has become a staple on the online shopping site ShopBop, too. "With major brands like Alexander Wang and Mara Hoffman designing activewear collections, the trend shows no signs of slowing down," said Lauren Edelstein, ShopBop's style director.

Athleisure sales have mushroomed, taking a bite out of denim sales. According to The NPD Group, men's and women's activewear sales, which include tops, bottoms, and athleisure, were up 17 percent to $35.4 billion for the year ending June 2015. During the same period, men's and women's sales of blue jeans were down 4 percent to $13.1 billion.

Room to Grow Athleisure is only the beginning, many say, of a movement to fuse fashion with athletics. Denim makers, envious of athleisure's popularity, are eyeing ways to incorporate some of those technical fabrics used in athletic wear into denim clothing.

Paul Guez, a longtime denim guru who started Sasson jeans and was instrumental in getting Joe's Jeans off the ground, said denim jeans used to have rigid fabric but they are incorporating softer fabrics with more give. "American Eagle Outfitters has super, super stretch jeans. And Replay made a huge ad, hiring five soccer guys to show you can exercise and do different moves in their jeans," he said.

People are demanding comfort in all their clothes, not just in the athleisure category. Rosemary Brantley, chair of the fashion design department at Otis College of Art and Design in Los Angeles, recently visited Nike's headquarters and sat in on meetings where the talk was about how to translate the comfort of athleisure into workwear that uses technical fabrics and elements. "Clothes that go to work are taking on more gussets that breathe and arms that stretch," she said. "In this meeting, everyone was talking about how this workwear movement is even more powerful than athleisure."

While women have embraced the athleisure concept, it still hasn't been snapped up by the children's and men's markets. But that will soon change. "I think men's is about to explode. We haven't even seen the tip of the iceberg," said Vargas of WGSN. "And we are going to see a boom in kids' sportswear, which is more of an extension of how parents dress."

Source: Deborah Belgum, "Athleisure—Fad or Fashion for the Long Haul?," *California Apparel News,* August 13, 2015, https://www.apparelnews.net/news/2015/aug/13/athleisurefad-or-fashion-long-haul/ (accessed February 7, 2016). Courtesy of California Apparel News.

Changing technology resulted in the decline of CD sales with the growth in demand for downloadable music. Retailing View 10.2 questions whether athleisure is a fad, a fashion, or a staple.

Seasonal merchandise is inventory whose sales fluctuate dramatically according to the time of the year. Both fashion and staple merchandise usually have seasonal influences. For instance, wool sweaters sell in fall and winter, whereas staples such as lawn mowers and garden tools are popular in spring and summer. Retailers carefully plan their purchases and deliveries to coincide with seasonal demand. Armed with information about where an item or a category is in its life cycle, retailers develop their sales forecast.

LO4 Setting Objectives for the Merchandise Plan

Retailers cannot hope to be financially successful unless they preplan the financial implications of their merchandising activities. Financial plans start at the top of the retail organization and are broken down into categories, while buyers and merchandise planners develop their own plans and negotiate up the organization. Top management looks at the overall merchandising strategy. They set the merchandising direction for the company by:

- defining the target market
- establishing performance goals
- deciding, on the basis of general trends in the marketplace, which merchandise classifications deserve more or less emphasis

Buyers and merchandise planners, on the other hand, take a more micro approach. They study their categories' past performance, look at trends in the market, and try to project the assortments for their merchandise categories for the coming seasons. The planning process is similar for smaller retailers. Although there aren't as many layers of management involved in planning and negotiations, they still start with the firm's overall financial goals and break them down into categories.

The resulting merchandise plan is a financial buying blueprint for each category. It considers the firm's financial objectives along with sales projections and merchandise flows. The merchandise plan tells the buyer and planner how much money to spend on a particular category of merchandise in each month so that the sales forecast and other financial objectives are met. Once the merchandise plan is set, the buyers and planners develop the assortment plan. The buyers work with vendors to choose merchandise, negotiate prices, and develop promotions. The merchandise planners break down the overall financial plan into how many of each item to purchase and how they should be allocated to stores. As you can imagine, there's a great deal of negotiating at each step.

DID YOU KNOW?

The best negotiator isn't the big-talking powerful personality. The best negotiator is armed with information, backed by research, and reinforced by facts and figures. Negotiation is more detective work than it is anything else. When you can go into a negotiation with the right *information*, then you have all that you need to win.[8]

Merchandise managers and buyers compete with each other over the size of their merchandise budgets.

Please note the following information is courtesy of © 2010 Oliver Wyman. Used with permission. All rights reserved.

As well, retailers have more information than ever about their suppliers and customers, from high-level score cards to detailed point-of-sale data covering every transaction. But in practice, this often leads to information overload rather than improved knowledge about the business; paradoxically, retailers are drowning in data but missing key insights. Taking full advantage of the wealth of data available is no simple task, and many retailers still rely on figures provided by their suppliers—ceding too much control of their categories in the process.

Retailers can and should exploit the information they possess, because it can give them a significant edge during negotiations, and can also change the terms of the entire discussion. Partnering with your suppliers is a good thing; letting them run your business is not. Answering the five questions below is one way to begin this process. They cover a broad spectrum, but have one thing in common: all rely on making more effective—in this context, one might say more aggressive—use of the rich vein of data that retailers possess. Senior executives should not rest easy until they know their category managers can answer these questions.

1. How Well Does Each Item Use Your Shelf Space?

Everyone knows different items generate different sales and cash margin per foot of shelf space, but few retailers make systematic and detailed comparisons across all competing products. Pointing out variations in financial performance can help get better terms from suppliers whose products underperform. Products with low cash margins must move faster, and conversely the slow movers must produce higher-than-average margins. If a supplier won't offer lower prices, the retailer should take action to improve cash margin per foot in other ways—ways that the supplier may not like. A detailed understanding of space productivity enables the retailer to drive a productive, fact-based discussion with the supplier. Exhibit 10–5 shows an example generated by linking planograms to sales

Exhibit 10–5
Space Productivity

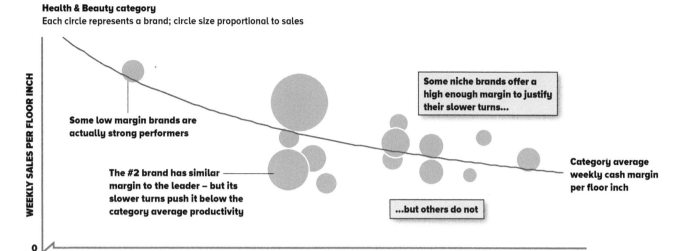

Health & Beauty category
Each circle represents a brand; circle size proportional to sales

(y-axis) WEEKLY SALES PER FLOOR INCH

Some low margin brands are actually strong performers

Some niche brands offer a high enough margin to justify their slower turns...

The #2 brand has similar margin to the leader – but its slower turns push it below the category average productivity

...but others do not

Category average weekly cash margin per floor inch

0

(x-axis) MARGIN %

Source: © 2010 Oliver Wyman. Used with permission. All rights reserved.

data to compare how well each supplier uses shelf space compared to the rest of the category and store. Furthermore, comparing shelf profitability often reveals differences between suppliers that are much greater than variations in percentage margin. This can justify asking for a better deal from underperforming suppliers.

2. Which Promotions Drive Value for the Retailer, not Just the Supplier?

Retailers often lose sight of a key fact when discussing promotions: their interests and the supplier's interests are not aligned. Brand switching means incremental sales to the supplier but cannibalization for the retailer; the reverse is true for store switching. If a large part of promotional volume comes from other items on the same shelf, the promotion likely reduces the retailer's sales and margin. Retailers need to understand the true economics of the promotions they run, including all effects: uplift, discount, cannibalization, purchase pull-forward, store switching effects, and supplier funding. Once they have this information, category managers usually discover that many promotions are not funded adequately by suppliers. As a result, category managers are able to make a convincing argument that they are better off stopping unproductive promotions if funding levels do not increase.

3. Which Brands and Items do Customers Really Value?

When negotiating with suppliers, the ultimate sanction is removing items, or entire brands, from the shelf. But to make this threat credible, category managers need to be able to counter suppliers' claims that their products are customer favourites, and are therefore vital to the assortment. The key is to understand how willing customers are to switch one item for another, by measuring their past purchasing behaviour. This will show that a few items are indeed essential, but in most cases if a retailer delists a product it will regain the lost sales through substitute products. Making this clear to suppliers dramatically strengthens a retailer's bargaining position. Exhibit 10–6 shows a switching matrix, which quantifies how much volume will be captured by other products if any given item is removed. It is based on actual transaction data, rather than surveys in which customers say how they behave.

4. How Much Profit Are You Generating for Your Suppliers?

When negotiating an item's cost, the strength of a category manager's bargaining position is defined by the financial contribution it makes to the business (see questions 1 and 2) and the importance that customers attach to it (see question 3). Of course, it is also vital to understand the strength of the supplier's bargaining position. Consumer goods

Exhibit 10–6
Brand Switching Matrix–Refrigerated Orange Juice

	Switchability: How much of today's sales would switch into other brands?	How much switched volume would go to each other brand?						
		Leading national brand	Private label	Premium brand 1	Premium brand 2	Second national brand	Regional brand 1	Economy brand 1
1.	Leading national brand — 21%		10%	27%	34%	29%	0%	0%
	Private label — 66%	69%		7%	10%	13%	0%	0%
	Premium brand 1 — 79%	78%	3%		12%	7%	0%	0%
	Premium brand 2 — 85%	74%	3%	9%		13%	0%	0%
2.	Second national brand — 85%	73%	5%	6%	16%		0%	0%
3.	Regional brand 1 — 86%	46%	20%	7%	10%	11%		0%
	Economy brand 1 — 91%	85%	0%	7%	4%	4%	0%	

1. The leading national brand is truly differentiated in customers' eyes, with low switchability into other brands. Of the volume that would switch, 10% would go to Private label, 27% to Premium brand 1, etc.
2. By contrast, the second best-selling brand has much lower loyalty – indicating sales "bought" with deep discount promotions.
3. Regional brand 1 has very low loyalty, and its volume is switchable into Private label, as well as the leading national brand.

Source: © 2010 Oliver Wyman. Used with permission. All rights reserved.

manufacturers typically run at higher gross margins than retailers (40 to 60 percent of sales); relatively speaking, volume matters more to them than to the retailer, and margin matters less. Using information from its own label suppliers, a retailer can build a simple model of each supplier's economics and predict what any deal looks like from the other side of the table. This helps the retailer adopt a negotiating position that is tough, but still advantageous to the other side. It also enables a retailer to determine how the proceeds of its growth are being shared with suppliers. Typically, the standard practices of the industry allow manufacturers to capture the lion's share of the profit created by a growing retailer, unless the retailer takes a strong stand.

Exhibit 10–7 shows how a retailer can use financial statements from publicly-traded companies to estimate the margin its suppliers make on additional volume. Most suppliers have far higher variable margins than retailers, and therefore have a stronger incentive to boost incremental volume. The supplier's trade funding is a key part of the economic picture, and is worth particular attention. Category managers are usually aware of how much trade funding they receive, but have no visibility into what suppliers are trying to achieve with these funds, and therefore how they can be used: what performance requirements exist, which funds can be moved into base cost and which cannot, and so on. We have seen situations where minor changes in merchandising unlock major increases in funding, but to achieve this a category manager needs a detailed understanding of the rules of the game.

5. How Do Your Negotiations With Supplier X Affect Your Colleagues?

Many suppliers span multiple categories, and often one category manager is not managing the entire portfolio of a given supplier. Indeed, it is not unusual for different category managers to have very different perspectives on a supplier's performance. It is therefore in the retailer's best interest to understand how the supplier's organization is structured. Does the same sales team call on several category managers? Do the supplier's business units operate independently or as a whole? Do funding structures vary across different business units? A holistic negotiating approach, with a defined "point person" to coordinate all category managers involved, ensures that everyone understands how their decisions affect the negotiations of their colleagues, and ultimately, the financial performance of the retailer as a whole. We often find that simply presenting a unified front to cross-category suppliers can unlock a great deal of value; if nothing else, the retailer prevents the supplier from offsetting savings offered to one category manager with a cost increases for another.

Exhibit 10–7
Supplier Volume Variable Margin

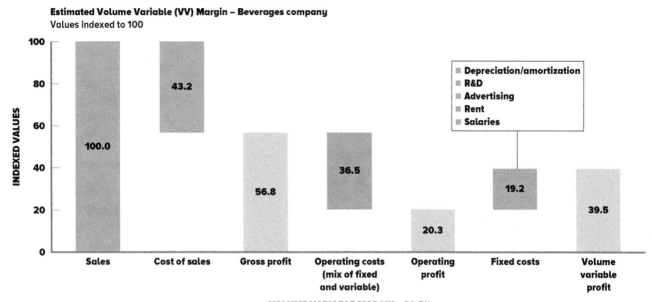

Estimated Volume Variable (VV) Margin – Beverages company
Values indexed to 100

VOLUME VARIABLE MARGIN = 39.5%

Source: © 2010 Oliver Wyman. Used with permission. All rights reserved.

Using data more intelligently and not depending on suppliers for information creates negotiating power. Supplementing category managers' trading instincts with solid analysis also opens up other opportunities. The retailer can restructure supplier panels, or offer more appealing incentives to top performers, while asking for more in return from those suppliers. SKU optimization ceases to be a hazardous experiment, followed by numerous "corrections" to address customer complaints. Ultimately, retailers exist to serve customers, not suppliers—and the way trading decisions are made should reflect this fundamental truth.

The questions described here obviously cover only a fraction of the things a category manager needs to know. A retailer's ultimate aim should be to gain the upper hand in the negotiating process by building a comprehensive understanding of its customers and suppliers. Better use of information allows a retailer to talk about its own customers, not about national averages; to present its own insights in negotiations, rather than listening to pitches from suppliers; and to rely on data from its own stores, not external reporting services.

Lo5 Developing an Assortment Plan

All retailers face the fundamental strategic question of what type of retail format to maintain to achieve a sustainable competitive advantage. A critical component of this decision is determining what merchandise assortment will be carried. Merchandise decisions are constrained by the amount of money

> **DID YOU KNOW?**
>
> A typical Walmart superstore carries approximately 142 000 SKUs.[9]

available to invest in inventory and the amount of space available in the store. Based on the financial objectives that have been set at the top and that have trickled through the retail organization, decisions regarding variety, assortment, and product availability must be made.

After forecasting sales for the category, the next step in the merchandise management planning process is to develop an assortment plan. An assortment plan is a list of SKUs that a retailer will offer in a merchandise category. The assortment plan thus reflects the breadth and depth that the retailer plans to offer in a merchandise category. After forecasting sales for the category, the next step in the merchandise management planning process is to develop an assortment plan (see Exhibit 10–2).

Category Breadth and Depth

The variety of a retailer's merchandise (also called *breadth*) is the number of different merchandising categories within a store or department. The retailer's depth of merchandise is defined as the number of SKUs within a category.

Services retailers also make assortment decisions. For example, some health clubs offer a large variety of activities and equipment from exercise machines to swimming, wellness programs, and New Age lectures. Others, like World Gym, don't offer much variety but have deep assortments of body-building equipment and programs. Some hospitals, such as big municipal hospitals found in most urban areas, offer a large variety of medical services, whereas others specialize in services such as trauma or prenatal care. For services retailers, the level of product availability is a sales forecasting issue.

Assortment planning involves decisions concerning the amount of merchandise choice that is available to the customer. Overstocking merchandise results in lower turnover and reduced profits; understocking may mean lost sales and unhappy customers who will take their business elsewhere. The ideal situation is the right merchandise, in the right quantity, at the right price, and at the right time.

Breadth of stock refers to the number of SKUs, which could be the variety of brands, sizes, or colours available to the customer.

depth The amount of a particular item of merchandise that a retailer will stock, reflecting attributes such as brand, size, or colour.

- A broad assortment will include numerous choices.

- A narrow assortment will provide the customer with only a few choices.

Depth of merchandise, or the amount of a particular item that a retailer will stock, includes the attributes of brand, size, or colour; for example, the number of styles of a specific brand of bicycle.

- A deep assortment refers to a large quantity of a single item.

- A shallow assortment consists of only a few of a single item.

Examples of merchandise with different levels of variety and depth include the following:

- *Broad and shallow assortment planning* is typical of the fashion retailer Club Monaco, which stocks a broad assortment of styles to satisfy the style-conscious consumer but does not carry depth in any particular item. The fashion customer is more selective about style, size, and colour, and changes with the newest trends.

- *Narrow and deep assortment planning* is an assortment typical of the mass merchandisers, such as Walmart. The assortment mix has only a few choices in a particular category, but it is stocked in considerable depth so it is seldom out of stock within that product group. There may be, for example, three brands.

- *Square assortment planning* is a moderate assortment strategy that is adopted by traditional department stores. In order to provide customers with a greater product selection than the mass merchandisers, Hudson's Bay and Sears adopt a square assortment plan. This assortment strategy is planned to have limited depth within the categories to avoid having an overstock situation that could result in markdowns and a loss of revenue at the end of the season.

In the context of merchandise planning, the concepts of breadth and depth are applied to a merchandise category rather than a retail firm. At the category level, variety reflects the number of different types of merchandise, and assortment is the number of SKUs per type. For example, the

Exhibit 10–8
Assortment Plan for Girls' Jeans

Styles	Traditional	Traditional	Traditional	Traditional	Traditional	Traditional
Price levels	$20	$20	$35	$35	$45	$45
Fabric composition	Regular denim	Stonewashed	Regular denim	Stonewashed	Regular denim	Stonewashed
Colours	Light blue Indigo Black	Light blue Indigo Black	Light blue Indigo Black	Light blue Indigo Black	Light blue Indigo Black	Light blue Indigo Black
Styles	**Boot-Cut**	**Boot-Cut**	**Boot-Cut**	**Boot-Cut**		
Price levels	$25	$25	$45	$45		
Fabric composition	Regular denim	Stonewashed	Regular denim	Stonewashed		
Colours	Light blue Indigo Black	Light blue Indigo Black	Light blue Indigo Black	Light blue Indigo Black		

assortment plan for girls' jeans in Exhibit 10–8 includes ten varieties (traditional or boot-cut, regular denim or stonewashed, and three price points reflecting different brands). For each type, there are 81 SKUs (3 colours × 9 sizes × 3 lengths). Thus, this retailer plans to offer 810 SKUs in girls' jeans.

Determining Breadth and Depth

The process of determining the breadth and depth for a category is called editing the assortment. When editing the assortment for a category like jeans, the buyer considers the following factors: the firm's retail strategy, the effect of assortments on GMROI, the complementarities between categories, the effects of assortments on buying behaviour, and the physical characteristics of the store.

<aside>

DID YOU KNOW?

Supermarkets typically stock 30 000 to 40 000 SKUs in a store, with less than 5 percent accounting for more than half the store's sales. However, the typical household buys only about 400 SKUs in an entire year. Month after month, customers buy the same items.[10]

</aside>

Retail Strategy The number of SKUs offered in a merchandise category is a strategic decision. For example, Costco focuses on customers who are looking for a few SKUs in a category (see Retailing View 10.3). In contrast, Best Buy focuses on consumers interested in comparing many alternatives in specific consumer electronic categories and thus offers more SKUs in each category.

The breadth and depth of the assortment in a merchandise category can affect the retailer's brand image.[11] Retailers might increase the assortment in categories that are closely associated with their image. For example, Costco typically has few SKUs per category, but it has a broad and deep assortment of wines in its US stores because its offering in this category reinforces its image of offering quality products with good value.

Assortments and GMROI In developing the assortment plan, buyers need to be sensitive to the trade-off of increasing sales by offering greater breadth and depth but, at the same time, potentially reducing inventory turnover and GMROI because of the increased inventory investment. Increasing assortment breadth and depth also can decrease gross margin. For example, the more SKUs offered, the greater the chance of **breaking sizes**—that is, stocking out of a specific size or colour SKU. If a stockout occurs for a popular SKU in a fashion merchandise category and the buyer cannot reorder during the season, the buyer will typically discount the entire merchandise type, thus reducing gross margin. The buyer's objective is to remove the merchandise type from the assortment altogether so that customers will not be disappointed when they do not find the size and colour they want.

> **breaking sizes** Stocking out of a specific size or colour SKU.

Complementary Merchandise When buyers develop assortment plans, they need to consider the degree to which categories in a department complement each other.[12] For instance, DVD players may have a low GMROI, suggesting that the buyer

Costco Goes for Variety, or Does It?

The Costco experience is often described as a treasure hunt. Products can include everything from blue jeans, air conditioners, and computer games one day, to books, children's toys, and diamond rings the next, plus a huge selection of food products. Costco keeps customers on their toes by offering a wide variety of merchandise that changes from day to day. This is the place where individual and business customers pay $55 to $110 per year for a membership to buy 24 rolls of toilet paper or none at all. This is where laundry detergent and Italian olive oil come in extra-large sizes, and where a 1000-piece lot of Ralph Lauren golf jackets, selling at 75 percent below retail, will vanish in an afternoon. In Costco's 4-acre stores, you can also visit the meat counter with its onsite butchers, order a cake from the bakery, and pick up a prescription and talk to the resident pharmacist to receive health advice.

All of these disparate categories provide an illusion of expansive variety. A Walmart Supercentre carries as many as 125 000 items; a grocery store will stock approximately 40 000. Not so at Costco, where you will find just 3800 to 4000 carefully chosen products. This makes it easier for the company to manage inventory and to monitor prices obsessively. Three-quarters of the merchandise is basic stock, such as canned tuna and paper towels; the other items are discretionary, often with high-end brands such as Godiva chocolates and Waterford

Niloo/Shutterstock.com.

crystal. The store's periphery offers a variety of services, including film development, an optical centre, a pharmacy, and a tire shop.

Costco's successful strategy is planned so that a pallet of product must bring in a specific amount of cash or it is out; it is about volume per item, operating with a margin of about 8 percent, and how to increase the volume per item. Traditional category management does not apply to Costco; for example, because Costco sells computer printers does not mean that it will sell printer paper. Unusual product juxtapositions, such as face creams next to crackers, are all part of a selling formula that homes in on the middle-class tastes for cross-shopping and impulse purchases.

The typical Costco customer is 35 to 55 years old and earns on average $100 000 in family income, about double the income of most Canadians. Costco's Canadian customers number about 3.5 million households, with up to 35 percent of its business in grocery. There are 60 Canadian Costco stores, whose average size is 165 000 square feet, with sales figures averaging about $118 million per store. Overall, Costco has approximately 10 million Canadian members and enjoys average annual sales of approximately $15 billion.

Sources: Julia Drake, "Welcome to the Big Time: Big Stores, Big Products, Big Savings, Big Profits: They're All Part of the Costco Experience," *Canadian Grocer*, May 2001; Ann Zimmerman, "Costco Goes for Variety, or Does It?" *Retailing* (McGraw-Hill Ryerson); "The Costco Story," *Costco*, http://www.costco.ca/about-us.html (accessed May 20, 2016).

carry a limited assortment. But customers who buy a DVD player might also buy complementary products and services such as accessories, cables, and warranties that have a high GMROI. Thus, the buyer may decide to carry more DVD-player SKUs to increase the more profitable accessory sales.

Effects of Assortment Size on Buying Behaviour

Offering large assortments provides a number of benefits to customers. First, increasing the number of SKUs that customers can consider increases the

chance they will find the product that best satisfies their needs. Second, large assortments are valued by customers because they provide a more informative and stimulating shopping experience due to the complexity associated with numerous products and the novelty associated with unique items. Third, large assortments are particularly appealing to customers who seek variety—those who want to try new things.

However, offering a large assortment can make the purchase decision more complex and time-consuming.[13] Research has shown that customers

The Chippery in Vancouver rates high on depth and low on breadth. It is the place to get fresh potato (or beet or yam) chips, a selection of gourmet dips, and fruit smoothies. And that's it!

Courtesy of Shikatani Lacroix Design Inc.

L06 Setting Inventory and Product Availability Levels

After developing the assortment plan, the third step in the merchandise planning process is to determine the model stock plan for the category.

Model Stock Plan

The **model stock plan**, illustrated in Exhibit 10–9, is the number of each SKU in the assortment plan that the buyer wants to have available for purchase in each store. For example, the model stock plan in Exhibit 10–9 includes nine units of size 1, short, which represent 2 percent of the 429 total units for girls' traditional $20 denim jeans in light blue. Note that there are more units for more popular sizes.

Retailers typically have model stock plans for the different store sizes in a chain. For example, retailers typically classify their stores as A, B, and C stores on the basis of their sales volume. The basic assortment in a category is stocked in C stores. For the larger stores, because more space is available, the number of SKUs increases. The larger A and B stores may have more brands, colours, styles, and sizes.

Product Availability

The number of units of **backup stock**, also called *buffer* or *safety stock*, in the model stock plan determines product availability. **Product availability** is defined as the percentage of the demand for a particular SKU that is satisfied. For instance, if 100 people go into a PetSmart store to purchase a small, Great Choice, portable kennel, but only 90 people can make the purchase before the kennel stock is depleted, the product availability for that SKU is 90 percent. Product availability is also referred to as the **service level**, or *level of support*.

The model stock plan needs more backup stock if the retailer wants to increase product availability, that is, increase the probability that customers

model stock plan A summary of the desired inventory levels of each SKU stocked in a store for a merchandise category.

backup stock The inventory used to guard against going out of stock when demand exceeds forecasts or merchandise is delayed; also called *safety stock* or *buffer stock*.

product availability A measurement of the percentage of demand for a particular SKU that is satisfied.

service level A measure used in inventory management to define the level of support or level of product availability; the number of items sold divided by the number of items demanded. Service level should not be confused with customer service. Also called *level of support*.

actually buy more if there are modest reductions of redundant items in assortments, such as reductions in the number of different ketchup bottle sizes or low-share brands carried by a supermarket.[14]

Physical Characteristics of the Store Buyers need to consider how much space to devote to a category. More space is needed to display categories with large assortments. In addition, a lot of space is needed to display individual items in some categories, and this limits the number of SKUs that can be offered in stores. For example, furniture takes up a lot of space, so furniture retailers typically display one model of a chair or sofa and then have photographs and cloth swatches or a virtual room on a computer to show how the furniture would look with different upholstery.

Multichannel retailers address the space limitations in stores by offering a greater assortment through their Internet and catalogue channels than they do in stores. For example, Staples offers more types of laptop computers and printers on its Internet site than it stocks in its stores. If customers do not find the computer or printer they want in the store, sales associates direct them to the company's website and can even order the merchandise for them from a POS terminal.

Exhibit 10–9
Model Stock Plans

LENGTH			SIZE								
			1	2	4	5	6	8	10	12	14
Short	%		2	4	7	6	8	5	7	4	2
	units		9	17	30	26	34	21	30	17	9
Medium	%		2	4	7	6	8	5	7	4	2
	units		9	17	30	26	34	21	30	17	9
Long	%		0	2	2	2	3	2	2	1	0
	units		0	9	9	9	12	9	9	4	0
	Total 100%										
	429 units										

will find the product they want when they visit the retailer's store. Choosing an appropriate amount of backup stock is critical to successful assortment planning. If the backup stock is too low, the retailer will lose sales and possibly customers too when they find that the products they want are not available from the retailer. If the level is too high, scarce financial resources will be wasted on needless inventory rather than being more profitably invested in increasing variety or assortment.

Exhibit 10–10 shows the trade-off between inventory investment and product availability. Although the actual inventory investment varies in different situations, the general relationship shows that extremely high level of product availability results in a prohibitively high inventory investment.

Several factors need to be considered to determine the appropriate level of backup stock and thus the product availability for each SKU. Retailers often classify merchandise categories or individual

SKUs as A, B, or C items, reflecting the product availability the retailer wants to offer. The A items are best-sellers bought by many customers. For example, white dress shirts is an A item for Banana Republic, and copy paper is an A item for Staples. A retailer rarely wants to risk A-item stockouts because running out of these very popular SKUs would diminish the retailer's image and customer loyalty. On the other hand, lower product availability is acceptable for C items, which are purchased by a small number of customers and are not readily available from other retailers. Some other factors considered in determining backup stock levels and product availability are the fluctuations in demand, the lead time for delivery from the vendor, the fluctuations in vendor lead time, and the frequency of store deliveries. These factors are discussed in the next section.

The trade-off among variety, assortment, and product availability is a crucial issue in determining a retailer's merchandising strategy. Buyers have a limited budget for the inventory investments they can make in a category. Thus, they are forced to

Exhibit 10–10
Relationship Between Inventory Investment and Product Availability

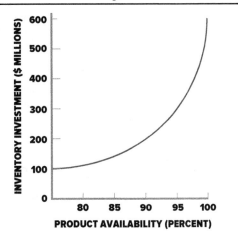

Banana Republic tries to be the one-stop shop for its target market. It carries a large variety of merchandise categories.
© McGraw-Hill Education/Andrew Resek.

sacrifice breadth of merchandise if they opt to increase depth, or they must reduce both depth and breadth to increase product availability.

Establishing a Control System for Managing Inventory

The first three steps in the merchandise planning process—forecasting SKU and category sales, determining the assortment plan, and establishing product availability (see Exhibit 10–2) quantify the buyer's sales expectations and service level. The fourth step in the merchandise management process is to establish a control system for how the orders, deliveries, inventory levels, and merchandise sales will evolve over time. The objective of this control system is to manage the flow of merchandise into the stores so that the amount of inventory in a category is minimized but the merchandise will still be available when customers want to buy it. The differences between the control systems for staple and fashion merchandise are discussed in the following sections.

Retailing View 10.4 describes how some retailers are using server-based merchandise management systems.

10.4	RETAILING VIEW

Retailers Use State-of-the-Art Merchandise Management Systems

SAS has developed an integrated system to maximize retailers' profitability using several modules. The system provides a merchandise planning and forecasting module that forecasts sales and provides buyers with suggestions about how much of a particular category to buy. It also helps planners determine assortments, plan space in stores, and allocate merchandise to stores. Its revenue optimization module helps buyers determine optimal initial prices on the basis of costs, regional demand patterns, and competitive price information. This module also helps buyers determine optimal prices for promotions and markdowns.

The Children's Place has been an SAS customer since 2005. It uses the software to optimize regular and clearance pricing strategies, promotion decisions, and preseason planning. The system also allows its buyers to make adjustments throughout the selling season and review actual performance with respect to planned performance.

The Aldo Group has experienced greater margins and overall profitability as a result of using Oracle's retail merchandising application, which competes with SAS's systems. This type of application allows the retailer to recognize underperforming merchandise categories and make changes faster to increase inventory turnover. As a

Sam Dao/Alamy.

result, customers can have the best selection of merchandise available. "Oracle Retail Markdown Optimization allows our buyers to maintain focus on the positive aspects of the assortment," says Lucia Cimaglia, general manager supply chain for the Aldo Group. Buyers feel assured the systems and procedures in place will work, which will "help manage in-season inventory and make the right decisions for the business, and that in turn frees time to look ahead to new seasons," adds Cimaglia.

Sources: "ALDO Group Implements Oracle® Retail Solution to Optimize In-Season Inventory Management," Oracle press release, April 25, 2011, http://www.oracle.com/us/corporate/press/365790 (accessed February 24, 2013); http://www.sas.com/industry/retail/merchandise/ (accessed October 24, 2007); "The Children's Place Retail Stores Inc. Chooses SAS for Advanced Merchandise Planning at Disney Store North America," SAS press release, March 7, 2007.

When planning the amount of inventory to order for a staple merchandise category such as outdoor furniture, Lowe's buyers must consider current inventory, customer demand, lead time for replenishment, and backup stock needed to avoid stockouts in the department.

© Valentino Visentini | Dreamstime.com.

Exhibit 10–11
Merchandise Flow of a Staple SKU

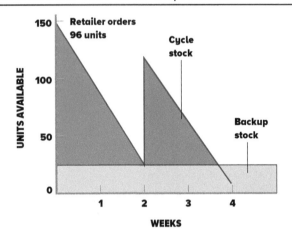

Control System for Managing Inventory of Staple Merchandise

SKUs in a staple merchandise category are sold month after month, year after year. Lowe's sales of purple paint this month will be about the same as they were during the same month a year ago. If the sales of purple paint are below forecast this month, the excess inventory of purple paint can be sold during the following month. Thus, an automated continuous replenishment control system is used to manage the flow of staple merchandise SKUs and categories. The continuous replenishment system monitors the inventory level of each SKU in a store and automatically triggers a reorder of an SKU when the inventory falls below a predetermined level.

Flow of Staple Merchandise   Exhibit 10–11 illustrates the merchandise flow in a staple merchandise management system. At the beginning of week 1, the retailer had 150 units of the SKU in inventory and the buyer or merchandise planner placed an order for 96 additional units. During the next two weeks, customers purchased 130 units, and the inventory level decreased to 20 units. At the end of week 2, the 96-unit order from the vendor arrived, and the inventory level jumped up to 116 units. The continuous replenishment system placed another order with the vendor that will arrive in two weeks, before customer sales decrease the inventory level to zero and the retailer stocks out.

Inventory for which the level goes up and down due to the replenishment process is called **cycle stock**, or *base stock*. The retailer hopes to reduce the cycle-stock inventory

cycle stock The inventory that goes up and down due to the replenishment process; also called *base stock*.

to keep its inventory investment low. One approach for reducing the cycle stock is to reorder smaller quantities more frequently. But more frequent, smaller orders and shipments increase administrative and transportation costs.

Because sales of the SKU and receipts of orders from the vendor cannot be predicted with perfect accuracy, the retailer has to carry backup stock, as a cushion, so that it doesn't stock out before the next order arrives. Backup stock is shown in yellow in Exhibit 10–11. Backup stock is the level of inventory needed to ensure merchandise is available in light of these uncertainties.

Determining the Level of Backup Stock   Several factors determine the level of backup stock needed for an SKU. First, the level depends on the product availability the retailer wants to provide. As discussed previously, more backup stock is needed when the retailer wants to reduce the chances of a stockout and increase the availability of the SKU. Thus, if Lowe's views white paint as an A item and rarely wants to stock out of it, a higher level of backup stock is needed. However, if melon paint is a C item and 75 percent product availability is acceptable, the level of backup stock can be lowered.

Second, the greater the fluctuation in demand, the more backup stock is needed. Suppose a Lowe's store sells an average of 30 gallons of purple paint in two weeks. Yet in some weeks, sales are 50 gallons, and in other weeks, they are only 10 gallons. When sales are less than average, the store ends up carrying a little more merchandise than it needs. But when sales are much more than average, there must be more backup stock to ensure that the store does not stock out. Note in Exhibit 10–11 that during week 4, sales were greater than average, so the retailer had to dip into its backup stock to avoid a stockout.

Third, the amount of backup stock needed is affected by the lead time from the vendor. **Lead time** is the amount of time between the recognition that an order needs to be placed and the point at which the merchandise arrives in the store and is ready for sale. If it took two months to receive a shipment of purple paint, the possibility of running out of stock is greater than it would be if the lead time was only two weeks. The shorter lead times inherent in collaborative supply chain management systems like CPFR (described in Chapter 9) result in a lower level of backup stock required to maintain the same level of product availability.

Fourth, fluctuations in lead time also affect the amount of backup stock needed. If Lowe's knows that the lead time for purple paint is always two weeks, plus or minus one day, it can more accurately plan its inventory levels. But if the lead time is one day on one shipment and then ten days on the next shipment, the stores must carry additional backup stock to cover this uncertainty in lead time. Many retailers using collaborative supply chain management systems require that their vendors deliver merchandise within a very narrow window— sometimes two or three hours—to reduce the fluctuations in lead time and thus the amount of required backup stock.

Fifth, the vendor's fill rate also affects the retailer's backup stock requirements. For example, Lowe's can more easily plan its inventory requirements if the vendor normally ships every item that is ordered. If, however, the vendor ships only 75 percent of the ordered items, Lowe's must maintain more backup stock to be certain that the paint availability for its customers isn't adversely affected. The percentage of complete orders received from a vendor is called the **fill rate**.

Automated Continuous Replenishment Once the buyer sets the desired product availability and determines the variation in demand and the vendor's lead time and fill rate, the continuous replenishment systems for staple SKUs can operate automatically. The retailer's information system determines the inventory level at each point in time, the **perpetual inventory**, by comparing the sales made through the POS terminals with the shipments received by the store. When the perpetual inventory level falls below the predetermined level, the system sends an EDI reorder to the retailer's distribution centre and the vendor. When the reordered merchandise arrives at the store, the level of inventory is adjusted up.

However, it is difficult to achieve fully automated continuous replenishment of staple merchandise because of errors in determining the actual inventory. For example, the retailer's information system might indicate that ten Gillette Fusion razors are in the store when, in fact, ten razors were stolen by a shoplifter and there are actually zero razors in the store. Since there are no razors in the store, there are no sales and the automated continuous replenishment system will never reorder razors for the store. Such inaccuracies can also arise when an incorrect number of units is inputted into the information system about a shipment from the distribution centre to the store. To address these problems, store employees need to periodically check the inventory recorded in the system with the actual inventory in the store.

Inventory Management Report The inventory management report provides information about the inventory management for a staple category. The report indicates the decision variables set by the buyer, such as product availability, the backup stock needed to provide the product availability, the order points and quantities plus performance measures such as planned and actual inventory turnover, the current sales rate or velocity, sales forecasts, inventory availability, and the amount on order. Exhibit 10–12 is an inventory management report for Rubbermaid bath mats.

The first five columns of Exhibit 10–12 contain the descriptions of each item, how many items are on hand and on order, and sales for the past 4 and 12 weeks. The first-row SKU is a Rubbermaid bath mat in avocado green. There are 30 units on hand and 60 on order. Thus, the quantity available of this SKU is 90. Sales for the past 4 and 12 weeks were 72 and 215 units, respectively.

Sales forecasts for the next 4 and 8 weeks are determined by the system using a statistical model

lead time The amount of time between recognition that an order needs to be placed and the point at which the merchandise arrives in the store and is ready for sale.

fill rate The percentage of an order that is shipped by the vendor.

perpetual inventory An accounting procedure whose objectives are to maintain a perpetual or book inventory in retail dollar amounts and to maintain records that make it possible to determine the cost value of the inventory at any time without taking a physical inventory; also known as *book inventory system or retail inventory method (RIM)*.

Exhibit 10–12
Inventory Management Report for Rubbermaid SKUs

In-Season Management - Worksheet: Inventory Mangement - Rubbermaid (Business View: 'Inventory Management : Global')

Worksheet   In-Season Management

Plan Edit View Tools Help

Skip To   Style

	Quantity On Hand	Quantity On Order	Sales Last 4 Wks	Sales Last 12 Wks	Forecast Next 4 Wks	Forecast Next 8 Wks	Product Availability	Backup Stock	Turnover Planned	Turnover Actual	Order Point	Order Quantity
RM- Bath												
RM Bath Mat - Avocado	30	60	72	215	152	229	99	18	12	11	132	42
RM Bath Mat - Blue	36	36	56	130	115	173	95	12	9	10	98	26
RM Bath Mat - Gold	41	72	117	325	243	355	99	35	12	13	217	104
RM Bath Mat - Pink	10	12	15	41	13	25	90	3	7	7	13	0

that considers the trends in past sales and the seasonal pattern for the SKU. However, in this case, the buyer made an adjustment in the forecast for the next 4 weeks to reflect an upcoming special promotion on avocado, blue, and gold bath mats.

The product availability is a decision variable input by the buyer. For the avocado bath mat SKU, the buyer wants 99 out of every 100 customers to find it in stock. But the buyer is less concerned about stocking out of pink bath mats and thus sets its product availability at 90 percent. The system then calculates the necessary backup stock for the avocado bath mat based on a predetermined formula— 18 units. This number is determined by the system based on the specified product availability, the variability in demand, the vendor delivery lead-time, and the variability in lead-time.

The planned inventory turnover for the SKU, 12 times, is a decision variable also set by the buyer on the basis of the retailer's overall financial goals; it drives the inventory management system. For this SKU, the system determined that the actual turnover, based on the cost of goods sold and average inventory, is 11.

Order Point The **order point** is the amount of inventory below which the quantity

Staple merchandise management systems are used for items like this rubber bath mat.
Courtesy of Rubbermaid.

available shouldn't go or the item will be out of stock before the next order arrives. This number tells the buyer that when the inventory level drops to this point, additional merchandise should be ordered. For this SKU, the buyer needs to place an order if the quantity in inventory falls to 132 or fewer units to produce the desired product availability.

Order Quantity When inventory reaches the order point, the buyer, or the system, needs to order enough units to ensure product availability before the next order arrives. Using the avocado bath mats in Exhibit 10–12 as an example, the order quantity is 42 units.

In the seven days before Christmas, retailers have marked peaks in their sales that can amount to as much of 40 percent of their December sales figures.
© Jackbluee/Dreamstime.com.

DID YOU KNOW?

More than 40 percent of retailers do not have a well-defined process for adjusting the four parameters of their inventory control system: product availability, order points, safety stock levels, and lead times.[15]

order point The amount of inventory below which the quantity available shouldn't go or the item will be out of stock before the next order arrives.

L07 Allocating Merchandise to Stores

After developing a plan for managing merchandise inventory in a category, the next step in the merchandise management process is to allocate the merchandise purchased and received to the retailer's stores. Research has found that these allocation decisions have a much bigger impact on profitability than does the decision about the quantity of merchandise to purchase.[16] In other words, buying too little or too much merchandise has less impact on category profit than making mistakes in allocating the right amount and type of merchandise to stores. Thus, many retailers have created positions called either "allocators" or "planners" to specialize in making store allocation decisions. As can be seen in Exhibit 10-13, allocating merchandise to stores involves three decisions: (1) how much merchandise to allocate to each store, (2) what type of merchandise to allocate, and (3) when to allocate the merchandise to different stores.

Amount of Merchandise Allocated

Retail chains typically classify each of their stores on the basis of annual sales. Thus, A stores would have the largest sales volume and typically receive the most **inventory**, while C stores would have the lowest sales volume and receive the least inventory for a category. In addition to the store's sales level, when making allocation decisions for a category, allocators consider the physical characteristics of the merchandise and the depth of assortment and level of product availability that the firm wants to portray for the specific store.

Type of Merchandise Allocated

The process of allocating merchandise to stores that was just described is useful for fashion merchandise and new staple items. As merchandise sells, it must be replenished, either by the vendor or through distribution centres. Retailers use either a pull or a push distribution strategy to replenish merchandise. With a **pull distribution strategy**, orders for merchandise are generated at the store level on the basis of demand data captured by point-of-sale terminals. With a **push distribution strategy**, merchandise is allocated to the stores on the basis of historical demand, the inventory position at the distribution centre, and the needs of the stores. A pull strategy is used by more sophisticated retailers because it's more responsive to customer demand.

In addition to classifying stores on the basis of their size and sales volume, retailers classify stores according to the characteristics of the stores' trading area. The profiles of trading areas are used in making store location decisions. Store trade area geodemographics are also used to develop merchandise assortments for specific stores. Consider the allocation decision of a national supermarket for its ready-to-eat cereal assortment. Some stores are located in areas dominated by segments called "Urban & Urbane," and other areas are dominated by the "Foundation of the Nation," as described in Exhibit 10–14.

The ready-to-eat breakfast cereal buyer would certainly want to offer different assortments for stores in these two areas. Stores with a high proportion of older retirees in their trading areas would have better results with an assortment of lower-priced, well-known brands and less expensive

inventory Goods or merchandise available for resale.

pull distribution strategy Strategy in which orders for merchandise are generated at the store level on the basis of demand data captured by point-of-sale terminals.

push distribution strategy Strategy in which merchandise is allocated to stores based on historical demand, the inventory position at the distribution centre, as well as the stores' needs.

Exhibit 10–13
Allocation Based on Sales Volume Breakdown by Store of Traditional $35 Denim Jeans

(1) Type of Store	(2) Number of Stores	(3) Percentage Of Total Sales, Each Store	(4) Sales per Store (total sales × col. 3)	(5) Store Type (col. 2 × col. 4)	(6) Unit Sales Per Store (col. 4/$35)
A	4	10.0%	$15 000	$60 000	429
B	3	6.7	10 000	30 000	286
C	8	5.0	7 500	60 000	214

Total sales $150 000

Exhibit 10–14
Example of Canadian Mosaics

Urban & Urbane	Foundation of the Nation
Hip and happening describe these 20–34 year old single and common-law people living in charming older apartments in the city. University and graduate degrees in visual and cultural arts, communications, life sciences, and technology are the catalysts for launching their careers in health, finance, and technical occupations. Being in metropolitan areas, they are high users of transit and commuting. Although incomes are well below average, they do not have children yet so household expenditures are low and they can spend time and money on themselves. They are moving up, moving on, and motivated!	West coast and Prairie cities are the home to this group of older people who rent an apartment or condominium and live alone. They are over 65 and likely collecting some type of retirement or government pension, with incomes coming in below $40 000. As they have already accumulated most material goods, their spending is low, especially on computer technology, however they are interested in keeping healthy, spending on medical supplies, prescribed medicines, and pharmaceuticals, and they contribute to public health plans. Reading newspapers keeps them informed and entertained, but they may take a chance on a lottery ticket just for fun! They are generous and give to charities in Canada. As they live in urban communities, they walk or take a short taxi ride to amenities.

private-label cereals. Stores in areas dominated by the Urban & Urbane geodemographic segment would do better with an assortment with higher-priced brands that are low in sugar, are organic, and contain whole wheat. President's Choice private-label brands would be favoured by an upwardly mobile market segment.

Even the sales of different apparel sizes can vary dramatically from store to store in the same chain. Exhibit 10–15 illustrates this point. Some stores sell significantly more large sizes and fewer small sizes than is average for the chain. If the buyer allocated the same size distribution of

merchandise to all stores in the chain, Store X would stock out of large sizes, have an oversupply of small sizes, or be out of some sizes sooner than other stores in the chain.

Timing of Merchandise Allocation

In addition to the need to allocate different inventory levels and types of merchandise across stores, differences in the timing of category purchases across stores need to be considered. To increase inventory turnover in the category, buyers need to recognize these regional differences and arrange for merchandise to be shipped to the appropriate regions when customers are ready to buy.

Retailers are considering the "paycheque cycle" when making merchandise allocation and promotion decisions, particularly in difficult economic times. Cash-strapped consumers are showing a tendency to make their largest purchases when they get their paycheques at the beginning of the month and to cut back on purchases as that money runs out toward the end of the month. Therefore, some supermarket chains devote more shelf space and promote larger-package sizes at the beginning of the month and small sizes at the end of the month.[17]

The issues involved in allocating merchandise inventory to stores, as just described, are particularly important for both fashion merchandise and new staple items. If merchandise sells and evolves into staple merchandise, it gets replenished over time, either by the vendor or through distribution centres.

Exhibit 10–15
Apparel Size Differences for Store X and the Chain Average

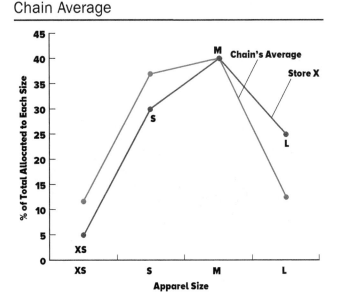

LO8 Analyzing Merchandise Management Performance

The next step in the merchandise planning process (see Exhibit 10–2) is to analyze the performance of the process and make adjustments, such as ordering more or less merchandise, lowering prices to increase sales, allocating different assortments to specific stores, or changing the assortment and model stock plans. Three types of analyses related to the monitoring and adjustment step are (1) sell-through analysis, (2) ABC analysis of assortments, and (3) multiattribute analysis of vendors. The first analysis provides an ongoing evaluation of the merchandise management plan compared with actual sales. The remaining two analyses offer approaches for evaluating and altering the assortment plan using the specific SKUs in the plan and the vendors that provide the merchandise to support the plan.

Sell-Through Analysis Evaluating Merchandise Plan

A **sell-through analysis** compares actual and planned sales to determine whether more merchandise is needed to satisfy demand or whether price reductions (markdowns) are required. Exhibit 10–16 shows a sell-through analysis for blouses for the first two weeks of the season.

These blouses are high-fashion items that experience significant uncertainty in sales. Thus, after two weeks in the stores, the buyer reviews sales and determines if adjustments are needed. The need to make adjustments depends on a variety of factors, including experience with the merchandise in the past, plans for featuring the merchandise in advertising, and the availability of **markdown money**

from vendors (funds that a vendor gives a retailer to cover lost gross margin dollars that result from markdowns).

In this case, the white blouses are selling significantly less well than planned. Examine the week 1 columns for the first SKU, the small white blouse. Planned sales were 20 units. The actual sales were 15 units. Therefore, the actual-to-plan percentage was −25 percent [(15 − 20)/20 = −25%]. This means that actual sales were 25 percent less than the planned sales. In fact, the actual-to-plan percentage is negative for all of the white blouses and positive for all of the blue blouses.

Therefore, the buyer makes an early price reduction to ensure that the merchandise isn't left unsold at the end of the season. The decision regarding the blue blouses isn't as clear. The small blue blouses are selling slightly ahead of the plan, and the medium blue blouses are also selling well, but the large blue blouses start selling ahead of plan only in the second week. In this case, the buyer decides to wait another week or two before taking any action. If actual sales stay significantly ahead of planned sales, a reorder might be appropriate.

Evaluating the Assortment Plan and Vendors

ABC Analysis An **ABC analysis** identifies the performance of individual SKUs in the assortment

sell-through analysis A comparison of actual and planned sales to determine whether early markdowns are required or whether more merchandise is needed to satisfy demand.

markdown money Funds provided by a vendor to a retailer to cover decreased gross margin from markdowns and other merchandising issues.

ABC analysis An analysis that rank orders SKUs by a profitability measure to determine which items should never be out of stock, which should be allowed to be out of stock occasionally, and which should be deleted from the stock selection.

Exhibit 10–16
Example of a Sell-Through Analysis for Blouses

Stock Number	Description		WEEK 1 Actual-to-Plan			WEEK 2 Actual-to-Plan		
			Plan	Actual	Percentage	Plan	Actual	Percentage
1011	Small	White silk V-neck	20	15	−25.0	20	10	−50.0
1011	Medium	White silk V-neck	30	25	−16.6	30	20	−33.0
1011	Large	White silk V-neck	20	16	−20.0	20	16	−20.0
1012	Small	Blue silk V-neck	25	26	4.0	25	27	8.0
1012	Medium	Blue silk V-neck	35	45	29.0	35	40	14.0
1012	Large	Blue silk V-neck	25	25	0	25	30	20.0

plan. It is used to determine which SKUs should be in the plan and how much backup stock and resulting product availability are provided for each SKU in the plan. In an ABC analysis, the SKUs in a merchandise category are rank-ordered by several performance measures, such as sales, gross margin, inventory turnover, and GMROI. Typically, this rank order reveals the general 80–20 principle; namely, approximately 80 percent of a retailer's sales or profits come from 20 percent of the products. This principle suggests that retailers should concentrate on the products that provide the biggest returns.

After rank-ordering the SKUs, the next step is to classify the items. On the basis of the classification, the buyer determines whether to maintain the items in the assortment plan and, if so, what level of product availability to offer. For example, a men's dress shirt buyer might identify the A, B, C, and D SKUs by rank-ordering them by sales volume. The A items account for only 5 percent of the SKUs in the category but represent 70 percent of sales. The buyer decides that these SKUs should never be out of stock and thus plans to maintain more backup stock for A items, such as keeping more sizes of long- and short-sleeved white and blue dress shirts than of the B and C items.

The B items represent 10 percent of the SKUs and 20 percent of sales. These items include some of the other better-selling colours and patterned shirts and contribute to the retailer's image of having fashionable merchandise. Occasionally, the retailer will run out of some SKUs in the B category because it does not carry the same amount of backup stock for B items as it does for A items.

The C items account for 65 percent of SKUs but contribute to only 10 percent of sales. The planner may plan to carry some C items only in very small or very large sizes of the most basic shirts, with special orders used to satisfy customer demand.

Finally, the buyer discovers that the remaining 20 percent of the SKUs, D items, have virtually no sales until they are marked down. Not only are these items excess merchandise and an unproductive investment, but they also distract from the rest of the inventory and clutter the store shelves. The buyer decides to eliminate most of these items from the assortment plan.

Multiattribute Analysis Method for Evaluating Vendors

The **multiattribute analysis method** for evaluating vendors uses a weighted-average score for each vendor. The score is based on the importance of various issues and the vendor's performance on those issues. This method is similar to the multiattribute approach that can be used to understand how customers evaluate stores and merchandise, as we discussed in Chapter 3. Retailing View 10.5 describes Home Depot's system for vendor evaluation.

To better understand the multiattribute analysis method of evaluating vendors, either current or proposed, consider the example in Exhibit 10–17 for vendors of men's casual slacks.

A buyer can evaluate vendors using the following five steps:

1. Develop a list of issues to consider in the evaluation (column 1).[18]

2. In conjunction with the GMM, determine the importance weights for each issue in column 1 on a scale from 1 to 10 (column 2), where 1 equals not important and 10 equals very important. For instance, the buyer and the merchandise manager believe that vendor reputation should receive a 9 because it's very important to the retailer's image. Merchandise quality receives a 5 because it's moderately important. Finally, a vendor's selling history is less important, so it could be rated 3.

3. Make judgments about each individual brand's performance on each issue (remaining columns). Note that some brands have high ratings on some issues but not on others.

4. Develop an overall score by multiplying the importance of each issue by the performance of each brand or its vendor. For instance, vendor reputation importance (9) multiplied by the performance rating for brand A (5) is 45. Promotional

---

Which of these shirts is an A item? B item?
© Karinabak/Dreamstime.com.

multiattribute analysis method A method for evaluating vendors that uses a weighted average score for each vendor, which is based on the importance of various issues and the vendor's performance on those issues.

Home Depot Takes Vendor Evaluations Seriously

Home Depot's vendor evaluation program focuses on three categories of excellence. The first, behavioural, helps it protect the reputation of its brand while instilling social and environmental responsibility into its vendor relationships. The second, manufacturing, is designed to improve product quality, cost, and innovation. The third, the supply chain category, is intended to reduce overall costs through process integration and standardization.

Home Depot has high expectations in terms of product quality, innovation, availability, on-time delivery, safety in production and shipping, compliance with laws and codes of conduct, and sensitivity to brand reputation. Its system measures service and ensures compliance specifically through the Vendor Center website. It features continuously updated information about how to do business with Home Depot, including the corporate performance policy, updates, news, information on events and training, and scorecards.

Included in the laundry list of expectations is Home Depot's Social and Environmental Responsibility (SER) program, which addresses a wide range of issues related to vendors' proper treatment of their workers and the environment, including age requirements, wages, working conditions, emergency planning, health and safety, and prohibitions against forced labour, fraud, and discrimination. The program combines regular audits of vendor factories with extensive education to help vendors understand the retailer's expectations.

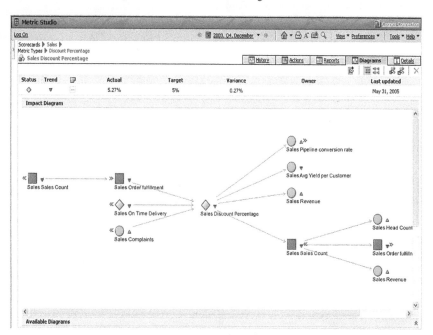

Home Depot's vendor analysis scorecard gives everyone a quick view of how the vendor is doing. Green is good, but red isn't.

© Cognos, an IBM Company.

Home Depot posts online vendor scorecards, providing graphical representations of their performance levels. Each participating vendor is rated on criteria such as compliance with shipping-platform standards and import on-time delivery. The vendors and Home Depot can observe trends over 13-month periods. Green, yellow, and red "lights" for each category let vendors know how they have been rated at a glance.

Although Home Depot's compliance program focuses on education instead of punishment, vendors pay a price if they fail to meet the company's strict requirements. Fines for non-compliance with its shipping standards amount to $10 000 for the first violation and $25 000 each time thereafter.

Sources: "Retail Supply Chains: 'Back End' or Business Value?" http://www.Cognos.com, November 29, 2006; Robert J. Bowman, "Home Depot Turns Its Attention to Vendor Performance Management," *SupplyChainBrain.com*, June 2006.

Exhibit 10–17
Multiattribute Analysis Method for Evaluating Vendors

Issues (1)	Importance Evaluation of Issues (I) (2)	PERFORMANCE EVALUATIONS OF INDIVIDUAL BRANDS ACROSS ISSUES			
		Brand A (P_a) (3)	Brand B (P_b) (4)	Brand C (P_c) (5)	Brand D (P_d) (6)
Vendor reputation	9	5	9	4	8
Service	8	6	6	4	6
Meets deliver dates	6	5	7	4	4
Merchandise quality	5	5	4	6	5
Markup opportunity	5	5	4	4	5
Country of origin	6	5	3	3	8
Product fashionability	7	6	6	3	8
Selling history	3	5	5	5	5
Promotional assistance	4	5	3	4	7
Overall evaluation a $\sum_{i-1}^{n} I_j \times P_{ij}$		280	298	212	341

$\sum_{i-1}^{n}$ = Sum of the expression

I_j = Importance weight assigned to the ith dimension.

P_{ij} = Performance evaluation for jth brand alternative on the ith issue.

1 = Not important

10 = Very important

assistance importance (4) multiplied by the performance rating (7) for vendor D is 28. This type of analysis illustrates an important point: It doesn't pay to perform well on issues that retailers don't believe are very important. Although vendor D performed well on promotional assistance, the buyer didn't rate this issue highly in importance, so the resulting score was still low.

5. To determine a vendor's overall rating, add the products for each brand for all issues. In Exhibit 10–17, brand D has the highest overall rating (341), so D is the preferred vendor.

This chapter provides an overview of the merchandise management planning process. Merchandise is broken down into categories for planning purposes. Buyers and planners manage these categories, often with the help of their major vendors.

The key performance measures used to assess merchandise management are GMROI and its components, sales-to-stock ratio, inventory turnover, and gross margin. High inventory turnover is important for a retailer's financial success. But if the retailer attempts to push inventory turnover to its limit, stockouts and increased costs may result.

The steps in the merchandise management process are (1) forecasting category sales, (2) developing an assortment plan, (3) determining appropriate inventory levels and product availability, (4) developing a plan for managing inventory, (5) allocating merchandise to stores, and (6) monitoring and evaluating performance and making adjustments.

Buying systems for staple merchandise are very different from those for fashion merchandise. Because staple merchandise is sold month after month and the sales levels are predictable, an automated continuous replenishment system is often used to manage staple merchandise categories.

The sales forecast and inventory turnover work together to drive the merchandise budget plan for fashion merchandise. The sales forecast is broken down by month, based on historical seasonality patterns. It's necessary to purchase more in months when sales are forecast to be higher than average. Planned inventory turnover is converted to stock-to-sales ratios and used in the merchandise budget plan to determine the inventory level necessary to support sales. Monthly stock-to-sales ratios are then adjusted to reflect seasonal sales patterns. The end product of the merchandise budget planning process is the dollar amount of merchandise a buyer should purchase each month for a category if the sales forecast and inventory turnover goals are to be met.

The open-to-buy system begins where the merchandise budget plan and staple goods inventory management systems leave off. It tracks how much merchandise is purchased for delivery in each month. Using an open-to-buy system, buyers know exactly how much money they have spent compared to how much they plan to spend.

Once the merchandise is purchased, merchandise buyers in multistore chains must allocate the merchandise to stores. The buyers must not only look at the differences in sales potential among stores, but also consider the differences in the characteristics of the customer base.

The performance of buyers, vendors, and individual SKUs must be determined. Three different approaches can evaluate merchandise performance. The sell-through analysis is more useful for examining the performance of individual SKUs in the merchandise plan. The buyer compares actual with planned sales to determine whether more merchandise needs to be ordered or whether the it should be put on sale. In an ABC analysis, merchandise is rank-ordered from highest to lowest. The merchandising team uses this information to set inventory management policies. For example, the most productive SKUs should carry sufficient backup stock to never be out of stock. Finally, the multi-attribute method is most useful for evaluating vendors' performance.

Key Terms

ABC analysis
backup stock
breaking sizes
category captain
category life cycle
category management
classification
continuous replenishment
cycle stock
department
depth

fashion merchandise category
fill rate
forecast
inventory
lead time
markdown money
merchandise category
merchandise group
merchandise management
model stock plan
multiattribute analysis method

order point
perpetual inventory
product availability
pull distribution strategy
push distribution strategy
seasonal merchandise category
sell-through analysis
service level
staple merchandise category
stock keeping unit (SKU)

Get Out & Do It!

1. **CONNECT EXERCISE** The Vendor Evaluation Model uses the multiattribute analysis method for evaluating vendors, as described in the chapter. Access your Student Resources in Connect and click on Vendor Evaluation Model in the additional resources for this chapter. There are two spreadsheets. Open the first spreadsheet, *vendor evaluation 1.xls*. This spreadsheet is the same as Exhibit 10–15. If you were selling Brand A to the retailer, which numbers would change? Change the numbers in the matrix and see the effect on the overall evaluation. Go to the second spreadsheet, labelled *evaluation 2.xls*. This spreadsheet can be used to evaluate brands or merchandise you might stock in your store. Assume you own a bicycle shop. List the brands you might consider stocking and the issues you would consider in selecting brands to stock. Fill in the importance of the issues (10 = very important, 1 = not very important) and the evaluation of each brand on each characteristic (10 = excellent, 1 = poor). Determine which is the best brand for your store.

2. **INTERNET EXERCISE** Go to the home page of the following three retail trade publications: *WWD* at http://www.wwd.com, *Chain Store Age* at http://www.chainstoreage.com, and *Retailing Today* at http://www.retailingtoday.com. Find an article in each that focuses on managing merchandise. How can these articles help retailers with merchandise planning decisions?

3. **INTERNET EXERCISE** Go to http://www.sas.com/resources/brochure/sas-merchandise-intelligence-overview.pdf. How does the SAS Merchandise Intelligence product provide retailers with information to support merchandise planning, forecasting, and measurement?

4. **GO SHOPPING** Visit a big-box office supply store and then a discount store to shop for school supplies. Contrast the breadth and depth offered at each. What are the advantages and disadvantages of breadth versus depth from each retailer's perspective? What are the advantages and disadvantages from the consumer's perspective?

DISCUSSION QUESTIONS AND PROBLEMS

1. Inventory shrinkage can be a problem for many retailers. How does the merchandise budget planning process account for inventory shrinkage?

2. Using the 80–20 principle, how can a retailer make certain that there is enough inventory of fast-selling merchandise and a minimal amount of slow-selling merchandise?

3. What is the order point and how many units should be reordered if a food retailer has an item with a seven-day lead time, ten-day review time, and daily demand of eight units? Say 65 units are on hand and the retailer must maintain a backup stock of 20 units to maintain a 95 percent service level.

4. A buyer at a sporting goods store in Vancouver receives a shipment of 400 ski parkas on October 1 and expects to sell out by January 31. On November 1, the buyer still has 375 parkas left. What issues should the buyer consider in evaluating the selling season's progress?

5. How and why would you expect variety and assortment to differ between a traditional bricks-and-mortar store and its Internet counterpart?

6. Simply speaking, increasing inventory turnover is an important goal for a retail manager. What are the consequences of turnover that is too slow? Too fast?

7. Assume you are the grocery buyer for canned fruits and vegetables at a five-store supermarket chain. Del Monte has told you and your boss that it would be responsible for making all inventory decisions for those merchandise categories. Del Monte will now determine how much to order and when shipments should be made. It promises a 10 percent increase in gross margin dollars in the coming year. Would you take Del Monte up on its offer? Justify your answer.

8. A buyer at Old Navy has received a number of customer complaints that he has been out of stock on some sizes of men's T-shirts. The buyer subsequently decides to increase this category's product availability from 80 percent to 90 percent. What will be the impact on backup stock and inventory turnover? Would your answer be the same if the product category were men's fleece sweatshirts?

9. Variety, assortment, and product availability are the cornerstones of the merchandise planning process. Provide examples of retailers that have done an outstanding job of positioning their stores on the basis of one or more of these issues.

10. A buyer is trying to decide from which vendor to buy a certain item. The item can be purchased as either a manufacturer brand or private-label brand. Using the following information, determine which vendor the buyer should use.

Issues	PERFORMANCE EVALUATIONS OF BRANDS		
	Importance Weight	Manufacturer Brand	Private-Label Brand
Vendor reputation	8	5	5
Service	7	6	7
Meets delivery dates	9	7	5
Perceived merchandise quality	7	8	4
Markup opportunity	6	4	8
Demand-generating ability	5	7	5
Promotional assistance	3	6	8

CHAPTER ELEVEN

Buying strategies

BUY NOW

LEARNING OBJECTIVES

Lo1   Determine what branding options are available to retailers.

Lo2   Explore the issues retailers should consider when sourcing internationally.

Lo3   Examine how retailers prepare for and conduct negotiations with their vendors.

Lo4   Investigate why retailers (buyers) are building strategic relationships with their vendors (sellers).

SPOTLIGHT ON RETAILING

PARTNERING FOR POSITIVE IMPACT

There is a shift taking place in the relationships and strategic partnerships that businesses in just about every sector are forming. The smaller, more interconnected and competitive the world gets, the more businesses are forming deeper, more genuine, and mutually beneficial partnerships based on shared values and goals. And few sectors are as well positioned to both drive this shift and benefit from it than the retail sector because relationships have always been at the core of its expertise and triumphs over marketplace adversity and challenges.

"Over the years, good retailers have made a huge effort to build relationships with staff and suppliers, but even more so with the community," says Paul McElhone, executive director of the University of Alberta's School of Retailing. "It's a big part of their success and it's more important than ever. Today's consumers are frustrated by companies that take and take from the community but don't give back. They're now supporting that with their wallets by supporting companies they feel are doing great work in the communities."

A CSR shift. Not that long ago, however, corporate social responsibility (CSR)—doing great work in the community—typically consisted of a retailer giving donations and/or volunteer hours to charitable causes. It was a philanthropic act that felt right but often seemed primarily a one-way street of giving. In the case of smaller retailers, frequently it didn't even have the added marketing benefit of being perceived as one of the good guys because many, such as Longo Brothers Fruit Markets Inc. (Longo's), simply didn't toot their own horn.

"Our founders, the Longo family, have always supported charities and community events since they founded the store in 1956," says Rob Koss, Longo's VP of marketing. "But they have been very humble about it."

In these days of public awareness and interest in social and environmental issues, retailers can no longer be humble. As consumers increasingly align themselves with retailers whose values they share, retailers have to let consumers know about what they stand for and show them that they walk the talk. In this, the non-profit sector has much to offer, especially when it comes to organizations that have developed a strong brand. Habitat for Humanity Canada, whose brand researchers have been put in the same league of strength as Starbucks, knows that its brand helps to strengthen the brand of its corporate partners, even ones with an already strong brand, such as Home Depot Canada. Longo's, which formed a strategic partnership with GE Appliances and Evergreen in 2011 to sponsor the not-for-profit's Evergreen Brick Works community environmental centre, is also aware of the benefits of a partnership with a strong non-profit brand.

"Evergreen is respected and recognized, so it also helps the business brand," says Koss. "We do a lot of great things in the community and working with Evergreen is a nice way to advertise that we do help out without it being crass advertising."

For the greater good. Forming relationships and partnerships that allow retailers to communicate with consumers with informative and helpful interaction, versus blatant advertising, is part of the shift that's going on, as the culture of social media spreads into the offline world, according to RedFlagDeals.com's founder, Derek Szeto. "We do encourage business large and small to come in and answer questions and help our users, but

© Deanpictures | Dreamstime.com.

we have to be careful with them coming in with a hard sell because that might have a negative effect and wouldn't serve the retailer well. We're trying to do an education piece on how we can all help each other."

Aware of the influence and strength of their own brands, some non-profits are developing a new type of relationship with retailers: one of supplier. An example of this is Mothers Against Drunk Driving, which in December 2011 launched a new line of non-alcoholic beverages, called MADD Virgin Drinks, to raise funds for the organization, educate on the need for designated drivers, and provide a non-alcoholic option for them. Not only do the retailers selling it benefit from the good CSR associated with the MADD brand, but they "also make a profit off the product," says Andrew Murie, MADD Canada's CEO. "It's a business type of donation rather than a charitable product. We benefit, our marketing partner benefits, and so does the retailer, and the customer has the satisfaction of knowing it's a win-win for everyone."

Identifying need and potential. The relationships that retailers such as Longo's and Home Depot are forming, however, are far more complex than simply about the power of brand. In the case of Longo's, the retailer joined forces with appliance manufacturer GE and top Toronto chefs to host demonstration-style cooking classes at its downtown Toronto store—with plans to expand the series to other stores across the GTA.

"It really comes down to the power of together. On the surface, it may seem strange for us to align with an appliance manufacturer, but when you peel it back, we have similar values, so it really makes sense," says Koss.

The partnership was born when GE's Philippe Meyersohn met Anthony Longo at a trade show. "We started talking and realized our organizations share similar values, including buying local and supporting local farmers. It's that commitment to our values that's resulted in it being so successful."

In order to remain competitive, says Koss, "I think we have to look at different ways. You have to understand your target demographics to make sure they align with a potential partner. For us the customer experience is first and foremost. We will never compromise our customer experience. So when we look at a partnership, we look at whether it will benefit the consumer."

Similarly, when it comes to Home Depot's support for Habitat ReStores, which sell gently used and new building materials to raise funds for Habitat's programs, the mutual benefits are multifold. Home Depot donates the majority of its return product to the ReStores. "We don't have a great way of tracking it but we estimate it represents $4.5 million to us," says Rob Voisin, director, ReStore Services. "We attribute a huge part of our success to our partnership with Home Depot. We can take problem product off their hand, whether it's returned product, or incorrectly ordered product, or discontinued product, so Home Depot doesn't have to have them shipped somewhere, including a landfill."

Home Depot has leveraged its partnership with Habitat to also help its own suppliers. "We have a few vendors who had established partnerships separately with Habitat and a couple of years ago they asked if they could use Home Depot stores as a hub to allow Habitat affiliates to come in and take some of that material. Now they're able to leverage their product donation through our stores and save money by using the existing structure."

Pushing the agenda. In other cases, retailers are forming strategic partnerships to push forward causes that affect the environment and society as well as their industry. David Smith, Sobeys' VP of retail strategy and sustainability, embarked on a leadership role back in 2008 to push sustainable seafood forward. It's a journey that has led the chain to initiate discussions and collaboration with a large network of players—from fishermen to NGOs, government, suppliers, and consumers. "This isn't consumer-driven, so it's up to us as retailers to lead the way," says Smith.

From Sobeys' perspective, the movement toward sustainable seafood has been slow, and as a result, it's a niche market. "The mainstream consumer is not really prepared to make a sacrifice for it," says Smith. "So you have to think of sustainability as a value-add. The issue needs a mainstream adoption. We have over 50 sustainable certified products, but also we're involved as a catalyst for change in the supply chain."

To that end, Sobeys held a national supplier summit with 150 of its suppliers to educate them on the issues of sustainable seafood and has also worked with partners on a website called ThisFish.info, which allows consumers to trace the journey of the fish they've purchased through the supply chain right to the fisherman who caught it.

Ultimately, Sobeys' leadership and partnerships for sustainable seafood, similar to the efforts being made by other retailers across the country, are about embracing the new strategic business mindset, which is all about collaboration that combines pragmatism and good business sense with shared values that can help create a sustainable and better future for earth, mankind—and retailer.

Source: Alexandra Lopez Pacheco, "Partnering for Positive Impact," *Canadian Retailer*, Spring 2012, Volume 22, Issue 2, pp. 40–41. Canadian Retailer, a publication of Retail Council of Canada.

The preceding chapter outlined the merchandise management process and the steps in the process that buyers go through to determine what and how much merchandise to buy. After creating an assortment plan for the category, forecasting sales, and developing a plan outlining the flow of merchandise (how much merchandise needs to be ordered and when it needs to be delivered), the next step in the merchandise management process is to acquire the merchandise. The process for acquiring merchandise differs for well-known national brands and private-label brands that are available exclusively from the retailer. Thus, the first strategic decision that needs to be made is to determine the type of brands to buy for the category.

When buying merchandise, buyers meet with vendors at wholesale marketing or in their offices and negotiate many issues such as prices, delivery dates, payment terms, and financial support for advertising and markdowns. The buying process for private-label merchandise is often more complex. Some retailers have their own design and sourcing departments that work with buyers to specify the merchandise designs and then negotiate with manufacturers to produce the merchandise. Because merchandise is often manufactured outside of Canada, these retailers need to deal with the complexities of international business transactions. In other cases, buyers might negotiate with national-brand vendors or manufacturers to buy merchandise designed by the supplier exclusivity for the retailer.

Although buyers meet and negotiate with national-brand vendors and private-label manufacturers each season concerning new merchandise, there is a trend toward developing long-term strategic relationships with key suppliers. These partnerships enable the collaboration needed to develop the efficient supply chains discussed in Chapter 9, as well as joint merchandise and marketing programs.

manufacturer brand
A line of products designed, produced, and marketed by a vendor; also called a *national brand*.

Lo1 Branding Strategies

Retailers and their buyers face a strategic decision about the mix of national brands and private-label brands sold exclusively by retailers. They can buy manufacturer brands such as Levi's, Kellogg's, or Black & Decker. Or they can develop their own private labels such as Old Navy jeans, President's Choice cookies from Loblaws, or Craftsman tools from Sears. Some use a mix of the two. In this section, we examine the relative advantages of these branding decisions, which are summarized in Exhibit 11–1.

Manufacturer Brands

A **manufacturer brand**, also known as a *national brand*, is a product designed, produced, and marketed by a vendor and sold to many different retailers. The manufacturer is responsible for developing the merchandise and establishing an image for the brand. In some cases, the manufacturer will use an umbrella or family-branding strategy in which its name appears as part of the brand name for a specific product, such as Kellogg's Corn Flakes. However, some manufacturers, such as Philip Morris—owner of Kraft Foods, Miller Brewing Company, as well as Philip Morris (tobacco products)—don't associate their name with the brand.

Some retailers organize some of their categories around their most important national brands. For instance, buyers in department stores are responsible for brands, such as Clinique or Estée Lauder, rather than for products, such as lipstick and fragrances. Clothing is also often organized by manufacturer brand (e.g., Polo/Ralph Lauren, Levi's, Liz Claiborne, or DKNY). These brands often have their own boutique within stores. Managing a category by national brand,

DID YOU KNOW?

Health and beauty (74 percent), pet care (47 percent), breakfast cereal (63 percent), and laundry detergent (69 percent) are the categories where brand names far outpace rival private labels as the preferred choice for consumers.[1]

Exhibit 11–1

Relative Advantages of Manufacturer versus Private Brands

Impact on Store	TYPE OF VENDOR	
	Manufacturer Brands	Private-Label Brands
Store loyalty	?	+
Store image	+	+
Traffic flow	+	+
Selling and promotional expenses	+	−
Restrictions	−	+
Differential advantages	−	+
Margins	?	?

+ advantage to the retailer, − disadvantage to the retailer, ? depends on circumstances.

rather than a more traditional classification scheme, is useful so that merchandise can be purchased in a coordinated manner around a central theme.

Buying from vendors of manufacturer brands can help store image, traffic flow, and selling/promotional expenses. Retailers buy from vendors of manufacturer brands because they have a customer following—people go into the store and ask for them by name. Loyal customers of manufacturer brands generally know what to expect from the products and feel comfortable with them, as with Samsonite luggage.

Manufacturers devote considerable resources to creating demand for their products. As a result, relatively less money is required by the retailer for selling and promotional expenses for manufacturer brands. For instance, Guess? Inc., manufacturer of jeans and other casual clothing, attempts to communicate a constant and focused message to the consumer by coordinating advertising with in-store promotions and displays.

DID YOU KNOW?

The number of shoppers who think brand-name packaging is more attractive than private-label packaging decreased 14 percent in 2011.[2]

Manufacturer brands typically have lower realized gross margins than private-label brands. These lower gross margins are due to the manufacturer assuming the cost of promoting the brand and increased competition among retailers selling these brands. Typically, many retailers offer the same manufacturer brands in a market, so customers compare prices for these brands across stores. Retailers often offer significant discounts on some manufacturer brands to attract customers to their stores.

Stocking national brands may increase or decrease store loyalty. If the manufacturer brand is available through a limited number of retail outlets (e.g., Lancôme cosmetics or Diesel jeans), customers loyal to the manufacturer brand will also become loyal to the stores selling the brand. If, on the other hand, manufacturer brands are readily available from many retailers in a market, customer loyalty may decrease because the retailer can't differentiate itself from the competition.

Another problem with manufacturer brands is that they can limit a retailer's flexibility. Vendors of strong brands can dictate how their products are displayed, advertised, and priced. Jockey, for instance, tells retailers exactly when and how its products (such as underwear) should be advertised.

Licensed Brands A special type of manufacturer brand is a **licensed brand**, in which the owner of a well-known brand name (licensor) enters into a contract with a licensee to develop, produce, and sell the branded merchandise. The licensee may be either the retailer that contracts with a manufacturer to produce the licensed product or a third party that contracts to have the merchandise produced and then sells it to the retailer. For example, fashion designers often license their name to sunglass and perfume companies.

Licensed brands' market share has grown increasingly large in recent years. Owners of trade names not typically associated with manufacturing have also gotten into the licensing business. For instance, the manufacturer of the sweatshirt or baseball cap emblazoned with your university or college's logo pays your school a licensing fee. If it didn't, it would be infringing on the school's logo (a trademark) and therefore would be involved in counterfeiting.

Private-Label Brands

Private-label brands, also called *store brands*, are products developed by a retailer and available for sale only from that retailer. Victoria's Secret and The Gap are among the top 20 private-label brands. Exhibit 11–2 gives examples of more private-label

licensed brand Brand for which the licensor (owner of a well-known name) enters into a contractual arrangement with a licensee (a retailer or a third party). The licensee either manufactures or contracts with a manufacturer to produce the licensed product and pays a royalty to the licensor.

Exhibit 11–2
Examples of Private-Label Brands

Industry	Store	Brand
Grocery stores	Metro	Irresistibles, Selection
	Loblaws	President's Choice, no name, Joe Fresh, Exact
	Sobeys	Compliments, Gourmet Minute
Mass merchandisers	Walmart	Great Value, Equate, Our Finest
	Giant Tiger	Giant Value
Department stores	Hudson's Bay	1670, Lord & Taylor, Hudson's Bay Signature Collection, Black Brown 1826, Gluckstein Home
	Sears	Kenmore, Craftsman, Martha Stewart
Specialty stores	Canadian Tire	Mastercraft
	Holt Renfrew	Holts, Miss Renfrew, hr2
	Home Depot	Husky, Ryobi, BEHR

brands. Retailers typically develop specifications for the merchandise and then contract with manufacturers who are often located in countries with developing economies to produce the products. But the retailer, not the manufacturer, is responsible for promoting the brand.

The size of retail firms has increased through consolidation, and private labels have assumed a new level of significance by establishing distinctive identities among retailers. Some retailers, such as The Gap and Club Monaco, sell their own labels exclusively as an integral element of their distinctiveness. Other retailers, such as Hudson's Bay and Sears, successfully mix manufacturer brands with their own retailer brands to project their unique image statement.

Private-branded products now account for an average of 18 percent of the purchases in Canada and roughly 26 percent in Europe. Switzerland has the highest consumption rate of private label goods, which currently stands at 45 percent of consumer packaged goods (CPG).[3] Private-label dollar volume in supermarkets, drug chains, and mass merchandisers is increasing twice as fast as national brands. Retailing View 11.1 describes Asda's private-label strategy.

Private labels have always added value to retailers, and Hudson's Bay, Shoppers Drug Mart, and Loblaws are clearly leading the way. Hudson's Bay claims 60 percent of its apparel assortment is private brand, and this trend is expected to grow. Holt Renfrew, a retailer that earns most of its profit from carrying powerful, high-fashion brand names, has 25 percent of its apparel inventory in private brands with desirable price points.

Consumer attitudes are driving the trend. Consumers are replacing more expensive brands with private brands from retailers. The trend seems to be about price rather than designer label: 80 percent of the jeans sold in Canada are under $39.

Offering private labels provides a number of benefits to retailers, as Exhibit 11–1 shows.

generic branding A branding strategy that targets a price-sensitive segment by offering a no-frills product at a discount price.

- The exclusivity of strong private labels boosts store loyalty. For instance, the MotoMaster line of auto parts and accessories in Canadian Tire are not found at other stores.

- Private labels enhance store image if the brands are of high quality and fashionable.

- Successful private-label brands can draw customers to the store. They can be a good

deal—10 to 18 percent less expensive than national brands in Canada, and as much as 25 percent cheaper in Europe.[4]

- Retailers that purchase private-label brands don't have the same restrictions on display, promotion, or price that often encumber their strategy with manufacturer brands. Retailers purchasing private brands also have more control over manufacturing, quality control, and distribution of the merchandise.

- Gross margin opportunities may be greater with private-label brands.

But there are drawbacks to using private-label brands. Although gross margins may be higher for private-label brands than for manufacturer brands, there are other expenses that aren't readily apparent. Retailers must make significant investments to design merchandise, create customer awareness, and develop a favourable image for their private-label brands. When private-label manufacturers are located outside Canada, the complications become even more significant. Sales associates may need additional training to help them sell private-label brands against better-known brands. If the private-label merchandise doesn't sell, the retailer can't return the merchandise to the manufacturer. These problems are most severe for high-fashion merchandise. Since the financial meltdown of 2008, private-label market share has been stagnant due to shoppers increasingly turning to promotions to save, and name brands have driven more sales through savvy pricing strategies.[5]

Private-Label Options[6]   Retail branding strategies have run the gamut from closely imitating manufacturer-brand packaging and products to distinct brand images, from low product quality and prices to premium positioning, and from non-existent promotion and merchandising to intense activity. We group private brands into four broad categories: generic, premium, parallel, and exclusive.

Generic branding targets a price-sensitive segment by offering a no-frills product at a discount price. Known as *generic* or *house brands*, such unbranded, unadvertised merchandise is found mainly in drug, grocery, and discount stores. These products are used typically for commodities like milk or

> **DID YOU KNOW?**
>
> In Switzerland, 45 percent of Consumer Package Goods (CPG) dollars go to store-brand products. By comparison, private-label penetration in Canada is 18 percent, slightly higher than the global average of 16.5 percent.[7]

U.K.'s Asda Loves Private Labels

The British supermarket retailer Asda, owned by Walmart, has a private-label portfolio that accounts for 45 percent of its grocery and 50 percent of its non-food sales. Asda has extended its own label into such categories as healthy eating, organics, and food for kids, and now is placing more emphasis on developing premium-priced private labels.

Asda offers six private-label brands in the food, health and beauty, and household categories. In addition, it has its successful George private-label clothing brand and a selection of Asda-branded financial services, including home, motor, and life insurance. Some of its brands include:

Asda, a U.K. chain owned by Walmart, developed George, a private-label apparel and footwear brand. Although very successful in the U.K, it has not been as successful in Walmart stores in the U.S. and Canada.
© Ashley Cooper/CORBIS.

- Smart Price—Economy-value, no-frills food and general merchandise essentials.
- Best-in-Market—Everyday food and general merchandise items at low prices.
- Good for you!—Foods with lower fat content than standard Asda brand alternatives.
- Organic—Best-value organic "everyday" products.
- Onn—Mid-level eclectic brand with stylized designs.
- Extra Special—Asda's premium private-label food brand.

- More for Kids—Healthier, fun products for kids across the food and health and beauty categories.

The Extra Special premium private-label brand has grown from 40 SKUs in 2000 to more than 750 across categories that include confectionery, soft drinks, snacks, trifles, specialty breads, prepared meat and fish meals, and a wide range of cheeses and sliced meats. The criteria for an Extra Special branded product include better taste and the finest ingredients compared with standard alternatives or national premium equivalents, but affordable at a 10 to 15 percent lower price than competitors' premium private-label equivalents.

Asda's private-label clothing and footwear brand, George, is the fourth-largest apparel brand in the United Kingdom. Created by George Davies, the former owner of a successful chain of British apparel stores, George merchandise comprises sleek but inexpensive clothing, accessories, and undergarments for women and men. Walmart is importing George merchandise and selling it as part of its effort to upgrade its apparel offering. But George merchandise has not been as successful in the United States and Canada.

Sources: http://www.asda.co.uk (accessed October 16, 2007); "Odin Drives ASDA 'Extra Special' Range onto Shelves," *The Retail Bulletin*, August 30, 2007; Bill Condie, "Asda Plans to Spruce Up Tired George Label as Growth Slows Down," *Knight Ridder Tribune Business News*, September 14, 2007.

eggs in grocery stores and underwear in discount stores. Once the mainstay of private-label brands, the sales of generics have been declining. These products are labelled with the name of the commodity and thus actually have no brand name distinguishing them.

Premium branding offers the consumer a private label at a comparable manufacturer-brand quality, usually with modest price savings. Examples of premium labels include Loblaw's President's Choice, Tesco's Finest (U.K.), Marks & Spencer's St. Michael (U.K.), Woolworth's Select (Australia), Pick and Pay's Choice (South Africa), and Albert Heijn's AH Select (Netherlands).[8] The premium brand attempts to match or exceed the product quality standard of the prototypical manufacturer brand in its category. There is no intention to duplicate the packaging or to trade off the brand equity of a particular manufacturer brand. However, consumers frequently perceive the retailer premium labels as competing manufacturer brands.

Retailer premium brands, with the appearance of comparability, compete directly with manufacturer national brands. To succeed, the retailer must commit the resources in

premium branding A branding strategy that offers the consumer a private label at a comparable manufacturer-brand quality, usually with a modest price savings.

market research, product development, quality control, and promotion in its market area commensurate with its manufacturer-brand competitors. Consequently, development of a premium branding program precludes many retailers that have few resources from diverting to this strategy. President's Choice, Loblaw's premium private label, competes on quality, not on price. Kellogg's has two scoops of raisins in its cereal, but President's Choice cereal has four and is still cheaper. The Decadent chocolate chip cookie under the President's Choice label has 39 percent chocolate chips by weight, compared with 19 percent in Chips Ahoy! In addition, it uses real butter instead of hydrogenated coconut oil and quality chocolate instead of artificial chips. The resulting product is Canada's market leader in chocolate chip cookies, despite being sold in only 20 percent of the market held by Loblaws.[9]

The development of super-premium and luxury private-label ranges are becoming part of retailers' multi-tier pricing strategies as they attract the attention of consumers seeking luxury at an affordable price. Loblaw Companies, marketer of the first and oldest Canadian premium private-label range under the President's Choice brand, was the first to announce its new and fairly extensive Black Label super-premium line. This new line is positioned as gourmet yet still affordable indulgences and luxuries and includes a range of product categories such as confectionery, cheese, pasta, and cookies.

In the summer of 2011, Walmart Canada test-marketed and launched its own black-label line of private-label food and beverages, which it named Our Finest. Its new premium-positioned private-label range features close to 200 SKUs. Other retailers have been developing and promoting new private-label brands in the super-premium and luxury brand segments, including Shoppers Drug Mart (Life Premium Gourmet) and Jean Coutu (Desir Lait line of boxed chocolates). This strategy has helped increase overall customer traffic and spending in stores in the face of an increasingly competitive grocery retailing landscape.

Parallel branding represents private labels that closely imitate the packaging and product attributes of leading manufacturer brands but with

parallel branding A branding strategy that represents a private label that closely imitates the trade dress (packaging) and product attributes of leading manufacturer brands but with a clearly articulated "invitation to compare" in its merchandising approach and on its product label.

exclusive co-brand A brand developed by a national brand vendor, often in conjunction with a retailer, and sold exclusively by the retailer.

a clearly articulated "invitation to compare" in its merchandising approach and on its product label. This invitation to compare on the product label was the basis for legal action. Like copycat branding, parallel branding seeks to benefit from the brand equity of the manufacturer brand by closely imitating the national brand's packaging and product qualities. However, the invitation to compare leaves little doubt that different manufacturers produce the two products. Consequently, the imitative packaging does not constitute a trademark infringement. Nevertheless, patent considerations can be an issue if appropriate discretion is not used.

Parallel branding is a leveraging strategy used to bolster a retailer's private-brand sales. The closer two products are in form, logo, labelling, and packaging, the more they are perceived as substitutes. Parallel brands attempt to produce a product and packaging so similar to the manufacturer brand that the only noticeable difference between the two is price. This promotes the view that the parallel brand provides better value for the consumer. Manufacturer brands produce store traffic, and the parallel brand leverages this traffic into parallel brand sales through similar packaging and aggressive store signage, displays, and shelf location. For instance, Shoppers Drug Mart's Life brand products are placed next to the manufacturer's brands and often look like them.

An **exclusive co-brand** is developed by a national brand vendor, often in conjunction with a retailer, and is sold exclusively by the retailer. The simplest form of an exclusive co-brand is when a national brand manufacturer assigns different model numbers and has different exterior features for the same basic product sold by different retailers. For example, LG appliances sold at Home Depot might have different model numbers than LG appliances with similar features available at The Brick. These exclusive models make it difficult for consumers to compare prices for virtually the same appliance sold by different retailers. Since the retailers are less likely to compete on prices when selling these exclusive co-brands, their margins for the products reach higher, and they are motivated to devote more resources toward selling the exclusive co-brands than they would for similar national brands.[10]

A more sophisticated form of exclusive co-branding is when a manufacturer develops an exclusive product or product category for a retailer. For example, Canadian manufacturer Gracious Living Group sells Eon Decking exclusively at The

Only at Hudson's Bay

Hudson's Bay Company (HBC), which was incorporated in 1670 by a British royal charter under King Charles II, is Canada's leading department store. HBC offers well-edited assortments of national, private, and exclusive popular fashion, beauty, home, and accessory designers and brands. HBC operates 92 stores in 8 provinces across Canada, as well as its website, www.thebay.com. HBC's portfolio also includes Lord & Taylor, a department store with 48 full-line store locations in the United States, and Home Outfitters, Canada's largest home specialty superstore with 69 locations.

While Hudson's Bay (or The Bay) carries many high-profile brands such as Coach, the retailer is building a strong portfolio of private in-house and exclusive brands at its Bay and Lord & Taylor chains. In fall 2013, the company introduced a new private brand called 1670 for contemporary men's and women's apparel at "moderate price-points." It expanded its Lord & Taylor line in 2014 beyond cashmere fashions to a wide assortment of goods. The other labels include the Hudson's Bay Signature Collection, Gluckstein Home, and Black Brown 1826. These private-label brands complement the company's current offering of national brands and "fill some gaps" in the overall assortment in terms of faster response time to shifting trends and the flow and timing of merchandise shipments.

The push on its own private-label brands also gives the company more latitude in setting prices without having to match competitors' discounts, and it scales back on middlemen, which in turn helps to generate higher margins and keeps customers from going to its vendors' rival stores. "As you watch the proliferation of vendors opening their own stores, you're seeing the reverse proliferation of retailers doing their own product," said Marc Metrick, HBC's chief marketing officer. Fate is in the hands of the company itself, ensuring profitability, which is the most important factor to ensure market success. HBC has set a five-year goal for private-label sales to reach 15 percent of its overall $3.9 billion in annual revenue (excluding the sold-off Zellers chain), up from 9 percent, according to its securities filings.

On May 1, 2014, HBC opened its first Kleinfeld Bridal store in Canada. Kleinfeld is the largest luxury bridal retailer in the world and is featured on the reality show *Say Yes to the Dress* on the TLC cable network. Ronald Rothstein, co-owner of Kleinfeld, said it was attracted to Hudson's Bay because of its strong wedding registry business, its track record in selling luxury designer lines at The Room, and the savvy of Bonnie Brooks (past president of Hudson's Bay) and Richard Baker (chief executive officer of Hudson's Bay).

According to Brooks, "Bringing Kleinfeld to Canada further supports [the] overall product differentiation strategy for Hudson's Bay, which is to deliver new, relevant, and exclusive brands and concepts to the marketplace. This incredible partnership will further [HBC's] position as Canada's headquarters and leading destination for gift registry, and now for designer bridal wear." The store located on the seventh floor of Toronto's flagship Hudson Bay store is a 20 000-square-foot Kleinfeld flagship salon, with future locations in the downtown Vancouver and Montreal stores. Kleinfeld reportedly generates an estimated $1000 of sales per square foot per year, which could mean an additional $20 million per year for the Queen Street flagship store.

Sources: Marina Strauss, "Hudson's Bay Says 'Yes' to Kleinfeld's Dresses," *The Globe and Mail*, March 26, 2013 (accessed May 3, 2013); "Hudson's Bay Company to Eliminate Most Private Label Brands," *Retail Insider,* December 13, 2012, http://www.retail-insider.com/2012/12/hudsons-bay-company-to-eliminate-most.html (accessed May 3, 2013); Marina Strauss, "HBC Putting Its Own Stripe on Merchandise with Private Labels," *The Globe and Mail*, December 10, 2012 (accessed May 1, 2013); "Hudson's Bay Says 'Yes' to Kleinfeld," CNW news release, March 26, 2013, http://www.newswire.ca/en/story/1135757/hudson-s-bay-says-yes-to-kleinfeld# (accessed May 5, 2013); http://www.thebay.com; http://www.kleinfeldbridal.com; "Kleinfeld Bridal Opens 1st Canadian Location," *Retail Insider,* May 1, 2014, http://www.retail-insider.com/retail-insider/2014/4/kleinfeld-may-1st (accessed February 10, 2016).

Home Depot Canada. Eon is a complete alternative decking system composed of plastic, dramatically reducing the need for wood. As the only 100 percent plastic product with a wood grain finish at The Home Depot, Eon is positioned as a premium product in their lumber and building materials assortment.[11] Levi's has also developed the Signature brand jeans for sale at Walmart. And Hudson's Bay's exclusive brands, as discussed in Retailing View 11.2, are not available from its competitors.

A Brand or a Store?

The distinction between a store and a brand has become blurred in recent years. Some large retailers have developed strong private-label merchandise.

Other retailers, such as Roots, have such a strong brand name that the average consumer cannot make a distinction between store and brand. Roots, the Canadian casual clothing retailer, has capitalized on its strong name recognition by widening the variety of merchandise offered at its stores. It now sells a range of products, including home decorating items. Manufacturers are trying to emulate the success of retailers such as Zara, whose name has become a brand in its own right.

A natural extension of the retailer's brand strategy is to exploit strong retail name recognition by selling its products through channels other than its own stores. Starbucks made one of the most aggressive moves by a retailer to broaden its customer base. The coffee shop retailer that brought North America the "decaf latte" teamed up with PepsiCo to market Frappuccino, a coffee-and-milk blend sold through traditional grocery channels. Starbucks also engaged in a joint venture with Dreyer's Grand Ice Cream to distribute Starbucks coffee-flavoured ice cream, and entered into a long-term licensing agreement with Kraft Foods, Inc., to accelerate the growth of the Starbucks brand in the grocery channel.

On the other side of the distribution spectrum, several firms that have traditionally been exclusively manufacturers have become retailers. Examples are Apple, Guess?, Calvin Klein, Ralph Lauren, Levi's, Harley-Davidson, Sony, and Nike. Why have these manufacturers chosen to become retailers?

- First, by becoming retailers they have total control over the way their merchandise is presented to the public. They can price, promote, and merchandise their line with a unified strategy. They don't have to worry about retailers cherry-picking certain items or discounting the price, for instance.

- Second, they can use these stores to test new merchandise and merchandising concepts. Based on these tests' results, they can better advise other retailers what to buy and how to merchandise their stores.

- Third, these manufacturers/retailers use their stores to showcase their merchandise to the public as well.

- Finally, although these stores often compete with stores that carry the same merchandise, some would argue that having a stronger retail presence creates a name recognition and synergy between the manufacturer and retailer that benefits both parties.

Lo2 International Sourcing Decisions

A decision closely associated with branding decisions is determining where the merchandise is made. Retailers involved in private branding are faced with many challenges related to international sourcing decisions. Retailers buying manufacturer brands usually aren't responsible for determining where the merchandise is made, but a product's country of origin is often used as a signal of quality. Certain items are strongly associated with specific countries, and products from those countries, such as gold jewellery from Italy or cars from Japan, often benefit from those linkages.

In this section, we will first examine the cost implications of international sourcing decisions. Initially, it often looks like retailers can get merchandise from foreign suppliers more cheaply than from domestic sources. Unfortunately, there are lots of hidden costs, including managerial issues, associated with sourcing globally that make this decision more complicated. We then examine the trend toward sourcing closer to home or actually reversing the trend toward international sourcing by buying "made in Canada." This section concludes by exploring ethical issues associated with retailers who buy from vendors engaged in human rights and child-labour violations.

Costs Associated with Global Sourcing Decisions

A direct reason for sourcing globally rather than domestically is to save money. Retailers must examine several cost issues when making these decisions. The cost issues discussed in this section are country-of-origin effects, foreign currency fluctuations, tariffs, free trade zones, inventory carrying costs, and transportation costs.

Country-of-Origin Effects

The next time you are buying a shirt made in Western Europe (e.g., Italy, France, or Germany), notice that it's probably more expensive than a comparable shirt made in a developing country such as Hungary, Ecuador, or Cambodia. These Western

DID YOU KNOW?

Toronto is home to more than 550 apparel manufacturers, with wholesale shipments totalling nearly $1.4 billion annually, or 16 percent of the $9 billion Canadian market.[12]

European countries have a reputation for high fashion and quality. Unfortunately for the Canadian consumer, however, the amount of goods and services that can be purchased from those countries is significantly less than the amount of merchandise that can be purchased from developing countries for the same amount of money. When making international sourcing decisions, therefore, retailers must weigh the savings associated with buying from developing countries with the image associated with buying merchandise from a country that has a reputation for fashion and quality.

Other countries might have a technological advantage in the production of certain types of merchandise and can therefore provide their products to the world market at a relatively low price. For example, Japan has always been a leader in the development of consumer electronics. Although these products often enter the market at a high price, the price soon drops as Japanese manufacturers learn to produce the merchandise more efficiently.

Foreign Currency Fluctuations An important consideration when making global sourcing decisions is fluctuations in the currency of the exporting firm. Unless currencies are closely linked, for example, between Canada and the United States, changes in the exchange rate will increase or reduce the cost of the merchandise.

Suppose, for instance, that Hudson's Bay was purchasing watches from Swatch in Switzerland for $100 000, which would be equivalent to 150 000 Swiss francs (SFr) if the exchange rate were 1.5 SFr for each dollar. If the dollar fell to, say, 1.1 SFr before the firm had to pay for the watches, it would end up paying $136 364 (or 150 000 SFr ÷ 1.1). The euro has all but eliminated this problem among the participating European countries.

Tariffs A tariff, also known as a *duty*, is a tax placed by a government on imports.[13] Import tariffs have been used to shield domestic manufacturers from foreign competition and to raise money for the government. In general, since tariffs raise the cost of imported merchandise, retailers have always had a strong incentive to reduce them. The General Agreement on Tariffs and Trade (GATT), the North American Free Trade Agreement (NAFTA), and foreign trade zones all reduce tariffs.

World Trade Organization The World Trade Organization (WTO) replaced GATT in 1996. With 144 member-countries, the WTO has become the

Maquiladoras are manufacturing plants in Mexico that make goods and parts or process food for export. They are very popular because their costs are lower than those of their Canadian and U.S. counterparts.

Danita Delimont/Alamy.

global watchdog for free trade. As a result of the WTO and its predecessor GATT, worldwide tariffs have been reduced from 40 percent in 1947 to an estimated 4 percent in 2000.[14] The WTO will continue to push for tariff reductions on manufactured goods as well as for liberalization of trade in agriculture and services.

North American Free Trade Agreement The ratification of NAFTA on January 1, 1994, created a tariff-free market with 364 million consumers. NAFTA members are currently Canada, the United States, and Mexico. NAFTA is expected to strengthen North America's position when negotiating with the European Union.

Canadian retailers gain from NAFTA for two reasons. First, Mexican labour is relatively low-cost and abundant. Thus, retailers can either search for low-cost suppliers in Mexico or begin manufacturing merchandise there themselves. **Maquiladoras**—plants in Mexico that make goods and parts or process food for export—are plentiful, have lower costs than their Canadian counterparts, and are located throughout Mexico, particularly in border towns such as Nogales and Tijuana. Second, with the growing importance of quick response inventory systems, the time it takes to get merchandise into stores becomes ever more critical. Transit times are shorter and managerial control problems are reduced when sourcing from Mexico, compared to the Far East or Europe.

Free Trade Zones Retailers involved in foreign sourcing of merchandise can lower import tariffs by using free trade

maquiladoras
Manufacturing plants in Mexico that make goods and parts or process food for export to North America.

free trade zone A special area within a country that can be used for warehousing, packaging, inspection, labelling, exhibition, assembly, fabrication, or transshipment of imports without being subject to that country's tariffs.

opportunity cost of capital The rate available on the next-best use of the capital invested in the project at hand. The opportunity cost should be no lower than the rate at which a firm borrows funds, since one alternative is to pay back borrowed money. It can be higher, however, depending on the range of other opportunities available. Typically, the opportunity cost rises with investment risk.

zones. A **free trade zone** is a special area within a country that can be used for warehousing, packaging, inspection, labelling, exhibition, assembly, fabrication, or transshipment of imports without being subject to that country's tariffs.

To illustrate how a free trade zone can benefit retailers, consider how German cars are imported to a foreign trade zone in Guatemala for distribution throughout Central America. The duty for passenger vehicles is 100 percent of the landed cost of the vehicle. The duty for commercial vehicles, however, is only 10 percent. The German manufacturer imports commercial vans with no seats or carpeting, and with panels instead of windows. After paying the 10 percent import duty, it converts the vans to passenger station wagons in the free trade zone in Guatemala and sells them throughout Latin America.

Inventory Carrying Cost The cost of carrying inventory is likely to be higher when purchasing from suppliers outside Canada than from domestic suppliers.

$$\begin{array}{c}\text{Cost of}\\\text{carrying}\\\text{inventory}\end{array} = \begin{array}{c}\text{Average}\\\text{inventory}\\\text{value}\\\text{(at cost)}\end{array} \times \begin{array}{c}\text{Opportunity}\\\text{cost of capital}\end{array}$$

The **opportunity cost of capital** is the rate available on the next best use of the capital invested in the project at hand. It would include the cost of borrowing money for a similar investment, plus insurance and taxes.

Transportation Costs In general, the farther merchandise has to travel, the higher the transportation cost will be for any particular mode of transportation. For instance, the cost of shipping a container of merchandise by ship from China to Vancouver is significantly higher than the cost from Panama to Vancouver. Quick delivery via air express will increase end costs significantly.

Managerial Issues Associated with Global Sourcing Decisions

In the previous section, we examined the specific costs associated with global sourcing decisions.

In most cases, retailers can obtain hard cost information that will help them make their global sourcing decisions. The managerial issues discussed in this section—quality control and developing strategic partnerships—are not as easily evaluated.

Quality Control When sourcing globally, it's harder to maintain and measure quality standards than when sourcing domestically. Typically, these problems are more pronounced in countries that are far away and underdeveloped. For instance, it's easier to address a quality problem if it occurs on a shipment of dresses from Costa Rica to Canada than if the dresses were shipped from Jakarta because Costa Rica is much closer than Indonesia.

There are both direct and indirect ramifications for retailers if merchandise is delayed because it has to be remade due to poor quality. Suppose Hudson's Bay is having pants made in Haiti. Before the pants leave the factory, Hudson's Bay representatives find that the workmanship is so poor that the pants need to be remade. This delay reverberates throughout the system. Hudson's Bay could have extra backup stock to carry it through until the pants can be remade, however it's more likely that the company won't have advance warning of the problem, so the stores will be out of stock.

A more serious problem occurs if the pants are delivered to the stores without the problem having been detected. This could happen if the defect is subtle, such as inaccurate sizing. Customers can become irritated and question merchandise quality. Also, markdowns ensue because inventories become unbalanced and shopworn.

Building Strategic Partnerships The importance of building strategic partnerships is examined later in this chapter. It is typically harder to build these alliances when sourcing globally, particularly when the suppliers are far away and in underdeveloped countries. Communications are more difficult. There is often a language barrier, and there are almost always cultural differences. Business practices—everything from terms of payment to the issues of trade practices such as commercial bribery—are different in a global setting. The most important element in building a strategic alliance—maintaining the supplier's trust—is more arduous in an international environment.

Source Close to Home or Buy "Made in Canada"?

Some retailers are shifting suppliers from Asia and Europe to nearby Central American and Caribbean countries, or they are seeking products made in Canada. There are four reasons for this shift:

1. It may be more profitable for the reasons detailed above.

2. Quick response delivery systems and sourcing globally are inherently incompatible, yet both are important and growing trends in retailing. Quick response systems are based on short and consistent lead times. Vendors provide frequent deliveries with smaller quantities. There's no room for defective merchandise. For a quick response system to work properly, a strong alliance is needed between vendor and retailer that is based on trust and a sharing of information through electronic data interchange (EDI) or radio frequency identification data (RFID) and collaborative planning, forecasting, and replenishment (CPFR). In the preceding section, we argued that each of these activities is more difficult to perform globally than domestically. Further, the level of difficulty increases with distance and the vendor's sophistication. Catalogue and Internet retailer Coldwater Creek (www.coldwatercreek.com), for instance, sources about 75 percent of its merchandise from North America, so it can purchase relatively small orders and receive quick delivery.[15]

3. Some customers prefer products that are made in Canada. Retailers are simply reacting to their customers' quality perceptions.

4. It's easier to police potential violations of human rights and child labour. Hudson's Bay, Ralph Lauren, The Gap, Nordstrom, J. Crew, The Limited, and others have had to publicly deflect allegations about human rights, child labour, or other abuses involving factories and countries where their goods are made.[16]

Long the target of anti-globalization movements, Gap Inc. released a report in the spring of 2004 outlining its monitoring and enforcement of labour standards among its global suppliers. The report detailed by region the compliance efforts at the hundreds of factories in its supply chain. Walmart has notified its global suppliers that it will immediately drop them if they subcontract their work to factories that haven't been authorized by the retailer. The

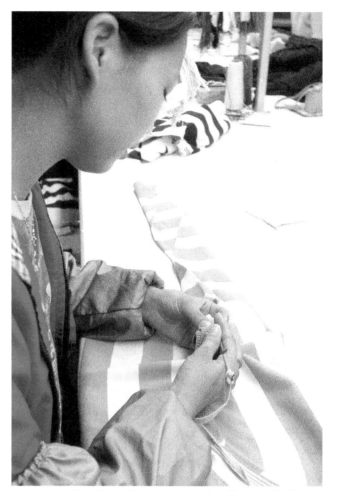

In response to the anti-sweatshop movement, high-profile companies like Reebok, Nike, and Liz Claiborne Inc. are publishing reports about audits undertaken in their factories.

Ingram Publishing/SuperStock.

stricter measure comes from increasing calls for better safety oversight following the factory collapse and deadly fire in 2012 at Bangladesh factories that supplied clothing to Walmart and other retailers. Walmart has moved to have employees stationed in countries where it subcontracts to ensure compliance, rather than relying on third-party agents as it has in the past. Further, Walmart intends to list the factories that are not authorized to manufacture goods for Walmart on its website. "We want the right accountability and ownership to be in the hands of the suppliers," says Rajan Kamalanathan, vice president of ethical sourcing at Walmart.[18]

DID YOU KNOW?

The United States is Canada's third-largest supplier of apparel, after China and Bangladesh. Asian suppliers of low-cost apparel constitute the strongest foreign competition for US apparel exporters to Canada.[17]

DID YOU KNOW?

Walmart Canada is one of the founding members of the Responsible Trade Committee—an advisory council of the Retail Council of Canada established to create a dialogue and share intelligence on issues of ethical sourcing in corporate Canada and to encourage the adoption of responsible trade practices by Canadian retailers. Visit www.retailcouncil.org/advocacy to learn more.[19]

Canadian consumers must understand that they are going to have to balance their desire for low prices with their concern for social responsibility before Third World sweatshop conditions improve dramatically. Unfortunately, there has been very little effort from the majority of Canadian retailers to improve Third World labour conditions.[20]

Connecting with Vendors

Now that we have examined the different branding decisions available to retailers and the issues surrounding global sourcing, we will concentrate on how and where retailers connect with their vendors. Retailers "go to market" to see the variety of available merchandise and to buy. A **market**, from the retail buyer's perspective, is a concentration of vendors within a specific geographic location, perhaps even under one roof or over the Internet. These markets may be Internet exchanges, permanent wholesale market centres, or temporary trade fairs. Retailers may also buy on their own turf, either in stores or at corporate headquarters. Finally, buyers can use resident buying offices that prearrange opportunities for buyers to visit vendors in major market centres in North America and abroad. Buyers of fashion apparel and accessory categories typically make major buying decisions five or six times a year, six months before the beginning of a season. Buyers of staple merchandise replenish the merchandise on a continuous basis. A listing of over 3000 trade shows and market weeks for the fashion industry can be viewed at Infomat (www.infomat.com).

market A group of vendors in a concentrated geographic location or even under one roof or over the Internet; also known as a *central market*.

trade shows Temporary concentrations of vendors that provide retailers opportunities to place orders and view what is available in the marketplace; also known as a *merchandise show* or *market week*.

Wholesale Market Centres

For many types of merchandise, retailers can do much of their buying in established market centres. Wholesale market centres have permanent vendor sales offices that retailers can visit throughout the year. Probably the world's most significant wholesale market centre for many merchandise categories is in New York City. The Fashion Centre, also known as the Garment District, is located from Fifth to Ninth Avenues and from 35th to 41st Streets. An estimated 22 000 apparel buyers visit every year for five market weeks and 65 annual related trade shows. The Garment District has 5100 showrooms and 4500 factories.[21] In Toronto, the Garment District is located in the Spadina Avenue and Queen Street West area.

The United States also has a number of regional wholesale market centres. The Dallas Market Centre, the world's largest, is a 7 million square-foot complex of six buildings.[22] Over 26 000 manufacturers and importers display their international products in its 2200 permanent showrooms and 460 000 square feet of temporary spaces. Some regional centres have developed into national markets for specific merchandise categories (for example, the Miami Merchandise Mart for swimwear).

Trade Shows

Many wholesale market centres host **trade shows**, also known as *merchandise shows* or *market weeks*. Permanent tenants of the wholesale market centres and vendors leasing temporary space participate. Here retailers place orders and get a concentrated view of what's available in the marketplace.

Although the high profile prêt-à-porter (ready to wear) trade shows are most obvious in New York, London, Milan, and Paris, Toronto was also quickly becoming an established fashion centre. One of the most anticipated events on Toronto's fashion calendar, the New Labels show, gave new designers the chance to showcase their innovations during the annual Fashion Week events.[23] Although the twice-yearly Toronto Fashion Week was cancelled in July 2016 due to lack of funding, a Toronto Men's Fashion Week and Toronto Women's Fashion Week were scheduled to take place in 2017.

Another annual Canadian event is the Canadian Gift and Tableware Association's CGTA Gift Show. With three locations across Canada (Toronto, Edmonton, and Montreal), it offers attendees a unique, one-stop-shop experience. The event features an expansive selection of quality gift products with over 2000 exhibitors nationwide and over 30 000 qualified buyers visiting the exhibits.[24]

Support Services for the Buying Process

Two services available to buyers that can help them more effectively acquire merchandise are resident buying offices and Internet exchanges.

Resident Buying Offices

Resident buying offices are organizations located in major buying centres that provide services to help retailers buy merchandise.

To illustrate how buying offices operate, consider how David Smith, owner of a Canadian prestige menswear store, uses his resident buying offices when he goes to market in Milan. Smith meets with market representative Alain Bordat of the Doneger Group, a buying office. Bordat, an English-speaking Italian, knows Smith's store and his upscale customers, so in advance of Smith's visit he sets up appointments with Italian vendors he believes would fit the Canadian store's image.

When Smith is in Italy, Bordat accompanies him to the appointments and acts as translator, negotiator, and accountant. Bordat informs Smith of the cost of importing the merchandise into Canada, taking into account duty, freight, insurance, processing costs, and so forth.

Once the orders are placed, Bordat writes the contracts and follows up on delivery and quality control. The Doneger Group also acts as a home base for buyers like Smith, providing office space and services, travel advisers, and emergency aid. Bordat and his association continue to keep Smith abreast of what is happening on the Italian fashion scene through reports and constant communication. Without the help of a resident buying office, it would be difficult, if not impossible, for Smith to penetrate the Italian wholesale market.

Internet Exchanges

Retail exchanges are providers of Internet-based solutions and services for retailers. The software and services offered by exchanges help retailers, manufacturers, and their trading partners reduce costs and improve efficiency by streamlining and automating sourcing and supply chain processes. They provide an opportunity for vendors and retailers to interact electronically rather than meeting face-to-face in a physical market. Retail exchanges can increase the efficiency of the buying process by offering software to support several of the systems discussed in previous chapters, such as reverse auctions; supply chain management; and collaborative planning, forecasting, and replenishment.

Two major retail exchanges, WorldWide Retail Exchange (WWRE) (http://wwre.globalsources.com) and GlobalNetXchange (GNX), were launched in 2000 as non-profit organizations owned and supported by groups of large retailers. The objective of these exchanges was to promote collaboration between retailers and vendors. They planned to provide a single, central hub that connected trading partners. Retailers would have unlimited access to their vendors' production data, and vendors would have instant access to retailers' sales projections.

The original vision of GNX and WWRE had a number of flaws. First, the exchanges underestimated the technological complexity of building such an exchange. Although some companies such as Walmart and Liz Claiborne had built effective private exchanges, they were designed to connect one trading partner to many, not many to many, as GNX and WWRE envisioned. Second, the cost of the software to provide some services, such as reverse auctions, dropped in price to the point that individual retailers could afford to administer their own reverse auctions. Third, the retail industry is extremely competitive, and retailers are reluctant to share information, preferring instead to keep their data and plans secret.[25]

In 2005, the two exchanges merged and is currently known as NeoGrid. The combined entity includes about 50 food, drug, and apparel retailers, including Carrefour SA, Sears Holdings Corp., Walgreen Co., Kroger Co., and Federated Department Stores Inc. Executives of the newly merged exchanges continue to hope that by creating a bigger and more sophisticated marketplace, retailers will be better equipped to face off against Walmart. The combined exchange will facilitate transactions for a retail group with about $1 trillion in combined annual sales.[26]

Using Internet Exchanges to Facilitate Buying

Retailers are exploring many strategies that provide consumers with the tools they need to purchase merchandise and services from them. Retailers also use the Internet for doing research for buying merchandise or services.

retail exchanges Electronic marketplaces operated by organizations that facilitate the buying and selling of merchandise using the Internet.

DID YOU KNOW?

Bangladesh has grown to be the second-largest apparel producer in the world behind China, with 3.6 million workers in the sector and some 4000 garment factories. Loblaw manufactures goods at 47 of them, and accounts for about 1 percent of the country's total apparel production.[27]

One of the most innovative and potentially useful developments stemming from retailers' growing level of sophistication with the Internet is retail exchanges. Retail exchanges are electronic marketplaces operated by organizations that facilitate the buying and selling of merchandise using the Internet. They provide an opportunity for vendors and retailers to interact electronically rather than meet face to face in a physical market. Retail exchanges can increase the efficiency of the buying process by integrating systems such as EDI with the ability to view merchandise and negotiate prices online. Although exchanges will never replace going to markets and interacting with vendors, they now make it possible for buyers to access any type of merchandise information with a mouse click.

Functions of Exchanges

Retail exchanges are still evolving. As such, we still do not know which functions or activities will become the most valuable to retailers. Some of the more prominent exchange functions are directory, selection, pricing, collaboration, and content.

Directory No longer do buyers have to wander trade shows or showrooms. Retail exchanges enable them to search for merchandise by vendor or type of product electronically.

Selection Buyers can then narrow the search to a particular vendor. Much of what used to be accomplished in the vendor's showroom can now be done online. Buyers can view individual SKUs. With technology improving all the time, they can be increasingly confident in the online catalogue's picture quality and colour. To help determine order quantities, buyers can obtain sales history from prior seasons for specific SKUs or for complementary products. Rather than travelling to Paris or Milan, buyers can replay runway fashion shows and obtain 360-degree views of merchandise from the comfort of their offices.

reverse auction
Auction conducted by retailer buyers. Known as a reverse auction because there is one buyer and many potential sellers. In reverse auctions, retail buyers provide a specification for what they want to a group of potential vendors. The competing vendors then bid down the price at which they are willing to sell until the buyer accepts a bid.

Pricing Retail exchanges use several pricing methods. In fact, the same exchange may use more than one pricing method depending on the situation. Merchandise can be offered at a fixed price where everyone pays the same amount. Or, the price of merchandise can be negotiated; in this case, the exchange acts as a broker between vendors and retailers. Finally, merchandise can be auctioned.

In traditional auctions like those conducted by eBay, there is one seller and many buyers. An auction conducted by retailer buyers is called a **reverse auction** because there is one buyer and many potential sellers. In reverse auctions, retail buyers provide a specification for what they want to a group of potential vendors. The competing vendors then bid down the price at which they are willing to sell until the buyer accepts a bid.[28] However, the retailer is not required to place an order with the lowest bidder. The retailer can choose to place the order at the price of the vendor who the retailer feels will provide the merchandise in a timely manner at the specified quality.

Reverse auctions have not been very popular with vendors. Few want to be anonymous contestants in bidding wars where price alone, not service or quality, is the sole basis for winning the business. Strategic relationships are also difficult to nurture when the primary interactions with vendors are through electronic auctions.[29]

The most common application for reverse auctions is to buy products and services used in retail operations rather than merchandise for resale. For example, a number of retailers work together to develop a specification for POS terminal paper tape and then pool their buying power to run a reverse auction and find a low-cost supplier that meets all of their needs. Other operating materials that are frequently bought on reverse auctions are store carpeting, fixtures, and supplies. Retailers can also use reverse auctions to procure private-label merchandise, commodities, and seasonal merchandise such as lawn furniture.

Collaboration Collaboration with vendors on every phase of the production and distribution process may become the most important benefit of retail exchanges. EDI, quick response inventory systems, and CPFR are integral components of retail exchanges.

The fashion world, where a short time period from idea conception to store shelf is a key success factor, stands to benefit significantly from retail exchanges. Although retailers have always provided design input to their vendors, it is the speed and clarity with which collaboration is facilitated with exchanges that is important. Suppose a buyer spots a potentially hot item on the street or in a movie. She snaps a digital picture and sends it simultaneously to a designer in Hong Kong and a fabric supplier in Thailand. The designer works out the specifications for the item, while the supplier sends both parties electronic versions of the fabric. All three parties collaborate on fine-tuning the design and product specifications. Not only does this collaborative effort shorten the lead time to market, but it minimizes the potential for errors.

Collaboration with other retailers for sourcing merchandise also has potential, but it may be difficult to achieve. Competing retailers aren't used to talking to each other. In fact, antitrust legislation may prohibit them from so doing.

Content Exchanges can even be an excellent source of general information. Many provide the latest industry news, trends, and fashions.

Types of Exchanges There are three basic types of exchanges: consortium, private, and independent. These types of exchanges are defined in terms of who owns and operates the exchange.

Consortium Exchanges A consortium exchange is a retail exchange that is owned by several firms within one industry. A firm must be a member of the consortium to participate in the exchange. Two consortium exchanges are 1SYNC and Neogrid.

- **1SYNC** is a customer-driven organization focused on accelerating adoption and implementation of the Global Data Synchronization Network (GDSN). As the leader in establishing and promoting standards and tools for the GDSN, 1SYNC helped launch solutions in multiple industries including alcohol, beverage, food service, general merchandise, hardlines (hard goods), health care, and retail. As a not-for-profit subsidiary of GS1US, 1SYNC's goal to ensure its over 5000 members make use of industry standards in the development of powerful tools to synchronize information and break the barriers that hinder the transfer of information in a business-to-business environment.[30]

- **Neogrid** provides B2B supply chain management solutions that are rapid to implement, easy-to-use, and complementary to existing systems, making supply chains more intelligent

and flexible to continuously improve the flow of goods. NeoGrid's SaaS model, integrated on a single cloud-based platform, enables collaboration among suppliers, manufacturers, distributors, and retailers, to synchronize every link of the supply chain and align supply with real demand. Currently Neogrid connects over 350 000 companies worldwide.[31]

The potential advantages of these exchanges are that retailers can pool their buying power to get better prices, and the fixed cost of developing the software and administering the exchange is shared across member-firms. However, coordinating the activities of different firms, and in some cases competing firms, has been difficult. There are often conflicting agendas among the founding members. Although not all members are in competition with one another, some are, making communication and goal setting complicated.[32] Also, since these exchanges are in competition with one another, companies are hesitant to back one for fear that it might be the wrong one. Finally, several major players have opted out of these consortia, including Walmart, Costco, Home Depot, Aldo, and Staples, to name a few.

Private Exchanges Private exchanges are exchanges that are operated for the exclusive use of a single firm. Although currently relatively small in number, they represent large players such as Walmart and Dell Computer. These larger companies have the size and scale to develop and operate their own exchanges. For example, Walmart moved its existing information system, Retail Link, to the Internet.[33] Retail Link was built during the 1990s at an estimated cost of US$1 billion. Walmart's private network enables its 10 000 suppliers to get information about sales and inventory levels in every store. The company's plans are to use its private exchange to consolidate purchasing worldwide, create global collaboration with its vendors, and bring suppliers online to compete for contracts. Although this and other exchanges are clearly designed to benefit the operator/owner, the vendors benefit from the strategic relationship and immediate access to sales and inventory data for planning purposes, such as CPFR.

Independent Exchanges An independent exchange is a retail exchange owned by a third

---

consortium exchange
A retail exchange that is owned by several firms within one industry.

private exchanges
Exchanges that are operated for the exclusive use of a single firm.

independent exchange
A retail exchange owned by a third party that provides the electronic platform to perform the exchange functions.

party that provides the electronic platform to perform the exchange functions. For example, a retailer is interested in running a reverse auction for an air-conditioning system. It contacts an independent exchange, such as Ariba. In the previous weeks, the retailer's purchasing agent and prospective suppliers prepare for the auction with the help of Ariba. Now, the purchasing agent and the 12 suppliers log on to an Ariba secure private network, and the bidding begins. Within minutes, the purchasing agent has saved thousands of dollars from its historic spending level. New bids come in every couple of minutes, driving the unit price lower and lower. In the ensuing hours, more than 250 interactive bids are received, saving the retailer more than US$400 000—a 16 percent savings below its historic spending level of US$2.5 million.[34, 35]

Lo3 Strategic Sales Planning

Negotiations are as basic to human nature as eating or sleeping. A negotiation takes place any time two parties confer with each other to settle some matter. For example, negotiations take place between parents and their children about issues such as allowances, and people negotiate with their friends about what to do on the weekend.

Business negotiations occur daily. People negotiate for higher salaries, better offices, and bigger budgets. Negotiations are crucial in buyers' discussions with vendors. Keeping this in mind, this section will look at negotiations from both the buyer's and seller's perspective. You may end up in either of these positions and need to know how to act based on your role in the sales process.

No one should go into a negotiation without intensive planning. We first provide guidelines from the seller's perspective regarding a successful sale. Next we discuss some tips for conducting negotiations from the vendor's perspective. Lastly we introduce a non-traditional negotiation process that a seller and buyer may want to consider instead of using traditional processes.

Guidelines for a Seller in the Negotiation Process

Planning and developing a process to create a win–win scenario for both the seller and buyer is critical to ensure a prosperous long-term relationship. A seller needs to take the following steps prior to engaging in the negotiation process (obtaining commitment) with a buyer.

Prospecting   Part of a salesperson's job is to prospect, which is forced behaviour due to churn (attrition). Salespeople typically will lose 10 to 20 percent of their portfolio annually due to churn. Thus, part of a salesperson's ongoing job is to be on the lookout for prospects. Prospects can come from a variety of places, including (but not limited to):

- networking events
- referrals from satisfied clients
- social media
- trade-shows (fairs, merchandising markets)
- cold calling

Planning the Sales Call   The seller needs to collect as much information as possible on the company she wishes to call prior to *any* communication. This will provide the seller with a perspective of the buying company, enabling her to create a profile of the prospect. What information should salespeople collect? Anything related to the seven Ps in the marketing mix and any macro (e.g., legal, social cultural trends, technology) or micro (e.g., competitors, customers, suppliers, or customers) environmental force they feel may be beneficial to gain the buyers interest in the salesperson's products or services.

Once the seller has all the information in place and has crafted a profile, he is ready to make the initial phone call to set up an appointment to present his products or services to the buyer. The key at this stage is to have something that will provide *value* to the purchaser. What that could be? Quite simply, the value must enhance one of the seven Ps in the marketing mix. Examples could include making a *process* more efficient, improving the quality of materials used in a *product*, or simply offering a better *price* on a product or service.

Making the Sales Call   At this stage (dependent upon the policies of the buying company), the seller physically meets the buyer in hopes of making a presentation at a later date. This is another data collection period. The seller is simply going in to learn as much as she can about the buyer and the organization via primary data collection. After this meeting, the seller takes the additional information acquired and gets ready to make a presentation to the buyer in the near future. Sometimes salespeople have to make the presentation at the same time as they make the initial call. If possible, a separate meeting is preferred to give the seller time to prepare properly for the next step, the presentation.

Making the Presentation This is the seller's opportunity to meet the buyer and present the product or service. One of the main things to remember at this stage is to explain to the buyer why they should commit to the product or service. The key here is to articulate the *value* the product or service will provide the buyer with. How will the product make the buyer's life "easier"?

Dealing with Objections Objections are not to be taken lightly. Objections will cause the seller to lose the deal if he is unable to address them in a timely and professional manner. To better deal with objections, a salesperson should anticipate potential objections and have a plan for dealing with them. To learn more about common objections, along with ways to deal with them, go to http://sbinformation.about.com/od/sales/tp/common-sales-objections.htm.

Obtaining Commitment At this stage, the buyer and seller are in the negotiation process. The seller tries to acquire the buyer's business by using an effective commitment method. such as:

- direct request – simply ask for the business
- benefit summary – remind the buyer of reasons why the buyer should do business
- balance sheet method – list the pros and cons of the buyer's proposal on a sheet of paper

Now that we can see how the seller has to prepare strategically for a sales process, let's use a hypothetical buying exercise between Sears and Tommy Hilfiger to see what the buyer should be thinking about during this process.

Tips for Buyers—Planning Negotiations with Vendors (Sellers)

Consider the hypothetical situation in which a men's designer shirt buyer at Sears is preparing to meet with a salesman from Tommy Hilfiger in the office in New York. The Sears buyer is ready to buy Tommy Hilfiger's spring line, but has some merchandising problems yet to be resolved from last season. Let's go over seven general guidelines for planning a negotiation session and for conducting a face-to-face negotiation session.

Knowledge is power! The more the buyer knows about the vendor, the better her negotiating strategy will be.

Consider History Buyers need a sense of what has occurred between the retailer and vendor in the past (if there is a history between the two entities). Sears and Tommy Hilfiger have had a long, profitable relationship; a sense of trust and mutual respect has been established. But the buyer must be careful; just because a relationship exists doesn't mean it will be smooth sailing going forward. In fact, in B2B relationships over 80 percent of partnerships dissolve within a decade.

Assess Where Things Are Today Although Tommy Hilfiger shirts have been profitable for Sears in the past, three patterns sold poorly last season. Some vendors believe that once they have sold merchandise to the retailer, their responsibility ends. This is a short-term perspective, however. If the merchandise doesn't sell, a good vendor, like Tommy Hilfiger, will arrange to share the risk of loss. The Sears buyer will ask to return some merchandise or provide markdown money— funds a vendor gives a retailer to cover lost gross margin dollars due to markdowns and other merchandising issues—usually in the form of a credit to the Sears account.

> **DID YOU KNOW?**
>
> The most dangerous mistake of a negotiation is not identifying what you want. If you prepare for nothing, then you are prepared to lose everything. Make a list of your desired outcomes, and rank them in order of importance. Make this list as specific as possible, including numbers and prices.[36]

Set Goals Besides taking care of last season's leftover merchandise, the Sears buyer has set goals in six areas for the upcoming sales meeting: additional markup opportunities, terms of purchase, transportation, delivery and exclusivity, communications, and advertising allowances. Keep in mind these are not exclusive criteria, but are based on this exercise with Sears and Tommy Hilfiger. A buyer could consider other factors as well. Having these goals in place prior to meeting with a seller will help ensure a well planned and executed meeting and a greater chance of a win–win situation.

Additional Markup Opportunities Vendors may have excess stock (manufacturers' overruns) due to order cancellations, returned merchandise from retailers, or simply an overly optimistic sales forecast. To move this merchandise, vendors offer it to retailers at lower-than-normal prices. Retailers can then make a higher-than-normal gross margin or pass the savings on to the customer. Since Sears is noted as a popular menswear store, it probably isn't interested in any excess inventory that Tommy Hilfiger has to offer. Off-price retailers such as Winners or Internet retailer Bluefly.com specialize in purchasing manufacturers' overruns (see Retailing View 11.4). Another opportunity for additional markups is with private-label merchandise, as previously discussed.

Terms of Purchase It's advantageous for buyers to negotiate for a long time period in which to pay for merchandise. Long terms of payment improve the firm's cash flow position, lower its liabilities (accounts payable), and can cut its interest expense if it has borrowing money from financial institutions to pay for its inventory. According to the *Competition Act*, however, a vendor can't offer different terms of purchase or prices to different retailers unless the difference can be cost-justified. But buyers would be remiss if they didn't ask for the best terms of purchase available.

Transportation Transportation costs can be substantial, though this doesn't pose a big problem with the Tommy Hilfiger shirts due to their high unit cost and small size. Nonetheless, the question of who pays for shipping merchandise from vendor to retailer can be a significant negotiating point.

Delivery and Exclusivity In retailing in general, and in fashion in particular, timely delivery is essential. Being the only retailer in a market to carry certain products helps a retailer hold a fashion lead and achieve a differential advantage. The buyer for Sears wants to be certain that shipment of the new spring line arrives as early in the season as possible, and that some shirt patterns won't be sold to competing retailers.

Communication Vendors and their representatives are excellent sources of market information. They generally know what is and isn't selling. Providing good, timely information about the market is an indispensable and inexpensive marketing research tool, so the Sears buyer plans to spend at least part of the meeting talking about market trends to the Hilfiger sales representative.

Advertising Allowances Retailers have the choice of advertising any product in the store. They can sometimes share the cost of advertising through a cooperative arrangement with vendors known as co-op advertising—a program undertaken by a vendor in which the vendor agrees to pay all or part of a pricing promotion. By giving retailers advertising money based on a percentage of purchases, vendors can better represent their product to consumers. Under the *Competition Act*, vendors are allowed to give advertising allowances on an equal basis—the same percentage to everyone—usually based on a percentage of the invoice cost. As a fashion retailer, Sears advertises heavily and would like Tommy Hilfiger to support a number of catalogues with a generous ad allowance.

Know the Vendor's Goals and Constraints

Negotiation can't succeed in the long run unless both parties believe they have won. By understanding what's important to Tommy Hilfiger, the Sears buyer can plan for a successful negotiating session. Generally, vendors are interested in providing a continuous relationship, testing new items, facilitating good communications, and providing a showcase to feature their merchandise.

A Continuous Relationship Vendors want to make a long-term investment in their retailers. For seasonal merchandise such as men's designer shirts, they have to plan their production in advance, so it's important to Tommy Hilfiger that certain key retailers such as Sears continue their support. The buyer plans to spend some time at the beginning of the meeting reviewing their mutually profitable past and assuring the Tommy Hilfiger sales rep that Sears hopes to continue their relationship.

Testing New Items There is no better way to test how well a new product will sell than to put it in a store. Retailers are often cautious with new items due to the risk of markdowns and the opportunity cost of not purchasing other, more successful merchandise. Yet vendors need their retailers to provide sales feedback for new items. Sears has always been receptive to some of Tommy Hilfiger's more avant-garde styles. If these styles do well in certain Sears stores, they will likely succeed in similar stores around the country.

Communication Just as Tommy Hilfiger can provide market information, Sears can share sales information. Also, the Sears buyer travels the world market and on one buying trip to England, found an attractive scarf, bought the scarf, and gave it to Tommy Hilfiger, who had it copied for a shirt. It was a big success!

Showcase In certain urban centres—notably Toronto, New York, London, Milan, and Paris—vendors use large stores to showcase their merchandise. For instance, many North American buyers go to market in New York. Most stop at the major retailers to see what's new, what's selling, and how it's displayed.

A good understanding of the legal, managerial, and financial issues that constrain a vendor will facilitate a productive negotiating session. For instance, the Sears buyer should recognize from past experience that Tommy Hilfiger normally doesn't allow merchandise to be returned, but does provide markdown money. If the Hilfiger rep initially says that giving markdown money is against company policy, the Sears buyer will have strong objective ammunition for her position.

Plan to Have at Least As Many Negotiators as the Vendor There is power in numbers. Even if the vendor is more powerful, aggressive, or important in the marketplace, the retailer will have a psychological advantage at the negotiating table if the vendor is outnumbered. At the very least, the negotiating teams should be of equal number. The Sears buyer plans to invite a merchandise manager into the discussion if the Tommy Hilfiger rep comes with a sales manager.

Choose a Good Place to Negotiate The Sears buyer may have an advantage in the upcoming meeting since it will be in the Sears office. The buyer will have everything at her fingertips, such as information plus secretarial and supervisory assistance. From a psychological perspective, people generally feel more comfortable and confident in familiar surroundings. On the other hand, if the negotiation were to be in Hilfiger's office, Sears would be able to learn a lot about the Hilfiger company. In the end, the preferable location for a negotiation is a personal choice.

Be Aware of Real Deadlines To illustrate the importance of deadlines, consider when labour strikes are settled. An agreement is often reached one minute before everyone walks out. There is always pressure to settle a negotiation at the last minute. The Sears buyer recognizes that the Tommy Hilfiger sales rep must go back to the office with an order in hand since there is a quota to meet by the end of the month. The Sears buyer must get markdown money or permission to return the unsold shirts by the end of the week or there will not be sufficient open-to-buy to cover the orders the buyer wishes to place. Recognizing these deadlines will help Sears come to a decisive closure in the upcoming negotiation.

The Art of Negotiation

One might argue there is an artistic element to negotiations. A strategic mapping process is highly recommended when negotiating on a B2B level. This isn't to say a negotiator (buyer or seller) has to read *The Art of War* by Sun Tzu prior heading into negotiations, but the person/team still needs to have a strategy or game plan in place to have the best chance of reaching a level of commitment both parties will be happy with.

A current challenge with negotiations is the learned organizational culture and history associated with the negotiation process. A survey of salespeople revealed the following about their internal negotiations processes:

- 85 percent report that they still use a "reactive" approach to negotiations
- 85 percent say they have no predetermined strategy for irrational competitor behaviour
- 71 percent report poor internal alignment on negotiation goals or processes
- 81 percent say they have no formal negotiation process[37]

So What is the Game Plan? Brian Dietmeyer, author of *Strategic Negotiation*, looks at the negotiation process in a different light. Two components of his overall strategy include:

- consequence of no agreement (CNA)
- trades

Exhibit 11-3 shows the consequences of not reaching an agreement.

In starting this process, you need to appreciate the logic behind the consequence of no agreement (CNA), which basically boils down to what possible outcomes could be reached with the other person (team) your are negotiating with. You need to look at this from your perspective (as a seller) and theirs

Exhibit 11-3

Consequences of not Reaching an Agreement

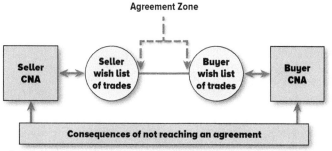

Source: Dietmeyer B.J. and Kaplan R., "Strategic Negotiation," 2004, Kaplan Publishing, USA.

(as a buyer). From the seller's perspective, there is basically one consequence: you will lose the sale. From the buyer's perspective, three things could happen if CNA occurs:

- go to another competitor
- resolve the issue/problem/opportunity with internal resources
- simply walk away and do nothing[38]

It is important to keep in mind that the entity that has less to lose has more power.

Since a negotiation process was started, we can assume both parties would like to be able to reach an agreement, to develop a contract. The question is, how does the seller strategically manage their side of the negotiation process to ensure the buyer doesn't consider their CNA options?

At this point it is up to both parties to identify potential *trades* that each might consider in order to ensure CNA isn't reached. Exhibit 11-4 outlines these possible trades.

Pricing is always a major element of the negotiation process, but there are other variables to consider that may allow a deal to occur. These variables include the following:

- terms
- quality of materials used
- timelessness of completion dates of contract variables
- depth of warranties and guarantee
- length of warranties and guarantees
- transportation options of finished goods
- level of service
- length of contract

These items can move in and out of the negotiation process to help identify items of benefit for both parties, allowing them to reach an agreement.

Dietmeyer's process involves providing multiple offers to a buyer. As a result, the seller may show the buyer up to three different "doors" or "options" with different price points and elements at a given time. This would allow the buyer to look at the list of options to see what fits better for them, in hopes that the buyer does not opt for a CNA resolution.[39]

Another key thing the seller needs to consider before the CNA process even starts is what are the seller's minimal, median, and maximum outcomes? Let's call this a three M analysis.

Sellers' (or Buyers') Commitment Positions Sellers and buyers should sit down prior to the start of a negotiation process to meet the other party and reflect on their minimal, median, and maximum levels of commitment positions for a deal. What is the minimal return the seller or buyer would find acceptable in order for a deal to proceed? What would be their median and maximum return?

- **Minimal** – This is the least favourable option the seller or buyer would agree to. The deal is still profitable, but the returns are minimal (a short-term contract or thin margins, for example). This type of deal may cover a salesperson's targets for a couple of weeks, perhaps a month.
- **Median** – This option is a more satisfactory agreement for either partly. The returns are better (longer contract, more profitable). This type of deal could cover off a salesperson's sales target for several months.
- **Maximum** – This is the best option either could hope for, and can include a lengthy contract or perhaps an extremely profitable or lucrative deal. This type deal could cover off a salesperson's targets for an entire year. It may also help position the salesperson in line for promotions or industry recognition.

These ranges gives the seller context and a place of reference. When the seller is in the middle of the negotiations, he or she can then reflect back on what his three commitment points are and use this to help him negotiate a better deal. This process ensures that the party using three M analysis doesn't get caught up in the "heat of the moment" while negotiating and make a rash emotional decision.

Exhibit 11-4
Trades

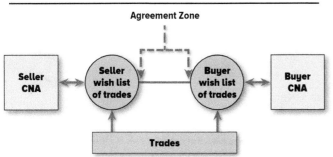

Source: Dietmeyer B.J. and Kaplan R., "Strategic Negotiation," 2004, Kaplan Publishing, USA.

LO4 Establishing and Maintaining Strategic Relationships with Vendors

Maintaining strong vendor relationships is an important method of developing a sustainable competitive advantage. In previous chapters, we discussed some of the ways partnering relations can improve information, exchange, planning, and the management of supply chains. For example, electronic data interchange could not be accomplished without the vendor and retailer making a commitment to work together and have a trusting relationship. In the same way, category management using category captains and CPFR (collaborative planning, forecasting, and replenishment) would be impossible without partnering relationships. In this section, we examine how retailers can develop strategic relationships and the characteristics of a successful long-term relationship.

Defining Strategic Relationships

Relationships between retailers and vendors are often based on arguing over splitting up a profit pie.[40] This is basically a win–lose relationship because when one party gets a larger portion of the pie, the other party gets a smaller portion. Both parties are interested exclusively in their own profits and are unconcerned about the other party's welfare. These relationships are common when the products are commodities and have no major impact on the retailers' performance. Thus, there is no benefit to the retailer to entering into a strategic relationship.

A **strategic relationship**, also called a *partnering relationship*, exists when a retailer and vendor are committed to maintaining the relationship over the long term and investing in opportunities that are mutually beneficial to the parties. In these relationships, it's important for the partners to put their money where their mouth is. They have taken risks to expand the pie—to give the relationship a strategic advantage over other companies.

Thus, a strategic relationship is a win–win relationship. Both parties benefit because the size of the pie has increased—both the retailer and vendor increase their sales and profits. Strategic relationships are created explicitly to uncover and exploit joint opportunities. Members in strategic relationships depend on and trust each other heavily; they share goals and agree on how to accomplish those goals; and they are willing to take risks, share confidential information, and make significant investments for the sake of the relationship.

A strategic relationship is like a marriage. When businesses enter strategic relationships, they are wedded to their partners for better or worse. For example, the U.K.'s Marks & Spencer had jointly developed a kitchen product with a vendor.[41] Four months after the product's introduction, the manufacturer realized that it had miscalculated the product's cost and, as a result, had underpriced the product and was losing money on the deal. It was a big hit at Marks & Spencer because it was underpriced. Marks & Spencer decided not to raise the price because the product was already listed in its catalogue. Instead, it helped the vendor re-engineer the product at a lower cost, cut its own gross margin, and gave that money to the manufacturer. It took a profit hit to maintain the relationship.

Maintaining Strategic Relationships

The four foundations of successful strategic relationships are mutual trust, open communication, common goals, and credible commitments.

Mutual Trust The glue in strategic relationships is trust. **Trust** is a belief that a partner is honest (reliable, stands by its word, sincere, fulfills obligations) and is benevolent (concerned about the other party's welfare).[42] When vendors and buyers trust each other, they are more willing to share relevant ideas, clarify goals and problems, and communicate efficiently. Information shared between the parties becomes increasingly comprehensive, accurate, and timely. There is less need for the vendor and buyer to constantly monitor and check up on each other's actions because each believes the other won't take advantage, given the opportunity.[43]

Strategic relationships and trust are often developed initially between the leaders of organizations. For example, when Walmart started to work with Procter & Gamble to coordinate its buying activities, Sam Walton got together with P&G's vice-president of sales on a canoeing trip. They discussed the mutual benefits of cooperating and the potential risks associated with altering their normal business practices.

> **strategic relationship** Long-term relationship in which partners make significant investments to improve both parties' profitability; also called a *partnering relationship*.
>
> **trust** A belief that a partner is honest (reliable, stands by its word, sincere, fulfills obligations) and is benevolent (concerned about the other party's welfare).

In the end, they must have concluded that the potential long-term gains were worth the additional risks and short-term setbacks that would probably occur as they developed the new systems.

Open Communication   In order to share information, develop sales forecasts together, and coordinate deliveries, Walmart and P&G have to have open and honest communication. This may sound easy in principle, but most businesses don't like to share information with their business partners. They believe it is none of the other's concern. But open, honest communication is a key to developing successful relationships. Buyers and vendors in a relationship need to understand what is driving each other's business, their roles in the relationship, each firm's strategies, and any problems that arise over the course of the relationship.

Common Goals   Vendors and buyers must have common goals for a successful relationship to develop. Shared goals give both members of the relationship incentive to pool their strengths and abilities and to exploit potential opportunities between them. There is also assurance that the other partner won't do anything to hinder goal achievement within the relationship.

For example, Walmart and P&G recognized that it was in their common interest to remain business partners—they needed each other—and to do so, both had to be allowed to make profitable transactions. Walmart can't demand prices so low that P&G can't make money, and P&G must be flexible enough to accommodate the needs of its biggest customer. With a common goal, both firms have incentive to cooperate because they know that by doing so, each can boost sales.

Common goals also help to sustain the relationship when expected benefit flows aren't realized. If one P&G shipment fails to reach a Walmart store on time due to an unfortunate event such as misrouting by a trucking firm, Walmart won't suddenly call off the whole arrangement. Instead, Walmart is likely to view the incident as a simple mistake and will remain in the relationship; this is because Walmart and P&G are committed to the same goals in the long run.

Credible Commitments   Successful relationships develop because both parties make credible commitments to the relationship. Credible commitments are tangible investments in the relationship. They go beyond just making the hollow statement, "I want to be a partner." Credible commitments involve spending money to improve the supplier's products or services provided to the customer.[45] For example, one of the strengths of the Walmart/P&G partnership is the obvious and significant investments both parties have made in EDI systems, CPFR forecasting systems, and material handling equipment.

Building Partnering Relationships

Although not all retailer–vendor relationships should or do become strategic partnerships, the development of strategic partnerships tends to go through a series of phases characterized by increasing levels of commitment:

- **Awareness.** No transactions have taken place. This phase might begin with the buyer seeing some interesting merchandise at a retail market or in an ad in a trade magazine. Reputation and image of the vendor can play an important role in determining if the buyer moves to the next stage.

- **Exploration.** The buyer and vendor begin to explore the potential benefits and costs. At this point, the buyer may make a small purchase and try to test the demand for the merchandise in several stores. In addition, the buyer will get information about how easy it is to work with the vendor.

- **Expansion.** The buyer has collected enough information about the vendor to consider developing a longer-term relationship. The buyer and the vendor determine that there is a potential for a win–win relationship. They begin to work on joint promotional programs, and the amount of merchandise sold increases.

- **Commitment.** Both parties continue to find the relationship mutually beneficial, and it moves to the commitment stage and becomes

DID YOU KNOW?

On a canoe trip in the mid-1980s, Lou Pritchett, P&G's vice president for sales, met with the Sam Walton (founder of Walmart) to mend a strained relationship. This meeting lead to the strategic partnership building an advanced EDI system. The system helped the two companies improve efficiencies and customer satisfaction, leading to a more profitable relationship and partnership.

DID YOU KNOW?

Walmart Canada has partnered with New York–based Mint-X Corp to introduce Great Value Mint-X Raccoon Repellent Garbage Bags.[44]

a strategic relationship. The buyer and vendor make significant investments in the relationship and develop a long-term perspective toward it.

It is difficult for retailer–vendor relationships to be as committed as some supplier–manufacturer relationships. Manufacturers can enter into monogamous (sole source) relationships with other manufacturers. However, an important function of retailers is to provide an assortment of merchandise for their customers. Thus, they must always deal with multiple, sometimes competing, suppliers. Regardless of which partner-building phase a retailer is in with a supplier, it is constantly involved in the give-and-take process of negotiations.

Legal and Ethical Issues for Buying Merchandise*

Given the many negotiations and interactions between retail buyers and vendors, ethical and legal issues are bound to arise. In this section, we will view ethical and legal issues from both retailers' and vendors' perspectives (see, for example, Retailing View 11.3 for a discussion of socially responsible buying). The most fundamental question is whether a retailer and vendor have a binding contract for a particular transaction. If they do, the next question is how to resolve disputes under that contract. In addition, retailers should not take advantage of their position of power in the marketing channel. In this regard, we will examine chargebacks, commercial bribery, slotting allowances, buybacks, and category management.

To protect their customers' interests and their own reputation, retailers must be cognizant of whether the merchandise is counterfeit or from the diverted market (the grey market). Vendors aren't likely to become legally entangled with their retailers so long as they sell to whoever wants to buy, sell whatever they want, and sell at the same price to all. But since most vendors don't want to be this free with their merchandise, we will look at exclusive territories, exclusive dealing agreements, tying contracts, and refusals to deal.

Contract Disputes

Contract formation in the retail context is usually straightforward. The retailer places an order with a vendor that in most cases the vendor accepts. This

*This section was developed with the assistance of Professor Ross Petty, Babson College.

creates a binding mutual obligation for the vendor to deliver the promised goods in exchange for the retailer agreeing to pay the specified price. Disputes arise when one party does not perform or when the parties disagree about details of the transaction such as the precise specifications of the goods.

Most retailers and vendors are more interested in continuing sales relationships than expensive litigation over legal rights. For this reason, many disputes are simply settled by negotiation and agreement between the two parties. It is common to include **alternative dispute resolution** provisions in contracts. Such provisions can include methods of settling the dispute that the parties agree upon, such as mediation, arbitration, or med-arb:

- **Mediation** involves selecting a neutral mediator to assist the parties in reaching a mutually agreeable settlement.
- **Arbitration** involves the appointment of an arbitrator who considers the arguments of both sides and then makes a decision that is usually agreed upon in advance as binding.
- **Med-arb** involves an initial attempt at mediation followed by binding arbitration if the mediation is unsuccessful.

Overworked courts routinely enforce alternative dispute resolution contract provisions in the United States.

Chargebacks

A **chargeback** is a practice used by retailers in which they deduct money from the amount they owe a vendor. There are two reasons for a chargeback. The first occurs when the retailer deducts money from an

alternative dispute resolution A provision included in a contract between retailer and vendor to help avoid litigation in the case of a dispute. Can include methods of settling the dispute that the parties agree upon, such as mediation, arbitration, or med-arb.

mediation Used in the case of a dispute between retailer and vendor that involves selecting a neutral party—the mediator—to assist the parties in reaching a mutually agreeable settlement.

arbitration Used in the case of a dispute between retailer and vendor that involves the appointment of a neutral party—the arbitrator—who considers the arguments of both sides and then makes a decision that is usually agreed upon in advance as binding.

med-arb Used in the case of a dispute between retailer and vendor that involves an initial attempt at mediation followed by binding arbitration if the mediation is unsuccessful. See *mediation* and *arbitration*.

chargeback A practice used by retailers in which they deduct money from the amount they owe a vendor.

Study: 81 Percent of Consumers Say they Will Make Personal Sacrifices to Address Social, Environmental Issues

Global consumers feel a personal accountability to address social and environmental issues and look to companies as partners in progress, according to findings from the 2015 Cone Communications/Ebiquity Global CSR Study.

Near-universal in their demands for companies to act responsibly, 9 in 10 consumers expect companies to do more than make a profit, but also operate responsibly to address social and environmental issues. Global consumers echo that high standard in their own lives and shopping behaviour: 84 percent of consumers globally say they seek out responsible products whenever possible, though 81 percent cite availability of these products as the largest barrier to not purchasing more.

The study, a follow-up to the 2011 and 2013 global studies on consumer attitudes, perceptions, and behaviours around corporate social responsibility (CSR), was conducted by Cone Communications and independent marketing analytics specialist, Ebiquity. The research reflects the sentiments of nearly 10 000 citizens in nine of the largest countries in the world by GDP: the United States, Canada, Brazil, the United Kingdom, Germany, France, China, India, and Japan.

"The research has revealed an increasingly sophisticated consumer," says Jennifer Ciuffo Clark, research director at Ebiquity. "Global consumers have high demands for companies to address social and environmental issues, but they now also understand they have an obligation to make change, as well. It's critical for companies to understand the nuanced drivers, barriers and opportunities that resonate among discerning global audiences."

Consumer CSR understanding, empowerment grows As CSR becomes firmly grounded in many global citizens' daily routines and considerations, consumers have a better understanding and are more optimistic overall about their own ability to make a positive

Big Cheese Photo/SuperStock.

impact. In fact, nearly three-quarters (72 percent) believe their purchases make a moderate-to-significant positive impact on social or environmental issues. This positive outlook may stem from a growing command of CSR terms and language: Consumer confusion of company CSR messages has dropped from 71 percent in 2011 to 65 percent in 2015.

As personal accountability and sophistication grow, consumers are also considering their own role in addressing social and environmental issues. Global consumers surveyed state they are willing to make personal sacrifices for the greater good: Four-in-five are willing to consume or purchase fewer products to preserve natural resources (81 percent) or buy a product from an unknown brand if it has strong CSR commitments (80 percent). Consumers are even willing to forgo elements such as ownership or quality to push progress forward:

- 61 percent would be willing to borrow or share products rather than buy new ones
- 57 percent would purchase a product of lesser quality or efficacy if it was more socially or environmentally responsible

"Companies shouldn't take consumers' willingness to make sacrifices as a signal to cut corners," says Cone EVP Alison DaSilva. "Rather, this is an opportunity to

Source: This article first appeared on SustainableBrands.com on May 27, 2015. Reprinted with permission from Sustainable Brands®.

engage consumers more fully in new CSR solutions, collaborating to push the boundaries of responsible consumption and lifestyle."

Consumers seek more options to engage in CSR efforts

The leading ways consumers want to get engaged with companies' CSR efforts are actions tied directly to their wallets, with 9 in 10 just as likely to purchase (89 percent) as to boycott (90 percent) based on companies' responsible practices. However, consumers view their role in creating social and environmental change as extending well beyond the cash register. If given the opportunity:

- 80 percent would tell friends and family about a company's CSR efforts
- 76 percent would donate to a charity supported by a company they trust
- 72 percent would volunteer for a cause supported by a company they trust
- 72 percent would voice their opinions directly to a company about CSR efforts

Despite their good intentions, the leading ways consumers actually engage with companies remain transactional, as shopping (63 percent), donating (61 percent), and boycotting a product (53 percent) are the top reported behaviours taken over the last 12 months.

"Companies are still relying on traditional forms of consumer engagement primarily tied to the product shelf, yet consumers are looking for more diverse ways to get involved with CSR efforts," says DaSilva. "Companies can serve as a catalyst for sparking donations, volunteerism and advocacy by giving consumers a spectrum of ways to get involved."

Bottom-line benefits from CSR engagement

CSR remains a boon to brand reputation and affinity. In line with 2013 results, when companies support social or environmental issues, consumer affinity overwhelmingly upsurges:

- 93 percent of global citizens will have a more positive image of that company
- 90 percent will be more likely to trust that company
- 88 percent will be more loyal (i.e., continue buying products or services)
- more than 8 in 10 consider CSR when deciding what to buy or where to shop (84 percent), which products and services to recommend to others (82 percent), which

companies they want to see doing business in their communities (84 percent) and where to work (79 percent)

CSR is also a powerful differentiator at the register, as 90 percent of global consumers would switch brands to one that is associated with a good cause, given similar price or quality. This inclination to shop with an eye toward greater good has remained strong since 2011.

Breaking through to the empowered consumer

Although global consumers factor social and environmental considerations into many daily decisions, breaking through is proving to be harder than ever. Yet, the consequences of not reaching consumers are high. Two-thirds (64 percent) of consumers say they only pay attention to company CSR efforts if an organization is going above and beyond what other companies are doing. Meanwhile, half (52 percent) will assume a company is not acting responsibly until they hear information otherwise.

The onus is on companies to ensure their CSR efforts and results are being delivered and heard in a way consumers understand.

- 88 percent expect companies to report on the progress of CSR efforts
- 86 percent believe if companies make CSR commitments, they must be held accountable forproducing and communicating results
- 89 percent believe companies need to do a better job showing how social and environmental commitments are personally relevant
- 64 percent will ignore a company's CSR messages altogether if they use terms they don't understand

Even as consumers expect companies to communicate results, companies should not rely solely on CSR reports to convey information, as only a quarter of global citizens have read a CSR report in the past 12 months. Companies should look to leverage and communicate data in new ways to stay relevant. Consumers say both stories and data related to impact are equally important (59 percent). They prefer to see CSR data in the form of:

- brief written summaries: 43 percent
- interactive websites: 34 percent
- videos: 31 percent
- infographics: 25 percent

The 2015 Cone Communications/Ebiquity Global CSR Study also reveals an increasing democratization of preferred communications channels. Once relegated to one

Continued

or two traditional sources, global consumers are now looking to a number of channels to get CSR information, from media and advertising to company websites and social media. Product packaging (19 percent), media (15 percent), and advertising (14 percent) remain the most effective ways to reach consumers, but social media and mobile channels combined continue to gain traction, nearly doubling from 10 percent in 2011 to 18 percent in 2015.

- on the product or its package/label: 19 percent (vs. 22 percent in 2011)
- media (e.g., stories or interviews): 15 percent (vs. 21 percent in 2011)
- advertising (print, broadcast, online): 14 percent (vs. 16 percent in 2011)
- social media (Facebook, Twitter): 13 percent (vs. 7 percent in 2011)
- mobile: 5 percent (vs. 3 percent in 2011)

"The consumer mindset of 'guilty until proven responsible' puts new pressure on companies to ensure their CSR messages are breaking through," DaSilva says. "As the communications landscape continues to become more diverse, companies must take an integrated approach to conveying CSR efforts. They need to strike a balance of hyper-targeting CSR content to consumers in ways that are personally relevant, while creating cohesive, always-on communications to break apart from the pack."

Social media leads CSR conversation

Consistent with 2013 results, consumers continue to see social media as an important way to learn, voice their opinions, and speak directly to companies around CSR issues, especially in developing countries. Three-in-five (61 percent) global consumers use social media to address or engage with companies around CSR issues, with usage skyrocketing in China (89 percent), India (88 percent), and Brazil (84 percent). Consumers are primarily using social media to share positive information or learn more about issues:

- 34 percent of consumers use social media to share positive information about companies and issues
- 30 percent use social media to learn more about companies or issues
- 25 percent use social media to share negative information

Global nuances Although there is strong support for CSR initiatives from all countries surveyed, the emerging markets of India, China, and Brazil again remain the most enthusiastic and unwavering in their support:

- **Emerging markets are more likely to feel the impact of company efforts:** Consumers in India (48 percent), China (36 percent), and Brazil (36 percent) are more likely to believe companies have made a significant impact on social and environmental issues (vs. 27 percent global average).
- **Citizens in emerging markets are more likely to seek out products and switch brands:** Consumers in India (95 percent), China (94 percent), and Brazil (93 percent) say they seek out responsible products wherever possible (vs. 84 percent global average) and are above-average in their desire to switch brands to one that supports a cause (China 97 percent, Brazil 96 percent, India 95 percent).
- **Consumers in emerging markets are more likely to follow through with purchases:** Consumers in China (84 percent), India (80 percent), and Brazil (76 percent) are more likely to have bought a product with a social or environmental benefit in the past 12 months (vs. 63 percent global average).

"This study reveals a higher level of understanding, awareness and support of corporate social responsibility efforts from the world's consumers. Despite distinctiveness on a country-by-country level, global consumers remain steadfast as open-minded partners for collaboration to drive forward social and environmental progress," DaSilva says. "Now companies must advance CSR beyond a peripheral brand attribute to create an entirely new CSR experience."

---

invoice because merchandise isn't selling. The second reason is vendor mistakes such as shoddy labelling, lost billings, wrong-size boxes or hangers, missing items, and late shipments. Although often legitimate contract disputes, chargebacks are frequently viewed as being unjustified by vendors. Retailers can use chargebacks as a profit centre. For instance, one senior executive at a large department store chain was told to collect US$50 million in chargebacks.[46] What makes chargebacks especially difficult for vendors is that once the money is deducted from an invoice, and the invoice is "paid," it is difficult to get the missing amount back, and negotiations or threats of litigation often appear to fall on deaf ears.

Commercial Bribery

Commercial bribery occurs in retailing when a vendor or its agent offers to privately give or pay a retail buyer "something of value" to influence purchasing decisions. Say a sweater manufacturer takes a department store buyer to lunch at a private club and then proposes a ski weekend in Banff. The buyer enjoys the lunch but graciously turns down the ski trip. These gifts could be construed as bribes or kickbacks, which are illegal unless the buyer's manager is informed of them (and is also not receiving private payments or gifts). In fact, the government doesn't allow money paid for bribes to be deducted as a business expense. From an ethical perspective, there is a fine line between the social courtesy of a free lunch and an elaborate free vacation.

To avoid these problems, many companies forbid employees from accepting any gifts from vendors. They want their buyers to decide on purchases based solely on what is best for the retailer. One major US discount store chain specifically forbids the taking of "bribes, commissions, kickbacks, payments, loans, gratuities, or other solicitations, including any item of value from suppliers to the company." But many companies have no policy against receiving gifts, and some unethical employees accept and even solicit gifts, even if their company has a policy against it. A good rule of thumb is to accept only limited entertainment or token gifts, such as flowers or a bottle of wine, for Christmas, birthdays, or other occasions. When the gift or favour is perceived to be large enough to influence a buyer's purchasing behaviour, it's considered to be commercial bribery and therefore is illegal.

Slotting Allowances

A **slotting allowance**, also called a *slotting fee* when viewed from the vendor's perspective, is a fee paid by a vendor for space in a retail store.[47] It differs from commercial bribes in that it is made to the retailer itself rather than to an individual buyer. This is considered to be a legal form of competition among vendors for shelf space in Canada.

Here's an example. When Kraft or any other consumer packaged goods manufacturer wants to introduce a new product, it often pays a slotting allowance to grocery and discount store chains for the space (slot) on the shelf. The fee varies depending on the nature of the product and the relative power of the retailer. Products whose brand names command relatively low customer loyalty pay the highest slotting allowances. Likewise, large grocery chains can demand higher slotting allowances than small, independent stores. Industry reports estimate the total amount spent on slotting fees in the United States to be between US$8 and US$16 billion per year.[48] The fees can range from a few hundred dollars to $25 000 per item per store or $3 million per supermarket chain.[49]

Slotting fees are not only present in the food industry. They are becoming prevalent in other retail venues, such as those that sell over-the-counter drugs, apparel, magazines, and computer software. In the music industry, for instance, retailers regularly charge vendors for the right to display and sell their merchandise.

Some retailers argue that slotting allowances are a reasonable method for ensuring that their valuable space is used efficiently. Such fees cover their costs of adding a new SKU to their computerized system of inventory, knowing that most new products fail and the SKU must later also be removed.

Concerns with slotting allowances arise when a dominant firm uses them to exclude rivals. If a dominant vendor pays large slotting fees that rivals cannot match, then the fees may have the effect of limiting competition among vendors. This may be particularly true when the vendor pays to obtain the best retail display space or to limit the space available to rivals.[50] Similarly, retail competition may be injured when large retailers extract much larger slotting allowances than those available to smaller retailers, giving the large firms a cost advantage.[51]

Buybacks

Similar to slotting allowances, the **buyback**, also known as a *stocklift* or *lift-out*, is a strategy vendors and retailers use to get products into retail stores. Specifically, a buyback can occur under two scenarios. The first and most ethically troubling is when a retailer allows a vendor to create space for its goods by "buying back" a competitor's inventory

commercial bribery A vendor's offer of money or gifts to a retailer's employee for the purpose of influencing purchasing decisions.

slotting allowance Fee paid by a vendor for space in a retail store; also called a *slotting fee*.

buyback A strategy vendors and retailers use to get products into retail stores, either when a retailer allows a vendor to create space for goods by "buying back" a competitor's inventory and removing it from a retailer's system, or when the retailer forces a vendor to buy back slow-moving merchandise; also called *stocklift* or *lift-out*.

and removing it from a retailer's system. In the second case, the retailer forces a vendor to buy back slow-moving merchandise.

Consider the following buyback scenario. At a national home improvement store chain, thousands of garden gloves manufactured by the store's main source of supply vanished almost overnight. The empty shelves were restocked with gloves made by another glove manufacturer. The second manufacturer purchased all of the original gloves in stock so it could fill the shelves with its own product. The purchased gloves were probably dumped into a sprawling underground pipeline for resale by faraway, perhaps foreign, retailers. There are about a half-dozen companies that provide buyback-type liquidation services.

Are buybacks illegal? Technically, a company with market power may violate laws if it stocklifts from a competitor so often as to shut it out of a market. But such cases brought under the *Competition Act* are difficult to prove.

Counterfeit Merchandise

Counterfeit merchandise includes goods made and sold without the permission of the owner of a trademark, a copyright, or a patented invention that is legally protected in the country where it is marketed. Trademarks, copyrights, and patents are all under the general umbrella of intellectual property. **Intellectual property** is intangible and is created by intellectual (mental) effort as opposed to physical effort. A **trademark** is any mark, word, picture, device, or nonfunctional design associated with certain merchandise (for instance, the crown on a Rolex watch and the GE on General Electric products). A **copyright** protects original work of authors, painters, sculptors, musicians, and others who produce works of artistic or intellectual merit. The copyright protects only the physical expression of the effort, not the idea. This book is copyrighted, so these sentences cannot be used by anyone without the consent of the copyright owners. However, anyone can take the ideas in this book and express them in different words. The owner of a patent controls the right to make, sell, and use a product for a period of 20 years or a design for 14 years.

intellectual property Property that is intangible and is created by intellectual (mental) effort as opposed to physical effort.

trademark Any mark, work, picture, or design associated with a particular line of merchandise or product.

copyright A regulation that protects original works of authors, painters, sculptors, musicians, and others who produce works of artistic or intellectual merit.

The nature of counterfeiting has changed over the past decade. Although manufacturers of high-visibility, strong-brand-name consumer goods are still tormented by counterfeiters, there is now a thriving business in counterfeit high-tech products such as software, CDs, and CD-ROMs. When considering software piracy, a study conducted by analyst firm International data Corp. for software maker Microsoft, identified pirated software in the workplace is costing enterprises more than $114 billion each year.[53] Why are software, CDs, and CD-ROMs so attractive to counterfeiters? They have a high unit value, are relatively easy to duplicate and transport, and have high consumer demand. For instance, suppose *Retailing Management* were available on a CD-ROM. It could be easily duplicated as a CD or reprinted as a book for a few dollars in a foreign country. Neither the publishers nor the authors would receive any money. In fact, it's likely that they wouldn't even know about the copyright infringement.

Retailers and their vendors have four avenues to pursue to protect themselves against the ravages of counterfeiting and intellectual property rights violations: product registration, legislative action, bilateral and multilateral negotiations, and measures taken by companies.[54]

First, the product must be trademarked, copyrighted, or patented in the countries in which it's sold. Unfortunately, registration in Canada provides no protection in another country, although treaties and other international agreements allow for prompt and easy registration in other countries based on initial registration in Canada.

The second method of protection is through legislative action. Several laws protect businesses against counterfeiting. Counterfeiting is a criminal rather than a civil offence.

Third, the Canadian government is engaged in bilateral and multilateral negotiations and education to limit counterfeiting. For instance, the WTO has rules on intellectual property protection.

Finally, companies are aggressively taking steps to protect themselves. The International Anti-Counterfeiting Coalition is a group of 375 firms that lobbies for strong legal sanctions worldwide. Individual companies are also taking an aggressive stance against counterfeiting.

DID YOU KNOW?

The RCMP conducts more than 400 investigations into counterfeit goods each year across the country. Canadian industry estimates the knockoffs cost it as much as $30 billion annually.[52]

Grey-Market and Diverted Merchandise

DID YOU KNOW?

Grey markets are significant as they now exceed $10 billion per year in North America and affect almost every major trademarked product. Grey markets are growing at a rate of more than 22 percent annually.[55]

A **grey-market good** is merchandise that possesses a valid North American registered trademark and is made by a foreign manufacturer, but is imported into North America without permission of the trademark owner. Grey-market merchandise is not counterfeit. This merchandise often is the same quality and may actually be identical to merchandise brought into the country through normal channels.

Selling grey-market merchandise may be legal in the United States. Recently, the Supreme Court ruled that American manufacturers cannot stop discount stores from buying North American products overseas and selling them domestically at reduced prices if the foreign manufacturer and domestic trademark owner fall under a common corporate umbrella.[56] Interestingly, the European Court of Justice decided to allow grey-market imports only from one member-state to another, but not from outside the European Union.[57]

Without realizing it, we see grey-market goods in the marketplace all the time. Some manufacturers of cars, jewellery, perfume, liquor, watches, cameras, crystal ware, ski equipment, tractors, baby powder, and batteries are all involved in grey marketing in the United States.

Here's an example of how the grey market for watches might work in the United States. To help create a prestigious image, to offset an unfavourable exchange rate, and to pad profit margins, Swiss watch manufacturers often charge a higher wholesale price in the United States than in Europe and other countries. A Swiss watchmaker such as Patek Philippe may sell 1000 watches to a retailer in Italy, whose price is about 30 percent less than an authorized retailer in the United States. The Italian retailer sells several of the more expensive watches that are slow sellers to a grey-market (unauthorized) retailer in the United States. Both the Italian and US retailers can make a profit, and the watches can still be sold to a US customer significantly below the manufacturer's suggested retail price (MSRP).

Diverted merchandise is similar to grey-market merchandise except it need not be distributed across international boundaries. Suppose, for instance, fragrance manufacturer Givenchy grants an exclusive territory to all Hudson's Bay stores. A discount store in Toronto purchases Givenchy products from a wholesale distributor in Las Vegas and sells it for 20 percent below the suggested retail price. The merchandise is diverted from its legitimate channel of distribution, and the wholesaler in this case would be referred to as a diverter.

Some discount store operators argue that customers benefit from the lack of restriction on grey-market and diverted goods because it lowers prices. Competition with retailers selling grey-market and diverted merchandise forces authorized dealers to cut their prices.

Traditional retailers, on the other hand, claim grey-market and diverted merchandise have a negative impact on the public. They believe that important after-sale service will be unavailable through retailers of grey-market or diverted goods, because they do not have adequate training or access to appropriate replacement parts. They also think that a less expensive grey-market or diverted product may hurt the trademark's image. Importantly, the grey-market product may be an out-of-date model or not work properly in a different country. For example, Philip Morris makes cartons of Marlboro cigarettes in the United States earmarked for foreign markets where prices are lower. These cigarettes often carry warning labels that are different from the required US Surgeon General's message. Further, the packages and formulation may be different as well.[58]

Vendors wishing to avoid the grey-market problem have several remedies. First, they can require all of their retail and wholesale customers to sign a contract stipulating that they will not engage in grey marketing. If a retailer is found in violation of the agreement, the vendor will refuse to deal with it in the future. Another strategy is to produce different versions of products for different markets. For instance, a camera manufacturer could sell the same camera in the United States and the European Union but with different names and warranties. This strategy would not prevent the European product from being sold in the United States, but distinctive packaging, design, instructions, and other features may discourage its sale.

grey-market good Merchandise that possesses a valid North American registered trademark and is made by a foreign manufacturer but is imported into North America without permission of the trademark owner.

diverted merchandise Merchandise that is diverted from its legitimate channel of distribution; similar to grey-market merchandise except it need not be distributed across international boundaries.

Where Did Winners Get Its Coach Handbags?

The national brands that off-price retailers like Marshalls and Winners sell at lower prices than their department and specialty store competition come from a variety of sources. Sometimes the merchandise comes directly from manufacturers like Coach, the luxury leather goods maker, because the item was last year's model, it didn't sell well at retail and was returned by its luxury retail customer, or Coach overestimated demand and therefore had excess inventory leftover. Coach in particular sells less than 1 percent of its bags to off-price stores. Although luxury manufacturers prefer not to have their merchandise sold in off-price stores, having these off-price stores provides an excellent opportunity to rid the luxury manufacturers of excess inventory.

Off-price stores like Winners regularly sell grey-market, but not counterfeit merchandise.
Torontonian/Alamy.

Another source of Coach bags for off-price retailers may be luxury retailers. These retailers may have bought too many bags or specific styles that did not sell and need to dispose of them at the end of a season. One alternative is for the retailers to mark down the price and put the handbags on sale. But sales on luxury products like Coach bags might damage the retailer's image. Also, Coach may not want their bags sold at a discount at luxury stores. So, the retailer might sell the excess inventory to off-price retailers like Winners. This diverting of merchandise to an unauthorized retailer is creating a grey market for the Coach bags. If Coach discovers that one of its luxury retailers is diverting its newer merchandise to off-price retailers, it might refuse to sell to the retailer in the future.

Luxury brands' vendors hope that their products don't end up in off-price outlets, but they definitely fight to make sure that counterfeit products are not sold anywhere. While it is relatively harmless for grey-market luxury, branded products to end up in an off-price store, it is quite harmful to the luxury brands if a counterfeit bag is sold in a Walmart store.

Since the sale of counterfeit goods is illegal, luxury brand vendors are taking steps to ensure that national retailers will not partake in their sale. Coach recently sued Target for selling counterfeit Coach bags in its stores. Similarly, the luxury conglomerate, LVMH, sued Walmart Stores for selling fake Fendi bags in its stores. In both of these cases, the vendors were very concerned that the image of their products will be damaged by having counterfeit merchandise sold in a discount store. Although it has not been confirmed that these products were authentic, the publicity surrounding these lawsuits raises the question in consumers' minds as to whether luxury brands sold in discount stores such as Walmart and Target are real.

Exclusive Territories

As noted in the diverted goods example above, vendors often grant **exclusive geographic territory** to retailers so that no other retailer in the territory can sell a particular brand. These territorial arrangements can benefit vendors by assuring them that "quality" retailers represent their products. In cases of limited supply, providing an exclusive territory to one retailer helps ensure that enough inventory can be carried to make a good presentation and offer the customer an adequate selection. For instance, by granting exclusive territories, the luxury Ferrari Automobile Company gives its dealers a monopoly for its products—a strong incentive to push Ferrari

exclusive geographic territory A policy in which only one retailer in a certain territory is allowed to sell a particular brand.

products. The dealers know there will be no competing retailers to cut prices, so their profit margins are protected. The retailer with an exclusive territory has the incentive to carry more inventory; use extra advertising, personal selling, and sales promotions; provide special displays and display areas; and develop special services for customers. The courts have tended to hold exclusive territories legal unless they restrict competition. Competition is restricted when other retailers have no access to similar products. For example, having exclusive Ferrari dealers wouldn't be a restraint of trade since other luxury cars are readily available to the public. On the other hand, if De Beers, the South African diamond cartel, granted exclusive territories to certain jewellery retailers, this would probably be seen as a restraint of trade because diamonds wouldn't be readily available through other sources and the De Beers dealers would not compete directly against each other because of their exclusive territories.

Exclusive Dealing Agreements

An **exclusive dealing agreement** occurs when a manufacturer or wholesaler restricts a retailer to carrying only its products and nothing from competing vendors. Again, the effect on competition determines these contracts' legality. For instance, suppose a retailer signs an agreement with Lee to sell only its jeans. There is no real harm done to competition because other manufacturers have many alternative retail outlets, and Lee's market share isn't large enough to approach monopolistic levels.

Tying Contracts

A **tying contract** exists when a vendor and a retailer enter into an agreement that requires the retailer to take a product it doesn't necessarily desire (the *tied product*) to ensure that it can buy a product it does desire (the *tying product*). Tying contracts are legal in Canada unless they substantially lessen competition or tend to create a monopoly, but the complaining party has the burden of proof. For example, a postcard jobber sued a postcard manufacturer for requiring that it purchase as many "local view" postcards as it did licensed Disney character postcards. The postcard manufacturer was the sole source for licensed Disney character postcards. The court dismissed the tying case because the jobber failed to prove a substantial lessening of competition.[59]

Refusal to Deal

The practice of refusing to deal (buy from or sell to) can be viewed from both suppliers' and retailers' perspectives. Generally, both suppliers and retailers have the right to deal or refuse to deal with anyone they choose. But there are exceptions to this general rule when there is evidence of anticompetitive conduct by one or more firms wielding market power.

A manufacturer may refuse to sell to a particular retailer, but it can't do so for the sole purpose of benefiting a competing retailer. For example, Mattel decided not to offer certain popular Barbie packages to wholesale clubs. This action in itself would have been legal. However, it was determined that Mattel agreed to do so as part of a conspiracy among ten toy manufacturers orchestrated by Toys "R" Us to prevent wholesale clubs from underselling the same toy packages that Toys "R" Us sells. The refusal to deal then became an illegal group boycott. After the U.S. Federal Trade Commission enjoined this conspiracy, the ten toy manufacturers agreed to settle private antitrust lawsuits by distributing money to states for children's charities and distributing toys directly to children's charities such as Toys for Tots.[60]

In summary, any time two parties interact, there is a potential for ethical and legal problems. Buyers face issues such as how much to charge a vendor for shelf space in their stores or whether they should accept a gift or favour from a vendor with no strings attached. An eye toward fairness and the desire to maintain a strong relationship should dictate behaviour in these areas. Retailers must also be concerned with the origin of their merchandise. Specifically, is it counterfeit or grey-market merchandise? Vendors encounter a different set of issues. In general, vendors need not worry about legal problems when selling to retailers so long as they sell whatever the retailers want, to whoever wants to buy, at the same price to all. But when vendors start making restrictions and exceptions, there may be legal violations.

exclusive dealing agreement Restriction a manufacturer or wholesaler places on a retailer to carry only its products and no competing vendors' products.

tying contract An agreement between a vendor and a retailer requiring the retailer to take a product it does not necessarily desire (the tied product) to ensure that it can buy a product it does desire (the tying product).

SUMMARY

Retail buying involves various issues, including determining a retailer's branding strategy, sourcing objectives, and vendor relationship strategies. The reality is that the bigger the retailer, the more buying clout it wields in dealing with suppliers. Long-term vendor relationships are created to establish a win–win situation that will develop a sustainable competitive advantage for both parties involved. To survive, retailers must be able to count on a predictable supply of merchandise at competitive prices and with sufficient promotional support.

Retailers can purchase either manufacturers' brands or private-label brands. Each type has its own relative advantages. Choosing brands and a branding strategy is an integral component of a firm's merchandise and assortment planning process.

A large percentage of the merchandise we buy is manufactured outside of Canada. The decision to buy from domestic manufacturers or source internationally is a complicated one. The cost, managerial, and ethical issues surrounding global sourcing decisions were discussed. Buyers and their merchandise managers have several opportunities to meet with vendors, view new merchandise, and place orders. They can use Internet exchanges or visit their vendors at wholesale market centres such as Toronto, New York, Paris, or Milan. Virtually every merchandise category has at least one annual trade show at which retailers and vendors meet. Buyers often meet with vendors on their own turf—in the retail store or corporate offices. Finally, meetings with vendors are facilitated by resident buying offices. Market representatives of these resident buying offices facilitate merchandising purchases in foreign markets.

Retailers should prepare for and conduct negotiations with vendors. Successful vendor relationships depend on planning for and being adept at negotiations.

Retailers that can successfully team up with their vendors can achieve a sustainable competitive advantage. There needs to be more than just a promise to buy and sell on a regular basis. Strategic relationships require trust, shared goals, strong communications, and a financial commitment.

With thousands of annual transactions taking place between retailers and their vendors, there is plenty of room for ethical and legal problems. The issues of charging vendors for shelf space or taking bribes was discussed. There are also problems associated with counterfeit and grey-market merchandise and issues that vendors face when selling to retailers, such as exclusive territories and tying contracts. Care should be taken when making restrictions on which retailers they will sell to, what merchandise, how much, and at what price.

Retailers face a plethora of discount/payment date combinations. A working knowledge of these terms of purchase is essential for any person involved in merchandising. More important, the most advantageous application of the terms can make a significant impact on corporate profits.

KEY TERMS

alternative dispute resolution
arbitration
buyback
chargeback
commercial bribery
consortium exchange
copyright
diverted merchandise
exclusive co-brand
exclusive dealing agreement
exclusive geographic territory
free trade zone

generic branding
grey-market good
independent exchange
intellectual property
licensed brand
manufacturer brand
maquiladoras
market
med-arb
mediation
opportunity cost of capital
parallel branding

premium branding
private exchanges
retail exchanges
reverse auction
slotting allowance
strategic relationship
trade shows
trademark
trust
tying contract

1. **GO SHOPPING** Go to your favourite department or discount store. Perform an audit of national and private brands. Interview a manager to determine whether the percentage of private brands has increased or decreased over the last five years. Ask the manager to comment on the store's philosophy toward national versus private brands. On the basis of what you see and hear, assess its branding strategy.

2. **INTERNET EXERCISE** Go to the WorldWide Retail Exchange (http://wwre.globalsources.com). The WorldWide Retail Exchange and Global Sources have formed a strategic alliance. What is the WorldWide Retail Exchange? What is the exchange designed to do? What value does membership to the exchange provide for retailers? For suppliers?

3. **GO SHOPPING** See if you can find some counterfeit, grey-market, or diverted merchandise. Compare it with the real thing.

DISCUSSION QUESTIONS AND PROBLEMS

1. Do retailers take advantage of their power positions by charging slotting fees, buybacks, and chargebacks?

2. Assume you have been hired to consult with The Gap on sourcing decisions for sportswear. What issues would you consider when deciding whether you should buy from Mexico or China, or find a source in Canada?

3. How would the decision to source outside Canada affect a retailer's need to carry backup stock?

4. Does your favourite clothing store have a strong private-brand strategy? Should it?

5. When setting goals for a negotiation session with a vendor, what issues should a buyer consider?

6. What do you think will be the future of retail exchanges?

7. What factors should a buyer consider when deciding with which vendors to develop a close relationship?

CHAPTER TWELVE

Retail pricing

LEARNING OBJECTIVES

Lo1 Explore the factors retailers consider when pricing merchandise.

Lo2 Examine the various pricing strategies retailers can use to influence consumer purchases.

Lo3 Look at how the Internet is changing the way retailers price their merchandise.

SPOTLIGHT ON RETAILING

PRICING WITHOUT BORDERS

Retailers across the country are facing massive challenges with respect to the price disparity between American and Canadian retail goods. Consumers aren't often aware of the reasons for this disparity, and more often than not believe that Canadian retailers are gouging them at the till.

"Canadian retailers are innovative and dedicated to bringing consumers the best product at the lowest price, but unfortunately they're operating on an uneven playing field that's tilted to favour American retailers," asserts Karen Pound, vice president of federal government relations for the Retail Council of Canada.

The retail sector is a major contributor in Canada, directly contributing $90.4 billion to the nation's gross domestic product in 2015. In addition, it plays a key role in bridging production and consumption, and affects other industries through the pioneering of innovative practices. In short, it's the foundation upon which the economy rests.

And yet, federal policies have conspired to put Canadian retailers at a disadvantage by ensuring that prices for consumer goods are consistently higher than they are south of the border.

According to Statistics Canada, in 2013, profit margins in the retail sector were just above 4.6 percent (store format). As such, it becomes clear that retailers play a very small part in determining final prices of the goods they sell and that there are significant external factors at play that contribute to the often vast differences in pricing of Canadian products versus identical products sold in the United States. These factors propel more people who live close to the border to dip into the United States to save the difference.

The steady flow of Canadians heading to the United States to shop turned into a flood in the wake of the federal government's decision to quadruple the exemption limit for goods being brought in from the United States. Since June 2012, returning travellers who have been outside of Canada for more than 24 hours but less than 48 hours have been able to bring back $200 worth of tax-exempt goods. That's up from $50. For those out of Canada for 48 hours or more, the exemption is also quadrupled, from $200 to $800.

Given that the vast majority of Canadians live within an hour's drive of the border, this issue affects not just border communities, but the national economy as an entirety.

"The real bottom line here is that there are areas where governments can take action to help retailers compete but they're not doing it. We want the government to help level the playing field, instead of doing things to tip the balance in favour of our neighbours to the south," says Karen Pound.

Governments and consumers need to understand the particular pressures on retailers who operate businesses on the border. During a session before the Senate, the Retail Council of Canada outlined the four significant factors faced by Canadian retailers that contribute to differences in retail pricing between Canada and the United States:

- import duties on finished goods
- supply management affecting prices of food products such as dairy and poultry
- vendor pricing in Canada
- regulatory harmonization

Country pricing. It would be easy to assume that suppliers provide their goods at a single international or North American price, providing for a level playing field for retailers on both sides of the border. Unfortunately, the reality is far different. Many multinational vendors and suppliers who sell to Canadian retailers do so by way of contracts that are negotiated specifically for the Canadian market.

"Volume comes into play here. The United States is a giant compared to Canada, and as a result, US retailers can get volume discounts more easily than Canadian retailers can," says Jamie Caswell, owner of Caswell's, a Niagara Falls clothing store. "I'm the second generation to operate the store; my son will be the third. In 53 years of business, we've never seen more challenging times because of the price disparity between our products and those sold across the river."

Caswell feels frustrated and hamstrung. Like most Canadian retailers, he works hard to provide his customers with the largest variety of products at the best available prices, but he's at the mercy of the suppliers who demand certain prices for their products. "I can't cut prices too much because the cost of doing business—rent, hydro, and so forth—remains the same," he says.

Country pricing is one of the largest contributors to the difference in pricing between Canada and the United States. The reality is that suppliers will charge Canadian retailers 50 percent more to buy their products than they charge retailers in the United States for identical products.

While the federal government may not have a direct role to play in the realm of country pricing, it is important that it does not perpetuate the ongoing misinformation to the Canadian public regarding the reasons for price differences. Suggesting that Canadian retailers are to blame for the difference in pricing is not only misleading, but it also acts to undermine the important relationships between Canadian retailers and their customers.

Pixeljoy/Shutterstock.com.

Sources: Adapted from from Andrew Hind, "Pricing Without Borders," *Canadian Retailer*, Summer 2012, Volume 22, Issue 3, p. 41, Canadian Retailer, a publication of Retail Council of Canada; Statistics Canada, "Gross Domestic Product at Basic Prices, by Industry (Monthly)," http://www .statcan.gc.ca/tables-tableaux/sum-som/l01/cst01/gdps04a-eng.htm (accessed February 18, 2016); Statistics Canada, "Table 080-0030: Annual Retail Trade Survey, Financial Estimates by North American Industry Classification System (NAICS) and Store Type Annual," http://www5.statcan. gc.ca/cansim/a26?lang=eng&retrLang=eng&id=0800030&pattern=080-0028..080-0032&tabMode=dataTable&srchLan=-1&p1=-1&p2=31 (accessed March 11, 2016). This does not constitute an endorsement by Statistics Canada of this product.

value Relationship between what a customer gets (goods/services) and what he or she has to pay for it.

The importance of pricing decisions is growing because today's customers demand good value. **Value** is the relationship between what the customer gets (goods/services) and what he or she has to pay for it.

$$\text{Value} = \frac{\text{Perceived benefit}}{\text{Price}}$$

DID YOU KNOW?

In a recent holiday survey, Accenture found that only 1 percent of respondents said a discount would negatively impact their impression of a luxury brand, while 70 percent said discounts were the biggest influence in their decision to purchase a luxury good.[1]

Thus, retailers can increase value and stimulate more sales (exchanges) by either increasing the perceived benefits offered or reducing the price. To some customers, good value means always getting a low price. Increasingly, Canadian consumers have become price-sensitive. Others are willing to pay extra as long as they believe they are getting their money's worth in terms of product quality or service.

If retailers set prices higher than the benefits they provide, sales and profits will decrease. In contrast, if retailers set prices too low, their sales might increase but profits might decrease due to the lower profit margin. In addition to offering an attractive value to customers, retailers need to consider the value proposition offered by their competitors and legal restrictions related to pricing. Thus, setting the right price can be challenging.

Retailers have responded to their customers' needs with retail formats that emphasize low prices as a means of creating a differential advantage. National discount store chains that offer everyday low prices, such as Walmart, dominate many markets in many product categories. A close competitor in the price-oriented market is the membership-only warehouse club, such as Costco. Another retail format is the off-price retailer (e.g., Winners), which purchases closeout and end-of-season merchandise at lower-than-normal prices and passes the savings on to the customer.

Some of the more mature retailing institutions, such as department stores and supermarkets, have come to grips with these forms of price competition by adopting a more aggressive pricing strategy, with a significant amount of their merchandise being sold below the manufacturer's suggested price through a strong promotion orientation. Finally, many retailers, such as Harry Rosen, have successfully maintained their market appeal by providing good value by offering customers high-quality merchandise and service without attempting to offer the lowest prices (see also Retailing View 12.1).

In the middle of this price competition among national giants are the smaller retailers. Typically unable to purchase in large quantities to receive lower prices like their larger competitors, mom-and-pop retailers have either learned to use other strategies to compete such as extending opening hours, or changing the level of personal service, the variety of goods, and services or the company image, or they have gone out of business. For instance, to compete with Walmart's low prices, small retailers have developed niche strategies by providing a broader assortment of merchandise within a given product category and better service.

Pricing decisions are also being affected by the development of electronic channels. Consumers can easily compare the prices for branded products sold by different retailers. The Internet also makes it easier for consumers to compare product attributes in addition to price.

The Internet has facilitated the use of an auction pricing mechanism. People have used auctions to facilitate trade for centuries. As eBay has demonstrated, no longer do auction participants have to be located at the same place.

Getting the right product onto store shelves at the right time and at the right price is the basic formula for success in retailing. Increased competition has made it more important than ever to get that formula right. Cost cutting issues might include the following:

- buying merchandise offshore to maintain higher profit potential due to higher Canadian dollar
- cutting packaging costs by including three languages—English, French, Spanish—to serve all North American markets
- retailers and suppliers partnering to maintain competitive prices
- using price optimization software technology to sell as much inventory as possible at the highest possible price

Although technology can help move products off store shelves quickly, the art of retailing lies in predicting demand patterns.

Luxury More Than Higher Prices

Ron White, president of The Foot Shoppe, which operates five shops located in tonier parts of the Greater Toronto Area, agrees.

"We're dealing with a world in which someone will buy a Gucci fanny pack for their 16-year-old," he says.

"(But) as a luxury retailer, you have to try to look to exclusivity in brands without the flash. Many luxury consumers we see don't want the Gucci or Louis Vuitton labels. They're more into understated elegance. They're the ones who will wear an $1100 T-shirt under a blazer that you never see."

Fred Singer, president of the Edmonton-based Henry Singer Fashion Group, adds that catering to diversified luxury tastes is a matter of understanding the best of all worlds.

"We deal with people who want very high-end, exclusive product with no labels, and others who won't buy a product unless it has the label they want. We have those who buy designer jeans for the fit and fabric, others for the brand. Everyone's perception is different. Some want to buy a product for what it is, others for what it says."

As far as balancing it all, he says, it starts with having the right product offerings, for the right customers and getting exclusivity where possible.

"More than anything else, it's about relationship development and being knowledgeable about your products. That's what all luxury customers really want—good products with good service and a sense of security that you know what you are talking about," he says.

Larry Rosen, president and CEO of Harry Rosen, one of the nation's better-known chains of high-end menswear stores, notes that the luxury shopper of today is not only savvier about products and fashion trends, there is also a growing number of younger consumers who appreciate the value of a cashmere sweater.

"They won't buy as many things, but they will certainly buy better-quality items," he says. "They're better informed. They're seeking the labels that represent luxury and trust. They're looking for the same from us retailers."

In response to that, he says a major investment for Harry Rosen is staff education and training. "Even when I'm shopping myself, I love to talk to someone who is really educated about what they are selling. That's certainly what our customers want. That's the value they are looking for."

Source: Excerpt from "Spotlight on Luxury Retailing: Redefining the Luxury Experience," *Canadian Retailer*, November/December 2007, pp. 44–45, http://www.retailcouncil.org/cdnretailer. Canadian Retailer, a publication of Retail Council of Canada.

Lo1 Approaches for Setting Prices

Retailers want to set prices to maximize long-term profits. To do this, they need to consider the following:

- cost, of the merchandise and services
- demand, the price sensitivity of consumers
- competition, because customers shop around and compare prices
- legal considerations

The following sections examine three approaches for setting retail prices—cost-oriented, demand-oriented, and competition-oriented—and describe how retailers determine how much they need to sell to break even.

Under the **cost-oriented method**, the retail price is determined by adding a fixed percentage to the cost of the merchandise. For instance, a family-owned women's specialty store might use the **keystone method** of setting prices, in which it simply doubles the cost of the merchandise to obtain the original retail selling price. If a dress costs $50, the original selling price is $100. With the **demand-oriented method**, prices are based on what customers expect or are willing to pay. In this case, the retailer may have found a particularly good value at $50, but believes that the profit-maximizing price is $115. The retailer is aware of the price sensitivity of the consumers. With the **competition-oriented method**, prices are based on competitors' prices.

Which method is best? The answer is, all three! The

cost-oriented method A method for determining the retail price by adding a fixed percentage to the cost of the merchandise; also known as *cost-plus pricing*.

keystone method A method of setting retail prices in which retailers simply double the cost of the merchandise to obtain the original retail selling price.

demand-oriented method A method of setting prices based on what the customers would expect or be willing to pay.

competition-oriented method A pricing method in which a retailer uses competitors' prices, rather than demand or cost considerations, as guides.

markup The increase in the retail price of an item after the initial markup percentage has been applied but before the item is placed on the selling floor.

cost-oriented method's strength is that it is quick, mechanical, and relatively simple to use. Retailers use it because they are making thousands of pricing decisions each week and cannot take the time to thoroughly analyze and determine the best price for each product.

As indicated by economic theory, the demand-oriented method's strength is that it allows retailers to determine which price will give them the greatest profit. But demand-oriented pricing is hard to implement, especially in a retailing environment with thousands of SKUs that require individual pricing decisions.

The competition-oriented method should be considered because it is always important to keep in mind what the competition is doing—after all, the customer does. The degree to which a retailer sets the market price or follows the market leader is, however, a complicated issue.

Retailers need to consider costs, demand, and competition in setting prices. The cost-oriented method would be the starting point for setting a price. The competition-oriented method provides an outside check on the marketplace. The demand-oriented method is then used for fine-tuning the strategy. Retailers would start with a price based on costs and their profit goals, consider competition, and then perform tests to determine if it's the most profitable price.

Service retailers face challenges that aren't as important to merchandise retailers.

The Cost-Oriented Method of Setting Retail Prices

This section explains how retail prices are set on the basis of merchandise cost. Unfortunately, the process isn't always as simple as doubling the cost, which we described earlier. For instance, the retail price at which the product is originally sold may not be the same as the final retail selling price due to markdowns. So retailers have devised methods of keeping track of changes in the retail price so that they can achieve their overall financial goals.

Recall that the retailer's financial goals are set by top management in terms of a target return on assets. In the strategic profit model, return on assets is calculated as net profit margin multiplied by asset turnover. Pricing goals are determined primarily from net profit margin.

For pricing decisions, the key component of net profit margin is gross profit margin percentage (Gross margin ÷ Net sales). Retailers set initial prices high enough so that after markdowns and other adjustments (known as reductions) are made, they will end up with a gross margin consistent with their overall profit goals (see Exhibit 12–1).

Markup Defined **Markup** is an important and fundamental concept that is used in retail operations. As a form of cost-oriented pricing, it is a widely-used pricing technique. Most retailers either use the MSRP (manufacturer's suggested retail price) or set prices by marking up the item's cost to yield a profitable gross margin. Then these cost-based prices are adjusted on the basis of insights about customer price sensitivity and competitive pricing.

When setting prices based on merchandise cost, retailers start with the following equation:

$$\text{Retail price} = \text{Cost of merchandise} + \text{Markup}$$

The markup is the amount added to the cost price in order to establish the retail price or the difference between the retail price and the cost of an item. Thus, if a sporting-goods retailer buys a tennis racquet for \$75 and sets the retail price at \$125, the markup is \$50. Markup often serves as a guide for the retailer when pricing merchandise and in providing the forecasted operating profit. The appropriate markup is determined to cover all of the retailer's operating expenses (labour costs, rent, utilities, advertising, etc.) needed to sell the merchandise and produce a profit for the retailer. Markup can be expressed as a dollar figure or as a percent. Retailers find working with ratios to be

Exhibit 12–1

Considerations in Setting Retail Prices

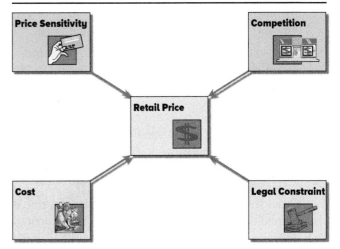

more meaningful as it allows for comparisons within or among classifications and departments, among stores within an ownership group, and among stores using a centralized buying office. For example, HBC might compare markup ratios in small electrics of Hudson's Bay with those of Home Outfitters.

Markup can be calculated as a percent of either the retail price or the cost price, but is typically calculated using the retail price. The calculation based on the retail price is more commonly used because retail expenses, markdowns, and profit are figured as dollars or percents of net sales, selling prices and discounts quoted to retailers by manufacturers are from retail list prices, and retail price data is more readily available than cost data. It is important to note that markup and expense data cannot be compared if they are not based on the same figures; both must be based either on cost or on retail figures. If a retailer buys a recliner chair for $200 and sells it for $600, the extra $400 covers operating costs and profit. The markup at retail is 66.7 percent or 200 percent at cost.

Calculating Markup Percent The difference is in the denominator when calculating markup as either a percentage at retail or at cost. The **markup percentage** is the markup as a percentage of the retail price unless otherwise stated:

$$\text{Markup percentage (at retail)} = \frac{\text{Retail selling price} - \text{Merchandise cost}}{\text{Retail selling price}}$$

Thus, the markup percentage for the tennis racquet is:

$$\text{Markup percentage} = \frac{\$125 - \$75}{\$125} = 40\%$$

The retail price based on the cost and markup percentage is:

Retail price = Merchandise cost + Markup

Retail price = Merchandise cost + Retail price × Markup percentage

$$\text{Retail price} = \frac{\text{Cost of merchandise}}{1 - \text{Markup percentage (as a fraction)}}$$

Thus, if a buyer for an office supply category specialist purchases calculators at $14 and needs a 30 percent markup to meet the financial goals for the category, the retail price needs to be:

$$\text{Retail price} = \frac{\text{Cost}}{1 - \text{Markup percent}} = \frac{\$14.00}{1 - 0.30} = 20$$

To calculate markup percentage at cost:

$$\text{Markup percentage (at cost)} = \frac{\text{Retail selling price} - \text{Merchandise cost}}{\text{Merchandise cost}}$$

The markup on retail is always less than 100 percent, while markup on cost may exceed 100 percent. As markup goes up, the gap between the retail and cost percentages grows. Consider our furniture retailer in the previous example who buys a recliner chair for $200 and considers selling it for $300, $400, $500, or $600. The $300 price generates a markup at retail of 33.3 percent and 50 percent at cost, the $400 price a 50 percent markup at retail and 100 percent at cost, the $500 price a 60 percent markup at retail and 150 percent at cost, and the $600 price a markup of 66.7 percent at retail and 200 percent at cost.

A retail buyer can work with markup in three different ways:

- calculating markup percent when cost and retail are known
- calculating retail when cost and markup percent are known
- calculating cost when retail and markup percent are known

Markup % = $ Markup ÷ $ Retail

$ Retail = $ Cost ÷ Cost %

$ Cost = $ Retail × Cost %

> **markup percentage**
> The markup as a percent of retail price.

When calculating markup percent when cost and retail are known, a buyer must determine if the markup achieved is sufficient to reach the department's planned goal. To find markup percent, find the markup dollars by subtracting $ cost from $ retail and then divide by retail dollars. A retailer's markup percentage can also be determined by taking into consideration planned retail operating expenses, profit, and net sales.

What is the markup percent on a sweater that costs $52 and retails for $115?

Markup % = $ Markup ÷ $ Retail

= $63 ÷ $115

= 54.78%

What is the planned markup for a sporting goods store that estimates its yearly operating expenses to be $65 000? The desired profit is $55 000 per year, including the owner's salary. Net sales are forecasted to be $300 000.

$$\text{Markup \%} = \frac{\text{Planned operating expenses} + \text{Planned profit}}{\text{Planned net sales}}$$

$$= \frac{\$65\,000 + \$55\,000}{\$300\,000}$$

$$= 42\%$$

Complete the Concept Check to help develop skill in learning the principles presented.

1. Calculate the markup percent on a ladies Guess watch that costs $45 and retails for $110.

2. The ladies accessory buyer at Hudson's Bay has sourced some hand-painted silk scarves for $240 a dozen at cost. (a) What is the retail price if a 50 percent markup is expected? (b) What is the retail price if a markup of 70 percent is expected?

3. Samantha buys a safari dress from the specialty store Cassis for $210. Determine the markup percent on the dress if it cost the store $80.

4. What is the cost price on the queen-size Serta mattress set that Kelly just purchased at Sleep Country for $2400 and provided the store with a 58 percent markup?

5. The paint department at Rona receives a shipment for a paint promotion that cost $8 for each litre can of white primer and would retail for $24.99 each. Find (a) the markup percent and (b) the cost percent for a litre of white primer.

6. Find the markup percent on the following order of Tommy Hilfiger sportswear for Hudson's Bay store 138.

	$Cost	$Retail
14 capri pants	$26.25 each	$75.00 each
14 safari shorts	$15.75 each	$45.00 each
25 halter tops	$7.00 each	$20.00 each
40 V-neck T-shirts	$15.25 each	$35.00 each

7. The buyer for toddler boys at Old Navy needs to buy a group of T-shirts for an upcoming top sale. She sources 50 dozen striped T-shirts at $42/dozen, 12 dozen collared tees at $60/dozen, and 40 dozen scoop-neck tees at $45/dozen. If she plans on retailing them all at a sale price of $8 each, what markup percent will she realize on the merchandise?

8. The men's buyer at Old Navy needs to buy three different styles of shorts for an upcoming promotion. He buys 200 units of style 1032 for $12 each, 200 units of style 1034 for $16 each, and 200 units of style 1036 for $20 each. Much like the toddler buyer in #5, he would like to sell the shorts all at the same advertised price point. What unit retail price point will he be able to charge if he wants a 58 percent markup?

initial markup The retail selling price initially placed on the merchandise less the cost of goods sold.

When calculating retail price when cost and markup percent are known, a buyer must evaluate the retail prices placed on the merchandise and take into account both the cost price and the markup percent needed. Buyers also need to evaluate the retail price to determine if consumers would be willing to buy the merchandise at that price. If the cost price and the markup percentage is known, it is necessary to find the cost percentage or cost complement before the retail price can be calculated. The complement of markup percent is 100 percent less markup percent on retail.

Calculate the retail price on a snowboard that costs $380 and has a markup of 56 percent.

$ Retail = $ Cost ÷ Cost %
= $380 ÷ 44%
= $864

Determine the cost of a men's dress shirt that retails for $78 and has a 55 percent markup.

$ Cost = $ Retail × Cost %
= $78 × 45%
= $35.10

Determining Initial Markup Initial markup can be calculated with percents or with specific dollar amounts. The same equation to calculate initial markup can be used when working with percents or dollar amounts since net sales always equals 100 percent. As all other percents are based on net sales, **initial markup** is the difference between the merchandise cost (COGS) and the original retail price placed on the goods, expressed as a percentage or dollar amount of retail value. Therefore, a loss can occur for a retailer if the initial markup placed on the goods (item or group of items) does not cover expenses and reductions. Retail reductions are things that reduce the retail value of goods, such as markdowns, employee discounts, special customer discounts, and inventory shrinkage.

There are other factors, such as workroom/alteration costs and cash discounts, that can affect the initial markup of merchandise. Workroom/alteration costs can increase the retail value of goods by adding additional value to the finished product (such as alterations to a suit or the cost of putting a table together). Cash discounts on the other hand represent a reduction in the cost of the goods (such as given to the store by the vendor for paying invoices early).

Initial markup

$$= \frac{\text{Expenses} + \text{Profit} + \text{Reductions} + \text{Alterations} - \text{Cash}}{\text{Net sales} + \text{Reductions}}$$

Determine the necessary initial markup percent for a retailer that has these planned figures.

Net sales	$200 000
Expenses	60 000
Reductions	15 000
Alteration costs	500
Cash discounts	250
Profit	7 550

Intial markup

$$= \frac{\text{Expenses} + \text{Profit} + \text{Reductions} + \text{Alterations} - \text{Cash discounts}}{\text{Net sales} + \text{Reductions}}$$

$$= \frac{60\,000 + 7550 + 15\,000 + 500 - 250}{200\,000 + 15\,000}$$

$$= \frac{82\,800}{215\,000}$$

$$= 38.5\%$$

Determine the necessary initial markup percent for the following retailer. Calculate initial markup using $ and % values.

Net sales	$220 000
Expenses	30%
Markdowns	3.2
Employee discounts	5.3
Shortages	1.0
Alteration costs	.5
Cash discounts	.25
Profit	$16 500

Intial markup

$$= \frac{\text{Expenses} + \text{Profit} + \text{Reductions} + \text{Alterations} - \text{Cash discounts}}{\text{Net sales} + \text{Reductions}}$$

$$\% = \frac{30 + 7.5 + 9.5 + .5 - .25}{100 + 9.5} = 43.15\%$$

$$\$ = \frac{\$66\,000 + \$16\,500 + \$20\,900 + 1100 - 550}{\$220\,000 + \$20\,900} = 43.15\%$$

(Note that the same answer is obtained using both $ and % values.)

Determining Maintained Markup Maintained markup is the actual sales realized for the merchandise when it is sold by the retailer minus its costs and is reported as a percent. Gross cost of goods sold does not reflect deductions for cash discounts and workroom costs. Gross cost of goods sold includes the following items from the income statement: opening inventory, gross purchases, less returns from vendor, net purchases, freight forward, and total merchandise handled. This differs from total cost of goods sold, which also includes cash discounts earned, net cost of merchandise sold, and net alteration/workroom costs. **Maintained markup** can be difficult to predict because it is based on the actual prices received rather than on planned sales. As a result, it is often calculated whenever the operating statement is prepared. Rather than calculating maintained markup on an individual purchase or a few items, retailers calculate it on the activity of an entire classification, department, or store for a given period or quarter.

maintained markup
The amount of markup the retailer wishes to maintain on a particular category of merchandise; net sales minus cost of goods sold.

Maintained markup $ = Net sales − Gross cost of goods sold

Maintained markup % = Maintained markup $ ÷ Net sales $

Determining the Initial Markup from Maintained Markup and Gross Margin Initial markup is always greater than maintained markup as long as there are any reductions. Also, as discussed above, initial markup is expressed either in dollars or as a percentage of retail price. This is because retailers using the retail inventory method (RIM) of inventory accounting think of their inventory in "retail" rather than "cost" terms. Also, expressing initial markup as a percentage of retail price closely resembles the other accounting conventions of expressing net profit, gross margin, and maintained markup as percentages of net sales, which are, of course, at retail. Retailers recognize maintained markup as the more meaningful ratio when comparing initial markup to maintained markup because it is a more accurate reflection of actual movement of merchandise. Retailers cannot determine maintained markup in advance as they do with initial markup, although they do try to maintain the amount of profit (markup) on a particular classification, department, or store.

Maintained markup and gross margin are both percentages that are calculated on net sales figures rather than on original retail prices. The difference in the calculation lies in the COGS number. Maintained markup is the difference between net sales and gross cost of goods sold, while gross margin is the difference between net sales and the total cost of goods sold. In other words, gross margin takes into consideration cash discounts and alteration/workroom costs into the calculation. If a retailer does not have any cash discounts or workroom or alteration costs for the specified period, gross margin and maintained markup are the same. Thus, the only difference between the two terms is the workroom costs (such as alterations to a suit or the cost of putting a table together) and cash discounts (given to the store by the vendor for paying invoices early).

Why do retailers make this distinction between maintained markup and gross margin? In many retail organizations, these workroom costs aren't controlled by the person who makes the pricing decision. For instance, the furniture buyer doesn't have control over costs associated with assembling a dining room table. In the same way, a buyer typically has no control over whether the accounting department takes the cash discounts offered to the company from its vendors for paying invoices early. But remember that, conceptually, maintained markup and gross margin are similar. Moores Clothiers has done an excellent job by collecting fees for alterations, a cost recovery.

The performance measure usually used to evaluate pricing decisions is gross margin. Exhibit 12–2 summarizes its components. We use the traditional accounting definition of gross margin:

Gross margin \$ = Net sales − Total cost of goods sold

Gross margin % = Gross margin \$ ÷ Net sales

Remember that gross margin is a financial term that expresses the difference between net sales (the price that the customer pays for merchandise) and the cost of the merchandise (the cost that the retailer paid for the merchandise). The gross margin return on investment (GMROI) is the financial ratio of gross margin dollars divided by the average cost of stock on hand.

The term *maintained markup* is very descriptive. It's the amount of profit (markup) a retailer plans to maintain on a particular category of merchandise. For example, in Exhibit 12–2, planned maintained markup is $62 000 on sales of $120 000, or 51.67 percent ($62 000 ÷ $120 000). In other words, to meet its profit goals, this retailer must obtain a 51.67 percent maintained markup.

reductions Markdowns; discounts to employees and customers; and inventory shrinkage due to shoplifting, breakage, or loss.

A retailer's life would be relatively simple if the amount of markup it wanted to maintain (maintained markup) were the same as the initial markup.

Exhibit 12–2

Sample Income Statement Showing Gross Margin

Net sales	$120 000
− Cost of goods sold	58 000
= Maintained markup	62 000
− Alteration costs + Cash discounts	3 000
= Gross margin	$ 59 000

Initial markup
= Retail selling price initially placed on the merchandise minus total cost of goods sold (COGS)

whereas,

Maintained markup
= The actual sales that you get for the merchandise minus gross cost of goods sold (COGS)

Why is there a difference? A number of reductions to the value of retail inventory occur between the time the merchandise is originally priced (initial markup) and the time it's sold (maintained markup). **Reductions** include markdowns, discounts to employees and customers, and inventory shrinkage (due to shoplifting, breakage, or loss). Initial markup must be high enough so that after reductions are taken out, the maintained markup is left. Thus, there is a difference between the initial and the maintained markup.

The difference between the initial and maintained markup is illustrated in Exhibit 12–3. The item illustrated costs $0.60, and the initial price for the item is $1.00, so the initial markup cost is $0.40, and the initial markup percentage is 40 percent. However, the average actual sale price for the item is $0.90. The reductions are $0.10, so the maintained markup is $0.30, and the maintained markup percentage is 33 percent (0.30/0.90).

The relationship between initial markup and maintained markup is

Initial markup = Maintained markup (as a % of net sales) + Reductions (as a % of net sales)/100% + Reductions (as a % of net sales)

Thus, if the buyer setting the price for the item shown in Exhibit 12–3 planned on reductions of 10 percent of actual sales and wanted a maintained markup of 33 percent, the initial markup should be:

Initial markup percentage = 33% + ($0.10/$0.90)
= 11.111%/100% + 11.111%
= 40%

The initial retail price should be:

Initial retail price = Cost/1 − Initial markup percentage
= $0.60/1 − 0.40 = $1.00

Exhibit 12–3
Difference Between Initial Markup and Maintained Markup

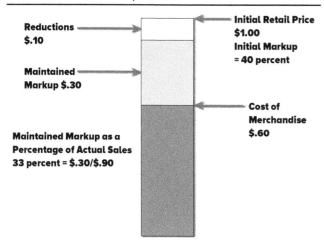

Reductions $.10

Maintained Markup $.30

Maintained Markup as a Percentage of Actual Sales
33 percent = $.30/$.90

Initial Retail Price
$1.00

Initial Markup
= 40 percent

Cost of Merchandise
$.60

The Demand-Oriented Method of Setting Retail Prices

Demand-oriented pricing should be used in conjunction with the cost-oriented method to determine retail prices. Using this method, retailers not only consider their profit structure but also pay close attention to the effect that price changes have on sales. For instance, if customers are extremely price-sensitive, then a price cut can increase demand so much that profits actually increase. Alternatively, if customers are insensitive to price, raising the price also can boost profits, since sales likely won't decrease. Demand-oriented pricing seeks to determine the price that customers are willing to pay and that will maximize profits.

To illustrate how an initial retail price is set using the demand-oriented method, we will use a hypothetical situation of Aritzia's new ribbed sleeveless T-shirt for women. Assume that the fixed cost of developing the product is $300 000 and the variable cost is $5 each. One benefit of private-label merchandise is the flexibility of being able to set any retail price. Aritzia decides to test the T-shirt in four markets at different prices. Exhibit 12–4 shows the pricing test's results. It's clear (from column 5) that a unit price of $10 is by far the most profitable ($450 000).

Although determining the optimal price based on a demand analysis is simple for one product, most retailers carry so many products that these tests become a very expensive proposition. Also, a

12.2 | CONCEPT CHECK

Complete the Concept Check to help develop skill in learning the principles presented.

1. A specialty store had the following planned figures. What is the initial markup?

Net sales	$124 000
Profit	$4 000
Expenses	$60 000
Employee discounts	$240
Markdowns	$3 200
Shortages	$1550

2. A specialty store had the following planned figures. What is the initial markup?

Net sales	100%
Profit	3.6%
Expenses	41%
Employee discounts	7.2%
Markdowns	4.8%
Shortages	1.0%

3. Calculate the initial markup using the following figures.

Net sales	$180 000
Expenses	38%
Employee discounts	8.3%
Markdowns	4%
Shortages	1%
Alterations	$124
Cash discounts	$280
Profit	12%

4. Calculate the maintained markup percent, using the following operating results for a specialty retailer.

Net sales		$375 000
Cost of goods sold		$35 000
Gross purchases	$185 000	
Less, returns to vendor	−6 500	
Net purchases	$178 500	
Freight inward	+3 500	
Total merchandise handled	$182 000	
Closing inventory		−52 000
Gross cost of merchandise sold		$130 000
Cash discounts earned		−6 800
Net cost of merchandise sold		$123 200
Net alteration/ workroom costs		+2 500
Total cost of merchandise sold		−125 700
Gross margin		$249 300

5. Calculate maintained markup and gross margin percent from the following operating results.

Net sales	$1 200 500
Cash discounts	$12 200
Alteration costs	$3 100
Gross cost of merchandise sold	$605 500

Exhibit 12–4
Results of Pricing Test

Market	(1) Unit Price	(2) Market Demand at Price (in units)	(3) Total Revenue (col. 1 × col. 2)	(4) Total Cost of Units Sold ($300 000 fixed cost + $5 variable cost)	(5) Total Profits (col. 3 − col. 4)
1	$ 8	200 000	$1 600 000	$1 300 000	$300 000
2	10	150 000	1 500 000	1 050 000	450 000
3	12	100 000	1 200 000	800 000	400 000
4	14	50 000	700 000	550 000	150 000

retailer must have multiple outlets to be able to manipulate prices in this manner.

A more sophisticated method of determining the most profitable price is a *pricing experiment*. In a pricing experiment, a retailer actually changes the price in a systematic manner to observe changes in purchases or purchase intentions. Exhibit 12–5 shows an example of a simple experiment—a classic before/after experiment with control group design. Two stores are similar in size and customer characteristics. Their weekly sales for a compact microwave oven are almost identical (10 and 12 units per week), and the ovens are selling at the same price, $100. The price at the first store is changed to $80, but the second store's price is left at $100. Thus, the second store is used as a control to make sure that any change in sales is due to the price change rather than to some outside force such as competition or weather. Now sales at the first store jump to 21 units per week, while sales at the control store hit 13 units. Barring any circumstances unknown to the retailer, the change in sales is due to the price cut. And, by the way, the $100 price is more profitable than the $80 price in the second store! Since product cost is $50, the $100 retail price provides a $650 gross margin [($100 − $50) × 13 units], whereas the $80 price provides a $630 gross margin [($80 − $50) × 21 units].

In the past, these pricing experiments weren't regularly applied because of the time and expense

of administering them. But now any retailer with point-of-sale terminals can run large-scale experiments. Retailers can use the data warehouses derived from their loyalty programs in conjunction with sales and price data to run experiments. These records cover what customers have purchased, prices paid, and conditions of sale (such as coupon usage and price specials). Demographic information on customers makes it possible to correlate price sensitivity with customer profiles.

Retailers and their vendors can also buy from private firms. For one of its many products, InfoScan, the company purchases information from individual supermarket chains on price and promotion activity that has been scanned through their POS terminals; it then aggregates data by region, chain, or market area.

The Competition-Oriented Method of Setting Retail Prices

As the name implies, when retailers use competition-oriented pricing, they set their prices on the basis of their competition rather than cost or demand considerations. Retailers can price either above, below, or at parity with the competition. The chosen strategy must be consistent with the retailer's overall strategy and its relative market position. Consider, for instance, Walmart and Birks, as we did previously. Walmart's overall strategy is to be the low-cost retailer for the merchandise it sells. It tries to price products it sells below competition. Birks, on the other hand, offers significant benefits to its customers including high quality, unique merchandise, impeccable service, and elegant locations. Those little blue boxes stamped with the Birks logo symbolize quality service and jewellery. Due to the unique nature of Birks' offering, it is able to set prices higher than its competitors'.

Exhibit 12–5
A Pricing Experiment

	Before	After
Store 1	10 units @ $100 Gross margin = $500	21 units @ $80 Gross margin = $630
Store 2 (Control)	12 units @ $100 Gross margin = $600	13 units @ $100 Gross margin = $650

Market leaders cannot, however, ignore their small competitors. Suppose that a sporting goods store in North Bay, Ontario, consistently underprices Walmart on fishing gear. Walmart will adjust its prices to meet or even beat the competitor in that market.

What should small competitors do to compete with market leaders? A jewellery store could price at parity or below Birks. Additionally, it could strive for competitive advantages in assortment or service. A more difficult question is how a casual wear store can compete against Walmart's prices. It cannot compete head to head with Walmart on every item. To do so would probably put it out of business because it cannot achieve the buying quantities of scale of Walmart. Instead, it should pick items that are very visible to customers and generate margin on items that customers cannot readily compare. If Walmart is advertising jeans at $19.99, then the casual wear store should either carry other brands of jeans or bite the bullet and price with or below Walmart.

Collecting and Using Competitive Price Data[2]

Retailers work to provide a consistent shopping experience, and part of that requires consistency between a retailer's market strategy and its pricing position within a market. Most large retailers routinely collect competitive price data from competitors to see if they need to adjust their prices to remain competitive.

Competitive price data are typically collected using store personnel, third-party providers, and vendor representatives (whose interests often bias the data). Costing between $0.15 and $2.00 per price point to collect, competitive price comparisons are typically still performed using pen and paper and sometimes without the consent of the competitor. Because the costs associated with collecting and then managing the data are significant, retailers need to be very strategic when structuring competitive price projects.

How Retailers Reduce Price Competition

Retailers have two fundamental strategies available to them for reducing price competition:

- First, they can adopt an EDLP strategy. Conditioning customers to expect a fair and relatively low price on a typical market basket of merchandise enables a retailer to charge slightly higher prices on some individual items.
- Second, they can use some of the branding strategies described previously. For instance,

they can develop lines of premium private-label merchandise. Since the competition doesn't have such merchandise, it is difficult for the customer to comparison shop.

Profit Impact of Setting a Retail Price: The Use of Break-Even Analysis

Now that we have examined how retailers set prices on the basis of the cost-, demand-, and competition-oriented methods, let's look at how retailers determine the volume of sales necessary for them to make a profit. A useful analytical tool is **break-even analysis**, which analyzes the relationship between total revenue and total cost to determine how much merchandise needs to be sold to achieve a break-even (zero) profit. For example, a retailer might want to know:

- break-even volume and dollars for a new product, product line, or department
- break-even sales change needed to cover a price change
- break-even sales to cover a target profit
- change in profit based on change in sales volume

Let's look more closely at the first two: the break-even volume of a new private-label product and the break-even sales change needed to cover a price change.

Calculating Break-Even for a New Product

Suppose PetSmart is considering the introduction of a new private-label, dry dog food targeting owners of older dogs. The cost of developing this dog food is $700 000, including salaries for the design team and testing the product. Because these costs don't change with the quantity of product that is produced and sold, they are known as **fixed costs**. PetSmart plans to sell the dog food for $12 a bag—the unit price. The **variable cost** is the retailer's expenses that vary directly with the quantity of product produced and sold. Variable costs often include direct labour and materials used

break-even analysis A technique that evaluates the relationship between total revenue and total cost to determine profitability at various sales levels.

fixed costs Costs that are stable and don't change with the quantity of product that's produced and sold.

variable cost A cost that varies with the level of sales and that can be applied directly to the decision in question.

break-even point (BEP) The quantity at which total revenue equals total cost and beyond which profit occurs.

contribution margin Gross margin less any expense that can be directly assigned to the merchandise.

in producing the product. PetSmart will be purchasing the product from a private-label manufacturer. Thus, the only variable cost is the dog food's cost, $5, from the private-label supplier. The **break-even point (BEP)** quantity is the quantity at which total revenue equals total cost, and then profit occurs for additional sales.

Break-even quantity

$$= \frac{\text{Fixed cost}}{\text{Actual unit sales price} - \text{Unit variable cost}}$$

$$= \frac{\$700\ 000}{\$12 - \$5} = 100\ 000 \text{ bags}$$

Thus, PetSmart needs to sell 100 000 bags of dog food to break even, or make zero profit, and for every additional bag sold, it will make $7 profit.

Now assume that PetSmart wants to make $100 000 profit from the new product line. The break-even quantity now becomes:

$$\frac{\text{Break-even}}{\text{quantity}} = \frac{\text{Fixed cost}}{\text{Actual unit sales price} - \text{Unit variable cost}}$$

$$= \frac{\$700\ 000 + \$100\ 000}{\$12 - \$5} = 114\ 286 \text{ bags}$$

Calculating Break-Even Sales A closely related issue to the calculation of a break-even point is determining how much unit sales would have to increase to make a profit from a price cut or how much sales would have to decline to make a price increase unprofitable.[3] Continuing with the PetSmart example, assume the break-even quantity is 114 286 units based on the $700 000 fixed cost, the $100 000 profit, a selling price of $12, and a cost of $5. Now PetSmart is considering lowering the price of a bag of dog food to $10. How many units must it sell to break even if it lowers its selling price by 16.67 percent to $10? Using the formula,

$$\frac{\text{Break-even}}{\text{quantity}} = \frac{\text{Fixed cost}}{\text{Actual unit sales price} - \text{Unit variable cost}}$$

$$= \frac{\$700\ 000 + \$100\ 000}{\$12 - \$5} = 160\ 000 \text{ bags}$$

So if PetSmart decreases its price by 16.67 percent from $12 to $10, unit sales must increase by 40 percent: (160 000 − 114 286) ÷ 111 286.

For another example of break-even sales, let's use the T-shirts from Aritzia and assume the break-even quantity is 57 143 units (based on the $300 000 fixed cost, the $100 000 profit, a selling price of $12, and a cost of $5). How many T-shirts must Aritzia sell to break even if it lowers its selling price by 16.6 percent to $10? Using the formula:

$$\frac{\%\text{break-even}}{\text{sales change}} = \frac{-\%\text{ price change}}{\%\text{CM} + \%\text{price change}} \times 100$$

where %CM stands for percentage contribution margin. **Contribution margin** is gross margin less any expense that can be directly assigned to the merchandise. In this example, since there are no variable costs besides the cost of the shirt, the contribution margin is the same as the gross margin. Also, don't forget the minus sign in the formula's numerator.

Contribution margin (CM) = Selling price − Variable costs
CM = $12 − $5 = $7
%CM = (CM ÷ Selling price) × 100
%CM = ($7 ÷ $12) × 100 = 58.33%

Substituting the %CM into the formula, we can calculate the break-even sales change:

$$\frac{\%\text{break-even}}{\text{sales change}} = \frac{-(-16.6)}{58.33 + (-16.6)} \times 100 = 39.78\%$$

$$\frac{\text{Unit break-even}}{\text{sales change}} = 39.78\% \times 57\ 143 \text{ units} = 22\ 731 \text{ units}$$

Thus, if Aritzia reduces its price to $10, it must sell an additional 22 731 units to break even. It should come as no surprise that when we add the break-even quantity at $12 to the break-even sales change to $10, we get 79 874 units (57 143 + 22 731)—almost the same break-even point of 80 000 units that we obtained using the first formula. (The difference is due to rounding.) The same formula can be used to determine the sales change necessary to break even with a price increase.

Price Adjustments

In Canada, retailers are relatively free to promote adjustments to the initial retail price with the hope of generating sales. In this section, we will examine markdowns, coupons, rebates, price bundling, multiple-unit pricing, variable pricing, and some special Internet pricing issues. Retailing View 12.2 describes how some retailers are trying to raise their gross margin percentage by avoiding markdowns.

Get Them While They're Hot

For years, retailers have lured customers into stores with sales and markdowns. Shoppers know when items will go on sale and often wait for bargains. Although this policy helps retailers sell more merchandise, it also decreases their gross margins. Frequent sales also may signal to customers that there might be something wrong with the merchandise or that it isn't good quality. Frequent sales can also damage a retailer's overall image. So retailers have devised tactics to reverse this cycle and encourage more customers to pay full price.

One method of reducing markdowns is to better control the quantities bought. By adopting a just-in-time inventory policy, in which small amounts of merchandise arrive just in time to be sold, customers perceive a scarcity and purchase at full price. Even if there are adequate quantities of merchandise available in the stockroom or in a distribution centre, displaying just a few items on the sales floor sends a signal to the customer to "buy them now, while they last!" If retailers simply change their displays frequently, customers will perceive that the merchandise is new and available in limited quantities.

Some retailers, such as Walmart, advertise everyday low prices, which implies that their products are already at low prices and therefore will not be further discounted. Even Hudson's Bay, long known for its everyday sales, is promoting "Every Day Value," or "Bay Value" items on many of its racks. Costco doesn't need to advertise its

Kristoffer Tripplaar/Alamy.

low prices; loyal customers return time after time to look for low-priced treasures.

A handful of retailers, like Coach, Lululemon, and Apple, have taken a dramatically different approach. They focus on quality and image and therefore simply don't have sales! Customers accept this full-price message. It is an enviable position, to which most retailers can only aspire.

These tactics for preventing bargain hunting increase gross margins as well as inventory turnovers. When more products are sold at full price, gross margins naturally increase. As retailers trim their inventories to give a feeling of "buy now or be sorry," sales also will increase, and inventory will decrease, thus resulting in greater inventory turnover.

Sources: Allison Kaplan, "Rough Weather Behind Them, Retailers Are Starting to Trim Their Sales," *St. Paul Pioneer Press*, January 26, 2007 (accessed January 25, 2008); Jayne O'Donnell, "Retailers Try to Train Shoppers to Buy Now," *USA TODAY*, September 25, 2006 (accessed January 25, 2008); Linda Whitaker, *Managing Markdowns: Why Prevention Is Better than the Optimization Cure* (Carlsbad, CA: Quantum Retail Technology, 2007), (accessed January 25, 2008); Kris Hudson, "Turning Shopping Trips into Treasure Hunts," *The Wall Street Journal*, August 27, 2007, p. B1; Timothy Taylor, "The Final Stretch," *Report on Business*, December 2011, pp. 27–31.

Markdowns

Markdowns are price reductions from the initial retail price. Markdowns are initiated because the lower price induces price-sensitive customers to buy more merchandise.

Reasons for Taking Markdowns A retailer's decision to take markdowns can be classified as either clearance (to dispose of merchandise) or promotional (to generate sales).

DID YOU KNOW?

Marked-down goods, which accounted for just 8 percent of department-store sales three decades ago, have climbed to around 20 percent, according to the National Retail Federation.[4]

Clearance Markdowns When merchandise is slow-moving, obsolete, at the end of its selling season, or priced higher than competitors' goods, it generally gets marked down for clearance purposes. This merchandise can become an eyesore and impair the store's image. Further, even if the merchandise can be sold in the following season, it may become shopworn or out of style. Also, the cost of carrying inventory is significant. If a buyer has to carry $10 000 of unwanted inventory at cost for a year with an annual inventory carrying cost of 35 percent, the cost would be $3500 (or $10 000 × 0.35)—not a trivial amount!

markdowns The price reductions in the initial retail price.

Fashion retailers tend to order more merchandise than they forecast selling because they are more concerned about selling out of a popular item before the end of the season than about over-ordering and having to mark down excess merchandise. Stocking out of popular merchandise can have a detrimental effect on a fashion retailer's image, whereas discounting merchandise at the end of the season merely reduces maintained markup.

Markdowns are part of the cost of doing business, and thus retailers plan for markdowns. They set an initial markup high enough so that after markdowns and other reductions are considered, the planned maintained markup will be achieved. Thus, a retailer's objective shouldn't necessarily be to minimize markdowns. If markdowns are too low, the retailer is probably pricing the merchandise too low, not purchasing enough merchandise, or not taking enough risks with the merchandise being purchased.

Promotional Markdowns Using a high/low pricing strategy described earlier in this chapter, retailers employ markdowns to promote merchandise to increase sales. A buyer may decide to mark down some merchandise to make room for something new. An additional benefit is that the markdown sale generates cash flow to pay for new merchandise. Markdowns are also taken to increase customers' traffic flow. Retailers plan promotions in which they take markdowns for holidays, for special events, and as part of their overall promotional program. In fact, small portable appliances (such as toasters) are called *traffic appliances* because they are often in a *leader pricing* program and sold at reduced prices to generate in-store traffic. Retailers hope that customers will purchase other products at regular prices while they are in the store. Another opportunity created by markdowns is to increase the sale of complementary products. For example, a supermarket's markdown on hot dog buns may be offset by increased demand for hot dogs, mustard, and relish—all sold at regular prices.

merchandising optimization software Set of algorithms (computer programs) that monitors merchandise sales, promotions, competitors' actions, and other factors to determine the optimal (most profitable) price and timing for merchandising activities, especially markdowns.

Optimizing Markdown Decisions Retailers have traditionally created a set of arbitrary rules for taking markdowns.[5] One retailer, for instance, flags markdown candidates when their weekly sell-through percentages fall below a certain value. Another retailer cuts prices on the basis of how long the merchandise has been in the store—marking products down by 20 percent after eight weeks, then by 30 percent after 12 weeks, and finally by 50 percent after 16 weeks.

Such a rules-based approach, however, is limited in several ways:

- It assumes that all the items within a category exhibit the same, consistent behaviour. So it treats a cashmere sweater the same way it treats a wool sweater.

- It follows a fixed schedule; it's not sophisticated enough to determine how shifts in sales trends or other factors such as promotions or holidays will affect demand.

- It fails to take gross margin into consideration; its only goal is to clear inventory.

Instead of relying on rules developed from averages, a retailer can benefit significantly from **merchandising optimization software**, a set of algorithms that monitors merchandise sales, promotions, competitors' actions, and other factors to determine the optimal (most profitable) price and timing for merchandising activities, especially markdowns. This software is currently being used by a growing number of major retailers and is commercially available from a number of specialty firms such as SAP.

The optimization software works by constantly refining its pricing forecasts on the basis of actual sales throughout the season. For example, the software recognizes that in early November, a winter item's sales are better than expected, so it delays taking a markdown that had been planned. Each week, as fresh sales data become available, it readjusts the forecasts to include the latest information. It computes literally thousands of scenarios for each item—a process that is too complicated and time-consuming for retailers to do on their own. It then evaluates the outcomes based on expected profits and other factors and selects the action that produces the best results.

Making good markdown decisions isn't all about relying on sophisticated computer software. Retailers must also work closely with their vendor partners to coordinate deliveries and help share the financial burden of taking markdowns.

Reducing the Amount of Markdowns by Working with Vendors Retailers can reduce the amount of markdowns by working closely with their vendors to time deliveries with demand. Merchandise that arrives before it is needed takes up valuable selling space and can get shopworn or damaged. On the other hand, when merchandise arrives too late, retailers may have trouble selling it without extensive markdowns. Quick response inventory systems reduce the lead time for receiving merchandise so that retailers can more closely monitor changes in trends and customer demand, thus reducing markdowns.

Vendors have a vested interest in retailers' success. Vendors that are knowledgeable about the market and competition can help with stock selections. Of course, a retailer must also trust its own taste and intuition; otherwise, its store will have the same merchandise as all other stores. Retail buyers can often obtain markdown money—funds a vendor gives the retailer to cover lost gross margin dollars that result from markdowns and other merchandising issues. For instance, assume a retailer has $1000 worth of ties at retail that are given a 25 percent markdown. Thus, when the ties are sold, the retailer receives only $750. But if the vendor provides $250 in markdown money, the maintained markup is unaffected. In this way, the vendor helps share the risk. According to the *Competition Act,* markdown money should be provided to all retailers on a proportionally equal basis, typically as a percentage of purchases. (Markdown money falls under the umbrella of potentially illegal price discrimination discussed in Appendix 12A, available on Connect.)

Determining Markdown Percent

Markdowns are expressed as a percent of net sales and cannot be calculated until the merchandise is sold. To determine markdown percent, the dollar markdown must first be found by subtracting the new, reduced price from the previous price and then the net sales is divided into the dollar markdown number. Net sales equals the original retail price minus markdowns.

Markdown $ = Previous price − New, reduced price

Markdown % = Markdown $ ÷ Net sales $

A sporting goods retailer receives six Burton snowboards that retail for $800. All six snowboards are reduced to $580 for a weekend "Winter Wonderland Sale." What is the markdown percent on this snowboard?

Markdown $ = Previous price − New, reduced price
$$= 6 \times (\$800 - \$580)$$
$$= 6 \times \$220$$
$$= \$1320$$

Sales from this snowboard $= 6 \times \$580 = \$3480$

Markdown % = Markdown $ ÷ Net sales
$$= \$1320 \div \$3480$$
$$= 37.93\%$$

If December markdowns for the women's accessory department total $24 360 and net sales for the same month are $98 245, what is the markdown percent?

Markdown % = Markdown $ in December ÷ Net sales for December
$$= \$24\,360 \div \$98\,245$$
$$= 24.8\%$$

Calculate net sales for the produce department if markdowns for boxed strawberries are 59.6 percent of net sales and the markdown dollar amount is $37.25.

Net sales = Markdown $ ÷ Markdown %
$$= \$37.25 \div 59.6\%$$
$$= \$62.50$$

Liquidating Markdown Merchandise

No matter what markdown strategy a retailer uses, some merchandise may still remain unsold. A retailer can use one of five strategies to liquidate this merchandise:

- "Job-out," or sell the remaining merchandise to another retailer.
- Consolidate the unsold merchandise.
- Place the remaining merchandise on an Internet auction site such as eBay, or have a special clearance location on the retailer's website.
- Give the merchandise to charity.
- Carry the merchandise over to the next season.

Selling the remaining marked-down merchandise to another retailer has been very popular among retailers. For instance, Winners purchases end-of-season merchandise from other retailers and sells it at deep discounts. This strategy enables the retailer to have a relatively short markdown period, provides space for new merchandise, and at the same time eliminates the often unappealing sale atmosphere. The problem with this strategy is that the retailer can recoup only a small percentage of the merchandise's cost—often a mere 10 percent.

Marked-down merchandise can be consolidated in a number of ways. First, the consolidation can be made into one or a few of the retailer's regular locations. Second, marked-down merchandise can be consolidated into another retail chain or an outlet

first-degree price discrimination Charging customers different prices based on their willingness to pay.

second-degree price discrimination Charging different prices to different people on the basis of the nature of the offering.

coupons Documents, electronic or hard copy, that entitle the holder to a reduced price or X cents off the actual price of a product or service.

store under the same ownership. Holt Renfrew (Last Call) uses this strategy. Finally, marked-down merchandise can be shipped to a distribution centre or a rented space such as a convention centre for final sale. This practice encourages a successful yet relatively short markdown period. Consolidation sales can be complex and expensive due to the extra transportation and recordkeeping involved.

The Internet is expected to be increasingly useful for liquidating marked-down merchandise. For example, an electronics store is partnering with eBay to sell goods it has received from trade-ins.

Giving clearance merchandise to charities is also an increasingly popular practice. Charitable giving is always a good corporate practice. It is a way of giving back to the community and has strong public relations benefits. Also, the cost value of the merchandise can be deducted from income.

The final liquidation strategy—to carry merchandise over to the next season—is used with high-priced nonfashion merchandise, such as furniture. Generally, however, it's not worth carrying over merchandise because of excessive inventory carrying costs. Retailers need to be well aware of consumers' propensity to check out "value" on the Internet—for example, www.selloffvacations.com and www.autotrader.com.

12.3 | CONCEPT CHECK

Complete the Concept Check to help develop skill in learning the principles presented.

1. During the month of May, the markdowns for shoes at Aldo totalled $18 600. Shoe sales for the month were $122 480. What was the markdown percent for May?

2. Children's Place six-month merchandise plan for the Guildford Town Centre, Surrey store indicates planned sales of $680 500 and planned markdowns of 30.6 percent. Find the planned markdown dollars.

3. Old Navy sold 200 pairs of men's shorts for $36 during their Victoria Day weekend sale. The shorts went back to their regular price of $45 after the weekend. What was the markdown percent?

Markdowns and Price Discrimination Ideally, retailers would like to have the opportunity to charge customers as much as they would be willing to pay. This practice is called **first-degree price discrimination**. For instance, if a wealthy customer wants to buy something, the retailer charges more. If a price-sensitive customer comes in, the retailer charges less. Although this practice is legal and is widely used in some retail sectors, such as by automobile and antiques dealers (see Appendix 12A, available on Connect), it is impractical in a retail store with 20 000 SKUs and prices that are displayed for everyone to see. Recently, however, customers are initiating first-degree price discrimination by haggling.

Consider price discrimination versus market segmentation. For example, service retailers (kitchen companies, painting contractors, landscape companies) often spend time "sizing up" or qualifying the prospect and determining the scope of work, including expanding the request, before submitting a proposal.

> ### DID YOU KNOW?
>
> Price discrimination can occur online. Researchers at Northeastern University confirmed major e-commerce websites show some users different prices and a different set of results, even for identical searches![6]

Markdowns and the other widely used retail adjustment practices described in the next section are known as **second-degree price discrimination**—charging different prices to different people on the basis of their willingness to do something. For example, early-bird specials at a restaurant offer lower-priced meals before 6 p.m.

Price Codes Traditionally the price of an item has usually ended with .99; why do you think you occasionally see prices ending with a 7 (.97) or a 4 (.94) or some other number? Chances are these are price-tag code numbers that are used to differentiate whether or not an item is at full price or has been discounted. Various retailers use different numbering schemes to communicate internally whether or not an time is being discounted and what type of discount is being applied. For example, Costco uses .99 for full or regular priced items and .97, .88, or .00 for markdowns.

Coupons

Coupons offer a discount on the price of specific items when they're purchased. Coupons are considered to be a second-degree price discrimination because they provide an incentive for price-sensitive customers to purchase more merchandise. Coupons are issued by manufacturers and retailers in newspapers, on products, on the shelf, at the cash register, over the Internet, and through the mail. Coupons are used because they are thought to induce customers to try products for the first time, convert those first-time users to regular users, encourage large purchases, increase usage, and protect market share against competition.

The evidence on the overall profitability of issuing coupons is mixed, depending on the product category. Since coupons have the seemingly positive effect of encouraging larger purchases than without coupons, the coupon promotion may be stealing sales from a future period without any net increase in sales. For instance, if a grocery store runs a coupon promotion on sugar, households may buy a large quantity of sugar and stockpile it for future use. Thus, unless the coupon is used mostly by new buyers, the net impact on sales will be negligible, and there will be a negative impact on profits because of the amount of the redeemed coupons and the cost of coupon redemption procedures. Unfortunately, it's very hard to isolate a market for new users without allowing current users to take advantage of the coupon promotion. If, on the other hand, the coupon is for a DVD or other product whose demand is not controlled by the degree of everyday usage, it might increase overall consumption (see Retailing View 12.4).

DID YOU KNOW?

Consumers who use digital coupons shop more and spend more than the average shopper. According to the *Digital Coupon Redeemer: Shopper Trends* report, heavy digital coupon users shop 47 percent more often than the average shopper. The average shopper spends $41.17 per shopping trip on grocery and household items annually, while heavy digital coupon users spend $63.97.[7]

Rebates

A **rebate** is a portion of the purchase price returned to the buyer. Generally, the customer sends a proof of purchase to the manufacturer or a rebate clearinghouse that processes rebates for the manufacturer, and the customer is sent a rebate cheque. Rebates are most useful when the dollar amount is relatively large. Otherwise, it's not worth the customer's time and postage to redeem the rebate. For instance, rebates are often offered on cars, major and portable appliances, computers, and electronic products.

From the retailer's perspective, rebates are more advantageous than coupons since they increase demand in the same way coupons do, but the retailer has no handling costs. Manufacturers like rebates because many consumers never bother to redeem them, allowing manufacturers to offer, in effect, phantom discounts.[8] Many advertisements prominently proclaim low prices, noting the requirement to send in for rebates in microscopic letters. Consumers are drawn to the store and purchase the product, but only 5 to 10 percent claim the rebate. As a result, consumer advocates hate rebates.

Manufacturers also like rebates because they let them offer price cuts to consumers directly. With a traditional price cut, retailers can keep the price on the shelf the same and pocket the difference. Rebates can also be rolled out and shut off quickly. That allows manufacturers to fine-tune inventories or respond quickly to competitors without actually cutting prices. Finally, because buyers are required to fill out forms with names, addresses, and other data, rebates become a great way to build a customer data warehouse. Retailers must comply with the Canadian privacy laws in effect when collecting customer information.

Price Bundling

Price bundling is the practice of offering two or more different products or services for sale at one price. For instance, McDonald's offers a value-meal bundle of a sandwich, french fries, and a soft drink at a discount compared with buying the items individually. Price bundling increases both unit and dollar sales by increasing the amount of merchandise bought during a store visit. The practice is an example of second-degree price discrimination because it offers more price-sensitive customers a lower-priced alternative.

Multiple-Unit Pricing

Multiple-unit pricing (or quality discounts) is similar to price bundling in that the lower total merchandise price increases sales, but the products or services are similar rather than different.[9] For example, a grocery store may sell three litres of fruit drink for $2.39 when

rebate Money returned to the buyer in the form of cash based on a portion of the purchasing price.

price bundling The practice of offering two or more different products or services for sale at one price.

multiple-unit pricing Practice of offering two or more similar products or services for sale at one price.

the price per unit is 99 cents—a savings of 58 cents. Like price bundling, this strategy is used to increase sales volume. Depending on the type of product, however, customers may stockpile for use at a later time. Multiple-unit pricing is an example of second-degree price discrimination because customers who buy and consume more of a product are presumably more price-sensitive and thus attracted by the lower prices if they buy more units.

Variable Pricing[10]

Variable pricing means charging different prices in different stores to different demographic segments, a practice referred to as third-degree price discrimination. For example, movie theatres have lower ticket prices for seniors and students. Both groups are price-sensitive. For instance, Barnes & Noble discounted its prices on the Internet compared to its bricks-and-mortar stores in order to compete with Amazon.com. Although this may be necessary in the short run because of these highly competitive, commodity-type products, it could cause ill will among customers who become accustomed to shopping in multiple channels.

Zone pricing refers to the practice of charging different prices in different stores, markets, or regions to address different competitive situations. Food retailers may have up to four or five pricing zones in a single city. They will have one zone if they are next to a Walmart and another zone if they are next to a less price-competitive regional chain. Prices can vary as much as 10 percent depending on the competition and the economic health of the neighbourhood.[11]

Variable pricing is easier in the food and drug retail sectors than for other stores because many do not **item price**—put a price tag on each item. It is easy to have different prices in various stores because it is so easy to change them—just scan the bar code on the shelf tag, change the price in the store's price database, and replace the shelf tag with a new label.

Variable pricing also doesn't conflict with retailers' promotional strategy because many newspapers print different editions or can use different freestanding inserts (FSI), which are ads printed at the retailer's expense and distributed as an insert in the newspaper. Even if the newspaper doesn't use zones, a store might carry 40 000 SKUs, advertise 1000, and still have 39 000 left for variable pricing.

There are problems associated with variable pricing in traditional stores. First, as for multichannel retailers, if customers shop in more than one price zone, they will tend to be confused and annoyed. Also, third-degree price discrimination based on income and age is considered to be an unethical practice by many.

Pricing Strategies

In today's retail market, two opposing pricing strategies prevail: everyday low pricing and high/low pricing.[12] We will describe these two strategies and the conditions under which each is used.

Everyday Low Pricing

Many retailers have adopted an everyday low pricing (EDLP) strategy. This strategy emphasizes continuity of retail prices at a level somewhere between the regular non-sale price and the deep-discount sale price of the retailer's competitors. The term *everyday low pricing* is therefore somewhat of a misnomer. Low doesn't necessarily mean lowest. Although retailers using EDLP strive for low prices, they aren't always the lowest price in the market. At any given time, a sale price at a competing store or a special purchase at a warehouse club store may be the lowest price. A more accurate description of this strategy is therefore everyday *same* prices because the prices don't have significant fluctuations.

A couple of the biggest Canadian retailers—Walmart and Staples—have adopted EDLP. In supermarket retailing, Loblaws, including Fortinos and Zehrs, is positioned as an EDLP store.[13] Although these retailers embrace EDLP as their strategy, they do occasionally have sales. They are just not as frequent as their high/low competitors.

Since it is difficult to always have the lowest prices, some retailers have adopted a **low-price guarantee policy** in which they guarantee that they will

variable pricing Charging different prices in different stores, markets, or zones.

zone pricing Charging different prices for the same merchandise in different geographic locations to be competitive in local markets.

item price The practice of marking prices only on shelves or signs and not on individual items.

low-price guarantee policy A policy that guarantees that the retailer will have the lowest possible price for a product or group of products, and usually promises to match or better any lower price found in the local market.

DID YOU KNOW?

The following Canadian retailers will beat competitors prices by 10 percent:

- Best Buy
- Canadian Tire
- Lowes
- Home Depot
- Rona[14]

have the lowest possible price for a product or a group of products. The guarantee usually promises to match or better any lower price found in the local market. The promise normally includes a provision to refund the difference between the seller's offer price and the lower price.

Canadian Tire currently uses a hybrid approach. While some of their items are EDLP, they have other items in the store that incorporate a high/low pricing model.

High/Low Pricing

In a **high/low pricing** strategy, retailers offer prices that are sometimes above their competition's EDLP, but they use advertising to promote frequent sales. The sales undertaken by retailers using high/low strategies have become more intense in recent years. In the past, fashion retailers would mark down merchandise at the end of a season, and grocery stores and drugstores would have sales only when their vendors offered them special prices or when they were overstocked. Today, many retailers respond to increased competition and a more price-conscious customer by promoting more frequent sales.

Deciding Which Strategy Is Best

The EDLP approach has a number of advantages, including the following:

- **Reduced price wars.** Many customers are skeptical about initial retail prices. They have become conditioned to buying only on sale—the main characteristic of a high/low pricing strategy. A successful EDLP strategy enables retailers to withdraw from highly competitive price wars with competitors. Once customers realize that prices are fair, they will buy more each time and buy more frequently.

- **Reduced advertising.** The stable prices caused by EDLP limit the need for weekly sale advertising used in the high/low strategy. Instead, retailers can focus on more image-oriented messages. In addition, EDLP retailers do not have to incur the labour costs of changing price tags and signs and putting up sales signs.

- **Reduced stockouts and improved inventory management.** An EDLP strategy reduces the large variations in demand caused by frequent sales with large markdowns. As a result, retailers can manage their inventory with more certainty. Fewer stockouts mean more satisfied

Which store is using a high/low pricing strategy, and which is using everyday low pricing?

(left) © AP Photo/Mark Lennihan; **(right)** © Annette Coolidge/PhotoEdit

customers, higher sales, and fewer rain checks. (A **rain check** is given to customers when merchandise is out of stock; it is a written promise to sell customers merchandise at the sale price when the merchandise arrives.) In addition, a more predictable customer demand pattern enables the retailer to improve inventory turnover by reducing the average inventory needed for special promotions and backup stock.

The high/low pricing strategy also has advantages, including the following:

- **Increase profit through price discrimination.** A high/low strategy allows retailers to charge higher prices to customers who are not price-sensitive and lower prices to price-sensitive customers. When fashion merchandise first hits the store, it's offered

high/low pricing A strategy in which retailers offer prices that are sometimes above their competition's everyday low price, but they use advertising to promote frequent sales.

rain check When sale merchandise is out of stock, a written promise to customers to sell them that merchandise at the sale price when it arrives.

yield management The practice of adjusting prices up or down in response to demand to control sales generated.

at its highest price. Fashion leaders, those who are less sensitive to price, and hard-to-fit customers often buy as soon as the merchandise is available. As the season progresses and markdowns are taken, more price-sensitive customers enter the market and pay a lower price for the same merchandise. Finally, hard-core bargain hunters enter the market for the end-of-season deep-discount sales at the end of each season—25 percent off merchandise that has already been marked down 33 to 50 percent.

- **Sales create excitement.** A "get them while they last" atmosphere often occurs during a sale. Sales draw crowds, and crowds create excitement. Some retailers augment low prices and advertising with special in-store activities such as product demonstrations, giveaways, and celebrity appearances.

- **Sales move merchandise.** All merchandise will eventually sell—the question is, at what price? Frequent sales enable retailers to move the merchandise, even though profits erode. The reasons retailers put certain merchandise on sale are discussed later in this chapter.

- **Emphasis is on quality.** A high initial price sends a signal to customers that the merchandise is high quality. When merchandise goes on sale, customers still use the original, or reference, price to gauge quality.

Pricing Services

Additional challenges arise when pricing services due to (1) the need to match supply and demand and (2) the difficulties customers have in determining service quality.[15]

Matching Supply and Demand

Services are intangible and thus cannot be inventoried. When retailers are selling products, if the products don't sell one day, they can be stored and sold the next day. However, when a plane departs with empty seats or a play is performed without a full house, the potential revenue from this unused capacity is lost forever. In addition, most services have limited capacity. For example, restaurants are limited in the number of customers that can be seated. Due to capacity constraints, services retailers might encounter situations in which they cannot realize as many sales as they could make.

To maximize sales and profits, many services retailers engage in yield management.[16] **Yield management** is the practice of adjusting prices up or down in response to demand to control the sales generated. Airlines are masters at yield management. Using sophisticated computer programs, they monitor the reservations and ticket sales for each flight and adjust prices according to capacity utilization. Prices are lowered on flights when sales are below forecasts and there is significant excess capacity. As ticket sales approach capacity, prices are increased.

Other services retailers use less sophisticated approaches to match supply and demand. For example, more people want to go to a restaurant for dinner or see a movie at 7:00 PM than at 5:00 PM. As a result, restaurants and movie theatres might not be able to satisfy the demand for their services at 7:00 PM but have excess capacity at 5:00 PM. Thus, restaurants and movie theatres often price their services lower for customers who use them at 5:00 PM compared with 7:00 PM in an effort to shift demand from 7:00 PM to 5:00 PM.

Theatres use a variety of strategies to try to ensure that the seats are sold and sold at prices equivalent to what customers are willing to pay. Targeted direct mail coupons are often used when the play opens, and two-for-one tickets are introduced about halfway through the run. In some cities, like Toronto and Stratford, theatres partner with half-price ticket brokers, which sell unsold tickets for 50 percent off the ticket price, but only for performances that same day.

Priceline.com offers a unique pricing scheme for booking airline flights, hotel rooms, and rental cars that helps service providers match supply and demand and captures some profit through price discrimination. Customers can visit its website and specify the price they are prepared to pay and the acceptable range of times, days, and/or quality for a particular leisure travel service. For example, a customer can indicate she wants to fly from Montreal to Vancouver, anytime between 6:00 AM and 10:00 PM on September 14 or stay in any four-star hotel in Maui from January 15 to January 20. Thus, the service for which the customer is paying is opaque; the customer does not know the specific nature of the service that will be offered. Then, Priceline.com accesses databases of participating suppliers to determine whether it can fulfill the

Haggling for a Better Price

While out shopping a few weeks ago, Regina Ranonis was trying to decide between trendy low-heeled boots or a more conservative style. Then the sales associate spoke up: If she would spring for both pairs, he would knock $270 off the total price.

Does this sound like the local flea market? It wasn't. A number of retailers are hoping to reel in sales by allowing haggling, or some form of it. The practice isn't entirely new—and it remains officially denied by most companies—but good consumers say they're getting deals every-where, from Home Depot to Best Buy. Big-name stores such as Saks and Macy's say savvy shoppers who can cite competitors' prices may also find some wiggle room.

If you think you can't haggle for a better price at national chain stores, think again.
© Getty Images.

The Internet has given a real boost to haggling for bargains. Fashion sites such as RetailMeNot.com list pro-motional codes that can be used online at checkout. Because many retailers honour a lower price on the same item found at a competitor's store or Internet site, savvy customers use search engines to find the best deal.

Some retailers offer special prices to their best cus-tomers, either while in the store or through an email alert. At Neiman Marcus, for instance, customers are regularly invited to "midday dash" sales that last for two hours. Customers receive an email about the sale earlier the same day. They can purchase at 50 percent off by click-ing on a link in the email message.

Customers in most countries, except the United States, Canada, Australia, and parts of England, are expected to haggle. Chinese con-sumers even have taken haggling to a new level—group haggling! The practice, called *tuangou*, or team purchase, begins in Internet chat rooms, where consumers devise plans to buy items like appliances, food, or even cars in bulk. Next, they show up together at the stores and demand discounts.

Many of the biggest US retail-ers, from The Gap to Pottery Barn, say they are sticking to firm no-haggling policies. Many retailers use cash registers that won't accept unauthor-ized discount prices without managerial approval. Some even have video cameras not only to watch shoppers, but also to make sure the employees aren't cutting sweet-heart deals for their friends.

Some of the best negotiating territory is at fran-chises, where owners have the flexibility to operate more like mom-and-pop shops. But even at major department stores and small chains, a growing number of managers are now authorized to lower a price to meet the competi-tion or throw in free alterations or delivery. Many stores take pains to insist that haggling is off-limits, even as customers and sales associates say it goes on all the time. The policy is, "Try not to come down in price too much, but don't let the business walk out."

Sources: Susan Reda, "Do You Haggle?" Stores, June 2009, p. 6; Marianne Rohrlich, "Adventures in Haggling the Retailers' View," *New York Times*, January 29, 2009, p. D7; Jeanine Poggi and Lily-Hayes Kaufman, "How to Find Secret Shopping Savings," *Forbes*, April 7, 2009; Stephanie Rosenbloom, "High-End Retailers Offering More Discounts," *New York Times*, August 1, 2009; Matt Richtel, "Even at Megastores, Hagglers Find No Price Is Set in Stone," *New York Times*, March 23, 2009, p. A1.

customer's offer and whether it wants to accept the price designated by the consumer. Consumers agree to hold their offers open for a specified pe-riod of time (generally, not longer than a minute) to determine whether they can or want to accept the offer. Once fulfilled, offers generally cannot be cancelled, making such purchases nonrefundable.

The service that Priceline.com offers benefits both buyers and sellers. Price-sensitive buyers save money, and sellers generate incremental revenue by selling their services at below retail prices but without disrupting their existing retail pricing struc-tures.[17] Retailing View 12.3 provides another exam-ple of how the Internet has enabled price-sensitive buyers to save money.

Determining Service Quality

Due to the intangibility of services, it is often di-fficult for customers to assess service quality,

leader pricing A pricing strategy in which certain items are priced lower than normal to increase the traffic flow of customers or to increase the sale of complementary products.

price lining A pricing policy in which a retailer offers a limited number of predetermined price points within a classification.

especially when other information is not available.[18] Thus, if consumers are unfamiliar with a service or service provider, they may use price to make quality judgments. For example, most consumers have limited information about lawyers and the quality of legal advice they offer. They may therefore base their assessment of the quality of legal services offered on the fees they charge. They may also use other non-diagnostic cues to assess quality such as the size and decor of the lawyer's office.

Another factor that increases the dependence on price as a quality indicator is the risk associated with a service purchase. In high-risk situations, many of which involve credence services such as medical treatment or legal consulting, the customer will look to price as a surrogate for quality.

Because customers depend on price as a cue of quality and because price creates expectations of quality, service prices must be determined carefully. In addition to being chosen to manage capacity, prices must be set to convey the appropriate quality signal. Pricing too low can lead to inaccurate inferences about the quality of the service. Pricing too high can set expectations that may be difficult to match in service delivery.

Lo2 Using Price to Stimulate Retail Sales

In this section, we examine three techniques used by retailers to increase sales. Each of these techniques—leader pricing, price lining, and odd pricing—makes the processing of price information easier for consumers and therefore facilitates sales.

Leader Pricing

In **leader pricing**, certain items are priced lower than normal to increase customers' traffic flow or to boost sales of complementary products. Reasons for using leader pricing are similar to those for coupons. The difference is that with leader pricing, merchandise has a low price to begin with, so customers, retailers, and vendors don't have to handle coupons.

Some retailers call these products *loss leaders*. In a strict sense, loss leaders are sold below cost. But a product doesn't have to be sold below cost for the retailer to be using a leader-pricing strategy.

Walmart, Amazon, and Target use leader pricing to sell top-selling books. Prices for the books are nearly 70 percent below cover prices.[19] Since publishers charge 50 percent of a hardcover book's cover price, these mega-retailers are losing money on these sales. The purpose of this leader-pricing structure is to attract customers to the company's online site, where they may then order additional items. The danger is that independent booksellers or eBay merchants could purchase multiple copies for resale. To prevent independent bookstores from buying the best-sellers for resale, Walmart, Amazon, and Target have set purchasing limits on these books.

The best items for leader pricing are frequently-purchased products such as white bread, milk, and eggs, or using well-known brand names such as Coke as loss leaders. Customers take note of ads for these products because they are purchased weekly. The retailer hopes consumers will also purchase their weekly groceries while buying loss leaders.

One problem with leader pricing is that it might attract shoppers referred to as cherry pickers, who go from one store to another, buying only items that are on special. These shoppers are clearly unprofitable for retailers.[20]

Price Lining

In **price lining**, retailers offer a limited number of predetermined price points within a classification. For instance, a tire store may offer tires only at $49.99, $69.99, and $89.99. Both customers and retailers can benefit from such a strategy for several reasons:

- Confusion that often arises from multiple price choices is essentially eliminated. The customer can choose the tire with either the low, medium, or high price. (There need not be three price lines; the strategy can use more or fewer than three.)

- From the retailer's perspective, the merchandising task is simplified. That is, all products within a certain price line are merchandised together. Further, the firm's buyers can select their purchases within the predetermined price lines.

- Price lining can also give buyers greater flexibility. If a strict formula is used to establish the initial retail price (initial markup), there could be numerous price points. But with a price-lining strategy, some merchandise may be bought below or above the expected cost for a price line. Of course, price lining can also limit retail buyers' flexibility. They may be forced to pass up potentially profitable merchandise because it doesn't fit into a price line.

- Although many manufacturers and retailers are simplifying their product offerings to save distribution and inventory costs and to make the choice simpler for consumers, price lining can be used to get customers to "trade up" to a more expensive model. Research indicates a tendency for people to choose the product in the middle of a price line. So, for example, if a camera store starts carrying a "super deluxe" model, customers will be more likely to purchase the model that was previously the most expensive. Retailers must decide whether it's more profitable to sell more expensive merchandise or save money by paring down their stock selection.[22]

DID YOU KNOW?

Each extra syllable in a price reduces the chances of it being recalled by 20 percent.[21]

Odd Pricing

Odd pricing refers to the practice of using a price that ends in an odd number, typically a nine.[23] Odd pricing has a long history in retailing. In the nineteenth and early twentieth centuries, odd pricing was used to reduce losses due to employee theft. Because merchandise had an odd price, salespeople typically had to go to the cash register to give the customer change and record the sale. This reduced salespeople's chances to take money for an item from a customer, keep the money, and never record the sale. Odd pricing was also used to keep track of how many times an item had been marked down. After an initial price of $20, the first markdown would be $17.99, the second markdown $15.98, and so on.

Although results of empirical studies in this area are mixed,[24] many retailers believe that odd pricing can increase profits. By assuming that shoppers in a grocery store don't notice the last digit of a price, the retailer is free to round a price up to the nearest nine. So, if the price would normally be $2.90, the retailers would round up to $2.99. This tactic would increase sales by 3 percent, more than most grocery stores' entire profit margin, with no

Many retailers set prices to end in 9s because they believe customers will perceive the prices as lower than they actually are.
John Crowe/Alamy.

increase in costs (increase in sales: $2.99 − $2.90 = $0.090 or $0.090 ÷ $2.99 = 3% of sales).

For products that are believed to be sensitive to price, many retailers will round the price down to the nearest nine to create a positive price image. If, for example, the price would normally be $3.09, many retailers will lower the price to $2.99. This practice is so prevalent that when planning new-product introductions, many manufacturers plan their cost to retailers such that the retail price will be rounded to a nine or a ninety-nine. Some of the more sophisticated price optimization systems (discussed earlier in this chapter) are capable of taking these factors into account, using ending numbers to optimize profits and price image.

DID YOU KNOW?

ShopSavvy allows consumers to use their Android phone's camera to scan barcodes to find the best online and local prices.[25]

Lo3 The Internet, Mobile Devices, and Price Competition

The growth of the electronic channel has changed the way consumers get and use information to make purchasing decisions based on price. Traditionally, price competition between store-based retailers offering the same merchandise was reduced by geography because consumers typically shop at the stores and malls closest to where they live and work. However, using the Internet, consumers can search

odd pricing The practice of ending prices with an odd number (such as 69 cents) or just under a round number (such as $98 instead of $100).

search engines
Computer programs that simply search for and provide a listing of all Internet sites selling a product category or brand with the price of the merchandise offered; also called *shopping bots.*

for merchandise across the globe at a low cost. Internet sites such as Shopzilla, RedLaser, TheFind, ShopStyle, and Price-Grabber.com allow customers to compare prices across a range of retailers.[26]

Searching for the lowest prices is facilitated by shopping bots. **Search engines** or *shopping bots* are computer programs that search for and provide a list of all Internet sites selling a product category or price of specific brands offered. To limit price comparisons, electronic retailers initially made it hard for customers to go from one Internet site to another. The electronic retailers used different interfaces so that customers needed to learn how to search through the offerings at each new site they visited. In addition, some Internet retailers electronically prevented shopping bots from accessing their sites, collecting information about the products sold at the site, or using these collected data to compare the prices offered at different electronic retailing sites.[27] Although these strategies made it more difficult to compare prices, they also made it more difficult to attract customers to websites.

Although consumers shopping electronically can collect price information with little effort, they can get a lot of other information about the quality and performance of products at a low cost. For instance, an Internet site that offers custom-made Oriental rugs can clearly show real differences in patterns and materials used in construction.

Retailers using an electronic channel can reduce the emphasis on price by providing better services and information. Because of these services, customers might be willing to pay higher prices for the merchandise. For example, Amazon.ca provides a customer with the table of contents and synopsis of a book, as well as reviews and comments by the author, or authors, and people who have read the book. When the customer finds an interesting book, Amazon's system is programmed to suggest other books by the same author or the same genre. Finally, customers can tell Amazon about their favourite authors and subjects and then receive emails about new books that might be of interest. The classic response to the question, What are the three most important things in retailing? used to be "location, location, location." In the world of electronic retailing, the answer is "information, information, information."[28]

Using shopping bots such as Bottomdollar.com, consumers can easily collect and compare prices for branded merchandise sold through an electronic retail channel.

Courtesy of Price-Grabber.com.

Group Buying Sites

Group buying sites such as WagJag, Groupon, and LivingSocial have surged in popularity. Many buying sites negotiate steep discounts on retail, services, and cultural events to subscribers in a generally free daily email, which are activated when a certain number of people agree to buy. Consumer trust in the wisdom of crowds may be the reason why consumers eagerly participate in group buying now, when a number of group buying sites failed ten years ago. Potential purchasers are, most often, asked for credit card details, which will be charged only when a required number of purchasers register for the deal.

There are two basic types of group buying vendors: those who primarily target offers to a local audience and those who focus on national offers. Groupon and WagJag, for example, primarily serve local markets with their listings targeted at the city and sometimes the neighbourhood level. If they run national deals, they are usually local deals run in multiple markets. For instance, The Gap participated in a Groupon promotion during the summer of 2010 that generated over $10 million in sales in one day.

Most group buying sites work on a revenue-sharing model where they take some percentage of the discounted price of every offer sold. The revenue share is negotiated between the buying site and the vendor. It could look like this:

Retail price	$100
Discount (%)	40%
Discount ($)	$40
Offer price (customer pays)	$60
Revenue share (%)	35%
Revenue share ($) (group buying site gets this amount)	$21
Retailer share	$39

There are three fundamental variables to any offer: product, what is being sold; discount, how much is the discount; and quantity, how many are sold or can be sold. Ideally, an offer is one that is profitable after the discount and revenue share, attracts potential buyers, doesn't diminish the brand, and appeals to the type of customer who is likely to become a repeat customer.

For many retailers, the offer could take one of several different forms:

- **Excess inventory.** Group buying sites offer a channel beyond many retailers' physical or virtual presence when they have excess inventory to unload quickly.
- **Dollars for credits.** This common deal offer is where a customer pays, for example, $5 to use toward any good or service for 50 percent of $10.
- **Discounts on specific goods or service.** This is a more targeted discount on a specific good or service—for example, $20 for a pedicure, regularly $40.
- **Significant discount or loss leader.** Some retailers may offer a product near or below cost with the hopes of upselling customers to more expensive or continued purchases—for example, cosmetic clinics that discount the first Botox treatment as a way to acquire new customers for regular treatments.

Group buying websites make local marketing at scale accessible to retailers. But they don't make them instantly profitable or ultimately worthwhile. Retailers need to be smart about their offers, thoughtful about the customer experience, and rigorous in their measurement.

Sources: Alyshah Hasham, "Groupon and Other Group Buying Sites such as WagJag and LivingSocial Benefit from Consumer 'Herd Mentality': Study," *Toronto Star*, February 23, 2012, http://www.thestar.com/printarticle/1135326 (accessed October 6, 2012); "The Other Contenders in the Group Buying Clone Wars," *CNBC*, December 6, 2010, http://www.cnbc.com/id/40495538/The_Other_Contenders_in_the_Group_Buying_Clone_Wars (accessed October 6, 2012); Alex Cohen, "The Ultimate Guide to Group Buying Sites," *SIM Partners*, September 19, 2012, http://searchenginewatch.com/article/2206458/The-Ultimate-Guide-to-Group-Buying-Sites (accessed October 6, 2012).

SUMMARY

Canadian consumers are becoming increasingly price-sensitive; they put pressure on retailers to offer pricing strategies such as everyday low prices. Retailers must remember that value is the relationship between what the customer gets and what he or she has to pay. Price competition among retailers is a growing trend, often resulting in escalating lower prices ending in a price war in which there are few winners. Successful retailers will make pricing decisions to match their retail strategy objectives, and acknowledge store image, merchandise mix, and customer service offerings. Using the Internet, consumers can now search for merchandise across the globe. The number of stores that a consumer can visit to compare prices is no longer limited by physical distance.

In this chapter, we have answered several questions. First, what fundamental pricing strategies are retailers adopting? Retailers lie on a continuum from using pure everyday low pricing to pure high/low strategies, where prices start high but decrease with frequent sales. However, most EDLP retailers must resort to occasional sales, and most high/low pricers are attempting to create an image of providing customers good value.

Second, how do retailers set retail prices? There are three primary approaches for establishing prices: the cost-, demand-, and competition-oriented methods. Each method has its merits, but a mix of methods is best. In making pricing decisions, retailers also use break-even analyses to determine the volume of sales necessary for them to make a profit.

Third, since the initial retail price isn't necessarily the price at which the merchandise is finally sold, how do retailers adjust the initial retail price and how do these adjustments affect profits? Retailers have several tactics available, including markdowns, coupons, rebates, bundling, multiple-unit pricing, variable pricing, and special Internet pricing.

Finally, how do retailers use price to stimulate sales without resorting to price discrimination? Three strategies are prevalent: price lining, leader pricing, and odd pricing.

Additional challenges arise when pricing services, due to the need to match supply and demand and the difficulties customers have in determining service quality. Retailers use yield management techniques to match supply and demand for services.

Legal issues that impact pricing decisions come from two sides. Those that affect the buying of merchandise include price discrimination and vertical price-fixing. The legal pricing issues that affect consumers are horizontal price-fixing, predatory pricing, comparative price advertising, bait-and-switch, and scanned versus posted prices. These issues are considered in Appendix 12A, available on Connect.

KEY TERMS

break-even analysis
break-even point (BEP)
competition-oriented method
contribution margin
cost-oriented method
coupons
demand-oriented method
first-degree price discrimination
fixed costs
high/low pricing
initial markup
item price

keystone method
leader pricing
low-price guarantee policy
maintained markup
markdowns
markup
markup percentage
merchandising optimization software
multiple-unit pricing
odd pricing
price bundling

price lining
rain check
rebate
reductions
search engines
second-degree price discrimination
value
variable cost
variable pricing
yield management
zone pricing

1. **INTERNET EXERCISE** Price bundling is very common in the travel and vacation industry. Go to the website for Sandals (http://www.sandals.com) and see what you can get—all for one price.

2. **GO SHOPPING** Go to a retailer who retails through bricks and clicks and examine the cost of items in the store and on the website. Do you find the same merchandise for sale in the store and online? Describe any differences observed.

3. **GO SHOPPING** Go to two different types of stores and try to bargain your way down from the tagged price. Describe your experience. Was there any difference in your success rate as a result of type of store or type of merchandise? Did you have better luck when you spoke to a manager?

4. **GO SHOPPING** Go to five different types of stores and ask the manager of each how he or she determines when to take markdowns and how much the markdown should be. What rule-based approaches are they using? Are any using merchandising optimization software?

5. Go to your favourite food store and your local Walmart to find the prices for the market basket of goods below. What was the total cost of the market basket at each store? How did the prices compare? Did Walmart live up to its slogan of "Always lower prices"?

COMPETITIVE PRICING: GROCERY STORE VS. WALMART						
Item	**Size**	**Brand**	**Grocery**	**Walmart**	**Price Difference**	**Percent Savings**
Grocery						
Ground coffee	369 g can	Tim Hortons				
Raisin Bran	675 g box	Kellogg's				
Pet Supplies						
Puppy Chow	1.6 kg bag	Purina				
Cleaning						
Liquid laundry detergent	1.47 l bottle	Tide				
Dryer sheets	80 count	Bounce				
Liquid dish detergent	591 ml bottle	Palmolive				
Health and Beauty						
Shampoo	355 ml bottle	Dove				
Toothpaste	170 ml tube	Colgate Total				
Total Cost of the Market Basket of Goods						

DISCUSSION QUESTIONS AND PROBLEMS

1. How does merchandising optimization software help buyers make better markdown decisions?

2. Simple examination of markdowns could lead us to believe that they should be taken only when a retailer wants to get rid of merchandise that's not selling. What other reasons could a retailer have to take markdowns?

3. Do you know any retailers that have violated any of the legal issues discussed in Appendix 12A, available on Connect? Explain your answer.

4. Which of the pricing strategies discussed in this chapter are used by your favourite retailer? Do you think they are used effectively? Can you suggest a more effective strategy?

5. What is the difference in the pricing strategies of ebay.com, priceline.com, and staples.com? Which firm do you think will be the strongest in ten years? Why?

6. A department's maintained markup is 38 percent, reductions are $560, and net sales are $28 000. What is the initial markup percentage?

7. Maintained markup is 39 percent, net sales are $52 000, alterations are $1700, shrinkage is $500, markdowns are $5000, employee discounts are $2000, and cash discounts are 2 percent. What are gross margin in dollars and initial markup as a percentage? Explain why initial markup is greater than maintained markup.

8. Cost of a product is $150, markup is 50 percent, and markdown is 30 percent. What's the final selling price?

9. Manny Perez bought a tie for $9 and priced it to sell for $15. What was his markup on the tie?

10. Answer the following:

   a) The Gap is planning a new line of leather jean jackets for fall. It plans to retail the jackets for $100. It is having the jackets produced in the Dominican Republic. Although The Gap does not own the factory, its product development and design costs are $400 000. The total cost of the jacket, including transportation to the stores, is $45. For this line to be successful, The Gap needs to make $900 000 profit. What is its break-even point in units and dollars?

   b) The buyer has just found out that Club Monaco, one of The Gap's major competitors, is bringing out a similar jacket that will retail for $90. If The Gap wishes to match Club Monaco's price, how many units will it have to sell?

11. The manager of a sporting goods department planned to purchase $8400 worth of merchandise at cost. This merchandise was to retail at $14 000. At Supplier A he purchased $4340 at cost, with a retail value of $7000. At Supplier B he purchased $3720 at cost, with a retail value of $6300. What markup percentage must the buyer take on purchases from a third supplier, C, to meet the overall markup objective?

CHAPTER THIRTEEN

Human resource management and staff training issues

LEARNING OBJECTIVES

Lo1 Review how retailers build a sustainable competitive advantage by developing and managing their human resources.

Lo2 Explore how organizational structure identifies the activities and tasks that need to be performed by employees and how these tasks determine the lines of authority and responsibilities in a retail firm.

Lo3 Review various ways in which store managers compensate, motivate, train, evaluate, recruit, and select their employees.

Lo4 Discuss the trends in human resource management that are impacting retailers today.

Lo5 Understand the importance of shrinkage and the relationship between employee theft and customer and store visitor theft.

SPOTLIGHT ON RETAILING

ATB DEVELOPING A POSITIVE EMPLOYEE EXPERIENCE

In an industry that has an annual turnover rate of approximately 17.5 percent, and a churn cost per employee averaging anywhere between $45 000 and $55 000, banks are looking at various ways to enhance the "work environment" in the hopes of reducing turnover.

Look no further than to ATB to develop a strategy for churn.

ATB has been acknowledged as a leader in employee satisfaction. This is reinforced by numerous employer awards, which include:

- 2013 Canada's Best 50 Employers
- 2013 Alberta's Top 10 Employers
- 2014 Canada's Best 50 Employers
- 2014 Alberta's Top 65 Employers
- 2015 Canada's Best 50 Employers
- 2015 Alberta's Top 70 Employers

- 2015 One of the 50 Most Engaged Workplaces in North America
- 2015 Best Workplaces for Millennials
- 2016 Alberta's Top 70 Employers

Why is ATB recognized so highly? Below are some of the reasons:

- Health benefits have a buy and sell option for vacations. People who work for ATB can switch up to one week of vacation for other benefit credits, or they can use benefit credits to purchase an additional week of vacation time.

- ATB has a grant program which allows employees to give back to the communities they work in. This past year employees have volunteered more

Toker + Associates Architecture Industrial Design Ltd.

than 11 000 hours (during company time) in their local communities.

- The company rewards healthy behaviour through programs such as *People First Initiative,* which is an online platform that records wellness activities and goals.

- ATB encourages employees to balance work and their personal lives through flexible work hours, telecommuting, and shortened and compressed work week options.

- Employees working at ATB Financial's head office can take advantage of a variety of onsite amenities, including a cafeteria (with healthy menus), an employee lounge (which features video games, foosball and table tennis), subsidized access to an onsite fitness facility, and deliveries of fresh fruit twice a week.

Not convinced? Here are the types of things that employees of ATB are saying:

Culture of the organization is great, lots of fun activities, and you can work remotely. Your boss trusts you to be able to do you work outside the office. Good work is rewarded in a timely way and often.

Exceptional at ensuring a work-life balance.

They have flex hours and there are opportunities to work from home.

To have this type of culture and "good feelings" starts at the top. Dave Mowat, president and CEO of ATB, instills this in the culture of ATB. David has been in his position with ATB for the past eight years and in 2014 won the prestigious Alberta Venture award "Alberta's Business Person of the Year." With an employee approval rating of 98 percent on glassdoor.com, the Alberta Venture award seems appropriate.

David Mowat provides a leadership style that is evident in great leaders and has fostered a culture at ATB to reflect that style.

Sources: http://www.canadianbusiness.com/lists-and-rankings/best-jobs/2015-best-employers-top-50/; http://www.compensationforce.com/2015/03/2014-turnover-rates-by-industry.html; https://www.pwc.com/ca/en/people-change/publications/pwc-workforce-performance-canadian-banking-2012-02-en.pdf; http://www.atb.com/about/Pages/our-history.aspx; http://www.atb.com/about/Pages/default.aspx; http://www.huffingtonpost.ca/2013/11/16/albertas-top-employers-best-companies_n_4270040.html; http://www.canadastop100.com/alberta/alberta2014.pdf; http://content.eluta.ca/top-employer-atb; http://albertaventure.com/2014/12/albertas-business-person-year-atb-financials-dave-mowat/; https://www.glassdoor.ca/Reviews/ATB-Financial-Reviews-E331202.htm; http://www.macleans.ca/economy/business/canadas-best-employers/; http://www.atb.com/SiteCollectionDocuments/Community/CSR-Report-2015.pdf.

This chapter focuses on the organization and management of employees—the retailer's human resources. Howard Schultz, chairman and chief global strategist of Starbucks, emphasizes that "the relationship that we have with our people and the culture of our company is our most sustainable competitive advantage."[1]

Store managers, due to their daily contact with customers, have the best knowledge of customer needs and competitive activity. From this unique vantage point, store managers play an important role in formulating and executing retail strategies. Buyers can develop exciting merchandise assortments and procure them at low cost, but the retailer only realizes the benefits of the buyers' efforts when the merchandise is sold. Good merchandise doesn't sell itself. Store managers must make sure that the merchandise is presented effectively and offer services that stimulate and facilitate customer buying decisions.

Retailers achieve their financial objectives by effectively managing their five critical assets:

- employees
- locations
- merchandise inventory
- stores
- customers

Human resource management is particularly important in retailing because employees play a major role in performing critical business functions. Retailing and other service businesses remain labour-intensive. Retailers rely on people to perform the basic retailing activities such as buying, displaying merchandise, and providing service to customers.

The activities undertaken to implement the retailer's human resource strategy, including recruiting, selecting, training, supervising, evaluating, and compensating sales associates, are typically undertaken by store management.

Store Management Responsibilities

Store managers are responsible for increasing the productivity of three of the retailer's principal assets: the firm's investments in its employees, its inventory, and its real estate. Most of this chapter is devoted to increasing labour productivity—namely, the sales generated by each store employee—by effectively managing them through recruiting and selecting good employees, training them to be more effective, and motivating them to perform at high levels (see Retailing View 13.1).

In addition to increasing labour productivity, store managers affect their stores' profits by controlling costs. The major costs are compensation and benefits for employees. Store managers are responsible for controlling these costs by efficiently scheduling labour. But store managers are also responsible for costs associated with operating and maintaining their buildings. Retailers are engaging in innovative cost-cutting initiatives that are also friendly to the environment. Another important retail cost-controlling activity is reducing inventory shrinkage resulting from shoplifting and employee theft.

Exhibit 13–1 outlines the steps in the employee management process that affect store employees' productivity: (1) recruiting and selecting effective people, (2) improving their skills through socialization and training, (3) motivating them to perform at higher levels, (4) evaluating them, and finally, (5) compensating and rewarding them.[2] Store managers also need to develop employees who can

Exhibit 13–1
Steps in the Process of Managing Store Employees

1. Recruit and select employees
2. Socialize and train new employees
3. Motivate and manage employees to achieve store performance goals
4. Evaluate employee performance and provide feedback
5. Compensate and reward employees

Recruiting Top Talent for Your Small Business

The recession and evolving demographics have forever changed the way that retailers recruit talent. Slowed profitability in North America and increased competition in both urban and suburban markets have resulted in the development of increasingly complex recruitment and retention initiatives by some retailers. But the impact of these influences has been felt by retailers of all sizes, presenting challenges with respect to recruitment of talented, service-oriented employees. In years past, prospective employees joined the retail industry to gain disposable income or experience. Now, candidates are looking not only for a job in the industry, but also a career.

These trends have posed a challenge to small retailers that, despite their lack of resources, must compete directly with larger retail chains (to say nothing of other sectors) for the best and brightest talent. To meet this challenge, independent retailers across the country are using innovative HR approaches and best practices to successfully recruit top-end talent and chart a course for continued success.

From Customer to Associate. Heather Wolsey, owner of Seasons Gift Shop in St. Albert, Alberta, has never in her 12 years in business had any trouble finding employees, despite the fierce competition for labour taking place in Canada. The recipe for her success is a relatively simple one: Hire from amongst regular customers, stir in a great working atmosphere, add a dash of "targeted recruitment" (a pleasant term for poaching), and allow them to settle into a thriving business.

"I always hire my customers," Wolsey explains. "You already know their personality, they're familiar with your business, and you know they are passionate about the store and what it carries. A salesperson has to love what they sell, after all. That's the benefit of a small store in a small city: You build a relationship with customers."

She also instinctively knows that in order to attract the best talent in Canada today, retailers must enhance their value proposition by increasing their reputation as "the place to work" in the communities in which they operate. To that end, Wolsey ensures that the store is an extremely positive workplace. "Customers pick up on that," she asserts, "which makes Seasons Gift Shop a much-sought-after place to be employed.

"I want all my staff to have well-rounded lives, so I'm very flexible in accommodating my staff with scheduling requests. And I provide a number of perks, such as a bonus at Christmas, membership to a gym in the same strip mall, and, best of all, trips to trade shows in Vegas and other spots," she says, explaining her success in attracting and retaining salespeople.

Source: Andrew Hind, "Recruiting Top Talent for Your Small Business," *Canadian Retailer*, Spring 2013, Volume 23, Issue 2, pp. 32–33. Canadian Retailer, a publication of Retail Council of Canada.

assume more responsibility and be promoted to higher-level management positions. By developing subordinates, managers help both their firms and themselves. The firm benefits from having more effective managers, and the manager benefits because the firm has a qualified replacement when the manager is promoted (see Exhibit 13–2).

It is important to clarify the term *management* as opposed to leadership or coaching. **Management** refers to the strategic approach of an organization to achieve its objectives by developing policies and plans and allocating resources. Human resource management then links the people with the strategic goals of the company. The term **leadership** refers to the ability of an individual to influence, motivate, and enable others to contribute toward the effectiveness and success of the organization. A good leader will act as a guide and lead by positive example. **Coaching** is the activity of supporting people so that they can achieve their goals, with goal setting, training, advising, encouraging, and rewarding their successes. Both John Stanton from Running Room and Chip Wilson (founder of Lululemon) use leadership and coaching activities in their very successful retail strategies. They both actively lead and coach staff and customers to achieve their fitness, professional, and personal goals, as well as meet the strategic goals of the company.

management A strategic approach of an organization to achieve its objectives by developing policies and plans for allocating resources.

leadership The process by which a person attempts to influence another to accomplish some goal or goals.

coaching The activity of supporting people to achieve their goals by goal setting, training, advising, encouraging, and rewarding their successes.

Exhibit 13–2
Responsibilities of Store Managers

MANAGING STORE EMPLOYEES
Recruiting and selecting
Socializing and training
Motivating
Evaluating and providing constructive feedback
Rewarding and compensating

CONTROLLING COSTS
Increasing labour productivity
Reducing maintenance and energy costs
Reducing inventory losses

MANAGING MERCHANDISE
Displaying merchandise and maintaining visual standards
Working with buyers
    Suggesting new merchandise
    Buying merchandise
    Planning and managing special events
    Marking down merchandise

PROVIDING CUSTOMER SERVICE

average sale per transaction (AST) A measure that evaluates productivity by looking at the number of transactions processed per store or department and the average dollar sale per transaction.

sales per employee hour A common measure of productivity that retailers use by dividing net sales by the total number of hours worked by the employee or employees during the specified time frame.

Lo1 Gaining Competitive Advantage through Human Resource Management

Human resource management can be the basis of a sustainable competitive advantage for three reasons:

- Labour costs account for a significant percentage of a retailer's total expenses. Thus, the effective management of employees can produce a cost advantage.

- The experience that most customers have with a retailer is determined by the activities of employees who select merchandise, provide information and assistance, and stock displays and shelves.

- These potential advantages, such as exceptional service, are difficult for competitors to duplicate.

Objectives of Human Resource Management

The strategic objective of human resource management is to align the capabilities and behaviours of employees with the short-term and long-term goals of the retail firm.[3] The productivity of human resource management can be measured in a number of ways, including average sale per transaction, sales per employee hour, sales per full-time equivalent, selling cost percent, and employee turnover.

Average sale per transaction (AST) is a measure that evaluates productivity by looking at the number of transactions processed per store or department and the average dollar sale per transaction.[4] A sale transaction can include several items rung up at the till at one time or one item. Since dollar amount of sales does not tell the whole story, this measure relates total gross sales to the number of transactions processed. When this dollar amount increases, the store is doing a better job of selling merchandise to the customer. In order to calculate average sale per transaction, divide the gross sales by the number of transactions.[5]

For example, if on Saturday gross sales of the shoe department were \$36 800 and there were 225 transactions, the average sale per transaction would be:

$$\text{Average sale per transaction} = \text{Gross sales} \div \text{Number of transactions}$$
$$= \$36\ 800 \div 225$$
$$= \$163.56$$

A performance measure that is often used for performance review is the sales per employee hour or average sales per labour hour measure. This performance measure looks at the sales for a period to the number of hours employee(s) have worked during that period and can be calculated per shift, week, month, quarter, or year for a single employee or for more. **Sales per employee hour** is calculated by dividing net sales by the total number of hours worked by the employee or employees during the specified time frame.[6]

For example, if Sally worked 30 hours during the past week and her net sales for the week were $3480, her sales per employee hour for the week would be:

$$\text{Sales per employee hour} = \text{Net sales} \div \text{Number of employee work hours}$$
$$= \$3480 \div 30$$
$$= \$116.00$$

During the same week, the net sales in the shoe department where Sally worked equalled $152 461. During that week, employees worked 1275 hours. The sales per employee hour for the week for the department would be:

$$\text{Sales per employee hour} = \text{Net sales} \div \text{Number of employee work hours}$$
$$= \$152\ 461 \div 1275$$
$$= \$119.67$$

In this example, Sally is underperforming relative to the rest of the department in terms of her sales per employee hour productivity number as she sold $3.58 less than the total employee average per hour for every hour that she worked that week.

Another common measure of productivity that retailers use is **sales per full-time employee**. As retailers employ a large number of part-time workers, a method is needed to make sense of the many ways in which salary costs can accumulate. One method is to convert hours worked into a **full-time equivalent**, or FTE. A full-time employee as defined by Statistics Canada is a worker who is employed on a year-round basis and who works 35 to 40 hours per week. (The industry standard for a full-time work week is 40 hours per week or 2080 hours per year.) Having a standard way to measure is very important when making internal comparisons between departments or externally to other companies. Employment figures from Statistics Canada are expressed as FTEs, making this method especially useful when benchmarking. Sales per full-time employee equivalent is therefore the relationship between net sales for a specified period of time and the number of full-time equivalent employees who worked during that specified period of time.[7]

For example, a coffee shop in the mall had weekly sales of $43 296. Six part-time employees worked a total of 320 hours and two full-time employees worked 37.5 hours each. Calculate the sales per full-time equivalent.

Sales per full time equivalent
$$= \text{Net sales} \div \text{Number of full-time equivalents}$$
$$= \$43\ 296 \div 10.53$$
$$= \$4111.68$$

To determine the number of full-time equivalents (10.53), divide the number of part-time hours worked (320) by the number of hours that the retailer considers a full-time workweek (37.5), and then add the number of full-time employees (2).

Selling cost is the relationship between sales productivity and wages and can be calculated for an individual salesperson, a department, and the entire store.[8] This productivity measure is useful when scheduling salespersons on the selling floor to ensure profitability.

For example, if a department manager wanted to calculate the selling cost percentage for a salesperson who made $10 per hour and worked 20 hours last week when net sales were $4320, he would calculate:

Selling cost %
$$= \text{Gross wages} \div \text{Net sales}$$
$$= \$200 \div \$4320$$
$$= 4.63\%$$

While **employee productivity** is directly related to the retailer's short-term profits, employee attitudes such as job satisfaction and commitment have important effects on customer satisfaction and subsequent long-term performance of the retailer. In addition to

sales per full-time employee A method used by retailers to calculate the many ways in which salary costs can accumulate.

full-time equivalent (FTE) The relationship between net sales for a specified period of time and the number of full-time equivalent employees who worked during that specified period of time.

selling cost The relationship between sales productivity and wages; can be calculated for an individual salesperson, a department, and the entire store.

employee productivity Output generated by employee activities. One measure of employee productivity is the retailer's sales or profit divided by its employee costs.

DID YOU KNOW?

Retail labour costs (compared to store sales) are approximately 15 percent in the apparel sector, 13 percent in the grocery sector, and 14 percent in the specialty sector.[9]

DID YOU KNOW?

A CAP study found it costs, on average, US$3328 to find, hire, and train a replacement for a $10/hour retail employee.[10]

employee turnover The number of employees occupying a set of positions during a period (usually a year) divided by the number of positions.

employee survey measures of these attitudes, a behavioural measure of these attitudes is employee turnover. **Employee turnover** is a ratio comparison of the number of employees a company must replace in a given time period to the average number of total employees. When a retailer must replace a worker, the retailer incurs direct and indirect expenses such as the cost of advertising to find a replacement, human resources costs, lost productivity, and new hire training. Many factors play a role in employee turnover rate and can stem both from employees and from the employer. Retailers use such factors as wages, benefits, family days, sick days, and job performance reviews to reduce their employee turnover.

A failure to consider both long- and short-term objectives can result in mismanagement of human resources and a downward performance spiral, as shown in Exhibit 13–3. Often, when retailers' sales and profits decline due to increased competition, they respond by decreasing labour costs. They reduce the number of sales associates in stores, hire more part-timers, and spend less on training. Although these actions may increase short-term productivity and profits, they have an adverse effect on long-term performance because employee morale and customer service decrease.[13]

Managing both employee and customer expectations is not an easy task, but is necessary for success. Researchers have been able to demonstrate that happy, satisfied employees, working in the best interests of the company, have a positive influence on a retailer's overall performance.

DID YOU KNOW?

In ATB Financial's 2015 Corporate Social Responsibility Report, 89 percent of team members said they wouldn't hesitate to recommend ATB to a friend seeking employment. Additionally, 91 percent said they were proud to be a part of ATB.[11]

DID YOU KNOW?

A survey by Citigroup and *Seventeen* magazine found that nearly four out of five US students—including those in high school, community college, online college, or traditional college or university—work while in school. The average working student puts in 19 hours a week during the school year.[12]

13.1 CONCEPT CHECK

Complete the Concept Check to help develop skill in learning the principles presented.

1. If sales for the week are $26 386 and sales associates work 240 hours, figure the sales per employee hour.

2. Last week, specialty retailer Boathouse had total gross sales of $128 320 with 720 transactions in its Cambridge, Ontario, store. What was the average sale per transaction (AST) for that Boathouse store location?

3. Figure the FTE on the basis of the following information: Coffee Time has 4 full-time employees who work 40 hours per week, and 16 part-time employees who work an average of 20 hours each per week; total weekly sales for Coffee Time are $47 324.

4. If a Canadian Tire store had weekly net sales of $56 986 in its sporting goods department and paid $4258 in gross wages, what would be the selling cost percentage for the sporting goods department?

5. If the lingerie department at Sears has gross wages of $16 238 for the month of July and a selling cost percentage of 8.7 percent, what are the net sales for the department for the month of July?

The Human Resource Triad

Retailers such as Canadian Tire believe that human resources are too important to be left solely to the HR department.[14] The full potential of a retailer's human resources is realized when three elements of the human resource triad work together—HR professionals, store managers, and employees.

HR professionals, typically working out of the corporate office, have specialized knowledge of HR practices and labour laws. They are responsible for establishing HR policies that reinforce the retailer's strategy and provide the tools and training used by line managers and employees to implement the policies. The line managers, who primarily work in the stores, are responsible for

Exhibit 13–3
Downward Performance Spiral

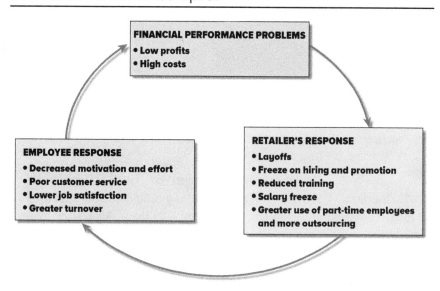

bringing the policies to life through their daily management of employees working for them (see Retailing View 13.2). The employees also share in the management of human resources. They can play an active role in providing feedback on the policies, managing their own careers, defining their job function, and evaluating the performance of their managers and co-workers.

Special HR Conditions Facing Retailers

Human resource management in retailing is very challenging due to the following conditions:

- the need to use part-time employees
- an emphasis on expense control
- the changing demographics of the workforce

Retailers operating in international markets face additional challenges because of differences in work values, economic systems, and labour laws.

Part-Time Employees Most retailers are open long hours and weekends to respond to the needs of family shoppers and working people. In addition, peak shopping periods occur during lunch hours, at night, on weekends, and during sales promotions. To deal with these peak periods and long hours, retailers have to complement their one or two shifts of full-time (35 to 40 hours per week) store employees with part-time workers. Retailers use computerized scheduling systems that are designed to boost service and trim costs by matching staff size to customer traffic, hour by hour. These systems can factor the effects of store promotions, sporting events, graduations, and even the weather to determine the right staffing for different hours and days. To minimize costs, the systems suggest that retailers complement their full-time store employees with part-time employees. Further, they are usually offered no health or retirement benefits and little job security.

Expense Control Retailers often operate on thin margins and must control expenses. Thus, they are cautious about paying high wages to hourly employees who perform low-skill jobs. To control costs, retailers often hire people with little or no experience to work as sales associates, bank tellers, and waiters. High turnover, absenteeism, and poor performance often result from the use of inexperienced, low-wage employees.

Overtime banked hours in Canada are 1.5 hours for each hour worked. This has become an issue in the contractor field where the government is auditing various companies and determining that too many employees are putting only one hour in the bank for each hour of overtime worked. This has led to large payouts by employers when this practice has been going on for many years. This practice can become a financial liability for businesses.

The lack of experience and motivation among many retail employees is particularly troublesome because these employees are often in direct contact with customers. Unlike manufacturing workers on an assembly line, the lowest-paid retail employees work in areas that are highly visible to customers. Poor appearance, manners, and attitudes can have a negative effect on sales and customer loyalty.

Employee Demographics As the retail consumer landscape continues to evolve and change, diverse communities are becoming a more important part of the total buying power. Research has indicated that having an employee population that reflects the consumer population can forge lasting connections, improve service outcomes,

Did You Know That You Can Reduce Staff Turnover and Increase Performance by Hiring the Right People?

It all begins, and sometimes ends, with your staff—a friendly greeting, knowledgeable advice, efficient service, and an appreciative smile. Your success in achieving better staff performance begins with your ability to hire properly. So how do you hire properly? Let's look at some quick tips that will help you select the right staff.

Reduce Your Staff Turnover First! The first step in a strategic approach to recruiting is to slow down your turnover rates. Here's how you do it:

- Start figuring out why employees are leaving. Conduct exit interviews. You can't fix the problem if you don't know what it is.
- Spend more time coaching and talking with each member of your team. In the process, you will improve your relationship, meaning they will stay with you longer.
- Make them successful. People typically don't quit when they're winning. Give them the training they need to succeed.
- Do a comprehensive job of on-boarding new employees. Give them everything they need to feel comfortable and to be successful in the first month of employment.

Get Out of Your Store and Find Your Next Employees. If you wait for candidates to show up on your doorstep, you will wait a long time. Go visit the other stores in your shopping area and get the word out that you're looking for great staff. Networking will get you great results when you invest time in doing it.

Look for Candidates Like Your Top Performers. Figure out what similarities exist between your best performers, including education, previous job experience, and even personality types. Then, look to hire candidates that match that profile. It doesn't guarantee they will be successful, but it certainly improves your odds.

Conduct a Minimum of Two Interviews. You can't accurately predict a candidate's success after spending just 20 minutes with them. Also, what message are you sending to the candidate if they get the job after a 15- to 20-minute interview? How important do you think they will believe the job is? Make them earn it.

Standardize Your Interviews. All candidates must go through the same process and be asked the same questions. You can't compare candidates accurately unless you ask them the same questions. Figure out what the best questions to ask are and stick to them. No shortcuts!

Use Assessments. Eliminate as much subjectivity as possible in the interview by having the candidate complete objective assessments that could include sales and service aptitude assessments, personality profiles, integrity assessments, and leadership profiles.

Check References. Take the time to call previous employers to gather as much supporting evidence as possible about the candidate you're about to hire. Would they hire them again? What responsibilities did they have? Were they successful in meeting those responsibilities? The best indicator of future performance is past performance.

Source: Retail Council of Canada and Graff Retail Group, "Did You Know That You Can Reduce Staff Turnover and Increase Performance by Hiring the Right People?" *Canadian Retailer*, Spring 2013, p. 48. Canadian Retailer, a publication of Retail Council of Canada.

and potentially enhance financial performance. Recent research by Deloitte Touche Tohmatsu Limited[15] indicates that retailers have a huge opportunity to leverage a diverse workforce for the following reasons:

- Diverse employees provide access to better consumer insights as they understand the cultural nuances firsthand.

- A workforce that reflects key characteristics of shoppers motivates improved loyalty as those consumers feel more comfortable doing business with people who understand them and mirror their "community."

- The employee base is further strengthened by development of a pipeline of the best recruits.

Exhibit 13-4
Tasks Performed in a Retail Firm

STRATEGIC MANAGEMENT

- Develop a retail strategy
- Identify the target market
- Determine the retail format
- Design organizational structure
- Select locations
- Scan the retail enivronment
- Strategize brand development and repositioning
- Plan for succession (a major priority for senior management)

MERCHANDISE MANAGEMENT

- Buy merchandise
  - Locate vendors
  - Evaluate vendors
  - Negotiate with vendors
  - Place orders
- Control merchandise inventory
  - Develop merchandise budget plans
  - Allocate merchandise to stores
  - Review open-to-buy and stock position
- Price merchandise
  - Set initial prices
  - Adjust prices

STORE MANAGEMENT

- Recruit, hire, train store personnel
- Plan work schedules
- Evaluate performance of store personnel
- Maintain store facilities
- Locate and display merchandise
- Sell merchandise to customers
- Repair and alter merchandise
- Provide services such as gift wrapping and delivery
- Handle customer complaints
- Take physical inventory
- Prevent inventory shrinkage

ADMINISTRATIVE MANAGEMENT (OPERATIONS)

- Promote the firm, its merchandise, and services
  - Plan communication programs
  - Develop communication budget
  - Select media
  - Plan special promotions
  - Design special displays
  - Manage public relations
- Manage human resources
  - Develop policies for managing store personnel
  - Recruit, hire, train managers
  - Plan career paths
  - Keep employee records
- Distribute merchandise
  - Locate warehouses
  - Receive merchandise
  - Mark and label merchandise
  - Store merchandise
  - Ship merchandise to stores
  - Return merchandise to vendors
- Establish financial control
  - Provide timely information on financial performance
  - Forecast sales, cash flow, profits
  - Raise capital from investors
  - Bill customers
  - Provide credit

Lo2 Designing the Organization Structure for a Retail Firm

The **organization structure** identifies the activities to be performed by specific employees and determines the lines of authority and responsibility in the firm. The first step in developing an organization structure is to determine the tasks that must be performed. Exhibit 13–4 shows tasks typically performed in a retail firm. These tasks are divided into four major categories:

- strategic management
- administrative management (operations)
- merchandise management
- store management

To illustrate the connection between the tasks performed and the organization structure, the tasks are colour-coded. Orange is used to represent the strategic tasks, gold for the merchandise management tasks, green for the store management tasks, and blue for the administrative management tasks.

The strategic market and finance decisions are undertaken primarily by senior management: the CEO, COO, vice-presidents, and the board of directors representing shareholders in publicly-held firms. Administrative tasks are performed by corporate staff employees who have specialized skills in human resource management, finance, accounting, real estate, distribution, and management information systems (MIS). People in these administrative functions develop plans, procedures, and information to assist operating managers in implementing the retailer's strategy.

In retail firms, the primary operating or line managers are involved in merchandise management and store management. These operating managers implement the strategic plans with the assistance of administrative personnel. They make the day-to-day decisions that directly affect the retailer's performance.

Organization Design Considerations

Once the tasks have been identified, the retailer groups them into jobs to be assigned to specific individuals and determines the reporting relationships.[17]

organization structure
A plan that identifies the activities to be performed by specific employees and determines the lines of authority and responsibility in the firm.

DID YOU KNOW?

Retail provides one out of every eight Canadian jobs.[16]

Specialization Rather than performing all the tasks shown in Exhibit 13–4, individual employees are typically responsible for only one or two tasks. **Specialization**, or focusing employees on a limited set of activities, enables employees to develop expertise and increase productivity. For example, a real estate manager can concentrate on becoming expert at selecting retail sites, while a benefit manager can focus on becoming expert in developing creative and cost-effective employee benefits. Through specialization, employees work only on tasks for which they were trained and have unique skills.

But employees may become bored if they are assigned a narrow set of tasks, such as putting price tags on merchandise all day long, every day. Also, extreme specialization may increase labour costs. For example, salespeople often don't have many customers when the store first opens, mid-afternoon, or at closing. Rather than hiring a specialist for stocking shelves and arranging merchandise, many retailers have salespeople perform these tasks during slow selling periods.

Responsibility and Authority Productivity increases when employees have the proper amount of authority to effectively undertake the responsibilities assigned to them. For example, buyers who are responsible for the profitability of a merchandise category need to have the authority to make decisions that will enable them to fulfill this responsibility. They should have the authority to select and price merchandise for their category and determine how the merchandise is displayed and promoted.

Sometimes the benefits of matching responsibility and authority conflict with benefits of specialization. For example, buyers rarely have authority over how their merchandise is sold in the stores or through the Internet. Other employees, such as store managers who specialize in management of salespeople or designers who specialize in constructing websites, have this authority.

Reporting Relationships After assigning tasks to employees, the final step in designing the organization structure is determining the reporting relationships. Productivity can decrease when too many or too few employees report to a supervisor. The effectiveness of supervisors decreases when they have too many employees reporting to them. On the other hand, if managers are supervising very few employees, the number of managers increases and costs go up. The appropriate number of subordinates ranges from four to 12, depending on the nature of their tasks, skills, and location.

Matching Organization Structure to Retail Strategy The design of the organization structure needs to match the firm's retail strategy. For example, category specialists and warehouse clubs such as Best Buy and Costco target price-sensitive customers and thus are very concerned about building a competitive advantage based on low cost. They minimize the number of employees by having decisions made by a few people at corporate headquarters. These centralized organization structures are very effective when there are limited regional or local differences in customer needs.

On the other hand, high-fashion clothing customers often aren't very price-sensitive, but can be extremely demanding, and consumer preferences vary across the country. Retailers targeting these segments tend to have more managers and decision making at the local store level. By having more decisions made at the local store level, human resource costs are higher, but sales also increase since merchandise and services are tailored to meet the needs of local markets.

Retail Organization Structures and Design Issues

Retail organization structures differ according to the type of retailer and the size of the firm. For example, a retailer with a single store will have an organization structure quite different from a national chain. See the expanded discussion in Appendix 13A (available on Connect) on the organization of a single-store retailer and a regional department store.

Two important issues in the design of a retail organization are:

- the degree to which decision making is centralized or decentralized
- approaches used to coordinate merchandise and store management

In the context of a department store chain, the first issue translates into whether the decisions concerning activities such as merchandise management, information and distributions systems, and human resource management are made by the regional department stores or the corporate headquarters. The second issue arises because retailers divide the merchandise and store management activities into different organizations within the firm. Thus, they need to develop ways for coordinating these interdependent activities.

Centralization versus Decentralization

Centralization occurs when authority for retailing decisions is delegated to corporate managers rather than to geographically dispersed regional, district, and store managers; **decentralization** occurs when authority for retail decisions is assigned to lower levels in the organization.

Retailers reduce costs when decision making is centralized in corporate management. For example:

- Overhead falls because fewer managers are required to make the merchandise, human resource, marketing, and financial decisions. Centralized retail organizations can similarly reduce personnel in administrative functions such as marketing and human resources.

- By coordinating buying across geographically dispersed stores, the company achieves lower prices from suppliers. The retailer can negotiate better purchasing terms by placing one large order rather than a number of smaller orders.

- Centralization provides an opportunity to have the best people make decisions for the entire corporation. For example, in a centralized organization, people with the greatest expertise in areas such as MIS, buying, store design, and visual merchandise can have all stores benefit from their skills.

- Centralization increases efficiency. Standard operating policies are used for store and personnel management; these policies limit the decisions made by store managers. For example, corporate merchandisers do considerable research to determine the best method for presenting merchandise. They provide detailed guides for displaying merchandise to each store manager so that all stores look the same throughout the country. Because they offer the same core merchandise in all stores, centralized retailers can achieve economies of scale by advertising through national media rather than more costly local media.[18]

Decentralization also has strengths, including the following:

- Although centralization has advantages in reducing costs, the disadvantage of centralization is that it makes it more difficult for a retailer to adapt to local market conditions.

- In addition to problems with tailoring merchandise to local needs, the centralized retailer also may have difficulty responding to local competition and labour markets. Since pricing is established centrally, individual stores may not be able to respond quickly to competition in their market.

- Centralized personnel policies can make it hard for local managers to pay competitive wages in their area or to hire appropriate types of salespeople.

> **centralization** The degree to which authority for making retail decisions is delegated to corporate managers rather than to geographically dispersed regional, district, and store management.

> **decentralization** When authority for retail decisions is made at lower levels in the organization.

However, centralized retailers are relying more on their information systems to react to local market conditions. By looking at buying patterns across a large number of stores, the centralized buyer might uncover opportunities that local managers would not see.

DID YOU KNOW?

The median number of stores in Canada per district manager is 11.[19]

Large retailers are using their information systems to make more and more merchandise and operations decisions at corporate headquarters. For example, the corporate staff at Holt Renfrew is taking responsibility for operational activities such as distribution, information systems, private-brand merchandise, and human resource management policies. However, each Holt Renfrew store division is still responsible for the management of merchandise.

Coordinating Merchandise and Store Management

Small independent retailers have little difficulty coordinating their stores' buying and selling activities. Owner–managers typically buy the merchandise and work with their salespeople to sell it. Being in close contact with customers, the

extrinsic rewards
Rewards (such as money, promotion, and recognition) given to employees by their manager or the firm.

intrinsic rewards Non-monetary, intangible rewards employees get from doing their jobs.

owner–managers know what their customers want.

On the other hand, large retail firms organize the buying and selling functions into separate divisions. Buyers specialize in buying merchandise and have limited contact with the store management responsible for selling it. Although this specialization increases buyers' skills and expertise, it makes it harder for them to understand customers' needs. Below, we discuss four approaches large retailers use to coordinate buying and selling.

Improving Appreciation for Store Environment

Fashion-oriented retailers use several methods to increase buyers' contact with customers and to improve informal communication between buyers and store personnel who sell the merchandise they buy. Management trainees, who eventually become buyers, are required by most retailers to work in the stores before they enter the buying office. During this six- to ten-month training period, prospective buyers gain appreciation for the activities performed in the stores, the problems salespeople and department managers encounter, and the needs of customers.

Making Store Visits
Another approach to increasing customer contact and communication is to have buyers visit the stores and work with the departments they buy for. At Walmart, all managers (not just the buyers) are required to visit stores frequently and practise the company philosophy of CBWA (coaching by wandering around). This face-to-face communication provides managers with a richer view of store and customer needs than they can get from impersonal sales reports from the company's management information system. Spending time in the stores improves buyers' understanding of customer needs, but this system is costly because it reduces the time the buyer has to review sales patterns, plan promotions, manage inventory, and locate new sources of merchandise.

Assigning Employees to Coordinating Roles
Some retailers have people in the merchandise division (the planners who work with buyers) and the stores (the managers of sales and merchandise who work for the store managers) who are responsible for coordinating buying and selling activities. Many national retail chains have regional and even district staff personnel to coordinate buying and selling activities.

Involving Store Management in Buying Decisions
Another way to improve coordination between buying and selling activities is to increase store employees' involvement in the buying process. This process would be more typical of smaller retail chains in which a decentralized buying process would assist the retailer in offering the newest trend for a specific target market. In some cases, the involvement of staff will not only provide a retail opportunity but also has the potential to build staff loyalty.

Besides developing an organization structure, human resource management undertakes a number of activities to improve employee performance, build commitment in employees, and reduce turnover. In the following two sections of this chapter, we examine these human resource management activities.

Lo3 Compensating and Motivating Retail Employees

A critical task of human resource management is to motivate employees to work toward achieving the firm's goals and implementing its strategy. The task is often difficult because employees' goals may differ from those of the firm. For example, a sales associate might find it more personally rewarding to creatively arrange a display than to help a customer. Retailers generally use three methods to motivate their employees' activities: policies and supervision, incentives, and organizational culture.

Store employees receive two types of rewards from their work: extrinsic and intrinsic. **Extrinsic rewards** are rewards provided by either the employee's manager or the firm, such as compensation, promotion, and recognition. **Intrinsic rewards** are rewards employees get personally from doing their job well. For example, salespeople often like to sell because they think it's challenging and fun. Of course, they want to be paid, but they also find it rewarding to help customers and make sales.[20]

Policies and Supervision

Perhaps the most fundamental method of coordination is to:

- prepare written policies that indicate what tasks employees are responsible for
- have supervisors/managers enforce these policies

For example, retailers may set policies on when and how merchandise can be returned by customers. If employees use the written policies to make these decisions, their actions will be consistent with the retailer's strategy.

However, strict reliance on written policies can reduce employee motivation. Employees might have little opportunity to use their own initiative to improve performance of their areas of responsibility. As a result, they eventually might find their jobs uninteresting. In addition, relying on rules as a method of coordination leads to a lot of red tape. Situations will arise that aren't covered by a rule. Then employees will need to talk to a supervisor before they can deal with the situation.

Incentives

The second method of motivating and coordinating employees uses incentives to motivate them to perform activities consistent with the retailer's objectives. For example, buyers will be motivated to focus on the firm's profits if they receive a bonus based on the profitability of the merchandise they buy.

Some of the criteria that managers and employees could be measured on include customer satisfaction, average order dollar amount, market share, sales growth, top-of-mind awareness in a market, promotion from within, employee development, ideas and suggestions from staff that are implemented, and revenue per square foot. It should be remembered that there can be a negative impact with a straight commission program with respect to the credibility of a manager or sales associate's worth to the company. For example, the financial industry will now need to disclose how much they are going to be paid by a fund if the customer purchases that fund.

Types of Incentive Compensation
There are two types of incentives:

- A **commission** is compensation based on a fixed formula, such as 2 percent of sales. For example, many retail salespeople's compensation is based on a fixed percentage of the merchandise they sell.
- A **bonus** is additional compensation awarded periodically based on an evaluation of the employee's performance. For example, store managers often receive bonuses at the end of the year based on their store's performance relative to its budgeted sales and profits.

Besides incentives based on individual performance, retail managers often receive additional income based on their firm's performance. These *profit-sharing* arrangements can be offered as a cash bonus based on the firm's profits or as a grant of stock options that link additional income to performance of the firm's stock.

A number of retailers such as Walmart and Home Depot use *stock incentives* to motivate and reward all employees, including sales associates. Employees are encouraged to buy shares in their companies at discounted prices through payroll deduction plans. These stock incentives align employees' interests with those of the company and can be very rewarding when the company does well. However, if growth in the company's stock price declines, employee morale declines too, corporate culture is threatened, and demands for higher wages and more benefits develop.[21]

An **incentive compensation plan** rewards employees on the basis of their productivity. Many retailers now use incentives to motivate greater sales productivity by their employees. With some incentive plans, a salesperson's income is based entirely on commission—called a **straight commission**. For example, a salesperson might be paid a commission based on a percentage of sales made minus the merchandise returned.

Incentive plans may include a fixed salary plus a commission on total sales, or a commission on sales over quota. For example, a salesperson might receive a salary of $200 per week plus a commission of 2 percent on all sales over a quota of $50 per hour.

Incentive compensation plans are a powerful motivator for salespeople to sell merchandise, but they have a number of disadvantages. For example, it's hard to get salespeople who are compensated totally by commission to perform non-selling activities. Also, salespeople will concentrate on the more expensive, fast-moving merchandise and neglect other merchandise. Sales incentives can also discourage salespeople from providing services to customers. Finally, salespeople compensated primarily by incentives don't develop loyalty to their

commission Compensation based on a fixed formula, such as percentage of sales.

bonus Additional compensation awarded periodically, based on a subjective evaluation of the employee's performance.

incentive compensation plan A compensation plan that rewards employees on the basis of their productivity.

straight commission A form of salesperson's compensation in which the amount paid is based on a percentage of sales made minus merchandise returned.

drawing account A method of sales compensation in which salespeople receive a weekly cheque based on their estimated annual income.

quota Target level used to motivate and evaluate performance.

quota–bonus plan Compensation plan that has a performance goal or objective established to evaluate employee performance, such as sales per hour for salespeople and maintained margin and turnover for buyers.

employer. The employer doesn't guarantee them an income, so they feel no obligation to the firm.

Under a straight commission plan, salespeople's incomes can fluctuate from week to week, depending on their sales. Because retail sales are seasonal, salespeople might earn most of their income during the Christmas season but much less during the summer months. To provide a steadier income for salespeople who are paid by high-incentive plans, some retailers offer a **drawing account**. With a drawing account, salespeople receive a weekly cheque based on their estimated annual income, and commissions earned are credited against the weekly payments. If the draw exceeds the earned commissions, the salespeople return the excess money they have been paid, and their weekly draw is reduced. If the commissions earned exceed the draw, salespeople are paid the difference.

Quotas are often used with compensation plans. A **quota** is a target level used to motivate and evaluate performance. Examples include sales per hour for salespeople or maintained margin and inventory turnover for buyers. For department store salespeople, selling quotas vary across departments due to differences in sales productivity levels.

A **quota–bonus plan** provides sales associates with a bonus when their performance exceeds their quota. A quota–bonus plan's effectiveness depends on setting reasonable, fair quotas, which can be difficult. Usually, quotas are set at the same level for everyone in a department, but salespeople in the same department may have different abilities or face different selling environments. Newly hired salespeople might have a harder time achieving a quota than more experienced salespeople. Thus, a quota based on average productivity may be too high to motivate the new salesperson and too low to effectively motivate the experienced salesperson. Quotas should be developed for each salesperson on the basis of his or her experience and the nature of the store area in which the salesperson works.[24]

Group Incentives To encourage employees in a department or store to work together, some retailers provide additional incentives based on the performance of the department or store as a whole. For example, salespeople might be paid a commission based on their individual sales and then receive additional compensation according to the amount of sales over plan, or quota, generated by all salespeople in the store. The group incentive encourages salespeople to work together in their non-selling activities and handling customers so that the department sales target will be achieved.[25]

Setting the Commission Percentage Assume that a specialty store manager wants to hire experienced salespeople. To get the type of person she wants, she feels she must pay $12 per hour. Her selling costs are budgeted at 8 percent of sales. With compensation of $12 per hour, salespeople need to sell $150 worth of merchandise per hour ($12 divided by 8 percent) for the store to keep within its sales cost budget. The manager believes the best compensation would be one-third salary and two-thirds commission, so she decides to offer a compensation plan of $4 per hour salary (33 percent of $12) and a 5.33 percent commission on sales. If salespeople sell $150 worth of merchandise per hour, they will earn $12 per hour ($4 per hour in salary plus $150 multiplied by 5.33 percent, which equals $8 per hour in commission).

$$\text{Commission } \$ = \text{Net sales} \times \text{Commission} \%$$

In addition to competitive salary, vacation, and tuition reimbursement as a retailer's key retention strategies, keeping your best requires attention to each employee as an individual. Retailers will need to be creative to keep their best employees eager to advance to become future company leaders.

Organizational Culture

The final method for motivating and coordinating employees is to develop a strong organizational

DID YOU KNOW?

73 percent of consumers attribute their best customer service experience to store employees. Conversely, 81 percent of consumers attribute their worst customer service experience to employees.[22]

DID YOU KNOW?

The mistake most retailers make is seeing everyone age 50 and over as one type of consumer with their brand habits set in stone.[23]

culture. An **organizational culture** is the set of values, traditions, and customs in a firm that guides employee behaviour. These guidelines aren't written in a set of policies and procedures; they are traditions passed along by experienced employees to new employees.[26]

Many retail firms have strong organizational cultures that give employees a sense of what they ought to do on their jobs and how they should behave to be consistent with the firm's strategy (see Retailing View 13.3). For example, Harry Rosen's strong organizational culture emphasizes customer service, while Walmart's organizational culture focuses on reducing costs so that the firm can provide low prices to its customers.

An organizational culture often has a much stronger effect on employees' actions than rewards offered in compensation plans, directions provided by supervisors, or written company policies.

Harry Rosen emphasizes the strength of organizational culture in the policy manual given to new employees. The manual has one rule: Use your best judgment to do anything you can to provide service to our customers. Lack of written rules doesn't mean that Harry Rosen employees have no guidelines or restrictions on their behaviour. Its organizational culture guides employees' behaviour. New salespeople learn from other employees that they should always wear clothes sold at Harry Rosen, that they should park their cars at the outskirts of the parking lot so that customers can park in more convenient locations, and that they should offer to meet busy executives at their offices with new menswear trend items.

Developing and Maintaining a Culture

Organizational cultures are developed and maintained through stories and symbols.[27] See http://stservicemovie.com for the story of Johnny, the grocery store bagger.

Disney strengthens its organizational culture through the labels it uses for its employees and by steeping employees in the culture during the selection process. Management and employees view themselves as part of a team whose job is to produce a very large show. Applicants are trying out for a role in the cast rather than being hired for a job. For hourly jobs, the casting director (the person in charge of recruiting) interviews applicants to determine if they can adapt to the company's strong organizational culture. Do they understand and accept the fact that Disney has strict grooming requirements (no facial hair for men, little makeup for women)? Is the applicant willing to work on holidays? After the initial screening, the remaining applicants are judged on how well they might fit in with the show. Current employees participate in the entire process—they assess the applicant's behaviours and attitudes while also providing first-hand information on their role in the "production."

organizational culture A firm's set of values, traditions, and customs that guide employee behaviour.

job analysis Identifying essential activities and determining the qualifications employees need to perform them effectively.

Job Analysis

The **job analysis** identifies essential activities and is used to determine the qualifications of potential employees. For example, retail salespeople's responsibilities vary from company to company and from department to department within a store.

Managers can obtain the information needed for a job analysis by observing employees presently doing the job and by determining the characteristics of exceptional performers. Exhibit 13–5 lists some questions that managers should consider in a job analysis for sales associates. Information

Exhibit 13–5
Questions for Undertaking a Job Analysis

- How many salespeople will be working in the department at the same time?
- Do the salespeople have to work together in dealing with customers?
- How many customers will the salesperson have to work with at one time?
- Will the salesperson be selling on an open floor or working behind the counter?
- How much and what type of product knowledge does the salesperson need?
- Does the salesperson need to sell the merchandise or just ring up the orders and provide information?
- Is the salesperson required to make appointments with customers and develop a loyal customer base?
- Does the salesperson have the authority to negotiate price or terms of the sale?
- Does the salesperson need to demonstrate the merchandise?
- Will the salesperson be expected to make add-on sales?
- Is the appearance important? How should an effective salesperson look?
- Will the salesperson be required to perform merchandising activities such as stocking shelves and setting up displays?
- To whom will the salesperson report?
- Under what compensation plan will the salesperson be working?

Corporate Culture

It comes down to clarity. If we're clear about what we're doing and what our business objectives are, and we keep that communication open and we keep people involved, it becomes easier to be that purveyor of corporate culture. Many of our best ideas are coming from the field. Who knows better what the customer wants, what's working and what's not than that person who's dealing every day with a customer?

Tina Shane, vice-president, retail and customer experience, western Canada, Chapters

The strategic plan really helps to develop the corporate culture. It needs to be communicated to all employees, even the part-timers.

Rafik Louli, regional director, central regional office #3, LCBO

The store manager is the lynchpin of a retail operation. How do you make sure the store manager is equipped to be purveyor of the corporate culture at the store level?

As the company, you have to clearly define what that expectation is for your customer service and your corporate culture. Next is training. Most retailers are at a new company every six months due to attrition, so that corporate culture training and expression of ongoing expectations needs to be constant. Most people want to know what the expectations of them are so that when they go home at night they've got a sense of contribution and success.

Ron Hornbaker, interim CEO, Golf Town

It starts with the recruitment process. The Body Shop brand and the brand values are always a part of the hiring process. When you seek out those who already believe in the values that your organization stands for, the transition to become what we call a brand ambassador is really a natural one. Our rule here is to make sure we keep managers at every level engaged and informed in the evolution of the brand so that they always feel like they are a part of that process.

Carmela Aita, director, human resources, The Body Shop

Most of our store managers are brought up through the organization, so the culture and the understanding of how to represent Future Shop is handed down from generation to generation, through our managers, through our district managers, and through all of the things that we do.

Mike Hickey, general manager, Future Shop, Calgary

Source: Excerpt from Robert Price, "Recruiting, Retaining, and Empowering Store Managers," Canadian Retailer, Winter 2012, Volume 22, pp. 36–39. *Canadian Retailer,* a publication of Retail Council of Canada.

collected in the job analysis is then used to prepare a job description.

Job Description

A **job description** includes activities the employee needs to perform and the performance expectations expressed in quantitative terms. The job description is a guideline for recruiting, selecting, training, and eventually evaluating employees.

Locating Prospective Employees

Staffing stores is becoming a critical problem because changing demographics are reducing the size of the labour pool.[28] Here are some suggestions being used by retailers to recruit employees in this tight labour market, in addition to placing ads in local newspapers and posting job openings on websites such as Monster.ca:

- Look beyond the retail industry.
- Use your employees as talent scouts.
- Provide incentives for employee referrals.
- Recruit from minority communities, immigrants, and seniors.
- Use the Internet to locate prospective employees. Today you cannot survive in business without computer skills. Employees comfortable with basic computer applications such as Word, Excel, and PowerPoint are not going to be challenged by point-of-purchase sales systems.
- Recruit from LinkedIn and other social networking sites.

Social Recruiting

It is not sufficient to just post job vacancies on online job boards such as Monster.ca or Workopolis. Job boards such as these should continue to be part of the recruiting mix a retailer uses, but the potential for LinkedIn and other social networking sites to play major roles in retail recruiting strategies is continuing to grow. Millions of potential employees profile themselves on these sites each year. Social recruiting isn't really new anymore. Some interesting stats regarding social recruiting include:

- The vast majority of recruiters (94 percent) use, or plan to use, social media for recruiting.
- Employers who used social media to hire found a 49 percent improvement in candidate quality.
- An Aberdeen study found that 73 percent of 18–34 year olds found their last job through a social network.
- Fully 30 percent of all Google searches, about 300 million per month, are employment related.
- Most recruiters (89 percent) report having hired someone through LinkedIn.
- While 94 percent of *recruiters* use social media for their jobs, only 39 percent of *employers* use social media for recruiting and hiring.
- About half (51 percent) of workers who currently have a job are either actively seeking, or open to a new job.
- The majority (94 percent) of recruiters are active on LinkedIn, but only 36 percent of candidates are. Job seekers, by a wide margin, prefer Facebook, with 83 percent reporting they are active there, compared to just 65 percent of recruiters.[30]

See Retailing View 13.4 for more information about the legal guidelines for recruiting using social media.

Screening Applicants to Interview

The screening process matches applicants' qualifications with the job description. Many retailers use automated prescreening programs as a low-cost method of identifying qualified candidates. Applicants either interact with a web-enabled store kiosk or call a toll-free telephone number, and a computer program asks some basic questions that the applicants answer using the keyboard or telephone buttons.

The questions are tailored to the retailer's specific needs and environment. For example, a mall-based chain selling music-themed merchandise asks, "Would you work in an environment where loud alternative music is played?" The response time for answering the questions is monitored and follow-up questions are asked when the answers are unusually slow. When applicants pass this automated pre-screen, additional information is collected using application forms, reference checks, and tests.[31]

job description A description of the activities the employee needs to perform and the firm's performance expectations.

DID YOU KNOW?

Almost all surveyed employers (93 percent) say they search social media profiles during the interview process. 42 percent of those employers say they have changed their mind about whether or not to hire someone based on what they have found online.[29]

Social Media Recruiting: Understand the Legal Guidelines

By: Melanie Berkowitz, Esq.

There's no question that social media is changing the way business works—and the trend goes well beyond marketing. Savvy companies are looking to social media trends to assist with their recruiting and hiring.

Lest you think social media is too complicated or just a phase, remember, a decade ago, using background screening to help with recruiting was still a novel idea. Before you jump in, make sure you understand the legalities of social media. Using a bit of common sense never hurts either.

Keep your Candidate Research Legal One of the easiest ways to use social media for recruiting to review an applicant's public postings and accounts, providing a better picture of him or her as a potential employee. But be careful. Once you review a candidate's online profile, a court will assume you are aware of that person's "protected characteristics" that are often part of their online postings.

These characteristics include gender and race as well as those that are not always evident in a face-to-face interview such as religion, age, sexual orientation or disability. In such cases employers need to be particularly careful not to expand their interview questions or decision-making beyond legal interview limits.

But what if a candidate's profile suggests that he or she may not be appropriate for the position—or even shows a lack of candor about their background or abilities? Here are a few such scenarios:

- A female candidate has numerous postings on her Facebook account about her "pig" of an ex-husband who constantly skips his time with their children, causing her to miss work at her current job.

- An applicant has applied for a job that requires heavy lifting and a lot of walking but whose online profiles reveals that he uses a cane.

"If you choose to review social media as part of your hiring practices, it's a better practice to wait until after you've met a candidate face to face," says David Baffa, labor and employment partner at national law firm Seyfarth Shaw, LLP. By using social media in this more targeted way, says Baffa, "you are less likely to be accused of making snap selection decisions or of relying on protected characteristics evident from a social network profile." Mr. Baffa also counsels consistency:

- If you decide to use social media in your recruiting process, make sure you conduct the same searches at the same point in the process for every applicant.

- Be sure to print or save screen shots if you see something that causes you to question the candidate's candor, professionalism or judgement.

- If you use an outside company to perform the background check, you must adhere to the requirements of the "Fair Credit Reporting Act."

Use Social Media Info Legally There is plenty of lawful information to be had from social media, though. Does your candidate have a Twitter account that she regularly updates with thoughtful "tweets"? Does his social media presence demonstrate a deeper interest in the type of job he is pursuing?

While social media should not be used to make final employment decisions, it can be used as an extension of the resume, a conversation starter that gives the interviewer a deeper understanding of the candidate. This is particularly true if familiarity with social media in business is needed for

Copyright 2016 – Monster Worldwide, Inc. All Rights Reserved. You may not copy, reproduce or distribute this article without the prior written permission of Monster Worldwide. This article first appeared in the Monster Resource Center. Visit Hiring.Monster.com and click on the Resource Center tab.

job application form A form a job applicant completes that contains information about the applicant's employment history, previous compensation, reasons for leaving previous employment, education and training, personal health, and references.

Application Forms A job application form contains information about the applicant's employment history, previous compensation, reasons for leaving previous employment, education and training, and references. This information enables the manager to determine whether the applicant meets the minimum qualifications and also provides information for interviewing the applicant.[32]

References A good way to verify the information given on an application form is to contact the applicant's references. Contacting references is also helpful for collecting additional information from people who have worked with the

the position at issue. A candidate for a marketing job who knows how to market herself via Facebook should stand out among otherwise equally-qualified job seekers.

Review and Audit Your Own Social Media Presence

When it comes to using social media to research, remember, it goes both ways. Assume that applicants and new hires could be searching you and your company and even trying to figure out the identity of possible interviewers ahead of time.

Of course it would be ideal to have a strong social media presence that creates a strong company brand and supports your small business marketing strategy so that consumers and job seekers have useful information about your company. But not every business has the time or resources to generate a social media marketing plan and online content strategy.

At minimum, make sure that whatever materials you have are accurate and legal. Things to consider:

- Make sure that your company's profile states that the business is an "equal opportunity employer."

- Do not make statements that could be construed as a promise of employment or business opportunity; particularly if the site is "live" and uses employees to add comments or blog postings. For example a job posting that states, "This is a great place to work," is fine. Promising that "All applicants will be hired," is obviously not.

- Know exactly who in your company or whether a third-party vendor is able to add to or change the content on the company's profile; make sure that it is consistent with other marketing and advertising messages.

Treat "Bad" Social Media Information Delicately

Social media law is constantly evolving as in the ground-breaking NLRB Facebook case.

Although such cases will certainly give employers pause, an attorney familiar with employment issues, privacy, and the evolving law of social media can help determine the best course of action.

While it's not always entirely clear what a potential employer can legally do with a candidate who has denounced his or her current boss on a social media site, you can create a social media policy as part of your social media strategy.

What about the more run-of-the-mill negative information that reflects poorly on the job candidate's professional image—such as pictures of a job applicant getting drunk and acting stupid, or comments that reveal ignorance or bigotry? Treat it the same way you would if you had gained the knowledge via the interview or in a resume.

But remember, a candidate may not control every image posted on a social media site, so consider the overall context. If you have lingering questions, consider consulting an attorney who is well-versed in social media before relying on negative information to justify an employment decision.

Give the Job Applicant Fair Notice

It's not necessary to have an applicant sign a waiver that allows you to review his or her social media accounts; it is a best practice to give them a "heads up" that you will be reviewing any and all "publicly posted social media accounts."

Chances are, if a candidate uses social media as an effective job-hunting tool, or has interesting things to say via social media, he or she is likely going to publicize their online presence anyway.

Legal Disclaimer: None of the information provided herein constitutes legal advice on behalf of Monster.

DID YOU KNOW?

A retailer incurs an additional $7000 to $10 000 of expenses in medical costs, absences, turnover, and lost productivity when it hires a drug user.[34]

applicant. In addition, store managers should check with former supervisors not listed as references. Due to potential legal problems, however, many companies have a policy of not commenting on past employees.[33]

Store managers generally expect to hear favourable comments from an applicant's references or even from previous supervisors who may not have thought highly of the applicant. One approach for reducing the positive bias is to ask the reference to rank the applicant relative to others in the same position. For example, the manager might ask, "How would you rate Pat's customer service skill in relation to other retail sales

DID YOU KNOW?

67 percent of retailers check references as part of the selection process; 54 percent do drug screening; and 35 percent use paper-and-pencil honesty tests.[35]

associates you have worked with?" Another approach is to use a positively toned scale ranging from "somewhat effective" to "extremely effective."

The Internet has become an excellent source of information on prospective employees. A quick look at someone's Facebook entry can often reveal more about the person than a face-to-face interview. A Google search can also be useful for finding out information that may not appear on the job application or emerge through contacts with references.

Testing Intelligence, ability, personality, and interest tests can provide insights about potential employees. For example, intelligence tests yield data about the applicant's innate abilities and can be used to match applicants with job openings and to develop training programs. However, tests must be scientifically and legally valid. They can be used only when the scores have been shown to be related to job performance. It is illegal to use tests assessing factors that are not job-related or that discriminate against specific groups.

Some retailers use tests to assess applicants' honesty and ethics. Paper-and-pencil honesty tests include questions to find out if an applicant has ever thought about stealing and if he believes other people steal ("What percentage of people take more than $1 from their employer?").[36] The use of lie detectors in testing employees is prohibited.

Realistic Job Preview Turnover is reduced when the applicants understand both the attractive and unattractive aspects of the job. Many retailers want their new hires to have previous retail experience. They have found that experience, even if the previous job was significantly different than the new opportunity, gives the applicant an appreciation for what a life in retailing is all about. For example, PetSmart, a pet supply category specialist, has each applicant view a ten-minute video that begins with the advantages of being a company employee and then shows scenes of employees dealing with irate customers and cleaning up animal droppings. This type of job preview typically screens out 15 percent of the applicants who would most likely quit within three months if they were hired.[37]

Screening Employers

The majority of analysis on screening seems to always be from the employer's perspective. But what about you, the job seeker—should you be screening your potential employer? "Today's job seekers know their worth and are aware of the competitive landscape. They see opportunities everywhere, and if one employer takes too long to respond or makes it difficult to apply, seekers will quickly pass it up for another job opening."

"Savvy candidates evaluate company brands before applying to or accepting a job, much in the same way they evaluate consumer brands when shopping. They research organizations as much as the employer is researching them, so employers need to use their website as a strong tool for engaging talent. Company websites are a key job hunting source for candidates. These company storefronts serve as a one-stop shop where job hunting begins. It is critical to develop a well-designed career site to deliver a consistent brand image that includes the company values, mission, etc. The company brand experience, in combination with detailed job descriptions and an online application, engages job seekers and helps them determine proactively if they are a cultural fit to the organization, and whether to apply."[38] (see Retailing View 13.5 for more information for employers)

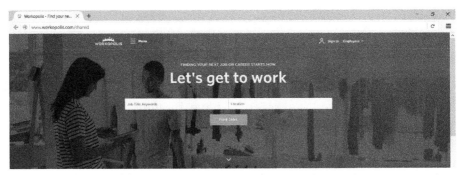

Internet sites such as workopolis.com can be useful recruiting tools and ensure that job applicants are computer-literate.

Used with permission from workopolis.com. Screenshot taken September 9, 2016.

Are You Using Social Media So Candidates Can Find You?

By: Emily Bennington

Raise your hand if you've ever heard of or experienced a good social media cautionary tale. You know, the one where Potential Employer A searches for Candidate B online, only to be confronted with an image of him mooning a crowd during Spring Break or holding an arsenal of weapons? (Both of these are true, by the way.)

There are a million stories and articles out there about how companies are using social media to screen candidates, and as the business owner or hiring manager, you may feel like you have all of the control, right? Not so fast.

Naturally, candidates can *use the same tools to screen you* and, *just like you,* if they don't like what they see, they move on. Any guesses on where they begin their research?

Google That's right. So if you don't have a Google alert set for both your name and your company's name, stop right now and <u>sign up.</u> Google alerts are free. But when it comes to keeping you informed about what others are saying on the web, they are priceless. Even if you have an alert set, though, it's still a best practice to Google yourself and your business every few weeks to see what's ranking high in the results. Since prospects are searching for you on Google, you want to be hyperaware of what they're finding.

Facebook While Facebook can certainly be considered the most social of all social media sites, your business should still be here as well. If you're not convinced Facebook is the place for social media recruiting, consider the most basic rule of marketing, i.e., *go where your customers are.* Certainly when it comes to college students, you will find them on Facebook. The question is: Will they find you?

To get started, simply set up a page for your company and post industry updates, events, photos and so on, and do so a minimum of every 2–3 days. Once you have a pretty lively page going, it's worth testing a few ads on Facebook that specifically target the demographic you're trying to reach. Assuming you have a compelling message and photo, Facebook ads can really drive traffic to your page and make it easier for potential hires to find you.

Twitter For businesses, Twitter represents a huge opportunity to directly engage with your audience. However, many companies are too scared to fully utilize the site for fear that someone may post something negative about their experience.

Meanwhile, users are posting anyway and, if you're not part of the conversation, you miss a key chance to respond. So, if your business is not on Twitter, sign up and jump in. Use the site to communicate with your clients, find out about HR best practices, offer deals to your followers, launch exclusive promotions, be a resource to your industry, or—ideally—all of the above. Your next great hire may be watching so understand that it's okay to be a Twit, just this once. Really.

LinkedIn The first rule of thumb with LinkedIn is to actually *have a presence* on the site. If you don't know where to start, see what your competitors are doing... then top it.

Blogging Blogging is a great way to give your company a voice in the marketplace today. In fact, with the right content and design, it could become the *linchpin of your marketing strategy.* That's because we all want to pull back the curtain on our favorite companies and a blog is the perfect format for this. So develop and embrace a company blog and use it as a way to distinguish yourself from the competition. For examples of how businesses have successfully leveraged their blogs, check out Michael Hyatt as well as Zappos.

As you can see, it's smart to turn the tables and take a hard look at your own web presence once in a while, particularly from the standpoint of a valuable potential hire. But remember: Do not be afraid. NO, you won't have 100% control of the message *and that's okay.* The benefits of putting your company "out there" and having a positive, online message far outweigh the negatives. In other words, Pandora is out of the box and she's not looking back. Neither should you.

Legal Disclaimer: None of the information provided herein constitutes legal advice on behalf of Monster.

Copyright 2016 – Monster Worldwide, Inc. All Rights Reserved. You may not copy, reproduce or distribute this article without the prior written permission of Monster Worldwide. This article first appeared in the Monster Resource Center. Visit Hiring.Monster.com and click on the Resource Center tab.

discrimination An illegal action of a company or its managers that results when a member of a protected class (women, minorities, etc.) is treated differently from non-members of that class (see *disparate treatment*) or when an apparently neutral rule has an unjustified discriminatory effect (see *disparate impact*).

disparate treatment In the case of discrimination, when members of a protected class are treated differently than non-members of that class, such as when a qualified woman (protected class) does not receive a promotion given to a less qualified man.

disparate impact In the case of discrimination, when an apparently neutral rule has an unjustified discriminatory effect, such as when a retailer requires high school graduation for all its employees, thereby excluding a larger proportion of disadvantaged minorities, when at least some of the jobs (e.g., custodian) could be performed just as well by people who did not graduate from high school.

Selecting Applicants

After screening applications, the selection process typically involves a personal interview. Since the interview is usually the critical factor in the hiring decision, the store manager needs to be well prepared and to have complete control over the interview.

Preparation for the Interview

The objective of the interview is to gather relevant information, not simply to ask a lot of questions. The most widely used interview technique, called the *behavioural interview*, asks candidates how they handled actual situations they have encountered in the past, situations requiring skills outlined in the job description. For example, applicants applying for a job requiring them to handle customer complaints would be asked to describe a situation in which they were confronted by someone who was angry with something they had done. Candidates are asked to describe the situation, what they did, and the outcomes of their actions. These situations also can be used to interview references for the applicants.[39]

DID YOU KNOW?

67 percent of job seekers using social media use Facebook, 45 percent use Twitter, while 40 percent use LinkedIn.[40]

An effective approach to interviewing involves some planning by the managers, but also allows some flexibility in selecting questions. Managers should develop objectives for what they want to learn about the candidate. Each topic area covered in the interview starts with a broad question, such as "Tell me about your last job," designed to elicit a lengthy response. The broad opening question is followed by a sequence of more specific questions, such as "What did you learn from that job?" or "How many subordinates did you have?"

Finally, managers must be careful to avoid asking questions that are discriminatory.[41]

Managing the Interview Exhibit 13–6 shows questions the manager might ask. Here are some suggestions for questioning the applicant during the interview:

- Encourage long responses by asking questions such as "What do you know about our company?" rather than "How familiar are you with our company?"
- Avoid asking questions that have multiple parts.
- Avoid asking leading questions such as "Are you prepared to provide good customer service?"
- Be an active listener. Evaluate the information that is being presented and sort out the important comments from the unimportant ones. Some techniques for active listening are repeating or rephrasing information, summarizing the conversation, and tolerating silences.[42]
- Observe the applicant's behaviour in the interview—attitude, appropriate dress, eagerness to learn. Some managers interview candidates while giving them a tour through the store. When the manager sees a display that's out of order, he or she might say, "While we're talking, would you help me straighten this out?" Some candidates will stand back; others will jump right in and help out. (*Hint*: You want to hire candidates from the second group.)

Legal Considerations in Selecting and Hiring Store Employees

Heightened social awareness and government regulations emphasize the need to avoid discrimination in hiring. Discrimination is specifically prohibited in the following human resource decisions: recruitment, hiring, discharge, layoff, discipline, promotion, compensation, and access to training.

Discrimination arises when a member of a protected class (women, minorities, etc.) is treated differently than non-members of that class (**disparate treatment**) or when an apparently neutral rule has an unjustified discriminatory effect (**disparate impact**).

Exhibit 13–6
Interviewing Questions

EDUCATION

What were your most favourite and least favourite subjects in university? Why?

What types of extracurricular activities did you participate in? Why did you select those activities?

If you had the opportunity to attend school all over again, what if anything, would you do differently? Why?

How did you spend the summers during university?

Did you have any part-time jobs? Which of your part-time jobs did you find most interesting? What did you find most difficult about working and attending college or university at the same time? What advice would you give to someone who wanted to work and attend university at the same time?

What accomplishments were you most proud of?

PREVIOUS EXPERIENCE

What's your description of the ideal manager? Subordinate? Co-worker?

What did you like most/least about your last job?

What kind of people do you find it difficult/easyto work with? Why?

What has been your greatest accomplishment during your career to date?

Describe a situation at your last job involving pressure. How did you handle it?

What were some duties on your last job that you found difficult?

Of all the jobs you've had, which did you find the most/least rewarding?

What is the most frustrating situation you've encountered in your career?

Why do you want to leave your present job?

What would you do if ...?

How would you handle ...?

What would you like to avoid in future jobs?

What do you consider your greatest strength/weakness?

What are your responsibilities in your present job?

Tell me about the people you hired on your last job. How did they work out? What about the people you fired?

What risks did you take in your last job and what were the results of those risks?

Where do you see yourself in three years?

What kind of reference will your previous employer give?

What do you do when you have trouble solving a problem?

QUESTIONS THAT ARE DISCRIMINATORY AND CANNOT BE ASKED

Do you have plans for having children/a family? What are your marriage plans? What does your husband/wife do? What happens if your husband/wife gets transferred or needs to relocate? Who will take care of your children while you're at work? (Asked of men) How would you feel about working for a woman?

How old are you? What is your date of birth? How would you feel working for a person younger than you? Where were you born? Where were your parents born?

Do you have any handicaps? As a handicapped person, what help are you going to need to do your work? How severe is your handicap?

What's your religion? What church do you attend? Do you hold religious beliefs that would prevent you from working on certain days of the week?

Do you feel that your race/colour will be a problem in your performing the job? Are you of _____ heritage/race?

An example of disparate treatment occurs when a qualified woman does not receive a promotion given to a less qualified man. Disparate impact occurs when a retailer requires high school graduation for all its employees, thereby excluding a larger proportion of disadvantaged minorities, when at least some of the jobs (e.g., custodian) could be performed just as well by people who did not graduate from high school. In such cases, the retailer is required to prove the imposed qualification is actually needed to be able to perform the job.

Finally, legislation opens up job opportunities for the disabled by requiring employees to provide accommodating work environments. A **disability** is defined as any physical or mental impairment that substantially limits one or more of an individual's major life activities or any condition that is regarded as being such an impairment. Although merely being HIV positive does not limit any life activities, it may be perceived as doing so and is therefore protected as a disability. Similarly, extreme obesity may be either actually limiting or perceived as such and also is protected as long as the obese person can perform the duties of the job. (See Retailing View 13.6 for a discussion of recent retail requirements dictated by changes to the *Accessibility for Ontarians with Disabilities Act.*)

disability Any physical or mental impairment that substantially limits one or more of an individual's major life activities or any condition that is regarded as being such an impairment.

Ensuring Accessibility in Ontario's Retail Environment

The first day of 2013 was the deadline for store operators to comply with revised regulations of the *Accessibility for Ontarians with Disabilities Act* (AODA), which dealt not with ramps or the size of doorways, but rather with the way that consumers with mental and physical challenges should be treated by staff. That the changes demanded of retailers have more to do with employee behaviour than structural changes makes the adjustment less costly, though perhaps no less tricky, to pull off.

Thus, it's understandable that Ontario retailers are cautious in their appraisal of AODA customer service regulations and their potential impact. Where some see a headache-inducing bureaucratic hoop to jump through, others see an opportunity to improve overall customer service while targeting a specific—and growing—consumer segment.

The government of Ontario would certainly like retailers to see the AODA customer service standards in the more positive light, arguing that the changes required make as much sense in financial terms as they do morally. The act's literature makes the claim that people with disabilities will account for 40 percent of all income earned in the province within 20 years time, and refers to a Martin Prosperity Institute study that suggests that the AODA could spur a $9.6 billion increase in Ontario retail revenue.

According to the act, all retailers have to do to cash in on this supposed windfall is make a few additions to their customer service routine, such as making sure to accommodate service animals, providing written services for customers with hearing deficits, and speaking slowly and clearly to persons with developmental challenges. To comply, businesses with fewer than 20 employees are required to create an enhanced customer service plan and train staff on how to serve consumers with disabilities. Retailers with 20 or more employees must take the added steps of making paper copies of their customer service plans available to those who ask to see it and filing a compliance report to the Ontario government.

John Milloy, Ontario's former minister of community and social services, has referred to AODA compliance as "easy to do" in press documents. Certainly, most of the customer service directives—such as simply asking a person in a wheelchair how they might be best served—seem based in common sense. And the government has supplied sample customer service plan templates, training videos, and guides to help facilitate the process.

Shoppers Drug Mart, for example, has bought into the idea of AODA customer service standards as good business strategy.

"Given that Canada has an aging population, it is expected that more and more people will be living with some form of disability, be it loss of hearing or mobility, and it is important that we ready ourselves to serve that growing demographic," says Tammy Smitham, director of communications and corporate affairs for Shoppers Drug Mart. Shoppers Drug Mart has posted its accessibility standards and accessible customer service practice on its website and, according to Smitham, complied with all other aspects of the legislation.

Dave Waye, human resources and compliance officer for Curry's Art Store, says his company has also managed to comply with AODA regulations without much difficulty. Furthermore, he says the process of doing so represented an opportunity to reaffirm the importance of customer service in general.

"In the broad sense, I don't think we see (the AODA standards) as a negative for the business, and in some ways you could even say it's a positive. It makes your staff more aware that customer service is number one," says Waye.

When it comes specifically to dealing with customers with disabilities, Waye says the AODA-mandated training may actually instill a greater confidence among employees.

"You know, we're in retail. Some of our staff are young. Some of them are high school students or first-year university students," he says. "They're part-timers and it's possible they've never come across someone with a disability.

"I don't think anyone would ever do something intentionally to offend, but they might do something just out of ignorance."

Waye believes this kind of accidental offence is less likely now that his staff have absorbed practical lessons on how to address different disabilities. But he stops short of saying that Curry's is looking to leverage its service of Ontarians with disabilities in its marketing initiatives.

"I wouldn't say that I view it that way, and that wasn't the way I presented it to the staff either," says Waye. "If this incents us to improve our levels of customer service, I guess it could well be a competitive advantage if others aren't doing the same. But I just think it's the right thing to do, and if it ends up being an advantage for us, too, that's great."

Source: Matthew Semansky, "Ensuring Accessibility in Ontario's Retail Environment," *Canadian Retailer,* Winter 2012, Volume 22, Issue 1, pp. 46–47. Canadian Retailer, a publication of Retail Council of Canada.

Private-sector retailers appear to be taking a wait-and-see approach to the AODA customer service requirements and any knock-on business effects. For the Liquor Control Board of Ontario (LCBO), however, the AODA is old hat. As a government organization, the LCBO was mandated to comply with the regulations in 2010.

Chris Layton, media relations co-ordinator for the LCBO, says the corporation's experience has been positive and that other retailers should look at the law as a boon to business.

"I think as a retailer you have to look at the regulations in something like the *Accessibility for Ontarians with Disabilities Act* as something that can help you create a more customer-friendly environment," says Layton. "We have not found compliance to be a challenge, but rather a way to better satisfy customers. And obviously having more satisfied customers has a positive effect on business."

Implementing AODA customer service standards does not appear to have been difficult for Ontario retailers and demographic trends to indicate that customers with disabilities represent a large and growing market. Whether this translates into increased revenue for retailers depends on many factors, including the degree to which employees effectively adhere to their training. For this reason, even those retailers who see potential opportunity couch their hopes in caution.

The AODA may bring with it great benefits, but for now it's just something that has to be done.

AODA Customer Service Standards
What retailers have to do to comply depends on their size. Retailers with fewer than 20 employees must create, implement, and train staff in a plan that does the following:

- takes into account different communication requirements (Braille for the vision-impaired, for example) of people with disabilities
- allows and creates space for devices such as wheelchairs and walkers, and service animals such as seeing-eye dogs
- welcomes support persons for people with disabilities
- informs customers when accessible services—for example, a ramp that is temporarily out of use—are unavailable
- invites feedback from customers with disabilities

Retailers are also advised to take stock of their stores and make simple changes, such as putting items within reach of people in wheelchairs and making changes to return policies out of consideration for the fact that some disabilities make it impossible to use fitting rooms. Retailers should also develop a system for responding to feedback.

Retailers with more than 20 employees must follow the same steps, but must also put their policies on paper and make them available to customers.

Better Service, More Revenue?
The government of Ontario has put forth the case that adopting AODA customer service regulations will result in increased revenue for retailers. Here are some key numbers from a Martin Prosperity Institute study assessing the economic impact of the AODA:

- Fifteen percent of Ontarians identified as persons with a disability in 2006, up from 14 percent in 2001. However, more than 31 percent of respondents in a Canadian Community Health Survey said that they had some difficulty with hearing, climbing stairs, or other challenges, so the number may be higher. **31%**

- Disability rates increase with age, and in Ontario, the percentage of the population over 55 is expected to increase from 23 percent to 33 percent by 2031. **23% 2011**

33% 2031

- The income controlled by Ontarians with, or at risk of, disability will rise 33 percent to $536 billion by 2031.

$536 billion

$403 billion

- By 2031, 40 percent of all income in the province will be controlled by persons with disabilities or over the age of 55. **40%**

- AODA implementation could spur an increase of $3.8 billion to $9.6 billion in retail sales in Ontario in the next five years alone.

$9.6 billion

$3.8 billion

Building Employee Commitment

An important challenge in retailing is to reduce turnover.[43] High turnover reduces sales and increases costs. Sales are lost because inexperienced employees lack the skills and knowledge about company policies and merchandise to interact effectively with customers. Costs increase due to the need to continually recruit and train new employees.

To reduce turnover, retailers need to build an atmosphere of mutual commitment in their firms. When a retailer demonstrates its commitment, employees respond by developing loyalty to the company. Employees improve their skills and work hard for the company when they feel the company is committed to them over the long run, through thick and thin. Some approaches that retailers take to build mutual commitment are as follows:

- developing employee skills through selection and training
- empowering employees
- creating a partnering relationship with employees[44]

Research indicates that engaging in these human resource management practices increases the firm's financial performance.[45]

Developing Skills

Two activities that retailers undertake to develop knowledge, skills, and abilities in their human resources are selection and training. Retailers that build a competitive advantage through their human resources are very selective in hiring people and make significant investment in training.

Selective Hiring The first step in building a committed workforce is recruiting the right people. Singapore Airlines, one of Asia's most admired companies, is consistently ranked among the top airlines in terms of service quality. Since its flight attendants are the critical point of contact with its customers, senior management is personally involved in their selection. Only 10 percent of the applicants make the initial screen; only 2 percent are hired.[46]

socialization The steps taken to transform new employees into effective, committed members of the firm.

The job requirements and firm strategy dictate the type of people hired. Simply seeking the best and the brightest often is not the best approach. For example, at a category killer in outdoor gear, the motto is "You live what you sell." Outdoor enthusiasts are hired as sales associates so that they can help customers and serve as a resource for the buying staff. Similarly, Chapters wants avid readers in its workforce.[47]

Socialization and Training After hiring employees, the next step in developing effective employees is introducing them to the firm and its policies. Retailers want the people they hire to become involved, committed contributors to the firm's successful performance. On the other hand, newly hired employees want to learn about their job responsibilities and the company they've decided to join. **Socialization** is the set of steps taken to transform new employees into effective, committed members of the firm. Socialization goes beyond simply orienting new employees to the firm. A principal objective of socialization is to develop a long-term relationship with new employees to increase productivity and reduce turnover costs (see Retailing View 13.7).[48]

A key factor in socializing new employees is to create a training and work environment that articulates the retailer's culture and strategy. Training is particularly important in retailing because more than 60 percent of retail employees have direct contact with customers. They are responsible for helping customers satisfy their needs and resolve their problems. Two keys to success for a retailer are how it treats its employees and its emphasis on training.

Investing in developing employee skills tells employees that the firm considers them important. In response to the difficulty in finding qualified service workers, Marriott has made a considerable investment in recruiting and training entry-level workers. The training goes beyond the basics of doing the job to include grooming habits and basic business etiquette such as calling when you can't come to work.

Starbucks creates strong commitment in its employees through an organizational culture based on standards for coffee preparation and a supportive, empowering attitude toward employees. Starbucks has created a partnership with Kids and Company, an organization that provides child care at a number of facilities in Ontario, Quebec, and Alberta. For a small annual membership fee paid by the

Retention

We do an employee attitude survey every two years where they tell us what they're feeling, both from an attitude point of view and a satisfaction and engagement point of view. We don't only ask. We then have committees who identify areas of opportunities and work towards improving those deficiencies that are noted.

Rafik Louli, regional director, central regional office #3, LCBO

I think in retail, too much of the time the torch isn't passed along properly, the experiences aren't passed along, and that engagement and that empowerment isn't handed down to people often enough to give them that sense of belonging. I think that's one thing Future Shop does very well in retail. If someone comes up with a suggestion and presents it and the company goes with it, we make sure we celebrate it across all levels of the organization so that people know about it.

Mike Hickey, general manager, Future Shop, Calgary

From where you sit, why is retention so difficult for retailers? What is it that retailers, on the whole, aren't getting? What's missing from the current equation?

When we talk about retention, it comes down to engagement and development. Often the focus is on the front end of recruitment but for some, the longer term component of retention becomes a lesser priority. At The Body Shop, we identify succession plans and career paths for all associates to keep them engaged.

Carmela Aita, director, human resources, The Body Shop

Fundamentally, if an employee connects with the organization that they're working for and if they connect with what they're doing within the organization, then retention becomes less of an issue because the employee is already committed. For me, I've been promoted and I've moved from one coast to another and I've been recognized, and we do this all the time. Let's recognize people and provide feedback and make sure they know they have a future with us and that they are contributing to the company. That creates retention. Who doesn't want to feel valued? Who doesn't want to have a say?

Tina Shane, vice-president, retail and customer experience, western Canada, Chapters

What causes the issue of low retention is the fact that if people don't see a clear career path they tend to become frustrated and disillusioned. For a lot of retailers, they look at career paths as being defined, and unless somebody dies above me I have no chance of getting to that level. What retailers can do is change that thought process. Once that basic need for survival is met, the next thing people want to be is taught. If you take out that barrier to learning, you're going to keep people.

Ron Hornbaker, interim CEO, Golf Town

Source: Excerpt from Robert Price, "Recruiting, Retaining, and Empowering Store Managers," Canadian Retailer, Winter 2012, Volume 22, pp. 36–39. *Canadian Retailer,* a publication of Retail Council of Canada.

In this structured training program, newly hired Moores salespeople learn about merchandise they will be selling.

Lars A. Niki.

company, Starbucks partners can have access to spots for their children. The company had a number of partners off on maternity leave who were unable to return to work because they couldn't find affordable child care. According to Sara Presutto, director of partner resources for Starbucks, the idea of keeping HR costs down isn't always a matter of deciding where to make the biggest cuts. As with the child care for its partners, it cuts recruiting and training costs by bringing back loyal partners who understand the corporate culture and the expectations of the job.[49]

Orientation Programs Orientation programs are critical in overcoming entry shock and socializing new employees.[50] Orientation programs can last from a few hours to several weeks. The orientation and training program for new salespeople might be limited to several hours, during which the new salesperson learns the retailer's policies and procedures and how to use the POS terminal. On the other hand, the orientation program for management trainees might take several weeks.

Effective orientation programs need to avoid information overload and one-way communication. When new hires are confronted with a stack of forms and company policies, they get the impression the company is very bureaucratic. Large quantities of information are hard to absorb in a short period of time. New employees learn information best when it's parcelled out in small doses.

Store managers need to foster two-way communication when orienting new employees. Rather than just presenting information about their firm, managers need to give newly hired employees a chance to have their questions and concerns addressed.

The orientation program is just one element in the overall training program. It needs to be accompanied by a systematic follow-up to ensure that any problems and concerns arising after the initial period are considered.

Structured Program During the structured program, new employees are taught the basic skills and knowledge they will need to do their job. For example, salespeople learn what the company policies are, how to use the point-of-sale terminal, and how to perform basic selling skills; stockroom employees learn procedures for receiving merchandise. This initial training might include lectures, audio-visual presentations, manuals, and correspondence distributed to the new employees.

The initial structured program should be relatively short so that new employees don't feel they are simply back in school. Effective training programs bring new recruits up to speed as quickly as possible and then get them involved in doing the job for which they have been hired.

On-the-Job Training The next training phase emphasizes on-the-job training. New employees are assigned a job, given responsibilities, and coached by their supervisor. The best way to learn is to practise what is being taught. New employees learn by doing activities, making mistakes, and then learning how not to make those mistakes again. Information learned through classroom lectures tends to be forgotten quickly unless it's used soon after the lecture.[51]

Employee Evaluation Most retailers evaluate employees annually or semi-annually. Feedback from evaluations is the most effective method for improving employee skills. Thus, evaluations should be done more frequently when managers are developing inexperienced employees' skills. Managers should supplement these formal evaluations with frequent informal ones. Evaluations are only meaningful if employees know what they are required to do, what level of performance is expected, and how they will be evaluated. Exhibit 13–7 shows a specialty store's criteria for evaluating sales associates.

An employee's overall evaluation is based on subjective evaluations made by the store manager and assistant managers. It often places equal weight on individual sales/customer relations activities and activities associated with overall store performance. By emphasizing overall store operations and performance, assessment criteria can motivate sales associates to work together as a team.

Exhibit 13-7
Factors Used to Evaluate Associates at a Specialty Store

50%
SALES/CUSTOMER RELATIONS

1. Greeting. Approaches customers within 1 to 2 minute with a smile and friendly manner. Uses open-ended questions.

2. Product knowledge. Demonstrates knowledge of product, fit, shrinkage, and price and can relay this information to the customer.

3. Suggests additional merchandise. Approaches customers at fitting room and cash/wrap areas.

4. Asks customers to buy and reinforces decisions. Lets customers know they've made a wise choice and thanks them.

25%
OPERATIONS

1. Store appearance. Demonstrates an eye for detail (colour and finesse) in the areas of display, coordination of merchandise on tables, floor fixtures, and wall faceouts. Takes initiative in maintaining store presentation standards.

2. Loss prevention. Actively follows all loss prevention procedures.

3. Merchandise control and handling. Consistently achieves established requirements in price change activity, shipment processing, and inventory control.

4. Cash/wrap procedures. Accurately and efficiently follows all register policies and cash/wrap procedures.

25%
COMPLIANCE

1. Dress code and appearance. Complies with dress code. Appears neat and well groomed. Projects current fashionable image.

2. Flexibility. Able to switch from one assignment to another, open to schedule adjustments. Shows initiative, awareness of store priorities and needs.

3. Working relations. Cooperates with other employees, willingly accepts direction and guidance from management. Communicates to management.

Analyzing Successes and Failures Every new employee makes mistakes. Store managers should provide an atmosphere in which salespeople try out different approaches to providing customer service and selling merchandise. Store managers must recognize that some of these new approaches are going to fail, and when they do, managers shouldn't criticize the individual salesperson. Instead, they should talk about the situation, analyze why the approach didn't work, and discuss how the salesperson could avoid the problem in the future.

Empowering Employees

Empowerment is the process of managers sharing power and decision-making authority with employees (see Retailing View 13.8). When employees have the authority to make decisions, they are more confident in their abilities, have greater opportunity to provide service to customers, and are more committed to the firm's success.

The first step in empowering employees is to review employee activities that require a manager's approval.

Each store in the Whole Foods chain is a profit centre, with the store employees organized in ten self-managed teams. The teams are responsible and accountable for the store's performance. For example, the store manager recommends new hires. It takes a two-thirds vote of the team to actually hire the candidate. The team members pool their ideas and come up with creative solutions to problems. Empowerment of retail employees transfers authority and responsibility for making decisions to lower levels in the organization. These employees are close to the retailer's customers and in a good position to know what it takes to satisfy customers. For empowerment to work, managers must have an attitude of respect and trust, not control and distrust.[52]

empowerment The process of managers sharing power and decision-making authority with employees.

Employee Feedback Survey

One of the primary benefits of an employee survey is to provide an opportunity for employees to give feedback to the retail organization. A well-designed employee survey can provide significant benefits in improving retention and organizational communication. In addition, if employees think that their personal needs and ideas are valued, this can build trust and commitment between managers and associates.

Employee feedback enables the retailer to identify gaps between organizational goals and actual policies. It helps align the retailer's goals and employee satisfaction by making employees

FISH! Empowers Employees

FISH! is a management philosophy developed by ChartHouse and inspired by the Pike Place Fish Market in Seattle. The selling atmosphere at Pike Place is unusual. Employees, known as fishmongers, throw fish over the counter to co-workers for wrapping. The fishmongers also invite customers to get in on the action and try to catch fish. What could be a dull store is transformed into a place where customers and employees are smiling, laughing, and connecting with one another, while keeping an eye out for flying fish.

Amy's Ice Cream (a 13-store chain of premium ice cream shops in Austin, San Antonio, and Houston, Texas) has similarly transformed what could be a boring transaction into a fun experience. Visit an Amy's store, and you'll see employees performing in a manner you won't forget. They juggle with their serving spades, toss scoops of ice cream to one another behind the counter, and break-dance on the freezer top. If there's a line out the door, they might pass out samples or offer free ice cream to any customer who'll sing or dance or recite a poem or mimic a barnyard animal or win a 60-second cone-eating contest.

The four FISH! principles are:

1. Choose your attitude—look for the worst and you'll find it; choose to look for the best and you'll find opportunities heretofore unimagined;
2. Be there—being fully present for one another and diving into every task with your whole heart;
3. Make their day—small kindnesses turn even routine encounters into special memories;

By giving employees the freedom to have fun at work, Pike Place Fish Markets employees reduce the delivery gap and improve customer service.
© David Kadlubowski/DIT/Corbis.

4. Play—serious tasks are made fun through spontaneity and creativity.

By empowering employees to implement the FISH! principles the best way they can, companies facilitate great customer service. For example, "choose your attitude" can empower employees to effect change from within themselves. Positive attitudes spread to other employees and onto customers. Empowering employees to "play" on the job makes the working and buying atmosphere fun, and happy customers buy more.

Sources: http://www.charthouse.com (accessed November 12, 2007); http://www.amysicecream.com (accessed November 11, 2007); Laura Gee, "Some Companies Work to Put Fun in the Office," October 23, 2007, http://www.dailypress.com; Tanya Rutledge, "Amy Miller, Sweet Success," *Austin Business Journal*, December 24, 2004, p. 16; Marcia Hicks, "Revitalizing Your Call Center Via FISH! Philosophy," *Direct Marketing Magazine*, December 1, 2003; Stephen C. Lundin, Harry Paul, and John Christensen, *Fish! A Remarkable Way to Boost Morale and Improve Results* (New York: Hyperion, 2000).

participants in the process of business improvement and success.

All questionnaires must be anonymous and take no more than 30 minutes to complete. For larger retailers electronic or Web-based questionnaires are the most efficient and cost-effective format. When designing a questionnaire, maintain consistency of question format, and use unbiased check boxes as an effective way to control responses. Open-ended responses allow employees to share their thoughts on issues. Retailers must act on the collected results of any survey. Never let data go unused. The value of employee feedback cannot be overstated.

Developing Partnering Relationships with Employees

Four human resource management activities that build commitment through developing partnering relationships with employees are as follows:

- reducing status differences
- promoting from within
- enabling employees to balance their careers and families
- enabling employees to pursue outside interests such as athletics and community activities

Retailers such as RBC and Canadian Tire not only support Canada's Olympic athletes through financial contributions, but also provide them with employment that recognizes their demanding training schedules.

Reducing Status Differences Many retailers attempt to reduce status differences between employees. With limited status differences, employees feel that they play an important role in the firm's achieving its goals and that their contributions are valued.

Status differences can be reduced symbolically through the use of language and cut substantively by lowering wage differentials and increasing communications between managers at different levels in the company. For example, hourly workers at Walmart are referred to as associates and managers are called partners, a practice that Sam Walton adopted when he started Walmart.

Whole Foods has a policy of limiting executive compensation to less than eight times the compensation of the average full-time salaried employee.

All Home Depot senior executives spend time in the stores, wearing the orange apron, talking with customers and employees. This "management by walking around" makes employees feel that their inputs are valued by the company and reinforces the customer service culture.

Promotion from within Promotion from within is a staffing policy that involves hiring new employees only for positions at the lowest level in the job hierarchy and then promoting employees for openings at higher levels in the hierarchy. Home Depot, Costco, and Walmart have had promotion-from-within policies.

Promotion-from-within policies establish a sense of fairness. When employees do an outstanding job and then outsiders are brought in over them, employees feel that the company doesn't care about them. Promotion-from-within policies also commit the retailer to developing its employees.[53]

Balancing Careers and Families The increasing number of two-income and single-parent families makes it difficult for employees to effectively do their jobs and manage their households. Retailers build employee commitment by offering services such as job sharing, child care, and employee assistance programs to help their employees manage these problems.

Flextime is a job scheduling system that enables employees to choose the times they work.

With **job sharing**, two employees voluntarily are responsible for a job that was previously held by one person. Both programs let employees accommodate their work schedules to other demands in their life such as being home when children return from school.[54]

Many retailers offer child care assistance. Sears' corporate headquarters has a 20 000 square-foot daycare centre. At Eddie Bauer, a catalogue retailer in Seattle, the corporate headquarters cafeteria stays open late and prepares takeout meals for time-pressed employees. Some companies will even arrange for a person to be at an employee's home waiting for the cable guy to come or to pick up and drop off dry cleaning.[55]

Retailing View 13.9 outlines the supports that store managers require from the organization to do their job well.

promotion from within A staffing policy that involves hiring new employees only for positions at the lowest level in the job hierarchy and then promoting employees for openings at higher levels in the hierarchy.

flextime A job scheduling system that enables employees to choose the times they work.

job sharing When two or more employees voluntarily are responsible for a job that was previously held by one person.

managing diversity A set of human resource management programs designed to realize the benefits of a diverse workforce.

Lo4 Trends in Retail Human Resource Management

In this final section, we discuss three trends in human resource management:

- the increasing importance of having a diverse workforce
- the growth in legal restrictions on HR practices
- the use of technology to increase employee productivity

Managing Diversity

Managing diversity is a human resource management activity designed to realize the benefits of a diverse workforce. Today, diversity means more than differences in skin colour, nationality, and gender.

Minority groups now embrace their differences and want employers to accept them for who they are. The appropriate metaphor is a salad bowl. Each ingredient in the salad is distinctive,

Nuts and Bolts of Store Management

I don't like the buzzwords. But empowerment is key—the freedom to make a decision. Store managers need to know that if they make a decision, they aren't going to get chastised for making the decision. In fact, I want them to make a decision. If it gets to me, it's too late. They should have taken care of the customer long before it gets to me. As long as they feel free to make a decision, and you've clearly defined what your expectations for those decisions are, more often than not they're going to make the right one.

Ron Hornbaker, interim CEO, Golf Town

They need to be provided with a very clear set of expectations and support on how to achieve those expectations. They also need a comprehensive training program on everything from understanding their role in the business, understanding how to analyze results, enhancing their product knowledge, and to understand and be able to execute the desired customer experience that we're looking to provide as an organization.

Carmela Aita, director, human resources, The Body Shop

And if we talk about the nuts and bolts of store management. What do store managers need most from the organization to do their job well?

Every employee needs clear goals, short-term and long-term. That comes from our business plans—we have five-year business plans and annual business plans, clearly communicated, not only to store managers, but to every employee in the organization.

Rafik Louli, regional director, central regional office #3, LCBO

Store managers need three things. One is support from the organization to know they have the autonomy to make choices and make decisions that may not help the customer in the short-term, but will help them in the long-term. Second, they need the opportunity to learn and grow within an organization because nobody wants to become stale or stagnant. Third, you have to have the mindset that the customer needs to always come first. And, within your organization's structure your associates have to come first before everything.

Mike Hickey, general manager, Future Shop, Calgary

There needs to be that open-door policy so that if the store manager knows what you want but isn't clear about how to get there or what tools they might need to make it easier, they feel comfortable and understand that upper management will be ready and available to help at any time. That open communication needs to be extended out to others within the organization as well—that can help immensely.

Tina Shane, vice-president, retail and customer experience, western Canada, Chapters

Source: Excerpt from Robert Price, "Recruiting, Retaining, and Empowering Store Managers," Canadian Retailer, Winter 2012, Volume 22, pp. 36–39. *Canadian Retailer,* a publication of Retail Council of Canada.

preserving its own identity, but the mixture of ingredients improves the combined taste of the individual elements.[56] Diversity and equity in the workplace always make good business sense. Consider the Canadian population, comprising more than 200 ethnic groups with multiple ties around the world. Businesses that embrace diversity are well positioned to be more competitive in world markets.[57]

Some legal restrictions promote diversity in the workplace by preventing retailers from practising discrimination based on non–performance-related employee characteristics. But retailers now recognize that promoting employee diversity can improve financial performance. By encouraging diversity in their workforce, retailers can better understand and respond to the needs of their customers and deal with the shrinking labour market.

Retail customers' racial and ethnic backgrounds are increasingly diverse. To compete in this changing marketplace, retailers need management staffs that match the diversity of their target markets. For example, 85 percent of the men's clothing sold in department stores is bought by women, and over 50 percent of Home Depot's sales are made to women. To better understand customer needs, department store and home improvement retailers feel that they must have women in senior management positions—people who really understand their female customers' needs.

The fundamental principle of managing diversity is the recognition that employees have different needs and require different approaches to accommodating those needs. Managing diversity goes beyond meeting equal employment opportunity laws. It means accepting and valuing differences. Some programs that retailers use to manage diversity involve offering diversity training, providing support groups and mentoring, and managing career development and promotions.[58]

Diversity Training Diversity training typically consists of two components: developing cultural awareness and building competencies. The cultural awareness component teaches people about how their own culture differs from the culture of other employees and how stereotypes they hold influence the way they treat people, often in subtle ways they might not realize. Then, role-playing is used to help employees develop better interpersonal skills, including showing respect and treating people as equals.

Support Groups and Mentoring A **mentoring program** assigns higher-level managers to help lower-level managers learn the firm's values and meet other senior executives.[59]

Career Development and Promotions Although laws provide entry-level opportunities for women and minority groups, these employees often encounter a glass ceiling as they move through the corporation. A **glass ceiling** is a figurative barrier that makes it difficult for minorities and women to be promoted beyond a certain level.

Similarly, women in the supermarket business have traditionally been assigned to peripheral departments such as bakery and deli, while men were assigned to the critical departments in the store: meat and grocery. Even in the supermarket chain corporate office, women traditionally have been in staff-support areas such as human resource management, finance, and accounting, while men are more involved in store operations and buying. To make sure that more women have an opportunity to break through the glass ceiling in the supermarket industry, firms are placing them in positions critical to the firm's success.[61]

Legal and Regulatory Issues in Human Resource Management

In Canada, all employers and all employees must comply with the *Employment Standards Act*, which identifies standards based on provincial legislation. Historically, collective agreements helped shape employment standards that today apply to about two-thirds of Canadian workers who are not involved in a unionized work environment. Each of Canada's ten provinces and three territories developed its own employment standards legislation, all based on a common set of issues. The *Employment Standards Act* is a law that establishes minimum entitlements pertaining to such issues as wages; paid holidays and vacations; leave for maternity, parental care, and adoption; bereavement leave; termination notice; overtime pay; and limits on the maximum

DID YOU KNOW?

Of 180 businesses survey in Canada (both large and small), 87 percent contribute money directly to causes while 51 percent support an employee volunteering program. Approximately 47 percent of businesses support employee-matching donations programs.[60]

mentoring program The assigning of higher-level managers to help lower-level managers learn the firm's values and meet other senior executives.

glass ceiling A figurative barrier that makes it difficult for minorities and women to be promoted beyond a certain level.

number of hours of work permitted per day or week.[62] Managing in this complex regulatory environment requires expertise in labour laws and skills in helping other managers comply with these laws. The major legal and regulatory issues involving the management of retail employees are as follows:

- equal employment opportunity
- compensation
- labour relations
- employee safety and health
- sexual harassment
- employee privacy

Equal Employment Opportunity   Canadian employment equity legislation is not about favouring anybody—women, persons with disabilities, Aboriginal persons, or visible minorities. The law is about identifying and eliminating employment barriers. It is also about instituting positive policies and practices and making reasonable accommodations to ensure that persons in the designated groups achieve a degree of workforce representation that reflects their representation in Canadian society.[63] **Illegal discrimination** is the actions of a company or its managers that result in members of a protected class being treated unfairly and differently than others. A protected class is all of the individuals who share a common characteristic defined by the law. Companies cannot treat employees differently simply based on their race, colour, religion, sex, national origin, age, or disability status. There is a very limited set of circumstances under which employees can be treated differently. For example, it is illegal for a restaurant to hire only young, attractive servers because that is what its customers prefer. Such discrimination must be absolutely necessary, not simply preferred.

In addition, it is illegal to engage in a practice that disproportionately excludes a protected group even though it might seem to be non-discriminatory. For example, suppose that a retailer uses scores on a test to make hiring decisions. If a protected group systematically performs worse on the test, the retailer is illegally discriminating even if there was no intention to discriminate.

illegal discrimination The actions of a company or its managers that result in members of a protected class being treated unfairly and differently than others.

Compensation   Laws relating to compensation define the 40-hour workweek, the pay rate for working overtime, and the minimum wage, and they protect employee investments in their pensions. In addition, they require that firms provide the same pay for men and women who are doing equal work of equal value.

DID YOU KNOW?

55 percent of consumers will pay extra for products and services from companies committed to positive social and environmental impact.[64]

Labour Relations   Labour relations laws describe the process by which unions can be formed and the ways in which companies must deal with the unions. They precisely indicate how negotiations with unions must take place and what the parties can and cannot do.

Employee Safety and Health   The basic premise of these laws is that the employer is obligated to provide each employee with an environment that is free from hazards that are likely to cause death or serious injury. According to Kerri O'Neill, a disability and wellness consultant at Staples Canada, health and safety is a concern for everybody. Retailers who are able to "work health and safety into daily aspects of the job and make it part of the culture instead of something they have to do," can "look at trends, be proactive and support a better trend." Examples of ways that managers can encourage a healthier lifestyle among workers by sponsoring gym memberships, offering employee discounts on health-related items, hosting in-store seminars with health experts, and paying in part or full for smoking cessation programs.[65]

Sexual Harassment   Sexual harassment includes unwelcome sexual advances, requests for sexual favours, and other verbal and physical conduct. Harassment isn't confined to requests for sexual favours in exchange for job considerations such as a raise or promotion. Simply creating a hostile work environment can be considered sexual harassment. For example, actions that are considered sexual harassment include lewd comments, joking, and graffiti, as well as showing obscene photographs, staring at a co-worker in a sexual manner, alleging that an employee got rewards by engaging in sexual acts, and commenting on an employee's moral reputation.

Customers can engage in sexual harassment as well as supervisors and co-workers. For example, female pharmacists find that some male customers demand lengthy discussions when they buy condoms. Pharmacists have difficulty dealing with these situations because they want to keep the person as a customer and also protect themselves from abuse.

Employee Privacy Employees' privacy protection is very limited. For example, employers can monitor email and telephone communications, and search an employee's work space and handbag. However, employers cannot discriminate among employees when undertaking these activities unless they have a strong suspicion that employees are acting inappropriately.

Developing Policies The human resource department is responsible for developing programs and policies to make sure that managers and employees are aware of these restrictions and know how to deal with potential violations. These legal and regulatory requirements are basically designed to treat people fairly. Employees want to be treated fairly and companies want to be perceived as treating their employees fairly. The perception of fairness encourages people to join a company and leads to trust and commitment of employees to a firm. When employees believe they are not being treated fairly, they can either complain, stay and accept the situation, stay but engage in negative behaviour, quit, or complain to an external authority and even sue the employer.

Perceptions of fairness are based on two factors:

- **Distributive justice**, which arises when outcomes received are viewed as fair with respect to outcomes received by others. However, the perception of distributive justice can differ across cultures. For example, in the individualistic culture of Canada, merit-based pay is perceived as fair, whereas in collectivist cultures such as China and Japan, equal pay is viewed as fair.

- **Procedural justice**, which is based on fairness of the process used to determine the outcome. Canadian workers consider formal processes as fair whereas group decisions are considered fairer in collectivist cultures.[66]

Lo5 Store Security Management

An important issue facing store management is reducing inventory losses due to employee theft, shoplifting, mistakes, inaccurate records, and vendor errors. Examples of employee mistakes are failing to ring up an item when it's sold and miscounting merchandise when it's received or during physical inventories. Inventory shrinkage due to vendor mistakes arises when vendor shipments contain less than the amount indicated on the packing slip.

According to the PwC's *Canadian Retail Security Survey 2012*, a rate of internal theft of 33.4 percent (as shown below) emphasizes the need for retailers to invest in strong internal policies and procedures, as the criminal activity appears to be gaining momentum from within the core of retailers' operations.

Shrinkage Incidents	2012	2008
Internal theft	33.4%	19.0%
External theft	43.0%	65.0%
Paperwork errors	19.9%	16.0%
Vendor fraud	3.7%	no data

Source: PwC Canada.

In developing a loss prevention program, retailers confront a trade-off between providing shopping convenience and a pleasant work environment on the one hand, and preventing losses due to shoplifting and employee theft on the other. The key to an effective loss prevention program is determining the most effective way to protect merchandise while preserving an open, attractive store atmosphere and a feeling among employees that they are trusted. Loss prevention requires coordination among store management, visual merchandising, and store design.

Merchandise Categories

Given the diverse group of respondents in the *Canadian Retail Security Survey 2012*, 25 different merchandise categories were identified that contribute most to shrinkage. The top three categories identified (in order) were alcohol, ladies apparel, and cosmetics and fragrances. Each of the categories is a high-volume and high-value category that appeals to criminal activity, both internal and external in nature (see Exhibit 13–8).

Calculating Shrinkage

Shrinkage is the difference between the recorded value of inventory (at retail prices) based on merchandise bought and

distributive justice Exists when outcomes received are viewed as fair with respect to outcomes received by others.

procedural justice An employee's perception of fairness (how he or she is treated) that is based on the process used to determine the outcome.

shrinkage An inventory reduction that is caused by shoplifting by employees or customers, by merchandise being misplaced or damaged, or by poor bookkeeping.

Exhibit 13-8

The Top Merchandise Categories That Contribute Most to Shrinkage

Alcohol	Garden
Women's apparel	Gloves
Cosmetics and fragrance	Intimate apparel
Health and beauty	Jewellery
Denim	Ladies' accessories
Food/confectionery	Lighters
Men's apparel	Lumber
Footwear	Pens
Handbags	Power tools
Kids and baby	Sporting goods
Pharmacy/razor blades	Sunglasses
Bath and shower	Wallets
Electronics/DVDs	

Source: PwC Canada.

received and the value of the actual inventory (at retail prices) in stores and distribution centres, divided by retail sales during the period. For example, if accounting records indicate inventory should be $1 500 000, the actual count of the inventory reveals $1 236 000, and sales were $4 225 000, the shrinkage is 6.2 percent.

Shrinkage

$$= \text{(Book inventory} - \text{Actual inventory)} \div \text{Net sales}$$

$$= (\$1\ 500\ 000 - \$1\ 236\ 000) \div \$4\ 225\ 000$$

$$= 6.2\%$$

Reducing shrinkage is an important store management issue. Retailers' annual loss from shrinkage averages about 1.6 percent of sales.[68] Every dollar of inventory shrinkage translates into a dollar of lost profit.

Although more than 70 percent of shoplifting is performed by amateurs, professional shoplifters now account for an estimated $15 to $30 billion in losses annually, representing almost 25 percent of reported shoplifting cases. These gangs of professional thieves concentrate in over-the-counter medications, infant formula, health and beauty aids, electronics, and specialty clothing. This stolen merchandise is often sold by shoplifters on Internet auction sites.

DID YOU KNOW?

The Ontario Service Safety Alliance reports that, over just eight years, Ontario employers paid more than $3.3 billion in direct costs because of musculoskeletal disorders, a common type of injury among retail workers.[67]

With identity theft and payment fraud on the rise due to bogus purchases appearing on credit card statements or missing funds from bank accounts via credit card fraud, retailers increasingly see chargebacks at the point-of-sale as a necessity of doing business. The generous returns policy instituted by many retailers has attracted criminals seeking a low-risk, high-reward way to make money.

On January 1, 2004, the *Personal Information and Protection of Electronic Documents Act* (PIPEDA) took effect in Canada. This privacy legislation outlines the responsibilities of Canadian businesses to the customers they serve.

The top three risks that companies face related to privacy damage are the following:

- damage to reputation of the business
- loss of customers
- litigation costs

Canadian retailers need to launch employee training programs and develop privacy statements for display in the store and on their websites. Transparency is critical to the success of retail privacy policy guidelines.

For additional information, visit the office of the Privacy Commissioner of Canada at http://www.priv.gc.ca.

DID YOU KNOW?

It costs a retailer $20 to $30 to process a paper HR form, but processing the form over an intranet only costs $0.05 to $0.10.[69]

DID YOU KNOW?

Canadian retailers are losing about $4 billion a year to shrinkage, which equates to an average estimated loss of $10.8 million per shopping day, according to PwC's *2012 Canadian Retail Security Survey*, completed in conjunction with the Retail Council of Canada (RCC).

Detecting and Preventing Shoplifting

Losses due to shoplifting can be reduced by store design, merchandise policies, special security measures, personnel policies, and prosecution of shoplifters.[70]

Store Design The following store design issues are used to reduce inventory shrinkage:

- Do not place expensive or small merchandise near entrance.
- Keep the height of fixtures low and arranged with no "blind spots" to maintain open sight lines to store entrances and dressing rooms so employees can see customers in the store and watch for shoplifters while providing better service.

- Use mirrors. Strategically placed one-way observation mirrors and hanging mirrors can help store employees observe customers.
- Because cash wraps are always staffed, they should be near areas that theft is likely to occur. Cash wraps are the places in a store where customers can buy their purchases and have them "wrapped"—placed in a bag.
- Alternate clothing hanger directions. Professional shoplifters can steal a tremendous amount of clothing by grabbing it off the rack. If the hangers are alternated, it is difficult for thieves to steal a lot at once.

Merchandise Policies   The following merchandise policies are used to reduce inventory shrinkage:

- Require a receipt for all returns, because many shoplifters steal with the intent of returning the merchandise for a cash refund.
- Lock up small, expensive items. Expensive apparel items can be chained. While locking merchandise in a cabinet or chaining expensive apparel decreases shrinkage, it may decrease sales by making it more difficult for customers to look at merchandise of interest.

Security Measures   Store employees can be the retailer's most effective tool against shoplifting. They should be trained to be aware, visible, and alert to potential shoplifting situations. Exhibit 13–9 outlines rules for spotting shoplifters. Perhaps the best deterrent to shoplifting is an alert employee who is very visible. Exhibit 13–10 describes security measures that retailers can use. Another

Exhibit 13–9
Spotting Shoplifters

DON'T ASSUME THAT ALL SHOPLIFTERS ARE POORLY DRESSED
To avoid detection, professional shoplifters dress in the same manner as customers patronizing the store. Over 90 percent of all amateur shoplifters arrested have either the cash, cheques, or credit to purchase the merchandise they stole.

SPOT LOITERERS
Amateur shoplifters frequently loiter in areas as they build up the nerve to steal something. Professionals also spend time waiting for the right opportunity, but less conspicuously than amateurs.

LOOK FOR GROUPS
Teenagers planning to shoplift often travel in groups. Some members of the group divert employees' attention while others take the merchandise. Professional shoplifters often work in pairs. One person takes the merchandise and passes it to a partner in the store's restroom, phone booths, or restaurant.

LOOK FOR PEOPLE WITH LOOSE CLOTHING
Shoplifters frequently hide stolen merchandise under loose-fitting clothing or in large shopping bags. People wearing a winter coat in the summer or a raincoat on a sunny day may be potential shoplifters.

WATCH THE EYES, HANDS, AND BODY
Professional shoplifters avoid looking at merchandise and concentrate on searching for store employees who might observe their activities. Shoplifters' movements might be unusual as they try to conceal merchandise.

Exhibit 13–10
Activities Used to Manage Loss Prevention Efforts 2008 and 2012

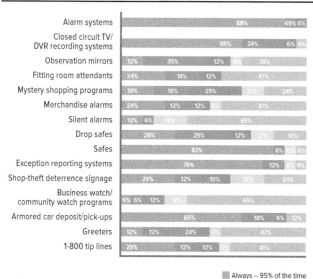

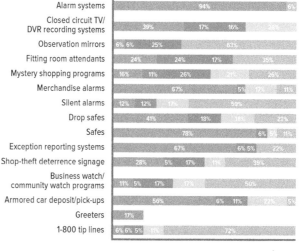

Always – 95% of the time   Occasionally – 35% to 60%   Never – 0%
Frequently – 60% to 95%   Infrequently – less than 35%

Source: PwC Canada.

electronic article surveillance (EAS) system A loss-prevention system in which special tags placed on merchandise in retail stores are deactivated when the merchandise is purchased. The tags are used to discourage shoplifting.

approach to deterring shoplifting is to embed dye capsules in the merchandise. If the capsules aren't removed properly by a store employee, they break and damage the merchandise.

By placing convex mirrors at key locations, employees can observe a wide area of the store. Closed-circuit TV cameras can be monitored from a central location, but purchasing the equipment and hiring people to monitor the system can be expensive. Some retailers install non-operating equipment that looks like a TV camera to provide a psychological deterrent to shoplifters.

Although these security measures reduce shoplifting, they can also make the shopping experience more unpleasant for honest customers. The atmosphere of a fashionable department store is diminished when guards, mirrors, and TV cameras are highly visible. Customers may find it hard to try on clothing secured with a lock-and-chain or an electronic tag. They can also be uncomfortable trying on clothing if they think they are secretly being watched via a surveillance monitor. Thus, when evaluating security measures, retailers need to balance the benefits of reducing shoplifting with the potential losses in sales.

Electronic article surveillance is a promising approach to reducing shrinkage with little effect on shopping behaviour. In an **electronic article surveillance (EAS) system**, special tags are placed on merchandise. When the merchandise is purchased, the tags are deactivated by the POS scanner. If a shoplifter tries to steal the merchandise, the active tags are sensed when the shoplifter passes a detection device at the store exit and an alarm is triggered.[71]

EAS tags do not affect shopping behaviour because customers do not realize they are on the merchandise. Due to the effectiveness of tags in reducing shoplifting, retailers can increase sales by displaying theft-prone, expensive merchandise openly rather than behind a counter or in a locked enclosure.

Some large national retailers insist that vendors install EAS tags during the manufacturing process because the vendors can install the tags at a lower cost than the retailers. In addition, retail-installed tags can be removed more easily by shoplifters. Vendors are reluctant to get involved with installing EAS tags because industry standards have not been adopted. Without these standards, a vendor would have to develop unique tags and merchandise for each retailer.[73]

Personnel Policies   The following personnel policies may help deter shoplifting:

- Use mystery and honesty shoppers—people posing as real shoppers—to watch for employee and customer theft.
- Have store employees monitor fitting rooms. Fitting rooms provide a good environment for stealing.
- Train store employees to be aware, visible, and alert to potential shoplifting situations.
- Provide excellent customer service. If employees know the customers and offer assistance, shoplifters will be deterred.

Prosecution   Many retailers have a policy of prosecuting all shoplifters. They feel a strictly enforced prosecution policy deters shoplifters. Some retailers also sue shoplifters in civil proceedings for restitution of the stolen merchandise and the time spent in the prosecution.

Reducing Employee Theft   The most effective approach to reducing employee theft and shoplifting is to create a trusting, supportive work environment. When employees feel they are respected members of a team, they identify their goals with the retailer's goals. Stealing from their employer becomes equivalent to stealing from themselves or their family, and they go out of their way to prevent others from stealing from the "family." Thus, retailers with a highly committed workforce and low turnover typically have low inventory shrinkage. Additional approaches to reducing employee theft are carefully screening employees, creating an atmosphere that encourages honesty and integrity, using security personnel, and establishing security policies and control systems (see Retailing View 13.10).

Screening Prospective Employees As mentioned previously, many retailers use paper-and-pencil honesty tests and make extensive reference checks to screen out potential employee theft problems.

Using Security Personnel In addition to uniformed guards, retailers use undercover shoppers to discourage and detect employee theft. These

DID YOU KNOW?

A dishonest employee typically takes over $1000 worth of goods and cash, whereas the average customer shoplifter takes $128 in merchandise.[72]

Holt Renfrew Uses Fingerprint Biometrics

Biometrics such as fingerprint recognition can be used for controlled access to POS systems, for manager approvals, and for transaction overrides. Holt Renfrew employees sign in with their fingertips, using biometrics scanning. Holt Renfrew is currently one of the only Canadian retailers using biometrics to track employee activities as part of their workforce management strategy. The concept eliminates problems of misplaced pass cards, shared passwords, and payroll discrepancies because fingerprint recognition is tied into the store's time and attendance system.

Biometrics such as fingerprint recognition can be used for controlled access to POS systems, for manager approvals, and for transaction overrides. This could also pave the way for consumer applications such as biometric payment at the POS.

Courtesy of NCR Corporation.

undercover security people pose as shoppers. They make sure salespeople ring up transactions accurately.

Establishing Security Policies and Control Systems To control employee theft, retailers need to adopt policies relating to certain activities that may facilitate theft. Some of the most prevalent policies include the following:

- Randomly search containers such as trash bins where stolen merchandise can be stored.

- Require store employees to enter and leave the store through designated entrances.

- Assign salespeople to specific POS terminals and require all transactions to be handled through those terminals.

- Restrict employee purchases to working hours.

- Provide customer receipts for all transactions.

- Have all refunds, returns, and discounts co-signed by a department or store manager.

- Change locks periodically and issue keys to authorized personnel only.

- Have a locker room where all employee handbags, purses, packages, and coats must be checked.

Retailers use EAS tags to reduce shoplifting. The tags (top) contain a device that is part of the price tag. If the tags are not deactivated when the merchandise is purchased, the stolen merchandise will be detected when the shopper passes through the sensor gates (bottom) at the store exit.

(top) © Aliaksandr Mazurkevich | Dreamstime.com; **(bottom)** Courtesy of Checkpoint Systems, Inc.

Recruitment

It comes down to how you bring them into the organization. Realizing that a lot of talent will be leaving our organization, about four years ago we made it a priority to set up a succession plan. We developed what's called the Onboarding Program, a week-long residential program, and a mentor program to keep new hires on track and successful.

Rafik Louli, regional director, central regional office #3, LCBO

When I interview people for a retail manager position, more often than not they're coming from another retailer. Maybe the challenge is to articulate the advantages of being in retail and delivering that message at the university level. It's also important to recognize that we work within a really dynamic and exciting industry—retailers can attract people from other industries who have similar skill-sets and competencies.

Ron Hornbaker, interim CEO, Golf Town

The recruitment of top talent continues to be a priority within the retail industry. What can retailers, individually or as an industry, do to attract more people to retail?

Use employee networks. We use referrals from associates. Referrals who come into the store do better because they already know someone in the company. They can ask friends questions that maybe they can't ask during the interview: How's the leadership team? Does the company actually care about you?

Mike Hickey, general manager, Future Shop, Calgary

At The Body Shop, we work to highlight career paths and options within our organization to potential candidates that come on board so they understand what their potential path can look like. We as employers should be able to highlight career paths for those up-and-coming students and grads looking at retail as a career.

Carmela Alta, director, human resources, The Body Shop

From my perspective, retail is always about recruiting, and you have to always be ahead of the curve. How we do that is by spending a lot of time looking at overall compensation. So not just looking at wages or salary but other things we offer like benefits and recognition. The other piece is fit. If you start from the point of connecting with the right fit to the right offer, you start a few steps ahead of where you want to take people over the long-term.

Tina Shane, vice-president, retail and customer experience, western Canada, Chapters

Source: Excerpt from Robert Price, "Recruiting, Retaining, and Empowering Store Managers," Canadian Retailer, Winter 2012, Volume 22, pp. 36–39. *Canadian Retailer,* a publication of Retail Council of Canada.

Human resource management plays a vital role in supporting a retailing strategy. The organization structure defines supervisory relationships and employees' responsibilities. The four primary groups of tasks performed by retailers are strategic decisions by the corporate officers, administrative tasks by the corporate staff, merchandise management by the buying organization, and store management.

In developing an organization structure, retailers must make trade-offs between the cost savings gained through centralized decision making and the benefits of tailoring the merchandise offering to local markets—benefits that arise when decisions are made in a decentralized manner.

Two critical human resource management issues are the development of a committed workforce and the effective management of a diverse workforce. Building a committed workforce is critical in retailing because high turnover has a major impact on profitability. A key factor in reducing turnover is developing an atmosphere of mutual commitment.

Effective store management can have a significant impact on a retail firm's financial performance. Store managers increase profits by increasing labour productivity, decreasing costs through labour deployment decisions, and reducing inventory loss by developing a dedicated workforce.

A well-crafted, well-executed employee feedback survey can provide significant benefits to improve employee satisfaction and retention, as well as organizational communications that ultimately improve the retailer's success.

Increasing store employees' productivity is challenging because of the difficulties in recruiting, selecting, and motivating store employees. Employees typically have a range of skills and seek a spectrum of rewards. Effective store managers need to motivate their employees to work hard and to develop skills so that they improve their productivity. Store managers must establish realistic goals for employees that are consistent with the store's goals.

Store managers also must control inventory losses due to employee theft, shoplifting, and clerical errors. Managers use a wide variety of methods in developing loss prevention programs, including security devices, employee screening during the selection process, and building employee loyalty to increase attention to shoplifting.

The human resource department is responsible for making sure that the firm complies with the laws and regulations that prevent discriminatory practices against employees and ensure that they have a safe work environment.

KEY TERMS

average sale per transaction (AST)
bonus
centralization
coaching
commission
decentralization
disability
discrimination
disparate impact
disparate treatment
distributive justice
drawing account
electronic article surveillance (EAS) system
employee productivity

employee turnover
empowerment
extrinsic rewards
flextime
full-time equivalent (FTE)
glass ceiling
illegal discrimination
incentive compensation plan
intrinsic rewards
job analysis
job application form
job description
job sharing
leadership
management

managing diversity
mentoring program
organization structure
organizational culture
procedural justice
promotion from within
quota
quota–bonus plan
sales per employee hour
sales per full-time employee
selling cost
shrinkage
socialization
specialization
straight commission

GET OUT & DO IT!

1. GO SHOPPING Go to a store and meet with the person responsible for personnel scheduling.

- How far in advance is the schedule made?
- How are breaks and lunch periods planned?
- How are overtime hours determined?
- What is the total number of budgeted employee hours for each department based on?
- How is flexibility introduced into the schedule?
- How are special requests for days off handled?
- How are peak periods planned for?
- What happens when an employee calls in sick at the last minute?

2. GO SHOPPING Go to a store and talk to the person responsible for human resource management to find out how salespeople are compensated and evaluated for job performance.

- What are the criteria for evaluation?
- How often are they evaluated?
- How much importance does the store place on a buyer's or manager's merchandising skills versus his or her ability to work with people?
- For an associate, what action is taken if the person does not meet sales goals? Can goals be adjusted? Can associates be moved to another area or type of function?
- Do salespeople have quotas? If they do, how are they set?
- Do sales associates make a commission? If yes, how does the commission system work? What are the advantages and disadvantages of the system?
- If there is no commission system, are any incentive programs offered? Give an example of a specific program or project used by the store to boost employee morale and productivity.

3. GO SHOPPING Go to a store, observe the security measures in the store, and talk with the manager about the store's loss prevention program.

- Are there surveillance cameras? Where are they located?
- What is the store's policy against shoplifters?
- What are the procedures for approaching a suspected shoplifter?
- How are shoplifters handled?
- How are sales associates and executives involved in the security programs?
- Is employee theft a problem? Elaborate.
- How is employee theft prevented in the store?
- How is shrinkage prevented in the store?
- How is customer service related to loss prevention in the store?

4. INTERNET EXERCISE Go to http://www.hrreporter.com. *Canadian HR Reporter* is an online guide to human resources management. Each issue provides real-world solutions to HR situations. Find and summarize the conclusions of articles addressing the HR challenges that retailers are facing, such as the management of a diverse workforce, international expansion, and the use of technology to increase productivity.

5. INTERNET EXERCISE Go to a national chain retailer's website and find its employment application form for sales associate. Assess the form for experience, education, and references.

1. Describe the similarities and differences in the organization of small and large retail companies. Why do these similarities and differences exist?

2. How can national retailers such as Best Buy and LaSenza, which both use a centralized buying system, make sure that their buyers are aware of the local differences in consumer needs?

3. What are the positive and negative aspects of employee turnover? How can a retailer reduce the turnover in its sales associates?

4. To motivate employees, several major department stores are experimenting with incentive compensation plans. Frequently, compensation plans with a lot of incentives don't promote good customer service. How can retailers motivate employees to sell merchandise aggressively and at the same time not jeopardize customer service?

5. Three approaches to motivating and coordinating employee activities are policies and supervision, incentives, and organization culture. What are the advantages and disadvantages of each?

6. Why should retailers be concerned about the needs of their employees? What can retailers do to satisfy the needs of employees?

7. How do on-the-job training and classroom training differ? What are the benefits and limitations of each approach?

8. Give examples of a situation in which a manager of a McDonald's restaurant must use different leadership styles.

9. Job descriptions should be in writing so employees clearly understand what's expected of them. But what are the dangers of relying too heavily on written job descriptions?

10. What's the difference between extrinsic rewards and intrinsic rewards? What are the effects of these rewards on the behaviour of retail employees? Under what conditions would you recommend that a retailer emphasize intrinsic rewards over extrinsic rewards?

11. Many large department stores are changing their salespeople's reward system from a traditional salary to a commission-based system. What problems can incentive compensation systems cause? How can department managers avoid these problems?

12. When evaluating retail employees, some stores use a quantitative approach that relies on checklists and numerical scores. Other stores use a more qualitative approach that requires less time checking and adding and more time discussing strengths and weaknesses in written form. Which is the better evaluation approach? Why?

13. What are the different methods for compensating employees? Discuss which methods you think would be best for compensating a sales associate, store manager, and buyer.

14. In addition to competitive salary, vacation, and tuition reimbursement as a retailer's key retention strategies, in what other ways can a retailer optimize employee satisfaction?

15. Discuss how retailers can reduce shrinkage from shoplifting and employee theft.

CHAPTER FOURTEEN

Building customer loyalty: customer relationship management and service strategies

LEARNING OBJECTIVES

Lo1   Define customer relationship management.

Lo2   Examine how retailers determine who their best customers are.

Lo3   Explore how retailers can build customer loyalty and increase their share of wallet.

Lo4   Discuss how customer service can build a competitive advantage.

Lo5   Determine the types of activities a retailer undertakes to provide high-quality customer service.

Lo6   Review how retailers can recover from a service failure.

SPOTLIGHT ON RETAILING

LOYALTY PROGRAMS: BIG INFORMATION BUSINESS

Customer loyalty management has become a pivotal component of a retailer's strategy to maximize a customer's lifetime value. In order to achieve sustainable business growth, retailers know it is imperative to make shopping experiences enjoyable, with customer benefits and communications targeted so that customers want to return. Loyalty programs are often part and parcel of a comprehensive customer loyalty management strategy. A loyalty program is a structured and long-term marketing effort that provides incentives to repeat customers who demonstrate loyal buying behaviour.

The transactional part of a loyalty program—make a purchase, pick up points—is not what loyalty is about. Retailers want loyalty from their customers, but a lot of businesses have confused loyalty programs with points-based initiatives. The retailer gives the reward points in exchange for information. For example, it is the ability of the business to learn their customers' needs and wants and to tailor not just their merchandise to them, but also the retail experience.

Sophisticated databases compile information to help retailers refine their merchandising mix and marketing strategy to gain a bigger market share. Information is power, and thanks to the data amassed from loyalty programs, inquiring marketers know what music we listen to, what restaurants we prefer, and what brand names gain our loyalty. This valuable information allows the retailer to tailor its marketing programs to specific customer segments and to concentrate on profitable customers who will generate the most revenue. Retaining a current customer is far less costly than finding a new one. It is estimated that it costs ten times more for a company to attract a new customer. Only 12 to 15 percent of customers are loyal to a single retailer, according to the Center for Retail Management at Northwestern University. But that set of shoppers generates between 55 and 70 percent of company sales.

While retail loyalty programs have many purposes, the greatest value that is created for retailers is the ability to convert a faceless footfall into an identifiable customer and to measure and understand their individual behaviours. According to crmtrends.com, the basic benefits that form the basis of all loyalty program initiatives are the following:

© The Canadian Press.

- **Shift.** Acquire new customers.
- **Lift.** Increase the spending of existing customers.
- **Retention.** Improve the natural churn rate of customers.
- **Profit mix.** Shift spending to higher-margin products.

Hence, a winning loyalty program should enable customer acquisition, provide understanding of customer behaviour, increase customer spending, and enhance business profitability and customer service across various channels used by customers to interact with retailers, such as the store, Web, mobile, kiosk, and paper.

Canadian consumers are quite familiar with loyalty programs as Canada is among the most mature and developed loyalty markets in the world. There are 120 million loyalty program memberships in Canada, with 90 percent of Canadians belonging to at least one loyalty program (compared to 74 percent in the United States and, for global comparison, 42 percent in India). Canadian loyalty memberships are on the rise. Between 2012 to 2014, loyalty memberships were up 8.1 percent.

Even with growth, the loyalty industry in Canada is facing challenges that occur or that are similar to those in every mature marketplace. A plethora of options has made Canadian consumers even more selective about which programs they join and actually use. Canadian savvy, combined with a crowded market, means that retail loyalty programs must deliver much more relevance to attract and engage the Canadian consumer.

As the loyalty market has matured and grown, so too have the ways to earn rewards and the kinds of rewards that can be redeemed. In the past, Canadians based their purchasing decisions on value, price, and convenience. Today, consumers have shifted, to some extent, away from a desire for possessions to a desire for experiences. Overall, consumers are looking for the meaningful, which includes value, engagement, and relevance.

At Aeroplan, for instance, more than 90 percent of members collect miles for travel, says David Klein, vice-president, marketing and innovation. But to further serve its customers, in 2012, Aeroplan launched a digital media store where members can turn miles into media downloads, a loyalty industry first in Canada.

In February 2013, the AIR MILES for Social Change program added to its list of ways to earn rewards by partnering with the federal government and 15 YMCAs across Canada. The partnership enables families to earn AIR MILES reward miles in ways that encourage physical activity, such as registering their children for day camps, using participating fitness facilities, or buying YMCA memberships.

Other recent trends that inject an element of fun and engagement for members of loyalty programs involve the use of social media and gamification. Gamification is the application of game thinking and game mechanics—including points, badges, or similar incentives—in non-game contexts to affect behaviour. Companies of all kinds are finding ways to put the structures and rules of games to work in business; consider Air Canada's frequent flyer status levels, Shoppers Drug Mart Optimum points, and Canadian Tire money (both paper and digital).

Loblaws is integrating smartphone technology and sophisticated data collection and processing into its new PC Plus digital loyalty program. PC Plus offers a number of innovations, both for Loblaws and for its customers, such as cutting back on the cost and waste of paper flyers and offering customized deals that better match up with shoppers' actual buying habits. Loading offers to their PC Plus cards on their mobile devices allows members to earn points when they buy the qualifying items at participating Loblaws stores. Members also get bonus offers, flyer offers, and in-store offers to enjoy. The more offers they take advantage of, the more points they can earn: 1000 points is equivalent to $1. Once they accumulate 20 000 points, they can redeem $20 off of their grocery bill. It's a prime example of mobile, social gamification working today for a major Canadian company.

AIR MILES used gamification to kick start its location-based (mobile) loyalty partnerships with merchants. Its main challenge was getting members to "check-in" (visit) the retail operations of its partners with their AIR MILES app active on their mobile devices. By creating a contest among members to see who would visit the most partner locations, they leveraged gamification to get members engaged and help them understand the new programs.

The challenge for all loyalty programs is that people want to simplify their lives, to discard things that aren't absolutely essential. If a loyalty program does not maintain sufficient engagement with increasingly discerning customers and becomes only an extra card in the wallet, or an extra app on a mobile device, it will be dispensed.

Sources: Barbara Farfan, "Customer Loyalty Program," About.com, http://retailindustry.about.com/od/glossary/g/customerloyalty.htm (accessed July 2, 2013); Jeff Berry, "Lonely at the Top: The 2013 COLLOQUY Loyalty Census: Growth and Trends in Canadian Loyalty Program Action," COLLOQUY/a Loyalty One research group, July 2013; PostMedia News, "Canadians Find Value in Loyalty Programs," *Vancouver Sun*, April 11, 2013; "Harper Government Partners with Air Miles Reward Program and YMCAs in Canada to Promote Healthy Living," http://www.phac-aspc.gc.ca/media/nr-rp/2013/2013_0220-eng.php (accessed July 3, 2013); "New YMCA Partnership with Air Miles and the Government of Canada," http://www.ymca.ca/en/what's-new/new-ymca-partnership-with-air-miles-and-the-government-of-canada.aspx (accessed July 3, 2013); and Mark Hayes, "How to Use Gamification to Increase Sales," *Shopify*, May 30, 2013, http://www.shopify.com/blog/7988857-how-to-use-gamification-to-increase-sales#ixzz2ZVPCS1SL (accessed July 3, 2013).

Business press and companies are talking a lot about the importance of managing customer relationships. Companies are spending billions of dollars on computer systems to help them collect and analyze data about their customers. Putting customers at the centre of the business equation pays off in retail profits. Companies around the world are focusing on new and innovative ways to serve their customers.

Customer service is the activities and programs developed by retailers to make the shopping experience for their customers special. Customers base their evaluations of store service on their perceptions. Although these perceptions are affected by the actual service provided, service (due to its intangibility) is often hard to evaluate accurately. Five customer service characteristics that customers use to evaluate service quality are reliability, assurance, tangibility, empathy, and responsiveness.[1] Some cues that customers use to assess these service characteristics are the following:

- **Reliability.** Accuracy of billing, meeting promised delivery dates
- **Assurance (trust).** Guarantees and warranties, return policy
- **Tangibility.** Appearance of store, salespeople
- **Empathy.** Personalized service, receipts of notes and emails, recognition by name
- **Responsiveness.** Returning calls and emails, giving prompt service.

Employees can play an important role in customer perceptions of service quality.[2] Customer evaluations of service quality are often based on the manner in which store employees provide the service, not just the outcome. Consider the following situation: A customer goes to a store to return an electric toothbrush that isn't working properly. In one case, company policy requires the employee to ask the customer for a receipt, check to see if the receipt shows the toothbrush was bought at the store, examine the toothbrush to see if it really doesn't work properly, ask a manager if a refund can be provided, complete some paperwork, and finally give the customer the amount paid for the toothbrush in cash. In a second case, the store employee simply asks the customer how much he paid and gives him a cash refund. The two cases have the same outcome: The customer gets a cash refund. But the customer might be dissatisfied in

share of wallet
The percentage of total purchases made by a customer in a store.

the first case because the employee appeared not to trust the customer and took so much time providing the refund. In most situations, employees have a great effect on the process of providing services and, thus, on the customer's eventual satisfaction with the services.

Customer relationship management (CRM) is a business philosophy and set of strategies, programs, and systems that focus on identifying and building loyalty with a retailer's most valued customers. CRM is based on the philosophy that retailers can increase their profitability by building relationships with their better customers. By effectively managing merchandise inventory and adding services, stores provide extra value that supports the objective of building customer loyalty to increase their share of wallet. The goal of CRM is to develop a base of loyal customers who patronize the retailer frequently. In the following sections of this chapter, we discuss in more depth the objective of CRM programs and the elements in the CRM process.

Lo1 The CRM Process

Traditionally, retailers have focused their attention on encouraging customers to visit their stores, look through their catalogues, and visit their websites. To accomplish this objective, they have traditionally used mass media advertising and price promotions, treating all their customers the same. Now retailers are beginning to concentrate on providing more value to their best customers, using targeted promotions and services to increase their **share of wallet**—the percentage of the customers' purchases made from the retailer—with these customers. This change in perspective is supported by research indicating that it costs over six times more to sell products and services to new customers than to existing customers, and that small increases in customer retention can lead to dramatic increases in profits.[3]

What Is Loyalty?

Customer loyalty, the objective of CRM, is more than having customers make repeat visits to a retailer and being satisfied with their experiences and the merchandise they purchased. Customer loyalty to a retailer means that customers are committed to purchasing merchandise and services from the retailer and will resist the activities of competitors

When guests check into five-star hotels like the Ritz-Carlton, they are greeted by name. Their preferences are known based on past visits. Everything possible is done to meet their needs and wants.

© Jim Cummins/Getty Images.

attempting to attract their patronage. They have a bond with the retailer, and the bond is based on more than a positive feeling about the retailer.[4]

An early example of CRM in the retail Canadian market can be traced back to Harry Rosen. In fact, you could argue that Harry Rosen was a pioneer in CRM. In the 1950s, Harry would record the purchase information of his customers on cue cards. He then expected his sales force to familiarize themselves with these cards before future customer visits. This ensured the salesperson would provide the customer with a personalized shopping experience, long before the development of database software, computers, and a CRM process!

Loyal customers have an emotional connection with the retailer. Their reasons for continuing to patronize a retailer go beyond the convenience of the retailer's store or the low prices and specific brands offered by the retailer. They feel such goodwill toward the retailer that they will encourage their friends and family to buy from it.

Programs that encourage repeat buying by simply offering price discounts can be easily copied by competitors. In addition, these types of price promotion programs encourage customers to be always looking for the best deal rather than developing a relationship with one retailer. However, when a retailer develops an emotional connection with a customer, it is difficult for a competitor to attract the customer.[5]

All the elements of the retail mix contribute to the development of customer loyalty (Exhibit 14–1) and repeat-purchase behaviour. Customer loyalty can be enhanced by creating an appealing brand image and providing convenient locations, attractive merchandise at compelling prices, and an engaging shopping experience. However, personal attention is one of the most effective methods for developing loyalty. For example, many small, independent restaurants build loyalty by functioning as neighbourhood cafés, where waiters and waitresses recognize customers by name and know their preferences.

The report titled "2015 Colloquy Loyalty Census Canada" indicates that membership growth in Canada is on the rise (as shown in Exhibit 14–1) . Several industries of note, which are up since 2012, include: retail (up 12.3 percent); financial (up 6.5 percent); coalition (up 3.75 percent); and travel and other (up 1.7 percent).[7]

Harry Rosen sales associates will take new menswear collections to the offices of their busy loyal customers and provide personalized services

DID YOU KNOW?

In the United States, coalition loyalty programs are not very prevalent. The two most common coalition program in Canada are AIR MILES and Aeroplan.[6]

Exhibit 14–1

Loyalty Census Snapshot:
Canada, 2012–2015

Source: COLLOQUY, owned by LoyaltyOne, is a leading provider of loyalty marketing research, publishing and education.

for their styling and tailoring needs. Providing such memorable experiences is an important avenue for building customer loyalty.[8]

Overview of the CRM Process

Exhibit 14–2 illustrates that CRM is an iterative process that turns customer data into customer loyalty through four activities:

- collecting customer data
- analyzing the customer data and identifying target customers
- developing CRM programs
- implementing CRM programs

The process begins with the collection and analysis of data about a retailer's customers and the identification of target customers. The analysis translates the customer information into activities that offer value to the targeted customers. Then these activities are executed through communication programs undertaken by the marketing department and customer service programs implemented by customer contact employees, typically sales associates. Each of the four activities in the CRM process (Exhibit 14–2) is discussed in the following sections.

customer database
The coordinated and periodic copying of data from various sources, both inside and outside the enterprise, into an environment ready for analytical and informational processing. It contains all of the data the firm has collected about its customers and is the foundation for subsequent CRM activities; also called *customer data warehouse*.

Collecting Customer Data

The first step in the CRM process is constructing a **customer database**. This database, referred to as a *customer data warehouse*, contains all of the data the firms have collected about its customers and is the foundation for subsequent CRM activities.

Customer Database

Ideally, the database should contain the following information:

- **Transactions.** A complete history of the purchases made by the customer, including the purchase date, the price paid, the SKUs purchased, and whether the merchandise was purchased in response to a special promotion or marketing activity.

- **Customer contacts.** A record of the interactions that the customer has had with the retailer, including visits to the retailer's website, inquiries made through in-store kiosks, and telephone calls made to the retailer's call centre, plus information about contacts initiated by the retailer, such as catalogues and direct mail sent to the customer.

Customers' sales information is recorded at POS terminals, stored in data warehouses, and used in CRM systems.
© Don Mason/Corbis.

Exhibit 14–2
The CRM Process Cycle

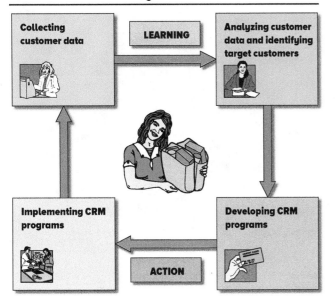

Collecting customer data → **LEARNING** → Analyzing customer data and identifying target customers → Developing CRM programs → **ACTION** → Implementing CRM programs →

- **Customer preferences.** What the customer likes, such as favourite colours, brands, fabrics, and flavours, as well as apparel sizes.
- **Descriptive information.** Demographic and psychographic data describing the customer that can be used in developing market segments.
- **Responses to marketing activities.** The analysis of the transaction and contact data provides information about the customer's responsiveness to marketing activities.

Different members of a household might have interactions with a retailer. Thus, to get a complete view of the customer, retailers need to be able to combine the individual customer data from each member of a household. For example, without these household-level data, a supermarket retailer might underestimate the importance of a household with several people who shop at the store.

The analysis of the customer database can provide important insights for planning merchandise assortment. For example, a supermarket chain sells over 300 types of cheese. Feta cheese ranked 295th in sales, which suggested it should not have a favourable position in the cheese department and might even be a candidate for elimination from the assortment. However, further analysis uncovered that feta cheese ranked 25th in sales for the supermarket's best customers.[10]

DID YOU KNOW?

The average Canadian has four loyalty program cards in their wallet, and 6 out of 10 choose loyalty programs that come free-of-charge.[9]

With today's technology, even small, independent retailers can create and use a customer database. For example, Gary Mead, a 34-year-old entrepreneur, uses his customer database to take on the giants: Domino's, Little Caesar's, and Pizza Hut. With a $2500 computer system, he keeps track of the purchase history of customers patronizing his restaurant. If customers don't order for 60 days, the system spits out a postcard with a discount to lure them back. Other promotions encourage customers to try all of the dishes offered by suggesting pasta dishes to pizza lovers. The database has 8500 customers in a town of 11 000; business has been increasing 25 to 30 percent each year.[11]

Loblaws unveiled a new loyalty program in May 2013 aimed at smartphone users. The PC Plus app lets customers collect points that can be redeemed for money off their grocery bill, create shopping lists, browse flyers, link recipes to shopping lists on the go, and receive personalized offers based on products that the system determines each customer wants, based on past purchase history. For shoppers who do not have a smartphone, the program is also available in card form. Both the card and the app are free. Loblaws spent two-and-a-half years developing PC Plus, which incorporates points from the supermarket chain's long-standing PC Financial credit card rewards program.[12] Retailing View 14.1 describes a British grocer's take on a similar customer-centric reward strategy.

Identifying Information

Constructing this database is relatively easy for catalogue and Internet shoppers and customers who use the retailer's credit card when buying merchandise in stores. Customers buying merchandise through non-store channels must provide their contact information (their name and address) so that the purchases can be sent to them. Since some retailers issue their own credit cards, they can collect the contact information for billing when

Frequent shopper cards are becoming so common that consumers cannot carry all of the cards in their wallets; key tags are an easy alternative.
David Wei/Alamy.

Tesco Uses Data Collected from Its Frequent-Shopper Program

Tesco, the largest supermarket chain in the United Kingdom and the third largest in the world, has been very effective at analyzing and exploiting the data it collects through its Clubcard frequent-shopper program. To encourage customers to enroll in the program, Tesco gives them points for every pound they spend in its stores, on its website, and at its gas stations. Customers who spend 25 pounds a week for 10 weeks get double points. The points are redeemed by reducing the shopping bill when customers check out.

In addition, customers can get more benefits by joining one of Tesco's clubs. For example, members of the Baby and Toddler Club get expert advice and exclusive offers to help them through the stages of parenting from pregnancy to childhood (tesco.com/babyclub). Members get discount coupons on baby essentials, a permit allowing them to park nearer to the store, and a free Pampers Hamper filled with baby items and special treats for the mother.

Analysis of the sales transactions identified six customer segments, such as the "Finer Foods" segment, which includes affluent, time-strapped shoppers who buy upscale products, and the "Traditional" segment, which represents shoppers who are homemakers and have time to cook meals. Unique marketing programs are developed for each of the segments.

Tesco frequently sends personalized coupon packages to Clubcard members. Some coupons are for products the customer normally buys, and others are for products that the retailer believes the customer would like to try. More than 1 million unique sets of coupons are distributed for each promotion. Between 15 and 20 percent of

Tesco uses retail analytics to alter its merchandise selection in stores, develop new products, and target specific customer groups.
Courtesy of Tesco Stores Limited.

the coupons are redeemed, compared with the industry average redemption rate of 1 to 2 percent.

Based on an analysis of the data, Tesco introduced "World Foods," which features Asian herbs and other ethnic food, into stores located in Indian and Pakistani neighbourhoods. However, when Tesco looked at the locations from which the customers travelled to buy the unique merchandise in these stores, it found that more than 25 percent of customers were coming from other neighbourhoods. This discovery led Tesco to add an assortment of World Foods to other stores.

Tesco also introduced a premium private-label brand, Tesco Finest, which includes duck pâté and premium wines and cheeses, because it discovered, through retail analytics, that its affluent customers were not buying wine, cheese, fruit, and other higher-priced–higher-margin items from Tesco.

Sources: Yan Ma, Jianxun Ding, and Wenxia Hong, "Delivering Customer Value Based on Service Process: The Example of Tesco.Com," *International Business Research 3,* no. 2 (2010), pp. 131–135; Andrew Smith and Leigh Sparks, "Reward Redemption Behaviour in Retail Loyalty Schemes," *British Journal of Management 20,* no. 2 (2008), pp. 204–218; http://www.Tesco.com (accessed July 1, 2010).

customers apply for the card. In these cases, the identification of the customer is linked to the transaction.

However, identifying most customers who are making in-store transactions is more difficult because they often pay for the merchandise with a debit card, cash, or a third-party credit card such as Visa and MasterCard. Common approaches that

store-based retailers use to overcome this problem are:

- asking customers for the identifying information
- offering loyalty card programs
- offering co-branded credit cards (e.g., Scotia Scene Visa, Walmart MasterCard, RBC Shoppers Optimum MasterCard)

Asking for Identifying Information Some retailers such as The Source, Nine West, and the Container Store have their sales associates ask customers for identifying information such as their phone number, name, postal code, and/or when they ring up a sale.[13] This information is then used to create the transaction database for the customer. However, this approach has two limitations. First, some customers may be reluctant to provide the information and feel that the sales associates are violating their privacy. Second, sales associates might forget to ask for the information or decide not to spend the time getting and recording it during a busy period.

Offering a Frequent Shopper Card A **frequent shopper program**, also called a **loyalty program**, is a program that identifies and provides rewards for customers who patronize a retailer. Some retailers issue customers a frequent shopper card, whereas others use a **private-label credit card**—a credit card that has the store's name on it—or a co-branded third-party credit card. In these cases, customer information is automatically captured when the card is scanned at the point of sale terminal. When customers enrol in one of these programs, they provide some descriptive information about themselves or their household and are issued a card with an identifying number. The customers then are offered an incentive to show the card when they make purchases from the retailer. Research has shown that customers generally prefer to get something extra—a reward—for their purchases, rather than lower prices.[14] Canadian consumers are more patient than their American counterparts. They are more willing to accumulate points and miles that yield free travel, in-store merchandise, or free reward catalogue redemptions. For example, a supermarket might offer frequent shoppers a point for every dollar spent in the store. The points can be redeemed for items in a gift catalogue or for free groceries. From the retailer's perspective, frequent shopper programs offer two benefits:

- Customers provide demographic and other information when they sign up for the program and then are motivated to identify themselves at each transaction.

- Customers are motivated by the rewards offered to increase the number of visits to the retailer and the amount purchased on each visit.

The major problems with using frequent shopper cards for identification are that the card is often squeezed out of the customer's wallet by other cards, the customer might forget to bring it to the store when shopping, or the customer might decide not to show it if he or she is in a hurry. Thus, retailers are recognizing that the optimal solution for interacting with today's customers will require a multichannel mix, including traditional media, direct mail, SMS, voice, email, and apps.[15] For instance, mobile applications can serve as a replacement for the traditional loyalty card or key fob, offering a new way to load, accrue, and redeem rewards (see Retailing View 14.2).

Founded in 1992, AIR MILES, Canada's premier coalition loyalty program, induces consumers to shop and collect air miles as a reward for loyalty to the retailer. Miles can be earned with purchases made at more than 120 stores as well as 100 more online retailers. The AIR MILES' databases compile information about customers and their shopping habits to assist retailers in tailoring merchandise and marketing strategies. According to Kelly Hlavinka of Colloquy Consulting, a loyalty consulting practice, AIR MILES accounts for a 70 percent penetration level among the nation's households. No such national coalition exists in the United States.[16]

Frequent flyer programs such as AIR MILES and Aeroplan are much more than simple loyalty programs. Both Aeroplan and AIR MILES are coalition programs because they have commercial partners. Aeroplan, for example, has more than 70 commercial partners in financial, retail, and travel sectors and makes money from the sale of its Aeroplan Miles to those commercial partners. Every time an Aeroplan member flies on Air Canada (partner), or uses a TD Aeroplan Visa (partner), or fills up a car with gas at an Imperial Oil (Esso) gas station (partner), the customer "earns" Aeroplan reward miles and the Aeroplan's commercial partners buy miles from Aeroplan. The partners are paying for the benefits of belonging and Aeroplan makes money on the spread between what

frequent shopper program A reward and communication program used by a retailer to encourage continued purchases from the retailer's best customers.

loyalty program A program set up to reward customers with incentives such as discounts on purchases, free food, gifts, or even cruises or trips in return for their repeated business.

private-label credit card A credit card that has the store's name on it and is issued by the retailer.

> **DID YOU KNOW?**
>
> On average, Americans now belong to 29 loyalty programs but are active, meaning they have had any sort of participation at all over the past year, in only 12 of those.[17]

Retailers Increase Focus on Mobile Applications to Enhance Customer Loyalty, Reveals IDC Retail Insights

As the retail industry begins to recover from economic instability, customer loyalty applications and CRM innovations become the key drivers of retailers' go-to-market strategies. In a 2011 report, IDC Retail Insights discussed why and how retailers are accessing their CRM technology and loyalty schemes to deliver an immersive shopping experience.

The study drew upon extensive IDC Retail Insights resources, including previous research and interviews with vendors and retail end users. A related IDC consumer survey on CRM and loyalty found that the top three customer expectations from loyalty programs include transparent management of loyalty programs, access to special services and personalized promotions, and access to a wider range of products matching personal preferences. These findings confirm retailers' attention toward integrating their current CRM with the latest technology innovations to enhance the overall customer experience and increase business benefits generated by loyalty.

Innovation is the basis of this retail transition, from traditional reward schemes to an omni-channel loyalty transparency. In order to address consumers' expectations and add value to the "earn points to redeem" schemes, it is imperative to look at loyalty management within its wider ecosystem. The report highlights that retailers must identify the right approach to implement innovative loyalty schemes.

For instance, multi-retailer loyalty schemes have become a successful example of partnership among several retailers. Key findings of this study show that:

- Loyalty is moving beyond points and discounts to become an integral part of a more encompassing customer experience that will support same-shopper sales and gain of market share to increase or recover competitive advantage.
- Omni-channel retailers use insights to identify and understand a core group of their most-valued customers. From there, they can predict what might motivate changes in shopping behaviour that will make them even more loyal.
- Mobile loyalty applications represent an element of innovation that meets customer's demand for real-time, profile-relevant, and location-based information. Along with existing mobile loyalty card apps, allowing customers to be recognized, receive more personalized offers, and earn points, "first mover" retailers are taking into consideration the current opportunities represented by near-field communication (NFC) technology, which enables contactless payments through mobile devices.

"The mobile targeted retailing and rewarding approach is most likely what customers expect from a leading customer-centric retailer," says Ivano Ortis, international head of IDC Retail Insights. "We believe that the ability to create and foster loyalty, enhanced by the delivery of new services, is the key issue for retailers to obtain repeated and long-term customer engagements. With better insight into demand dynamics and customer behaviour provided by loyalty applications, retailers can measure the real increase in customer retention, providing an opportunity to drive repeated, larger, and more profitable customer transactions. Retailers must choose the loyalty management applications that deliver higher flexibility, scalability, and responsiveness to optimize the customer experience."

Source: Adapted from "Retailers Increase Focus on Mobile Applications to Enhance Customer Loyalty, Reveals IDC Retail Insights," *International Data Group,* August 1, 2011, http://idg.com/www/pr.nsf/ByID/PKEY-8MAL7R.

it sells its points for and what it costs the program to buy the relevant reward. It also makes money by managing the rewards program for Air Canada. It further benefits from what is known in the industry as breakage, which is the estimated 17 percent of Aeroplan miles that will never be redeemed.[18]

Privacy and CRM Programs

Although detailed information about individual customers helps retailers provide more benefits to their better customers, consumers are concerned about retailers violating their privacy when they collect this information.

Privacy Concerns   The degree to which consumers feel their privacy has been violated depends on:

- their control over their personal information when engaging in marketplace transactions — Do they feel they can decide on the amount and type of information collected by the retailer?

- their knowledge of the collection and use of personal information — Do they know what information is being collected and how the retailer will be using it? Will the retailer be sharing the information with other parties?[19]

These concerns are particularly acute for customers using an electronic channel because many of them do not realize the extensive amount of information that can be collected without their knowledge. In addition to collecting transaction data, electronic retailers can collect information by placing cookies on visitor's hard drives.

Cookies are text files that identify visitors when they return to a website. Due to the data in the cookies, customers do not have to identify themselves and use passwords every time they visit a site. However, the cookies also collect information about other sites the person has visited and what pages they have downloaded.[20]

Protecting Customer Privacy   Canada's privacy law went into effect on January 1, 2004. The federal privacy legislation changed the way companies do business and how marketers collect, use, or disclose customer information in the course of a commercial activity within Canada. In order to be compliant with the legislation, organizations must appoint a privacy officer and implement detailed procedures to protect personal information. The *Privacy Act* is all about relationships with customers and employees and is based on ten principles for the protection of personal

DID YOU KNOW?

Research from SAS has found that nearly three-quarters of Canadians expect that, when they give a company personal information, such as their age, email address, income, or birth date, the company will use that information to tailor promotions to them personally.[21]

cookies Computer text files that identify visitors when they return to a website so that customers do not have to identify themselves or use passwords every time they visit the site. Cookies also collect information about other sites the person has visited and what pages have been downloaded.

Sears provides a detailed description of its privacy policy on its website.
Used with permission of Sears Canada, Inc.

information. The Canadian Marketing Association outlines the basic principles:

1. *Accountability*—An organization will be responsible for ensuring that personal information in its possession, including information that has been transferred to a third party for processing, is secure and that the third party is compliant with the law.

2. *Identifying purposes*—How you plan to use customer data must be identified at the time of, or prior to, collection of the individual's information. If you want to use information already collected for a new purpose, you will have to identify the new purpose to your customer and obtain new consent.

3. *Consent*—You must have consent for the collection, use, or disclosure of personal data.

4. *Limiting collection*—If you make marketing lists available to third parties, you will have an obligation to ensure that you have obtained consent from consumers prior to passing their personal information on to third parties. You will also need to keep records of having received that consent.

5. *Limiting use, disclosure, and retention*—If you are using customer data as part of your marketing activities, you can retain this information as long as the individual is an active customer, or for the length of the marketing campaign.

6. *Accuracy*—Marketers are obligated to keep personal information on consumers as accurate and up-to-date as possible.

7. *Safeguard security*—All those who are involved in the transfer, rental, sale, or exchange of mailing lists are responsible for protecting the data and taking appropriate measures to ensure against unauthorized access.

data mining Technique used to identify patterns in data found in data warehouses, typically patterns that the analyst is unaware of prior to searching through the data.

8. *Openness*—Organizations should undertake to develop privacy policies, train staff on the company's privacy practices, and make information available to the public concerning their privacy policy.

9. *Individual access*—Marketers will need to make customers' personal information available upon their request.

10. *Challenging compliance*—Marketers will be required to establish formal inquiry and complaint-handling procedures and make this known to consumers who enquire.

The Canadian Standards Association has developed an electronic resource, "The Privacy Code: A Matter of Privacy —Understanding and Applying the New Canadian Privacy Law," for any organization that needs assistance in making a smooth transition toward privacy law compliance.[22]

In summary, there is growing consensus that personal information must be fairly collected; the collection must be purposeful; and the data should be relevant, maintained as accurate, essential to the business, subject to the rights of the owning individual, kept reasonably secure, and transferred only with the permission of the consumer. To address these concerns, many retailers that collect customer information have privacy policies. They must clearly state what information is collected from each visitor and how it will be used, give consumers a choice as to whether they give information, and allow them to view and correct any personal information held by an online retail site. Retailers using an electronic channel must also ensure that consumer information is held securely and is not passed on to other companies without the permission of the customer.[23]

Lo2 Analyzing Customer Data and Identifying Target Customers

The next step in the CRM process is analyzing the customer database and converting the data into information that will help retailers develop programs for building customer loyalty. Data mining is one approach commonly used to develop this information. **Data mining** is a technique used to identify patterns in data, typically patterns that the analyst is unaware of prior to searching through the data. For example, Eddie Bauer uses predictive modelling to decide who receives specialized mailings and catalogues. Each year, Eddie Bauer features an outerwear special, and—thanks to data mining—it can determine which customers are most likely to buy it. Data mining allows Eddie Bauer to determine seasonal buying habits as well. Then the company can identify people with similar characteristics who don't normally buy outerwear and target them with mailings to bring them into the store or encourage them to buy from the catalogue. As a result, customer spending has increased by 30 to 50 percent annually.[24]

Market basket analysis is a specific type of data analysis that focuses on the composition of the basket, or bundle, of products purchased during a single shopping occasion. This analysis is often useful for management in suggesting where to place merchandise in a store. For example, based on market basket analyses, Fortinos changed the traditional location of several items. For example:

- Since bananas are the most common item in grocery carts, Fortinos Supercentres sell bananas next to the corn flakes as well as in the produce section.

- Kleenex tissues are in the paper-goods aisle and also mixed in with cold medicine.

- Measuring spoons are in housewares and also hanging next to baking supplies such as flour and Crisco shortening.

- Flashlights are in the hardware aisle and also with a seasonal display of Halloween costumes.

Identifying Market Segments

Traditionally, customer data analysis has focused on identifying market segments—groups of customers who have similar needs, purchase similar merchandise, and respond in a similar manner to marketing activities. For example, when Eddie Bauer analyzed its customer database, it discovered two types of shoppers. One group it calls "professional shoppers"—people who love fashion and value good customer service. The other group it calls "too busy to shop people"—people who want the shopping experience over as quickly as possible. The professional shoppers tended to use the alteration service, call the customer service desk, and seek out the same salesperson when they made purchases in the stores. On the other hand, the people too busy to shop typically shop from the catalogue and website. Eddie Bauer uses this information to develop unique advertising programs targeting each of these segments.

Eddie Bauer also discovered that morning shoppers are more price-sensitive and like to buy products on sale more than evening shoppers. Evening shoppers tend to be in the professional shopper segment. Using this information, Eddie Bauer installed electronic window posters in some test stores that allow different images to be displayed at different times of the day. In the morning, the displays feature lower-priced merchandise and items on sale; in the evening, the more expensive and fashionable merchandise is displayed.[25]

Home Depot realized that 70 to 80 percent of its kitchen renovation department was coming from 20 to 30 percent of the department's customers.[26] It speculated that these heavy spenders might spend even more if it organized the department around meeting their needs. It knew that heavy-spenders want lots of choices and information. So it added more assortment, better-trained associates, a computer-aided design system, and suites of innovative kitchen layouts arranged so that customers could readily sense what their kitchen would look like after a renovation. The results—higher sales and profit per square foot than traditional departments designed to satisfy all customers.

market basket analysis Specific type of data analysis that focuses on the composition of the basket (or bundle) of products purchased by a household during a single shopping occasion.

lifetime customer value (LTV) The expected contribution from the customer to the retailer's profits over his or her entire relationship with the retailer.

Identifying Best Customers

Using information in the customer database, retailers can develop a score or number indicating how valuable the customers are to the firm. This score can then be used to determine which customers to target.

Lifetime Value   A commonly used measure to score each customer is called lifetime customer value. **Lifetime customer value (LTV)** is the expected contribution from the customer to the retailer's profits over his or her entire relationship with the retailer.

LTV is estimated by using past behaviours to forecast future purchases, gross margin from these purchases, and costs associated with servicing the customers. Some of the costs associated with a customer are the cost of advertising and promotions used to acquire the customer and the cost of processing merchandise that the customer has returned. Thus, a customer who purchases $200 on groceries from a supermarket every other month would have a lower LTV for the supermarket than a customer who buys $30 on each visit and shops at the store three times a week. Similarly, a customer who buys apparel only when it's on sale in a department store would have a lower LTV than a customer who typically pays full price and buys the same amount of merchandise.

These assessments of LTV are based on the assumption that the customer's future purchase behaviours will be the same as they have been in the

DID YOU KNOW?

In 1906, Italian economist Vilfredo Pareto created a mathematical formula to describe the unequal distribution of wealth in his country. He observed that 20 percent of the people owned 80 percent of the wealth. In the late 1940s, Dr. Joseph M. Juran inaccurately attributed the 80–20 Rule to Pareto, calling it Pareto's Principle. While it may be misnamed, Pareto's Principle, or Pareto's Law as it is sometimes called, can be a very useful tool to help retailers manage effectively.[27]

past. Sophisticated statistical methods are typically used to estimate the future contributions from past purchases. For example, these methods might consider how recently purchases have been made. The expected LTV of a customer who purchased $600 on one visit six months ago is less than the LTV of a customer who has been purchasing $100 of merchandise every month for the last six months. Go to http://customerlife-timevalue.co/ to calculate what the LTV of a consumer could be!

Customer Pyramid Most retailers realize that their customers differ in terms of their profitability or LTV. In particular, they know that a relatively small number of customers account for the majority of their profits. This realization is often called the **80–20 rule**— 80 percent of the sales or profits come from 20 percent of the customers. Thus, retailers could group their customers into two groups based on the LTV scores. One group would be the 20 percent of the customers with the highest LTV scores, and the other group would be the rest. However, this two-segment scheme, "best" and "rest," does not consider important differences among the 80 percent of the customers in the "rest" segment.[28]

A commonly used segmentation scheme divides customers into four segments, illustrated in Exhibit 14–3. This scheme allows retailers to develop more appropriate strategies for each of the segments. Each of the four segments is described below.

- **Platinum segment.** This segment is composed of the retailer's customers with the top 25 percent of LTVs. Typically, these are the most loyal customers who are not overly concerned about merchandise price and place more value on customer service.

- **Gold segment.** The next 25 percent of the customers in terms of their LTV make up the gold

80–20 rule A general management principle stating that 80 percent of the sales or profits come from 20 percent of the customers.

Exhibit 14–3
The Customer Pyramid

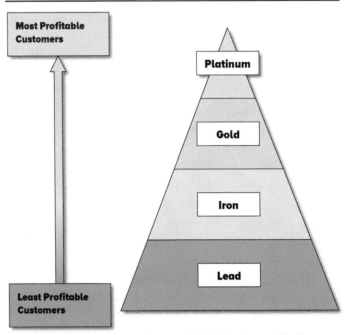

Source: Valerie Zeithaml, Roland Rust, and Katherine Lemon, "The Customer Pyramid: Creating and Serving Profitable Customers," *California Management Review* 43 (Summer 2001), p. 124. Reprinted with permission.

segment. These customers have a lower LTV than platinum customers because they are more price-sensitive. Even though they buy a significant amount of merchandise from the retailer, they are not as loyal as platinum customers and probably patronize some of the retailer's competitors.

- **Iron segment.** Customers in this third tier probably do not deserve much special attention from the retailer due to their modest LTV.

- **Lead segment.** Customers in the lowest segment can cost the company money. They often demand a lot of attention but do not buy much from the retailer. For example, real estate agents often encounter people who want to spend their weekends looking at houses but are really not interested in buying one.

The segmentation scheme described above differs from the segments of passengers in airline frequent flyer programs because it is based on LTV rather than miles flown. Thus, it recognizes that some customers who fly a lot of miles might be taking low-cost flights, whereas other customers, although flying the same number of miles, might be much more profitable because they fly first class and don't seek discount fares.

Another common segment scheme, called **decile analysis**, breaks customers into ten deciles according to their LTV rather than the quartiles illustrated above. When using decile analysis, the 10 percent of the customers with the highest LTV would be in the top.

RFM Analysis RFM (recency, frequency, monetary) analysis, often used by catalogue retailers and direct marketers, is a scheme for segmenting customers according to how recently they have made a purchase, how frequently the y make purchases, and how much they have bought. Exhibit 14–4 is an example of an RFM analysis done by a catalogue apparel retailer that mails a catalogue each month to its customers.

The catalogue retailer divides its customers into 32 groups or segments based on how many orders the customer has placed during the last year, how much merchandise the customer has purchased, and the last time the customer placed an order. Each segment is represented by one cell in Exhibit 14–4. For example, the customers in the upper-left cell have made one or two purchases in the last year, made a purchase within the last two months, and purchased less than $50 of merchandise.

Catalogue retailers often use this type of analysis to determine which customer groups should be sent catalogues. For each of the RFM groups, they will determine the percentage of customers in the group who made a purchase from the last catalogue sent to them. For example, 5 percent of the customers in the upper-left corner of

Exhibit 14–4 placed an order from the last catalogue sent to them. With information about the response rate of each cell and the average gross margin from orders placed by customers in the cell, the catalogue retailer can calculate the expected profit from sending catalogues to the customers in each cell. For example, if the average gross margin from orders placed by customers in the upper-left cell is $20 and the cost of sending a catalogue to customers in the cell is $0.75, the company would make $0.25 per customer from each catalogue mailed to the customers in the cell.

$$\$20.00 \text{ contribution} \times 0.05 \text{ response}$$
$$= \$1.00 \text{ expected contribution} - \$0.75 \text{ cost}$$
$$= \$0.25 \text{ per customer}$$

RFM analysis is basically a method of estimating the LTV of a customer using recency, frequency, and monetary value of past purchases. Exhibit 14–5 illustrates how RFM can be used for developing customer target strategies.

Customers who have made infrequent, small purchases recently are considered to be first-time customers. The objective of CRM programs directed toward this segment of customers is to convert them

decile analysis A method of identifying customers in a CRM program that breaks customers into ten deciles based on their LTV (lifetime customer value). When using decile analysis, the top 10 percent of the customers would be the most-valued group.

RFM (recency, frequency, monetary) analysis Often used by catalogue retailers and direct marketers, a scheme for segmenting customers based on how recently they have made a purchase, how frequently they make purchases, and how much they have bought.

Exhibit 14–4
RFM Analysis for a Catalogue Retailer

| Frequency | Monetary | RECENCY | | | |
		0–2 months	3–4 months	5–6 months	Over 6 months
1–2	<$50	5.0%*	3.5%	1.0%	0.1%
1–2	Over $50	5.0	3.6	1.1	0.1
3–4	<$150	8.0	5.0	1.5	0.6
3–4	Over $150	8.8	5.0	1.7	0.8
5–6	<$300	10.0	6.0	2.5	1.0
5–6	Over $300	12.0	8.0	2.7	1.2
Over 6	<$450	15.0	10.0	3.5	1.8
Over 6	Over $450	16.0	11.0	4.0	2.0

*Percentage of customers in the cell who made a purchase from the last catalog mailed to them.

Source: Reprinted by permission of Harvard Business School Press. Adapted from Robert Blattberg, Gary Getz, and Jacquelyn Thomas, *Customer Equity: Building and Managing Relationships as Valuable Assets* (Boston: Harvard Business School Press, 2001), p. 18. Copyright © 2001 by the Harvard Business School Publishing Corporation; all rights reserved.

Exhibit 14-5
RFM Target Strategies

Frequency	Monetary	RECENCY			
		0–2 months	3–4 months	5–6 months	Over 6 months
1–2	<$50	First-time customers		Low-value customers	
1–2	Over $50				
3–4	<$150	Early repeat customers		Defectors	
3–4	Over $150				
5–6	<$300	High-value customers		Core defectors	
5–6	Over $300				
Over 6	<$450				
Over 6	Over $450				

Source: Reprinted by permission of Harvard Business School Press. Adapted from Robert Blattberg, Gary Getz, and Jacquelyn Thomas, *Customer Equity: Building and Managing Relationships as Valuable Assets* (Boston: Harvard Business School Press, 2001), p. 18. Copyright © 2001 by the Harvard Business School Publishing Corporation; all rights reserved.

into early repeat customers and eventually high-value customers. CRM programs directed toward customers in the high-value segment (high frequency, recency, and monetary value) attempt to maintain loyalty, increase retention, and gain a greater share of wallet by selling more merchandise to them. On the other hand, customers who have not purchased recently either have low lifetime value and are not worth pursuing or are committed to another retailer and may be difficult to recapture. CRM programs designed to realize these objectives are discussed in the following section.

Lo3 Developing CRM Programs

Having segmented customers according to their future profit potential, the next step in the CRM process (see Exhibit 14–2) is to develop programs for the different customer segments. In the following sections, we discuss programs retailers use for retaining their best customers, converting good customers into high-LTV customers, and getting rid of unprofitable customers.

Customer Retention

Retailers use four approaches to retain their best customers:

* frequent shopper programs
* special customer services
* personalization
* community

Frequent Shopper Programs As mentioned previously, frequent shopper programs are used both to build a customer database by identifying customers with transactions and to encourage repeat purchase behaviour and retailer loyalty.[30] Retailers provide incentives to encourage customers to enroll in the program and use the card. These incentives are either discounts on purchases made from the retailer or points for every dollar of merchandise purchased. The points are then redeemable for special rewards. Some recommendations concerning the nature of the rewards offered are outlined in Exhibit 14–6.

Canadian Tire money is Canada's oldest loyalty program. The Canadian Tire Advantage loyalty card and key fob, which was rolled out in early 2012, offers customers 1 percent back, or one point per dollar, on the value of purchases. Those using the new card in conjunction with the company's proprietary credit card, the Options MasterCard, accrue three points for every dollar spent. The rate for the iconic Canadian Tire paper money is 0.4 percent. Rob Shields, senior vice-president of marketing, claims that the company would not be phasing out the paper-based program: "It is highly emotional [and] has terrific

> **DID YOU KNOW?**
>
> "Only 8 percent of consumers in a loyalty program feel they are actually receiving better offers as a result of sharing their personal details."[29]

> **DID YOU KNOW?**
>
> Only 13 percent of retail executives feel that frequent shopper programs are effective at building customer relationships.[31]

Exhibit 14-6
Recommendations for Frequent Shopper Reward Programs

Tiered Rewards should be tiered according to the volume of purchase to motivate customers to increase the level of their purchases. These tiers can be based on individual transactions or cumulative transactions. For example, HBC Points Card and Shoppers Optimum Program reward customers with cumulative points based on dollars spent. Customers generally accept the idea that people who spend more should receive greater rewards.

Offer Choices Not all customers value the same rewards. Thus, the most effective frequent shopper programs offer customers choices. For example, Coles Myer, a leading Australian retailer, originally offered customers air miles but shifted to a menu of rewards when it discovered that many customers did not value air miles. Tesco, a U.K. supermarket chain, lets customers cash in points for special discounts on entertainment, vacation packages, or sporting events. Sainsbury, a competitor, allows customers to use their points for vouchers that can be used to make purchases at a variety of retail partners such as British Gas.

Non-monetary incentives are very attractive to some customers. For example, Holt Renfrew offers loyal customers the opportunity to attend by-invitation-only special shopping events, a Sotheby auction, or an underwater expedition to see the *Titanic*.

Some retailers link their frequent shopper programs to charitable causes. For example, Target donates 1 percent of all purchases charged to Target's Guest Card to a program that benefits local schools. Although these altruistic rewards can be an effective part of a frequent shopper program, such incentives probably should not be the focal point of the program. Research indicates that the most effective incentives benefit the recipient directly, not indirectly, as is the case with charitable contributions.

Reward All Transactions To ensure the collection of all customer transaction data and encourage repeat purchases, programs need to reward all purchases, not just purchases of selected merchandise.

Transparency and Simplicity Customers need to be able to quickly and easily understand when they will receive rewards, what the rewards are, how much they have earned, and how they can redeem the points they have accumulated. The ground rules need to be clearly stated. There should be no surprises or confusion.

VIP Options Some customers are willing to pay a upfront load fee to have access to additional benefits. Amazon prime is an example of this. The consumer pays $79.00 Canadian to have a free two-day shipping option and also early access to deals (30 minutes sooner than other consumers).

Sources: Frank Badillo, *Customer Relationship Management* (Columbus, OH: Retail Forward, 2001); Stephan Butscher, *Customer Clubs and Loyalty Programmes* (Aldershot, Hampshire: Ashgate Publishing, Limited, 2002); Amazon.ca, https://www.amazon.ca/gp/prime/pipeline/landing?ie=UTF8&ref_=nav_logo_prime_join (accessed June 14, 2016).

brand presence and brand link and the tangible nature some people just love." He notes that while many customers are still attached to using the "money" coupons, they want more convenient options and to collect rewards through different platforms. The new program "really complements the credit card more than the paper base," he said. "From a customer standpoint, the value creation for them is very good."[32] A more complex loyalty program was required to better position the growing company against existing competitors and the arrival of new competitors. The new card program provides Canadian Tire much-needed data that other companies, such as Hudson's Bay, Petro-Canada, and Shoppers Drug Mart, have been mining for years.

Before the launch of the new program in 2012, Canadian Tire knew only about its credit card customers; everybody else was anonymous to them. "Loyalty programs are the most ubiquitous way that a retailer can actually start to understand who their customers are, how different they are, and [to] segment them," says Shields. "As a universal loyalty program across all tenders, we are [now] going to be capturing upwards of 70 percent of our transactions on a known customer basis."[33]

While Canadian Tire money was the most-loved loyalty program in Canada a decade ago, the *Major Markets Retail Survey* from KubasPrimedia found that AIR MILES was the top loyalty program in Canada in 2011, with 79 percent of survey respondents enrolled in it. Canadian Tire was tied for second place with HBC Rewards, at 56 percent, followed by Shoppers Optimum at 54 percent and Aeroplan at 44 percent.[34]

Shoppers Drug Mart's Optimum loyalty card program has approximately 10 million active card holders and rewards shoppers with 10 points for every dollar spent. Shoppers Optimum also offers a credit card backed by the Royal Bank of Canada. The marketing information derived from the cards' data banks allows Shoppers Drug Mart to recognize the significant differences among Canadian regions and cater to customers' unique circumstances and buying habits in each area and as unique individuals. In July 2013, Loblaw Companies announced it had reached a deal to buy Shoppers Drug Mart in a stock-and-cash deal valued at $12.4 billion. The deal brings together the country's largest grocer with Canada's largest pharmacy chain.[35]

Loblaw would not say how many customers it has in its points program, but said that when it launched its new PC Plus points program in 2013, it had a target of reaching about 15 million customers, which will be helped by the large base of Optimum members. Of particular value to Loblaw would be the customer database of Optimum customers in Quebec, where Shoppers runs its Pharmaprix stores and Loblaw has a smaller presence.[36]

Four factors limit the effectiveness of frequent shopping programs:

1. They can be expensive. For example, a 1 percent price discount can cost large retailers over $100 million a year. In addition, for a large retailer, the launch and maintenance investment (store training, marketing, fulfillment support, and information technology and systems costs) can be as high as $30 million. Annual maintenance costs can reach $5 million to $10 million when marketing, program support, offer fulfillment, customer service, and IT infrastructure costs are figured in. Then there are the marketing support costs needed to maintain awareness of the program.[37]

2. It is difficult to make corrections in programs when problems arise. Programs become part of the customer's shopping experience. Customers must be informed about even the smallest changes in programs. They react negatively to any perceived "take away" once a program is in place, even if they are not actively involved in it. The more successful the program, the greater the customer reaction to changes made by the retailer, and these negative reactions reduce customer trust and loyalty to the retailer.

3. It is not clear that these programs increase customer spending behaviour and loyalty toward the retailer.[38] For example, 48 percent of the customers enrolled in frequent shopper programs with supermarkets indicated they had spent more with the retailer than they would have if the program were not offered, but only 18 percent of customers enrolled in programs with apparel retailers indicated that the program increased spending.[39]

4. Perhaps most important, it is difficult to gain a competitive advantage based on frequent shopper programs. Since the programs are so visible, they can be easily duplicated by competitors. For example, Tesco and Safeway, two large supermarket chains in the United Kingdom, got into a loyalty card war. They played a game of "can you top this," which benefited their customers but reduced their profits until Safeway closed down its program.[40]

To avoid this problem, retailers are offering benefits to their best customers that are more personalized, based on their unique knowledge of the customer, and thus less visible to competitors. (See Retailing View 14.3 for a discussion of a health-driven loyalty partnership.)

Special Customer Services Retailers provide unusually high-quality customer service to build and maintain the loyalty of platinum customers. For example, the top-tier customers get calls from service reps several times a year for "a friendly chat" and get an annual call to wish them happy holidays. Due to these special services, the retention rates for top customers have increased 50 percent.

Sometimes these special services are very subtle. For example, at the retailer's website, only top-tier customers get the option to click on an icon that connects them to a live service agent for a phone conversation. Other customers never see this icon. When service reps bring up a customer's account, coloured squares flash on their computer screens. Green means the caller is a profitable customer and should be granted waivers and other special treatment. Reds are unprofitable customers who get no special treatment.[41]

Personalization An important limitation of CRM strategies developed for market segments, such as a platinum segment in the customer pyramid (Exhibit 14–3) or early repeat customers in the RFM analysis (Exhibit 14–4), is that each segment is composed of a large number of customers who are not identical. Thus, any strategy will be most appealing to only the typical customer in the segment, and not as appealing to the majority of customers in the segment. For example, customers in the platinum segment with the highest LTVs might include a 25-year-old single woman who has quite different needs than a 49-year-old working mother with two children.

With the availability of customer-level data and analysis tools, retailers can now economically offer unique benefits and target messages to individual customers. They now have the ability to develop programs for small groups of customers and even specific individuals. For example, a Harry Rosen salesperson can search the company's customer database, identify

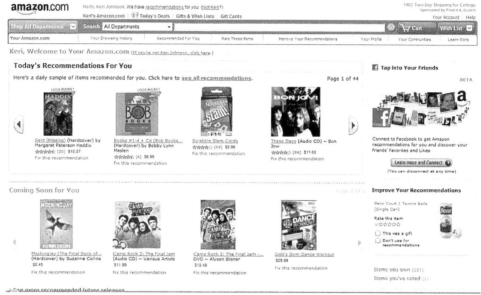

Amazon.com provides personalized recommendations based on past purchases.
Courtesy of Amazon.com.

customers who have bought Hugo Boss suits in the past, and send them an email informing them of the shipment of new suits that just arrived in the store. Developing retail programs for small groups or individual customers is referred to as **1-to-1 retailing**.

Many small, local retailers have always practised 1-to-1 retailing. They know each of their customers, greet them by name when they walk in the store, and then recommend merchandise they know the customers will like. These local storeowners do not need customer databases and data mining tools; they have the information in their heads. But most large retail chains and their employees do not have this intimate knowledge of their customers. Thus, the CRM process enables larger retailers to efficiently develop relationships similar to those that many small local retailers have.

The Internet channel provides an opportunity for retailers to automate the practice of 1-to-1 retailing. When registered customers log on to Amazon.com, the first page they see is personalized for them. Their name is displayed in a greeting, and products are displayed based on an analysis of their past purchase behaviour. For example, if a customer has bought mystery novels from Amazon.com in the past, the latest books from mystery book authors they have bought are presented.

These personalized rewards or benefits that customers receive are based on unique information possessed by the retailer and its sales associates. This information in the retailer's customer database cannot be accessed or used by competitors. Thus, it provides an opportunity to develop a sustainable competitive advantage.

The effective use of this information creates the positive feedback cycle in the CRM process. Increasing repeat purchases with a retailer increases the amount of data collected from the customer, which enables the retailer to provide more personalized benefits that in turn increase the customer's purchases from the retailer.

Retailing View 14.1 (earlier in this chapter) examined how U.K.-based Tesco uses the information collected through its Club card program to target promotions and tailor assortments in its stores to preferences of customers in the store's trading area. Mobile can also effectively connect members to on-the-go information, such as updated program information, program news, points accumulation, and reward announcements. Two examples of popular and successful loyalty programs that are multi-faceted and have efficiently blended multiple channels in one communication are Starbucks and Cineplex-Scene.

Community A fourth approach to building customer retention and loyalty is to develop a sense of community among customers. The Internet channel offers an opportunity for customers to exchange information using bulletin boards and to develop more personal relationships with each other and the retailer. By participating in such a community,

1-to-1 retailing
Developing retail programs for small groups or individual customers.

AIR MILES for Social Change—Rewards Motivate Canadians to be Healthy

Today's not-for-profit organizations are becoming more creative in their approaches to foster change and deliver against their mission. And AIR MILES for Social Change has proven that pairing change-driving initiatives with a rewards program can lead to unprecedented success. Canada's Heart and Stroke Foundation (HSF) is a case in point.

Background. According to the Heart and Stroke Foundation, nine out of ten Canadians have a risk factor for heart disease and stroke, and the incidence of these conditions is increasing at an alarming rate. To help combat these statistics, HSF partnered with AIR MILES for Social Change, rewarding Canadians with AIR MILES reward miles for participating in the following initiatives:

- Healthy Living mobile app
- Blood Pressure Action Plan
- E-tools such as risk assessment, online support, donations
- Heart Smart family e-newsletter
- Heart and Stroke Foundation lottery prize

Organizational challenges. HSF is one of the largest charities in Canada and has achieved significant results in advocacy, research, and education. HSF wanted to increase that impact by driving education and behaviour change with the Canadian population directly.

While many Canadians know they should reduce their risks for heart disease and stroke, only a small segment does so in a committed way. Only a third of Canadians eat five or more servings of vegetables and fruits a day, and 50 percent are physically inactive. Almost one-third of Canadian children are overweight or obese. As a result, 250 000 potential years of life are lost to these diseases.

Organizational objectives. To address the issue of consumer motivation, HSF clearly defined its goals for each initiative.

Mobile app objectives:

- Drive app downloads to build an installed user base.
- Empower Canadians with information and support to reduce risk of heart disease and stroke.

Blood Pressure Action Plan objectives:

- Equip Canadians aged 50 and over with tools to help them achieve and manage a healthy blood pressure.

E-tools objectives:

- Increase completions of the HSF "My Risk Assessment" and sign-ups for the HSF "My eSupport."
- Attract donations to HSF.

Heart Smart e-newsletter objectives:

- Drive online sign-ups.
- Provide practical, inspiring heart-healthy info, tips, and recipes for Canadian parents.

Heart and Stroke Foundation lottery objectives:

- Add more choice to prize options.

The engagement. AIR MILES for Social Change was called on to help HSF achieve all of these objectives

Source: Material copyright of LoyaltyOne, Inc.

---

customers become reluctant to leave the "family" of other people patronizing the retailer.

For example, in addition to offering merchandise for sale, a sporting goods retailer could provide an opportunity for organizers of local sporting events to post information about these events on its website. The volunteers organizing youth soccer and baseball leagues and tennis and golf tournaments could provide information about meetings and game dates, times, and places. Then the retailer could collect information about the participants in local leagues and offer discounts to encourage the teams to buy their uniforms and equipment and facilitate their transactions.

Converting Good Customers into Best Customers

In the context of the customer pyramid (Exhibit 14–3), increasing the sales made to good customers is referred to as *customer alchemy*—converting iron and gold customers into platinum customers.[42] Customer alchemy involves offering and selling more products and services to existing customers by incentivizing the population through tangible rewards. AIR MILES for Social Change is a division of the AIR MILES Reward Program, Canada's leading coalition loyalty program, which boasts more than two-thirds of Canadian households as members. Coalition loyalty programs reward members with miles for shopping at a variety of merchants. The miles can be redeemed for travel, merchandise, or cash discounts at the point of sale.

AIR MILES for Social Change designed an incentive-based offering specific to each of the foundation's initiatives.

- **Mobile app.** In 2012, users could earn 25 reward miles by downloading the app and completing setup.
- **Blood Pressure Action Plan.** In 2012, participants earned 20 reward miles for signing up.
- **E-tools.** In 2011, participants earned 10 reward miles for completing the HSF risk assessment and registering for the My Health eSupport tool. Donors earned 5 to 30 reward miles, based on donation levels.
- **Heart Smart e-newsletter.** In 2012, 20 reward miles were offered at sign-up.
- **Heart and Stroke Lottery.** In 2012, early-bird ticket purchasers were given the chance to win either $30 000 cash or 200 000 reward miles. Plus, 40 000 prize winners could choose to win a 325 AIR MILES reward miles bonus card. Almost 9 percent of all prize winners chose AIR MILES reward miles as their prize, surpassing the goal of 7 percent.

Proven solutions. The results for each initiative's program exceeded all expectations, including:

- Mobile apps experienced over 9000 successful completions and downloads in a four-week period. The

number of downloads after the launch of the first email was 13 times higher than before.

- Over 14 000 people signed up for the Blood Pressure Action Plan in the month of November, nearly all of which were AIR MILES collectors. This initiative exceeded the campaign goal by 281 percent.
- In the first four-and-a-half days, the partnership drove more e-tool risk assessment completions than HSF marketing had achieved in the preceding two-and-a-half years. An e-tool donation offer also drove a significant number of new, high-value donors to HSF.
- The Heart Smart e-newsletter had more than 31 000 sign-ups in four months, exceeding expectations.

Conclusions. The following conclusions were drawn as a result of the initiative:

- New marketing tools, such as a popular reward program targeting loyal members, can extend the power of an organization's existing communications initiatives.
- As a proven motivator for behavioural change, offering the right rewards can incentivize people to try a new activity, even if it requires effort or commitment.
- By offering the right reward via the right channels, an organization can also educate and attract new cash donors and new participants in fundraising efforts.

Going forward, AIR MILES for Social Change and the Heart and Stroke Foundation are continuing to grow the partnership, evolving from test-and-learn tactical programs toward long-term sustainable behaviour change solutions. And when it comes to health, sustainable change is the best reward of all.

---

and increasing the retailer's share of wallet with these customers. For example, Tesco, the U.K. supermarket chain, added a second tier to its frequent shopper program to increase share of wallet.

The first tier has a traditional design to gather customer data. The second tier, targeted at its better customers, is more innovative. Customers earn a "key" when they spend US$38 or more in a single transaction. Fifty keys make the customer a "keyholder," 100 keys a "premium keyholder." When customers achieve these higher levels, they get discounts on popular entertainment events, theatre

tickets, sporting events, and hotel vacations. The key program seeks to convert iron and gold customers into platinum customers. In the four years since starting the key program, Tesco has raised its market share from 13 percent to more than 17 percent.

The retailer's customer database reveals opportunities for cross-selling and add-on selling.

Cross-selling is selling a complementary product or service in a specific transaction,

cross-selling When sales associates in one department attempt to sell complementary merchandise from other departments to their customers.

add-on selling Selling additional new products and services to existing customers, such as a bank encouraging a customer with a chequing account to also apply for a home improvement loan from the bank.

near-field communications (NFC) A set of standards for smartphones and similar devices to establish radio communication with each other by touching them together or bringing them into close proximity, usually no more than a few inches.

SoLoMo (social, local, and mobile) The convergence of collaborative, location-based, and on-the-go technologies.

gamification The application of game theory concepts and techniques to non-game activities.

such as selling a customer a printer when he or she has decided to buy a computer. For example, a supermarket chain has a frequent shopper program, called the Gold Card program, for its best customers. When Gold Card member Debra Onsager enters the store, she "swipes" her card at a kiosk, and a high-speed printer provides a personalized shopping list with up to 25 deals. The deals offered are based on Debra's purchase history. If Debra's history shows she frequently purchases corn chips but does not buy dip, she will get a deal on bean dip printed on her shopping list to encourage her to try a new product. If she passes up the deal this time in the market, the next time the value of the bean dip coupon will be automatically increased.

Add-on selling is selling additional new products and services to existing customers, such as a supermarket chain that explored the opportunity to offer dry cleaning services in its supermarkets. To determine the stores and customers that would find this new service appealing, it looked through its customer database for households with two-income professionals, 25 to 35 years old, who sought one-stop shopping, as indicated by purchases of cosmetics, hosiery, and prepared meals.[43] Oprah Winfrey also builds add-on sales for her offerings through a strong emotional bond with her target market.

Predictive analytics can help create cross-sell and up-sell opportunities at the point of sale. For example, Loblaw's PC Plus program can make recommendations to members not only on their individualized purchase behaviour, but also on what other users with similar tastes have purchased and presumably enjoyed. The program will even create a grocery list and send recipes to the member's smartphone based on current promotions for that specific member. Harry Rosen associates use mobile CRM to provide real-time personalized service in-store and to update clients on new clothing items and events that match their specific interests.

In addition to these real-time recommendations, retailers can integrate other technologies into their loyalty programs, such as near-field communications or intelligent SoLoMo applications, as well as allow customers to use their smartphones to pay for purchases or redeem coupons.

Near-field communications (NFC) is a set of standards for smartphones and similar devices to establish radio communication with each other by touching them together or bringing them into close proximity, usually no more than a few inches. Present and anticipated applications include contactless transactions, data exchange, and simplified setup of more complex communications such as Wi-Fi.[44]

SoLoMo (social, local, and mobile) is the convergence of collaborative, location-based, and on-the-go technologies. SoLoMo applications allow advertisers to push notifications to potential customers who are geographically nearby. Examples of SoLoMo apps include Foursquare, AroundMe, and Yelp. Many of these services incorporate some aspects of gamification to encourage member retention.

Gamification is the application of game theory concepts and techniques to non-game activities. Generally speaking, the overarching goal of gamification is to engage participants with an activity they find fun in order to influence their behaviour. In marketing, a gamification initiative might address the cognitive and emotional aspects of game theory as well as the social ones by including a system of rules for participants to explore through active experimentation and discovery, awarding points or badges for levels of participation, displaying leaderboard scores to encourage competition, and offering prizes so that participants have a chance to win something of value.[45]

Dealing with Unprofitable Customers

In many cases, the bottom tier of customers actually have negative LTV. Retailers actually lose money on every sale they make to these customers. For example, catalogue retailers have customers who repeatedly buy three or four items and return all but one of them. The cost of processing two or three returned items is much greater than the profits coming from the one item that the customer kept. The process of no longer selling to these unprofitable customers can be referred to as "getting the lead out," in terms of the customer pyramid.[46] Two approaches for getting the lead out are offering less costly approaches for satisfying the needs of lead customers, and charging the

Getting the Lead Out

One source of unprofitable customers is the practice of fraudulent returns, which costs retailers more than $15 billion each year. Some examples of these costly returns include people who buy a large-screen television for their Super Bowl party and then return it after the game, or who buy an expensive dress for a special occasion and return it after they wear it once. Professional returners even use the Internet to make money on fraudulent returns. Some people steal merchandise from a store, return it for credit slips, and then turn the credit slips into cash by selling them at a discount on eBay or other online auction sites.

Retailers like The Limited and Best Buy are fighting back against such high-tech fraud with high-tech defences. Limited Express's return policy says consumers have up to 60 days to return items. However, the company's return policy also notes that it uses an industrywide service operated by Return Exchange to authorize returns and that "under certain circumstances we reserve the right to deny returns." Return Exchange, based in Irvine, California, analyzes Limited Express's customer database and identifies customers who have an unusually high propensity for returning merchandise. When these customers return merchandise, the POS terminal generates a slip of paper that says "RETURN DECLINED," and the sales associate tells the customer to call the toll-free number at the bottom for more information.

Best Buy is undertaking a strategy to focus on gold and platinum customers and get rid of lead customers. To lure high spenders, it is providing more effective customer service. To discourage undesirable customers, it is reducing promotions that tend to draw them into the store

and removing them from direct marketing lists. The trickiest challenge may be to deter bad customers without turning off good ones.

Best Buy's campaign against undesirable customers pits it against dozens of websites such as FatWallet.com, SlickDeals.net, and TechBargains.com that trade electronic coupons and tips from former clerks and insiders, hoping to gain extra advantages against the stores. At SlickDeals.net, whose subscribers boast about techniques for gaining hefty discounts, a visitor recently bragged about his practice of shopping at Best Buy only when he thinks he can buy at below the retailer's cost.

Best Buy cannot bar undesirable customers from its stores, but it is taking steps to put a stop to their most damaging practices. It is enforcing a restocking fee of 15 percent of the purchase price on returned merchandise. To discourage customers who return items with the intention of repurchasing them at a "returned merchandise" discount, it is experimenting with reselling returned merchandise over the Internet, so the goods don't reappear in the store where they were originally purchased. Best Buy also cut ties to FatWallet.com, an online "affiliate" that had collected referral fees for delivering customers to Best Buy's website.

Rejecting customers is a delicate business. Filene's Basement was criticized on television and in newspapers for asking two Massachusetts customers not to shop at its stores because of their frequent returns and complaints. Best Buy's CEO apologized in writing to students at a Washington, D.C., school after employees at one store barred a group of black students while admitting a group of white students.

Sources: Jennifer Davis, "Retailers Use Technology to Thwart Would-Be Thieves," *San Diego Tribune*, June 13, 2007; http://www.fashionera.com/Trends_2006/2006_spring_fashion_trends_returns_consumer_fraud.htm (accessed September 20, 2007); http://www.oracle.com/applications/retail/mom/retail-returns-management.html (accessed September 20, 2007).

customers for the services they are abusing. (See Retailing View 14.4.)

Implementing CRM Programs

Increasing sales and profits from the CRM programs is a challenge. For example, according to a study, 52 percent of the retailers surveyed indicated that they were engaged in some type of data mining, but 76 percent of those retailers undertaking

data mining indicated that the activity had made no contribution to the bottom line.[47]

This experience of retailers emphasizes that effective CRM requires more than appointing a manager of CRM, installing a computer system to manage and analyze a customer database, and making speeches about the importance of customers. The effective implementation of CRM programs requires the close coordination of activities by different functions in a retailer's organization. The MIS

Exhibit 14–7

Services Offered by Retailers

Acceptance of credit cards	Display of merchandise	Presentations on how to use merchandise
Alterations of merchandise	Dressing rooms	Provisions for customers with special needs (wheelchairs, translators)
Assembly of merchandise	Extended store hours	Repair services
ATM terminals	Facilities for shoppers with special needs (physically challenged)	Rest rooms
Bridal registry	Gift wrapping	Return privileges
Cheque cashing	Layaway plans	Rooms for checking coats and packages
Child care facilities	Parking	Shopping carts
Credit	Personal assistance in selecting merchandise	Signage to locate and identify merchandise
Delivery to home or work	Personal shoppers	Special orders
Demonstrations of merchandise	Play areas for children	Warranties

department needs to collect, analyze, and make the relevant information readily accessible to employees implementing the programs—the front-line service providers and sales associates and the marketers responsible for communicating with customers through impersonal channels (mass advertising, direct mail, and email). Store operations and human resource management need to hire, train, and motivate the employees who will be using the information to deliver personalized services.

Most retailers are product-centric, not customer-centric. Typically, there is no area of a retail firm organized by customer type—responsible for delivering products and services to types of customers. Perhaps in the future, retailers will have market managers to perform this coordinating function.

Lo4 Customer Service

Customer service is the set of activities and programs undertaken by retailers to make the shopping experience more rewarding for their customers. These activities increase the value customers receive from the merchandise and services they purchase. All employees of a retail firm and all elements of the retailing mix provide services that increase the value of merchandise.

For example, employees in the distribution centre contribute to customer service by making sure that the merchandise is in stock. The employees responsible for store design contribute by

customer service The set of retail activities that increase the value customers receive when they shop and purchase merchandise.

increasing the customer's convenience in getting to the store and finding merchandise and making shopping an enjoyable experience.

Exhibit 14–7 lists some of the services provided by retailers and/or shopping centres. Most of these services encourage customers to choose a specific retailer to buy products and services. Services, such as alterations and the assembly of merchandise, actually change merchandise to fit the needs of a specific customer. Some of these services are derived from the retailer's store design or website or from policies established by the retailer. However, this part of the chapter focuses on some of the most important personalized services provided by sales associates interacting directly with customers.

In the next section, we discuss retailers' opportunities to develop strategic advantage through customer service. Then we examine how retailers can take advantage of this opportunity by providing high-quality service.

DID YOU KNOW?

The word *service* is from the Latin term *servus*, meaning "slave."[48]

Strategic Advantage through Customer Service

Good service keeps customers returning to a retailer and generates positive word-of-mouth communication, which attracts new customers.[49]

Providing high-quality service is difficult for retailers. Automated manufacturing makes the quality of most merchandise consistent from item to item. But the quality of retail service can vary dramatically from store to store and from salesperson to salesperson within a store. It's hard for retailers to control the performance of employees who provide the service. A sales associate may provide good service to one customer and poor service to the next customer.

In addition, most services provided by retailers are intangible—customers can't see or touch them. Clothing can be held and examined, but the assistance provided by a sales associate or an electronic agent can't. Intangibility makes it hard to provide and maintain high-quality service because retailers can't count, measure, or check service before it's delivered to customers.

The challenge of providing consistent high-quality service provides an opportunity for a retailer to develop a sustainable competitive advantage. For example, Holt Renfrew devotes much time and effort to developing an organizational culture that stimulates and supports excellent customer service. Competing department stores would like to offer the same level of service but find it hard to match Holt Renfrew's performance.[50]

Customer Service Strategies

Customization and standardization are two approaches retailers use to develop a sustainable customer service advantage. Successful implementation of the customized approach relies on the performance of sales associates or the degree to which customer interactions can be customized using an electronic channel. The standardization approach relies more on policy, procedures, and store and website design and layout.[51]

Customization Approach The customization approach encourages service providers to tailor the service to meet each customer's personal needs.[52] For example, sales associates in specialty stores help individual customers locate appropriate apparel and accessories.

DID YOU KNOW?

Based on an American Express survey, "78 percent of consumers have bailed on a transaction or not made an intended purchase because of a poor service experience."[53]

Harry Rosen Does Customer Service Excellence in customer service is nothing new to Harry Rosen Inc. Known for delivering unprecedented levels of personalized service to its customers, the company's sales today account for nearly 40 percent of the high-end menswear market in Canada. Building on existing wireless technology, the retailer worked with Hewlett-Packard (HP) partner Technology Solutions International (TSI) to implement a wireless, Microsoft Windows–based solution on HP handheld devices. The retailer equipped all sales associates with the ability to access customer data and product preference information while on the sales floor, and gave managers insight into real-time sales data, so they could deliver consistent, excellent customer service to every customer entering the store—whether or not they had an appointment. Using the HP iPAQ hw6955 makes it easier to be able to figure out what the consumer wants, even if they aren't sure what they are looking for! This system enables sales representatives to stay engaged with consumers on the floor during the sales process. This is critical as it does not interrupt the flow of a sales presentation by having to physically leave the client to locate sales information on a different device.[54]

The customized approach typically results in most customers' receiving superior service. But the service might be inconsistent because service delivery depends on the judgment and capabilities of the service providers. Some service providers are better than others, and even the best service providers can have a bad day. In addition, providing the customized service is costly since it requires more well-trained service providers or complex computer software.

Standardization Approach The **standardization approach** is based on establishing a set of rules and procedures and ensuring they are implemented consistently. By strict enforcement of these procedures, inconsistencies in the service are minimized. For example, through standardization, customers receive the same food and service at McDonald's restaurants across the globe. The food may not be exactly what customers want, but it's consistent and served in a timely manner at a low cost.

Store or website design and layout also play an important role in the standardization approach. In many situations, customers don't need the services employees provide. They know what they want to buy,

DID YOU KNOW?

Shopping carts were first introduced in 1937 in a Humpty Dumpty store in Oklahoma City.[55]

standardization approach An approach used by retailers to provide customer service by using a set of rules and procedures so that all customers consistently receive the same service.

Customer Service at IKEA

IKEA is a global furniture retailer based in Sweden. Its concept of service differs from that of the traditional furniture store. The typical furniture store has a showroom displaying some of the merchandise sold in the store. Complementing the inventory are books of fabric swatches, veneers, and alternative styles that customers can order. Salespeople assist customers in going through the books. When the customer makes a selection, an order is placed with the factory, and the furniture is delivered to the customer's home in six to eight weeks. This system maximizes customization, but the costs are high.

In contrast, IKEA uses a self-service model based on extensive in-store displays. At information desks in the store, shoppers can pick up a map of the store, plus a pencil, order form, clipboard, and tape measure. After studying the catalogue and displays, customers proceed to a self-service storage area and locate their selections using codes copied from the sales tags. Every product available is displayed in over 70 room-like settings throughout the 19 000 square-foot warehouse store. Thus, customers don't need a decorator to help them picture how the furniture will go together. Adjacent to the display room is a warehouse with ready-to-assemble furniture in boxes that customers can pick up when they leave the store.

IKEA effectively uses a self-service method to provide customer service through signage and information in displays and on the merchandise.
© Getty Images.

Although IKEA uses a "customers do it themselves" approach, it does offer some services that traditional furniture stores do not, such as in-store child-care centres and information about the quality of the furniture. Toddlers can be left in a supervised ballroom filled with 50 000 brightly coloured plastic balls. There are changing rooms in each store, complete with bottle warmers and disposable diaper dispensers. Displays cover the quality of products in terms of design features and materials, with demonstrations of testing procedures.

Sources: John Kelly, "A Good Place by Design," *Washington Post*, December 23, 2004, p. C13; Mike Duff, "Late-Blooming IKEA U.S. Wears 20 Well," *DSN Retailing Today*, September 6, 2004, pp. 6–9.

---

and their objective is to find it in the store and buy it quickly. In these situations, retailers offer good service by providing a layout and signs that enable customers to locate merchandise easily, by having relevant information in displays, and by minimizing the time required to make a purchase.[56]

Retailing View 14.5 shows how IKEA uses a standardized, self-service approach with some unique elements.

Cost of Customer Service As indicated previously, providing high-quality service, particularly customized service, can be very costly. For over 100 years, the Savoy Hotel in London maintained a special place in the hearts of the world's elite. Maids switched off vacuum cleaners when greeting guests entering the hallway in the morning. Each floor had its own waiter on duty from 7 AM to 3 PM. Guests could get cotton sheets instead of the standard Irish linen sheets if they wished. Preferred fruits were added to the complementary fruit bowl in each room. Rooms were personally furnished for customers who regularly had extended stays at the hotel. At times, the hotel staff moved the customers' furniture, including personal pictures, from storage into their rooms when they arrived.

But this high level of personal attention is very costly to provide. The Savoy employed about three people for each of its 200 rooms, about double the average for a hotel. These services resulted in annual losses, and the hotel was eventually sold to a corporation that eliminated some of the services.

In many cases, however, good customer service can actually reduce costs and increase profits. A study by Andersen Consulting estimates that it costs 5 to 15 times more to acquire a new customer than to generate repeat business from present customers, and a 5 percent increase in customer retention can increase profits by 25 to 95 percent.[57] Thus, it costs a business much less to keep its existing customers satisfied and sell more merchandise to them than it does to sell to people who aren't buying from the business now.

Returns Rethink

Some people are admittedly shopaholics, which, when mixed with an indecisive nature, is disastrous for many retailers. These are the people who buy something one week, often wearing or using it, and expect to return it the next. These shoppers believe that anything is—and should be—returnable. Some customers may take advantage of a liberal return policy believing that the retailer wants the customer to be happy at any cost.

Harry Rosen has always upheld a policy of unconditional satisfaction for customers. They will even take back a well-worn, two-year-old suit if the customer becomes unhappy with it. The rationale: It's a way to bond with the customer and reinforce the relationship in a positive way. But many stores are taking a harder stance toward returns. The Gap now gives customers with a receipt 90 days (no receipt required if purchased with a credit card) to claim a full cash refund or exchange. New technology enabling customers to buy and burn their own copies caused HMV Canada to terminate its "no questions asked" policy, which used to include cash back for open CDs. The Retail Council of Canada concludes that a tougher position on returns can improve a retailer's profit by as much as 2 percent.[60]

Retailers need to consider the costs and benefits of service policies. For example, many retailers are reconsidering their "no questions asked" return policy. Home Depot's policy was to take back all merchandise and give cash back. Now, if customers don't have a receipt, they can get only a store credit. If they have a receipt, they can get cash back. With some consumer electronics products, customers must pay a 15 percent restocking charge for returned merchandise. Retailers are seeing too many big-screen TVs coming back the day after the Super Bowl, and too many prom dresses coming back the day after prom night.[61]

The easy return policy is an important selling feature for department stores. Customers will put up with a lack of other services, but the return policy is an established expectation and changing this liberal policy is difficult. Hudson's Bay allows a 30-day period for a cash refund with a receipt, after which a store credit is considered. The eagerness to please is also apparent at Sleep Country Canada, which offers a "comfort guarantee" that allows customers to return mattresses within 60 days. Despite many problems with returned merchandise, retailers strive to ensure many happy returns—for both sides of a sale. Remember that it is more cost-effective to keep a customer than to find a new one.

DID YOU KNOW?

According to a National Retail Federation consumer survey, one out of every three gift recipients (38 percent) returned at least one item during the 2014 holiday season.[59]

DID YOU KNOW?

About 8 percent of all merchandise purchased in stores is returned.[58]

Best Buy has tightened its return policies to help dissuade the least profitable customers who abuse return privileges.

© AP Photo/Janet Hostetter.

Lo5 Customer Evaluation of Service Quality

When customers evaluate retail service, they compare their perceptions of the service they receive with their expectations. Customers are satisfied when the perceived service meets or exceeds their expectations. They are dissatisfied when they feel the service falls below their expectations.[62]

Role of Expectations

Customer expectations are based on a customer's knowledge and experiences.[63] For example, customers do not expect to get an immediate response to a letter or even a telephone call, but they expect to get a response to an email the next time they turn on their computer.

Technology is dramatically changing the ways in which customers and firms interact. Customers now can interact with companies through automated voice response systems and place orders and check on delivery through the Internet. But customers still expect dependable outcomes, easy access, responsive systems, flexibility, apologies, and compensation when things go wrong. In other words, they still want good service. Now they just expect this level of service even when people are not involved.[64]

Expectations vary depending on the type of store. Customers expect a supermarket to provide convenient parking, to be open from early morning to late evening, to have a wide variety of fresh and packaged food that can be located easily, to display products, and to offer fast checkout. They don't expect the supermarket to have store employees stationed in the aisle to offer information about groceries or how to prepare meals. On the other hand, when these same customers shop in a specialty store, they do expect the store to have knowledgeable salespeople who can provide information and assistance.

Since expectations aren't the same for all types of retailers, a customer may be satisfied with low levels of actual service in one store and dissatisfied with high service levels in another store. For example, customers have low service expectations for self-service retailers such as discount stores and supermarkets. Walmart provides an unusual service for a discount store: An employee stands at the entrance to each store, greeting customers and answering questions. Because this service is unexpected in a discount store, customers evaluate Walmart's service positively, even though the actual level of service is far below that provided by a typical specialty store.

Department stores have many more salespeople available to answer questions and provide information than Walmart does. But customer service expectations are also higher for department stores. If department store customers can't locate a salesperson quickly when they have questions or want to make a purchase, they are dissatisfied.

When retailers provide unexpected services, they build a high level of customer satisfaction, referred to as *customer delight*.[65] Some examples of unexpected positive service experiences include the following:

- A restaurant sends customers who have had too much alcohol to drink home in a taxi and then delivers their car in the morning.
- A men's store sews numbered tags on each garment so that the customer will know what goes together.
- A gift store keeps track of important customer dates and suggests appropriate gifts.

Customer service expectations vary around the world. Although Germany's manufacturing capability is world renowned, its poor customer service is also well known. People wait years to have telephone service installed. Many restaurants do not accept credit cards, and customers who walk into stores near closing time often receive rude stares. Customers typically have to bag merchandise they buy themselves. Because Germans are unaccustomed to good service, they don't demand it. But as retailing becomes global and new foreign competitors enter, German retailers are becoming more concerned.

On the other hand, the Japanese expect excellent customer service. In Canada, it's said that "the customer is always right." In Japan, the equivalent expression is *okyakusama ha kamisama desu*, "the customer is God." When a customer comes back to a store to return merchandise, he or she is dealt with even more cordially than when the original purchase was made. Customer satisfaction isn't negotiable. The customer is never wrong! Even if the customer misused the product, retailers feel they were responsible for not telling the customer how to use it properly. The first person in the store who

service gap The difference between customers' expectations and perceptions of customer service, assessed in order to improve customers' satisfaction with their service.

knowledge gap The difference between customer expectations and the retailer's perception of customer expectations. This factor is one of four factors identified by the gaps model for improving service quality.

standards gap The difference between the retailer's perceptions of customers' expectations and the customer service standards it sets. This factor is one of four factors identified by the gaps model for improving service quality.

delivery gap The difference between the retailer's service standards and the actual service provided to customers. This factor is one of the four factors identified by the gaps model for improving service quality.

communication gap The difference between the actual service provided to customers and the service promised in the retailer's promotion program. This factor is one of the four factors identified by the gaps model for improving service quality.

hears about the problem must take full responsibility for dealing with the customer, even if the problem involved another department.

The Gaps Model for Improving Retail Service Quality

The gaps model (see Exhibit 14–8) indicates what retailers need to do to provide high-quality customer service.[66] When customers' expectations are greater than their perceptions of the delivered service, customers are dissatisfied and feel the quality of the retailer's service is poor. Thus, retailers need to reduce the **service gap** (the difference between customers' expectations and perceptions of customer service) to improve customers' satisfaction with their service.

Four factors affect the service gap:

1. **Knowledge gap**: The difference between customer expectations and the retailer's perception of customer expectations.

2. **Standards gap**: The difference between the retailer's perceptions of customers' expectations and the customer service standards it sets.

3. **Delivery gap**: The difference between the retailer's service standards and the actual service provided to customers.

4. **Communication gap**: The difference between the actual service provided to customers and the service promised in the retailer's promotion program.

These four gaps add up to the service gap. The retailer's objective is to reduce the service gap by reducing each of the four gaps. Thus, the key to improving service quality is to:

- understand the level of service customers expect
- set standards for providing customer service
- implement programs for delivering service that meets the standards
- undertake communication programs to accurately inform customers about the service offered by the retailer

Exhibit 14–8
Gaps Model for Improving Retail Service Quality

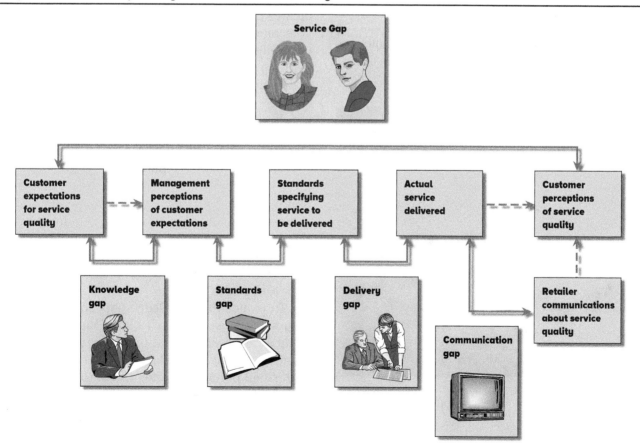

The following sections describe these gaps and methods for reducing them.

Knowing What Customers Want: Closing The Knowledge Gap

The most critical step in providing good service is to know what the customer wants. Retailers often lack accurate information about what customers need and expect. This lack of information can result in poor decisions. For example, a supermarket might hire extra people to make sure the shelves are stocked so that customers will always find what they want, but it may fail to realize that customers are most concerned about waiting at the checkout line. From the customer's perspective, the supermarket's service would improve if the extra employees were used to open more checkout lines rather than to stock shelves.

Retailers can reduce the knowledge gap and develop a better understanding of customer expectations by undertaking customer research, increasing interactions between retail managers and customers, and improving communication between managers and employees who provide customer service.

DID YOU KNOW?

80 percent of North Americans are willing to share personal information with companies if it means getting more personal service while shopping.[67]

The first step in providing good customer service is understanding customer expectations. This sales associate is conducting a survey to assess customer expectations.

Blend Images/Alamy.

Researching Customer Expectations and Perceptions

Market research can be used to better understand customers' expectations and the quality of service provided by a retailer. Methods for obtaining this information range from comprehensive surveys to simply asking some customers about the store's service.

DID YOU KNOW?

Only 39 percent of consumers surveyed say they would complain to the store manager if they received poor service.[68]

Gauging Satisfaction with Individual Transactions Another method for doing customer research is to survey customers immediately after a retail transaction has occurred. For example, Sears employees who deliver and assemble furniture in homes ask customers to complete a short survey describing how helpful, friendly, and professional the employees were. Airlines periodically ask passengers during a flight to evaluate the ticket-buying process, flight attendants, in-flight service, and gate agents.

Customer research on individual transactions provides up-to-date information about customers' expectations and perceptions. The research also indicates the retailer's interest in providing good service. Since the responses can be linked to a specific encounter, the research provides a method for rewarding employees who provide good service and correcting those who exhibit poor performance.

Focus Groups Rather than surveying many customers, retailers can use focus groups of eight to 12 customers to gain insights into expectations and perceptions. For example, store managers might meet three times a year for one-and-a-half to two hours with a select group of customers who are asked to provide information in a focus group about their experiences in the stores and to offer suggestions for improving service. The participants are rewarded with food and merchandise or money for their time and effort.

To reduce the knowledge gap, some managers may select customers who have made large and small purchases; they call these customers and ask them what they like and don't like about the store. With small purchasers, they probe to find out why the customers didn't buy more. Could they find everything they wanted? Did they get the assistance they expected from store employees?

Some retailers have consumer advisory boards composed of a cross-section of their preferred customers. Members of the board complete questionnaires three to four times a year on subjects such as holiday shopping problems, in-store signage, and service quality. In exchange for their input, members receive gift certificates. Restaurants and retailers often ask for comments regarding service.

Interacting with Customers Owner–managers of small retail firms typically have daily contact with their customers and thus have accurate first-hand information about them. In large retail firms, managers often learn about customers through reports, so they miss the rich information provided by direct contact with customers.

Stanley Marcus, founder of Neiman Marcus department stores, feels managers can become addicted to numbers and neglect the merchandise and customers. He uses suspenders as an example of how buyers can make poor decisions by only looking at the numbers. Originally, suspenders came in two sizes: short and long. By analyzing the numbers, buyers realized they could increase turnover by stocking one-size-only suspenders. The numbers looked good, but the store had a lot of dissatisfied customers. With only one size, short men's pants fell down, and the fit was uncomfortable for tall men. "It comes back to the fact that the day is still only 24 hours long, and if you're a retailer, you've still got to spend some of those 24 hours with your customers and your products. You can't allow the computer to crowd them out as crucial sources of information."[69]

Customer Complaints Complaints allow retailers to interact with their customers and acquire detailed information about their service and merchandise. Handling complaints is an inexpensive means of isolating and correcting service problems.[70]

Although customer complaints can provide useful information, retailers can't rely solely on this source of market information. Typically, dissatisfied customers don't complain. To provide better information on customer service, retailers need to encourage complaints and make it easy for customers to provide feedback about their problems. For example, some retailers set up a complaint desk in a convenient location where customers can get their problems heard and solved quickly.

Feedback from Store Employees Salespeople and other employees in regular contact with customers often have a good understanding of customer service expectations and problems. This information will improve service quality only if the employees are encouraged to communicate their experiences to high-level managers who can act on it.

Some retailers regularly survey their employees, asking questions such as:

- What is the biggest problem you face in delivering high-quality service to your customers?
- If you could make one change in the company to improve customer service, what would it be?

Using Customer Research

Collecting information about customer expectations and perceptions isn't enough. The service gap is reduced only when retailers use this information to improve service. For example, store managers should review the suggestions and comments made by customers daily, summarize the information, and distribute it to store employees and managers.

Feedback on service performance needs to be provided to employees in a timely manner. Reporting the July service performance in December makes it hard for employees to reflect on the reason for the reported performance.

Finally, feedback must be prominently presented so that service providers are aware of their performance.

Setting Service Standards: Closing The Standards Gap

After retailers gather information about customer service expectations and perceptions, the next step is to use this information to set standards and develop systems for delivering high-quality service. Service standards should be based on customers' perceptions rather than internal operations. For example, a supermarket chain might set an operations standard of a warehouse delivery every day to each store. But frequent warehouse deliveries may not result in more merchandise on the shelves or improve customers' impressions of shopping convenience.

To close the standards gap, retailers need to:

- commit their firms to providing high-quality service
- develop innovative solutions to service problems
- define the role of service providers
- set service goals
- measure service

Commitment to Service Quality

Service excellence occurs only when top management provides leadership and demonstrates commitment. Top management must be willing to accept the temporary difficulties and even the increased costs associated with improving service quality. This commitment needs to be demonstrated to the employees charged with providing the service. For example, the L.L. Bean website includes the following definition of *customer*:

What is a customer?

A customer is the most important person ever in this company–in person or by mail.

A customer is not dependent on us, we are dependent on him.

A customer is not an interruption of our work, he is the purpose of it.

We are not doing a favor by serving him, he is doing us a favor by giving us the opportunity to do so.

A customer is not someone to argue or match wits with. Nobody ever won an argument with a customer.

A customer is a person who brings us his wants. It is our job to handle them profitably to him and to ourselves.[71]

Top management's commitment sets service quality standards, but store managers are the key to achieving those standards. Store managers must see that their efforts to provide service quality are noticed and rewarded. Providing incentives based on service quality makes service an important personal goal. Rather than basing bonuses only on store sales and profit, part of store managers' bonuses should be determined by the level of service provided. For example, some retailers use results of customer satisfaction studies to determine bonuses.

Developing Solutions to Service Problems

Frequently, retailers don't set high service standards because they feel service improvements are either too costly or not achievable with available employees. This reflects an unwillingness to think creatively and to explore new approaches for improving service.

Innovative Approaches Finding ways to overcome service problems can improve customer satisfaction and, in some cases, reduce costs. For example, when customers complained about the long wait to check out, many hotels felt they couldn't do anything about the problem. Marriott, however, thought of a creative approach to address this service problem. It invented Express Checkout, a system in which a bill is left under the customer's door the morning before checkout and, if the bill is accurate, the customer can check out by simply using the TV remote or calling the front desk to have the bill charged automatically to his or her credit card. See Retailing View 14.6 for a discussion of emerging mobile payment technology.

Using Technology Many retailers are installing kiosks with broadband Internet access in the stores. In addition to offering customers the opportunity to order merchandise not available in the store, kiosks can provide routine customer service, freeing employees to deal with more demanding customer requests and problems. For example, customers can use kiosks to locate merchandise in the store and to indicate whether specific products, brands, and sizes are available in the store. Kiosks can also be used to automate existing store services such as gift registry management, rain checks, and credit applications, and preorder service for bakeries and delicatessens.

Customers can use a kiosk to find out more information about products and how they are used. For example, a Home Depot customer can go to a kiosk to find out how to install a garbage disposal and to get a list of all of the tools and parts that are needed for the installation. A Best Buy customer can use a kiosk to provide side-by-side comparisons of two Blu-ray players and to find more detailed information than is available from the shelf tag or from a sales associate. The customer can also access evaluations of the models as reported by *Consumer Reports*. The information provided by the kiosk could be tailored to specific customers by accessing the retailer's customer database. For example, a customer who is considering a new set of speakers might not remember the preamplifier purchased previously from Best Buy. This customer might not know whether the speakers are compatible with the preamplifier or what cables are needed to connect the new speakers. These concerns could be addressed by accessing the retailer's customer database through the kiosk.

Kiosks can also be used to provide customized solutions. For example, a customer, perhaps with the assistance of a salesperson, wants to design a

Adoption Problems Plague Digital Wallets

With published reports stating that 1 billion smartphones have already been sold worldwide, retailers are eyeing digital wallets as a way to complete mobile transactions. But first, retailers must overcome security, awareness, and integration issues.

Unlike traditional m-commerce, when a purchaser enters credit card information either through a mobile app or via a mobile site, digital wallets make use of technologies such as near-field communications (NFC). A mobile phone designed to work with NFC radio frequencies can enable a "contactless" payment in-store. Using this technology, MasterCard's PayPass, for example, enables a "tap-and-go" transaction at the point of sale (POS) through contactless readers. Similar to PayPass, Google has its own digital wallet, Google Wallet, which lets consumers virtually store their credit and debit account information in one place.

While still in its infancy, the market for digital wallets in Canada could reach $90 billion by 2017, up from $2 billion in 2010, according to Suretap Research. The typical user of mobile paying methods is between 30 and 44 years old, is university/college-educated, and has an above-average yearly salary.

However, before benefiting from this emerging market, merchants must overcome significant hurdles, according to Denee Carrington, a Forrester analyst and author of the report *U.S. Mobile Payments Forecast*. For starters, merchants must abide by the standards imposed by the US Europay, MasterCard, Visa (EMV) smartcard payment system. This is an internationally accepted standard that enables chip cards, POS terminals, and automated teller machines to securely authenticate credit and debit card transactions. The benefits are even greater since EMV payments also incorporate personal identification numbers to ensure that a mobile payment transaction was completed by the person who owns the mobile device.

Already, 22 countries, including many in Europe, as well as Mexico, Brazil, and Japan, have accepted EMV technology, according to the Smart Card Alliance. The United States, however, lags behind. One of the main reasons, according to MasterCard Advisors, could be the convenience factor. US merchants have gotten used to the current electronic payment infrastructure that has been in place for 30 years because it does "meet basic payment needs and maintains fraud at acceptable levels."

But because EMV paves the way for mobile transactions through chip-based technology, it will become an immediate priority for retailers in the years to come. Those merchants that fail to upgrade over the next couple of years could find themselves footing a majority of the bill, as opposed to the payment processor, should a fraudulent credit card transaction occur.

While merchants are not yet switching out their POS platforms to solely accommodate digital wallets, it would be a logical accompaniment to an EMV migration, as some analysts point out. "As long as they're doing a technology refresh, [merchants that] haven't upgraded to EMV...could incorporate capabilities like near-field communications, contactless readers, and rich graphical displays that would allow consumers to choose from a variety of payment instruments," observes Aaron McPherson, director of IDC's Financial Insights' Payments and Security Practice.

Retailers will also have to raise consumer awareness of digital wallets. While consumers might have heard of PayPal, Google Wallet, ISIS, V.me by Visa, and MasterCard PayPass Wallet, they don't necessarily know what each of the payment technologies accomplishes, according to *Digital Wallet Road Map 2013*, a mobile payment report by comScore. The study indicates that only 12 percent of consumers have used digital wallets other than PayPal. Of the 72 percent of respondents who were aware of PayPal's digital wallet, only 48 percent had used it.

"When we looked at future intent and presented people with a list of items that would increase their likelihood to use a digital wallet, security was number one and cost savings was next on the list," explains Andrea Jacobs, leader of comScore's Payments Practice. If a retailer provided a coupon or reward for local savings, 35 percent of people said it would increase their likelihood to use a digital wallet.

But as McPherson maintains, "hooking it all together on the back end and actually making the [rewards] offers will be a much trickier proposition because it's not so much a technology issue as it is a business and complexity issue." Rewards and loyalty will have a significant bearing on the payment methods that consumers choose. For instance, if a customer links a Citi Rewards card to a Google Wallet, and Citi offers rewards for usage, the vendors have to figure out if the rewards credits will appear in Google Wallet or in Citi's mobile app, according to McPherson.

Sources: Kelly Liyakasa, "Adoption Problems Plague Digital Wallets," *CRM Magazine*, April 2013, http://www.destinationcrm.com/Articles/Columns-Departments/Insight/Adoption-Problems-Plague-Digital-Wallets-88274.aspx (accessed July 8, 2013); CNW, "Suretap, Canada's Leading Open Digital Wallet, Expands Payment Options with Introduction of Virtual Reloadable Prepaid Card," September 8, 2015, http://www.newswire.ca/news-releases/suretap-canadas-leading-open-digital-wallet-expands-payment-options-with-introduction-of-virtual-reloadable-prepaid-card-525627421.html (accessed March 7, 2016); Statista, "Statistics and facts about Mobile Payments," http://www.statista.com/topics/982/mobile-payments/ (accessed March 7, 2016).

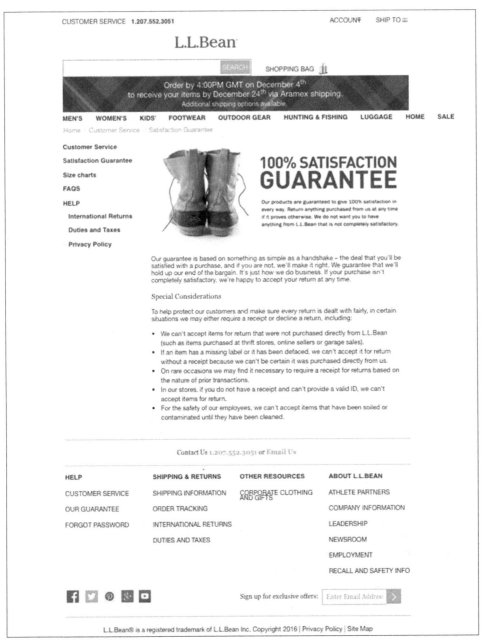

L.L. Bean search result page.

Source: http://www.llbean.com/customerService/aboutLLBean/guarantee.html.

home entertainment system. A kiosk could allow the customer to see what the system would look like after setup. Music store customers could use a kiosk to review and select tracks and make a custom compact disc. Kiosks also allow consumers the ability to search the company's inventory listing for specific products. Finally, customers could use a kiosk to see how different colours of cosmetics would look on them without having to apply the cosmetics. These types of applications could complement the efforts of salespeople and improve the service they can offer to customers.[72]

Defining the Role of Service Providers

Managers can tell service providers that they need to provide excellent service, but not clearly indicate what excellent service means. Without a clear definition of the retailer's expectations, service providers are directionless.

The Ritz-Carlton Hotel Company has its "Gold Standards" printed on a wallet-size card carried by all employees. The card contains the hotel's motto ("We Are Ladies and Gentlemen Serving Ladies and

Gentlemen"), the three steps for high-quality service (warm and sincere greeting, anticipation and compliance with guests' needs, and fond farewell), and 20 basic rules for Ritz-Carlton employees, including:

- Any employee who receives a complaint "owns" the complaint.
- Instant guest gratification will be ensured by all. React quickly to correct problems immediately.
- "Smile. We are on stage." Always maintain positive eye contact.
- Escort guests rather than giving directions to another area of the hotel.[73]

Setting Service Goals

To deliver consistent, high-quality service, retailers need to establish goals or standards to guide employees. Retailers often develop service goals based on their beliefs about the proper operation of the business rather than the customers' needs and expectations. For example, a retailer might set a goal that all monthly bills are to be mailed five days before the end of the month. This goal reduces the retailer's accounts receivable but offers no benefit to customers. Research undertaken by American Express showed customer evaluations of its service are based on perceptions of timeliness, accuracy, and responsiveness. Management then established goals (such as responding to all questions about bills within 24 hours) related to these customer-based criteria.

Employees are motivated to achieve service goals when the goals are specific, measurable, and participatory in the sense that they participated in setting them. Vague goals—such as "Approach customers when they enter the selling area" or "Respond to e-mails as soon as possible"—don't fully specify what employees should do, nor do such goals offer an opportunity to assess employee performance. Better goals would be "All customers should be approached by a salesperson within 30 seconds after entering a selling area" or "All emails should be responded to within three hours." These goals are both specific and measurable.

Employee participation in setting service standards leads to better understanding and greater acceptance of the goals. Store employees resent and resist goals arbitrarily imposed on them by management.

Measuring Service Performance

Retailers need to continuously assess service quality to ensure that goals will be achieved.[74] Many retailers do periodic customer surveys to assess service quality. Retailers also use mystery shoppers to assess their service quality. A **mystery shopper** is a professional shopper who "shops" a store to assess the service provided by store employees and the presentation of merchandise in the store. Some retailers use their own employees as mystery shoppers, but most contract with a firm to provide the assessment. Information typically reported by the mystery shoppers includes:

- How long did it take before a sales associate greeted you?
- Did the sales associate act as if he or she wanted your business?
- Was the sales associate knowledgeable about the merchandise?

mystery shopper
Professional shopper who "shops" a store to assess the service provided by store employees.

Mystery shoppers are professional shoppers who "shop" at a store to determine the service provided by store employees and the presentation of merchandise in the store.
© James Darell/Getty Images.

Retailers typically inform salespeople that they have "been shopped" and provide feedback from the mystery shopper's report. Some retailers offer rewards to sales associates who receive high marks and schedule follow-up visits to sales associates who get low evaluations.[75]

Meeting and Exceeding Services Standards: Closing The Delivery Gap

To reduce the delivery gap and provide service that exceeds standards, retailers must give service providers the necessary knowledge and skills, provide instrumental and emotional support, improve internal communications and reduce conflicts, and empower employees to act in the customers' and firm's best interests.[76] Chat rooms offered through an electronic channel enable customers to help the retailer to provide services to others.

Giving Information and Training

Store employees need to know about the merchandise they offer as well as their customers' needs. With this information, employees can answer customers' questions and suggest products. This also instills confidence and a sense of competence, which are needed to overcome service problems.

In addition, store employees need training in interpersonal skills. Dealing with customers is hard—particularly when they are upset or angry. All store employees, even those who work for retailers that provide excellent service, will encounter dissatisfied customers. Through training, employees can learn to provide better service and to cope with the stress caused by disgruntled customers.

Specific retail employees (salespeople and customer service representatives) are typically designated to interact with and provide service to customers. However, all retail employees should be prepared to deal with customers. For example, Walt Disney World provides four days of training for its maintenance workers, even though people can learn how to pick up trash and sweep streets in much less time. Disney has found that its customers are more likely to direct questions to maintenance people than to the clean-cut assistants wearing Ask Me, I'm in Guest Relations buttons. Thus, Disney trains maintenance people to confidently handle the myriad of questions they will be asked rather than responding, "Sorry, I don't know. Ask her."[77]

Toys "R" Us assesses customer satisfaction with checkout service by counting the number of abandoned shopping carts with merchandise left in the store because customers became impatient with the time required to make a purchase. After the firm noticed an alarming increase in abandoned carts, it developed a unique program to reduce customers' time in line waiting to pay. Cashiers' motions while ringing up and bagging merchandise were studied. Based on this research, a training program was developed to show cashiers how to use their right hand to record purchases on the POS terminal and their left hand to push merchandise along the counter. Counters were redesigned to have a slot lined with shopping bags in the middle of the counter. As the cashier pushes the merchandise along the counter, it drops into a bag. After the customer pays for the merchandise, the cashier simply lifts the bag from the slot and hands it to the customer, and a new bag pops into place.

Providing Instrumental and Emotional Support

Service providers need to have the **instrumental support** (the appropriate systems and equipment) to deliver the service desired by customers. For example, a hotel chain installed a computer system to speed up the checkout process. A study of the new system's effectiveness revealed that checkout time was not reduced because clerks had to wait to use the one stapler available to staple the customer's credit card and hotel bill receipts.

In addition to instrumental support, service providers need emotional support from their coworkers and supervisors. **Emotional support** involves demonstrating a concern for the well-being of others. Dealing with customer problems and maintaining a smile in difficult situations are psychologically demanding. Service providers need to be in a supportive, understanding atmosphere to deal with these demands effectively.[78]

instrumental support Support for retail service providers such as appropriate systems and equipment to deliver the service desired by customers.

emotional support Supporting retail service providers with the understanding and positive regard to enable them to deal with the emotional stress created by disgruntled customers.

Improving Internal Communications and Providing Support

DID YOU KNOW?

Two-thirds of customers who put merchandise into an electronic shopping cart at a website do not complete the transaction.[79]

When providing customer service, store employees must often manage the conflict between customers' needs and the retail firms' needs.[80] For example, many retailers have a no-questions-asked return policy. Under such a policy, the retailer will provide a refund at the customer's request even if the merchandise wasn't purchased at the store or was clearly used improperly. When Hudson's Bay inaugurated this policy, some employees refused to provide refunds on merchandise that had been worn or damaged by the customer. They were loyal Bay employees and didn't want customers to take advantage of their firm.

Retailers can reduce such conflicts by having clear guidelines and policies concerning service and by explaining the rationale for these policies. Once Bay employees recognized that the goodwill created by the no-questions-asked policy generated more sales than the losses due to customers' abusing the policy, they implemented the policy enthusiastically.

Conflicts can also arise when retailers set goals inconsistent with the other behaviours expected from store employees. For example, if salespeople are expected to provide customer service, they should be evaluated on the service they provide, not just on the sales they make.

Finally, conflicts can also arise between different areas of the firm. An auto dealer with an excellent customer service reputation devotes considerable effort to reducing conflict by improving communication among its employees. The dealership holds a town hall meeting in which employees feel free to bring up service problems. For example, the receptionist discussed her frustration when she couldn't locate a sales rep for whom a customer had called. The customer finally said, "Well, I'll just take my business elsewhere." She used this example to emphasize that sales reps should tell her when they slip out to run an errand. Now no one forgets that the front desk is the nerve centre of the dealership.

Empowering Store Employees

Empowerment means allowing employees at the firm's lowest level to make important decisions concerning how service is provided to customers. When the employees responsible for providing service are authorized to make important decisions, service quality improves.[82]

Nordstrom department stores provides an overall objective—satisfy customer needs—and then encourages employees to do whatever is necessary to carry out the objective. For example, a Nordstrom department manager bought 12 dozen pairs of hosiery from a competitor in the mall when her stock was depleted because the new shipment was delayed. Even though Nordstrom lost money on this hosiery, management applauded her actions to make sure customers found hosiery when they came to the store looking for it. Empowering service providers with only a rule such as "Use your best judgment" can cause chaos. At Nordstrom, department managers avoid abuses by coaching and training salespeople. They help salespeople understand what "Use your best judgment" means.

However, empowering service providers can be difficult. Some employees prefer to have the appropriate behaviours clearly defined for them. They don't want to spend the time learning how to make decisions or to assume the risks of making mistakes.

In some cases, the benefits of empowering service providers may not justify the costs. For example, if a retailer uses a standardized service delivery approach like McDonald's, the cost of hiring, training, and supporting empowerment may not lead to consistent and superior service delivery. Also, studies have found that empowerment is not embraced by employees in different cultures. For example, employees in Latin America expect their managers to possess all the information needed to make good business decisions. The role of employees is not to make business decisions; their job is to carry out the decisions of managers.[83]

DID YOU KNOW?

Google has developed a survey called "Googlegeist," which solicits feedback on hundreds of issues and then enlists volunteer employee teams across the entire company to solve the biggest problems.[81]

Providing Incentives

As we discussed, many retailers use incentives, such as paying commissions on sales, to motivate employees. But retailers have found that commissions on sales can decrease customer service and job satisfaction. Incentives can motivate high-pressure selling, which leads to customer dissatisfaction. However, incentives can also be used effectively to improve customer service. For example, in one retail chain, managers distributed notes to store employees when they solved a customer's problem. The notes could be converted into a cash bonus. This program was particularly effective because the reward was provided at about the same time the appropriate behaviour occurred.

Communicating the Service Promise: Closing The Communication Gap

A fourth factor leading to a customer service gap is a difference between the service promised by the retailer and the service actually delivered. Overstating the service offered raises customer expectations. Then if the retailer doesn't follow through, expectations exceed perceived service, and customers are dissatisfied. For example, if a store advertises that a customer will always be greeted by a friendly, smiling sales associate, customers may be disappointed if this doesn't occur. Raising expectations too high might bring in more customers initially, but it can also create dissatisfaction and reduce repeat business. The communication gap can be reduced by making realistic commitments and by managing customer expectations.

Realistic Commitments

Advertising programs are typically developed by the marketing department, while the store operations division delivers the service. Poor communication between these areas can result in a mismatch between an ad campaign's promises and the service the store can actually offer. This problem is illustrated by Holiday Inn's "No Surprises" ad campaign. Market research indicated hotel customers wanted greater reliability in lodging, so Holiday Inn's agency developed a campaign promising no unpleasant surprises. Even though hotel managers didn't feel they could meet the claims promised in the ads, top management accepted the campaign. The campaign raised customer expectations to an unrealistic level and gave customers who did confront an unpleasant surprise an additional reason to be angry. The campaign was discontinued soon after it started.

Managing Customer Expectations

How can a retailer communicate realistic service expectations without losing business to a competitor that makes inflated service claims? American Airlines' "Why Does It Seem Every Airline Flight Is Late?" ad campaign is an example of a communication program that addresses this issue. In print ads, American recognized its customers' frustration and explained some uncontrollable factors causing the problem: overcrowded airports, scheduling problems, and intense price competition. Then the ads described how American was improving the situation.

Information presented at the point of sale can be used to manage expectations. For example, theme parks and restaurants indicate the waiting time for an attraction or a table. Electronic retailers tell their customers if merchandise is in stock and when they can expect to receive it. Providing accurate information can increase customer satisfaction even when customers must wait longer than desired.[84]

Sometimes service problems are caused by customers. Customers may use an invalid credit card to pay for merchandise, may not take time to try on a suit and have it altered properly, or may use a product incorrectly because they failed to read the instructions. Communication programs can inform customers about their role and responsibility in getting good service and can give tips on how to get better service, such as the best times of the day to shop and the retailer's policies and procedures for handling problems.

Lo6 Service Recovery

As mentioned previously, delivery of customer service is inherently inconsistent, so service failures are bound to arise. Rather than dwelling on negative aspects of customer problems, retailers should focus on the positive opportunities they generate. Service problems and complaints are an excellent source of information about the retailer's offering (its merchandise and service). Armed with this information, retailers can make changes to increase customer satisfaction.

Service problems also enable a retailer to demonstrate its commitment to providing high-quality customer service. By encouraging complaints and handling problems, a retailer has an opportunity to strengthen its relationship with its customers.

Effective service recovery efforts significantly increase customer satisfaction, purchase intentions, and positive word of mouth. However, post-recovery satisfaction is less than that satisfaction prior to the service failure.[85]

Most retailers have standard policies for handling problems. If a correctable problem is identified, such as defective merchandise, many retailers will make restitution on the spot and apologize for inconveniencing the customer. The retailer will offer either replacement merchandise, a credit toward future purchases, or a cash refund.

In many cases, the cause of the problem may be hard to identify (did the salesperson really insult the customer?), uncorrectable (the store had to close due to bad weather), or a result of the customer's unusual expectations (the customer didn't like his haircut). In this case, service recovery might be more difficult. The steps in effective service recovery are:

- Listen to the customer.
- Provide a fair solution.
- Resolve the problem quickly.[86]

Listening to Customers

Customers can become very emotional over their real or imaginary problems with a retailer. Often this emotional reaction can be reduced by simply giving customers a chance to get their complaints off their chests. Store employees should allow customers to air their complaints without interruption. Interruptions can further irritate customers who may already be emotionally upset. It's very hard to reason with or satisfy an angry customer.

Customers want a sympathetic response to their complaints. Thus, store employees need to make it clear they are happy that the problem has been brought to their attention. Satisfactory solutions rarely arise when store employees have an antagonistic attitude or assume that the customer is trying to cheat the store.

In 2004, Hudson's Bay launched an online survey for customers at its 99 Bay stores as well as its 300 Zellers and 45 Home Outfitters stores. The customer's receipt invited the shopper to go online and fill out a questionnaire, thus earning a chance to win 1 million HBC reward points (equivalent to $100). Feedback from customers can pinpoint problems in specific departments, not enough sale items, or unfriendly service.

For many years, retailers have used mystery shoppers to provide feedback on customer services, but times have changed and customers are eager to log on and discuss their shopping experience. The advantage is that these are real customers who are in the store shopping and are not on the store's payroll. Customer service scores for the stores have improved since online feedback was initiated.[87]

Providing a Fair Solution

When confronted with a complaint, store employees need to focus on how they can get the customer back, not simply how they can solve the problem. Favourable impressions arise when customers feel they have been dealt with fairly. When evaluating the resolution of their problems, customers compare how they were treated in relation to others with similar problems or how they were treated in similar situations by other retail service providers. This comparison is based on observation of other customers with problems or on information about complaint handling learned from reading books and talking with others. Customers' evaluations of complaints' resolutions are based on distributive fairness and procedural fairness.[88]

Distributive Fairness Distributive fairness is a customer's perception of the benefits received compared to their costs (inconvenience or loss). Customers want to get what they paid for. The customer's needs can affect the perceived correspondence between benefits and costs. For example, one customer might be satisfied with a rain check for a food processor that was advertised at a discounted price but was sold out. This customer feels the low price for the food processor offsets the inconvenience of returning to the store. But another customer may need the food processor immediately. A rain check won't be adequate compensation for him. To satisfy this customer, the salesperson must locate a store that has the food processor and have it delivered to the customer's house.

Customers typically prefer tangible rather than intangible resolutions to their complaints. Customers may want to let off steam, but they also want to

distributive fairness Exists when outcomes received are viewed as fair with respect to outcomes received by others.

feel the retailer was responsive to their complaint. A low-cost reward, a free soft drink, or a discount communicates more concern to the customer than a verbal apology.

If providing tangible restitution isn't possible, the next best alternative is to let customers see that their complaints will have an effect in the future. This can be done by making a note, in front of the customer, to a manager about the problem or writing to the customer about actions taken to prevent similar problems in the future.

procedural fairness
The perceived fairness of the process used to resolve customer complaints.

Procedural Fairness **Procedural fairness** is the perceived fairness of the process used to resolve complaints. Customers consider three questions when evaluating procedural fairness:

- Did the employee collect information about the situation?

- Was this information used to resolve the complaint?
- Did the customer have some influence over the outcome?

Resolving Problems Quickly

Customers are more satisfied when the first person they contact can resolve a problem. When customers are referred to several different employees, they waste a lot of time repeating their story. Also, the chance of conflicting responses by store employees increases.

Customers should be told clearly and precisely what they need to do to resolve a problem. When American Express cardholders ask to have an unused airline ticket removed from their bill, they are told immediately that they must return the ticket to the airline or travel agency before a credit can be issued. Fast service often depends on providing clear instructions.

Customer relationship management is a business philosophy and set of strategies, programs, and systems that focus on identifying and building loyalty with a retailer's most valued customers. Loyal customers are committed to patronizing a retailer and are not prone to switching to a competitor. In addition to building loyalty, CRM programs are also designed to increase the share of wallet from the retailer's best customers.

CRM is an iterative process that turns customer data into customer loyalty through four activities:

- collecting customer data
- analyzing the customer data and identifying target customers
- developing CRM programs
- implementing CRM programs

The first step of the process is to collect and store data about customers. One of the challenges in collecting customer data is identifying the customer with each transaction and contact. Retailers use a variety of approaches to overcome this challenge.

The second step is analyzing the data to identify the most profitable customers. Two approaches used to rank customers according to their profitability are calculating the customer's lifetime value and categorizing customers on the basis of characteristics of their buying behaviour—recency, frequency, and monetary value.

Using this information about customers, retailers can develop programs to build loyalty in their best customers, increase their share of wallet with better customers (converting gold customers into platinum customers), and deal with unprofitable customers (getting the lead out).

Four approaches that retailers use to build loyalty and retain their best customers are:

- launching frequent shopper programs
- offering special customer service
- personalizing the services they provide
- building a sense of community

Retailers increase share of wallet through cross-selling and add-on selling. Unprofitable customers are dealt with by developing lower-cost approaches for servicing these customers. Effectively implementing CRM programs is difficult because it requires coordinating a number of different areas in a retailer's organization.

Due to the inherent intangibility and inconsistency of service, providing high-quality customer service is challenging. However, customer service also provides an opportunity for retailers to develop a strategic advantage. Retailers use two basic approaches to providing customer service: customization and standardization approaches. The customized approach relies primarily on sales associates. The standardized approach places more emphasis on developing appropriate rules and procedures and the store design.

Customers evaluate customer service by comparing their perceptions of the service delivered with their expectations. Thus, to improve service, retailers need to close the gaps between the service delivered and the customer's expectations. These gaps are reduced by knowing what customers expect, setting standards to provide the expected service, providing support so that store employees can meet the standards, and realistically communicating the service they offer to customers. Knowledge of service gaps can be determined by conducting focus groups.

Due to inherent inconsistency, service failures are bound to arise. These lapses in service provide an opportunity for retailers to build even stronger relationships with their customers.

KEY TERMS

1-to-1 retailing
80–20 rule
add-on selling
communication gap
cookies
cross-selling
customer database
customer service
data mining
decile analysis
delivery gap

distributive fairness
emotional support
frequent shopper program
gamification
instrumental support
knowledge gap
lifetime customer value (LTV)
loyalty program
market basket analysis
mystery shopper
near-field communications (NFC)

private-label credit card
procedural fairness
RFM (recency, frequency, monetary)
   analysis
service gap
share of wallet
SoLoMo (social, local, and mobile)
standardization approach
standards gap

GET OUT & DO IT!

1. GO SHOPPING Look in your wallet:
   a) What loyalty cards do you have?
   b) Why do you have these specific cards?
   c) Rate each card on a scale: 1 (poor) to 10 (fantastic).

2. INTERNET EXERCISE Contact the Canadian Marketing Association (CMA), a leading authority on privacy issues, at http://www.the-cma.org. What are the major issues confronting retailers? What seminars are being offered to assist retailers in understanding Canada's privacy legislation?

3. INTERNET EXERCISE Go to some of the retail sites that you frequent and compare their privacy policies. Which policies make you less concerned about violations of your privacy? Why? Which policies, or lack thereof, raise your concern? Why?

4. SHOPPING Are you a participant in a frequent shopper program? Why are you a member? Consider the Shoppers Optimum card program.
   a) How does a membership benefit the consumer?
   b) Would this membership card be of value to you personally? Explain why or why not.

5. INTERNET EXERCISE Visit http://www.airmilesshops.ca—the AIR MILES virtual shopping mall. What are the shopping options and special promotions for AIR MILES collectors? How does the website encourage you to participate and sign up for AIR MILES? What information does it request from you?

6. GO SHOPPING Go to a local store and be a customer. Ask for assistance and suggestions regarding a potential purchase. Write a report describing your shopping experience, and make suggestions for improving the store's customer service.

7. GO SHOPPING Go to a discount store such as Walmart, a department store, and a specialty store to buy a pair of jeans. Compare and contrast the customer service you receive in the stores. Which store made it easiest to find the pair of jeans you would be interested in buying? Why?

8. INTERNET EXERCISE Visit https://blog.kissmetrics.com/how-to-calculate-lifetime-value/ and answer the following questions:
   a) Based on the projections, what is the lifetime value of a Starbucks customer?
   b) What are the three types of formulas one could use to calculate LTV?
   c) What are the five variables which could be used to calculate LTV?

1. What is CRM?

2. Why do retailers want to determine the lifetime value of their customers?

3. Why do customers have privacy concerns about frequent shopper programs that supermarkets have, and what can supermarkets do to minimize these concerns?

4. What are examples of opportunities for add-on selling that might be pursued by (a) travel agents, (b) jewellery stores, and (c) dry cleaners?

5. How would you suggest that a dry cleaner build greater loyalty and retention with its best customers?

6. Which of the following types of retailers do you think would benefit most from instituting CRM: (a) supermarkets, (b) banks, (c) automobile dealers, or (d) consumer electronic retailers? Why?

7. Develop a CRM program for a local store that sells apparel with your college or university's logo. What type of information would you collect about your customers, and how would you use this information to increase the sales and profits of the store?

8. How can a real estate agent deal with people who are just looking and not ready to buy? What are the agent's potential benefits and risks in undertaking these actions?

9. What are the different approaches retailers can use to identify customers with their transactions? What are the advantages and disadvantages of each approach?

10. A CRM program focuses on building relationships with a retailer's better customers. Some customers who do not receive the same benefits as the retailer's best customers may be upset because they are treated differently. What can retailers do to minimize this negative reaction?

11. For each of these services, give an example of a retailer for which providing the service is critical to its success. Then give an example of a retailer for which providing the service is not critical: (a) personal shoppers, (b) home delivery, (c) money-back guarantees, (d) credit.

12. Holt Renfrew and McDonald's are noted for their high-quality customer service, but their approaches to providing this quality service are different. Describe this difference. Why have the retailers elected to use these different approaches?

13. Is customer service more important for store-based retailers or electronic retailers? Explain.

14. Providing customer service can be very expensive for retailers. When are the costs of providing high-quality services justified? What types of retailers find it financially advantageous to provide high-quality customer service? What retailers can't justify providing high-quality service?

15. Gaps analysis provides a systematic method of examining a customer service program's effectiveness. Top management has told an information systems manager that customers are complaining about the long wait to pay for merchandise at the checkout station. How can the systems manager use gaps analysis to analyze this problem and suggest approaches to reducing this time?

16. How could an effective customer service strategy cut a retailer's costs?

17. Employees play a critical role in customer perceptions of quality service. If you were hiring salespeople, what characteristics would you look for to assess their ability to provide good customer service?

18. a) What is a focus group?
    b) Design ten open-ended questions to use in a customer focus group to determine a retailer's customer service gaps and make improvements.

CHAPTER FIFTEEN

Appealing to the customer: retail communication mix

LEARNING OBJECTIVES

Lo1   Explore how retailers can build brand equity for their stores and their private-label merchandise.

Lo2   Examine the individual elements of a retail communication strategy and how each element contributes to a successful communication campaign.

Lo3   Review the strengths and weaknesses of different methods for communicating with customers.

Lo4   Examine the steps involved in developing a communication program.

Lo5   Review how retailers establish a communication budget.

SPOTLIGHT ON RETAILING

MOBILE IN THE NEW MILLENNIUM (BRANDS AND MILLENNIALS)

Catalyst and GroupM Next conducted original research examining when, where, and how Canadians are using their mobile devices.

Mobile continues to experience substantial growth in Canada, with smartphone ownership increasing by a staggering 24 percent year over year. The real story, however, is not in how mobile is growing, but rather how it is changing. The research reveals that as the Canadian mobile landscape expands, it is evolving in significant—and unexpected—ways.

As the largest generational cohort in Canada since the Baby Boomers, Millennials are a segment of the population that is of particular interest to marketers. Conventional wisdom is that Millennials are more connected and tech-savvy than members of older generations. And indeed, this study confirms that members of this cohort are playing a key role in the evolving mobile landscape.

The 2014 survey again asked respondents how they use their phones. The findings revealed that at-home smartphone usage has risen and on-the-go activity has declined—a surprising discovery given that mobility is one of the main advantages offered by mobile technology.

The reported smartphone frustrations also reveal a clear preference for larger screens over smaller screens. This preference makes sense in light of increasing at-home usage for activities like watching video and reading articles, which are easier to accomplish on a large screen. Recent large-screen smartphone models like the iPhone 6 Plus and the Samsung Galaxy Note 4 have both responded to and fed this market demand.

The study also examined how people in the youngest age demographic (18–24 years) compare with people in all other age demographics with regard to at-home usage across six common activities—getting directions, finding a new restaurant, reading emails, using Facebook, watching a short video, and checking the weather. Results are shown in the image below.

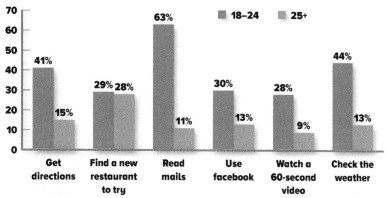

Growth In Share Of "At Home" Users Within Respondents Who Use Smartphone As Primary Device For Activity

Out of the six common activities, Millennials usage is much greater in five of the six categories. The exception is "finding new restaurants," in which the age groups are pretty much even.

Interestingly, compared to other age groups, the youngest of the Millennials are more likely to use apps and have a greater number of apps on their phone. In response to the question "How many of your apps have you used in the past month?," those in the 18-24 group reported an average of 8.88—more than any other age group.

Brands that are interested in reaching young people should take into account the fact that these consumers tend to be more engaged with their devices at home, and more active on mobile applications, than their elders. Appropriate allocation of resources (such as application development budget) may thus depend to some degree on the age of a brand's target market.

Growing screen sizes have turned the smartphone into an ideal device for at-home activities like watching video and reading articles, while ongoing frustrations with battery life and data caps have limited its utility for activities on the go. These same limitations have made real estate on the smartphone highly competitive, as more users are deleting or consolidating apps and turning to the browser instead. Millennials are a driving force behind the trend toward at-home smartphone usage, and are also more active than other age groups on mobile applications.

For brands operating in the Canadian market, this research can be distilled into four key strategic takeaways:

- With 68 percent smartphone penetration, mobile is no longer an option but a necessity. All forms of content (long-form, short-form, video, images, etc.) should be mobile-optimized.

- Mobile consumers are active at home as much as (or more than) they are on the go. Search and display advertising budgets may therefore yield better results on mobile during off-work hours versus during the day.

- Application development projects should be approached with care. This is a highly saturated space with a selective audience, so brands need to be able to provide a unique value proposition to app users.

- Millennials are especially active on mobile, including applications. Brands whose target market includes young people should be particularly concerned with offering mobile solutions across both the browser and, if applicable, the app.

In an increasingly connected world, competition is rife and attention is at a premium. The brands that succeed will be the ones that have a clear idea of who their target market is, and how to provide them with a convenient and hassle-free mobile experience that takes into account their ever-evolving habits.

Syda Productions/Shutterstock.
Source: Catalyst Canada.

Lo1   A critical step in the retail management decision-making process is developing and implementing a communication program to:

- build appealing brand images
- attract customers to stores and Internet sites
- encourage customers to buy merchandise

The communication program informs customers about the retailer as well as the merchandise and services it offers, and plays a role in developing repeat visits and customer loyalty.

brand A distinguishing name or symbol (such as a logo, design, symbol, or trademark) that identifies the products or services offered by a seller and differentiates those products and services from the offerings of competitors.

brand energy The concept that links the idea that a brand creates value through meaningful experiences rather than a focus on generating profits.

Communication programs can have both long-term and short-term effects on a retailer's business. From a *long-term perspective*, communication programs can be used to create and maintain a strong, differentiated image of the retailer and its store brands. This image develops customer loyalty and creates a strategic advantage. Thus, brand-image–building communication programs complement the objective of a retailer's CRM (customer relationship management) program.

On the other hand, retailers frequently use communication programs to realize the *short-term objective* of increasing sales during a specified time period. For example, retailers often have sales during which some or all merchandise is priced at a discount for a short time, for example, at the end of a season. Grocery stores usually place weekly ads with coupons that can be used to save money on purchases made during the week.

Using Communication Programs to Develop Brands and Build Customer Loyalty

A **brand** is the symbolic embodiment of all the information connected to the product and/or retailer and serves to create associations and expectations around it. A brand often includes a logo, fonts, colour schemes, symbols, and sound, which may be developed to represent implicit values, ideas, and even personality. In a retailing context, the name of the retailer is a brand that indicates to consumers the type of merchandise and services offered by the

Retail advertising can be used to achieve long-term objectives such as building a brand image, or short-term sales. The Payless ShoeSource ad (above) generates short-term sales through a special promotion.
Courtesy of the TJX Companies, Inc.

retailer. Some retailers develop private-label brands or store brands that are exclusively sold through their channels. In some cases this private-label merchandise bears the retailer's name, such as Shoppers Drug Mart aspirin. In other cases, special brand names are used, such as Hudson's Bay's Baycrest, Shoppers Drug Mart's Life, and Canadian Tire's Mastercraft.

A retailer develops a brand by associating an image with the product and services that is branded into the consciousness of consumers. A brand is therefore one of the most valuable elements in a retailer's advertising strategy. One goal in brand recognition is the identification of a brand without the name of the company present. It is therefore important that a brand be protected legally by patent or copyright. For example, the well-known brand of Apple is recognized for innovation in technology and has created immense success in the branding of iPhone and iTunes.

Brand energy is the concept that links the idea that the brand creates value through meaningful experiences rather than a focus on merely generating profits. The energy that flows throughout the business develops a consistent way of thinking, feeling, and behaving toward the retailer and its products and services in all employees; an example is Mountain Equipment Co-op, where customers become members for a nominal fee and embrace its environmental philosophy.

Attitude branding is the choice to represent a feeling that is not necessarily connected with the product or retailer—for example, Nike: "Just Do It"; The Body Shop: "Trade Not Aid"; and Dove: "Real Beauty." A great brand adds a sense of purpose to the experience. (Retailing View 15.2 explores more fully what Dell has done in terms of attitude branding.)

Value of Brand Image

Brands provide value to both customers and retailers. Brands convey information to consumers about the nature of the shopping experience—the retailer's mix—they will encounter when patronizing a retailer. They also affect customers' confidence in decisions made to buy merchandise from a retailer. Finally, brands can enhance customers' satisfaction with the merchandise and services they buy. Consumers feel different when wearing jewellery bought from Birks than from Claire' or lingerie from La Senza than from Walmart.

The value that brand image offers retailers is referred to as **brand equity**. Strong brand names can affect the customer's decision-making process, motivate repeat visits and purchases, and build loyalty. In addition, strong brand names enable retailers to charge higher prices and lower their marketing costs.

Customer loyalty to brands arises from heightened awareness of the brand and the emotional ties toward it. For example, some brands such as Canadian Tire are so well known by consumers that they are typically in a consumer's consideration set. In addition, customers identify and have strong emotional relationships with some brands. For example, Winners has an image of offering fashionable merchandise at bargain prices. Going to Winners is a cool experience, and everybody now considers it cool to save money. High brand awareness and strong emotional connnections reduce the incentive of customers to switch to competing retailers.

Styles vary by store. Jewellery only available at select locations. Visit winners.ca for locations near you.

It was love at first sight, at a price oh-so-right.

✉ f ▶ 🐦 ⬚

WINNERS®
Find Fabulous For Less

Winners uses advertising to build its image of offering fashionable merchandise at low prices.

Photographer – Juan Carlos Algarin, Model – Dani Seitz.

A strong brand image enables retailers to increase their margins. When retailers have high customer loyalty, they can engage in premium pricing and reduce their reliance on price promotions to attract customers. Brands with weaker images are forced to offer low prices and frequent sales to maintain their market share.

Finally, retailers with strong brand names can leverage their brand to successfully introduce new retail concepts with only a limited amount of marketing effort. For example, The Gap has efficiently extended its brand to GapKids and BabyGap, and Roots extended its brand name to Roots Kids. Virgin has extended its brand name into numerous areas including Air, Space travel, Wines, and Mobile services, to name a few!

attitude branding The choice of a symbol that represents a feeling that is not necessarily connected with the product or retailer.

brand equity The value that brand image offers retailers.

Bienvenue au Québec: How Outsiders Become Local Quebec Retailers

There's a little known fact about how Tim Hortons adapted to the Quebec market. The chain was first called Tim Horton's (notice the apostrophe). The apostrophe was later lost to Quebec's language law, which stipulates that unless a business name is simply a personal name, it must be translated into French. Tim Horton's would have become *Les beignes de Tim Horton*. Rather than producing separate signage and marketing materials for the Quebec market, Tim Horton's became Tim Hortons from coast to coast. While it changed its name to maximize efficiencies instead of adopting a distinctly Quebecois identity, and chose to offer essentially the same menu mix within the same restaurant environment, Tim Hortons has definitely struck a chord with Quebecers.

Headspace Marketing Inc., a Toronto-based marketing-communications consultancy helping clients build their brands in Quebec, asked 1000 Quebec men and women to rate how well or poorly 12 retail brands had adapted to their needs and expectations.[2] Of the 12 brands surveyed, three stand out as having best adapted to Quebecers' needs and wants.

Tim Hortons leads the pack with a 98 percent score. Canadian Tire follows with a score of 97 percent (see the graph below). With its green maple leaf logo, the "driving, playing, fixing, and living" store first opened in Quebec in

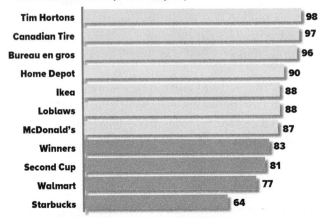

ADAPTATION SCORE (% well adapted)

Retailer	Score
Tim Hortons	98
Canadian Tire	97
Bureau en gros	96
Home Depot	90
Ikea	88
Loblaws	88
McDonald's	87
Winners	83
Second Cup	81
Walmart	77
Starbucks	64

Source: Used with permission of Headspace Marketing Inc.

1939. Proudly Canadian, the retailer doesn't appear to have done things differently in Quebec. The merchandise mix, the unique products, and the Canadian Tire money featuring the well-known Scotsman Sandy McTire appear as popular in Rivière-du-Loup as in Kamloops.

Staples Business Depot in Quebec is the destination for office supplies. But don't expect to find a Staples sign on the building or anything about a depot. *Bureau en gros*, which loosely translated means "wholesale office

Source: Headspace Marketing Inc.

DID YOU KNOW?

Canadian Tire "money" was introduced in 1958 at Canadian Tire gas bars and started being promoted in the stores in 1961 as a customer loyalty initiative.

A strong brand name creates a strategic advantage that is very difficult for competitors to duplicate. Many of the most brilliant marketers can be found in Canada, and many others around the world look to Canadian companies for best practices. For example, Hootsuite, a social media company currently operating in Vancouver, BC, offers services to over 10 million people world wide. Hootsuite offers software that allows businesses to manage multiple social media platforms with one software pack. Ryan Holmes saw the opportunity to create a better social media experience for businesses, and it is the world's most widely used social relationship platform.[1]

Building Brand Equity

The activities that a retailer needs to undertake to build brand equity for its firm or its private-label merchandise are as follows:

- Create a high level of brand awareness.
- Develop favourable associations with the brand name.
- Consistently reinforce the image of the brand.

supplies," is one of the top three brands among those tested that Quebecers felt best adapted to their needs. The name certainly has much to do with it, but the offer is no different. Mind you, Quebecers are often pleasantly surprised to be consistently asked at the checkout if they found everything they were looking for.

Home Depot, IKEA, Loblaws, and McDonald's all get scores in the high eighties. While many Quebecers call Loblaws *"Lobolah,"* its President's Choice products and made-in-Quebec advertising seem to be resonating well with a market that loves a new twist on Habitant pea soup as much as unpasteurized cheese.

In many towns in Quebec, McDonald's restaurants are as visible as the now mostly empty churches and, perhaps because of the *poutine* on the menu, its community involvement, or its support of Alexandre Despaties— *un p'tit gars d'ici*—the quick-service restaurant chain gets good marks from Quebecers.

IKEA, concentrated in Montreal, also gets good marks from Quebecers who obviously have no problem making the trip to the Swedish store.

Winners, with an 83 percent score, has apparently done well in Quebec with its off-pricing strategy. The formula is the same and for a while the advertising featured a local spokesperson, Geneviève Brouillette. Everyone loves a bargain, and Quebecers are no different. And unlike shoppers in the rest of Canada who are more likely to find shopping is a chore, Quebecers love it.

The giant Walmart gets a 77 percent score. Quebecers might like its everyday low prices and enjoy watching a TV spot featuring a young couple from Chicoutimi who bought all their Christmas decorations at the local Walmart; they seem to be less impressed by the corporation's labour relations.

So what can we learn from this? There don't appear to be universal rules. In some cases, having a French name, adapting the offering to Quebecers' tastes, or speaking their language through made-in-Quebec advertising might help increase a retailer's relevance and familiarity among shoppers in Quebec. Retailers should keep in mind, however, that the basics of retailing (fair pricing, quality products, clean and accessible stores, well-stocked shelves, and outstanding service) make the difference in Quebec as everywhere else. Other surveys have also consistently highlighted the importance Quebecers attach to customer service. For example, when asked what the retailers who have deployed self-checkout should do with the staff being reallocated, 72 percent of Quebecers said "having easily accessible personnel in aisle, at a greeter station, or at a customer service desk to help locate product, answer questions, etc." Only 58 percent of Ontarians said so.[3]

Quebecers will handsomely reward those retailers who cater to their needs in a manner that recognizes them as people and shoppers. Knowing whether to adopt, adapt, or create for Quebec is the key to success.

Brand Awareness **Brand awareness** is the ability of a potential customer to recognize or recall that the brand name is a type of retailer or product/service. Thus, brand awareness is the strength of the link between the brand name and type of merchandise or service in the minds of customers. There is a range of awareness from aided recall to top-of-mind awareness. **Aided recall** occurs when consumers indicate they know the brand when the name is presented to them. **Top-of-mind awareness**, the highest level of awareness, arises when consumers mention a brand name first when they are asked about the type of retailer, a merchandise category, or a type of service. For example, Best Buy has top-of-mind awareness if a consumer responds "Best Buy" when asked about retailers that sell consumer electronics. High top-of-mind awareness means that a retailer typically will be in the consideration set when customers decide to shop for a type of product or service.

Retailers build top-of-mind awareness by having memorable names; by repeatedly exposing their name to customers through advertising, locations, and sponsorships; and by using memorable symbols. Some brand names are

brand awareness The ability of a potential customer to recognize or recall that a particular brand name belongs to a retailer or product/service.

aided recall When consumers indicate they know the brand when the name is presented to them.

top-of-mind awareness The highest level of brand awareness; arises when consumers mention a brand name first when they are asked about a type of retailer, a merchandise category, or a type of service.

easy to remember. For example, the name Home Depot, because "Home" is in its brand name, is memorable and closely associated with home improvements, as is Canadian Tire with the automotive reference and the fact that this is a Canadian company.

Ian Dagnall/Alamy.

Tim Hortons has high awareness because of the large number of stores it has. Customers walk and drive by the stores all the time. The sheer number of stores provides substantial exposure to its brand. Most Canadians are well aware of the popular "roll up the rim to win" promotion.

Symbols involve visual images that typically are more easily recalled than words or phrases and thus are useful for building brand awareness. For example, the images of Colonel Sanders and the golden arches enhance the ability of customers to recall the names KFC and McDonald's.

Many Canadian retailers are finding that sponsorships are a cost-effective means of increasing their exposure as well as helping the communities that they serve. Take a Hike—an outdoor sporting goods store in Thunder Bay, Ontario—is passionate about sponsorships and participates in local festivals and outdoor activity workshops for the community. Its Socks for Shelter House program donates one pair of socks (retail value,

brand association
Anything linked to or connected with the brand name in a consumer's memory.

By using this symbol, Lululemon builds awareness for its offerings and makes it easier for customers to recall its name and image.

Rob Crandall/Alamy.

$16) for every four pairs sold; suppliers also get involved and contribute to the worthy cause.[4]

Associations   Building awareness is the first step in developing brand equity, but the value of the brand is largely based on the associations that customers make with the brand name. A **brand association** is anything linked to or connected with the brand name in a consumer's memory. For example, some of the associations that consumers might have with McDonald's are golden arches, fast food, clean stores, hamburgers, french fries, Big Mac, and Ronald McDonald. In the case of McDonald's, these links are so strong that when a consumer thinks of fast food, hamburgers, or french fries, they also think of McDonald's. These strong associations influence consumer buying behaviour. For example, when consumers think about camping, Mountain Equipment Co-op might immediately come to mind, stimulating a visit to a Mountain Equipment Co-op store or its website.

Some common associations that retailers develop with their brand name are as follows:

DID YOU KNOW?

Canada continues to be a leader in online engagement: first in page views and visits, second in hours per visitor.[5]

- **Merchandise category.** The most common association is to link the retailer to a category of merchandise. For example, Staples would like to have consumers associate its name with office supplies. Then, when a need for office supplies arises, consumers immediately think of Staples.

- **Price/quality.** Some retailers, such as Holt Renfrew, want to be associated with offering high prices and unique, high fashion merchandise. Other retailers, such as Walmart, want associations with offering low prices and good value.

- **Specific attribute or benefit.** A retailer can link its stores to attributes such as convenience (7-Eleven) or service (Harry Rosen).

- **Lifestyle or activity.** Some retailers associate their name with a specific lifestyle or activity. For example, The Nature Company, a retailer offering books and equipment to study nature, is linked to a lifestyle of interacting with the environment. Best Buy is associated with computers, software, and small office equipment.

The brand image is a set of associations that are usually organized around some meaningful themes.

Thus, the associations that a consumer might have with McDonald's might be organized into groups such as kids, service, and type of food. Mountain Equipment Co-op nurtures its brand image of selling high-quality, functional products and providing helpful service for outdoor activity.

Consistent Reinforcement The retailer's brand image is developed and maintained through the retailer's communication program as well as other elements of the communication mix, such as merchandise assortment and pricing, the design of its stores and website, and the customer service it offers. To develop a strong set of associations and a clearly defined brand image, retailers need to be consistent, presenting the same message to customers over time and across all of the elements of the retail mix.

Rather than creating unique communication programs for sales associates, retailers need to develop an **integrated marketing communication program**—a program that integrates all of the communication elements to deliver a comprehensive, consistent message. Without this coordination, the communication methods might work at cross-purposes. For example, the retailer's TV advertising campaign might attempt to build an image of exceptional customer service, but the firm's sales promotions might all emphasize low prices. If communication methods aren't used consistently, customers may become confused about the retailer's image and therefore not patronize the store.

An example of this is Koodo's character called "El Tabador," Koodo uses an integrated marketing communication program to reinforce its brand image associated with fun-loving teenagers and young adults. In 2010, an IMC campaign introduced a new champion to the cell phone market known as El Tabador. "A four-inch-tall animated luchador (an iconic Mexican wrestler)," El Tabador "would save customers from the injustice of long-term contracts with hard-hitting offers and new plans." The campaign was used in various medias at the same time, including print, outdoor, television, POS, an online mockumentary with wrestler Bret "Hitman" Hart, social media, and tiny muchacho action figures.[6]

Another spokesperson currently being used in the Canadian retail market is "Gary" from Canadian Tire. Gary was introduced to the Canadian consumer in the fall of 2012. At that time, Canadian Tire wanted a consistent message it could deliver across the plethora of Canadian Tire product offerings. The company wanted to move away from micro ad campaigns and focus their advertising dollars more on a macro campaign level across the country. Gary has been seen in numerous commercials pitching basically everything Canadian Tire sells in their various departments, including automotive, outdoor living, and tools and hardware (to name a few).[7]

> **integrated marketing communication program** The strategic integration of multiple communication methods to form a comprehensive, consistent message.

Extending the Brand Name

Retailers can leverage their brand names to support their growth strategies. For example, IKEA used its strong brand image to successfully enter the Canadian home furnishing retail market; Laura

Koodo has successfully used El Tabador as part of an integrated marketing communication strategy to reinforce its image associated with independent teenagers and young adults.

Koodo Mobile's materials used with permission. © 2016 TELUS. All rights reserved.

Harnessing the Power of Social Media to Make Customers Happy

Social media has revolutionized how companies communicate with, listen to, and learn from their customers. The volume of information generated can be a powerful tool for improving all business operations, including product design, technical support, and customer service, but it is also a very daunting task simply to make sense of it all! Consistent with its image as a global leader in computing, Dell is recognized as one of the top social media brands worldwide.

The company has always valued consumer input, according to founder and CEO Michael Dell: "One of Dell's founding principles was really about listening and learning from our customers, and being able to take that feedback to improve." Dell still offers traditional online support forums, which post questions and answers for different user groups and by topic. Now, however, social media channels like Facebook and Twitter have vastly accelerated that learning curve. Dell's mobile phone app also helps users stay connected on the road.

Each of Dell's multiple, highly developed social media channels differs qualitatively. They give the company and its customers the immediacy of instant chat and conversations through Facebook, LinkedIn, Twitter, and Google+, as well as Dell's flagship blog Direct2Dell.com and a host of other blogs.

Listening and analysis—or social media monitoring—is key. It enables Dell to identify salient customer input and trends. By teaming with social media monitor partner Salesforce Radian6, for example, Dell couples text analysis and high-volume, digital content-gathering technology methods to monitor approximately 25 000 conversations a day. In addition to customer support, the new media provide company and product news, as well as food for thought to its customers about digital business and digital life.

Dell gathers and monitors these online chats, posts responses or ideas, and engages in other discussions from its new social media listening command centre. The staff includes 70 trained employees who follow and respond to social media conversations in 11 languages. All tweets, Facebook posts, and other comments that warrant a Dell response are answered within 24 hours.

Sources: Andrea Edwards, "Dell—a Top Five Social Media Brand—Looking for Fresh Ideas," *SAJE Communication*, October 12, 2011; "Introducing Dell's Social Media Command Center," http://www.Dell.com; Ed Twittel, "How Dell Really Listens to Its Customers," *ReadWriteEnterprise*, July 22, 2011; "Social Media," http://www. Dell.com.

---

introduced a Laura II collection for women wearing plus-sizes and Laura Petites for small sizes; and the Pottery Barn launched its Pottery Barn Kids catalogue to target children. In other cases, retailers have pursued growth opportunities using a new and unrelated brand name. For example, The Gap used the brand name Old Navy for its value concept, and HBC named its new home store concept Home Outfitters.

There are pluses and minuses to extending a brand name to a new concept. An important benefit of extending the brand name is that minimal communication expenses are needed to create awareness and a brand image for the new concept. Customers will quickly transfer the original brand's awareness and associations to the new concept. However, in some cases, the retailer might not want to have the original brand's associations connected with the new concept. For example, Abercrombie & Fitch decided to invest in building new and different brand images for Gilly Hicks and Hollister Co. rather than branding them with a similar name.

These issues also arise as a retailer expands internationally. Associations with the retailer's brands that are valued in one country may not be valued in another. For example, French consumers prefer to shop at supermarkets that offer good service and high-quality grocery products, whereas German shoppers prefer supermarkets that offer low prices and good value. Thus, a French supermarket retailer with a brand image of quality and service might not be able to leverage its image if it decides to enter the German market.[8]

Retailers communicate using a mix of methods, such as advertising, sales promotion, publicity, email, blogs, and social media such as Twitter, Facebook, Pinterest, and YouTube. In large retail firms, the communication mix elements examined are managed by the firm's marketing or advertising department and the buying organization. The other elements, such as store atmosphere and salespeople, are managed by store personnel and the head office. The following sections of this chapter examine the methods that retailers use to communicate with their customers and how they plan and implement their communication programs to build brand equity as well as short-term sales.

Lo2 Methods of Communicating with Customers

For any communication campaign to succeed, the firm must deliver the right message to the right audience through the right media, with the ultimate goal of profiting from long-term customer relationships rather than just short-term transactions. Reaching the right audience is becoming more difficult, however; as the media environment grows, it becomes more complicated and fragmented.[9]

No single type of media is necessarily better than another. The goal of a retail communication strategy is to use media so that the sum exceeds the total of individual media types. However, advances in technology have led to a variety of new, along with traditional, media options for consumers, all of which vie for consumers' attention. Print media have also grown and become more specialized. This proliferation of media has led many retailers to shift their promotional dollars from advertising to direct marketing, use of Internet sites, and other forms of promotion in search of the best way to deliver messages to their target audiences.

We now examine the individual elements of a retail communication strategy and the way each contributes to a successful communication campaign (see Exhibit 15–1). The elements can be viewed on two axes: passive and interactive (from a consumer's perspective), and offline and online. Note that as the retailers' repertoire of communication elements has expanded, so too have the ways in which retailers can communicate with their customers; so, for instance, direct marketing appears in three of the four boxes. Firms have also expanded their use of traditional media (e.g., advertising, public relations, and sales promotions) from pure offline to a combination of offline and online.

Direct Marketing

Direct marketing is measureable, trackable, database-building marketing that communicates directly

Exhibit 15–1
Elements in an IMC Strategy

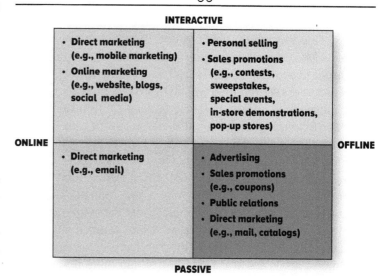

Source: Dhruv Grewal and Michael Levy, *Marketing*, 3rd ed. (New York: McGraw-Hill/Irwin, 2012).

with target customers to generate a response or transaction. Direct marketing contains a variety of traditional and new forms of marketing communication initiatives and is represented in three of the four quadrants in Exhibit 15–1. Traditional direct marketing includes mail and catalogues sent through the mail; today, it also includes Internet-enabled methods such as email and mobile marketing.

The increased use of customer databases has enabled retailers to identify and track consumers over time and across purchase situations, and this has contributed to the growth of direct marketing. Retailers have been able to build these databases, thanks to consumers' increased use of credit and debit cards, store-specific credit and loyalty cards, online shopping, contesting, and social media groups, all of which require the buyer to give the seller personal information that becomes part of its database. Because firms understand customers' purchases better when they possess such information, they can more easily focus their direct marketing efforts (call to action) appropriately. A **call to action** is the portion of the marketing or sales message that prompts potential consumers to perform a desired action within the desired time frame.

direct marketing A form of nonstore retailing in which customers are exposed to merchandise through print or electronic media; they then can purchase the merchandise by telephone, mail, or over the Internet.

call to action The portion of the marketing or sales message that prompts potential consumers to perform a desired action within the desired time frame.

Call-to-action phrases often use action verbs such as sign up, click here, register today, call now, or buy now. For example, American Eagle recently sent out this call to action via email to its AERewards customers: Get 'em while they are hot! Take an extra 50% off AE's summer sizzling clearance sale.

Direct marketing retailers try to carefully target their customers so that they will be more receptive to their messages. Shoppers Drug Mart's Optimum card, for example, has a digital deals program that sends weekly email deals and online printable coupons for items that Optimum cardholders have purchased previously, as well as identifies items that are in the current circular that match previous purchasing behaviour. "Generic marketing messages just don't resonate as much as we'd like them to," said David Harrington, the retailer's vice-president of business analytics and Optimum. "Customers demand much more of us. We have already got [them] as an engaged cardholder—it is kind of our obligation to send [targeted messaging] back to [them]."[10] These different forms of direct marketing demonstrate how this communication method can vary on both the interactivity and online/offline dimensions of Exhibit 15–1.

Direct Mail **Direct mail** includes any brochure, catalogue, advertisement, or other printed marketing material delivered directly to the consumer through the mail or by a private delivery company.[11] Retailers have communicated with their customers through the mail for as long as the mail has existed. The direct mail piece can go to all customers, to a subset of customers according to their previous purchases, or even on a personalized basis to individual customers.

Retailers frequently use data collected at point-of-sale (POS) terminals to target their direct mail promotions. For example, Hudson's Bay keeps a database of all purchases made by its credit card and loyalty card customers. With information about each customer's purchases, the retailer can then target direct mail about a new perfume to customers with a history of purchasing such merchandise. Further, many retailers encourage their salespeople to maintain preferred customer lists and use them to mail out personalized invitations or notes.

Retailers also can purchase a wide variety of lists that help them target consumers with specific demographic profiles, interests, and lifestyles. For example, a home furnishings store could buy a list of subscribers to *Architectural Digest* in its trading area and then mail a catalogue or specific information about home furnishings to those upscale consumers. Canada Post offers direct mail business solutions for businesses that do not have access to internal lists or consumer data.

Although relatively expensive on a per-customer basis (because of printing, mail costs, and a relatively low response rate), direct mail is still extensively used by many retailers because people respond favourably to personal messages.

Email **Email** is a direct marketing communication vehicle that involves sending messages over the Internet. Email, like other forms of electronic communications (e.g., websites, m-commerce), can be personalized to the specific consumer and thus is similar to communication delivered by salespeople. However, when the same message is delivered electronically to all recipients, electronic communications more closely resemble advertising. Retailers use email to inform customers of new merchandise and special promotions, confirm the receipt of an order, and indicate when an order has been shipped.

Email marketing can reduce the time and effort involved in structuring a direct-to-consumer campaign versus using common offline direct marketing communication (print postal mailings or telesales) techniques. Email allows for real-time messaging and personalized messages to consumers. Retailers can send unique birthday or anniversary messages to customers or send individual deals to customers based on their buying habits (e.g., PC Plus program from Loblaws). Because email takes less time to create and send than more traditional marketing mediums, communication with consumers can happen more frequently. Finally, email marketing has an exponentially greater ability to track sales and user engagement. Retailers are able to track how many people open an email, how many customers click a link in an email, which specific link within the email is clicked, and whether the email even made it to the customer's inbox.

Mobile Marketing **Mobile marketing**, also called *m-commerce* or *mobile commerce*, is marketing

direct mail Any brochure, catalogue, advertisement, or other printed marketing material delivered directly to the consumer through the mail or by a private delivery company.

email A paid personal communication vehicle that involves sending messages over the Internet.

mobile marketing Communicating with and selling to customers through wireless handheld devices, such as cellular telephones; also called *m-commerce* or *mobile commerce*.

DID YOU KNOW?

By the end of 2015, 75 percent of people who accessed the Internet went online via a mobile device.[13]

through wireless handheld devices, such as cellular telephones, and involves completing a transaction via cellphone.[12] Retailing View 15.3 provides insights up upcoming trends retailers need to consider when developing their mobile strategy. Smartphones have become far more than tools for placing calls; they offer a kind of mobile computer with the ability to obtain sports scores, weather, music, videos, and text messages, as well as to purchase

15.3 RETAILING VIEW

Trending Mobile Marketing Themes

Themes that could potentially influence a company's retail mobile journey over the next several years include the following:

1. Apps are becoming an integrated component of Digital Retail Marketing Strategy

Trends indicate that a brand's mobile apps will give traditional TV advertising a run for its money. Apps are projected to build loyalty, driving consumers to buy online via m-Commerce. Civic Science indicates that TV advertising influence dropped over 12 percent between 2014 and 2105. Marketers continue to influence time-deprived consumers and "travelling road warriors," and liberate online shoppers via apps. For example, using the Canadian Tire app, customers can scan any page of the hard copy catalogue to access a number of additional features, including videos and tutorials on how to use the product.

2. Mobile budgets and resources get serious

Canadian Tire has invested over $300 million dollars in data equipment and software housed in Winnipeg, Manitoba, to improve their digital experience with Canadian customers.

3. Indoor movements of customers in brick and mortar rising in prominence

A report recently released by the Canadian Marketing Association indicated that almost 60 percent of respondents use Beacon technology to enhance their shopping experience in a retail setting. In addition, over 80 percent of consumers are aware this technology exists.

4. Optimization of content is finding its home in the "technology stack"

As indicated by Michael Della Penna, "Content management and optimization across channels becomes a required component of any technology stack. While many marketers look to content as a critical component of their strategy, more often than not, brands lack the ability to effectively and efficiently optimize and distribute this content across channels."

5. Pedal to the metal, M-commerce is on the fast track

E-commerce in Canada continues to trend positively. *Canadian Business* is forecasting that e-commerce retail spending will equate to 10 percent of total retail spending in the Canadian marketplace by 2017, up from 6 percent in 2014.

6. Marketing is taking a hybrid route based on mobile, movement, and real-time exposure

Marketers need to think to rethink how they will communicate their message to consumers. Three important elements are movement, mobile, and locale. The message will have to access consumers via both physical and digital channels. Michael Della Penna, author of "10 Mobile Marketing Themes to Look Out for in 2016," states: "On the physical front, marketers have more tools at their disposal to target customers on the pre-visit via geo-fencing, during a visit through interactions with beacons, and post-visit with multichannel retargeting. Additionally, advancements in real-time mobile messaging enable orchestration with other channels including email, display, and even direct mail."

Sources: Michael Della Penna, "10 Mobile Marketing Themes to Look Out for in 2016," *ClickZ,* December 15, 2016, https://www.clickz.com/clickz/column/2437827/10-mobile-marketing-themes-to-look out-for-in-2016 (accessed March 14, 2016); "Insight Report: Social Media Now Equals TV Advertising in Influence Power on Consumption Decisions," *Civic Science,* October 16, 2014, https://civicscience.com/ourinsights/insightreports/social-media-equals-tv-advertising-in-influence-power-on-consumption-decisions/ (accessed September 24, 2016); Gary Ng, "Canadian Tire for iOS Brings Interactive Features to Company Catalogue [u]," *iPhone in Canada,* April 4, 2016, http://www.iphoneincanada.ca/app-store/canadian-tire-iphone-wow-guide/ (accessed September 24, 2016); Qasim Mohammad, "After Years in the Slow Lane, Canada's e-commerce Ecosystem is Booming," *Canadian Business,* February 22, 2016, http://www.canadianbusiness.com/innovation/canada-ecommerce-innovators/ (accessed September 24, 2016); John Lorinc, "How Canadian Tire is Pioneering Tomorrow's Retail Experience Now," *Canadian Business,* February 29, 2016, http://www.canadianbusiness.com/lists-and-rankings/most-innovative-companies/canadian-tire/ (accessed September 24, 2016).

merchandise. Smartphone usage has increased significantly and by 2018 it is projected that 65 percent of the Canada's population will be using a smartphone.[14] Ninety-nine percent of the Canadian population has access to wireless services. When looking at how retail activities relate to smartphone use, comScore has identified some interesting behaviour.

Based on application usage, the top three uses of smartphones are:

- creating a list for shopping
- locating stores
- identifying store deals or coupons

Based on browser usage, the top three uses of a smartphone are:

- locating stores
- finding product prices
- researching product attributes[15]

The RedLaser shopping comparison app for the iPhone takes a picture of a product's barcode and then lists the prices for that item at various retailers.

Courtesy of eBay. Used with permission.

DID YOU KNOW?

73 percent of people always have their mobile device with them![16]

Retailers' success with mobile marketing rests on integrating marketing communications with fun and useful apps that are consistent with consumer attitudes toward mobile devices (see Exhibit 15–2). In response, firms are steadily improving customers' potential experience with their mobile interfaces by creating applications for consumers. For example, McDonald's Pick-n-Play used a mobile Web URL to allow consumers to control a game of Pong on an interactive billboard to win coupons. Retailing View 15.4 describes another innovative use of mobile marketing.

The RedLaser shopping comparison application takes a picture of a product's barcode and lists the prices for that item at various local retailers. Google Shopper has the same capability for Android. NearbyNow and Amazon's mobile applications allow users to buy products and complete their transactions though their cellphones.

Foursquare and WeReward target mobile phone users and send them marketing messages on the basis of GPS technology. Started by a video game aficionado, Foursquare awards points to consumers who try local retailers, enabling them to unlock "badges" and earn titles, such as "Mayor" of a particular venue.[17] The badges and titles entitle the recipient to discounts or special offers. For example, Starbucks Mayors can unlock their offers to get a $1 discount on a Frappuccino.[18] The application is based on GPS locations, so users can recommend nearby retailers to friends in the area. Furthermore, the application's data analytics capabilities allow retailers to track the impact of mobile marketing campaigns.

Tim Hortons' *Chill to Win* contest was an online contest with two ways to play for a chance to win prizes. On the game cup was a label, which contained an alphanumeric code (PIN code). This PIN

Exhibit 15–2
Retail Activities on Smartphones

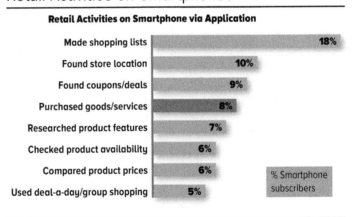

Retail Activities on Smartphone via Application

	% Smartphone subscribers
Made shopping lists	18%
Found store location	10%
Found coupons/deals	9%
Purchased goods/services	8%
Researched product features	7%
Checked product availability	6%
Compared product prices	6%
Used deal-a-day/group shopping	5%

Retail Activities on Smartphone via Browser

Found store location	28%
Compared product prices	20%
Researched product features	19%
Checked product availability	19%
Found coupons/deals	15%
Purchased goods/services	14%
Used deal-a-day/group shopping	6%
Made shopping lists	6%

Source: comScore, "2015 Canada Digital Future in Focus," March 27, 2015, https://www.comscore.com/Insights/Presentations-and-Whitepapers/2015/2015-Canada-Digital-Future-in-Focus (accessed March 14, 2016).

Sportsgirl

Sportsgirl is an Australian multichannel fashion retailer that used QR codes in its most recent digital strategy, creatively dubbed "Window Shop." Customers can make immediate purchases via their mobile devices (smartphone or tablet) by scanning the QR code on the Sportsgirl products that are displayed on the storefront's window. Sportsgirl updates the window weekly to feature the latest styles, creating a 24/7 shopping experience. All orders made via the QR codes are rewarded with a gift that is sent with the purchased product. According to the retailer, the aim of the Window Shop program is to bring Sportsgirl's superflagship-store product to all areas, providing greater choice for customers nationwide.

Ray Warren Backgrounds/Alamy.

Source: Adapted from Samantha Youl, "Sportsgirl Introduces Innovative QR Code Feature," *PowerRetail*, February 22, 2012, http://www.powerretail.com.au/multichannel/sportsgirl-qr-code-feature/#ixzz2VRqSmBJh (accessed June 1, 2013).

code could be played at the Peel 'n' Play online game at http://www.chilltowin.com or on the customer's mobile device (smartphone or tablet) at m.chilltowin.com.

The foundation of mobile marketing is short codes, which were introduced in Canada in July 2003.[19] Short codes allow consumers to interact with retailers via text messaging. Instead of sending text messages to the regular ten-digit phone number, cellphone users send it to a **short code**, a five- or six-digit number or word/brand name. A short code becomes a *common short code (CSC)* when the same code is activated across multiple mobile phone networks, which greatly extends its reach to many more mobile phone customers.[20] Retailers can lease dedicated short codes for a period of three, six, or twelve months. Cost varies for *random short codes* (completely random in selection) and *selected short codes*

Foursquare encourages consumers to buy at participating retailers by offering discounts and special offers.

© 2010 foursquare.

(specifically requested codes). For example, Victoria's Secret uses a selected short code: text "start" to ANGEL (26435) and expect exclusive discounts via text message from the retailer. Canadian Tire uses a random short code for its Jumpstart mobile donation campaign: "Give kids a sporting chance! You can help the Canadian Tire Jumpstart program by texting the word JUMP to short-code 45678 on your mobile phone. A $5.00 donation will be made on your behalf to the children which will be added your phone bill!" Exhibit 15–3 graphs the increased usage of short code texting, and shows the percent of the population that has sent or received a text message from an organization.

QR (quick response) codes are a specialized version of a two-dimensional (2D) barcode.[21] QR codes are intended

short code A five- or six-digit number or word used for messaging.

Exhibit 15–3
Use of Short Code Texting

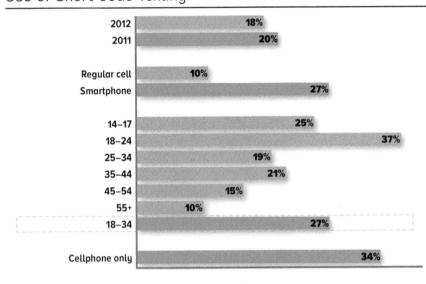

- Similar to 2011, one in five mobile phone users (18%) have sent or received a text message from an organization in the past.
- Just over one-quarter of mobile phone users (27%) between 18 and 34 have used short code texting this way in the past.
- Mobile users more likely to have used short code texting in the past are.
  - Smartphone owners (27%)
  - Cellphone only households (34%)
  - Those between 18 and 24 years old (37%)

Percent who have sent or received a text message from an organization

	Gender		Region					
	Male	Female	BC	AB	MB/SK	ON	QC	ATL
Have sent or received a text message from an organization	19%	17%	17%	19%	14%	16%	21%	22%

Source: Quorus Consulting Group, *2012 Cell Phone Consumer Attitudes Study*, April 23, 2012, p. 51, http://cwta.ca/wordpress/wp-content/uploads/2011/08/CWTA-2012ConsumerAttitudes.pdf (accessed June 1, 2013).

to be scanned by the camera on a mobile phone, providing a fast and easy way to transfer information.[22] There are several different types of 2D barcodes, but the two most used by retailers are the QR code format. QR codes have no licensing restrictions—so they will always be free—and are supported by a variety of readers.[23]

Retailers use QR codes in a variety of ways: product information, app-based user perks, discounts, sweepstakes, incentives, endorsement of the retail brand, check-in, instructions, sharing via social media, price comparison, and direct online shopping. Some QR codes are even linked to store inventories and can tell you the quantity, size, and colour currently in stock of the product scanned.[24]

Customers can use the QR reader on their smartphones to get detailed information about the product they are considering. They can read consumer reviews, compare features with similar products, and in some cases, even email details to a friend who might be giving advice.[25] Many stores

QR code
Lourens Smak/Alamy.

have designed their own smartphone apps. While signs could just publicize the apps, the QR codes make it quick and easy to acquire the app. In many cases, these apps go beyond just providing product information and include styling advice, loyalty programs, social media, or check-in incentives and location-based discounts.[26]

Incentivizing consumers to interact with the brand using a mobile phone by offering discounts, special offers, and opportunities to win prizes or gifts with purchase with a QR code not only promotes reciprocity but also enables the transaction to occur in one step. (See Exhibit 15–4 for survey data about using smartphones to make purchases.) Stores use QR codes to connect to social media by sharing, as well as by checking in on sites such as Foursquare and Facebook. A check-in explicitly endorses a product or retail brand to those connected to a user's profile. QR codes are also showing up in-store on shelf-talkers and price tags. QR codes provide the opportunity to add much more technical data than can fit on a retail package or tag. Best Buy uses QR codes to link the user to a specific mobile-optimized page for the product, while Sephora uses QR codes to offer demonstrations and instructions for cosmetics. Videos of this nature can also engage the consumer if a salesperson is not available for immediate assistance.[27]

According to a ClickIQ survey of 900 shoppers, half of all people who purchase products online first go to a bricks-and-mortar store to do their research.[28] Known as **showrooming**, this buzzword refers to the growing number of customers who browse the wares of traditional bricks-and-mortar retailers; feel, touch, and smell the merchandise; and then take out their smartphones and price around until they find the product they want for the lowest price—usually from an online retailer such as Amazon that doesn't have anywhere near the same overhead.[29] This trend makes it critical for retailers to provide an integrated shopping experience across multiple touchpoints through the path to purchase in order to maintain customers' loyalty to the brand and its products and services.

Retailers can harness QR code technology to add value for consumers and harness showrooming to impact their revenue, as in the following examples:[30]

- **Cross-sell.** A consumer can scan a QR code for a TV, and instantly receive a promotion for a free HDMI cable with the purchase of the TV in-store.

- **Bundling.** If consumers scan multiple QR codes during a single in-store visit, they could receive an offer for a gift card if a specific set of products or dollar amount is purchased in the store during that store visit.

showrooming Visiting a bricks-and-mortar store to research a product before purchasing it through electronic means after browsing online for the best price.

Exhibit 15–4
Interest in Mobile Payments

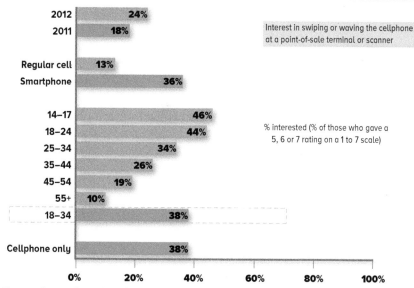

Interest in swiping or waving the cellphone at a point-of-sale terminal or scanner

% interested (% of those who gave a 5, 6 or 7 rating on a 1 to 7 scale)

- Almost one in four (24%) cellphone users are interested in the idea of swiping or waving their cellphone at a point-of-sale terminal or scanner. Interest in mobile payments increased significantly from 18% in 2011 to 24% in 2012.
- Nearly 4 in 10 respondents between 18 and 34 years old (38%) are interested in swiping or waving their phone for a purchase, a significant increase from 2011 (27%).
- Those more likely to be interested include:
  – Cellphone only households (38%)
  – Smartphone users (36%)
  – Men (29%)
  – Residents in BC and in Atlantic Canada (30%)
  – The younger respondents are, the more likely they are to be interested in this idea.

Source: Quorus Consulting Group, *2012 Cell Phone Consumer Attitudes Study*, April 23, 2012, p. 30, http://cwta.ca/wordpress/wp-content/uploads/2011/08/CWTA-2012ConsumerAttitudes.pdf (accessed June 1, 2013).

- **Behavioural.** A consumer that has scanned a QR code for a particular product type on a previous visit could trigger an alert if they scan a product in that product group during a subsequent visit. The alert could inform the customer that a brand within that product group is on sale.

- **Location/time specific.** Location data could be passed on if available to show exclusive deals only available at a specific store location, or content could be changed based on the time of day or weather.

- **Endless aisle.** Scanning a QR code for a jacket could provide a list of alternative sizes and colours that aren't stocked in that store. The consumer could then be offered the option of ordering the version she wants with just a few clicks on her smartphone or tablet and have it delivered to the store or her home.

© AP Photo-J. Pat Carter/The Canadian Press.

In June 2013, Walmart Canada introduced mobile stores inside 50 bus shelters in the city of Toronto. Customers used their mobile devices to scan posters with QR codes at these choice bus shelters to buy select items, including Pantene shampoo, Pampers diapers, and Tide detergent. The campaign was scheduled to run for four weeks and, according to Simon Rodrique, vice president of e-commerce for Walmart Canada, "allow[ed] [Walmart] to help Torontonians shop for essentials on the go, anywhere, at any time."[31]

Mobile shopping via smartphone is still in its infancy but is gaining traction with consumers. It is set to grow by around 40 percent year over year until around 2016.[32] Some larger retailers using mobile in their communication strategies reported significant rises in market share of mobile commerce transactions starting around the latter half of 2012. Add to that fact that people are spending more and more time on mobile apps (approximately 70 percent

of smartphone users have downloaded apps to their phones[33]), and that there were an estimated 10 billion mobile, Internet-enabled devices being used around the world by 2016,[34] and it is no surprise that retailers are embracing this as a method of communication (see Exhibit 15–5).

Online Marketing

Websites Retailers are increasing their emphasis on communicating with customers through their

Exhibit 15–5
Smartphone Shopping Adoption by Store Category

Smartphone Shopping Adoption by Store Category		Frequency of Use by Store	Mobile Influence Factor (2012)	Projected Influence Factor (2016)
Electronic/Appliances	49%	60.9%	8.3%	29.4%–33.7%
GM/Department/Warehouse	46%	52.5%	6.7%	23.8%–27.2%
Clothing/Footware	38%	56.2%	5.9%	21.1%–24.1%
Food/Beverage	35%	58.2%	5.7%	18.7%–23.0%
Books and Music	33%	57.1%	5.2%	17.3%–21.3%
Home Improvement/Garden	31%	53.5%	4.6%	15.2%–18.7%
Sporting Goods, Toys, Hobby	30%	56.7%	4.7%	15.6%–19.2%
Health/Personal Care/Drug	27%	58.4%	4.4%	14.5%–17.8%
Furniture/Home Furnishing	24%	58.7%	3.9%	12.9%–15.9%
Misc Including Office Supplies	22%	51.1%	3.1%	10.3%–12.7%
Convenience/Gas Station	19%	56.0%	3.0%	8.5%–11.2%
Weighted Average			5.1%	17.2%–20.6%

Note: The base for "Smartphone Shopping Adoption by Store Category" is survey respondents who own a smartphone and have ever used it to shop, either before they go to a store or in the store. The "Mobile influence Factor" applies to all store sales in that category.

Source: Deloitte Development, *The Dawn of Mobile Influence: Discovering the Value of Mobile in Retail*, 2012, p. 5, http://www.deloitte.com/assets/Dcom-UnitedStates/Local%20Assets/Documents/RetailDistribution/us_retail_Mobile-Influence-Factor_062712.pdf (accessed January 13, 2014).

websites. Retailers use their websites to build their brand images; to inform customers of store locations, special events, and the availability of merchandise in local stores; and to sell merchandise and services.

In addition, some retailers provide services that help garner customer loyalty and indirectly increase sales. Grand & Toy's website, for example, has a business solutions that provides advice and product knowledge. By providing this information, the company reinforces its image as the essential source of products, services, and information for businesses.

Other retailers devote areas of their websites to community building. These sites offer an opportunity for customers with similar interests to learn about products and services that support their hobbies and to share information with others. Visitors to these websites can also post questions seeking information and/or comments about issues, products, and services. For example, Mountain Equipment Co-op (MEC), an outdoor apparel and equipment retailer, offers planning resources for hiking trips, bike tours, paddling, adventure travel, and other trips. By doing so, MEC creates a community of customers who engage in activities using the merchandise that MEC sells. The community thus reinforces MEC's brand image.

Many retailers also encourage customers to post reviews of products they have bought or used, and they even have visitors to their websites rate the quality of the reviews. Research has shown that these online product reviews increase customer loyalty and provide a competitive advantage for sites that offer them.

Blogs   A **blog** (also called *weblog*) contains periodic posts on a common Web page. A well-received blog can communicate trends, announce special events, and create word-of-mouth, which is communication between people about a retailer.[35] Blogs connect customers by forming a community, allow the company to respond directly to customers' comments, and facilitate long-term relationships between customers and the company. By their very nature, blogs are supposed to be transparent and contain authors' honest observations, which can help customers

determine their trust and loyalty levels. Today, blogs are becoming more interactive as the communication between bloggers and customers has increased.

Many retailers use blogs as part of their communication strategy. A top-ranked retailer blog is Omnivoracious, Amazon's blog, which is, naturally, all about books. Dell, Apple, Sears, Best Buy, Lululemon, and QVC also have highly rated blogs.[36]

Social Media   **Social media** is media content distributed through social interactions. Social media leverage requires a good communication strategy coupled with appropriate content to reach out to the correct target audience and achieve the goals set out. Social media is not advertising; although it sounds simple and easy, social media is not easy and requires time and effort to make it useful. Content for social media platforms has to be engaging for online users or they will not be interested. Additionally, it has to come across as unbiased and focus on bringing out the best of the product and/ or service rather than emphasizing the brand or retailer.[37]

Five major online facilitators of social media for retailers are YouTube, Facebook, Pinterest, Twitter, and Instagram. As another online vehicle for word-of-mouth communication, online social media enable consumers to review, communicate about, and aggregate information about products, prices, and promotions. This type of social media also allows users to interact among themselves (e.g., form a community). Such online communities enable users to provide other like-minded consumers and retailers with their thoughts and evaluations about a retailer's products or services. A major benefit of social media is to have your customers share with their contacts, as 90 percent of consumers trust peer recommendations with only 10 percent trusting advertising.[38]

Retailers are using social media to engage their customers in a proactive dialogue. When a retailer provides content in

> **blog** A public website where users post informal journals of their thoughts, comments, and philosophies; also called *weblog*.

> **social media** Media content distributed through social interactions; major online facilitators of social media include YouTube, Facebook, Pinterest, and Twitter.

© Used with permission from MEC.

social media, people often begin sharing and commenting on it. The retailer then must monitor the feedback and respond if necessary—especially if the commentary is negative. When a retailer finds an unhappy customer, it should recognize the event as a prime customer experience opportunity, engage the consumer, and attempt to remedy the situation. By proactively engaging with its customers, a retailer can build stronger relationships. Furthermore, retailers can help cultivate their images through social media that depict them in a certain way, adding a human element that otherwise might not exist.

The social networking site Shopstyle.com features clothing and accessories from hundreds of Internet stores. Shoppers can browse different looks that feature items across several retailers, put together outfits on their own, and then share and discuss with friends.

Not all social media have positive results, though.[39] Social media eliminate boundaries, often exposing companies to customers' true (and sometimes mean) thoughts and behaviours. Consider the situation in which Kevin Smith, the popular director of films such as *Clerks* and *Dogma* and the actor who played Silent Bob in several movies, was removed from a Southwest Airlines flight because his large size required him to purchase two seats. Smith immediately tweeted about the situation to his more than 1.6 million Twitter followers.

Home Depot fosters its identity with instructional do-it-yourself videos on YouTube.
Courtesy of The Home Depot.

Southwest quickly responded on its blog, citing its longstanding rules and concern for other passengers. But other responses were equally split in support of the airline and Smith.[40]

YouTube On this video-sharing social media platform, users upload, share, and view videos. This medium gives retailers a chance to express themselves in a different way than they have before. A retailer like television home shopping network HSN can

Exhibit 15-6
Facebook

- Total number of Facebook users: 1.26 billion
- Total number of Facebook monthly active users: 1.19 billion
- Total number of Facebook daily active users: 728 million
- Percentage of millennials (15- to 34-year-olds) that use Facebook: 66%
- Number of times daily that the Facebook Like or Share buttons are viewed: 22 billion
- Eighty percent of social media users prefer to connect with brands through Facebook.
- Country with most active Facebook users: Canada

- More than half of all Canadians log onto Facebook at least once per month.
- On average, 61 percent of global users check Facebook at least once a day. In the U.S. 70 percent of them do; in Canada, it's 74 percent.
- Pages with the most Canadian Likes: eminem, Tim Hortons, Family Guy, YouTube, and The Simpsons
- Top brands by Likes: Tim Hortons, Subway, Skittles, Target Canada, and iTunes
- A whopping 77 percent of B2C companies and 43 percent of B2B companies acquired customers from Facebook.
- Seventy-four percent of marketers believe Facebook is important for their lead generation.

Sources: Jennifer Wadsworth, "Canadians Are the Most Active Facebook Users in the World," *InsideFacebook.com*, August 23, 2013, http://www.insidefacebook.com/2013/08/23/canadians-still-the-most-active-facebook-users-in-the-world; Ray C. He, "Introducing New Like and Share Buttons," Facebook Developer blog, November 6, 2013, https://developers.facebook.com/blog/post/2013/11/06/introducing-new-like-and-share-buttons; Brian Honigman, "100 Fascinating Social Media Statistics and Figures From 2012," *The Huffington Post*, November 29, 2012, http://www.huffingtonpost.com/brian-honigman/100-fascinating-social-me_b_2185281.html?; Michael Stelzner, *2013 Social Media Marketing Industry Report*, Social Media Examiner blog, May 21, 2013, http://www.socialmediaexaminer.com/social-media-marketing-industry-report-2013; Craig Smith, "By the Numbers: 64 Amazing Facebook User Statistics," Digital Marketing Ramblings blog, December 28, 2013, http://expandedramblings.com/index.php/by-the-numbers-17-amazing-facebook-stats/#.UtQ-6NK1yM4; Jeff Bullas, "46 Amazing Social Media Facts in 2013," October 25, 2013, http://www.jeffbullas.com/2013/10/25/46-amazing-social-media-facts-in-2013/#!AcpwvTuqjwz8bAc.99 (all accessed January 13, 2014); VLADGRIN/Shutterstock Royalty Free.

broadcast its own channel, that is, a YouTube portal that contains content relevant only to the company's own products.[41] YouTube also provides an effective medium for hosting contests and posting instructional videos. Home Depot attracts more than 4400 viewers per day with an array of videos detailing new products available in stores, as well as instructional-do-it-yourself videos, such as "How to Tips for Mowing Your Lawn" and "How to Repair a Toilet."[42] These videos maintain the core identity of the Home Depot brand while also adding value for consumers, who learn useful ways to improve their homes.

Facebook This social media platform with more than a billion active users gives companies a forum to interact with fans (see Exhibit 15–6). Retailers have access to the same features that regular users do, including a "wall" where they can post company updates, photos, and videos or participate in a discussion board.

An excellent example of a fan page is that of the discount clothing retailer Forever 21.[43] When a fan clicks to indicate that he or she "likes" a certain post, the message gets relayed into a news feed, so every friend of that user sees what he or she likes, creating a huge multiplier effect.[44] Accordingly, marketers must consistently update and maintain their fan pages to exploit them as the tremendous assets they can be.

Twitter This microblogging site, in which users are limited to 140-character messages, is also a platform to facilitate communication using social

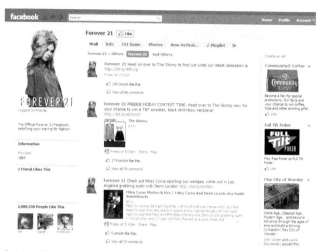

Retailers like Forever 21 are using Facebook to communicate with their customers and create a sense of community.
Courtesy of Forever 21.

media. Twitter provides another option for retailers and their customers to communicate using social media. Twitter has more than 228 million monthly active users (see Exhibit 15–7).

Twitter is actively used by both small and large retailers. Small retailers with limited marketing budgets love the immediate response they can induce by sending a promotional message. A local bakery tweets, "Two new scones: Lemon Blueberry and Chorizo Cheddar!" and gets responses from 400 Twitter followers—a huge captive audience for a local entity. Large retailers that have enough funds to mass-market through national campaigns use Twitter as a way to stay in personal touch with their customers. For instance, Best Buy (@BestBuy)

Exhibit 15–7
Twitter

- There are over 500 million total Twitter users.
- There are over 288 million active monthly Twitter users.
- On average, over 400 million tweets are sent per day.
- Fifty-six percent of customer tweets to companies are being ignored.
- Thirty-two percent of all Internet users are using Twitter.
- The most followed brand on Twitter is YouTube, with 19 million followers.
- Eleven accounts are created every second on Twitter.

- Sixty percent of Twitter users are using the social network via mobile.
- Thirty-four percent of marketers have generated leads using Twitter.
- Twitter's fastest growing age demographic is 55- to 64-year-olds with active users at 79 percent.
- Twenty-nine percent of under 35s use Twitter and 17 percent plan to start.
- The average millennial (15- to 34-year-olds) uses 2.5 social networks, with Facebook (66 percent), Twitter (29 percent), and Google+ (28 percent) the most popular.

Sources: Jeff Bullas, "46 Amazing Social Media Facts in 2013," October 25, 2013, http://www.jeffbullas.com/2013/10/25/46-amazing-social-media-facts-in-2013/#.IAcpwvTuqjwz8bAc.99; "Twitter 2012," Sirona Consulting blog, http://blog.sironaconsulting.com/.a/6a00d8341c761a53ef016767bafa2c970b-pi; Shea Bennett, "Why First Class Customer Service Is the Key to Social Media Success," AllTwitter blog, May 24, 2012, http://www.mediabistro.com/alltwitter/social-key-customer-service_b23050; Matt McGee, "Social Network Demographics: Pew Study Shows Who Uses Facebook, Twitter, Pinterest & Others," *MarketingLand.com*, September 14, 2012, http://marketingland.com/social-network-demographics-pew-study-shows-who-uses-facebook-twitter-pinterest-others-21594; Holly Richmond, "The Growth of Mobile Marketing and Tagging," *Microsoft Tag*, March 21, 2011, http://tag.microsoft.com/community/blog/t/the_growth_of_mobile_marketing_and_tagging.aspx; "Infographic: Social Media Statistics for 2012," DigitalBuzz blog, January 3, 2012, http://www.digitalbuzzblog.com/social-media-statistics-stats-2012-infographic/ (all accessed January 13, 2014); VLADGRIN/Shutterstock Royalty Free.

tweets in-store deals to its followers: an example of a promotional tweet could be something like this: *Save $200 on this Acer laptop: http://bbyurl.us/tgg in-store only for a limited time! @BestBuy_deals.*

Pinterest Pinterest is an online pinboard-style image-sharing website that is entirely driven by visuals. Users can share images found online, or they can directly upload images onto Pinterest. Using the Pin It button, users can share directly in their browser from any Web page and can also share their pins on Twitter and Facebook. Research shows that 80 percent of all pins are re-pins, which means only 20 percent are original pins.[45] Globally, the site is most popular with women. In 2012, it was reported that 83 percent of the global users were women,[46] and in February 2013, Reuters and ComScore stated that Pinterest had 48.7 million users.[47] The average time spent on the site by users is 98 minutes per month (see Exhibit 15–8).

This social media site offers retailers and their brands an effective visual communication platform. Jewellery and accessories website Boticca.com, which was co-founded by former eBay and private equity executives, compared 50 000 shoppers referred from Pinterest to 50 000 shoppers referred from Facebook and said the Pinterest users spent way more money—$185 versus $85—but less time browsing the site.[48] While both Pinterest and Facebook are social media sites consumers visit to connect with people who have similar styles and interests, Pinterest is more often a destination for shopping inspiration, tracking, and product discovery. Forty-three percent of Pinterest members agree that they use Pinterest to "associate with retailers or brands with which [they] identify." A greater percentage (55 percent) of Pinterest users have engaged with retailers and brands via Pinterest, compared to the percentage of Facebook users that engage retailers or brands on Facebook (48 percent). But how customers engage differs for each of the two social media platforms. Pinterest users are more likely to be "creators"—adding and sharing retailer/brand-related content—while Facebook users are more likely to be "participators"—interacting with promotional activities developed by retailers and brands.[49]

When Sephora, the beauty products retailer, revamped its website in April 2012, it was one of the first retailers to integrate the Pin It button throughout the site. Sephora coordinated the introduction of Pin It buttons with its "Paint the Town Sweepstakes" campaign. The company invited consumers to pin their beauty shopping lists. Pinners participating in the campaign were encouraged to re-pin the post on Sephora Sweepstakes Pinterest logo

Exhibit 15–8
Pinterest

- Pinterest's three most popular pins: Hasselback Garlic Cheesy Bread Recipe, Rainbow Fruit Kabobs Photo, and Lovely Framing Compositions.
- Percentage of shares by content: fashion, 10%; parenting, 16%; food, 18%
- People share with Pinterest three times more often on mobile than on a computer.
- Ninety-seven percent of the fans of Pinterest's Facebook page are women.
- Over 80 percent of pins are re-pins.
- Eighty percent of Pinterest users are women (66 percent in Canada), while 50 percent of all Pinterest users have children (38 percent in Canada).
- Thirty-five percent of Canadian Pinterest users have a household income of over $100 000 per year.
- Canada is the second-largest country of Pinterest users, following the United States.

- Pinterest referrals spend 70 percent more money than visitors referred from non-social channels.
- The average Pinterest user spends 98 minutes per month on the site, compared to 2.5 hours on Tumblr and 7 hours on Facebook.
- Sixty-nine percent of online consumers who visit Pinterest have found an item they've bought or wanted to buy, compared with 40 percent of Facebook users.
- The most popular age group on Pinterest is 25- to 34-year-olds.
- Forty-three percent of people prefer Pinterest to associate with retailers or brands; 24 percent chose Facebook.
- Nine percent of people have participated in contests or promotions via Pinterest.
- iPads are the Pinterest user's device of choice.

Sources: Bob Gilbreath, "New Data Insights on Pinterest's Potential," *MarketingLand.com*, August 16, 2013, http://marketingland.com/new-data-insights-on-pinterests-potential-52323; "Infographic: All About How People Share on Pinterest," *MarketingLand.com*, October 25, 2013, http://marketingland.com/infographic-how-people-share-on-pinterest-63052; "How Popular Is pinterest.com?" *Alexa.com*, n.d., http://www.alexa.com/siteinfo/pinterest.com#demographics; "Pinterest Demographics," Cahoots blog, March 21, 2013, http://cahootsblog.com/2013/03/21/pinterest-demographics/; "Facts Tagged with Pinterest," *FactBrowser.com*, n.d., http://www.factbrowser.com/tags/pinterest/; Catharine Smith, "Pinterest's 15 Most Popular Pins of All Time," *The Huffington Post*, April 17, 2012, http://www.huffingtonpost.com/2012/04/17/pinterest-most-popular-pins_n_1431564.html; "Infographic: How Users Interact on Pinterest," Wishpond blog, n.d., http://blog.wishpond.com/post/44155339712/infographic-how-users-interact-on-pinterest; Brian Honigman, "100 Fascinating Social Media Statistics and Figures From 2012," *The Huffington Post*, November 29, 2012, http://www.huffingtonpost.com/brian-honigman/100-fascinating-social-me_b_2185281.html? (all accessed January 13, 2014); VLADGRIN/Shutterstock Royalty Free.

board in order to win one of ten Sephora by OPI Tinsel Town Collector's sets. With only 12 original pins, Sephora Sweepstakes pinboard gained nearly 100 000 followers and 8415 users re-pinned the post.[50] Within a few short months, Pinterest became a top ten referring site for Sephora.com. Sephora's head of digital, Julie Bornstein, told *VentureBeat* in an interview that Pinterest members spent 15 times more on the company's products than Facebook fans.[51] Sephora uses its "Trending Now" board on Pinterest to showcase its newest products. Hashtags tie new products to a specific campaign, and all products lead back to its e-commerce site. Further, Sephora invites participation by asking fans/followers to upload their own tagged photos, which then exposes the product collection to new audiences.

Instagram "Instagram has become one of the most popular social media platforms among people of all ages, and savvy businesses are finding creative ways to tap into its potential as a new marketing channel."[52] Currently Instagram has over 400 million followers. With those kind of numbers, it was only a matter of time until retailers started using this application to inform consumers of products and service offerings. The purpose of Instagram is to share videos and photos. Instagram uses a follower model just like Twitter. Users can find their Facebook and Twitter friends and follow them on Instagram, and post and share photos and videos for others to follow.[53] (See Exhibit 15–9.)

Instagram normally doesn't let retailers have active link with pictures, but the app does let brands engage via different types of contests. People who follow the brands incorporate certain types of hashtags with their posts, hoping to win either gift cards or other types of prizes. "For example, Hudson's Bay Co.'s Lord & Taylor had a dress sell out quickly after 50 fashion influencers were paid to post photos and tag them #designlab to highlight its new collection." Credit Suisse's research on eleven retailers from the fashion industry, which includes H&M and Forever 21, had the biggest following (each having over 6 million followers). Regarding department stores, Nordstrom sets the pace as they have approximately 800 000 followers and have approximately 15 000 likes per photo.[54]

Retailing View 15.5 provides an example of how three retailers are effectively using social media.

Sales Promotions

Sales promotions are special incentives or excitement-building programs that encourage consumers to purchase a particular product or service; they are typically used in conjunction with other advertising or personal selling programs. Like personal selling and telemarketing, sales promotions are a form of offline/interactive communications (Exhibit 15–1). Many sales promotions, such as free samples or point-of-purchase (POP) displays, attempt to build short-term sales; others, such as loyalty programs, contests, and sweepstakes, have become integral components of retailers' long-term customer relationship management (CRM) programs, which they use to build customer loyalty. The tools used in sales promotions, along with their advantages and disadvantages, are presented in Exhibit 15–10 and then discussed.

> **sales promotions** Paid, impersonal communication activities that offer extra value and incentives to customers to visit a store or purchase merchandise during a specific period of time.

Exhibit 15–9
Instagram

- The Instagram community has grown to more than 400 million strong.
- More than 80 million photos per day are shared on Instagram.
- It represents a global community, with more than 75 percent living outside of the United States.
- The average Instagram user spends 21 minutes per day using the app.
- The app is more popular among younger people, with usage at 41 percent among those aged 16–24 and at 35 percent among those aged 24–34.

- Instagram first began testing sponsored posts in late 2013 in the United States with brands including Michael Kors, General Electric, Levi's, Lexus, and Ben & Jerry's.
- Currently the top five retail brands on Instagram are Zara, MAC cosmetics, Sephora, Topshop, and H&M. Video ads can be up to 30 seconds in length.
- Instagram rolled out sponsored posts to UK users on September 23, 2014 with Starbucks, Cadbury, Estée Lauder, Waitrose, Channel 4, and Rimmel among the brands included in the initial trials.

Sources: Instagram Blog, "Celebrating a Community of 400 Million," September 22, 2015, http://blog.instagram.com/post/129662501137/150922-400million; David Moth, "20+ Instagram Stats Marketers Need to Know," January 6, 2015, https://econsultancy.com/blog/65939-20-instagram-stats-marketers-need-to-know/; ICONOSQUARE, http://index.iconosquare.com/category/retail/ (all accessed March 15, 2016); VLADGRIN/Shutterstock Royalty Free.

Social Media 101-Multiple Platform Strategy at Its Finest

It goes without saying that if you wish to communicate with your customers in this millennium, you need to be active on social media.

Social media allows retailers to inform customers of new products offerings, augment customer service initiatives, and expand on brand promotion activities. Listed below are three companies that communicate with their customers on multiple social media platforms. Let's have a look at how they engage their customers.

Burberry

Regardless of the social media platform being used, Burberry is consist with their message, "mirroring elements such as the profile/cover images used for each account and the elegant swirly font used in graphics and videos, in addition to the consistently high quality of their visual content and acoustic backing tracks on their videos."

Ahead of the curve, in 2009 Burberry created their own social media platform, engaging consumers with it rather than using other available social media platforms at the time. The campaign used with their platform was called **Art of the Trench Coat.** Burberry customers were able to post pictures of themselves wearing the famous Burberry trench coat.

The concept behind developing their own platform was based on control. Burberry wanted to be able to have "control over the aesthetics of the site rather than being confined to a particular format—however, users could comment on them, 'like', and share the photos via Facebook, Twitter, and email."

Currently, approximately 60 percent of their marketing budget is dedicated to digital media. This pioneer of omnichannel retailing knows how to do it right! Let's take a look at how Burberry manages their social media platforms.

TWITTER With approximately 7 million followers (**@Burberry**), Burberry is most active on Twitter, tweeting on average five times per day. Their most popular posts are photos of new collections, which receive between 50 and 100 re-tweets and 100 to 200 favourites (acknowledgments). The use of interactive campaigns (London fashion week and new product releases) on this platform have been very well received by their followers. This platform could be considered the most influential of all their digital campaigns.

FACEBOOK Their great est following is on Facebook, with over 17 million likes and over 129 000 visits. Engagement is highest on this platform as well, with a typical post receiving anywhere between 2000 and 50 000 likes. Typically, Burberry posts once a day on this platform. "Facebook is a good platform for Burberry to exhibit full galleries of their collections and of catwalk shows, unlike the other platforms that are best for singular images."

INSTAGRAM Using their trademark trench coats in photographs around the London area, Burberry reinforces their branding strategy via **Instagram.** Their use of #cinemagraph showing "animated sketches from their LFW collection, catwalk makeup designs and moving images of scenes around London" confirms their ranking as one of the leading edge social media retailers. Having an average 35 000 likes per post related to #cinemagraph doesn't hurt either, nor does the 8 million followers.

TESCO

Tesco does a fantastic job communicating with their social media audience and leveraging their customer service initiates via various social media platforms. The significance of their social media strategy is evident, to the point that they publish their social media community rules online.

TWITTER Tesco has diluted its presence on Twitter by creating accounts for each area of its store, such as Tesco Bank, Tesco Media, Tesco Mobile, Tesco Food, and so on. The various accounts allow Tesco to create more direct and focused messages tailored to each customer segment.

The most popular Twitter handles, however, are the main Tesco account and the Tesco Offers account. The Tesco Offers account is, as the name suggests, dedicated

Sources: Annmarie Hanlon, "Retailers successfully using social media," *Evonomie,* http://www.evonomie.net/2015/01/28/social-media/retailers-successfully-using-social-media/ (accessed November 15, 2016); David Moth, "How Tesco uses Facebook, Twitter, Pinterest and Google+," *Econsultancy,* January 24, 2013, https://econsultancy.com/blog/61946-how-tesco-uses-facebook-twitter-pinterest-and-google/ (accessed November 15, 2016); Sarah Vizard, "M&S invests 20% of media spend in social media as it ups focus on storytelling," *Marketing Week,* June 4, 2015, https://www.marketingweek.com/2015/06/04/ms-invests-20-of-media-spend-in-social-media-as-it-ups-to posting all of the offers available from the store. The main Tesco account is used more as a channel to provide customer service—replying to various tweets from followers. Posts from **@Tesco** are also used as a way to highlight specific products and services and to comment on relevant topics. The posts are very light-hearted and often comical.

FACEBOOK With over 2.1 million likes on Facebook, it is easy to see the leverage Tesco has and employs via Facebook with their customers. Proof of this can be seen in their biography, which states "Customer query? Tell us on our timeline."

On average, Tesco posts twice a day on Facebook, typically about its products or the brand itself. The posts found on Facebook are mostly educational or entertaining in nature. They also include informative posts relating to such things as eating healthy and unique recipes.

Tesco uses other aspects of Facebook to communicate with their target audience. Take the "Notes" section in Facebook, for instance. This section is used to inform consumers about the terms and conditions of their contests. They also have a link on their Facebook page that redirects consumers back to their website's "contact us" page so consumers have access to various phone numbers and emails that they can use to reach out to customer service representatives.

PINTEREST Tesco states on their Pinterest page, "Follow us for delicious recipes, inspiring home ideas and helpful lifestyle hacks." With an array of topics including recipes, DIY holiday decorating suggestions, and home design ideas, the 44 000 followers who have access to 62 boards have plenty of options to become inspired and get their creative juices flowing! The pins used are a mixture of photos from Tesco's website, pins from other websites, and pins from other Pinterest account holders. By "posting third-party content Tesco will has gained greater exposure among Pinterest users, thereby increasing its number of followers."

MARKS & SPENCER

With approximately 20 percent of their marketing budget dedicated to storytelling and another 25 percent

dedicated to social media, it is interesting to see how this marketing strategy will play out in the long run. For several years now, M&S have employed a storytelling theme in a number of their campaigns. One popular campaign is their Christmas storytelling video, which can be viewed on several of their social media platforms including Facebook, Twitter, and **YouTube.**

"M&S spokeswoman says much of this spend on social media goes on sharing content and distributing campaigns on social media. She adds that the retailer has a very active fan base on social media and is looking to engage with them with timely and relevant content."

TWITTER M&S uses **Twitter** in a similar fashion as their Facebook page, informing consumers of products and promotions via photos and videos. With over 500 000 followers and over 2300 likes, Twitter definitely can be seen as a valuable platform for the M&S brand. One thing to note: there doesn't seem to be a customer service element on their Twitter page; instead, it seems to be based strictly on product information.

FACEBOOK With a variety of engagement tools including photos, videos, and articles, one may argue that M&S seems to know what they are doing with their social media platforms. With over 4.5 million likes on their **Facebook** page alone, it is clear that the retailer knows what content is important to the customer. A spokesperson for M&S indicated that "customer participation has been very successful for us and we want to continue that. Use of social media is increasingly important because customers respond to it incredibly well."

Though there are no longer brick and mortar locations in Canada, M&S still uses their social media platforms to drive traffic to their website where Canadians can purchase M&S products. On M&S's Facebook page, customers can find a hyperlink that directs them to the Canadian Marks & Spencer website.

Like Tasco, M&S also has a "Notes" page where they post terms and conditions for contests they are holding for their customers.

INSTAGRAM Similar to Burberry, M&S's **Instagram** page only shows photos similar to the ones customers would view in a campaign. The images do speak to the company's brand image, and both firms provide opportunities for

focus-on-storytelling/ (accessed November 15, 2016); Sarah Vizard, "M&S plans more 'savvy' social media marketing approach," *Marketing Week,* January 9, 2014, https://www.marketingweek.com/2014/01/09/ms-plans-more-savvy-social-media-marketing-approach/ (accessed November 15, 2016); "How Burberry Uses Social Media [CASE STUDY]", *Link Humans,* http://linkhumans.com/case-study/burberry (accessed November 15, 2016).

Continued

consumers to shop online via their Instagram platforms. Though M&S has a much smaller Instagram following (483 000) compared to Burberry, M&S still has sufficient traffic to warrant use of this platform.

IN CLOSING Marks & Spencer, Tesco, and Burberry are exemplars of companies that have been able to successfully develop communities around their brands via social media. Conscious of the importance of how the online and offline worlds connect, all three employ a consistent message ensuring optimal brand recognition and engagement. Omni-channel retailing is here to stay, and these three firms have solidified their existence in their product categories as a result of their commitment to social media.

Coupons Coupons offer a discount on the price of specific items when they're purchased. Coupons are issued by manufacturers and retailers in newspapers, on products, on the shelf, at the cash register, over the Internet, and through the mail. Retailers use coupons because they are thought to induce customers to try products for the first time, convert first-time users to regular users, encourage large purchases, increase usage, and protect market share against competition. Some retailers have linked coupons directly to their loyalty programs. Drugstore giant Shoppers Drug Mart, for instance, tracks its customers' purchases from its Optimum loyalty card and gives them coupons that are tailored just for them.

Coupon promotions, like all temporary promotions, may be stealing sales from a future period without any net increase in sales. For instance, if a supermarket runs a coupon promotion on sugar, households may buy a large quantity of sugar and stockpile it for future use. Thus, unless the coupon is used mostly by new buyers, the net impact on sale is negligible, and there will be a negative impact on profits due to the amount of redeemed coupons and cost of the coupon redemption procedures. Coupons may annoy, alienate, and confuse consumers and therefore do little to increase store loyalty.

Some stores, such as Loblaws, are making coupons more effective by customizing coupon content to alter customers' purchasing habits. For instance, if a customer typically spends a small amount during each shopping trip, the customer will receive coupons that encourage larger purchases, such as

Exhibit 15–10
Types of Sales Promotions

Promotion	Advantages	Disadvantages
Coupons	• Stimulate demand • Allow for direct tracing of sales	• Have low redemption rates • Have high cost
Rebates	• Stimulate demand • Increase value perception	• Are easily copied by competitors • May just advance future sales
Premiums (price or award)	• Build goodwill • Increase perception of value	• Consumers buy for premium, not product • Have to be carefully managed
Samples	• Encourage trial • Offer direct involvement	• Have high cost to the firm
POP displays	• Provide high visibility • Encourage brand trial	• Can be difficult to get a good location in the store • Can be costly to the firm
Special events	• Generate excitement and traffic	• Can be costly • Can distract customers from purchasing during the event
Pop-up stores	• Generate customer interest • Open up new markets and market segments	• Have high cost • Must hire store personnel • May take sales away from other company-owned stores

Christine (aka Coupon Christine) is passionate about couponing and saving money. With sold-out workshops across her hometown of London, Ontario, and a growing couponing Facebook group, she's helping others become passionate about saving money using coupons.

Used by permission of Coupon Christine.

"buy one, get one free." If another customer spends a lot each time she shops but shops sporadically, that customer will get coupons that expire relatively quickly. Unique coupons will also encourage customers to try new brands within categories that they normally purchase, or products that complement their usual purchases, such as shampoo to customers that purchase hair colour.[55]

Shopping bot sites, such as MyCoupons.com, provide customers with a large selection of coupons by bringing all the coupons available throughout the Internet onto one website. For instance, a customer might go to The Bay and find a KitchenAid mixer for $199.99. A cellphone scan of the bar code through ShopSavvy.com might find the same item at Walmart, which is a kilometre away, for $179.99. Then the customer might visit MyCoupons.com and see that Walmart is offering a $20 coupon, thus saving the customer $40 in a matter of minutes.

A new breed of coupon, printed from the Internet or sent to or accessed via mobile phones, is packed with information about the customer who uses it. While the coupons look standard, their bar codes can be loaded with a startling amount of data, including identification about the customer, Internet address, Facebook page information, and even the search terms the customer used to find the coupon in the first place. For instance, if a customer comes into a store with a coupon for T-shirts, the information on the coupon could reveal whether the customer was searching for "underwear" or "muscle shirts."

Rebates Rebates provide another form of discounts for consumers off the final selling price. In this case, however, the manufacturer, instead of the retailer, issues the refund as a portion of the purchase price returned to the buyer in the form of cash. Retailers generally welcome rebates from vendors because they generate sales in the same way that coupons do but the retailers incur no handling costs.

Many products, such as consumer electronics, offer rebates that may lower the price of the item significantly. Some vendors enjoy the added exposure of appearing on consumer websites, such as PriceGrabber.com and Nextag.com, that sort products by price and then link the customer to the retailer's website. Vendors offer such generous rebates because the likelihood that consumers will actually apply for the rebate is low. Other firms, such as Staples and Apple, have simplified the rebate redemption process with "Easy Rebates."[56]

Premiums A **premium** offers an item for free or at a bargain price to reward some type of behaviour, such as buying, sampling, or testing. Such rewards build goodwill among consumers, who often perceive high value in them. Premiums can be distributed in a variety of ways: They can be included in the product packaging, such as the toys inside cereal boxes; placed visibly on the package, such as a coupon for free milk on a box of Cheerios; handed out in the store; or delivered in the mail, such as the free-perfume offers Victoria's Secret mails to customers.

Samples **Samples** offer potential customers the opportunity to try a product or service before they make a buying decision. Distributing samples is one of the most costly sales promotion tools but also one of the most effective. Quick-service restaurants and grocery stores frequently use sampling. For instance, Loblaws, Sobeys, Metro, and Walmart all provide samples of products to customers. Costco uses so many samples that customers can often have an entire meal!

Point-of-Purchase (POP) Displays **Point-of-purchase (POP)** is a merchandise display that is located at the

premium A type of sales promotion whereby an item is offered free of charge or at a bargain price to reward some type of behaviour, such as buying, sampling, or testing.

samples A small amount or size of a product given to potential customers as an inducement to purchase.

point-of-purchase (POP) An area where the customer waits at checkout.

point of purchase, such as the checkout counter in a supermarket. Retailers have long recognized that the most valuable real estate in the store is at the POP. Customers see products like a magazine or a candy bar while they are waiting to pay for their items and impulsively purchase them. In the Internet version of point-of-purchase display, shoppers are stimulated by special merchandise, price reductions, or complementary products that Internet retailers feature on the checkout screen.

Special Events A **special event** is a sales promotion program comprising a number of sales promotion techniques built around a seasonal, cultural, sporting, musical, or some other special event.[57] Special events can generate excitement and traffic to the store. Apparel and department stores do trunk shows, made-to-measure events, and fashion shows. Sporting goods stores do demonstration of equipment, while grocery stores might have cooking classes. Bookstores do readings and book signings. Car dealerships can have rallies or shows of new or vintage models. Even if the sales registered during the event aren't significant, the long-term effect can be quite beneficial.

Pop-Up Stores An extreme type of sales promotion is a pop-up store. Pop-up stores are temporary storefronts that exist for only a limited time and generally focus on a new product or limited group of products offered by a retailer. They are also used by some retailers during the holiday season to increase exposure and convenience shopping for their customers without having to invest in a long-term lease.

Gucci, the Italian leather retailer and manufacturer, has opened pop-up stores named Gucci-Icon Temporary in New York's SoHo, Miami Beach, Tokyo, London, Berlin, Paris, and Hong Kong. The stores featured limited-edition sneakers retailing for $500 to $600, with classic Gucci design elements and some special features like a silver or gold dog tag.[58]

Although most sales promotions are effective at generating short-term interest among customers, they aren't very useful for building long-term loyalty. Customers who participate in a promotion might learn more about a store and return to it, but typically customers attracted by sales promotions are interested in the promoted merchandise, not the retailer. Unfortunately, when a specific promotion is effective for a retailer, competing retailers learn about it quickly and offer the same promotion, which prevents the innovating retailer from gaining any long-term advantage.

Personal Selling

Personal selling is a communication process in which sales associates help customers satisfy their needs through face-to-face exchanges of information. It is a form of offline/interactive communication (Exhibit 15–1). The cost of communicating directly with a potential customer is quite high compared with other forms of promotion, but it is simply the best and most efficient way to sell certain products and services. Customers can buy many products and services without the help of a salesperson, but salespeople simplify the buying process by providing information and services that save customers time and effort. In many cases, sales representatives add significant value, which makes the added expense of employing them worthwhile.

Advertising

Advertising entails the placement of announcements and persuasive messages purchased by retailers and other organizations that seek to inform and/or persuade members of a particular target market or audience about their products, services, organizations, or ideas.[59] Retailers are the largest group of national advertisers, spending almost $16 billion annually. McDonald's and Target are among the ten largest advertisers in the United States, each spending more than $1 billion a year.[60] Walmart dropped out of the list of top ten advertisers in 2011, spending 28.8 percent less than it did the previous year. In the United States, the ten largest retail advertisers represent 23.9 percent of the share of US sales and include Macy's, Target, Sears, Walmart, Home Depot, JCPenney, Best Buy, Lowe's, Kohl's, and Gap Inc.[61]

Mass advertising can entice consumers into a conversation with retailers, although it does not necessarily require much action by consumers, which places it on the passive end of the spectrum. Traditionally, advertising has been passive and offline (e.g., ads on TV, in magazines, and in newspapers; see Exhibit 15–1). However, recently there has been

special event Sales promotion program comprising a number of sales promotion techniques built around a seasonal, cultural, sporting, musical, or other event.

personal selling A communication process in which salespeople help customers satisfy their needs through face-to-face exchanges of information.

advertising Paid communications delivered to customers through non-personal mass media such as newspapers, television, radio, direct mail, and the Internet.

a growth in online advertising. This section reviews advertising's traditional media and examines a method of lowering the retailer's advertising cost through cooperative advertising with vendors.

Newspapers Retailing and newspaper advertising grew up together over the past century. But the growth in retail newspaper advertising has slowed recently as retailers have begun using other media. Still, 57 percent of newspapers' advertising dollars are generated by retailers.[62] In addition to displaying ads with their editorial content, newspapers distribute **freestanding inserts**. A freestanding insert (FSI), also called a *preprint*, is an advertisement printed at the retailer's expense and distributed as an insert in the newspaper. However, there are so many FSIs in some newspapers that readers can become overwhelmed. As a result, some retailers have reduced the number of FSIs they use because of the clutter and because young readers, who may be their primary target markets, don't regularly read newspapers.

Because newspapers are distributed in well-defined local market areas, they are effective at targeting specific retail markets. Newspapers also offer a quick response. There is only a short time between the deadline for receiving the advertisement and the time that the advertisement will appear. Thus, newspapers are useful for delivering messages on short notice.

Newspapers, like magazines, effectively convey a lot of detailed information. Readers can go through an advertisement at their own pace and refer to part of the advertisement when they want. But newspaper ads aren't effective for showing merchandise, particularly when it's important to illustrate colours, because of the poor reproduction quality.

The life of a newspaper advertisement is short because the newspaper is usually discarded after it has been read. In contrast, magazine advertising has a longer life because consumers tend to save magazines and read them several times during a week or month.

Finally, the cost of developing newspaper ads is relatively low. However, the cost of delivering the message may be high if the newspaper's circulation is broader than the retailer's target market, requiring the retailer to pay for exposure that won't generate sales. In a study conducted by the Newspaper Association of America (NAA) on how America shops and spends, findings clearly demonstrate the power of newspapers and news websites and the influence this media has on consumer purchasing and planning behaviours. Here are some of the insights and highlights from that study:[63]

- Six in ten consumers used newspapers in the past week to plan shopping and purchasing decisions.

- Eight in ten consumers took action on a newspaper insert (in the last 30 days), including comparison shopping, sharing with others, and taking it to purchase.

- Sixty-four percent of consumers use coupons from a newspaper versus 53 percent from direct mail.

- Newspaper website visitors are (compared to overall adults) 40 percent more likely to have purchased something online or in-store in the past 30 days, 62 percent more likely to go online for coupons, 79 percent more likely to use a mobile phone in a store to comparison shop, and 80 percent more likely to use a shopping app on a mobile device.

Magazines Advertising in magazines is mostly done by national retailers such as The Bay and The Gap. With the growth of local magazines, regional editions of national magazines, and specialized magazines, local retailers can take advantage of this medium. Retailers tend to use this medium for image advertising because the reproduction quality is high. Due to the lead time—the time between submitting the advertisement and publication—a major disadvantage of magazine advertising is that the timing is difficult to coordinate with special events and sales.

In April 2013, Walmart Canada and Rogers Media Inc. launched the country's newest magazine, *Walmart Live Better*, a multi-platform lifestyle brand. Top Canadian editors and contributors, including *Walmart Live Better's* editor-in-chief, Sandra Martin, provide readers the latest trends and tips in food, home, beauty, and fashion. The magazine is available for free at Walmart Canada Supercentres in English Canada, and is also available in digital formats for online, mobile, and iPad users. With a press run of 1 million

> **DID YOU KNOW?**
>
> Ad expenditure in Canada will be approximately US$15.5 billion in 2017, up from $13.2 billion in 2012.[64]

freestanding insert (FSI) An advertisement printed at the retailer's expense and distributed as an insert in the newspaper; also called a *preprint*.

copies per issue, it automatically became Canada's largest circulation magazine, according to Rogers.[65]

Produced by the Custom Content division within Rogers Media, the print edition of *Walmart Live Better* is published six times a year, while the website is updated regularly with exclusive, added-value content. In addition to print and digital, readers can engage with the Walmart brand through social media properties such as Walmart's Facebook page, the Live Better Pinterest page, or Twitter.[66]

Television

Television commercials can be placed on a national network or a local station. A local television commercial is called a spot. Retailers typically use TV for image advertising, to take advantage of the high production quality and the opportunity to communicate through both visual images and sound. Television ads can also demonstrate product usage. For example, TV is an excellent medium for car, furniture, and consumer electronics dealers.

In addition to its high production costs, broadcast time for national TV advertising is expensive. Spots have relatively small audiences, but they may be economical for local retailers. To offset the high production costs, many vendors provide modular commercials, in which the retailer can insert its name or a "tag" after information about the vendor's merchandise.

The average North American over the age of 2 spends more than 34 hours a week watching live television, says a Nielsen report, plus another three to six hours watching taped programs.[67]

Radio

Many retailers use radio advertising because messages can be targeted to a specific segment of the market.[68] Some radio stations' audiences are highly loyal to their announcers. When these announcers promote a retailer, listeners are impressed. The cost of developing and broadcasting radio commercials is relatively low.

One disadvantage of radio advertising, however, is that listeners generally treat the radio broadcast as background, which limits the attention they give the message. Consumers must get the information from a radio commercial when it's broadcast, so they can't refer to the advertisement for information they didn't hear or remember.

co-op advertising A program undertaken by a vendor in which the vendor agrees to pay all or part of a promotion for its products; also called *cooperative advertising.*

public relations (PR) A retail communication tool for managing communications and relationships to achieve various objectives, such as building and maintaining a positive image of the retailer, handling or heading off unfavourable stories or events, and maintaining positive relationships with the media.

Co-op Programs

Co-op advertising (or *cooperative advertising*) is a promotional program undertaken by a vendor and a retailer working together. The vendor pays for part of the retailer's advertising but dictates some conditions. For example, Ford wanted to get their 3200 US dealerships to do more digital advertising. In order to achieve this goal, Ford was willing to pay 50 percent of the digital media cost a dealership incurred.[69] In addition to lowering costs, co-op advertising enables a retailer to associate its name and well-known national brands and use attractive artwork created by national brands. Mattel's biggest customer is Walmart (19 percent of 2011 global sales), followed by Toys "R" Us (11 percent) and Target (8 percent). The toy marketer (Barbie, Fisher-Price) spent 11 percent of 2011 sales on ads and promotion.[70]

Co-op advertising has some drawbacks though. First, vendors want the ads to feature their products, whereas retailers are more interested in featuring their store's name, location, and assortment of merchandise and services offered. This conflict in goals can reduce the effectiveness of co-op advertising from the retailer's perspective. Second, ads developed by the vendor often are used by several competing retailers and may list the names and locations of all retailers offering their brands. Thus, co-op ads tend to blur distinctions between retailers. Third, restrictions that the vendor places on the ads may further reduce their effectiveness for the retailer. For example, the vendor may restrict advertising to a period of time when the vendor's sales are depressed, but the retailer might not normally be advertising during that time frame.

Outdoor Billboards

Billboards and other forms of outdoor advertising are effective vehicles for creating awareness and providing a very limited amount of information to a narrow audience. Thus, outdoor advertising has limited usefulness in providing information about sales. Outdoor advertising is typically used to remind customers about the retailer or to inform people in cars of nearby retail outlets.[71] For example, La Senza used sexy images on billboards in the Toronto area to promote Christmas sales of lingerie.

Public Relations

Public relations (PR) involves managing communications and relationships to achieve various objectives, such as building and maintaining a positive image of the retailer, handling or heading off unfavourable stories or events, and maintaining positive relationships with the media. In many cases, public relations activities support other promotional efforts by generating "free" media attention and general goodwill. The practice of PR is no longer dominated by one-way communication that seeks to simply transfer content from the retailer to the consumer. Retailers are getting creative with their PR strategies in light of the opportunities social media offers them. Many retailers are now using social media platforms such as Twitter, Facebook, blogs, Pinterest, Instagram, and others to promote, inform, and give feedback to engage in two-way conversations with their customers.

Clothes retailer Kenneth Cole, in a bid to encourage sales, started a provocative campaign on its own site asking customers to make a stand on controversial topics such as war, gay marriage, and guns. In the same fashion, the campaign encouraged customers to buy clothes based on what they think they look good in among what they wear. From a public relations perspective, it can be said that the retailer is brave to align such deep, serious societal issues with the current trends and choice of clothes people choose to wear; the opposite can also be said, that the retailer is insensitive and repulsive to even push out a campaign like this. What made matters worse was a tweet during the Egypt riots that jokingly said that the uproar in Cairo was due to the new spring collection that Kenneth Cole was pushing out, essentially encouraging people to buy more clothes while people are dying in Egypt.[72]

For years, Walmart did little to promote itself as a positive social force, believing its low prices would speak for themselves. But it increasingly has been subjected to public criticism from labour unions and environmentalists, so Walmart hired its first public relations firm. The public relations firm set up a war room to respond quickly to attacks or adverse news. Internet blogs and grassroots initiatives were developed to stimulate popular support for Walmart. The firm also looked for proactive opportunities to demonstrate Walmart's social consciousness. For example, after the devastating earthquake in Haiti, Walmart contributed more than $1.5 million in direct financial support as well as in-kind contributions, such as prepackaged food kits, blankets, and face masks. In addition, through various in-store and online fundraising campaigns, Walmart associates and customers globally have contributed more than $3 million for the relief effort.[73]

Walmart Canada is a corporate sponsor for three national charity partners (Children's Miracle Network, Breakfast Clubs of Canada, Canadian Red Cross and Evergreen) and has supported more than 1000 other community-directed charity grants, surpassing $200 million dollars since 1994. In 2013, Walmart Canada had raised $23 million dollars for community via fundraising and Walmart donations.[74]

Retailers also benefit when celebrities wear their fashions. For instance, when photos were posted on the Internet of First Lady Michelle Obama wearing a J.Crew cream-coloured cardigan and "dazzling dots" skirt on a visit to a cancer centre in London, the retailer's website sold out almost immediately.[75] Similarly, the placement of designer apparel at media events like the Oscars benefits the retailer, the designer, and the celebrity. And nothing happens by accident. Public relations people on both sides help orchestrate the events to get the maximum benefit for both parties.

Another very popular PR tool is event sponsorship. Event sponsorship occurs when corporations support various activities (financially or otherwise), usually in the cultural or sports and entertainment sectors. Some retailers sponsor sporting events such as the Kia Toronto Football Academy, while others buy naming rights to a sporting venue, such as the Air Canada Centre, which is home to the Toronto Maple Leafs hockey club, the Toronto Raptors basketball club, and the Toronto Rock lacrosse team.

When retailers and vendors use product placement, they pay to have their product included in non-traditional situations, such as in a scene in a movie or television program. For instance, Liz and Jack of *30 Rock* discuss whether McDonald's McFlurry is the best dessert in the world. On CBS's *The Big Bang Theory*, Sheldon says that he "needs access to the Cheesecake Factory walk-in freezer." In *The Biggest Loser*, the contestants have to run from one Subway restaurant to the next.

Lo3 Strengths and Weaknesses of Communication Methods

Communication methods differ in terms of control, flexibility, credibility, and cost (Exhibit 15–11).

Control

Retailers have more control when using paid versus unpaid communication methods. When using

Exhibit 15–11
Media Capability

Media	Targeting	Timeliness	Information Presentation Capacity	Life	Cost
Newspapers	Good	Good	Modest	Short	Modest
Magazines	Modest	Poor	Modest	Modest	High
Direct Mail	Excellent	Modest	High	Short	Modest
Television	Modest	Modest	High	Short	Modest
Radio	Modest	Good	Low	Short	Low
Internet					
Banner	Excellent	Excellent	Low	Modest	High
Website	Excellent	Excellent	High	Long	Modest
Email	Excellent	Excellent	Modest	Short	Low
Social Media					
Blog	Excellent	Excellent	High	Long	Low
Twitter	Excellent	Excellent	Low	Short	Modest
Facebook	Excellent	Excellent	High	Short	Modest
Pinterest	Excellent	Excellent	High	Short	Low
Outdoor Billboards	Modest	Poor	Very Low	Long	Modest
Shopping Guides	Modest	Modest	Low	Modest	Low
Yellow Pages	Modest	Poor	Low	Long	Low

advertising, sales promotions, online marketing, direct marketing, and store atmosphere, retailers determine the message's content; for advertising, direct marketing, and sales promotions, they control the time of its delivery. Since each salesperson can deliver different messages, retailers have less control over personal selling than other paid communication methods. Retailers have little control over the content or timing of publicity and word-of-mouth communications. Since unpaid communications are designed and delivered by people not employed by the retailer, they can communicate unfavourable as well as favourable information. For example, news coverage of food poisoning at a restaurant or discrimination at a hotel can result in significant declines in sales.

Flexibility

Personal selling is the most flexible communication method, because salespeople can talk with each customer, discover their specific needs, and develop unique presentations for them. Direct mail and online marketing are also very flexible because they can be personalized to specific customer interests. Other communication methods are less flexible. For example, traditional ads tend to deliver the same message to all customers.

Credibility

Because publicity and word-of-mouth are communicated by independent sources, their information is usually more credible than the information in paid communication sources. For example, customers see their friends and family as highly credible sources of information. In contrast, customers tend to doubt claims made by salespeople and in ads since they know retailers are trying to promote their merchandise.

Cost

Publicity and word-of-mouth are classified as unpaid communication methods, but retailers do incur costs to stimulate them. Paid impersonal communications often are economical. For example, a full-page ad in the *Toronto Star* costs about two cents per person to deliver the message in the ad. In contrast, personal selling, because of its flexibility, is more effective than advertising, but it is more costly. A ten-minute presentation by a retail salesperson paid $12 per hour costs the retailer $2—100 times more than exposing a customer to a newspaper, radio, or TV ad. Although maintaining a website on a server is relatively inexpensive, it is costly to design, to continuously update the site, and to promote the site to attract visitors. Direct marketing communication can be sent to customers for about $2 per person reached, but the people reached are more targeted and therefore the spend could be more cost-effective than other communication methods.

Due to the differences just described, communication methods differ in their effectiveness in performing communication tasks and their effectiveness in different stages of the customer's decision-making process. Typically, mass media advertising is most effective at building awareness. Online, direct, and newspaper advertising are effective for conveying information about a retailer's offerings and prices. Personal selling and sales promotion are most effective at persuading customers to purchase merchandise. Mass media and magazine advertising, publicity, online (websites, social media), and store atmosphere are most cost-effective at building the retailer's brand image and encouraging repeat purchases and store loyalty.

Lo4 Planning the Retail Communication Process

Almost every retail business needs to promote itself in some way, reaching out to customers and potential customers. Exhibit 15–12 illustrates the four steps in developing and implementing a retail communication program: establishing objectives, determining a budget, allocating the budget, and implementing and evaluating the mix.

Establishing Objectives

Retailers establish objectives for communication programs to provide the following:

- direction for people implementing the program
- a basis for evaluating its effectiveness

Some communication programs have a long-term objective, such as creating or altering a retailer's brand image. Other communication programs focus on improving short-term performance, such as increasing store traffic on weekends.

Communication Objectives While retailers' overall objective is to generate long- and short-term sales and profits, they often use communication objectives rather than sales objectives to plan and evaluate their communication programs. **Communication objectives** are specific goals related to the retail communication mix's effect on the customer's decision-making process.

Exhibit 15–13 shows hypothetical information about customers in the target market for a Zehrs grocery store. This information illustrates goals related to stages in the consumer decision-making process. Note that 95 percent of the customers are aware of the store (the first stage in the decision-making process) and 85 percent know the type of merchandise it sells. But only 45 percent of the customers in the target market have a favourable attitude toward the store, 32 percent intend to visit the store during the next few weeks, 25 percent actually visit the store during the next two weeks, and 18 percent regularly shop at the store.

communication objectives Specific goals for a communication program related to the effects of the communication program on the customer's decision-making process.

Exhibit 15–12
Steps in Developing a Retail Communication Program

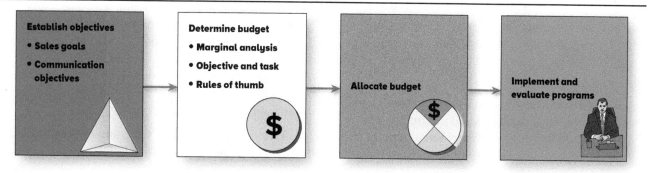

Exhibit 15–13
Communication Objectives and Stages in Consumers' Decision-Making Process at the Supermarket

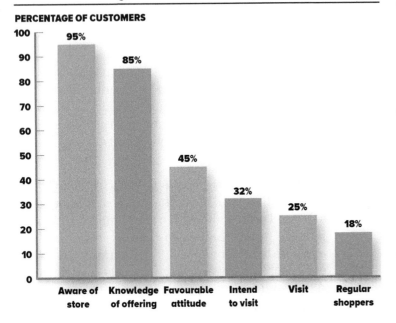

PERCENTAGE OF CUSTOMERS

In this hypothetical example, most people know about the store and its offerings. The major problem confronting the supermarket is the big drop between knowledge and favourable attitude. Thus, the store should develop a communication program with the objective of increasing the percentage of customers with a favourable attitude toward it.

To effectively implement and evaluate a communication program, objectives must be clearly stated in quantitative terms. The target audience for the communication mix needs to be defined, along with the degree of change expected and the time period over which the change will be realized.

For example, a communication objective for the grocery store's program might be to increase—from 45 percent to 55 percent within three months—the percentage of customers within a ten-kilometre radius of the store who have a favourable attitude toward the store. This objective is clear and measurable. It indicates the task the program should address. The people who implement the program know what they're supposed to accomplish.

The communication objectives and approaches used by vendors and retailers differ, and these differences can lead to conflicts. Some of these points of conflict are as follows:

- **Long-term versus short-term goals.** Most communication done by vendors (manufacturers) is directed toward building a long-term image of their products. On the other hand, most

retailer communication is typically used to announce promotions and special sales that generate short-term revenues.

- **Product versus location.** When vendors advertise their branded products, they don't care where the customer buys them. On the other hand, retailers don't care what brands customers buy as long as they buy them in their store.

- **Geographic coverage.** Since people tend to shop at stores near their homes or workplaces, most retailers use local newspapers, TV, and radio to target their communication. On the other hand, most vendors sell their brands nationally and thus tend to use national TV and magazines.

- **Breadth of merchandise offered.** Typically, vendors have a relatively small number of products to advertise. They can devote a lot of attention to developing consistent communication programs for each brand they make. Retailers offer a much broader set of products and often focus on building short-term sales.

Even though vendors and retailers have different goals, they frequently work together to develop mutually beneficial outcomes. An example is a coordinated program between Shoppers Drug Mart and Coppertone. The program offered a two-dollar-off coupon to the customer with the purchase of Coppertone sun care products. The addition of shelf-talker signs on shelves creates awareness by providing information about the promotion and encouraging customer participation. The co-marketing promotion benefits both Shoppers Drug Mart and Coppertone by building sun care customers' loyalty.

Consumer Rights In designing any consumer communication package, one of the objectives is to acknowledge and comply with consumer rights requirements. No retailer wants bad publicity as a result of consumer advocacy groups' negative press. Advances in consumerism have come in the form of federal and provincial legislation designed to protect the consumer and establish standards for manufacturers and retailers. The Consumers' Association of Canada (www.consumer.ca) seeks to uphold the following consumer rights:

- **The right to choice.** Consumers must have a choice of products offered by a variety of manufacturers and retailers. In fact, competition usually provides the benefit of lower prices to the consumer (*Competition Act*).

- **The right to be informed.** Consumers must have access to complete information about a product before buying it. For example, consider the importance of fabric content and care labelling, food ingredients and nutritional content (which are of extreme importance to people with food allergies), and information that will describe the potential dangers of using a product. Detailed information can be an asset in the case of lawsuits (*Packaging and Labelling Act, Textile Labelling Act, Weights and Measures Act*).

- **The right to safety.** The product must be safe for its intended use. This means that the product must be accompanied by instructions for its proper use and carry a guarantee of product quality and reliability as tested by the manufacturer. Federal agencies will take action to force businesses to recall defective products and issue public warnings (*Food and Drug Act, Hazardous Products Act*).

- **The right to be heard.** Someone will listen to consumers' complaints and take appropriate action to solve the problems. Many retailers have added customer service centres in the store to address customer concerns, and maintain a toll-free telephone number and/or a website so that customers can contact a service representative for immediate assistance.[76]

Developing the Promotional Message

Most retail promotional messages have a short life and are designed to have an immediate impact. This immediacy calls for a copywriting style that grabs the reader's attention. Exhibit 15–14 outlines specific suggestions for developing local newspaper ads.

Factors in Selecting Media   To convey their message with the most impact to the most consumers in the target market at the lowest cost, retailers need to evaluate media in terms of coverage, reach, cost, and impact of the advertising messages delivered through the medium.

DID YOU KNOW?

The average consumer sees over 2000 advertising messages per week.[77]

Coverage   Coverage refers to the number of potential customers in the retailer's target market that could be exposed to an ad in a given medium. For example, assume that the size of the target market is 100 000 customers. The local newspaper is distributed to 60 percent of the customers in the target market, 90 percent of the potential customers have a TV set that picks up the local station's signal, and 5 percent of the potential customers drive past

coverage The theoretical number of potential customers in the retailer's target market that could be exposed to an ad in a given medium.

Exhibit 15–14
Suggestions for Developing Local Ads

1. Have a dominant headline	The first question a consumer asks is, What's in it for me? Thus, retailers need to feature the principal benefit being offered in the headline along with a reason why the consumer should act immediately. The benefit can be expanded on in a subhead.
2. Use a dominant element	Ads should include a large picture or headline. Typically, photographs of real people attract more attention than drawings. Action photographs are effective in getting readers' attention.
3. Stick to a simple layout	The ad's layout should lead the reader's eye through the message from the headline to the illustration and then to the explanatory copy, price, and retailer's name and location. Complex elements, decorative borders, and many different typefaces distract the reader's attention from the retailer's message.
4. Provide a specific, complete presentation	Ad readers are looking for information that will help them decide whether to visit the store. The ad must contain all of the information pertinent to this decision, including the type of merchandise, brands, prices, sizes, and colours. Consumers are unlikely to make a special trip to the store on the basis of vague information. Broadcast ads, particularly radio ads, tend to be very creative but often leave the consumer thinking, Gee, that was a clever ad, but what was it advertising?
5. Use easily recognizable, distinct visuals	Consumers see countless ads each day. Thus, to get the consumers' attention, retailers must make their ads distinct from those of the competition. Ads with distinctive art, layout, design elements, or typeface generate higher readership.
6. Give the store's name and address	The store's name and location are the two most important aspects of a retail ad. If consumers don't know where to go to buy the advertised merchandise, the retailer won't make a sale. The retailer's name and location must be prominently displayed in print ads and repeated several times in broadcast ads.

Lowe's sponsorship for a NASCAR racing team generates publicity and builds brand awareness. However, this publicity could be unfavourable if its NASCAR team engaged in unsanctioned activities.

Courtesy of Lowe's.

a billboard. Thus, the coverage for newspaper advertising would be 60 000; for TV advertising, 90 000; and for the specific billboard, 5000.

Reach In contrast to coverage, **reach** is the actual number of customers in the target market exposed to an advertising medium. If, on any given day, 60 percent of the potential customers who receive the newspaper actually read it, then the newspaper's reach would be 36 000 (or 60 percent of 60 000). Retailers often run an ad several times, in which case they calculate the **cumulative reach** for the sequence of ads. For example, if 60 percent of the potential customers receiving a newspaper read it each day, 93.6 percent (or 1 minus the probability of not reading the paper three times in a row [0.40 × 0.40 × 0.40]) of the potential customers will read the newspaper at least one day over the three-day period in which the ad appears in the paper. Thus, the cumulative reach for running a newspaper ad for three days is 56 160 (or 93.6 percent × 60 000), which almost equals the newspaper's coverage.

When evaluating Internet advertising opportunities, the measure used to assess reach is the number of unique visitors—the number of different people who access the Web page on which the ad is located.

Cost The **cost per thousand (CPM)** measure is often used to compare media. Typically,

reach The actual number of customers in the target market exposed to an advertising medium.

cumulative reach The cumulative number of potential customers that would see an ad that runs several times.

cost per thousand (CPM) A measure that is often used to compare media. CPM is calculated by dividing an ad's cost by its reach.

impact An ad's effect on the audience.

frequency The number of times a potential customer is exposed to a promotional message.

CPM is calculated by dividing an ad's cost by its reach. Another approach for determining CPM is to divide the cost of several ads in a campaign by their cumulative reach. If, for instance, in the previous example, one newspaper ad costs $500 and three ads cost $1300, the CPM using simple reach is $13.89, or $500/(36 000/1000). Using cumulative reach, the CPM is $23.15, or $1300/(56 160/1000). Note that the CPM might be higher using cumulative reach rather than simple reach, but the overall reach is also higher, and many potential customers will see the ad two or three times.

CPM is a good method for comparing similar-size ads in similar media, such as full-page ads in the *National Post* and the *Barrie Examiner*. But CPM can be misleading when comparing the cost-effectiveness of ads in different types of media, such as newspaper and TV. A TV ad may have a lower CPM than a newspaper ad, but the newspaper ad may be much more effective at achieving the ad's communication objectives, such as giving information about a sale.

Impact **Impact** is an ad's effect on the audience. Due to their unique characteristics, different media are particularly effective at accomplishing different communication tasks. Exhibit 15–15 shows the effectiveness of various media for different communication tasks. TV is particularly effective at getting an audience's attention, demonstrating merchandise, changing attitudes, and announcing events. Magazines are particularly appropriate for emphasizing the quality and prestige of a store and its offering and for providing detailed information to support quality claims. Newspapers are useful for providing price information and announcing events. Websites are particularly effective for demonstrating merchandise and providing information. Outdoor advertising is most effective at promoting a retailer's name and location.

Determining Promotional Frequency and Timing

The frequency and timing of promotions determine how often and when customers will see the retailer's message.

Frequency **Frequency** is how many times the potential customer is exposed to a promotional message. Frequency for Internet advertising is typically assessed by measuring the number of times a Web

Exhibit 15–15

Effectiveness of Media by Communication Objective

Communication Task	Newspapers	Magazine	Direct Mail	TV	Radio	Websites	Email	Outdoor	Social
Getting attention	Low	Medium	Medium	Medium	Low	Low	High	Medium	Medium
Identifying name	Medium	High	Low	Low	Low	Low	Medium	High	High
Announcing events	High	Low	High	High	Medium	Low	High	Low	High
Demonstrating merchandise	Low	Medium	High	High	Low	Highest	Low	Low	Medium
Providing information	Low	High	High	Low	Low	Highest	Medium	Lowest	High
Changing attitudes	High	Medium	High	High	Medium	High	Low	Low	High
Building brand image	Low	Medium	High	High	Low	High	Low	Low	High

page with the message is downloaded during a visit to the site.

The appropriate frequency depends on the message's objective. Typically, several exposures to a promotional message are required to influence a customer's buying behaviour. Thus, campaigns directed toward changing purchase behaviour rather than creating awareness emphasize frequency over reach. Ads announcing a sale are often seen and remembered after one exposure. Thus, sale ad campaigns emphasize reach over frequency.

Timing Typically, a promotional message should appear on, or slightly precede, the days consumers are most likely to purchase merchandise. For example, if most consumers buy groceries Thursday through Sunday, then supermarkets should advertise on Thursday and Friday. Similarly, consumers often go shopping after they receive their paycheques at the middle and the end of the month. Thus, advertising should be concentrated at these times.

Lo5 Determine the Communication Budget

The second step in developing a retail communication program is determining a budget (see Exhibit 15–12). The economically correct method for setting the communication budget is

Email communications are very cost-effective in targeting messages to specific customers.

Image provided by Indigo Books & Music.

marginal analysis. Even though retailers usually don't have enough information to perform a complete marginal analysis, the method shows how managers should approach budget-setting programs.

The marginal analysis method for setting a communication budget is the approach retailers should use when making all of their resource allocation decisions, including the number of locations in a geographic area, the staffing of stores, and the floor and shelf space devoted to merchandise categories.

Marginal Analysis Method **Marginal analysis** is based on the economic principle that firms should increase communication expenditures so long as each additional dollar spent generates more than a dollar of additional contribution. The marginal analysis method is used to determine how much should be spent on the retailer's communication program.[78]

In Exhibit 15–16, the first column indicates 21 different communication expense levels. The retailer estimates store sales (column 2), gross margin (column 3), and other expenses (columns 4 and 5). Then the retailer calculates the contribution

marginal analysis A method of analysis used in setting a promotional budget or allocating retail space, based on the economic principle that firms should increase expenditures as long as each additional dollar spent generates more than a dollar of additional contribution.

Exhibit 15-16
Marginal Analysis for Setting a Retailer's Communication Budget

Level	Communication Expenses (1)	Sales (2)	Gross Margin Realized (3)	Rental Expense (4)	Personnel Expense (5)	Contribution Before Communication Expenses (6) = (3) − (4) − (5)	Profit After Communication Expenses (7) = (6) − (1)	
1	$0	$240 000	$96 000	$44 000	$52 200	$ (200)	$ (200)	
2	5 000	280 000	112 000	48 000	53 400	10 600	5 600	
3	10 000	330 000	132 000	53 000	54 900	24 100	14 100	
4	15 000	380 000	152 000	58 000	56 400	37 600	22 600	
5	20 000	420 000	168 000	62 000	57 600	48 400	28 400	
6	25 000	460 000	184 000	66 000	58 800	59 200	34 200	
7	30 000	500 000	200 000	70 000	60 000	70 000	40 000	Last year
8	35 000	540 000	216 000	74 000	61 200	80 800	45 800	
9	40 000	570 000	228 000	77 000	62 100	88 900	48 900	
10	45 000	600 000	240 000	80 000	63 000	97 000	52 000	
11	50 000	625 000	250 000	82 500	63 750	103 750	53 750	
12	55 000	650 000	260 000	85 000	64 500	110 500	55 500	
13	60 000	670 000	268 000	87 000	65 100	115 900	55 900	
14	65 000	690 000	276 000	89 000	65 700	121 300	56 300	Best profit
15	70 000	705 000	282 000	90 500	66 150	125 350	55 350	
16	75 000	715 000	286 000	91 500	66 450	128 050	53 050	
17	80 000	725 000	290 000	92 500	66 750	130 750	50 750	
18	85 000	735 000	294 000	93 500	67 050	133 450	48 450	
19	90 000	745 000	298 000	94 500	67 350	136 150	46 150	
20	95 000	750 000	300 000	95 000	67 500	137 500	42 500	
21	100 000	750 000	300 000	95 000	67 500	137 500	37 500	

DID YOU KNOW?

Based on research from the DMA (Direct Marketing Association), 21 percent of the companies surveyed send out emails to contacts three to four times per month.[79]

excluding expenses on communications (column 6) and the profit when the communication expenses are considered (column 7). To estimate the sales generated by different levels of communications, the retailer can rely on judgment and experience, or might analyze past data to determine the relationship between communication expenses and sales. Historical data also provide information about the gross margin and other expenses as a percentage of sales.

Notice that at low levels of communication expenses, an additional $5000 in communication expenses generates more than a $5000 incremental contribution. For example, increasing the communication expense from $15 000 to $20 000 increases contribution by $10 800 (or $48 400 − $37 600). When the communication expense reaches $65 000, further increases of $5000 generate less than $5000 in additional contributions. For example, increasing the budget from $65 000 to $70 000 generates only an additional $4050 in contribution ($125 350 − $121 300).

In this example, the retailer determines that the maximum profit would be generated with a communication expense budget of $65 000. But it notices that expense levels between $55 000 and $70 000 all result in about the same level of profit. Thus, the retailer makes a conservative decision and establishes a $55 000 budget for communication expenses.

In most cases, it's very hard to do a marginal analysis because often retail managers don't know the relationship between communication expenses and sales. Note that the numbers in Exhibit 15–16 are simply the retailer's estimates; they may not be accurate.

Sometimes retailers do experiments to get a better idea of the relationship between communication expenses and sales. Say, for example, a catalogue retailer selects several geographic areas in Canada with the same sales potential. The retailer then distributes 100 000 catalogues in the first area,

Exhibit 15–17

Illustration of Objective-and-Task Method for Setting a Communication Budget

Objective: Increase from 25 percent to 50 percent over the next 12 months the percentage of target market living or working within 10 kilometres of our store who know of our store's location and product.

Task: 480, 30-second radio spots during peak commuting hours (7:00 to 8:00 AM and 5:00 to 6:00 PM).	$12 300
Task: Sign with store name near entrance to mall.	$4 500
Task: Display ad in the Yellow Pages.	$500

Objective: Increase from 5 percent to 15 percent in 12 months the percentage of target market who indicate that our store is their preferred store to shop in.

Task: Develop TV campaign to improve image and run 50, 30-second commercials.	$24 000
Task: Hold four information seminars followed by a wine-and-cheese social.	$8 000

Objective: Selling merchandise remaining at end of season.

Task: Special event.	$6 000
Total budget	$55 300

200 000 in the second area, and 300 000 in the third area. Using the sales and costs for each distribution level, it could go through an analysis like the one in Exhibit 15–16 to determine the most profitable distribution level.

Other methods that retailers use to set communication budgets are the objective-and-task method and rules of thumb, such as the affordable, percentage-of-sales, and competitive parity methods. These methods are less sophisticated than marginal analysis but easier to use.

Objective-and-Task Method The **objective-and-task method** determines the budget required to undertake specific tasks for accomplishing communication objectives. To use this method, the retailer first establishes a set of communication objectives. Then the necessary tasks and their costs are determined. The sum total of all costs incurred to undertake the tasks is the communication budget.

Exhibit 15–17 illustrates how the retailer uses the objective-and-task method to complement the marginal analysis. The retailer establishes three objectives:

* to increase the awareness of the store

* to create a greater preference for his/her store among customers in the target market

* to promote the sale of merchandise remaining at the end of each season

The total communication budget the retailer requires to achieve these objectives is $55 300.

Besides defining the objectives and tasks, the retailer must also recheck the financial implications of the communication mix by projecting the income statement for next year using the communication budget (see Exhibit 15–18). This income statement includes an increase of $25 300 in communication expenses over last year. Upon examination, the retailer feels that this increase in the communication budget will boost annual sales from $500 000 to $650 000. Based on the retailer's projections, the increase in communication expenses will raise store profits.

The results of the marginal analysis and the objective-and-task methods suggest a communication budget between $55 000 and $65 000.

objective-and-task method A method for setting a promotion budget in which the retailer first establishes a set of communication objectives and then determines the necessary tasks and their costs.

Rule-of-Thumb Methods In the previous two methods, the communication budget is set by estimating communication activities' effects on the firm's future sales or communication objectives. The **rule-of-thumb methods** discussed in this section use an alternative logic.

rule-of-thumb methods A type of approach for setting a promotion budget that uses past sales and communication activity to determine the present communications budget.

Exhibit 15–18

Financial Implications of Increasing the Communication Budget

	Last Year	Next Year
Sales	$500 000	$650 000
Gross margin (realized)	200 000	260 000
Rental, maintenance, etc.	70 000	85 000
Personnel	60 000	64 500
Communications	30 000	55 300
Profit	$ 40 000	$ 55 200

Affordable Method When using the affordable budgeting method, retailers first forecast their sales and expenses, excluding communication expenses, during the budgeting period. The difference between the forecast sales and expenses plus desired profit is then budgeted for the communication mix expenses. In other words, the affordable method sets the communication budget by determining what money is available after operating costs and profits are budgeted.

The major problem with the affordable method is that it assumes that the communication expenses don't stimulate sales and profit. Communication expenses are just a cost of business, like the cost of merchandise. When retailers use the affordable method, they typically cut "unnecessary" communication expenses if sales fall below the forecast rather than increase communication expenses to increase sales.

Percentage-of-Sales Method The percentage-of-sales method sets the communication budget as a fixed percentage of forecast sales. Retailers use this method to determine the communication budget by forecasting sales during the budget period and using a predetermined percentage to set the budget. The percentage may be the retailer's historical percentage or the average percentage used by similar retailers.

The problem with the percentage-of-sales method is that it assumes the same percentage used in the past, or by competitors, is still appropriate for the retailer. Consider a retailer that hasn't opened new stores in the past but plans to open many new stores in the current year. It must create customer awareness for these new stores, so the communication budget should be much larger in the current year than in the past.

Using the same percentage as competitors also may be inappropriate. For example, a retailer might have better locations than its competitors. Due to these locations, customers may already have a high awareness of the retailer's stores. Thus, the retailer may not need to spend as much on communications as competitors with poorer locations spend.

One advantage of both the percentage-of-sales method

affordable budgeting method A budgeting method in which a retailer first sets a budget for every element of the retail mix except promotion and then allocates the leftover funds to a promotional budget.

percentage-of-sales method A method for setting a promotion budget based on a fixed percentage of forecast sales.

competitive parity method An approach for setting a promotion budget so that the retailer's share of promotion expenses is equal to its market share.

and the affordable method for determining a communication budget is that the retailer won't spend beyond its means. Since the level of spending is determined by sales, the budget will go up only when sales go up and the retailer generates more sales to pay for the additional communication expenses. When times are good, these methods work well because they allow the retailer to communicate more aggressively with customers. But when sales fall, communication expenses are cut, which may accelerate the sales decline.

Competitive Parity Method Under the competitive parity method, the communication budget is set so that the retailer's share of communication expenses equals its share of the market. For example, consider a sporting goods store in a small town. To use the competitive parity method, the owner–manager would first estimate the total amount spent on communications by all of the sporting goods retailers in town. Then the owner–manager would estimate his or her store's market share for sporting goods and multiply that market share percentage by the sporting goods stores' total advertising expenses to set its budget. Assume that the owner–manager's estimate of advertising for sporting goods by all stores was $5000 and the estimate of his or her store's market share was 45 percent. On the basis of these estimates, the owner–manager would set the store's communication budget at $2250 to maintain competitive parity.

Like the other rule-of-thumb methods, the competitive parity method doesn't allow retailers to exploit the unique opportunities or problems they confront in a market. If all competitors used this method to set communication budgets, their market shares would stay about the same over time (assuming that the retailers developed equally effective campaigns).

<aside>
DID YOU KNOW?

Supermarkets spend 1.1 percent of annual sales revenue on advertising, department store retailers spend 3.7 percent of sales, and women's apparel specialty retailers spend 4.7 percent of sales.[80]
</aside>

Allocating the Promotional Budget

After determining the size of the communication budget, the third step in the communication planning process is allocating the budget (see Exhibit 15–12). In this step, the retailer decides how much of its budget to allocate to specific communication elements, merchandise categories, geographic regions, or long- and short-term objectives. For example, a department store must decide how much of its communication budget to spend in each area where it has stores. Sears decides how much to allocate to appliances, hardware, and apparel. The sporting goods store owner–manager must decide how much of the store's $2250 communication budget to spend on promoting the store's image versus generating sales during the year and how much to spend on advertising and special promotions.

Research indicates that allocation decisions are more important than the decision on the amount spent on communications.[81] In other words, retailers often can realize the same objectives by reducing the size of the communication budget but allocating the budget more effectively.

An easy way to make such allocation decisions is just to spend about the same in each geographic region or for each merchandise category. But this allocation rule probably won't maximize profits because it ignores the possibility that communication programs might be more effective for some merchandise categories or for some regions than for others. Another approach is to use rules of thumb, such as basing allocations on the sales level or contribution for the merchandise category.

Allocation decisions, like budget-setting decisions, should use the principles of marginal analysis. The retailer should allocate the budget to areas that will yield the greatest return. This approach for allocating a budget is sometimes referred to as the **high-assay principle**. Consider a miner who can spend his time digging on two claims. The value of the gold on one claim is assayed at $20 000 per tonne, whereas the assay value on the other claim is $10 000 per tonne. Should the miner spend two-thirds of his time at the first mine and one-third of his time at the other mine? Of course not! The miner should spend all of his time mining the first claim until the assay value of the ore mined drops to $10 000 a tonne, at which time he can divide his time equally between the claims.

Similarly, a retailer may find that its customers have a high awareness and very favourable attitude toward its women's clothing but may not know much about the store's men's clothing. In this situation, a dollar spent on advertising men's clothing might generate more sales than a dollar spent on women's clothing, even though the sales of women's clothing are greater than the sales of men's clothing.

Planning, Implementing, and Evaluating Communication Programs—Three Illustrations

The final stage in developing a retail communication program is implementation and evaluation (see Exhibit 15–12). In this final section of the chapter, we illustrate the planning and evaluation process for three communication programs—an advertising campaign by a small specialty retailer, a sales promotion opportunity confronting a supermarket chain, and a communication program emphasizing direct marketing undertaken by a large retail chain.

Advertising Campaign   South Gate West is one of several specialty import home-furnishings stores competing for upscale shoppers. The store has the appearance of both a fine antiques store and a traditional home- furnishing shop, but most of its merchandise is new Asian imports.[82]

The owner realized that his communication budget is considerably less than the budget of the local Pier 1 store. (Pier 1 is a large international import home-furnishings chain.) He decides to concentrate his limited budget on a specific segment and use highly distinctive copy and art in his advertising. His target market is experienced, sophisticated consumers of housewares and home decorative items. His experience indicates the importance of personal selling for more seasoned shoppers because they make large purchases and seek considerable information before making a decision. Thus, the retailer spends part of his communication budget on training his sales associates.

The advertising program that the retailer develops emphasizes his store's distinctive image. He uses the newspaper as his major vehicle. Competitive ads contain line drawings of furniture with prices. His ads emphasize the imagery associated with Asian furniture by featuring off-the-beaten-path scenes of Asian countries with unusual art objects. This theme is also reflected in the store's atmosphere.

To evaluate his communication program, the retailer needs to compare the results of his program with the objectives he developed during the first part of the planning process. To measure his campaign's effectiveness, he conducts an inexpensive tracking

high-assay principle A method of allocating a communication budget that uses the principles of marginal analysis. The retailer should allocate the budget to areas that will yield the greatest return.

study. Telephone interviews are performed periodically with a representative sample of furniture customers in his store's trading area. Communication objectives are assessed using the following questions:

Communication Objective	Question
Awareness	What stores sell East Asian furniture?
Knowledge	Which stores would you rate outstanding on the following characteristics?
Attitude	On your next shopping trip for East Asian furniture, which store would you visit first?
Visit	Which of the following stores have you been to?

Here are the survey results for one year:

	Before Campaign	Six Months After	One Year After
Awareness (percentage mentioning store)	38%	46%	52%
Knowledge (percentage giving outstanding rating for sales assistance)	9	17	24
Attitude (percentage first choice)	13	15	19
Visit (percentage visited store)	8	15	19

The results show a steady increase in awareness, knowledge of the store, and choice of the store as a primary source of East Asian furniture. This research provides evidence that the advertising is conveying the intended message to the target audience.

Sales Promotion Opportunity Many sales promotion opportunities undertaken by retailers are initiated by vendors. For example, Colgate-Palmolive might offer the following special promotion to Loblaws: During a one-week period, Loblaws can order Fab laundry detergent in the 2-kg size at 15 cents below the standard wholesale price. However, if Loblaws elects to buy Fab at the discounted price, the grocery chain must feature the 2-kg container of Fab in its Thursday newspaper ad at $1.59 (20 cents off the typical retail price). In addition, Loblaws must have an end-aisle display of Fab.

Before Loblaws decides whether to accept such a trade promotion and then promote Fab to its customers, it needs to assess the promotion's impact on its profitability. Such a promotion may be effective for the vendor but not for the retailer.

To evaluate a trade promotion, the retailer considers the following:

- the realized margin from the promotion
- the cost of the additional inventory carried due to buying more than the normal amount
- the potential increase in sales from the promoted merchandise
- the potential loss suffered when customers switch to the promoted merchandise from more profitable private-label brands
- the additional sales made to customers attracted to the store by the promotion[83]

When Fab's price is reduced to $1.59, Loblaws will sell more Fab than it normally would. But Loblaws' margin on the Fab will be less because the required retail discount of 20 cents isn't offset by the wholesale discount of 15 cents. In addition, Loblaws might suffer losses because the promotion encourages customers to buy Fab, which has a lower margin than Loblaws' private-label detergent that customers might have bought. In fact, customers may stockpile Fab, buying several boxes, which will reduce sales of Loblaws' private-label detergent for some time after the special promotion ends. On the other hand, the promotion may attract customers who don't normally shop at Loblaws but who will visit to buy Fab at the discounted price. These customers might buy additional merchandise, providing a sales gain to the store that it wouldn't have realized if it hadn't promoted Fab.

Special Promotion Using a CRM/Campaign Management Tool A national retailer with 580 store locations uses its CRM/campaign management system to plan, design, evaluate, and implement a special Canada Day promotion.[84] The diagram of the system is shown in Exhibit 15–19. The retailer has a customer database with purchase information complemented with additional customer information acquired through external sources.

After an initial planning meeting, the retailer decides to use direct mail, mobile marketing, and email communication channels with supporting in-store promotions and existing advertising. Customers need to bring in a coupon to take advantage of the special promotion. The goal of the campaign is to generate a 10 percent increase in sales during the Canada Day period.

Using the campaign management tool in the system, the retailer examines a number of what-if scenarios, enabling the team to chart out all of the tasks, costs, and related deadlines to determine projected ROI. Initially, they want to target customers who have visited the stores and made a purchase within the last nine months. During the target market segmentation evaluation process, they determine that the counts are too low and increase the target criterion to customer purchases within the last 12 months. Using this criterion, the communication program is directed to 2.6 million customers. A review of past holiday promotion programs suggests a response rate of 2.5 percent.

Based on the 2.5 percent response rate for 2.6 million customers, the number of people projected to visit the stores is 65 000. The special promotion is a $49 item, but the average sale once people are in the store is $99. On the basis of this information, the Canada Day event special promotion is targeted to generate gross sales between $3.1 million and $6.4 million.

The cost for the direct-mail piece is $0.65/piece and the email piece is $0.03/email. To mail and email 2.6 million customers, the cost is $1 768 000. In determining the product costs on the special promotion item, a 75 percent markup is used. The campaign profitability margin is projected to be between $600 000 and $3.1 million. The financial analysis developed by the planning tool is shown in Exhibit 15–20.

Once the what-if analysis is completed and the campaign plan is built with all of the details and responsibilities of each department, it is set into action. The action plan includes all the required steps in the campaign process, along with the costs, responsibilities, and deadlines on the marketing production schedule. By putting the plan into production, all of the tasks are sent to the people responsible for completing them, so that deadlines and costs are tracked. Each department receives a series of tasks specific to that department's deliverables:

- The creative department is assigned the responsibility of designing the direct mail piece with the coupon. It also designs the email piece with a print coupon. Once the design process is completed and approved, the artwork is sent to the print vendor for printing and the marketing department for email distribution.

- The database marketing department is responsible for sending the list of customers in the target market analysis (the customers who have visited a store and made a purchase in the last 12 months) to the mail vendor. Each record in the customer database has a unique identifier so that the results of the campaign will be properly tracked and analyzed.

- The store promotions department has to make sure that the in-store promotional materials are consistent with the message in the campaign. Media services also have to verify consistency in all media with the campaign message.

Exhibit 15–19
CRM/Campaign Management System

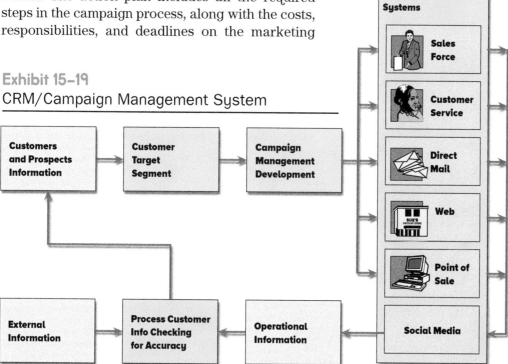

Exhibit 15–20
Financial Analysis of Special Canada Day Promotion

Campaign Planning Financials			
Target Market Count		**Campaign Costs**	
Records in 12-month period	2.6 million	Direct mail ($0.65/piece)	$1 690 000
2.5% response rate		E-mail ($0.03/e-mail)	$78 000
Project response count	65 000	Total cost	$1 768 000
Gross Revenue		**Net Revenue (less product cost of 25%)**	
Special promotion $49/each	$3 185 000	$2 388 750	
Average sale $99/each	$6 435 000	$4 826 250	
	Campaign Profitability		
	Special promotion	$620 750	
	Average sale	$3 058 250	

During the entire campaign process, a management view of the financial information and campaign deliverables/deadline information is available. As the stores report their customer sales, management's reports are automatically generated, and the response ROI is analyzed to determine if the marketing campaign was successful. The information from all of the customer touchpoints is collected, processed, and added to the customer database. The successful campaign is then templated for future use to save time in the planning phase for the next holiday campaign. The matrix solution allows management to optimize resources and manage deadlines and deliverables, thus increasing productivity, efficiency, and ROI.

SUMMARY

In today's economy, where good news is often quickly matched by an equal portion of bad news, effectively competing and winning customers every day is vital to a retailer's success. The best retailers maintain their loyal customers and win new ones, pursuing larger market share by communicating through education, building brand awareness, and developing experiential involvement. Consumers today are both online and offline, and sometimes online while shopping offline. Online they are sharing, friend-validating, researching, learning, and developing a point of view. Offline there is touching, brand comparing, and brand associating.

The communication program can be designed to achieve a variety of objectives for the retailer. Objectives include building a brand image of the retailer in the customer's mind, increasing sales and store traffic, providing information about the retailer's location and offering, and announcing special activities. Retailers need to be where their customers are with both their messaging and their products and/or services.

Retailers communicate with customers through advertising, sales promotions, websites, store atmosphere, publicity, personal selling, email, and word-of-mouth. These elements in the communication mix must be coordinated so that customers will have a clear, distinct image of the retailer and won't be confused by conflicting information. Also, consumer rights requirements must be acknowledged and complied with.

Many retailers use rules of thumb to determine the size of the promotion budget. Marginal analysis (the most appropriate method for determining how much must be spent to accomplish the retailer's objectives) should be used to determine whether the level of spending maximizes the profits that could be generated by the communications mix.

The largest portion of a retailer's communication budget is typically spent on advertising and sales promotions. A wide array of media can be used for advertising. Each medium has its pros and cons. Newspaper advertising is effective for announcing sales, whereas TV ads are useful for developing an image. Sales promotions are typically used to achieve short-term objectives, such as increasing store traffic over a weekend. Most sales promotions are supported in part by promotions offered to the retailer by its vendors. Publicity and word-of-mouth are typically low-cost communications, but they are very difficult for retailers to control.

Direct marketing contains a variety of traditional and new forms of marketing communication initiatives, including Internet-enabled methods such as mobile marketing. The increased use of customer databases has enabled retailers to identify and track consumers over time and across purchase situations, contributing to more personalized promotional activity.

KEY TERMS

advertising
affordable budgeting method
aided recall
attitude branding
blog
brand
brand association
brand awareness
brand energy
brand equity
call to action
communication objectives
competitive parity method
co-op advertising
cost per thousand (CPM)

coverage
cumulative reach
direct mail
direct marketing
email
freestanding inserts (FSI)
frequency
high-assay principle
impact
integrated marketing communication program
marginal analysis
mobile marketing
objective-and-task method
percentage-of-sales method

personal selling
point-of-purchase (POP)
premium
public relations (PR)
reach
rule-of-thumb method
sales promotions
samples
short code
showrooming
social media
special event
top-of-mind awareness

GET OUT & DO IT!

1. INTERNET EXERCISE Go to http://www.youtube.com/user/WestJet and explain the success of WestJet ads in communicating to the customer.

2. INTERNET EXERCISE Go to http://www.dove.ca and click on the link for Our Mission. Describe how Dove has connected to the female consumer through emotional messages with its Self-Esteem campaign.

3. INTERNET EXERCISE Review the trends at http://www.trendwatching.com for a future focus on advertising and consumer directions.

4. GO SHOPPING Go to a retail store and make a list of all of the specific elements and information in the store that communicate the store's image and the merchandise it is offering to customers.

5. GO SHOPPING Look though the freestanding inserts (FSIs) in your local newspaper. Evaluate the general use of FSIs, and select the FSIs that you think are most effective. Why are these FSIs more effective than the other ones?

6. INTERNET EXERCISE Visit the Consumers' Association of Canada at http://www.consumer.ca. Identify the eight consumer rights profiled on the site, and give a retail example of each.

7. INTERNET EXERCISE You can find more information about the use of radio as an advertising medium at the Radio Advertising Bureau site, http://www.rab.com. Based on this information, what types of retail messages can be delivered more effectively by radio compared to other media? How has the radio app Shazam potentially changed radio advertising opportunities for retailers?

DISCUSSION QUESTIONS AND PROBLEMS

1. How do brands benefit consumers? Retailers?

2. How can advertising, personal selling, and promotion complement each other in an integrated marketing communications program?

3. As a means of communicating with customers, how does advertising differ from publicity?

4. Why is the newspaper the favourite medium used by retailers for advertising? What are the advantages and disadvantages of newspaper advertising? Why is the use of newspaper decreasing and use of direct mail increasing?

5. For which of the following growth opportunities do you think the retailer should use its brand name when pursuing the opportunity? Why?

   a) McDonald's starts a new chain of restaurants to sell seafood in a sit-down environment competing with Red Lobster.

   b) Sears starts a chain of stand-alone stores that sell just home appliances.

   c) Netflix starts a chain of stores selling consumer electronics.

6. What factors should be considered in dividing up the budget among a store's different merchandise areas? Which of the following should receive the highest advertising budget: fashionable women's clothing, men's underwear, women's hosiery, or kitchen appliances? Why?

7. Outline some elements in a communication program to achieve the following objectives:

   a) Increase store loyalty by 20 percent.

   b) Build awareness of the store by 10 percent.

   c) Develop an image as a low-price retailer. How would you determine whether the communication program met the objective?

8. Some retailers direct their advertising efforts toward reaching as wide an audience as possible. Others try to expose the audience to an advertisement as many times as possible. When should a retailer concentrate on reach? When should a retailer concentrate on frequency?

9. A retailer plans to open a new store near a university. It will specialize in merchandise such as T-shirts, sweatshirts, and accessories. Develop an integrated communication program for the retailer. What specific advertising media should the new store use to capture the university market?

10. Cooperative (co-op) advertising is a good way for a retailer to extend an ad budget. Why is it not always in a retailer's best interests to rely extensively on co-op advertising?

CASES

Case	Title	Chapter
1	The Last Days of Target	1
2	Retailing in India—Impact of Hypermarkets	2
3	Sobeys Finds Its Fit with the Urban Crowd: Customer Behaviour	3
4	Attracting Generation Y to a Retail Career	3, 4, 13
5	Staples Inc.	9
6	Starbucks' Expansion into China	5, 7
7	Build-A-Bear Workshop: Where Best Friends Are Made	4
8	Supplementing for Success in the Canadian Market	4
9	Blue Tomato: Internationalization of a Multichannel Retailer	7
10	Vivah Jewellery: Location Strategy	5
11	Stephanie's Boutique: Store Strategy	5
12	Innovating the In-Store Experience	6
13	Building the Apple Store	6
14	Mountain Equipment Co-op: Revitalizing a Brand	7
15	Tiffany & Co. and TJX: Comparing Financial Performance	8
16	The Chocolate Shop	8
17	Walmart: Pioneer in Supply Chain Management	9
18	Lindy's Bridal Shoppe: Assortments	10
19	Merchandise Strategy: Process for Success	10
20	Hughes: Developing a Buying Plan	11
21	Capital Sportswear: Buying	11
22	How Much for a Good Smell? Pricing	12
23	Enterprise Rent-A-Car Focuses on Its People	13
24	Creating Loss Prevention Programs That Fit the Culture	13
25	HR Technology Is All about Connections	13
26	Preparing for Succession, Stitch by Stitch	13
27	Customer Service and Relationship Management at Nordstrom	14
28	Active Endeavors Analyzes Its Customer Database	14
29	Engaging with Customers through Social Media	14
30	Diamond in the Rough	14
31	Target Marketing with Google AdWords	15
32	Generating Advertising Revenue from a Digital Screen Network at Harrods of London	15

The grand opening of Target Canada was set to begin in one month, and Tony Fisher needed to know whether the company was actually ready. In February 2013, about a dozen senior-level employees gathered at the company's Mississauga, Ontario, headquarters to offer updates on the state of their departments. Fisher, Target Canada's president, was holding these meetings every day as the launch date crept closer. The news was rarely good. The company was having trouble moving products from its cavernous distribution centres and onto store shelves, which would leave Target outlets poorly stocked. The checkout system was glitchy and didn't process transactions properly. Worse, the technology governing inventory and sales was new to the organization; no one seemed to fully understand how it all worked. The 750 employees at the Mississauga head office had worked furiously for a year to get up and running, and nerves were beginning to fray. Three test stores were slated to open at the beginning of March, followed shortly by another 21. A decision had to be made.

Fisher, 38 years old at the time, was regarded as a wunderkind who had quickly risen through the ranks at Target's American command post in Minneapolis, from a lowly business analyst to leader of a team of 400 people across multiple divisions. Launching the Target brand in a new country was his biggest task to date. The news he received from his group that February afternoon should have been worrying, but if he was unnerved, Fisher didn't let on. He listened patiently as two people in the room strongly expressed reticence about opening stores on the existing timetable. Their concern was that with severe supply chain problems and stores facing the prospect of patchy or empty shelves, Target would blow its first date with Canadian consumers. Still, neither one outright advocated that the company push back its plans. "Nobody wanted to be the one to say, 'This is a disaster,'" says a former employee. But by highlighting the risks of opening now, the senior employees' hope was that Fisher would tell his boss back in Minneapolis, Target CEO Gregg Steinhafel, that they needed more time.

The magnitude of what was at stake began weighing on some of those senior officials. "I remember wanting to vomit," recalls one participant. Nobody disagreed with the negative assessment—everyone was well aware of Target's operational problems—but there was still a strong sense of optimism among the leaders, many of whom were US expats. The mentality, according to one former employee, was, "If there's any team in retail that can turn this thing around, it's us." The group was riding a wave of momentum, in fact. They had overcome seemingly endless hurdles and worked gruelling hours to get to this point, and they knew there were costs to delaying. The former employee says the meeting ultimately concerned much more than when to open the first few stores; it was about the entirety of Target's Canadian launch. Postponement would mean pushing back even more store openings. Everyone else in attendance expressed confidence in sticking to the schedule, and by the time the meeting concluded, it was clear the doors would open as promised. "That was the biggest mistake we could have made," says the former employee.

Roughly two years from that date, Target Canada filed for creditor protection, marking the end of its first international foray and one of the most confounding sagas in Canadian corporate history. The debacle cost the parent company billions of dollars, sullied its reputation, and put roughly 17 600 people out of work. Target's arrival was highly anticipated by consumers and feared by rival retailers. The chain, whose roots stretch back to 1902, had perfected its retail strategy and grown into a US$70-billion titan in its home country. Target was a careful, analytical, and efficient organization with a highly admired corporate culture. The corporation's entry into Canada was uncharacteristically bold—not just for Target, but for any retailer. Under Steinhafel, the company paid $1.8 billion for the leases to the entire Zellers chain in 2011 and formulated a plan to open 124 locations by the end of 2013. Not only that, but the chain expected to be profitable within its first year of operations.

Why Target Canada collapsed has been endlessly dissected by analysts, pundits, and journalists. But the people who know what happened best are the employees who lived through the experience. On the first anniversary of the company's bankruptcy filing, *Canadian Business* spoke to close to 30 former employees in Canada and the United States to find out how Target, one of the best retailers in North America, got it so wrong in Canada. (Target declined to comment on specific issues, pointing to previous statements it has made on its Canadian venture. The former employees interviewed for this story requested anonymity to preserve relationships in the industry.) Even those employees remain baffled by how Target Canada collapsed. But what emerged is a story of a company trapped by an overly ambitious launch schedule, an inexperienced leadership team expected to deal with the biggest crisis in the firm's history, and a sophisticated retail giant felled by the most mundane, basic, and embarrassing of errors.

In the fall of 2013, hundreds of Target Canada head office staff piled into the auditorium at the Mississauga Living Arts Centre for a state-of-the-union address from their leaders. The employees were weary and frustrated by this point. The bulk of the 124 stores had opened, and it was clear the launch had gone seriously awry. Consumers were frustrated when confronted with empty shelves, and the media and financial analysts were hammering the company for it. On stage, Fisher stated his conviction that Target Canada was making progress and that 2014 would be a greatly improved year. A Q&A session followed; one employee bravely asked Fisher what he would do differently if he could do the launch over again. A man in the front row stood up and offered to field the question. Taking the microphone, Steinhafel, Target's CEO, didn't hesitate with his answer: He would renegotiate the real estate deal that facilitated the company coming to Canada in the first place.

That deal started with Richard Baker, the executive chairman of Hudson's Bay Co. Although Baker is a retail executive, he is, at heart, a real estate man. His maternal grandfather started buying and selling real estate in New York City in 1932 and helped pioneer the concept of shopping malls. Baker's greatest business insight was to recognize the value of the property developed by both his grandfather and father. In the 1990s, he started selling some of it off to various companies, including Walmart. That relationship proved fortuitous in late 2010, when Walmart approached him and offered to buy the Zellers chain from HBC. Baker realized there was more value to Zellers' real estate than to the operation itself, since Walmart had soundly beaten the brand. An astute deal maker, Baker and his team reached out to Target to stoke the company's interest. (Baker, through a spokesperson, declined to comment.)

It was an open secret that Target was interested in the Canadian market. But the company had previously decided it wanted to grow as quickly as possible if it were to enter Canada, rather than pursue a slow, piecemeal expansion. The challenge was in acquiring enough real estate to make that possible. The Zellers sale provided just such an opportunity. After Baker's team let Target know Zellers was on the block—and Walmart was interested—the American company acted quickly to finalize its own offer.

Walmart would eventually back out, but Target put down $1.8 billion. Steinhafel bought everything, essentially committing the company to opening stores as quickly as possible to avoid paying rent on stores that weren't operational and leaving landlords without anchor tenants. The price Steinhafel paid raised eyebrows. "When the numbers got up as high as they did, we found that pretty surprising," says Mark Foote, the CEO of Zellers at the time.

But Steinhafel may have felt justified in making such a bold move. In the three years since he was appointed CEO, he'd boosted revenue 8.3 percent—not a huge number, but an impressive one, considering the United States was experiencing the worst recession since the Great Depression. Steinhafel had joined Target in 1979, and his entire professional career had been spent with the company. Target experienced steady growth during that time, and Steinhafel had simply become accustomed to succeeding. "The company had never really failed before," says a former employee who worked in both the US and Canada. There was no reason to think Target wouldn't be able to pull this off.

Almost immediately, employees in Minneapolis were seconded to work on the Canadian launch. It was considered a privilege to be recruited. "The company was pouring in resources left, right, and sideways, so it was palpably exciting in Minneapolis," says a former employee. But there was also immense pressure. "From the very beginning, there was a clock that was ticking," says the former employee. "And that clock was absurd." The company did everything it could to remove barriers that might slow progress and to ensure decisions could be made quickly. Timelines were hugely compressed. Building a new distribution centre from scratch, for example, might take a few years. Target was going to do it in less than two years—and it planned to construct three of them.

One of the most important decisions concerned technology—the systems that allow the company to order products from vendors, process goods through warehouses, and get them onto store shelves promptly. In the US, Target used custom technology that had been fine-tuned over the years to meet its exacting needs, and the corporation had developed a deep well of knowledge around how these systems functioned. Target faced a choice: Was it better to extend that existing technology to Canada or buy a completely new, off-the-shelf system?

Finding an answer was tricky. By using Target's existing technology, employees in Canada could draw on the large amount of expertise in the United States. That plan had shortcomings as well. The technology was not set up to deal with a foreign country, and it would have to be customized to take into account the Canadian dollar and even French-language characters. Those changes would take time—which Target did not have. A ready-made solution could be implemented faster, even if the company had little expertise in actually using it.

The team responsible for the decision went with a system known as SAP, made by the German enterprise software company of the same name. Considered the gold standard in retail, SAP is used by many companies around the world, from Indigo in Canada to Denmark's Dansk supermarket chain. It essentially serves as a retailer's brain, storing huge amounts of data related to every single product in stores. That data would be fed by SAP into Target's other crucial systems: software to forecast demand for products and replenish stocks, and a separate program for managing the distribution centres. After implementing SAP in Canada, Target wanted to eventually switch the US operations over as well, aligning the two countries and ensuring the entire company benefited from the latest technology.

While SAP might be considered best in class, it's an ornery, unforgiving beast. Sobeys introduced a version of SAP in 1996 and abandoned the effort by 2000. (It wasn't until 2004 that the grocery chain tried again.) Similarly, Loblaws started moving to SAP in 2007 and projected three to five years to get it done. The implementation took two years longer than expected because of unreliable data in the system. Target was again seeking to do the impossible: It was going to set up and run SAP in roughly two years. The company wasn't doing it alone, however, and hired Accenture (which also worked on Loblaws' integration) as the lead consultant on the project. Target believed the problems other retailers faced were due to errors in data conversion. Those companies were essentially taking information from their existing systems and translating it for SAP, a messy process in which it's easy to make mistakes. Target, on the other hand, was starting fresh. There was no data to convert, only new information to input.

By early 2012, with the planned opening still a year away, the nerve centre for the Canadian launch had moved from Minneapolis to Mississauga, and waves of American expats settled up north. Hiring was a top priority. Target has a unique, well-established corporate culture in the US, which the company views as one of the reasons for its success, and leaders sought to replicate that environment here. Target describes itself as "fast, fun, and friendly," to work for and it's a place where attitude and soft skills are of equal—if not more—importance to experience. "Target's motto was they could train you for the job, but they couldn't train culture," says a former employee.

In the US, the company prides itself on its development programs for even junior positions like business analysts, who help co-ordinate the flow of product, and merchandising assistants, who work with buyers to choose which products to stock and negotiate costs with vendors. Target typically recruits candidates for these positions straight out of school and prepares them for a career in retail. That's how Tony Fisher got his start—he joined the company as an analyst in 1999, after he was drafted by the Texas Rangers baseball organization and played for two years in the minor leagues. Young employees receive months of instruction and are paired with a mentor. Hiring for culture over experience works, essentially, because Target in the US provides ample training.

In Canada, the company succeeded in hiring people with the right personalities, but young staff received only a few weeks of training, according to former employees who worked at Target in both countries. The Canadian team lacked the institutional knowledge and time to properly mentor the new hires. "Everyone was stretched thin. We didn't have the manpower to get everything done in the time frame that was laid out," says a former employee. Another was surprised to see how green his colleagues were. "I was one of the older people there, and I was in my mid-30s," he says.

Target Canada would eventually learn what happens when inexperienced employees working under a tight timeline are expected to launch a retailer using technology that nobody—not even at the US headquarters—really understood.

Strange things started happening in 2012, once ordering began for the pending launch. Items with long lead times coming from overseas were stalled—products weren't fitting into shipping containers as expected, or tariff codes were missing or incomplete. Merchandise that made it to a distribution centre couldn't be processed for shipping to a store. Other items weren't able to fit properly onto store shelves. What appeared to be isolated fires quickly became a raging inferno threatening to destroy the company's supply chain.

It didn't take long for Target to figure out the underlying cause of the breakdown: The data contained within the company's supply chain software, which governs the movement of inventory, was riddled with flaws. At the very start, an untold number of mistakes were made, and the company spent months trying to recover from them. In order to stock products, the company had to enter information about each item into SAP. There could be dozens of fields for a single product. For a single product, such as a blender, there might be fields for the manufacturer, the model, the UPC, the dimensions, the weight, how many can fit into a case for shipping and so on. Typically, this information is retrieved from vendors before Target employees put it into SAP. The system requires correct data to function properly and ensure products move as anticipated.

A team assigned to investigate the problem discovered an astounding number of errors. Product dimensions would be in inches, not centimetres, or entered in the wrong order: width by height by length, instead of, say, length by width by height. Sometimes the wrong currency was used. Item descriptions were vague. Important information was missing. There were myriad typos. "You name it, it was wrong," says a former employee. "It was a disaster."

It was also something the company should have seen coming. The rush to launch meant merchandisers were under pressure to enter information for roughly 75 000 different products into SAP according to a rigid implementation schedule. Getting the details from suppliers largely fell on the young merchandising assistants. In the industry, information from vendors is notoriously unreliable, but merchandising assistants were often not experienced enough to challenge vendors on the accuracy of the product information they provided. (The staff were also working against the countdown to opening.) "There was never any talk about accuracy," says a former employee. "You had these people we hired, straight out of school, pressured to do this insane amount of data entry, and nobody told them it had to be right." Worse, the company hadn't built a safety net into SAP at this point; the system couldn't notify users about data entry errors. The investigative team estimated information in the system was accurate about 30 percent of the time. In the US, it's between 98 percent and 99 percent. (Accenture, which Target hired as a consultant on SAP, said in a statement: "Accenture completed a successful SAP implementation for Target in Canada. The project was reviewed independently and such review concluded that there is no Accenture connection with the issues you refer to.")

The investigating team went to Fisher and John Morioka, the senior vice-president of merchandising, with a drastic proposal: Shut down the entire merchandising division so everyone could comb through and verify every single piece of data in the system—manually. The team stressed there was simply no other way to get it done. Hiring an external consultant would take too long, and it was impossible to expect the employees to do such a painstaking, arduous task and their regular jobs at the same time. Fisher immediately gave the green light.

Thus, "data week" was held in the fall of 2012. Merchandisers essentially had to confirm every data point for every product with their vendors. A buyer might have 1500 products and 50 to 80 fields to check for each one. The more experienced employees had the foresight to keep records of verified information (dubbed "sources of truth"), which made the task a little easier. Others weren't so lucky. Complicating matters was the dummy information entered into the system when SAP was set up. That dummy data was still there, confusing the system, and it had to be expunged. "We actually sat there and went through every line of data manually," says a former employee. "It was terrible." Target anticipated how awful it would be and designed the week to help keep employees sane. To kick it off and rally spirits, a few employees performed a hip-hop song-and-dance routine on the first day. Ice cream and pizza flooded in to keep employees fuelled up, some of whom stayed well past midnight that week, squinting at screens through bleary eyes.

There was an entirely different process to ensure the correct data actually made it into SAP. The employees in Mississauga couldn't do so directly. Instead, the information was sent to a Target office in India, where staff would load it into SAP. Extra contractors had to be hired in India, too. "Sometimes even when we had the data correct, it got mixed up by the contractors in Target India," says a former employee. (Another former employee disputes this: "Sometimes the quality of their work wasn't so great, but for the most part they did a good job.") In any event, uploading took longer than expected, and data week stretched into two. Periodic data blitzes in individual departments became common into the following year.

But data week was successful on a number of fronts. It weeded out the worst of the errors and forced Target Canada to realize the importance of accurate data. It was also a bonding experience—as terrible as it was. "The company came together that week," says a former employee. "We were all in the trenches doing this unglamorous work."

On March 4, 2013, Tony Fisher led a gaggle of reporters through a new Target location in Guelph, Ontatio. The store officially opened the next day, along with two others in the province.

The company had been teasing consumers for a year at this point, starting with a pop-up shop in Toronto featuring designer Jason Wu. There had also been a high-profile ad during the Academy Awards to hype the Canadian launch, and actors Sarah Jessica Parker and Blake Lively were lined up to appear at the grand opening.

Workers were still stocking shelves at the time, and signs throughout the store read, "We're open (mostly)." The three Ontario stores were part of Target's soft launch, and the company explained in a press release that the goal was to use them to iron out kinks and "determine operational readiness" before opening 21 more locations as part of its official launch that month.

At the Guelph store, Fisher, wearing a red checkered shirt and a red tie, pointed out the bright lighting and wide aisles, and promised a quick, convenient checkout experience. "Not only have we brought that same Target brand experience," he said, referring to the US, "but we've actually enhanced it and made it better." Fisher sported a head of thick dark hair and could flash a camera-ready smile when he needed to. Some of his former employees dismiss him as just a media-friendly face, but others describe him as whip-smart, detail oriented, and incredibly dedicated to Target. More than a few people say Fisher "bled Target red." When he wasn't talking to reporters about the pending launch, he could have a stern, imposing demeanour (a defence mechanism to compensate for his young age, perhaps), so much so that employees would warn prospective hires about to interview with him not to be put off. It wasn't until Fisher got to know people that he warmed up.

His tour of the first store was breathlessly covered by media, and consumer anticipation was running high. In Guelph, customers lined up before the store opened at 8 a.m., and when they were finally let in, floor staff cheered and offered them

high-fives. News crews were ready to snag customers as they left and cajole them into showing off their purchases. (The first items bought at Target Canada? A Tarzan DVD and a Michael Bolton CD.)

The foot traffic in the early days was more than expected, which was encouraging, but it didn't take long for consumers to start complaining on social media about empty shelves. "Target in Guelph, please stock up and fill the shelves," wrote one aggrieved shopper on Facebook. "How can I or anyone purchase if there is nothing left for me to buy?" Target told the media that it was overwhelmed by demand and made assurances that it was improving the accuracy of product deliveries. The reality was that Target was still struggling with data quality problems that were hampering the supply chain, and it didn't have time to address the root causes before opening another wave of stores. Problems multiplied, and the public mood continued to turn against Target. Consumers soured on the brand when confronted with empty shelves—the exact scenario some senior employees warned of earlier in the year.

Ironically, even as consumers encountered barely stocked stores, Target's distribution centres were bursting with products. Target Canada had ordered way more stock than it could actually sell. The company had purchased a sophisticated forecasting and replenishment system made by a firm called JDA Software, but it wasn't particularly useful at the outset, requiring years of historical data to actually provide meaningful sales forecasts. When the buying team was preparing for store openings, it instead relied on wildly optimistic projections developed at US headquarters. According to someone with knowledge of the forecasting process in Minneapolis, the company treated Canadian locations the same way they did operational stores in the US and not as newcomers that would have to draw competitors away from rival retailers. Even if the stores were in out-of-the-way spots—and some of the locations in the Zellers portfolio certainly were—the company assumed the strength of the Target brand would lure customers. There was another element at play, too. "Once you signed up to do 124 Zellers locations, it felt like there was a point where it's like we have to assume sales will be good," says the former employee. "It's very backwards."

In Canada, some buyers also relied on vendors for guidance, but vendors fell under the Target spell like everyone else. "They would say, 'Because it's Target, they'll sell double what Zellers was selling.'

And that would be what we put in that initial forecast," says a former buyer. In consequence, Target ordered too much product that first year. It all hit the distribution centres at the same time, creating a severe bottleneck.

The depots were hampered by other factors, caused by lingering data problems and the learning curve associated with the new systems. Manhattan, the company's warehouse software, and SAP weren't communicating properly. Sometimes, the issues concerned dimensions and quantities. An employee at headquarters might have ordered 1000 toothbrushes and mistakenly entered into SAP that the shipment would arrive in a case pack containing 10 boxes of 100 toothbrushes each. But the shipment might actually be configured differently—four larger boxes of 250 toothbrushes, for example. As a result, that shipment wouldn't exist within the distribution centre's software and couldn't be processed. It would get set aside in what was designated as the "problem area." These sorts of hang-ups happen at any warehouse, but at Target Canada, they happened with alarming frequency. Warehouse workers got so desperate to move shipments they would sometimes slice open a crate that was supposed to contain, say, a dozen boxes of paper towels but only had 10, stuff in two more boxes, tape it shut and send it to a store that way.

By fall of 2013, Target's three distribution centres—approximately four million square feet in all—were overflowing with goods. Tractor-trailers sat idling in the yards, waiting to be unloaded. The situation got so bad that Target scrambled to rent a handful of storage facilities to accommodate all of the inventory flooding in. The process of determining which goods to send to these rented facilities was haphazard, making it difficult to track things down later. "It was like a massive black hole," says a former employee. Another recalls feeling shocked when visiting the rental warehouse in Vancouver. "It was the most rickety, Podunk thing you can imagine," says the former employee, likening it to the treacherous labyrinthine underworld in Indiana Jones and the Temple of Doom. American expats, accustomed to the efficiency of the US operations, were flabbergasted. Waves of senior staff were flown in from Minneapolis, but because they were unfamiliar with the technology Target Canada used, there wasn't much they could do.

The issues at the distribution centres caused havoc downstream. Stores might end up with an abundance of some products and a dearth of others. The auto-replenishment system, which keeps track of what a store has in stock, wasn't functioning properly, either. Like many other parts of retail, replenishment is an exacting science that can go haywire without correct data. At Target Canada, the technology relied on having the exact dimensions of every product and every shelf in order to calculate whether employees need to pull more products to fill an empty rack. Much of that data was still incorrect, and therefore the system couldn't be relied upon to make accurate calculations. The problem became immediately apparent when Target opened its first three test stores. Fisher made the call to shut off the system and replenish manually. That meant store employees had to literally walk the floor and check each shelf—a laborious, error-laden process. (Auto-replenishment wasn't switched back on until later that year.)

The Mississauga head office, meanwhile, didn't have a clear picture of how bad the situation was inside stores. The merchandising department's software often indicated items were in stock, but then the team would field confused and angry phone calls from employees responsible for store operations, demanding to know why they didn't have products. "We almost didn't see what the customer was seeing," says a former employee. "We'd look on paper and think we're OK. Then we'd go to the store, and it's like, 'Oh my god.'"

To add even more headaches, the point-of-sale system was malfunctioning. The self-checkouts gave incorrect change. The cash terminals took unusually long to boot up and sometimes froze. Items wouldn't scan, or the POS returned the incorrect price. Sometimes a transaction would appear to complete, and the customer would leave the store—but the payment never actually went through. The POS package was purchased from an Israeli company called Retalix, which worked closely with Target Canada to address the issues. Progress was maddeningly slow. In 2014, a Retalix team flew to Toronto to see first-hand what Target was dealing with. After touring a store, one of the Retalix executives remarked, "I don't understand how you're using this," apparently baffled the retailer managed to keep going with so many bugs. But Target didn't have time to find a new vendor and deploy another technology. "We were bound to this one bad decision," says a former employee. (Retalix was purchased in 2012 by NCR Corp., the American global payment transaction firm.) "When entering a new country, it is normal for retail software systems to require updates to tailor the solution to market needs and processes," NCR said in a statement in response to questions about Target's experience. "NCR was making progress to customize the solution for the market and Target's new operations until their decision to exit the country."

Unlike SAP, Retalix is not an industry standard, and why Target chose it isn't entirely clear. Former employees suggest that Retalix sold itself on its omnichannel capabilities, meaning it would be able to process payments on mobile devices. Time may have been another factor. "In the US, this never would have made it off the launching pad," says a former employee. "There would have been a robust process for testing."

Meanwhile, after a few rounds of store openings, the status update meetings Fisher held at headquarters had turned darkly comic. After the regular rundown of crippling operational problems, the president still ended each gathering with a pep talk of sorts, reiterating how proud he was of the team and all they had accomplished. Despite his stubborn optimism, those meetings had grown more tense too. Everyone knew the launch was a disaster and the company had to stop opening stores so it could fix its operational problems, but no one actually said so. "Nobody wanted to be the one person who stopped the Canadian venture," says a former employee. "It wound up just being a constant elephant in the room." There was also a sense of powerlessness. The Canadian expansion was ultimately driven by Minneapolis, and because of the real estate deal hatched by CEO Gregg Steinhafel, the company was committed to opening these stores. Speaking up wouldn't have changed much. "That's why, in the end, nobody fell on a sword. Because of the leases, it had to move forward."

The entire organization started to crack under the pressure. John Morioka, Target's head of merchandising, became emotional during meetings on more than one occasion. "I don't remember being brought to tears," he told *Canadian Business* but declined to elaborate. Tensions grew between Morioka and Bryan Berg, the senior vice-president of stores, and both leaders' direct reports attempted to sort out issues among themselves rather than involving their respective bosses. (Morioka says he "maintained respectful relations with my peers." Berg declined to comment.) Stress caused another former employee to crack a tooth from grinding his teeth during sleep. It took a toll on personal lives as well. "I was just so exhausted all the time," says yet another former employee. "When I came home, I was no one. I was a shell."

Tony Fisher felt it too. He was open about telling employees that he'd never managed through such a challenging situation before. Former employees say his background—primarily in merchandising—was ill-suited to helping him deal with the severe operational and technological problems Target Canada faced. Those close to Fisher say he took the company's troubles personally. In the early days, he was a constant sight on the floor of Target Canada's open-concept office, chatting with employees at all levels. But he and some of his leadership team became less visible as problems mounted. "For leaders who have experience with failure, that would be the last thing you do," says a former employee. "You would be front and centre, give confidence and reinforce the direction. That didn't happen." Others contend Fisher's schedule didn't allow him to be as visible. As the situation worsened, he was frequently in meetings, participating in conference calls, visiting stores, or flying to Minneapolis. (Fisher declined to comment.)

In February 2014, Target headquarters released its annual results, revealing a US$941-million loss in Canada. The company attributed the shortfall to growing pains, expansion costs, and—because of all that excess inventory sitting in warehouses—significant markdowns. "As we enter 2014 with a much cleaner inventory position, the team's number one operation focus is on in-stocks—ensuring we have the right quantity of each item in the right place at the right time," Steinhafel said on the earnings call. It was his last as Target CEO. A month prior, Target had disclosed a massive security breach in which hackers stole the personal information of 70 million customers in the US. Combined with the bleeding operations in Target Canada, Steinhafel's position was untenable, and he stepped down in May. (He walked away with US$61 million in compensation.) Fisher—hand-picked by Steinhafel—left the company two weeks later.

By the end, Fisher was practically a ghost. "He gave every last ounce of himself. He was just done. He had nothing left," says a former employee. His departure wasn't surprising, but it was deeply felt. "I loved Tony. He's probably one of the smartest people I've met," says someone who worked with him closely. "He absolutely took the fall for Target Canada." The reality is the odds were stacked against him from the start, given the extremely tight timeline and the thin margin for error. "Everyone was trying to execute Gregg Steinhafel's deal," says a former employee, "and once one thing went wrong, it was an impossible achievement."

But someone else now had to try.

It was Mark Schindele who took over as head of Target Canada. He was a 15-year company veteran and previously served as a senior vice-president of merchandising operations in Minneapolis. At one point, Target Canada had printed a weekly flyer in which nearly every single item featured on the front cover was out of stock, a situation that would have been unheard of in Minneapolis. When Schindele learned of it, according to a former employee, he remarked, "I can't believe it's as bad as it actually is."

A new crop of senior leaders arrived from US HQ with Schindele, replacing some of the exhausted execs who handled the launch. The biggest difference between the two groups was attitude: The new team had energy. Decisions were made faster as well. Under Fisher, the company had trouble making tough calls. "We had so much faith we could solve any problem. If we just work a little harder, we'll get to the resolution," says a former employee. "But then the thing in front of you explodes." For example, inventory started piling up in Target's distribution centres again in early 2014, and it became clear the company needed to rent additional storage sites. Discussions dragged on for months. The new leadership, however, quickly implemented a plan to rent more space.

Schindele brought increased focus to the company too. He prioritized what he called "mom's shopping list," which consisted of basic household items such as toilet paper, toothpaste, and detergent. Employees at all points along the supply chain were to ensure those items made it to stores and stayed in stock. Those particular products were important because Target Canada needed to change people's shopping habits and lure them away from Shoppers Drug Mart and Loblaws. But it didn't stand a chance if it couldn't offer the basics that bring people back to stores. Even so, the company planned to reduce its emphasis on groceries. Target used groceries as a traffic driver in the US and attempted to replicate that strategy here, failing to fully realize how competitive the category is in Canada. To further differentiate from other retailers, Schindele wanted to promote apparel and accessories, emphasizing Target's "cheap chic" image, in direct contrast to Walmart. A massive product revamp was planned for the fall.

Discussion about marketing and when it was appropriate to invite the consumer back into the stores after making a terrible first impression intensified. Those conversations started when Fisher was still in place. Around Target's first anniversary, the marketing team proposed an "apology" campaign of sorts—something to acknowledge that the company had learned a lot about Canadians during its year of operation, and that it was seeking to improve the shopping experience. Fisher was not in favour of the idea, according to two former employees. "Tony wouldn't allow the marketing team to say to the Canadian public that we made a mistake," says one. "I was in a meeting where he said, 'That's not who we are.'" Another former employee suggests the reluctance wasn't Fisher's alone; all public relations decisions had to be vetted by headquarters in the US at the time. Regardless, the idea was only hatched very shortly before Fisher left the company.

In June 2014, however, Target Canada released its apology on YouTube, which featured employees and executives reflecting on the challenges of the first year and confessing to their sins. "Maybe we didn't put our best foot forward when we entered into Canada," said Damien Liddle, the company's senior corporate counsel. "Certainly we know we've disappointed our Canadian guests." The video was remarkably candid as far as corporate mea culpas go, but maintained an optimistic note. "We're headed in the right direction now," said another employee in the video. "For sure."

By that time, the stores were indeed functioning better. For one thing, Target had a year of sales history from Canada. The company segmented stores based on performance, too, and focused intently on stocking up its top 25 locations, rather than treating all stores in the same manner.

A small group of employees also made an alarming discovery that helped explain why certain items appeared to be in stock at headquarters but were actually missing from stores. Within the chain's replenishment system was a feature that notified the distribution centres to ship more product when a store runs out. Some of the business analysts responsible for this function, however, were turning it off—purposely. Business analysts (who were young and fresh out of school, remember) were judged based on the percentage of their products that were in stock at any given time, and a low percentage would result in a phone call from a vice-president demanding an explanation. But by flipping the auto-replenishment switch off, the system wouldn't report an item as out of stock, so the analyst's numbers would look good on paper. "They figured out how to game the system," says a former employee. "They didn't want to get in trouble and they didn't really understand the implications." Two people involved in the discovery allow that human error may have been a component, too. Like SAP, the replenishment software was brand new to Target, and the company didn't fully understand how to use it. When Schindele was told of the problem, he ordered the function to be fully activated, which revealed for the first time the company's pitifully low in-stock percentages. From there, a team built a tool that reported when the system was turned on or off, and determined whether there was a legitimate reason for it to be turned off, such as if the item was seasonal. Access to the controls was taken away from the analysts, depending on the product.

The company had also been learning more about using SAP correctly. Former employees describe decoding SAP as like peeling an onion—it had multiple layers and made you want to cry. One initiative in particular greatly improved Target's data quality. A technology team was finally able to install an automatic verification feature to catch bad data before it could enter SAP and wreak havoc. If an employee entered a UPC that was short one digit, for example, the system wouldn't allow that purchase order to proceed until the code was correct. The technology Target used in the US has these checks and balances, as do other retailers who use SAP. Target Canada finally implemented a verification tool in 2014, according to a former employee who was involved, owing to time constraints. "This happened very late in the game."

There was yet another basic error Target Canada didn't discover until 2014. According to one former employee, there was a misunderstanding about shipping dates. What Target thought was the "in-DC date," meaning the date on which product would arrive at a distribution centre, was interpreted by some of its larger vendor partners as the day on which they would actually ship the product to Target. As a result, stock was constantly arriving late from Target's perspective but on time according to vendors. "It was like, 'Holy crap, how did we possibly not know this?'" says the former employee. (Others dispute this characterization and say the impact of the mix-up was limited.)

All of these improvements meant that by the latter half of 2014, Target could finally have some confidence that the right products would arrive at the right times, greatly improving the in-stock position of the stores—particularly during the all-important holiday season. Indeed, during December and January 2015, Target employees were beginning to feel like there was a light at the end of the tunnel. The company had a much better handle on its technology, its data, and the supply chain, and every day

no longer felt like a crisis. Target Canada was at last transitioning into a functional—almost normal—retailer. There were even big plans for 2015, such as implementing online shopping at Target.ca.

Despite the optimism, there was an undercurrent of unease. The parent company installed a new CEO to replace Gregg Steinhafel in 2014. The new head, Brian Cornell, was the first outsider to lead the company. Cornell had spent his career as an executive at PepsiCo and Walmart, where he ran the Sam's Club warehouse chain. With no existing ties to Target, he was free to make sweeping changes if needed. The retailer was still suffering from the fallout of the data breach months prior and accusations that it had lost its way in the US, where same-store sales were declining. Cornell cast a skeptical eye on the Canadian operations. "To succeed in Canada, we will need a major step-change in performance," he said on a conference call in November. "We need to see improved financial performance from every Target store in Canada over time."

There were more worrying signs in January. Schindele was suddenly nowhere to be seen. Meetings that had been scheduled with him were cancelled. Paralysis gripped the upper ranks in Canada, as executives had either disappeared in mysteriously long meetings or were busy speculating on what was going to happen. Cornell came to Canada that month to tour stores in Ontario. He noted that the shelves were stocked, but he was perturbed by the lack of actual customers, according to a report by Reuters. At Mississauga headquarters, employees were bracing themselves for a wave of layoffs and a massive number of store closings.

The news on January 15 was much worse: Target Canada was filing for bankruptcy protection. It had spent $7 billion on the expansion so far, and it didn't project turning a profit until at least 2021. Early that morning, Schindele's direct reports broke the news to their teams, who then informed their own departments. One of these leaders recalls moving through a fog and hyperventilating while struggling to remember how to dial in to a conference call. After running through the prepared script he was given, he broke down, crying. "These were people I'd hired. I'd impacted their lives. I'd become friends with them. So that was horrible," says the former employee. A press release went out at 8 a.m. By then, the entire company knew.

An all-employee meeting was held later that morning, and an emotional Schindele reiterated the reasons for the decision, choking up as he addressed employees. Shock permeated the building.

"It's heartbreaking for me, because I never, ever thought this would happen," says a former employee who uprooted his life in Minneapolis to move to Mississauga. Representatives for the bankruptcy monitor and the liquidators were in the building that day, and started meeting with employees, who were still trying to process the news, to discuss dismantling the operations. "They wanted advice on how to cut apart not only a corpse but my corpse," says a former employee. For others, there was a sense of relief that the endless marathon that was Target Canada was finally over. "All these insane projects we were working on simply didn't matter anymore," says another former employee. Investors were pleased Target had finally broken free of the black hole of the Canadian operations and gave the stock a 2 percent bump that day.

All 133 stores closed by April. Schindele soon returned to Target in Minneapolis, where he's now senior vice-president of Target properties. Fisher later resurfaced as a senior vice-president at a consumer health-care company also in Minneapolis. Steinhafel, the one who put the entire operation in motion and set it on a path toward self-destruction, has kept his head down. His LinkedIn profile simply lists him as a "retail professional." (He did not respond to requests for comment.)

Curiously, the US retailer has not abandoned the country entirely. In October, Target launched a small pilot project to ship goods ordered online to Canadians. The company that lost billions, suffered a humiliating defeat here, and endured an ordeal that left its employees drained, exhausted, and ultimately jobless, titled the website for Canuck shoppers "Target loves Canada."

Discussion Questions

1. Using the 7 P marketing mix model, analyze each P in terms of Target's move to the Canadian market. Indicate what went wrong with each of the seven marketing mix components.

2. Should Gregg Steinhafel, CEO of Target, have opened all 124 store locations at once? Why or why not? What was Steinhafel's rationale for opening all 124 stores at the same time?

3. You are the CEO for Target. What would you have done to ensure a smoother transition to the Canadian market? Make sure you elaborate on your rationale.

Source: Joe Castaldo, "The Last Days of Target," *Canadian Business*, http://www.canadianbusiness.com/the-last-days-of-target-canada/ (accessed June 14, 2016).

CASE 2 Retailing in India—Impact of Hypermarkets

The history of India contains a wealth of change and alteration, and the modern era is no different as the country blossoms into a major player in the global economy. Sizable economic growth during the past decade, particularly in the retail sector, has changed the way consumers behave. Although the size of the current Indian retail sector is impressive, its potential really speaks to what retailing will mean in the future. The retail market in India was approximately $353 billion in 2010, and by 2014 it was projected to reach $543 billion in total sales, with modern retailing accounting for 27 percent.

International retailers are slowly making their way into India. India's government allows foreign companies to open only single-brand stores. Large retailers with more than one brand are required to engage in a joint venture with an Indian company. Walmart, Tesco, and Carrefour have opened hypermarkets in India, but doing so was not an easy

process. Carrefour waited ten years to open its first store as a result of the restrictions. Hypermarkets—large retail outlets—combine the products found in a department store and supermarket, with the goal of turning shopping into an experience. The large store layouts and variety of merchandise force customers to spend more time in the stores, which in turn leads to more sales. The potential for hypermarkets in India sheds light on the country's changing retail landscape and the shopping habits of its consumers.

Before 2000, Indian consumers generally purchased many of their retail goods from local mom-and-pop stores called *kiranas*, which sold mainly provisions and groceries. Shopping at *kiranas* is easy and convenient, because the small stores serve specific neighbourhoods and establish personal relationships with their customers. The new infusion of hypermarkets threatens to rob local store owners of their customer base—approximately a 23 percent decrease in sales in one year.

There are over 300 hypermarkets and 6800 supermarkets in India. India has been experiencing 20 percent annual growth in retail markets. Hypermarket sales were expected to increase fivefold from 2009 to 2013, and supermarket sales were expected to increase 150 percent during the same period. Each new store opening may draw customers from 20 to 25 *kiranas* and fruit and vegetable stands, affecting over 100 000 vendors.

Most *kiranas* cannot compete with hypermarkets because these larger retail outlets create more efficiency within the supply chain. Much local produce in India currently gets wasted because the country lacks sufficient infrastructure. Even as it progresses through rapid development, India still lacks some amenities that Westerners take for granted, such as refrigeration in retail operations. If a large retailer wants to open a hypermarket in India, it will have to invest capital to ensure freshness throughout the supply chain and help reduce waste. The Indian government is expected to spend US$500 billion over the next few years to develop a world-class infrastructure, which should spur growth in the retail sector.

The lack of infrastructure underlies a related issue facing hypermarkets. Unlike in Western nations, India's rather poor roads and transportation systems do not allow retailers to locate on large plots of land on the outskirts of town, since fewer consumers can reach them. Therefore, hypermarkets must look for retail space in more urban areas, which provide little available real estate. Buying up space from existing stores means displacing local corner shops already inhabiting that space, and this may prompt protests from Indian consumers and store owners who value the Indian tradition that the *kiranas* represent. Yet larger retail outlets in India could have a dramatic impact on the economy, possibly creating millions of jobs in the next ten years. Although many Indians may not appreciate the notion of hypermarkets immediately, their presence is likely inevitable.

Much of the impetus for the emergence of hypermarkets in India also comes from changes among Indian consumers. The country's younger generations are exposed to a host of innovative products that were unknown to their parents. They are far more receptive to new products and ideas. In addition, this segment of the population reflects the shifting age demographics; more than half of India's current population is younger than 25 years of age. With such a large percentage of younger consumers,

it seems inevitable that India's cultural tastes will evolve. The strong and abundant local *kiranas* have been a cultural mainstay, but they cannot efficiently offer Indians access to new and technologically advanced products. Because hypermarkets combine department stores and supermarkets, they carry product lines that local vendors cannot. They sell brand-name products at affordable prices, thereby enabling Indians to purchase a wide assortment of goods that they otherwise could not have.

This shift, from local mom-and-pop stores to more organized retail outlets, is happening very quickly in India. It is embraced by many consumers despite the cultural and legal considerations associated with hypermarkets. Furthermore, because hypermarkets offer potential benefits for both the economy and the national infrastructure, local governments generally support the arrival of a hypermarket. The ultimate target market, however, is not the government but the consumers, and just as in any country at any time, the challenge lies in understanding what those consumers want and how to get it to them.

Discussion Questions

1. How might a hypermarket located in India appeal to consumers and orient them to shopping in larger stores?

2. Is the Indian government's willingness to spend $500 billion to improve the nation's infrastructure good news for international retailers? Why or why not?

3. Identify the main changes that mark Indian consumers. How can international retailers learn more about India's youthful demographic?

Sources: "Infra Red—India's Ambitious Development Plans Hinge on Attracting Private Capital," *The Economist*, July 8, 2010; "A Wholesale Invasion—a French Supermarket Chain Takes a Bet on India," *The Economist*, May 20, 2010; Armina Ligaya, "India Puts Squeeze on Hypermarkets," *National*, September 16, 2009; "India—Tier I & II Cities May Have 300 Hypermarkets by 2011," *RNCOS*, August 13, 2009; http://www.ibef.org/industry/retail. aspx (accessed July 15, 2010); "Coming to Market—Retailing in India," *The Economist*, April 15, 2006, p. 69; "Despite Growing Debt, the Indian Consumer Banks on Tomorrow," *India Knowledge@Wharton*, October 31, 2006; Ranjan Biswas, "India's Changing Consumers," *Chain Store Age*, May 2006; John Elliott, "Retail Revolution," *Fortune*, August 9, 2007, pp. 14–16; Amelia Gentleman, "Indians Protest Wal-Mart's Wholesale Entry," *New York Times*, August 10, 2007.

This case was written by Todd Nicolini, while an MBA student at Loyola College in Maryland, under the supervision of Professor Hope Corrigan, and Britt Hackmann, Babson College.

Venture into Sobeys' latest Urban Fresh grocery store in downtown Toronto and your senses are set ablaze. Rows and rows of colourful, local, and organic produce and fragrant, fresh meals are set against a backdrop of contemporary design elements that give the space a high-end, gourmet shop feel.

"Our shoppers are foodies and they like to experiment with food, so we give them a lot to get excited about," says Mary Dalimonte, general manager, Fresh Service Format for Sobeys.

With a diverse selection of gourmet and grocery item staples, the 20 000 square-foot store, located at the bottom of a city centre condo, maximizes space with the use of vertical merchandizing and smaller-scale packaging. "This store caters to a four- to five-block radius of shoppers who won't be buying the ten-pound bag of potatoes," says Dalimonte. "They are condo dwellers—mostly singles or couples—who don't have a lot of space to store food." Even the grocery carts are smaller. "This is the ultimate urban grocery shopper cart with a place to put your purse and your coffee," she adds.

But a lack of space doesn't limit the variety of food offerings by any means. The Urban Fresh store features an extensive salad bar, a sushi section, a made-to-order pizza and pasta component, numerous prepared meals to go, as well as a café offering gourmet coffees with a selection of tables and chairs to enjoy them. "We want this to be our customers' place to come for a coffee on a Sunday, so we purposely put the chairs and tables facing the window. Even the benches outside face out to the street so our customers can people-watch—it's really meant to be a neighbourhood destination," says Dalimonte. The space also fits a substantial deli, butcher, and fish counter, complete with a fishmonger who offers samples and suggestions for dinner options. "Most people don't know what they're making tonight for dinner so we make it easy for them," she says.

While the supermarket giant opened the first of its smaller-scale "urban" grocery stores several years ago in Toronto, the model has evolved into what is now a chic, European-style food destination with a focus on freshness and style. This is made apparent from the blades of glass painted on the storefront windows and potted grass throughout the store to the hand-cut green wallpaper complete with tree motifs that expertly camouflage the condo's otherwise unsightly building structure. The floors are the original concrete, but they are buffed and tinted black to provide the urban feel.

The store's focal point, however, is a giant chandelier in a rotunda that will be incorporated into the new format Urban Fresh stores going forward. "The chandelier inspired the contemporary yet classic feel of the store. There really is a mix of traditional and contemporary going on here," says designer Charlane Codner, partner/VP creative services for Fish Out of Water. A second rotunda with lights over the café creates another zone in the store, she adds.

Further exemplifying the classic feel are custom-made aisle ends made of painted medium density fibreboard, which resemble armoires that could easily pass for the ones found in someone's living space. Even the use of metro shelving to hold product throughout the store as opposed to traditional racks give the space a contemporary feel that the designers say really plays to the urban customer base.

"We also aimed to strike a balance between design and functionality," adds Codner. Case in point: the glass around the meat and seafood areas alleviates cool air flow from hitting the customer, but also features a visually enticing frosted vinyl layer imprinted with the wallpaper motif used throughout the rest of the store.

Even the signage throughout the space veers away from traditional grocery models by featuring a few super-size, vibrant graphics of food as opposed to lots of text. "It's subtle and sexy," says Codner. "It's food as romance. It has to speak for itself."

Lighting throughout the store is also used to emphasize the focus on food. Codner says high-intensity discharge lights throughout provide strong ambient light levels while metal halide lights give a punch in select areas.

Dalimonte says customer reaction to the store has been extremely positive. "We've been hearing really good things and those that come to visit that aren't from the area say they wish they had one of these stores near them," she says. "Customers like the ambience and really appreciate the attention to detail."

From a financial perspective, she says Sobeys is pleased with the performance of the Urban Fresh model so far. With 11 stores in Ontario and two in Alberta, she says "the sky's the limit" when it comes to future expansion. In fact, she says "Toronto residents will be very pleased at our next location."

Discussion Questions

1. Do you agree that stores in urban centres call for unique designs and product offerings? Why or why not?

2. Identify another retailer that has tailored its retail strategy and/or in-store design to meet the needs of the urban market.

Source: Rosalind Stefanac for the Retail Council of Canada, *Canadian Retailer,* January/February 2010, pp. 11–12. Canadian Retailer, a publication of Retail Council of Canada.

CASE 4   Attracting Generation Y to a Retail Career

The Diva Brand

Diva is a specialty retail store focused on fast-fashion jewellery and accessories. The brand's origins are in Australia, but recent years have seen rapid international expansion, and the brand now has stores in America, Russia, and Europe. Diva is predominantly located in shopping centres, with some stores in high-street locations, and is always positioned in/around apparel fashion clusters. The stores are clean, simplistic, and brightly lit, reflecting their fast-moving, funky, and vibrant product range targeted at the youth market (predominantly, 15- to 25-year-old females). Diva's positioning sees it as the only fashion jewellery/hair accessory specialist retailer in Australia.

Due to Diva's recent expansion, staff numbers have grown significantly. However, Diva is confronted with the problem of attracting and retaining experienced and talented people, particularly from Generation Y. In an attempt to counteract this problem, Diva has implemented several internal talent policies to provide a point of difference and be an employer of choice, including:

- training plans/workshops to fill skill gaps
- a career development program for top store managers
- a leadership development program for top regional managers
- increased salary package offers for certain roles to attract talent/skill
- global expansion, with new offers of career progression

Generational Differences in the Workforce

As a result of key demographic and lifestyle issues such as aging populations, declining fertility, delayed retirements, rising labour participation rates, and higher life expectancies, there is a demographic trough in the Asia Pacific workforce, in which there is soon to be smaller proportions of younger-aged members and larger cohorts of mature-aged workers. This is further compounded by a shrinking talent pool and the fact that retail is not perceived as a career of choice by the adult population, who have limited sight of career path opportunities "beyond the shop floor."

Although research acknowledges the pertinence of this issue in retailing today, it remains unclear how to effectively manage generational diversity in the workplace. This is not a new issue; however, wider age groups are culminating in less segregated work arrangements. In the past, older staff undertook senior managerial positions, while younger workers assumed front-desk or field positions. However, today it is common to see staff members from all age groups working together on projects, with senior employees managing across several generations or younger employees managing older generations. It is important to note that, if managed poorly, intergenerational impacts can cause conflict for employers and among employees, hampering workplace productivity and morale.

Retailers, as well as organizations from many other industries, therefore need to identify and adopt the best approaches in attracting and retaining staff across all retail functions, optimizing the experiences of mature-aged workers while capitalizing on the potential of young employees. This involves understanding each generation and its unique perspectives, communication styles, and working styles in order to provide tailored support. Each generation holds different perspectives of work, including the definition of an attractive working environment, leadership qualities, and preferred team-playing approaches, and has an individual information processing style. For example, Generation Y believes in having fluid work patterns and influencing job terms and conditions. Conversely, the Baby Boomer generation regards work as a primary security in life, while Generation X values a balance between work and life.

Generation Y

Born between 1981 and 2000, members of Generation Y were one of the key segments of focus in shop floor to boardroom given their sheer numbers and prospective employment in retail as recent or upcoming workforce entrants. While organizations have had time to understand Baby Boomers and Generation X-ers, determining the needs of Generation Y-ers has been challenging, especially given their vastly different values. This is particularly important given the significant career opportunities that exist for Generation Y in retailing. In better understanding the unique career motivations, perceptions, and aspirations of Generation Y, a number of focus groups were conducted with university students who were studying a business major and currently working in retail, and high school students who were studying retail-related subjects and currently working in retail or interested in doing so. In terms of perceptions of working in retail, research found that retail is simply not viewed as a career of choice by Generation Y. This is primarily due to the feeling that retail involves "just being a checkout chick," has limited or no career paths "beyond the shop floor" and is therefore a short-term employment solution, and has difficult conditions at times (e.g., long hours, repetitive tasks, low salaries). A related concern was that the retail industry is not generally perceived as prestigious in the eyes of the general public.

Despite such issues, there were a number of motivators (other than financial) for working in retail for Generation Y, such as improving one's social life and extending friendship circles, gaining work experience while studying, and following a particular passion (i.e., fashion). Generation Y-ers also reported a variety of career aspirations that were generally consistent with the courses or subjects they were studying. Despite the fact that few listed retail as their number-one career option, a strong desire was found for a career that could be facilitated by the retail industry, such as marketing, HR, or buying.

Focused on self-improvement, Generation Y-ers also expressed enjoyment in working for organizations that provide constant learning environments; they want to be involved in the organization's vision and mission, desire mobility and flexibility in the workplace, and seek instant gratification. Members of Generation Y also thrive on systematic feedback and value positive reinforcement at accelerated rates, as compared to previous generations. This is the primary reason that Generation Y questions starting at the bottom of the organizational ladder, having developed a strong desire for rapid career progression from years of high-level education.

Discussion Questions

1. How can Diva demystify what happens behind the scenes and make potential Generation Y employees aware of the opportunities available to them beyond the shop floor?

2. Diva has implemented a learning organizational culture in an attempt to attract and retain staff. Discuss the possible pros and cons of this strategy for Generation Y.

3. Give examples of how other organizations (perhaps even non-retailers) attract a Generation Y workforce. What could Diva learn from other organizations?

Source: This case was written by Sean Sands, Monash University, and Carla Ferraro, Monash University.

Staples operates in the highly competitive office products market. The office supply category specialists, including Staples, Office Depot, and OfficeMax (the big three), have dramatically changed the landscape of the office supply industry. First, they greatly expanded the use of retail stores and Internet channels as a means of distributing office supply products, capitalizing in part on the significant increase in the number of home offices. Prior to the mid-1980s, office supply customers primarily placed their orders through commissioned salespeople or catalogues.

Warehouse clubs, supermarkets, and full-line discount retailers also have begun taking market share away from the big three office supply retailers because of their ability to sell the bulk items at lower prices. Retailers such as Walmart and Costco offer low prices on office supplies, which forces the major office supply retailers to offer more than just products, such as extra services and greater customer service. The big three office supply stores have also expanded their business-to-business (B2B) efforts to sell to other companies, such as Wells Fargo or IBM. Staples Advantage, for example, offers a range of products and services to its B2B customers.

Company Background

Originally opened in 1986 by executive-turned-entrepreneur Tom Stemberg, Staples has reached sales of more than $25 billion. Staples also has been credited with pioneering the high-volume office products superstore concept. By evolving its original mission of slashing the costs and eliminating the hassles of running an office to one of making it easy to buy office products, Staples has become the world's largest office products company.

To distinguish itself in this competitive industry, Staples strives to provide a unique shopping experience to customers in all of its market segments. Central to maintaining customer satisfaction is developing strong customer relationship skills and broad knowledge about office products among all associates hired by the company. Therefore, Staples includes formal training as an integral part of the development of its associates.

Another truly important aspect of customer service is the availability of merchandise. In the office supply industry, customers have very specific needs, such as finding an ink cartridge for a particular printer, and if the store is out of stock of a needed item, the customer may never come back.

Staples uses various marketing channels to address the needs of its different segments. Smaller businesses are generally served by a combination of retail stores, the catalogue, and the Internet. Retail operations focus on serving the needs of consumers and small businesses, especially through an in-store kiosk that enables customers to order a product that may not be available in the store and receive the product via overnight delivery. In-store kiosks allow them to choose to have the product delivered to their home, business, or local store. If a customer does not want to shop in the store, he or she can visit Staples.com to order required products and select from a much larger assortment. The typical Staples retail store maintains approximately 8000 stockkeeping units (SKUs), but Staples.com offers more than 45 000 SKUs. This multichannel approach allows Staples to increase its productivity by stocking only more popular items in stores but not sacrificing product availability.

Multichannel Integration

Staples' overall goal has been to become the leading office products and services provider by combining its existing experience, extensive distribution infrastructure, and customer service expertise with web-based information technology. As a result, the integration of different channels of distribution into one seamless customer experience has been of particular interest to the company. Staples, like many other multichannel retailers, has found that many customers use multiple channels to make their Staples purchases and that sales increase when customers use more than one channel (e.g., customers who shop two channels spend twice as much as a single-channel shopper; a tri-channel shopper spends about three times as much as a single-channel shopper). Therefore, the greater the number of channels a particular customer shops, the greater the overall expenditures he or she is likely to make.

Staples faces several challenges in integrating its channels of distribution, though, most of which are related to its Internet channel. First, it must consider the extent to which the Internet may cannibalize its retail store sales. The most attractive aspect of the Internet is its potential to attract new customers and sell more to existing customers. But if overall sales are flat—that is, if online retailing only converts retail store sales to Internet sales—Staples suffers increased overhead costs and poorer overall productivity. Second, Staples must be concerned about the merchandise position of its retail stores compared with that of alternative channels. Because a retail store cannot carry as much merchandise as the Internet channel, the challenge is to keep an appropriate balance between minimizing stockouts and avoiding the proliferation of too many SKUs in retail stores. Finally, Staples has to contend with price competition, both within its own multichannel organization and from competitors.

Staples' Added Services

Such competition means that Staples must continue to differentiate itself from other office supply retailers by adding extra value to office supplies, which themselves represent commoditized products. For example, its Copy and Print centres within its big-box stores enable customers to order print jobs and receive the help of an in-store print specialist. To increase this business line further, Staples also has opened standalone Staples Copy and Print centres, which are approximately 2000 square feet, compared with its typical 30 000-square-foot, big-box

stores. The small size of these stores allows them to be located in metropolitan areas or places where there would not be sufficient space for a large, big-box store. Customers can order their copies through the Staples website, then pick them up in the store or have them delivered. The Copy and Print stores also sell basic office supply products that customers may need to pick up at the last minute when they come to collect their print orders.

Discussion Questions

1. Assess the extent to which Staples has developed a successful multichannel strategy. What factors have contributed to its success?

2. What are the advantages and disadvantages of using kiosks as a part of its approach?

3. How should Staples assess which SKUs to keep in its stores versus on the Internet?

4. How do the Staples Copy and Print centres differentiate it from the competition?

Sources: "Office Supply Stores in the US—Industry Report," *IBIS World*, March 23, 2010; 2012 Staples Annual Report; interview with Max Ward, vice president of technology at Staples; W. Caleb McCann, J. P. Jeannet, Dhruv Grewal, and Martha Lanning, "Staples," in *Fulfillment in E-Business,* eds. Petra Schuber, Ralf Wolfle, and Walter Dettling (Germany: Hanser, 2001) pp. 239–252 (in German); interview with Staples' Vice President of Stores Demos Parneros and Executive Vice President of Merchandising and Marketing Jevin Eagle.

This case was written by Jeanne L. Munger, University of Southern Maine; Britt Hackmann, Nubry.com; and Dhruv Grewal and Michael Levy, Babson College.

CASE 6 Starbucks' Expansion into China

Brand History/Growth

Starbucks, an American-based coffee company, opened its first store in Seattle, Washington, in 1971. The mission for this coffee shop was to not only have high-quality coffee, but to create a more relaxed environment where customers could meet and converse with friends. In 1987, Starbucks consisted of 11 stores and 100 employees, with a dream of becoming a national brand. Starbucks coffee shops were opening throughout the United States with 1015 stores by 1996. The Starbucks Corporation then set its sights on international expansion beginning in 1997, when the number of total stores was 1412. In 2012, the company operated 17 003 locations, with 37 percent outside of the United States in 40 countries. Starbucks' financial performance showed an

accelerated increase in revenue in the early 2000s because of the focus on international expansion.

Starbucks made the decision to concentrate in China in 1998, along with many other businesses. China is an emerging market because the middle class is in a state of constant growth, and companies want to capitalize on the opportunity the China market offers.

Starbucks quickly recognized that there were different cultures within China. Starbucks joined forces with three regional partners as a strategy to enter the emerging market and provide Chinese consumers with more localized products. In 1999, Starbucks launched a joint venture with Mei Da Coffee Company Limited in North China to open locations in Beijing. In this joint venture, both parties are equally invested in the project in terms of money and time. This was followed in 2000 with a joint venture in South China with Maxim's Caterers Limited. Starbucks also partnered with Uni-President in East China to further advance interests in Shanghai, Taipei, and Hong Kong.

Joining forces with Chinese business partners helped Starbucks gain insights into the tastes and preferences of local consumers. Entering a new market with established local partners enabled Starbucks to quickly learn about the different cultures in each individual region in China. It was not necessarily easy for coffee-centric Starbucks to grow its presence in a country that primarily drinks tea. Starbucks was faced with the challenge of creating a new marketing campaign that would revolutionize how the Chinese viewed and drank coffee. Total coffee consumption in China grew from 35.33 thousand metric tons in 2006 to 59.62 thousand metric tons in 2010.

Competitive Advantage

Product

Starbucks is known for selling premium coffee products. However, in China, Starbucks realized that the global brand needed to appeal to local tastes. Starbucks elected to tailor the menu to match the preferences of the local culture. Starbucks began introducing beverages that included regional ingredients, such as green tea. Additional products created specifically for the Chinese market included white tea, black sesame green tea, Frappuccino blended crème, iced rice dumplings, and Starbucks moon cakes. In China, this allowed for customers to select from a wide variety of products to meet their needs.

Promotion

Starbucks used a smart market entry strategy to grow in China. The first step was to select high-visibility and high-traffic locations to project its brand image and attract loyal consumers. Starbucks maintained a strong brand identity and marketed it as a lifestyle "symbol" rather than just a logo. Starbucks wanted consumers to see the green circle Siren logo and to think of sophistication and the ability to afford "personal luxury." One reason this strategy is working is that Starbucks didn't seem to be a threat to the "tea drinking" culture. The company used innovative marketing to create new demand for coffee and the experience that Starbucks stores offer customers.

Price

Starbucks kept its corporate pricing strategy that used premium pricing to ensure the desired profit margin. Starbucks believes in the quality of its products. Many competitors cut prices in order to compete in the Chinese market. Starbucks believes this is a losing strategy because companies cannot afford to "out-cut" the local Chinese competitors.

Placement

Starbucks brought the "Western coffee experience" to the Chinese market. This experience was the ability to go somewhere with friends and acquaintances, relax, and drink some favourite beverages. This proved to be a successful strategy when Starbucks first opened in China in January 1999. Many competitors did not offer air conditioning or the atmosphere of Starbucks, which provides a meeting place for business executives and friends. Starbucks' very comfortable environment allows for dine-in service instead of taking a coffee or tea on the go. This is quite different from the experience in the United States, where the majority of sales come from take-out orders. The experience that Starbucks strives to give is not just the comfortable chairs, upbeat music, and chic interior, but the feeling of a more modern lifestyle.

Human Resources

Starbucks has been incredibly successful at recruiting and training employees. The company sends baristas (brand ambassadors) to all new stores and trains employees to preserve its brand integrity. This ensures that, globally, employees stay true to the Starbucks brand. Because the overall experience is what differentiates Starbucks from competitors, this is a critical component. Annual employee turnover rates of 30 percent or higher are common in China, but Starbucks' turnover rate is much lower due to its attractive compensation packages, career paths, and working environment. Starbucks' exceptional service contributes to its success in China. In interviews with people in Shanghai, the majority of the population stated that they preferred the taste of products from competitors, but that they continue to choose Starbucks due to a high level of service.

China Today/Future

Starbucks believes that there is still an opportunity to expand in China. As of 2012, Starbucks had more than 570 stores in 48 cities with numerous additional cities for future growth. Starbucks has been in China for 13 years and has laid a foundation for continued development. Belinda Wong was appointed Starbucks' China president in July 2011. Wong's mission is to fulfill the target opening of 1500 outlets on mainland China by 2015. She believes this will continue to provide jobs and further demonstrate Starbucks' commitment to China.

Starbucks is not the only coffee company looking for continued growth in China. The market has attracted other businesses, such as British brands Costa Coffee and Pacific Coffee Company. Costa Coffee plans to expand to 2500 stores by 2018 with hopes of taking a third of the market share in China. Starbucks also faces competition from McDonald's, Caribou Coffee, and Dunkin' Brands. Dunkin' Brands anticipates increasing its investment in China and recently named the basketball player LeBron James as the brand ambassador for Asia. Dunkin' Brands added pork doughnuts to further customize the local menu.

In addition to increased competition, Starbucks also needs to pay careful attention to the average Chinese customer's income and discretionary spending. Chinese customers love the experience that Starbucks offers but may purchase only a coffee and spend all day in the store. However, a customer in the United States normally purchases coffee with a baked good. The Chinese consumer is more price sensitive and therefore tends to spend less.

Finally, Starbucks must ensure not to offend the Chinese population. In September 2012, Starbucks opened a store near the famed Buddhist temple in East China. Some people have expressed concerns over this store's location because it is seen as being disrespectful to the Chinese culture. This is also not the first time that a Starbucks location has created debate. In 2007, Starbucks was forced to close a store in Beijing's Forbidden City as a result of public outcries.

Wong is not concerned with these factors and stated, "We have never felt more confident about accelerating our growth momentum" after opening Starbucks' 100th store in Beijing in 2012. Chief Executive Officer Howard Schultz is also confident and believes that Starbucks will continue to be successful in China. Critics are not as confident that Starbucks will continue to be a success in China. In 2008, Starbucks closed 600 underperforming stores in the United States that had opened less than 18 months earlier. Time will tell if rapid expansion in China is a winning strategy for Starbucks.

Discussion Questions

1. Prepare a SWOT analysis based on the case to support Starbucks' expansion plans in China. Based on your SWOT analysis, what recommendations would you make to Starbucks' CEO with regard to the market development growth strategy for this country?

2. Give examples of how Starbucks was successful upon entering the China market. Use the following videos to frame your response:
   - Starbucks grows coffee in China, *Reuters Video*, available at: http://www.youtube.com/watch?v=BYSiGomkGdg
   - Starbucks in China, available at: http://www.youtube.com/watch?v=0A3rnWIEJY8
   - Starbucks wakes up to China, *Reuters Video*, available at: http://www.youtube.com/watch?v=CgWJAouxorg

3. Compare Starbucks' US and Chinese strategies. What are the similarities and differences? What generalities can you glean from this analysis to help the company expand into other global marketplaces? Use the case and the following article to frame your response:
   - "Starbucks' Quest for Healthy Growth: An Interview with Howard Schultz," *McKinsey Quarterly* 2 (2011), pp. 34–43, http://www.mckinseyquarterly.com/Strategy/Growth/Starbucks_quest_for_healthy_growth_An_interview_with_Howard_Schultz_2777.

Sources: "Agriculture Consumption and Production." *China Country Review*, 2012, pp. 159–161; "China: Brewing Up a Success Story," *Thai Press Reports,* March 5, 2012; "China Focus: Starbucks Outlet near Buddhist Temple Triggers Debate," *Xinhua News Agency,* September 24, 2012; "Don't Get Excited About Starbucks' Chinese Expansion Just Yet," *Forbes.com,* May 4, 2012; "Greater China," *News.starbucks.com,* 2012, http://news.starbucks.com/about+starbucks/starbucks+coffee+international/greater+china; "Localization Fuels Starbucks' Success in China," *Business Daily Update,* February 14, 2012; Shaun Rein, "Why Starbucks Succeeds in China and Others Haven't," *USA Today online,* February 10, 2012; Chris Sorensen, "Serving a Billion Latte Sippers," *Maclean's* 125, no. 17 (May 7, 2012), p. 41; "Starbucks Annual Report 1999–2011," *Starbucks Investor Relations,* http://investor.starbucks.com/phoenix.zhtml?c599518&p5irol-reportsannual; "Starbucks Believes That China Will Be Second Largest Market by 2014," *News.starbucks.com,* April 1, 2012; "Starbucks: Company Profile," http://www.starbucks.com/about-us/company; "Starbucks' Quest for Healthy Growth: An Interview with Howard Schultz," *McKinsey Quarterly* 2 (2011), pp. 34–43; Helen H. Wang, "Five Things Starbucks Did to Get China Right," *Forbes.com,* August 10, 2012.

This case was written by Bethany Wise and Samantha Leib, MBA students at Loyola University, Maryland, under the supervision of Professor Hope Corrigan.

Modern consumers want good value, low prices, and convenience, but they also appreciate a great shopping experience. Build-A-Bear Workshop usually locates its more than 425 stores in malls worldwide. It generates more than $390 million in annual sales by offering customers the opportunity to make their own stuffed animals, complete with clothing and accessories.

In 1997, Maxine Clark came up with the idea for Build-A-Bear Workshop and opened a storefront in St. Louis. She had plenty of experience in the corporate side of retailing, having worked for Payless ShoeSource and May Department Stores. Clark left corporate America on a mission to bring the fun back to retailing. Currently, the company has sold more than 70 million furry friends.

The bear-making process consists of eight steps: Choose Me, Hear Me, Stuff Me, Stitch Me, Fluff Me, Dress Me, Name Me, and Take Me Home. The stores mirror the chain's name in that customers, or builders, choose an unstuffed animal and, working with the retailer's staff, move through eight "creation stations" to build their own bear (or other animal). At the first station, the Stuffiteria, children can pick fluff from bins marked "Love," "Hugs and Kisses," "Friendship," and "Kindness." The stuffing is sent through a long, clear tube and into a stuffing machine. A sales associate holds the bear to a small tube while the builder pumps a foot peddle. In seconds, the bear takes its form. Before the stitching, builders must insert a heart. The builders follow the sales associates' instructions and rub the heart between their hands to make it warm. They then close their eyes, make a wish, and kiss the heart before putting it inside the bear. After selecting a name and having it stitched on their animal, builders take their bears to the Fluff Me station, where they brush their bears on a "bathtub" that features spigots blowing air. Finally, they move to a computer station to create a birth certificate.

Bears go home in Cub Condo carrying cases, which act as mini-houses complete with windows and doors. In addition to serving as playhouses, the boxes advertise Build-A-Bear Workshop to the child's friends. "[You] could buy a bear anywhere," says Clark, Chief Executive Bear. "It's the experience that customers are looking for." The experience isn't limited to the stores themselves. The retailer's website, buildabear.com, embraces the same theme. Build-A-Bearville (buildabearville.com) is an online virtual world where users can play with each other and play games. The bears that they bought at the store have a unique code that allows the user to redeem gifts while playing games in Build-A-Bearville.

Customers pay about $25 for the basic bear, but they can also buy music, clothing, and accessories. To keep the experience fresh, Build-A-Bear Workshop regularly introduces new and limited-edition animals. Clothes and accessories are also updated to reflect current fashion trends. Outfits for the bears complement the owner's interests and personalities with themes such as sports, colleges, hobbies, and careers. Some children and their parents hold in-store birthday parties, with music playing from the store's official CD. To ensure customers enjoy a great experience every time they visit, all sales associates attend a three-week training program at "Bear University," and the firm offers incentive programs and bonuses. The inventory in the stores changes frequently, with different bear styles arriving weekly. Build-A-Bear Workshops also feature limited-edition and seasonal merchandise, such as a Beary Businesslike Curly Teddy for Father's Day; mummy, wizard, and witch bears for Halloween; and a Sweet Hugs & Kisses Teddy for Valentine's Day.

In 2013, responding to the changing interests of children, Build-A-Bear announced a sweeping upgrade to its retail stores. Clark noted that developments in digital technology have changed how kids play: "[In 1997] children were playing board games. Now they're playing games online . . . Kids are being bombarded with the next new shiny objects. But they've always loved teddy bears and that's not going to change."[1]

Because the stores are a mix between the product (the teddy bear) and the experience of creating the teddy bear, the new design incorporates several digital upgrades. To help determine appropriate changes, the company enlisted several children, termed "Cub Advisors," and their moms for advice on the changes they would like to see in the stores.

Based on this research and advice, the stores are undergoing a massive redesign. Starting at the storefront, signage has been incorporated with Microsoft Kinect technology that enables kids to play with the signage before entering. The use of digital signage allows stores to highlight sales and new products, as well as several holiday themes. The revamped "Love Me" station allows kids to give their stuffed animals personalities at an interactive table using emoticons, which are pictorial representations of a facial expression like a happy face. The "Hear Me" station has a touchscreen that allows customers to choose and load prerecorded music and animal noises, or record their own voice. The "Stuff Me" station offers the option to add custom scents such as bubble gum, cotton candy, and chocolate chip. Finally, kids can wash their bears in a digital bathtub at the "Fluff Me" station. In an effort at contingency planning, "low-tech" options are being designed that can be put over the digital stations if computers act up.

Refact

The teddy bear came into being in 1903, when President Teddy Roosevelt refused to shoot a cub while bear hunting. The spared animal was thereafter referred to as the Teddy Bear.

Discussion Questions

1. Is the Build-A-Bear Workshop concept a fad, or does it have staying power?
2. Describe the target customer for this retailer.
3. What can Build-A-Bear Workshop do to generate repeat visits to the store?

Sources: http://www.buildabear.com; http://www.buildabearville. com; Sandy Smith, "Integration Specialists," *Stores*, January 2013; Tom Ryan, "Build-A-Bear Workshop Goes High-Tech," *Retail Wire*, October 8, 2012.

This case was written by Barton Weitz, University of Florida, and Scott Motyka, Babson College.

CASE 8 — Supplementing for Success in the Canadian Market

When award-winning US-based specialty retailer The Vitamin Shoppe started exploring the possibility of expanding its operations into the Canadian market in 2011, it already recognized the attractiveness of the robust retail industry in the country, particularly the health and wellness category. The supplement market is a $3 billion industry in Canada, which sees 70 percent of Canadian citizens taking supplements on a regular basis. The company also understood that there was clearly lots of room for another retailer of vitamins and health products to play. The questions they had, however, were far more philosophical in nature.

"We kicked off the official business effort internally about 18 months ago," explains Musab Balbale, The Vitamin Shoppe's director of business development. "There were two key questions that we asked initially. We first wanted to identify whether or not there was an opportunity for us to really create a compelling offering to the customer based on what our core values are—assortment, knowledge, and value. And the second was, do we have the organizational breadth internally to successfully execute against the opportunity?"

To answer its first question, the company, which branded itself as Vitapath for the Canadian market, didn't have to look any further than its product. It conducted a review of the competitive landscape in the country and identified a real opportunity to bring a unique offering to Canada.

"We view ourselves as a single destination in the market that serves the entire family," explains Balbale. "We carry not only vitamins and supplements focused on the health conscious consumer, but we also carry a strong line of sports supplements focused on the active consumer."

Whether the Vitapath customer is looking for gummy multivitamins for their kids, basic fish oils and supplements, or more obscure herbs for those people becoming more conscious about taking care of their health in specific ways, Balbale believes that the supplement retailer has it all. However, he points out that the product is only the beginning of the Vitapath experience.

"The level of assortment and breadth that we offer is unique to the market," he says. "That comes with a level of service and knowledge that engages the customer in conversation and imparts product value."

And because of this, Vitapath's store associates, called "health enthusiasts," are core to what the company is and what they do, which is serve customers.

"We want to wow our customers by impressing them by the level of engagement offered in our stores. We want that to be our differentiator."

To achieve this, the company knew that it needed to hire the right people—people who would believe in what the store stands for and become ambassadors for its products and values. It also knew that it could not stray from its objectives during the recruitment process.

"We hire on three filters—empathy, knowledge, and passion—and we never compromise on these core attributes when searching for talent," he says. "But we're particularly mindful of hiring people who want to serve customers and who are enthusiastic about good health and about nutritional education. We've found that if we hire with these criteria in mind, we get great people who are tremendous for our brand."

In its search for the right associates, the company talked to a lot of people and posted on job boards. But there was a very active aspect to its efforts, which included visiting nutritionist colleges and job fairs associated with nutritionist colleges to find talent. The company asked for recommendations from its suppliers and vendors in Canada, and also scoured LinkedIn to see if it could find interested people connected to the industry.

"In the end, we just talked to as many people as we possibly could," says Balbale. "And we're really pleased to say that we found the right people who fit our profile and who are enthusiastic about the opportunity."

The right people with the right attitude and knowledge level were hired to join the Canadian team; however, their journey was just beginning. Vitapath invited senior members of its store team, including the district manager and store managers, to spend three weeks in The Vitamin Shoppe's Buffalo stores close to the border to impart the softer cultural side of what the company is and what it aims to do. The team then entered into a sophisticated year-long training program that the company developed.

"We call it Vitapath University," explains Balbale. "It's an online training program that provides our health enthusiasts with the tools to become more knowledgeable and improve their customer service abilities."

The training combines online curriculum with in-store training exercises that focus on three things: (1) building category health knowledge, (2) building specific brand and product knowledge, and (3) focusing on developing empathetic customer engagement skills. Time is scheduled for each team member to train during store hours to complete three modules, each with three levels of learning within them, with a test at the end of each module and level.

The training program has been very well-received by the retailer's health enthusiasts as it prepares them to properly offer the service that Vitapath is building its brand on. And, what's more, the company has instituted a pay-for-knowledge program in which individuals receive an increase in pay for each level that they pass that's commensurate to the score with which they passed.

"Our store health enthusiasts really appreciate the program because it has real incentives for them to excel and grow and learn with the company," points out Balbale. "We think it provides the right feedback for all of the personal investment that our store health enthusiasts put into the company and serving our customers."

Aside from the customer and the health enthusiasts that serve them, the company also had to examine its internal breadth that Balbale speaks of to ensure that challenges related to expansion into Canada were met head on.

"This was our first expansion outside of the United States, and so we faced internally the challenges that any company does leaving its native market," explains Balbale. "We had to learn everything from managing multiple currencies, how to identify and comply with local regulations, whether it be financial or human resources related, finding local partners, our legal counsel, marketing partners, and folks that could build a construction for us and put our fixtures together in our stores."

The company tackled these challenges by making the expansion a company-wide effort. According to Balbale, Vitapath and its American parent The Vitamin Shoppe are both internally very operationally focused and have a pretty collaborative culture. The combination allowed them to tackle the challenges as they arose by making each of its business units responsible for delivering their respective solution in Canada.

"We worked really hard together to make sure that where those business units overlapped, we really understood the nuances and requirements so that we could deliver an exceptional experience for our Canadian customers."

What was most challenging for the company, however, was in developing operational processes that differ from those that they employ in the United States.

"In the United States we're a 582-store chain," says Balbale. "We have our own distribution centres, and we have all of the vendors ship to our distribution centres, which we then ship out to our stores. In Canada, because of our smaller scale with two initial stores, we chose to develop a direct-to-store delivery supply chain model."

The direct-to-store model involves product coming into the store that needs to be opened, counted, and audited, with all information communicated back to the vendor. Balbale admits that the process is not perfect, allowing too much room for error on both the store and vendor side, but that they are working through the challenges.

Another challenge faced by Vitapath in Canada, and another reason to implement the direct-to-store shipment of product, is in addressing challenges posed by Health Canada regulations, which differ significantly from those south of the border. In Canada, retailers offering supplements and other health food and vitamin products are required to sell only products that have been registered with Health Canada and that have received what's called a national products number. In addition to that, the full chain of control from manufacturing to delivery of product to the store needs to be licensed by Health Canada.

"In order to comply with Health Canada regulations, we're working primarily with Canadian brands and Canadian distributors—over 80 percent of our product is sourced locally."

This decision, however, was not only to simplify the sourcing strategy and to reduce the number of imports, but to ensure that Vitapath is a truly Canadian brand and Canadian distributor.

"It's a decision that we've come to be really proud of," says Balbale. "We'll continue to monitor our stores and will continue to listen to our customer. If there are gaps within our assortment that we can't fill from within Canada, we'll find brands and products in the US to help strengthen that assortment. But we're really proud of the fact that Vitapath is a Canadian business. One that supports other Canadian businesses."

And the decision to partner primarily with Canadian manufacturers was also made easier due to the fact that the company already had great relationships with Canadian vendors from their work in the US.

"We've had some really great relationships with Canadian brands even before we entered the market. They actually helped us in understanding their view of the market and have been incredibly helpful to us in providing market insight and advice. And quite honestly, working so closely together has helped strengthen our relationship with them and it continues to provide already strong Canadian brands with opportunities in our stores in the United States. We really look to our suppliers and vendors as business partners and work together to make both of our businesses better."

Vitapath opened its first stores in Canada, both in the Greater Toronto Area, in January [2013]. And though it may be too early to tell exactly how the company's being received by its Canadian consumer, Balbale is extremely optimistic concerning the progress of the stores.

"We're here for the long run. We plan to open additional stores later in 2013 and 2014 and are looking at real estate actively. Vancouver certainly is an exciting market for us to go next. It has a particular focus on health and wellness which in some ways looks a lot like the West Coast in the United States. But right now we're focused on building out Toronto and building enough scale to support our brand and the infrastructure in Canada.

Discussion Questions

1. What is Vitapath's retail strategy? What is its target market and how does it try to develop an advantage over its competition?

2. Describe Vitapath's retail mix: product, price, promotion, people, place, process. How does its retail mix support its strategy?

3. What factors in the environment provided the opportunity for The Vitamin Shoppe to develop a new and potentially successful retail chain in Canada? What insight did Balbale have that perhaps other players in the health and wellness category did not?

4. What do you think the Vitapath brand could mean to consumers? How have the Vitapath management tried to affect the value of its brand name?

5. What do you believe will be the major challenges facing Vitapath as it goes forward? Is the brand advantage sustainable going forward? Can Vitapath defend its position against other health and wellness specialty retailers?

6. What other potential Canadian markets do you believe would support the growth of the brand? Why?

Source: Sean C. Tarry, "Supplementing for Success in the Canadian Market," *Canadian Retailer,* Spring 2013, Volume 23, Issue 2, pp. 40–43. Canadian Retailer, a publication of Retail Council of Canada.

Blue Tomato: Internationalization of a Multichannel Retailer

The History of Blue Tomato: A Brick-and-Mortar Retailer

When Blue Tomato started, it was at the initiative of Gerfried Schuller, a former European snowboard champion who opened a snowboarding school in 1988 and then launched a small store for snowboarders in Schladming, an Austrian ski resort, in 1994. Since that time, Blue Tomato has opened eight brick-and-mortar stores throughout Austria and Germany. Three shops are located in ski areas, and five of them function in more urban locations. To expand its business activities, Blue Tomato has expanded the variety of merchandise its sells, including products for not just snowboarders but also surfers, skaters, and freeskiers.

Evolution of Blue Tomato into a Multichannel Retailer

The number of brick-and-mortar stores that a small company like Blue Tomato could open easily was relatively limited, which meant its potential customer contacts were limited, too. Therefore, it expanded into the online realm in 1997, allowing Austrian customers to place orders 24 hours a day, seven days a week. By 1999, its first large-scale Web store was online; in 2008, it relaunched its website (http://www.blue-tomato.com) to facilitate the product-ordering process and introduced a product finder, designed to help customers locate just the right snowboards, boot bindings, snow gear, and street wear. Using predetermined characteristics (e.g., preferred brands, size, price), this sophisticated product finder helps consumers identify their ideal product alternatives. For the company, the website relaunch was a great success, leading to sales increases of 35 percent in the first year. In general, Blue Tomato's Web store has enabled it to attract new customers without investing in finding, building, or stocking new stores. In addition, it has been able to offer far more products online than it could stock in any single brick-and-mortar outlet.

In 2002, Blue Tomato expanded its multichannel strategy even further by publishing a new, printed snowboard catalogue (with a print run of 130 000 in the first year), targeting convenience-oriented customers who avoid online shopping. This catalogue has expanded to a print run of 500 000; in addition, the company offers not just the snowboard catalogue but also a freeski catalogue (with a print run of 170 000 in 2013), a skate and street-styles catalogue (print run of 80 000 in 2013), and a surf/summer catalogue (print run of 350 000 in summer 2013). To distribute these catalogues, Blue Tomato uses direct mailings to selected customers, hands them out at events, and promoted them with flyers in snowboard, freeski, and surf magazines. Interested consumers also can request catalogues on the company's website, download them from its website, or view the pages online.

Although many of the company's sales come through its online orders, it relies on its brick-and-mortar stores to maintain close, direct contacts with its (potential) customers, in line with its overall corporate philosophy. To ensure direct customer contact and attract new customers, Blue Tomato also opened two test centres in ski resorts, which allow (potential) customers to try out new snowboards, boots, and bindings. The company hosts four snowboard schools in local ski areas, together with special events, such as its "Kids Days," during which children can attend its snowboard courses for free.

Synergies Across Distribution Channels

In addition to its individual strengths, Blue Tomato relies on the synergies it has created across its different distribution channels. Since 2011, it has installed media boxes, or kiosks, in its brick-and-mortar stores that allow consumers to look up personalized information about special offers in particular stores. They also can log on to their Facebook (or other social media) page, connect with their friends, and ask about how well the latest snowgear or streetwear suits them. Furthermore, customers can search for products in the printed or online catalogues and order them online, or vice versa. According to Blue Tomato, the printed catalogues have contributed to and extended its online business; the opportunity to view catalogues online might further boost its online sales. For the future, the company plans to add pickup and return services to its brick-and-mortar stores, enabling customers to order a product online and pick it up in their local store.

Challenges Coordinating Different Distribution Channels

The main challenge of operating multiple distribution channels is for Blue Tomato to provide a consistent face to customers across all contact points. For example, it seeks to reinforce its commitment to customer service throughout its Web store. To meet this challenge, it also standardizes all prices and communication. With regard to price, the company simply guarantees to offer the best price. If a consumer orders a product on the telephone after receiving a catalogue, but the product is listed at a cheaper price on the website because the price dropped since the catalogue was published, Blue Tomato charges the customer the lower price. Its return policy—customers can return products within 21 days—also is consistent in each channel. In terms of communication, Blue Tomato's devotion to snowboarding, skating, and freeskiing is manifested by employees in the brick-and-mortar stores, as well as through the events the company hosts. Beyond this content-oriented integration, the company's communication is formally integrated.

However, the product overlap across the different distribution channels is relatively minimal. Whereas the brick-and-mortar stores and catalogues offer limited merchandise variety and assortment, its website posts more than 450 000 products, from approximately 400 brands, available for purchase. This poor overlap might be a challenge for Blue Tomato in terms of reinforcing its retail brand image among customers.

Internationalization

To initiate its internationalization moves, in 1997, Blue Tomato installed international purchasing facilities on its website. The focus of these early internationalization efforts was on German-speaking countries (i.e., Germany and Switzerland) and German-speaking customers. The website thus was available only in German. This strategy represented an easy choice, because the language barriers between different German-speaking countries are negligible, nor did Blue Tomato face many barriers in terms of export or customs regulations. Austria and Switzerland participate in stable exchange rates, and Austria and Germany already relied on a common currency (the euro).

But this internationalization process also has expanded, particularly in the catalogue channel, in which catalogues are available in different languages (e.g., the snowboard catalogue is issued in five languages, and the surf/summer catalogue is offered in four). The relaunch of the company's website in 2008 also sparked advances in the internationalization process, because the online store was no longer restricted to German-speaking customers; today, it has been translated into 14 languages. Thus, customers from countries throughout the world can place an order with Blue Tomato. Its most important foreign markets remain geographically nearby, including Germany, Switzerland, Scandinavia, the Benelux countries, Great Britain, and Spain, but it also has received orders from exotic destinations such as Hawaii, Hong Kong, and Argentina. Furthermore, Blue Tomato has earned the distinction of offering the largest selection of snowboards in the world on its website. As a result, 70 percent of its online orders come from foreign markets. In 2011, its products were delivered to 65 countries.

By the end of 2012, Blue Tomato's internationalization remained focused solely on its Web store and printed catalogues. In these channels, it relies on direct exports. Furthermore, regardless of the channel used to support the internationalization, it has maintained its standardization strategy with respect to prices charged and communication. That is, the prices are the same for all customers in all countries, without any international price differentiation. The catalogue layout also remains standardized, though the specific products included in each catalogue issue vary slightly to reflect the varying appeal of certain brands in some international markets.

These eventual outcomes are not to suggest that the process of internationalization was easy. Blue Tomato has confronted several challenges, stemming largely from the complexity of the European market. Most countries in Europe are members of the European Union, but different legal conditions and tax rates arise in each member-state, and their cultural differences remain pertinent. Logistics costs and economic power also differ from country to country, with notable effects on the level of income of (potential) customers. Against this background, Blue Tomato decided to undertake some foreign direct investment in Germany: As of the end of 2012, the company had opened three brick-and-mortar stores in its neighbouring country.

Meanwhile, Blue Tomato ranks as the leading European multichannel retailer for board sports and related apparel. If it decides to expand its internationalization further, by opening stores in other countries, it clearly will need to invest additional financial and personnel resources. Regardless of the strategy it might choose for such a foreign market entry, tackling more markets, with more widely variant national, legal, tax, and logistic characteristics, could make it more difficult for the company to continue with its strategy of standardization.

In 2012, Blue Tomato was acquired by Zumiez Inc., a leading North American specialty retailer of action sports–related apparel, footwear, equipment, and accessories. Zumiez already operates more than 450 stores in the United States and Canada and maintains a Web store (http://www.zumiez.com). Despite this acquisition, Blue Tomato plans to continue to keep its headquarters in Austria, even as it seeks to meet its latest objective: to become the world leader in action sports retailing.

Discussion Questions

1. What strengths do the different distribution channels have from the company's perspective?

2. Which synergies has Blue Tomato created across different channels? What additional actions might it take to become an omnichannel retailer?

3. What key challenges remain for Blue Tomato in its efforts to coordinate these different channels?

4. Which challenges might Blue Tomato face as it expands its business activities internationally?

Source: This case was written by Professor Thomas Foscht and Assistant Professor Marion Brandstaetter, both of Karl-Franzens-University, Graz, Austria.

CASE 10 Vivah Jewellery: Location Strategy

In 1985, the first Vivah Jewellery store opened at Pickering Town Centre and heralded a new trend for Directions East—a wholesale distribution company that focused on gift items and art objects imported from the Far East. The company also carried jewellery items that were sold to select Canadian retailers and it wasn't long before jewellery, which represented 20 percent of the product lines, began to make up 80 percent of the sales. As a result, the decision was made to create a retail concept that would focus specifically on fashion jewellery and Vivah Jewellery was born.

The retail store was named after founder Zell Goodbaum's wife Vivah—an accomplished gold and silversmith with an artistic flair for jewellery design. The product lines reflected her preference for classic lines and simplicity, as well as a belief that fashion jewellery could be high quality and affordable. Vivah's love of handmade designs was embraced by retail customers who found that Vivah Jewellery offered a more affordable alternative to traditional jewellery stores such as Birks and Peoples and a step up from the fashion jewellery offerings of fashion retailers such as Suzy Shier and Reitmans. Major product lines include earrings, necklaces, bracelets, and rings—75 percent of which feature sterling silver and semi-precious stones.

The company cautiously began its retail concept with a kiosk location (approx. 200 square feet). The original kiosk location was extremely successful and more kiosk locations were added as the company began to slowly expand—opening in locations that provided sufficient customer traffic to suit their small space needs. Today, the company has 29 retail locations in Ontario, six in British Columbia, and two in Alberta.

Kiosks are the venue of choice for most Vivah outlets, but the company has a few traditional retail stores within shopping malls (referred to as in-line stores). The in-line stores are slightly larger than the kiosks (300 square feet on average) but small compared to most retail stores in malls. Surprisingly, kiosks may be small in size but the rental costs are not—kiosks, because of their central locations, can cost more than a traditional storefront location. Rental costs for kiosks and in-line mall locations vary depending on the mall's location and customer traffic.

Range of Monthly Rental Costs		
Ontario	**Low**	**High**
Kiosk	$3500	$5200
In-line store	$1700	$4500
British Columbia		
Kiosk	$2500	$9900
In-line store	$2900	$6500

In addition to the monthly rental cost, malls often demand a percentage of monthly sales as well as a monthly contribution to the mall's marketing budget. Vivah focuses on small to medium-sized malls for the most part, as kiosk space rents in some of the larger malls are substantial. For example, Vivah had a kiosk location at the Toronto Eaton Centre for several years and paid $12 000 a month in rent.

Vivah has also experimented with some nontraditional locations—a kiosk inside Credit Valley Hospital in Mississauga, a leased space inside Angie Strauss's Gallery in Niagara-on-the-Lake, and a retail store at the Fallsview Casino in Niagara Falls.

Due to the small physical size of the product lines (the average product takes up a half-inch of space) Vivah does not require a lot of space to carry a full product assortment. The average kiosk location is 200 square feet and carries 7000 to 8000 SKUs. Sales are fairly consistent through the year (with a spike during the Christmas season) as jewellery is often a special occasion purchase (Valentine's Day, Mother's Day, prom, graduation, weddings). On average, sales per square foot are $1500. Vivah offers a wide range of prices in its product lines, including one-of-a-kind designs that are sold at the higher end of the spectrum.

Price Range of Product Lines	
Earrings	$14.95–$149.95
Bracelets	$19.95–$499.95
Necklaces	$24.95–$999.99

Certain core product lines are carried at each Vivah location; however, store managers have the flexibility to adapt their product offerings to suit local market needs. The company continues to focus on sterling silver and semi-precious stones but has devoted more space to bridal jewellery product lines, which have proven to be an extremely successful addition to its retail offerings. The primary market for Vivah is women, 35 to 55 years of age, middle income, who appreciate jewellery but are not necessarily looking for cutting-edge or high-end items. The secondary market is the bride who is buying for herself as well as her wedding party.

The company spends a limited amount on advertising, relying on word of mouth, repeat customers, and the retail locations as the main form of promotion. To help reach the bridal market, the company advertises in *Wedding Bells* magazine and the magazine's website, and has access to the magazine's mailing and email lists.

The Vivah management team is well aware that the retail industry is continually changing and that new retail concepts are being introduced all the time. Retail is extremely competitive and current downward economic trends are serious causes for concern for many small retailers. Management is interested in new formats that may provide growth opportunities for the company beyond the traditional mall environment. For example, Vivah management has considered acquiring retail space on cruise ships. The company has also been approached by some US malls; however, at this point the retailer is wary of entering an even more competitive market where it has little experience and no brand awareness.

Discussion Questions

Vivah management has turned to your retail consulting firm to develop a retail strategy for the future.

1. In planning for the future, what kinds of information should Vivah seek out? Explain your answer.

2. What are Vivah's competitive advantages and disadvantages in comparison to other jewellery retailers? How can it reduce the disadvantages?

3. What other types of sites do you think Vivah should consider (besides those stated in the case)? Why?

Source: Courtesy of Terri Champion.

CASE 11 | Stephanie's Boutique: Store Strategy

Stephanie Wilson must decide where to open a ready-to-wear boutique she has been contemplating for several years. Now in her late 30s, she has been working in municipal government ever since leaving university, where she majored in fine arts. She is divorced with two children (ages five and eight) and wants her own business, at least partly to be able to spend more time with her children. She loves fashion, feels she has a flair for it, and has taken evening courses in fashion design and retail management.

Recently, she heard about a plan to rehabilitate an old arcade building in the downtown section of her city. This news crystallized her resolve to move now. She is considering three locations.

The Downtown Arcade

The city's central business district has been ailing for some time. The proposed arcade renovation is part of a master redevelopment plan, with a new department store and several office buildings already operating. Completion of the entire master plan is expected to take another six years.

Dating from 1912, the arcade building was once the centre of downtown trade, but it's been vacant for the past 15 years. The proposed renovation includes a three-level shopping facility, low-rate garage with validated parking, and a convention centre complex. Forty shops are planned for the first (ground) floor, 28 more on the second, and a series of restaurants on the third.

The location Stephanie is considering is 900 square feet and situated near the main ground floor entrance. Rent is $20.50 per square foot, for an annual total of $18 480. If sales exceed $225 000, rent will be calculated at 8 percent of sales. She will have to sign a three-year lease.

Tenderloin Village

The gentrified urban area of the city where Stephanie lives is nicknamed Tenderloin Village because of its lurid past. Today, however, the neat, well-kept brownstones and comfortable neighbourhood make it feel like a yuppie enclave. Many residents have done the remodelling work themselves and take great pride in their neighbourhood.

About 20 small retailers are now in an area of the Village adjacent to the convention centre complex. Most of them are trendy, affordable restaurants. There are also three small women's clothing stores. The site available to Stephanie is on the Village's main street on the ground floor of an old house. Its space is also about 900 square feet. Rent is $15 000 annually with no coverage clause. The landlord knows Stephanie and will require a two-year lease.

Appletree Mall

This suburban mall has been open for eight years. A successful regional centre, it has three department stores and 100 smaller shops just off a major highway about ten kilometres from downtown. Of its nine women's clothing retailers, three are in a price category considerably higher than what Stephanie has in mind.

Appletree has captured the retail business in the city's southwest quadrant, though growth in that sector has slowed in the past year. Nevertheless, mall sales are still running 12 percent ahead of the previous year. Stephanie learned of plans to develop a second shopping centre east of town, which would be about the same size and character as Appletree Mall. But groundbreaking is still 18 months away, and no renting agent has begun to enlist tenants.

The store available to Stephanie in Appletree is two doors from the local department store chain's mall outlet. At 1200 square feet, it's slightly larger than the other two possibilities. But it's long and narrow—24 feet in front by 50 feet. Rent is $24 per square foot ($28 820 annually).

In addition, on sales that exceed $411 500, rent is 7 percent of sales. There is an additional charge of 1 percent of sales to cover common-area maintenance and mall promotions. The mall's five-year lease includes an escape clause if sales don't reach $411 500 after two years.

Discussion Questions

1. Describe the pluses and minuses of each location.
2. What type of store would be most appropriate for each location?
3. If you were Stephanie, which location would you choose? Why?

Source: This case was prepared by Professor David Ehrlich, Marymount University.

CASE 12 | Innovating the In-Store Experience

Imagine riding an escalator in your favourite sports store on a Saturday morning. Suddenly, instead of the second-floor ski section destination you thought you were heading to, for a brief moment you are no longer on an escalator—or even in a sports store for that matter. Rather, you're riding a chairlift up a mountain and getting ready to mash some moguls in your mind. Sounds exciting, right?

This is just one of the many innovations and in-store surprises customers experience at Sport Chek's Retail Lab store in midtown Toronto, which opened in January 2013. While the store is only 12 000 square feet, thanks to 140 digital screens and other technology, it feels much bigger.

"People call it multichannel, or omni-channel, but to the consumer it's just shopping," explains

Michael Medline, president, FGL Sports. "You have to be consistent, but also exciting through all your channels. Our feeling is our stores can be very exciting for the consumer, which helps us compete with bricks-and-mortar and e-retailers as well. We wanted to take it to the next step."

A One-of-a-Kind Experience

In 2012, Sport Chek undertook a brand reformation captured by its new tagline, "Your Better Starts Here." The Yonge Street outlet in Toronto with its 140 digital screens, massive shoe wall with 500 different footwear styles, as well as a multitude of other in-store innovations, is a one-of-a-kind experience. It's also one that epitomizes Sport Chek's brand reinvention. And the company's "next step" in its evolution includes an ambitious strategic plan to grow the retail chain by 50 percent in terms of square footage over the next five years.

"We are not going to build ten lab stores, but we will take the learning from this test store and incorporate it into the flagship stores we are building and also retrofit it into many of our current stores as well," Medline adds.

It's this type of innovation that, in an ever-competitive, ever-changing shopping environment, is critical to a retailer's success. Despite technological advances and the rise of the online shopping channel, the in-store experience is still king; it's a key piece of a retailer's core business they can't afford to neglect.

Differentiating the Brand

When it comes to a brand's strength, it's also where retailers can really shine and truly separate themselves from their competitors to win the battle for customer loyalty. What is the added value you are giving them for choosing to shop at your store?

Joe Jackman, chief executive officer at Jackman Reinvention, partners with clients to help them build their brand and "become the most powerful version of themselves."

According to Jackman, there are two keys. The first is something he calls "core." This is a set of customer expectations of what they believe epitomizes a positive and productive service experience. The second is that unexpected part where there are opportunities to differentiate and build your brand. These two things need to work in tandem.

"The first is often overlooked and shouldn't be because it is foundational," Jackman explains. "I say that because you almost have to earn the permission to surprise and delight customers in unexpected ways by delivering what is first expected."

These customer expectations include all manner of touch points, including, but not limited to, the layout of the store, ease of navigation, access to the staff when they need them, displays that are not only easily accessed but also easy to understand, and a visual environment that is conducive to whatever the shopping occasions are.

"All of these things present opportunities to define the brand and take it to the next level, but the first job is to consistently deliver what the customer expects and that's the hardest part," Jackman adds.

Jackman points to Burberry's flagship store on Regent Street in London, England, which he had the opportunity to visit on a recent trip overseas, as one that epitomizes the ultimate in-store customer experience. What made it so special?

"They've created a stunning environment that celebrates not only their products but also their brand," he explains. "They've also integrated technology, but not in a superfluous way, which is one of the things that is happening now; technology for some equates to throwing a lot of screens in a store. But technology needs to be thoughtfully done and integrated.

"Burberry has done some amazing things to create a brand experience unlike any other," he adds. "The product looks amazing, and the staff are beyond good; they are brand ambassadors. That was my experience as someone who studies retail and as a customer."

Passionate People Drive the In-Store Experience

It's great to have the latest and greatest in technology, but all the digital screens and tablets alone do not equal a memorable in-store customer experience. You also need an all-star staff of passionate people who are knowledgeable and well-trained to emotionally connect with your shoppers; the end-goal is for them to forge long-term relationships with each customer who enters your store.

"We couldn't do the things we are trying to do and will do if we didn't have great staff," comments Medline. "If you don't have the best products and the most knowledgeable and passionate staff, even with great technology, you are not going to succeed."

Medline believes his operations team is the best in the business, and it all starts from an extremely simple principle.

"We hire people who are passionate about sports," he says. "If you go to the Lab Store, you will see that. The people serving you will be unbelievably knowledgeable, not just about the product, but on how you can use the products."

Sport Chek's staff not only have the ability to recommend the right pair of shoes, but they will get to know more about why customers are making that purchase by asking the right questions, such as are they planning to run competitively or just to get in shape? At the Toronto Lab Store, customers can also participate in a comprehensive gait analysis on a special treadmill that will help staff determine the perfect shoe that is customized to their running style. Then, Sport Chek staff can enhance that in-store experience further by adding their experience.

"Our staff can talk to that customer about why they are running, where the best running trails are in town, or when the next 5K is," Medline says. "That is the future of the store experience. To compete, you have to have that value add. You have to be able to build in some ways; it's very old-fashioned in terms of that one-on-one interaction with the customer."

Professional Expert Advice

Golf Town also understands the important role its people play when it comes to enhancing the customers' in-store experience. Ron Hornbaker, EVP of Golf Town Operations Canada, reveals that the big-box golf retailer has added a lot of things in the past year to make its store more "experiential," such as the latest in swing analysis, club-fitting technology, and hiring more full-time Class A CPGA professionals to give in-store lessons.

"We have the best teaching equipment you can get," Hornbaker reveals. "We use a three-camera video system to record your swing. This video can be immediately downloaded and sent directly to your smartphone, complete with the pro's commentary."

Hornbaker says the best part is the cost, so there should be no excuse for golf enthusiasts to take a lesson or two at one of their stores. Lessons are $39.99 for a half-hour video lesson with one of their professionals, $99.99 for a series of three lessons, and $149.99 for a series of five.

Golf Town continues to lead the way with its try-before-you-buy philosophy by placing an emphasis on club fitting. All Golf Town stores are now equipped with "master fitters," with each store having a minimum of two—and some as many as three—of these certified staff.

"Since January [2013], we've spent more than a half a million dollars in this area by putting in new launch monitors in all our stores," he explains. "Most of the major golf manufacturers out there use the same software systems to fit pros and many PGA Tour players.

"If you go into a Golf Town store, part of what we pride ourselves in is that we want you to feel like you are on the course," Hornbaker adds. "We paint our ceilings blue, it's not cheap to do, but we do it because we want the customer to have that feeling of space and being outdoors. We also picked green carpeting on purpose."

Training for Knowledge

The other big innovation Golf Town launched last year to enhance its customers in-store experience is something called "Green Jacket Selling," its proprietary sales training program.

"This surrounds the question: 'What is it to be a Golf Town customer in one of our stores?'" Hornbaker explains. "If I'm a customer, how do I want someone to assist me with my golf purchase: Some of our research included hiring a mystery shopper to give us an objective look, and we designed our entire staff training program around that."

The Green Jacket Selling experience has an online learning and development system. Each sales associate is also assigned a mentor.

From virtual reality to tablets to passionate staff and mentorship programs that help store staff bring their products to life, the in-store customer experience continues to evolve and expand. Retailers that recognize the components that contribute to an exceptional one will reap the rewards. "The future of retailing is definitely exciting stores, but that has got to be based on great products and great staff," admits Michael Medline. "Sports lends itself to an exciting customer experience, and we are turning it up a notch."

Discussion Questions

1. What is the key piece of a retailer's core business that they can't afford to neglect?

2. How can a brand's strength separate retailers from their competition and help them win the battle for customer loyalty?

3. How do passionate people drive the in-store experience?

Source: David McPherson, "Innovating the In-Store Experience," *Canadian Retailer,* Spring 2013, Volume 23, Issue 2, pp. 22–25. Canadian Retailer, a publication of Retail Council of Canada.

Founded in 1976 by Steve Jobs and Steve Wozniak, Apple has become an innovative leader in the consumer electronics industry. In addition to offering traditional desktop and laptop computers, all of which feature Apple's OS X operating system, Apple essentially founded the digital music player when it introduced the iPod and online music store markets with iTunes; launched easy-to-use iPhones and iPads with increasingly more features; and introduced online movie/TV services through AppleTV and publishing and multimedia software.

Before Apple Retail Stores

During the early 1990s, Apple struggled as computer sales began shifting from specialized computer stores to mainstream retail stores. Big-box retailers such as Best Buy and Circuit City could offer a wider selection of computers at lower prices, although they lacked adequate customer service and support. These big-box retailers and specialized stores faced even more competition in the form of mail-order outlets, including CompuAdd, Gateway, and Dell.

Beginning in 1990, Dell shifted from selling its computers in warehouse and specialized computer stores to operating as an online direct mail-order company. Dell facilitated its online operations with an efficient online store that could handle high-volume sales. The online Dell store (dell.com) represented a new strategy for manufacturing: Computers were built as they were ordered. In turn, Dell could reduce inventory, because it no longer produced computers in mass quantities and then pushed inventory through the channel to resellers.

While establishing its online store, Apple needed to balance its direct orders with the sales initiated by its channel partners, mail-order resellers, independent dealers, and CompUSA, with which it initiated a "stores within stores" strategy to focus on Apple's products. Apple's partnership with CompUSA paid off. When the San Francisco CompUSA store was equipped with Macs, Apple's sales jumped from 15 to 35 percent of overall store sales.

Apple also put its own employees to work in various retail outlets to help inform and educate customers, as well as ensure its products were being displayed in working order. The company estimated it spent between $25 000 and $75 000 per month on this initiative. Apple executives soon realized they could not compete with PC brands by selling just laptops and desktops in big-box retail stores, because retailers could earn greater profits by selling lower-quality PC models. They had little to no incentive to sell Macs. Without its own retail store, Apple would always be at the mercy of the independent dealers and partners that operated with different strategic goals.

Designing the Apple Store

To compete with the PCs sold by big-box retailers, Apple needed to shift from selling its electronics through intermediaries to offering products directly through Apple Stores. This shift would not come easily. Steve Jobs, Apple's dynamic founder, first looked to bring in new executives. Mickey Drexler, former CEO of The Gap and now CEO of J.Crew, was hired in 1999 as part of Apple's board of directors.

Next, Jobs brought in Ron Johnson, who had been a merchandising executive with Target, to run Apple's retail division as vice president of retail operations.

Instead of launching stores from the start, Drexler suggested that Jobs rent a warehouse and build a prototype store, coined Apple Store Version 0.0. Apple executives then continuously redesigned the store until they achieved a layout that would entice shoppers to not only enter, but also make purchases. The first store prototype was configured by product category, with hardware laid out according to the internal organization of the company rather than by how customers logically shop. Executives quickly decided to redesign the store to better match customer interests. Although the redesign cost Apple more than six months, the executives believed this time investment was necessary to achieve a successful store that could compete with well-established electronics retailers and remain consistent with the Apple brand. Its first store opened in Tyson's Corner, Virginia, in May 2001.

The Apple Store Layout

When considering a site for a retail store, Apple uses its customer base to forecast visitor volume and revenues. Most Apple Stores locate within existing shopping malls or lifestyle centres, where retail traffic is already present. There are two types of full-size stores: a street-facing building or an in-mall store. The stores range from 3600 to 20 000 square feet, although most fall in the 3000 to 6000 square-foot range. Storefronts are typically all glass with a backlit Apple logo, and the front display windows change occasionally to focus on the newest marketing campaign. Apple's internal team designs the window displays, often using slot and cable systems to suspend design elements within the window. In some cases, the swinging entrance doors are in the middle, but in other stores, a logo wall appears in the middle with two doors located on either side. Store interiors feature only three materials: glass, stainless steel, and wood.

In addition to the retail floor, Apple Stores have backroom areas that sometimes include a public restroom, offices, and the inventory area. At some sites that lack sufficient space, inventory storage is located at a separate facility, always within walking distance. The store layout changes multiple times throughout the year. Apple executives organize planograms to coincide with the introduction of new products or heavily marketed merchandise. The layouts depend on the size of the store. A typical in-mall store locates merchandise in the front half of the store and customer service and support areas in the rear. Apple Stores carry fewer than 20 products, and every display piece is available for hands-on use so that customers can get an accurate feel for the available hardware and software.

On tables along the right wall, iPhones and iPods take up the front half of the store. Along the left wall, tables hold various models of general and high-end desktop and laptop computers. These displays give way to The Studio, a newer section hosted by experts who will answer application-oriented, creative questions. Two to three island tables in the front centre display software on Apple computers; additional island tables exhibit peripherals such as iPod docking stations and printers. A small children's area houses Apple computers running children's software. The Genius Bar takes up the back wall, with stools before a counter staffed with Apple experts for repairs and consultations. Larger stores also have a theatre area in the back, featuring a rear-projection screen with an audience area of either U-shaped wooden benches or full theatre seats in rows. This store layout is typical for a store located in a super-regional mall.

Apple Stores thus follow a free-form layout, which allows customers to browse the store according to their own interests. Signage hanging from the ceiling, for greater visibility, directs customers to specific areas within the store. Bright lighting draws attention to merchandise and creates a sense of excitement. Highlighted merchandise also helps draw customers strategically through the store. As customers browse the products, employees wearing Apple T-shirts and lanyards make themselves available to answer any questions.

Through its intensive development efforts, Apple has created a unique, customer service–oriented shopping experience. Customers can schedule face-to-face appointments at an Apple Store to test-drive products. One-to-one personal training sessions help customers become familiar with the array of Apple products. The company also offers free one-hour instructional or informational workshops every day for iPod, iPhone, and Mac owners. It also offers support for business customers by providing insight and advice about how to create a presentation from start to finish using Apple products.

Discussion Questions

1. Have you ever visited an Apple Store? If yes, did you make a purchase? Why or why not?

2. Why are Apple's store layout and atmosphere important?

3. Visit your local Apple Store. Does the layout of the store help to provide you with an excellent customer experience? Explain.

Sources: Philip Elmer-Dewitt, "Apple Ranks No. 4 in E-Retailing Survey," *Fortune*, May 5, 2010, http://www.apple.com/retail (accessed July 14, 2010); Daniel Eran, "Apple's Retail Challenge," *RDM*, November 8, 2006, http://www.roughlydrafted.com/RD/Q4.06/1DDD598A-7CE0-479EA6F9-912777CAB484.html (accessed July 14, 2010); "The Stores," *IfoAppleStore.com*, http://www.ifoapplestore.com/the_stores.html (accessed July 14, 2010); Jerry Useem, "Apple: America's Best Retailer," *Fortune*, March 8, 2007.

This case was written by Brienne Curley, while an MBA student at Loyola College in Maryland, under the supervision of Hope Corrigan.

Mountain Equipment Co-op (MEC) is a Canadian-owned and co-operatively run retailer that makes and sells outdoor recreation gear, clothing, and services to support its members in being active outdoors. As a co-op, MEC sells only to customers who hold a membership, which is technically a share that can be purchased by anyone. Over four decades, MEC has grown from the original six members to 3.9 million and to become a member costs $5, the same as it did in 1971. MEC sells more than 28 000 products at 17 stores across the country. In 2012, it reported sales of $302 million. The co-op exists to inspire and enable everyone to lead active outdoor lifestyles in a way that does the least harm and the most good—environmentally, socially, and economically.

Relative to some, MEC is a large retailer and brand, but in reality it remains a relatively niche retailer in the larger sporting and leisure market. Technology is evolving rapidly, consumers are purchasing differently (online, mobile, and in-store), and the Canadian retail space is more competitive than ever. International retailers and new domestic competitors such as SAIL are opening across the country, coupled with the rise of e-commerce options such as Backcountry.com and Amazon. Supply chains are becoming more volatile and globally diverse. MEC itself has seen significant changes in their membership and recreation patterns, and an increase in urbanization. Today, 71 percent of its members live in urban centres.

In response to these changes, the co-op updated its five-year business sustainability strategy in 2012, with a focus on four pillars: product integrity, retail operations, member service, and community. The company expanded its product assortment, breaking it out into three categories (backcountry, active lifestyle, and lifestyle) to better serve its changing members in an authentic way. MEC invested in e-commerce to provide omni-channel access, and increased its outreach in stores to foster active communities through events, meet-ups, and clinics. Finally, it updated its social compliance strategy, which is dedicated to improving working conditions in factories that produce MEC-brand apparel and gear.

In summer 2013, David Labistour, MEC's CEO, wrote a blog post on the company's website to unveil the co-op's new brand identity and strategy. Entitled "Looking toward MEC's Future," he discussed how the co-op was evolving to include more urban activities and changing the iconic logo to remain vibrant and relevant to the 3.9 million members. Though MEC's largest change by far had already begun on the store shelves, the co-op's new mountain-free logo was the most polarizing transformation. According to MEC's Chief Marketing Officer Anne Donohoe, there was a need to modify the opinions of the current customer base and also acquire new customers. The best way to do that was through a modification of their logo. In order to realize new goals, a different logo needed to be created to reflect the new market segments. The new marketing campaign includes the tagline, "We are all outsiders," which celebrates yoga alongside rock climbing, backcountry skiing, and dog-walking. The idea is to shift the iconic brand from something perceived as elitist and exclusive to diversify the image, expanding the concept of what MEC is all about. The key is targeting segments who want to go outdoors, whether it be taking the dog for a walk or mountain biking.

Critics of both the new logo and MEC's new all-inclusive approach have been vocal on the company's social network. Tom Herbst, who served as CEO from 1974 to 1976 and again from 1978 to 1992, says the "mountain" in the name wasn't even there to begin with. Originally the name they were going to use for the company excluded the word mountain, but the BC Registry felt that the name would not be specific enough, thus they change it to include mountain in title.

All of MEC's decisions and operations according to its charter are geared toward a member-centric mentality and are guided by its values: adventure, creativity, quality, integrity, leadership, co-operation, humanity, stewardship, and sustainability.

Discussion Questions

1. Has MEC stayed relevant, even as more competitors have entered the marketplace?

2. Has MEC adequately responded to the changes in the market? Is it meeting the needs of its members?

3. What are the International Co-operative Alliance principals and how has MEC put these values into practice? Use the information provided at http://www.ica.coop/en/what-co-op/co-operative-identity-values-principles and http://www.mec.ca/AST/ContentPrimary/AboutMEC/AboutOurCoOp/MecCharter.jsp.

Sources: "What Matters and Why," *MEC*, http://www.mec.ca/AST/ ContentPrimary/AboutMEC/Sustainability/AccountabilityReport/ Economics.jsp (accessed January 28, 2014); Linda Nguyen, "Mountain Equipment Co-op unveils new logo, name to appeal to urban customers," *Canadian Business*, June 18, 2013, http://www.

canadianbusiness.com/business-news/mountain-equipment-co-op-unveils-new-logo-name-to-appeal-to-urban-customers/ (accessed January 28, 2014); "Looking toward MEC's future," MEC company blog, June 18, 2013, http://blog.mec.ca/?s=looking+toward+me c%27s+future (accessed January 28, 2014).

CASE 15 Tiffany & Co. and TJX: Comparing Financial Performance

The year 2012 marked the 175th anniversary of Charles Lewis Tiffany's opening of his store in downtown Manhattan in 1837. Tiffany & Co. is mostly known for its exquisite jewellery, but it also has additional luxury items in its product assortment. The Tiffany robin's egg "blue boxes" have become a ubiquitous status symbol, representing the company's brand quality and craftsmanship. Tiffany & Co. has a different strategy and marketing approach than other national retailers. Throughout its history, the company's mission has been to enrich the lives of its customers by creating enduring objects of extraordinary beauty that will be cherished for generations. Tiffany & Co. has accomplished this by crafting beautiful designs, using fine-quality materials and expert workmanship, and presenting those products to its customers at luxurious stores in high-end locations.

TJX Corporation, on the other hand, consists of a mix of stores under the names of TJ Maxx, HomeGoods, and Marshalls in the United States (with additional stores under different names in Canada and Europe). TJX strives to offer exceptional value through its four pillars of great fashion, brand, quality, and price. It works with a variety of national brands so that its merchandise assortments at these stores are ever-changing. It is willing to purchase less-than-full assortments of items, styles, sizes, and quantities from vendors and pass on the cost savings to its customers. So that it doesn't have to completely rely on merchandise from national-brand vendors for its assortment offerings, TJX offers some private-label merchandise, which is produced specifically for TJX only. TJX does not own any factories, but rather sources its private-label products with manufacturers. It keeps relatively low inventory levels, which has helped it produce relatively fast inventory turns while maintaining strong gross margins.

Discussion Questions

1. Calculate the following for both Tiffany and TJX using data from the abbreviated income statements and balance sheets in Exhibit 1.
   a. Gross margin percentage
   b. SG&A expense percentage
   c. Operating profit margin percentage
   d. Net profit margin (after taxes) percentage
   e. Inventory turnover
   f. Asset turnover
   g. Return on assets percentage

Exhibit 1

2011 Financial Data for Tiffany and TJX (in thousands)

	Tiffany (Year Ending 1/31/2012)	TJX (Year Ending 1/28/2012)
	Income Statement	**Income Statement**
Net sales	$3 642 937	$23 191 455
Less: Cost of goods sold	$1 491 783	$16 854 249
Gross margin	$2 151 154	$6 337 206
Less: SG&A expenses	$1 442 728	$3 890 144
Operating profit margin	$708 426	$2 447 062
Less: Interest expense	$48 578	$35 648
Other income	$5 099	$0
Net income before taxes	$664 951	$2 411 414
Less: Taxes	$255 761	$915 324
Net income after taxes	$439 190	$1 496 090
	Balance Sheet	**Balance Sheet**
Cash	$433 954	$1 507 112
Accounts receivable	$184 085	$204 304
Inventory	$2 073 212	$2 950 523
Other current assets	$198 424	$470 693
Total current assets	$2 889 675	$5 132 632
Fixed assets	$767 174	$2 706 377
Long-term assets	$502 143	$442 596
Current liabilities	$626 677	$3 063 423
Long-term liabilities	$186 802	$2 008 892
Stockholders' equity	$2 348 905	$3 209 290

2. Compare and contrast the calculated financial figures for Tiffany and TJX. Analyze and discuss why the percentages and ratios differ for the two retailers.

3. Analyze which retailer has the better overall financial performance.

4. Why is ROA a good measure of a retailers' financial performance?

Sources: Walmart Annual Report, 2012; Tiffany & Co. Annual Report, 2012.

This case was prepared by Nancy J. Murray, University of Wisconsin–Stout, and Michael Levy, Babson College.

CASE 16 | The Chocolate Shop

The Chocolate Shop (CS) is a specialty chocolate shop that retails delicious chocolate morsels. It is owned by Susie and has been in business for three years. At the beginning of January 2016, the shop moved its location to a small, quaint building in St. Jacob's that it shares with two other boutiques of complementary items. It does not produce any chocolate but instead buys from a local supplier.

Sales

CS sells to retail customers; recently, the shop has expanded into producing small gift baskets to sell to local businesses (B2B) for customer appreciation gifts. This B2B has grown to 30 percent of the shop's 2016 sales, and CS offers these clients net 30 days. The other 70 percent of the 2016 business was from retail. Only 30 percent of retail pays cash and the other 70 percent pays by credit card, which costs CS 3 percent of these sales. This will continue in 2017. Susie puts her credit card fees with other expenses (miscellaneous) when comparing to the SME reports.

In 2016, the shop's sales were projected to be $425 000 with the following seasonality patterns for the two segments of the business:

2016	Retail	B2B
January	3%	1%
February	21%	5%
March	16%	2%
April	9%	5%
May	2%	1%
June	4%	0%
July	4%	0%
August	4%	0%
September	2%	2%
October (est.)	12%	4%
November (est.)	8%	20%
December (est.)	15%	60%
Total	**100%**	**100%**

Susie is projecting that 2017 retail sales will rise by 2 percent as bus tours are expected to increase as the economy picks up. The B2B sales portion is projected to rise 5 percent as she continues to expand her sales through networking. Giving out samples at the October Chamber After Five was a great promotional tool for her this year. She believes the seasonality breakdown for the two segments will remain constant.

In 2018, Susie is projecting the same increases in the yearly sales again (2 percent for retail and 5 percent in B2B over 2017 sales).

Cost of Sales (Direct Costs)

Susie has developed a wonderful working relationship with her one supplier, Ascot Chocolates, which makes a full range of chocolate products. Turnaround is quick. She places orders, receives them, and pays COD one month in advance of the sales. She calculates that her cost of sales for her chocolate is 60 percent. She gets her packaging and wrapping material for 2 percent of her total revenue as she uses it (same month as sale). Again, she pays COD. That's all she considers to be direct expenses.

Advertising

Susie uses various methods of advertising but finds word of mouth is most reliable for her B2B segment. She does hire a window painter/decorator to merchandise her front window displays in January, March, May, September, and November. Each time it costs $200. Those same months, she prints brochures at a cost of $300 each time. In addition, she donates samples to the Chamber of Commerce and gift packages to various charities to a total of $1800 per year. She figures that occurs evenly throughout the year. She has a static website basically showing her location and product list. It was set up last year, and she estimates she will spend $300 in April 2017 to update it slightly. In July 2017, she intends to get a vehicle wrap done. It will cost her $2000, and she will write this off as an advertising expense.

There is an advertising fund for St. Jacob's stores that gives them additional mentions and ads in community advertising. She pays $4000 a year for her share. It is paid in March each year.

Memberships

Susie belongs to the local Chamber of Commerce and some of its subcommittees and spends $360 per year payable in July each year. Plus, she finds her $600 membership in the Boutique Retail Association of Canada, payable in September each year, well worth the cost.

Professional Fees

Susie's total lawyer and accountant fees for the year are about $3200. She pays this in equal payments in January, April, July, and October.

Salaries for Employees

Susie works in the business during busy times but she is also the main sales and delivery person to the business accounts. She also does the purchasing, and the bookkeeping for the business. It is usually 60+ hours per week. She is single with no dependents. She withdraws $1250 per month and has set up no benefits for herself.

Her long-time friend and one full-time employee earns $15 per hour and works 160 hours per month. In addition, Susie has payroll expenses and some benefits she pays to her, adding up to an additional 25 percent per month.

She hires part-time worker(s) January to April and October to December. She pays them an average of $11 per hour, and they work assigned shifts amounting to another 120 hours per month. Their payroll expenses are an additional 18 percent of the wages.

Lease and Location Expenses

In January 2016, Susie opened the new location with a five-year lease. When she moved in, she made a deal with the landlord to make leasehold improvements. Her share was $6000 in leasehold improvements that she is depreciating over the entire length of the lease.

Her rent is $30 per square foot for her 1200 square feet of retail space. In addition, she pays an additional $2 per square foot (on her 1200) for common area maintenance (CAM). CAM covers a common lunchroom, washrooms, two parking spots, signage, and all interior and exterior maintenance. Her only location costs are minor maintenance and cleaning costs of approximately $250 per month.

Delivery Expenses

Susie has decided to bring her van into the business as of January 2017. It is an older white cargo van valued at $13 000. She estimates it will have a salvage value of $1000 in four years. There will be no cash transaction. She is going to put all vehicle maintenance and operating costs in a delivery account. She figures that will amount to $300 per month plus an extra $250 in December as that is her busy month for deliveries to businesses.

Other Monthly Expenses

Other monthly cash expenses for 2017 are estimated to be as follows:

Bank charges	$40
Utilities	$150
Telephone/Internet	$250
Insurance (content)	$100
Other/miscellaneous	$3000

Financing Arrangements

Susie has a good working relationship with her local bank. She has a secured line of credit against her house with a $100 000 limit on it. She pays 3.5 percent interest on it anytime she uses it. For this forecasting, she assumes she pays the full month's interest on the borrowed amount from the previous month. She also assumes she pays back everything in the next month and again borrows anything she needs. She realizes this is slightly overestimating the interest, but finds it is the best way to track the interest and be conservative.

However, her house is for sale, meaning she will lose her secured line of credit, probably sometime in the summer of 2017. She may have cash reserves, or it might be tied up in legalities. She isn't planning to buy another house in the near future. For now, she is going to continue with her forecasting but this is troubling.

Her family has promised her a loan of $30 000 on January 1, 2017, to help with inventory expenses for Valentine's Day. They are charging her only 2.5 percent on any remaining principal. She has agreed to pay them $5000 principal and the yearly interest amount each December starting December 2017.

Depreciation (or Amortization)

Susie uses straight line depreciation for all her long-term assets. Anything associated with the building will be depreciated over the term of the lease.

Her store fixtures, cash register, etc. had an original value of $24 000 when she moved in January 2016 and were to be depreciated over six years; 2017 is their third year of usage. In addition, her computer equipment that she bought in January 2016 is worth $2000, and it should be depreciated over two years as she does like to keep up to date. She had no other depreciable items.

Balance Sheet Details

As of December 31, 2016, the shop's balance sheet included the following items:

- Cash on hand: $4000 (she likes to always keep a minimum monthly balance of $4000)
- Inventory on hand: $15 000
- Accounts receivable: $52 222 (will collect all of it in January 2017)
- Line of credit payable: $20 922
- Ending owner's equity: $72 100

Susie realizes it is important to have robust spreadsheets to help her with analysis and planning. She is looking to you to create this financial model and also use them to make sound recommendations to improve her business.

Discussion Questions

1. Prepare the following:
   a. Financial notes sheet(s) for all inputs and financial explanations used
   b. Monthly cash flow forecast for the year of 2017.
   c. Pro forma income statement for the year of 2017. It must compare the percentage of sales to the SME benchmarking for "confectionery and nut stores" for the whole industry of incorporated businesses in Canada in 2017.
   d. Pro forma balance sheet as at December 31, 2017, compared to the December 31, 2016, statement (on same sheet, side by side).

2. Susie is concerned with her cash flow management. Examine her current practices for collection of monies—what is it costing her and what would be some alternatives to consider. Then in your recommendations, state what you think she should do and back it up with the potential savings/cash flow Susie could expect.

3. Flowing from the analysis, prepare three justified recommendations for Susie to improve her business in 2017. (Justified means you have done the analysis and can now recommend specific actions backed up by estimates and figures.)

This case was written by Barbara Rice, Professor at Conestoga College.

CASE 17 | Walmart: Pioneer in Supply Chain Management

Walmart dominates the retailing industry in terms of its sales revenue, its customer base, and its ability to drive down costs and deliver good value to its customers. After all, the world's largest corporation takes pride in having received numerous accolades for its ability to continuously improve efficiency in the supply chain while meeting its corporate mandate of offering customers everyday low prices.

Tight inventory management is legendary at Walmart through its just-in-time techniques that allow the firm to boast one of the best supply chains in the world. Walmart has not only transformed its own supply chain, but also influenced how vendors throughout the world operate because the company has the economic clout to request changes from its vendor partners and to receive them. Recognized for its ability to obtain merchandise from global sources, Walmart also pioneered the strategy of achieving high levels of growth and profitability through its precision control of manufacturing, inventory, and distribution. Although the company is not unique in this regard, it is by far the most successful and most influential corporation of its kind and has put into practice various innovative techniques.

And when Walmart does something, it does it on a massive scale. Walmart's computer system, for example, is second only to that of the Pentagon in storage capacity. Its information systems analyze more than 10 million daily transactions from point-of-sale data and distribute their analysis in real time both internally to its managers and externally via a satellite network to Walmart's many suppliers, who use the information for their production planning and order shipment.

Much of the popularity of supply chain management has been attributed to the success of Walmart's partnership with Procter & Gamble. During the 1980s, the two collaborated in building one of the first collaborative planning, forecasting, and replenishment (CPFR) systems, a software system that linked P&G to Walmart's distribution centres, taking advantage of advances in the world's telecommunications infrastructure. When a Walmart store sold a particular P&G item, the information flowed directly to P&G's planning and control systems. When the inventory level of P&G's products at Walmart's distribution centre got to the point where it needed to reorder, the system automatically alerted P&G to ship more products. This information helped P&G plan its production. Walmart was also able to track when a P&G shipment arrived at one of its distribution warehouses, which enabled it to coordinate its own outbound shipments to stores. Both Walmart and P&G realized savings from the better inventory management and order processing, savings that in turn were passed on to Walmart's consumers through its everyday low prices.

A history of success doesn't mean Walmart executives can rest. Changes in social values, economic fluctuations, technology advances, and other marketplace factors demand that Walmart continue its search for innovative ways to keep consumer prices down.

Walmart's Innovations

Walmart has pioneered many innovations in the purchase and distribution processes of the products it sells. More than 20 years ago, Walmart drove the adoption of UPC bar codes throughout the retail industry; it also pioneered the use of electronic data interchange (EDI) for computerized ordering from vendors. Its hub-and-spoke distribution network ensures goods are brought to distribution centres around the country and then directed outward to thousands of stores, each of which is within a day's travel. Through the use of cross-docking, one of its best-known innovations, half the goods trucked to a distribution centre from suppliers ship to stores within 24 hours. The other half, called "pull stock" is stored at the distribution centre until needed at stores. In addition, Walmart uses a dedicated fleet of trucks to ship goods from warehouses to stores in less than 48 hours, as well as to replenish store inventories about twice a week. Thus, with flow-through logistics, the company speeds the movement of goods from its distribution centres to its retail stores around the world.

Today, the retail giant continues to push the supply chain toward greater and greater efficiency, prioritizing customer needs while employing new technologies and greener practices. One of the early adopters of RFID technology to increase efficiency in its supply chain, Walmart discovered the value of balancing vision with technology maturity levels after mandating that its suppliers apply RFID tags to crates and pallets bound for its stores. Some companies thrived using the new technology. Others, including Walmart itself, ran into trouble. At the time of the mandate, RFID technology was in its infancy, and costs for planning, hardware, software, and training were prohibitive for many suppliers. Additionally the technology was new enough that the industry lacked best practices for implementation. Indeed, it lacked any examples that might help newcomers avoid pitfalls. Walmart repealed its edict, but continues to probe the usefulness of the technology. Today, Walmart is slowly testing the usefulness of RFID tags with apparel.

In response to criticism from consumer groups, Walmart tackled environmental sustainability in its supply chain and, as is frequently the case because of the company's size, became a trendsetter for other retailers. After vowing to reduce its greenhouse gas emissions by the equivalent of taking nearly 4 million cars off the roads for a year, Walmart directed its suppliers to think green throughout the full product lifecycle. Suppliers are required to pay for sustainability efforts—a price most accept willingly to retain their relationship with Walmart. Many also recognize that reducing energy use will benefit them as energy costs rise. Harnessing energy, increasing recycling, reducing waste, and minimizing packaging and transportation all reduce cost in the supply chain in addition to appealing to today's eco-conscious consumers and preserving global resources.

In a third innovation, Walmart is consolidating its global sourcing. The new model focuses on increasing the percentage of products purchased directly from suppliers and buying from global merchandising centres rather than through individual countries. Third-party procurement providers, who previously enjoyed a substantial business from the retail giant, will find themselves increasingly bypassed in the supply chain. In addition to eliminating the cost of a middle party, this effort may give Walmart increased control over inbound freight. Better control, in turn, can lower inventory costs. Thus, Walmart's continuous use of innovations leads to lower inventory and operating costs, which enables Walmart to keep its lean costs.

Following the fire in a Bangladesh factory that supplied clothing to Walmart in November of 2012 that killed 112 workers, Walmart has further tightened its control over its supply chain. The clothing being made and supplied to Walmart in this factory was done without Walmart's knowledge; it was an unapproved subcontract by one of its vendors. As a result, Walmart has moved to a "zero tolerance" policy on suppliers subcontracting without Walmart's knowledge and approval.

Finally, responding to growing criticism that Walmart purchases too many products from foreign countries and does not do enough to support the American economy, it has announced a new initiative to hire 100 000 veterans and source more products from the United States. As of March 1, 2013, any honourably discharged veteran who applies for a job with Walmart will be given one. The plan is to reach its goal of 100 000 veteran hires in five years. Additionally, over the next 10 years, Walmart plans to purchase an additional $50 billion in US-made goods, increasing its already large share of US-made products. Currently, approximately 55 percent of Walmart's US sales come from items such as groceries, health and beauty products, household goods, and pet supplies, most of which are sourced in the United States.

Walmart continues to hone its management of the flow of products and information among its suppliers, distribution centres, and individual stores through technology to increase its control of logistics and inventory. Thoughtful use of innovation has put Walmart at the top of the retailing game. Not all organizations can pull this approach off as well. Walmart is a unique case in which a single, very powerful firm took primary responsibility for improving performance across its own supply chain. By developing a superior supply chain management system, it has reaped the rewards of higher levels of customer service and satisfaction, lower production and transportation costs, and more productive use of its retail store space. Fundamentally, it boils down to Walmart's ability to link together suppliers, distribution centres, retail outlets, and, ultimately, customers, regardless of their location. Although operational innovation isn't the only ingredient in Walmart's success, it has been a crucial building block for its strong competitive position.

Discussion Questions

1. How does an individual firm like Walmart manage a supply chain, particularly considering that supply chains include multiple firms with potentially conflicting objectives? Describe some of the conflicts that could arise in such a circumstance.

2. What are some of the ways that Walmart's supply chain management system has provided it the benefits of higher levels of product availability and lower merchandise acquisition and transportation costs? Provide specific examples of each benefit.

Sources: Mike Troy, "Wal-Mart's Inventory Equation," *Retailing Today*, September 11, 2006; "Financial Outlook: Restoring the Productivity Loop," *Retailing Today*, June 26, 2006; Sharon Gaudin, "Some Suppliers Gain From Failed Wal-Mart RFID Edict," *Computer World*, April 28, 2008; "RFID News: JC Penney CEO Says Retailer Going All in on RFID, Perhaps with Significant Impact on the Industry," *Supply Chain Digest,* August 15, 2012: William B. Cassidy, "Wal-Mart Tightens the Chain," *Journal of Commerce*, January 18, 2010; "Wal-Mart Tightens Rules for Suppliers," *CBC News*, January 22, 2013; "Walmart Announces $50 Billion Buy American Campaign," *Huffington Post*, January 15, 2013.

This case was written by Jeanne L. Munger, University of Southern Maine; Kate Woodworth; and Dhruv Grewal, Michael Levy, and Scott Motyka, all of Babson College.

CASE 18 | Lindy's Bridal Shoppe: Assortments

Located in Lake City (population 80 000), Lindy's Bridal Shoppe, a small bridal store, sells bridal gowns, prom gowns, accessories, and silk flowers. It also rents men's formal wear and performs various alteration services. Lindy Armstrong, age 33, has owned the store since its founding in March

2000. She is married to a high school teacher and is the mother of three young children. A former nurse, she found the demands of hospital schedules left too little time for her young family. An energetic, active woman with many interests, she wanted to continue to work but also have time with her children.

The silk flowers market enabled Lindy to combine an in-home career with child-rearing. She started Lindy's Silk Flowers with $75 of flower inventory in Vernon, a small town of about 10 000 people ten kilometres from Lake City. Working out of her home, she depended on word-of-mouth communication among her customers, mainly brides, to bring in business. As Lindy's Silk Flowers prospered, a room was added onto the house to provide more space for the business. Lindy was still making all the flowers herself.

Her flower-making schedule kept her extremely busy. Long hours were the norm. Lindy was approached by a young photographer named Dan Morgan, who proposed establishing a one-stop bridal shop. In this new business, Dan would provide photography, Lindy would provide silk flowers, and another partner, Karen Ross (who had expertise in the bridal market), would provide gowns and accessories. The new store would be located in Vernon in a rented structure. Shortly before the store was to open, Dan and Karen decided not to become partners and Lindy became the sole owner. She knew nothing about the bridal business. Having no merchandise or equipment, Lindy was drawn to an ad announcing that a bridal store in a major city was going out of business.

She immediately called and arranged to meet the owner. Subsequently, she bought all his stock (mannequins, racks, and carpet) for $4000. The owner also gave her a crash course in the bridal business. From March 2000 to December 2009, Lindy owned and operated a bridal gown and silk flowers store named Lindy's Bridal Shoppe in Vernon. The location was chosen primarily because it was close to her home. Although Vernon is a very small town, Lindy felt that location wasn't a critical factor in her store's success. She maintained that people would travel some distance to make a purchase as important as a bridal gown. Rent was $250 per month plus utilities. Parking was a problem.

During this period, Lindy's Bridal Shoppe grew. Bridal gowns and accessories as well as prom dresses sold well. As the time approached for Lindy to renew her lease, she wondered about the importance of location. A move to Lake City might be advisable. A much larger town than Vernon, Lake City is the site of a university. Lindy decided to move.

General Business Description

The majority of Lindy's Bridal Shoppe's current sales are made to individuals who order bridal gowns off the rack or from the catalogues of three major suppliers. At the time of the order, the customer pays a deposit, usually half of the purchase price. The balance is due in 30 days. Lindy would like payment in full at the time of ordering regardless of the delivery date. But payment is often delayed until delivery. Once ordered, a gown must be taken and the bill paid when delivered.

No tuxedos are carried in the store, so customers must order from catalogues. Fitting jackets and shoes are provided to help patrons size their purchases. Lindy's Bridal Shoppe rents its men's formal wear from suppliers. Payment from the customer is due on delivery. Certain times of the year see more formal events than others. Many school proms are held during late April and May, and June, July, and August are big months for weddings.

Since traditional dates for weddings are followed less and less closely, Lindy believes that the business is becoming less seasonal, though January and February are quite slow.

Promotion Practices

Lindy's Bridal Shoppe engages in various promotional activities but is constrained by her limited finances. The firm has no operating budget, which prevents any formal appropriation for advertising expenses. Newspaper ads constitute the primary promotional medium, though radio is occasionally used. Ads for prom dresses are run only during prom season. These ads usually feature a photograph of a local high school student in a Lindy's Bridal Shoppe gown plus a brief description of the student's activities.

Other promotional activities include bridal shows at a local mall. Lindy feels these have been very successful, though they are a lot of work. A recent prom show in a local high school used students as models. This proved to be an excellent way to stimulate sales. Lindy hopes to go into several other area high schools during the next prom season, though this will demand much planning.

Personnel

Lindy, the sole owner and also the manager of the firm, finds it hard to maintain a capable workforce. As a small company, Lindy's Bridal Shoppe can't offer premium salaries for its few positions. There is one full-time salesperson. The part-time staff includes a salesperson, alterations person, bookkeeper, and custodian. Lindy handles all the paperwork. Her responsibilities include paying bills, ordering merchandise and supplies, hiring and firing personnel, fitting customers, and selling various items. She makes all the major decisions that directly affect the firm's operations. She also makes all the silk flowers herself. It's time-consuming, but she isn't satisfied with how anyone else makes them.

Merchandise Offerings

Lindy's Bridal Shoppe's major product lines are new wedding, prom, and party gowns. No used gowns are sold. Discontinued styles or gowns that have been on the rack for a year are sold at reduced prices, primarily because discoloration is a major problem. Gowns tend to yellow after hanging on the racks for a year. A wide variety of accessories are provided. Lindy believes it's important that her customers not have to go anywhere else for them. These accessories include shoes, veils, headpieces, jewellery, and foundations. Slips may be rented instead of purchased. One room of Lindy's Bridal Shoppe is used only to prepare silk flowers.

Service Offerings

Lindy's Bridal Shoppe's major service offering is fitting and alteration. Most gowns must be altered, for which there is a nominal charge. Lindy feels that personal attention and personal service set her apart from her competitors. Emphasizing customer satisfaction, she works hard to please each customer. This isn't always easy. Customers can be picky, and it takes time to deal with unhappy people.

Location

Lindy's Bridal Shoppe is located at the end of Lake City's main through street. Initially, Lindy didn't think location was important to her bridal store's success, but she has changed her mind. Whereas business was good in Vernon, it's booming in Lake City. Vehicular traffic is high, and there is adequate, if not excess, parking. Lindy's Bridal Shoppe has a 12-year lease. Rent ($1800 per month) includes heat and water, but Lindy's Bridal Shoppe must pay for interior decoration. The physical facility is generally attractive, with open and inviting interior display areas. But some areas both inside and outside the store have an unfinished look.

Some storage areas require doors or screens to enhance the interior's appearance. The fitting room ceilings are unfinished, and the carpeting inside the front door may be unsafe. One other interior problem is insufficient space. There seems to be inadequate space for supporting activities such as flower preparation, customer fittings, and merchandise storage, which gives the store a cluttered look.

Several external problems exist. The signs are ineffective, and there is a strong glare on the front windows. This detracts from the effectiveness of the overall appearance and interior window displays. The parking lot needs minor maintenance. Parking lines should be painted and curbs must be repaired. Much should be done to add colour and atmosphere through basic landscaping.

Competition

Lindy's Bridal Shoppe is the only bridal shop in Lake City. Lindy believes she has four main competitors: Whitney's Bridal Shoppe is five kilometres from Lake City; Ender's Brides, a new shop with a good operation, is in Spartan City, 80 kilometres away; Carole's is a large, established bridal shop in Smithtown, 110 kilometres distant; and Gowns-n-Such is in Andersonville, 120 kilometres away. A new store in Yorktown (25 km away) is selling used gowns and discontinued styles at reduced prices. Lindy watches this new- and used-gown store closely.

Some of her potential customers are buying wedding gowns from electronic retailers such as The Knot (http://www.theknot.com) and the Wedding Channel (http://www.weddingchannel.com). Although these electronic retailers are not making significant sales in her trading area now, Lindy is concerned that some of the services offered by these electronic retailers (such as gift registries, email notices, wedding planning, and wedding picture displays) will attract her customers.

Financial Considerations

Basic financial information includes the following:

1. Markup: 50 percent
2. 2016 sales: $200 000 (estimated)
3. Average inventory: $70 000
4. Turnover: 3.0 (approximately)
5. Annual expenses are as follows:

Rent:	$19 200
Labour:	$24 000
Utilities:	$7 000
Supplies:	$12 000
Equipment:	$4 000
Miscellaneous:	$4 000

6. Estimated total costs ($200 000 sales): $170 200
7. Implied profit including owner's salary: $29 800
8. Capital invested (equipment, $8000; inventory, $70 000): $78 000
9. ROI: $5800/$78 000 = 7.4 percent (assume owner salary of $24 000 per year)

The Future

Lindy Armstrong is uncertain about the future. She enjoys the business, but feels that she's working very hard and not making much money. During all the years of Lindy's Bridal Shoppe's operation, she hasn't taken a salary. She works 60 hours or more a week. Business is excellent and growing, but she is tired. She has even discussed selling the business and returning to nursing.

Discussion Questions

1. Could Lindy change the emphasis of her merchandise mix to increase her sales?
2. Which products should have more emphasis? Which should have less?
3. What personnel decisions must Lindy face to improve her business?
4. How could someone like Lindy Armstrong balance the demands of her family and her business?
5. If one of Lindy's competitors were to offer her $150 000 for her business, should she sell?

Source: This case was prepared by Linda F. Felicetti and Joseph P. Grunewald, Clarion University of Pennsylvania.

CASE 19 | Merchandise Strategy: Process for Success

Tom has just started his new job as vice president of merchandise. He knows that the categories he is now responsible for have been declining in performance for several years and he has been hired to turn those categories around. Tom recognizes immediately that to accomplish this turnaround, he and his new team need to develop a sound merchandise strategy. Tom calls in his merchandising team, consisting of several groups, each representing a different category and composed of buyers, assistant buyers, and planners. He lays out a process to have each group gather valuable information on the categories for which it is responsible to be used in the creation of an overall merchandise strategy. Each group will gather information on customers, pricing, and products and evaluate the information to identify growth areas for their category. But first Tom requires each product category team group to develop a mission statement reflecting how the team will approach their business going forward.

Tom requests each category group, upon completion of their merchandise strategy, to prepare a brief presentation that expresses and supports their merchandise strategy, as well as their recommendations regarding areas for future growth. The presentations will be reviewed by Tom, the general merchandise manager, and the president. Each merchandise strategy presentation will include details regarding the following material as they relate to the groups' product category and should be arranged in the following order.

Mission Statement

The mission statement is designed to include the guiding principles of the group and would include the following:

- **Need:** Why does the company need this product category?
- **Integration with corporate:** How does this category further the corporate mission?

- **Objectives:** What are the short- and long-term goals for this category?
- **Strategy:** What will the group do to achieve all the above?

Customer Profile

The customer profile identifies the target consumer to drive merchandise decisions for the product category and would include the following:

- Customer demographics (e.g., age, sex, race, income)
- Customer spending and shopping habits (e.g., regular price vs. sale price, weekend vs. weekday)
- Customer product fashion dimension (e.g., fashion vs. basic)
- Customer quality preference dimension (e.g., low quality vs. high quality)
- Customer value dimension (e.g., low importance vs. high importance)
- Key volume price point triggers by product category (e.g., polo shirt @ $19.99)

Product Guidelines

The product guidelines define characteristics that best suit the target consumer for the product category and would be based on the following information:

- **Style:** Look, feel, colour, shape, fashion direction (forward or laggard)
- **Sourcing:** Domestic, international, branded, private label, co-brand, designer
- **Quality:** Standards, material use, workmanship
- **Price:** Opening price points, mid-range price points, and high-end price points
- **Assortment:** Breadth versus depth of product assortment in the category

Pricing Strategy

The pricing strategy defines the price range of key product lines in the category in relation to the competition and helps define product sourcing and product hierarchy decisions. Pricing strategy should also reduce intra-company competition. Pricing strategy addresses internal and external competition and includes the following:

- **Assortment:** Product pricing by category to address internal competition
- **Competition:** Product pricing by category to address external competition

Recommended Growth Strategy

Opportunities for future growth are determined by the group and should be fully supported by the information the group compiled. The growth strategy includes the following:

- category and sub-category development
- new or expanded assortments
- reduced or eliminated products, categories, or sub-categories

Student Instructions

Each group should begin by selecting a retailer. The group should profile the retailer, its place in the industry, its position on merchandise assortments, and its positioning against its competition. Information at the corporate level that can be gathered that relates to the merchandise strategy (e.g., mission statement) should be included in the presentation. Bearing in mind the retailer selected, each team should select a product category or sub-category to be the focus of the merchandise strategy. For example:

- **Retailer:** Hudson's Bay
- **Product category:** Men's sportswear
- **Product sub-category:** Men's woven sport shirts

This selection scheme can be developed for any type of retailer. The goal is to select a category that is big enough but not so large as to require multiple strategies. (For example, menswear would require multiple strategies.) It may be best to review your selection with your instructor. Throughout the merchandise strategy process, you may need to use public industry data to fill in for information you will not be able to gather from the retailer directly. This may include store trips and online searches.

It is recommended that an initial meeting be held by the group to develop the mission statement. The mission statement sets the direction of the group in the process of gathering the appropriate information and analyzing the product, customer, pricing, and areas of growth.

When all the information is gathered, each group should again meet to develop the recommended growth strategy based on the mission statement and the data assembled from all group members. Next, each group should develop a brief PowerPoint-style presentation detailing their findings regarding mission statement, customer profile, product guidelines, pricing strategy, and recommended growth strategy. Each presentation should be structured in this order and address, at a minimum, each of the points outlined

for each topic. Group members can use the notes section for each slide to detail the information they gathered, how it was obtained, and how they came to their conclusions. If information is obtained from published materials, proper citation should be given.

Discussion Questions

1. Which of the main components of a merchandise strategy are most valuable? Why?

2. Why is a mission statement so important to a merchandise strategy?

3. Does every merchant team have a merchandise strategy? Why or why not?

Source: This case was written by Robert P. Jones, University of Tennessee, and Michael Levy, Babson College.

CASE 20   Hughes: Developing a Buying Plan

In this hypothetical case, a well-established, medium-sized Canadian department store, Hughes, reflects consumers' needs by featuring popular names in fashion for the individual consumer, family, and home. It tries to offer a distinctive, wide assortment of quality merchandise with personalized customer service. The many customer services include personal shoppers; credit with in-house charge, MasterCard, and Visa; and an interior design studio. Hughes' pricing policy permits it to draw customers from several income brackets. Moderate-income consumers seeking value and fashion-predictable soft goods are target customers, as are upscale customers with a special interest in fashion.

The department store is implementing new marketing strategies to prepare for continuing growth and expansion. Hughes' merchandising philosophy is to attract the discerning middle-market customer who comprises 70 percent of the population as well as sophisticated fashion-conscious consumers who expect to buy high-quality, brand-name merchandise at competitive prices.

One portion of Hughes' buying staff is responsible for the Oriental rug department within home furnishings. The open-to-buy figure for this classification within the home furnishings division will be based on last year's sales history (Exhibit 1).

Exhibit 1
Last Year's Fall/Winter Sales Results for Oriental Rugs

Sales volume: Markup:	$120 000 51.5%			
	Size	Percentage of Sales	Fabrication	Percentage of Sales
	3′ × 5′	20%	Silk	15%
	4′ × 6′	40	Cotton	25
	6′ × 9′	15	Wool	60
	8′ × 10′	10		
	9′ × 12′	15		

Exhibit 2
Ghuman's Wholesale Price List

	FABRICATION		
Size	Silk	Wool	Cotton
3' × 5'	$ 400	$ 250	—
4' × 6'	700	500	$200
6' × 9'	850	700	275
8' × 10'	1200	1000	350
9' × 12'	1400	1300	500

Colours: Background colours available are navy, burgundy, black, and cream.

Quantities required for purchase: No minimum orders required.

Payment plan: Payment can be made in Canadian dollars or Indian rupees. Letter of credit needs to be established prior to market trip.

Delivery: Air freight—10 to 14 days, delivery time; cost is usually 25 percent of total order.

Ocean freight: 39 days plus inland time is necessary; cost is usually 8–10 percent of total order.

Customer loyalty: Loyalty to customers is exceptional. Damaged shipments can be returned. Ghuman's philosophy is to help the retailers obtain a profit on their product lines.

It has been projected that a 15 percent increase over last year's sales volume can be attained due to oriental rugs' continued popularity. This year's open-to-buy for fall/winter will be $66 200. The buying staff will be making its purchases for fall/winter in Amritsar, India, a city known for top-quality carpets. Ghuman Export Private, Ltd., of Amritsar, Punjab, India, is the manufacturer the buyers will contact.

Exhibit 2 shows information about Ghuman to use in the decision-making process.

Discussion Question

1. Work up a buying plan to use when buying from Ghuman. Decide how to distribute the allotted open-to-buy dollars among the available sizes, colours, and fabrications. Since it's an overseas manufacturer, consider additional costs such as duty and shipping, which also need to be covered by the allocated open- to-buy dollars.

Source: This case was prepared by Professor Ann Fairhurst, Indiana University.

CASE 21 Capital Sportswear: Buying

"We need to have vendors who can take this burden off of us," said Ken Joynes, Capital Sportswear inventory manager. "We have had a sales increase of 20 percent over the last two years and my people can't keep up with it anymore."

In this hypothetical case, Keith Wilson, general manager of Capital Sportswear, reviewed the colourful chart showing the sales trend and replied, "I never thought I would have to complain about a sales increase, but it is obvious that the sales are well beyond our control. Something has to be done and that is why we are meeting today."

Capital Sportswear was founded by George Wilson in 1963 in a major metropolitan area. For years, Capital Sportswear has been successful in the sportswear market. In 2000, George Wilson retired, and his son, Keith Wilson, was appointed general manager. From the beginning, Keith Wilson has been a real go-getter. Recently completing his MBA, he has wasted no time in locating new markets for Capital Sportswear. He immediately contacted major universities and colleges and gained four-year

exclusive contracts for apparel purchases made by the sports teams of their athletic departments.

Soon after, Capital's sportswear became popular among students. This growing demand for the company's products motivated Wilson to open two more retail stores. During the fall of 2013, sales had increased beyond expectations. Although the company achieved a successful reputation in the marketplace, sales growth has generated major problems.

In the beginning, operations were fairly smooth and the company's inventory control department updated most of its procedures. Joynes emphasized the crucial role of routinization in the overall inventory maintenance process to keep up with the increasing turnover. The sales increase was 20 percent, as opposed to the 12 percent that had been forecasted for 2014. It was this increase that initiated a series of problems in the inventory control department. To temporarily alleviate the backlog, Wilson authorized Joynes to lease an additional warehouse (see the replenishment level for July 2013

Exhibit 1

Sales for Capital Sportswear in 2013

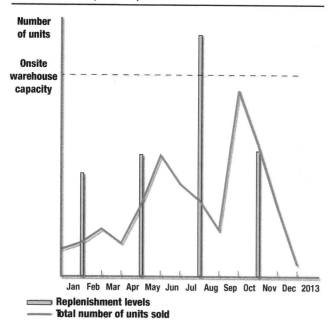

- ▭ Replenishment levels
- ── Total number of units sold

in Exhibit 1). It was decided that a maximum of 16 percent of the total inventory carrying costs was going to be dedicated to the off-premise inventory.

Worrying about not being able to meet demand on time, Joynes met with suppliers and asked them to provide more timely delivery schedules to Capital Sportswear. When he stated that the company was not going to tolerate any reasons for future delays, two major suppliers expressed their concerns about his lack of flexibility and requested price concessions. They simply indicated that Joynes's demand had to be supported by providing cash or reducing quantity discounts. Joynes ignored these comments and indicated how serious he really was by stating that Capital Sportswear could always find new suppliers.

By the end of a long discussion, arguments were beyond the manageable point and the two large suppliers decided to quit dealing with the company. After the meeting, Joynes received a memo from Wilson. Wilson was very concerned about the potential reactions of the rest of the vendors. He stated in his memo that since Capital Sportswear was continuously growing, it was expected to present a more supportive attitude to its suppliers. He expressed his belief that the company needed a cohesive atmosphere with the rest of the channel members, especially with its vendors.

During the next six months, Joynes had limited success in locating one or more large suppliers that would be able to deliver the products to Capital

Sportswear on a timely basis. Faced with growing demand from the surrounding colleges and universities, he had to accumulate excess stock to avoid possible shortages. At the end of the six-month period, a memo from the accounting department of the company indicated the financial significance of the problem. In his memo, accounting manager Roger Boles simply addressed the high costs of inventory maintenance/security functions (for details, see Exhibit 2). He advised finding a substitute inventory policy to lower these cost figures.

Specifically, he stated that the rental cost for the additional warehouse had levelled off at 16 percent, well beyond the maximum. Keith Wilson immediately scheduled a meeting and asked the top managers to come up with the alternative plans to eliminate this problem. "I should have never let those

Exhibit 2

Comparative Statement of Profit and Loss for Years Ended December 31

	2014 (forecast)	2013	2012
Net sales	$165 000	$120 000	$100 000
Cost of sales			
Beginning inventory	7 000	6 000	4 000
Purchases(net)	140 000	92 000	62 000
	147 000	98 000	66 000
Ending inventory	9 000	7 000	6 000
	138 000	91 000	61 000
Gross profit	27 000	29 000	39 000
Expenses			
Stock maintenance	7 500	5 250	750
Rent	2 500	1 250	250
Insurance	4 500	3 500	500
Interest	4 500	2 500	1 000
Selling	3 500	2 500	2 000
Promotion	7 500	5 500	4 000
Supplies	2 750	1 500	250
Miscellaneous	2 250	1 500	250
	35 000	23 500	10 000
Net profit from operations	(8 000)	5 500	29 000
Other income			
Dividends	925	750	450
Interest	825	600	350
Miscellaneous	650	400	200
	2 400	1 750	1 000
Net profit before taxes	(5 600)	7 250	130 000
Provision for income taxes	1 008	1 305	8 100
Net profit after taxes	(4 592)	5 945	21 900

suppliers quit," said Joynes. "It had a negative effect on our image, and now we all see the results."

"It's too late to worry about that," admonished Wilson. "Instead, we have to come up with a strategy to meet the demand effectively without increasing our costs to the detriment of profits. You realize that the university contracts will expire at the end of the year."

"That's the crucial fact," said Boles. "We simply cannot afford to stock up beyond the current level; it is just too expensive. It is well beyond the funds we have had even from the increased sales."

"In other words, the elimination of the excess inventory is necessary. Who are the vendors that we have at the moment?" asked Wilson.

"There are only three suppliers remaining after the last meeting," replied Joynes. "They are fairly small businesses, but we've been dealing with them for quite some time. They have been successful in keeping up with us, and the details of their operations are summarized in their report."

"It seems like we have a good selection here," said Wilson, after looking at the report in front of him. "If they mostly work with us, we should be able to influence the future direction of their operations. In other words, it should not be difficult to convince them that they need to upgrade their deliveries in such a way that we can eliminate our excess inventory."

"That would cut down the rental costs that we incur from the additional warehouse," said Boles.

"Obviously!" Wilson replied impatiently. "We will probably need to provide those vendors with a comprehensive support program. If we can convert the floor space of the warehouse from storage to sales, we will have additional funds in retail operations. We can invest a portion of these funds in supporting our vendors and improve our image by forming a cohesive network with them. Of course, there will be a limit to this support. After all, it will be expensive for us to make the transition, too. Therefore, I would like you to come up with an analysis for converting the existing system to a more efficient one. I would like to know what we can do and how we can do it. To be very honest, gentlemen, I do not want to increase the sales if we do not know how to handle that increase."

Discussion Questions

1. What is relationship management?

2. Explain how relationship management can benefit both retailer and supplier?

3. How might the use of a quick response system affect the financial performance of Capital Sportswear?

4. What problems would Wilson have implementing a quick response system with vendors?

Source: This case was prepared by S. Altan Erdem, University of Minnesota–Duluth.

CASE 22 How Much for a Good Smell? Pricing

For the past two Christmas seasons, Courtney's, an upscale gift store, has carried a sweet-smelling potpourri in a plastic bag with an attractive ribbon. Heavily scented with cloves, the mixture gives a pleasant holiday aroma to any room, including the store.

Two years ago, the mixture cost $4.50 a bag. Courtney's (the only store in town that carried it) sold 300 pieces for $9.50. Courtney's supply ran out ten days before Christmas, and it was too late to get any more.

Last year, the manufacturer raised the price to $5.00, so Courtney's raised its retail price to $9.95. Even though the markup was lower than the previous year, the store owner felt there was "magic" in the $10 price. As before, the store had a complete sellout, this time five days before Christmas. Sales last year were 600 units.

This year, the wholesale price has gone up to $5.50, and store personnel are trying to determine the correct retail price. The owner once again wants to hold the price at $10 ($9.95), but the buyer

disagrees: "It's my job to push for the highest possible markup wherever I can. This item is a sure seller, as we're still the only store around with it, and we had some unsatisfied demand last year. I think we should mark it at $12.50, which will improve the markup to 56 percent. Staying at $10 will penalize us unnecessarily, especially considering the markup would be even lower than last year. Even if we run into price resistance, we'll only have to sell 480 to maintain the same dollar volume."

The owner demurs, saying, "This scent is part of our store's ambiance. It acts as a draw to get people into the store, and its pleasant smell keeps them in a free-spending state of mind. I think we should keep the price at $9.95, despite the poorer markup. And if we can sell many more at this price, we'll realize the same dollar gross margin as last year. I think we should buy 1000. Furthermore, if people see us raising a familiar item's price 25 percent, they might wonder whether our other prices are fair."

Discussion Questions

1. What prices caused Courtney's new charges?

2. Which price would result in the highest profit?

3. What other factors should Courtney's consider?

4. What price would you charge, and how many units would you order?

Source: This case was written by Professor David Ehrlich, Marymount University.

CASE 23   Enterprise Rent-A-Car Focuses on Its People

Enterprise is the largest and most profitable car rental business (by sales $19.4 billion), and fleet (1.7 million vehicles) worldwide. There are more than 9,000 offices located conveniently where people live and work in the United States, Canada, the United Kingdom, Ireland, Germany, France, and Spain, with additional franchised business partners worldwide. More than 6,000 of these offices are in the US alone, and there are currently more than 600 locations in Canada. This includes a network of airport and neighbourhood locations. Enterprise is a $3.5 billion company in Canada, with more than 5,200 Canadian employees and a fleet that exceeds 83,000 vehicles.

When Jack Taylor started Enterprise in 1957, he adopted a unique strategy. Most car rental firms targeted business- and leisure-travel customers who arrived at an airport and needed to rent a car for local transportation. Taylor decided to target a different segment—individuals whose own cars are being repaired, who are driving on vacation, or who for some other reason simply need an extra car for a few days. The traditional car rental companies have to charge relatively high daily rates because their locations in or near airports are expensive. Although the airport locations are convenient for customers travelling by air, they are inconvenient for people seeking a replacement car while theirs is in the shop or an extra car to drive for a few days. So Enterprise locates its rental offices in downtown and suburban areas, where much of its target market lives and works. The firm provides local pickup and delivery service at no cost in most areas.

Enterprise's human resource strategy is a key to its success. The company fosters a sense of ownership among its employees. For example, its management training program starts by defining a clear career path for each management trainee. Then it teaches employees how to build their own business. Their compensation is tied directly to the financial results of the local operation. Employees from the rental branch offices often advance to the highest levels of operating management.

The firm hires college and university graduates for its management trainee positions because it feels that these graduates demonstrate intelligence and motivation. Rather than recruiting the students with the highest marks, it focuses on hiring people who were athletes or actively involved in campus social activities, or who held part-time job. Enterprise wants people who were social directors or high-ranking officers of social organizations, such as student governments and campus clubs, because they typically have the good interpersonal skills needed to effectively deal with Enterprise's varied customers.

Jack Taylor's growth strategy was based on providing high-quality, personalized service so that customers would return to Enterprise when they needed to rent a car again. One of his often-quoted sayings summarizes his philosophy: "If you take care of your customers and employees, the bottom line will take care of itself." But because operating managers were initially compensated on the basis of sales growth, not customer satisfaction, service quality declined.

The first step Enterprise took to improve customer service was to develop a customer satisfaction measure. The questionnaire, called the Enterprise Service Quality Index, was developed on the basis of input from the operating managers. Thus managers felt ownership of the measurement tool. As the index gained legitimacy, Enterprise made a big deal about it. It posted the scores for each location prominently in its monthly operating reports—right next to the net profit numbers that determined managers' pay.

The operating managers were able to track how they were doing and how all their peers were doing, because all of the locations were ranked. To increase the motivation of managers to improve the service at their location, Enterprise announced that managers could be promoted only if their customer satisfaction scores were above the company average. Then it demonstrated that it would abide by this policy by refusing to promote some star performers who had achieved good growth and profit numbers but had below-average satisfaction scores.

To provide a high level of service, new employees generally work long hours as they, like all Enterprise managers, are expected to jump in and help wherever needed. But all this hard work can pay off. Enterprise does not hire outsiders for entry-level jobs—every position is filled by promoting someone already inside the company. Thus Enterprise employees know that if they work hard and do their best, they may very well succeed in moving up the corporate ladder and earn a significant income. The results of this strategy are impressive and they include many accolades and awards for Enterprise. They ranked in the top ten of *BusinessWeek*'s first-ever list of "Customer Service Champs," and they were ranked number five by *BusinessWeek* as one of the "50 Best Places to Launch a Career."

Discussion Questions

1. What are the pros and cons of Enterprise's human resource management strategy?

2. Would you want to work for Enterprise? Why or why not?

3. How does its human resource strategy complement the quality of customer service delivered by its representatives?

Source: This case was written by Barton Weitz, University of Florida, with Canadian revisions provided by Samantha Boucher, talent acquisition specialist human resources, and updates from Enterprise websites.

CASE 24 Creating Loss Prevention Programs That Fit the Culture

Based upon yoga principles of healthy living and integrity, Lululemon's asset protection program is intended to leverage the inherent goodness in people.

"In most asset management protection programs, 90 percent of the message is usually directed at the 1 percent who would actually steal. That creates an adversarial relationship and doesn't speak to most people," explains Rich Groner, Lululemon's asset protection regional manager, east US. "At Lululemon, our asset protection program begins with the assumption that most people are smart and have integrity. That's an important distinction. People tend to respond well when treated this way."

Unlike at many retailers where asset protection involves creating additional rules and safeguards, Lululemon resisted the urge to control stores from head office or put more procedures in place. Instead, it decided to focus on encouraging "great behaviour."

"Rather than enforcing a set of controls that by definition assume people are inclined to be dishonest, we try to empower our associates to act in harmony with one another and our customers. This is accomplished through creating a culture with three core principles: gratitude, integrity, and *Asteya,* a yoga term for non-stealing," explains Groner.

Appealing to the Goodness

Fostering a sense of gratitude for what one has in life—whether it be a job, material possessions, or relationships—is important. It invigorates people and creates a happy workforce, and is the opposite of entitlement, the main cause of theft.

Integrity encourages self-control and honesty, which is far more effective in reducing shrinkage than any corporate system or procedure could ever be.

Asteya is a root principle of yoga and has been adopted by Lululemon. Yoga, after all, is not just stretching but also a mantra for a healthy way of living. *Asteya* speaks to what you restrain yourself from doing. It's not just about stealing material objects, but also what you can steal from people—respect, confidence, reputation, and so on.

"We spend 80 percent of our time speaking to associates about these principles as opposed to any other asset protection message," says Groner. "It's all about exploring the question, 'What does it mean to be a great person?' It's a unique training program designed specifically to fit the healthy living culture of our company."

Loss prevention means securing your investments and securing your future. Retailers approach this in many different ways, but one commonality is that their loss prevention programs are founded on the belief that a company's greatest assets are its associates.

Discussion Questions

1. How does Lululemon's asset management program differ from that of other retailers?

2. What is the main cause of internal theft?

3. What does the *Asteya* principle adopted by Lululemon have to do with internal theft?

Source: Excerpt from Andrew Hind, "Protecting Assets, the Bottom Line," *Canadian Retailer,* Store 2012, Volume 22, Issue 4, p. 59. Canadian Retailer, a publication of Retail Council of Canada.

There are countless Web-based resources coming to the fore that can help retailers of any size manage any or all HR functions, from recruiting, scheduling, and payroll, to workforce management and training. It's just a matter of how you apply them.

The Social Side of Recruitment and Retention

At IKEA Canada, Paul Clark, recruitment and succession manager in Burlington, Ontario, believes networking online is the way of the future. In fact, it has become a major part of his company's HR duties, including management recruiting. "The traditional way of posting jobs and advertising in newspapers is long gone," he says.

LinkedIn is a go-to resource for recruiting management and executive talent. That's a bonus for an organization that has 35 to 40 management positions in each location. "It lets you tap into a very specific talent pool and access and communicate with nonactive job seekers," Clark says.

The most talented people aren't necessarily looking for jobs, confirms Danielle Restivo, manager of corporate communications for LinkedIn Canada. That's why businesses would benefit from being more proactive. "'What retailers are looking for is the most efficient way to find the best talent, and this is a lot better than the 'post and pray' method."

Stephanie Corker, head of recruitment for Lululemon Athletica in Vancouver, says social networking at her operation may begin with recruitment, but it carries on once employees are on board. "Social media has helped us attract the right skill sets, and keep them."

The retailer leverages LinkedIn, Facebook, and Twitter to create a connected community. Each store's Facebook page, for example, is used for everything from product notification and local community news to sharing goals and showcasing employee achievements.

"People are excited to share their stories through Lululemon and hear what other employees are blogging about," Corker says. "Social media is also a great on-boarding tool for new recruits."

Time and Money

Two of the most labour-intensive functions that keep managers on-site long after the doors close for business are scheduling and payroll. Whether running an operation with a few employees or a nationwide chain, online access to automated scheduling and payroll services is growing by leaps and bounds.

Anthony Rinella, CEO of Algrin Technologies Inc., a developer of SkedX, says communication is always a big challenge for retailers when it comes to scheduling. "Vacation days get lost, availability goes missing—it all leads to employee disengagement, bad customer service, and shortages on the floor."

With online scheduling services, employees know when they are working and managers know when they can work, notes Rinella. They can get to information through a computer or mobile device, and use text or email to send out schedules and alerts electronically, post shifts to find replacements, or send notices to employees. "A retailer could easily reduce scheduling time from one to one-and-a-half hours to ten minutes a week for less than $5 per employee, per month," says Rinella.

Kerina Elliott, vice president, human resources, store operations and administration for M&M Meat Shops, has dispensed with her paper scheduling processes and is now using SkedX. "It used to take a few hours a month to arrange schedules and create all sorts of nuisance when it came to making changes with our old paper-based and call-in processes. Now it takes us half the time."

For payroll on a small scale, retailers are looking to features within mainstays such as QuickBooks to ease the time burden. "It's hard to stay on top of all the legislative changes, from TD1 forms and records of employment to amendments and T4s," says Brad Card, payroll senior product manager for Intuit Canada Ltd. "With an automated payroll system, regardless of how many employees you have, it literally takes two to three minutes to do your payroll."

"Once you get started, it's a very efficient way to do things, and it's much easier to keep information organized and in compliance with the government," agrees Maureen Burleson, president of The Montana Group, a provider of bookkeeping services to retailers and other businesses.

Subscribing to the Whole Nine Yards

On a grander scale, subscription-based online services are rapidly turning workforce management solutions into a viable option. "Regardless of whether you have 5, 50, or 500 employees, full workforce management is now affordable," says Bryan Gault, regional vice president for Payworks Canada. "You can use online services to track scheduling payroll, vacation information, training, work history, skill sets, and sick days—and to report on all that."

And the benefits to the retailer can be increased exponentially when working from a unified database through which all information can flow and populate other applications. "Whether you're looking at HR, time and attendance, or payroll, you only need to enter information once because it's the same database," Gault explains. "You don't have to re-create the wheel and duplicate entries. A retailer can even offer self-serve options for employees to view their information electronically."

Golf Town has been working with Payworks since 2009 to centralize workforce management functions for its 60 stores, says Susan Gilpin, director of HR. "Before, every store ran its own payroll. The biggest challenge was people moving between stores, because it meant processing it as a termination and new hire."

With an integrated workforce management approach, she says Golf Town can achieve the consistency it wants, knowing that information is accurate across the board, and that all the proper employment standards and practices are kept. "We took the administrative end away from managers, and that helps to keep them on the sales floor. That's a huge plus." She adds that in her world, Web-based services have changed HR for administrators. "I came from an environment where a lot of resources were needed to run payroll. Now we can do it all with one analyst. And we've barely skimmed the surface of what the technology can do."

Accelerating the Learning Curve

The advent of sophisticated graphics and easy login access over high-speed networks has also changed the training picture dramatically, says Cara Danielson, associate vice president, learning &

development, for Canadian Tire Corp. She reports it has managed to reduce 26 hours of learning to six for new Mark's Work Wearhouse employees by dispensing with manuals and binders in favour of an e-learning system. "It's also a lot more effective, so when our people hit the floor they're a lot more confident," she says.

The system can track "pretty much everything," Danielson adds. "Every module includes an assessment and a test, so we can upload progress, results, and test scores."

Mark's started out with 40 modules in 2009, and has grown the library to 376 modules that cover orientation, customer service, and product knowledge. Over time, Mark's has moved more and more into a graphic-rich gaming experience, from exercises in dressing a mannequin to navigating a virtual store online. "We're also introducing a social media aspect to share comments and learning experiences," Danielson says.

She reports that close to 85 percent of employees have completed e-learning training. "They love it, and we don't have any trouble getting them to take it." For Danielson, e-learning is a game-changer for getting more effective employees on the floor quicker. "Even before a new employee steps on the floor, they are ready to help customers. It creates an amazing learning environment."

Discussion Questions

1. What are the two most labour-intensive functions for human resource managers?

2. How have the following retail organizations used Web-based resources to manage parts of their HR functions?
   - Lululemon
   - M & M Meat Shops
   - Golf Town
   - Canadian Tire Corp.

Source: Denise Deveau, "HR Technology Is All about Connections," *Canadian Retailer*, Winter 2012, Volume 22, Issue 1, pp. 40–43. Canadian Retailer, a publication of Retail Council of Canada.

CASE 26 | Preparing for Succession, Stitch by Stitch

Before Jennifer Baird had even completed her studies at university, she had already started on the journey toward realizing her dream of becoming president of her family's business. Just eight years and a lot of hard work later, that dream has become

a reality. At the ripe age of 30, Jennifer is now the president of Stitch It Clothing Alterations, the only national alterations company in North America with stores coast-to coast in Canada as well as a finger in the US market. However, despite her youth, she explains that getting to this point is the result of a well-thought-out ten-year plan that her father Alain built. She also admits that if it had been up to her, the path to succession may have looked a little different.

When Jennifer eventually graduated from the halls of academia, she felt as though she was ready to take on the world. She had gained valuable experience working two different part-time retail jobs throughout her post-secondary years. She also believed that she already possessed an intimate knowledge of the industry and the business she was to one day run. With a business degree under her belt, to boot, she felt well and truly prepared to step into an office role at the company.

"Because I had already worked quite a bit in Stitch It stores during university, I thought that I had earned my stripes. I thought I could move right into head office," she explains. "Thank goodness my dad knew better. As soon as I graduated, he put me right back into the stores. He knew that I needed a deeper understanding of the basics of the business."

The First Stitch

Jennifer vividly remembers the beginning of her journey, "like it was yesterday," she quips, when she sat down with her father to create the ten-year succession plan that would result in an opportunity for her to run the family's national company. It was a plan that she recognized immediately as one that would clearly involve a lot of hard work focused on gaining the respect of Stitch It's 650 associates.

The plan started while Jennifer was in her second year of university at a time when the Baird family was given the opportunity to buy Stitch It back from the retail powerhouse that helped Alain grow the business in its early years. Alain, however, had no interest in buying the company back for himself. He was only interested in doing so if there were some succession planning involved. He asked Jennifer if it was something that she would consider.

"It was a big decision for me to make at the age of 21," she explains. "But I already possessed a passion for retail. And I already loved this company—I loved what it was about and how it was started. I didn't have to think about it too long. My immediate reaction was a resounding 'yes!'"

Hard Work and Understanding

Though her reaction may have been immediate, she was well aware that her rise to ascendancy within the company would not be. It was going to require a lot of hard work—hard work, at the insistence of her father, that involved working in every role and covering every aspect of the company, from office administrator to area supervisor. She even moved to Chicago where she was responsible for overseeing the opening of the company's six stores there.

"I've learned so much during this experience about production, training, hiring, and building a region. I've worked within an HR function, have worked customer service in our stores, have managed stores, and have led operations. I've pretty much worked within all of the facets of the business leading up to where I am today. Doing things this way has afforded me fantastic learning opportunities and prepared me for my role as president."

It's the skills that Baird has picked up while working in all of these capacities that she credits for her early successes. She also explains that the intimate knowledge of the company and all of its facets that she now possesses could never be learned in school or anywhere else.

"There is no substitute for learning your business from the ground up," she says. "The in-store experiences taught me so much about our business, including the fact that running a successful service business is not just about serving your external customer. It's about serving your internal customers as well. Our associates are the face of Stitch It; by working the front lines, I feel connected to both sets of our customers."

Baird goes on to explain her deep appreciation for her earlier experiences gained in the stores—experiences that help her today in her role as president.

"When I visit stores today, I know enough about the processes to test out new concepts and programs," she explains. "There have been many times when we come up with a great idea at head office but it just doesn't work when I get into a store. Unfortunately, this lesson is something that can go stale if you do not stay connected. I try to get into the stores as much as possible and hope to do even more of it as I get settled into my new role."

Openness and Communication

Beyond taking this step-by-step—or stitch-by-stitch—tactical approach to succession, which has given Baird the opportunity to learn all of the ins and outs of her family's business, she stresses open and honest communication as the other critical element to an effective succession plan.

"Communication is critical," she asserts. "I knew right away that it was going to be important for my father and me both to commit to keeping open and honest communication between us. That was the only way this was going to work. In family businesses, we often take communication for granted. It's easy to assume that family members will be on the same page, but that isn't always the case. Having structured conversations around the succession plan and how well it is going is crucial. We may be family, but we are not mind-readers."

The communication between Baird and her father continues to this day, allowing her to at all times be within reach of advice from the man who started the company and the benefits of this advice are not lost on Baird.

"My father and I have a meeting every single week where we talk about what's happening. We're in a transition period right now. I have taken over the president's role, but Alain is staying on full-time for two years to continue to mentor me. He makes sure that things are going well and allows me to make some mistakes while ensuring that 'both of his babies' are staying on the right course."

Discussion Questions

1. Why is succession planning becoming increasingly critical in retail?

2. How does Stitch It manage to meet the needs of its customers?

3. Where do you think the challenges and opportunities are for Stitch It?

Source: Sean C. Tarry, "Preparing for Succession, Stitch by Stitch," *Canadian Retailer,* Winter 2013, Volume 23, Issue 1, pp. 12–16. Canadian Retailer, a publication of Retail Council of Canada.

CASE 27	Customer Service and Relationship Management at Nordstrom

Nordstrom's unwavering customer-focused philosophy traces its roots to founder Johan Nordstrom's values. Johan Nordstrom believed in people and realized that consistently exceeding their expectations would lead to success and a good conscience. He built his organization around a customer-oriented philosophy. The organization focuses on people, and its policies and selections are designed to satisfy people. As simple as this philosophy sounds, few of Nordstrom's competitors have truly been able to grasp it.

A Focus on People

Nordstrom employees treat customers like royalty. Employees are instructed to do whatever is in the customer's best interest. Customer delight drives the values of the company. Customers are taken seriously and are at the heart of the business. Customers are even at the top of Nordstrom's so-called organization chart, which is an inverted pyramid. Moving down from the customers at the top of the inverted pyramid are the salespeople, department managers, and general managers. Finally, at the bottom is the board of directors. All lower levels work toward supporting the salespeople, who in turn work to serve the customers.

Employee incentives are tied to customer service. Salespeople are given personalized business cards to help them build relationships with customers. Uniquely, salespeople are not tied to their respective departments but to the customer. Salespeople can travel from department to department within the store to help their customer, if that is needed. For example, a Nordstrom salesperson assisting a woman shopping for business apparel helps her shop for suits, blouses, shoes, hosiery, and accessories. The salesperson becomes the "personal shopper" of the customer to show her merchandise and provide fashion expertise. This approach is also conducive to building long-term relationships with customers, as over time the salesperson comes to understand each customer's fashion sense and personality.

The opportunity to sell across departments enables salespeople to maximize sales and commissions while providing superior customer service. As noted on a *60 Minutes* segment, "[Nordstrom's service is] not service like it used to be, but service that never was."

Despite the obsession with customer service at Nordstrom, ironically, the customer actually comes second. Nordstrom understands that customers will be treated well by its employees only if the employees themselves are treated well by the company. Nordstrom employees are treated almost like the extended Nordstrom family, and employee satisfaction is a closely watched business variable.

Nordstrom is known for promoting employees from within its ranks. The fundamental traits of a successful Nordstrom salesperson (e.g., commitment to excellence, customer service) are the same traits emphasized in successful Nordstrom executives.

Nordstrom hires people with a positive attitude, a sense of ownership, initiative, heroism, and the ability to handle high expectations. This sense of ownership is reflected in Nordstrom's low rate of shrinkage. Shrinkage, or loss due to theft and record-keeping errors, at Nordstrom is under 1.5 percent of sales, roughly half the industry average. The low shrinkage can be attributed in large part to the diligence of salespeople caring for the merchandise as if it were their own.

Employees at all levels are treated like businesspeople and empowered to make independent decisions. They are given the latitude to do whatever they believe is the right thing, with the customers' best interests at heart. All employees are given the tools and authority to do whatever is necessary to satisfy customers, and management almost always backs subordinates' decisions.

In summary, Nordstrom's product is its people. The loyal Nordstrom shopper goes to Nordstrom for the service received—not necessarily the products. Of course, Nordstrom does offer quality merchandise, but that is secondary for many customers.

Customer-Focused Policies

One of the most famous examples of Nordstrom's customer service occurred in 1975 when a Nordstrom salesperson gladly took back a set of used automobile tires and gave the customer a refund, even though Nordstrom had never sold tires! The customer had purchased the tires from a Northern Commercial Company store, whose retail space Nordstrom had since acquired. Not wanting the customer to leave the Nordstrom store unhappy, the salesperson refunded the price of the tires.

Nordstrom's policies focus on the concept of the *lifetime value of the customer*. Although little money is made on the first sale, when the lifetime value of a customer is calculated, the positive dollar amount of a loyal customer is staggering. The lifetime value of a customer is the sum of all sales and profits generated from that customer, directly or indirectly. To keep its customers for a lifetime, Nordstrom employees go to incredible lengths. In a Nordstrom store in Seattle, a customer wanted to buy a pair of brand-name slacks that had gone on sale. The store was out of her size, and the salesperson was unable to locate a pair at other Nordstrom stores. Knowing that the same slacks were available at a competitor nearby, the sales clerk went to the rival, purchased the slacks at full price using petty cash from her department, and sold the slacks to the customer at Nordstrom's sale price. Although this sale resulted in an immediate loss for the store, the investment in promoting the loyalty of the happy customer went a long way.

Nordstrom's employees try to never say no to the customer. Nordstrom has an unconditional return policy. If a customer is not completely satisfied, he or she can return the new and generally even heavily used merchandise at any time for a full refund. Ironically, this is not a company policy; rather, it is implemented at the discretion of the salesperson to maximize customer satisfaction. Nordstrom's advice to its employees is simply, "Use good judgment in all situations." Employees are given the freedom, support, and resources to make the best decisions to enhance customer satisfaction. The cost of Nordstrom's high service, such as its return policy, coupled with its competitive pricing would, on the surface, seem to cut into profit margins. This cost, however, is recouped through increased sales from repeat customers, limited markdowns, and, if necessary, the "squeezing" of suppliers.

Nordstrom's vendor relationships also focus on maximizing customer satisfaction. According to former CEO Bruce Nordstrom, "[Vendors] know that we are liberal with our customers. And if you're going to do business with us, then there should be a liberal influence on their return policies. If somebody has worn a shoe and it doesn't wear satisfactorily for them, and we think that person is being honest about it, then we will send it back." Nordstrom realizes some customers will abuse the unconditional return policy, but it refuses to impose that abuse back onto the vendors. Here again, the rule of "doing what is right" comes into play.

Nordstrom's merchandising and purchasing policies are also extremely customer-focused. A full selection of merchandise in a wide variety of sizes is seen as a measure of customer service. An average Nordstrom store carries roughly 150 000 pairs of shoes with a variety of sizes, widths, colours, and models. Typical shoe sizes for women range from 2½ to 14, in widths of A to EEE. Nordstrom is fanatical about stocking only high-quality merchandise. Once when the upper parts of some women's shoes were separating from the soles, *every* shoe from that delivery was shipped back to the manufacturer.

Discussion Questions

1. What steps does Nordstrom take to implement its strategy of providing outstanding customer service?

2. How do these activities enable Nordstrom to reduce the gaps between perceived service and customer expectations, as described in Chapter 14?

3. What are the pros and cons of Nordstrom's approach to developing a competitive advantage through customer service?

Source: This case was written by Alicia Lueddemann, the Management Mind Group, and Sunil Erevelles, University of North Carolina, Charlotte.

CASE 28 | Active Endeavors Analyzes Its Customer Database

Active Endeavors is an outdoor apparel and accessory retailer located in Iowa City, Iowa. The store is locally owned and has been in business for 13 years, and it has a reputation for high quality and product innovation. Its target market is high-income individuals with an interest in outdoor activities and travel.

Ken Stuart, the founder of the store, has felt pressure on profit margins and increased competition, especially due to the emergence of the Internet. He tries to remain on top of competition by offering new products and a wide and deep assortment, but he thinks there might be an opportunity to increase the store's market position by using a transactional database of its customers. The store has the customers' transaction records, which include customer name and address, transaction date, products and quantity purchased, and purchase price. He is thinking of using the transactional database to design and target a direct mail campaign designed to increase traffic.

Ken analyzed the customers' past purchase behaviour using the RFM analysis and classified the customers into six groups (Exhibit 1). The cut-off figures for the classifications were unique to the store. He is now contemplating the customer profile and what to do with it.

Discussion Questions

1. Describe the type of customers in each group.

2. What would you recommend Active Endeavors do to get more business from each group?

Source: This case was written by Edward Rhee, Stonehill College.

Exhibit 1
Customer Classification Based on Purchase History

Customer Group	Recency	Frequency	Monetary
1	Purchased within the last 3 months	Purchased 4 or more times	Purchased $337.63 or more
2	Purchased within the last 3 months	Purchased once	Purchased $18.90 or less
3	Purchased between the last 3 months and a year	Purchased 4 or more times	Purchased $338.63 or more
4	Purchased between the last 3 months and a year	Purchased once	Purchased $18.90 or less
5	Purchased more than a year ago	Purchased 4 or more times	Purchased $337.63 or more
6	Purchased more than a year ago	Purchased once	Purchased $18.90 or less

Leveraging social media to engage potential customers and better understand their preferences and needs can seem like a daunting task. Where should retailers start?

Retailers need to understand that the use of social media is not a fad that will disappear within the next six to twelve months. The number of users on social networking sites increases every day. There are approximately 1.25 billion users on Facebook, 500 million users of Twitter, and more than 100 million people use the Snap-chat app each day.

Retailers need to choose the website that will benefit the specific needs of their business. Facebook is a great tool to help retailers become involved in conversations with customers about their own product or service. Twitter, on the other hand, represents one of the quickest and easiest ways to generate word of mouth among customers concerning sales, promotions, and new product releases.

Interacting with consumers on a day-to-day basis within an environment that encourages communication and sharing is vital to understanding consumer attitudes toward retailer brands and the company's reputation. Engaging with customers online allows retailers to extend their reach beyond their physical storefront. The promotional and marketing capabilities of social media offer retailers enormous opportunity to engage customers where they are and present them with real-time information regarding sales and services that can have an immediate effect on visits to the store. Whether their customer is located in a different town, city, province, or even country—leveraging social media will allow retailers to connect with that customer within seconds.

A website that best suits the specific needs of the business needs to be chosen, and retailers need to explore it to become comfortable with the tools. Getting staff involved and providing tutorials for those who may not be engaged in social media is also a good idea. The more the retailer and their staff know about the medium, the more effective tool it will be.

Management and staff need to understand the objectives behind using social media. A clear, concise description of the way the websites and their tools are to be used and how to communicate and connect within them is important. Uploading fresh and current content on a consistent basis will grab the attention and interest of customers and get them into the store. For example, Facebook allows retailers to upload video, audio, and images, which can be used to create really dynamic marketing content that will add great value to the online experience of the customer, increasing the effectiveness of the retailer's engagement with them.

Social media dismantles the old "retailer to customer" one-way interaction. Now, retailers can reach customers and engage with them in meaningful and live conversation, enabling them to become more proactive in their approach, giving them the opportunity to adjust their operations, products, or services to suit the needs and expectations of the customer. Online tools such as Google Alerts, Technorati, and Twitter Search are great ways to find out what customers are saying about them and the products and services they provide. Once they have listened and heard, they can respond to the attitudes of the consumer through improved pricing, product availability, or anything else that might help improve the shopping experience of their clientele.

Discussion Questions

1. Will social media become an essential part of the corporate marketing strategy for retailers?

2. What benefits can a retailer gain from using social media?

3. If you were assigned the task of improving the marketing efforts of a new Internet retailer, would you use social media? Why or why not? Does it depend on what the company is selling?

4. Have you ever followed a retailer on Twitter or belonged to a retailer's Facebook group? Was it a positive or negative experience? Did it affect your buying decision? In what ways?

Sources: Retail Council of Canada, *Canadian Retailer*, January/February 2010, p. 46; Jeff Bullas, "46 Amazing Social Media Facts in 2013," JeffBullas.com blog, October 25, 2013, http://www.jeffbullas.com/2013/10/25/46-amazing-social-media-facts-in-2013/#IAcpwvTuqjwz8bAc.99 (accessed January 28, 2014); Sarah Frier, "Snapchat User 'Stories' Fuel 10 Billion Daily Video Views," *Bloomberg Technology*, April 28, 2016, http://www.bloomberg.com/news/articles/2016-04-28/snapchat-user-content-fuels-jump-to-10-billion-daily-video-views (accessed July 22, 2016). Canadian Retailer, a publication of Retail Council of Canada.

Ruth Diamond, president of Diamond Furriers, is concerned that sales in her store appeared to have flattened out. She is considering establishing a different method for compensating her salespeople. Diamond is located in an affluent suburb of Montreal. Ruth's father had founded the company 40 years earlier, and she had grown up working in the business. After his retirement in 1980, she moved the store into an upscale shopping mall not far from its previous location and sales boomed almost immediately, rising to just over $1 million in five years. However, once it reached that sales volume, it remained there for the next three years, making Ruth wonder whether her salespeople had sufficient incentive to sell more aggressively.

Diamond's staff is all women, ranging in age from 27 to 58 years. There are four full-timers and four part-timers (20 hours a week), all of whom have at least three years of experience in the store. All of them are paid at the same hourly rate ($15) with liberal benefits. Employee morale is excellent, and the entire staff displays strong personal loyalty to Diamond.

The store is open 78 hours a week, which means that there is nearly always a minimum staff of three on the floor, rising to six at peak periods. Diamond's merchandise consists exclusively of fur coats and jackets, ranging in price from $750 to more than $5000. The average unit sale is about $2000. Full-timers' annual sales average about $160 000, and the part-timers' are a little over half of that.

Diamond's concern about sales transcends her appreciation for her loyalty toward her employees. She asks them, for example, to maintain customer files and call their customers when new styles come in. Although some of them are more diligent about this than others, none of them appear to want to be especially aggressive about promoting sales.

She began to investigate commission systems and discussed them with some of her contacts in the trade. All suggested lowering the salespeople's base pay and installing either a fixed or a variable commission rate system.

One idea was to lower the base hourly rate from $15 to $12 and let them make up the difference through a 4 percent commission on all sales, to be paid monthly. Such an arrangement would allow them all to earn the same as they currently do.

However, she also realized that such a system would provide no incentive to sell the higher-priced furs, which she recognized might be a way to improve overall sales. So she also considered offering to pay 3 percent on items priced below $2000 and 5 percent on all those above.

Either of these systems would require considerable extra bookkeeping. Returns would have to be deducted from commissions. And she was also concerned that disputes might arise among her people from time to time over who had actually made the sale. So she conceived of a third alternative, which was to leave the hourly rates the same but pay a flat bonus of 4 percent of all sales over $1 million and then divide it among the salespeople on the basis of the proportion of hours each had actually worked. This "commission" would be paid annually, in the form of a Christmas bonus.

Discussion Questions

1. What are the advantages and disadvantages of the various alternatives Ruth Diamond is considering?

2. Do you have any other suggestions for improving the store's sales?

3. What would you recommend? Why?

Source: This case was prepared by Professor David Ehrlich, Marymount University.

Australia's oldest retailer evolved from Appleton and Jones in 1835 to David Jones in 1838. Today, David Jones, or simply DJs, has dozens of department stores, predominantly in Australia's capital cities. Similar to many retailers, and despite having a mail-order business since the late 1800s, DJs suffered a few missteps with its online presence in the early 2000s. Now, however, the David Jones website, davidjones.com.au, is integral to DJs' daily operations.

Chris Taylor, a recent university graduate, manages DJs' online presence. Thanks to its successful website and changing media habits, David Jones is considering online advertising to drive targeted traffic to the website. Given the prominence of Google and sponsored search, Chris would like to test Google AdWords.

Starting late last century, search engines began to develop interactive advertising models based on user interests, such as keywords typed into a search engine. The concept, *sponsored search*, aligns online advertisements with search engine queries. In sponsored search—also known as paid search, keyword advertising, pay-per-click (PPC) advertising, and search advertising—advertisers pay for search engine traffic to their websites via link-based ads that search engines display in response to user queries. Thus, if a user searches Google using the keyword *retailers*, AdWords ads that mention retailing would appear. If the user clicks on an ad, the user then goes to a specific web page—the landing page—on the advertiser's website.

As the leading search engine, Google has driven developments in sponsored search beyond search engine results. In addition to placing advertisements on Google and affiliated search engine results, such as AOL.com and Ask.com, advertisers can place AdWords on other websites. Via its content network, Google dynamically matches ads to a web page's content and pays the website owner if a visitor clicks on the ad. Google's content network includes millions of websites in over 100 countries and 20 languages, such as the British travel site Lonely Planet and the French television channel M6. In the United States, for example, the *New York Times* earns revenue by placing AdWords on its web pages. Thus, advertisers can place AdWords on search engine results and on the millions of websites in Google's content network.

AdWords are simple text-based ads with four lines of copy predominantly in the right-hand column and at the top of Google search results. The first line, or headline, has a maximum of 25 characters. The next two lines and the final line with the website address have a maximum of 35 characters each. Two sample AdWords advertisements for David Jones are shown in Exhibit 1. The copy is identical except for the first half of the third line,

"Great holiday specials" versus "Expanded holiday hours." The ad on the left should interest value-conscious market segments, while the one on the right should attract consumers seeking after-hours shopping.

In addition to their simple and non-intrusive nature, AdWords' advantages over traditional advertising such as print or television include better segmentation and more direct targeting. Advertisers select the keywords and the geographic location of the person doing the search. For geographic segmentation, David Jones might want its ads to appear only for people in a key source market, such as Sydney or Melbourne.

To target consumer interests, David Jones could use keywords such as *Christmas*, *holidays*, *shopping*, and *retailers*. But these keywords could be too expensive because they are so generic. Although generic terms may attract clicks on an AdWords advertisement, many of these clicks may be from random rather than targeted David Jones web shoppers. Unlike a cost-per-thousand model based on impressions, this contextual advertising based on keywords charges advertisers on a cost-per-click basis. Chris and her team want to pay for targeted clicks.

To minimize paying for unwanted clicks, online advertisers also include negative keywords such as *cheap* or *free*. Including the negative keyword *cheap* alongside the keywords *Christmas* and *shopping* means that no AdWords ads will show on search results for users keying in the three keywords *cheap*, *Christmas*, and *shopping*.

Furthermore, advertisers bid on the cost per click in a dynamic auction. When many advertisers bid on generic terms such as *Christmas* and *shopping*, this drives the cost up for these keywords. Thus clever advertisers bid on specific phrases such as *Christmas shopping* rather than on *Christmas* and *shopping*.

Chris and her team use four Google websites to understand and determine applicable content network websites, keywords, and estimated keyword costs:

- Google AdWords Glossary (https://adwords. google.com/support/bin/topic.py?topic=29)
- Google Content Network (http:www.google. com/adwords/contentnetwork/)
- Google Keyword Tool (https://adwords.google. com/select/KeywordToolExternal)
- Google Traffic Estimator (https://adwords. google.com/select/TrafficEstimatorSandbox)

Exhibit 1
Sample AdWords

Christmas at David Jones	Christmas at David Jones
Convenient major city locations	Convenient major city locations
Great holiday specials; visit now	Expanded holiday hours; visit now
DavidJones.com.au	DavidJones.com.au

As AdWords accounts are easy to set up and manage, the testing possibilities are many. Major considerations that Chris and her team would like to test include:

- appropriate keywords, keyword phrases, and negative keywords
- geographic segmentation
- advertising copy and appeals
- keyword pricing
- Google's content network
- aligning the landing page with the AdWords copy

The final point above—the landing page—leads to a key aspect of David Jones' online presence, its website. As davidjones.com.au illustrates, the website serves many target markets and offers many products. For example, online visitors may find information on store events, employment, publicly traded stock shares, and registration for email alerts and bridal registries, as well as traditional department store products such as clothing. Effective AdWords align the advertising copy with the landing page. That is, the advertisement directs consumers to a relevant web page rather than to the David Jones home page at davidjones.com.au. The left-column ad in Exhibit 1, which focuses on holiday specials, would take visitors to a landing page with holiday specials. Similarly, the right-column ad in Table 1 would take visitors to a landing page featuring expanded holiday hours.

Discussion Questions

1. On the basis of your review of the David Jones website at davidjones.com.au, use examples to explain how different sections of the home page serve different audiences. What other audiences would you suggest David Jones serve via its website? Why?

2. On the basis of your review of the David Jones website, davidjones.com.au, design three separate AdWords advertisements.

Source: This case was written by Jamie Murphy, Murdoch Business School; Meghan O'Farrell, Google; and Alex Gibelalde, Google.

CASE 32 — Generating Advertising Revenue from a Digital Screen Network at Harrods of London

Retailers have slowly been implementing digital screen networks. In most instances, the messages are focused on branding and impacting the customer shopping experience. Very few networks, such as Walmart's SMART Network and, to a lesser extent, Target's Channel Red, have also been able to generate a stream of advertising revenue. In the department store category, Harrods is the only high-end luxury store to successfully sell advertising on its in-store digital signage network. Factors such as a solid and consistent customer base and the store's unique environment have contributed to the success of the signage.

It is difficult to imagine any retail environment as unique as Harrods. It is a key destination for millions of visitors who come to the United Kingdom every year (it is the UK's third-largest tourist attraction). It houses the world's finest luxury brands across a million square feet of retail space. It has a history dating back to 1849 and can count the rich and famous from all corners of the globe as its customers. The brand is synonymous with luxury, the "finer things in life," and a range of merchandise unequalled under one roof. Average daily traffic is 45 000 customers (occasionally rising to 100 000 on special days). Many of them are high-net-worth individuals, including royalty from around the world, as well as celebrities and billionaires.

Advertisements on the network are sold to premium brands, such as Armani and Cartier. The medium is often sold as part of an integrated marketing campaign, which often includes other media such as posters, lift-wraps (signage on elevator doors), windows, and even pages in the Harrods magazine. Combined with other in-store media, screens are an integral part of the campaign, providing impact, awareness, and, often, directional signage leading customers to the "heart of the promotion"—the place where the product and the customer meet.

The specific location of each screen was carefully considered so that each customer would have a multiscreen sight line. In most cases, customers see more than one screen within their view. The same content appears simultaneously on each screen in the network, so the advertisers have high impact with their ads appearing several times at once.

In most cases, screens are positioned on the sides of escalators in the store. Unlike the case at many transport hubs, most customers in Harrods stand still on the moving steps. As they glide up to the next floor, they take in the view, which includes the digital screens. Each advertiser has a 15-second slot.

Harrods' digital screen network is all managed in-house. There is a dedicated ad sales team, operations team, and technical and creative team who are all committed Harrods employees who live and breathe the brand. These employees believe in and are included in how and what is being marketed. They sit in the building and pass by the media that they are selling and marketing 20 times a day. They also see with their own eyes the audience that they are selling to the advertisers. They see the clothes they are wearing, the limos that deliver them to the store, and the number of Harrods' famous green bags they are carrying. They can see the impact that the screens can have on a consumer purchasing decision, or even simply see customers watching content through their Dior sunglasses as they glide up an escalator.

Network staff also have relationships with the brands and the advertisers. They have a relationship which has been nurtured and developed so that they are working "alongside" a brand to find marketing solutions to drive brand sales and awareness, which in turn benefits not only the brand, but also Harrods as a store.

The store is continuously changing, and as part of that development, additional digital screens are introduced as part of new departments and remodels. When Harrods first introduced its digital signage network, it realized that it had to do something special to integrate the screens into the environment. It didn't want screens hanging from ceilings above walkways that look tacky, amateur, and cheap. It invested heavily in each screen installation, with customized reinforced glass, polished steel bezels, additional cooling fans, and colour schemes that are consistent with the store's decor. This gave the screens a look of luxury. A lot of care, thought, and attention have been invested in each location to give the advertiser the optimum in presentation.

Harrods monitors the effectiveness of a campaign via sales data. It has some impressive results from advertisers who have enjoyed double-digit sales increases during and following a digital campaign in the store. You would naturally ask the question, "Well, why isn't everyone advertising on the screens?" The answer to this question involves many factors including, among other things, the following:

- The medium is new and many vendors are unfamiliar with its benefits.
- Vendors are not always sure about where the funding of digital screen ads should come from. That is, is it a marketing/advertising expenditure or an in-store promotional expenditure?
- There are creative challenges associated with messages. For instance, is the message capturing the attention of the customers? Does it have a call to action or an offer?

If there is one way to deter advertisers, then it's to have blank, malfunctioning screens. It seems obvious, but so many networks in retail lumber on with as many as 25 percent of the screens non-operational. No wonder they find selling ads a struggle! Harrods has a zero-tolerance strategy within the operations team, resulting in the team's touring the store every morning before the store opens checking that all is as it should be. As well, it has invested heavily in preventive maintenance contracts, and has a backup stock of spare screens available should a screen die and require replacement.

Digital networks can make money for a retailer. Harrods has realized both ad sales revenue and increased sales of advertised products. However, such results take significant investments in time, resources, and money. The future success for generating advertising sales is dependent on improvements in technical reliability of the hardware and software, combined with more investment in content and creativity. Interactivity via mobile/smartphones is clearly part of the future. Harrods is investing in the latest technology, implementing new and unique content that captures people's imagination, and working alongside brands that are prepared to invest to realize the benefits.

Discussion Questions

1. What are the reasons that Harrods has been successful at selling advertising on its digital signage network and other retailers have not? Why would consumer product manufacturers be interested in advertising on Harrods' network?

2. What are the pluses and minuses for a retailer offering a digital network in its stores?

Source: This case was written by Steven Keith Platt, Platt Retail Institute, and Guy Cheston, Director of Advertising Sales and Sponsorship, Harrods.

1-to-1 retailing Developing retail programs for small groups or individual customers.

80–20 rule A general management principle stating that 80 percent of the sales or profits come from 20 percent of the customers.

ABC analysis An analysis that rank orders SKUs by a profitability measure to determine which items should never be out of stock, which should be allowed to be out of stock occasionally, and which should be deleted from the stock selection.

accessibility (1) The degree to which customers can easily get into and out of a shopping centre; (2) ability of the retailer to deliver the appropriate retail mix to the customers in the segment.

accounts payable The amount of money owed to vendors, primarily for merchandise inventory.

accounts receivable The amount of money due to the retailer from selling merchandise on credit.

accrued liabilities Liabilities that accumulate daily but are paid only at the end of a period.

actionability Means that the definition of a market segment must clearly indicate what the retailer should do to satisfy its needs.

adaptability A company's recognition of cultural differences and adaptation of its core strategy to the needs of local markets.

add-on selling Selling additional new products and services to existing customers, such as a bank encouraging a customer with a chequing account to also apply for a home improvement loan from the bank.

advance shipping notice (ASN) An electronic document received by a retailer's computer from a supplier in advance of a shipment.

advertising Paid communications delivered to customers through nonpersonal mass media such as newspapers, television, radio, direct mail, and the Internet.

affordable budgeting method A budgeting method in which a retailer first sets a budget for every element of the retail mix except promotion and then allocates the leftover funds to a promotional budget.

aided recall When consumers indicate they know the brand when the name is presented to them.

alternative dispute resolution A provision included in a contract between retailer and vendor to help avoid litigation in the case of a dispute. Can include methods of settling the dispute that the parties agree upon, such as mediation, arbitration, or med-arb.

amount and quality of parking facilities A store having enough parking spaces, close enough to the building, so that the store is ideally accessible to customers, but not so many open spaces that the store is viewed as being unpopular. A standard rule of thumb is 5.9 spaces per 1000 square feet of retail store space.

analogue approach A method of trade area analysis, also known as the *similar store* or *mapping approach*, that is divided into four steps: (1) describing the current trade areas through the technique of customer spotting; (2) plotting the customers on a map; (3) defining the primary, secondary, and tertiary area zones; and (4) matching the characteristics of stores in the trade areas with the potential new store to estimate its sales potential.

anchors Major retailers located in a shopping centre.

arbitration Used in the case of a dispute between retailer and vendor that involves the appointment of a neutral party—the arbitrator—who considers the arguments of both sides and then makes a decision that is usually agreed upon in advance as binding.

artificial barriers In site evaluations for accessibility, barriers such as railroad tracks, major highways, or parks.

asset turnover Net sales divided by total assets.

assets Economic resources, such as inventory or store fixtures, owned or controlled by an enterprise as a result of past transactions or events.

atmospherics The design of an environment via visual communications, lighting, colour, music, and scent to stimulate customers' perceptual and emotional responses and ultimately to affect their purchase behaviour.

attitude branding The choice of a symbol that represents a feeling that is not necessarily connected with the product or retailer.

average sale per transaction (AST) A measure that evaluates productivity by looking at the number of transactions processed per store or department and the average dollar sale per transaction.

backup stock The inventory used to guard against going out of stock when demand exceeds forecasts or merchandise is delayed; also called *safety stock* or *buffer stock*.

bargaining power of vendors A competitive factor that makes a market unattractive when a few vendors control the merchandise sold in it. In these situations, vendors have an opportunity to dictate prices and other terms, reducing retailer's profits.

barriers to entry Conditions in a retail market that make it difficult for firms to enter the market.

benefit segmentation A method of segmenting a retail market on the basis of similar benefits sought in merchandise or services.

big-box stores Large, limited-service retailers.

blog A public website where users post informal journals of their thoughts, comments, and philosophies; also called *weblog*.

bonus Additional compensation awarded periodically, based on a subjective evaluation of the employee's performance.

bootleg The sale of imitation goods where there is little or no attempt to hide the fact that the product is counterfeit.

bottom-up planning When goals are set at the bottom of the organization and filter up through the operating levels.

brand A distinguishing name or symbol (such as a logo, design, symbol, or trademark) that identifies the products or services offered by a seller and differentiates those products and services from the offerings of competitors.

brand association Anything linked to or connected with the brand name in a consumer's memory.

brand awareness The ability of a potential customer to recognize or recall that a particular brand name belongs to a retailer or product/service.

brand energy The concept that links the idea that a brand creates value through meaningful experiences rather than a focus on generating profits.

brand equity The value that brand image offers retailers.

brand images Sets of associations consumers have about a brand that are usually organized around some meaningful themes.

brand loyalty Indicates customers like and consistently buy a specific brand in a product category. They are reluctant to switch to other brands if their favourite brand isn't available.

break-even analysis A technique that evaluates the relationship between total revenue and total cost to determine profitability at various sales levels.

break-even point (BEP) The quantity at which total revenue equals total cost and beyond which profit occurs.

breaking bulk A function performed by retailers or wholesalers in which they receive large quantities of merchandise.

breaking sizes Stocking out of a specific size or colour SKU.

bullwhip effect The buildup of inventory in an uncoordinated channel.

buyback A strategy vendors and retailers use to get products into retail stores, either when a retailer allows a vendor to create space for goods by "buying back" a competitor's inventory and removing it from a retailer's system, or when the retailer forces a vendor to buy back slow-moving merchandise; also called *stocklift* or *lift-out*.

buying process The stages customers go through to purchase merchandise or services.

buying situation segmentation A method of segmenting a retail market based on customer needs in a specific buying situation, such as a fill-in shopping trip versus a weekly shopping trip.

call to action The portion of the marketing or sales message that prompts potential consumers to perform a desired action within the desired time frame.

catalogue channel A non-store retail format in which the retailer communicates directly with customers using catalogues sent through the mail.

category captain A supplier that forms an alliance with a retailer to help gain consumer insight, satisfy consumer needs, and improve the performance and profit potential across the entire category.

category life cycle A merchandise category's sales pattern over time.

category management The process of managing a retail business with the objective of maximizing the sales and profits of a category.

category signage Signage within a particular department or sector of the store designed to identify types of products offered; usually located near the goods to which they refer.

category specialist A discount retailer that offers a narrow but deep assortment of merchandise in a category and thus dominates the category from the customers' perspective. Also called *category killer*.

central business district (CBD) The traditional downtown business area of a city or town.

centralization The degree to which authority for making retail decisions is delegated to corporate managers rather than to geographically dispersed regional, district, and store management.

chargeback A practice used by retailers in which they deduct money from the amount they owe a vendor.

checking The process of going through goods upon receipt to make sure that they arrived undamaged and that the merchandise received matches the merchandise ordered.

checkout areas The places in a store where customers can purchase merchandise and have it "wrapped"—placed in a bag; also called *cash-wrap areas*.

classification A group of items or SKUs for the same type of merchandise, such as pants (as opposed to jackets or suits), supplied by different vendors.

closeout retailers Off-price retailers that sell a broad but inconsistent assortment of general merchandise as well as apparel and soft home goods, obtained through retail liquidations and bankruptcy proceedings.

co-op advertising A program undertaken by a vendor in which the vendor agrees to pay all or part of a promotion for its products; also called *cooperative advertising*.

coaching The activity of supporting people to achieve their goals by goal setting, training, advising, encouraging, and rewarding their successes.

collaborative planning, forecasting, and replenishment (CPFR) A collaborative inventory management system in which a retailer shares information with vendors. CPFR software uses data to construct a computer-generated replenishment forecast that is shared by the retailer and vendor before it's executed.

combination stores Retailers that sell both food and non-food items.

commercial bribery A vendor's offer of money or gifts to a retailer's employee for the purpose of influencing purchasing decisions.

commission Compensation based on a fixed formula, such as percentage of sales.

communication gap The difference between the actual service provided to customers and the service promised in the retailer's promotion program. This factor is one of the four factors identified by the gaps model for improving service quality.

communication objectives Specific goals for a communication program related to the effects of the communication program on the customer's decision-making process.

comparable store sales growth The sales growth in stores that have been open for over one year; also called *same-store sales growth*.

competition-oriented method A pricing method in which a retailer uses competitors' prices, rather than demand or cost considerations, as guides.

competitive parity method An approach for setting a promotion budget so that the retailer's share of promotion expenses is equal to its market share.

competitive rivalry The frequency and intensity of reactions to actions undertaken by competitors.

composite segmentation A method of segmenting a retail market using multiple variables, including benefits sought, lifestyles, and demographics.

congestion The amount of crowding of either cars or people.

consideration set The set of alternatives the customer evaluates when making a merchandise selection.

consignment When the vendor owns the merchandise until it is sold by the retailer, at which time the retailer pays for the merchandise.

consortium exchange A retail exchange that is owned by several firms within one industry.

continuous replenishment A system of continuously monitoring merchandise sales and generating replacement orders, often automatically, when inventory levels drop below predetermined levels.

contribution margin Gross margin less any expense that can be directly assigned to the merchandise.

convenience stores Stores that provide a limited variety and assortment of merchandise at a convenient location with speedy checkout.

conventional supermarket A self-service food store that offers groceries, meat, and produce with limited sales of non-food items, such as health and beauty aids and general merchandise.

cookies Computer text files that identify visitors when they return to a website so that customers do not have to identify themselves or use passwords every time they visit the site. Cookies also collect information about other sites the person has visited and what pages have been downloaded.

copyright A regulation that protects original works of authors, painters, sculptors, musicians, and others who produce works of artistic or intellectual merit.

corporate social responsibility (CSR) Voluntary actions taken by a company to address the ethical, social, and environmental impacts of its business operations and the concerns of its stakeholders.

cost of goods sold Amount on an income statement that represents the cost of purchasing raw materials and manufacturing finished products.

cost per thousand (CPM) A measure that is often used to compare media. CPM is calculated by dividing an ad's cost by its reach.

cost-oriented method A method for determining the retail price by adding a fixed percentage to the cost of the merchandise; also known as *cost-plus pricing.*

counterfeit merchandise Goods that are made and sold without permission of the owner of a trademark, a copyright, or a patented invention that is legally protected in the country where it is marketed.

coupons Documents, electronic or hard copy, that entitle the holder to a reduced price or X cents off the actual price of a product or service.

coverage The theoretical number of potential customers in the retailer's target market that could be exposed to an ad in a given medium.

cross-docked Items that are unloaded from the shippers' truck and within a few hours reloaded onto trucks going to stores. These items are prepackaged by the vendor for a specific store, such that the UPC labels on a carton indicate the store to which it is to be sent.

cross-sectional ratio analysis The analysis of a financial ratio of a company with the same ratio of different companies in the same industry.

cross-selling When sales associates in one department attempt to sell complementary merchandise from other departments to their customers.

cross-shopping A pattern of buying both premium and low-priced merchandise or patronizing expensive, status-oriented retailers and price-oriented retailers.

culture The meaning and values shared by most members of a society.

cumulative attraction The principle that a cluster of similar and complementary retailing activities will generally have greater drawing power than isolated stores that engage in the same retailing activities.

cumulative reach The cumulative number of potential customers that would see an ad that runs several times.

current assets Cash or any assets that can normally be converted into cash within one year.

current liabilities Debts that are expected to be paid in less than one year.

customer database The coordinated and periodic copying of data from various sources, both inside and outside the enterprise, into an environment ready for analytical and informational processing. It contains all of the data the firm has collected about its customers and is the foundation for subsequent CRM activities; also called *customer data warehouse.*

customer loyalty Customers' commitment to shopping at a store.

customer relationship management (CRM) A business philosophy and set of strategies, programs, and systems that focuses on identifying and building loyalty with a retailer's most valued customers.

customer returns The value of merchandise that customers return because it is damaged, it doesn't fit, and so forth.

customer service The set of retail activities that increase the value customers receive when they shop and purchase merchandise.

cycle stock The inventory that goes up and down due to the replenishment process; also called *base stock.*

data mining Technique used to identify patterns in data found in data warehouses, typically patterns that the analyst is unaware of prior to searching through the data.

data warehouse The coordinated and periodic copying of data from various sources, both inside and outside the enterprise, into an environment ready for analytical and informational processing. It contains all of the data the firm has collected about its customers and is the foundation for subsequent CRM activities.

decentralization When authority for retail decisions is made at lower levels in the organization.

decile analysis A method of identifying customers in a CRM program that breaks customers into ten deciles based on their LTV (lifetime customer value). When using decile analysis, the top 10 percent of the customers would be the most-valued group.

delivery gap The difference between the retailer's service standards and the actual service provided to customers. This factor is one of the four factors identified by the gaps model for improving service quality.

demalling The activity of revitalizing a mall by demolishing a mall's small shops, scrapping its common space and food courts, enlarging the sites once occupied by department stores, and adding more entrances to the parking lot.

demand-oriented method A method of setting prices based on what the customers would expect or be willing to pay.

demographic segmentation A method of segmenting a retail market that groups consumers on the basis of easily measured, objective characteristics such as age, sex, income, and education.

department A segment of a store with merchandise that represents a group of classifications the consumer views as being complementary.

department store A retailer that carries a wide variety and deep assortment, offers considerable customer services, and is organized into separate departments for displaying merchandise.

depth The amount of a particular item of merchandise that a retailer will stock, reflecting attributes such as brand, size, or colour.

depth interview An unstructured personal interview in which the interviewer uses extensive probing to get individual respondents to talk in detail about a subject.

depth of merchandise The number of SKUs within a merchandise category; also called *assortment* and *depth of stock.*

destination stores Retail stores in which the merchandise, selection, presentation, pricing, or other unique feature acts as a magnet for customers.

digital signage Signs whose visual content is delivered digitally through a centrally managed and controlled network and displayed on a television monitor or flat-panel screen.

direct investment The investment and ownership by a retail firm or a division or subsidiary that builds and operates stores in a foreign country.

direct mail Any brochure, catalogue, advertisement, or other printed marketing material delivered directly to the consumer through the mail or by a private delivery company.

direct marketing A form of nonstore retailing in which customers are exposed to merchandise through print or electronic media; they then can purchase the merchandise by telephone, mail, or over the Internet.

direct selling A retail format in which a salesperson, frequently an independent distributor, contacts a customer directly in a convenient location (either at a customer's home or at work), demonstrates merchandise benefits, takes an order, and delivers the merchandise to the customer.

direct store delivery (DSD) A method of delivering merchandise to stores in which vendors distribute merchandise directly to the stores rather than going through distribution centres.

direct-response advertising Advertisements on TV and radio that describe products and provide an opportunity for customers to order them.

disability Any physical or mental impairment that substantially limits one or more of an individual's major life activities or any condition that is regarded as being such an impairment.

discount store A general merchandise retailer that offers a wide variety of merchandise, limited service, and low prices; also called *mass merchandiser* and *full-line discount store*.

discrimination An illegal action of a company or its managers that results when a member of a protected class (women, minorities, etc.) is treated differently from non-members of that class (see *disparate treatment*) or when an apparently neutral rule has an unjustified discriminatory effect (see *disparate impact*).

disparate impact In the case of discrimination, when an apparently neutral rule has an unjustified discriminatory effect, such as when a retailer requires high school graduation for all its employees, thereby excluding a larger proportion of disadvantaged minorities, when at least some of the jobs (e.g., custodian) could be performed just as well by people who did not graduate from high school.

disparate treatment In the case of discrimination, when members of a protected class are treated differently than non-members of that class, such as when a qualified woman (protected class) does not receive a promotion given to a less qualified man.

dispatcher A person who coordinates deliveries from the vendor to the distribution centre or stores, or from the distribution centre to stores.

distribution centre A warehouse that receives merchandise from multiple vendors and distributes it to multiple stores.

distribution channel A set of firms that facilitate the movement of products from the point of production to the point of sale to the ultimate consumer.

distributive fairness Exists when outcomes received are viewed as fair with respect to outcomes received by others.

distributive justice Exists when outcomes received are viewed as fair with respect to outcomes received by others.

diversification opportunity A strategic investment opportunity that involves an entirely new retail format directed toward a market segment not presently being served.

diverted merchandise Merchandise that is diverted from its legitimate channel of distribution; similar to grey-market merchandise except it need not be distributed across international boundaries.

downtown location The central business district located in the traditional shopping area of smaller towns, or a secondary business district in a suburb or within a larger city, generally featuring lower occupancy costs, fewer people, fewer stores, smaller overall selection of goods or services, and fewer entertainment and recreational activities than more successful primary central business districts.

drawing account A method of sales compensation in which salespeople receive a weekly cheque based on their estimated annual income.

drop-shipping A supply chain system in which retailers receive orders from customers and relay these orders to a vendor and then the vendor ships the merchandise ordered directly to the customer; also called *consumer direct fulfillment*.

drugstore Specialty retail store that concentrates on pharmaceuticals and health and personal grooming merchandise.

electronic article surveillance (EAS) system A loss-prevention system in which special tags placed on merchandise in retail stores are deactivated when the merchandise is purchased. The tags are used to discourage shoplifting.

electronic data interchange (EDI) The computer-to-computer exchange of business documents from retailer to vendor and back.

electronic retailing A retail format in which the retailers communicate with customers and offer products and services for sale over the Internet. Also called *e-tailing, online retailing,* and *Internet retailing*.

email A paid personal communication vehicle that involves sending messages over the Internet.

emotional support Supporting retail service providers with the understanding and positive regard to enable them to deal with the emotional stress created by disgruntled customers.

employee productivity Output generated by employee activities. One measure of employee productivity is the retailer's sales or profit divided by its employee costs.

employee turnover The number of employees occupying a set of positions during a period (usually a year) divided by the number of positions.

empowerment The process of managers sharing power and decision-making authority with employees.

end caps Display fixtures located at the end of an aisle.

ethics A system or code of conduct based on universal moral duties and obligations that indicate how one should behave.

everyday low pricing strategy (EDLP) A pricing strategy that stresses continuity of retail prices at a level somewhere between the regular non-sale price and the deep-discount sale price of the retailer's competitors.

exclusive co-brand A brand developed by a national brand vendor, often in conjunction with a retailer, and sold exclusively by the retailer.

exclusive dealing agreement Restriction a manufacturer or wholesaler places on a retailer to carry only its products and no competing vendors' products.

exclusive geographic territory A policy in which only one retailer in a certain territory is allowed to sell a particular brand.

expenses Costs incurred in the normal course of doing business to generate revenues.

extended problem solving A buying process in which customers spend considerable time at each stage of the decision-making process because the decision is important and they have limited knowledge of alternatives.

external sources of information Information provided by the media and other people.

extrinsic rewards Rewards (such as money, promotion, and recognition) given to employees by their manager or the firm.

factory outlets Outlet stores owned by a manufacturer.

fair trade Purchasing practices that require producers to pay workers a living wage, well more than the prevailing minimum wage, and offer other benefits, such as on-site medical treatment.

fashion merchandise category Category of merchandise that typically lasts several seasons, and sales can vary dramatically from one season to the next.

fashion/specialty centre A shopping centre that is composed mainly of upscale apparel shops, boutiques, and gift shops carrying selected fashions or unique merchandise of high quality and price.

feature areas Areas designed to get the customer's attention that include end caps, promotional aisles or areas, freestanding fixtures and mannequins that introduce a soft goods department, windows, and point-of-sale areas.

fill rate The percentage of an order that is shipped by the vendor.

financial resources Resources that enable companies to make strategic decisions, such as expansion into international markets, requiring significant and ongoing financial commitment, often at the expense of short-term profit.

first-degree price discrimination Charging customers different prices based on their willingness to pay.

fixed assets Assets that require more than a year to convert to cash.

fixed costs Costs that are stable and don't change with the quantity of product that's produced and sold.

flextime A job scheduling system that enables employees to choose the times they work.

floor-ready merchandise Merchandise received at the store ready to be sold, without the need for any additional preparation by retail employees.

focus group A marketing research technique in which a small group of respondents is interviewed by a moderator using a loosely structured format.

forecast To estimate or calculate in advance: predict the future.

four-way fixture A fixture with two cross-bars that sit perpendicular to each other on a pedestal. Also known as a *feature fixture*.

franchisees The owner of an individual store in a franchise agreement.

franchising A contractual agreement between a franchisor and a franchisee that allows the franchisee to operate a retail outlet using a name and format developed and supported by the franchisor.

franchisors The owner of a franchise in a franchise agreement.

free trade zone A special area within a country that can be used for warehousing, packaging, inspection, labelling, exhibition, assembly, fabrication, or transshipment of imports without being subject to that country's tariffs.

free-form layout A store design, used primarily in small specialty stores or within the boutiques of large stores, that arranges fixtures and aisles asymmetrically. Also called *boutique layout*.

freestanding fixtures Fixtures and mannequins located on aisles that are designed primarily to get customers' attention and bring them into a department.

freestanding insert (FSI) An advertisement printed at the retailer's expense and distributed as an insert in the newspaper; also called a *preprint*.

freestanding site A retail location that is not connected to other retailers.

freight forwarders Companies that purchase transport services. They then consolidate small shipments from a number of shippers into large shipments that move at a lower freight rate.

frequency The number of times a potential customer is exposed to a promotional message.

frequent shopper program A reward and communication program used by a retailer to encourage continued purchases from the retailer's best customers.

frontal presentation A method of displaying merchandise in which the retailer exposes as much of the product as possible to catch the customer's eye.

full-time equivalent (FTE) The relationship between net sales for a specified period of time and the number of full-time equivalent employees who worked during that specified period of time.

gamification The application of game theory concepts and techniques to non-game activities.

generic branding A branding strategy that targets a price-sensitive segment by offering a no-frills product at a discount price.

gentrification A process in which old buildings are torn down or are restored to create new offices, housing developments, and retailers.

geodemographic segmentation A market segmentation system that uses both geographic and demographic characteristics to classify consumers.

geographic information system (GIS) Computerized systems that enable analysts to visualize information about their customers' demographics, buying behaviour, and other data in a map format.

geographic segmentation Segmentation of potential customers by where they live. A retail market can be segmented by countries, provinces, cities, and neighbourhoods.

glass ceiling A figurative barrier that makes it difficult for minorities and women to be promoted beyond a certain level.

global culture A company's embracing a multicultural perspective and developing an infrastructure that makes maximal use of local management.

global strategy Replicating a retailer's standard retail format and centralized management throughout the world in each new market.

globally sustainable competitive advantage One of the characteristics of retailers that have successfully exploited international growth opportunities.

gondola An island type of self-service counter with tiers of shelves, bins, or pegs.

grey-market good Merchandise that possesses a valid North American registered trademark and is made by a foreign manufacturer but is imported into North America without permission of the trademark owner.

grid layout A store design, typically used by grocery stores, in which merchandise is displayed on long gondolas in aisles with a repetitive pattern.

gross margin The difference between the price the customer pays for merchandise and the cost of the merchandise (the price the retailer paid the supplier of the merchandise). More specifically, gross margin = net sales − cost of goods sold (= maintained markup) − alteration cost + cash discounts; also called *gross profit*.

gross margin return on investment (GMROI) A financial ratio that assesses a buyer's contribution to return on assets: gross margin dollars divided by average (cost) inventory.

habitual decision making A purchase decision involving little or no conscious effort.

hedonic benefit Shopping for pleasure, entertainment, and/or to achieve an emotional or recreational experience.

hedonic needs Needs motivating consumers to go shopping for pleasure.

high-assay principle A method of allocating a communication budget that uses the principles of marginal analysis. The retailer should allocate the budget to areas that will yield the greatest return.

high/low pricing A strategy in which retailers offer prices that are sometimes above their competition's everyday low price, but they use advertising to promote frequent sales.

Huff gravity model A trade area analysis model used to determine the probability that a customer residing in a particular area will shop at a particular store or shopping centre.

hypermarkets Large combination food (60–70 percent) and general merchandise (30–40 percent) retailers.

idea-oriented presentation A method of presenting merchandise based on a specific idea or the image of the store.

identifiability Permits a retailer to determine a market segment's size and with whom the retailer should communicate when promoting its retail offering.

illegal discrimination The actions of a company or its managers that result in members of a protected class being treated unfairly and differently than others.

impact An ad's effect on the audience.

impulse products Products that are purchased by customers without prior plans. These products are almost always located near the front of the store, where they are seen by everyone and may actually draw people into the store.

in-store kiosks Spaces located within stores containing a computer connected to the store's central offices or to the Internet.

incentive compensation plan A compensation plan that rewards employees on the basis of their productivity.

independent exchange A retail exchange owned by a third party that provides the electronic platform to perform the exchange functions.

infomercials TV programs, typically 30 minutes long, that mix entertainment with product demonstrations and solicit orders placed by telephone from consumers.

information search The stage in the buying process in which a customer seeks additional information to satisfy a need.

ingress/egress The means of entering/exiting the parking lot of a retail site.

initial markup The retail selling price initially placed on the merchandise less the cost of goods sold.

input measure A performance measure used to assess the amount of resources or money used by the retailer to achieve outputs.

instrumental support Support for retail service providers such as appropriate systems and equipment to deliver the service desired by customers.

integrated marketing communication program The strategic integration of multiple communication methods to form a comprehensive, consistent message.

intellectual property Property that is intangible and is created by intellectual (mental) effort as opposed to physical effort.

interest The amount charged by a financial institution to borrow money.

interest income The income a retailer can generate through proprietary credit cards, bank deposits, bonds, treasury bills, fixed income investments, and other investments.

internal sources of information Information in a customer's memory such as names, images, and past experiences with different stores.

intertype competition Competition between retailers that sell similar merchandise using different formats, such as discount and department stores.

intratype competition Competition between retailers of the same type (e.g., Loblaws versus Sobeys).

intrinsic rewards Non-monetary, intangible rewards employees get from doing their jobs.

inventory Goods or merchandise available for resale.

inventory turnover Net sales divided by average retail inventory; used to evaluate how effectively managers use their investment in inventory.

item price The practice of marking prices only on shelves or signs and not on individual items.

job analysis Identifying essential activities and determining the qualifications employees need to perform them effectively.

job application form A form a job applicant completes that contains information about the applicant's employment history, previous compensation, reasons for leaving previous employment, education and training, personal health, and references.

job description A description of the activities the employee needs to perform and the firm's performance expectations.

job sharing When two or more employees voluntarily are responsible for a job that was previously held by one person.

joint venture An entity formed when the entering retailer pools its resources with a local retailer to form a new company in which ownership, control, and profits are shared.

keystone method A method of setting retail prices in which retailers simply double the cost of the merchandise to obtain the original retail selling price.

kiosk A small selling space offering a limited merchandise assortment.

knockoff A copy of the latest styles displayed at designer fashion shows and sold in exclusive specialty stores. These copies are sold at lower prices through retailers targeting a broader market.

knowledge gap The difference between customer expectations and the retailer's perception of customer expectations. This factor is one of four factors identified by the gaps model for improving service quality.

lead time The amount of time between recognition that an order needs to be placed and the point at which the merchandise arrives in the store and is ready for sale.

leader pricing A pricing strategy in which certain items are priced lower than normal to increase the traffic flow of customers or to increase the sale of complementary products.

leadership The process by which a person attempts to influence another to accomplish some goal or goals.

leased department An area in a retail store leased or rented to an independent company. The leaseholder is typically responsible for all retail mix decisions involved in operating the department and pays the store a percentage of its sales as rent.

liabilities Obligations of a retail enterprise to pay cash or other economic resources in return for past, present, or future benefits.

licensed brand Brand for which the licensor (owner of a well-known name) enters into a contractual arrangement with a licensee (a retailer or a third party). The licensee either manufactures or contracts with a manufacturer to produce the licensed product and pays a royalty to the licensor.

lifestyle centre A shopping centre with an outdoor, traditional streetscape layout with sit-down restaurants and a conglomeration of specialty retailers.

lifestyle segmentation A method of segmenting a retail market based on consumers' lifestyles.

lifetime customer value (LTV) The expected contribution from the customer to the retailer's profits over his or her entire relationship with the retailer.

limited problem solving A purchase-decision process involving a moderate amount of effort and time. Customers engage in this type of buying process when they have some prior experience with the product or service and their risk is moderate.

limited-assortment supermarkets Supermarkets offering a limited number of SKUs; also called *extreme-value food retailers*.

locavore movement A movement whose adherents' primary source of food originates within a specified radius of where they live.

logistics Part of the supply chain process that plans, implements, and controls the efficient, effective flow and storage of goods, services, and related information from the point of origin to the point of consumption to meet customers' requirements.

long-term liabilities Debts that will be paid after one year.

low-price guarantee policy A policy that guarantees that the retailer will have the lowest possible price for a product or group of products, and usually promises to match or better any lower price found in the local market.

loyalty program A program set up to reward customers with incentives such as discounts on purchases, free food, gifts, or even cruises or trips in return for their repeated business.

m-commerce The purchase of products and services through mobile devices.

macro-environment The external environment that the retailer cannot control, including competition, economic stability of the trade area, the technology that will make retailing more efficient, the regulatory and ethical environment in which the business operates, and social trends, including consumer behaviour and lifestyle and demographic trends.

maintained markup The amount of markup the retailer wishes to maintain on a particular category of merchandise; net sales minus cost of goods sold.

mall A shopping centre with a pedestrian focus where customers park in outlying areas and walk to the stores.

management A strategic approach of an organization to achieve its objectives by developing policies and plans for allocating resources.

managing diversity A set of human resource management programs designed to realize the benefits of a diverse workforce.

manufacturer brand A line of products designed, produced, and marketed by a vendor; also called a *national brand*.

maquiladoras Manufacturing plants in Mexico that make goods and parts or process food for export to North America.

marginal analysis A method of analysis used in setting a promotional budget or allocating retail space, based on the economic principle that firms should increase expenditures as long as each additional dollar spent generates more than a dollar of additional contribution.

markdown money Funds provided by a vendor to a retailer to cover decreased gross margin from markdowns and other merchandising issues.

markdowns The price reductions in the initial retail price.

market A group of vendors in a concentrated geographic location or even under one roof or over the Internet; also known as a *central market*.

market basket analysis Specific type of data analysis that focuses on the composition of the basket (or bundle) of products purchased by a household during a single shopping occasion.

market expansion opportunity A strategic investment opportunity that employs the existing retailing format in new market segments.

market penetration opportunity An investment opportunity strategy that focuses on increasing sales to present customers using the present retailing format.

markup The increase in the retail price of an item after the initial markup percentage has been applied but before the item is placed on the selling floor.

markup percentage The markup as a percent of retail price.

med-arb Used in the case of a dispute between retailer and vendor that involves an initial attempt at mediation followed by binding arbitration if the mediation is unsuccessful. See *mediation* and *arbitration*.

mediation Used in the case of a dispute between retailer and vendor that involves selecting a neutral party—the mediator—to assist the parties in reaching a mutually agreeable settlement.

mentoring program The assigning of higher-level managers to help lower-level managers learn the firm's values and meet other senior executives.

merchandise budget plan A plan used by buyers to determine how much money to spend in each month on a particular fashion merchandise category, given the firm's sales forecast, inventory turnover, and profit goals.

merchandise category An assortment of items (SKUs) the customer sees as reasonable substitutes for each other.

merchandise group A group within an organization managed by the senior vice presidents of merchandise and responsible for several departments.

merchandise management The process by which a retailer attempts to offer the right quantity of the right merchandise in the right place at the right time while meeting the company's financial goal.

merchandising optimization software Set of algorithms (computer programs) that monitors merchandise sales, promotions, competitors' actions, and other factors to determine the optimal (most profitable) price and timing for merchandising activities, especially markdowns.

micro-environment All of the things within the retailer's control, including the retail product that will be sold, the price for the product, the store location, the promotion and visual image of the store, the processes, and human resource management decisions.

mission statement A broad description of the scope of activities a business plans to undertake.

mixed-use development (MXD) Development that combines several uses in one complex—for example, shopping centre, office tower, hotel, residential complex, civic centre, and convention centre.

mobile marketing Communicating with and selling to customers through wireless handheld devices, such as cellular telephones; also called *m-commerce* or *mobile commerce*.

model stock plan A summary of the desired inventory levels of each SKU stocked in a store for a merchandise category.

multiattribute analysis method A method for evaluating vendors that uses a weighted average score for each vendor, which is based on the importance of various issues and the vendor's performance on those issues.

multiattribute attitude model A model of customer decision making based on the notion that customers see a retailer or a product as a collection of attributes or characteristics. The model can also be used for evaluating a retailer, product, or vendor. The model uses a weighted average score based on the importance of various issues and performance on those issues.

multichannel retailer Retailer that sells merchandise or services through more than one channel.

multilevel system A retail format in which people serve as master distributors, recruiting other people to become distributors in their network.

multinational strategy A strategy that involves changing a retailer's products and image to reflect the international marketplace, using a decentralized format, learning about the country's culture, and changing the retail concept to adapt to cultural differences and cater to local market demands.

multiple-unit pricing Practice of offering two or more similar products or services for sale at one price.

mystery shopper Professional shopper who "shops" a store to assess the service provided by store employees.

natural barriers Barriers, such as rivers or mountains, that affect accessibility to a site.

near-field communications (NFC) A set of standards for smartphones and similar devices to establish radio communication with each other by touching them together or bringing them into close proximity, usually no more than a few inches.

net profit A measure of the overall performance of a firm; revenues (sales) minus expenses and losses for the period.

net profit margin The profit (after tax) a firm makes divided by its net sales.

net sales The total number of dollars received by a retailer after all refunds have been paid to customers for returned merchandise.

North American Industry Classification System (NAICS) Classification of retail firms into a hierarchical set of six-digit codes based on the types of products and services they produce and sell.

notes payable Current liabilities representing principal and interest the retailer owes to financial institutions (banks) that are due and payable in less than a year.

objective-and-task method A method for setting a promotion budget in which the retailer first establishes a set of communication objectives and then determines the necessary tasks and their costs.

odd pricing The practice of ending prices with an odd number (such as 69 cents) or just under a round number (such as $98 instead of $100).

off-price retailer A retailer that offers an inconsistent assortment of brand-name, fashion-oriented soft goods at low prices.

omni-channel retailing Seamless integration between all channels so that shoppers can shop any way they want with the exact same results.

operating expenses Costs, other than the cost of merchandise, incurred in the normal course of doing business, such as salaries for sales associates and managers, advertising, utilities, office supplies, and rent.

opportunity cost of capital The rate available on the next-best use of the capital invested in the project at hand. The opportunity cost should be no lower than the rate at which a firm borrows funds, since one alternative is to pay back borrowed money. It can be higher, however, depending on the range of other opportunities available. Typically, the opportunity cost rises with investment risk.

order point The amount of inventory below which the quantity available shouldn't go or the item will be out of stock before the next order arrives.

organization structure A plan that identifies the activities to be performed by specific employees and determines the lines of authority and responsibility in the firm.

organizational culture A firm's set of values, traditions, and customs that guide employee behaviour.

outlet centres Typically feature stores owned by retail chains or manufacturers that sell excess and out-of-season merchandise at reduced prices.

outlet stores Off-price retailers owned by a manufacturer or a department or specialty store chain.

output measure Measure that assesses the results of retailers' investment decisions.

outsource Obtain a service from outside the company that had previously been done by the firm itself.

overstored trade area An area having so many stores selling a specific good or service that some stores will fail.

owners' equity The amount of assets belonging to the owners of the retail firm after all obligations (liabilities) have been met; also known as *net worth* and *shareholders' equity*.

parallel branding A branding strategy that represents a private label that closely imitates the trade dress (packaging) and product attributes of leading manufacturer brands but with a clearly articulated "invitation to compare" in its merchandising approach and on its product label.

party plan system Salespeople encourage people to act as hosts and invite friends or co-workers to a "party" at which the merchandise is demonstrated. The host or hostess receives a gift or commission for arranging the meeting.

percentage-of-sales method A method for setting a promotion budget based on a fixed percentage of forecast sales.

perpetual inventory An accounting procedure whose objectives are to maintain a perpetual or book inventory in retail dollar amounts and to maintain records that make it possible to determine the cost value of the inventory at any time without taking a physical inventory; also known as *book inventory system* or *retail inventory method (RIM)*.

personal selling A communication process in which salespeople help customers satisfy their needs through face-to-face exchanges of information.

pick ticket A document that tells the order filler how much of each item to get from the storage area.

planogram A diagram created from photographs, computer output, or artists' renderings that illustrates exactly where every SKU should be placed.

point-of-purchase (POP) An area where the customer waits at checkout.

point-of-sale (POS) areas Areas where the customer waits at checkout. This area can be the most valuable piece of real estate in the store, because the customer is almost held captive in that spot; also called *point-of-purchase (POP) areas.*

point-of-sale signage Signs placed near the merchandise they refer to so that customers know the price and other detailed information.

polygons Trade areas whose boundaries conform to streets and other map features rather than being concentric circles.

pop-up stores Stores in temporary locations that focus on new products or a limited group of products.

popping the merchandise Focusing spotlights on special feature areas and items.

positioning The design and implementation of a retail mix to create in the customer's mind an image of the retailer relative to its competitors; also called *brand building*.

post-purchase evaluation The evaluation of merchandise or services after the customer has purchased and consumed them.

power centre Shopping centre that is dominated by several large anchors, including discount stores, off-price stores, warehouse clubs, or category specialists.

power perimeter The area around the outside walls of a supermarket that have fresh-merchandise categories.

premium A type of sales promotion whereby an item is offered free of charge or at a bargain price to reward some type of behaviour, such as buying, sampling, or testing.

premium branding A branding strategy that offers the consumer a private label at a comparable manufacturer-brand quality, usually with a modest price savings.

price bundling The practice of offering two or more different products or services for sale at one price.

price lining A pricing policy in which a retailer offers a limited number of predetermined price points within a classification.

primary zone The geographic area from which the store or shopping centre derives 60 to 65 percent of its customers; also called *primary trade area*.

private exchanges Exchanges that are operated for the exclusive use of a single firm.

private-label brands Products developed and marketed by a retailer and available for sale only by that retailer; also called *store brands*.

private-label credit card A credit card that has the store's name on it and is issued by the retailer.

procedural fairness The perceived fairness of the process used to resolve customer complaints.

procedural justice An employee's perception of fairness (how he or she is treated) that is based on the process used to determine the outcome.

product availability A measurement of the percentage of demand for a particular SKU that is satisfied.

productivity measure The ratio of an output to an input determining how effectively a firm uses a resource.

promotion from within A staffing policy that involves hiring new employees only for positions at the lowest level in the job hierarchy and then promoting employees for openings at higher levels in the hierarchy.

promotional aisle or area Aisle or area of a store designed to get the customer's attention. An example might be a special "trim-the-tree" department that seems magically to appear right after Halloween every year for the Christmas holidays.

promotional allowances Payments made by vendors to retailers to compensate the latter for money spent in advertising a particular item.

promotional signage Describes special offers and may be displayed in windows to entice the customer into the store.

proprietary store credit card system A system in which credit cards have the store's name on them and the accounts receivable are administered by the retailer; also known as an *in-house credit system*.

psychographics Refers to how consumers live, how they spend their time and money, what activities they pursue, and their attitudes and opinions about the world they live in.

public relations (PR) A retail communication tool for managing communications and relationships to achieve various objectives, such as building and maintaining a positive image of the retailer, handling or heading off unfavourable stories or events, and maintaining positive relationships with the media.

public warehouses Warehouses that are owned and operated by a third party.

pull distribution strategy Strategy in which orders for merchandise are generated at the store level on the basis of demand data captured by point-of-sale terminals.

pull supply chain Strategy in which orders for merchandise are generated at store level on the basis of demand data captured by point-of-sale terminals.

push distribution strategy Strategy in which merchandise is allocated to stores based on historical demand, the inventory position at the distribution centre, as well as the stores' needs.

push supply chain Strategy in which merchandise is allocated to stores on the basis of historical demand, the inventory position at the distribution centre, and the stores' needs.

pyramid scheme When a firm and its program are designed to sell merchandise and services to other distributors rather than to end users.

quick response (QR) delivery system A system designed to reduce the lead time for receiving merchandise, thereby lowering inventory investment, improving customer service levels, and reducing distribution expenses; also known as a *just-in-time inventory management system*.

quota Target level used to motivate and evaluate performance.

quota–bonus plan Compensation plan that has a performance goal or objective established to evaluate employee performance, such as sales per hour for salespeople and maintained margin and turnover for buyers.

racetrack layout A type of store layout that provides a major aisle to facilitate customer traffic that has access to the store's multiple entrances. Also known as a *loop*.

radio frequency identification (RFID) A technology that allows an object or person to be identified at a distance by means of radio waves.

rain check When sale merchandise is out of stock, a written promise to customers to sell them that merchandise at the sale price when it arrives.

reach The actual number of customers in the target market exposed to an advertising medium.

rebate Money returned to the buyer in the form of cash based on a portion of the purchasing price.

receiving The process of filling out paperwork to record the receipt of merchandise that arrives at a store or distribution centre.

reductions Markdowns; discounts to employees and customers; and inventory shrinkage due to shoplifting, breakage, or loss.

reference group One or more people whom a person uses as a basis of comparison for his or her beliefs, feelings, and behaviours.

region In retail location analysis, refers to a part of the country, a particular city, or a census metropolitan area (CMA).

regional centre Shopping mall that provides general merchandise (a large percentage of which is apparel) and services in full depth and variety.

regression analysis A statistical approach based on the assumption that factors that affect the sales of existing stores in a chain will have the same impact on stores located at new sites.

Reilly's law of retail gravitation A model used in trade area analysis to define the relative ability of two cities to attract customers from the area between them.

related diversification opportunity A diversification opportunity strategy in which the retailer's present offering and market share something in common with the market and format being considered.

retail chain A firm that consists of multiple retail units under common ownership and usually has some centralization of decision making in defining and implementing its strategy.

retail exchanges Electronic marketplaces operated by organizations that facilitate the buying and selling of merchandise using the Internet.

retail format The retailers' type of retail mix (product, price [value], promotion [communication], place, people, and processes).

retail format development opportunity An investment opportunity strategy in which a retailer offers a new retail format—a format involving a different retail mix—to the same target market.

retail market A group of consumers with similar needs (a market segment) and a group of retailers using a similar retail format to satisfy those consumer needs.

retail market segment A group of customers whose needs will be satisfied by the same retail offering because they have similar needs and go through similar buying processes.

retail strategy A statement that indicates (1) the target market toward which a retailer plans to commit its resources, (2) the nature of the retail offering that the retailer plans to use to satisfy the needs of the target market, and (3) the bases upon which the retailer will attempt to build a sustainable competitive advantage over competitors.

retailer A business that sells products and services to consumers for their personal or family use.

retailer loyalty Indicates that customers like and habitually visit the same retailer to purchase a type of merchandise.

retailing A set of business activities that adds value to the products and services sold to consumers for their personal or family use.

retailing concept A management orientation that holds that the key task of a retailer is to determine the needs and wants of its target markets and to direct the firm toward satisfying those needs and wants more effectively and efficiently than competitors do.

retained earnings The portion of owners' equity that has accumulated over time through profits but has not been paid out in dividends to owners.

return on assets (ROA) Net profit after taxes divided by total assets.

reverse auction Auction conducted by retailer buyers. Known as a reverse auction because there is one buyer and many potential sellers. In reverse auctions, retail buyers provide a specification for what they want to a group of potential vendors. The competing vendors then bid down the price at which they are willing to sell until the buyer accepts a bid.

reverse logistics The process of capturing value from and/or properly disposing of merchandise returned by customers and/or stores.

RFM (recency, frequency, monetary) analysis Often used by catalogue retailers and direct marketers, a scheme for segmenting customers based on how recently they have made a purchase, how frequently they make purchases, and how much they have bought.

road condition Includes the age, number of lanes, number of stoplights, congestion, and general state of repair of roads in a trade area.

road pattern A consideration used in measuring the accessibility of a retail location via major arteries, highways, or roads.

rounder A round fixture that sits on a pedestal. Smaller than the straight rack, it is designed to hold a maximum amount of merchandise. Also known as a *bulk fixture* or *capacity fixture*.

rule-of-thumb methods A type of approach for setting a promotion budget that uses past sales and communication activity to determine the present communications budget.

sales per employee hour A common measure of productivity that retailers use by dividing net sales by the total number of hours worked by the employee or employees during the specified time frame.

sales per full-time employee A method used by retailers to calculate the many ways in which salary costs can accumulate.

sales per linear foot A measure of space productivity used when most merchandise is displayed on multiple shelves of long gondolas, such as in grocery stores.

sales per square foot A measure of space productivity used by most retailers since rent and land purchases are assessed on a per-square-foot basis.

sales promotions Paid, impersonal communication activities that offer extra value and incentives to customers to visit a store or purchase merchandise during a specific period of time.

samples A small amount or size of a product given to potential customers as an inducement to purchase.

satisfaction A post-consumption evaluation of the degree to which a store or product meets or exceeds customer expectations.

saturated trade area A trade area that offers customers a good selection of goods and services, while allowing competing retailers to make good profits.

scale economies Cost advantages due to the size of a retailer.

scrambled merchandising The offering of merchandise not typically associated with the store type, such as clothing in a drugstore.

search engines Computer programs that simply search for and provide a listing of all Internet sites selling a product category or brand with the price of the merchandise offered; also called *shopping bots*.

seasonal merchandise category Category of inventory whose sales fluctuate dramatically according to the time of the year.

second-degree price discrimination Charging different prices to different people on the basis of the nature of the offering.

secondary zone The geographic area of secondary importance in terms of customer sales, generating about 20 percent of a store's sales; also called *secondary trade area*.

security policy The set of rules that applies to activities in the computer and communications resources that belong to an organization.

sell-through analysis A comparison of actual and planned sales to determine whether early markdowns are required or whether more merchandise is needed to satisfy demand.

selling cost The relationship between sales productivity and wages; can be calculated for an individual salesperson, a department, and the entire store.

selling, general, and administrative expenses (SG&A) Operating expenses, plus the depreciation and amortization of assets.

service gap The difference between customers' expectations and perceptions of customer service, assessed in order to improve customers' satisfaction with their service.

service level A measure used in inventory management to define the level of support or level of product availability; the number of items sold divided by the number of items demanded. Service level should not be confused with customer service. Also called *level of support.*

services retailer Organization that offers consumers services rather than merchandise. Examples include banks, hospitals, health spas, doctors, legal clinics, entertainment firms, and universities.

servuction system A design that includes both a visible and invisible area which provides value to the consumer.

share of wallet The percentage of total purchases made by a customer in a store.

shareholders' equity The amount of assets belonging to the owners of the retail firm after all obligations (liabilities) have been met.

shopping centre A group of retail and other commercial establishments that is planned, developed, owned, and managed as a single property.

short code A five- or six-digit number or word used for messaging.

showrooming Visiting a bricks-and-mortar store to research a product before purchasing it through electronic means after browsing online for the best price.

shrinkage An inventory reduction that is caused by shoplifting by employees or customers, by merchandise being misplaced or damaged, or by poor bookkeeping.

situation audit An analysis of the opportunities and threats in the retail environment and the strengths and weaknesses of the retail business relative to its competitors.

skeletal statement An analysis of the five key categories found in all operating statements.

SKU (stock keeping unit) The smallest unit available for keeping inventory control. In soft goods merchandise, an SKU usually means size, colour, and style.

slotting allowance Fee paid by a vendor for space in a retail store; also called a *slotting fee.*

social media Media content distributed through social interactions; major online facilitators of social media include YouTube, Facebook, Pinterest, and Twitter.

socialization The steps taken to transform new employees into effective, committed members of the firm.

SoLoMo (social, local, and mobile) The convergence of collaborative, location-based, and on-the-go technologies.

special event Sales promotion program comprising a number of sales promotion techniques built around a seasonal, cultural, sporting, musical, or other event.

specialization The organizational structure in which employees are typically responsible for only one or two tasks rather than performing all tasks. This enables employees to develop expertise and increase productivity.

specialty store Store concentrating on a limited number of complementary merchandise categories and providing a high level of service in an area typically under 8000 square feet.

standardization approach An approach used by retailers to provide customer service by using a set of rules and procedures so that all customers consistently receive the same service.

standards gap The difference between the retailer's perceptions of customers' expectations and the customer service standards it sets. This factor is one of four factors identified by the gaps model for improving service quality.

staple merchandise category A category of inventory that has continuous demand by customers over an extended period of time; also called *basic merchandise category.*

stock keeping unit (SKU) The smallest unit available for keeping inventory control. In soft goods merchandise, an SKU usually means a size, colour, and style.

stock-to-sales ratio Specifies the amount of inventory that should be on hand at the beginning of the month to support the sales forecast and maintain the inventory turnover objective.

stockout A situation occurring when an SKU that a customer wants is not available.

store advocates Customers who like a store so much that they actively share their positive experiences with friends and family.

straight commission A form of salesperson's compensation in which the amount paid is based on a percentage of sales made minus merchandise returned.

straight rack A type of fixture that consists of a long pipe suspended with supports going to the floor or attached to a wall.

strategic alliance Collaborative relationship between independent firms. For example, a foreign retailer might enter an international market through direct investment but develop an alliance with a local firm to perform logistical and warehousing activities.

strategic profit model (SPM) A tool used for planning a retailer's financial strategy based on both margin management (net profit margin), asset management (asset turnover), and financial leverage management (financial leverage ratio). Using the SPM, a retailer's objective is to achieve a target return on owners' equity.

strategic relationship Long-term relationship in which partners make significant investments to improve both parties' profitability; also called a *partnering relationship.*

strategic retail planning process The steps a retailer goes through to develop a strategic retail plan. It describes how retailers select target market segments, determine the appropriate retail format, and build sustainable competitive advantages.

strengths and weaknesses analysis A critical aspect of the situation audit in which a retailer determines its unique capabilities—its strengths and weaknesses relative to its competition.

strip centre A shopping centre that usually has parking directly in front of the stores and does not have enclosed walkways linking the stores.

subculture A distinctive group of people within a culture. Members of a subculture share some customs and norms with the overall society but also have some unique perspectives.

supercentres Large stores (160 000 to 200 000 square feet) combining a discount store with a supermarket.

superregional centre Similar to a regional centre, but because of its larger size, it has more anchors and a deeper selection of merchandise, and it draws from a larger population base.

superstore A large supermarket between 35 000 and 45 000 square feet in size.

supply chain management The set of approaches and techniques firms employ to efficiently and effectively integrate their suppliers, manufacturers, warehouses, stores, and transportation intermediaries to efficiently have the right quantities at the right locations, and at the right time.

sustainable competitive advantage A distinct competency of a retailer relative to its competitors that can be maintained over a considerable time period.

SWOT analysis An analysis of strengths, weaknesses, opportunities, and threats, designed to assess both the micro- and macro-environments and their relation to the retailer.

symbiotic store A store that does not create its own traffic and whose trade area is determined by the dominant retailer in the shopping centre or retail area; also called a *parasite store.*

target market The market segment(s) toward which the retailer plans to focus its resources and retail mix.

tariff A tax placed by a government upon imports; also called *duty.*

television home shopping A retail format in which customers watch a TV program demonstrating merchandise and then place orders for the merchandise by phone; also called *teleshopping.*

tertiary zone The outermost ring of a trade area that includes customers who occasionally shop at the store or shopping centre; also called *tertiary trade area.*

ticketing and marking Procedures for making price labels and placing them on the merchandise.

time-series analysis A comparison of a variable to itself over time.

tonnage merchandising A display technique in which large quantities of merchandise are displayed together.

top-down planning One side of the process of developing an overall retail strategy where goals are set at the top of the organization and filter down through the operating levels.

top-of-mind awareness The highest level of brand awareness; arises when consumers mention a brand name first when they are asked about a type of retailer, a merchandise category, or a type of service.

trade area A geographic sector that contains potential customers for a particular retailer or shopping centre.

trade shows Temporary concentrations of vendors that provide retailers opportunities to place orders and view what is available in the marketplace; also known as a *merchandise show* or *market week.*

trademark Any mark, work, picture, or design associated with a particular line of merchandise or product.

traditional strip centre A shopping centre that is designed to provide convenience shopping for the day-to-day needs of consumers in their immediate neighbourhood.

traffic flow The balance between a substantial number of cars and not so many that congestion impedes access to the store.

trust A belief that a partner is honest (reliable, stands by its word, sincere, fulfills obligations) and is benevolent (concerned about the other party's welfare).

tying contract An agreement between a vendor and a retailer requiring the retailer to take a product it does not necessarily desire (the tied product) to ensure that it can buy a product it does desire (the tying product).

understored trade area An area that has too few stores selling a specific good or service to satisfy the needs of the population.

Universal Product Code (UPC) The black-and-white bar code found on most merchandise that is used to collect sales information at the point of sale using computer terminals that read the code. This information is transmitted computer to computer to buyers, distribution centres, and then to vendors, who in turn quickly ship replenishment merchandise.

unrelated diversification Diversification in which there is no commonality between the present business and the new business.

utilitarian benefit A motivation for shopping in which consumers accomplish a specific task, such as buying a suit for a job interview.

utilitarian needs Needs motivating consumers to go shopping to accomplish a specific task.

value Relationship between what a customer gets (goods/services) and what he or she has to pay for it.

value retailers General merchandise discount stores that are found in low-income urban or rural areas and are much smaller than traditional discount stores, less than 9000 square feet.

variable cost A cost that varies with the level of sales and that can be applied directly to the decision in question.

variable pricing Charging different prices in different stores, markets, or zones.

variety The number of different merchandise categories within a store or department; also called *breadth.*

vending machine retailing A non-store format in which merchandise or services are stored in a machine and dispensed to customers when they deposit cash or use a credit card.

vendor-managed inventory (VMI) An approach for improving supply chain efficiency in which the vendor is responsible for maintaining the retailer's inventory levels in each of its stores.

vertical integration An example of diversification by retailers involving investments by retailers in wholesaling or manufacturing merchandise.

vertical merchandising A method whereby merchandise is organized to follow the eye's natural up-and-down movement.

visibility The customers' ability to see the store and enter the parking lot safely.

visual merchandising The presentation of a store and its merchandise in ways that will attract the attention of potential customers.

warehouse club A retailer that offers a limited assortment of food and general merchandise with little service and low prices to ultimate consumers and small businesses.

weeks of inventory The number of months of supply times four weeks.

wholesale-sponsored voluntary cooperative group An organization operated by a wholesaler offering a merchandising program to small, independent retailers on a voluntary basis.

yield management The practice of adjusting prices up or down in response to demand to control sales generated.

zone pricing Charging different prices for the same merchandise in different geographic locations to be competitive in local markets.

Chapter 1

1. http://www.runningroom.com/hm/inside.php?lang=1&id=2669 (accessed December 13, 2015).
2. For a more detailed discussion of distribution channels, see Louis W. Stern, Adel I. El-Ansary, Erin Anderson, and Anne T. Coughlan, *Marketing Channels* (Englewood Cliffs, NJ: Prentice Hall, 2002).
3. http://catalyst.ca/2015-canadian-smartphone-market/ (accessed December 15, 2015).
4. http://www.bsr.org (accessed May 21, 2007).
5. "Corporate Social Responsibility Practices Present Opportunity for Canadian Retailers," *Canadian Retailer,* September/October 2009, http://www.retailcouncil.org/cdnretailer, p. 4.
6. Luciano Barin Cruz and Eugenio Avila Pedrozo, "Corporate Social Responsibility and Green Management: Relation between Headquarters and Subsidiary in Multinational Corporations," *Management Decision 47,* no. 7 (2009), pp. 1174–1199.
7. http://corp.canadiantire.ca/EN/CorporateCitizenship/Pages/default.aspx (accessed December 15, 2015).
8. Christopher Daniel and Tony Hernandez, *The CSCA retail 100* (Centre for the study of Commercial Activity 2014).
9. Christopher Daniel & Tony Hernandez, *The CSCA retail 100,* p. 2 (Centre for the Study of Commercial Activity 2014).
10. Ibid., Exhibit 1-5, p. 2.
11. Ibid.
12. Ibid.
13. Marina Strauss, "Aldo's Global Footprint," *The Globe and Mail,* September 3, 2010; Marina Strauss, "Loblaw's Joe Fresh Hooks Up with JC Penney," *The Globe and Mail,* July 25, 2012; *Consumer Trends Update: Canada's Changing Retail Market,* p. 13.
14. *Global Powers of Retailing 2015 – Embracing innovation,* Deloitte,http://www2.deloitte.com/content/dam/Deloitte/global/Documents/Consumer-Business/gx-cb-global-powers-of-retailing.pdf, p. G20.
15. Ibid., p. G20.
16. *Global Powers of Retailing 2015 – Embracing innovation,* Deloitte, http://www2.deloitte.com/content/dam/Deloitte/global/Documents/Consumer-Business/gx-cb-global-powers-of-retailing.pdf, p. G21.
17. "Ingvar Kamprad," en.wikipedia.org/wiki/Ingvar_Kamprad (accessed May 25, 2007).
18. http://www.retailcouncil.org/media/newsreleases/retail-council-of-canada-honours-excellence-and-innovation-at-store-2015 (accessed December 17, 2015).
19. http://www.leons.ca/about-us (accessed December 17, 2015).
20. Sarah Butler, "Would You Like a Bag with That, Madam?" *London Times,* October 7, 2006.

Chapter 2

1. Pierre Mercier, Rune Jacobsen, and Andy Veitch, "Ten Trends That Are Reshaping the Retail Industry," BCG Perspectives, August 9, 2012, https://www.bcgperspectives.com/content/articles/retail_digital_economy_retail_2020_competing_in_changing_industry/(accessed October 13, 2012).
2. Christopher Daniel & Tony Hernandez, *The CSCA Retail 100,* Centre for the Study of Commercial Activity 2015, p. 8.

3. Larry Greenberg, "Hudson's Bay Faces Challenges from Southern Rival," *The Wall Street Journal,* May 24, 1996, p. B4.
4. http://www.dollarama.com/about_us/our_history/ (accessed December 18, 2015).
5. http://www.macleans.ca/economy/economicanalysis/off-target-how-a-u-s-retail-giant-misread-the-canadian-market/ (accessed December 18, 2015).
6. Carlta Vitzthum, "Just-in-Time Fashion-Spanish Retailer Zara Makes Low-Cost Lines in Weeks by Running Its Own Show," *The Wall Street Journal,* May 18, 2001, p. B1; and Benjamin Jones, "Madrid: Zara Pioneers Fashion on Demand," *Europe,* September 2001, pp. 43–44.
7. Marianne Wilson, "Disposable Chic at H&M," *Chain Store Age,* May 2000, pp. 64–66.
8. http://www.visa.ca/en/aboutcan/mediacentre/news/mobile_ecommerce.jsp#.Vl8jTr9v_eI "(accessed December 14, 2015).
9. Hollie Shaw, "Landlord Rivalries at Root of Store Wars," *National Post,* July 16, 2003.
10. Denise Deveau, "Big Box Shrinkage in a Post-Internet World," *Canadian Retailer,* spring 2012, Vol. 22, Issue 2, pp. 46–47.
11. David P. Schulz, "Triversity Top 100 Retailers: The Nation's Biggest Retail Companies," http://www.stores.org, 2001.
12. http://www.retail-insider.com/retailinsider/2014/8/bloomingdales (accessed December 16, 2015).
13. Christopher Daniel & Tony Hernandez, *The CSCA retail 100* pg. 8 (Centre for the Study of Commercial Activity 2015).
14. Tracie Rozhon, "Main Street's Latest Threat," *New York Times,* June 14, 1999, p. A25; "Annual Report of Categories," *Drug Store News,* May 17, 1999; and "Annual Report on Drug Chains," *Drug Store News,* April 26, 1999.
15. http://business.financialpost.com/news/retail-marketing/why-the-rexall-pharmacy-chain-is-a-hot-acquisition-target (accessed December 22, 2015).
16. https://en.wikipedia.org/wiki/Shoppers_Drug_Mart (accessed December 22, 2015).
17. http://www.murale.ca/en-ca/Stores-and-Events.aspx (accessed December 22, 2015).
18. https://www.tjx.com/business/businesses_winners.html (accessed December 22, 2015).
19. Hollie Shaw, "Spending Spree Will Continue," *National Post,* January 6, 2003.
20. Leanne Delap, "Hard-Core Winners Addicts Tell All," *Globe and Mail,* February 28, 2004.
21. https://www.tjx.com/business/businesses_marshalls_ca.html (accessed December 22, 2015).
22. http://www.factorydirect.ca/AboutUs.aspx (accessed December 22, 2015)
23. Marina Strauss, "Dollarama turns up heat on Walmart," *Globe and Mail,* September 15, 2011.
24. Debby Garbato Stankevich, "More Value to a Dollar: With Traditional Discounters Concentrating Market," *Retail Merchandiser,* October 2001, pp. 21–23.
25. http://calgaryherald.com/business/local-business/pop-up-stores-becoming-a-popular-retail-trend?__lsa=a006-8658 (accessed December 22, 2015).
26. http://supermarketnews.com/top-25-global-food-retailers-2013 (accessed December 22, 2015).
27. http://marketrealist.com/2015/02/competitive-forces-walmart-dominates-grocery-industry/ (accessed December 22, 2015).

28. Hollie Shaw, "Supermarket Offers Health Club," *Canadian Press Newswire*, November 8, 1999.

29. "Food Industry Glossary: Conventional Supermarket," Food Marketing Institute, http://www.fmi.org/research-resources/fmi-research-resources/food-industry-glossary/'c'-supermarket-terms (accessed September 27, 2013).

30. http://www.fmi.org/docs/facts_figs/grocerydept.pdf.

31. "Low-end grocery stores carve out niche," *The (Harrisburg, PA) Patriot-News*, October 13, 2004, http://www.tmcnet.com/usubmit/2007/10/13/3012485.htm (accessed September 27, 2013).

32. "About M&M," M&M Meat Shops website, http://www.mmmeatshops.com/en/aboutmm/index.asp?curURL=%2Fen%2Findex%2Easp (accessed September 27, 2013).

33. *Language of the Food Industry* (Washington, DC: Food Marketing Institute, 1998).

34. "Voting with your Trolly," *The Economist*, December 7, 2006.

35. Pete Russell, "No market share growth for private label in Canada," *Canadian Grocer*, March 21, 2011, http://www.canadiangrocer.com/uncategorized/no-market-share-growth-for-private-label-in-canada-5277 (accessed September 27, 2013).

36. Tyghe and Kohbodi, "Loblaw Companies Ltd.," p. 9.

37. Ibid., p. 10.

38. Ibid., p. 10.

39. "Markets in Motion," in "66th Annual Report of the Grocery Industry," *Progressive Grocer*, April 1999, p. 31.

40. Shaw, "Supermarket Offers Health Club."

41. *Language of the Food Industry.*

42. Personal communication, Bryan Gildenberg, M. Ventures, February 2002.

43. "About Us: History," Loblaw Companies Limited website, http://www.loblaw.ca/English/About-Us/history/default.aspx (accessed September 27, 2013).

44. Tyghe and Kohbodi, "Loblaw Companies Ltd.," p. 19.

45. Sandra J. Skrovan, "Industry Brief: Warehouse Clubs," PricewaterhouseCoopers, June 2001, p. 7.

46. Jamie Sturgeon, "Here's who's really winning Canada's grocery wars," http://globalnews.ca/news/1678970/heres-whos-really-winning-canadas-grocery-wars/ (accessed December 22, 2015).

47. George Strachan, Keith Wills, and Yukihiro Moroe, "Retail Surprises: A Look Back from 2005," Goldman Sachs, December 2000, pp. 9–10.

48. Fiscal Year 2014 - Consolidated Financial Statements, April 27, 2014), http://corpo.couche-tard.com/wp-content/uploads/2014/06/EF-annuels-anglais-2014_FINAL.pdf (accessed December 22, 2015).

49. 2014 Annual Report - "Our Business" http://corpo.couche-tard.com/wp-content/uploads/2014/06/WEB-Rapport-annuel-EN.pdf, (accessed December 22, 2015).

50. http://www.eatzis.com.

51. Peter O'Dowd, "The British Are Coming to Change Our Grocery Stores," ABC News Business Unit, April 19, 2007; Jennifer Halterman, "Tesco's U.S. Invasion Update" (Columbus, OH: Retail Forward, September 2006).

52. "A Supermarket Business Survey of Consumers Shows That the More Prepared Foods They Buy, the Bigger the Ring at the Checkout," *Supermarket Business*, July 15, 2001, pp. 37, 40+.

53. Personal communication, Jo Natale, Wegmans, February 2002.

54. *The Canadian Food Retail Sector: Opportunities for Swiss Companies*, p. 12.

55. "Retail Ecommerce Sales in Canada to Near C$30 Billion" eMarketer, January 15, 2015, http://www.emarketer.com/Article/Retail-Ecommerce-Sales-Canada-Near-C30-Billion/1011853 (accessed December 23, 2015).

56. Sean Silcoff, "What keeps online retail in Canada from clicking?" *The Globe and Mail*, May 12, 2012, http://www.theglobeandmail.com/report-on-business/what-keeps-online-retail-in-Canada-from-clicking/article4178807/?page=all (accessed February 9, 2012); and Hollie Shaw, "Canadian shoppers, bricks-and-mortar retailers finally embracing the Web," *Financial Post*, December 8, 2012, http://www.business.financialpost.com/2012/12/08/canada-embraces-online-retail-shopping/ (accessed February 9, 2012).

57. Maddy Keith, "Global eCommerce Sales, Trends and Statistics 2015," September 2, 2015, http://www.remarkety.com/global-ecommerce-sales-trends-and-statistics-2015 (accessed December 22, 2015).

58. Silcoff, "What keeps online retail in Canada from clicking?"

59. Ibid.

60. Lindsay Shugerman, "Catalog merchandise marketing," Catalogs.com Info Library, http://www.catalogs.com/info/b2b/catalog-merchandise.html, data from U.S. Census Bureau (accessed October 19, 2009).

61. Eve Lazarus, "Loyalty: Beyond Points and Discounts," *Canadian Retailer*, spring 2012, Vol. 22, Issue 3, pp. 48–49.

62. IKEA Canada Launches New 2016 Catalogue Celebrating the Little Moments Around the Kitchen, Corporate News, 05-08-2015 http://www.ikea.com/ca/en/about_ikea/newsitem/2015_2016catalogue (accessed December 23, 2015).

63. Laurens Bianchi, "IKEA Adds Interactivity to Its Cataogues," ViralBlog, July 23, 2012, http://www.viralblog.com/mobile-and-apps/ikea-adds-interactivity-to-its-catalogues/ (accessed September 27, 2013).

64. Retail Council of Canada, *Retail Technology in Canada* report.

65. Jeffery Ball, "In Digital Era, Marketers Still Prefer a Paper Trail," *Wall Street Journal*, October 16, 2009.

66. Ibid.

67. Dirk Perrefort and Susan Silvers, "Inside the Mall, a Class of Cultures," *McClatchy-Tribune Business News*, January 7, 2010.

68. http://www.dsa.ca/content/industry/news.php.

69. Ibid.

70. http://dsa.org/pubs/numbers/.

71. http://www.dsa.org/pubs/numbers/calendar05factsheet.pdf (accessed June 7, 2007).

72. Ibid.

73. "T-commerce! On Sale Now for a Limited Time!" *Cableworld*, December 4–17, 2006; "Will Viewers Buy into Shopping Via TV Ads?" *NMA*, October 13, 2005.

74. "Smartphones," *State of the Media: Social Media Report 2012*, Nielsen. http://www.nielsen.com/US/en/reports/2012/state-of-the-media-social-media-report-2012.html.

75. "2001 State of the Vending Industry Report," *Automatic Merchandiser*, http://www.amonline.com/current/industryreports.shtml.

76. Ibid.

77. "Looking ahead: Innovation a must for Canadian vending operators," *Canadian Vending*, Spring 2012, http://www.canadianvending.com/content/view/2970/136/.

78. Dana Flavelle, "New Fit for Vending Machines," *Toronto Star*, January 15, 2010, (accessed July 26, 2013).

79. "Vending Machine Operators in Canada: Market Research Report" *IBIS World* May 2016 http://www.ibisworld.ca/industry/default.aspx?indid=1113 (accessed July 27, 2016).

80. Valarie Zeithaml, A. Parasuraman, and Leonard Berry, "Problems and Strategies in Services Marketing," *Journal of Marketing*, 49 (Spring 1985), pp. 33–46; and Stephen W. Brown and Mary Jo Bitner, "Services Marketing," *AMA Management Handbook*, 3rd ed. (New York: AMACOM Books, 1994).

81. This section is based on material in Lyda Hyde, "Multi-Channel Integration: The New Retail Battleground," PricewaterhouseCoopers, 2001; and Joseph Alba, John Lynch, Barton Weitz, Chris Janiszewski, Richard Lutz, Alan Sawyer, and Stacy Woods, "Interactive Home Shopping: Consumer, Retailer, and Manufacturers Incentives to Participate in Electronic Markets," *Journal of Marketing, 61* (July 1997), pp. 38–53.

82. David Moin, "Getting Personal," *Women's Wear Daily Internet Supplement,* May 2000, pp. 10–17.

83. "40+ years in the making; the new "Shop MEC" iPhone app is now available," MEC website, news release, December 17, 2012, http://mediaroom.mec.ca/2012/12/40-years-in-the-making-the-new-shop-mec-iphone-app-is-now-available.

84. Rachel Ledford, "The Connected Customer," *E-Retailing Intelligence Update* (Columbus, OH: Retail Forward, November 2001), p. 6.

85. Reid Claxton, "Customer Safety: Direct Marketing's Undermarketed Advantage," *Journal of Direct Marketing* 9 (Winter 1995), pp. 67–78.

86. *Deloitte's Store 3.0 Survey: The Next Evolution,* Deloitte, September 2011, p. 7.

87. *Deloitte's 2012 Retail Study: The Rise of the Connected Consumer,* 2012 Edition, Deloitte, p. 17.

88. Deloitte Digital, "Navigating the New Digital Divide: Capitalizing on digital influence in retail," http://www2.deloitte.com/content/dam/Deloitte/us/Documents/consumer-business/us-cb-navigating-the-new-digital-divide-v2-051315.pdf, 2015, p.3.

89. *Deloitte Digital: The Dawn of Mobile Influence, 2012,* Deloitte, p. 4.

90. Catalyst, "With Growth Comes Change: The Evolving Mobile Landscape in 2015," http://catalyst.ca/2015-canadian-smartphone-market/ (accessed December 22, 2015).

91. Google/IPSOS OTX MediaCT, "The Mobile Movement. Understanding Smartphone Users," April 2011.

92. *Deloitte Digital: The Dawn of Mobile Influence, 2012,* p. 5.

93. Deloitte Digital, "Navigating the New Digital Divide: Capitalizing on digital influence in retail," http://www2.deloitte.com/content/dam/Deloitte/us/Documents/consumer-business/us-cb-navigating-the-new-digital-divide-v2-051315.pdf, 2015, p.8 (accessed December 27, 2015).

94. *Deloitte Digital: The Dawn of Mobile Influence, 2012,* p. 5.

95. Deloitte Digital, "Navigating the New Digital Divide: Capitalizing on digital influence in retail," http://www2.deloitte.com/content/dam/Deloitte/us/Documents/consumer-business/us-cb-navigating-the-new-digital-divide-v2-051315.pdf, p. 8 (accessed December 2015).

96. "The Shopping Channel Celebrates 25 Years of Great Shopping with Big Birthday Celebration," news release, February 1, 2012, http://www.newswire.ca/en/story/914233/the-shopping-channel-celebrates-25-years-of-great-shopping-with-big-birthday- celebration.

97. Darren Hitchcock, "Five ways to embrace omni-channel retailing," Econsultancy.com, August 29, 2012 (accessed October 2, 2013).

98. Michael de Kare-Silver, "Multi-Channel vs. Omni-Channel," *Digital Prospects,* www.dekaresilver.com/downloads/multi-channel-vs-omni-channel.pdf (accessed July 30, 2013).

99. Brian Kilcourse, "Gaming Google: The Growing Importance of Omni-channel," *Retail Systems Research,* March 1, 2011 (accessed July 30, 2013).

100. Deloitte, "Omni-channel: Rethink, reshape, revalue Retail Study 2014," http://www.retailcouncil.org/sites/default/files/documents/Deloitte-RCC-Retail-Study.pdf, p. 4.

101. Ibid.

102. Ibid.

103. Fortna, "5 Steps to Designing Omni-channel Fulfillment Operations," http://www.fortna.com/whitepapers/designing-omnichannel-fulfillment-operations-en.pdf (accessed December 27, 2015).

104. Andrew Solmssen, "Omni-Channel Marketing: Your Next Challenge," *ClickZ,* August 17, 2012, http://www.cmo.com/content/cmo-com/home/articles/2012/8/17/omnichannel-marketing-your-next-challenge.fram.html (accessed October 2, 2013).

105. Kenneth Clow, David Kurtz, John Ozment, and Beng Soo Ong, "The Antecedents of Consumer Expectations of Services: An Empirical Study across Four Industries," *Journal of Services Marketing* 11 (May–June 1997), pp. 230–248; and Ann Marie Thompson and Peter Kaminski, "Psychographic and Lifestyle Antecedents of Service Quality Expectations," *Journal of Services Marketing* 7 (1993), pp. 53–61.

106. Susan Stellin, "Online Customer Service Found Lacking," *New York Times,* January 3, 2002, p. C1.

107. Mary Jo Bitner, "Self-Service Technologies: What Do Customers Expect? In This High-Tech World, Customers Haven't Changed—They Still Want Good Service," *Marketing Management,* Spring 2001, pp. 10–15.

108. Timothy Keiningham and Terry Vavra, *The Customer Delight Principle* (Chicago: American Marketing Association, 2002).

109. Parsuraman and Valarie Zeithaml, "Understanding and Improving Service Quality: A Literature Review and Research Agenda," in B. Weitz and R. Wensley, eds., *Handbook of Marketing* (London: Sage, 2002).

110. Michael Harline and O. C. Ferrell, "The Management of Customer-Contact Service Employees: An Empirical Investigation," *Journal of Marketing* 60 (October 1996), pp. 52–70; and Lois Mohr and Mary Jo Bitner, "The Role of Employee Effort in Satisfaction with Service Transactions," *Journal of Business Research* 32 (March 1995, pp. 239–252).

111. Russ Martin, "Canadian Tire joins digital incubator to improve retail and online offering," *Marketing Magazine,* March 21, 2013, http://www.marketingmag.ca/news/marketer-news/canadian-tire-joins-digital-incubator-to-improve-retail-and-online-offering-74899.

112. Paul Lima, "Instant Gratification," *Profit,* April 2002, p. 56; Sandra Guy, "Stores Juggle Service with High-Tech Savvy," *Chicago Sun-Times,* July 1, 2002, p. B12; Julie Clark, "The Importance of Kiosks in Retail Has Grown," *Display and Design Ideas,* September 2001, p. 18; and Ken Clark, "Confused about Kiosks," *Chain Store Age,* November 1, 2000, p. 96.

113. http://retailindustry.about.com, April 4, 2001.

114. Bob Tedeschi, "Bricks-and-Mortar Merchants Struggling to Assess Web Sidelines," *New York Times,* September 3, 2001, p. C3.

115. "Organizing for Cross-Channel Retailing," white paper, J.C. Williams Group, Toronto, 2008; "Customer Centricity Drives Retail's Multichannel Imperative," white paper, IBM Global Business Services, Armonk, NY, 2008.

116. "The Next Evolution: Store 3.0: An executive perspective on retailer readiness for tomorrow's store," Deloitte, 2011, p. 2.

117. Google, "Our Mobile Planet: Canada," May 2012.

118. "Will Smarter Phones Make for Smarter Shoppers?" Deloitte, June 2011.

119. Sebastian Van Baal and Christian Dach, "Free Riding and Customer Retention across Retailers' Channels," *Journal of Interactive Marketing* 19 (Spring 2005), pp. 75–85.

120. Dun and Bradstreet Corporate Starts (New York: Dun and Bradstreet, 1998).

121. Jim Simmons and Shizue Kamikihara, "Commercial Activity in Canada," Centre for the Study of Commercial Activity, Ryerson University, Report 2009-02, p. 53.

122. Bill Quinn, *How Wal-Mart Is Destroying America (and the World): And What You Can Do About It* (Berkeley, CA: Ten Speed Press, 2000).

Chapter 3

1. For a detailed discussion of customer behaviour, see J. Paul Peter and Jerry C. Olson, *Consumer Behavior and Marketing Strategy*, 6th ed. (New York: McGraw-Hill, 2002); and Michael R. Solomon, *Consumer Behavior: Buying, Having, and Being*, 5th ed. (Upper Saddle River, NJ: Prentice Hall, 2002).

2. Article by LS Retail, inspired by Daniel Levine's keynote during LS Retail's conference conneXion 2015.

3. Ibid.

4. Ibid.

5. Ibid.

6. Ibid.

7. Liz C. Wang, Julie Baker, Judy A. Wagner, and Kirk Wakefield, "Can a Retail Website be Social?" *Journal of Marketing* 71, no. 3 (2007), pp. 143–157; Gianluigi Guido, Mauro Capestro, and Alessandro M. Peluso, "Experimental Analysis of Consumer Stimulation and Motivational States in Shopping Experiences," *International Journal of Market Research* 49, no. 3 (2007), pp. 365–386.

8. Guido, Capestro, and Peluso, "Experimental Analysis"; Woonbong Na, Youngseok Son, and Roger Marshall, "Why Buy Second-Best? The Behavioral Dynamics of Market Leadership," *Journal of Product & Brand Management* 15, no. 1 (2007), pp. 16–22; Min-Young Lee, Kelly Green Atkins, Youn-Kyung Kim, and Soo-Hee Park, "Competitive Analyses Between Regional Malls and Big-Box Retailers: A Correspondence Analysis for Segmentation and Positioning," *Journal of Shopping Center Research*, April 2006, pp. 81–98.

9. Sylvie Morin, Laurette Dube, and Jean-Charles Chebat, "The Role of Pleasant Music in Servicescapes: A Test of the Dual Model of Environmental Perception," *Journal of Retailing* 83, no. 1 (2007), pp. 115–130; Nicole Bailey and Charles S. Areni, "When a Few Minutes Sound Like a Lifetime: Does Atmospheric Music Expand or Contract Perceived Time?" *Journal of Retailing* 82, no. 3 (2006), pp. 189–202; Michael A. Jones and Kristy E. Reynolds, "The Role of Retailer Interest on Shopping Behavior," *Journal of Retailing* 82, no. 2 (2006), pp. 115–126; Shu pei Tai, "Impact of Personal Orientation on Luxury-Brand Purchase Value," *International Journal of Marketing Research* 47, no. 4 (2005), pp. 429–454.

10. Jess W.J. Weltrereden, "Substitution or Complementarity? How the Internet Changed City Centre Shopping," *Journal of Retailing and Consumer Services* 14, no. 3 (2007), pp. 192–207; Shun Yin Lam, Albert Wai-Lap Chau, and Tsunhin John Wong, "Thumbnails as Online Product Displays: How Consumers Process Them," *Journal of Interactive Marketing* 21, no. 1 (2007), pp. 36–59.

11. Teresa Lindeman, "Retailers Try to Convince Customers to Stick Around," *Miami Herald*, April 26, 2007.

12. Melody Vargas, "Frequent Leisure Time Shoppers Spend More per Trip," *About Retailing*, July 11, 2006.

13. Brian T. Ratchford, Debabrata Talukdar, and Myung-Soo Lee, "The Impact of the Internet on Consumers' Use of Information Sources for Automobiles: A Re-Inquiry," *Journal of Consumer Research* 34, no. 1 (2007), pp. 111–119; Glenn J. Browne, Mitzi G. Pitts, and James C. Wetherbe, "Cognitive Shopping Rules for Terminating Information Search in Online Tasks," *MIS Quarterly* 31, no. 1 (2007), pp. 89–104; John Graham, "How to Profit from Customer Buying-Cycle Basics," *Printer and Publisher* 69, no. 2 (2006).

14. http://www.nearbynow.co (accessed June 27, 2007).

15. Capgemini, "Cars online 2014 Generation Connected," https://www.capgemini.com/sites/default/files/annual-report/768636/img/Cars_Online_2014_Final_Web_Group.pdf (accessed December 29, 2015).

16. John P. Mello Jr., "Solo Hunters, Social Gatherers and the Online Marketplace," *E-Commerce Times*, May 25, 2007 (accessed December 24, 2007); Helene F. Jaillet, "Web Metrics: Measuring Patterns in Online Shopping," *Journal of Consumer Behavior* 2, no. 4 (2003), pp. 369–381.

17. Bob Tedeschi, "Shopping Site Offers a Way to Raid a Celebrity's Closet," *The New York Times*, November 13, 2006 (accessed December 24, 2007); Steven Bellman, Eric J. Johnson, Gerald L. Lohse, and Naomi Mandel, "Designing Marketplaces of the Artificial with Consumers in Mind: Four Approaches to Understanding Consumer Behavior in Electronic Environments," *Journal of Interactive Marketing* 20, no. 1 (2006), pp. 21–33.

18. Bob Tedeschi, "A Richer Trip to the Mall, Guided by Text Messages," *The New York Times*, March 5, 2007 (accessed December 24, 2007); Alice Z. Cuneo, "'Yard' Sale? Sprite Talks to Teens with Mobile Promotions," *Advertising Age* (Midwest region edition), June 11, 2007, p. 23.

19. Paul Dwyer, "Measuring the Value of Electronic Word of Mouth and its Impact in Consumer Communities," *Journal of Interactive Marketing* 21, no. 2 (2007), pp. 63–79; Pallavi Gogoi, "Retailers Take a Tip from MySpace," *BusinessWeek*, February 13, 2007.

20. Cecilie Rohwedder, "For a Delicate Sale, a Retailer Deploys 'Stocking Fellas,'" *The Wall Street Journal*, December 21, 2006, p. A1.

21. Manu De Ros, "The rise of omni-channel retail: definition and 5 tips," Selligent.com, http://www.selligent.com/en/blogs/tips-practices/the-rise-of-omni-channel-retail-definition-and-5-tips/ (accessed October 18, 2013).

22. Teresa F. Lindeman, "Macy's Sees Food as the Way to the Wallet," *Boston Globe*, May 14, 2007.

23. Chris T. Allen, Karen A. Machleit, Susan Schultz Kleine, and Arti Sahni Notani, "A Place for Emotion in Attitude Models," *Journal of Business Research* 58, no. 4 (2005), pp. 494–499; Armin Scholl, Laura Manthey, Roland Helm, and Michael Steiner, "Solving Multiattribute Design Problems with Analytic Hierarchy Process and Conjoint Analysis: An Empirical Comparison," *European Journal of Operational Research* 164, no. 3 (2005), pp. 760–777; Richard Lutz, "Changing Brands Attitudes through Modification of Cognitive Structure," *Journal of Consumer Research* 1, no. 1 (1975), pp. 125–136.

24. Dong-il Yoo and Hiroshi Ohta, "Optimal Pricing and Product Planning for New Multiattribute Products based on Conjoint Analysis," *International Journal of Production Economics* 38, no. 2, 3 (1995), pp. 245–253; Richard J. Lutz and James R. Bettman, "Multi-Attribute Models in Marketing: A Bicentennial Review," in *Consumer and Industrial Buying Behaviour*, eds. A.G. Woodside, J.N. Sheth, and P.D. Bennett (New York: Elsevier-North Holland, 1977), pp. 13–50; William L. Wilkie and Edgar D. Pessimier, "Issues in Marketing's Use of MultiAttribute Attitude Models," *Journal of Marketing Research*, November 1973, pp. 428–441.

25. Pat West, P. Brockett, and Linda Golden, "A Comparative Analysis of Neural Networks and Statistical Methods for Predicting Consumer Choice," *Marketing Science* 16, no. 4 (1997), pp. 370–391.

26. Peter R. Darke, Amitava Chattopadhyay, and Laurence Ashworth, "The Importance and Functional Significance of Affective Cues in Consumer Choice," *Journal of Consumer Research* 33, no. 3 (2006), pp. 322–328; David Bell, Tech-Hua Ho, and Christopher Tang, "Determining Where to Shop: Fixed and Variable Costs of Shopping," *Journal of Marketing Research* 35 (August 1998), pp. 352–370.

27. John G. Lynch and Gal Zauberman, "Construing Consumer Decision Making," *Journal of Consumer Psychology* 17, no. 2 (2007), pp. 107–112; Wayne D. Hoyer and Steven Brown, "Effects of Brand Awareness of Choice for a Common, Repeat-Purchase Product," *Journal of Consumer Research,* September 1990, pp. 141–149.

28. Pallavi Gogoi, "I Am Woman, Hear Me Shop," *BusinessWeek,* February 14, 2005, p. 23.

29. Peter N. Child, Suzanne Heywood, and Michael Kliger, "Do Retail Brands Travel?" *McKinsey Quarterly,* no. 1 (2002), pp. 25–34.

30. Andras Vag, "Simulating Changing Consumer Preferences: A Dynamic Conjoint Model," *Journal of Business Research* 60, no. 8 (2007), pp. 904–911; Richard J. Lutz, "Changing Brand Attitudes through Modification of Cognitive Structure," *Journal of Consumer Research* 1 (March 1975), pp. 49–59.

31. Jeanette Borzo, "From Lands' End to Fair Trade," *Business 2.0,* December 2006, p. 31.

32. Joan Voight, "Getting a Handle on Customer Reviews," *Adweek* 48, no. 26 (June 25–July 2, 2007), pp. 16–17; Nanda Kumar and Izak Benbasat, "The Influence of Recommendations and Consumer Reviews on Evaluations of Websites," *Information Systems Research* 17, no. 4 (2006), pp. 425–441; Bob Tedeschi, "Help for the Merchant in Navigating a Sea of Shopper Opinions," *The New York Times,* September 4, 2006.

33. Ibid.

34. Claire Cain Miller, "Closing the Deal at the Virtual Checkout Counter," *The New York Times,* October 12, 2009.

35. NewAd Media.

36. "Beware of Dissatisfied Consumers: They Like to Blab," *Knowledge@Wharton,* March 8, 2006, based on "Retail Customer Dissatisfaction Study 2006," conducted by the Jay H. Baker Retailing Initiative at Wharton and The Verde Group (accessed December 24, 2007); "The Lowdown on Customer Loyalty Programs: Which Are the Most Effective and Why," *Knowledge@Wharton,* September 6, 2006; Sandra Kennedy, "Keeping Customers Happy," *Chain Store Age,* February 2005, p. 24; Heiner Evanschitzky, Gopalkrishnan Iyer, Josef Hesse, and Dieter Ahlert, "E-Satisfaction: A Re-Examination," *Journal of Retailing* 80, no. 3 (2004), pp. 239–252; Emin Babakus, Carol Bienstock, and James Van Scotter, "Linking Perceived Quality and Customer Satisfaction to Store Traffic and Revenue Growth," *Decision Sciences* 35 (Fall 2004), pp. 713–738; Jarrad Dunning, Anthony Pecotich, and Aron O'Cass, "What Happens When Things Go Wrong? Retail Sales Explanations and Their Effects," *Psychology & Marketing,* July 2004, pp. 553–568; Richard Oliver, Roland Rust, and Sajeev Varki, "Customer Delight: Foundations, Findings, and Managerial Insights," *Journal of Retailing* 73 (Fall 1997), pp. 311–336; Chezy Ofir and Itamar Simonson, "The Effect of Stating Expectations on Customer Satisfaction and Shopping Experience," *Journal of Marketing Research* 44, no. 1 (2007), pp. 164–174.

37. Piyush Sharma, Bharadhwaj Sivakumaran, and Roger Marshall, "Impulse Buying and Variety Seeking: A Trait-Correlates Perspective," *Journal of Business Research* 63 (March 2010), pp. 276–283; David H. Silvera, Anne M. Lavack, and Fredric Kropp, "Impulse Buying: The Role of Affect, Social Influence, and Subjective Wellbeing," *Journal of Consumer Marketing* 25, no. 1 (2008), pp. 23–33; Ronan De Kervenoael, D. Selcen, O. Aykac, and Mark Palmer, "Online Social Capital: Understanding E-Impulse Buying in Practice," *Journal of Retailing and Consumer Services* 16 (July 2009), pp. 320–328.

38. "Let's Play Shopping," *Marketing Week,* November 22, 2001, pp. 45–47; Conway Lachman and John Lanasa, "Family Decision-Making Theory: An Overview and Assessment," *Psychology & Marketing* 10 (March–April 1993), pp. 81–94; and Robert Boutlier, "Pulling the Family Strings," *American Demographics,* August 1993, pp. 44–48.

39. Jean Darian, "Parent-Child Decision Making in Children's Clothing Stores," *International Journal of Retail & Distribution Management* 26 (October 1998), pp. 421–432; Kay Palanand and Robert Wilkes, "Adolescent-Parent Interaction in Family Decision Making," *Journal of Consumer Research* 24 (September 1997), pp. 159–171; Christy Fisher, "Kidding around Makes Sense," *Advertising Age,* June 27, 1994, pp. 34, 37; and Sharon Beatty and Salil Talpade, "Adolescent Influence in Family Decision Making: A Replication with Extension," *Journal of Consumer Research* 31 (September 1994), pp. 332–341.

40. "Bring the Family . . . Bring the Kids," *Travel Agent Caribbean and Bahamas Supplement,* April 7, 1997.

41. Dianne Pogoda, "It's a Matter of Time: Stores Keep Traffic Moving, Cash Flowing," *Women's Wear Daily,* April 9, 1996, pp. 1, 8.

42. Susan Reda, "What Are Shoppers Saying About You?" *Stores,* February 2007.

43. Bruce Horovits, "Alpha Moms Leap to Top of Trendsetters," *USA Today,* March 27, 2007; Alexander Frenzel Baudisch, "Consumer Heterogeneity Evolving from Social Group Dynamics: Latent Class Analysis of German Footwear Consumption 1980-1991," *Journal of Business Research* 60, no. 8 (2007), pp. 836–847; Julie Juan Li and Chenting Su, "How Face Influences Consumption: A Comparative Study of American and Chinese Consumers," *International Journal of Market Research* 49, no. 2 (2007), pp. 237–256.

44. Susan Reda, "What Are Shoppers Saying about You?," *Stores,* February 2007.

45. Judy Waytiuk, "Discounter Diversity," *Marketing Magazine,* May 19, 2003; David Chow, "Reaching New Canadians," *Strategy Magazine,* September 22, 2003; Natalie Rivard, "Reaching Tween Girls in Quebec," *Strategy Magazine,* December 1, 2003.

46. Soyeon Shim and Mary Ann Eastwick, "The Hierarchical Influence of Personal Values on Mall Shopping Attitudes and Behaviors," *Journal of Retailing* 74 (Spring 1998), pp. 139–160.

47. Cyndee Miller, "Top Marketers Take a Bolder Approach in Targeting Gays," *Marketing News,* July 4, 1994, pp. 1–2.

48. Market Access Secretariat, Global Global Analysis Report, "Consumer and Retail Trends in China March 2014," http://www5.agr.gc.ca/resources/prod/Internet-Internet/MISB-DGSIM/ATS-SEA/PDF/6457-eng.pdf (accessed December 30, 2015).

49. Robert Verdisco, "Gender-Specific Shopping," *Chain Store Age,* February 1999, pp. 26–28; Matthew Klein, "He Shops, She Shops," *American Demographics,* March 1998, pp. 34–40; and Suein Hwang, "From Choices to Checkout, the Genders Behave Very Differently in Supermarkets," *The Wall Street Journal,* March 22, 1994, pp. A1, A4.

50. Donna Myers, "Cater to Women Shoppers, Ask What They Want," *Casual Living,* August 2009.

51. Nielsen, *State of the Media: The Social Media Report,* December 4, 2012, p. 6, http://www.nielsen.com/us/en/insights/reports-downloads/2012/state-of-the-media-the-social-media-report-2012.pdf (accessed October 21, 2013).

52. "AOL Research Findings Determines Driving Forces behind Women's Online Content Consumption," BusinessWire, April 14, 2011, http://www.businesswire.com/news/home/20110414006018/en/AOL-Research-Findings-Determines-Driving-Forces-Women%E2%80%99s (accessed October 16, 2013); http://advertising.aol.com.

53. *Retailing 2015: New Frontiers,* PricewaterhouseCoopers and TNS Retail Forward, 2007, p. 3, www.pwc.com/es_CL/cl/publicaciones/assets/retailing2015.pdf (accessed October 16, 2013).

54. Ibid., p. 8.
55. Faith Popcorn, *Evolution* (New York: Hyperion Press, 2000); David Foot and Daniel Stoffman, *Boom Bust & Echo 2000* (Toronto: Macfarlane Walter & Ross, 1998); Oliver Bertin, "Harley-Davidson's Great Ride to the Top," *Globe and Mail*, July 4, 2003; Don Tapscott, Growing Up Digital (New York: McGraw-Hill, 1998); Brad Adgate, "Everything You'd Care to Know about Teens," *Horizon Media*, October 29, 2003.
56. http://www5.statcan.gc.ca/cansim/a26?lang=eng&retrLang =eng&id=0510001&&pattern=&stByVal=1&p1=1&p2=31&t abMode=dataTable&csid= (accessed December 30, 2015).
57. Michael J. Weiss, *The Clustered World* (Boston: Little, Brown, 2000).
58. http://www.statista.com/statistics/433692/generation-z-media-usage-canada/ (accessed December 31, 2015).
59. http://www.tetrad.com/demographics/canada/environics/prizmc2.html.
60. GD Sourcing, "Research and Retrieval," *The Business Newsletter*, June 26, 2003, gdsourcing.com; Michael Adams, *Better Rich Than Happy* (Toronto: Penguin Books, 2000).
61. John Lorinc, "The Autonomous Rebel," *U of T Magazine*, Winter 2011, http://www.magazine.utoronto.ca/all-about-alumni/michael-adams-environics-stayin-alive-book/ (accessed October 16, 2013).
62. Deena M Amato-McCoy, "A Point of Differentiation," *Chain Store Age*, January 2007, pp. 26–27; Jeff Zabin, "The Importance of Being Analytical," *Brandweek*, July 24, 2006, p. 21; Mindy Fetterman, "Best Buy Gets in Touch with Its Feminine Side," *USA Today*, December 20, 2006.

Chapter 4

1. Roger Evered, "So What Is Strategy?" *Long Range Planning* 16 (Fall 1983), p. 120.
2. See David Aaker, *Strategic Market Management*, 6th ed. (New York: John Wiley, 2001); and A. Coskun Samli, *Strategic Marketing for Success in Retailing* (Westport, CT: Quorum Books, 1998).
3. Michael Porter, *On Competition* (Boston: Harvard Business School Press, 1998); and Michael Porter, "What Is Strategy?" *Harvard Business Review*, November–December 1996, pp. 61–78.
4. Bridget Finn and Gary Heavin, "How to Grow a Chain That's Already Everywhere," *Business 2.0*, March 2005, p. 52; Clarke Canfield, "No-Frills Fitness Club Takes Its Alternative Route to Small Towns," *Los Angeles Times*, November 26, 2004, p. C4.
5. http://www.mafazineluiza.com.br (accessed April 4, 2010); Guillermo D'Andrea, "Latin American Retail: Where Modernity Blends with Tradition," International Review of Retail, Distribution and Consumer *Research* 20 (February 2010), pp. 85–101; Rob Katz, "How Magazine Luiza Courts the Poor," *HBS Working Knowledge*, April 18, 2007.
6. Anthony Boardman and Aidan Vining, "Defining Your Business Using Product-Customer Matrices," *Long Range Planning* 29 (February 1996), pp. 38–48; and R.L. Rothschild, *How to Gain and Maintain Competitive Advantage in Business* (New York: McGraw-Hill, 1984).
7. Cynthia Montgomery, "Creating Corporate Advantage," *Harvard Business Review*, May-June 1998, pp. 71–80; Shelby Hunt and Robert Morgan, "The Comparative Advantage Theory of Competition," *Journal of Marketing* 59 (April 1995), pp. 1–15; Kathleen Conner and C.K. Prahalad, "A Resource-Based Theory of the Firm: Knowledge versus Opportunism," *Organizational Science* 7 (September-October 1996), pp. 477–501; David Collins and Cynthia Montgomery, "Competing on Resources: Strategy for the 1990s," *Harvard Business Review* 73 (July–August 1995), pp. 118–128; William Werther and Jeffrey Kerr, "The Shifting Sands of Competitive Advantage," *Business*

Horizons 38 (May–June 1995), pp. 11–17; "10 Quick Wins to Turn Your Supply Chain into a Competitive Advantage," January 2002, http://retailindustry.about.com/library/bl/bl_ksa0112.htm?terms=competitive+advantage; and "Multi-Channel Integration: The New Retail Battleground," Retail Forward, Inc., March 2001, http://www.pwcris.com.
8. Jeffrey H. Dyer and Harbir Singh, "The Relational View: Cooperative Strategy and Sources of Interorganizational Competitive Advantage," *Academy of Management Review* 23 (October 1998), pp. 660–679; Robert M. Morgan and Shelby Hunt, "Relationship-Based Competitive Advantage: The Role of Relationship Marketing in Marketing Strategy," *Journal of Business Research* 46 (November 1999), pp. 281–290; Shelby D. Hunt and Robert M. Morgan, "The Comparative Advantage Theory of Competition," *Journal of Marketing* 59 (April 1995), pp. 1–15.
9. Gerrard Macintosh and Lawrence Lockshin, "Retail Relationships and Store Loyalty: A Multi-Level Perspective," *International Journal of Research in Marketing* 14 (1997), pp. 487–497.
10. Jo Marney, "Bringing Consumers Back for More," *Marketing Magazine*, September 10, 2001, p. 33; Kathleen Seiders and Douglas Tigert, "Impact of Market Entry and Competitive Structure on Store Switching/Store Loyalty," *International Review of Retail, Distribution and Consumer Research* 7, no. 3 (1997), pp. 234–256; and Niren Sirohi, Edward McLaughlin, and Dick Wittink, "A Model of Consumer Perceptions and Store Loyalty Intentions for a Supermarket Retailer," *Journal of Retailing* 74 (June 1998), pp. 223–247.
11. http://www.llbean.com/customerService/about LLBean/guarantee.html?nav=hp-guaranteefooter (accessed January 4, 2016).
12. Richard Czerniawski and Michael Maloney, *Creating Brand Loyalty: The Management of Power Positioning and Really Great Advertising* (New York: AMACOM, 1999); S. Chandrasekhar, Vinod Sawhney, Rafique Malik, S. Ramesh Kumar, and Pranab Dutta, "The Case of Brand Positioning," *Business Today*, June 7, 1999, pp. 131–140; Bernard Schmitt, Alex Simonson, and Joshua Marcus, "Managing Corporate Image and Identity," *Long Range Planning* 28 (October 1995), pp. 82–92; Tim Ambler, "Category Management Is Best Deployed for Brand Positioning," *Marketing*, November 29, 2001, p. 18; and Harriet Marsh, "Why New Look Must Take Stock," *Marketing*, March 29, 2001, p. 17.
13. Amy Merrick, "Tired of Trendiness, Former Shoppers Leave Gap, Defect to Competitors," *The Wall Street Journal*, December 6, 2001, p. B1.
14. Mary Jo Bitner, "Self-Service Technologies: What Do Customers Expect?" *Marketing Management*, Spring 2001; Mary Jo Bitner, Steven W. Brown, and Matthew L. Meuter, "Technology Infusion in Service Encounters," *Journal of the Academy of Marketing Science*, March 2000; Mary Jo Bitner and Valerie Zeithaml, *Services Marketing*, 2nd ed. (Burr Ridge, IL: McGraw-Hill/Irwin, 1999); Leonard Berry, "Relationship Marketing of Services Growing Interest: Emerging Perspectives," *Journal of the Academy of Marketing Science* 23 (Fall 1995), pp. 236–245; and Mary Jo Bitner, "Building Service Relationships: It's All about Promises," *Journal of the Academy of Marketing Science* 23 (Fall 1995), pp. 246–251.
15. Brian Jackson, "Canadians' love of loyalty rewards is swayed most by this digital channel," http://www.itbusiness.ca/news/canadians-love-of-loyalty-rewards-is-swayed-most-by-this-digital-channel/54790 (accessed January 4, 2016).
16. Brian Jackson, "Canadians' love of loyalty rewards is swayed most by this digital channel," http://www.itbusiness.ca/news/canadians-love-of-loyalty-rewards-is-swayed-most-by-this-digital-channel/54790 (accessed January 4, 2016).

17. Hollie Shaw, "Harry Rosen Dons New Look for Expansion: CEO's Pragmatic View," *Financial Post*, September 3, 2008; Shaun Proulx, "Harry Goes Lofty, Large and Luxe," The *Globe and Mail*, September 3, 2008; Denise Power, "Harry Rosen Embracing Technology," *Daily News Record*, February 12, 2007, p. 16.

18. S.A. Shaw and J. Gibbs, "Procurement Strategies of Small Retailers Faced with Uncertainty: An Analysis of Channel Choice and Behaviour," *International Review of Retail, Distribution and Consumer Research* 9, no. 1 (1999), pp. 61–75.

19. "Global Brands Face Up to International Retailing," *Marketing Week*, October 26, 2000, p. 32.

20. Richard Cuthbertson, Gerd Islei, Peter Franke, and Balkan Cetinkaya, "What Will the Best Supply Chains Look Like in the Future?" *European Retail Digest*, Summer 2006, pp. 7–15; "Competitive Advantage through Supply Chain Innovation," *Logistics & Transport Focus*, December 2004, pp. 56–59.

21. Werther and Kerr, "The Shifting Sands of Competitive Advantage."

22. Roger Kerin, Vijay Mahajan, and P. Rajan Varadarajan, *Contemporary Perspectives on Strategic Market Planning* (Boston: Allyn & Bacon, 1991), Ch. 6. See also Susan Mudambi, "A Topology of Strategic Choice in Retailing," *International Journal of Retail & Distribution Management*, 1994, pp. 22–25.

23. Erin White, "Abercrombie Seeks to Send Teeny-Boppers Packing," *The Wall Street Journal*, August 30, 2001, pp. B1, B4.

24. Sarah Ellison, "Carrefour Finds It Difficult to Build Single Global Brand," *The Wall Street Journal*, August 30, 2001, http://www.wsj.com.

25. Hollie Shaw, October 16, 2014, "Amazon.ca sells four times as much as its biggest online rivals in Canada," *Financial Post*, http://business.financialpost.com/news/retail-marketing/amazon-ca-sells-four-times-as-much-as-its-biggest-online-rivals-in-canada (accessed January 5, 2016).

26. http://www.tescocorporate.com/page.aspx?pointerid=3DB554FCAE344BD88EEEEFA63D71B831 (accessed July 30, 2007).

27. The Alfano Group, "25 Interesting facts about Home Depot, the world's biggest home repair store," http://thealfanogroup.blogspot.ca/2015/01/25-interesting-facts-about-home-depot.html (accessed January 5, 2016).

28. Anita McGahan, "Sustaining Superior Profits: Customer and Supplier Relationships," *Harvard Business Online*, http://harvardbusinessonline.hbsp.harvard.edu, March 1, 1999, pp. 1–7; and Randolph Beard, "Regulation, Vertical Integration and Sabotage," *Journal of Industrial Economics* 49, no. 3, (2001), pp. 319–333.

29. http://www.businessweek.com/magazine/content/05_46/b3959003.htm (accessed July 30, 2007).

30. Donald Lehman and Russell Winer, *Analysis for Marketing Planning*, 5th. ed. (Burr Ridge, IL: McGraw-Hill/Irwin, 2001).

31. Andrew Campbell, "Mission Statements," *Long Range Planning* 30 (December 1997), pp. 931–935.

32. Alfred Rappaport, *Creating Shareholder Value: The New Standard for Business Performance* (New York: Wiley, 1988); Robert C. Higgins and Roger A. Kerin, "Managing the Growth-Financial Policy Nexus in Retailing," *Journal of Retailing* 59, no. 3 (Fall 1983), pp. 19–47; and Roger Kerin, Vijay Mahajan, and P. Rajan Varadarajan, *Contemporary Perspectives on Strategic Market Planning* (Boston: Allyn & Bacon, 1991), Ch. 6.

33. See Linda Gatley and David Clutterbuck, "Superdrug Crafts a Mission Statement," *International Journal of Retail and Distribution Management* 26 (October–November 1998),

pp. 10–11, for an interesting example of the process used by a U.K. drugstore chain to develop a mission statement.

34. David Aaker, *Strategic Market Management*, 6th ed. (New York: John Wiley, 2001).

35. Michael Porter, "Strategy and the Internet," *Harvard Business Review*, March 2001, pp. 63–78; and Michael Porter, *Competitive Strategy* (New York: Free Press, 1980).

36. "The Estée Lauder Companies Inc.," *Hoovers Online*, 2002, http://www.hoovers.com/premium/profile/8/0,2147,40148,00.html.

37. "L'Oréal SA," *Hoovers Online*, 2002, http://www.hoovers.com/premium/profile/2/0,2147,41772,00.html.

38. Terry Clark, P. Rajan Varadarajan, and William M. Pride, "Environmental Management: The Construct and Research Propositions," *Journal of Business Research* 29, no. 1 (January 1994), pp. 23–39; James Lang, Roger Calantone, and Donald Gudmundson, "Small Firm Information Seeking as a Response to Environmental Threats and Opportunities," *Journal of Small Business Management*, January 1997, pp. 11–29; and Masoud Yasai-Ardekani and Paul Nystrom, "Designs for Environmental Scanning Systems: Tests of a Contingency Theory," *Management Science* 42 (February 1996), pp. 187–204.

39. Bill Quinn, *How Wal-Mart Is Destroying America (and the World): And What You Can Do About It* (Berkeley, CA: Ten Speed Press, 2000).

40. Erin White, "Retail Brand Buys Brooks Brothers from Marks & Spencer for $225 Million," *The Wall Street Journal*, November 23, 2001; and Andrew Ross Sorkin, "Owner of Casual Corner Chain in Deal for Brooks Brothers," *New York Times*, November 23, 2001.

41. David Aaker, *Strategic Market Management*, 6th ed. (New York: John Wiley, 2001); G. Stalk, "Competing on Capabilities: The New Rules of Corporate Strategy," *Harvard Business Review*, March–April 1992, pp. 51–69; and Donna Cartwright, Paul Boughton, and Stephen Miller, "Competitive Intelligence Systems: Relationships to Strategic Orientation and Perceived Usefulness," *Journal of Managerial Issues* 7 (Winter 1995), pp. 420–434.

42. Blair Cameron, "The Recession Hangover: How Inflation Is Changing Canadian Retail," Joint Research from Loyalty One and the Retail Council of Canada, August 2011, p. 5, http://www.retailcouncil.org/training/research/industry/RecessionHangover.pdf (accessed October 21, 2013).

43. Brendan Soucie, "March 2012–Canadian eCommerce Monthly Trends Report," Demac Media, April 5, 2012, http://www.demacmedia.com/canadian-ecommerce-monthly-trends/canadian-ecommerce-statistics-series-march-2012/ (accessed October 21, 2013).

Chapter 5

1. Hiawatha Bray, "Microsoft Takes Page from Apple Retail Plan," *Boston Globe*, July 18, 2009.

2. Michael E. Porter, *Competitive Strategy: Techniques for Analyzing Industries and Competitors* (Simon & Schuster Trade, 1998).

3. Nima Ghodratpour, "Are Canada's Competitive Rents Helping Drive Retail Expansion?," *Retailer-Insider*, Aug. 2014 http://www.retail-insider.com/retail-insider/2014/8/rents (accessed January 6, 2016).

4. Robert W. Buckner, *Site Selection: New Advancements in Methods and Technology* (New York: Lebhar-Friedman Books, 1998), p. 18.

5. Karen A. Machleit, Sevgin A. Eroglu, and Susan Powell Mantel, "Perceived Retail Crowding and Shopping Satisfaction: What Modifies This Relationship?" *Journal of Consumer Psychology* 9, no. 1 (2000), p. 29.

6. Buckner, *Site Selection*, pp. 31–32.

7. Buckner, *Site Selection.*

8. Business value of geospatial industry, http://geospatial-world.net/Professional/ViewBlog.aspx?id=304, September 17, 2013 (accessed January 7, 2016).

9. David L. Huff, "Defining and Estimating a Trade Area," *Journal of Marketing* 28 (1964), pp. 34-38; and David L. Huff and William Black, "The Huff Model in Retrospect," *Applied Geographic Studies* 1, no. 2 (1997), pp. 22–34.

10. Tammy Drezner and Zvi Dressner, "Validating the Gravity-Based Competitive Location Model Using Inferred Attractiveness," *Annals of Operations Research* 111 (March 2002), pp. 227–441.

11. Conseil Quebecois du Commerce de Detail (CQCD). "Vive la difference!" *Canadian Retailer,* March/April, 2004.

12. Buckner, *Site Selection,* Ch. 15.

13. List of largest enclosed shopping malls in Canada, https://en.wikipedia.org/wiki/List_of_largest_enclosed_shopping_malls_in_Canada (accessed January 7, 2016).

14. Marina Strauss, "Store wars: Retail landlords battle for high-end tenants," http://www.theglobeandmail.com/globe-investor/store-wars-retail-landlords-battle-for-high-end-tenants/article9862235/, *Globe and Mail,* March 17, 2013 (accessed January 7, 2016).

15. Eddie Baeb, "A Mall Struggles to Defend Its Glitz," *Crain's Chicago Business* 23, no. 9 (February 29, 2000), p. 3; Elin Schoen Brockman, "As Malls Die, the Next Generation Re-Creates the Past," *New York Times,* August 8, 1999, p. 4; Kevin Kenyon, "Power Moves: New Formats Help Developers Rejuvenate Enclosed Centers," *Shopping Centers Today,* October 8, 1999; and Herb Greenberg, "Dead Mall Walking," *Fortune* 141, no. 9 (May 1, 2000), p. 304.

16. CTV News, "New megamall to come with concert hall, footbridge over Decarie," http://montreal.ctvnews.ca/new-megamall-to-come-with-concert-hall-footbridge-over-decarie-1.2380914, May 19, 2015 (accessed January 7, 2016).

17. Debra Hazel, "Demalling for Dollars," *Shopping Centers Today,* January 2, 2001; and Suzette Hill, "To De-Mall or EMall? Shaping Web Shopping," *Apparel Industry Magazine* 61, no. 2 (February 2000), pp. 36–38.

18. Patricia Williams, "$355M Vaughan Mall Built on Themes: Innovative Design Reflects Canadian Culture," *Daily Commercial News and Construction Record,* Vol. 76: June 19, 2003; and Rebecca Sullivan, "Construction Begins on Vaughan Mills," Canada Newswire, Ottawa: June 16, 2003.

19. Julie Elliott, "Retail Gets a Breath of Fresh Air," *National Post,* November 3, 2003.

20. Edmund Mander, "Defining a Hot Concept Lifestyle Centers Elude Classification," *Shopping Centers Today,* August 2001, pp. 1, 44–45.

21. Lois Huff and Stephanie Shamroski, "Outlet Centers: The Search for Value," Retail Forward, Inc., May 2001.

22. Ray A. Smith, "Outlet Centers in the U.S. Turn Upmarket in Amenities," *The Asian Wall Street Journal,* June 8, 3002, p. 11.

23. "Simon Property Group and Calloway REIT Celebrate the Start of Construction on Toronto Premium Outlets® With Groundbreaking Ceremony on April 25," Simon Property Group, news release, April 10, 2012.

24. Jennifer Steinhauser, "It's a Mall ..., It's an Airport," *New York Times,* June 10, 1998, pp. C1, C4.

25. Connie Robbins Gentry, "The Rebirth of City Development," *Chain Store Age,* May 2000, pp. 83–90.

26. CBC News, "Downtown living the 'new normal,' report says Employers move to urban cores to attract qualified workers, retail follows," http://www.cbc.ca/news/business/downtown-living-the-new-normal-report-says-1.2815490, October 28, 2014 (accessed January 6, 2016).

27. http://www2.thebay.com/theroom/history/(accessed January 6, 2016).

Chapter 6

1. "Canada GDP Annual Growth Rate," *Trading Economics,* http://www.tradingeconomics.com/canada/gdp-growth-annual (accessed June 23, 2013).

2. Store Improvements: Remodels, Refreshes and More, http://www.chainstoreage.com/article/store-improvements-re-models-refreshes-and-more#. November 23, 2015 (accessed January 13, 2016).

3. Mitchell Mauk, "The Store as Story," *VM & SD,* October 2000, pp. 23, 25.

4. Joseph Sirgy, Dhruv Grewal, and Tamara Mangleburg, "Retail Environment, Self-Congruity, and Retail Patronage: An Integrative Model and a Research Agenda," *Journal of Business Research* 49, no. 2 (August 2000), pp. 127–138.

5. Kathleen Purvis, "It's Scary: Your Supermarket Shopping Is Done by Design," *Seattle Times,* June 19, 2002, based on research by Kevin Kelly.

6. Julia Werdigier, "To Woo Europeans, McDonald's Goes Upscale," *The New York Times,* August 25, 2007 (accessed December 28, 2007).

7. Linda Matchan, "The Sleek, Smooth Design of Apple's iPod Is Now Mirrored in the Architecture of Some of the Company's High-Profile Stores," *Boston Globe,* June 29, 2006.

8. Eileen Bridges and Renée Florsheim, "Hedonic and Utilitarian Shopping Goals: The Online Experience," *Journal of Business Research* 61 (April 2008), pp. 309–314; Ravindra Chitturi, Rajagopal Raghunathan, and Vijay Mahajan, "Delight by Design: The Role of Hedonic versus Utilitarian Benefits," *Journal of Marketing* 72 (May 2008), pp. 48–63; Andrew Smitha and Leigh Sparks "It's Nice to Get a Wee Treat If You've Had a Bad Week," *Journal of Business Research* 62 (May 2009), pp. 542–547.

9. Stacey Menzel Baker, Jonna Holland, and Carol Kaufman-Scarborough, "How Consumers with Disabilities Perceive 'Welcome' in Retail Servicescapes: A Critical Incident Study," *Journal of Services Marketing* 21, no. 3 (2007), pp. 160–173; Robert Pear, "Plan Seeks More Access for Disabled," *New York Times,* July 16, 2008, p. 11: Rosemary D. F. Bromley and David L. Matthew, "Reducing Consumer Disadvantage: Reassessing Access in the Retail Environment," *International Review of Retail, Distribution & Consumer Research* 17, no. 5 (2007), pp. 483–501; Marianne Wilson, "Accessible Fixtures," *Chain Store Age* 83, no. 2 (February 2007).

10. See, for example, *Disabled in Action of Metropolitan New York, Inc. et al. v. Duane Reade, Inc.,* U.S. District Court, Southern District of New York, Civil Action No. 01 Civ. 4692 (WHP), 2004; *Californians for Disability Rights v. Mervyn's, Superior Court of California,* No. 2002-051738 (RMS), 2003; *Shimozono, et al. v. May Department Stores Co. d/b/a Robinsons-May,* Federal Court, Central District of California, Case No. 00-04261 (WJR), 2001; *Access Now, et al., v. Burdines, Inc.,* Federal Court, Southern District of Florida, Case No. 99-3214 (CIV), 2000.

11. Michael Barbaro, "Department Stores Settle Disability Lawsuit," *Washington Post,* February 9, 2005, p. E02.

12. McColl and L. Jongbloed (eds.), "Disability and Social Policy in Canada" (2nd ed.), *Captus University Publications,* 2006, Concord, ON; Michael Prince, "Does Canada Need a National Disability Act?" *Public Lecture,* 2007; Michael J. Prince, *Absent Citizens: Disability Politics and Policy in Canada,* University of Toronto Press, Toronto, 2009.

13. Mary Ann McColl, Mike Schaub, Lauren Sampson, and Kevin Hong, "A Canadians With Disabilities Act?" *Canadian Disability Policy Alliance Secretariat,* Summer 2010.

14. http://www.aodacompliance.com (accessed June 2013).

15. http://www.osler.com/NewsResources/Details.aspx?id=3236 (accessed June 2013).

16. http://www.aodacompliance.com (accessed June 2013).

17. Claire Wilson, "The Harlem Revival Brings in the Shops," *The New York Times*, April 18, 2007 (accessed January 4, 2008).

18. Joseph Weishar, "Moving Targets." *Visual Merchandising and Store Design*, September 1990.

19. "International Interior Store Design Competition," *Visual Merchandising and Store Design*, February 1996, pp. 35–76.

20. Fiona Soltes, "It's the Message, Not the Medium," *Stores*, October 2007, p. 26; Michael Curran, "Now Playing: Interactive Retail Marketing 2.0," *Stores*, August 2007, p. 92; Katherine Field, "Digital Signage: A Powerful New Medium," *Chain Store Age*, May 2006, p. 204; Steven Keith Platt, Kingshuck Sinha, and Barton Weitz, *Implications for Retail Adoption of Digital Signage Systems* (Chicago, IL: Platt Retail Institute, 2004).

21. Raymond R. Burke, "Behavioral Effects of Digital Signage," *Journal of Advertising Research* 49 (June 2009), pp. 180–186.

22. "Five Easy Steps," *VM & SE*, June 2000, pp. 42–43.

23. Mindy Fetterman and Jayne O'Donnell, "Just Browsing at the Mall? That's What You Think," *USA Today*, September 1, 2006; Paco Underhill, *Why We Buy: The Science of Shopping* (New York: Simon and Schuster, 2000).

24. IMS, "The Ultimate Retail-Consumers are the new POS Disruption," http://www.imsresultscount.com/resultscount/2015/03/the-ultimate-retail-disruption-consumers-are-the-new-pos.html, March 27, 2015 (accessed January 17, 2016).

25. Joseph Weishar, "The Business of the Wall," *Visual Merchandising and Store Design*, October 1985.

26. Sara Bauknecht, "Smart Mirror Matches Fashion Rather Than Reflect," *Pittsburgh Post-Gazette*, December 14, 2009.

27. Bo Begole, Takashi Matsumoto, Wei Zhang, Nicholas Yee, Juan Liu, and Maurice Chu, "Designed to Fit: Challenges of Interaction Design for Clothes Dressing Room Technologies," in *Human-Computer Interaction: Interacting in Various Application Domains* (Berlin/Heidelberg: Springer, 2009); Jeanine Poggi, "Dressing Rooms of the Future," *Forbes*, July 22, 2008.

28. The concept of atmospherics was introduced by Philip Kotler, "Atmosphere as a Marketing Tool," *Journal of Retailing* 49 (Winter 1973), pp. 48–64. The definition is adapted from Richard Yalch and Eric Spangenberg, "Effects of Store Music on Shopping Behaviour," *Journal of Service Marketing* 4, no. 1 (Winter 1990), pp. 31–39.

29. Pierre Chandon, J. Wesley Hutchinson, Eric T. Bradlow, and Scott H. Young, "Does In-Store Marketing Work? Effects of the Number and Position of Shelf Facings on Brand Attention and Evaluation at the Point of Purchase," *Journal of Marketing* 73 (November 2009), pp. 1–17.

30. Eric R. Spangenberg, David E. Sprott, Bianca Grohmann, and Daniel L. Tracy, "Gender-Congruent Ambient Scent Influences on Approach and Avoidance Behaviors in a Retail Store," *Journal of Business Research* 59, no. 12 (2006), pp. 1281–1287; Anna S. Mattila and Jochen Wirtz, "Congruency of Scent and Music as a Driver of In-Store Evaluations and Behavior," *Journal of Retailing* 77, no. 2 (Summer 2001), pp. 273–289.

31. Mintel, "Over A Third Of US Millennial Women Say Social Media Is A Top Influencer For Clothing Purchases," http://www.mintel.com/press-centre/fashion/over-a-third-of-us-millennial-women-say-social-media-is-a-top-influencer-for-clothing-purchases June 9th 2015 (accessed January 17, 2016).

32. Marina Strauss, "Aldo's global footprint," http://www.theglobeandmail.com/report-on-business/small-business/going-global/aldos-global-footprint/article601117/?page=all, August 23, 2012 (accessed January 17, 2016).

33. Brooks Barnes, "Disney's Retail Plan Is a Theme Park in Its Stores," *New York Times*, October 13, 2009.

34. http://www.charthouse.com (accessed July 1, 2010).

35. "Atmosphere as a Marketing Tool," *Journal of Retailing* 49 (Winter 1973), pp. 48–64. The definition is adapted from Richard Yalch and Eric Spangenberg, "Effects of Store Music on Shopping Behavior," *Journal of Service Marketing* 4, no. 1 (Winter 1990), pp. 31–39.

36. Anna S. Mattila and Jochen Wirtz, "Congruency of Scent and Music as a Driver of In-Store Evaluations and Behavior," *Journal of Retailing* 77, no. 2 (Summer 2001), pp. 273–289.

37. Teresa A. Summers and Paulette R. Hebert, "Shedding Some Light on Store Atmospherics; Influence of Illumination on Consumer Behavior," *Journal of Business Research* 54, no. 2 (November 2001), pp. 145–150.

38. Susan Franke, "Architects, Experts Say Proper Design Can Propel Shoppers into Stores," *Pittsburgh Business Times*, July 12, 2002.

39. For a review of this research, see Joseph A. Bellizzi and Robert E. Hite, "Environmental Color, Consumer Feelings, and Purchase Likelihood," *Psychology and Marketing* 9, no. 5 (September-October 1992), pp. 347–363.

40. Duncan Herrington and Louis Capella, "Effects of Music in Service Environments: A Field Study," *Journal of Services Marketing* 10, no. 2 (1996), pp. 26–41.

41. Richard F. Yalch and Eric R. Spangenberg, "The Effects of Music in a Retail Setting on Real and Perceived Shopping Times," *Journal of Business Research* 49, no. 2 (August 2000), pp. 139–148; Michael Hui, Laurette Dube, and Jean-Charles Chebat, "The Impact of Music on Consumers' Reactions to Waiting for Services," *Journal of Retailing* 73, no. 1, (1997), pp. 87–104; and Julie Baker, Dhruv Grewal, and Michael Levy, "An Experimental Approach to Making Retail Store Environmental Decisions," *Journal of Retailing* 68 (Winter 1992), pp. 445–460.

42. Maxine Wilkie, "Scent of a Market," *American Demographics*, August 1995, pp. 40–49.

43. Anna S. Mattila and Jochen Wirtz, "Congruency of Scent and Music as a Driver of In-Store Evaluations and Behavior," *Journal of Retailing* 77, no. 2 (Summer 2001), pp. 273–290.

44. Cathleen McCarthy, "Aromatic Merchandising: Leading Customers by the Nose," *Visual Merchandising and Store Design*, April 1992, pp. 85–87.

45. Velitchka Kalchteva and Barton Weitz, "How Exciting Should a Store Be?" *Journal of Marketing*, Winter 2006, pp. 34–62.

46. Ibid.

47. Jung-Hwan Kim, Minjeong Kim, and Jay Kandampully, "The Impact of Buying Environment Characteristics of Retail Websites," *Service Industries Journal* 27, no. 7 (2007), pp. 865–880; David Cunningham, Liz Thach, and Karen Thompson, "Innovative E-Commerce Site Design: A Conceptual Model to Match Consumer MBTI Dimensions to Website Design," *Journal of Internet Commerce* 6, no. 3 (2007), pp. 1–27.

48. James J. Cappel and Zhenyu Huang, "A Usability Analysis of Company Websites," *Journal of Computer Information Systems* 48, no. 1 (2007), pp. 117–123.

49. Benjamin P.C. Yen, "The Design and Evaluation of Accessibility on Web Navigation," *Decision Support Systems* 42, no. 4 (2007), pp. 219–235.

50. "Tips on Improving the Checkout Process," http://www.e-consultancy.com, August 17, 2007.

51. Ibid.

52. Formisimo, Hazel Bolton, "Shopping Cart Abandonment Rate Statistics," http://www.formisimo.com/blog/shopping-cart-abandonment-rate/ February 20, 2015 (accessed January 17, 2016).

Chapter 7

1. Jamie Sturgeon, "It's official, Tim Hortons, Burger King become one," http://globalnews.ca/news/1724238/its-official-tim-hortons-burger-king-become-one/, December 12, 2014 (accessed January 17, 2016).
2. Lawrence Stevenson, Joseph Shlesinger, and Michael Pearce, Power Retail (Whitby, ON: McGraw-Hill Ryerson, 1999); and Jonathan Reynolds and Christine Cuthbertson, Retail Strategy: The View from the Bridge (Amsterdam: Elsevier, 2004).
3. "2013 Global Powers of Retailing," Stores, January 2013, pp. G17–G21.
4. Frank Badillo, "Global Retail Outlook," Retail Forward, May 2009; 2009 Global Development Index (New York: Kearney, 2009).
5. Ian Bremmer, "The new world of business," Fortune, http://fortune.com/2015/01/22/the-new-world-of-business/, January 22, 2015 (accessed January 18, 2016).
6. "China's Retail Revolution: An Interview with Walmart's Ed Chan," BusinessWeek, October 2009.
7. Han Ben-Shjabat, Mike Moriarty, and Deepa Bahgara, Windows of Hope for Global Retailing (Chicago: Kearney, 2009); Ken Schepy, "Retailing in India: Challenges and Opportunities," Chain Store Age, July 2008; Mehul Srivastava, "Big Retailers Still Struggle in India," BusinessWeek India, October 16, 2009.
8. Brenda Sternquist, International Retailing, ABC Media Inc., 1998; "A Tiger, Falling behind a Dragon," The Economist, June 21, 2003; "Two Systems, One Grand Rivalry," The Economist, June 21, 2003.
9. Jane Barrett, "Designer Heralds Upturn as Retail Sales Rise 9%," National Post, April 14, 2004.
10. "Big in Beijing," W Magazine, September 2012, http://www.wmagazine.com/travel/2012/09/giorgio-armani-beijing-recommendations (accessed November 18, 2013).
11. Bernard Wysocki, Jr., "In Developing Nations, Many Youth Are Big Spenders," The Wall Street Journal, June 26, 1997, pp. A1, A11.
12. Elisabeth Rosenthal, "Buicks, Starbucks and Fried Chicken. Still China?" New York Times, February 25, 2002, http://www.nytimes.com/2002/02/25/international/asia/25CHIN.html?pagewanted=all (accessed November 18, 2013).
13. David Woodruff, "For French Retailers, a Weapon against Wal-Mart," The Wall Street Journal, September 27, 1999, pp. B1, B4; and David Woodruff, "Carrefour Is Mounting a Push into Japanese Markets," The Wall Street Journal, June 15, 1999, p. B7.
14. Deloitte, "Global Powers of Retailing 2016 Navigating the new digital divide," http://www2.deloitte.com/ru/en/pages/consumer-business/articles/global-powers-of-retailing-2016.html (accessed January 19, 2016).
15. Deloitte, "Global Powers of Retailing 2016 Navigating the new digital divide," http://www2.deloitte.com/ru/en/pages/consumer-business/articles/global-powers-of-retailing-2016.html 2016 (accessed January 19, 2016).
16. Geoff Wissman, "Critical Issues: The Top 100 Retailers Worldwide 2000," Retail Forward, Inc., August 2001, p. 16.
17. Deloitte, "Global Powers of Retailing 2016 Navigating the new digital divide," http://www2.deloittc.com/ru/en/pages/consumer-business/articles/global-powers-of-retailing-2016.html (accessed January 19, 2016).
18. "The World Is Not Their Oyster," Chain Store Age, May, 2001, p. 60.
19. This section is adapted from "Winning Moves on a Global Chessboard: Wal-Mart and Costco in a Global Context," Goldman Sachs Investment Research, May 12, 2000.
20. Lisa Penaloza and Mary Gilly, "Marketer Acculturation: The Changer and the Changed," Journal of Marketing 63 (Summer 1999), pp. 84–95.
21. Sarah Ellison, "Carrefour Finds It Difficult to Build Single Global Brand," The Wall Street Journal, August 30, 2001.
22. Erik Gordon, "Taking the Plunge?" Chain Store Age Supplement, December 1997, pp. 14–23; and "Shopping the World," The Economist Newspaper, June 18, 1999, pp. 1–2.
23. "Handcuffs on High Street," The Economist, May 13, 2000, p. 62.
24. Deloitte, "Global Powers of Retailing 2016 Navigating the new digital divide," http://www2.deloitte.com/ru/en/pages/consumer-business/articles/global-powers-of-retailing-2016.html (accessed January 19, 2016).
25. "Handcuffs on High Street," The Economist, May 13, 2000, p. 62.
26. Ibid.
27. Colliers International "Nation Retail Report Canada Spring 2015".
28. Jean-Pierre Jeannet and H. David Hennessey, Global Marketing Strategies, 5th ed., (Boston: Houghton Mifflin, 2000); and "What's the Best Way to Set up Shop?" Chain Store Age Global Retailing Supplement, December 1997, pp. 32–35.
29. Greg Silverman and David Wasserman, "Retailing in Latin America," Global Retail Forward, July 2001, p. 13; Stephanie Shamroski, "Retailing in Turkey," Global Retail Forward, January 2000, p. 6; Ira Kalish and Stephanie Shamroski, "Global Retail Intelligencer," Global Retail Forward, April 2001, p. 2; Philip Walker, "Retailing in India," Global Retail Forward, March 2000, p. 12; Lois Huff and Stephanie Shamroski, "Retailing in the United Kingdom," Global Retail Forward, December 2000, p. 17; and Marianne Wilson, "Thinking Big," Chain Store Age, July 1, 2001, p. 47.
30. "An Opening Door Policy," Chain Store Age, January 2000, pp. 62–63.
31. http://www.marksandspencer.com
32. Stats Canada, http://www.statcan.gc.ca/daily-quotidien/141205/t141205b001-eng.htm (accessed January 20, 2016).
33. "Wal around the World," The Economist, December 8, 2001, p. 8; and "Pooled Assets," Chain Store Age, June 1, 2001, p. 50.
34. Rob Deloney, "McDonald's Banks on Franchising in China," National Post, September 9, 2003.
35. Alex Gillis, "Spanish Armada," National Post, October 1, 1999.
36. Erik Gordon, "Taking the Plunge?" Chain Store Age Global Retailing Supplement, Ernst & Young, December 1997, pp. 14–23.
37. "Chain Stores in India," The Economist, May 29, 2008.
38. Statista, https://habitat.inkling.com/project/sn_ee8e/files/s9ml/chapter007/ch07_reader_5.html (accessed January 1, 2016).
39. Deloitte, "Global Powers of Retailing 2016: Navigating the new digital divide," January 2016, http://www2.deloitte.com/sg/en/pages/consumer-business/articles/global-powers-of-retailing.html (accessed January 20, 2016).
40. Deloitte, "Global Powers of Retailing 2016: Retail Beyond," January 2016, p. 23, http://www2.deloitte.com/sg/en/pages/consumer-business/articles/global-powers-of-retailing.html (accessed January 20, 2016).
41. Ibid., p. 20.
42. Ibid., p. 23.
43. Ibid., p. 20.
44. Ibid., p. 28.
45. Ibid., p. G17.
46. Ibid., p. 34.
47. Ibid., p. 29.
48. http://www.bloomberg.com/bw/articles/2014-08-28/for-world-donut-domination-its-tim-hortons-vs-dunkin-donuts (accessed January 22, 2016).

49. Jacqueline Thorpe, "India the Jewel in Global Market," *National Post*, April 16, 2004.

50. Christopher Daniel & Tony Hernandez, *The CSCA retail 100*, p. 6 (Centre for the Study of Commercial Activity, 2015).

51. ABC News, "China Big in Counterfeit Goods," http://abcnews.go.com/WNT/story?id=130381&page=1 (accessed January 23, 2016).

52. Ibid.

53. The Vancouver Sun, "B.C. storeowner slapped with record fine for selling fashion fakes," http://www.canada.com/vancouversun/story.html?id=3aefc0d4-a63c-4a87-ac14-da4a0b225d70, June 2008 (accessed January 23, 2016).

54. http://www.rcmp-grc.gc.ca/fep-pelf/ipr-dpi/faq-eng.htm (accessed January 23, 2016).

Chapter 8

1. Patrick Dunne and Robert Lusch, *Retailing*, 5th ed. (Mason, OH: Southwest, 2000) pp. 39–40.

2. "Diversity at McDonald's: A Way of Life," *Nation's Restaurant News*, January, 2005, pp. 92–95.

3. 2007 annual report, Lululemon Athletica Inc., April 8, 2008, http://files.shareholder.com/downloads/LULU/0x0xS909567-08-415/1397187/filing.pdf.

4. Stanley B. Block, Geoffrey A. Hirt, and Douglas J. Short, *Foundations of Financial Management*, 8th ed. (Whitby ON: McGraw-Hill Ryerson, 2009), pp. 23, 28.

5. http://cbdd.wsu.edu/kewlcontent/cdoutput/TOM505/page25.htm, Chapter 8: Analysis of Financial Statements.

6. Lawrence J. Gitman, *Principles of Managerial Finance*, 12th ed. (Upper Saddle River, NJ: Pearson Prentice Hall), p. 118.

7. Lululemon Athletica Inc., 2015 annual report, March 26, 2015, http://investor.lululemon.com/secfiling.cfm?filingID=1397187-15-16 (accessed January 27, 2016).

8. http://www.loblaw.ca/.

9. BDC, "Controlling your retail business's overhead," https://www.bdc.ca/en/articles-tools/money-finance/manage-finances/pages/standard-costs-retail-industry.aspx (accessed January 29, 2016)

10. Jane O'Donnel, "Retailers Want a Place in Your Wallet," *USA Today*, July 10, 2006.

11. Average retail inventory is estimated from the balance sheet inventory. Assume the end-of-year inventory on the balance sheet is average cost inventory: Average retail inventory = Average cost inventory/(1 – Gross margin percent (expressed as a decimal)).

12. To illustrate, suppose Net sales = $50,000 and Average inventory at retail = $10,000; Inventory turnover = $50,000 ÷ $10,000 = 5. To convert inventory turnover expressed at retail to turnover at cost, we multiply by the cost complement, which is the percentage of net sales represented by the cost of goods sold. If the gross margin is 40 percent, the cost complement is 60 percent (100% – 40%). By multiplying the numerator and denominator by 60 percent, the result is cost of goods sold divided by the average inventory at cost. Thus, inventory turnover is 5 whether it is calculated using retail or cost figures.

13. The rationale behind this equation is as follows: The sales-to-stock ratio is expressed with the numerator at retail and the denominator at cost. To get inventory turnover, both numerator and denominator must be at either retail or cost. 100% – Gross margin % is the percentage of net sales represented by the cost of goods sold (also known as the cost complement). By multiplying the sales-to-stock ratio by the cost complement we, in essence, convert the numerator (sales) to the cost of goods sold and therefore have numerator and denominator both expressed at cost.

14. James Surowiecki, "The Most Devastating Retailer in the World," *The New Yorker*, September 18, 2000, p. 74.

15. This section is adapted from William R. Davidson, Daniel J. Sweeney, and Ronald W. Stampfl, *Retailing Management*, 5th ed. (New York: John Wiley & Sons, 1984).

16. Terry Pristin, "Owning Your Retail Space Is Not Just for The Big Guys Anymore," *The New York Times*, March 29, 2006.

17. Although the use of asset turnover presented here is helpful for gaining appreciation of the performance ratio, capital budgeting or present value analyses are more appropriate for determining the long-term return of a fixed asset.

18. Bryan Gildenberg, Mventures, personal communication, February 2002.

19. All categories of shares, including preferred shares, paid-in capital, and treasury shares, are included with common shares for simplicity.

20. "A Strong and Useful Light," *Harvard Business Review* 80, no. 5 (May 2002), p. 12.; John D. Sterman and Nelson P. Repenning, "Nobody Ever Gets Credit for Fixing Problems That Never Happened: Creating and Sustaining Process Improvement," *Harvard Business Online*, July 1, 2001; Loren Gary, "The Right Kind of Failure," *Harvard Management*, update article, January 1, 2002; Gary Sutton, *The Six-Month Fix: Adventures in Rescuing Failing Companies* (New York: John Wiley & Sons, November 2001); and Bernard Salanie, *The Microeconomics of Market Failures* (Boston: MIT Press, November 2000).

21. Daniel J. Sweeney, "Improving the Profitability of Retail Merchandising Decisions," *Journal of Marketing*, January 1973, pp. 60–68.

Chapter 9

1. David Simchi-Levi, Philip Karminsky, and Edith Simchi-Levi, *Designing and Managing the Supply Chain: Concepts, Strategies, and Case Studies*, 4th ed. (New York: McGraw-Hill/Irwin, 2010); Roberta S. Russell, *Operations Management: Creating Value along the Supply Chain*, 7th ed. (Hoboken, NJ: Wiley, 2010); Barbara Flynn, Michiya Morita, and Jose Machuca, *Managing Global Supply Chain Relationships: Operations, Strategies and Practices* (Hauppauge, NY: Nova Science, 2010); Faustino Taderera, *Logistics and Supply Chain Management: Warehousing, Distribution* (Saarbrücken, Germany: Lap Lambert Academic, 2010); Jayaraman Vaidyanathan, "Creating Competitive Advantages through New Value Creation: A Reverse Logistics Perspective," *Academy of Management Perspectives* 21, no. 2(2007), pp. 56–73.

2. Lee Holman and Greg Buzek, "What's the Deal with Out-of-Stocks?" *IHL Group*, December 2008.

3. Holman and Buzek, "What's the Deal with Out-of-Stocks?"

4. "Bharti Enterprises and Walmart Join Hands in Wholesale Cash-and-Carry to Serve Small Retailers, Manufacturers and Farmers," PR Newswire, August 6, 2007.

5. Jesper Aastrup and Herbert Kotzab, "Forty Years of Out-of-Stock Research—and Shelves Are Still Empty," *International Review of Retail, Distribution and Consumer Research*, February 20, 2010, pp. 147–164; Jesper Aastrup and Herbert Kotzab, "Analyzing Out-of-Stock in Independent Grocery Stores: An Empirical Study," *International Journal of Retail & Distribution Management* 37, no. 9 (2009), pp. 765–789; Mike Griswold, "Out of Stock," *Forbes*, December 14, 2006.

6. "Bar Codes Change the Way Retailers Stocked, Priced Products," *Boston Globe*, June 29, 2004, p. C1.

7. Aemilia Madden, "19 Fascinating Facts You Never Knew About Zara," http://www.popsugar.com/fashion/Zara-Facts-37094189#photo-37099916 *Pop Sugar* October 23, 2015 (accessed February 3, 2016).

8. Constance Hays, "What Walmart Knows about Customers' Habits," *New York Times*, November 14, 2004, p. C1.

9. Council of Supply Chain Management Professionals, http://cscmp.org/ (accessed August 18, 2007).

10. Susan Elzey, "Location Part of Store Closing," *Knight Ridder Tribune Business News*, July 19, 2007; Dollar General Corporation, 10-K form, filed with the SEC on February 2, 2007; Amy Sung, "Dollar General Cites Progress with Store Receiving System," *Supermarket News*, October 10, 2005, p. 49.

11. http://www.businessdictionary.com/definition/freight-forwarder.html (accessed June 19, 2010).

12. Oliver E. Williamson, "Outsourcing: Transaction Cost Economics and Supply Chain Management," *Journal of Supply Chain Management* 44, no. 2, pp. 5–16; Salla Lutza and Thomas Ritter, "Outsourcing, Supply Chain Upgrading and Connectedness of a Firm's Competencies," *Industrial Marketing Management* 38 (May 2009), pp. 387–393; Erin Anderson and Barton Weitz, "Make or Buy Decisions: Vertical Integration and Marketing Productivity," *Sloan Management Review* 27 (Spring 1986), pp. 3–19.

13. Huaqin Zhang and Guojie Zhao, "Strategic Selection of Push-Pull Supply," *Modern Applied Science* 2, no. 1 (2008).

14. Andreas Otto, Franz Josef Schoppengerd, and Ramin Shariatmadari, *Direct Store Delivery: Concepts, Applications and Instruments* (New York: Springer, 2009).

15. Eric P. Jack, Thomas L. Powers, and Lauren Skinner, "Reverse Logistics Capabilities: Antecedents and Cost Savings," *International Journal of Physical Distribution & Logistics Management* 40, no. 3 (2010), pp. 228–246; S. Dowlatshahia, "A Cost-Benefit Analysis for the Design and Implementation of Reverse Logistics Systems: Case Studies Approach," *International Journal of Production Research* 48, no. 5 (January 2010), pp. 1361–1380; James Stock and J. P. Mulki, "Product Returns Processing: An Examination of Practices of Manufacturers, Wholesalers/Distributors, and Retailers," *Journal of Business Logistics* 30, no. 1 (2009), pp. 33–63; Michael Bernon and John Cullen, "An Integrated Approach to Managing Reverse Logistics," *International Journal of Logistics: Research & Applications* 10, no. 1 (2007), pp. 41–56.

16. David Blanchard, "Supply Chains Also Work in Reverse," *Industry Weekly*, May 1, 2007 (accessed January 8, 2008).

17. Adam Robinson, "Top 3 Benefits of a Reverse Logistics Management Program," *Cerasis*, February 27, 2014, http://cerasis.com/2014/02/27/reverse-logistics-management/ (accessed February 5, 2016).

18. Keith Regan, "Toys 'R' Us Wins Right to End Amazon Partnership," *E-Commerce Times*, March 3, 2006.

19. "Top 12 Drop-Shipping Best Practices," *Multichannel Merchant*, October 27, 2009; Karen E. Klein, "How Drop-Shipping Works for Retailers and Manufacturers," *BusinessWeek*, September 23, 2009; and Elliot Rabinovich, Manus Rungtusanatham, Timothy M. Laseter, "Physical Distribution Service Performance and Internet Retailer Margins: The Drop-Shipping Context," *Journal of Operations Management* 26 (November 2008), pp. 767–781.

20. Zack Rutherford, "Hard Facts about the Drop Shipment Business," SaleHOO, http://www.salehoo.com/blog/hard-facts-about-the-drop-shipment-business (accessed February 5, 2016).

21. "Benefits of Supply Chain Collaboration," http://www.supplytechnologies.com/blog/the-importance-of-supply-chain-collaboration (accessed February 5, 2016).

22. Huynh Trung Luong and Nguyen Huu Phien, "Measure of Bullwhip Effect in Supply Chains: The Case of High Order Autoregressive Demand Process," *European Journal of Operational Research* 183, no. 1 (2007), pp. 197–209; Hau Lee, V. Padmanabhan, and Seungjin Whang, "The Bullwhip Effect in Supply Chains," *Sloan Management Review*, Spring 1997, pp. 93–102.

23. Seung-Kuk, Paik, and Prabir K. Bachi, "Understanding the Causes of the Bullwhip Effect in a Supply Chain," *International Journal of Retail & Distribution Management* 35, no. 4 (2007), pp. 308–324.

24. http://www.ecrnet.org (accessed June 4, 2009).

25. V.G. Narayanan and Ananth Raman, "Aligning Incentives in Supply Chains," *Harvard Business Review*, November 2004, pp. 94–102.

26. Lora Cecere, "EDI: Workhorse of the Value Chain," http://www.gxs.co.uk/wp-content/uploads/EDI-Workhorse_of_the_Value_Chain.pdf (accessed February 5, 2016).

27. http://www.i2.com/industries/consumer_industries/vmi/vendor_managed_inventory.cfm (accessed June 15, 2010).

28. Lisa Harrington, "The Consumer Products Supply Chain: Shopping for Solutions," http://inboundlogistics.com, August 2006; Jamie Swedberg, "Collaboration Can Speed Fashion Cycle," *Apparel Magazine*, June 2004, p. 33.

29. Chang, Tien-Hsiang, Hsin-Pin Fu, Wan-I Lee, Yichen Lin, and Hsu-Chih Hsueh, "A Study of an Augmented CPFR Model for the 3C Retail Industry," *Supply Chain Management* 12, no. 3 (2007), pp. 200–209; Attaran and Attaran, "Collaborative Supply Chain Management."

30. "Flow-Through DC Yields Savings for Fred Meyer," *Chain Store Age*, October 1995, pp. 64–66; quote by Mary Sammons, senior vice-president, Fred Meyer.

31. "The history of QR Codes," http://www.qrcodesinmarketing.net/history-of-qr-codes.html (accessed February 5, 2016).

32. *Canadian Low Cost Country Sourcing Survey*, Supply Chain and Logistics Association, 2007.

33. Barbara E. Kahn and Leigh McAlister, *Grocery Revolution: The New Focus on the Consumer* (Reading, MA: Longman, Addison-Wesley, 1997).

34. James Surowiecki, "The Most Devastating Retailer in the World," *The New Yorker*, September 18, 2000, p. 74; and William Echikson, "The Mark of Zara," *BusinessWeek*, May 29, 2000, p. 98.

35. Ken Clark, "Coping with Returns," *Chain Store Age*, November 1, 2000, p. 124; based on focus group research by the Reverse Logistics Executive Council and the University of Nevada's Center for Logistics Management.

36. "30 Amazing Facts About RFID Technology," http://cybra.com/30-amazing-facts-about-rfid-technology/, September 28, 2015 (accessed February 5, 2016).

37. Gary McWilliams, "Walmart's Radio-Tracked Inventory Hits Static," *Wall Street Journal*, February 15, 2007, p. B1.

38. Ibid.; Zeynep Ton, Vincent Dessain, and Monika Stachowiak-Joulain, "RFID at the Metro Group," *Harvard Business School Publications* (9-606-053), November 9, 2005.

39. Hardgrave, S. Langford, M. Waller, and R. Miller, "Measuring the Impact of RFID on Out of Stocks at WalMart," *MIS Quarterly Executive* 7, no. 4 (2008).

40. Claire Swedberg, "Intel Unveils RFID System for Retailers," *RFID Journal*, September 2015, http://www.rfidjournal.com/articles/view?13517 (accessed February 5, 2016).

41. Rhonda Ascierto, "IBM Updates Web Sphere RFID with Drug ePedigree," *CBR*, August 9, 2007.

42. FDA 2006 Compliance Policy Guide for the Prescription Drug Marketing Act.

43. B. Hardgrave, Matthew Waller, and R. Miller, "Does RFID Reduce Out of Stocks? A Preliminary Analysis," Sam M. Walton College of Business, University of Arkansas, Information Technology Research Institute, November 2005, http://itri.uark.edu/research/display.asp?articles=ITRI-WP058-1105.

44. RFID Journal, https://www.rfidjournal.com/faq/show?85 (accessed February 5, 2016).

45. Lynn A. Fish and Wayne C. Forrest, "A Worldwise Look at RFID," *Supply Chain Management Review*, April 2007, pp. 48–55.

46. Michael Cohen, "Canadians ready for beacon technology," *CMA*, September 23, 2015, http://www.the-cma.org/about/blog/canadians-ready-for-beacon-technology (accessed February 5, 2016).
47. Ibid.
48. Ibid.
49. Ibid.

Chapter 10

1. Sharon Bailey, "Nordstrom's inventory management better than that of its peers," *Market Realist*, February 15, 2015, http://marketrealist.com/2015/02/nordstroms-inventory-management-better-than-that-of-peers/ (accessed February 7, 2015).
2. Jesper Aastrup, David B. Grant, and Mogens Bjerr, "Value Creation and Category Management through Retailer-Supplier Relationships," *International Review of Retail, Distribution and Consumer Research*, December 2007, pp. 523–545.
3. Jonathan O'Brien, *Category Management in Purchasing: A Strategic Approach to Maximize Business Profitability* (London: Logan Page, 2009).
4. Dal-Young Chun and Jack M. Cadeau, "How Supplier Category Management Policy Influences Category Sales Performance," *Asia Pacific Journal of Marketing and Logistics* 22, no. 2 (2010), pp. 222–231; Arto Lindblom and Rami Olkkonenb, "An Analysis of Suppers' Roles in Category Management Collaboration," *Journal of Retailing and Consumer Services 15* (January 2008), pp. 1–8.
5. Subir Bandyopadhyay, Anna Rominger, and Savitri Basaviaha, "Developing a Framework to Improve Retail Category Management through Category Captain Arrangements," *Journal of Retailing and Consumer Services* 16 (July 2009), pp. 315–319.
6. Joshua D. Wright, "Antitrust Analysis of Category Management: *Conwood v United Tobacco*," *Supreme Court Economic Review* 17, no. 1 (2009), pp. 27–35.
7. Walter S. Mossberg, "Palm's New Hand-Held Goes Mano a Mano with Blackberry," *Wall Street Journal*, January 31, 2002, p. B1.
8. Neil Patel, "5 Facts That Will Help You Win Any Negotiation," *Forbes*, July 16, 2015, http://www.forbes.com/sites/neilpatel/2015/07/16/5-facts-that-will-help-you-win-any-negotiation/#53f22e5b2cb7 (accessed February 8, 2016).
9. SCDigest Editorial Staff, "Supply Chain News: Walmart to Reverse SKU Count Reductions, Bring Back 8500 Items to Shelves," *Supply Chain Digest* April 14, 2011, http://www.scdigest.com/ontarget/11-04-14-2.php?cid=4438 (accessed February 8, 2016).
10. Herb Sorensen, "How Supermarkets Manage the 'Long Tail' of In-Store Media?" *Retail Wire*, November 5, 2008.
11. Stephan Hamilton and Timothy Richards, "Product Differentiation, Store Differentiation, and Assortment Depth Management," *Management Science* 55 (August 2009), pp. 1368–1376.
12. Ram Bezawada, S. Balachander, P.K. Kannan, and Venkatesh Shankar, "Cross-Category Effects of Aisle and Display Placements: A Spatial Modeling Approach and Insights," *Journal of Marketing* 73 (May 2009), pp. 99–110.
13. Tammy Worth, "Too Many Choices Can Tax the Brain, Research Shows Having a Wealth of Options Can Lead to Poor Decision Making, Experts Say," *Los Angeles Times*, March 16, 2009.
14. Susan Broniarczyk, "Product Assortment," in *Handbook of Consumer Psychology*, eds. Curtis Haugtvedt, Paul Herr, and Frank Kardes (New York: Psychology Press, 2008), pp. 708–755.
15. "Inventory Management 2003: An Overview," *Chain Store Age*, December 2003, p. 3A.

16. Murali Mantrala, P. Sinha, and A. Zoltners, "Impact of Resource Allocation Rules on Marketing Investment-Level Decisions and Profitability," *Journal of Marketing Research* 29, no. 2 (May 1992), pp. 162–175.
17. Anjali Cordeiro, "Consumer Goods Makers Heed 'Pay-check Cycle,'" *Wall Street Journal*, February 23, 2009.
18. These issues were taken from Janet Wagner, Richard Ettenson, and Jean Parrish, "Vendor Selection among Retail Buyers: An Analysis by Merchandise Division," *Journal of Retailing* 65, no. 1 (Spring 1989), pp. 58–79.
19. Joel Warady, "Asda Takes the 'Pulse of the Nation,'" *Retail Wire*, July 16, 2009.
20. Jinhong Xie and Steven Shugan, "Advance Selling," in *Handbook of Pricing Research in Marketing*, ed. V. Rao (Northhampton, MA: Edward Elgar, 2009), pp. 451–477.
21. This section was developed with the assistance of KhiMetrics.

Chapter 11

1. "Private Label: Battles with brand names over quality and price," *Checkout*, The Integer Group and M/A/R/C Research (http://www.shopperculture.com), May 2012, p. 3.
2. Ibid., p. 2.
3. Nielsen, "The State of Private Label Around the World," November 2014, http://www.nielsen.com/content/dam/nielsenglobal/kr/docs/global-report/2014/Nielsen%20Global%20Private%20Label%20Report%20November%202014.pdf (accessed February 9, 2016).
4. Rusch, "Private Labels: Does Branding Matter?"; and http://www.brandchannel.com/features-effect.asp?id=94.
5. Nielsen, "The State of Private Label Around the World," November 2014, http://www.nielsen.com/content/dam/nielsenglobal/kr/docs/global-report/2014/Nielsen%20Global%20Private%20Label%20Report%20November%202014.pdf (accessed February 9, 2016).
6. Michael Harvey, "The Trade Dress Controversy: A Case of Strategic Cross-Brand Cannibalization," *Journal of Marketing Theory and Practice* 6, no. 2 (Spring 1998), pp. 1–15.
7. Carman Allison, "Picking up private label," *Canadian Grocery*, March 24, 2015, http://www.canadiangrocer.com/blog/picking-up-private-label-51204 (accessed February 9, 2016).
8. "Best Global Brands 2007," *BusinessWeek*, August 6, 2007.
9. Kumar and Steenkamp, *Private Label Strategy*.
10. Mark Beren, Shantanu Dutta, and Steven Shugan, "Branded Variants: A Retail Perspective," *Journal of Marketing Research*, February 1996, pp. 9–20.
11. http://www.eonoutdoor.com/decking.php.
12. http://www.gbmabc.com/canada/en/retailapparelmarketin-canada2010.pdf.
13. Export tariffs are used in some less developed countries to generate additional revenue. For instance, the Argentine government may impose an export tariff on wool that is exported. An export tariff actually lowers the competitive ability of domestic manufacturers, rather than protecting them, as is the case with import tariffs.
14. "Border Battles," *The Economist*, October 3, 1998, p. 6.
15. Personal communication, David Gunter, director of corporate communications, Coldwater Creek, July 2002.
16. Steven Greenhouse, "18 Major Retailers and Apparel Makers Are Accused of Using Sweatshops," *New York Times*, January 14, 1999, p. A9.
17. Anne D'Innocenzio, "Wal-Mart Warns Suppliers on Stricter Measures," Associated Press, January 22, 2013, http://bigstory.ap.org/article/wal-mart-warns-suppliers-stricter-measures (accessed December 9, 2013).
18. http://www.walmart.ca/wms/microsite/CorpVal/Annual%20Report/WM_CSR08_En4.pdf.

19. http://www.gbmabc.com/canada/en/retailapparelmarketin-canada2010.pdf.

20. "Labor Forces Review," *Daily News*, April 26, 1998.

21. http://www.fashioncenter.com.

22. http://www.dallasmarketcenter.com.

23. Erin Silver, "Fashion Week in Toronto: A Day for the New Guys," Toronto Fashion, March 21, 2002.

24. https://www.cangift.org/en/home/

25. Dan Scheraga, "Collaboration Evolves," *Chain Store Age*, July 2005, p. 58.

26. Janet Adamy, "Retail Exchanges Plan Merger to Vie with Wal-Mart," *Wall Street Journal*, April 26, 2005, p. B7.

27. Hollie Shaw, "Loblaw pledges to stay in Bangladesh, improve safety after building collapse," *Financial Post*, May 2, 2013, http://business.financialpost.com/2013/05/02/loblaw-pledges-to-stay-in-bangladesh-improve-safety-after-building-collapse.html (accessed May 3, 2013).

28. Sandy Jap, "Online Reverse Auctions: Issues, Themes, and Prospects for the Future," *Journal of the Academy of Marketing Science* 30, no. 4 (Fall 2002); forthcoming M.L. Emiliani, "Business-to-Business Online Auctions: Key Issues for Purchasing Process Improvement," *Supply Chain Management: An International Journal* 5, no. 4 (2000), pp. 176–186.

29. Richard Wise and David Morrison, "Beyond the Exchange: The Future of B2B," *Harvard Business Review*, November–December 2000, pp. 86–96.

30. Technology Executives Club, http://www.technology-executivesclub.com/sponsorpages/1sync.php (accessed February 10, 2016).

31. https://www.neogrid.com/en/our-history

32. Tim Laseter, Brian Long, and Chris Capers, "B2B Benchmark: The State of Electronic Exchanges," *strategy+business*, 4th quarter, 2001, http://www.strategy-business.com/search/Archives.

33. Ibid.

34. Adapted from V. Kasturi Rangan, "FreeMarkets Online," Harvard Business School case #9-598-109, February 1999.

35. http://www.ariba.com/about

36. Neil Patel, "Facts That Will Help You Win Any Negotiation," *Forbes*, July 16th 2015, http://www.forbes.com/sites/neilpatel/2015/07/16/5-facts-that-will-help-you-win-any-negotiation/#4d272f682cb7 (accessed February 12, 2016).

37. Dietmeyer, B.J. and Kaplan, R. "Strategic Negotiation," 2004, Kaplan Publishing, USA.

38. Ibid.

39. Ibid.

40. Barton Weitz and Sandy Jap, "Relationship Marketing and Distribution Channels," *Journal of the Academy of Marketing Sciences* 23 (Fall 1995), pp. 305–320; and F. Robert Dwyer, Paul Shurr, and Sejo Oh, "Developing Buyer-Seller Relationships," *Journal of Marketing* 51 (April 1987), pp. 11–27.

41. Nirmalya Kumar, "The Power of Trust in Manufacturer-Retailer Relationships," *Harvard Business Review*, November-December 1996, pp. 92–106.

42. Erin Anderson and Anne Coughlan, "Structure, Governance, and Relationship Management," in *Handbook of Marketing*, eds. B. Weitz and R. Wensley (London: Sage, 2002).

43. Erin Anderson and Barton Weitz, "The Use of Pledges to Build and Sustain Commitment in Distribution Channels," *Journal of Marketing Research* 29 (February 1992), pp. 18–34.

44. http://www.plstorebrands.com.

45. Ibid.

46. Thomas J. Ryan, "Financial Forum: Chargeback Debate Roars on as Practice Remains Fact of Life," *WWD*, June 1, 1998, pp. 14, 16.

47. Similar types of fees charged to vendors are display fees (paid for special merchandising and display of products) and pay-to-stay fees (paid to continue stocking and displaying a product).

48. Bizshift-Trends. "War for Retail Shelf Space; Battle for Shelf Placement; Fight for Slotting Fees: It's All About– Pay-4-Space, Position, Leverage...," May 18, 2014, http://bizshifts-trends.com/2014/05/18/war-retail-shelf-space-battle-shelf-placement-fight-low-slotting-fees-position-mindshare/ (accessed February 16, 2016).

49. Marcia O'Connor, "Export Basics - Listing Fees or Slotting Allowances (Pay-to-stay fees)," June 2014, http://www1.agric.gov.ab.ca/$Department/deptdocs.nsf/all/trade11223/$FILE/4_listing_fees2014.pdf (accessed February 16, 2016).

50. *Conwood Company, LLP v United States Tobacco Co.*, 2002 Fed App/0171P (6th Cir. 2002).

51. Federal Trade Commission, "World's Largest Manufacturer of Spice and Seasoning Products Agrees to Settle Price Discrimination Charges," FTC press release, March 8, 2000.

52. http://www.cbc.ca/news/background/consumers/counterfeit.html.

53. It World Canada, "Software piracy costs businesses $114B: IDC," March 11, 2013, http://www.itworldcanada.com/article/software-piracy-costs-businesses-114b-idc/47517 (accessed February 16, 2016).

54. This section draws from Michael R. Czinkota and Ilkka A. Ronkainen, *International Marketing*, 6th ed. (Cincinnati: South-Western, 2000).

55. Irvine Clarke III and Margaret Owens, "Trademark Rights in Gray Markets," *International Marketing Review* 17, no. 2/3 (2000), p. 272.

56. *Kmart Corp. v. Cartier, Inc.*, 486 U.S. 281 (1988).

57. *Sebao Inc. v. GB Unic. SA*, 1999 E.T.M.R. 681.

58. Suein L. Hwant, "Tobacco: As Cigarette Prices Soar, a Gray Market Booms," *Wall Street Journal*, January 28, 1999, p. B1.

59. *Southern Card & Novelty v. Lawson Mardon Label*, 138 F.3d 869 (1998).

60. *In re Toys R Us Antitrust Litigation*, 191 F.R.D. 347 (E.D.N.Y. 2000).

Chapter 12

1. *2010 Accenture Holiday Luxury Shopping Survey*, quoted in Tom Jacobson, Ray Florio, and Tiago Salvador, "The Premium of Value: Pricing and Promoting Luxury to the New Consumer," Accenture, p. 4.

2. This section was developed with the assistance of KhiMetrics.

3. This section is based on Thomas T. Nagle and Reed K. Holden, *The Strategy and Tactics of Pricing: A Guide to Profitable Decision Making* (Prentice Hall, 2002).

4. Amy Merrick, "Priced to Move: Retailers Try to Get Leg Up on Markdowns with New Software," *Wall Street Journal*, August 7, 2001, p. A1.

5. Soman, "Does Holding on to a Product Result in Increased Consumption Rates?" *Advances in Consumer Research* 24 (1997), pp. 33–35; Brian Wansink, "Do We Use More When We Buy More? The Effects of Stockpiling on Product Consumption," *Advances in Consumer Research* 25 (1998), pp. 21–22; and Valerie S. Folkes, Ingrid M. Martin, and Kamal Gupta, "When to Say When: Effects of Supply on Usage," *Journal of Consumer Research* 20, no. 3, (December 1992), pp. 467–477.

6. Kara Brandeisky, "How to Beat Online Price Discrimination," *Time*, October 23, 2014, http://time.com/money/3534651/price-discrimination-travelocity-orbitz-home-depot/ (accessed February 21, 2016).

7. "Levi Strauss Reacquires a Pair of Jeans, at Markup," *Wall Street Journal*, May 29, 2001, p. 13A.

8. William M. Bulkeley, "Rebates' Big Appeal: Many People Neglect to Redeem Them," *Wall Street Journal*, February 10, 1998, pp. B1–B2.

9. Carl Shapiro, Carol Shapiro, and Hal R. Varian, *Information Rules: A Strategic Guide to the Network Economy* (Harvard Business School Publishing, 1998).

10. This section was developed with the assistance of KhiMetrics.

11. Dan Scheraga, "One Price Doesn't Fit All," *Chain Store Age*, March 2001, pp. 104–105; taken from research by Mark Husson, who tracks the supermarket sector for Merrill Lynch.

12. Christopher S. Tang, David R. Bell, and Teck-Hua Ho, "Store Choice and Shopping Behavior: How Price Format Works," *California Management Review* 43, no. 2 (Winter 2001), pp. 56–74; and Alan Sawyer and Peter Dickson, "Everyday Low Prices vs. Sale Price," *Retailing Review* 1, no. 2 (1993), pp. 1–2, 8.

13. Christopher S. Tang, David R. Bell, and Teck-Hua Ho, "Store Choice and Shopping Behavior: How Price Format Works," *California Management Review* 43, no. 2 (Winter 2001).

14. Doug Murray, "These 15 Stores Have the Best Price Match Guarantees in Canada," *Slice*, July 24, 2015, http://www.slice.ca/money/photos/stores-with-the-best-price-match-guarantees/#!Leons_ (accessed February 22, 2016).

15. Valarie A. Zeithaml and Mary Jo Bitner, *Service Marketing: Integrating Customer Focus across the Firm*, 4th ed. (New York: McGraw-Hill, 2005)

16. Arvind Sahay, "How to Reap Higher Profits With Dynamic Pricing," *MIT Sloan Management Review* 48, no. 4 (2007), pp. 53–60; Barry Berman, "Applying Yield Management Pricing to Your Service Business," *Business Horizons* 48 (March/April 2005), pp. 169–182; Ramao Desiraju and Steven Shugan, "Strategic Service Pricing and Yield Management," *Journal of Marketing* 63 (January 1999), pp. 44–56.

17. Priceline.com 10-K report, filed with the Securities and Exchange Commission, December 26, 2006.

18. Thomas T. Nagle and Reed K. Holden, *The Strategy and Tactics of Pricing*, 3rd ed. (Upper Saddle River, NJ: Pearson, 2002); Glenn Voss, A. Parasuraman, and Dhruv Grewal, "The Roles of Price, Performance and Expectations in Determining Satisfaction in Services Exchanges," *Journal of Marketing* 62, no. 4 (October 1998), pp. 46–61.

19. Jeffrey A. Trachtenberg and Miguel Bustillo, "Amid Price War, Three Retailers Begin Rationing Books," *Wall Street Journal*, October 30, 2009.

20. Leigh McAlister, Edward I. George, and Yung-Hsin Chien, "A Basket-Mix Model to Identify Cherry-Picked Brands," *Journal of Retailing* 85, no. 4 (2009), pp. 425–436.

21. Marc Vanhuele, Gilles Laurent, and Xavier Dreze, "Consumers; Immediate Memory for Prices," *Journal of Consumer Research* 33, no. 2 (2006), pp. 163–172.

22. Itamar Simonson, "Shoppers Easily Influenced Choices," *New York Times*, November 6, 1994, p. 311; based on research by Itamar Simonson and Amos Tversky, http://www.nytimes.com.

23. This section was developed with the assistance of KhiMetrics.

24. This discussion has been going on for at least 70 years; see Louis Bader and James De. Weinland, "Do Odd Prices Earn Money?" *Journal of Retailing* 8 (1932), pp. 102–104. For recent research in this area, see Karen Gedenk and Henrik Sattler, "The Impact of Price Thresholds on Profit Contribution—Should Retailers Set Nine-Ending Prices?" *Journal of Retailing* 75, no. 1 (1999), pp. 33–57; Robert M. Schindler and Patrick N. Kirby, "Patterns of Rightmost Digits Used in Advertised Prices: Implications for Nine-Ending Effects," *Journal of Consumer Research* 24 (September 1997), p. 192–201; and Mark Stiving and Russell S. Winer, "An Empirical Analysis of Price Endings with Scanner Data," *Journal of Consumer Research* 24 (June 1997), pp. 57–67.

25. https://play.google.com/store/apps/details?id=com.biggu.shopsavvy&hl=en.

26. Claire Cain Miller, "Mobile Phones Become Essential Tool for Holiday Shopping," *New York Times*, December 18, 2009; Geoffrey A. Fowler and Yukari Iwatani Kane, "Price Check: Finding Deals with a Phone: New Mobile Applications Use Bar-Code Scanners, GPS to Help Comparison-Shoppers" *Wall Street Journal*, December 16, 2009.

27. Rebecca Quick, "Web's Robot Shoppers Don't Roam Free," *Wall Street Journal*, September 3, 1998, pp. B1, B8.

28. Xing Pan, Brian Ratchford and Venkatesh Sankar, "Why Aren't the Prices for the Same Items the Same at Me.com and You.com? Drivers of Price Dispersion among E-Tailers," working paper, Robert H. Smith Business School, University of Maryland, 2001; Erik Brynjolfson and Michael Smith, "Frictionless Commerce? A Comparison of Internet and Conventional Retailer," *Management Science* 46, no. 4, April 2000), pp. 563–585.

Chapter 13

1. Susan Jackson and Randall Schuler, *Managing Human Resources through Strategic Relationships*, 8th ed. (Mason, OH: Southwestern, 2003), p. 5.

2. John Bernardin, *Human Resource Management: An Experiential Approach,* 4th ed. (Burr Ridge, IL: McGraw-Hill, 2006); Raymond Noe, John Hollenbeck, Barry Gerhart, and Patrick Wright, *Fundamentals of Human Resource Management,* 2nd ed. (Burr Ridge, IL: McGraw-Hill, 2006).

3. Michael Bergdal, "Our 'People' Culture Is a Major Competitive Asset," *Stores*, April 1999, pp. 114–115; Raphael Amit, "Human Resources Management Processes: A Value-Creating Source of Competitive Advantage," *European Management Journal*, April 1999, pp. 174–182; Tim Ambler, "Valuing Human Assets," *Business Strategy Review* 10 (Spring 1999), pp. 57–58; Tony Grundy, "How Are Corporate Strategy and Human Resources Strategy Linked?" *Journal of General Management* 23 (Spring 1998), pp. 49–73; and Gerard Farias, "High Performance Work Systems: What We Know and What We Need to Know," *Human Resource Planning* 21 (June 1998), pp. 50–55.

4. Shari Waters, "Measuring Retail Performance and Productivity: Tracking Retail Sales," http://retail.about.com.od/marketingsalespromotion/a/measuring_sales.htm.

5. Cynthia R. Easterling, Ellen L. Flottman, Marian H. Jernigan, amd Beth E.S. Wuest, *Merchandising Mathematics for Retailing*, 4th ed. (Upper Saddle River, New Jersey: Pearson), p. 78.

6. T.J. Schier, "Sales per Employee," http://ezinearticles.com/?sales-per-employee&id=312758.

7. Bradley James Bryant, "How to Calculate FTE Hours," eHow.com, http://www.ehow.com/how_5096086_calculate-fte-hours.html.

8. Easterling, Flottman, Jernigan, and Wuest, *Merchandising Mathematics for Retailing*, p. 76.

9. "Measuring up Retail Benchmarking Survey," *PWC*, November 2013, http://www.retailcouncil.org/sites/default/files/documents/pwc-benchmarking-study-2013-11-en.pdf (accessed April 24, 2016).

10. Heather Boushey and Sarah Jane Glynn, "There Are Significant Business Costs to Replacing Employees ," *Centre for American Progress* November 16, 2012, https://www.americanprogress.org/wp-content/uploads/2012/11/CostofTurnover.pdf (accessed February 24, 2016).

11. ATB Financial 2015 Corporate Social Responsibility Report, http://www.atb.com/SiteCollectionDocuments/Community/CSR-Report-2015.pdf (accessed February 24, 2016).

12. Quentin Fottrell, "80% of students work at least part-time," *Market Watch*, August 8, 2013, http://www.marketwatch.com/story/nearly-4-out-of-5-students-work-2013-08-07 (accessed February 24, 2016).

13. Jeffrey Pfeffer, *The Human Equation* (Boston: Harvard Business School Press, 1998), pp. 26–28.

14. Roth, "My Job at the Container Store," *Fortune*, January 10, 2000, pp. 74–78.

15. Alison Kenney Paul, Thom McElroy and Tonie Leatherberry, "Diversity as an Engine of Innovation: Retal and Consumer Goods Companies Find Competitive Advantage in Diversity," *Deloitte Review* issue 8, 2011.

16. "A Changing Retail Landscape: An Analysis of Emerging Human Resource Trends," November 2009. Presented in partnership Retail Council of Canada and Human Resources and Social Development Canada, p. 9.

17. Michael Gold and Andrew Campbell, "Do You Have a Well-Designed Organization?" *Harvard Business Review*, March 2002, pp. 117–125; and Richard L. Daft, *Essentials of Organization Theory and Design*, 2nd ed. (Cincinnati: South-Western College Publishing, 2000).

18. Walter Loeb, "Unbundling or Centralize: What Is the Answer?" *Retailing Issues Letter* (College Station: Center for Retailing Studies, Texas A&M University, May 1992).

19. Dave Crisp, "Human Resources Keeps Evolving," *Canadian Retailer*, November/December 2003.

20. Carol Sansone and Judith M. Harackiewicz, *Intrinsic and Extrinsic Motivation: The Search for Optimal Motivation and Performance* (San Diego: Academic Press, 2000).

21. Patricia Sellers, "Can Home Depot Fix Its Sagging Stock?" *Fortune*, March 4, 1996, pp. 139–145; and Bob Ortega, "What Does Wal-Mart Do If Stock Drop Cuts into Workers' Morale?" *Wall Street Journal*, January 4, 1995, pp. A1, A5.

22. James Fitzsimmons and Mona Fitzsimmons, *Service Development: Creating Memorable Experiences* (Thousand Oaks, CA.: Sage Publications, 2000); and Suzanne Barry Osborn, "Is Your Customer Being SERVED?" *Chain Store Age*, November 1, 2000, p. 52.

23. Mitchell Brown, "The New Old," *Canadian Retailer*, March/April 2009, p. 36.

24. David Good and Charles Schwepker, "Sales Quotas: Critical Interpretations and Implications," *Review of Business*, 22 (Spring-Summer 2001), pp. 32–37.

25. Todd Zenger and C. R. Marshall, "Determinants of Incentive Intensity in Group-Based Rewards," *Academy of Management Journal* 43 (April 2000), pp. 149–63.

26. Susan Jackson and Randall Schuler, *Managing Human Resources through Strategic Relationships*, 8th ed. (Mason, OH: Southwestern, 2003), p. 141.

27. Beverly Kaye and Betsy Jacobson, "True Tales and Tall Tales: The Power of Organizational Storytelling," *Training & Development* (March 1999), pp. 44–51; and Nancy L. Breuer, "The Power of Storytelling," *Workforce* (December 1998), pp. 36–42.

28. Aaron Bernstein, "Too Many Workers? Not for Long," *BusinessWeek*, May 20, 2002, p. 126.

29. Peter Harris, "The top three things that employers want to see in your social media profiles," *Workopolis*, April 5, 2015, http://careers.workopolis.com/advice/the-three-things-that-employers-want-to-find-out-about-you-online/.

30. JP Medved, "Top 15 Recruiting Statistics for 2014," *Capterra*, February 14, 2014, http://blog.capterra.com/top-15-recruiting-statistics-2014/ (accessed February 24, 2016).

31. Debby Stankevich, "Retailers Focus on Optimizing Technology," *Retailer Merchandiser*, March 2002, pp. 55–58; Ginger Koloszyc, "Tight Labor Market Spurs High-Tech Employment Screening," *Stores*, July 1998, pp. 77–81; and David Schulz, "Small Retailers Turn to Pre-Employment Screening Services," *Stores*, May 1998, pp. 72–74.

32. Sarah Fister, "Separating Hires from Liars," *Training*, July 1999, pp. 22–24.

33. Jane Bahls, "Available Upon Request," *HR Magazine*, January 1999, pp. S2–S7.

34. Paul Taylor, "Providing Structure to Interviews and Reference Checks," *Workforce, Workforce Tools Supplement*, May 1999, pp. S11–S55; and Allen Huffcutt and David Woehr, "Further Analysis of Employment Validity: A Quantitative Evaluation of Interviewer-Related Structuring Methods," *Journal of Organizational Behaviour* 20 (July 1999), pp. 549–556.

35. Richard C. Hollinger and Amanda Adams, *2006 National Retail Security Survey* (Gainesville: University of Florida, 2007), p. 16.

36. John Bernardin and Donna Cooke, "Validity of an Honesty Test in Predicting Theft among Convenience Store Employees," *Academy of Management Journal* 36 (October 1993), pp. 1097–1099.

37. Kal Lifson, "Turn Down Turnover to Turn Up Profits," *Chain Store Age*, November 1, 1996, pp. 64–66.

38. Nicole Fallon Taylor, "Hiring in the Digital Age: What's Next for Recruiting?," *Business News Daily*, January 11, 2016, http://www.businessnewsdaily.com/6975-future-of-recruiting.html#sthash.yP5C7lzE.dpuf (accessed February 24, 2016).

39. John Bible, "Discrimination in Job Applications and Interviews," *Supervision*, November 1998, pp. 9–12; Laura Williamson, James Campion, Mark Roehling, Stanley Malos, and Michael Campion, "Employment Interview on Trial: Linking Interview Structure with Litigation Outcomes," *Journal of Applied Psychology* 82 (December 1997; pp. 900–913; and Peter Burgess, "How Those 'Innermost Thoughts' Are Revealed," *Grocer*, March 9, 1996, pp. 60–62.

40. "Job Seeker Nation Study 2015 - Inside the Mind of the Modern Job Seeker," *Jobvite*, https://www.jobvite.com/wp-content/uploads/2015/01/jobvite_jobseeker_nation_2015.pdf (accessed February 24, 2016).

41. Lucette Comer and Tanya Drollinger, "Active Empathetic Listening and Selling Success: A Conceptual Framework," *Journal of Personal Selling and Sales Management* 9 (Winter 1999), pp. 15–29; and C. David Sheppard, Stephen Castleberry, and Rick Ridnour, "Linking Effective Listening with Sales Performance: An Exploratory Investigation," *Journal of Business and Industrial Marketing* 12 (1997), pp. 315–321.

42. John McKinnon, "Retailers Beware!" *Florida Trend*, June 1996, pp. 20–21.

43. This section is based on Chapter 3 in Jeffrey Pfeffer, *The Human Equation* (Boston: Harvard Business School Press, 1998).

44. Gary Dessler, "How to Earn Your Employees' Commitment," *Academy of Management Executive* 13 (May 1999), pp. 58–59; Deb McCusker, "Loyalty in the Eyes of Employers and Employees," *Workforce*, November 1998, pp. 23–28; and David L. Stum, "Five Ingredients for an Employee Retention Formula," *HR Focus*, September 1998, pp. S9–S11.

45. Shari Caudron, "How HR Drives Profits: Academic Research and Real-World Experience Show How HR Practices Affect the Bottom Line," *Workforce*, December 2001, pp. 26–30; and "HR's New Role: Creating Value," *HR Focus*, January 2000, pp. 1–4.

46. Ling Sing Chee, "Singapore Airlines: Strategic Human Resource Initiatives," in *International Human Resource Management: Think Globally and Act Locally*, ed. Derek Torrington (New York: Prentice Hall, 1994), pp. 314–330.

47. "State of the Industry Operational Management," *Chain Store Age*, August 1, 1998, p. 17A.

48. Daniel Cable and Charles Parson, "Socialization Tactics and Person-Organization Fit," *Personnel Psychology* 54 (Spring 2001), pp. 1–24; and Cheri Young and Craig Lundberg, "Creating a First Day on the Job," *Cornell Hotel and Restaurant Administration Journal*, December 1996, pp. 26–29.

49. "A Tall Order," *retailHR, Canadian Retailer,* March/April 2009, p. 25.

50. John Wanous and Arnon Rechers, "New Employee Orientation Program," *Human Resource Management Review* 10 (Winter 2000), pp. 435–452; and Charlotte Garvey, "The Whirland of a New Job," *HR Magazine* 46 (June 2001), pp. 110–116.

51. Bert Versloot, Jan Jong, and Jo Thijssen, "Organisational Context of Structured on-the-Job Training," *International Journal of Training and Development* 5 (March 2001), pp. 2–23.

52. Graham L. Bradley and Beverley A. Sparks, "Customer Reactions to Staff Empowerment: Mediators and Moderators," *Journal of Applied Social Psychology,* May 2000, pp. 991–1003; Martin Beirne, "Managing to Empower? A Healthy Review of Resources and Constraints," *European Management Journal,* April 1999, pp. 218–226; and Mohammed Rafiq, "A Customer-Oriented Framework for Empowering Service Employees," *Journal of Services Marketing* 12 (May–June 1998), pp. 379–397.

53. Shankar Ganesan and Barton Weitz, "The Impact of Staffing Policies on Retail Buyer Job Attitudes and Behaviors," *Journal of Retailing,* Spring 1996, pp. 231–245.

54. Janet Wiscombe, "Flex Appeal—Not Just for Moms," *Workforce,* March 2002, p. 18; Leslie Faught, "At Eddie Bauer You Can Work and Have a Life," *Workforce,* April 1997, pp. 83–88; and Davan Maharaj, "A Suitable Schedule: Flextime Gains as Employers Agree There's More to Life than Work," *Los Angeles Times,* July 10, 1998, p. D2.

55. Charles J. Hobson, Linda Delunas, and Dawn Kesic, "Compelling Evidence of the Need for Corporate Work/Life Balance Initiatives: Results from a National Survey of Stressful Life-Events," *Journal of Employment Counseling,* March 2001, pp. 38–42; and Jeffrey Hill, Alan J. Hawkins, Maria Ferris, and Michelle Weitzman, "Finding an Extra Day a Week: The Positive Influence of Perceived Job Flexibility on Work and Family Life Balance," *Family Relations,* January 2001, pp. 49–57.

56. Roosevelt Thomas, "From Affirmative Action to Diversity," *Harvard Business Review,* March–April 1990, pp. 107–117.

57. Michael Petrou, "Employment Equity Is about Hiring the Best," *Ottawa Citizen,* December 21, 2003.

58. Kathleen Iverson, "Managing for Effective Workforce Diversity," *Cornell Hotel & Restaurant Administration Quarterly,* April 2000, pp. 2–7; Parshotam Dass, "Strategies for Managing Human Resource Diversity: From Resistance to Learning," *Academy of Management Executive* 13 (May 1999), pp. 68–69; and Philip Rosenzweig, "Strategies for Managing Diversity," *Financial Times,* March 6, 1998, pp. 6–9.

59. Audrey J. Murrell, Faye J. Crosby, and Robin J. Ely, eds., *Mentoring Dilemmas: Developmental Relationships within Multicultural Organizations* (Mahwah, NJ: Erlbaum, 1999); Max Messmer, "Mentoring: Building Your Company's Intellectual Capital," *HR Focus,* September 1998, pp. S11–S13; and Erik Van Slyke, "Mentoring: A Results-Oriented Approach," *HR Focus,* February 1998, pp. 14–15.

60. Julia Howell, "Bottom Line of Corporate Community Investment," *Imagine Canada* 2012, http://www.imaginecanada.ca/sites/default/files/www/en/misc/bottom_line_corporate_community_investment_10222012.pdf (accessed February 25, 2016).

61. Linda Wirth, *Breaking through the Glass Ceiling: Women in Management* (Washington DC: International Labour Office, 2001); Sheila Wellington, "Cracking the Ceiling," *Time,* December 7, 1998, p. 187; Alison Maitland, "Cracks Appear in Glass Ceiling," *Financial Times,* April 8, 1999, p. 22; and Tammy Reiss, "More Cracks in the Glass Ceiling," *BusinessWeek,* August 10, 1998, p. 6.

62. Ontario Federation of Labour, Employment Standards Act, October 2000.

63. Gary Dessler, Nina Cole, Patricia Goodman, and Virginia Sutherland, *Fundamentals of Human Resources Management in Canada,* Toronto: Pearson, 2004.

64. "Doing Well by Doing Good," *Nielsen,* June 2014, http://www.nielsen.com/content/dam/corporate/us/en/reports-downloads/2014%20Reports/global-corporate-social-responsibility-report-june-2014.pdf (accessed February 28, 2016).

65. Robert Price, "Feeling Groovy (… and How to Make Sure Your People Stay that Way)," *Retailer's Guide for Independent Retailers and Store Managers: Health & Safety,* 5, no. 3.

66. Colquitt, "On the Dimensionality of Organizational Justice: A Construct Validation of a Measure," *Journal of Applied Psychology* 86 (2001), pp. 386–400.

67. Price, "Feeling Groovy …."

68. http://www.retailcouncil.org/cdnretailer, *Canadian Retailer,* March/April 2009, p. 7.

69. Mary Wagner, "Don't Call Us," *Internet Retailer,* June 2002, pp. 8–9.

70. Mike Delaney, "How to Beat Shoplifting," about.com, April 26, 2006, accessed January 25, 2008; Ronald Bond, "Preventing Retail Theft," http://www.entrepreneur.com, July 1, 2007 (accessed January 25, 2008).

71. "Combating Shrink at the Source," *Chain Store Age,* December 2000, p. 152.

72. Timothy Henderson, "Loss Prevention Software Aids in Retail Fight against Costly Employee Theft," *Stores,* March 2001, pp. 68–72.

73. Ginger Koloszyc, "Supermarkets Find Growing Payoff in EAS Anti-Shoplifting Systems," *Stores,* February 1999, pp. 28–30; and "Sales Up, Shrink Down with Source Tagging," *Chain Store Age,* August 1998, p. 84.

Chapter 14

1. Parsuraman and Valarie Zeithaml, "Understanding and Improving Service Quality: A Literature Review and Research Agenda," in eds. B. Weitz and R. Wensley, *Handbook of Marketing* (London: Sage, 2002).

2. Michael Hartline and O.C. Ferrell, "The Management of Customer-Contact Service Employees: An Empirical Investigation," *Journal of Marketing* 60 (October 1996), pp. 52–70; and Lois Mohr and Mary Jo Bitner, "The Role of Employee Effort in Satisfaction with Service Transactions," *Journal of Business Research* 32 (March 1995), pp. 239–252.

3. Fredrick Reichfeld, *The Loyalty Effect* (Cambridge, MA: Harvard Business School Press, 1996).

4. See Stephanie Coyles and Timothy Gokey, "Customer Retention Is Not Enough," *McKinsey Quarterly* 2 (2002), pp. 3–14.

5. Anna S. Mattila, "Emotional Bonding and Restaurant Loyalty," *Cornell Hotel and Restaurant Administration Quarterly,* December 2001, pp. 73–80; and Susan Fournier, Susan Dobscha, and David Glen Mick, "Preventing the Premature Death of Relationship Marketing," *Harvard Business Review,* January–February 1998, pp. 42–50.

6. Ibid.

7. Jeff Berry, "The 2015 Loyalty Census - Big Nimbers Big Hurdles," *Colloquy Report,* February 2015, https://www.colloquy.com/resources/pdf/reports/2015-loyalty-census.pdf (accessed March 2, 2016).

8. Joseph Pine and James Gilmore, *Experience Economy: Work Is Theatre and Every Business a Stage* (Boston: Harvard-Business Press, 1999).

9. Brian Jackson, "Canadians' love of loyalty rewards is swayed most by this digital channel," *itbusiness.ca,* March

31, 2015, http://www.itbusiness.ca/news/canadians-love-of-loyalty-rewards-is-swayed-most-by-this-digital-channel/54790 (accessed March 2, 2016).

10. Frank Badillo, *Retail Perspectives on Customer Relationship Management* (Columbus, OH: Retail Forward, February 2001), p. 33.

11. "Cooking Up a Deep-Dish Database," *BusinessWeek*, November 20, 1995, p. 160.

12. "Loblaw's loyalty program aims for the smartphone age," *Canadian Grocer*, May 6, 2013, www.canadiangrocer.com/top-stories/loblaw-launches-all-digital-loyalty-program-25407? (accessed July 8, 2013); Denise Brunsdon, "Loblaws' new 'PC Plus' loyalty program is really a game in disguise," *Canadian Business*, May 9, 2013, www.canadian-business.com/blogs-and-comment/loblaw-pc-plus-gamification (accessed July 8, 2013); Marina Strauss, "Loblaw targets a well-oiled loyalty program," *The Globe and Mail*, February 28, 2012, www.theglobeandmail.com/globe-investor/loblaw-targets-a-well-oiled-loyalty-program/article4171761 (accessed July 8, 2013).

13. Lorie Grant, "Why Do Cashiers Want Your Digits?" *USA Today*, April 23, 2002, p. B1.

14. http://www.cmbinfo.com/pdf/WSI_Nordstrom.pdf (accessed September 8, 2007).

15. Mark Friedman and Kelly Hlavinka, "Fully Charged: Delivering the Mobile Advantage Throughout the Customer Lifecycle," *PARTNERtalk LoyaltyOne/Colloquy*, January 2013, p. 4.

16. http://www.businesswire.com/cgi-bin.cgi?eid=5542833 (accessed May 10, 2010).

17. Jeff Berry, "2015 & Beyond," *Colloquy-Loyalty Talks*, November/December, 2015, p. 4, https://www.colloquy.com/resources/pdf/magazines/20151216-mag.pdf (accessed March 2, 2016).

18. http://www.cbc.ca/consumer/story/2009/08/06/f-reward-cards.html#ixzz0oOPFyDeU (accessed May 10, 2010).

19. George Milne, "Privacy and Ethical Issues in Database/Interactive Marketing and Public Policy: A Research Framework and Overview of the Special Issue," *Journal of Public Policy and Marketing* 19 (Spring 2000), pp. 1–7.

20. Dan Scheraga, "Courting the Customer," *Chain Store Age*, January 2000, p. 88; Ro Panepinto, "Preventative Customer Care," *Response*, October 1999, pp. 46–53; and Steve Larsen, "Personalization Without Privacy Won't Sell: Build Trust by Keeping Customers Informed," *Internet Retailer*, November 1999, p. 70.

21. Shawn Smith, "Big Data = Big Opportunities for Canadian Retailers," http://www.sas.com/en_ca/insights/articles/big-data/big-data-retail.html, *SAS* (accessed March 2, 2016).

22. Jill Clayton, "Employers Brace for Privacy Law," *National Post*, December 15, 2003; Matthew McClearn, "Full Disclosure," *Canadian Business*, Vol. 76, November/December 2003; "New Privacy Law Takes Effect January 1, 2004," Canada NewsWire, Ottawa: December 1, 2003; and Amanda Maltby, "Adapting to Canada's New Privacy Rules," *Marketing Magazine*, November 3, 2003.

23. Christopher Robertson and Ravi Sarathy, "Digital Privacy: A Pragmatic Guide for Senior Managers Charged with Developing a Strategic Policy for Handling Privacy Issues," *Business Horizons* 45 (January-February 2002), pp. 2–6.

24. Christophe Giraud-Carrier, "Success Stories in Data/Text Mining," *Brigham Young University*, http://dml.cs.byu.edu/~cgc/docs/mldm_tools/Reading/DMSuccessStories.html (accessed March 3, 2016).

25. Frank Badillo, *Retail Perspectives on Customer Relationship Management* (Columbus, OH: Retail Forward, February 2001), p. 25.

26. George Stalk Jr., "In Praise of the Heavy Spender," *Globe and Mail*, May 21, 2007.

27. F. John Reh, "Pareto's Principle - The 80-20 Rule," *About Money*, http://management.about.com/bio/F-John-Reh-229.htm (accessed March 3, 2016).

28. Valarie Zeithaml, Roland Rust, and Katherine Lemon, "The Customer Pyramid: Creating and Serving Profitable Customers," *California Management Review* 43 (Summer 2001), p. 124.

29. The Canadian Press, "Canadians Unhappy With Their Loyalty Programs, Aimia Survey Finds," http://www.huffingtonpost.ca/2015/09/08/loyalty-programs-canada-survey_n_8102692.html (accessed March 3, 2016).

30. See Werner Reinartz and V. Kumar, "On the Profitability of Long-Life Customers in a Noncontractual Setting: An Empirical Investigation and Implications for Marketing," *Journal of Marketing* 64 (October 2000).

31. Ken Gofton, "Pinpointing Loyalty," *Marketing*, January 21, 1999, p. 65.

32. Hollie Shaw, "New Canadian Tire loyalty program may challenge iconic paper tender," *Financial Post*, February 15, 2012 (accessed July 2, 2013).

33. Ibid.

34. Ibid.

35. Linda Nguyen, "Loblaw and Shopper's say Optimum loyalty program to stay the same," Canadian Press, July 15, 2013.

36. Ibid.

37. James Cigliano, Margaret Georgladis, Darren Pleasance, and Susan Whalley, "The Price of Loyalty," *McKinsey Quarterly* 4 (2000), p. 73.

38. Graham Dowling and Mark Uncles, "Do Customer Loyalty Programs Really Work?" *Sloan Management Review* 38 (Summer 1997), pp. 71–82.

39. James Cigliano, Margaret Georgladis, Darren Pleasance, and Susan Whalley, "The Price of Loyalty," *McKinsey Quarterly* 4 (2000), p. 70.

40. "Loyalty: At What Cost?" *Marketing*, May 16, 2002, pp. 48–50.

41. "Why Service Stinks," *Business Week Online*, October 23, 2000.

42. Roland Rust, Valarie Zeithaml, and Katherine Lemon, *Driving Customer Equity* (New York: Free Press, 2002), Ch. 13.

43. Frank Badillo, *Retail Perspectives on Customer Relationship Management* (Columbus, OH: Retail Forward, February 2001), pp. 33–34.

44. http://en.wikipedia.org/wiki/Near_field_communication#cite_ref-WhatIsNFC_1-0.

45. http://searchcloudapplications.techtarget.com/definition/gamification.

46. Roland Rust, Valarie Zeithaml, and Katherine Lemon, *Driving Customer Equity* (New York: Free Press, 2002), Ch. 13.

47. "Retail IT 2001," *Chain Store Age*, October 1, 2001, p. 24.

48. Murray Raphael, "Tell Me What You Want and the Answer Is Yes," *Direct Marketing*, October 1996, p. 22.

49. Valarie Zeithaml, Leonard Berry, and A. Parasuraman, "The Behavioral Consequences of Service Quality," *Journal of Marketing* 60 (April 1996), pp. 31–46.

50. Robert Spector and Patrick McCarthy, *The Nordstrom Way: The Inside Story of America's #1 Customer Service Company*, 2nd ed. (New York: John Wiley, 2001).

51. Odekerken-Schroder, K. De Wulf, H. Kasper, M. Kleijnen, J. Hoekstra, and H. Commandeur, "The Impact of Quality on Store Loyalty: A Contingency Approach," *Total Quality Management* 12 (May 2001), pp. 307–322; and Benjamin Schneider and David Bowen, *Winning the Service Game* (Boston: Harvard Business School Press, 1995).

52. Banwari Mittal and Walfried Lassar, "The Role of Personalization in Service Encounters," *Journal of Retailing* 72 (Spring 1996), pp. 95–109.

53. Shankar Ganesan and Barton Weitz, "The Impact of Staffing Policies on Retail Buyer Job Attitudes and Behaviors," *Journal of Retailing*, Spring 1996, pp. 231–245.

54. http://www.hp.com/canada/portal/smb/success_stories/stories/harry_rosen.html (accessed July 10, 2013).

55. "Retailers Join the War Effort," *Chain Store Age,* June 1994, p. 15.

56. Roger Bennett, "Queues, Customer Characteristics and Policies for Managing Waiting-Lines in Supermarkets," *International Journal of Retail and Distribution Management* 26 (February–March 1998), pp. 78–88; and Julie Baker and Michaelle Cameron, "The Effects of the Service Environment on Affect and Consumer Perceptions of Waiting Time: An Integrative Review and Research Propositions," *Journal of the Academy of Marketing Science* 24 (Fall 1996), pp. 338–349.

57. Amanda Stillwagon, "Did You Know: A 5% Increase in Retention Increases Profits by Up to 95%," *Small Business Trends,* September 11, 2014, http://smallbiztrends.com/2014/09/increase-in-customer-retention-increases-profits.html (accessed March 4, 2016).

58. "2015 Consumer Returns in the Retail Industry," *The Retail Equation,* 2015, http://www.theretailequation.com/Retailers/IndustryReports (accessed March 4, 2016).

59. Ibid.

60. Rebecca Eckler, "Sometimes ... You Have to Test Drive It," *National Post,* August 26, 2003; and Deirdre McMurdy, "Returns Rethink," *National Post,* December 21, 2002.

61. Martha McNeil Hamilton and Dina El Boghdady, "The Spirit of Giving Back; Shoppers Discover Stricter Policies for Returning Gifts," *Washington Post,* December 27, 2001, p. E01; and "Retailers Get Strict on Merchandise Returns," *St. Louis Post-Dispatch,* May 17, 2002, p. C1.

62. Parsuraman and Valarie Zeithaml, "Understanding and Improving Service Quality: A Literature Review and Research Agenda," in eds. B. Weitz and R. Wensley, *Handbook of Marketing* (London: Sage, 2002); and Praveen Kopalle and Donald Lehmann, "Strategic Management of Expectations: The Role of Disconfirmation Sensitivity and Perfectionism," *Journal of Marketing Research,* August 2001, pp. 386–401.

63. Kenneth Clow, David Kurtz, John Ozment, and Beng Soo Ong, "The Antecedents of Consumer Expectations of Services: An Empirical Study across Four Industries," *Journal of Services Marketing* 11 (May–June 1997), pp. 230–248; and Ann Marie Thompson and Peter Kaminski, "Psychographic and Lifestyle Antecedents of Service Quality Expectations," *Journal of Services Marketing* 7 (1993), pp. 53–61.

64. Mary Jo Bitner, "Self-Service Technologies: What Do Customers Expect? In This High-Tech World, Customers Haven't Changed—They Still Want Good Service," *Marketing Management,* Spring 2001, pp. 10–15.

65. Timothy Keiningham and Terry Vavra, *The Customer Delight Principle* (Chicago: American Marketing Association, 2002).

66. The following discussion of the gaps model and its implications is based on Deon Nel and Leyland Pitt, "Service Quality in a Retail Environment: Closing the Gaps," *Journal of General Management* 18 (Spring 1993), pp. 37–57; Valarie Zeithaml, A. Parasuraman, and Leonard Berry, *Delivering Quality Customer Service* (New York: Free Press, 1990); and Valarie Zeithaml, Leonard Berry, and A. Parasuraman, "Communication and Control Processes in the Delivery of Service Quality," *Journal of Marketing* 52 (April 1988), pp. 35–48.

67. http://retailindustry.about.com, April 4, 2001.

68. "Driving Customers Away," *Chain Store Age,* June 2001, p. 39.

69. "Merchant Prince: Stanley Marcus," *Inc.,* June 1987, pp. 41–44.

70. Chapman and George Argyros, "An Investigation into Whether Complaining Can Cause Increased Consumer Satisfaction," *Journal of Consumer Marketing* 17, 2000, pp. 9–19; Tibbett L. Speer, "They Complain Because They Care," *American Demographics,* May 1996, pp. 13–15; and Jagdip Singh and Robert Wilkes, "When Customers Complain: A Path Analysis of Key Antecedents of Customer Complaint Response Analysis," *Journal of the Academy of Marketing Science* 24 (Fall 1996), pp. 350–365.

71. http://www.llbean.com/customerService/aboutLLBean/company_values.html?nav=ln

72. Sandra Guy, "Stores Juggle Service with High-Tech Savvy," *Chicago Sun-Times,* July 1, 2002, p. B12; Julie Clark, "The Importance of Kiosks in Retail Has Grown," *Display and Design Ideas,* September 2001, p. 18; and Ken Clark, "Confused about Kiosks," *Chain Store Age,* November 1, 2000, p. 96.

73. Paul Hemp, "My Week as a Room-Service Waiter at the Ritz," *Harvard Business Review,* June 2002, pp. 50-62; and Len Berry, *On Great Customer Service* (New York: Free Press, 1995), pp. 73–74.

74. See Chuck Chakrapani, *How to Measure Service Quality and Customer Satisfaction: The Informal Field Guide for Tools and Techniques* (Chicago: American Marketing Association, 1998).

75. David Lipke, "Mystery Shoppers," *American Demographics,* December 2000, pp. 41–44; and "Mystery Shopping's Lightweight Reputation Undeserved," *International Journal of Retail and Distribution Management* 27 (February–March 1999), pp. 114–117; Rachel Miller, "Undercover Shoppers," *Marketing,* May 28, 1998, pp. 27–30; and Jennifer Steinhauer, "The Undercover Shoppers," *New York Times,* February 4, 1998, p. D1.

76. See Jim Poisant, *Creating and Sustaining a Superior Customer Service Organization: A Book about Taking Care of the People Who Take Care of the Customers* (Westport, CT: Quorum Books, 2002); "People-Focused HR Policies Seen as Vital to Customer Service Improvement," *Store,* January 2001, p. 60; Michael Brady and J. Joseph Cronin, "Customer Orientation: Effects on Customer Service Perceptions and Outcome Behaviors," *Journal of Service Research,* February 2001, pp. 241–251; and Michael Hartline, James Maxham III, and Daryl McKee, "Corridors of Influence in the Dissemination of Customer-Oriented Strategy to Customer Contact Service Employees," *Journal of Marketing* 64 (April 2000), pp. 25–41.

77. Disney Institute and Michael Eisner, *Be Our Guest: Perfecting the Art of Customer Service* (New York: Disney Editions, 2001).

78. Alicia Grandey and Analea Brauburger, "The Emotion Regulation behind the Customer Service Smile," in *Emotions in the Workplace: Understanding the Structure and Role of Emotions in Organizational Behavior,* eds. R. Lord, R. Klimoski, and R. Kanfer (San Francisco: Jossey-Bass, 2002); and Mara Adelman and Aaron Ahuvia, "Social Support in the Service Sector: The Antecedents, Processes, and Consequences of Social Support in an Introductory Service," *Journal of Business Research* 32 (March 1995), pp. 273–282.

79. Moria Cotlier, "Adieu to Abandoned Carts," *Catalog Age,* October 2001, p. 39.

80. Mark Johlke and Dale Duhan, "Supervisor Communication Practices and Service Employee Job Outcomes," *Journal of Service Research,* November 2000, pp. 154–165.

81. Alan Randolph, and Marshall Sashkin, "Can Organizational Empowerment Work in Multinational Settings?" *Academy of Management Executive* 16 (February 2002), pp. 102–116.

82. Conrad Lashley, *Empowerment: HR Strategies for Service Excellence* (Boston: Butterworth/Heinemann, 2001).

83. Alan Randolph, and Marshall Sashkin, "Can Organizational Empowerment Work in Multinational Settings?" *Academy*

of Management Executive 16 (February 2002), pp. 102–116; and Graham Bradley and Beverly Sparks, "Customer Reactions to Staff Empowerment: Mediators and Moderators," *Group and Organization Management* 26 (March 2001), pp. 53–68.

84. Piyush Kumar, Manohar Kalawani, and Makbool Dada, "The Impact of Waiting Time Guarantees on Customers' Waiting Experiences," *Marketing Science* 16, no. 4 (1999), pp. 676–785.

85. James Maxham, "Service Recovery's Influence on Consumer Satisfaction, Positive Word-of-Mouth, and Purchase Intentions," *Journal of Business Research*, October 2001, pp. 11–24; and Michael McCollough, Leonard Berry, and Manjit Yadav, "An Empirical Investigation of Customer Satisfaction after Service Failure and Recovery," *Journal of Service Research*, November 2000, pp. 121–137.

86. "Correcting Store Blunders Seen as Key Customer Service Opportunity," *Stores*, January 2001, pp. 60–64; Stephen W. Brown, "Practicing Best-in-Class Service Recovery: Forward-Thinking Firms Leverage Service Recovery to Increase Loyalty and Profits," *Marketing Management*, Summer 2000, pp. 8–10; Stephen Tax, Stephen Brown, and Murali Chandrashekaran, "Customer Evaluations of Service Complaint Experience: Implications for Relationship Marketing," *Journal of Marketing* 62 (April 1998), pp. 60–76; Amy Smith and Ruth Bolton, "An Experimental Investigation of Customer Reactions to Service Failures and Recovery Encounters: Paradox or Peril?" *Journal of Services Research* 1 (August 1998), pp. 23–36; and Cynthia Webster and D.S. Sundaram, "Service Consumption Criticality in Failure Recovery," *Journal of Business Research* 41 (February 1998), pp. 153–159.

87. Marina Strauss, "Mining Customer Feedback, Firms Go Undercover and Online," *Globe and Mail*, May 13, 2004.

88. Ko de Ruyter and Martin Wetsel, "The Impact of Perceived Listening Behavior in Voice-to-Voice Service Encounters," *Journal of Service Research*, February 2000, pp. 276–284.

Chapter 15

1. https://hootsuite.com/about

2. Survey conducted by Headspace Marketing Inc. from August 17 to 21, 2005. For the survey, a representative randomly selected sample of 2000 adult Quebecers were interviewed by telephone. With a sample of this size, the results are considered accurate to within ±3.1 percentage points, 19 times out of 20, of what they would have been had the entire adult Quebec population been pulled. The data were weighted to ensure the sample's regional and age/sex composition reflects that of the actual Quebec population. This survey reviewed twelve retailer brands in Quebec. The results in no way reflect an exhaustive assessment of all retailer brands conducting business in Quebec. They serve to better understand the variables that influence Quebecers' perceptions of those retailers' ability to adapt to the needs and expectations of Quebec shoppers. Given that awareness levels have a significant impact on the results, they have been adjusted to eliminate the effect of brand awareness on brand evaluation. The rating scale therefore represents a brand's perceived ability to adapt based only on the rating of those respondents able to assess the brand.

3. Ipsos-Reid/NCR survey conducted from September 10 to September 13, 2004.

4. Denise Deveau, "Spreading the Good Word through Sponsorships," *Canadian Retailer*, March/April 2004.

5. http://www.comscore.com/

6. Strategy Staff, "CASSIES Gold: El Tabador boosts Koodo," *Strategy*, January 28, 2013, http://strategyonline.ca/2013/01/28/cassies-gold-el-tabador-boosts-koodo/ (accessed March 14, 2016).

7. Jeffrey Alan Payne, "Old Canadian Tire Guy vs New Canadian Tire Guy," *Chill*, September 17, 2015, http://www.ichill.ca/articles/old-canadian-tire-guy-vs-new-canadian-tire-guy (accessed March 14, 2016).

8. Peter Childs, Suzanne Heywood, and Michael Kliger, "Do Retail Brands Travel?" *McKinsey Quarterly* 1 (2001), pp. 12–16.

9. Chris Barrows, "Unauthorized Verses," *Inventing the Future, Honoring the Past: Journal of Integrated Marketing Communications 2009*, pp. 27–30 (Evanston, IL: Northwestern University).

10. Hollie Shaw, "Loblaw debuts digital loyalty program amid Target, Walmart competition," *Financial Post*, May 6, 2013, http://business.financialpost.com/2013/05/06/loblaw-debuts-loyalty-smartphone-app-as-grocery-retail-war-heats-up (accessed January 13, 2014).

11. http://www.frederiksamuel.com/blog/ad-dictionary (accessed October 29, 2007).

12. Fareena Sulta and Andrew J. Rohm, "How to market to Generation (M)obile," *MIT Sloan Management Review*, Summer 2008.

13. Heidi Cohen, "2016 Mobile Marketing Trends Every Marketer Needs, January 11, 2016, http://heidicohen.com/2016-mobile-marketing-trends/ (accessed March 16, 2016).

14. Mobile, "Over Half of Canada's Population to Use Smartphones in 2015," *eMarketer*, January 6, 2015, http://www.emarketer.com/Article/Over-Half-of-Canadas-Population-Use-Smartphones-2015/1011759 (accessed March 14, 2016).

15. comScore, "2015-Canada-Digital-Future-in-Focus," March 27, 2015, https://www.comscore.com/Insights/Presentations-and-Whitepapers/2015/2015-Canada-Digital-Future-in-Focus (accessed March 14, 2016).

16. Facebook IQ, "The Thumb Is in Charge," October 26, 2015, http://insights.fb.com/2015/10/26/the-thumb-is-in-charge/ (accessed March 16, 2016).

17. Shane Snow, "Inside Foursquare: Checking In Before the Party Started," *Wired* magazine, May 24, 2010, http://www.wired.com/business/2010/05/inside-foursquare-checking-in-before-the-party-started-part-i/all (accessed January 13, 2014).

18. Ludovic Pricat, "When Cliché Becomes Reality: Starbucks Coupons for Foursquare Mayors," http://www.gpsbusiness-news.com/When-Cliche-Becomes-Reality-Starbucks-Coupons-for-Foursquare-Mayors_a2265.html, May 26, 2010.

19. Canadian Wireless Telecommunications Association, "Mobile Marketing," http://www.txt.ca/english/business/marketing.php (accessed June 1, 2013).

20. Ibid.

21. "QR Code Essentials," Denso ADC, 2011, http://www.nacs.org/LinkClick.aspx?fileticket=D1FpVAvvJuo%3D&tabid=1426&mid=4802 (accessed June 3, 2013).

22. RetailGeek.com, "Best Buy Deploys QR Codes to Enhance Shopping Experience," September 15, 2010, http://retailgeek.com/best-buy-deploys-qr-codes-to-enhance-shopping-experience (accessed June 3, 2013).

23. Ibid.

24. "Retail QR Codes," Business Card QR Codes website, www.businesscardsqrcode.com/retail-qr.html (accessed June 3, 2013).

25. "Retailers Use of QR Codes," nellymoser website, http://www.nellymoser.com/action-codes/qr-codes-retail-stores/retailers-use-of-qr-codes (accessed June 3, 2013).

26. Ibid.

27. Ibid.

28. ScanLife, "The Showrooming Effect: How Retailers Can Use QR Codes to Create Opportunity," October 2012, p. 2, http://www.scanlife.com/blog/wp-content/uploads/2012/10/

Showrooming-Whitepaper_ScanLife_FINAL.pdf (accessed January 13, 2014).

29. Eve Lazarus, "Unpacking Showrooming," *Canadian Retailer*, spring 2013, Volume 23, Issue 2, pp. 37–38.

30. Scanlife, "The Showrooming Effect," p. 4.

31. Jennifer Kwan, "Wal-Mart invades Toronto bus stops," Yahoo! Canada, June 7, 2013, http://ca.finance.yahoo.com/blogs/insight/wal-mart-invade-toronto-bus-stops-190600620.html (accessed June 13, 2013).

32. David Mercer, "The 3 best shopping carts for mobile e-Commerce (m-commerce)," SME Pals, September 19, 2012, wsm4b.com/mobile-ecommerce/3-best-shopping-carts-mobile-ecommerce-m-commerce (accessed June 3, 2013).

33. Quorus Consulting Group, *2012 Cell Phone Consumer Attitudes Study.*

34. David Mercer, "The 3 best shopping carts for mobile e-Commerce (m-commerce)."

35. Greet Van Hoye and Filip Lievens, "Social Influences on Organizational Attractiveness: Investigating If and When Word of Mouth Matters," *Journal of Applied Social Psychology* 37, no. 9 (2007), pp. 2024–2047; Robert East, Kathy Hammond, and Malcolm Wright, "The Relative Incidence of Positive and Negative Word of Mouth: A Multi-Category Study," *International Journal of Research in Marketing* 24, no.2 (2007), pp. 175–184; Tom Brown, Thomas Barry, Peter Dacin, and Richard Gunst, "Spreading the Word: Investigating Antecedents of Consumers' Positive Word-of-Mouth Intentions and Behaviours in a Retailing Context," *Journal of the Academy of Marketing Science* 33 (Spring 2005), pp. 123–139.

36. Erin Jo Richey, "15 Top Internet Retailers Who Blog," flatfrogblog.com, January 7, 2010.

37. Eastwest Public Relations, "Social Media: A #PR Perspective," April 30, 2013, http://www.eastwestpr.com/2013/04/social-media-a-pr-perspective/#sthash.7W8ippXH.dpuf (accessed January 13, 2014).

38. The Nielsen Company, "Global Advertising Consumers Trust Real Friends and Virtual Strangers the Most," July 7, 2009, http://www.nielsen.com/us/en/newswire/2009/global-advertising-consumers-trust-real-friends-and-virtual-strangers-the-most.html (accessed May 6, 2013).

39. Chrysanthos Dellarocas, "Strategic Manipulation of Internet Opinion Forums: Implications for Consumers and Firms," *Management Science* 52 (October 2006), pp. 1577–1593; Liyun Jin, "Business Using Twitter, Facebook to Market Goods," *Pittsburgh Post-Gazette*, June 21, 2009.

40. Christi Day, "Not So Silent Bob," Nuts About Southwest blog, February 14, 2010, http://www.blogsouthwest.com/blog/not-so-silent-bob.

41. "Brand Channels," YouTube, http://www.gstatic.com/youtube/engagement/platform/autoplay/advertise/downloads/YouTube_BrandChannels.pdf (accessed April 2010).

42. Home Depot Branded Channel, http://www.youtube.com/user/homedepot?blend=2&ob=4#p/a (accessed June 2013).

43. Forever 21 Facebook Fan Page, http://www.facebook.com/#!/Forever21?ref=ts (accessed June 6, 2013).

44. Ibid.

45. M. Michalik, "Pinterest statistics, interaction and engagement," http://www.viralblog.com/social-media/pinterest-statistics-users-interaction-and-engagement/.

46. "Pinterest: A Review of Social Media's Newest Sweetheart," Engauge blog, March 21, 2012, http://blog.engauge.com/2012/03/paper-pinterest-a-review-of-social-medias-newest-sweetheart/ (accessed January 2, 2013).

47. "Start-up Pinterest wins new funding, $2.5 billion valuation," Reuters, February 20, 2013.

48. Laura Hazard Owen, "Pinterest vs. Facebook: Whose users spend more?" GigaOm blog, May 8, 2012 (accessed June 2, 2013).

49. "Pinterest vs. Facebook: Which Social Sharing Site Wins at Shopping Engagement?" bizrateinsights.com, October 15, 2012.

50. Lum, "7 Interesting Pinterest Marketing Campaigns," May 2, 2012, http://www.creativeguerrillamarketing.com/social-media-marketing/5-interesting-pinterest-marketing-campaigns/.

51. http://venturebeat.com/company/sephora/ and http://venturebeat.com/2013/02/27/sephora-our-pinterest-followers-spend-15x-more-than-our-facebook-followers/.

52. Hanna West, "Top Instagram Tips for Retailers," *SnapRetail*, February 18, 2015, http://www.snapretail.com/top-instagram-tips-for-retailers/ (accessed March 16, 2016).

53. Jon Mitchell "What Is the Point of... Instagram?" *readwrite* April 28, 2012, http://readwrite.com/2012/04/18/what_is_the_point_of_instagram (accessed March 16, 2016).

54. Jonathan Ratner, "How Instagram is becoming a must-have for retailers," *Financial Post*, April 13, 2015, http://business.financialpost.com/investing/trading-desk/how-instagram-is-becoming-a-must-have-for-retailers?__lsa=8a29-9995 (accessed March 15, 2016).

55. Sarah Mahoney, "Study: Coupons Make Consumers Blush," *Marketing Daily*, February 17, 2009; personal communication with Rob Price, VP of retail marketing, CVS, June 16, 2009.

56. http://www.stapleseasyrebates.com/img/staples/paperless/pages/Landing.html (accessed June 6, 2013).

57. http://www.marketingpower.com/_layouts/Dictionary.aspx?dLetter=S (accessed June 28, 2010).

58. http://www.freshnessmag.com/2009/08/06/gucci-sneakers-pop-up-shop-gucci-icon-temporary/ (accessed July 2, 2010).

59. American Marketing Association, *Dictionary of Marketing Terms* (Chicago: American Marketing Association, 2008).

60. "100 Leading National Advertisers," *Advertising Age*, Volume 83, Number 26, June 25, 2012, p. 21.

61. Ibid., p. 24.

62. Newspaper Association of America, *PEW Research Center's Project for Excellence in Journalism 2012 State of the News Media*, http://stateofthemedia.org/2012/newspapers-building-digital-revenues-proves-painfully-slow/newspapers-by-the-numbers/ (accessed June 4, 2013).

63. "2013 NAA Study: How America Shops and Spends," Omniture Site Catalyst, April 2013, EnquirerMedia.com, http://www.enquirermedia.com/images/NAA2013.pdf (accessed June 6, 2013).

64. Statista, http://www.statista.com/statistics/235212/media-ad-spending-in-canada/ (accessed March 16, 2016).

65. Linda Barnard, "Walmart Canada launches glossy magazine," *Toronto Star*, April 8, 2013, http://www.thestar.com/life/2013/04/08/walmart_canada_launches_glossy_magazine.html.

66. "Rogers Media and Walmart Canada Unveil Walmart Live Better Multiplatform Magazine," news release, CNW, April 8, 2013, http://www.newswire.ca/en/story/1142077/rogers-media-and-walmart-canada-unveil-walmart-live-better-multiplatform-magazine.

67. David Hinckley, "Americans spend 34 hours a week watching TV, according to Nielsen numbers," *New York Daily News*, September 19, 2012, http://www.nydailynews.com/entertainment/tv-movies/americans-spend-34-hours-week-watching-tv-nielsen-numbers-article-1.1162285.

68. "Maximizing the Potential of Audio Advertising," *Chain Store Age*, March 1995, p. B13.

69. David Barkholz, "Ford co-op program pushes more digital ads," *Automotive News*, January 13, 2014, http://www.autonews.com/article/20140113/RETAIL/301139986/ford-co-op-program-pushes-more-digital-ads (accessed March 16, 2016).

70. "100 Leading National Advertisers," p. 14.

71. Cyndee Miller, "Outdoors Gets a Makeover," *Marketing News,* April 10, 1995, pp. 1–26; and Teresa Andreoli, "From Retailers to Consumers: Billboards Drive the Message Home," *Discount Store News,* September 19, 1994, p. 14.

72. EASTWEST Public Relations, "Social Media: A #PR Perspective."

73. http://www.walmartstores.com/haiti (accessed July 3, 2010).

74. http://www.walmartcanada.ca/article/supporting-families-in-need and http://cdn.corporate.walmart.com/eb/b2/e92a6 adf4e428d71d20d0f6e1c13/2014-global-responsibility-report-canadian-supplement.pdf (accessed March 16, 2016).

75. Nicole Carter, "Michelle Obama J.Crew Outfits in London Prompt Shopping Frenzy Stateside," *New York Daily News,* April 3, 2009.

76. "Flow-Through DC Yields Savings for Fred Meyer," *Chain Store Age,* October 1995, pp. 64–66; quote by Mary Sammons, senior vice-president, Fred Meyer.

77. Gary Witkin, "Effective Use of Retail Marketing Database," *Direct Marketing,* December 1995, pp. 32–35.

78. Stephen Smith, Narendra Agrawal, and Shelby McIntyre, "A Discrete Optimization Model for Seasonal Merchandise Planning," *Journal of Retailing* 74 (Summer 1998), pp. 193–222; Scott Neslin and John Quilt, "Developing Models for Planning Retailer Sales Promotions: An Application to Automobile Dealerships," *Journal of Retailing* 63 (Winter 1987), pp. 333–364; and Arthur Allaway, J. Barry Mason, and Gene Brown, "An Optimal Decision Support Model for Department-Level Promotion Mix Planning," *Journal of Retailing* 63 (Fall 1987), pp. 216–241.

79. "National client email report 2015," The Direct Marketing Association(UK), April 2015, http://www.dma.org.uk/uploads/ckeditor/National-client-email-2015.pdf (accessed January 14, 2014).

80. George Belch and Michael Belch, *Advertising and Promotion,* 5th ed. (New York: McGraw-Hill, 2001), pp. 227–228.

81. Murali Mantralla, "Allocating Marketing Resources," in eds. Barton Weitz and Robin Wensely, *Handbook of Marketing* (London: Sage, 2002), pp. 409–435.

82. This example is adapted by William R. Swinyard, professor of business management, Brigham Young University, from the "Overseas Airlines Service" case.

83. Ronald Curhan and Robert Kopp, "Obtaining Retailer Support for Trade Deals: Key Success Factors," *Journal of Advertising Research* 27 (December 1987-January 1988), pp. 51–60.

84. This illustration was provided by Kathy Perry, senior vice-president, Matrix Technology Group, Inc., http://www.mxtg.net.

Name Index

Subject Index